Berkeley Sr.

SCOTT, FORESMAN

HISTORY AND LIFE

America's most popular
world history text

Now in its 4th edition

NEW CONTENT

NEW SKILLS

NEW COMPONENTS

**—ALL RECOMMENDED
BY TEACHERS!**

WESTERN HERITAGE

NON-WESTERN CIVILIZATIONS

MAP AND GEOGRAPHY SKILLS

CRITICAL THINKING

READABILITY

TEACHER'S EDITION

PROGRAM COMPONENTS

EXPANDED COVERAGE OF OUR WESTERN HERITAGE

For high school students coming to grips with the important issues of their lives—who they are, what they want to be, the kind of contributions they can make—*History and Life* provides insights into the past that students can relate to today. Between the past and the present, there is not a gulf but a continuum, and nowhere is this sense of continuity more important than in the expanded coverage of our Western heritage. No matter what their background has been, all students are directly influenced by the culture, language, religion, technology, and political values of Western

civilization. As they mature, today's students are in the process of learning about, and joining, the traditions of the past.

More about democracy

To help students understand, appreciate, and put into practice the traditions of democracy, the 4th edition of *History and Life* offers four more chapters, which permit expanded coverage of these

crucial aspects of our Western tradition:

■ Ancient Greece, the cradle of democracy

■ The American and French revolutions, the forge of democracy

■ The world since World War II, the globalization of democracy

More primary sources

For students to experience what it has meant for people to take part in the development of both Western and non-Western civilizations, *History and Life* presents an abundance of primary source material.

■ Each chapter contains "From the Archives," a feature

that highlights primary source quotations—from letters, literature, songs, speeches—as a means of continually grounding theory and narrative in actual human experience.

■ The text includes excerpts from such fundamental documents as the English Bill of Rights, the American Declaration of Independence, and the French Declaration of the Rights of Man and of the Citizen.

■ "Highlights of Civilization," at the end of each chapter, examines such crucial Western developments as the signing of the Magna Carta, the influence of the United States Constitution, and nonviolent resistance movements for democratic change.

FULL TREATMENT OF NON-WESTERN CIVILIZATIONS

History and Life enables teachers to give their courses the emphasis they want by including material that fosters genuine understandings of international issues. This new 4th edition emphasizes the contributions of significant non-Western cultures— African, Asian, New World, and Middle Eastern—to a

world that is increasingly interdependent.

The structure of the new 4th edition reflects parallel cultural developments throughout the world. The three parts —Civilizations Forming, Civilizations Connecting, and Civilizations Interacting— culminate in a final unit, The Era of Global Interdependence, which covers the rise of independence in, and interdependence among, the nations of Europe, Asia, Africa, the Middle East, and Latin America.

Throughout the text, the contributions of different civilizations provide a rich texture of multi-cultural diversity. More than four chapters are devoted to the history of China and the Middle East, while eight chapters examine the history of Africa and the Americas.

For teachers whose classes are organized on a global approach, *History and Life* provides the scope they need.

ENHANCED MAP SKILLS AND GEOGRAPHIC CONCEPTS

History and Life helps teachers build students' understanding of important skills and concepts in geography. Maps, globes and other features enable students to see important relationships between geography and the course of human events.

Among the many map and geographic features offered:

■ The text consistently builds map skills. Maps are supported by captions that stimulate learning by posing questions that are answered on-page in the Teacher's Edition.

■ The new 4th edition features nearly twice as many

topics as Nile Currents, the Steppe and the Mongols, and Geopolitics and the Caribbean Basin.

■ Many chapters begin with a section on the influence of geography on history.

EQUATOR

TROPIC OF CAPRICORN

Tropical rainforest
Savanna
Humid subtropical
Mediterranean
Marine west coast
Desert
Steppe
Highlands

N

0   400   800 1200   Kilometers
0   400   800   Miles

"Geography: A Key to History" essays as the 3rd edition did. With two of these features per unit, students will explore such geographically intriguing

■ More than 120 maps featured in the text reflect the latest scholarship and most recent events.

■ The type of map projection employed for world and large-area maps is always identified.

■ A new atlas at the back of the text provides an immediate reference to present-day maps.

■ Geography skills worksheets in the Teacher's Resource File augment and reinforce the presentation of skills in the text.

T7

QUESTIONS AND ACTIVITIES THAT INVITE TRUE CRITICAL THINKING

History and Life provides a carefully developed program of critical thinking questions that guides students to compare, analyze, and make independent judgments. Learning how to evaluate past experience enables students to appreciate other times and other ways of living. It also encourages insights that help them cope with the problems of their own world.

The critical-thinking program in *History and Life* is thorough. There is one critical-thinking question in every Section Review, and two in every Chapter and Unit Review.

Chapter Reviews also include critical thinking skills in the Chapter Skills and Activities.

To promote a lifetime of sound reasoning, *History and Life*

helps to develop these critical-thinking skills:

■ Making hypotheses

■ Analyzing comparisons

■ Evaluating sources of information

■ Predicting effects

■ Making decisions

■ Identifying assumptions

■ Assessing cause and effect

■ Recognizing values

■ Making generalizations

For more information on the *History and Life* approach to critical thinking, see the

monograph by Professor John Barell on page T26.

READING STRATEGIES THAT PROMOTE STUDENT SUCCESS

Every year, many thousands of students succeed with the *History and Life* program, in large part because the program helps them to organize their study.

How is this accomplished? By careful text organization, presentation, and review. In addition, the readability expert who helped design the text has provided guided reading strategies for each chapter. These strategies include pre-reading, reading, and post-reading steps. Because the text is organized according to these steps, students are motivated to read and to comprehend what they have read.

Further evidence of *History and Life* readability:

■ Each chapter introduction sets a purpose for reading and is followed by a reading preview.

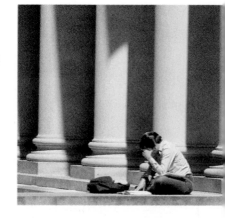

■ New vocabulary is bold-faced and defined at first appearance. It also is summarized in the glossary.

■ The standard Thorndike Barnhart pronunciation

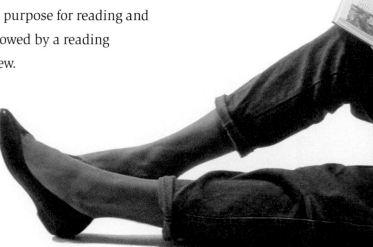

system is used for difficult or foreign words.

History and Life is structured for student success. The new 4th edition is divided into three parts for clarity and greater manageability. With section titles and subtitles stated in complete sentences, the text virtually outlines itself. And the help for students does not stop there. For further practice and reinforcement,

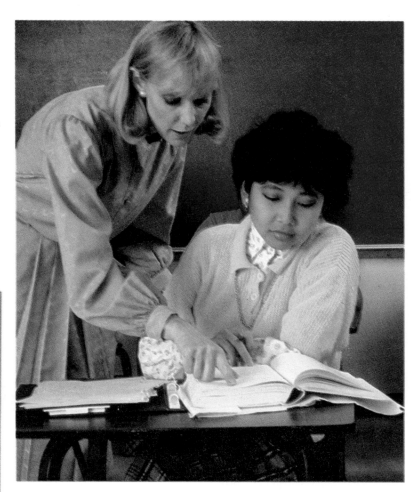

the Management Book in the Teacher's Resource File contains a number of blackline masters on reading strategies and gives optional strategies tailored to each chapter.

For a complete explanation of the program's reading strategies, from organization through testing, see the monograph by reading expert Lorraine Gerhart on page T28.

STATE-OF-THE-ART TEACHER'S EDITION

History and Life helps teachers share their historical knowledge and insights by means of a simple, three-part lesson plan. This plan presents all the information teachers need on special tinted columns in the Teacher's Edition.

Teacher's Edition columns appear beside large (90% of full size) reproductions of the student pages to which they refer.

Objectives
Clearly stated learning objectives are provided for each section.

Focus and Motivate
This material forms a bridge from students' past experience and learning to the subject matter at hand, in ways that stimulate interest.

Teach
Activities suggested here relate to the objectives, although they are not limited to them.

---

2 Lesson Plan

Essential Learning Objectives

Students will learn to:
- describe the Germanic invasions of the Roman Empire.
- explain the factors that helped the eastern Roman Empire remain strong.

1 FOCUS AND MOTIVATE

Call students' attention again to Tacitus' description of the German warrior in the chapter introduction. Ask students to describe Tacitus' view of the German warrior and speculate on whether his description is based on personal observation or on hearsay. (personal observation)

2 TEACH

- On an outline map of Europe and Asia from the Geography Skills book, have students indicate the approximate places where these Germanic tribes originally lived: East Goths, West Goths, Vandals, Lombards, Alemanni, Burgundians, Franks, Jutes, Angles, Saxons.

- Discuss the way of life, religion, and government of the Germanic peoples. Have students compare the behavior of the Romans as victors to the behavior of victorious Germanic peoples. Ask students to speculate on why Germanic warriors did not enslave people they conquered.

- Using the map on page 182, have students deduce which migrations of German tribes resulted because of the threat of an invasion by the Huns and which might have been caused

Germanic Invasions, A.D. 150–568

🌐 **MAP STUDY** The map shows the path of the major Germanic invasions that destroyed the western Roman Empire. It also shows the route of the Huns, a people from Central Asia. What country is the farthest west the Huns reached?

2 The Roman Empire collapsed under attacks from Germanic tribes.

While the Church was growing stronger, the once mighty government of the Caesars was crumbling. Internal problems of the Roman Empire, such as corruption and disunity, made it easier for external forces to destroy it. Then came the final crushing blows—attacks by Germanic tribes.

German tribes pressed against the Roman frontier.

In the 4th century A.D., most Germanic peoples in Europe lived east of the **Rhine** and north of the **Danube** rivers. To the west and north of the Black Sea were Gothic peoples, that is, the East Goths—Ostrogoths—and the West Goths—Visigoths. To the west of these tribes and extending over a large area east of the Rhine, were the Vandals, Lombards, Alemanni, Burgundians, and Franks. In and near present-day Denmark lived the Jutes, Angles, and Saxons. (Study the map above to locate the places and peoples discussed in this section.)

These Germanic groups were seminomads, that is, they both herded their cattle and farmed for a living. They were energetic and vigorous, and as a people prized strength and courage in battle. They worshiped many gods, including Tiw [tē'ü], the god of war; Wotan, the chief of the gods; Thor, the god of thunder; and Freya [frā'ə], the goddess of fertility. (The names of these gods live on today in the English words Tuesday, Wednesday, Thursday, and Friday.)

The Germanic peoples governed themselves through tribal assemblies made up of voting freemen. Their laws were based on long-established customs. These political practices, especially the use of assemblies, had a strong influence later in

ANSWER TO MAP STUDY Gaul—present-day France

182

Lesson–plan features that teachers will profit from day after day are called out below.

In addition, special planning pages that picture optional ancillaries have been inserted

before each Unit and Chapter to help teachers plan activities and adjust teaching time.

---

medieval England, where they laid a foundation for parliamentary government and English common law.

For hundreds of years, Romans and Germans had fought each other on the borders of the Roman Empire. Still, there were long periods of war and long periods of peace. During the peaceful periods, Roman and Germanic peoples mixed with one another. Some Germans entered the Roman Empire and settled on vacant lands. Others, captured in war, became slaves on Roman estates, and still others became soldiers in the legions. If this process had been allowed to continue, the Germans might have been gradually absorbed into the empire. However, the German tribes, under attack by other tribes and aware of the decay and weakness of the Roman Empire, took advantage of the opportunity. They turned the gradual mixing into an overwhelming invasion.

German tribes forced their way into all parts of the western Roman Empire.

The German tribes were forced into motion by a group of people called the Huns, whom you read about in Chapter 8. During the 4th century, the Huns moved out of their territory in Central Asia into China, India, and Europe. (See the map, page 182.) Mounted on swift horses, they attacked with lightning ferocity. Crossing the Dnieper [nē′pər] River, they conquered the Ostrogoths in eastern Europe. The Visigoths in the path of the Huns, fearing attack also, sought safety by attacking and occupying Roman settlements.

In 378 the Roman emperor Valens led a large army against the Visigoths at Adrianople in present-day Bulgaria. Surprisingly, the Visigoths won the battle of Adrianople, scattered the Roman forces, and killed the emperor. This battle is considered one of the most decisive in history because it left the Roman Empire defenseless. It was the first major battle that Rome had lost in hundreds of years. German tribes outside the empire began to round up their cattle, mobilize their fighting men, and move toward the Roman borders.

Thirty-two years after the battle of Adrianople, in 410 the Visigothic general, Alaric, led the Visigoths to Rome itself, which they sacked and looted. By that time, other German tribes—the

BACKGROUND St. Jerome wrote of the Germanic movements around A.D. 400: "Nations innumerable and most savage have invaded all Gaul. The whole region . . . has been devastated. . . ."

Franks, Vandals, and Burgundians—were also moving into the empire. About 450, German tribes from northwest Europe—the Angles, Saxons, and Jutes—sailed to Britain, where they killed or enslaved some of the Britons and forced others to retreat into Wales and Scotland. (See the map, page 182.) The Romans, who had previously occupied Britain, had withdrawn their troops earlier to protect the empire nearer Italy.

The **Anglo-Saxon** invaders destroyed Roman civilization in Britain and set up rival kingdoms. For the next 600 years, Anglo-Saxon England had a weak central government. However, the people did develop a strong tradition of participation in local government, which was a seed for later democratic government in the area, that is, a government run by the common people.

To add to the violence and confusion, the Huns, led by **Attila** [at′l ə], also invaded the empire, threatening to enslave or destroy both Romans and Germans. So, forgetting their own differences for a while, the Romans and Germans united against their common enemy, the Huns. Romans and Ger-

The Anglo-Saxons made elaborate jewelry, such as the gold purse lid (right) and the silver and enamel brooch (below). Both pieces were found in England.

183

---

by other factors, such as population increases, scarcity of arable land, harsh climate, or ambitious leaders.

- Draw a time line extending from A.D. 300–600 and add the following dates at the top: A.D. 378, A.D. 410, A.D. 451, A.D. 453, A.D. 476. Have students name and describe the event that occurred on each date.

GUIDED PRACTICE
Have students write several sentences on why the eastern part of the Roman Empire endured and was not invaded. Also for guided practice:

 Overhead Transparency 19

3   ASSESS AND CLOSE

ASSESS
1. Who was the feared leader of the Huns? (Attila)
2. What tribe was the victor at the battle of Adrianople? (Visigoths)

OPTIONAL RETEACHING
Have students write summary statements on the Germanic invasions of the western part of the Roman Empire.

OPTIONAL ENRICHMENT
1. Have students research and write a summary of the famous battle in the Teutoburg Forest in A.D. 9 during which Arminius, a Cheruscan prince, defeated Varus, a provincial Roman governor. (average)
2. Assign students to research and write a short paper on the revival of learning and literature under Theodoric, including the contributions of the scholars Boethius and Cassiodorus. (challenging)

Assess and Close
This section offers:
■ questions and activities that check students' comprehension of the section;
■ optional reteaching activities;
■ optional enrichment activities;
■ independent practice/homework suggestions;
■ a short summary statement with which the teacher can leave students at the conclusion of the section.

INDEPENDENT PRACTICE/ HOMEWORK
Assign the Section Review, Activities page 54, or Workbook page 36.

CLOSURE
To summarize the lesson tell students that the downfall of the Roman Empire, partly brought about by the Germanic invasion, spawned a new civilization based on Christianity. This civilization was a blend of old and new.

Answers to Section 2 Review

Identify
Key Terms, People, and Places are defined on pages indicated in parentheses. Also see the Glossary and Biographical Dictionary.
Rhine (182), Danube (182), Anglo-Saxons (183), Attila (183), Constantinople (184)

Main Ideas
1. They fought along the borders of the Roman Empire but also mixed with each other during times of peace.
2. The Huns from Central Asia conquered the Ostrogoths and threatened the Visigoths, pushing them into Roman territory where they attacked the Romans, defeating them at the Battle of Adrianople. Germanic tribes then spread through the empire.
3. In that year Odoacer, a German leader, deposed the Roman emperor.

Critical Thinking
Statement erroneously assumes that because the Germans conquered a highly civilized people—the Romans—they were wandering barbarians with little valuable culture of their own.

---

mans stood togeth (present-day Franc tle of Chalons [shä

The western em
Meanwhile, the em weak that they we Many Roman soldi one, Odoacer [ō′də of the Roman arm of the puppet Ro named Romulus A

Odoacer was the officially approved 476 is often given Rome. In a strict "fall." The decline been slow and con rupt officials, and diers into the legio

Since the early d eral emperors at weakness of the we Chapter 6, in 330 E his capital to the ci renamed **Constant** the empire. By the Empire had become peror ruled in the Still, the two sectio arated, continued t

In fact, the we breaking up. By th came the Roman been established i inces. The Anglo-S sigoths ruled Spai had established a k controlled Gaul. It fare, and in 493 it was ravaged by civ aly, which had bee man Empire, woul government until t

The eastern part collapse or give w sions. With its c Byzantine Empire

184

T13

ADDITIONAL COMPONENTS THAT BRING HISTORY ALIVE—*AND* EASE TEACHING LOADS

TEACHER'S RESOURCE FILE

Five ancillaries in this handy file are filled with teaching help and student enrichment. The result? Classes go more smoothly and profitably.

The Teacher's Resource File for *History and Life* contains:

■ **Activities** 164 general worksheets, one for each section; 40 reteaching activities (one for each chapter); 40 enrichment activities (one for each chapter)

■ **Geography Skills** One pretest to gauge students' general knowledge of place geography; 40 geography worksheets accompanying 40 outline maps (one worksheet and one map for each chapter); 40 map lessons (one for each chapter)

■ **One-Day Plays** Five plays on historic trials that may be performed by students in class to provide historical insights and enrichment. The five plays are "The Trial of Socrates," "The Trial of Joan of Arc,"

"The Trial of Atahualpa," "The Trial of Gandhi," "The Trial of Adolph Eichmann."

■ **Management book** A wealth of worksheets on reading comprehension, critical thinking skills, and social studies skills; PLUS skills scope and sequence chart and classroom accountability charts

■ **Tests** One pretest to gauge students' general knowledge of world history; 40 chapter tests and 40 alternates; 9 unit tests and 9 alternates; one midterm test and one alternate; one final exam and one alternate. In addition to testing students' knowledge of key terms, people, places, and main ideas in world history, each test also includes a critical thinking question.

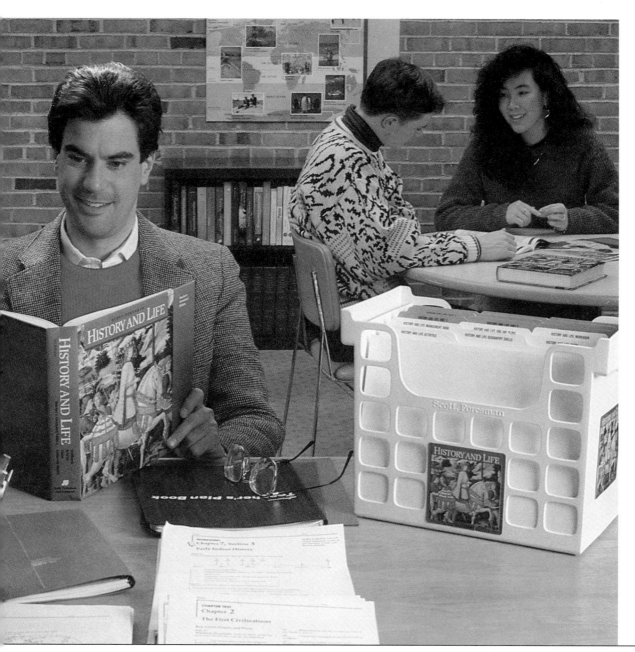

SOURCE READINGS

Titled *Treasures of the World,* this lively four-color illustrated book offers two source readings per chapter. Excerpts from documents, laws, letters, diaries, and songs provide a total of eighty true-life insights into the way it was for people of the past.

OVERHEAD TRANSPARENCIES

Eighty full-color overhead transparencies provide maps and charts from the text, as well as new visuals for enrichment.

WORKBOOK

This workbook, a true study manual, provides one worksheet for each section of the text (164 sheets in all) to review, reinforce, and enrich understanding of main ideas, people, and places.

TEST GENERATOR

The test generator provides a bank of 40 questions for each chapter. Versions are available for use with Apple or IBM computers.

Authors

T. Walter Wallbank is the author of numerous articles and books in the field of world history. He pioneered the development of civilization and world history courses in high schools and colleges and has studied and taught extensively in Europe, Africa, and Asia.

Arnold Schrier has written extensively and taught courses in the fields of European and world history. In 1988 and 1989, he was President of the World History Association. He is an authority on Russian history and does research and teaching on the subject in this country and abroad. He also works with public high schools in the development of social studies curriculum.

Donna Maier has served as an African studies consultant for encyclopedia and trade book publishers. She has traveled and studied widely in Africa, the Middle East, and Europe. She is the author of a number of books and articles on African culture and is presently lecturing in African history and world history.

Patricia Gutierrez-Smith has participated widely in the formation of curriculum materials for urban schools and students. She has been a social studies teacher in several Chicago high schools and is presently teaching world history and Latin American history.

Philip A. Roden has taught in Nigeria, at Chicago's Marshall High School, and at Northwestern University. He is coauthor of two United States history texts and has written numerous teaching materials.

Academic Consultants

Dr. Gerald A. Danzer
Professor of History
University of Illinois at Chicago
Chicago, Illinois

Dr. Ghada Talhami
Associate Professor of History
Lake Forest College
Lake Forest, Illinois

Linda S. Wojtan
Mid-Atlantic Region Japan-in-the-Schools Program
University of Maryland
College Park, Maryland

Critical Thinking

Dr. John Barell
Professor, Department of Curriculum
Montclair State College
Upper Montclair, New Jersey

Reading Comprehension

Robert A. Pavlik
Chairperson, Reading-Language Arts Department
Cardinal Stritch College
Milwaukee, Wisconsin

Lorraine Gerhart
Cardinal Stritch College
Milwaukee, Wisconsin

Teacher Consultants

Linda Black
Teacher of World History
Langham Creek High School
Houston, Texas

Karen Clark
Teacher of World History
Johnson High School
Savannah, Georgia

Timothy M. Helmus
Teacher of World History
City High School
Grand Rapids, Michigan

Katie Ivey
Teacher of World History
Dimmitt High School
Dimmitt, Texas

Lynda Prejean
Teacher of World History
Clear Creek High School
League City, Texas

Kenneth R. Ridenour
Teacher of World History
Camelback High School
Phoenix, Arizona

Joyce L. Stevos
Social Studies Area Supervisor
Department of Public Schools
Providence, Rhode Island

SCOTT, FORESMAN

HISTORY AND LIFE

4th Edition

Teacher's Annotated Edition

T. Walter Wallbank, *University of Southern California*

Arnold Schrier, *University of Cincinnati*

Donna Maier, *University of Northern Iowa*

Patricia Gutierrez-Smith, *Roberto Clemente High School,
Chicago, Illinois*

Philip A. Roden, *Evanston Township High School,
Evanston, Illinois*

Scott, Foresman and Company

Editorial Office: Glenview, Illinois
Regional Offices: Sunnyvale, California • Atlanta, Georgia
Glenview, Illinois • Oakland, New Jersey • Dallas, Texas

12345678910-VHJ-95949392

Contents

Teacher's Annotated Edition

*The Skills Scope and Sequence Chart and Reading Strategies and
Critical Thinking Worksheets are in the Management Book of the
Teacher's Resource File.*

PART ONE

CIVILIZATIONS FORMING   1

UNIT ONE

Civilization Begins   2

UNIT TWO

The Age of Classical Civilizations   56

PART TWO

CIVILIZATIONS CONNECTING   172

UNIT THREE

The Era of Regional Civilizations: Christendom and Islam   175

The Era of Regional Civilizations: Asia, Africa, and the Americas

UNIT FOUR

PART THREE

CIVILIZATIONS INTERACTING   348

The Early Modern Era: Europe's Transformation and Expansion

UNIT FIVE

The Early Modern Era: Asia, Africa, and the Americas

UNIT SIX

Students and the Teaching of World History

As all world history teachers know, two challenges are always with us. One is finding an effective way to organize world history; the other is teaching it to students. Young people offer a challenge, because they are notoriously present-minded. What happened before the dawn of their own consciousness seems so distant as to be irrelevant to their present concerns. Such indifference produces the one-dimensional, ahistoric personality whose vision and understanding are crabbed by the brevity of a single lifetime. To overcome that shortsightedness and instill a sense of identity in the flow of time is one of the great tasks confronting every teacher of history.

Yet, the very youthfulness that induces mental myopia also can create a psychological predisposition for history. This may sound paradoxical, but consider this. What student has not had the experience of meeting someone for the first time and, wanting to find out who the new acquaintance is, asking "Where are you from?" or "Where did you grow up?" or "Where did you go to school?" There is a natural assumption that the new acquaintance will answer with some kind of personal chronology. Describing one's background is a logical way of identifying oneself. The logic that attunes a student to learn about other individuals through personal histories is easily applied to learning about other peoples and societies through their histories.

Another psychological problem has to do with the way hindsight can distort the actual process of history. To a student it seems so logical and, therefore, so easy to believe that what *has* happened *had* to happen, and that it had to happen in precisely the way it did. Such a view ignores the role of chance and accident in history, the unpredictability of individual behavior, or the fact that when decisions have to be made there are usually many options from which to choose. The task facing all teachers of history is to demonstrate that nothing is cut and dried at the time it happens—it only seems that way in the hindsight of the next generation.

Calvin and Hobbes   by Bill Watterson

The other challenge, that of organizing world history, is one that every textbook author must meet. Some do it with a topical approach. Most others, including this one, do it with a chronological framework. One of the great advantages of a chronological approach is that, if the time frame chosen is truly worldwide, students have an opportunity to compare developments taking place simultaneously among various peoples of the world. They are in a position to compare and contrast differences in social and political institutions, levels of literacy and technology, ethical and religious ideas, cultural attainments, and economic developments. Such comparisons, especially if made between Western and non-Western civilizations in the same time segment, should help reduce the Europocentrism so common to world history courses. They also should demonstrate the resourcefulness of human beings in organizing societies and coping with the environment. In addition, there is an opportunity to explore the spread of plants, animals, foods, technology, medicines, ideas, and institutions from one civilization to another in the same historical era. Students thus can be introduced to the concept of cultural diffusion. As one approaches modern times, students are in a position to see how the tempo or diffusion speeds up and how widely separated areas of the world have become increasingly interdependent. Students then should be better prepared to evaluate how the policies and programs of one society have affected other societies.

It is this kind of worldwide time frame that forms the basic organizational scheme for *History and Life.* The overall theme of this text is that we humans have come a long way, from living in comparative isolation 10,000 years ago to living in a global village today. To make the theme clearer, the text has been divided into Parts covering large slices of time. In Part One, stretching over the longest period of time, civilizations were slowly forming. Once civilizations had formed, changes came faster—history "speeded up." Therefore Part Two covers only 1,000 years, during which civilizations reached out over larger areas and made wider connections. Part Three covers the last 500 years, a time when civilizations increasingly interacted with one another until, by the mid-20th century, we had reached a condition of global interdependence.

Each of the Parts has been subdivided into Units, which cover somewhat smaller slices of time, and each Unit has been further subdivided into Chapters on specific civilizations and developments. The arrangement of Units gives us a way of seeing what was happening around the world in the same time period, while the individual Chapters describe what was unique and distinctive in the development of particular societies.

Of course, no organizational scheme by itself can resolve all problems for all teachers. Ultimately, it is the individual teacher who must decide what goals he or she wishes to achieve, and then choose content that seems most conducive to the realization of those goals.

Arnold Schrier, Professor
University of Cincinnati

How to Teach the Course You Want

As an author of *History and Life,* and as a college professor who receives and teaches your students after you have taught and prepared them, I would like to see students exposed to all of the material in *History and Life* so that they become better informed citizens of their community and the world. However, school systems have differing curriculum and syllabus requirements in their social studies programs, some emphasizing our Western cultural heritage in a "Western civilization" course, and some taking more of a non-Western or international studies approach. Then again, some teachers are not required to emphasize a particular approach, but for individual reasons such as background, experience, or the nature of their student body, they prefer to pursue one approach instead of another. For these reasons we are providing some guidelines to assist you in using this book to teach the course you want or need, depending on whether you prefer to emphasize Western or non-Western civilizations.

WESTERN CIVILIZATION EMPHASIS

The justification for teaching world history to American students with an emphasis on Western civilization, or on our Western heritage, is that no matter who you are in America—a tenth-generation descendant of a Mayflower passenger, an American Indian, a newly arrived Vietnamese refugee, a black American, or a third-generation European immigrant—European culture, language, religion, technology, and political values dominate American society today. No one can excel or function well in the United States without knowledge and awareness of our Greco-Roman, Judeo-Christian, and European heritage. If this is the emphasis that your school system encourages, or if you are very limited in time and feel that these are the fundamentals you wish to impart to your

students first, the following chart will guide you to select the chapters in this book that will form a comprehensive Western civilization course. If time permits, omitted non-Western chapters can be used toward the end of the school year.

Naturally, it is impossible to teach a comprehensive Western civilization course without learning about the deep impact made on Europe by ideas from Southwest Asia, especially the Jewish religion, which first flourished in a Middle Eastern environment. For this reason Empires and Religion in the Middle East (Chapter 3), has been marked for inclusion in a Western civilization course. Also necessary for a well-structured Western civilization course is an examination of Europe's encounter with, and subsequent dominating influence on, the rest of the world. For this reason certain chapters, such as The Age of Exploration (Chapter 20), The Formation of Latin America (Chapter 25), The Surge of Imperialism (Chapter 30), and Nationalism, Revolution, and Dictatorship (Chapter 33), have been marked for inclusion in a Western civilization course. Generally, Russian history is considered today to be an essential part of European history, though it is often included in world civilization courses in order to expose American students to a culture quite different from that of the United States. Chapters about Russian and Soviet history have, therefore, also been marked for inclusion in both Western and non-Western courses.

NON-WESTERN CIVILIZATION EMPHASIS

The justification for a world civilization course is, first, that despite the dominance of European cultures in the United States, it is not just a transplanted Europe. Our nation has drawn on a myriad of other cultures—American Indian, African, Chinese, Islamic, and Polynesian, to name just a few—and is far richer for it. Furthermore, the world is rapidly

"shrinking." Instantaneous telecommunications, the potential of nuclear war, and environmental problems on a global scale all demonstrate our dependence on decisions made by all nations and peoples. Thus, well-educated high school students, if they are to be prepared to face and solve the problems of life in the United States and the world today, must be aware of the rich heritage of the whole world and its contemporary interdependence. This belief is implicit in the overall structure of *History and Life* with its division into three parts: Civilizations Forming, Civilizations Connecting, and Civilizations Interacting, as well as in the last unit, The Era of Global Interdependence.

If an emphasis on non-Western history is what you or your school system has chosen, the following chart will guide you to select the chapters in this book that will help you achieve that emphasis. The selections, for a non-Western course, are based on the assumption that the students in your class have already had a course in Western civilization. By teaching the chapters that are checked "non-Western civilization," you will expose students to the major world cultures of past and present while excluding European development. If your students have had no previous course in Western civilization, or if their background in it needs to be reinforced, the ideal solution is to teach all chapters of the text.

Of course, it is impossible to teach a good world civilization course without dealing with the recent confrontation of Western European culture and non-Western societies. For this reason you will notice that some chapters concerning European history are also checked in the non-Western civilization column, in particular The Age of Exploration (Chapter 20), The Surge of Imperialism (Chapter 30), and Nationalism, Revolution, and Dictatorship (Chapter 33).

CONCLUSION

Whatever the emphasis you wish to apply, other considerations such as school calendar, personal preference, and student interest also should guide you in selecting units, chapters, cultures, and historical eras to explore with your class. We hope you find the lesson plans and supplementary materials that we have provided in this Teacher's Annotated Edition and in the Teacher's Resource File useful in expanding and developing your chosen chapters and topics.

Donna J. E. Maier, Professor
University of Northern Iowa

Unit		Chapter		Western Civilization	Non-western Civilization
ONE — Civilization Begins Prehistory–500 B.C.	1	Early Humans		■	■
	2	The First Civilizations		■	■
	3	Empires and Religions in the Middle East		■	■
TWO — The Age of Classical Civilizations 3000 B.C.–A.D. 500	4	The Rise of Greek Civilization		■	
	5	The Greek Achievements		■	
	6	The Roman Legacy		■	
	7	The Flowering of Civilization in India			■
	8	China Reaches a Golden Age			■
	9	Africa and the Americas in the Classical Age			■
THREE — The Era of Regional Civilizations: Christendom and Islam 500–1500	10	Rome and the Rise of Christendom		■	
	11	The Formation of Europe		■	
	12	The Growth of National Monarchies		■	
	13	The Byzantine Empire and the Formation of Russia		■	■
	14	The Rise and Expansion of Islam			■
	15	Islamic Civilization			■
FOUR — The Era of Regional Civilizations: Asia, Africa, and the Americas 500–1500	16	China's Predominance in Asia			■
	17	The Emergence of Japan			■
	18	Empires in Africa and the Americas			■
FIVE — The Early Modern Era: Europe's Transformation and Expansion 1500–1800	19	The European Renaissance		■	
	20	The Age of Exploration		■	■
	21	The Reformation and National Power		■	
	22	The Scientific Revolution		■	
SIX — The Early Modern Era: Asia, Africa, and the Americas 1500–1800	23	Muslim Empires in Turkey, Persia, and Africa			■
	24	China and Japan in Seclusion			■
	25	The Formation of Latin America		■	■
SEVEN — The Sweep of Revolutions in the West 1500–1900	26	Democratic Revolutions in England and North America		■	
	27	Revolutions in France and Latin America		■	
	28	The Industrial Revolution		■	
	29	Revolutions in Everyday Life and Politics		■	
EIGHT — The Interval of Western Dominance 1750–1945	30	The Surge of Imperialism		■	■
	31	World War I		■	■
	32	The Soviet Union: The First Communist State		■	■
	33	Nationalism, Revolution, and Dictatorship		■	■
	34	World Depression and World War II		■	■
NINE — The Era of Global Interdependence 1945–Present	35	Europe, the Cold War, and the Superpowers		■	■
	36	The Assertion of Independence in Asia			■
	37	The Struggle for Self-Rule in Africa			■
	38	Economic Growth and International Tension in the Middle East			■
	39	The Struggle for National Development in Latin America		■	■
	40	An Interdependent World		■	■

Critical Thinking in History

History is a record of how different peoples have acted alone and in collaboration with others to reach certain goals. The men and women depicted on the pages of *History and Life* have faced significant problems. They have responded to their needs or problems with a wide variety of plans, strategies, and alternative courses of action. Critical thinking in studying history is making reasoned judgments about these actions.

The readers of *History and Life* face the important task of attempting to make the historical record meaningful by perceiving the relationships within and among different events and making connections with their own lives. Thinking about particular events, such as the American, French and Russian revolutions, brings to mind many different kinds of questions that the critical reader or interpreter should ask in order to achieve understanding. Some of these questions include the following:

"What kinds of problems led to these drastic upheavals in each nation?"

"What caused these problems?"

"Given these circumstances why did people choose to act as they did?"

"Could they have acted otherwise with different consequences?"

"What conclusions do I draw about the meaning and significance of these events, based upon the information I have?"

"How are these events related to others I know of both in history and in my own life?"

When thinking about events, students also should be encouraged to use imaginative projection. Any event allows us to imagine ourselves as participants in that event and to ask, "How would I think and feel were I Patrick Henry at this moment?" When we do this we gain a much greater appreciation for the conditions under which people solved their problems with the specific courses of action they chose.

These questions present a problem-solving context for critical thinking in history. The specific skills that we use in *History and Life* may be described as follows.

MAKING DECISIONS

Here we can enter into the thinking of the various historical actors by analyzing how they identified problems, designed alternative solutions, made decisions based upon evidence and a set of criteria and implemented these decisions. For example, we will grapple with understanding the actions of the American colonists in their rebellion against the British.

ASSESSING CAUSE AND EFFECT AND MAKING HYPOTHESES

In all history we are interested in why things happen. Why did some people in France think, for example, that they could no longer live under the Bourbon monarchy? Here we establish hypotheses that might provide a causal explanation. We then search for evidence to support one or more reasons why we think this occurred. We also look for counter evidence against our own hypotheses. In so doing we will be identifying needs and problems faced by persons that led to or motivated certain courses of action. In this way historians are acting like scientists when, for example, they attempt to figure out why the planets behave as they do.

EVALUATING SOURCES OF INFORMATION

Not all accounts of events are good enough to be used in drawing conclusions about what happened at a given moment in time. We need to examine the evidence to ensure that it is reliable, objective, accurate, and unbiased. We need to search for evidence that favors our conclusion, for example, that the colonists were motivated by economic reasons and for evidence that contradicts this point of view. Otherwise our conclusions about the reasons for revolution will be distorted and our reasoning will, therefore, be slanted in inappropriate directions.

IDENTIFYING ASSUMPTIONS

When attempting to figure out the causes and results of a complex set of events we often must be certain to uncover the assumptions we are making about these events. We want to know what we are taking for granted—what we are assuming to be true about the actors and their actions and to verify it against the best information available.

PREDICTING EFFECTS

As we attempt to predict effects, we are in a sense projecting ourselves into the historical scene and thinking, "What would happen if a certain action were taken? The American colonists had several options. What would have happened had they done something different than the course they followed?" Here we are determining causal relations by being able to reason from knowledge of similar patterns, and this gives us a sense of being actors on the historical stage that have options or choices to make.

ANALYZING COMPARISONS

In making comparisons we are striving to make separate events more meaningful by discovering linkages or connections such

events might have with similar events in history and in our own lives. For example, we might ask, "In what ways was the storming of the Bastille similar to or different from the actions of the Bolsheviks in Russia? How are these events similar to those in our lives?" We make these comparisons by identifying similar characteristics and those that are different and then discussing the relationships among these characteristics. Our conclusions will lead us to a broader interpretation of historical events by being able to recognize patterns and make generalizations.

MAKING GENERALIZATIONS

When we examine one set of events we often look for patterns of relationships in order to understand the actions more comprehensively. A pattern is a repetition of relationships. For example, we can ask, "Do all revolutions proceed as those in America, France, and Russia did—from festering discontent to an initial spark that ignited passions and led to prolonged violence with long-term consequences?" If we can identify these kinds of sequential relationships, then we can understand events and apply patterns to other historical phenomena. Such patterns can be expressed as generalizations. A generalization results when we find likenesses amongst many, different events and, for example, draw the general conclusion that revolutions are caused by raising people's levels of expectation. Generalizations help us think productively because we can refer to many different events at one time.

RECOGNIZING VALUES

In thinking of why people have acted as they have, we begin to appreciate their motives and that these are often strongly conditioned by values, beliefs, or strongly held points of view. Most of our actions are influenced by values (established ideals to which we give worth,

such as honesty), even though they are not often clearly stated or even acknowledged by the actors themselves.

CONCLUSION

One cannot think well in any subject without possessing certain supportive attitudes or dispositions. Those that will foster more productive inquiry in history are the following: an openness to different points of view, a desire for objectivity and accuracy, a spirit of questioning, not accepting all things at face value or from authority, not acting impulsively, a willingness to suspend judgment until as much evidence as possible has been gathered, and, finally, an ability to empathize with the actors on the historical stage.

Critical thinking skills and questions have been interwoven throughout *History and Life,* the Teacher's Annotated Edition, and the Teacher's Resource File. These skills and questions have been designed to aid teachers in helping students make reasoned judgments about the vast scope of historical events presented in this program.

John Barell, Professor
Montclair State College

Improving Reading Comprehension

Most high school students read a history assignment word for word at the same rate of about 250 words per minute from the beginning of the assignment to the end. When they have finished a chapter, the students feel that they have successfully completed the reading assignment. The students have gathered as many facts and dates as they can remember and often have made no connections between them. They may have only a vague knowledge of key events and related ideas. The students often feel they are unable to comprehend the chapter without the class discussion that the teacher will provide.

With a little help, students can become strategic readers and comprehend much more information about the world and its history. Students can learn how to predict which events and ideas are important and to set purposes for reading that will enable them to decide which facts are most relevant. When students have been able to comprehend the chapter and identify the important understandings, class discussions become much more lively. Students who are strategic readers are able to expand the meaning of the information by contributing ideas, asking questions, and providing additional examples from their own experience or previous reading. A student who is a strategic reader may say, "I can't agree with that idea. This chapter built a case for...."

INTRODUCING HISTORY AND LIFE

Classroom teachers can promote the effective use of the textbook by reviewing the overall organization of the book. Spend a few minutes when making the first reading assignments to note the table of contents, how the units are divided, the divisions of the chapters into sections, the special features in each chapter, and the special sections of the book.

Classroom teachers can help students read effectively by explaining that a strategic reader does not read everything word for word at the same speed. A strategic reader previews the assignment, activates what he or she already knows about the subject, thinks about the structure of the text and the ideas, and adjusts the reading speed.

Reading can be divided into three stages: pre-reading, reading, and post-reading. The pre-reading stage often determines how well the student comprehends the text.

PRE-READING COMPREHENSION FEATURES

Have students open *History and Life* and examine the first chapter to note the following pre-reading features:

Advance Organizer is the chapter introduction, which sets the background for what students are going to read.

Reading Preview lists the title of each section of a chapter and provides an overview of the main ideas of the entire chapter.

Section Opener consists of a paragraph which introduces the main ideas of the section. When a student thinks about the opener and the structure of the chapter, the student's mind is becoming ready to recognize and accept new information.

Titles, Heading and Subheading Statements, and Captions can help students preview the information they are about to read.

Pictures, Maps, and Tables can clarify ideas and motivate students to raise questions, such as: "Which paragraphs relate to this picture?" "How does this map, table, or picture fit in with the main ideas?"

READING COMPREHENSION FEATURES

Next, select one section and lead students to identify the following qualities of the writing style and specific cues that make the text easier to read and understand:

Main Ideas are usually the first sentences in the paragraphs.

Action Verbs are used in many sentences to stimulate the students' visual, auditory, and kinesthetic backgrounds.

Nouns are used after indefinite words such as "this," "these," "those," or "some" to help students refer to the preceding information.

Cue Words such as "therefore," "next," or "also" help students see the relationships between two or more main ideas.

Key Terms, People, or Places in Boldface are defined in the context directly, and the other information in the paragraph helps to expand the meaning of the term.

Heading and Subheading Statements develop the structure of the text by highlighting the important ideas. Secondary ideas are further highlighted by subheadings.

POST-READING COMPREHENSION FEATURES

Lastly, identify and explain how to use the post-reading features:

Section Reviews reinforce comprehension of each section by reviewing the Key Terms, People, or Places, and restating the main ideas in question form.

Critical Thinking questions at the end of each section help students reorganize and evaluate the information they have read.

Chapter Reviews at the end of each chapter summarize the main points from the chapter and review the important understandings.

Titles, Headings, Subheadings, and Captions, which are useful for pre-reading and reading, also are important when reviewing the main ideas.

Pictures, Maps, and Tables help the student to expand the main ideas and to synthesize the information contained in the chapter.

GUIDING STRATEGIC READING OF HISTORY AND LIFE

Guided Reading Strategies for each chapter, in the Management Book of the Teacher's Resource File, contain pre-reading, reading, and post-reading steps. When you are giving the class a reading assignment, take a few minutes to review the pre-reading, reading, and post-reading steps that will aid students in becoming strategic readers. Emphasize that the pre-reading stage often determines how well they will understand the reading assignment. This review will help students to use the steps automatically and effectively.

In the pre-reading steps for each chapter, the student is directed to answer three important questions:

1. What do I already know about this topic?
2. What kind of information am I going to read?
3. What are my purposes for reading?

The reading steps for each chapter include a reading strategy based on the organization of the particular chapter the student is about to read. You will find an activity selected from one of these four reading strategies:

What's the Question?
Vocabulary Interview
You Are the Historian
Relationship-Web

Each strategy provides the student with specific directions for concentrating on the main ideas of the chapter, interacting with the information, reorganizing the information for better understanding, and expanding the meaning beyond the printed page. When a strategy is introduced for the first time, have students complete one of the four strategy worksheets in the Management Book of the Teacher's Resource File. When using the strategy in later reading assignments, students may be directed to construct their own strategy sheet to be part of a notebook or as notes to

PEOPLE UNCLEAR ON THE CONCEPT

be saved. The post-reading steps for each section are a means of reviewing, comparing, evaluating, and synthesizing the information from the reading assignment.

APPLYING THE FOUR READING STRATEGIES

A strategic reader interacts with the text before, during, and after reading. To help your students become strategic readers and to operate independently, have them learn the strategies in three stages: knowledge, application, and independent control.

Knowledge level. Inform students about the strategy and introduce it using familiar, easy, material. Students will be able to learn how to use the strategy without concentrating on the content. After students know how to use the strategy, concentration will be shifted more to the content and less on the strategy itself. When discussing and modeling the strategy, "think out loud." Talk through the steps of the strategy and point out where problems might arise and how to solve them.

Application level. Monitor student application of the strategy. Discuss the use of the strategy with students. Ask students to explain the steps, how they put the steps into practice, any difficulties they may have had, and if they changed any part of the strategy. Why did they make changes and did these changes help them to read more effectively?

Independent control level. Prompt students to share the possible ways a strategy can be used and the variations that might be applied. The students might suggest a variation that is helpful to them personally. It helps students if you relate how you have used a strategy to read more effectively or tell them about your own struggles to comprehend difficult material.

Eventually, students will apply the strategies to reading assignments appropriately with little or no teacher guidance. Students will activate background, preview, and set purposes for reading. They will stop reading word for word and will automatically begin reading for ideas. Your efforts will have given your students the opportunity to be independent readers.

Lorraine Gerhart
Cardinal Stritch College

Barr Films
P.O. Box 5667
3940 East Foothill Boulevard
Pasadena, CA 91107

Beacon Films
c/o University of Illinois
Film Center
1325 South Oak
Champaign, IL 61820

Centron Educational Films
1621 West 9th Street
Lawrence, KS 66044

Cornerstone Production
c/o University of Illinois
Film Center
1325 South Oak
Champaign, IL 61820

Coronet
Division of Esquire, Inc.
65 E. South Water Street
Chicago, IL 60601

**[EB] Encyclopaedia Britannica
Education Corporation**
425 North Michigan Avenue
Chicago, IL 60611

Films, Inc.
1144 Wilmette Ave.
Wilmette, IL 60091

Heritage Visuals
c/o University of Illinois
Film Center
1325 South Oak
Champaign, IL 61820

Indiana University
c/o University of Illinois
Film Center
1325 South Oak
Champaign, IL 61820

**International Film
Foundation**
200 West 72nd Street
Room 64
New York, NY 10023

Journal Films, Inc.
930 Pitner Avenue
Evanston, IL 60202

**Learning Corporation
of America**
Division of W. F. Hall
Printing Co.
1350 Avenue of the Americas
New York, NY 10019

Lucerne Films Inc.
7 Bahama Road
Morris Plains, NJ 07950

McGraw Hill
110 15th Street
Del Ray, CA 92014

National Geographic Society
17th and M Streets N.W.
Washington, D.C. 20036

**[PBS VIDEO]
PBS Broadcasting Service**
1320 Braddock Place
Alexandria, VA 22314

**Time/Life Films Multimedia
Division**
43 West 16th Street
New York, NY 10011

**University of Illinois
Film Center**
1325 South Oak
Champaign, IL 61820

Voyager Company
2139 Manning Avenue
Los Angeles, CA 90025

**[WETAVISION] WETA Vision
Educational Activities**
Box 2626
Washington, D.C. 20013

SCOTT, FORESMAN

HISTORY AND LIFE

4th Edition

SCOTT, FORESMAN

HISTORY AND LIFE

4th Edition

T. Walter Wallbank, *University of Southern California*

Arnold Schrier, *University of Cincinnati*

Donna Maier, *University of Northern Iowa*

Patricia Gutierrez-Smith, *Roberto Clemente High School, Chicago, Illinois*

Scott, Foresman and Company

Editorial Office: Glenview, Illinois
Regional Offices: Sunnyvale, California • Atlanta, Georgia
Glenview, Illinois • Oakland, New Jersey • Dallas, Texas

Cover and facing page: The young rider, thought to be Lorenzo de' Medici, a member of the powerful Florentine family, appears in a fresco painted in 1459 by Benozzo Gozzoli.

Authors

T. Walter Wallbank is the author of numerous articles and books in the field of world history. He pioneered the development of civilization and world history courses in high schools and colleges and has studied and taught extensively in Europe, Africa, and Asia.

Arnold Schrier has written extensively and taught courses in the fields of European and world history. In 1988 and 1989, he was President of the World History Association. He is an authority on Russian history and does research and teaching on the subject in this country and abroad. He also works with public high schools in the development of social studies curriculum.

Donna Maier has served as an African studies consultant for encyclopedia and trade book publishers. She has traveled and studied widely in Africa, the Middle East, and Europe. She is the author of a number of books and articles on African culture and is presently lecturing in African history and world history.

Patricia Gutierrez-Smith has participated widely in the formation of curriculum materials for urban schools and students. She has been a social studies teacher in several Chicago high schools and is presently teaching world history and Latin American history.

Teacher Consultants

Linda Black
Teacher of World History
Langham Creek High School
Houston, Texas

Karen Clark
Teacher of World History
Johnson High School
Savannah, Georgia

Timothy M. Helmus
Teacher of World History
City High School
Grand Rapids, Michigan

Kenneth R. Ridenour
Teacher of World History
Camelback High School
Phoenix, Arizona

Joyce L. Stevos
Social Studies Area Supervisor
Department of Public Schools
Providence, Rhode Island

Academic Consultants

Dr. Gerald A. Danzer
Professor of History
University of Illinois at Chicago
Chicago, Illinois

Dr. Ghada Talhami
Associate Professor of History
Lake Forest College
Lake Forest, Illinois

Linda S. Wojtan
Mid-Atlantic Region Japan-in-the-Schools Program
University of Maryland
College Park, Maryland

Critical Thinking

Dr. John Barell
Professor, Department of Curriculum
Montclair State College
Upper Montclair, New Jersey

Reading Comprehension

Robert A. Pavlik
Chairperson, Reading-Language Arts Department
Cardinal Stritch College
Milwaukee, Wisconsin

Lorraine Gerhart
Cardinal Stritch College
Milwaukee, Wisconsin

Copyright © 1993
Scott, Foresman and Company, Glenview, Illinois.
All Rights Reserved. Printed in the United States of America.
This publication is protected by Copyright and permission should be obtained from the publisher prior to any prohibited reproduction, storage in a retrieval system, or transmission in any form or by any means, electronic, mechanical, photocopying, recording, or otherwise. For information regarding permission, write to: Scott, Foresman and Company, 1900 East Lake Avenue, Glenview, Illinois 60025.
ISBN: 0-673-35168-8

Acknowledgments for quoted matter and illustrations are included in the acknowledgments section on pages 855–856. The acknowledgments section is an extension of the copyright page.

The authors and publishers would like to thank the above consultants for their reviews of *History and Life* during its developmental stage. They contributed valuable comments, chapter by chapter, on both the content and level of difficulty. Their assistance has helped make *History and Life* a practical classroom text.

CONTENTS

PART ONE

CIVILIZATIONS FORMING   1

Prehistory–A.D. 500
Enormous change occurred during the time covered in Part One, which begins in prehistoric times. The earliest civilization arose about 3500 B.C., while five of the major world religions, along with the classical age civilizations of China, India, Greece, and Rome, developed between 1500 B.C. and A.D. 500.

UNIT ONE

Civilization Begins *Prehistory–500 B.C.*   2

PART TWO

CIVILIZATIONS CONNECTING   172

A.D. 500–1500

Part Two covers a time in which rich and powerful centers of civilization came into existence not only in Europe and Asia, but in Africa and the Americas as well. No one of them was able to predominate over the others. In each of these civilizations, there was a pattern of widening connections, primarily through religion and trade.

UNIT THREE

The Era of Regional Civilizations: Christendom and Islam *500–1500*   174

The Era of Regional Civilizations: Asia, Africa, and the Americas *500–1500* 290

PART THREE

CIVILIZATIONS INTERACTING　　348

1500–Present
Since 1500 the world increasingly has become a place of communication and interaction between civilizations, with vast networks for transporting goods and people, transmitting ideas and technologies, and extending military power and political control. In our era technology has brought about a global economy and an interdependent world.

Maps, Charts, Fine arts, and Special lessons

MAPS, CHARTS, FINE ARTS, AND SPECIAL LESSONS

From the Archives

Highlights of Civilization

Mystery in History

Geography: A Key to History

Daily Life

HOW TO USE *History and Life*

History and Life has been organized so that you will find it easy to use. The book is divided into three Parts, with nine units and 40 chapters. Special features, fine arts, and a variety of maps appear regularly throughout the text. You will also find an extensive atlas and reference section at the back of the book.

Part Organization

The overall theme of this text is that we humans have come a long way, from living in comparative isolation 10,000 years ago to living in an interdependent world today. To make this theme clearer, the text has been divided into three Parts, each of which covers a large slice of time. Part One includes the long stretch of time from prehistory to A.D. 500, Part Two covers A.D. 500 to A.D. 1500, and Part Three takes us from 1500 to the present. Each Part opens with a brief introduction, an illustrated time line, and a large map showing the major civilizations that occurred during that time.

Unit Organization

Each of the Parts is subdivided into units, which cover somewhat smaller slices of time and correspond to well-defined historical periods. Each of the nine units opens with a full-page photograph, an overview of the main ideas in that unit, and a list of the chapters contained within it. At the end of each unit is a two-page Unit Review. This includes a chapter-by-chapter summary, an in-book practice test, and a Using Writing Skills activity that will help you develop and improve writing techniques that relate to the study of history.

UNIT ONE

Chapter Organization

Each of the units is further subdivided into chapters, which cover specific civilizations and developments. Each chapter opens with an introduction, a locator map to help you determine the general area discussed in the chapter, two or three key dates, an introduction, and a large photograph. Each chapter also has a Reading Preview that includes a guiding statement and a list of the sections in the chapter. The end of each chapter features a two-page Chapter Review that includes Section Summaries, a Review Dates time line, and an in-book practice test.

Section Organization

Each section of the chapters includes a number of subsections that begin with a heading in the dark type. These subsections correspond to the main ideas in the section. All Key Terms, People, and Places also appear in dark type within the text. The study of world history includes many terms, people, and places, some of which may be unfamiliar to you. Many of these new names will be followed by their pronunciations. A guide to pronunciation can be found on page 835.

History and Life features more than 120 maps. Each map in a section has a Map Study caption, which asks questions to help you grasp the map's meaning and practice your map-reading skills.

At the end of each section is a Section Review. Completing the Section Review will help you

1 *Scientists worked out*

MAP STUDY

identify key terms, people, and places, and review the main ideas of the section. Each section review concludes with a question that will ask you to put your critical thinking skills to work.

Highlights of Civilization

A Highlights of Civilization appears at the end of each chapter right before the Chapter Review. This feature explores significant and enduring cultural or scientific contributions of many of the world's cultures to civilization. For example, some of the Highlights of Civilization that you will read include Roman Engineering, Islamic Calligraphy, Blue-and-White Chinese Porcelain, Benin Bronzes, The Telescope and the Microscope, Mughal paintings, Indonesian Batik, and Latin American Literature. Each full-page feature is identified in your textbook with the symbol at right.

From the Archives

A From the Archives selection appears within each chapter. The selections include excerpts both of important documents from world history and of poems, speeches, novels, and diaries. For example, you will find selections by or from The Ten Commandments, Homer's *Odyssey*, the Analects of Confucius, an oral history of King Sundiata, Joan of Arc, Sor Juana Inés de la Cruz, and Chairman Mao's *Little Red Book*.

Geography: A Key to History

Two Geography: A Key to History lessons appear in each unit to help you to understand the geographic features of places around the world, along with basic geographic principles. Each full-page essay includes a map that explains some aspect of geography that has affected history. Some Geography: A Key to History features include Nile Currents and the Etesian Wind, the Steppe and the Mongols, and Geopolitics and the Caribbean Basin. Each feature is identified with the symbol at right.

Mystery in History

A Mystery in History appears within each unit, setting forth a historical mystery with its clues and interpretations. This feature allows you to see how a historian's work is often like that of a detective, as he or she seeks out clues in government records, diaries, newspapers, and objects that lie buried in the earth. Some mysteries you will explore are Who Was the Queen of Sheba? Did Robin Hood Really Exist? and Did the Potato Change History? Each Mystery in History is identified with the symbol at right.

Atlas and Reference

An extensive Atlas and Reference Section begins on page 781. It includes the following:

Atlas. Twenty detailed political, physical, and historical maps are featured in the Atlas. There are also a List of Rulers throughout history and a selection of charts about historical subjects.

Facts About Countries. This eight-page section features a complete and updated list of the nations of the world with a flag and geographical data for each. Refer to this section to check a nation's capital, area, population, major languages, and important products.

Glossary/Biographical Dictionary. This section provides definitions and biographical information for each of the key terms and people listed in the text, along with the page on which they first appear.

Index. The Index provides general and specific references to help you locate text information quickly and easily. Each of the key places listed in the text can be found in the Index, along with its latitude and longitude.

WHAT IS HISTORY?

The following statements deal with the subject of history—what it is, what the historian does, and why history is valuable. Opinions about these matters vary, and in no sense do the authors of *History and Life* agree with them all. Indeed, it would be impossible to do so. Nevertheless, a sampling of opinions shows how history has been the object of speculation and controversy since people first begin to record their actions and thoughts. Some of the quoted passages date from ancient times, and others come from modern writers.

Definitions of History

It is somewhat unfortunate that the word history *should be used in several different senses. In its origin (Greek . . .) it meant learning by inquiry. The historian . . . was a searcher after knowledge, an investigator. But by a subtle transformation the term came to be applied to the record or narrative of what had been learned by investigation; and in this sense it passed over into the Latin* historia *and into modern speech. . . . Meantime another ambiguity . . . caused confusion in thought. The word* history *is used to denote not only the record of what has been learned by inquiry, but also the course of events themselves.*

Allen Johnson, *The Historian and Historical Evidence*, 1926

Human history is in essence a history of ideas. **H. G. Wells, *Outline of History*, 1920**

History is . . . the record of what one age finds worthy of note in another.

Jakob Burckhardt, 1818–1897, Swiss historian

My image of History would have . . . at least two persons, talking, arguing, always listening to the other as they gestured at their books; and it would be a film, not a still picture, so that you could see that sometimes they wept, sometimes they were astonished, sometimes they were knowing, and sometimes they laughed with delight.

Natalie Zemon Davis, American historian, 1988, on the complexity and multiple vision of history

History . . . is indeed little more than the register of crimes, follies, and misfortunes of mankind.

Edward Gibbon, *Decline and Fall of the Roman Empire*, 1776–1788

History is made out of the failures and heroism of each insignificant moment.

Franz Kafka, 1883–1924, Czech novelist

The history of all hitherto existing society is the history of class struggles.

Karl Marx and Friedrich Engels, *The Communist Manifesto*, 1848

The history of the world is the record of [people] in quest of . . . daily bread and butter.

Hendrik Van Loon, *The Story of Mankind*, 1921

History is the witness of the times, the light of truth, the life of memory, the teacher of life, the messenger of antiquity.

Marcus Tullius Cicero, 106–43 B.C., Roman statesman

The history of the world is but the biography of great men.

Thomas Carlyle, *Heroes and Hero-Worship*, 1841

The subject of history is the life of peoples and of humanity.

Count Leo Tolstoy, *War and Peace*, 1865–1872

The Role of the Historian

Historians ought to be precise, truthful, and quite unprejudiced, and neither interest or fear, hatred nor affection, should cause them to swerve from the path of truth, whose mother is history.

Miguel de Cervantes, *Don Quixote*, 1605–1615

History repeats itself, says the proverb, but that is precisely what it never really does. It is the historians (of a sort) who repeat themselves.

Clement F. Rogers, 1866–1949, British theologian

The whole past . . . consists of the infinite number of things which each person who ever lived has said, thought, and done. . . . Historians select a few of these thoughts, words, and deeds that seem to have general significance, and these become history as we ordinarily think of it. Because . . . ideas of what is significant change from time to time and because new knowledge frequently becomes available[,] history is constantly being rewritten.

Bernard Norling, *Towards a Better Understanding of History*, 1960

Faithfulness to the truth of history involves far more than a research, however patient and scrupulous, into special facts. Such facts may be detailed with the most minute exactness, and yet the narrative, taken as a whole, may be unmeaning or untrue. The narrator must seek to imbue himself with the life and spirit of the time. He must study events in their bearings near and remote; in the character, habits, and manners of those who took part in them. He must himself be, as it were, a sharer or a spectator of the action he describes.

Francis Parkman, *Pioneers of France in the New World*, 1865

The Uses of History

To enable [people] to understand the society of the past and to increase [their] mastery over the society of the present is the dual function of history.

Edward H. Carr, *What Is History?*, 1962

For policy making, history offers no blueprint, no specific solution to problems. One of its lessons is the folly of expecting such, for the essence of history is change. Still, history reveals much about human behavior; its possibilities and its limits, what may be expected under certain conditions, the danger signs to be considered, the aspirations to be taken into account, the scourges of pride and dogma, and the fruits of endurance and attention to detail.

Paul A. Gagnon, American historian, 1988

Our custom of taking records and preserving them is the main barrier that separates us from the scatter-brained races of monkey. For it is this extension of memory that permits us to draw upon experience and which allows us to establish a common pool of wisdom. . . . Knowledge of things said and

done . . . is a knowledge which not merely sees us through the trivial decisions of the moment, but also stands by in the far more important time of personal or public crisis.

Sherman Kent, *Writing History*, 1941

The study of history is said to enlarge and enlighten the mind. Why? Because . . . it gives it a power of judging of passing events, and of all events, and a conscious superiority over them, which before it did not possess.

John Henry Cardinal Newman, *On the Scope and Nature of University Education*, 1852

Study the past if you would divine the future.   **Confucius, Chinese philosopher, 500s B.C.**

Those who cannot remember the past are condemned to repeat it.

George Santayana, 1863–1952, American philosopher

I teach kings the history of their ancestors so that the lives of the ancients might serve them as an example, for the world is old, but the future springs from the past.

Djeli Mamoudou Kouyaté, an African griot (historian), 1950s

PART ONE

Civilizations Forming

3500 Sumerians move into Mesopotamia	3000 Corn is cultivated in Mexico

| 3500 B.C. | 3000 | 250 |

Sumerian plaque, from around 2600 B.C.

Prehistory—A.D. 500

Part One covers a vast sweep of time, from the appearance of the first human beings to about A.D. 500. The earliest civilization arose around 3500 B.C., and the great classical age civilizations of China, India, Greece, and Rome took shape between 1500 B.C. and A.D. 500. Most of the major world religions and philosophical traditions also came into existence during this period: Hinduism, Buddhism, Confucianism, Judaism, and Christianity. The one exception was Islam, which developed after A.D. 600. Today, the majority of the world's peoples live in cultures directly influenced by these classical civilizations and their religious and philosophical traditions.

A key characteristic of this period is that the early civilizations formed independently of one another. Although there was some contact between them, this was a time when the main cultural centers were generally isolated from each other. As you read through Part One, consider how the classical age civilizations differed from one another and what made each of them unique.

ARCTIC OCEAN

NORTH AMERICA

PACIFIC OCEAN

MAYA

MOCHE

SOUT AMERI

Classical Age Civilizations, to A.D. 500

Han China, 202 B.C.–A.D. 220

Gupta India, A.D. 320–500

Greece, 750 B.C.–150 B.C.

Roman Empire, 27 B.C.–A.D. 476

Kush, 900 B.C.–A.D. 350

Axum, A.D. 300–700

Maya, A.D. 300–900

Moche, A.D. 100–700

1700	1200	750	492	1	395
Shang dynasty emerges in China	Moses leads Jews out of Egypt	Kush begins to flourish	Age of Pericles begins in Greece	Jesus is born	Roman Empire splits into two parts

| 2000 | 1500 | 1000 | 500 | A.D. 1 | 500 |

Bronze ceremonial vessel, Shang dynasty China

Kushite nobles

Roman Colosseum, built around A.D. 80

ARCTIC OCEAN

EUROPE

ASIA

ROMAN EMPIRE

GREEK EMPIRE

HAN CHINA

GUPTA INDIA

ATLANTIC OCEAN

KUSH

AFRICA

AXUM

PACIFIC OCEAN

INDIAN OCEAN

AUSTRALIA

N

| 0 | 2000 Miles |
| 0 | 2000 Kilometers |

1

Civilization Begins

OVERVIEW

This unit covers the beginnings of life on earth, early civilizations, and Middle Eastern empires and religions before 500 B.C.

ADDITIONAL TEACHING AIDS FOR UNIT ONE

Literature for the Teacher

Aldred, Cyril. *Akhenaton: King of Egypt.* London: Thames & Hudson, 1988.

Cohen, Eugene N. and Edwin Eames. *Cultural Anthropology.* Glenview: Scott, Foresman and Co., 1982.

Cotterell, Arthur. *The Encyclopedia of Ancient Civilizations.* New York: Mayflower Books, 1980.

Fagan, Brian M. *People of the Earth: An Introduction to World Prehistory* (6th edition). Glenview: Scott, Foresman and Co., 1989.

Grant, Michael. *History of Ancient Israel.* New York: Charles Scribner's Sons, 1984.

Winstone, H. V. F. *Uncovering the Ancient World.* New York: Facts on File Publications, 1986.

Literature for the Student

Aldred, Cyril. *The Egyptians.* London: Thames & Hudson, 1984. (challenging)

Burgess, Robert. *Man: 12,000 Years Under the Sea.* New York: Dodd, Mead & Co., 1980. (easy)

Campbell, Bernard G. *Humankind Emerging.* Glenview: Scott, Foresman and Co., 1988. (challenging)

Cavendish, Richard. *Prehistoric England.* New York: British Heritage Press, 1983. (challenging)

Fagan, Brian M. *Archaeology: A Brief Introduction* (3rd edition). Glenview: Scott, Foresman and Co., 1988. (challenging)

Fagan, Brian M. *New Treasures of the Past.* New York: Quarto Publications, 1987. (average)

Romant, Bernard. *Life in Egypt in Ancient Times.* Minerva, 1978. (easy)

Romer, John. *People of the Nile: Everyday Life in Ancient Egypt.* New York: Crown Publishing, 1982. (easy)

Van Loon, Hendrik Willem. *The Story of Mankind.* Liveright Publishing Corp., 1972 (average)

Wedgewood, C. V. *The Spoils of Time.* New York: Doubleday, 1985. (challenging)

Whitten, Phillip, and David E. K. Hunter. *Anthropology: Contemporary Perspectives.* Glenview: Scott, Foresman and Co., 1987 (challenging)

Audio-Visual Materials*

Dr. Leakey and the Dawn of Man. Film, 26 minutes, color, [National Geographic Society], 1966. Reviews the fossil record of human development in Europe and Asia and documents the lifework of the Leakeys

The Making of Mankind. Film, 6 programs (2 reels each), 55 minutes, color, [Time-Life], 1981. "In the Beginning"—Richard Leakey gives an overview of prehistory. "One Small Step"—explores the significance of the oldest human footprints. "A Human Way of Life"—visits to one of the few hunter-gatherer groups still extant. "Beyond Africa"—speculates about the spread of humans from Africa. "A New Dawn"—reviews 1960 discovery of "missing-link" human skull. "Setting Dawn"—reviews problems

Stonehenge: Mystery in the Plain. Video, 24 minutes, color, [EB], 1980. Looks at the desolate beauty of Stonehenge and its myths and legends

Tut: The Boy King. Video or film, 50 minutes, color, [Films, Inc.], 1977. Orson Welles narrating an up-close view of the treasures of the tomb

* For a complete listing of sources of audio-visual materials see page T30.

OPTIONAL WRITING ASSIGNMENTS

1. You are a reporter for *New Stone Age* magazine. Your speciality is writing articles that are featured each month in your magazine. For the next issue, write an article explaining the changes that have taken place in the lives of people since the Old Stone Age.

2. You produce filmstrips for use in New Stone Age schools. Prepare a captioned filmstrip explaining and demonstrating some of the new tools available since the Old Stone Age. Your filmstrip should consist of at least nine frames:

Frame 1 - Title Frame
Frame 2 - Introduction (text only)
Frame 3 - Explanation of a tool (how it is made and used)

Frame 4 - Drawing of the tool
Frame 5 - Explanation
Frame 6 - Drawing
Frame 7 - Explanation
Frame 8 - Drawing
Frame 9 - Summary

3. Write a speech for delivery at your next tribal council meeting. In the speech you should try to convince the council members to abandon their nomadic lives and settle in one place.

4. You are an inventor attending a Bronze Age inventors' conference. Write a letter to a friend describing your invention and some of the other inventions that you saw at the conference.

5. You are a newspaper reporter for the *Mesopotamian Message*. Write an article on the new codes proposed by Hammurabi. Be sure to explain the codes and give your readers an understanding of ways the codes might impact their lives.

6. You are a visitor from Mars who has landed along the Nile River. Write a post card to a friend back on Mars explaining what you have seen during your short stay in this strange place.

7. You are taking a five-day boat trip up the Huang River in ancient China. Write an entry in your diary for each day of your trip describing what you have seen and learned.

UNIT TESTS
IN THE TEACHER'S RESOURCE FILE

Unit Test, pp. 17–18

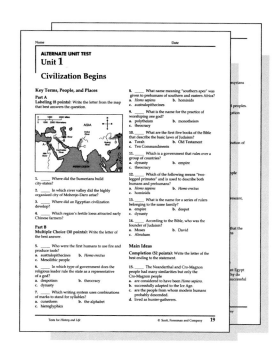

Alternate Unit Test, pp. 19–20

FINE ART IN UNIT ONE

Fine art forms an integral part of the historical record of events portrayed in this textbook. A listing of the paintings, drawings, sculpture, historic photographs, architecture, and other works of fine art selected to illustrate this unit follows. Students may be asked to research the artists and their works and report their findings to the entire class. Students also may be asked to write one or more paragraphs describing what they see upon a detailed study of a work of art and what the artist was attempting to communicate.

Civilization Begins

Themes and Patterns How did it all come about? Today we see and read about many nations and all kinds of people with different ways of life and different forms of government. How did people come to be this way? For an explanation, we must look at history—at the story of how people lived, what they did and said, how they solved their problems, and what ideas and customs they developed.

For the earliest people, life was difficult. They had to learn how to find food and shelter, protect themselves, and develop rules and customs that would make group living possible. The way in which various peoples have solved these basic problems is called their culture.

A great advance in human culture came when people began to farm, to establish governments and laws, to make metal tools, to build cities, and to write. This kind of culture is called civilization. The period before recorded history is said to be prehistoric because people did not have a record-keeping system.

Civilization first began in four river valleys, shown on the map on page 22. Along the shores of the Tigris-Euphrates [tī′gris yü frā′tēz] rivers in Southwest Asia and the Nile river in Africa, civilization began to develop as early as 3500 B.C. Between 2500 and 2000 B.C., civilization also developed in the Indus [in′dəs] River Valley in India and along the Huang [hwäng′] River in China.

Civilization also developed independently in various places in the Americas and Africa south of the Sahara after 2000 B.C. The early civilizations of North and South America and of sub-Saharan Africa will be discussed in Unit 2.

A photographer's light in the Lascaux cave reveals a painting made more than 20,000 years ago by a Cro-Magnon artist. This is one of the earliest paintings ever made, yet it reveals the skill of an accomplished artist.

Chapters in This Unit

3

Chapter

1 Early Humans

OVERVIEW

This chapter describes the development of
the first life forms, human advances during
the Stone Ages, and the cultural achievements that formed the basis of civilization.

PLANNING CHART

Section	Text Pages	Key Concept	Suggested Teaching Time
1 Life began on ancient Earth.	6–8	The formation of the earth and of the first living things took place over billions of years.	One day **More time?** Use *Overhead Transparency 1* and *Source Reading 1A*.
2 People developed basic skills in the Old Stone Age.	8–11	Early humans developed increasingly complex skills and tools for survival in harsh environments.	One day **Less time?** Use the material in Sections 2 and 3 to teach the major developments of each period of the Stone Ages in one lesson. **More time?** Use *Source Reading 1B*.
3 People made great advances in the Middle Stone Age and the New Stone Age.	11–14	People learned to make better use of natural resources, became food producers, and established communities.	One day
4 Important inventions appeared during the Bronze Age.	14–16	The use of metal tools and other inventions produced the surplus food supplies that made specialization of labor possible.	One day **More time?** Use *Overhead Transparency 2*.

ANCILLARIES

Materials that may be used with this chapter
to reinforce, reteach, enrich, and assess
learning are pictured on the following pages.

Teacher's Resource File

ACTIVITIES

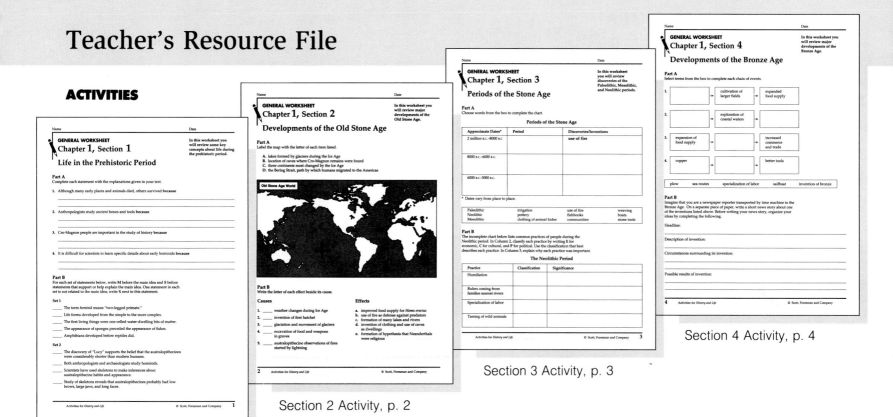

Section 1 Activity, p. 1

Section 2 Activity, p. 2

Section 3 Activity, p. 3

Section 4 Activity, p. 4

Chapter 1 Reteaching, p. 5

Chapter 1 Enrichment, p. 6

Teacher's Resource File

GEOGRAPHY SKILLS

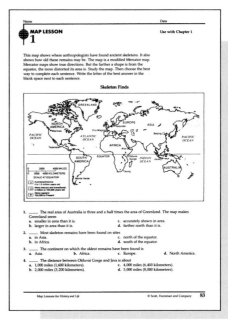

Chapter 1 Geography
Worksheet/Map, pp. 3–4

Chapter 1 Map Lesson, p. 83

TESTS

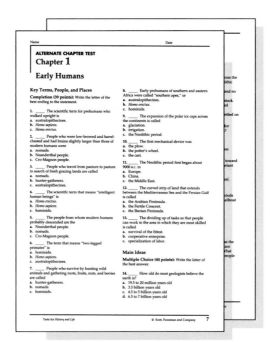

3c

Chapter Test, pp. 5–6

Alternate Chapter Test, pp. 7–8

Other Optional Ancillaries

WORKBOOK

Section 1 Worksheet, p. 1

Section 2 Worksheet, p. 2

Section 3 Worksheet, p. 3

Section 4 Worksheet, p. 4

SOURCE READINGS

Source Reading 1A
Source Reading 1B

TEST GENERATOR

40 multiple-choice questions for Chapter 1

OVERHEAD TRANSPARENCIES

Overhead Transparency 1
Overhead Transparency 2

1

Early Humans

Prehistory—3000 B.C.

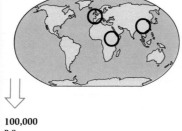

100,000 B.C.

c. 50,000 B.C. Modern humans begin to spread across the world

c. 9000 B.C. Agriculture begins in Middle East

c. 3500 B.C. Bronze metalworking begins in Middle East

2000 B.C.

1000 B.C.

One day in 1879, 12-year-old María de Sautuola and her father, Don Marcelino de Sautuola, were exploring the cave of Altamira on his estate in northern Spain. Suddenly Don Marcelino heard María cry out, "Toros! Toros!" (Bulls! Bulls!) He found her staring at the ceiling of the cavern. It was covered with huge bison, painted in red and black. They were drawn so dramatically that they seemed almost alive. Don Marcelino also found pictures of horses, deer, and wild boars. He was convinced that the pictures had been painted by primitive people many centuries earlier.

María's discovery made the cave of Altamira famous. However, the scientists of the time were skeptical. They thought that the pictures could not have been painted by primitive people because the paintings were so skillfully made. The scientists claimed that the paintings had been recently made and that the Spanish noble was trying to deceive people.

However, a few years later, in 1895, a French scholar reported the discovery of other prehistoric paintings on the walls of a cave in Lascaux [läs kō′], France. During the next two years, yet other cave paintings were discovered in France and Spain. By 1900 scientists generally accepted these examples of cave art as the work of prehistoric people. It is now believed that the cave paintings at Altamira are around 15,000 years old.

Since that first discovery at Altamira, scientists have developed many new techniques for studying the distant past. Using special equipment, teams of scientists analyze the remains and tools of early people to determine how they lived.

Some of these scientists are physical anthropologists. They study the physical remains of prehistoric peoples to try to determine how they looked and lived. Archaeologists specialize in the excavation and study of the artifacts, or objects, that remain from ancient sites. Through a variety of techniques, such as the analy-

4

A Cro-Magnon artist carved this ivory horse around 30,000 years ago from a mammoth tusk.

sis of animal bones, seeds, beads, and pieces of pottery, archaeologists form theories explaining what people ate, what tools they used, and with whom they traded. Another technique, called radiocarbon dating, helps these scientists learn when ancient people lived.

Physical anthropologists and archaeologists work with other specialists—such as chemists, botanists, physicists, and geologists—to reconstruct the past. Not surprisingly, there are many competing theories to describe the age of various sites, the kind of society various peoples lived in, and what these ancient peoples looked like. No one today knows, for example, why the prehistoric cave paintings were made—for religious reasons, perhaps, or to record certain events. This is only one of the many mysteries surrounding the story of human prehistory, mysteries that are only beginning to be solved.

Reading Preview

In this chapter you will learn about the beginnings of human history.

1. *Life began on ancient Earth.*
2. *People developed basic skills in the Old Stone Age.*
3. *People made great advances in the Middle Stone Age and the New Stone Age.*
4. *Important inventions appeared during the Bronze Age.*

1 Lesson Plan

Essential Learning Objectives

Students will learn to:

Do in Learning Log (handwritten)

- ✓ describe when and how the earth and its oceans were formed.
- ✓ list the stages in the development of living things.

1 FOCUS AND MOTIVATE

Draw a horizontal time line the entire length of the chalkboard. Ask students how long this line should be if one inch represented one year of the earth's age. (The line would circle the earth more than three times.)

2 TEACH

Divide the time line that you drew on the chalkboard into proportional sections with labels above the line as follows: FORMATION OF EARTH (4.5 to 5 billion years ago), FIRST LIFE FORMS (4 billion years ago), EARLY HOMINIDS (4 million to 100,000 years ago). Possible details under the first heading: flaming mass of gas and steam, cooling and hardening, clouds, rain, oceans. Under the second heading, make separate lists of water- and land-dwelling forms of life. Emphasize the increasing complexity of each type of life form. Details under the third heading should include australopithecines, *Homo erectus,* and *Homo sapiens.*

GUIDED PRACTICE

Tell students to make a chart that *(handwritten: Copy gruby)* gives the years, sites, skeletal evidence, and characteristics of each of the hominids listed above.

---

1 Life began on ancient Earth.

How old is the earth? How long have people lived on it? Scientists have studied these questions for many years. In the past few decades, astronomers, physicists, chemists, geologists, and other scientists have begun to gather information that may help answer these important questions.

The earth was formed about 5 billion years ago.

Most geologists now believe that the earth is approximately 4.5 to 5 billion years old. According to most scientific theories, the planet began as a glowing cloud of gas and dust that slowly formed into a ball of molten rock. Heavier materials such as iron sank to the center of the planet while lighter gases such as nitrogen and water vapor moved to the surface, forming the earth's atmosphere and oceans.

After hundreds of millions of years had passed, most of the planet was covered by deep oceans and shallow seas. It was in these oceans and seas that living things first appeared; and with them begins the story of life on earth.

Living things developed from simple to more complex forms.

Most scientists believe that the first living things—which existed about 4 billion years ago—were simple one-celled, water-dwelling plants and animals. These tiny bits of living matter had no bony structures. More advanced, multi-celled life forms then developed. Sponges, jellyfish, snails, crabs, and then fish appeared in the water.

All the earliest animal life forms lived in water. From them developed amphibians, which are frog-like creatures that could live on land as well as in the water. Later, reptiles such as snakes and lizards appeared, and after a long time, birds and more complex animals. Each of these stages of animal development took tens of millions of years.

To survive, these early life forms had to struggle against other living things and against changing environmental conditions. Many early plants and animals did not survive. Others became stronger as new generations adapted to meet changing condi-

---

tions on the earth. Some animals changed a great deal. For example, most scientists believe that millions of years ago horses were only about one foot high. They had four-toed front feet and three-toed hind feet. Today horses are from 5 to 6.5 feet high and have only one toe on each foot.

Skeletons give clues to the appearance of early humans.

There are many theories about the origin of human beings. However, most scientists believe that

(handwritten: In Log term)

Important History Terms

age a long or short span of time, often associated with a person or distinctive condition: *the Stone Age, the space age.*

B.C. and A.D. Western cultures use the Gregorian calendar, which dates events from the birth of Jesus. B.C. means "*before Christ,*" and A.D. means *anno domini,* which is Latin for "in the year of our Lord," and refers to the years after the birth of Jesus.

century a 100-year period. The A.D. 1900s are the 20th century A.D. The Chinese philosopher Confucius lived in the 500s B.C., which is the 6th century B.C.

civilization advanced stage of social development usually characterized by farming, a legal system, metal tools, cities, and writing.

culture the customs, techniques, and arts of a people or nation.

decade a 10-year period.

era a period in history; an age: *the Romantic era.*

generation the average span of time from the birth of children to the birth of their children; about 25 years. People who share experiences are often considered members of a "generation": *the revolutionary generation, the postwar generation.*

history the branch of knowledge that deals with the record and interpretation of past events.

millennium a 1,000-year period. The plural is "millennia."

period a long or short span of time; age; era: *the period of Ottoman rule, a period of economic growth.*

prehistory the period before recorded history

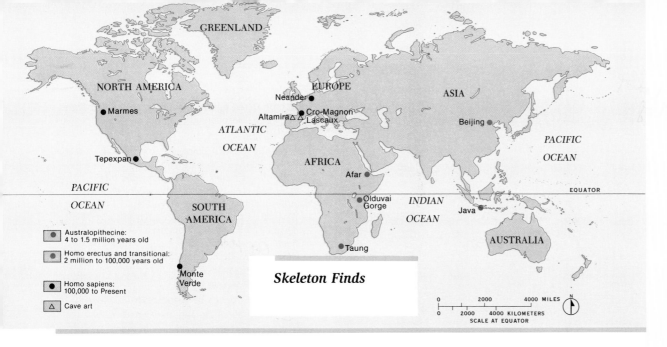

NORTH AMERICA
• Marmes
• Tepexpan

GREENLAND

EUROPE
Neander •
Altamira△ △ • Cro-Magnon
           Lascaux

ASIA
Beijing •

ATLANTIC
OCEAN

PACIFIC
OCEAN

PACIFIC
OCEAN

AFRICA
Afar •

EQUATOR

SOUTH
AMERICA

• Olduvai
  Gorge

INDIAN
OCEAN

Java •

AUSTRALIA

Monte
Verde

• Taung

Skeleton Finds

● Australopithecine:
  4 to 1.5 million years old

● Homo erectus and transitional:
  2 million to 100,000 years old

● Homo sapiens:
  100,000 to Present

△ Cave art

0   2000   4000 MILES
0   2000   4000 KILOMETERS
        SCALE AT EQUATOR

 MAP STUDY   This map shows important skeleton finds mentioned in Chapter 1 as well as three early finds from the Americas. On what continent were the australopithecine skeletons found?

Homo sapiens [hō′mō sā′pē enz], that is, human beings, came into existence about 100,000 years ago. Ancient skeletons suggest that other beings, similar to humans, lived nearly 4 million years before that time. Both humans and these prehuman creatures are called **hominids**, which means "two-legged primates."

The anthropologists who study these ancient bones have developed some ideas about what the prehumans may have looked like. They are also trying to learn about their diet and culture from the plant and animal remains and tools found with the skeletal remains.

Anthropologists have named these early prehumans **australopithecines** [ô′strə lō pith′ə sēns], which means "southern apes." Skeletal remains of hundreds of australopithecines have been found in eastern and southern Africa. Judging from remains such as teeth, skulls, and even footprints embedded in ancient mud, scientists believe that this small hominid had a low brow, a long face and large jaws, and walked upright. The oldest-known

australopithecine skeleton, discovered in Afar, Ethiopia, is that of a female, nicknamed Lucy. She was probably 3.5 feet tall and may have lived about 4 million years ago.

Living at the same time as some of the later australopithecines were larger creatures more like modern humans. Scientists call these creatures **Homo erectus** [hō′mō ə rek′təs]. The word *Homo*, from the Latin word for human being, is the scientific term for humans. The word *erectus* means that they walked upright. More than 5 feet tall, *Homo erectus* made use of fire and produced tools, including the first true hand-ax. The oldest-known *Homo erectus* fossil is the skull of a 2- or 3-year-old child. It was found on Java and is thought to be almost 2 million years old.

Human beings had larger brains than other hominids.

The use of stone tools came with an expansion in brain size. The average brain size of *Homo erectus* was 1,000 cubic centimeters, nearly twice that of

ANSWER TO MAP STUDY Africa

Answers to Section 1 Review

Identify

Key Terms, People, and Places are defined on pages indicated in parentheses. Also see the Glossary and Biographical Dictionary.
Homo sapiens (7), hominids (7), australopithecines (7), *Homo erectus* (7), Neanderthal people (8), Cro-Magnon people (8)

Main Ideas

1. Earth is 4.5 to 5 billion years old. First life was probably in the sea.
2. one-celled plants and animals; Animals became more complex and moved onto the land.
3. Remains show evidence of low brows, long faces, large deep jaws, upright posture. *Homo erectus* was taller, used fire, and produced tools.
4. Their brains were larger, their teeth smaller, and their legs longer and straighter.

Critical Thinking

The only remains from the distant past are physical remains, such as skeletons, stone tools, and footprints. There is little remaining evidence that indicates what prehumans and early humans looked like, what their family life was like, if they talked, and other such details.

Above are the remains of Lucy, the oldest-known australopithecine. She is believed to have lived around 4 million years ago.

the early australopithecines. Modern human brain size averages 1,350 cubic centimeters. The study of skeletal remains shows the changes that took place over hundreds of thousands of years. The brain became larger, the teeth became smaller, and the legs became longer and straighter.

Skeleton finds from the Neander Gorge in Germany and the Cro-Magnon [krō mag′nən] cave in France show these changes. Scientists labeled the skeletons first discovered at these sites *Homo sapiens*, which means "intelligent human beings." The people named after the places where these remains were found are called **Neanderthal people** [nē an′dər thôl] and **Cro-Magnon people**. They are considered the first true humans.

Both the Neanderthal people and the Cro-Magnon people seem to have lived about l00,000 years ago in Africa, Europe, and Asia. Although Neanderthal people are considered *Homo sapiens*, they differed in appearance from modern humans—they were barrel-chested and low browed, and their brains were slightly larger. Apparently Neanderthal people died out around 40,000 years ago, but nobody knows why. The Cro-Magnon people, from whom modern humans probably descend, became the main type of human being about this time.

Section 1 Review

Identify *Homo sapiens*, hominids, australopithecines, *Homo erectus*, Neanderthal people, Cro-Magnon people

Main Ideas

1. According to most geologists, how old is the earth? Where did the earliest life forms probably dwell?
2. Which living things probably appeared first on earth? What changes probably took place in the kinds of animals that live on earth?
3. What clues do bones and other remains give about the appearance of australopithecines? How did *Homo erectus* differ from the australopithecines?
4. How did Neanderthal and Cro-Magnon people differ from earlier people?

Critical Thinking

Evaluating Sources of Information: Why will specific details about the appearance and customs of early peoples probably always be a mystery?

---

2 People developed basic skills in the Old Stone Age.

Generally, the time from about 2 million B.C. to about 3000 B.C. is called the Stone Age because people of this time made many of their weapons and tools from stone. Almost all of this long period is also called "prehistoric" because writing was not invented until around 3000 B.C. Archaeologists divide the Stone Age into three broad periods, mainly according to the kinds of stone working done in each period. The earliest is called the Old Stone Age, or **Paleolithic period**. It lasted from about 2 million B.C. to about 8000 B.C. The Middle Stone Age, or **Mesolithic period**, lasted from about 8000 B.C. to about 6000 B.C. The New Stone Age, or **Neolithic period**, lasted from about 6000 B.C. to about 3000 B.C.

During these very long periods of time, humans developed and improved their ability to think. They were able to learn from experience and to devise new ways of doing things. Another important trait was their ability to talk—to exchange ideas with others. Such abilities have helped humans live in a variety of environments.

Homo erectus made tools and cooked with fire.

One of the first advances toward civilization was the development of crude tools and weapons. The prehumans called *Homo erectus* found ways to fashion rocks into useful sizes and shapes. For example, they made the fist hatchet by using one rock to chip another. With such weapons, *Homo erectus* could hunt animals larger than those that could be killed with bare hands alone, thus improving both their food supply and their defense against predators.

Most anthropologists believe that it took hundreds of thousands of years for prehumans to learn how to control the use of fire. Australopithecines probably knew of fire because they saw grass or trees burning where lightning struck. They may have picked up flaming sticks and used them to frighten off dangerous animals.

Eventually, prehumans probably learned to keep a fire burning by adding wood or leaves. They also learned to cover the fire with ashes at night so that there would be coals glowing in the morning to rekindle the flames. Many anthropologists believe that *Homo erectus* was the first prehuman to learn how to actually start a fire and to use it to cook.

Neanderthal and Cro-Magnon people adapted to the Ice Age.

During the last million years of the Old Stone Age, fire became very important in regions affected by the great continental ice sheets, or glaciers, that covered much of the Northern Hemisphere. During the **Ice Age**, the era between about 1.5 million B.C. and 8000 B.C., there were at least four long periods of **glaciation**, that is, four times when the polar ice caps gradually expanded across the continents.

Each of these glacial periods lasted around 40,000 to 60,000 years, and they were separated by interglacial periods (warm periods) that lasted some 40,000 years. During the glacial periods, massive sheets of ice, measuring two miles thick in some places, covered much of North America and Europe and parts of Asia. Refer to the map on page 10 to see the regions covered by ice.

As the glaciers moved across the landscape, they transported trillions of tons of stones and boulders that scraped and gouged the land like monstrous bulldozers. In North America, glaciers carved out what became the Great Lakes, and water from melting ice formed the Ohio and Missouri river valleys. About 50,000 years ago, the glaciers stopped moving; about 20,000 years ago, they began melting. The end of the Ice Age is usually considered to be about 10,000 years ago, that is, around 8000 B.C. However, some scientists think that the ice sheets will come again.

During the Ice Age, many people and animals died from exposure or starvation. Others moved to warmer regions or adapted to the cold. Some animals, such as the woolly mammoth and woolly rhinoceros, developed thick hides or coats of fur.

Neanderthal and Cro-Magnon people were also able to adapt. They lived in caves and wore animal skins to keep warm. To make such clothing, they had to invent new tools—stone knives for skinning and bone tools for scraping the flesh and fat from the inner side of animal skins.

Neanderthal people may have been the first to fasten handles to chipped stones to make crude knives and spears. They may also have been the first to develop religious beliefs. Remains of food and weapons found in graves suggest to many anthropologists that Neanderthal people may have believed in some kind of life after death.

Both Neanderthal and Cro-Magnon people lived entirely by hunting wild animals and gathering roots, berries, fruits, and nuts. People who live this way are called **hunter-gatherers**. In our time, a few remote groups in isolated parts of the world still live mainly as hunter-gatherers.

Cro-Magnon people developed fine tools, fitted clothing, art, music, and trade.

Late in the Ice Age, about 30,000 years ago, the Cro-Magnon people increased in numbers. They invented finer and more sophisticated tools than those of the Neanderthal people. For example, the Cro-Magnon people made spears with fine flint points and harpoons of reindeer horn and bone. To sew skins together, they developed bone needles, which they used to make fitted clothing.

The Cro-Magnon people were also artists. They carved figures of animals from horn and bone, molded statues in clay, and carved and painted the walls of caves. Anthropologists generally believe

< 8000 BC

2 Lesson Plan

Essential Learning Objective

Students will learn to describe how prehumans and humans learned skills and adapted to harsh conditions in the Stone Age.

1 FOCUS AND MOTIVATE

Ask what people do today to survive extreme temperature differences. (use machines to heat or cool environment, wear more or less clothing) Tell students that a million years ago the climate became much colder as an Ice Age began. Ask students how prehumans and humans might have adapted.

2 TEACH

- Draw a long horizontal time line on the chalkboard to illustrate the years of the Paleolithic period and the Ice Age. At correct intervals, add the names of the hominids that lived during those years. Allow students to direct the placement of the information.

- Discuss the methods used by *Homo erectus* and by Neanderthal and Cro-Magnon people in making stone tools and weapons. List all of the items used by Paleolithic hominids on the chalkboard. Emphasize the continual improvements made over time, pointing out the human traits that made these innovations possible. Stress also how the changing environment of the Ice Age influenced people to learn to adapt or migrate to survive.

GUIDED PRACTICE

Have students rank the abilities and skills developed by hominids from most important to least important, and to explain and defend their rankings.

1. How did early humans get food? (hunting and gathering)
2. How may *Homo sapiens* have migrated to the Americas? (across the Bering Strait)

OPTIONAL RETEACHING

Assign groups of students to draw or write descriptions of the types of tools and weapons used by Australopithecine, *Homo erectus,* Neanderthal, and Cro-Magnon hominids.

OPTIONAL ENRICHMENT

1. Have students prepare a written or oral report on the effects of the Ice Ages on areas of the United States. (average)
2. Have students research one of the sites where prehistoric cave paintings have been found. The report should include a description or sketches of the paintings, their age, and their location in the site. (challenging)
3. Also for enrichment:

 Source Reading 1B

INDEPENDENT PRACTICE/ HOMEWORK

Assign the Section Review, Activities page 2, or Workbook page 2.

CLOSURE

Tell students that during the years of the Old Stone Age or Paleolithic period, 2 million B.C. to 8,000 B.C., prehumans made crude fist hatchets and learned to use fire. Neanderthal and Cro-Magnon developed ways of surviving during the Ice Ages. Cro-Magnon, like modern humans, created art forms, traded with other groups, and lived in many areas of the world.

The Ice Age

MAP STUDY Between 2 million B.C. and 8000 B.C. there were four periods of glaciation. On which continents did the glaciers most expand? Which continents were not greatly covered by glaciers?

that this Cro-Magnon art was made for religious purposes. A 30,000-year-old bone flute discovered in France suggests that the Cro-Magnon people may have been the first to make musical instruments. They also began to trade with each other across long distances, and the items traded, such as beads and seashells, indicate that they probably decorated themselves with jewelry. This combination of inventiveness, artistic ability, and willingness to trade made them different from other early humans.

During the late Paleolithic period, perhaps 50,000 years ago, *Homo sapiens* began migrating to various parts of the world. The glaciers froze so much water that ocean levels fell. Two land bridges were exposed, one between Asia and Australia, the other between Asia and Alaska. By about 30,000 B.C. humans were able to travel to every continent except Antarctica.

This lively horse was painted on a wall in the cave of Altamira.

ANSWER TO MAP STUDY North America, Europe, Asia, Antarctica; South America, Africa, Australia

Section 2 Review

Identify Paleolithic period, Mesolithic period, Neolithic period, Ice Age, glaciation, hunter-gatherers

Main Ideas

l. What advances did *Homo erectus* make toward the development of civilization?

2. List three ways that Neanderthal and Cro-Magnon people adapted to the Ice Age.

3. What three traits made Cro-Magnon people different from Neanderthals and other early humans? When did modern humans begin migrating to various parts of the world?

Critical Thinking

Identifying Assumptions: Why do you think that anthropologists would consider the burial customs of Neanderthal people to be evidence that they had religious beliefs?

---

3 | People made great advances in the Middle Stone Age and the New Stone Age.

Toward the end of the Old Stone Age, the glacial ice receded to the north, and forests and grasslands grew in its place. About 8000 B.C. another stage in human progress toward civilization began—the Middle Stone Age, or Mesolithic period.

Mesolithic people invented pottery and fishing equipment and tamed wild dogs.

One very important Mesolithic advance was the first crude pottery. Pots made of sunbaked clay were used to store food. By about 7000 B.C., oven-fired clay bowls and jars were used to store water. Since many Mesolithic peoples lived along shores of water, fish and shellfish were their main foods. Mesolithic people invented the fishhook and many types of nets, and they learned to hollow out logs to make boats. They also invented the bow and arrow and made fine stone spearheads.

During Mesolithic times people tamed the wild dogs, such as jackals, that followed groups of humans. Dogs became valuable for hunting and for guarding property. They were probably the first animals to be domesticated, or tamed.

FROM THE ARCHIVES The Blanchard Bone is described in *The Roots of Civilization*, by Alexander Marshack (New York: McGraw-Hill, 1972), and in *National Geographic*, January, 1975. In interpreting the bone calendar, concentrate on the twisting

[margin handwritten note:] Some people now any like the

From the Archives

The Blanchard Bone

Archives are organized collections of records. In modern times, records are usually on paper or in the memory banks of computers. A different kind of record is pictured in the photograph at right. This ancient record is the Blanchard bone, found in a rock shelter in France. The bone may have been carved by a Cro-Magnon person 30,000 years ago to record the passage of time. If so, it is thus one of the earliest examples of humans' ability to measure time, create a record, and make symbols for that purpose.

Archaeologist Alexander Marshack decoded the markings on the bone. The drawing at right illustrates his theory that the notations stand for the waxing and waning of the moon over a period of two and a half months.

Neolithic people invented agriculture and improved their living conditions.

The Middle Stone Age gradually gave way to the New Stone Age, or Neolithic period, but at different times in different places. In the **Middle East**, for example, the Neolithic period began as early as 9000 B.C., but in Europe it did not begin until about 3000 B.C.

Farming and herding. During the Neolithic period, people found that seeds placed in the earth would grow into plants that would furnish both food and many more seeds. **Agriculture**—the deliberate cultivation of crops and the raising of live-

and turning of the line as a whole and disregard the shapes of individual marks. Full moons are represented by two looping turns toward the top; new moons are looping turns at the bottom.

Answers to Section 2 Review

Identify

Key Terms, People, and Places are defined on pages indicated in parentheses. Also see the Glossary and Biographical Dictionary. Paleolithic period (8), Mesolithic period (8), Neolithic period (8), Ice Age (9), glaciation (9), hunter-gatherers (9)

Main Ideas

1. *Homo erectus* made tools and weapons that increased food supply and used fire for cooking.

2. They lived in caves, wore animal skins, and invented new tools for skinning and scraping hides.

3. inventiveness, artistic ability, willingness to trade. Possibly modern humans began migrating around 50,000 years ago.

Critical Thinking

Anthropologists assume that burying food and weapons with the dead indicates that people believe in life after death, a form of religious belief.

---

3 | *Lesson Plan*

Essential Learning Objectives

Students will learn to:

• give examples of human progress during the Mesolithic and Neolithic periods.

• describe the importance of agriculture in the development of community cultures.

1 | FOCUS AND MOTIVATE

Ask students to share their ideas about how farming might have begun. Elicit the conditions that would have been necessary for the development of agriculture. (People might have observed sprouting seeds of foods that were already part of their diet. Fertile soil and plentiful rainfall or sources of water also were needed.)

2 TEACH

- List advances of the Mesolithic period, checking to be sure that students grasp the relationship between living near water and the inventions that took advantage of that resource.

- Point out that the Mesolithic period gave way to the Neolithic period at different times in different areas. List the Neolithic advances under these subheadings: Agriculture, Communities, and Textiles. Discuss how agriculture created communities, leading to government, law, and the development of a priesthood.

GUIDED PRACTICE

Ask students to suggest some new situations that would have required regulations in early farming communities. (water supplies, irrigation projects, storage and distribution of surplus crops, property lines, inheritance rights)

Stone Age Advances

The Stone Age was a time of major discoveries and inventions. Here is a list of the most important advances made during each broad period of the Stone Age.

Paleolithic
(c. 2 million B.C. to c. 8000 B.C.)

hunting, gathering, and
  fishing
use of tools and weapons
use of fire
language
clothing
religious beliefs
art and music
trade

This hand-axe was made by *Homo erectus* around 300,000 years ago.

---

stock—was thus developed in this period. Agriculture is one of the greatest inventions of all time. Human beings were now able to produce their food as well as find existing supplies.

Between 9000 B.C. and 6000 B.C., small farming villages sprang up in present-day Turkey, Iraq, Syria, Israel, and Jordan. (See map, page 794.) These are the oldest-known farming villages yet discovered in the world. The first crops were wheat and barley because those plants grew wild in this region and their seeds were easily gathered.

About the same time, Neolithic people learned to tame such wild animals as sheep, goats, pigs, and cattle so that they could have meat when they needed it. When herds and flocks of these domesticated animals ate most of the grass supply near a camping place, the people and animals moved to fresh grazing lands. This way of life is called nomadic, and the people who travel from pasture to pasture are called **nomads**. In some parts of Asia and Africa, people still follow this way of life.

Settled communities. With this new knowledge of raising plants and herding animals, human beings could produce their own food. They no longer had to depend on luck. People became less likely to starve, and the human population in-creased. People began living in larger, settled communities. With a reliable food supply, people could also turn their attention to other ways of improving their lives. For example, they greatly improved their material culture: they made their houses strong, their clothes comfortable, and their pottery beautiful. They also found time to practice **specialization of labor**, which means dividing up work so that those people most skilled in a particular task perform only that task, while others specialize in other jobs.

Weaving and other improvements. During the New Stone Age, people learned to spin and weave. The earliest-known woven fabrics are linen fabrics found in Egypt that date from about 5000 B.C. Linen is made from flax, a plant whose long stalk fibers are spun into thread and then woven into cloth. Other people learned to spin the fleece from sheep into yarn and weave it into woolen cloth. During this period people also learned to press and roll animal hairs together to make felt blankets.

During the Neolithic period, other important discoveries were made at an ever faster rate. Farming led to the invention of hoes and other stone tools for cultivating the soil. Milling stones were invented for grinding grain. Potters learned to make

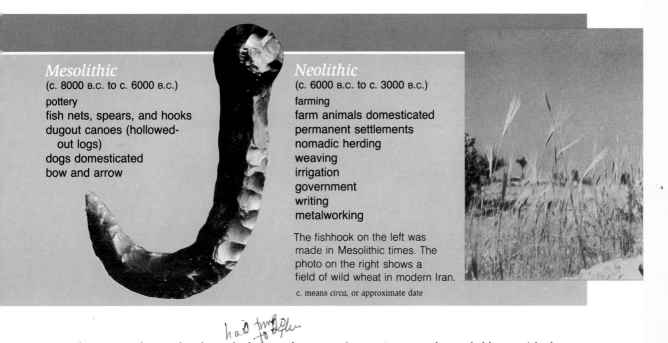

Mesolithic
(c. 8000 B.C. to c. 6000 B.C.)

pottery
fish nets, spears, and hooks
dugout canoes (hollowed-
out logs)
dogs domesticated
bow and arrow

Neolithic
(c. 6000 B.C. to c. 3000 B.C.)

farming
farm animals domesticated
permanent settlements
nomadic herding
weaving
irrigation
government
writing
metalworking

The fishhook on the left was
made in Mesolithic times. The
photo on the right shows a
field of wild wheat in modern Iran.

c. means *circa*, or approximate date

3 | ASSESS AND CLOSE

ASSESS

1. Name two ways in which New Stone Age people produced their own food. (by farming and herding)
2. Where did the Neolithic Revolution first take place? (Middle East)

OPTIONAL RETEACHING

Assign students to list items that might have been used by a group of Mesolithic people living along a seacoast. Have them add items that could have been added to their way of living during the Neolithic period.

OPTIONAL ENRICHMENT

Have students do research and indicate on a world map from the Geography Skills book the dates at which farming began in: the Middle East, Europe, India, China, and the Americas. The first food crops grown in each area could also be shown. (average)

INDEPENDENT PRACTICE/ HOMEWORK

Assign the Section Review, Activities page 3, or Workbook page 3.

CLOSURE

Tell students that humans have been struggling to gain control over their environments since before the Ice Age and that with the development of farming, people had formed the basis for civilization.

a wide variety of cups, bowls, and plates and to decorate them with multi-colored designs.

Neolithic people developed more complex governments and religions.

Far back into the Paleolithic period—no one knows just how far—people had learned to help each other in hunting, gathering, and caring for their families. Groups of families joined together for this purpose, forming simple communities.

When farming began in the Middle East, the early farmers established permanent settlements. Some farmers began to think of the land they farmed as belonging to them or their group, and to protect their fields and animals from intruders, they established villages and small towns. Perhaps the armed people who defended these towns also served as the local government.

In several of the more advanced food-producing regions, **irrigation**—supplying crops with water—was essential for agriculture. The local government was probably run by members of the families who lived closest to the river and controlled the water supply. An important member of such a family would become the ruler of a small city and the surrounding farmlands.

Stone Age people probably punished most wrongdoers by humiliating them. People living in small groups were dependent on each other for survival. Therefore, unpopularity was a severe form of punishment. However, even within small groups, some offenses, such as murder, were probably punished in more drastic ways. After the group decided that a person was guilty, the wrongdoer was executed or banished. As groups became larger, more offenses were punished formally.

Religion, too, became more elaborate as the size of groups increased. People turned to certain men and women in their group who seemed to be skilled at praying and understanding what others needed. These special persons often formed a priesthood. It was their job to pray and to try to prevent droughts, plagues, and other misfortunes.

The development of agriculture and other changes that came about in the Neolithic period were so important that some scholars refer to these changes as the Neolithic Revolution. That may be stretching the meaning of the word "revolution" too far because the changes took place over thousands of years. However, there is no doubt that the introduction of agriculture was the greatest single change in the history of humanity.

13

Identify
Key Terms, People, and Places are defined on pages indicated in parentheses. Also see the Glossary and Biographical Dictionary.
Middle East (11), agriculture (11), nomad (12), specialization of labor (12), irrigation (13)

Main Ideas
1. pottery; fishing equipment such as fishhooks, nets, and log boats; domestication of wild dogs
2. invention of farming and herding; settled villages with improved material culture; inventions such as weaving, hoes, milling stones
3. became more complex

Critical Thinking
The water supply needed regulation by officials. Dependable water for farms produced abundant food. The population grew and specialization of labor increased. Government and law became more elaborate.

leads to civ.

4 Lesson Plan

Essential Learning Objective
Students will learn to describe Bronze Age improvements in tools, farming, transportation, and pottery.

1 FOCUS AND MOTIVATE
Ask students to imagine life today without metals. Ask them to name items that would not exist.

2 TEACH
Make columns on the board titled: Farming, Transportation, Commerce. Have students identify the stages in the early development of each.

cov mays use paper

These elegant containers, found in present-day Israel, were made on a potter's wheel around 1700 B.C.

The invention of agriculture permanently altered the way people lived. Without the food produced by farmers, cities could not exist, and urban life as we know it would be impossible.

Section 3 Review

Identify Middle East, agriculture, nomad, specialization of labor, irrigation

Main Ideas
1. Name three important advances made during the Mesolithic period.
2. How did Neolithic people dramatically change the way they lived?
3. How did the Neolithic Revolution affect local government, laws, and religion?

Critical Thinking
Making Hypotheses: Why do you think that more complex governments first developed in areas that needed irrigation?

4 Important inventions appeared during the Bronze Age.

As long as people were dependent upon stone tools, they were limited in the kinds of work they could do because stone tools and weapons were easily broken. To make better tools, people needed a more durable material that could be molded into different sizes and shapes.

People learned to make metal tools and weapons.

Toward the end of the New Stone Age, people in the Middle East found that they could use copper found in the ground in an almost pure metallic state to make tools and weapons. At first, they hammered the copper to shape it, but they later learned that they could melt the copper and pour the liquid metal into molds. In this way they could make tools and weapons of any size or shape.

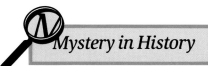

Mystery in History

WHY WAS STONEHENGE BUILT?

On a windswept plain in southern England stands a strange grouping of massive stone slabs called Stonehenge. Dating from about 2000 B.C., Stonehenge is the most famous monument of its kind. Similar megaliths, or large stone monuments, are found on continental Europe, Asia, and Africa.

Who raised the megaliths at Stonehenge? How did they raise them, and for what purpose? Archaeologists, studying the site, concluded that Neolithic and Bronze Age peoples built Stonehenge between 2000 and 1400 B.C. during three major periods of building and rebuilding. How they quarried the stones and put them in place is as yet unknown.

The photograph and diagram of Stonehenge show that huge stone slabs were placed in a circle, with a circle of smaller slabs inside. All the large, upright slabs forming the outer circle were once capped by horizontal slabs, or lintels. The circles enclose a horseshoe-shaped grouping of colossal stones, another horseshoe of smaller stones, and the Altar Stone, a 16-foot long block of sandstone that fell over in 1620. A rough stone called the Heel Stone is outside the photograph along the path at the upper right.

After careful study, scholars learned in the 1960s that 24 different alignments of the stones correlated either with a sunrise, a sunset, a moonrise, or a moonset. Was Stonehenge then an observatory, designed to mark the change of seasons or to predict eclipses? Or did the builders intend Stonehenge to be a religious temple? We may never know the answer to this mystery.

Standing ■
Missing ▭
Fallen ▨
Lintels ▭

Altar Stone

This aerial view of Stonehenge shows the circular arrangement of the megaliths.

Early metalworkers made another advance when they discovered that tin and copper, melted together in the right amounts, made a reddish-brown metal called **bronze.** Bronze was far superior to copper as a useful metal because it was easier to shape and gave a stronger and sharper cutting edge than copper alone. Because bronze was the chief metal in the Middle East for about 2,000 years, the period in which it was used there is called the Bronze Age. This age began in the Middle East about 3500 B.C. However, bronze was not known in China until about 1800 B.C., and in the Americas it was not invented until about A.D. 1100.

Progress was made in farming, transportation, and commerce.

Along with bronze tools came other inventions. One of these inventions was the plow drawn by animals. At first, farmers planted seeds in holes made with a digging stick. Then they learned to make a simple hoe that they pulled through the soil with a rope. The next step was to harness an animal, such as an ox, to an improved hoe, which in turn led to the development of the plow. The invention of the plow was a major advance because it enabled farmers to cultivate large fields instead of small plots.

Another important aid to farming was the development of better ways to control and use water for crops. In places where there was little rainfall, farmers learned to irrigate their fields by digging ditches that connected them to lakes and streams. They also learned to protect fields from floods.

One problem for early people was finding ways to transport heavy loads. Mesolithic people had used a crude sled. Later, an ox was used to pull the sled. Someone may have learned that a sled could be pulled more easily if poles or logs were put under it so that the sled moved forward as the logs rolled along the ground. Many experiments were probably made before people invented the wheel, which led to the development of carts.

Another important invention from this period that also improved transportation was the sailboat, which made it possible to move heavy loads by water. Bronze Age people began to explore the coastal waters of the Mediterranean Sea, developing sea routes that linked people in distant places.

Yet another important Bronze Age invention was the potter's wheel, the world's first mechanical device. The **potter's wheel** is a small, flat wheel that is set on top of a vertical axle. The potter throws a lump of wet clay onto the wheel and then, while turning the wheel, shapes the clay with his or her hands. The potter's wheel made possible the production of more pots of a more uniform shape and size than had been possible to make before.

All of these new discoveries called for specialized labor. Meanwhile, the expansion of the food supply made it possible for more workers to be freed from the job of producing food. No longer were all people hunters and gatherers, farmers, or herders. Some became potters, metalworkers, sailors, or tradespeople. Commerce and trade gradually increased as jobs became more specialized.

Middle Eastern people pioneered Bronze Age advances.

It was the people of the Middle East, especially those living in the **Fertile Crescent**—the curved strip of land that extends between the Persian Gulf and the Mediterranean Sea—who pioneered the most important technological advances of the Bronze Age. They had learned how to make and shape metals (a skill called metallurgy), how to use the wheel and the plow, how to harness oxen, and how to design sailing boats. Together these inventions and discoveries transformed the economies of the societies in the Fertile Crescent and made possible the rise of the first urban civilizations, about which you will read in Chapter 2.

Section 4 Review

Identify bronze, potter's wheel, Fertile Crescent
Main Ideas
1. In what ways was bronze better than copper for making tools and weapons?
2. What improvements in farming, transportation, and pottery making took place during the Bronze Age?
3. How did the Bronze Age inventions in the Middle East transform the economies of the people there?

Critical Thinking
Making Hypotheses: What effect do you think an invention like the sailboat might have on the cultures of people living near a navigable river or a harbor?

The First Farmers

Mathematics, astronomy, the calendar, writing, the growth of cities—in short, what we call civilization—came about when people learned how to grow crops and raise animals for food. Sometime around 9000 B.C., the first farmers, in different parts of the world, began to scratch the soil with simple tools and plant different kinds of seeds or roots.

The simple hand mill, or quern (bottom), was once used to grind grain in Iraq. The large stone that forms the lower part of the mill would have been too heavy to carry from one hunting camp to another. Stone Age farmers, however, could build permanent homes, such as the 6000 B.C. house in Iraq whose stone foundation is shown at the middle left.

Bone fossils of Neolithic pigs have been found at the same Iraqi site, evidence that pigs have provided humans with meat, lard, and hides for more than 8,000 years. Like sheep, goats, and cattle, pigs are hoofed animals. Such animals graze or browse for food and possess a strong herding instinct, thus making them easy to capture and domesticate.

Signs of a settled existence for early peoples include (top left) a pottery vessel in the shape of a pig, 5600 B.C.; (middle left) the foundation of an Iraqi farmhouse; (bottom) a quern and pestle, 7000 B.C.

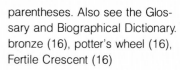 parentheses. Also see the Glossary and Biographical Dictionary. bronze (16), potter's wheel (16), Fertile Crescent (16)

Main Ideas

1. easier to shape, stronger and sharper cutting edge
2. invention of the plow, various irrigation techniques, the wheel, the sailboat, the potter's wheel
3. made possible the rise of the first urban civilizations

Critical Thinking

People could trade ideas and techniques across long distances, helping spread knowledge about new inventions like the plow, the wheel, and the potter's wheel.

CW spread by trade, war

HIGHLIGHTS OF CIVILIZATION

The rise and spread of agriculture around the world are the subject of *The First Farmers*, by Jonathan Norton Leonard (New York: Time-Life Books, 1973).

Ask students why pottery and bread making are signs of a change from a hunting and gathering life to a more settled existence. (Pottery would be likely to break with constant moving, so hunters and gatherers often use woven baskets or wooden bowls. Making bread also involves spending time in one place.)

Point out to students that both a mill and a beehive-shaped oven are shown in the foundation of the Iraqi farmhouse. The circular object beneath the pottery pig is probably a stone found at the site. Because of its potential usefulness as a grinding stone, the house was built nearby. The circular object at the upper right-hand corner of the photograph is the remains of a beehive-shaped oven.

Answers to Test Yourself

Key Terms, People, and Places
The key terms, people, and places tested here were introduced in the chapter sections and reviewed in the Section Reviews. For definitions see the page references at the appropriate Section Reviews. Also see the Glossary and Biographical Dictionary.

Main Ideas
The main ideas tested here were introduced in the sections of this chapter and reviewed in the Section Reviews. For answers to these questions, see the appropriate Section Reviews.

Critical Thinking
1. The development of agriculture, a transportation system, crafts, and organized government all contributed to the rise of cities.
2. Adaptation to cold led to the use of fire and clothing. Living near water led to improved fishing and sailing. Warmer weather and fertile soil encouraged farming and the development of pottery.

CHAPTER 1 REVIEW

Section Summaries

Section 1
Life began on ancient Earth.
According to many geologists, the earth was formed about 4.5 to 5 billion years ago from a cloud of gas and dust. Seas and oceans formed, and gradually early forms of life appeared in them. Most scientists believe that modern *Homo sapiens* came quite late in the long span of the development of life on earth.

Section 2
People developed basic skills in the Old Stone Age.
From studies of bones, tools, and other remains, physical anthropologists and archaeologists suggest that during the Old Stone Age, which lasted from about 2 million B.C. to about 8000 B.C., prehumans learned to make stone tools and to use fire. An early type of human being, the Neanderthal people, wore skins to keep warm and may have had religious beliefs. The first modern humans, the Cro-Magnon people, made major advances in tools, developed art and music, and traded across long distances.

Section 3
People made great advances in the Middle Stone Age and the New Stone Age.
The Middle Stone Age began at the end of the Ice Age, about 8000 B.C. During this period people made the first pottery; invented fishhooks, nets, and other fishing equipment; and tamed wild dogs. In the New Stone Age, which began about 6000 B.C., people learned to farm and herd, to build settled communities, and to spin and weave. They established villages and towns for protection, developed governments and laws, and introduced more elaborate forms of religion.

Section 4
Important inventions appeared during the Bronze Age.
During the Bronze Age, which began in the Middle East around 3500 B.C., people made bronze tools. They also invented the plow, the wheel, the sailboat, and the potter's wheel; improved irrigation techniques; and developed trade and commerce. These inventions transformed society in the Middle East and led to the rise of urban civilizations.

Test Yourself

Key Terms, People, and Places
Identify the significance of each of the following:
Section 1

a. *Homo sapiens*	**d.** *Homo erectus*
b. hominids	**e.** Neanderthal people
c. australopithecines	**f.** Cro-Magnon people

Review Dates

c. 50,000 B.C.
Modern humans begin to spread across the world

c. 9000 B.C.
Agriculture Begins in Middle East

c. 6000 B.C.
Neolithic period begins

c. 5000 B.C.
Earliest known woven fabrics found in Egypt

c. 3500 B.C.
Bronze metalworking begins in Middle East

| 10,000 B.C. | 5000 B.C. | A.D 1 | | |

Answers to Chapter Skills and Activities

Practicing Study and Research Skills
1. Paleolithic, b,d,e,f; Mesolithic, c,h,j; Neolithic, g; Bronze Age, a,i

Linking Past and Present
Some possible answers: People lived in caves and constructed skin clothes. Today people might build specialized homes, design clothing similar to that of astronauts, and grow food indoors.

Learning History Through Maps
Answers: United States, Mexico, Chile, West Germany, Tanzania, China, and Indonesia

Section 2
a. Paleolithic period   **d.** Ice Age
b. Mesolithic period   **e.** glaciation
c. Neolithic period   **f.** hunter-gatherers

Section 3
a. Middle East   **d.** specialization of labor
b. agriculture   **e.** irrigation
c. nomads

Section 4
a. bronze   **c.** Fertile Crescent
b. potter's wheel

Main Ideas
Section 1
1. According to most geologists when was the earth formed? Where did the earliest forms of life live?
2. What were the first living things to exist on earth? In what ways did the animals change over time?
3. How do scientists think australopithecines looked? In what ways did *Homo erectus* differ from the australopithecines?
4. How were Neanderthal and Cro-Magnon people different from earlier people?

Section 2
1. In what ways did *Homo erectus* advance toward the development of civilization?
2. How did the Neanderthal and Cro-Magnon people adapt to the Ice Age?
3. How did Cro-Magnon people differ from Neanderthals and other early humans? When did modern humans begin migrating to various parts of the world?

Section 3
1. Which important advances were made during the Mesolithic period?
2. What changes did the Neolithic people make in the way they lived?
3. Why did the Neolithic people develop more complex government, laws, and religions?

Section 4
1. What were the advantages of using bronze rather than copper for making tools and weapons?
2. How did farming, transportation, and pottery making improve during the Bronze Age?

3. How was the economy of the people in the Middle East transformed by the Bronze Age inventions?

Critical Thinking
1. Assessing Cause and Effect How did changes during the Bronze Age lead to the rise of cities?
2. Making Hypotheses How did environmental conditions lead to the inventions that early humans made during the Ice Age, and the Mesolithic, Neolithic and Bronze ages?

Chapter Skills and Activities

Practicing Study and Research Skills
Making a Time Line
Time lines show you the chronology of events so that you can see what happened in relation to other events. Make a time line placing the tool, weapon, or development in the correct period: Paleolithic, Mesolithic, Neolithic, or Bronze Age.
a. developed the potter's wheel
b. made first hatchet
c. invented the fishhook
d. used fire
e. developed religious beliefs
f. sewed skins to make fitted clothing
g. developed agriculture
h. used bow and arrow
i. used a plow drawn by animals
j. tamed dogs

Linking Past and Present
The Ice Age caused many changes in the lives of early humans. Some scientists think that today we live in an interglacial period and that the ice sheets will come again. What changes were caused by the Ice Age? What changes do you think would happen if it occurred again?

Learning History Through Maps
Use the map on page 7 called Skeleton Finds. Compare the places labeled Marmes, Tepexpan, Monte Verde, Neander, Olduvai Gorge, Beijing, and Java to the World Political map on page 782–783. What are the modern names of the countries where these places are located?

CRITICAL THINKING QUESTION LEVEL 1. easy; 2. challenging

2 The First Civilizations

OVERVIEW

This chapter tells how civilization began by tracing its development in four river valley cultures of the Middle East and Asia.

PLANNING CHART

Section	Text Pages	Key Concept	Suggested Teaching Time
1 The oldest civilization began in Mesopotamia.	22–26	Climate and geography challenged the peoples of Mesopotamia to create the first civilization.	One day **More time?** Use *Overhead Transparency 3* or *Source Reading 2A.*
2 An Egyptian civilization arose along the Nile River.	26–34	Egypt built the world's longest-lasting civilization with skills and talents developed through farming and trade.	Two days **More time?** Use *Overhead Transparency 4* or *Source Reading 2B.*
3 An ancient city revealed the early Indus Valley civilization.	34–36	The Indus Valley civilization enjoyed economic prosperity until environmental changes and mysterious attackers brought it to an end.	One day **Less time?** Combine the lesson on Mesopotamia with the material on the Indus Valley by emphasizing the trading relationships between the two cultures.
4 Chinese civilization developed along the Huang River.	37–38	Chinese culture originated in the advances made by the scholars and artisans of the Huang River Valley.	One day

ANCILLARIES

Materials that may be used with this chapter to reinforce, reteach, enrich, and assess learning are pictured on the following pages.

Teacher's Resource File

ACTIVITIES

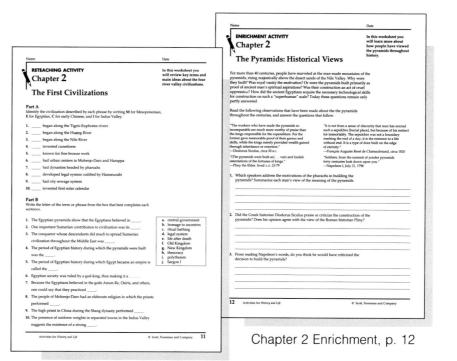

Section 1 Activity, p. 7

Section 2 Activity, p. 8

Section 3 Activity, p. 9

Section 4 Activity, p. 10

Chapter 2 Reteaching, p. 11

Chapter 2 Enrichment, p. 12

Teacher's Resource File

GEOGRAPHY SKILLS

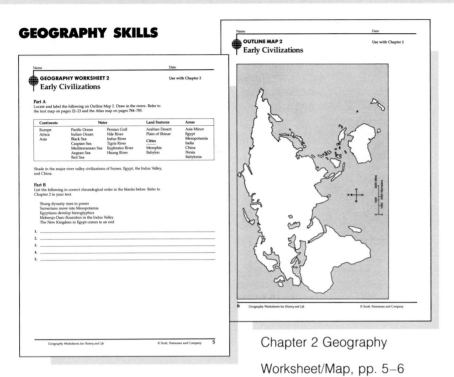

Part A
Locate and label the following on Outline Map 2. Draw in the rivers. Refer to text map on pages 22–23 and the Atlas map on pages 784–785.

Continents	Water		Land Features	Areas
Europe	Pacific Ocean	Persian Gulf	Arabian Desert	Asia Minor
Africa	Indian Ocean	Nile River	Plain of Shinar	Egypt
Asia	Black Sea	Indus River		Mesopotamia
	Caspian Sea	Tigris River	**Cities**	India
	Mediterranean Sea	Euphrates River	Memphis	China
	Aegean Sea	Huang River	Babylon	Persia
	Red Sea			Babylonia

Shade in the major river valley civilizations of Sumer, Egypt, the Indus Valley, and China.

Part B
List the following in correct chronological order in the blanks below. Refer to Chapter 2 in your text.

Shang dynasty rises to power
Sumerians move into Mesopotamia
Egyptians develop hieroglyphics
Mohenjo-Daro flourishes in the Indus Valley
The New Kingdom in Egypt comes to an end

1. _____
2. _____
3. _____
4. _____
5. _____

Geography Worksheets for History and Life   © Scott, Foresman and Company   5

---

6   Geography Worksheets for History and Life   © Scott, Foresman and Company

Chapter 2 Geography Worksheet/Map, pp. 5–6

The first civilizations in the world developed along great river systems where the soil was fertile and water was available for irrigation. Study the map. Choose the best answer to each question. Write its letter on the line.

Early Civilizations

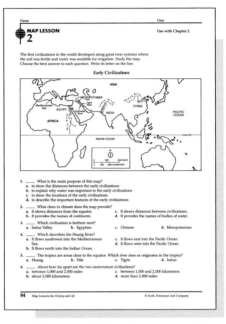

1. _____ What is the main purpose of this map?
   a. to show the distances between the early civilizations
   b. to explain why water was important to the early civilizations
   c. to show the locations of the early civilizations
   d. to describe the important features of the early civilizations

2. _____ What clues to climate does the map provide?
   a. It shows distances from the equator.   c. It shows distances between civilizations.
   b. It provides the names of continents.   d. It provides the names of bodies of water.

3. _____ Which civilization is farthest west?
   a. Indus Valley   b. Egyptian   c. Chinese   d. Mesopotamian

4. _____ Which describes the Huang River?
   a. It flows southwest into the Mediterranean Sea.   c. It flows east into the Pacific Ocean.
   b. It flows north into the Indian Ocean.   d. It flows west into the Pacific Ocean.

5. _____ The tropics are areas close to the equator. Which river rises or originates in the tropics?
   a. Huang   b. Nile   c. Tigris   d. Indus

6. _____ About how far apart are the two easternmost civilizations?
   a. between 1,000 and 2,000 miles   c. between 1,000 and 2,000 kilometers
   b. about 2,000 kilometers   d. more than 2,000 miles

84   Map Lessons for History and Life   © Scott, Foresman and Company

Chapter 2 Map Lesson, p. 84

TESTS

Key Terms, People, and Places

Part A
Matching (22 points): Write the letter of the key term from the box that best fits the definition.

1. _____ a government in which the religious leader rules the state as a representative of a god
2. _____ kind of writing invented by the Sumerians
3. _____ the practice of worshiping many gods and goddesses
4. _____ a government that rules over a group of countries
5. _____ the worship of one god
6. _____ a small country consisting of a city and the surrounding territories depending on it
7. _____ a temple in the form of a massive, stepped tower
8. _____ a series of rulers belonging to the same family
9. _____ an Egyptian ruler
10. _____ a form of picture writing developed by the Egyptians
11. _____ fine, rich soil formed from deposits of dust

a. city-state	g. theocracy
b. ziggurat	h. polytheism
c. cuneiform	i. monotheism
d. dynasty	j. hieroglyphics
e. pharaoh	k. loess
f. empire	

Part B
Yes/No (18 points): Write Y if the key person or place is used correctly. Write N if it is not.

12. _____ **Hammurabi** was a ruler of China who is remembered for a written code of laws.
13. _____ **King Menes** united Upper Egypt and Lower Egypt, forming the world's first national government.

14. _____ **Mesopotamia** was the western portion of the Fertile Crescent.
15. _____ Civilization emerged along the Nile River in Egypt.
16. _____ The **Indus Valley**, in what is now Pakistan and western India, had a highly organized way of life 4,500 years ago.
17. _____ In **China** early civilization developed along the Huang River.

Main Ideas

Multiple Choice (48 points): Write the letter of the best answer.

18. _____ How did the Sumerians organize their society?
   a. They divided the region into independent city-states.
   b. They chose a royal family and built a dynasty.
   c. They established the world's first national government.
   d. They created an empire and gave the ruling power to the priests.

19. _____ What did the Sumerians NOT invent?
   a. the arch   b. the plow
   c. the solar calendar   d. writing

20. _____ Why did Sumerian civilization last for thousands of years?
   a. Natural barriers kept Mesopotamia isolated.
   b. Conquerors took on and adapted Sumerian ways.
   c. The military defeated all enemies.
   d. A strong Sumerian dynasty united the nation.

21. _____ For what do scholars now credit Hammurabi?
   a. enforcing laws that punished all people equally
   b. creating the first written code of laws
   c. modifying a written code of laws developed by the Sumerians
   d. forming the first national government

Tests for History and Life   © Scott, Foresman and Company   9

Chapter Test, pp. 9–10

Key Terms, People, and Places

Part A
Yes/No (22 points): Write Y if the key term is used correctly. Write N if it is not.

1. _____ A government in which a religious leader rules as a god's representative is a **theocracy**.
2. _____ **Cuneiform** was a kind of writing invented by the Sumerians.
3. _____ The worship of one god is called **polytheism**.
4. _____ An **empire** is a government that rules over a complete continent.
5. _____ The practice of worshiping many gods and goddesses is called **monotheism**.
6. _____ A **city-state** was a small country consisting of a city and the surrounding territories depending on it.
7. _____ A **ziggurat** was a type of pyramid.
8. _____ A **dynasty** is made up of a series of unrelated rulers.
9. _____ An Egyptian ruler was a **pharaoh**.
10. _____ **Hieroglyphics** is the name given to the earliest form of cuneiform.
11. _____ The **loess** found in China is a fine, rich soil formed from deposits of dust blown from Central Asia during the Ice Age.

Part B
Matching (18 points): Refer to the box in the next column. Write the letter of the key person or place that best fits the definition.

12. _____ the ruler of Babylonia who is remembered for a written code of laws
13. _____ the Egyptian ruler who united Upper Egypt and Lower Egypt, forming the world's first national government
14. _____ the eastern portion of the Fertile Crescent; the "land between the rivers"

15. _____ the country where the Nile River valley civilization developed
16. _____ the area of what is now Pakistan and western India that had a highly organized way of life 4,500 years ago
17. _____ the country where civilization grew up along the Huang River

a. Hammurabi	d. Egypt
b. Indus Valley	e. King Menes
c. Mesopotamia	f. China

Main Ideas

Completion (48 points): Write the letter of the best ending to the statement.

18. _____ In southern Mesopotamia, the Sumerians organized their society by
   a. dividing the region into independent city-states.
   b. choosing a royal family and building a dynasty.
   c. establishing the world's first national government.
   d. creating an empire and giving the ruling power to the priests.

19. _____ The Sumerians did NOT invent
   a. writing.
   b. the plow.
   c. the arch.
   d. the solar calendar.

20. _____ Sumerian civilization lasted for thousands of years because
   a. conquerors took on and adapted Sumerian ways.
   b. natural barriers kept Mesopotamia isolated.
   c. a strong military defeated all enemies.
   d. a strong dynasty united the nation.

21. _____ Scholars now credit Hammurabi with
   a. creating the first written code of laws.
   b. modifying the Sumerian written code of laws.
   c. enforcing laws that punished all people equally.
   d. forming the first national government.

Tests for History and Life   © Scott, Foresman and Company   11

Alternate Chapter Test, pp. 11–12

Other Optional Ancillaries

WORKBOOK

Name _____ Date _____

WORKSHEET
Chapter 2, Section 1

In this worksheet you will review some aspects of Mesopotamian civilization.

Civilization of the Mesopotamians

Part A
Only three of the four items in each group are related in some way. Circle the item that does not belong and explain how the remaining three items are related.

1. Tigris and Euphrates rivers   plain of Shinar   Hammurabi   Mesopotamia

2. stylus   cuneiform   wedge   arch

3. ziggurat   city-state   tower   irrigation

4. plow   arch   calendar   wheeled vehicles

5. Sargon 1   Hammurabi   legal code   harsh punishments

Part B
Imagine that Hammurabi had buried a time capsule to give future generations a clear picture of the way his people lived. What things might he have included in his time capsule?

Worksheets for History and Life   © Scott, Foresman and Company   **5**

Section 1 Worksheet, p. 5

Name _____ Date _____

WORKSHEET
Chapter 2, Section 2

In this worksheet you will review important developments in Egyptian history.

The Early Egyptians

Part A
Number the events in the order in which they happened.

___ The last Egyptian dynasty was overthrown by the Greeks.
___ Egypt reached the height of its power under Thutmose III.
___ The world's first solar calendar was invented.
___ The Hyksos invaded and conquered Egypt.
___ King Menes united Upper and Lower Egypt.
___ The restoration of Egyptian rule began the New Kingdom.

Part B
Complete each statement with explanations given in your text.

1. The development of irrigation by Egyptian farmers may be regarded as an early form of local government **because**

2. Egypt was well protected from invasion **because**

3. Despite the humiliation of Hyksos rule, the Egyptians benefited in some ways from the invaders **because**

4. The Nile flood was a welcome event to the Egyptians **because**

5. Throughout much of Egyptian history, the pharaohs had absolute power over their subjects **because**

6. Egyptian priests succeeded in persuading Egyptians to return to polytheism after Akhenaton's death **because**

6   Worksheets for History and Life   © Scott, Foresman and Company

Section 2 Worksheet, p. 6

Name _____ Date _____

WORKSHEET
Chapter 2, Section 3

In this worksheet you will review the Indus Valley civilization.

The Indus Valley Civilization

Part A
Write C next to each phrase that correctly completes the unfinished sentence. (Each incomplete sentence may have more than one correct ending.)

1. People of the Indus Valley developed a complex civilization that
   ___ had well-planned cities.
   ___ covered an area of about 1,000 miles
   ___ had a uniform administration over several towns.
   ___ had the world's first solar calendar.
   ___ had a standardized system of weights.

2. The economy of the Indus Valley was
   ___ based on farming and trade.
   ___ highly productive, as evidenced by the size of the uniform weights for grain.
   ___ enriched by trade with Sumerians, Babylonians, and Mesopotamians.
   ___ based on cattle as a symbol of wealth.

3. The Indus Valley civilization slowly declined as
   ___ Mohenjo-Daro was repeatedly overrun by mud.
   ___ constant rebuilding reduced the will and energy of the people.
   ___ trade with other civilizations was ordered to stop.
   ___ an unknown disaster struck about 1500 B.C.

Part B
On a separate piece of paper, write a letter that an archaeologist might have written to a friend shortly after the discovery of Mohenjo-Daro. Your letter should show the significance of at least four findings. Before writing your letter, fill out the chart below to help organize your ideas.

Finding   Significance

Worksheets for History and Life   © Scott, Foresman and Company   **7**

Section 3 Worksheet, p. 7

Name _____ Date _____

WORKSHEET
Chapter 2, Section 4

In this worksheet you will review the Chinese civilization that developed along the Huang River.

Early China

Part A
For each set of statements below, write M before the main idea and S before statements that support or help explain the main idea. One statement in each set is not related to the main idea; write X next to this statement.

Set 1
___ According to legend, Yu fought a mighty river to save his people from floods.
___ Loess is a fine, rich soil.
___ Ban Ku used a hammer and chisel to make the universe.
___ The Chinese have many myths and legends about ancient times.

Set 2
___ The Chang River is also known as the Yangtze.
___ Geography influenced early Chinese civilization.
___ The Huang River, called "China's Sorrow," brought life as well as destruction to its valley.
___ The fertile Huang River plains provided productive farming, including the growing of millet.

Set 3
___ Although nobles controlled the distant parts of the kingdom, the Shang king was a powerful leader.
___ In addition to being the military leader, the Shang king was the high priest.
___ The Chinese during the Shang dynasty had a polytheistic religion.
___ The people believed the king governed by the command of heaven.

Part B
Write the letter of the term or name from the box next to its definition or identifying phrase.

1. ___ oldest collection of Chinese poetry
2. ___ best known product of Shang artisans
3. ___ used to foretell the future
4. ___ main economic activity of Chinese during the Shang period
5. ___ river along which early Chinese first grew millet
6. ___ artificial pools for cultivation of rice
7. ___ river along which early Chinese first grew rice
8. ___ skill advanced by Chinese women

a. paddies
b. Book of Odes
c. Chang
d. bronze work
e. bones and shells
f. silkworm cultivation
g. farming
h. Huang

8   Worksheets for History and Life   © Scott, Foresman and Company

Section 4 Worksheet, p. 8

SOURCE READINGS

Source Reading 2A
Source Reading 2B

TEST GENERATOR

40 multiple-choice questions for Chapter 2

OVERHEAD TRANSPARENCIES

Overhead Transparency 3
Overhead Transparency 4

Chapter

2

The First Civilizations

3500 B.C.–1600 B.C.

4000 B.C.	
3500 B.C.	Sumerians move into Mesopotamia
3100 B.C.	Upper and Lower Egypt are united
2500 B.C.	Urban life in Indus Valley begins
1700 B.C.	Shang dynasty emerges in China
1000 B.C.	
A.D. 1	

The world's first civilizations developed along four great river systems where the soil was fertile and water was easily available for irrigation. The map on pages 22–23 shows the four river valleys where these favorable conditions existed: the Tigris-Euphrates in Mesopotamia, the Nile in Egypt, the Indus in India, and the Huang in China. However, civilization did not begin simultaneously in these four regions. Archaeological evidence reveals that the world's oldest civilization—that of Sumer—began in Mesopotamia about 3500 B.C. In Egypt civilization emerged around 3100 B.C., in India around 2500 B.C., and in China around 1700 B.C.

In the Americas civilization developed independently on a coastal plain several hundred years later. There the earliest civilization, the Olmec, first emerged in Mexico around 1200 B.C.

In the early river valley civilizations of Mesopotamia and Egypt, the rivers were so important to the lives of the people who lived along them that they were worshiped as gods.

Every September the Nile flooded, bringing huge amounts of water for irrigation. As the flood waters gradually receded, the fields along the Nile were enriched with layers of mud and silt that provided a fertile soil for growing bountiful crops. These conditions were the same for thousands of years.

Along the Tigris-Euphrates, the Nile, the Indus, and the Huang, abundant harvests encouraged the population to grow. Not everyone had to work at getting food; some people were free to spend their lives in other kinds of work. As a result, over thousands of years these river valley peoples gradually developed what we call civilization.

As you learned in Chapter 1, civilization is the advanced stage of human society in which people have cities and organized governments. There is a specialization of labor with a variety of occupations. Some people are farmers, but others are weavers, pot-

These statues were found in the ruins of Sumerian temples. Made around 2500 B.C., they were probably given to a god or goddess as part of a prayer or religious ceremony.

ters, bakers, merchants, soldiers, and so on. Civilizations also usually have a system of writing and counting, developed at first in order to keep records of property. Another important feature of a civilization is the building of large structures, such as temples, palaces, and city walls. The first two civilizations—that of Sumer and of Egypt—developed near each other in the Middle East. They were in contact with each other and influenced each other's development in various ways. Somewhat later, complex societies developed independently in India and China, giving rise to unique civilizations there. The rise of these four early civilizations will be discussed in Chapter 2.

Reading Preview

In this chapter you will read about the world's four oldest civilizations.

1. *The oldest civilization began in Mesopotamia.*
2. *An Egyptian civilization arose along the Nile River.*
3. *An ancient city revealed the early Indus Valley civilization.*
4. *Chinese civilization developed along the Huang River.*

Lesson Plan

Essential Learning Objectives

Students will learn to:

- describe Sumerian society and its contributions to world civilization.
- explain how Sumerian culture influenced other peoples of the Middle East.

1 FOCUS AND MOTIVATE

Briefly discuss with students the aspects of human life that represent civilization and how those aspects might have started.

2 TEACH

- Clarify the concept of the city-state. List and explain the functions of each level in Sumerian society.

- Identify Sumerian inventions asking students to discuss the importance of each development. Emphasize that although the Sumerians were vulnerable to conquest, the most valuable aspects of their culture were adopted and even improved by invading peoples.

- Discuss the importance of Hammurabi's Code. Elicit from students the values of Babylonian culture that can be learned by studying their laws. (Class differences were upheld, efforts were made to treat the poor fairly, farming was of major importance.)

GUIDED PRACTICE

Direct students to name as many occupations as possible that they can identify from the list of Sumerian inventions. (mathematicians, engineers, cart makers, wheelwrights)

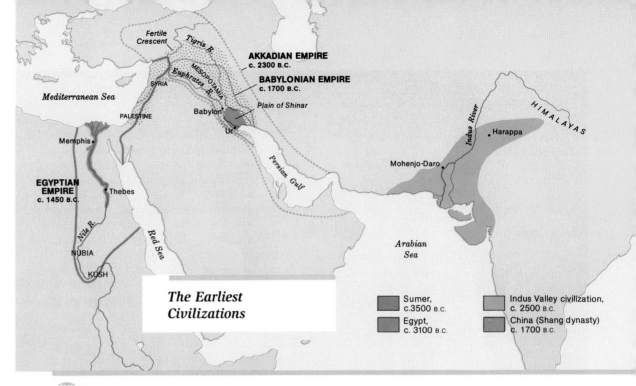

The Earliest Civilizations

Sumer, c.3500 B.C.
Egypt, c. 3100 B.C.
Indus Valley civilization, c. 2500 B.C.
China (Shang dynasty) c. 1700 B.C.

 MAP STUDY The map shows the approximate locations of the four earliest civilizations. Each one developed in a fertile river valley. Name the rivers where these civilizations developed.

1 The oldest civilization began in Mesopotamia.

Mesopotamia, which means "land between the rivers," was the eastern portion of the Fertile Crescent, the well-watered region that extends in an arc from the Mediterranean Sea to the Persian Gulf.

The Sumerians built city-states in southern Mesopotamia.

About 3500 B.C. a people known as the Sumerians moved into the southern portion of the fertile plain of Shinar between the Tigris and Euphrates rivers. This area is in present-day Iraq where the Tigris and Euphrates rivers flow into the Persian Gulf. The Sumerians probably migrated from the southeast, for their language is unrelated to those of the Semitic peoples of Mesopotamia who lived to the northwest.

The Sumerians were farmers and city builders. Since rainfall was sparse in this desertlike area, the Sumerians dug canals and ditches to control the spring floods of the Tigris and Euphrates and to irrigate the land. They then built cities along the rivers and their branches. These tributaries carved up the land into so many isolated regions that each Sumerian city became an independent **city-state**, that is, a small country consisting of a city and the surrounding territories that depended on it.

Each city-state had its own local gods who, the Sumerians believed, had the power to destroy their city through floods. To please and calm the gods, the Sumerians built a splendid temple in the center of each city. By 2000 B.C. the temple had become a **ziggurat**, a massive stepped tower that dominated the city. It was the first monumental architecture in Mesopotamia.

The temple and its priests owned a large portion of the city's territory, but they did not rule the city.

BACKGROUND The term "Semitic" refers to a language family, not a racial group. Various Semitic languages were, and still are, spoken in Mesopotamia and the Arabian peninsula. Other language families mentioned often in this text are Indo-

European, Indo-Aryan, Germanic, Turkic, and Bantu. Each of these language families includes a number of languages.

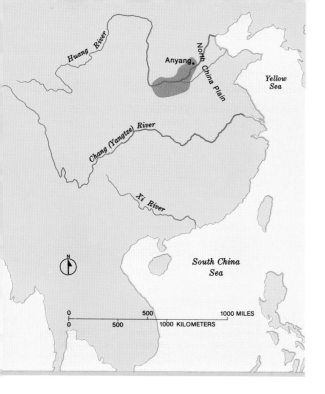

inventions that we use today, for example, writing.

As far as is known, the Sumerians were the first people on earth to invent writing, which they invented sometime before 3000 B.C. Scholars think that Sumerian writing began as marks drawn to represent clay tokens (see the diagram at left on page 24). Such tokens had been in use as early as 9000 B.C. as receipts showing that a payment had been made to a worker or an official. The Sumerians did not have pen or paper but instead used a stylus, or pointed stick, to make impressions on soft clay bricks or tablets. The tablets were then baked to give them permanent form.

The Sumerians' writing is called **cuneiform** [kyü nē'ə fôrm], meaning "wedge-shaped," because of the shape of the marks made by the stylus. Each combination of marks stood for a syllable. Sumerian cuneiform writing was later adopted by the other peoples of the Fertile Crescent. The Egyptians developed their writing system from Sumerian writing.

The plain of Shinar lacked stones for building. However, clay was everywhere, so the Sumerians

This Sumerian ziggurat was built at Ur in present-day Iraq around 2000 B.C. A temple once crowned the top of the ziggurat.

Political control was in the hands of the king, a war leader who was originally elected to power. However, wars between the city-states were so frequent that eventually the kingship became hereditary. As the supreme ruler in the city, the king held much land, as did the temple priests and other high-ranking people, called nobles. The lands of these nobles were worked by slaves, as well as by free men and women called clients. In addition, there were free citizens known as commoners who also owned land. They belonged to large patriarchal families (ruled by a male family head), participated in the political affairs of the city, and had full protection under the law.

The Sumerians made immense contributions to civilization.

The Sumerians were a highly creative people who made lasting contributions to human society. We owe a great debt to the Sumerians for a number of

BACKGROUND Point out to students that the four civilizations discussed in Chapter 2 began as Neolithic cultures. The invention of writing by the Sumerians around 3000 B.C. marks the transition between "prehistory" and "history," but, of course, all peoples did not learn to write then. Some peoples did not have a written language until recent times.

used sun-dried clay bricks to build their houses and temples. Their invention of the arch was a major contribution to architecture, because an arch can support heavy walls over openings for doorways and windows.

The Sumerians invented the plow, and they probably were the first to develop wheeled vehicles. The Sumerians were also skilled mathematicians; in fact, they invented many mathematical ideas that we still use today. For example, the division of a circle into 360 degrees, and the hour into 60 minutes, and a minute into 60 seconds is based on the Sumerian system.

The Sumerians also developed a literature that had a lasting impact on world civilization. Their hymns and odes to their gods became part of the literary heritage of the Middle East. Many of the hymns in the Bible, for example, have a style that is related to stylistic forms invented by the Sumerians. See, for example, the hymn to Inanna, the goddess of the morning star on page 25. Over time, the Sumerians also developed a legal code that became the basis of the legal systems of many other peoples of the Middle East, including the Babylonians and Israelites.

Other peoples took over and adapted Sumerian civilization.

Mesopotamia had no natural barriers against invasion, and, as a result, the individual city-states were easy to attack. However, in spite of frequent invasions, Sumerian civilization lasted for thousands of years because the conquerors took on Sumerian ways. These conquerors further developed the Mesopotamian civilization pioneered by the Sumerians.

Among the many peoples who were directly influenced by Sumerian ideas and ways of life were the Akkadians, the Babylonians, the Hittites, the Israelites, the Assyrians, the Chaldeans, and the Persians. These peoples will be discussed both in this chapter and the next.

About 2300 B.C. the Sumerian city-states were forcibly united by Sargon I, an invader from Akkad in northern Mesopotamia. Historians believe that he built the world's first empire, which extended east to Persia (present-day Iran), north to the Black Sea, and west to the Mediterranean. Find these places on the map on pages 22–23. Notice how much larger Sargon's empire was than Mesopotamia. Sargon's descendants ruled after him for

3 | ASSESS AND CLOSE

ASSESS

1. What kind of political system did the Sumerians develop? (hereditary rule of kings who controlled city-states)

2. Name the invention that enabled the Sumerians to build doors and windows in clay-brick structures. (the arched opening)

The Earliest Writing

3000 B.C.

3000 B.C.

| sheep | wool | numeral 1 | legal decision |

Above, Sumerian writing may have developed from clay tokens (top line). *At right,* early picture writing evolved into cuneiform symbols (see photo detail).

The Development of Cuneiform Writing

	3000 B.C.		600 B.C.
Bird			
Fish			
Sun			
Orchard			

about 180 years and did much to spread Sumerian civilization throughout the Middle East.

Hammurabi, the king of Babylonia, expanded the Sumerian legal code.

Six hundred years later, about 1700 B.C., a king named **Hammurabi** [ham′ü rä′bē], who came from what is now Syria, brought all of southern Mesopotamia under one rule. His capital was the city of Babylon [bab′ə lən], and all of southern Mesopotamia became known as Babylonia [bab′ə-lō′nē ə], which means "gate of the gods." Locate Babylonia on the map on pages 22–23.

Hammurabi is best remembered for a written code of laws that extended the legal system developed by the Sumerians. Hammurabi's Code was discovered in 1901 by a team of French archaeologists digging at Susa in present-day Iran. They found three pieces of black stone with writing on them, which, when put together, formed an eight-foot column.

The discovery of this column excited archaeologists and historians because the writing was found to be a code of laws, the earliest ever to be deciphered. At first, Hammurabi was given credit for creating the Code, but scholars now believe that he modified a code that was first developed by the Sumerians.

Hammurabi stated on the column that his goal was "to cause justice to prevail in the land, to destroy the wicked and the evil, to prevent the strong from oppressing the weak . . . and to further the welfare of the people." The nearly 300 sections of the Code tried to accomplish these goals by dealing strictly with violations of the law, which shows how serious these problems were in Mesopotamian society.

To promote justice and further the welfare of the people, merchants and other businessmen and women had to guarantee the quality of their goods and services and set fair prices. Doctors and veterinarians were to charge poor people less for medical and surgical services than they charged rich people. Slavery for debt was limited to four years.

Those farmers who failed to keep irrigation canals and ditches in good repair had to pay all costs for damaged crops. In a civilization where farming was so important, these strict laws on agriculture

From the Archives

Hymn to Inanna

Thousands of clay tablets, now housed in museums throughout the world, allow the ancient Sumerians to speak to us today. Most tablets contain business or legal records. Others hold myths, epic tales, fables, proverbs, and hymns—the oldest significant body of literature yet uncovered. The verse below is from a hymn to Inanna, who was the Goddess of the Morning and Evening Star and the chief goddess of the city-state of Uruk.

Mighty, majestic, and radiant,
You shine brilliantly in the evening,
You brighten the day at dawn,
You stand in the heavens like the sun and
  the moon,
Your wonders are known both above and
  below,
To the greatness of the holy priestess of
  heaven,
To you, Inanna, I sing!

often resulted in bumper crops, which helped the population grow and prosper.

Crimes of theft and violence were punished harshly, but the punishment depended on social class. Among equals, the Code demanded that the punishment fit the crime. However, if an aristocrat committed a crime against a commoner, the aristocrat was punished less severely. As the Code stated it: "If a man has knocked out the eye of a noble, his eye shall be knocked out," whereas if the same man knocked out the eye of a commoner, he was only required to pay a fine.

Hammurabi's Code became the basis for other legal systems long after his death. Since law is one of the main ways that people establish and keep social order, the Code represents a major advance in civilization.

FROM THE ARCHIVES The "Hymn to Inanna" is from *Inanna, Queen of Heaven and Earth: Her Stories and Hymns from Sumer,* by Diane Wolkstein and Samuel Noah Kramer (New York: Harper and Row, 1983).

Encourage students to speculate about the relationship between the Sumerians and their gods that is implied in this portion of the hymn.

Identify
Key Terms, People, and Places are defined on pages indicated in parentheses. Also see the Glossary and Biographical Dictionary. Mesopotamia (22), city-state (22), ziggurat (22), cuneiform (23), Hammurabi (25)

Main Ideas
1. The desert environment laced with irrigation canals divided the land into isolated city-states. Sumerian society was divided into classes headed by a king and landowning priests and nobles. Land was worked by clients and slaves. Free citizens known as commoners had political power.
2. communication—writing; architecture—the arch; agriculture—the plow; transportation—wheeled vehicles; mathematics—the division of the circle into 360°; literature—forms of hymns; law—a legal system
3. Sargon I and other conquerors overran the region and took on Sumerian ways. These conquerors spread Sumerian civilization throughout the Middle East.
4. a code of laws which served to promote justice and further the welfare of all the people. The code is considered a major advance in civilization because it helps establish and keep social order.

Critical Thinking
Justice, protection of the weak, and the welfare of society were the goals of the Code. The maintenance of the irrigation system was essential to society. Slavery and a class system were considered normal but needed to be regulated.

Section 1 Review

Identify Mesopotamia, city-state, ziggurat, cuneiform, Hammurabi

Main Ideas
1. What geographic conditions led to the development of Sumerian city-states? How was Sumerian society organized?
2. What contributions did the Sumerians make to civilization in the fields of communication, architecture, agriculture, transportation, mathematics, literature, and law?
3. How did Sumerian civilization spread throughout the Middle East?
4. What was the goal of Hammurabi's legal code? Why does it represent an important advance in civilization?

Critical Thinking
Recognizing Values: Every society has its own ideas about what is right and wrong. Judging from the description in the text of Hammurabi's Code, what kinds of social problems was it probably designed to solve?

---

2 | *An Egyptian civilization arose along the Nile River.*

Look at the map on pages 22–23. You can see where **Egypt** is in relation to Mesopotamia. By 5000 B.C. Neolithic people living along the Nile had learned to farm barley and wheat and to raise cattle. However, it took another 2,000 years for a fully developed Egyptian civilization to emerge.

Egyptian farmers began to develop a civilization.

The farmers of Egypt relied on the September flood of the Nile to bring new soil and water to their fields. The new soil kept the land fertile for growing crops. During other months farmers dug irrigation ditches to bring Nile water to their fields.

In order to dig the ditches, keep them in repair, and build dams for the benefit of all, the farmers formed work teams. Each team had a male leader who directed the work and made rules for the workers to follow. In time, as the work became more complicated and the work teams contained more people, the leader grew more powerful. He directed the work of planting and harvesting crops, and he decided whether to store or distribute crop surpluses. He employed administrators to help supervise the workers and keep track of the harvests. These organized cooperative efforts probably were the earliest form of local government in Egypt.

Because the farmers needed to plan for planting and harvesting, they counted the days between the

Farm scenes from a tomb wall depict a husband and wife (below) harvesting grain and (middle) pulling flax for linen and (bottom) a grove of date palms.

arrivals of the Nile floods. They studied the paths of the sun, moon, and stars to learn when to expect the spring planting season. Their studies led to the invention of the world's first solar (yearly) calendar around 4000 B.C.

The Egyptians noticed that on one day each year about flood time, a bright star—now known as Sirius [sir′ē əs]—appeared in the eastern sky before sunrise. By counting the days between appearances of this star, they figured that the length of a year is 365 days. They divided the year into 12 months and gave each month 30 days, with five feast days added at the end of the year.

With some modifications, this calendar served the Egyptians well for several thousand years and is the direct ancestor of the calendar we use today. Year One of the Egyptian calendar is our date of 4236 B.C. Therefore, if we had continued to follow the dating system established by this calendar, we would now be approaching the year 6236 instead of the year 2000.

The development of irrigation, the rise of local governments, and the invention of a calendar all took place between 5000 and 3100 B.C. During this period the Egyptians also devised a system of writing and discovered how to make copper tools. About 400 years after the Sumerians invented the plow, the Egyptians also developed one, which greatly increased crop production.

Egyptian history is divided into broad periods.

Ancient Egyptian history is divided into periods: the Old Kingdom, the Middle Kingdom, and the New Kingdom. Each of these periods ended in eras of foreign invasion or civil war. The years that preceded the Old Kingdom period are known as Predynastic Egypt.

Predynastic Egypt. At first, Egypt simply consisted of a number of small independent villages. Gradually, local rulers gained control first of nearby villages and then of larger areas, thus forming small kingdoms. As generations passed, a ruling class of nobles and princes emerged.

By 3100 B.C. two separate kingdoms had developed, one in the Nile Delta region called Lower Egypt and one along the river called Upper Egypt. **King Menes** [mē′nēz], the ruler of Upper Egypt,

united the two kingdoms, forming the world's first national government. Menes located his capital city at Memphis, near present-day Cairo. (See the map on pages 22–23.)

The accession of King Menes to the throne of the united kingdom marks the beginning of the First Dynasty [dī′nə stē]. A **dynasty** is a series of rulers belonging to the same family. Altogether thirty dynasties reigned in Egyptian history, the last one ending in 332 B.C. when Egypt became part of Alexander the Great's empire. Ancient Egypt existed as a separate country for almost 3,000 years, the world's longest national history.

The Old Kingdom (c. 2700 B.C.–c. 2200 B.C.). Little is known about the first few hundred years of Egyptian history. The Old Kingdom, or Pyramid Age, began about 2700 B.C. with the Third Dynasty, and it lasted about 500 years. During this period six dynasties ruled Egypt. Each was headed by a ruler called a **pharaoh**, meaning "royal house."

During the period of the Old Kingdom, merchant ships sailed up and down the Nile, and expeditions left the Nile Valley to trade with peoples in other parts of Africa and the Mediterranean. Artists carved fine statues, and craftworkers wove soft linen cloth and made pottery with the use of a potter's wheel. Workers continued to use stone tools, but they also made some tools from copper.

Egypt's geography allowed the Old Kingdom to enjoy many centuries of peace. Unlike Mesopotamia, which suffered from constant warfare because the land was exposed to frequent invasions, Egypt was closed off from the outside world. On both the east and the west, the Nile was protected by grim deserts, on the south by the Nile cataracts (steep waterfalls), and on the north by the Mediterranean Sea. In the northeast, Egypt was most vulnerable to invasion by land from western Asia. As a result,

What's in a Name?

THE NILE The name Nile probably comes from the Semitic word *nahal*, meaning "river," which the Greeks changed to Neilos. The ancient Egyptians called the river Ar, meaning "black."

Essential Learning Objectives

Students will learn to:

- discuss the major achievements of each period of Egyptian civilization.
- identify the functions of individuals in the class structure of Egyptian society.
- examine the importance of religion in Egyptian culture

1 FOCUS AND MOTIVATE

Discuss with students what they know of ancient Egypt. Write responses on the chalkboard. Ask students to formulate questions based on each response. (Example: Egyptians built pyramids. When and why were the pyramids built?) Questions still unanswered after studying the section may be assigned for extra credit.

- Identify for students the periods of ancient Egyptian history: Predynastic, Old, Middle, and New Kingdoms. Point out the approximate years and characteristics of each period.

- Name the groups that made up the three classes in Egyptian society. Stress the religious aspects of the pharaoh's power and clarify the concepts of theocracy and polytheism.

- In discussing Egyptian achievements, elicit the practical purposes of writing, mathematics, building, and medicine in daily life.

GUIDED PRACTICE

Distribute copies of outline maps of Africa from the Geography Skills Book. Direct students to indicate and label the Nile river; major cities of the Old, Middle, and New Kingdoms; trade routes to Europe and Asia; and the extent of the Egyptian empire.

The Pyramids at Giza were built during the Old Kingdom as tombs for pharaohs. They are guarded by the Great Sphinx, which modern workers are trying to save from the ravages of pollution.

the Old Kingdom had no standing army, and, in times of need, used local guard units for defense.

The Great Pyramids were built during the Old Kingdom as tombs for the pharaohs. To build these gigantic tombs, the pharaohs used thousands of peasants as laborers. The largest pyramid, built at the town of Giza [gē′zə] for King Cheops [kē′ops], is immense—about 450 feet high and 750 feet wide at each base. It is said that it took 20 years and the work of 100,000 people to build this mighty pyramid. The larger stone blocks weigh several tons each. To quarry, transport, and raise these massive blocks into place with almost no machinery was a remarkable engineering feat.

The Middle Kingdom (c. 2000 B.C.–c. 1800 B.C.). Around 2200 B.C. civil war brought the collapse of the Old Kingdom, and for more than 200 years, rival leaders fought among themselves for wealth and power. Eventually princes from the city of Thebes [thēbz] reunified the country, beginning the period known as the Middle Kingdom, which lasted between 2000 and 1800 B.C.

The princes from Thebes became the new pharaohs, and they made Egypt strong and prosperous. They encouraged art and literature and began new irrigation projects that greatly increased the crop area. Pharaohs of the Middle Kingdom built a canal that joined the business centers of the Nile Valley with the trade routes of the Red Sea. Look at the map on pages 22–23 to see where Thebes was in relation to the Red Sea. During the Middle Kingdom period, Egypt conquered Nubia, the kingdom to its south, and it expanded trade with Palestine and Syria in the Fertile Crescent.

Around 1800 B.C. Egypt was again wracked by a long period of civil war. About 1750 B.C., while weak from internal disorder, Egypt was conquered by nomadic invaders from western Asia called the Hyksos [hik′sos]. An ancient record speaks of the invaders savagely burning cities, destroying

Egyptian temples, and treating the people with great cruelty. This domination by foreigners humiliated the Egyptians and ignited their feelings of superiority. A prince of Thebes declared,

> No man can settle down, when despoiled by the taxes of the Asiatics. I will grapple with him, that I may rip open his belly! My wish is to save Egypt and to smite the Asiatics!

The Hyksos ruled Egypt for about 100 years. During this time the Egyptians learned from them how to make superior bows and arrows and to wage war with horse-drawn chariots that the Hyksos had introduced into Egypt. This knowledge proved useful to the Egyptians in the next period of their history, when they embarked on a program of aggressive expansion.

The New Kingdom (c. 1600 B.C.–c. 1100 B.C.). Leaders from Thebes drove the Hyksos out and restored Egyptian rule to Egypt. This marked the beginning of the New Kingdom, or empire, which lasted from 1600 to 1100 B.C. An **empire** is a government that rules over a group of countries.

During the era of the New Kingdom, the pharaohs attacked neighboring peoples and extended Egyptian rule into southwestern Asia, as far north as the Euphrates River. For a 20-year-period between 1490 and 1469 B.C., Egypt was ruled by its only female pharaoh, Queen Hatshepsut [hat'shepsüt], who gained the throne in a coup (an unlawful seizure of government). Her reign was marked by building programs and the expansion of trade to East Africa. She also attempted to make succession to the throne pass through the female line. However, after she died the next pharaoh, King Thutmose [thüt'mō sə] III, had Queen Hatshepsut's statues destroyed and her name erased from all monuments. As a result, her name does not appear on official lists of Egyptian rulers.

Egypt reached the height of its power around 1450 B.C. during the reign of King Thutmose III. The map on pages 22–23 shows the extent of the Egyptian empire around 1450 B.C. Find Thebes, the capital city.

For about 450 years after the overthrow of the Hyksos, increased trade and tribute (forced payments) from conquered countries made Egypt rich. The capital, Thebes, became a city of statues, temples, and palaces. Egyptian ships carried products, such as wheat and linens, across the Mediterranean to Europe and Asia. The ships returned with lumber and metal weapons, which Egypt needed but did not produce.

By about 1100 B.C., Egypt had again grown weak from quarrels among its leaders, rebellions among its conquered peoples, and costly battles with for-

DAILY LIFE

A procession of bearers bringing offerings is a favorite scene on tomb walls. The frequency of such scenes indicates the importance of animals in the daily life and religion of ancient Egypt. In the scene at left, bearers from the conquered land of Kush are offering tribute to Ramses II. Among their gifts are cattle, gazelles, a lion, leopards, and a giraffe. Leopards and lions were sometimes trained as pets or used in hunting.

BACKGROUND Be sure students realize that historians believe that early Egyptian administrators were always men, so that students come to see that terms such as "he" and "she" have very precise meanings in this text.

eign enemies. Hundreds of years of civil war and foreign invasions followed. The last Egyptian dynasty, the Thirtieth, was overthrown by the Greeks in 332 B.C., and a Greek dynasty, known as the Ptolemies, soon took over the government. This event marks the end of almost 3,000 years of rule by the pharaohs of Egypt.

Egyptian society was ruled by a god-king and divided into classes.

Throughout much of Egyptian history, the pharaohs had absolute power over their subjects—partly because most of these rulers governed justly, but mainly because people believed that the pharaohs were descended from a god and were gods themselves. A government in which the religious leader rules the state as a god's representative is called a **theocracy** [thē ok′rə sē].

In theory, the pharaoh owned all the land, commanded the army, and controlled the irrigation system. Since no person could administer such a huge kingdom, the pharaoh appointed officials to assist him. However, he was personally responsible for making all the important decisions of government. Beginning with the Old Kingdom, Egyptians created a complex but efficient government that supported the absolute power of the pharaoh.

Egyptian society was divided into three broad classes. The upper class of people was made up of the priests, the court nobility, and the landed nobility. The men and women who were priests performed religious ceremonies, especially those having to do with the burial of the dead. The court nobles advised the pharaoh and the queen and carried out their orders, and the landed nobility managed their great estates.

From writings and pictures on tombs and temples, scholars have learned a great deal about life among the upper class. They lived in palatial

Below is a tomb painting of Osiris, the king of the dead. At right is a golden mask of King Tutankhamen, who died at the age of 19.

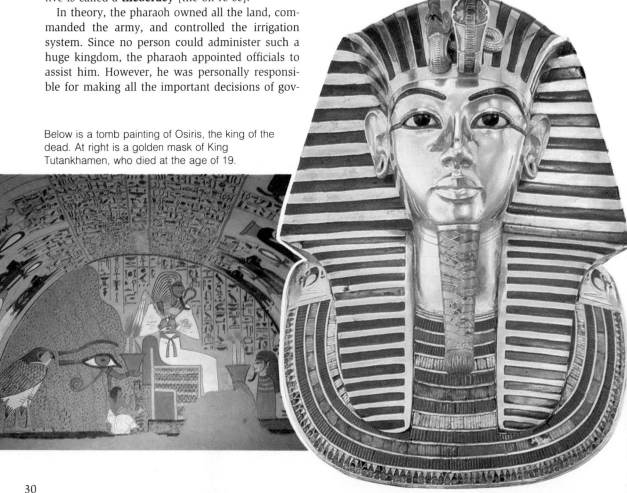

homes, with luxurious furnishings, elaborate gardens, and sumptuous food.

The middle class included men and women who became rich through trade. Skilled artisans, who made furniture and jewelry, worked with leather and cloth, and directed the building of tombs and palaces, were also in the middle class. So were professional people such as teachers, artists, doctors, and scribes. Scribes, who wrote letters and documents for a living, held an important place in Egypt because few people could read or write.

The lower class, to which the great mass of Egyptians belonged, was made up of two groups—slaves and peasants. The slaves were usually prisoners of war. Like the peasants, they worked on farms, irrigation systems, roads, and building projects. The peasants, heavily burdened by taxes and forced labor, had few political rights. They lived poorly in small, mud-brick homes with few furnishings. However, it was possible for smart and ambitious young Egyptians to rise to higher rank.

Sometimes loyal and able slaves were given their freedom. On a few occasions, a talented slave rose to become a government official. The most famous example is the story of Joseph in the Bible. He came to Egypt as a slave and rose to be the second most powerful official, next to the pharaoh.

Religion in Egypt was concerned with life after death and good conduct.

Egyptians reasoned that just as plants decline in the autumn and reappear in the spring, so too people must have life after death. They believed that the human body should be preserved after death, as a mummy, in order for the soul to live on. Preserving the body became a highly skilled art. Beliefs about the afterlife led the Egyptians to build large tombs in which to keep the mummified bodies of their dead rulers.

Good conduct was also thought necessary for immortality, or life after death. The god Osiris was the king of the dead and it was he who decided whether a person had lived justly enough to deserve eternal life. In the *Book of the Dead*, a collection of New Kingdom writings, the soul of a deceased man says to Osiris:

> Here am I: I come to thee; I bring to thee
> Right and have put a stop to wrong.

> I am not a doer of wrong to men.
> I am not one who slayeth his kindred.
> I am not one who telleth lies instead of truth.
> I am not conscious of treason.
> I am not a doer of mischief.

The Egyptians worshiped many gods and goddesses, a practice called **polytheism** [pol′ē-thē′iz′əm]. The most important deities were Amon-Re [ä′mən rā], the sun god, and Osiris [ō-sī′ris], the god of the underworld and lord of the afterlife. Egyptian gods and goddesses were often pictured as beings with human bodies and the heads of animals. The Egyptians also worshiped certain animals, including cows, monkeys, crocodiles, and serpents.

During the reign of pharaoh Akhenaton [äk′ə-nä′tn], a new faith was temporarily born. Akhenaton, who ruled from 1379 to 1362 B.C., believed in one supreme god, Aton [ä′ton], the sun. Akhenaton outlawed the worship of all gods except Aton and took government support away from the priests of other gods.

However, the priests were many and powerful. They succeeded in terrifying the already fearful people into believing that if they obeyed Akhenaton they would suffer the wrath of the gods. While Akhenaton lived, his orders were not openly disobeyed, but after his death, the priests persuaded Egyptians to return to polytheism.

Akhenaton's goals are the subject of historical controversy. Did he want to establish the worship of one God, **monotheism**, or was he merely attempting to raise up Aton above all the other gods? Because of this uncertainty, Akhenaton's place in the history of religion is not established. Whatever the case, his attempt to bring religious reform to Egypt is known to have failed because Akhenaton tried to impose an unpopular religion from above. Unlike Jewish monotheism (see Chapter 3), the worship of the sun god as the only god was not a religion deeply felt and cherished by a whole people.

The Egyptians made major advances in literature, mathematics, and other fields.

Sometime before 3000 B.C., the Egyptians developed **hieroglyphics** [hī′ər ə glif′iks], a form of picture writing that was probably stimulated by early

BACKGROUND The word *hieroglyphics* comes from the Greek words *hieros,* meaning "sacred," and *glyphe,* meaning "a carving."

31

ASSESS

1. On what did the Egyptians base their calendar year? (the 365-day interval between sightings of the star Sirius)
2. What was King Menes' major accomplishment? (He united Egypt and founded the first dynasty.)
3. When did Egypt conquer an empire? (during the New Kingdom)

OPTIONAL RETEACHING

Direct selected students to write short paragraphs about the activities of the groups in Egyptian society. Provide time for students to read their work aloud.

OPTIONAL ENRICHMENT

1. Have students research and write reports or prepare maps illustrating the sources and extent of the Nile river. (average)
2. Ask a group of students to prepare a large chart of the names and roles of Egyptian gods. (challenging)
3. Also for enrichment:

 Overhead Transparency 4

 Source Reading 2B

INDEPENDENT PRACTICE/ HOMEWORK

Assign the Section Review, Activities page 8, or Workbook page 6.

CLOSURE

Summarize the lesson by telling students that because of its secure geographical location Egypt enjoyed long periods of peace and prosperity. The Egyptians adopted some aspects of their culture from others, but their major accomplishments in art, religion, and building are admired today as they have been throughout history.

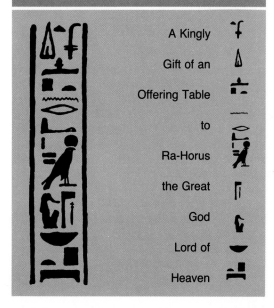

Egyptian Hieroglyphics

A Kingly

Gift of an

Offering Table

to

Ra-Horus

the Great

God

Lord of

Heaven

Sumerian writing. The first writings consisted of pictures of objects. Gradually picture signs came into use for ideas as well as objects. For example, a picture of an eye could mean "sight" or "eye."

In time, Egyptian writers also used picture signs to indicate sound. These developments were only the beginnings of a true alphabet. A true alphabet is a set of letters, each representing only sounds and no meanings. Scholars believe that the Phoenicians, who invented the first true alphabet around 1000 B.C., developed the symbols from Egyptian hieroglyphics.

The first Egyptian books were written on material made from papyrus [pə pī′rəs], a reed plant. Papyrus is the origin of the English word "paper." Egyptian books consisted of long rolls of papyrus pasted together. The earliest books were about religion, but during the Middle Kingdom, some adventure stories were written. These works were probably the first works of fiction ever published.

The Egyptians were extremely inventive mathematicians. Because Nile floods washed away markers for land boundaries, the Egyptians surveyed the land often, developing geometry to measure the boundaries. They invented addition, subtraction, and division, but never learned how to multiply except by adding. They also discovered how to compute the areas of triangles, circles, and other shapes. Their engineers used mathematics to work out the precise measurements necessary in the construction of the pyramids and temples. They probably learned some of their practical problem-solving techniques from the Mesopotamians.

The Egyptians were outstanding builders in stone, and both sculptors and engineers liked to think big. The Great Pyramids and the Sphinx are examples of the Egyptian fondness for mammoth structures.

Religion inspired the building of Egyptian tombs and temples. The most famous temple was that of the sun god Amon-Re, at Karnak, built in the 1200s B.C. Part of this great temple still stands. Its hall is larger than a football field and is 80 feet high. The roof was supported by rows of giant columns. The Egyptians were the first to support roofs with columns rather than with walls.

As Egyptians studied ways to preserve the human body after death, their doctors became familiar with its anatomy and the healing properties of certain herbs. They made many medical advances: they knew how to heal certain wounds, set broken bones, and perform simple surgery. It is not until the 19th century A.D., when the role of microbes in spreading disease was discovered, that medicine advanced much beyond the level achieved by the ancient Egyptians.

As you read on page 27, the Nile Valley was blessed with natural geographic barriers that provided much security against invasion. The regularity of the Nile flood, with its life-giving deposits of silt and its dependable irrigation water, also gave the Egyptians a sense of security and a confident outlook. Their religion reflected this confidence. The pharaoh, thought to be a god, watched over the people in this life and in the hereafter. The confident and optimistic outlook of the Egyptians found expression not only in their religion but also in their art, architecture, and daily life. These qualities enabled the Egyptians to build a civilization that lasted longer than that of any other people, ancient or modern.

GEOGRAPHY

A Key to History

NILE CURRENTS AND THE ETESIAN WIND

About 5,000 years ago, the Egyptians learned to use the regular summer winds to move sailboats. As a result, they greatly expanded trade and travel along the Nile River.

In the summer the air above the North African desert becomes hot. As the air heats, it expands, becomes lighter, and rises. The air above the Mediterranean stays cooler than that above the desert. Because the cooler air is heavier, it stays close to the ground. The cool air flows south to replace the hot air rising from the desert, and this flow of air toward the desert forms the wind.

Etesian [i tē′zhən] is the name given to the wind that blows across the Mediterranean Sea each summer into eastern Mediterranean regions and Egypt. The wind blows from mid-May to mid-September. During the day, the wind sometimes reaches speeds of 40 miles an hour. During the cooler nights, the wind dies down.

By harnessing the power of the wind, the Egyptians carried on a two-way trade along the Nile. The river current carried boats northward (downstream) toward the Mediterranean. The etesian wind pushed sailboats southward (upstream) toward Karnak and Thebes. Thus, the Egyptians found a way to solve the problem that faces all river traders: how to move goods upstream against the current.

REVIEW
1. How do differences in the air temperature over land and over water affect the wind currents over the Nile River?
2. Why is it important for traders to be able to ship goods in two directions?

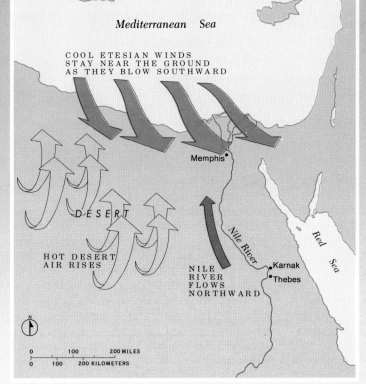

Mediterranean Sea

COOL ETESIAN WINDS STAY NEAR THE GROUND AS THEY BLOW SOUTHWARD

DESERT

HOT DESERT AIR RISES

Memphis

NILE RIVER FLOWS NORTHWARD

Nile River

Karnak
Thebes

Red Sea

N

0   100   200 MILES
0   100   200 KILOMETERS

If you were sailing on the Nile, in what direction would the river currents carry your boat? In what direction would your boat be carried by the estesian wind?

33

Identify

Key Terms, People, and Places are defined on pages indicated in parentheses. Also see the Glossary and Biographical Dictionary.
Egypt (26), King Menes (27), dynasty (27), pharaoh (27), empire (29), theocracy (30), polytheism (31), monotheism (31), hieroglyphics (31)

Main Ideas

1. Leaders of irrigation teams became heads of local governments; calendar, writing, copper tools, plow
2. Old Kingdom: period of peace, trade and crafts, Great Pyramids; Middle Kingdom: period of prosperity, art, literature, irrigation projects, canal to Red Sea, conquest of Nubia; New Kingdom: period of conquest, empire, temples and palaces, sea trade
3. a god with absolute power who owned all land and controlled the army and irrigation system. Egyptian society had an upper, middle, and lower class of peasants and slaves.
4. a belief in many gods and preserving the body for life after death.
5. developed hieroglyphics; adventure stories; geometry, addition, subtraction, division; huge structures, columns; healing wounds, setting broken bones, and simple surgery. Their civilization reflected optimism and confidence.

Critical Thinking

Their experience with fighting the Hyksos and their new knowledge of advanced military techniques may have introduced a militaristic outlook into their society. A study of their writings and inscriptions on monuments might help answer this question.

Section 2 Review

Identify Egypt, King Menes, dynasty, pharaoh, empire, theocracy, polytheism, monotheism, hieroglyphics

Main Ideas

1. How did the farming methods of the early Egyptians lead to the development of local governments? What important skills and techniques were invented between 5000 and 3100 B.C.?
2. Into what broad periods is ancient Egyptian history divided? Briefly describe the major characteristics of each period.
3. Describe the role of the pharaoh in the Egyptian government. Into what classes was Egyptian society divided?
4. What were the outstanding features of the Egyptian religion?
5. Describe ancient Egypt's contribution to writing, mathematics, architecture, and medicine. How did the Egyptians' sense of security affect their civilization?

Critical Thinking

Making Hypotheses: Why do you think that the Egyptians became so warlike after they freed themselves from the Hyksos? What evidence might you need to answer this question convincingly?

---

3 An ancient city revealed the early Indus Valley civilization.

Refer again to the map on pages 22–23. Around 4,500 years ago, people living in the **Indus Valley** in what is now Pakistan and western India had a highly organized way of life. Yet practically nothing was known about this early civilization until recent times.

Archaeologists discovered a lost civilization.

In the 1850s engineers began to build a railroad in the Indus Valley near the town of Harappa [hə-rap′ə]. As workers prepared the area, they uncovered large numbers of baked bricks, which they used to lay the railroad bed. They also uncovered many ornaments and small figures that were generally ignored or carried off as mementos by the local villagers. Little did the railroad workers or villagers know that they were destroying remains from one of the world's oldest civilizations.

No one thought much about the bricks and ornaments for 70 years. Then, in the 1920s, the British government began to study the area. Archaeologists discovered enough remains to learn that the bricks that the railroad workers had found were from the ruins of an ancient city, which archaeologists named Harappa after the modern town. In the course of their diggings, archaeologists also found delicate golden jewelry, small sculptures of what appeared to be a mother goddess, and copper and bronze tools. It soon became apparent that the people of this ancient city had developed a complex civilization that rivaled that of Mesopotamia and Egypt.

The Indus Valley civilization, which now is believed to have lasted between 2500 B.C. and 1500 B.C., covered a huge area that extended inland for about 1,000 miles from the Arabian Sea to the foothills of the Himalaya Mountains. Find this region on the map on pages 22–23.

Life in Mohenjo-Daro was highly organized.

In the years since Harappa was discovered, remains of several hundred towns and villages have since been found, and British, American, Pakistani, and Indian archaeologists have learned much about this ancient culture. The best source of information is Mohenjo-Daro [mō hen′jō dä′rō], a city in southern Pakistan 400 miles southwest of Harappa. The site of this ancient city is also shown on the map on pages 22–23.

The city of Mohenjo-Daro was laid out in rectangles, much like many modern cities. The city was divided into manufacturing, business, and residential districts, and the streets were paved with baked bricks and lined with shops. The windows of houses faced interior courtyards, not the street. Staircases led to the roof, where the families enjoyed the cool night air. Most houses had indoor toilets, and some of the larger houses had baths. Neat brick-lined sewers along the streets carried off sewage and rainwater. In fact, the city sewage system was so well planned that it had no equal in the modern world until the mid-19th century.

In the center of Mohenjo-Daro was a thick-walled, mud-brick citadel, or fort, that guarded the city. Inside were public buildings that included a granary for grain storage and a large bath that was probably used for religious rituals.

Life for members of the upper class seems to have been quite luxurious. Their wooden furniture was decorated with carefully crafted bone, shell, and ivory inlays, and tiles lined their bathtubs. Their copper and bronze tools and gold and silver jewelry were attractive and well made. As far as is known, the Indus Valley people were the first to grow cotton and to weave it into cloth.

Archaeologists also found numerous toys and stamp seals in the ruined city. Toy birds, miniature clay bulls tethered to tiny carts, marbles, balls, and rattles amused the children of Mohenjo-Daro. The stamp seals were small pieces of stone carved with carefully detailed pictures and about 400 symbols that seem to indicate some kind of writing. So far this writing has not been deciphered. Many of the seals had small rings on the back, indicating that they might have been worn on thongs as ornaments. It is thought that the seals were pressed into soft material, such as wax or clay, and used to show ownership.

The people of Mohenjo-Daro had an elaborate religion.

Many female statues have been found in the ruins of the Indus Valley civilization. They seem to indicate that the people worshiped a goddess. Sculpture and carvings on the stamp seals suggest that the people burned incense or candles to their goddess and that animals were included in their religion. The great bath house, with its huge public bathing area surrounded by smaller private baths, also had living quarters. These private baths and living quarters suggest that a priest class lived in luxury and celebrated ritual bathings. Today many Indians who follow the Hindu religion, which you will read about in Chapter 7, still practice ritual bathing. It is possible that this custom began with the Indus Valley people.

The economy of the Indus civilization depended on farming and trade.

Farming was the most important economic activity in the Indus Valley civilization. Located in Mohenjo-Daro were huge round platforms where an organized labor force pounded grain. Along with farming, trade was important, too, as shown by the many standardized weights discovered. Quartz weights, many of them exactly the same size, indicate that the people used standard weights to measure goods in their business deals. Some weights are so small they must have been used to weigh gold. Others were used by grocers who sold spices. The largest ones, made of stones so heavy they had to be hauled into place by ropes, may have been used to weigh large amounts

The writing of the early Indus Valley people has not been deciphered. The three seals below were probably used to identify personal property.

Essential Learning Objectives

Students will learn to:
- give examples of archaeological evidence found in Mohenjo-Daro.
- describe the economy and culture of Indus Valley civilization.

1 FOCUS AND MOTIVATE

Direct students to describe aspects of our civilization that may still exist 4,000 years from now. Ask what future archaeologists might determine about our culture from these finds.

2 TEACH

Divide the chalkboard vertically into two sections. In one section list the archaeological evidence found in Mohenjo-Daro; in the other section, write down what each bit of evidence indicates about the culture. Categories should include city planning, residential design, personal possessions, writing, religion, and trade.

GUIDED PRACTICE

Give students outline maps of the world from the Geography Skills Book. Direct them to indicate possible trade routes to Mesopotamia. Have them also identify cultures in the Fertile Crescent that existed at the same time as the Indus Valley.

3 ASSESS AND CLOSE

ASSESS

What evidence exists that the people of Mohenjo-Daro had invented writing? (carved seals or stamps with pictures and 400 symbols)

Here are the ruins of the huge public bath at Mohenjo-Daro. It was surrounded by smaller private baths and living quarters for priests.

of grain. The presence of these uniform weights in widely separated towns suggests to archaeologists that the entire area was under the control of a strong central government.

Although Harappa and Mohenjo-Daro were 400 miles apart, the Indus River made trade and a uniform administration possible over a wide area. Camels and ox-drawn carts carried goods overland to the mountains west of the Indus Valley. Evidence also indicates that the Indus Valley people traded by sea with many distant groups, including the Sumerians, Babylonians, and other Mesopotamians. Thus were goods and ideas carried back and forth between the early civilizations.

The Indus Valley civilization had two major seaport cities. Huge piers and warehouses indicate that the cities must have once sat right on the water. Today, however, these cities are 30 miles inland from the Arabian Sea. This change in their position relative to the sea is the result of geological changes that have taken place over thousands of years. Slowly the shape of the Indian coastline has been shifting. Layers of rock deep in the

earth's surface have moved, raising up mud flats to become land where once the sea waters lapped.

History is silent about the end of the Indus Valley civilization.

Little is known about the decline or destruction of this ancient civilization. The city of Mohenjo-Daro seems to have been slowly overrun by mud from a nearby lake, formed from the earth's shifting surface. Over and over, houses were rebuilt on platforms raised to higher, safer levels. Some archaeologists believe that this constant work reduced the will and energy of the people. We do know that the oldest buildings, found 40 feet below the mud surface, were much better built than those above. Dikes and banks seem to have been neglected, and prosperity declined.

Then disaster struck. About 1500 B.C. some terrible misfortune hit Mohenjo-Daro and possibly all the Indus Valley people. Skeletons were found in groups, some showing axe or sword cuts, as though these people had huddled together for comfort in the face of a terrible massacre. What happened, however, remains a mystery. The name Mohenjo-Daro means "the place of the dead."

Section 3 Review

Identify Indus Valley

Main Ideas

1. What finds led to the discovery that an ancient civilization had once flourished in the Indus Valley?
2. Describe four features of Mohenjo-Daro that indicate that life in the city was highly organized.
3. What religious beliefs and organization do archaeological finds seem to indicate?
4. What was the basis of the economy of the Indus Valley civilization? What evidence indicates that the Indian coastline has changed greatly in the last 4,000 years?

Critical Thinking

Making Hypotheses: Archaeological evidence indicates that copper and bronze were generally used for tools. From this scholars have concluded that the Indus Valley civilization was a peaceful one. If this theory is correct, make a hypothesis as to why the Indus Valley people were peaceful.

4 Chinese civilization developed along the Huang River.

Like other peoples, the Chinese have many myths and legends about ancient times. One such legend describes the first man, Ban Ku, who used a hammer and chisel for 18,000 years to make the universe. He finished the job 2,229,000 years ago.

Other legends describe early princes called the Xia [shya], who ruled over a number of small kingdoms between 2200 and 1700 B.C. Yu, the first prince, is described as being brave and strong, a sort of superhero. According to legend, he fought a mighty river to save his people from floods. An early Chinese saying claims that, "But for Yu, we should all have been fishes." Such legends are unreliable as historical evidence, but they often contain important clues about the early settlement of a region. It is true that Neolithic peoples settled in the Huang River Valley in early times. The region is shown on the map on pages 22–23.

Geography influenced early Chinese civilization.

In the cold, dry areas of northern **China** were vast treeless plains of fertile **loess** [les], a fine rich soil formed from deposits of dust blown into China from Central Asia during the Ice Age. The Huang, which means "yellow" in Chinese, ran through these plains carrying large amounts of silt, from whose yellowish color the river gets its name. The silt continually built up the river bed until its banks became higher than the surrounding plain. From time to time the river overflowed, causing tragic floods, so that the river came to be called "China's Sorrow." In spite of this, its waters brought life to the valley. It was on these fertile plains that the Chinese began to farm, perhaps as early as 5000 B.C.

By 4500 B.C. Chinese farmers were growing millet, a cereal grass that is eaten today by about one-third of the world's population. A thousand years later, soybeans were cultivated, and pigs were raised for food and for scavenging, to keep farmyards clean.

By 3500 B.C. Chinese women were also raising silkworms, spinning the unraveled cocoons into fine silk thread, and weaving silk cloth. Throughout history, people have considered Chinese silk to be among the finest textiles in the world.

Around 2000 B.C. people who had migrated southward to the mouth of the Chang [chäng] River learned to grow rice in the semitropical climate. (Note that the Chang River is also known as the Yangtze [yang′tsē] River.) Because rice needs to have its roots underneath water, these people developed the elaborate farming methods that are still used in much of East and Southeast Asia today. They made artificial pools, called paddies, by building dikes around low-lying land and diverting water from nearby streams. Then they sowed the rice seeds in dry land and transplanted them to the paddies by hand, a plant at a time, when the shoots were about a foot high.

These early Chinese lived in villages near their fields. Walls of pounded earth protected their villages. Their houses were walled cones placed over circular areas dug out of the ground. The roof was supported by six posts cut from tree trunks, and it was made of wooden beams covered with straw and earth. The door was an opening in the roof.

The people of the Shang civilization made elaborate bronze vessels like this container in the shape of an elephant.

BACKGROUND Today the Pinyin system for spelling Chinese names is commonly used in atlases, newspapers, and reference books. To do library research, however, your students may need to know the Wade-Giles spelling of Chinese names.

Following are the Pinyin names in this chapter and, in parentheses, the same names with the Wade-Giles spelling: Huang River (Hwang Ho), Xia princes (Hsia princes), Chang River (Yangtze River).

4. farming and trade; major seaports now located 30 miles from the sea

Critical Thinking
The economy seemed to provide wealth by means of farming and trade. Perhaps there were no major threats to the civilization until warlike invaders came and wiped it out in a terrible massacre.

4 Lesson Plan

Essential Learning Objectives
Students will learn to:
- identify the effects of geography on farming societies of China.
- describe the political structure and culture of Shang China.

1 FOCUS AND MOTIVATE

Have students compare the latitudes of the United States and China on Atlas maps on pages 789 and 795. Discuss the effect of climate on ways of life in the northern and southern states of the United States.

2 TEACH

- List separately the characteristics of northern and southern China. Name the rivers, climatic conditions, types of soil, and crops.
- Discuss the basis of the Shang kings' power. Give examples of archaeological finds of the period and elicit from students the skills necessary to produce each item.

GUIDED PRACTICE
Direct students to name the food crops grown in the Shang period. (millet and soybeans)

ASSESS

Why have no large buildings or temples from Shang China been found? (Wood and earth structures deteriorated.)

OPTIONAL RETEACHING

Distribute copies of the outline map of ancient China in the Geography Skills book. Have students label the two river systems, color the major physical features appropriately, and indicate the crops grown in each area during the Shang period.

Students also may be assigned Activities reteaching page 11.

OPTIONAL ENRICHMENT

1. Have students report on the historical background of silkworm culture in China. (average)
2. Suggest that students research the methods used in casting bronze vessels in Shang China. (challenging)

Students also may be assigned Activities enrichment page 12.

INDEPENDENT PRACTICE/ HOMEWORK

Assign the Section Review, the Chapter Review items, Activities page 10, or Workbook page 8.

CLOSURE

Tell students that civilization in China began in the Huang River Valley and also developed later in the Chang River Valley. Written history began about 1500 B.C.

Answers to Section 4 Review

Identify

Key Terms, People, and Places are defined on pages indicated in

Shang kings were religious leaders (1700 B.C.–1027 B.C.).

The written history of China begins about 1700 B.C. with the rise of the Shang [shäng] dynasty. The Shang capital was north of the Huang River, near the present city of Anyang, shown on the map on pages 22–23. The Shang kings controlled only a small area around their capital, and strong nobles ruled the distant parts of the kingdom. However, the nobles recognized the Shang king as the head of the armies and as the religious leader. They believed that he governed by the command of heaven. As high priest, the king paid homage to his ancestors and made animal sacrifices to the gods to bring about good harvests.

Much of the knowledge of Shang history comes from excavations, begun in 1928, of sites near Anyang. Archaeologists have found no great monuments or palaces. Stone was scarce in China, and buildings were made from perishable wood and packed earth. A poem from the *Book of Odes,* the oldest collection of Chinese poetry, tells how the people built a temple:

He called upon his overseer of public works,
He called upon his Minister of Education,
And charged them to build dwellings.
They leveled all the land by skillful measuring,
They built wooden frames which rose straight and high,
The temple of our ancestors grew mightily.
Armies of men brought earth in baskets
And, shouting joyfully, poured it into the frames.
They rammed it in with great ringing blows,
They leveled off the walls and these resounded mightily,
They built up five thousand cubits [about 1.5 miles] at once,
And so well did they labor
That the rolling of the great drum
Would not cover the noise thereof.

Writing, bronze making, and other skills advanced during the Shang period.

One important source of information about the early Chinese is the writing on pieces of animal bones and tortoise shells. Priests wrote questions about the future on the bones and shells. Then they heated the bones and interpreted the cracks that appeared as answers from gods or ancestors.

BACKGROUND The wood of the furniture disintegrated, but the decorations did not. Archaeologists found the decorations on the floor where the furniture had been.

Questions were asked on many subjects, and they tell us much about the Shang civilization. The bones ask about what to sacrifice to the spirits, when will be a good day for an important journey, and when will be a good time for the army to attack. Priests asked about the harvest and the weather, about when the time was good to go hunting or fishing. Also, the priests told the spirits about their enemies' misdeeds, about how many people had been killed or taken prisoner, so that the spirits could punish their enemies.

The inscriptions show that Chinese writing was well advanced at this time. Shang writing had about 2,000 symbols. In addition to writing on bones and shells, the people kept records on tablets of wood and bamboo.

The people of the Shang period are best known for their very fine bronze work. Artisans made bronze vessels of different shapes for cooking or for ceremonial uses. These vessels were elaborately decorated with scrolls, spirals, and the faces of dragons and other imaginary creatures.

In addition to the bronze work, pieces of carved ivory and jade, marble sculptures, dagger-axes, and chariot fittings have been found at Shang sites. These discoveries also show a high level of technology. The Shang people, however, were conquered in 1027 B.C. by a less civilized group of nomads who invaded the country from the northwest.

Section 4 Review

Identify China, loess

Main Ideas

1. How did geography influence the development of early Chinese civilization?
2. Why did the strong nobles accept the Shang kings? What responsibilities did the kings have?
3. What major advances in skills and technology took place during the Shang period?

Critical Thinking

Analyzing Comparisons: Both the Shang kings and the Egyptian pharaohs were religious leaders who ruled over a class of nobles. What similarities and differences were there in the kinds of power held by these rulers?

HIGHLIGHTS OF CIVILIZATION

Early Mathematics

The Sumerians and the ancient Egyptians were inventive, sophisticated people. To construct their towering ziggurats and massive pyramids, Sumerians and Egyptians had to be expert mathematicians.

At first, mathematics was used only for counting and measuring. Later, the Sumerians and Egyptians learned to solve many practical problems through geometry—the branch of mathematics measuring such two-dimensional figures as squares, circles, and triangles and such three-dimensional figures as cubes, spheres, and pyramids.

The Sumerians based their system of calculation on 60. Many numbers can be divided into 60, so this proved a practical choice. We follow the Sumerian system when we use 60 as a base number to divide hours and degrees in a circle.

The Egyptians added and subtracted as we do, but they multiplied by doubling and redoubling. Although this method was awkward, the Egyptians calculated the volume of pyramids with a remarkably small margin of error.

In the cuneiform tablet at left, a Sumerian dealt with the measurement of circles, rectangles, and triangles. In the scene below, Egyptian farmers are using a knotted rope to measure their fields.

Main Ideas

1. The rich loess soil and waters of the Huang River promoted millet farming in the north; the semitropical climate and waters of the Chang River promoted rice growing in the south. Both rivers often flooded.
2. Nobles believed the king governed by command of heaven. As high priest the king paid homage to his ancestors and made sacrifices to bring good harvests.
3. 2,000 symbols used in writing; finely cast bronze vessels; carved ivory and jade, marble sculpture

Critical Thinking

Rulers in both cultures were believed to derive their power from the gods. In Egypt, however, pharaohs were considered to be gods themselves. Shang kings shared power with nobles whereas pharaohs had absolute power.

HIGHLIGHTS OF CIVILIZATION

Ask students why Egyptian architects and engineers would need to calculate the volume of a pyramid. (to determine how much weight the base would have to support) For extra credit, have students research Snefru's Pyramid at Meidum and the Bent Pyramid at Dahshur, where the Egyptians gained practical experience in pyramid building.

Key Terms, People, and Places
The key terms, people, and places tested here were introduced in the chapter sections and reviewed in the Section Reviews. For definitions see the page references at the appropriate Section Reviews. Also see the Glossary and Biographical Dictionary.

Main Ideas
The main ideas tested here were introduced in the sections of this chapter and reviewed in the Section Reviews. For answers to these questions, see the appropriate Section Reviews.

Critical Thinking
1. Cuneiform used symbols to stand for syllables; hieroglyphics used pictures to stand for ideas and syllables; the Phoenician alphabet used symbols to stand for individual sounds.
2. Possible answers might include: Egypt had a long period of peace; Sumer had a code of law; Mohenjo-Daro had well-developed cities; China had a high level of technology.

CHAPTER 2 REVIEW

Section Summaries

Section 1
The oldest civilization began in Mesopotamia.
The Sumerians created city-states ruled over by kings. Society was a mixture of classes that included nobility, commoners, and slaves. The Sumerians developed writing, mathematics, the plow, the arch, and the use of wheeled vehicles. Around 1700 B.C. Hammurabi adapted the Sumerian legal system and made a code of laws.

Section 2
An Egyptian civilization arose along the Nile River.
Around 3100 B.C. King Menes unified Egypt. During the Old Kingdom period, which began around 2700 B.C. and ended in civil war around 2200 B.C., the Great Pyramids were built, and trade flourished. Around 2000 B.C. princes from Thebes began the Middle Kingdom, another era of unity and prosperity. Following 100 years of Hyksos rule, around 1600 B.C. the New Kingdom began, and Egypt became an empire.

Section 3
An ancient city revealed the early Indus Valley civilization.
Excavations at Mohenjo-Daro, Harappa, and other sites in modern-day India and Pakistan revealed a large, unified civilization based on farming and trade. The Indus Valley people developed highly organized cities and possibly a strong central government. They developed a form of writing and had advanced methods of sewage disposal, and they traded with Sumerians and other Mesopotamians.

Section 4
Chinese civilization developed along the Huang River.
The Shang dynasty was the first Chinese dynasty (1700 B.C.–1027 B.C.). Shang kings were high priests recognized by nobles in the Huang River Valley. The Shang people are known for their advances in writing, their finely cast bronze vessels, and their well-made carvings and sculptures.

Test Yourself

Key Terms, People, and Places
Identify the significance of each of the following:

Section 1
a. Mesopotamia   d. cuneiform
b. city-state   e. Hammurabi
c. ziggurat

Review Dates

4000 B.C. Egyptians develop the first solar calendar

3500 B.C. Sumerians move into Mesopotamia

3100 B.C. Upper and Lower Egypt are united

2500 B.C. Urban life in Indus Valley begins

1700 B.C. Shang dynasty emerges in China

332 B.C. Greeks end the rule of the Egyptian dynasties

4000 B.C. 3000 B.C. 2000 B.C. 1000 B.C. A.D. 1 A.D. 1000

Practicing Study and Research Skills
Students should make charts that reflect their understanding of the chapter content.

Linking Past and Present
Possible answers might include the views of religion on nature, the use of irrigation, and the concern of using the winds to aid trade in the early civilizations. Today's answers might include the differences in sources of power, in construction, and scientific explanations for occurrences.

Learning History Through Maps
greatest impact in Egypt and Pakistan; least impact in China and Iraq

Section 2
a. Egypt   f. theocracy
b. King Menes   g. polytheism
c. dynasty   h. monotheism
d. pharaoh   i. hieroglyphics
e. empire

Section 3
a. Indus Valley

Section 4
a. China   b. loess

Main Ideas

Section 1
1. How did geographic conditions result in the development of Sumerian city-states? In what way was Sumerian society organized?
2. How did the Sumerians contribute to civilization in the areas of communication, architecture, agriculture, transportation, mathematics, literature, and law?
3. What caused the spread of Sumerian civilization throughout the Middle East?
4. What was the purpose of Hammurabi's legal code? What is its significance in advancing civilization?

Section 2
1. In what ways did the farming methods of the early Egyptians lead to the development of local governments? Describe the important skills and techniques which were devised between 5000 and 3100. B.C.
2. What are the major periods of ancient Egyptian history? Describe the major characteristics of each.
3. What was the pharaoh's role in the Egyptian government? What classes divided Egyptian society?
4. Describe the outstanding features of the Egyptian religion.
5. How did ancient Egypt contribute to writing, mathematics, architecture, and medicine? How did its sense of security affect its culture?

Section 3
1. How was an ancient civilization discovered in the Indus Valley?
2. What features of Mohenjo-Daro show that life in the city was highly organized?
3. What do archaeological finds seem to indicate about religious beliefs and organization in the Indus Valley civilization?
4. Describe the economic basis of the Indus Valley civilization. Why do archaeologists believe the Indian coastline has changed greatly in the last 4,000 years?

Section 4
1. In what ways did geography influence the development of early Chinese civilization?
2. Why did nobles accept the rule of the Shang kings? Describe the responsibilities of the kings.
3. What significant changes in skills and technology occurred during the Shang period?

Critical Thinking
1. **Analyzing Comparisons** How do Sumerian cuneiform, Egyptian hieroglyphics, and the Phoenician alphabet differ?
2. **Recognizing Values** Which of the early river valley societies would you have preferred to live in? What are your reasons?

Chapter Skills and Activities

Practicing Study and Research Skills
Working with Charts
It is often difficult to compare the similarities and differences between societies. One way to make this easier is to devise a chart, comparing things in similar categories. Select five topics such as religion, government, and inventions, and compare them for each of the four earliest civilizations.

Linking Past and Present
Life in the four earliest civilizations was greatly controlled by nature and the weather. Do the climate and weather patterns still greatly control our lives today? Give reasons for your answer.

Learning History Through Maps
Compare the map of the four earliest civilizations on pages 22–23 with the World Physical and World Population Maps in the Atlas section of this book. Do the rivers still have the same effect on the population distribution of the four regions? Where do they seem to have the greatest and least impact?

CRITICAL THINKING QUESTION LEVEL 1. average; 2. easy

41

Chapter

3 Empires and Religions in the Middle East

OVERVIEW

This chapter describes the achievements of the Phoenicians and the Jews in the period of independence that ended when the Assyrians, Neo-Babylonians, and Persians established empires.

PLANNING CHART

Section	Text Pages	Key Concept	Suggested Teaching Time
1 The Phoenicians expanded trade and established colonies.	43–44	Phoenician ships carried ideas as well as trade goods to the people of the Mediterranean area and beyond.	One day **Less time?** Assign Section 1 to be read with Section 2 and teach both sections in one class period. **More time?** Use *Overhead Transparency 5*.
2 The Jews developed a distinct culture of enduring significance.	45–47	The ancient Jews endured many hardships while developing a religious ethic valued by many cultures today.	One day **More time?** Use *Source Reading 3A*.
3 The Assyrians, Chaldeans, and Persians built large empires.	49–50	Assyrian and Neo-Babylonian empires rose and fell in the Middle East, but fair and efficient policies helped the Persians become a major power.	One day **More time?** Use *Overhead Transparency 6* and *Source Reading 3B*.

ANCILLARIES

Materials that may be used with this chapter to reinforce, reteach, enrich, and assess learning are pictured on the following pages.

Teacher's Resource File

ACTIVITIES

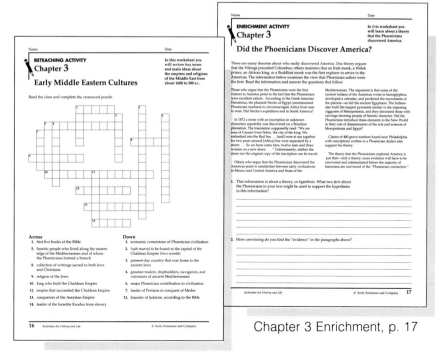

Section 1 Activity, p. 13

Section 2 Activity, p. 14

Section 3 Activity, p. 15

Chapter 3 Reteaching, p. 16

Chapter 3 Enrichment, p. 17

Teacher's Resource File

GEOGRAPHY SKILLS

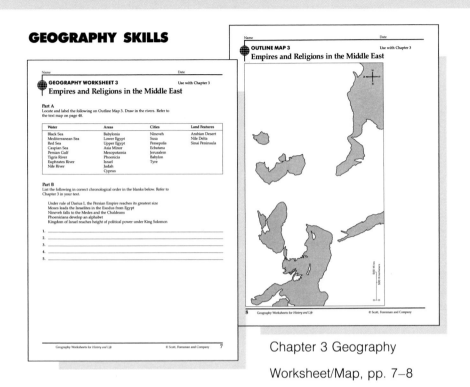

GEOGRAPHY WORKSHEET 3   Use with Chapter 3

Empires and Religions in the Middle East

Part A

Locate and label the following on Outline Map 3. Draw in the rivers. Refer to the text map on page 48.

Water	Areas	Cities	Land Features
Black Sea	Babylonia	Nineveh	Arabian Desert
Mediterranean Sea	Lower Egypt	Susa	Nile Delta
Red Sea	Upper Egypt	Persepolis	Sinai Peninsula
Caspian Sea	Asia Minor	Ecbatana	
Persian Gulf	Mesopotamia	Jerusalem	
Tigris River	Phoenicia	Babylon	
Euphrates River	Israel	Tyre	
Nile River	Judah		
	Cyprus		

Part B

List the following in correct chronological order in the blanks below. Refer to Chapter 3 in your text.

Under rule of Darius I, the Persian Empire reaches its greatest size
Moses leads the Israelites in the Exodus from Egypt
Nineveh falls to the Medes and the Chaldeans
Phoenicians develop an alphabet
Kingdom of Israel reaches height of political power under King Solomon

1. _____
2. _____
3. _____
4. _____
5. _____

OUTLINE MAP 3   Use with Chapter 3

Empires and Religions in the Middle East

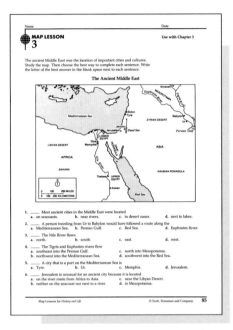

**Chapter 3 Geography
Worksheet/Map, pp. 7–8**

MAP LESSON 3   Use with Chapter 3

The ancient Middle East was the location of important cities and cultures. Study the map. Then choose the best way to complete each sentence. Write the letter of the best answer in the blank space next to each sentence.

The Ancient Middle East

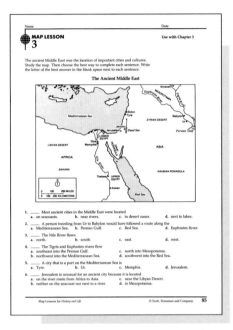

1. _____ Most ancient cities in the Middle East were located
   a. on seacoasts.   b. near rivers.   c. in desert oases.   d. next to lakes.

2. _____ A person traveling from Ur to Babylon would have followed a route along the
   a. Mediterranean Sea.   b. Persian Gulf.   c. Red Sea.   d. Euphrates River.

3. _____ The Nile River flows
   a. north.   b. south.   c. east.   d. west.

4. _____ The Tigris and Euphrates rivers flow
   a. southeast into the Persian Gulf.   c. north into Mesopotamia.
   b. northwest into the Mediterranean Sea.   d. southwest into the Red Sea.

5. _____ A city that is a port on the Mediterranean Sea is
   a. Tyre.   b. Ur.   c. Memphis.   d. Jerusalem.

6. _____ Jerusalem is unusual for an ancient city because it is located
   a. on the river route from Africa to Asia.   c. near the Libyan Desert.
   b. neither on the seacoast nor next to a river.   d. in Mesopotamia.

Chapter 3 Map Lesson, p. 85

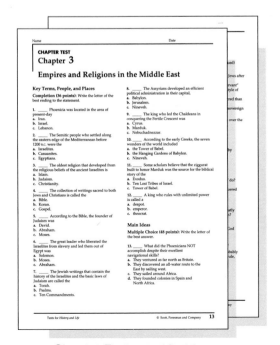

CHAPTER TEST

Chapter 3

Empires and Religions in the Middle East

Key Terms, People, and Places

Completion (36 points): Write the letter of the best ending to the statement.

1. _____ Phoenicia was located in the area of present-day
   a. Iran.
   b. Israel.
   c. Lebanon.

2. _____ The Semitic people who settled along the eastern edge of the Mediterranean before 1200 B.C. were the
   a. Israelites.
   b. Canaanites.
   c. Egyptians.

3. _____ The oldest religion that developed from the religious beliefs of the ancient Israelites was
   a. Islam.
   b. Judaism.
   c. Christianity.

4. _____ The collection of writings sacred to both Jews and Christians is called the
   a. Bible.
   b. Koran.
   c. Gospel.

5. _____ According to the Bible, the founder of Judaism was
   a. David.
   b. Abraham.
   c. Moses.

6. _____ The great leader who liberated the Israelites from slavery and led them out of Egypt was
   a. Solomon.
   b. Moses.
   c. Abraham.

7. _____ The Jewish writings that contain the history of the Israelites and the basic laws of Judaism are called the
   a. Torah.
   b. Psalms.
   c. Ten Commandments.

8. _____ The Assyrians developed an efficient political administration in their capital,
   a. Babylon.
   b. Jerusalem.
   c. Nineveh.

9. _____ The king who led the Chaldeans in conquering the Fertile Crescent was
   a. Cyrus.
   b. Marduk.
   c. Nebuchadnezzar.

10. _____ According to the early Greeks, the seven wonders of the world included
    a. the Tower of Babel.
    b. the Hanging Gardens of Babylon.
    c. Nineveh.

11. _____ Some scholars believe that the ziggurat built to honor Marduk was the source for the biblical story of the
    a. Exodus.
    b. Ten Lost Tribes of Israel.
    c. Tower of Babel.

12. _____ A king who rules with unlimited power is called a
    a. despot.
    b. emperor.
    c. theocrat.

Main Ideas

Multiple Choice (48 points): Write the letter of the best answer.

13. _____ What did the Phoenicians NOT accomplish despite their excellent navigational skills?
    a. They ventured as far north as Britain.
    b. They discovered an all-water route to the East by sailing west.
    c. They sailed around Africa.
    d. They founded colonies in Spain and North Africa.

Chapter Test, pp. 13–14

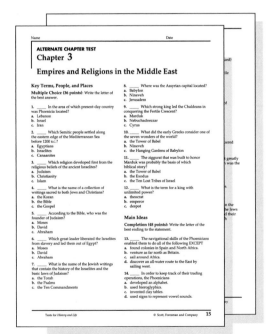

ALTERNATE CHAPTER TEST

Chapter 3

Empires and Religions in the Middle East

Key Terms, People, and Places

Multiple Choice (36 points): Write the letter of the best answer.

1. _____ In the area of which present-day country was Phoenicia located?
   a. Lebanon
   b. Israel
   c. Iran

2. _____ Which Semitic people settled along the eastern edge of the Mediterranean Sea before 1200 B.C.?
   a. Egyptians
   b. Israelites
   c. Canaanites

3. _____ Which religion developed first from the religious beliefs of the ancient Israelites?
   a. Judaism
   b. Christianity
   c. Islam

4. _____ What is the name of a collection of writings sacred to both Jews and Christians?
   a. the Koran
   b. the Bible
   c. the Gospel

5. _____ According to the Bible, who was the founder of Judaism?
   a. Moses
   b. David
   c. Abraham

6. _____ Which great leader liberated the Israelites from slavery and led them out of Egypt?
   a. Moses
   b. David
   c. Abraham

7. _____ What is the name of the Jewish writings that contain the history of the Israelites and the basic laws of Judaism?
   a. the Torah
   b. the Psalms
   c. the Ten Commandments

8. _____ Where was the Assyrian capital located?
   a. Babylon
   b. Nineveh
   c. Jerusalem

9. _____ Which strong king led the Chaldeans in conquering the Fertile Crescent?
   a. Marduk
   b. Nebuchadnezzar
   c. Cyrus

10. _____ What did the early Greeks consider one of the seven wonders of the world?
    a. the Tower of Babel
    b. Nineveh
    c. the Hanging Gardens of Babylon

11. _____ The ziggurat that was built to honor Marduk was probably the basis of which biblical story?
    a. the Tower of Babel
    b. the Exodus
    c. the Ten Lost Tribes of Israel

12. _____ What is the term for a king with unlimited power?
    a. theocrat
    b. emperor
    c. despot

Main Ideas

Completion (48 points): Write the letter of the best ending to the statement.

13. _____ The navigational skills of the Phoenicians enabled them to do all of the following EXCEPT
    a. found colonies in Spain and North Africa.
    b. venture as far north as Britain.
    c. sail around Africa.
    d. discover an all-water route to the East by sailing west.

14. _____ In order to keep track of their trading operations, the Phoenicians
    a. developed an alphabet.
    b. used hieroglyphics.
    c. invented clay tables.
    d. used signs to represent vowel sounds.

Alternate Chapter Test, pp. 15–16

41c

Other Optional Ancillaries

WORKBOOK

Section 1 Worksheet, p. 9

Section 2 Worksheet, p. 10

Section 3 Worksheet, p. 11

SOURCE READINGS

Source Reading 3A
Source Reading 3B

TEST GENERATOR

40 multiple-choice questions for Chapter 3

OVERHEAD TRANSPARENCIES

Overhead Transparency 5
Overhead Transparency 6

Empires and Religions in the Middle East

1600–500 B.C.

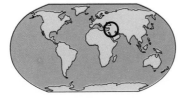

1600 B.C.

c. 1200 B.C. Moses leads the Jews out of Egypt

c. 1000 B.C. Phoenicians develop the alphabet

562 B.C. Nebuchadnezzar dies, and the Persian Empire begins its rise

500 B.C.

400 B.C.

About 1600 B.C., a century after the death of Hammurabi, the Hittites, an Indo-European people from Asia Minor (present-day Turkey), destroyed Babylon and gradually became a major power. After 1450 B.C. energetic Hittite kings created a highly centralized government and extended their empire to include Syria, recently lost by the Egyptian pharaoh Akhenaton. The Egyptian ruler Ramses II tried to win back Syria, but the Hittites were stronger. They forced Ramses back to Palestine and persuaded him to make peace and enter into an alliance of friendship. For a time the Hittite-Egyptian alliance helped both parties fend off new threats from barbarian invasions.

At its height the Hittite civilization was impressive. The Hittites were the first people of the Middle East to use iron tools and weapons. With the spread of this new technology, the Bronze Age gave way to the Iron Age. It would be hard to imagine what our lives would be like today without products made of iron and its refinement—steel.

Building on the superior Mesopotamian civilizations of the peoples they conquered, the Hittites developed law codes of their own and adopted the cuneiform script for their own language. They excelled in the organization and administration of the empire. They ruled wisely and were sensible enough to seek peace by means of an alliance with Egypt. Together the two empires brought an interlude of peace to most of the ancient world.

Shortly after 1200 B.C., a new wave of invaders swept down from the north and in from the Mediterranean, destroying the Hittite Empire. There followed a period of roughly 500 years during which several small states developed flourishing civilizations that left an indelible mark on world history. Then, as we shall see, they lost their independence but not their identity when new mighty empires arose—first the Assyrian, followed by the Chaldean (or Neo-Babylonian), and then the Persian.

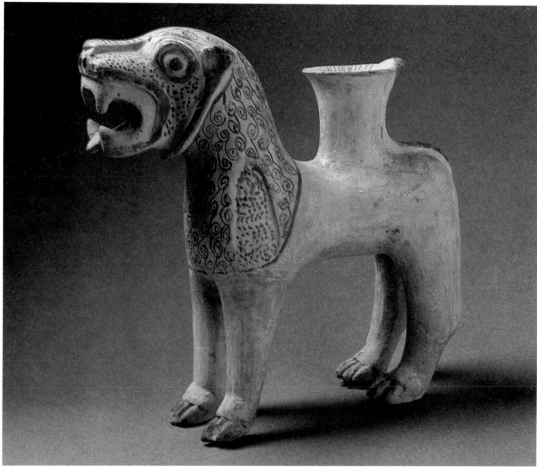

This early lion-shaped Hittite vase (c. 1800 B.C.) was reserved for libations, those liquids used in offerings to a god.

Reading Preview

In this chapter you will read how the Phoenicians, Jews, Assyrians, Chaldeans, and Persians developed important civilizations.

1. The Phoenicians expanded trade and established colonies.

2. The Jews developed a distinct culture of enduring significance.

3. The Assyrians, Chaldeans, and Persians built large empires.

BACKGROUND Phoenicia is the name the Greeks gave to the people who lived along the Mediterranean coast of present-day Lebanon. The word *Phoenicia* is Greek for "land of purple" and refers to the purple dye the natives extracted by a

 The Phoenicians expanded trade and established colonies.

Located in the area of present-day **Lebanon**, Phoenicia [fə nē′shə] was one of the small nations that rose to prominence after the destruction of the Hittite Empire and the decline of Egypt.

The Phoenicians were great sea traders.

The Phoenicians were actually a branch of a Semitic people known as **Canaanites** who had settled

secret process from shellfish. Throughout the ancient world, purple-dyed cloth from Phoenicia was much in demand by kings and wealthy citizens, thus the term "royal purple" we sometimes hear today.

43

1 **Lesson Plan**

Essential Learning Objective

Students will learn to locate Phoenicia and identify goods and cultural elements exchanged in its sea trade.

1 FOCUS AND MOTIVATE

Ask students how a teenager in another culture might be affected by hearing rock and roll music or seeing fashions worn in U.S. high schools. (They might like or want them.) Tell students to look for ways in which the Phoenicians also spread cultural ideas.

2 TEACH

- Point out the location of Phoenicia on the map on page 44. Emphasize how pressure from Arameans and Jews and geographic conditions caused the Phoenicians to turn to the sea.

- Stress that Phoenicians imported raw materials and turned them into products that they sold for a profit. Check to be sure that students grasp how important colonies and military posts are to the expansion and protection of trade.

- Refer to the chart on page 45 and identify relationships between the Phoenician and later alphabets.

GUIDED PRACTICE

Have students list the benefits of trade to the Phoenicians and their trading partners. (profit, cultural exchange, access to a variety of goods)

ASSESS

Why did the Phoenicians become navigators and sea traders? (Expansion by land was blocked by other peoples and mountains.)

OPTIONAL RETEACHING

Hand out outline maps of the Mediterranean area from the Geography Skills book. Have students draw routes to show sources of raw materials for Phoenician products.

OPTIONAL ENRICHMENT

1. Have students research and write a report on the Phoenician colony at Carthage, including a time line of the major events in its history. (average)
2. Assign a written report on the navigational skills of Phoenician sailors, the types of ships built, and the extent of their explorations. (challenging)
3. Also for enrichment:

 Overhead Transparency 5

INDEPENDENT PRACTICE/ HOMEWORK

Assign the Section Review, Activities page 13, or Workbook page 9.

CLOSURE

Tell students that Phoenician navigators and sea traders, using the stars to guide their ships, colonized the Mediterranean and sailed around Africa. Phoenician ships carried raw materials home from Africa, Britain, and Spain and made them into fine products much in demand by the nobility and kings of neighboring countries. Even more important was the influence of the Phoenicians in exporting new ideas and inventions such as the alphabet.

ANSWER TO MAP STUDY Byblos, Sidon, Tyre; Israel, Judah

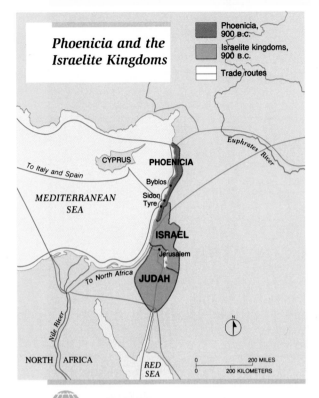

Phoenicia and the Israelite Kingdoms

- Phoenicia, 900 B.C.
- Israelite kingdoms, 900 B.C.
- Trade routes

MAP STUDY Phoenicia was divided into city-states. What were the names of its three main cities? What were the names of the Israelite kingdoms to the south?

along the eastern edge of the Mediterranean. After about 1200 B.C., much of the Canaanites' land was conquered by the Arameans (ancient Syrians) in the north and the ancient Jews in the south. Hemmed in by the Lebanon Mountains to the east, the Phoenicians turned to the sea to seek their fortune. They quickly became the greatest traders, shipbuilders, navigators, and colonizers of the Mediterranean region. Their culture flourished between about 1200 and 300 B.C., when they were conquered by the Greeks. The Phoenicians never formed a united nation, but lived in small independent city-states like the Sumerians. Sailing out from their home ports of Tyre [tīr], Sidon [sī′dən], and Byblos [bib′ləs], Phoenician traders ventured

BACKGROUND Trading goods manufactured at home and gathered from all over the Middle East, Phoenician ships brought back tin from Britain, copper and silver from Spain,

BACKGROUND The Phoenicians occupied the islands of Cyprus and Rhodes, and they set up military posts in Malta, Sicily, Sardinia, and Corsica to protect their trading ships.

beyond the Mediterranean and into the Atlantic as far north as Britain. They founded colonies at Cadiz in Spain and Carthage in North Africa and traded goods such as glass and metalware for British tin, African ivory, and Spanish silver.

The Phoenicians developed the art of navigation, guiding their ships by the stars, to the point where it was safe to sail beyond the sight of land. Venturing into the oceans, they sailed around Africa some 2,000 years before Vasco da Gama. (See Chapter 20.) More important than the articles of trade, the Phoenicians took with them the arts and sciences of Mesopotamia and Egypt and spread them in Greece, North Africa, Italy, and Spain.

The Phoenicians developed the alphabet.

Among the many contributions of the Phoenicians to civilization, the development of the alphabet around 1000 B.C. is of special importance. To keep track of their trading operations, the Phoenicians needed a more efficient system of writing than that used by the Sumerians or Egyptians. Their answer was to make an alphabet from signs that represented sounds. The word **alphabet** comes from their first two letters—"aleph" and "bet."

The Phoenician alphabet was made up of 22 consonant symbols. Around 800 B.C. the Phoenicians introduced this alphabet to the Greeks, who added vowel sounds. From this combination of consonant and vowel signs came the alphabet we use today. The chart on the facing page shows some of the many alphabets derived from the Phoenician alphabet. Along with the alphabet, the Phoenicians carried westward knowledge of the Babylonian numbering system based on 60, which we use today in dividing a circle.

Section 1 Review

Identify Lebanon, Canaanites, alphabet

Main Ideas

1. In what activity did the Phoenician cities excel?
2. How did the Phoenicians solve the problem of record keeping?

Critical Thinking

Making Hypotheses: Why were the Phoenician cities such important carriers of civilization?

ivory from Africa, and lead, gold, and iron from the south shores of the Black Sea.

BACKGROUND Tell students that the alphabet we use to write English is called the "Roman alphabet." Small (lower-case) letters were invented around 800 A.D.

BACKGROUND At first the term *Jew* referred to the people of the kingdom of Judah. Later it applied to all people whose religion is Judaism.

The Evolution of the Alphabet

This table shows how many of the world's languages use alphabets derived from the Phoenician alphabet. The English alphabet is based on the Greek version; it came to us by way of Etruscan and Latin. The Russian Cyrillic alphabet was taken directly from the Greek. Note that Hebrew also developed from the Phoenician alphabet.

Phoenician	Early Hebrew	Early Aramaic	Early Greek	Classical Greek	Etruscan	Early Latin	Classical Latin	Russian-Cyrillic	German-Gothic	English
				A	A	A	A	A		A a
				B		B	B	Б		B b
				Γ		C	C	Г		C c
				Δ	E	D	D	Д		D d
						F	F	Е		E e
						F	F	Ф		F f
				Γ			G	Г		G g
				H	I	H	H	И		H h
						I	I	I		I i
										J j
				K	К	K	K	К		K k

BACKGROUND Point out to students that the Phoenicians and Jews were also Mesopotamians, and their language and customs were similar to those of other peoples in the region. However, the Jewish religion was unique because it emphasized one God who demanded moral behavior from all people on earth.

2 The Jews developed a distinct culture of enduring significance.

South of Phoenicia, in present-day Israel, was the land of the ancient Jews, or Israelites. Their language was Hebrew, a Semitic language closely related to Phoenician and written in the same script. Although the ancient Jews shared many cultural traditions with other Mesopotamians, their religion was quite different. The religious ideas they developed are known as **Judaism**, which grew into one of the world's great religions.

Judaism profoundly influenced two other major religions, Christianity and Islam. The religious and ethical values of the West are deeply rooted in Judaism. Whatever your religious beliefs, chances are that your ideas of right and wrong and of justice derive from the teachings of the ancient Jews.

The Israelites fled slavery and established the kingdom of Israel.

Early Jewish history is recorded in the **Bible**, a collection of writings sacred to both Jews and Christians. The Jewish writings, written in Hebrew, are known as the Old Testament to distinguish them from the New Testament, which deals with the teachings of Jesus. According to the Bible, the founder of Judaism was the patriarch **Abraham**, who led his people out of Mesopotamia into Canaan around 1900 or 1800 B.C. This was shortly before the time of Hammurabi's rule in Babylon. Abraham and his followers reached the land of Canaan, the biblical name for Palestine, which according to the Bible was the land promised to Abraham's descendants.

Three generations later, under the leadership of Jacob, many of the Jews left Canaan and migrated into northeastern Egypt to escape drought and famine. Jacob was also called "Israel," and his descendants later organized themselves into a confederation of 12 tribes, called Israelites. The Israelites, or ancient Jews, remained in Egypt for more than 400 years. At first they prospered as cattle herders, but then they were enslaved by the pharaoh and forced to build monuments for the Egyptians.

According to the Bible, a great leader named **Moses** liberated the Israelites from slavery in the 1200s B.C. and led them out of Egypt back toward the promised land of Canaan. Known as the Exodus, the liberation of the Israelites from slavery is a cornerstone of Jewish history and religion.

Returning to Canaan, the task of winning the land from the Canaanites fell to Moses' successor, Joshua. The conquest of Canaan took about 200

45

Answers to Section 1 Review

Identify
Key Terms, People, and Places are defined on pages indicated in parentheses. Also see the Glossary and Biographical Dictionary.
Lebanon (43), Canaanites (43), alphabet (44)

Main Ideas
1. sea-going commerce
2. with an alphabet that was a great advance over cuneiform writing

Critical Thinking
Because Phoenicians were great traders, their cities reflected the diverse culture acquired in residents' travels.

2 Lesson Plan

Essential Learning Objectives

Students will learn to:
- describe the struggles of the early Jews in establishing the Kingdom of Israel.
- discuss the importance of the teachings of Judaism.

1 FOCUS AND MOTIVATE

Ask students to name actions that our society teaches are right or wrong. List them in two columns on the chalkboard. Guide students in identifying the underlying moral standards of the actions listed. (Example: Murder and stealing cause harm to others or to property.) While reading this section, students should look for values inherited from the Jewish religion.

- Identify the location and language of the early Jews.

- Explain that the Old Testament is sacred to Jews, Christians, and Muslims and is also an important source of historical information. Stress the significance of the Jews' belief in one God at a time when belief in many nature gods was common.

- Make a time line that illustrates events in Jewish history from Abraham (1900–1800 B.C.) to the Prophets (750–550 B.C.). Emphasize the repeated efforts of the Jews to return to Canaan.

GUIDED PRACTICE

Use the feature, "From the Archives," page 47, to discuss the significance of the Ten Commandments as a code of laws. Guide students in grasping the ancient values that underlie modern social and legal structures.

3 ASSESS AND CLOSE

ASSESS

Why was Moses an important figure in Jewish history? (He led the Jews out of Egypt and received the Ten Commandments.)

OPTIONAL RETEACHING

Have students name the Jewish leaders discussed in this section, identify the role of each, and write leaders' names and identifications on the chalkboard in chronological order.

OPTIONAL ENRICHMENT

1. Assign a report on the historical background of the Jewish holiday of Passover. This might be done with library research or by interviewing an authority on Judaism. (average)

years, and during this time the Israelites found themselves facing a new and more powerful enemy, the Philistines, a people armed with iron weapons who had moved into southern Canaan around 1200 B.C. In their hour of desperation, the Israelite leaders, who were called judges, decided to unify their tribes under a king. They chose a young soldier named Saul, who became the first king of Israel. He ruled from 1020 to 1000 B.C.

David and Solomon ruled a united kingdom.

Saul was followed on the throne by David, who captured Jerusalem and made it the capital of his kingdom. Under David's son Solomon, who ruled from 972 to 932 B.C., the kingdom of Israel reached the height of its political power.

Solomon, who is renowned for his wisdom, began a vast building program. He built a magnificent Temple in Jerusalem—the first for the worship of one God—as well as cities, palaces, fortresses, and roads. He sent ships to trade in distant places and maintained good relations with neighboring states. To pay for his ambitious build-

ing program, Solomon levied very heavy taxes. After his death, the ten northern tribes revolted against this heavy taxation and set up the independent kingdom of Israel. The southern tribes made up the kingdom of Judah, which was ruled from Jerusalem by the descendants of David. Although the two kingdoms divided, the people considered themselves a single people and followed the same religion. The word Jew comes from the name of the people of Judah—the Judeans.

This image of a Canaanite man shows a style of dress also worn in Phoenicia and Israel around 1000 B.C.

The two kingdoms are shown on the map on page 44. Weakened by the division, both kingdoms were open to invaders. In 722 B.C. the Assyrians conquered the northern kingdom and scattered its inhabitants throughout the vast Assyrian Empire. Absorbed by other peoples, they lost their identity and became known to history as the Ten Lost Tribes of Israel. In 586 B.C. the Chaldeans conquered the southern kingdom, burned the Temple at Jerusalem, and carried the citizens off into exile in Babylon. They remained there for about 50 years until Cyrus the Persian conquered the Chaldeans and permitted the Jews to return home. However, many thousands remained in Babylon, where their descendants formed a large Jewish community that lasted until the 20th century.

Moses taught the high spiritual and ethical standards of Judaism.

From the time of Abraham, the Israelites worshiped one God, who held them to a very high standard of ethical and ritual behavior. According to Judaism, there is only one God in the universe who rules over all peoples and who demands high moral conduct from all peoples. This belief in one God is called monotheism. It stood in sharp contrast to the beliefs of neighboring peoples—Egyptians and Mesopotamians—who worshiped many gods.

Moses was a major figure in the development of monotheism and of the Jewish faith. During the Exodus from Egypt, Moses taught the Israelites that they had made an eternally binding covenant, or formal agreement, with God. The covenant assured them of God's love and protection but made them especially accountable for their sins and shortcomings.

The Bible describes how God gave Moses the Ten Commandments on Mount Sinai and accepted the Israelites as His chosen people. As you can see from the excerpt on the facing page, the Ten Commandments required the Jews to worship one God and to follow a strict code of conduct. They were forbidden to steal, murder, lie, or commit adultery. They were also to honor their parents and to observe the Sabbath, the seventh day of the week, as a holy day of rest and worship.

Starting with Moses, a code of Jewish law and

BACKGROUND The Jews who returned to Jerusalem rebuilt the Temple but did not gain political independence. From 539 to 332 B.C., they remained under the rule of Persia. Thereafter they were ruled in turn by Alexander the Great, the Ptolemies of Egypt, and the Roman Empire.

From the Archives

The Ten Commandments

The Ten Commandments as revealed to Moses are rules for living and for worship. The commandments are not numbered in the Bible, and their numbering and the exact wording differ slightly in the different versions of the Bible.

I am the Lord thy God, who brought thee out of the land of Egypt, out of the house of bondage.

    Thou shalt have no other gods before Me.

    Thou shalt not make unto thee a graven image, nor any likeness of anything that is in heaven above, or that is in the earth beneath, or that is in the water under the earth. . . .

    Thou shalt not take the name of the Lord thy God in vain. . . .

    Remember the sabbath day, to keep it holy. . . .

    Honor thy father and thy mother. . . .

    Thou shalt not kill.

    Thou shalt not commit adultery.

    Thou shalt not steal.

    Thou shalt not bear false witness against thy neighbor.

    Thou shalt not covet [desire] thy neighbor's house; thou shalt not covet thy neighbor's wife, nor his manservant, nor his maidservant, nor his ox, nor his ass, nor anything that is thy neighbor's.

Exodus 20:2–17

custom evolved from the Ten Commandments. Much of this code was recorded in the Bible, the outstanding literary achievement of the Jews. The Bible is divided into 24 books. The first five books— Genesis, Exodus, Leviticus, Numbers, and Deuteronomy—make up the Jewish **Torah** and contain the early history of the Israelites as well as the basic laws of Judaism. The Torah, which means "teaching," emphasizes the ideas of the promised land and the covenant with God. A second group of books develops this message with

FROM THE ARCHIVES The Ten Commandments are found in Exodus, as indicated in the reference following the reading. Ask students which of the Ten Commandments are reflected in past or present laws of our country. (Commandments 6, 7, 8,

BACKGROUND The dream of an independent Jewish state never died, and in 1948, after a lapse of nearly 20 centuries, a new State of Israel was created under United Nations auspices.

the words of the Prophets, and the remaining books contain various writings, such as Psalms, Ruth, and Job.

The Prophets taught a new concept of Judaism.

Between 750 and 550 B.C., Judaism was further refined by a series of great prophets—religious leaders who claimed to communicate God's will to the people. According to Jeremiah, for example, God demanded righteousness and protection for the weak and helpless. The prophet Micah emphasized mercy and justice:

> He has shown you, O Man, what is good; and what does the Lord require of you but to do justice, and to love kindness, and to walk humbly with your God.

The prophets saw Jewish history and, indeed, all history as being governed by the sovereign will of God. According to their view, the Assyrian and Chaldean conquests was God's way of punishing the Jews for their sins. The prophet Isaiah, who lived to see the end of the Babylonian Exile, declared that Israel was God's "righteous servant," purified through suffering and ready now to guide the world to the worship of God. Thus, the Jews who returned from the Babylonian Exile gained a faith in their destiny that would sustain and inspire them through the centuries.

Section 2 Review

Identify Judaism, Bible, Abraham, Moses, Torah

Main Ideas

1. Describe briefly the events leading to the establishment of the kingdom of Israel.
2. Which of Saul's successors ruled over a united kingdom? Why was the kingdom divided?
3. What role did Moses play in the development of Judaism?
4. How did the prophets influence Judaism?

Critical Thinking

Predicting Effects: Observance of the Sabbath as a day of rest and worship was an important Jewish contribution to civilization. How might life in the United States be different if the need for rest from labor at least once a week were not generally accepted?

and 9) Ask what Commandment 9 means. How is it reflected in the laws of our country? (Do not accuse wrongly; laws against libel and slander)

2. Assign a student to research and report on the Old City of Jerusalem— its history, religious sites, and present condition. (challenging)

3. Also for enrichment:

📖 *Source Reading 3A*

INDEPENDENT PRACTICE/ HOMEWORK

Assign the Section Review, Activities page 14, or Workbook page 10.

CLOSURE

Tell students that the religious teachings of the ancient Jews helped form the moral standards of Western culture. Throughout their long history, as the tribes of Israel suffered many hardships, Jewish leaders developed and taught a unique value system.

Answers to Section 2 Review

Identify

Key Terms, People, and Places are defined on pages indicated in parentheses. Also see the Glossary and Biographical Dictionary. Judaism (45), Bible (45), Abraham (45), Moses (45), Torah (47)

Main Ideas

1. Descendants of Abraham went to Egypt, became slaves, returned to Canaan, fought Canaanites and Philistines, and united under King Saul.
2. David and Solomon. Solomon's heavy taxes led northern tribes to rebel.
3. taught Israelites of the covenant with God
4. Prophets demanded righteousness, protection of the weak, mercy, and justice.

Critical Thinking

fewer recreational, leisure, and cultural activities; less emphasis on family life; more health problems

GEOGRAPHY

A Key to History

THE FERTILE CRESCENT

History began in the Fertile Crescent, the thin semicircle of fertile land stretching from Israel and Judah on the Mediterranean Sea to the Persian Gulf. The western horn of the crescent curves along the Mediterranean coast. The eastern horn follows the Tigris and Euphrates rivers to the Persian Gulf. Each winter, melting snow and rain send a renewing ripple of water and soil down the Tigris and the Euphrates rivers. The meltwater flows from mountains to the northeast and the northwest.

When forests were cut down in the watershed areas, the runoff came much faster. This sometimes created raging floods, especially on the Tigris River. Sometimes the waters would follow one course, sometimes another.

Silt carried by the floodwaters piled up at the mouths of the rivers each year, creating marshes and reed swamps and eventually dry land. The city-state of Ur on the Euphrates River was once on the gulf. On modern maps, its ruins are shown many miles from the gulf as the river has continued to create new land.

In ancient times, the rulers of the land between the Tigris and Euphrates rivers were able to build dams and canals to control the floodwaters. The fertile land could then be irrigated to grow crops.

In places this is still being done. However, many more acres could be placed into production if the flood control devices were rebuilt and if deforestation and grazing of animals in the watershed areas was controlled.

REVIEW

1. In ancient times, the Tigris and the Euphrates rivers reached the sea separately, as this map shows. Today, the rivers join to form one channel. How might this change affect agriculture in the area?
2. What factors could help make agriculture within the Fertile Crescent more productive today?

Follow the paths of the Tigris and the Euphrates rivers from the mountains of Asia Minor to the Persian Gulf. Why have river valleys sheltered early civilizations in dry regions?

The Fertile Crescent

Black Sea

Caspian Sea

ASIA MINOR

HITTITES

MESOPOTAMIA

Tigris

Euphrates

Nineveh

CYPRUS

SYRIA

River

River

Mediterranean Sea

Sidon
Tyre

PHOENICIA

ISRAEL

SYRIAN DESERT

Babylon

BABYLONIA

Ecbatana

NILE DELTA
Jerusalem
LOWER EGYPT

JUDAH

Susa
SUMERIANS

Ur

SINAI PENINSULA
UPPER EGYPT

Nile River

Red Sea

Persian Gulf

Fertile Crescent

N

| 0 | 200 | 400 MILES |
| 0 | 200 | 400 KILOMETERS |

48

3 The Assyrians, Chaldeans, and Persians built large empires.

The era of small, independent states such as Phoenicia and the Israelite kingdoms came to an abrupt end with the rise of new Middle Eastern empires. The first of these was the Assyrian, followed by the Chaldean (or Neo-Babylonian), and then the Persian.

The Assyrians relied on terror.

A people of Semitic origin, the Assyrians were long established in the upper Tigris Valley. They began to push toward the Mediterranean in the 9th century B.C. and conquered Babylon in the 8th century. By 671 B.C. they ruled the Fertile Crescent and had annexed Egypt.

The Assyrian army was impressive indeed. With its chariots, mounted cavalry, and siege equipment that enabled it to conquer walled cities, the Assyrian army was the most terrifying yet seen in the ancient world. Few conquerors in history have been as cruel and heartless. Conquered peoples who refused to bow to the Assyrian will were brutally tortured or burned alive. Mass deportations, like that of the Israelites, were used to destroy national feeling and prevent uprisings.

The Assyrians developed an efficient political administration that served as a model for their successors, especially the Persians and Alexander the Great. The fine library of clay tablets in the Assyrian capital, **Nineveh** [nin′ə və], helped preserve much of our knowledge of Mesopotamia.

However, because the Assyrians were such cruel rulers, the peoples they conquered longed for revenge. In 612 B.C. the Assyrian Empire fell to the Chaldeans from Babylonia and the Medes from Persia. Everywhere in the empire people rejoiced because their cruel Assyrian masters were overthrown.

A Neo-Babylonian Empire arose (605–550 B.C.).

With the fall of Nineveh, Babylonia became powerful for the first time since Hammurabi, more than 1,000 years earlier. (The Chaldean Empire is therefore also known as the Neo-Babylonian Empire.) The Chaldeans, guided by their strong king

The Assyrian and Chaldean (Neo-Babylonian) Empires

Assyrian Empire, about 670 B.C.

Chaldean (Neo-Babylonian) Empire, about 562 B.C.

MAP STUDY The Assyrian Empire extended from the Persian Gulf to Egypt and the island of Cyprus. On what river was Nineveh, its capital, located? Did the Chaldean Empire include Egypt and Cyprus?

Nebuchadnezzar [neb′yə kəd nez′ər], built the Chaldean Empire by conquering the Fertile Crescent. Refer to the map above to compare the Chaldean Empire with the earlier Assyrian Empire.

Nebuchadnezzar rebuilt Babylon, making it the most impressive city of its day. Among its many marvels were the famous **Hanging Gardens of Babylon**, lush roof-top gardens regarded by the Greeks as one of the seven wonders of the world. Nebuchadnezzar also built a ziggurat, or temple-tower, in honor of Marduk, the chief god of the Chaldeans. Some scholars believe this was the source for the story in the Bible of the **Tower of Babel.**

The Chaldeans, building on the work of earlier people, studied the stars as well as the sun, moon, and planets. Without any telescopes or accurate time-recording instruments, they used mathematics to work out detailed tables of the movements of these bodies and thus made important contributions to the science of astronomy.

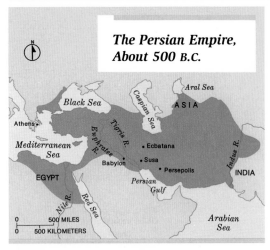

The Persian Empire, About 500 B.C.

 MAP STUDY The Persian Empire reached all the way from Europe to India. Did it extend as far as the shores of the Black, Caspian, and Aral seas?

The Chaldeans believed it was possible to tell the future by studying the stars. They charted the movements of stars to help them predict the future. Thus they began the study of astrology, still found in daily newspapers.

The Chaldean Empire was the last great Mesopotamian empire whose culture was directly influenced by the Sumerian civilization. Although once powerful, the Chaldean Empire began to decay when Nebuchadnezzar died in 562 B.C. It was soon succeeded by the Persian Empire.

The Persians built a vast empire (525–331 B.C.).

In 550 B.C. a Persian general named Cyrus the Great led attacks on his neighbors, the Medes. This was the beginning of the Persian Empire, which soon expanded across the Middle East. (See the map above.) Unlike the Assyrian rulers, the Persian kings allowed conquered peoples to worship their own gods, to use their own languages, and to keep their own customs.

The Persian government, like the Assyrian and Chaldean governments, was ruled by a **despot**, or a king with unlimited power. Under Darius I, who

ruled from 521 to 486 B.C., the Persian Empire reached its largest size. Four capital cities—Susa, Ecbatana, Babylon, and Persepolis—were set up in different parts of the empire.

To improve communications throughout the huge empire, the Persian kings maintained a network of fine roads. Along these highways rode the king's messengers, changing horses every 14 miles. These horsemen could cover 1,500 miles in a little more than a week. Ordinary travelers took three months to travel the same distance.

The Persian kings supported farming and encouraged trade in the whole empire, partly because they wanted all districts to be able to pay taxes. The tax burden, however, was not heavy. Throughout the empire, a money system of gold and silver coins was used.

The Persian kings treated other peoples fairly, in part because of the influence of the Persian religion. Founded by Zoroaster in the 7th century B.C., this religion asked its followers to choose and obey Ahura Mazda, the god of good, over Ahriman, the god of evil. In time, the Zoroastrians believed, the world would come to an end. All people would then face a last judgment, and the righteous would go to heaven and the wicked to hell. These ideas influenced Judaism, Christianity, and Islam all of which believe in a final judgment. In addition, Christianity and Islam came to accept the view that the wicked are condemned to hell.

Section 3 Review

Identify Nineveh, Nebuchadnezzar, Hanging Gardens of Babylon, Tower of Babel, despot

Main Ideas
1. How did reliance on terror contribute to Assyria's rise and later decline?
2. Why is the Chaldean Empire sometimes called the Neo-Babylonian Empire?
3. How did the Persians govern their empire?

Critical Thinking
Recognizing Values: Although the Persian government was ruled by a despot, it treated its peoples far more leniently than other empires we have studied. Why, then, do we in the United States consider a despot a bad kind of ruler?

The Torah

A non-Jew once asked Hillel—a famous rabbi of the late 1st century B.C.—to teach him the entire Torah while he was standing on one foot. Hillel replied, "That which is hateful to you, do not do to your neighbor. This is the entire Torah; the rest is commentary."

The Torah—the first five books of the Bible—contains numerous passages that illustrate Hillel's assertion. For example, the Ten Commandments, found both in the

The Torah scroll (below) is read at Sabbath services. Symbols on the 4th-century Roman glass (below right) include a menorah—a seven-branched candelabrum said to symbolize the seven days of Creation.

book of Exodus and in the book of Deuteronomy, are a set of laws that demand that people deal morally with family members, friends, servants, employees, and neighbors.

Although the Ten Commandments are the most famous of the Torah's teachings, other laws in the Torah set similar ethical standards. For example, a law in the book of Leviticus states, "When you reap the harvests of your land, you shall not gather the gleanings of your harvest. . . . [instead] you shall leave them for the poor." In this way Jews were required to help the needy in their communities. The Torah further demands that people treat not only their neighbors with kindness, but also deal kindly with people they do not know.

Finally the statement "Love your neighbor as yourself," is the source of the maxim Hillel presented as the Torah's key teaching. This verse, found in Leviticus, Chapter 19, has become the cornerstone not only of Judaism, but the main ethical principle for peoples who follow other religions throughout the Western world.

2. Chaldeans made Babylon a capital city again after 1,000 years.
3. Subject peoples could worship their own gods, speak their own language, and keep their own customs. Empire had fine roads to maintain good communications.

Critical Thinking
Modern ideas of government reject unlimited authority; one despot may be just, but others may not.

HIGHLIGHTS OF CIVILIZATION
Point out the photograph of the Torah. Explain that it is handwritten in Hebrew on parchment scrolls by learned scribes. The Torah reading is the focus of Jewish Sabbath services. During the service the Torah is removed from the cabinet, or Ark, partially unrolled, and read aloud in Hebrew. The Torah is divided into 52 portions, one for each week of the year. At the end of the year, the Torah is rerolled in a joyous holiday called *Simchat Torah.*

The Torah ark shown on the plate between guardian lions contains the first five books of the Bible. Other objects shown on the plate are the amphora with oil for the Menorah, the *etrog* (citrus fruit used during the Feast of Tabernacles), and the *shofar* (ram's horn, blown to announce the New Year on Rosh Hashanah).

The first menorah was said to have been fashioned following precise instructions from Moses, inspired by a revelation from God. Several attempts have been made to interpret the symbolism of the seven branches. Different views hold that the seven lamps symbolize the seven heavens, the seven planets, or the six weekdays and the Sabbath, together representing the seven days of the Creation.

Answers to Test Yourself

Key Terms, People, and Places
The key terms, people, and places tested here were introduced in the chapter sections and reviewed in the Section Reviews. For definitions see the page references at the appropriate Section Reviews. Also see the Glossary and Biographical Dictionary.

Main Ideas
The main ideas tested here were introduced in the sections of this chapter and reviewed in the Section Reviews. For answers to these questions, see the appropriate Section Reviews.

Critical Thinking
1. archaeological evidence, including ancient writing, on-site studies of ancient cities and dwellings, murals and other art, old coins.
2. Persian religion was like a conscience; based on the teachings of Zoroaster, it said a day of judgment was coming.

CHAPTER 3 REVIEW

Section Summaries

Section 1
The Phoenicians expanded trade and established colonies.
The strength of Phoenicia rested on overseas commerce. To facilitate trade, colonies were established along the trade routes, and the art of navigation was developed. To ease record keeping, the Phoenicians developed an alphabet that became the basis for the alphabet we use today.

Section 2
The Jews developed a distinct culture of enduring significance.
Jewish history centers around monotheism—the belief in one God who rules the universe—and the attempt to establish a nation in Israel in keeping with a divine covenant. After a period of slavery in Egypt, the Israelites established the kingdom of Israel with Jerusalem as its capital. The kingdom flourished under David and Solomon. After Solomon's death it divided into two kingdoms that were later conquered, one by the Assyrians and the other by the Chaldeans. The Jewish religion provided a moral and ethical base that greatly influenced other religions, especially Christianity and Islam.

Section 3
The Assyrians, Chaldeans, and Persians built large empires.
Using terror as a weapon of conquest, the Assyrians brought political unity to the Mesopotamian area, bringing to an end the independence of small states. Harsh treatment of subject peoples led to rebellion and the defeat of the Assyrians at the hands of the Chaldeans. The Chaldeans, or Neo-Babylonians, built an impressive capital at Babylon and kept alive some aspects of the old Sumerian culture. With the fall of the Chaldeans, the Persians built a vast empire. The Persian government was ruled by a despot, but it treated its peoples humanely. An efficient government and an excellent communication system brought stability to the empire.

Review Dates

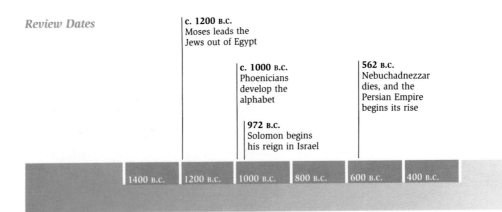

c. 1200 B.C.
Moses leads the Jews out of Egypt

c. 1000 B.C.
Phoenicians develop the alphabet

972 B.C.
Solomon begins his reign in Israel

562 B.C.
Nebuchadnezzar dies, and the Persian Empire begins its rise

1400 B.C. | 1200 B.C. | 1000 B.C. | 800 B.C. | 600 B.C. | 400 B.C.

Test Yourself

Key Terms and People
Identify the significance of each of the following:

Section 1
a. Lebanon
b. Canaanites
c. alphabet

Section 2
a. Judaism
b. Bible
c. Abraham
d. Moses
e. Torah

Section 3
a. Nineveh
b. Nebuchadnezzar
c. Hanging Gardens of Babylon
d. Tower of Babel
e. despot

Main Ideas

Section 1
1. What economic activities were important in Phoenicia?
2. What innovations in record keeping began with the Phoenicians?

Section 2
1. What events led to the establishment of the kingdom of Israel?
2. Under which kings did the Israelites flourish? What caused the kingdom to divide into two parts?
3. Why is Moses of such importance in Jewish history?
4. How did the prophets influence Judaism?

Section 3
1. What part did the use of terror play in the rise and fall of Assyria?
2. Why is the Chaldean Empire also called the Neo-Babylonian Empire?
3. How did the Persians govern their vast realm?

Critical Thinking
1. Evaluating Sources of Information   Much of what we know about the early history of the Jews comes from the Bible. What other sources of information can be used to learn about the various events described in the Bible?

2. Recognizing Values   The Persians governed better than most of the earlier empires that flourished in Mesopotamia. What influence may their religious beliefs have had on their style of governing?

Chapter Skills and Activities

Practicing Study and Research Skills
Using Your School Library
In his poem *The Destruction of Sennacherib* [sə nak′ər-ib], the 19th-century English poet Lord Byron described in vivid language how the Assyrian invaders appeared to their victims.

> The Assyrian came down like the wolf on the fold.
> And his cohorts were gleaming in purple and gold
> And the sheen of their spears was like stars on the
>   sea,
> When the blue wave rolls nightly on deep Galilee.

Suppose you wanted to read all of Lord Byron's poem. Where would you go to find it? Probably the best place to start is your school library's card catalog. If you need help, ask the school librarian. If you know how to use the library, look in the card catalog under the poet's name. You will discover some interesting information about Lord Byron's name. If your library has Byron's collected works, you need look no farther. If not, ask the librarian to guide you to anthologies (collections) of English literature. A poem as well known as this one is often included in anthologies.

Linking Past and Present
Make a list of names, terms, and ideas found in Chapter 3 that were already somewhat familiar to you because they are either still in common use or because you have come across them in other subjects you have studied. You will be surprised how long your list will be.

Learning History Through Maps
Use the map on page 44 of Phoenicia and the Israelite Kingdoms and the one on page 49 of the Assyrian and Chaldean (Neo-Babylonian) empires to explain why the small states were unlikely to remain independent with the rise of great empires.

CRITICAL THINKING QUESTION LEVEL 1. average; 2. challenging

UNIT ONE

REVIEW

Summarizing the Unit

Chapter 1
Early Humans
Many scientists believe that prehumans called hominids began to emerge about 4 million years ago. Modern *Homo sapiens* are believed to have come quite late in the long span of the development of life on earth, about 100,000 B.C. They learned to make tools, trade, domesticate plants and animals, and develop rules to make group living possible.

Chapter 2
The First Civilizations
The four earliest civilizations developed in river valleys in the Middle East, in India, and in China. These early civilizations developed between about 3500 B.C. and 1600 B.C. During this period people began to build cities, establish governments and laws, make metal tools, and write.

Chapter 3
Empires and Religions in the Middle East
Civilization progressed with the creation of great empires, some built by peaceful means, others by the use of force. Two lasting achievements, the Phoenician alphabet and the Jewish religion, which is based on monotheism and the view that God demands high moral conduct from all people, developed during this period.

Using Writing Skills

The skill of effective writing is important in the study of history. It helps define, explain, describe, compare, analyze, evaluate, or persuade. The process used in writing about history topics is the same as that used for any writing. Four steps take you through from beginning to end: prewriting, writing, revising, and presenting. These steps need not be isolated. Writing may take place as you prewrite, prewriting and revising as you write, and writing as you revise. The following guidelines will introduce you to the writing process. In later unit reviews, other features will help you develop effective writing skills.

(1) Prewriting involves choosing an appropriate topic and developing ideas about your purpose, audience, and facts.
(2) Writing is putting your first draft on paper as quickly as possible without worrying about spelling or grammar.
(3) Revising involves several activities intended to turn your first draft into a well-written final copy.
(4) Presenting, or publishing, means sharing your work with your chosen audience.

Activity. Writers often need a nudge to begin their work. One effective warm-up is freewriting, in which a writer spends a set amount of time writing down anything that comes to mind. In effect, the writer is thinking on paper. To experience freewriting, select any general topic from this unit (for example, early humans, early governments, early inventions, or early religions). Take ten minutes to write down everything that comes to mind about that or a related topic. Don't worry about spelling or punctuation, and don't think that you have to know how a sentence or passage is going to turn out before you begin to write it. Just write down your ideas without stopping.

Test Yourself

Key Terms and People
Match each term or person with the correct definition.
1. leader who extended the legal system developed by the Sumerians
2. human beings
3. leader who founded Judaism
4. periods of expansion of the polar ice caps
5. leader who established the Chaldean Empire
6. the worship of one God
a. *Homo sapiens*
b. Hammurabi
c. Ice Age
d. Abraham
e. monotheism
f. Nebuchadnezzar

Key Dates

Match the letters on the time line with the events for which they stand:

3600 B.C.　3150 B.C.　2700 B.C.　2250 B.C.　1800 B.C.　1350 B.C.　900 B.C.

A　B　C　D　E　F

___ Urban life in the Indus Valley begins.
___ Moses leads the Jews out of Egypt.
___ Bronze metalworking begins in the Middle East.
___ The Shang dynasty emerges in China.
___ The Phoenicians develop the alphabet.
___ Upper and Lower Egypt are united.

Key Places

Match the letters on the map with the places described below:

___ place where the first cave paintings were discovered
___ place where the Pyramids were built
___ location of the earliest civilization
___ place where Shang dynasty was established
___ location of the ancient city of Mohenjo-Daro

Main Ideas

1. Cro-Magnon people were different from other earlier people because ___
a. they used fire for warmth.
b. they traded across long distances.
c. they used bronze tools.
d. they developed an irrigation system.
2. The rise of cities probably occurred because ___
a. there was a reliable food supply.
b. there was a need for trade.
c. there was a need for defense.
d. there was a desire to give up nomadic life.
3. The river civilization that was dependent on yearly flooding was the ___
a. Huang.
b. Tigris-Euphrates.
c. Nile.
d. Indus.
4. The first form of writing is known as ___
a. papyrus.
b. monotheism.
c. cuneiform.
d. theocracy.
5. Western religious beliefs of justice and ideas of right and wrong originated with ___
a. Islam.
b. Christianity.
c. Zoroastrianism.
d. Judaism.

Critical Thinking

1. Making Hypotheses What role has trade had on the development of society, starting with the earliest human beings? Support your answer with evidence.
2. Assessing Cause and Effect What early inventions or ideas are still in practice in modern times? Give examples.

CRITICAL THINKING QUESTION LEVEL 1. challenging; 2. average

The Age of Classical Civilizations

OVERVIEW

This unit describes classical and other civilizations throughout the world that developed and flowered from 2000 B.C. to A.D. 500.

ADDITIONAL TEACHING AIDS FOR UNIT TWO

Literature for the Teacher

Bowman, Alan. *Egypt After the Pharaohs 332 B.C.–A.D. 642.* Berkeley: University of California Press, 1986.

Gernet, Jacques. *A History of Chinese Civilization.* New York: Cambridge University Press, 1986.

Grant, Michael. *The Rise of the Greeks.* New York: Charles Schribner's Sons, 1987.

McGregor, Malcolm. *The Athenians and Their Empire.* Vancouver: University of British Columbia Press, 1987.

Scullard, H. H. *Roman Britain: Outpost of an Empire.* London: Thames & Hudson, 1979.

Stuever, Stuart, and Felicia Holton and Antonelli Koster. *Americans in Search of Their Prehistoric Past.* NAL, 1985.

Titus, Livy. *Rome and Italy.* Penguin, 1982.

Turner, Geoffrey. *Indians of North America.* Poole: Blandford Press, 1979.

Wolpert, Stanley. *A New History of India* (second edition). New York: Oxford University Press, 1982.

Literature for the Student

Arnold, Guy. *Datelines of World History.* New York: Warwick Press, 1983 (easy)

Bradford, E. Hannibal. *The General from Carthage.* McGraw-Hill, 1981. (average)

Cotterell, Arthur. *The First Emperor of China.* New York: Holt, Rinehart, 1981. (easy)

Pirazzoli-t' Serstevens, Michèle. *The Han Dynasty.* New York: Rizzoli, 1982. (challenging)

Stuart, Gene S. *America's Ancient Cities.* National Geographic Society, 1988. (average)

Wood, Michael. *In Search of the Trojan War.* New York: Facts on File Publications, 1985. (challenging)

Audio-Visual Materials*

Digging Into the Past. Film, 14 minutes, color, [Coronet], 1976. Unearthing the remains of an ancient Indian culture, including sorting, analysis, and carbon dating, with information discovered about 8,000 years of human life

Early American Civilizations (second edition). Video or film, 22 minutes, color, [Coronet], 1987. Architecture, culture, cities, and agriculture of the Olmecs, Mayas, Toltecs, Aztecs, and Incas

The Glory That Remains. Film, 30 minutes, color, [Time-Life], 1969. Rise and fall of Persia under the Archaemenid dynasty

The Glory That Was Greece. Films, 3 titles, 38–40 minutes each, color, [Time-Life], 1967. "The Age of Civil War"—Peloponnesian War recounted. "The Age of Victory"—traces the history of the Persian Wars. "The Age of Monos"—explores Greek legends

Greece: The Golden Age. Video or film, 29 minutes, color, [McGraw-Hill], 1963. Greek civilization that shaped the western world through its philosophy, literature, political ideas, and art

The Immortals: Socrates. Video or film, 26 minutes, color, [Coronet], 1987. Ed Asner portrays Socrates. Depicts him, imprisoned and awaiting judgment, reviewing principles upon which his life has been based

The Louvre: Volume 3, Antiquities. Video, color, [The Voyager Company]. Discusses Greek, Roman, Egyptian, and Near Eastern relics

Rise and Decline of the Roman Empire (revised). Video or film, 19 minutes, color, [Coronet], 1980. Traces the development of Rome from early tribal communities to the decline of its mighty empire

Seeking the First Americans (Odyssey Series). Video, 60 minutes, color, [PBS Video], 1980

* For a complete listing of sources of audio-visual materials see page T30.

55a

OPTIONAL WRITING ASSIGNMENTS

1. You are a theater critic for an Athenian newspaper. Write a review of a play (your choice) from that new playwright, Sophocles. Be sure also to describe the kinds of people attending, the theater, and the play.

2. You are a visitor to Rome at the time of Julius Caesar. Write a postcard to a friend describing what you have seen. On the back of the postcard, draw a picture of a Roman scene.

3. You are a newspaper advice columnist for the *Indian Informer* newspaper. Write responses to two letters that you received. One letter, from a member of a lower caste, complains of the unfairness of the caste system. The second letter seeks your advice in ways to handle a prearranged marriage. Your responses must be compassionate and yet defend the existing social order in India.

4. You are a travel agent in ancient China during its Golden Age. Prepare an itinerary for a group tour of your land. Be sure to identify interesting places that you will visit and describe the importance of these places.

5. You are an employment recruiter for the Greek shipping industry in the year 500 B.C. Write a speech that you will soon deliver to young Greeks encouraging them to seek employment on Greek ships. Be sure to emphasize what they will gain from their work aboard the ships.

UNIT TESTS
IN THE TEACHER'S RESOURCE FILE

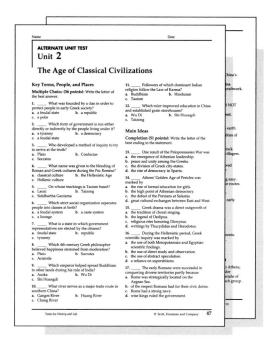

Unit Test, pp. 45–46

Alternate Unit Test, pp. 47–48

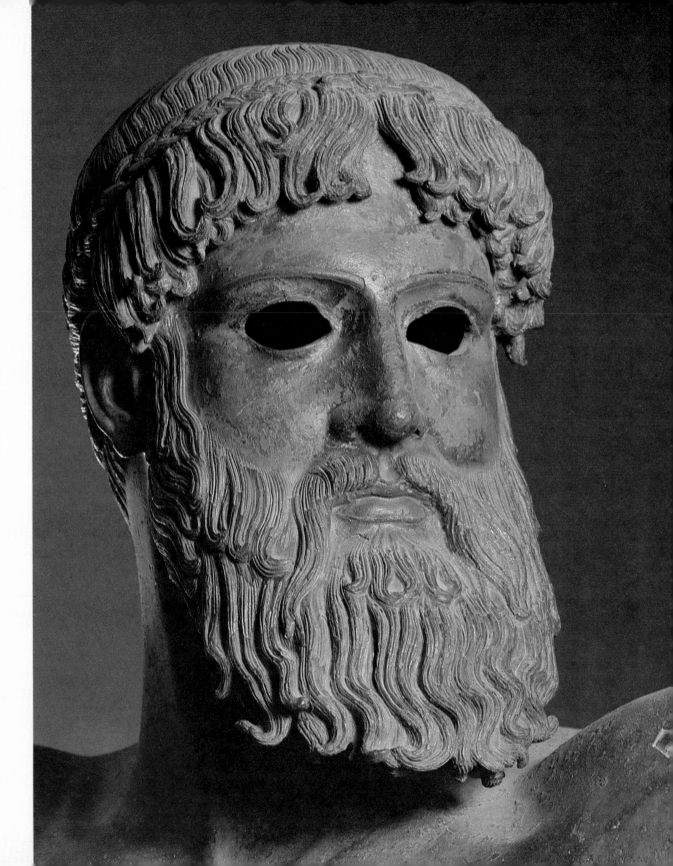

FINE ART IN UNIT TWO

Fine art forms an integral part of the historical record of events portrayed in this textbook. A listing of the paintings, drawings, sculpture, historic photographs, architecture, and other works of fine art selected to illustrate this unit follows. Students may be asked to research the artists and their works and report their findings to the entire class. Students also may be asked to write one or more paragraphs describing what they see upon a detailed study of a work of art and what the artist was attempting to communicate.

The Age of Classical Civilizations

Themes and Patterns Around 1000 B.C. major civilizations began to emerge in Greece, Italy, India, and China. These civilizations have undergone many changes in the past 3,000 years but they are still considered a standard, or ideal, by many peoples. That is why they are called "classical."

Each of the four classical civilizations made important contributions to world civilization in the areas of religion, democracy, law, government, culture, science, and technology. Greece was the home of democracy, the cradle of Western civilization. Rome preserved and spread Greek culture and was the place where Christianity originated. Meanwhile, in India and China, the major religions of Hinduism, Buddhism, Confucianism, and Taoism developed. Professional schools also began during these classical times, and some of the finest art and architecture in all human history was produced.

Although the four major classical civilizations achieved distinctive patterns of internal development, one outstanding feature of the age as a whole was an increase in trade and communication between the civilizations. Another feature of this age was the growth of brilliant civilizations beyond Eurasia, in Africa and the Americas. The cultural achievements of the Axum in East Africa and the Maya of the Yucatán peninsula rank as high points in each of those civilizations during the classical age.

p. **106,** Pompeiian bedroom, 1st century B.C., The Metropolitan Museum of Art

p. **109,** Colosseum, built by Vespasian and Titus, A.D. 75–80, Rome

p. **113,** Pannini, Giovanni Paolo, *The Interior of the Pantheon* (detail), c. 1740, The National Gallery of Art, Washington, D.C.

p. **117,** Siva Nataraja bronze statue, Nelson Gallery of Art, Atkins Museum, Kansas City, MO

p. **122,** Brahma stone statue, c. 11th century, The Metropolitan Museum of Art

p. **139,** Bronze vessel, Zhou dynasty, China

p. **151,** Sloan, Richard, *Shadow of the Ruins,* 1988, Private collection

p. **167,** Temple of the Warriors, Maya c. 1000, Chichén Itzá

This exquisite bronze statue of Zeus, the ruler of the gods in Greek mythology, represents both the artistic and cultural achievements of the age of classical civilizations. The statue dates from 470 to 450 B.C.

Chapters in This Unit

4 The Rise of Greek Civilization

OVERVIEW

This chapter covers Greek civilization from its earliest beginnings in Crete through its Hellenic and Hellenistic phases and points out its lasting contributions to Western culture.

PLANNING CHART

Section	Text Pages	Key Concept	Suggested Teaching Time
1 Aegean civilization developed from sea trade.	60–63	A combination of factors—geographic location, trade, exposure to and adoption of ideas and technologies—led to the rise of an Aegean culture.	One day **More time?** Use *Overhead Transparency 7*
2 The Greeks expanded to control the eastern Mediterranean.	64–68	Independent, democratic city-states arose, and eventually, the Greeks became leaders of the eastern Mediterranean.	Two days **More time?** Use *Overhead Transparency 8* or *Source Reading 4A.*
3 Defeat of the Persians led to Athens' recognized leadership.	69–72	Greek culture thrived as the Greeks were threatened by the Persians and by the city-state rivalries, which eventually led to their weakening.	One day **Less time?** Assign Section 3 to be read before class and teach it together with Section 4. Refer to the maps of Ancient Greece and of Alexander's Empire to illustrate the events of these two sections.
4 The Macedonians conquered the Greeks, and the Hellenistic Age began.	72–74	The weakened city-states became part of Alexander's empire, and Greek culture diffused and mixed with other cultures in the empire.	One day **More time?** Use *Source Reading 4B.*

ANCILLARIES

Materials that may be used with this chapter to reinforce, reteach, enrich, and assess learning are pictured on the following pages.

Teacher's Resource File

ACTIVITIES

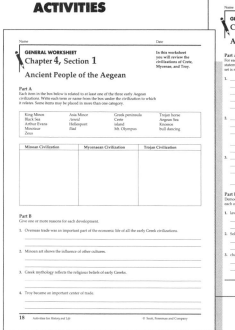

Section 1 Activity, p. 18

Section 2 Activity, p. 19

Section 3 Activity, p. 20

Section 4 Activity, p. 21

Chapter 4 Reteaching, p. 22

Chapter 4 Enrichment, p. 23

Teacher's Resource File

GEOGRAPHY SKILLS

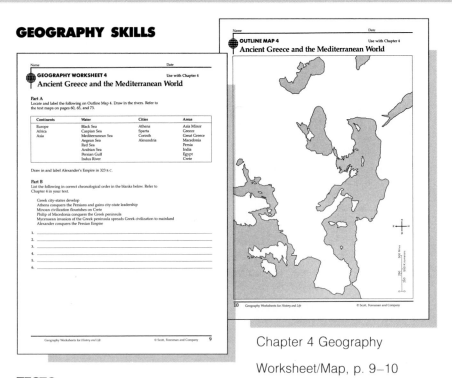

Chapter 4 Geography
Worksheet/Map, p. 9–10

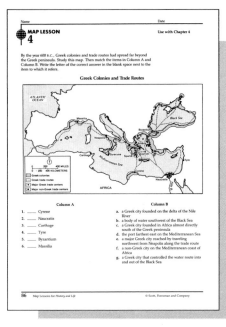

Chapter 4 Map Lesson, p. 86

TESTS

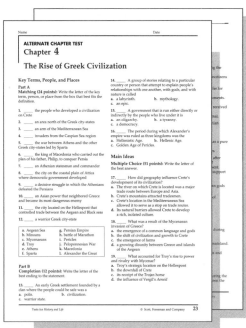

Chapter Test, pp. 21–22

Alternate Chapter Test, pp. 23–24

Other Optional Ancillaries

WORKBOOK

Section 1 Worksheet, p. 12

Section 2 Worksheet, p. 13

Section 3 Worksheet, p. 14

Section 4 Worksheet, p. 15

SOURCE READINGS

Source Reading 4A
Source Reading 4B

OVERHEAD TRANSPARENCIES

Overhead Transparency 7
Overhead Transparency 8

TEST GENERATOR

40 Multiple-choice questions for Chapter 4

4

CHAPTER INTRODUCTION

Call students' attention to the accomplishments of the Greeks. Ask students to give opinions as to which of these accomplishments has had the greatest long-term effects.

LOCATOR GLOBE

Call students' attention to the globe, which indicates the general area of the world discussed in this chapter. (A detailed map appears on page 60.)

TIME LINE

Have students use the time line to figure out how many years passed between the Mycenaean invasion of Greece and the beginning of the "Age of Pericles."

The Rise of Greek Civilization

2000 B.C. – 150 B.C.

2000 B.C.

1900 B.C.   Mycenaeans invade Greece

492 B.C.   "Age of Pericles" begins

338 B.C.   Hellenic dominance ends

300 B.C.

200 B.C.

In ancient Greece, the birthplace of democracy, a group of people lived spread among several isolated, protected settlements. These communities were located not only on the mountainous peninsula that we today know as modern Greece, but also on the many islands in the Aegean Sea and along the western coast of Asia Minor. They were constantly in conflict both with one another and with powerful and corrupt influences from within. They were also vulnerable to invading forces.

Yet within this complex environment, the model for modern democracy was created and the forms of architecture, sculpture, history, philosophy, drama, and poetry that we today consider classic were developed. Modern science also began in these isolated city-states, with the study of physics, mathematics, biology, and medicine.

By the 5th century B.C., one Greek city-state, Athens, had reached the height of its glory and power. In the year 431 B.C., Pericles [per'ə klēz'], a general and statesman, was chosen by his fellow Athenians to present the annual funeral oration, or speech, which was given to honor those citizens lost in war during the past year. Pericles' words are still remembered because they describe the democratic government and way of life of Athens in the 5th century B.C.

> Our government is not copied from our neighbors. We are an example to them. Our constitution is called a democracy because power is in the hands not of the few but of the whole people. When it is a question of settling private disputes, everyone is equal before the law. No talented man is kept out of public service because he is poor or from the wrong class. We have no dark words or angry looks for our neighbor if he enjoys himself in his own way. We are open and friendly in our private, day-to-day relations with each other. In our public affairs we keep strictly to the law.

The painting above (1600–1400 B.C.) is from the Minoan civilization on Crete. Ancient Greek culture owes much to the Minoans, among the earliest peoples of the Aegean.

In Athens the successful experiment with democratic government did not occur quickly or easily but was instead an evolutionary process with its own failures and excesses. Indeed, success in Greece was not reserved for Athens alone. Sparta, its rival city-state, developed an efficient military government that left behind many of its own lasting contributions.

Reading Preview

In this chapter, you will read about ancient Greece and its early democratic experience.

1. Aegean civilization developed from sea trade.

2. The Greeks expanded to control the eastern Mediterranean.

3. Defeat of the Persians led to Athens' recognized leadership.

4. The Macedonians conquered the Greeks, and the Hellenistic Age began.

1 *Lesson Plan*

Essential Learning Objective

Students will learn to identify the factors that led to the development of the Aegean civilization.

1 FOCUS AND MOTIVATE

Ask students to name the civilizations with which the peoples of the Aegean probably had contact. Have them speculate which achievements of these civilizations probably had an impact on the peoples of the Aegean. (Egyptians: mathematics, medicine; Hittites: laws, knowledge of how to work iron; Phoenicians: shipbuilding, navigation, alphabet)

2 TEACH

- Discuss how the peoples of the Aegean civilization used their geographic location to compensate for the lack of arable lands.

- Outline and discuss the important contributions of the Minoans and Mycenaeans to Greek civilization.

GUIDED PRACTICE

Have students list the types of information that a study of their myths might reveal about a people. (religious beliefs, social attitudes and values, technological facts, history) Also for guided practice:

 Overhead Transparency 7

Ancient Greece, 2000–450 B.C.

 MAP STUDY As you can see from the map above, ancient Greece included more area than the peninsula of modern Greece. Locate the islands of Crete, Rhodes, and Samothrace. How might the many islands of the Aegean aid Greek civilization but hinder Greek unity?

 1 *Aegean civilization developed from sea trade.*

To early people, the sea meant mystery and danger. In small boats they may have ventured into water with caution, staying close to the shoreline by day and taking refuge in harbors at night. However, the sea slowly became less frightening and began to become an important highway for trade and exposure to different people and ideas.

The Phoenicians, whom you learned about in Chapter 3, were among the early traders who dared to sail the open waters. Others who met the challenge of the deep were the people who lived on the islands of the **Aegean Sea** [i jē′ən] and along its shores. Find the Aegean Sea, an arm of the Mediterranean, on the map above. The irregu-

lar coastline of the Greek peninsula holds many deep harbors and covers about 400 miles. The rugged, mountainous land of Greece lacks sufficient farmland, so the trading for food and other goods was born out of necessity.

Crete developed a flourishing culture.

Historians believe that Crete [krēt], an island located southeast of Greece in the Mediterranean Sea, was settled as early as 6000 B.C. Neolithic peoples from southwestern Asia were the first inhabitants, later joined by some Egyptians around 3100 B.C. Between 2000 and 1400 B.C., Crete developed into a strong, wealthy power in the ancient world, serving as a stop on the trade routes between Europe and Africa and between Africa and Asia. The civilization that developed is called **Minoan** [mi nō′ən] for the legendary King Minos [mīn′əs].

ANSWER TO MAP STUDY Isolation allowed groups to develop without much interference from enemy groups but also hindered the acceptance of outside groups.

60

Ancient Greek legends contain a number of references to Minoan civilization. One of the most famous stories concerns the Minotaur [min'ə tôr], a flesh-eating monster with the head of a bull and the body of a man. According to legend, King Minos was forbidden by the gods to kill the Minotaur because the monster's death would mean the destruction of Crete. Minos turned for help to a masterful Greek engineer named Daedalus [ded'l əs]. Daedalus designed an elaborate labyrinth [lab'ə-rinth'], a bewildering mazelike series of passageways, in which the Minotaur could be kept.

The eventual defeat of the Minotaur is one of the best-known stories of ancient Greece. After King Minos' son was killed while in Athens, the king declared that Athens' punishment would be to send seven girls and seven boys into the labyrinth to feed the Minotaur every ninth year. Out of pity for the children, a Greek hero named Theseus [thē'sē əs] offered himself as one of the victims.

Upon his arrival on Crete, however, Theseus found himself the object of the love of King Minos' daughter Ariadne [ar'ē ad'nē]. Ariadne promised to help Theseus kill the Minotaur, thereby betraying her father, if he would agree to take her back to Athens as his wife. Theseus agreed. He used a magic ball of thread and the plans to the maze, which Daedalus had left with Ariadne, to make his way in and out of the labyrinth, slaying the Minotaur in the process.

Until the late 19th century, the Minoan civilization was known only through legends. No artifacts or other evidence that might have proven the existence of this civilization had ever been found. In 1894, however, Sir Arthur Evans, a British archaeologist, began excavations on Crete. He found inscribed clay tablets, which revealed that an early civilization—the Minoans—had existed. They had developed a system of writing and made bronze tools and weapons that showed an advanced stage of technology. A major find was the ruins of the royal palace at Knossos [nos'əs]. Sprawling across six acres, the palace, like the legendary labyrinth of the Minotaur, was a giant maze with many rooms and corridors. The palace had an ingenious underground plumbing system as well.

The Minoans were the first people in history to sail on long voyages over the open sea. As a result, Crete became rich from its overseas trade, which included such exports as olive oil, wine, pottery, and metalworks. Because of their trade, the Minoans reflected many foreign influences in their art while maintaining their own graceful forms of architecture, painting, and sculpture.

Their art reveals a cheerful, pleasure-loving people who enjoyed sports and the world of nature. In addition, Minoan women enjoyed a freedom and social status equal to that of the men. The chief Minoan deity was the earth goddess who ruled over the entire universe. She was served by priestesses, and sacrifices of animals and grain were made in her honor at major festivals.

Among the discoveries unearthed by Evans were wall paintings picturing a real thrill of many Minoans—the dangerous sport of "bull dancing." This sport called upon a man or woman to meet a

The dangerous Minoan sport of "bull dancing" is illustrated by the wall painting below, located on a wall at the Palace of Knossos.

61

ASSESS

Why were the Mycenaeans a unifying force in Greece? (spoke a common language and worshipped the same gods)

OPTIONAL RETEACHING

Have students write two paragraphs, one describing the skills and achievements of the Minoans and the other those of the Mycenaeans, by making inferences based on their artifacts and myths.

OPTIONAL ENRICHMENT

1. Have students do research on what is known about the daily life of the Minoans and write a few paragraphs explaining how archaeologists deduced this knowledge from artifacts. (average)
2. Assign students to read a synopsis of *The Odyssey of Homer*. Have interested students read the entire epic and present reports on one of the following parts: Books i–iv, Books v–viii, Books ix–xii, and Books xiii–xxiv. (challenging)

INDEPENDENT PRACTICE/ HOMEWORK

Assign the Section Review, Activities page 18, or Workbook page 12.

CLOSURE

Summarize the lesson by telling students that the Aegean civilization developed as a result of trade and a borrowing of ideas and technologies from societies on the Mediterranean Sea. The invasion of the Greek peninsula by the Mycenaeans unified the Greeks by introducing a common language and worship of the same gods.

charging bull in the arena, grasp its horns and somersault over its body into the arms of a companion. Bull dancing, which may have been a religious ceremony, was held in crowded amphitheaters.

Mycenaean invaders spread Greek civilization to the mainland.

About 1900 B.C. people from the Caspian Sea region invaded the Greek peninsula. The newcomers came to be known as **Mycenaeans** [mī′sə-nē′ənz], and they spoke an early form of Greek. They built fortified cities, such as Mycenae [mī-sē′nē]. Around the fortresses were villages of peasants, who worked for the Mycenaean princes. Their civilization began to engage in trade, borrowing heavily from the Minoans. About 1450 B.C. the Mycenaeans captured Knossos, and during the following century, they also attacked and destroyed other cities on Crete.

In 1400 B.C., however, the Minoans drove the Mycenaeans off their island. Minoan trade and city life revived somewhat, but commercial leadership in the Aegean had already passed to Mycenae.

From 1400 to 1200 B.C., Mycenae became a unifying force in Greece and the islands of the Aegean. The many peoples began to speak a common language and worship the same gods. These gods were Zeus [züs], the most powerful god, and his family of other gods and goddesses. These gods were believed to live on Mt. Olympus, an actual mountain in northeastern Greece.

Like societies throughout history, the people of Greece developed many stories about their gods and goddesses. These stories, called myths, attempted to explain people's relationship with one another, with the gods, and with nature. As a whole, the group of myths relating to a particular country or person is called **mythology**. The mythology of ancient Greece reflects its early religious beliefs. Greek mythology includes many explanations for such questions as how the world began and why the sun rises.

Greek and Roman Divinities

Greek	Roman	Greek	Roman
Aphrodite [af′rə dī′tē] Goddess of love and beauty	**Venus** [vē′nəs]	**Hades** [hā′dēz] God of the underworld, ruler of the dead	**Pluto** [plü′tō], **Dis** [dis]
Apollo [ə pol′ō] God of the sun, music, poetry, prophecy, and healing	**Apollo** [ə pol′ō]	**Hephaestus** [hə fes′təs] God of fire and metalworking	**Vulcan** [vul′kən]
Ares [er′ēz] God of war	**Mars** [märz]	**Hera** [hir′ə] Queen of the gods	**Juno** [jü′nō]
Artemis [är′tə mis] Goddess of the hunt, the forests, wild animals, and the moon	**Diana** [dī ä′nə]	**Hermes** [hėr′mēz] Messenger of Zeus, god of merchants, gamblers, and thieves	**Mercury** [mėr′kyər ē]
Athena [ə thē′nə] Goddess of wisdom, warfare, the arts, and industry	**Minerva** [mə nėr′və]	**Hestia** [hes′tē ə] Goddess of the hearth	**Vesta** [ves′tə]
Demeter [di mē′tər] Goddess of agriculture	**Ceres** [sir′ēz]	**Persephone** [pər sef′ə nē] Goddess of the underworld, ruler of the dead	**Proserpina** [prō sėr′pə nə]
Dionysus [dī′ə nī′səs] God of wine	**Bacchus** [bäk′əs]	**Poseidon** [pə sīd′n] God of the sea	**Neptune** [nep′tün]
		Zeus [züs] God of the sky, king of the gods	**Jupiter** [jü′pə tər], **Jove** [jōv]

From the Archives

An Odyssey

Homer's Odyssey—one of the world's greatest adventure stories—has long been enjoyed for its timeless expression of life's triumphs and defeats. In the passage below, Odysseus is struggling against a storm that Poseidon, the sea god, has hurled against him.

[All] my days are consumed in longing—to travel home and see the day of my arrival dawn. If a god must shatter me upon the wine-dark sea, so be it. I shall suffer with a high heart; for my courage has been tempered to endure all misery. . . .

[Poseidon] drove the clouds into a heap and, trident in hand, tossed together the desolate waters. He summoned all the violent gusts that were in all the winds and let them loose, blind-folding sea and land with storm-clouds. Night leaped into heaven. Mightily the surge rolled up, for east wind clashed upon south wind, the ill-blowing west with the north wind from the upper sky. Therefore the knees and warm heart of Odysseus shook and heavily did he commune with his own high courage.

Mycenae and Troy became rival centers of Aegean civilization.

Aegean civilization also included parts of Asia Minor. The city of **Troy**, situated in what is now Turkey, was especially important because it was strategically located on the Hellespont [hel′i spont]. The Hellespont, now called the Dardanelles [därd′n elz′], is a strait, or narrow channel, connecting the Aegean and Black seas. Because of its location, Troy controlled the trade between these two seas, a profitable trade that involved the valuable food products of the fertile lands around the Black Sea.

After about 1300 B.C., Mycenaean trade began to decline for reasons that are still not fully understood. Trade contacts with Egypt and the eastern Mediterranean were broken. In addition, the Mycenaean lords fought with one another.

This time of crisis is revealed in the *Iliad* [il′ē-əd] and the *Odyssey* [od′ə sē], two epic poems thought to have been composed later in the 800s B.C. by the blind Greek poet Homer. Homer probably had grown up hearing about past Greek heroes and decided to write about his heritage. The *Iliad* tells of the anger of a warrior named Achilles [ə kil′ēz] and its tragic results, an episode in a war between some Mycenaeans and Troy. The *Odyssey* describes the many adventures of the soldier, Odysseus [ō dis′ē əs] on his 10-year trip home after the end of the Trojan War.

The most famous story about Troy's destruction was written between 30 and 19 B.C., more than 700 years after Homer's time, by the Roman poet Vergil. His epic poem, the *Aeneid* [i nē′id], was based on Greek sources and includes the story of how ingenious Mycenaean invaders built a huge wooden horse and left it outside of Troy's gates. The Trojans were impressed with this immense statue, which they believed to be a gift from the gods. They moved it into their city only to discover—too late—that enemy soldiers were hidden inside this Trojan horse.

Section 1 Review

Identify Aegean Sea, Minoans, Mycenaeans, mythology, Troy

Main Ideas

1. How did Crete's location aid the development of its rich civilization?
2. How did the Mycenaean invasion change the history of Greece?
3. Why did the location of Troy allow the city to become the principal Mycenaean rival?

Critical Thinking

Recognizing Values: The cultures of the ancient peoples of the Aegean changed as trade expanded and contacts were made with ideas from other civilizations. Give examples of how the culture or values of the United States have been influenced by other cultures.

FROM THE ARCHIVES The excerpt from the *Odyssey* is from *The Odyssey of Homer, Newly Translated into English Prose* (New York: Oxford University Press, 1932), pp. 75–77. Have students find words and phrases showing Homer's use of vivid language. (Possible answers: verbs such as "shatter," "drove," etc.; imagery such as "wine-dark sea," "desolate waters," etc.

Answers to Section 1 Review

Identify

Key Terms, People, and Places are defined on pages indicated in parentheses. Also see the Glossary and Biographical Dictionary. Aegean Sea (60), Minoans (60), Mycenaeans (62), mythology (62), Troy (63)

Main Ideas

1. Its location as an island in the Aegean Sea allowed Crete to serve as a stop on various trade routes. This economic activity, along with the Minoans' own trading efforts, brought riches to Crete.
2. The Mycenaean invasion shifted civilization and growth to the mainland of Greece. The Mycenaeans gathered people in protective communities where all spoke a common language and began to believe in the same gods.
3. Troy, located at the strategic Hellespont, was able to control the profitable trade passing between the Aegean and Black seas.

Critical Thinking

The United States has been a "melting pot" of many cultures. Examples of outside influences have been felt in ethnic food, music, and art. The United States also imports goods and uses technology from other countries to improve U.S. products.

2 *Lesson Plan*

Essential Learning Objectives

Students will learn to:

- describe the development of city-states.
- compare the democracy of Athens with the government of Sparta.

1 | FOCUS AND MOTIVATE

Call students' attention to Pericles' speech on democracy in the chapter introduction. Have them compare the Greeks' belief in the rights of the individual with the beliefs of the Indo-Aryans, as expressed through the caste system. Ask students to provide examples of effects on present-day cultures of these divergent beliefs.

2 | TEACH

- List on the chalkboard and discuss the changes that occurred on the Greek peninsula between 1200 B.C. and 700 B.C. (Dorian invasion, displacement of Mycenaeans and resettlement around Athens, intermarriage between Dorians and Mycenaeans, formation of communities, revival of art of writing, change in type of government) Have students hypothesize why little is known about the period called the "Dark Ages of Greek history." (Sample hypotheses: Few artifacts from this period have been found. Written records do not exist.)

BACKGROUND Four major types of government were known to and named by the Greeks: monarchy, oligarchy, tyranny, and democracy.

2 | The Greeks expanded to control the eastern Mediterranean.

Throughout its existence, the Mycenaean civilization had been threatened by outside forces. About 1200 B.C. the warlike Dorians invaded the Greek peninsula from the north. The Mycenaean civilization was already tottering, and they were driven from their cities. Many of the survivors settled around the city of Athens, but others took refuge on islands in the Aegean and on a strip of seacoast in Asia Minor known as Ionia [ī ō′nē ə]. See the map on page 60 to find Ionia, on the eastern shore of the Aegean. In turn, the Dorians settled in the southwest area of Greece.

Little is known about this period, called the "Dark Ages of Greek history." However, when the curtain was lifted from this time of transition, radical changes had taken place.

The Dorians and the remaining Mycenaeans had intermarried and had formed communities. Slowly, the people of Athens and other settlements had begun to cooperate with each other for protection, trade, and religion. The art of writing, which had been learned from the Minoans and subsequently lost, was revived in a different form learned from the Phoenicians. The heroic kings recounted by the poet Homer had been replaced by changing forms of government. By 700 B.C. Greek had become a universal language among the Aegean people. Greeks began to cooperate, and they held religious festivals where all the city-states gathered for worship and games.

From this spirit of cooperation and competition emerged the Olympic Games, which began in 776 B.C. as a festival to honor Zeus. The games began as a single day of racing and wrestling, but in the 7th century B.C., chariot-racing and single-horse races were added as well. The winners received crowns of wild olive leaves, and upon their return home, were escorted with great ceremony.

The Greeks called themselves Hellenes [hel′ēns] because they believed their common ancestor was Hellen, a god in Greek mythology. The great era of expansion that followed the "Dark Ages" is called the Hellenic [he len′ik] period, which lasted from about 750 to 338 B.C.

BACKGROUND The first modern Olympics were held at Athens in 1896. The first winter games were held at Chamonix, France, in 1924.

BACKGROUND The English word democracy comes from the Greek words *demos* meaning "people" and *kratos* meaning "rule."

Independent city-states were formed on the Greek peninsula.

Early Greek society was quite simple. The people grouped into clans, which were ruled by a king or tribal chief. Each clan founded a settlement, known as a **polis** [pō′lis], where the people would be safe from attack. The countryside around the polis was used for farming and grazing.

The development of city-states. The geographic isolation of these settlements led to the growth of small city-states, which were independent states consisting of a city and the territories depending on it. The members of each city-state were proud of their home city, and jealously guarded its independence. The city-states rarely cooperated with one another except when invaders threatened their safety.

One of the greatest contributions of the city-states to civilization was democratic government. A **democracy** is a government that is run by the people who live under it, either in a direct or indirect fashion. In early Greek society, however, only male landowners born in a particular city-state could become full citizens, with all the rights of the democracy. Women and foreign-born men were therefore excluded.

Democratic government evolved gradually in the Greek city-states. The first step toward democracy was most often the formation by a group of nobles of an oligarchy [ol′ə gär′kē], which is a government in which a few people have the ruling power.

The goddess Arethusa, wreathed in olive leaves, adorns this coin (479 B.C.) from the Greek city of Syracuse. The dolphins represent the seas.

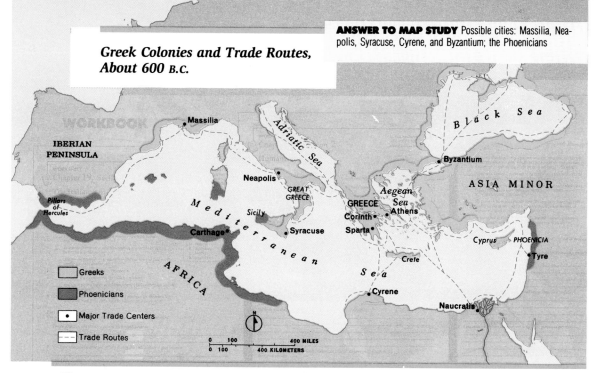

Greek Colonies and Trade Routes, About 600 B.C.

ANSWER TO MAP STUDY Possible cities: Massilia, Neapolis, Syracuse, Cyrene, and Byzantium; the Phoenicians

MAP STUDY Locate three Greek cities on the map that were not located on the Greek peninsula. What other strong power is shown to be a force around the Mediterranean?

With their increased power, the nobles wrote law codes that ensured that justice was no longer a matter of whim or guess. Penalties were set by law rather than by a judge, and the laws were available for all to see. Thus, the common people benefited.

The development of colonies. By the middle of the 700s B.C., however, the nobles who held power in the Greek world had become corrupt. They had increased their wealth through control of the farmland, and small farmers had been forced to mortgage their land or sell themselves into slavery to pay their debts. Many farmers gave up the land in favor of small-scale manufacturing. Soil erosion and a lack of good land also contributed to the decline of farming.

In contrast to the decline of farming, the making of pottery, textiles, and bronze weapons and tools flourished. As a result, the Greeks eventually needed more markets for their goods. In addition, a growing population placed increasing demands on the available food supply, leading to a search for new sources of food. The Greeks realized that migration to other parts of the region would give people a chance to have more economic and political freedom. For these reasons, the Greeks began to establish colonies.

Each new colony was bound by social and religious ties to its parent city-state. Thus, the city-states became less isolated and more in tune with the larger world. Colonies were established in places far and wide. They could be found all along the Aegean and Black sea coasts, and as far west as the Iberian peninsula and North Africa. The colonies established are on the map above.

The power of the nobility was challenged by tyrants.

The establishment of colonies did not end the discontent in Greece however. Three important trends brought about the fall of the nobility. The first trend was the development of a heavily armed infantry of citizens. The power of the infantry,

BACKGROUND Plato described colonies thus, "When men who have nothing, and are in need of food,... follow their leaders in an attack ... on the rich—these ... are sent away by the [ruler] in a friendly spirit as far as he is able; and this ... is termed a colony." The colonies were politically independent, despite social and religious ties.

- Trace the evolution of government from kingship in early Greek society to democracy in Athens as described in Pericles' speech of 431 B.C. Have students cite the reforms that occurred under Solon, Pisistratus, and Cleisthenes. Explain the difference between direct democracy and indirect (or representative) democracy. Have students name some countries where representative democracy is practiced today.

- Discuss the chains of cause and effect created by a decline in agriculture on the Greek peninsula. (search for food sources—migration and colonization; increase in small-scale manufacturing—search for new markets; increase in trade and markets—exposure to new ideas and inventions; adoption of use of money in trade—accumulation of wealth without land ownership; appearance of wealthy business class—demand for voice, or power, in government)

- Chart and compare differences in economies, governments, and social values between Sparta and Athens. Have students point out Spartan practices that would be abhorred and practices that would be admired by people of present-day Western societies.

GUIDED PRACTICE
Have students write a few sentences explaining why democracy as defined by Pericles—a government in which power is in the hands of not a few but of the whole people—was not actually practiced in Athens.

1. What three trends brought about the fall of the nobility through revolutions? (development and growth in power of heavily armed infantry that supported demands of the common people for better living conditions; development and use of coinage in Lydia, which was adopted in Greece; appearance of business class that became wealthy and demanded a voice in the government)
2. What practice begun by Cleisthenes allowed citizens to banish officials and other citizens who were considered dangerous to the Athenian state? (ostracism)

OPTIONAL RETEACHING

1. Outline the development of city-states and the evolution of democracy.
2. Have students write one or more paragraphs contrasting the city-state of Athens with the city-state of Sparta.

OPTIONAL ENRICHMENT

1. Have students research the migrations of the Mycenaeans after the Dorian invasion of about 1200 B.C. Students should draw a map showing the islands and areas where the Mycenaeans resettled. (average)
2. Assign interested students to research and present an oral report on the invention and use of the phalanx, and its profound influence on the Spartan way of life. (challenging)
3. Also for enrichment:

 Overhead Transparency 8

 Source Reading 4A

The Acropolis in Athens still contains many of the famous buildings from ancient times. At left is the temple of Athena Nike, and at right is the Parthenon.

which was made up of troops trained, equipped, and organized to fight on foot, grew until they proved to be a match for the cavalry, or soldiers on horseback, that supported the nobles. With its growing power, the infantry demanded better living conditions for the common people.

The second trend was that the development of coinage in Lydia [lid′ē ə], a country in Asia Minor, quickly spread to Greece. (Find Lydia on the map on page 60.) With money, a family could rise socially without owning much land. This condition led to the third trend, which was the appearance of an important new group—a business class of merchants, shipowners, and artisans. This group, emboldened by the accumulation of money, demanded a voice in government.

As a result of this unrest, a number of revolutions took place between 650 and 500 B.C in

Greece. Many city-states came under the rule of tyrants who had taken power unlawfully. To the Greeks "tyranny" simply meant one-man rule. A tyrant was not always a cruel or oppressive ruler, as the word means today. Often he was a noble who had become democratic in outlook and to whom the people turned for leadership. In Greece the rise of tyrants was the first step toward government by the people.

Democratic government developed in Athens.

On the dusty coastal plain of Attica [at′ə kə] in southeastern Greece lay the city of **Athens**. (Locate this city on the map on page 65.) The city hugged the slopes of a hill known as the Acropolis [ə krop′ə lis], upon which the Athenians built their forts and temples. Sailors and merchants from faraway countries brought trade and many different ideas to Athens.

From the 700s to the 500s B.C., the government in Athens was controlled by a council of nobles. The most important public official was the chief magistrate, a government official who had the power to uphold the laws. The chief magistrate was elected every year from among the nobles. During these two centuries, various groups of citizens in Athens became increasingly unhappy with

What's in a Name?
___

ATHENS Athens is named after Athena, daughter of Zeus, who was the patron goddess of the city. She was the deity of wisdom and a guardian of cities. She was also the goddess of war and peace, fertility, and the arts and crafts.

their social and political conditions. One of these groups consisted of peasant farmers. Many farmers were so badly in debt that they had become like slaves to the nobles who supported them.

The beginnings of internal reform. The council of nobles gradually realized that if they did not heed the people's cries for reforms, they would most likely be overthrown by a tyrant, as had been happening in other Greek city-states. In 594 B.C., therefore, the nobles elected Solon [sō′lən] chief magistrate and gave him broad powers to make changes. Solon was a noble who had both an understanding of the farmers' needs and a strong sense of justice.

Solon canceled the farmers' debts and outlawed the practice of debt slavery, but he resisted the farmers' demands to redistribute the land. He enlarged the council and included not only the nobles but also rich property owners. This Council of 400 drew up new laws, and an assembly of all citizens voted on them. In addition, Solon offered citizenship to craftsworkers who had not been born in Athens, provided that they and their families would settle in the city. He also encouraged trade.

However, discontent still had a place in Athens. Shepherds within the city-state were unhappy because they owned no land. They managed to find a leader in Pisistratus [pī sis′trə təs], a distant relative of Solon. Pisistratus took over from Solon in 560 B.C. and ruled as tyrant for more than 30 years. He solved economic problems by banishing many nobles, forcing them to leave Athens, and redistributing their lands among the poor. He also encouraged trade and the development of the arts.

The next important tyrant in Athenian history was Cleisthenes [klīs′thə nēz], who came to power in 508 B.C. Under Cleisthenes, the practice of ostracism was begun. Ostracism was a system that once a year gave the 6,000 citizens of Athens a chance to vote to temporarily banish any citizens or officials they viewed as dangerous to the Athenian state. In addition, Cleisthenes strengthened the growth of democracy by setting up new political districts and increasing the number of members in the council to 500. These changes allowed more people to take part in politics and guaranteed that a greater variety of local interests would be represented in government.

Solon, Pisistratus, and Cleisthenes were all champions of the people. With their reforms, Athens took large steps toward becoming a democracy. Gradually, other city-states followed the lead of Athens, and by 500 B.C., democratic governments were being formed in many Greek city-states.

The contributions of Athens to civilization. During the 500s and 400s B.C., the city-state of Athens made important strides in the development of democratic government. In doing so, they also made significant contributions to Western civiliza-

For the practice of ostracism, begun under Cleisthenes, broken bits of pottery and later, small bronze discs were used to vote.

tion. The statesman Pericles spoke of these important contributions in a speech given in 431 B.C., which included the following:

1. The Greek government, in which citizens were equal before the law, became a model for Western democracy.

2. Public service, that is, working for the community good, was thought to be an honorable and necessary part of every citizen's life.

3. Citizens were free to live their lives, to come and go as they pleased, to speak their minds openly.

4. An awareness of beauty enhanced Greek life. As Pericles said: "Our love of what is beautiful does not lead to extravagance; our love of the things of the mind does not make us soft."

5. Public debates were held before the state took action.

Sparta became a warrior state.

The city-state of **Sparta** was an important exception to the trend toward popular government. Sparta lay on the Peloponnesus [pel′ə pə nē′səs], the peninsula that makes up the southern part of

INDEPENDENT PRACTICE/ HOMEWORK

Assign the Section Review, Activities page 19, or Workbook page 13.

CLOSURE

Summarize the lesson by telling students that the Dorians invaded the Greek peninsula in 1200 B.C., driving the Mycenaeans from their cities. The conquered people and the Dorians intermarried and established settlements, which developed into city-states. A new type of government developed in Athens and all other city-states but Sparta. All city-states originally had an agrarian economy that changed to a trade economy, with the exception of Sparta whose economy remained agricultural.

Identify

Key Terms, People, and Places are defined on pages indicated in parentheses. Also see the Glossary and Biographical Dictionary.

polis (64), democracy (64), Athens (66), Sparta (67)

Main Ideas

1. The city-states gradually moved toward a democratic form of government, first with an oligarchy in which open law codes were developed.

2. Solon was elected by other nobles to rule Athens, and he canceled farmers' debts and outlawed debt slavery. The council of nobles was enlarged to include wealthy landowners. Pisistratus helped the landless by banishing many nobles and distributing their land to the poor. Under Cleisthenes, the membership of the council was increased to 500, allowing more people to have a voice in the government.

3. When the Spartans (Dorians) settled and built Sparta, they made serfs of the people who already lived there. Those inhabitants were the helots. Other measures, such as secret police and military training for all males, may have caused dissension, making a strong government necessary.

Critical Thinking

The emerging Greeks shared a language and gods. They were independent, but knew that in times of crisis they could depend on their neighbors. Friendly athletic competition encouraged them to interact with each other.

Greece. When the ancestors of the Spartans came to the Peloponnesus, they subdued the natives, whom they called helots. Allowed to remain on the land as farmers, the helots grew food for the conquerors, but were not allowed to become citizens. Sparta's growth began in the 700s B.C., when they took over neighboring Messenia [mə sē′nē ə]. As a result, Sparta had sufficient amounts of land and was therefore not attracted by colonization and trade. However, the never ending threat of rebellion by the Messenians and the helots remained an important element in the shaping of the Spartan government.

In about 600 B.C., the Spartans set up a constitution whose purpose was to maintain the military strength of the state. An assembly of citizens was created, but it had little power. Instead, control of the state was held by a small group of citizens called the Council of Elders.

Sparta was set up much like a military camp. To maintain high health standards, only the strong and healthy babies who passed state inspection were allowed to live. At age 7, boys were taken from their homes and put in a "pack" governed by teenage youths. Each pack engaged in physical training, and lived on a simple diet. To add to their food supply, the boys were taught to live off the land and encouraged to steal, but they were beaten if caught.

Each year in Sparta, the boys in the packs were flogged to test their powers of physical endurance. At age 20, the young men became field soldiers, and were then allowed to marry, but they continued to live in the barracks. At age 30, men were admitted to the assembly and given various government posts. Finally, at age 60, they were dismissed from the army and allowed to live with their families.

Girls were trained to be strong, healthy mothers of warriors. They were given vigorous training in running, wrestling, and javelin throwing. As their men marched off to war, Spartan women are said to have told their sons and husbands: "Come back with your shield or on it." To this day, the English word *spartan* refers to someone who is courageous, disciplined, and leads a simple life.

In sharp contrast to the Spartan citizens, the helots were looked upon as state property and were treated little better than slaves. To spy on them and to stop revolt, the Spartans set up a secret police force. Once a year, the government legalized the killing of any helot, and thus ensured that the troublemakers were always wiped out.

The highly trained Spartan army was used against its neighbors with some success. It was diplomacy, however, backed by force, that allowed Sparta to extend its influence over its neighbors. To this end, in the 400s B.C., Sparta formed the Peloponnesian League, a military alliance with nearby states in the south of Greece.

Section 2 Review

Identify polis, democracy, Athens, Sparta

Main Ideas

1. How did the city-states on the Greek peninsula contribute to the development of a democratic government?
2. What reforms of Solon, Pisistratus, and Cleisthenes helped bring Athens closer to democracy?
3. Why did the Spartans install their military-type government?

Critical Thinking

Recognizing Values: When the Greeks emerged from their "Dark Ages," the people had adopted certain values and shared things in common that to a certain degree unified them. Give examples of these value changes.

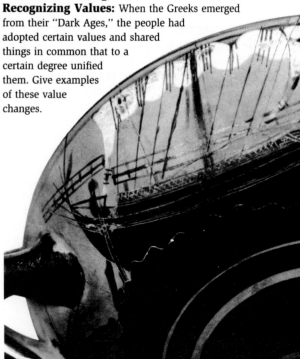

3 Defeat of the Persians led to Athens' recognized leadership.

The Greeks, through their development of trade and founding of colonies, which extended all around the Black Sea and westward all the way to Spain, were bound to come into conflict with another major power. Ultimately, the adjacent Asian power, the **Persian Empire**, became their most dangerous enemy. Locate the Persian Empire on the map on page 60.

Defeat of the Persians ensured the leadership of Athens.

The hostilities that developed between the Greeks and the Persians began to arise along the eastern coast of the Aegean Sea. Here, in Ionia, lived the descendants of the Greek colonists who had settled the area around the 700s B.C. These Ionian Greeks were vital to Greece's economic and cultural strength. After Persian victories in the area placed the Ionian Greeks under Persian rule, the Greeks revolted. They felt that they had been given a lesser role in the government and resented their Persian-appointed leadership. They set up their own governments and appealed to Athens for help.

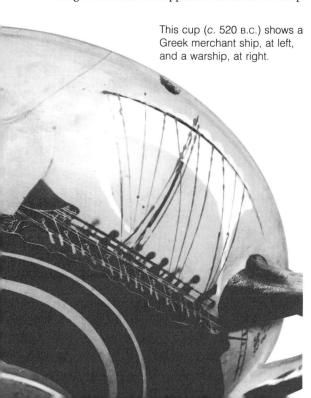

This cup (c. 520 B.C.) shows a Greek merchant ship, at left, and a warship, at right.

The Athenians came to their aid, but the Greeks were nonetheless defeated. As a result, the Athenians began to build a navy to protect their own city. The Persians, at the same time, were determined to conquer the Greek mainland and punish the Athenians for helping the Ionian Greeks.

Battles at Marathon and Salamis. Darius I, the Persian king, knew that Ionia was vulnerable as long as Athens remained free to persuade its allies to revolt, so in 490 B.C., he sent a Persian force to defeat the Athenians. The force of about 20,000 men sailed to the Bay of Marathon, located close to Athens. The Greeks, however, were ready for his attack. Athens and Sparta had earlier agreed to an alliance to fight the Persians. The Athenians sent a runner to Sparta to tell of the Persians' approach, but the superstitious Spartans refused to march until the next full moon.

Without the aid of the Spartans, the Athenians faced the Persians outnumbered two to one. However, their superior weapons and strategy made the Greek armed forces victorious at the **battle of Marathon**.

A Greek legend recounts the feat of one Greek soldier, Pheidippides, who was said to have run about 26 miles from the battlefield at Marathon to Athens to report the victory. He died of exhaustion as he arrived with his message, "Rejoice! We conquer!" This courageous act was commemorated with the marathon run when the modern Olympic Games were revived in Athens in 1896.

The battle of Marathon destroyed the notion of the Persians' strength. In addition, the victory at Marathon gave the Greeks confidence to believe in their ability to defend themselves against any future attacks from the Persians.

Ten years later, Xerxes [zėrk′sēz′], the son of Darius, attacked Greece. The independent Greeks, under the loose alliance of the Peloponnesian League, appointed Sparta to lead the defense against the Persian army. The Spartans set up a defense at the narrow pass of Thermopylae [thər-mop′ə lē], shown on the map on page 60, but were defeated. The Persians moved on to Athens. Here, Xerxes won easily, taking the city and burning the Acropolis.

The Athenians, however, still had an effective navy. After losing Athens, they took to their ships

- Have students compare the aims of education in Athens with the present-day aims of education in the United States. Point out that some slaves were taught mathematics and to read and write because they needed those skills to perform jobs that are today carried out by business and professional people.

- Elicit reasons for the establishment of the Delian League, Athens' power within the League, and its use of power for its own gain. Discuss the Peloponnesian War. Ask students to predict the long-term effects of the war on Greece.

GUIDED PRACTICE

Have students identify three factors that led to Athens' rise in power from the time of the Persian Wars to the formation of the Delian League. (superior navy, winning decisive battles, prestige among city-states)

3 | ASSESS AND CLOSE

ASSESS

1. Why was the Peloponnesian League formed? (to defend Greece against Persian invaders)
2. What three groups of people could not become citizens of Athens? (women, foreigners, slaves)

BACKGROUND The Greeks won at Salamis because they were better sailors than the Persians and had smaller, more maneuverable ships.

and fought the army of Xerxes in the harbor of the island of Salamis [sal′ə mis]. This sea battle was a disaster for the Persians, and Xerxes was forced to return to Asia Minor. The Greeks had proved themselves the masters of the Aegean.

The Golden Age of Pericles. After the defeat of the Persians, Athens took the lead in holding many of the city-states together in a defensive alliance called the Delian [dē′lē ən] League. To maintain a strong navy for the league, each member state was assessed ships or money, the amount dependent upon its wealth. Athens, from the beginning, dominated the league. Its power and wealth were based on a thriving trade, supremacy at sea, and prestige.

Under **Pericles**, an Athenian statesman and military commander, Athens reached the high point of its democracy. This era of prosperity was called the Golden Age of Pericles. During this time, from 460 to 429 B.C., the Parthenon [pär′thə non], a beautiful temple to Athena, was built, and Greek arts and literature flourished.

In Athens at this time, the real power of government lay in the assembly. All male citizens over 18 years old were members. The assembly passed laws, decided important issues, and elected an executive board of ten generals. The generals were controlled by the assembly, which could reelect them, exile them, or put them to death. Pericles was president of this board of generals.

The Council of 500, which drew up laws for the assembly to pass, was divided into committees dealing with matters such as public buildings and street repairs. Everyone serving the state was paid for his work, a rule that guaranteed that even poor men were able to serve.

Athenian democracy was based on the principle that all citizens were equal.

Athenian law allowed that nearly every citizen could hold one or more public offices during his life. The mass participation of citizens in political life is known as pure or direct democracy. Governments in which the citizens elect representatives to act for them are called representative democracies.

However, it is important to remember that most people in Athens could not be citizens. Women, foreigners, and slaves could not be, and these groups far outnumbered the citizens. Therefore,

significant limits to the idea of equality did exist in Greece. In fact, centuries would pass before the ideals of democracy and equality that we hold sacred today would become generally accepted among large numbers of people.

The Athenians either bought their slaves or captured them as prisoners of war. The slaves who worked in the silver mines did so in chains and suffered under their Greek rulers. House slaves, however, were often treated well, almost as members of the family. Some slaves even became free noncitizens. There were about 100,000 slaves in Athens, about 25 percent of the total population. This huge number made possible the Hellenic idea of leisure. While slaves did the work, citizens had time to cultivate their minds.

Athens' legal system was also guided by the principle of equal rights for citizens. To ensure that every accused person was given a fair trial, Athens had juries of the court, with paid jurors chosen by lot, to try cases.

To prevent a situation in which all the jurors could be bribed, the size of the jury varied from 201 citizens to as many as 2,001, depending upon the wealth and status of the accused. Compared to the jury of today's American court, with its 12 members, these Athenian juries were enormous.

There were other differences between Athenian and modern American juries as well. In Athens the cases were decided by majority vote, not a unanimous decision as in the United States. There were also no full-time judges or lawyers in Athens. In addition, if the accused were found guilty, the punishment was determined in a unique way. Each side, for and against the accused, suggested a punishment and the jury voted for whichever punishment it judged to be fair.

A liberal education was stressed in Athens.

Education in Athens was considered important to maintaining a healthy democratic government. The aim of Athenian education was therefore to help students develop both fine bodies and an appreciation for the arts, to learn to think for themselves, and to become good Athenian citizens.

Education in Athens was quite different for boys and girls. Although citizens were expected to educate their sons, their daughters were generally not given the same opportunities. The state did not provide schools, so parents instead hired tutors, most of whom taught large groups of children and were generally poorly paid. Athenian boys started school when they were 6 years old and continued until they were 16 or older. Most boys learned to play musical instruments, such as the flute or lyre [līr], an ancient stringed instrument somewhat like a small harp. Then, at age 14, boys began going to a gymnasium. Here they were trained in running, wrestling, boxing, and other athletic skills. Here, too, they studied geometry, astronomy, natural history, geography, and public speaking.

Women in Athens did not take part in political affairs, so the education of girls was more limited. Girls did not receive the formal education that the boys did, but they studied in their homes to learn to read, write, and play a musical instrument. Girls also learned many other skills, such as weaving and pottery-making. Athenian homes were often self-sufficient workshops run by women. In the politics of Athens, women were considered unimportant. They did not have any legal standing in court, so if a woman wanted the protection of the law, she had to find a male citizen to represent her in court.

City-state rivalries undermined Greek power.

As Athenian strength grew, and the Persian threat receded, many of Athens' allies in the Delian League wanted to drop out of the league. Athens, still wary of the Persians, fought any attempts to secede from the alliance and ultimately created an empire to force these allies to remain under Athenian control. In this fashion, Athens prevented the Delian League from being a true union of democratic states. Instead, the Athenians forced the other city-states to pay taxes to them, and Athenian settlers took over some of their lands. In addition, Athenian traders received special commercial advantages.

During the last years of Pericles' rule, the other city-states, who considered Athens to be a tyrant city, tried to bring about the downfall of Athens. Gradually corruption crept into the Athenian government. Pericles' successors had neither his intellect nor his high morals, and instead used the government bodies for their own gain.

In 431 B.C. the resentment of the other city-states developed into open war. With Sparta in the lead, the city-states fought Athens in the disastrous **Peloponnesian War**. After a long and costly struggle, Sparta finally defeated Athens in 404 B.C. Wars

DAILY LIFE

Women in ancient Greece were responsible for running the household and raising the children. In wealthy families, that job meant supervising the slaves, who did most of the work and took care of the children. In most families, however, wealthy or not, women spun thread and wove cloth. The vase at left, from about 560 B.C., shows women working the wool. In households without their own water source, women used the common wells, far left, both for getting water and for socializing with other women.

Answers to Section 3 Review

Identify

Key Terms, People, and Places are defined on pages indicated in parentheses. Also see the Glossary and Biographical Dictionary. Persian Empire (69), battle of Marathon (69), Pericles (70), Peloponnesian War (71)

Main Ideas

1. Persian takeover of the Ionian Greeks led the Greeks to revolt and call for aid from Athens. Persian anger at Athens led them to send a fleet to the Greek mainland. Eventual Athenian victory gave Athens confidence to defend their city-state.
2. Athens achieved the highest point of its democracy. The Parthenon was built and art and literature flourished.
3. All citizens could hold office and participate in government. The city-state's legal system ensured the equality of all accused by using large juries and fair punishment.
4. Boys received a more liberal education from tutors and in schools in music, physical training, and academic subjects. Girls were taught at home to read, write, and play a musical instrument.
5. Athens tried to make the Delian League a base for its empire. It forced other city-states to pay taxes, and Athenian settlers took over some of their land. Jealousy among other city-states resulted in civil war.

Critical Thinking

Women, foreigners, and slaves in Athens were not citizens and, therefore, had no voice in government. The United States has no slaves, allows women to vote, and even foreigners may demonstrate, object, and voice their opinions.

---

among the city-states continued, however, and eventually brought about the collapse of Spartan leadership. The Peloponnesian War left the Greeks weakened and divided. Meanwhile, to the north, a new power was gaining strength.

Section 3 Review

Identify Persian Empire, battle of Marathon, Pericles, Peloponnesian War

Main Ideas

1. What circumstances led to the clash between the Greeks and the Persians at the battle of Marathon? What did the victory mean to the Athenians?
2. What were some achievements that took place in Athens following their victory at Salamis during the Age of Pericles?
3. In what ways did Athenian democracy guarantee that all citizens were equal?
4. In what ways did the training of an Athenian boy differ from that of an Athenian girl?
5. What caused the decline in Athens' power?

Critical Thinking

Analyzing Comparisons: The ancient Athenians considered their government a democracy. Discuss a feature of the Athenian government that we would consider undemocratic today and compare it to the government of the United States. (Use the opening portion of the chapter including Pericles' speech on page 58 to help you answer the question.)

---

 4 *The Macedonians conquered the Greeks, and the Hellenistic Age began.*

In an area north of the Greek city-states, known as **Macedonia**, the expected threat to Athenian supremacy was strengthening. Locate Macedonia on the map on page 73. The leader of this Macedonian threat was a young king named Philip, who claimed the throne in 359 B.C. at the age of 23. As a youth, Philip had been a hostage in the Greek city of Thebes [thēbz] and had learned to respect Greek culture and admire its military training. As a result, he used his new authority to organize an

---

army of professional soldiers to augment the fine cavalry provided by his Macedonian nobles.

Philip also centralized the administration of his kingdom and established cities. These cities were organized like the Greek city-states except that they were firmly under Philip's royal control. Philip himself was known as a ruthless leader, willing to use bribery, lies, and other treacherous means to reach his goals. These goals included the formation of a strong kingdom in which the weakened Greek city-states would be under his rule.

Philip's conquest of the Greeks ended the Hellenic period.

Early in 338 B.C., the growing Macedonian threat led Athens and Thebes to form an alliance to protect themselves. In the summer of that year, these two city-states attacked Philip, but the Macedonian king was prepared for them and almost destroyed the Greek army in the battle of Chaeronea [ker'ə-nē'ə]. His young son Alexander led the cavalry while Philip coordinated the infantry. This clash marked the end of the power of the city-states, and Philip soon controlled all of the Greek peninsula except Sparta.

Within a year, Philip called together delegates from the major city-states of Greece (except Sparta) at Corinth. There the so-called Hellenic League was formed. The city-states received a large degree of self-government, but each had to agree to give Philip military support should any of the other city-states threaten the peace. Then, in 336 B.C., after preparing to invade Persia, Philip was assassinated.

However, Philip had prepared his successor for the task of ruling. His son, Alexander, had been given the finest education available, including a period of tutoring by the famous Greek philosopher, Aristotle [ar'ə stot'l]. While Alexander was still in his early teens, Philip had shared state secrets with him. Therefore, when Alexander mounted the throne at age 20, he proved himself a strong leader who eventually earned the illustrious name **Alexander the Great**.

Alexander conquered the Persian Empire.

The young Alexander decided to carry out his father's plan to conquer Persia. He fervently admired

BACKGROUND Philip was assassinated by a noble with a personal grudge.

Alexander's Empire, 323 B.C.

MACEDONIA
Danube River
Black Sea
GRANICUS
Sardis
ROUTE OF ALEXANDER
Issus
Arbela
SYRIA
Ecbatana
Mediterranean Sea
Tyre
Alexandria
Jerusalem
Babylon
Susa
P E R S I A
Memphis
E G Y P T
A R A B I A
Persepolis
ROUTE OF ALEXANDER
Red Sea
Persian Gulf
Arabian Sea
Caspian Sea
Aral Sea
Jaxartes River
Oxus River
Bactra
BACTRIA
Indus River
I N D I A

x Battles

0   200   400 MILES
0   200   400 KILOMETERS

MAP STUDY The map above shows the extent of Alexander's large empire. Locate the red line that indicates Alexander's route. From what region did he depart? Use the map of Europe on page 792 to determine which modern-day countries lie in that same area.

Hellenic civilization and wanted to spread it abroad. His own ambition burned within him as well, and he was convinced that he was destined to rule the world. In 334 B.C., with more than 30,000 infantry and 5,000 cavalry, he marched eastward. It was a journey from which Alexander would never return.

Early in his journey, Alexander won a major triumph at the battle of Granicus. As you can see from the map above, this battle was a first step into Asia. The victory encouraged the Greeks in Asia Minor to revolt against their Persian rulers. The next year, Alexander's forces met the armies of the Persian ruler, Darius III, at Issus [is′əs]. After a number of battles, Alexander's soldiers roundly defeated the Persians. Alexander then marched on to Babylon and then Persepolis, where he took his seat on the throne of Persia. So ended 200 years of Persian domination of the eastern Mediterranean world.

Alexander then moved east through Persia to India, where he met the young ruler Chandragupta Maurya. After some time, however, his homesick and weary soldiers forced him to turn back. In 323 B.C., on what should have been his triumphant return to Macedonia, Alexander died in Babylon, a victim of fever. In truth, many of his military successes were in part the result of the disorganized state of the Persian Empire, but Alexander was indeed a skillful general and a gallant leader in his own right.

To following generations, Alexander's idea of "one world" was of great importance. He envisioned a blend of Greek and Persian culture, a blend that had the Greek language and Greek law as strong bonds. Marriages between his soldiers and the women of the Persian Empire were encouraged, and Alexander himself married two Persian princesses. In addition, a standard system of money was used throughout the lands that he

ANSWER TO MAP STUDY Macedonia; Greece, Albania, Yugoslavia, Bulgaria, and Romania

4 Lesson Plan

Essential Learning Objective

Students will learn to describe the changes that occurred in Greece and Persia after their conquest by Philip of Macedonia and Alexander the Great.

1 FOCUS AND MOTIVATE

Ask students to speculate how the history of Greece might have been different had Sparta and Athens ended their rivalry and united Hellas.

2 TEACH

• Outline the major events during the reigns of Philip of Macedonia and Alexander the Great in Greece, Egypt, and Persia. Have students name the outstanding qualities of both leaders.

• Discuss Alexander's policy of Hellenization. Have students describe his vision of a blended Greek and Persian culture.

GUIDED PRACTICE

Have students write a paragraph describing the experiences and training received by the young Alexander that helped him become a strong leader.

3 ASSESS AND CLOSE

ASSESS

How was Alexander's Empire divided after his death? (into three kingdoms)

OPTIONAL RETEACHING

Have students list changes that took place in Greece and Persia during the Hellenistic Age.

Students also may be assigned Activities reteaching page 22.

73

Alexander the Great is pictured in this intricate Pompeiian mosaic, a careful copy of a famous Hellenistic painting.

conquered and the Persian system of administrative districts remained almost the same. More than 70 new cities were founded, and their governing bodies were staffed by Persians as well as Greeks and Macedonians. In short, Alexander believed in the creation of a strong world government in which all peoples were equal.

Commerce and culture spread during the Hellenistic Age.

Upon the death of Alexander, the empire was left with no heirs to govern it. As a result, it was divided into three parts, each ruled by one of Alexander's generals. Antigonus [an tig′ə nəs] ruled the kingdom of Macedonia, which continued to hold partial control over Greece. Ptolemy [tol′ə-mē] ruled Egypt, and Seleucus [sə lü′kəs] controlled Syria and Persia. Dynasties were established in these kingdoms, and the three parts made up what was called the Hellenistic world. The period of these kingdoms, called the **Hellenistic Age**, lasted for almost 200 years after Alexander's death.

Hellenistic Greeks were generally tolerant of the many different religions in the Middle East. Jews living in Hellenistic cities, for example, were free to practice their religion. Many Jews in Alexandria spoke Greek, so that the Torah and other Jewish writings were translated into Greek. In the 2nd century B.C., however, Seleucid kings did try to suppress the Jewish religion in Judea, in an effort to impose cultural unity. As a result, the Jews revolted under the leadership of the Maccabee family and preserved their religion. This victory, which saved Judaism, is celebrated in the Jewish holiday of Hanukkah.

The Hellenistic Age was a time of much economic growth and of cultural exchange between East and West. The network of cities founded by Alexander created new markets for a variety of goods and acted as centers for the spread of Greek culture. The greatest city of this time was Alexandria, Egypt, with a population of more than half a million people. The city had wide, beautiful streets and an impressive library of 750,000 books.

The Hellenic and Hellenistic phases of Greek civilization were different from each other in one basic respect. During the Hellenic Age, Greek culture was confined to the Mediterranean and Black Sea areas. In the Hellenistic Age, by contrast, Greek culture spread to other parts of the world known to the Greeks at that time, especially the Middle East, India, and China.

Section 4 Review

Identify Macedonia, Alexander, Hellenistic Age
Main Ideas
1. How did Philip's conquest of the Greeks affect the city-states?
2. How did Alexander the Great apply his idea of "one world" to the conquered Persian Empire?
3. How were the Hellenistic Greeks different from those in the Hellenic period?

Thinking Critically
Making Hypotheses: Alexander the Great had a dream of "one world." Can you describe what your concept of a unified world would be? Would it work? Why or why not? What factors would lead to success or failure?

BACKGROUND The Hellenistic Age ended when the Romans conquered Macedonia and Greece around 148 B.C. However, some people date the end of the Hellenistic Age to the Roman defeat of Cleopatra, the last Ptolemy, in 31 B.C.

HIGHLIGHTS OF CIVILIZATION

Greek Architecture

The ancient Greeks built magnificent temples to honor their gods. Most temples followed the same simple plan, which consisted of a stepped platform with a row of graceful fluted (grooved) columns on each side. Above these columns were marble panels depicting religious and historical themes. The columns enclosed a chamber called the cella that held a statue of a god.

The measurements of all the parts were governed by strict rules that produced a feeling of dignified, elegant harmony. The columns pictured in the diagram show the three basic styles—Doric, Ionic, and Corinthian. The Doric style was massive and severe. The Ionic and Corinthian styles gave an airier appearance and were more ornamental. Both the Doric and Ionic styles derived from an earlier version know as Aeolic [ē ä′lik], also shown, from eastern Greece. The scrolls were meant to imitate the foliage of the acanthus, a flowering herb grown in that region.

The Parthenon at Athens, pictured here, is the supreme example of a Doric temple. Its grace and beauty remain apparent despite its ruined state. Built during the rule of Pericles, between 448–432 B.C., the Parthenon held at its center a beautiful gold and ivory statue of Athena, goddess of wisdom, by the noted sculptor Phidias (fid′ē əs).

Many details contributed to the perfection of the Parthenon. The columns tilt slightly inward and are not uniformly spaced. Hardly a single straight line exists in the building. All these variations were deliberately planned by the architects to enhance the grace and harmony of the building.

Doric Aeolic

Ionic Corinthian

The Parthenon at the Acropolis in Athens is shown at left. The diagrams above depict four Greek capitals—the top part of the columns.

were loyal, trading colonies. During the Hellenistic period, Alexander spread Greek influence throughout the known world.

Critical Thinking
Students' answers should demonstrate an understanding of Alexander's "one world" concept.

HIGHLIGHTS OF CIVILIZATION
Explain that Athena was glorified at a great annual festival, the Panathenaea, during which celebrants moved in procession from the gates of the city and around the Parthenon. The building was preserved for many centuries, first as a Christian church and later as a Turkish mosque. It was severely damaged in 1687 when Turkish gunpowder stored in the Parthenon was detonated during a war with the Venetians. Ask students why they think the Athenians might devote so much time and money to building a temple for Athena. (Possible answers: Athena was the chief goddess of Athens; she represented wisdom; in celebrating Athena, the Athenians were celebrating themselves and their victories over barbarian enemies.)

Answers to Test Yourself

Key Terms, People, and Places
The key terms, people, and places tested here were introduced in the chapter sections and reviewed in the Section Reviews. For definitions see the page references at the appropriate Section Reviews. Also see the Glossary and Biographical Dictionary.

Main Ideas
The main ideas tested here were introduced in the sections of this chapter and reviewed in the Section Reviews. For answers to these questions, see the appropriate Section Reviews.

Critical Thinking
1. Students should select a legend and explain what, if any, elements of truth exist in the story.
2. In their responses, students should consider the effects of Philip's and Alexander's rules before their deaths. Their answers should reflect an understanding of each man's ambitions and talents.

CHAPTER 4 REVIEW

Section Summaries

Section 1
Aegean civilization developed from sea trade.
Among the first people to travel on open waters were the Phoenicians, but another civilization that developed early because of its sea trade was that of the Minoans on Crete. The Mycenaeans spread the Aegean civilization to the mainland.

Section 2
The Greeks expanded to control the eastern Mediterranean.
The Mycenaean civilization fell to the Dorians, who moved into the Greek peninsula and drove the Mycenaeans into Ionia. During the "Greek Dark Ages," the Dorians and remaining Mycenaeans intermarried to become the Greeks. When they emerged from this period, these Greeks formed a number of independent city-states, including Athens and Sparta.

Section 3
Defeat of the Persians led to Athens' recognized leadership.
During the Hellenic age, 750–338 B.C., Athens became the most powerful city-state and the leader of the Delian League. Athens reached its height during the Golden Age of Pericles. Jealousy and rivalry among city-states led the Greeks to civil war.

Section 4
The Macedonians conquered the Greeks, and the Hellenistic Age began.
The Greek city-states became part of the Macedonian empire. Philip, the king of Macedonia, was assassinated in 336 B.C., but his son Alexander the Great conquered many parts of Asia.

Test Yourself

Key Terms, People, and Places
Identify the significance of each of the following:

Section 1
a. Aegean Sea
b. Minoans
c. Mycenaeans
d. mythology
e. Troy

Section 2
a. polis
b. democracy
c. Athens
d. Sparta

Section 3
a. Persian Empire
b. battle of Marathon
c. Pericles
d. Peloponnesian War

Section 4
a. Macedonia
b. Alexander (the Great)
c. Hellenistic Age

Review Dates

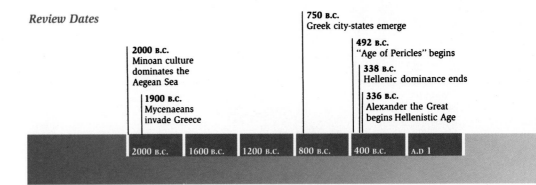

2000 B.C.
Minoan culture dominates the Aegean Sea

1900 B.C.
Mycenaeans invade Greece

750 B.C.
Greek city-states emerge

492 B.C.
"Age of Pericles" begins

338 B.C.
Hellenic dominance ends

336 B.C.
Alexander the Great begins Hellenistic Age

2000 B.C. 1600 B.C. 1200 B.C. 800 B.C. 400 B.C. A.D 1

Main Ideas

Section 1

1. How was Crete's location important to the economic and cultural development of the Minoan civilization?

2. What changes did the Mycenaean invasion cause to Greek civilization?

3. How was Troy's location valuable strategically?

Section 2

1. How did Greek city-states move toward democracy?

2. What were some of the important reforms that helped Athens become more democratic?

3. What conditions led to the development of a strong military government in Sparta?

Section 3

1. How did the Greeks and Persians come into conflict with one another?

2. Why were the years of Pericles' rule called the Golden Age?

3. How did the Athenian government ensure that all citizens were treated as equals?

4. What were the differences in the education of Athenian boys and girls?

5. Why did the power of Athens decline?

Section 4

1. What requirements were placed upon the Greek city-states because of Philip's conquest?

2. How did Alexander try to achieve his dream for "one world"?

3. What were the differences between the Hellenic and Hellenistic Greeks?

Critical Thinking

1. Evaluating Sources of Information From the findings of modern archaeologists, we have learned that certain parts of Greek legends did indeed chronicle actual people and real events. Think about a legendary figure or event with which you have grown up. (Robin Hood, the battle of the Alamo, the ride of Paul Revere, and Johnny Appleseed are suggestions.) Research one legend to separate fact from fiction.

2. Predicting Effects Philip was assassinated after 23 years of rule. Alexander ruled only 13 years. What do you think would have happened if either of these Macedonian kings had held power for more time?

Chapter Skills and Activities

Practicing Study and Research Skills

Using the Card Catalog

The key to any library is the card catalog. By knowing how to use it, you can unlock the wealth of information the library has to offer. The card catalog is arranged alphabetically. It contains at least three cards for each book in the library—an author card, a title card, and a subject card. Each card contains similar information—title, author, publisher, and date of publication. The contents of each book are usually briefly described.

Each card in the card catalog has a number that indicates where in the library the book (or pamphlet, tape cassette, or film) can be found. Most libraries use either the Dewey decimal system or the Library of Congress system of arranging their nonfiction books according to subject. Fiction is usually arranged alphabetically by author's last name.

When you need a specific book, look for the title or author card in the catalog. If you have a topic but no specific title, look up the subject. If you don't find the subject, think of another way of stating it ("Ionians" might be under "Greece," for example), or ask the librarian. What type of card would you look for in the card catalog to find each of the following?

a. a book on the early Greek Olympics

b. a biography of Alexander the Great

c. The *Aeneid*

d. a book by the Greek poet Homer

Linking Past and Present

Our modern Olympic Games are fashioned from the Ancient Greek competitions. In what ways are they the same? What additions have the modern games made to reflect different or new areas of athletics?

Learning History Through Maps

In this chapter we have studied many different stages of the growth of civilization. Each time a change came, another city became most prominent. Find each of these cultural centers using the maps on pages 60, 65, and 73. Then look at a current map to see if any of these cities still exist.

CRITICAL THINKING QUESTION LEVEL 1. average; 2. easy

Answers to Chapter Skills and Activities

Practicing Study and Research Skills

a. subject
b. subject
c. title
d. author

Linking Past and Present

Students' responses should reflect some knowledge or research about the different events of the modern and historic Olympic games. Most of the events of the modern Olympics, however, were not a part of the ancient games.

Learning History Through Maps

Students should find the following cities: Tyre, Knossos, Mycenae, Troy, Athens, Sparta, Alexandria. These cities still exist: Athens, Alexandria.

Chapter

5 The Greek Achievements

OVERVIEW

This chapter focuses on the works of Greek
philosophers, scientists, and artists as they
sought the true meanings of the universe,
human life, and beauty.

PLANNING CHART

Section	Text Pages	Key Concept	Suggested Teaching Time
1 The Greeks laid the foundation for philosophy.	79–82	Different schools of philosophy examined the nature of existence.	One day **More time?** Use *Source Reading 5A* or the One-Day Play, *The Trial of Socrates*.
2 The Greeks produced impressive literature.	82–84	Writers developed various explanations for the causes of events in drama and history.	One day **Less time?** Combine Sections 2 and 3. Treat Greek literature and art as one lesson.
3 The Greeks made important advances in science and art.	84–86	The use of reason helped Greek scientists to discover the physical world. Artists created ideals of beauty in statues and temples.	One day **More time?** Use *Overhead Transparencies 9 and 10* or *Source Reading 5B*.

ANCILLARIES

Materials that may be used with this chapter
to reinforce, reteach, enrich, and assess
learning are pictured on the following pages.

Teacher's Resource File

ACTIVITIES

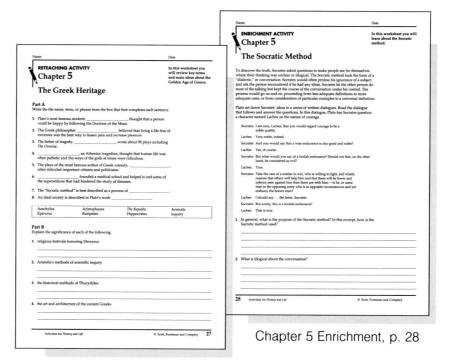

Section 1 Activity, p. 24

Section 2 Activity, p. 25

Section 3 Activity, p. 26

Chapter 5 Reteaching, p. 27

Chapter 5 Enrichment, p. 28

Teacher's Resource File

GEOGRAPHY SKILLS

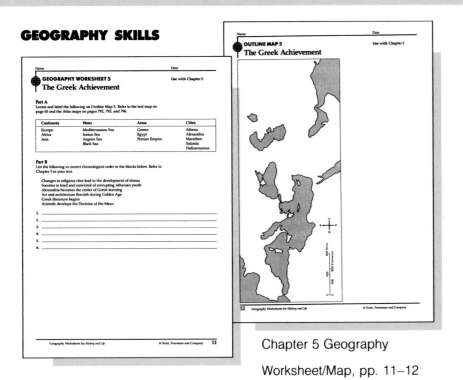

Chapter 5 Geography
Worksheet/Map, pp. 11–12

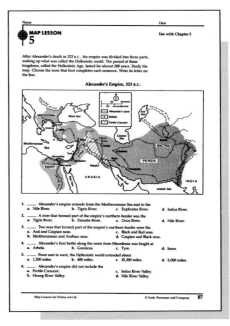

Chapter 5 Map Lesson, p. 87

TESTS

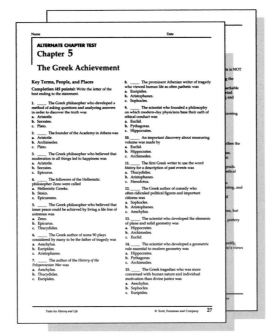

ONE-DAY PLAYS

The Trial of Socrates

Chapter Test, pp. 25–26   Alternate Chapter Test, pp. 27–28

Other Optional Ancillaries

WORKBOOK

WORKSHEET
Chapter 5, Section 1

Greek Philosophy

In this worksheet you will review contributions of the Greeks to philosophy.

Part A

Write the term or name from the box that best completes each statement.

1. A famous school in Athens that was started by Plato and existed for over 900 years was the _____
2. The discipline that seeks to understand the universe and the individual's place within it is called _____
3. The work of Plato that describes an imaginary land where each man and woman performs the task to which he or she is best suited is _____
4. Asking the right questions and systematically seeking answers is _____
5. The school of philosophy whose founder believed in increasing pleasure by avoiding extremes was _____
6. The philosophy which taught that true happiness comes when one finds one's proper place in nature was _____
7. The philosopher who taught the Doctrine of the Mean was _____

| philosophy | The Republic | inquiry | Epicureanism |
| Academy | Stoicism | Aristotle | |

Part B

Complete each statement with the explanations given in your text.

1. Socrates was known as "the gadfly" because
2. Socrates was put on trial because
3. Socrates advocated a persistent questioning of all ideas because
4. Compared to Plato, Aristotle seemed more down-to-earth because

16 Worksheets for History and Life   © Scott, Foresman and Company

Section 1 Worksheet, p. 16

WORKSHEET
Chapter 5, Section 2

Greek Literature

In this worksheet you will review Greek literature of the Golden Age.

Read the clues below and complete the crossword puzzle using the terms in the box.

Across

1. author of *History of the Persian Wars*
6. the subject about which Thucydides wrote
9. Greek god of wine
10. central character in a play by Sophocles
11. historian who looked for human causes of the Greek wars

Down

2. type of Greek literature
3. author of *Oedipus Rex*
4. writer of Greek comedy
5. form of drama in which direct endings are unhappy or disastrous
7. last of three great Athenian tragedians
8. father of tragedy

drama	history	Euripides	tragedy
Aristophanes	Dionysus	Aeschylus	Herodotus
Oedipus	Sophocles	Thucydides	

Worksheets for History and Life   © Scott, Foresman and Company   17

Section 2 Worksheet, p. 17

WORKSHEET
Chapter 5, Section 3

Greek Science and Art

In this worksheet you will review Greek achievements in science and art.

Part A

Only three of the four items in each group are related in some way. Circle the item that does not belong and explain how the remaining three items are related.

1. Euclid — astronomy — geometry — Pythagoras
2. oath — Archimedes — Hippocrates — medicine
3. Alexandria — drawings — pottery — paintings
4. Phidias — Athena — pottery — sculpture
5. "Laocoon" — "Apollo Belvedere" — "Winged Victory" — Corinthian painting

Part B

For each set of statements below, write M for the main idea and S before statements that support or help explain the main idea. One statement in each set is not related to the main idea; write X next to this statement.

1. ___ Aristotle argued that new truths could be acquired through induction and deduction.
   ___ The Greek scientist Hippocrates founded a medical school.
   ___ This new breed of philosophers believed that direct study and observation enabled one to find the truth.
   ___ During the Hellenistic Age, Greek philosopher-scientists introduced new methods of scientific inquiry.

2. ___ The mathematical breakthroughs of Euclid form the foundation of plane and solid geometry.
   ___ Only parts of the work of Phidias still remain.
   ___ Greek scientists made important discoveries that advanced human knowledge.
   ___ Archimedes discovered the method of water displacement to measure volume.
   ___ High-school students today study the Pythagorean theorem.

18 Worksheets for History and Life   © Scott, Foresman and Company

Section 3 Worksheet, p. 18

SOURCE READINGS

Source Reading 5A
Source Reading 5B

TEST GENERATOR

40 multiple-choice questions for Chapter 5

OVERHEAD TRANSPARENCIES

Overhead Transparency 9
Overhead Transparency 10

Chapter 5

The Greek Achievement

750 B.C.–150 B.C.

500 B.C.

c. 430 B.C. Sophocles writes *Oedipus Rex*

c. 370 B.C. Plato writes the *Republic*

334 B.C. Aristotle founds the Lyceum

300 B.C.

200 B.C.

In summing up the meaning of Greece to the modern world, the 19th-century English poet Shelley proclaimed, "We are all Greeks, our laws, our literature, our religion, our arts have their roots in Greece." Our Founding Fathers would have agreed with Shelley. The writers of our Constitution, in an effort to establish a government that would strike a balance between liberty and authority, debated issues first argued in Athens in the 5th century B.C.

Most of the delegates to the Constitutional Convention in 1787 had been schooled in the classics—Greek and Roman studies. They had studied Homer and could read the *Iliad* and the *Odyssey* in the original Greek. From their study of history, these early American leaders were familiar with the deeds of Pericles, the plays of the Greek dramatists, and the art of imperial Athens.

Our budding young nation looked to ancient Greece for inspiration. As a result, the curriculum in the first American colleges stressed classical studies. Thomas Jefferson, himself an architect, turned to Greek models when he designed his home at Monticello and buildings for the University of Virginia.

Other Presidents, including Madison and Monroe, followed Jefferson's example. A walk today through our nation's capital, Washington, D.C., should be sufficient to convince anyone that the buildings that crowned the Acropolis in the days of Pericles set a standard of beauty and proportion that is still admired and copied after 25 centuries.

Important and obvious though the Greek influences are in the art and architecture of the modern world, the most significant impact of Greece on later centuries has been in the realm of ideas—in philosophy, politics, science, literature, and in religion. Little wonder then that the famous modern historian of world civilizations, Arnold Toynbee, should say of Greece, here was "the finest flower of the species that has ever yet come to pass."

Pottery often provides glimpses into ancient Greek religion. Here Persephone, a daughter of Zeus, sits with her husband, Hades, ruler of the underworld.

Reading Preview

In this chapter you will read about important Greek achievements.

1. The Greeks laid the foundation for philosophy.

2. The Greeks produced impressive literature.

3. The Greeks made important advances in science and art.

 1 | *The Greeks laid the foundation for philosophy.*

After the defeat of Persia, the Greeks entered upon the richest period of their history. Although most of the Greek world was involved, Athens became the cultural center, serving as a magnet that attracted artists, poets, and philosophers from all over the Greek world.

1 **Lesson Plan**

Essential Learning Objective

Students will learn to identify Greek philosophers who had lasting influence on Western civilization.

79

The Greeks sought answers about people's lives through reason.

The contributions made by the Greeks to philosophy—that is, to an understanding of the universe and the individual's place within it—surpassed that of most other peoples. They advanced theory after theory to explain the nature of the world and everything in it.

By the middle of the 5th century B.C., Greek thinkers turned away from speculations about the nature of the physical world and began to center their attention on matters that directly affected people. The lead was taken by a group of teachers who were referred to collectively as the **Sophists** [sof′ists].

One of the leading Sophists was **Protagoras** [prō tag′ər əs], who summed up the Sophist philosophy in the phrase "man is the measure of all things." He seemed to be saying that such things as truth, beauty, and justice are not absolutes. They differ from time to time, from place to place, and from person to person. The Sophists argued that society should judge right from wrong and determine what was just in any given situation.

The Sophists were very popular with the younger generation of Athens. Their views, however, brought a strong reaction from their critics. Many Athenians feared that the views of the Sophists, if widely accepted, would undermine society. The result would be anarchy and an attack on religion.

A new school of philosophy arose in Athens.

To counter the Sophists' views, a new school of philosophy developed that was destined to be the most influential of all. The new school held to the view that truth is not something relative to time and place, as the Sophists maintained. They believed that truth is real and unchanging. Absolute standards of right and wrong and of good and evil exist and can be discovered by using the right method. Their method was that of inquiry, of asking the right questions and systematically seeking answers. Their leaders were three of the most famous men in the history of philosophy—Socrates, Plato, and Aristotle.

Socrates [sok′rə tēz′] lived in the 5th century B.C. He was known to other Athenians as "the

From the Archives

Aristotle's *Politics*

The goal of the state, in Aristotle's view, was human happiness. He wanted the leaders of Athens to study political theory so they would strive to govern in the best possible way. For this reason, he urged them to consider the origin and purpose of governments.

Every state is a community of some kind, and every community is established with a view to some good; for mankind always act in order to obtain that which they think good. But if all communities aim at some good, the state or political community, which is the highest of all, and which embraces all the rest, aims at good in a greater degree than any other, and at the highest good. . . .

Our purpose is to consider what form of political community is best of all for those who are most able to realize the ideal of life. We must therefore examine not only this but other constitutions, both such as actually exist in well-governed states, and any theoretical forms which are held in esteem; that what is good and useful may be brought to light.

gadfly" because his persistent questioning of all ideas and acts stung his listeners into thinking. In fact, the so-called "Socratic method" consisted of asking questions and then carefully analyzing the answers to try to arrive at the truth. Socrates might begin by asking the question, What is the beautiful and what is the ugly? Each answer would be questioned, and further questions would be posed until agreement was reached by the participants about the exact meaning of the terms. Socrates' advice to everyone was "know thyself."

Some Athenians believed that Socrates was a bad influence on his students because he encouraged young men to question the acts of Athenian leaders. As a result, Socrates was put on trial in

FROM THE ARCHIVES The excerpt is from *Politics* in *The Works of Aristotle*, Vol. II, translated by W. D. Ross (Chicago: Encyclopaedia Britannica, Inc., 1952), pp. 445, 455. Ask students to discuss the purpose of the state according to Aristotle.

80

(realizing the "good life") Can the "good life" be realized under different forms of government? (yes, if the people are willing to accept the form of government and the laws are just and promote the "common good.")

399 B.C., charged with corrupting the youth of the city and showing disrespect for religious traditions.

In his defense at the trial, Socrates justified his actions with pride but was convicted by a wide margin. As you learned in Chapter 4, Greek defendants proposed their own punishment to go along with the proposal of the state. Socrates, who believed that he had only acted virtuously, suggested that he deserved to be fed by the state for life. After persuasion from some friends, however, Socrates proposed a fine of a miniscule amount. Socrates' claims incensed the court, and the jury voted to sentence him to death. After a month in jail, Socrates took a drink of poisonous hemlock.

The most famous pupil of Socrates was **Plato** [plā′tō], who lived from 430 B.C. to 347 B.C. He started the Academy, a famous school in Athens that existed for more than 900 years. His best known work is *The Republic*, which describes an imaginary land in which each man or woman does the work that suits that individual best. In this imaginary land, all young people would be given 20 years of education, and no job would be closed to women.

Plato believed that there should be three classes of people—workers to produce the necessities of life, soldiers to guard the state, and philosophers to rule in the interests of all. Private property would be abolished, and education would be set up for the benefit of the rulers.

Plato's most famous pupil was the 4th century philosopher, **Aristotle** [ar′ə stot′l]. He was a brilliant thinker with wide interests, writing about biology, mathematics, astronomy, physics, ethics, logic, and politics.

Like most Athenians, Aristotle believed that a person could be happy by being moderate in all things. He taught that people should strike a balance or mean point, between rash action and inactivity. According to the Doctrine of the Mean, the best way to meet danger is through brave action—brave action being the mean, or halfway point between two extremes, between foolhardiness and cowardice.

In his book, *Politics,* Aristotle wrote about the good and bad features of different kinds of governments: monarchy, aristocracy, and democracy. You will find an excerpt from *Politics* in the "From

the Archives" feature at left. Unlike Plato, Aristotle did not describe an imaginary state, nor did he find a single ideal system. As a work, *Politics* serves to point out an important difference between Plato and Aristotle. Plato often appeared to deal only with abstract ideas, but Aristotle, in contrast, seemed more down-to-earth.

Hellenistic philosophers sought the good life.

Two major schools of Greek philosophy came out of the Hellenistic Age. These were Epicureanism

Aristotle was one of the most influential thinkers of all time. As a philosopher and a scientist, he broke through barriers and set new standards.

[ep′ə kyù rē′ə niz′əm] and Stoicism [stō′ə siz′əm]. The first was developed by **Epicurus**, a man who believed that living a life free of extremes was the best way to lessen pain and increase pleasure.

Some of his followers misinterpreted his ideas about pleasure. They thought Epicurus meant that one should only eat, drink, and be merry. For this reason, Epicureanism is often misrepresented as meaning that pleasure, instead of the mental activity that Epicurus emphasized, is a way of gaining inner peace.

Another Hellenistic philosopher, Zeno [zē′nō], developed a philosophy known as Stoicism. He taught that true happiness, or inner peace, can be reached by people when they find their proper places in nature. His followers were called **Stoics**, because they often met on a *stoa,* or porch.

Believing all nature to be good, the Stoics thought that people must accept poverty, disease, and even death as the will of God. This philosophy led them to be indifferent toward all kinds of experience, good or bad. Today, the word "stoic" means a person who does not show feelings or emotions.

This ivory statuette shows the elaborate exaggeration of Greek theater costumes.

2 The Greeks produced impressive literature.

As we saw in Chapter 4, Greek literature began in the 800s B.C. with the epic poetry attributed to Homer. The literature of the Golden Age drew heavily on this tradition and on the Greek religious heritage, also from the distant past.

By the time of Pericles, the Greeks had invented innumerable stories and legends about the gods. The people honored the gods but were free to accept any account of them they wished. Greek religion became an important part of community life, and honoring the gods was seen as an important civic duty. The stories and legends about the gods were a continuing source of inspiration for poets, dramatists, and historians.

The Greeks invented drama.

Greek drama began as part of the religious rites that were held at festivals honoring the god of wine, Dionysus [dī′ə nī′səs]. A chorus of men chanted hymns and performed dances in praise of the god. In the 6th century B.C., changes in the rites eventually led to the development of drama. Individual actors were separated from the chorus and given roles to play, and dialogue was used. Most important was the use of new themes based on heroic legends not related to Dionysus. You will

A professional Greek poet recites his work in a performance, continuing the literary tradition of Homer.

learn more about Greek drama in the "Highlights of Civilization" feature on page 87.

By the 5th century B.C., two distinct forms of drama—tragedy and comedy—had evolved in Athens. For the most part, the writers of tragedy borrowed from the old familiar legends of the gods and heroes for their plots. They reinterpreted these themes in the light of the values and problems of their own times. The chorus remained a basic part of the play, commenting on the action as it took place. Both men's and women's roles were played by men. Greek tragedy dealt with serious matters, and the plays always had unhappy or disastrous endings.

Athenian playwrights excelled in tragic and comedic drama.

The most famous authors of tragedies among the Greeks were three Athenian poets who lived in the 5th century B.C.. They were Aeschylus, Sophocles, and Euripides.

Aeschylus [es′kə ləs], considered by many to be the father of tragedy, wrote some 90 plays, of which only seven have survived. He found inspiration in contemporary themes as well as the old myths and legends.

In *The Oresteia,* a series of three plays, Aeschylus drew his material from the Trojan War and its aftermath. The hero Agamemnon [ag′ə mem′non] returns home safely from the war only to be murdered by his wife Clytemnestra [klī′təm nes′trə]. His son Orestes [ô res′tēz] and daughter Electra avenge their father's death with Orestes' murder of his mother. In turn, however, Orestes is made to pay for his crime when he goes insane. In this way the tragic cycle of murder, revenge, and retribution is carried out.

Sophocles [sof′ə klēz′], the most important of the Greek tragedians, was concerned more with human nature and individual motivation than with the working out of divine justice. He illustrated the strength of the human spirit by depicting people who experienced painful tragedy.

The most famous of his surviving plays, *Oedipus Rex* ("Oedipus the King") centers around the tragic consequences when Oedipus [ed′ə pəs], not knowing the true identity of his parents, kills his father and subsequently marries his mother.

Euripides [yù rip′ə dēz′], the last of these prominent Athenian writers of tragedy, reflected the more critical spirit that prevailed in the wake of the Peloponnesian War. To him, human life was often pathetic, and the ways of the gods at times ridiculous. Euripides' popularity lasted long after the Golden Age, probably because of his use of everyday speech in his writings and his modern critical outlook toward life.

Comedy, which is an amusing play or a play with a happy ending, also began in the festivals of Dionysus. The most famous author of comedy was **Aristophanes** [ar′ə stof′ə nēz], another 5th century Greek. Since no laws protected Athenians from false or damaging statements, Aristophanes often ridiculed important citizens and politicians in his plays.

The Greeks wrote the first true histories.

So far as we know, the word *history* was first used for a description of past events by **Herodotus** [hə rod′ə təs], a 5th century B.C. Greek. His masterpiece, *History of the Persian Wars,* is filled with anecdotes, legends, and many entertaining bits of odd information that are not always reliable as historical evidence. Herodotus does, however, let the reader know when he is describing events he can verify.

2 TEACH

- Explain the development of drama from early festivals honoring Dionysus to the acting out of legends. Stress the purpose of the chorus and that men played all roles.
- Discuss the distinctive character of the works of each major Greek playwright.
- Clarify the difference in method used by Herodotus and Thucydides. Help students grasp the importance of unbiased reporting by historians but point out that it is difficult if not impossible to avoid bias entirely.

GUIDED PRACTICE

Have pairs of students write paragraphs describing a historical or current event using the methods of either Herodotus or Thucydides.

3 ASSESS AND CLOSE

ASSESS

1. Which playwright emphasized the human nature and motivations of his characters? (Sophocles)
2. Who were targets of the jokes in Aristophanes' comedies? (important people and public officials)

OPTIONAL RETEACHING

Ask if the plots of any of the Greek plays are similar to any dramas that students have seen. Discuss the universality of drama themes.

OPTIONAL ENRICHMENT

1. Have students draw a plan of an early Greek theater illustrating the various structures found in a typical theater. (average)
2. Assign a student to research and report on the drama contests held in ancient Athens. (challenging)

Assign the Section Review, Activities
page 25, or Workbook page 17.

CLOSURE

Summarize the lesson by telling students that the greatest literature of
Greece was its drama. Playwrights
used religious legends and stories of
heroes as themes for their plays.

Answers to Section 2 Review

Identify

Key Terms, People, and Places are
defined on pages indicated in parentheses. Also see the Glossary
and Biographical Dictionary.
Aeschylus (83), Sophocles (83), Euripides (83), Aristophanes (83), Herodotus (83), Thucydides (84)

Main Ideas

1. Individual actors were separated
from the chorus and given roles.
New themes were introduced based
on heroic legends.
2. Aeschylus, considered the father
of Greek tragedy; Sophocles, the finest tragic dramatist; Euripides, noted
for his critical and modern outlook;
Aristophanes, noted for comedy
3. Herodotus wrote history that did
not always separate fact from fiction;
Thucydides' history was more reliable and objective.

Critical Thinking

As historians, one purpose would be
to praise their fellow Greeks in order
to inspire them. An objective account
makes for better history but does not
necessarily inspire patriotism.

The use of masks, popular in ancient Greek drama,
is carried to modern times in this production of
Aeschylus' *Oresteia* in Britain.

The other important Greek historian of the 5th
century was **Thucydides** [thü sid′ə dēz′]. Like Herodotus, Thucydides wrote only one book, the *History of the Peloponnesian War.* In it, he only used
material that he felt was important to the history.
A faithful historian, Thucydides judged evidence
and only used facts he had carefully checked.

Thucydides looked for the human causes of the
Greek wars. He did not believe that human events
could be explained as fate or as acts of the gods.
Thucydides' *History of the Peloponnesian War* became a model for other historians.

Section 2 Review

Identify Aeschylus, Sophocles, Euripides,
Aristophanes, Herodotus, Thucydides

Main Ideas

1. How did the festivals honoring Dionysus lead to the
   development of drama?
2. Who were the most famous writers of tragedy and
   comedy? For what are they remembered?
3. Who were the leading Greek historians and what
   kind of history did they write?

Critical Thinking

Evaluating Sources of Information: Imagine that
you are a Greek historian during the Golden Age.
Would you try to be objective about your country's and
ruler's activities even when appealing to the patriotism
of your readers? Why?

---

3 The Greeks made important advances in science and art.

Just as they did in philosophy and literature, the
Greeks broke new ground and set high standards
in science and art. The Greeks absorbed the heritage of earlier peoples and advanced it far beyond
any of their predecessors.

Greek scientists introduced new methods of inquiry.

Building on the work of earlier philosophers,
Greek scientists of the 5th and 4th centuries B.C.
made remarkable progress. They began looking at
the world around them with an open mind, in an
effort to explain its mysteries by reason rather
than by myth and legend. Aristotle was far and
away the ideal of this new breed of philosopher-scientist. He not only dominated his age but also
provided the foundation for the remarkable scientific advances of the Hellenistic period and for
many centuries to come. True knowledge, he argued, could be obtained only as a result of the
painstaking collection and organization of particular facts.

In his famous work *Organon*, Aristotle set forth
two ways in which new truths could be acquired.
The first, induction, moves from particular facts to
general truths. In other words, the scientist collects
a body of facts, studies them, and then reaches at
least a tentative conclusion as to where these facts
lead. Deduction, on the other hand, moves from
the general to the particular. In using this method,
the scientist begins with an idea that appears to
have validity, then goes in search of the specific
examples that support it.

Using these methods, Aristotle and his assistants
investigated such diverse fields as biology, mathematics, astronomy, physics, literary criticism, rhetoric, logic, politics, ethics, and metaphysics. In science he uncovered facts that would not be
discovered again until the intellectual revolution of
the 17th and 18th centuries.

The Hellenistic Greeks added to scientific knowledge.

Building on the work of Aristotle and others,
Greek science continued to advance in the 3rd cen-

BACKGROUND Egyptian ruler, Ptolemy I, with the aid of one of Aristotle's students, built a library in Alexandria.

Called the Museum, the library was the largest in the ancient world, containing more than a half million volumes.

tury B.C. Greek concern for direct study and observation, instead of abstract speculation, reached its peak during the Hellenistic period. The new center of learning was now Alexandria, Egypt.

Scientists flocked to Alexandria to carry on research and study with other scientists. Based on direct observation of natural phenomena, their discoveries broke new ground in several key areas. In mathematics **Euclid** [yü′klid] laid down the elements of plane and solid geometry. In the area of physics, **Archimedes** [är′kə mē′dēz] made an important discovery about measuring volume. According to legend, Archimedes was asked by Hiero, the king of Syracuse, to figure out whether a goldsmith had cheated him by making a crown that was not pure gold. In solving the problem, Archimedes determined how to find the volume of an object by measuring the amount of water it displaced in a container. He also discovered that the goldsmith had in fact tried to cheat the king.

Two other Greeks made important achievements that have endured to this day. **Pythagoras** [pə thag′ər əs] stated the geometric rule that is essential to any high-school geometry course, the Pythagorean [pə thag′ə rē′ən] theorem, above right.

The Pythagorean Theorem
The square of the hypotenuse of a right triangle (z) equals the sum of the squares of the other two sides.

The other scientist, **Hippocrates** [hi pok′rə tēz′], founded a medical school. "Every disease has a natural cause," he said. His work helped end some of the superstitions and belief in magic that had stood in the way of the study of disease. Physicians today swear an oath of ethical conduct, called the Hippocratic oath, based on one that Hippocrates drew up.

Art and architecture flourished throughout the Greek world.

The most striking evidence of the splendor of Greek civilization is provided by the art and architecture of the 5th century B.C. Even in a state of ruin, as so much of it is, the artistic achievement of the Golden Age is an inspiration.

The porch of the Maidens (c. 421–409 B.C.) still stands in Athens. A modern replica forms a wall of Chicago's Museum of Science and Industry.

BACKGROUND In astronomy Aristarchus put forth the theory that the earth rotates on its axis and moves in an orbit around the sun. In geography Eratosthenes drew parallels of latitude and lines of longitude on his map of the inhabited world.

He also calculated the circumference of the earth to within 200 miles of the correct figure.

3 *Lesson Plan*
Essential Learning Objectives
Students will learn to:
- describe Aristotle's inductive and deductive methods.
- identify Hellenistic scientists, artists, and sculptors.

1 FOCUS AND MOTIVATE

Explain that because the Greeks were geographically located near Mesopotamia and Egypt, they were in a position to learn from earlier peoples. Discuss how ideas travel.

2 TEACH

- Guide students to give examples of how the inductive and deductive methods of Aristotle are used. Point out the connection between the works of Greek philosophers and scientists. Help students to see that these thinkers shared an interest in the nature of the physical world.
- Point out that the works of Greek artists told about life in Greece in addition to setting new standards of beauty, harmony, and balance.

GUIDED PRACTICE
Have students use the Glossary and Biographical Dictionary to find the dates of each Greek scientist's life. Arrange the dates on a time line and indicate which scholars could have worked together or whose work might have helped later scholars.

3 ASSESS AND CLOSE

ASSESS
On what did Aristotle believe that true knowledge must be based? (the collection and organization of facts)

The Winged Victory (c. 190 B.C.), prominently displayed at the Louvre in Paris, was skillfully carved from a solid eight-foot block of marble.

Parthenon, is now gone, and only remnants of his other works remain.

Hellenistic sculptors continued and intensified the realistic approach of the Golden Age, adding dramatic and emotional elements. Outstanding surviving examples from the Hellenistic period include the "Laocoön," the "Apollo Belvedere," the "Venus de Milo," and the "Winged Victory."

As you learned in the "Highlights of Civilization" feature in Chapter 4, classical Greek architecture reflected harmony and proportion. All relationships, such as column spacing and height and the curvature of floor and roof lines, were calculated and executed with remarkable precision to achieve a perfect balance.

The host of new cities that sprang up in Hellenistic times served as a tremendous impetus to architecture. The new cities benefited from town planning, with streets laid out on a rectangular grid. The impressive public buildings were elaborate and highly ornamented. The much more elaborate Corinthian columns were preferred over the simple Doric and Ionic.

Greek painting, pottery, and sculpture all reflected high artistic standards. The value of Greek pottery for the student of the past is as much or more in the drawings and paintings on the vases as in the pottery itself. In many instances these illustrations tell us about aspects of everyday life in ancient Greece that we can learn in no other way.

Greek sculpture also reflected the high artistic standards of Greek civilization. The most famous sculptor of the age was Phidias [fid'ē əs]. His masterpiece—Athena, which once stood inside the

Section 3 Review

Identify Euclid, Archimedes, Pythagoras, Hippocrates
Main Ideas
1. What new methods of inquiry did Greek scientists introduce?
2. What contributions did the Hellenistic Greeks make to scientific knowledge?
3. In which of the arts did the Greeks excel?

Critical Thinking
Assessing Cause and Effect: Imagine that you are a Greek scientist during the Hellenistic period. Do you think that you would join the many scientists who traveled to Alexandria to study? What advantages might you see in a community of scholars? Might there be disadvantages?

86

HIGHLIGHTS OF CIVILIZATION

Greek Drama

Tragedy, Aristotle said, excites pity and awe, thereby bringing about a sense of emotion purged and purified. Thus, the Greek philosopher explained the power of tragedy to lift an audience to heights of intense pleasure.

So powerful was the work of the ancient Greek dramatists that audiences as large as 30,000 would gather for their performances. Although it combined acting, poetry, music, and dance, the theater was much more than a form of entertainment among the ancient Greeks. Performances were also a means of celebrating the most profound religious and civic beliefs held by citizens.

The difficulty of the actors in being heard in open-air theaters before large audiences led to the construction of theaters on hillside sites, where banks of stone seats surrounded a circular stage called the orchestra. The actors wore masks with speaking tubes that may have worked something like a megaphone to enhance the sound of their voices.

The magnificent theater at Epidaurus in Peloponnesus, below left, now partially restored, is the best preserved theater building of classical times. The theater provides seats for 12,000 people, all within direct line of sight and sound with the stage.

In the earliest Greek theaters, all the dramatic action took place within the orchestra circle. In an effort to make themselves more easily heard, the actors later began to speak some of their lines from a raised stage. By the time the theater at Epidaurus was built in the 4th century B.C., the actors often performed on a raised, two-level stage, the ruins of which can be seen in the background of the photograph. The chorus, however, remained in the orchestra.

The theater at Epidaurus is noted for its almost perfect acoustics—the structural features that determine how well sounds can be heard. A quiet audience can hear a pin dropped at the center of the orchestra.

The theater at Epidaurus, Greece, dates from the 4th century B.C. The ancient Greek dramas are performed here each summer.

parentheses. Also see the Glossary and Biographical Dictionary. Euclid (85), Archimedes (85), Pythagoras (85), Hippocrates (85)

Main Ideas
1. Methods based on reason, especially Aristotle's inductive and deductive reasoning
2. They emphasized direct study and observation of nature.
3. probably sculpture and architecture

Critical Thinking
Students might mention that scientists together might share ideas, but also might discourage individuals from following certain ideas.

HIGHLIGHTS OF CIVILIZATION
The Greek Way to Western Civilization, by Edith Hamilton, will help able students appreciate the Greek contributions (New York: Mentor Books).

You might explain that the actors and the chorus performed in the orchestra. The actors also used a two-level stage, the ruins of which can be seen in the background of the photograph.

Ask students why they think the Greeks enjoyed watching tragedies. (Opinion: possibly because tragedy gets beneath the surface of life and explores the deepest human emotions that have universal impact)

Key Terms, People, and Places
The key terms, people, and places tested here were introduced in the chapter sections and reviewed in the Section Reviews. For definitions see the page references at the appropriate Section Reviews. Also see the Glossary and Biographical Dictionary.

Main Ideas
The main ideas tested here were introduced in the sections of this chapter and reviewed in the Section Reviews. For answers to these questions, see the appropriate Section Reviews.

Critical Thinking
1. Students should consider the values of the Epicureans, many of whom have misrepresented Epicurus' ideas that life should be without extremes to mean that pleasure in such things as eating and drinking would lead to inner peace. They should also consider the Stoics, who believed that people must accept whatever experience nature handed them, good or bad. They should then decide which ideas fit best with the modern American culture.
2. They might be making the assumption that the forms of architecture, drama, and art followed by the Greeks were superior to other forms, and should be a part of our culture today.

CHAPTER 5 REVIEW

Section Summaries

Section 1
The Greeks laid the foundation for philosophy.
The Greeks made many significant contributions to the study of philosophy. The philosophers of the 5th century B.C. centered their attention on matters that directly affect people. The Sophists argued that standards were relative and that each society should judge what is best for itself. Socrates, Plato, and Aristotle rejected the Sophist view, arguing that absolute standards do exist and can be discovered by reason. Hellenistic thinkers sought a philosophy that would lead to the good life.

Section 2
The Greeks produced impressive literature.
Greek drama began as a religious ceremony then evolved into a religious-civic festival. Aeschylus, Sophocles, and Euripides were the most outstanding writers of tragedy. Aristophanes, on the other hand, was famous for his comedies. In the writing of history, Herodotus produced interesting narrative accounts but was less exacting and accurate than the other important historian of the time, Thucydides.

Section 3
The Greeks made important advances in science and art.
Advances made by Greek scientists resulted from their uses of new methods of inquiry. They viewed the world with an open mind and sought rational explanations for what they observed. Aristotle's introduction of the inductive and deductive methods gave scientists more reliable methods in their search for answers. Hellenistic scientists made practical applications of these theories and achieved important results in mathematics, physics, astronomy, and biology. Greek art and architecture reflected the high artistic standards of their civilization.

Test Yourself

Key Terms, People, and Places
Identify the significance of each of the following:

Section 1
a. Sophists
b. Protagoras
c. Socrates
d. Plato
e. Aristotle
f. Epicurus
g. Stoics

Section 2
a. Aeschylus
b. Sophocles
c. Euripides
d. Herodotus
e. Thucydides

Section 3
a. Euclid
b. Archimedes
c. Pythagoras
d. Hippocrates

Review Dates

c. 430 B.C. Sophocles writes *Oedipus Rex*

c. 400 B.C. Hippocrates founds medical school

399 B.C. Socrates is sentenced to death

c. 370 B.C. Plato writes the *Republic*

334 B.C. Aristotle founds the Lyceum

c. 300 B.C. Euclid produces *Elements*

500 B.C.   450 B.C.   400 B.C.   350 BC.   300 B.C.   250 B.C.

Main Ideas

Section 1
1. What had become the major focus of Greek philosophy by the 5th century B.C.?
2. What did Socrates, Plato, and Aristotle think of the Sophists' ideas?
3. How did the Hellenistic philosophers think the good life could be achieved?

Section 2
1. What part did the festivals honoring Dionysus play in the development of drama?
2. Who were the major writers of tragedy and comedy? Describe some of their plays.
3. How were the kinds of history written by the two Greek scholars Herodotus and Thucydides different?

Section 3
1. What methods did Aristotle and other Hellenistic Greeks use in their scientific work?
2. How was science advanced during the Hellenistic period?
3. What achievements did the Greeks make in the areas of art and architecture?

Critical Thinking
1. **Recognizing Values** Which philosophy do you think would have more appeal in the United States today—the Epicurean or the Stoic? Why?
2. **Identifying Assumptions** What assumptions do you think people who design buildings, write plays, or sculpt statues today in the styles of ancient Greece might hold?

Chapter Skills and Activities

Practicing Study and Research Skills
Using a Table of Contents

Suppose that you've started to work on a research paper. Once your search through the card catalog has yielded a number of books, how do you decide which books would be the best for your topic? One quick way to decide is to consult the book's Table of Contents, which is always located near the front of the book. The Table of Contents lists chapter titles, subsection titles—if used, and page numbers. Use the Table of Contents for this book to answer the following questions:
1. On what page would you find the "Highlights of Civilization" for Chapter 5? What is the topic of this particular "Highlights" feature?
2. How many pages does this book have on ancient Greece?
3. In which chapter would you expect to find information on modern Europe after 1945?

Linking Past and Present
Study the photograph above of the Jefferson Memorial, standing today in Washington, D.C. In what ways does this memorial to Thomas Jefferson, the third president of the United States, dedicated in 1943, reflect the ancient Greek style of architecture?

Learning History Through Maps
As you have learned in this chapter, Alexandria, Egypt, was the major center of scientific learning during the Hellenistic period. Using the political and physical maps of Africa in the Atlas on pages 796–797, locate two bodies of water—including rivers—near which Alexandria was located.

CRITICAL THINKING QUESTION LEVEL 1. challenging; 2. average

89

Chapter

6 The Roman Legacy

OVERVIEW

This chapter covers the rise of the Roman Republic to an empire, its eventual decline, and its lasting contributions to Western civilization.

PLANNING CHART

Section	Text Pages	Key Concept	Suggested Teaching Time
1 The Roman Republic arose on the Italian peninsula.	92–96	A combination of factors, including geography, values, military strength, and leadership, enabled Rome to control central and southern Italy.	One day
2 The republic became a far-flung empire.	96–101	Rome became a vast empire that controlled almost all the lands bordering the Mediterranean Sea.	One day **Less time?** Assign Section 2 to be read before class and teach it together with Section 3. Use the map on page 102 to illustrate the grown of the Empire. **More time?** Use *Source Reading 6A*.
3 The Roman Empire lasted for many centuries.	101–105	In spite of often incompetent leadership, the Roman Empire held together for more than 400 years.	One day **More time?** Use *Overhead Transparency 11*.
4 The Romans developed a lasting Greco-Roman culture.	105–112	Most roots of Western civilization can be traced to the culture that flourished in the Roman Empire from about 27 B.C. to A.D. 180.	One day **More time?** Use *Overhead Transparency 12* or *Source Reading 6B*.

ANCILLARIES

Materials that may be used with this chapter to reinforce, reteach, enrich, and assess learning are pictured on the following pages.

Teacher's Resource File

ACTIVITIES

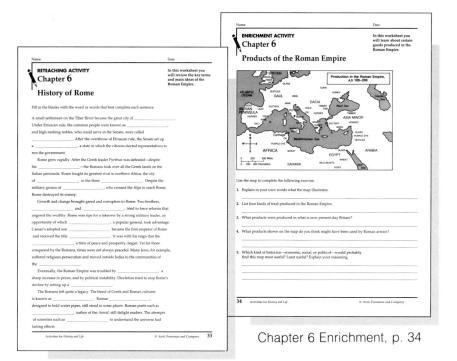

Section 1 Activity, p. 29

Section 2 Activity, p. 30

Section 3 Activity, p. 31

Section 4 Activity, p. 32

Chapter 6 Reteaching, p. 33

Chapter 6 Enrichment, p. 34

Teacher's Resource File

GEOGRAPHY SKILLS

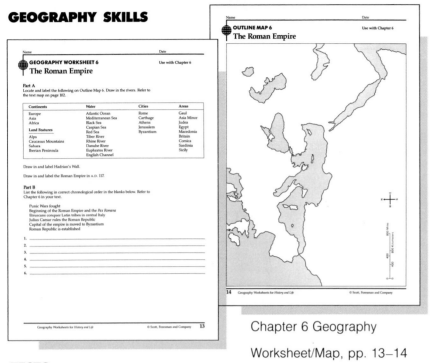

Chapter 6 Geography
Worksheet/Map, pp. 13–14

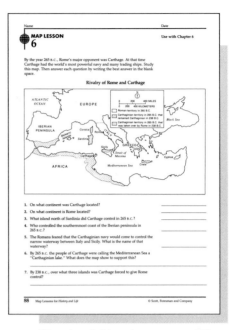

Chapter 6 Map Lesson, p. 88

TESTS

Chapter Test, pp. 29–30

Alternate Chapter Test, pp. 31–32

Other Optional Ancillaries

WORKBOOK

Name _____ Date _____

WORKSHEET
Chapter 6, Section 1

In this worksheet you will review important events in the early history of Rome.

Early Roman History

Part A
Using the numbers 1 through 7, arrange the events in chronological order. On the lines after each event, tell why it was an important happening.

a. ____ The Gauls invade Rome.

b. ____ Pyrrhus leads attack against Rome.

c. ____ The Roman Senate sets up a republic.

d. ____ Plebeians win the right to have written laws.

e. ____ Rome forms the Latin League with Latin tribes.

f. ____ The plebeian assembly wins the right to make laws for all citizens.

g. ____ Members of the Latin League revolt against Rome.

Part B
Write the number of each event from Part A and its exact date on the proper place on the time line.

550 B.C.   500   450   400   350   300   250 B.C.

Worksheets for History and Life   © Scott, Foresman and Company   19

Section 1 Worksheet, p. 19

Name _____ Date _____

WORKSHEET
Chapter 6, Section 2

In this worksheet you will review the ways in which Rome changed from a republic to an empire.

From Republic to Empire

Part A
For each statement below, write two or three sentences that support or provide details for that statement.

1. Rome's greatest rival in the region of northern Africa was Carthage.

2. As Rome expanded, political and economic changes at home led to civil war.

3. Julius Caesar used his popularity with the plebeians and the army to take control of Rome.

4. Octavian became the first emperor of Rome.

Part B
What do you think might have happened in Rome if Julius Caesar had NOT crossed the Rubicon? Write a paragraph explaining your answer.

20   Worksheets for History and Life   © Scott, Foresman and Company

Section 2 Worksheet, p. 20

Name _____ Date _____

WORKSHEET
Chapter 6, Section 3

In this worksheet you will review some facts and opinions about the Roman Empire and its decline.

The Roman Empire

Read the statements below and write F for fact and O for opinion before each one. For each opinion, explain one other point of view that people might hold.

1. ____ Augustus was the greatest emperor of Rome.

2. ____ The *Pax Romana* was a peaceful period during which people lived happily under enlightened Roman rule.

3. ____ Rome declined primarily for economic reasons.

4. ____ Both Diocletian and Constantine were humane despots.

5. ____ After the death of Theodosius I, the Roman Empire was divided into eastern and western halves.

6. ____ The Roman emperor's decision to reduce the gold and silver content of the money supply was wise, since it saved the empire's dwindling supply of precious metal.

7. ____ The following words of Marcus Aurelius reflect the influence of the Stoic philosophy: "Blot out vain pomp; check impulse; quench appetite; keep reason under its own control."

8. ____ Had Romans followed the Stoic philosophy, the decline of Rome could have been prevented.

Worksheets for History and Life   © Scott, Foresman and Company   21

Section 3 Worksheet, p. 21

Name _____ Date _____

WORKSHEET
Chapter 6, Section 4

In this worksheet you will review lasting contributions of the Romans.

The Roman Heritage

Part A
Present at least two specific facts from your text to support each statement.

1. Latin's lasting influence is evident in the words people use today.

2. Roman law provided the basis for many systems of law today.

3. The classical culture was a blend of Greek and Roman culture.

4. The Romans did not slavishly copy Greek art and architecture.

Part B
Write the letter of the name of the person from the box that best matches the description.

1. ____ author of a history of Rome

2. ____ a scholar, astronomer, and mapmaker

3. ____ author of a study of Germanic tribes

4. ____ author of *Commentaries on the Gallic Wars*

5. ____ author of the *Aeneid*

6. ____ physician who studied the role of the arteries

7. ____ author of *Parallel Lives*

a. Julius Caesar	e. Plutarch
b. Vergil	f. Ptolemy
c. Livy	g. Galen
d. Tacitus	

22   Worksheets for History and Life   © Scott, Foresman and Company

Section 4 Worksheet, p. 22

SOURCE READINGS

Source Reading 6A
Source Reading 6B

TEST GENERATOR

40 multiple-choice questions for Chapter 6

OVERHEAD TRANSPARENCIES

Overhead Transparency 11
Overhead Transparency 12

The Roman Legacy

750 B.C. — A.D. 395

800 B.C.

753 B.C. Legendary founding of Rome

509 B.C. Roman Republic is established

27 B.C. Augustus became first Roman emperor

A.D. 100

A.D. 200

A.D. 300

To Edward Gibbon, an 18th-century English historian and author of *Decline and Fall of the Roman Empire*, "the period in the history of the world during which the condition of the human race was most happy and prosperous" was the 2nd century A.D. It was during this century that the Roman Empire reached its greatest extent and was, according to Gibbon, "governed by absolute power, under the guidance of virtue and wisdom." A Roman subject of the 2nd century agreed and had this to say about the era:

> The whole world keeps holiday; the age-long curse of war has been put aside; mankind turns to enjoy happiness. Strife has been quieted, leaving only the competition of cities, each eager to be the most beautiful and the most fair. Every city is full of gymnastic schools, fountains and porticos, temples, shops, and schools of learning. The whole earth is decked with beauty like a garden.

There were those who would disagree. Some thought Roman rule was a mixed blessing at best, and others felt it was oppressive and tyrannical, a rule in which the Romans used their military power cruelly and unjustly. A 20th-century British historian, Arnold Toynbee, called the 2nd century A.D. a time of stalemate when the world "lay more or less passive under the pall" of Roman power. Writing in the 2nd century, the Roman historian Tacitus [tas′ə təs] quoted the words of a British chieftain: "They [the Romans] make a desert and call it peace." The Jews, whose country was destroyed by the Romans, would generally have agreed.

A difference of opinion is a good point at which to begin to look at Roman history. In truth, military conquest did make Rome a world state. The boundaries of the empire expanded as the Roman armies scored victory after victory. Yet force alone was not enough to maintain a unified state. Skillful diplomacy, effective government, a flexible system of law, a widespread network of

Rome's reliance on the sea is evident in this exquisite floor mosaic, found in a seaside Pompeian home. In the mosaic, brightly colored pieces of stone detail the wide variety of sealife in the waters around Rome.

roads and commercial towns—all of these factors helped Rome bring together within one empire a great number of peoples of diverse backgrounds.

For more than two centuries, from 27 B.C. to A.D. 180, the Romans maintained the *Pax Romana*, or "Roman Peace," throughout their far-flung domain.

Reading Preview

In this chapter you will read how Rome grew from a small Italian city-state to a vast empire.

1. The Roman Republic arose on the Italian peninsula.

2. The republic became a far-flung empire.

3. The Roman Empire lasted for many centuries.

4. The Romans developed a lasting Greco-Roman culture.

Lesson Plan

Essential Learning Objectives

Students will learn to:

- describe the steps in Rome's development from an Etruscan province to master of central and southern Italy.
- explain the factors that helped Rome become strong militarily.

Have students read the chapter opener to find two positive and two negative opinions about Rome. (Positive: Gibbon and a Roman subject. Negative: Toynbee and a German chieftain.) Point out that modern historians also do not agree about the effects of Roman rule. Ask students to keep these conflicting opinions in mind as they study this section, and the chapter as a whole, and to look for evidence that supports either point of view.

- Provide students with outline maps of Europe from the Geography Skills book. Have students label: Rome, Etruscans, Alps, Latin League, Gauls, Greek Colonies. Use color-coding to indicate (a) geographical features, (b) groups that invaded Rome, and (c) peoples conquered by Rome.

- An outline of the structure of the Roman Republic would include: Government, Class, Family Values, Military Strength, Leadership, Plebeian Rights. Add details to ensure that students grasp how each factor contributed to Rome's strength.

1   *The Roman Republic arose on the Italian peninsula.*

Between 2000 and 1000 B.C., about the time that the Greek-speaking tribes were moving into their future homeland, another branch of Indo-Europeans moved south through the Alps into the Italian peninsula. Most important among these peoples were the Latins, a group of tribes who settled in the Tiber [tī′bər] River Valley of western Italy. About 750 B.C., the Latins built a small settlement near the Tiber River. Over time, the city of **Rome** grew from this modest beginning.

Early Rome was ruled and influenced by the Etruscans.

In the 7th century B.C., the Latin tribes were conquered by their powerful neighbors to the north, the Etruscans. Little is known about the Etruscans, but they are believed to have come from Asia Minor. They drained the marshes around Rome, encouraged trade, and taught the Latins to write with the Greek alphabet and to use arches in their buildings. In addition, the Romans began to worship some of the Etruscans' gods and to make statues of these gods as the Etruscans had.

Many important features of Roman government developed under Etruscan rule. The Etruscans were responsible for bringing the first city-state civilization to Italy. A king of Etruscan descent ruled the state and was elected to his office by the Latin tribal chieftains. He served as high priest, as well as chief magistrate (a government official who has the power to uphold the laws), and chose a group of nobles, called the Senate, to advise him. These high-ranking freemen were usually large landowners and were known as **patricians** [pə-trish′əns], or fathers of the state. In contrast, the small farmers and tradespeople were known as **plebeians** [pli bē′əns], or common people.

Consuls and the Senate led the Roman Republic.

In the 7th and 6th centuries B.C., an Etruscan family named Tarquin ruled Rome. A bitter rivalry for power developed in the family until eventually,

The Chimera [kə mir′ə], the most famous example of prized Etruscan bronzework, is a mythical monster with a lion's body, goat's head, and serpent's tail.

The detail of an Etruscan fresco above depicts a splendid banquet with musicians and dancers, a popular event among the Etruscan nobility. The fresco is from the Tomb of the Leopards and dates from the early 5th century B.C.

GUIDED PRACTICE
Have students list five aspects of their culture that the Romans learned from the Etruscans. (Greek alphabet, gods, arches, city-state government, Senate)

one member, Tarquin the Proud, murdered the king and declared himself ruler. A tyrant, he was despised by the people and was finally deposed by the Senate in 509 B.C.

The Senate then set up a **republic**, a state in which the citizens elect representatives to run the government. As in early Greece, power in the Roman Republic was held tightly by those people at the top of the social scale.

The new republic was governed by two consuls, who were the chief magistrates, and the Senate.

What's in a Name?

ROME Legend has it that Rome is named for Romulus. He and Remus were brothers who, the story goes, were raised by a wolf. More likely, the city's name comes from *groma*, a Latin word meaning "crossroads."

The consuls could serve for only one year, a provision that kept them from becoming too powerful. In wartime or other emergencies, however, a dictator, or absolute ruler, could rule in place of the consuls, but the term of office was limited to six months. The Senate was made up of 300 patricians appointed for life by the consuls. This powerful group of senators conducted foreign policy, proposed the laws, handled the government's finances, and nominated the consuls for office.

Rome expanded within the Italian peninsula.

Soon after Tarquin and the Etruscans were overthrown in 509 B.C., Rome and the nearby Latin tribes got together to form a defensive alliance known as the Latin League. By the beginning of the 4th century B.C., Rome and the league successfully controlled the central Italian peninsula.

Soon, however, two setbacks to Roman expansion occurred. The first was the invasion in 390

93

B.C. by the Gauls, who were fierce, fair-haired warriors who came from what is now France and northern Italy. The Gauls destroyed the Roman army, almost burned Rome to the ground, and held a small group of Romans under siege for seven months. Although the Gauls left after they were paid a huge ransom in gold, the damage to Roman prestige was serious. In the long run, however, the defeat served to strengthen the Romans by leading them to fortify their city and army.

The second setback took place in 340 B.C., when other members of the Latin League, jealous of Rome, revolted. After two years of war, Rome defeated its former allies, dissolved the league, and forced each tribe to sign a separate treaty. The Romans then turned north and conquered the Etruscans, who were weak from repeated attacks by the Gauls. For protection against the Gauls, a defensive line on the Arno River was set up to stop future attacks. (See map, page 102.)

The only serious rivals to Roman rule left on the Italian peninsula were the Hellenistic Greeks in southern Italy and Sicily [sis′ə lē]. Their city-states, first settled during the 700s B.C., were flourishing centers of Greek culture. The Greeks steadily became alarmed at the growing power of Rome. To help stop the Roman expansion, they called upon Pyrrhus [pir′əs], a relative of Alexander the Great and an ambitious military leader from northern Greece. In 280 B.C., with an army of 25,000 men and 20 elephants, he defeated the Romans in battle. The war elephants, unknown in Italy at the time, crushed the enemy forces much like tanks have done in modern battles.

Pyrrhus then invited the former members of the Latin League to join forces with him against Rome. They refused. Stunned, he made a peace offer to Rome, but it was rejected. Pyrrhus then launched a second successful attack, but his losses were so great that he exclaimed, "Another such victory and we are lost." To this day, a costly victory is known as a **pyrrhic victory**.

When a third battle failed to force the Romans to make peace, Pyrrhus returned to Greece. The Romans then quickly conquered the Greek lands on the Italian peninsula. By 270 B.C., less than 250 years after the founding of the republic, Rome was master of all central and southern Italy.

Many factors contributed to the military success of the Romans.

The Romans succeeded in both conquering and managing diverse peoples and territories because of four basic reasons. These reasons relate to Rome's favorable geography, strong family values, great military strength, and wise leadership.

Geography. In conquering the hostile peoples surrounding Rome—Etruscans in the north, hill tribes in central Italy, and Greeks in the south—the Romans were favored by geography. One important advantage was the city's central location on the Italian peninsula. This position gave the Romans a strategic advantage over their enemies, who had difficulty uniting successfully.

Another advantage resulted from the mountainous terrain of the Italian peninsula. The Alps to the north kept all but the most determined invaders from entering the peninsula. In addition, the Romans were not hurt by the Apennines, which run down most of the Italian peninsula. These mountains were not as rugged as those found in Greece and therefore did not work against Rome's unification of the area. (See the map, page 102.)

Family values. Most of the early Romans were farmers. They lived simply, worked hard, and fought well. In general, the Roman family was a close-knit group held together by affection, the necessities of a frugal life, and the strict authority of parents. Both parents played important roles in family activities and taught their children loyalty, courage, and self-control. Most Romans took their civic and religious duties seriously.

The stern virtues prized by Roman family life were a source of strength to the early republic. In later years, when increasing power and wealth began to undermine family life, some people were unhappy about the passing of the old order. "Rome stands built upon the ancient ways of life," warned a poet of the 3rd century B.C. who felt the need for a return to the strong family values of the past.

Military strength. The success of the Roman conquests was largely the result of a well-trained army of citizen-soldiers. The basic military unit was the legion [lē′jən], an infantry force of 6,000 men at full strength. Each legion was divided into groups of 120 men. At first only Roman property owners could be soldiers. However, as Rome ex-

3 **ASSESS AND CLOSE**

ASSESS

1. Whose settlements in southern Italy did Rome conquer? (the Greeks)
2. What political rights were won by the plebeians? (the veto, written laws, right to hold office)

This stone monument from a young boy's tomb illustrates the family values held by the early Romans. The mural shows several stages of the boy's life, moving from his mother's arms (on the far left) to the company of a tutor (on the far right).

panded and the need for soldiers increased, conquered peoples were forced to supply troops for the army.

In addition to enriching a strong army, Rome's military strength also aided its political goals. New military roads, such as the Appian Way, connected Rome to other cities on the Italian peninsula. These new roads, intended to speed the movement of troops, also opened up trade and communication among Italian cities.

Wise leadership. The Romans had great talents for organization. For example, they gave full privileges of Roman citizenship to some of their conquered peoples. This select group of conquered people could vote and hold political office in Rome. Others were given less important rights, such as the right to own property.

In addition, Rome granted a large measure of independence to the peoples it conquered. They were free to run their own affairs, set up their own assemblies, and elect their own magistrates. Rome, however, controlled the administration of justice and handled city-to-city affairs. As a result, the Roman Republic maintained stability.

The plebeians fought for equal rights within Rome.

Soon after the founding of the republic, the plebeians began to demand a greater role in government.

As Rome's territory expanded, its need for loyal and well-trained citizen-armies grew. As a result, the plebeians, who made up the bulk of the army, were able to gain a greater voice and role in the government over time.

Under pressure from dissatisfied plebeians, the Roman government allowed the plebeians to establish their own assembly. This assembly, called the *Concilium Plebis* ("gathering of the plebeians"), was governed by plebeian-elected leaders called tribunes. At first, this assembly lacked power and influence, but over time its power began to grow.

In addition to dealing with plebeian concerns in their own assembly, the tribunes also sat in on Senate discussions. They could not take part in the debates or vote, but if they felt that the laws under discussion would not be in the plebeians' favor, they could cry out *"Veto,"* which meant, "I forbid." Although at first the veto did not stop the Senate from passing laws, it did encourage senators to rethink unpopular legislation.

About 450 B.C. the plebeians won the right to have the laws of the republic written down and available for all to see. This prevented judges from making different decisions on similar cases in order to favor patrician interests. These written laws were called the Law of the Twelve Tables. They were carved on twelve bronze tablets and hung in the forum, a central, open-air meeting place.

Answers to Section 1 Review

Identify

Key Terms, People, and Places are defined on pages indicated in parentheses. Also see the Glossary and Biographical Dictionary. Rome (92), patricians (92), plebeians (92), republic (93), pyrrhic victory (94)

Main Ideas

1. introduction of city-state government and its system of rulers, arches, gods, and its writing system
2. consuls and senators, patricians
3. throughout the Italian peninsula, the Latin League
4. Rome was favored by geography, strong family values, military strength, and wise leadership. Rome's central location prevented its enemies from unifying, and the Alps stopped most invaders coming from the north.
5. The plebeians filled Rome's growing need for soldiers. They were successful in gaining the right of veto, in the establishment of the Law of the Twelve Tables, and in gaining entry to important Senate and other government positions.

Critical Thinking

Students should consider the positive and negative effects of granting such privileges to conquered peoples. Some positive effects: a feeling of strong loyalty for Rome among the conquered, respect for Rome, unity within the republic. Some negative effects: such privileges could possibly keep the conquered peoples strong, Romans might not approve.

From the Archives

The Law of the Twelve Tables

The Romans' earliest and most important body of written law was the Law of the Twelve Tables. The following excerpts are fragments quoted in the works of Roman authors.

TABLE III

1. A person found guilty of breaking the law by verdict of the praetor [judge] shall have 30 days grace.
2. At their expiration, the person bringing the lawsuit shall serve a summons on the accused person and take him before the praetor.

TABLE IV

2. If a son shall be sold into slavery three times by his father, he shall be freed from his father's authority.

TABLE VIII

3. If anyone, with or without a weapon, shall break a bone of a free man, he shall be fined 300 Roman coins; if of a slave, he shall be fined 150 coins.

Little by little, the plebeians made more gains. The veto power of the tribunes became more effective, and by the 4th century B.C., a plebeian held one of the consulships. In addition, plebeians became eligible for membership in the Senate and other government offices that had previously been reserved for patricians. Two such offices were the praetors [prē'tərz], who were judges in charge of the law courts, and censors [sen'sərz], who upheld the moral code of the republic and registered citizens for tax and voting purposes.

In 287 B.C. a law made the plebeian assembly into a popular assembly that made laws that were binding on all citizens. The old distinctions between patrician and plebeian were wiped away. However, a rising class of rich plebeians, whose wealth had come from trade, industry, or marriage,

eventually took control of the assembly. As a result, the struggle for political power and social equality did not come to an end. In the centuries ahead, differences in wealth and status continued to play an important part in the story of Rome.

Section 1 Review

Identify Rome, patricians, plebeians, republic, pyrrhic victory

Main Ideas

1. In what ways did the Etruscans influence the development of Rome?
2. What were the two main leadership positions of the Roman Republic? Were these positions generally filled by patricians or plebeians?
3. Where did Rome's first expansion efforts take place? What defensive alliance first attempted to unify the region around Rome?
4. Why was Rome able to be a military success? How did the geography of Italy help Rome?
5. Why were the plebeians able to demand equal rights in the Roman government? Give two examples in which they were successful.

Critical Thinking

Assessing Cause and Effect: Imagine that you are a Roman general who is conquering foreign lands. Would you choose to grant the defeated the kinds of privileges that the Romans usually granted? Why or why not?

2
The republic became a far-flung empire.

Once the Romans had dominated the Italian peninsula, they turned to the northern coast of Africa, where the city of **Carthage** remained as Rome's only rival. Carthage had been founded in 814 B.C. by Phoenicians and had grown into a rich and large commercial power from sea trade in the western Mediterranean. The Carthaginian domain included territory in north Africa and the Iberian peninsula (present-day Spain and Portugal) and trading centers on the islands of Sardinia, Corsica, and Sicily. The strong Carthaginian navy, made up of mercenary soldiers who fought primarily for money, blocked Roman expansion in the Mediterranean.

FROM THE ARCHIVES The portion of the Law of the Twelve Tables adapted here, together with other fragments that were modernized or distorted, may be found in *Remains of Old Latin,* edited and translated by E. H. Warminston (Cambridge, MA:

Harvard University Press, 1961). Ask students whose rights were being protected by the laws in Table IV. (sons sold into a form of slavery by their fathers) Who was protected by the laws in Table VIII? (victims of personal injuries)

A strong rivalry between Rome and Carthage led to the Punic Wars.

Between 264 and 146 B.C., Carthage and Rome maintained a bitter rivalry and fought three major wars for control of the western Mediterranean. These wars are known as the **Punic** [pyü'nik] **Wars**, from the Latin *Punici* for "Phoenicians."

The First Punic War. This first of many struggles centered around the Carthaginian settlement on the northeastern tip of Sicily. The Carthaginians feared that once the Romans had conquered the Greek cities of southern Italy, they would move to control Sicily as well. The Romans, on the other hand, were concerned that Carthage's strong navy could use the Strait of Messina as a short bridge from Sicily onto the Italian peninsula.

The contest between Rome and Carthage was clearly unequal. The odds favored Carthage, which was rich in gold, manpower, and ships. The Romans, with a strong army, were not a seafaring people, but they realized that Carthage could be defeated only if its navy were smashed. With amazing determination, the Romans built up a navy. In a series of naval battles, several Roman fleets were destroyed. Finally, however, the Romans defeated the Carthaginians in 241 B.C.

Sicily became the first Roman province and was made to pay an annual tribute of grain to Rome. Later, the islands of Sardinia and Corsica were conquered and made into a single province. No longer was Roman power restricted to the Italian peninsula, and the Roman navy proved supreme in the western Mediterranean.

The Second Punic War. This next war of revenge took place 22 years after the first ended. It has been called a "conflict between the nation Rome and the man Hannibal." **Hannibal** was a young and ambitious Carthaginian general whose military genius has been rated as equal to that of Alexander the Great. He is said to have sworn on a sacred altar to his father, also a general, to remain Rome's enemy for life.

Hannibal forced Rome to declare war in 219 B.C. by attacking a Roman ally, the city of Sagento in Spain. With cavalry, African war elephants, and about 40,000 infantrymen, Hannibal then crossed through southern Gaul and over the Alps into Italy. Trace this route on the map on page 102. The

BACKGROUND The Romans lost 200,000 people in the first naval battles against the Carthaginians.

The two faces of this ancient coin show the Carthaginian leader Hannibal and one of the troop of war elephants he led to face the Romans.

difficult journey cost Hannibal about half of his men, much of his equipment, and all but one elephant. With the Gauls of northern Italy enlisted as allies, Hannibal began to march south.

To meet the emergency, the Romans made Fabius Maximus dictator. He was a cautious leader who refused to risk an all-out battle. Although his policy of watchful waiting succeeded in frustrating Hannibal, it was also unpopular with the many Romans who wanted a face-to-face battle.

Their opportunity finally came at Cannae [kan'ā] in southern Italy. There, in 216 B.C., Hannibal encircled the Romans and wiped out a force at least a third larger than his own. He was stopped however, from inflicting a mortal blow upon Rome. He dared not lay siege to Rome without reserves of manpower and supplies. Because the Romans and their loyal allies controlled the seas, Hannibal was cut off from his resources.

Finally, the Romans decided to open up another front under the bold leadership of Scipio [sip'ē ō] the Elder. Scipio was a general believed to be Hannibal's match in terms of military strategy. Roman forces invaded north Africa, and Hannibal was forced to return home to defend Carthage. At Zama in 202 B.C., Hannibal was defeated and fled to the east to save his life. The peace terms dictated by the Romans were harsh—Carthage gave up its navy, lost its freedom in foreign affairs, paid annual tribute to Rome, and surrendered Spain. Despite these terms, the Romans were still afraid that Carthaginian power would grow once again.

The Third Punic War. True to the Romans' suspicion, over the next 50 years, Carthage slowly

2 *Lesson Plan*
Essential Learning Objectives

Students will learn to:
- identify the areas that were added to Rome's territory through conquests and alliances.
- evaluate the causes of the political and economic changes that led to the end of the republic.

---

1 FOCUS AND MOTIVATE

Ask students to give examples of Roman strengths and weaknesses from what they have learned thus far. (Examples of strengths might be Rome's large army, loyal citizens, good leaders; weaknesses, the conflict between rich and poor) Have students predict what Rome's next course of action might be. (further conquest)

- Have students add to the outline maps used in Section 1 the areas that were conquered or allied to Rome through the Punic Wars, eastward expansion, and Caesar's conquests.

- Chart the widening political and economic differences between the patricians and the plebeians as the Senate gained power at the expense of the tribunes and as small farmers lost their lands. Compare the policies of the Gracchus brothers, Sulla, and Caesar that attempted to solve Rome's problems. Discuss how Octavian finally restored order at the expense of the republic.

GUIDED PRACTICE

Have students identify the factors that caused Rome to change from a republic to a virtual monarchy.

regained its power. Roman resentment of this growing strength reached a peak when, in 149 B.C., Rome sent an ultimatum to Carthage demanding that the Carthaginians abandon their city and settle away from the coast. Since this demand was equal to a death sentence for such a commercial power, the Carthaginians had to refuse.

Rome responded by attacking Carthage and laying siege to the city, an act that kept food from coming into Carthage and led to widespread starvation. When the Romans finally entered Carthage, they burned the city to the ground and are said to have destroyed the fertility of the soil by throwing salt into plowed fields. Thus, in 146 B.C., the Third Punic War ended and the Carthaginians were bro-

ken. The few who survived were sold into slavery, and the Carthaginian lands in north Africa became the Roman province of Africa.

Roman expansion led to changes within the republic.

Shortly after the end of the Second Punic War, Roman expansion turned eastward. After a series of wars, they defeated the Macedonians, and in 146 B.C., made Macedonia a Roman province. In the same year, the Romans burned Corinth and made the other Greek city-states subject to Rome.

The Romans began their move into the lands that are now considered the Middle East when, in 133 B.C., the king of Pergamum in Asia Minor

This relief suggests how Roman military ships might have been used, with soldiers on deck, ready to attack, and slaves working the oars below.

willed his kingdom to Rome. The king apparently feared that the discontented masses in his kingdom would revolt unless Rome, with its reputation for maintaining law and order, took over. In addition, Egypt and other nearby countries allied themselves with Rome and later became Roman territories. By 100 B.C., Rome controlled almost every land that bordered the Mediterranean, which the Romans called *Mare Nostrum* — "Our Sea."

Political changes. As Rome became increasingly involved in foreign affairs, the Senate grew in power and prestige by conducting state negotiations. The popular assembly had the power to ratify, or approve, treaties and to declare war, but, in reality, this body acted merely to confirm the decisions of the senators. Political power had become concentrated in the Senate, and the tribunes had become pawns of the senators. Corruption in government increased, particularly in the provinces, where officials often used their jobs to make themselves rich.

Economic changes. In addition to politics, the wars also hurt farming in the Italian peninsula. The small landowners of the republic, whose spirit had made Rome so strong, saw their lands either devastated by Hannibal's army or left unattended because of frequent calls into military service. To add to their problems, large supplies of cheap grain were coming in from Sicily.

Many small landowners who found that they couldn't compete in this changing market drifted to Rome in search of jobs. However, jobs were scarce. The large landowners around Rome were already using slaves who had been captured in the wars to work their land, and there was no large-scale industry offering other jobs. An unhappy, out-of-work mob thus developed in the city.

In contrast to the poverty and unemployment of the masses, the riches of war pouring into Rome made some people wealthy for the first time. Wealthy landowners, who had plentiful slave labor, were encouraged to buy more and more land. Many stopped growing grain and switched to the more profitable production of olive oil and wine, or of sheep and cattle. This new wealth changed Roman attitudes toward the state. The traditions of public duty and self-discipline gradually gave way to greed and soft living.

Civil war. Two brothers of a prominent Roman family, **Tiberius** [tī bir′ē əs] **and Gaius** [gī′yəs] **Gracchus** [grak′əs], came to the support of the dissatisfied masses. In 133 B.C. Tiberius was elected tribune. He believed that the decline of the Roman character could be stopped if the backbone of the old Roman society, the small landowner, were restored to its old strength.

To help this become a reality, Tiberius proposed a law that would divide the farmlands gained in war among the out-of-work farmers. He also wanted to make it against the law for any person to own more than a certain amount of land. Since his proposal would have taken away land from some of the richest families, a group of rich men had Tiberius murdered.

Ten years later, Gaius was elected tribune and worked on his brother's reforms. He was able to pass a land reform bill, and the wealthy were again alarmed. Many of Gaius' supporters were attacked. Gaius himself committed suicide.

Rome was now the scene of bitter rivalry between the People's party, supported by the plebeians and the masses, and the Senate, the agent of the rich patricians. The country was divided by violence and civil war.

Finally, Sulla [sul′ə], an able general and strong supporter of the Senate, restored order. Appointed dictator by the Senate, he doubled the size of this ruling council and limited the power of the veto. Sulla's changes wiped out many of the gains made by the plebeians in their struggle for equality. In 79 B.C. Sulla retired, believing that his work would be permanent. He had brought peace to the republic, but his changes didn't last.

Julius Caesar became dictator of Rome.

During the time of civil strife, the army had changed. Traditionally, the Roman army had been made up of citizens who fought because of a duty to the state. Now the army included volunteer soldiers from the landless class who expected to get rich from the gains of war. They were willing to serve for long periods of time and were loyal to their military leader. Under these conditions, a popular general could easily use his military power to gain political power. Such a man was the brilliant general **Julius Caesar** [sē′zər].

The marble statue of Julius Caesar above, located in Rome, is his best surviving full-length portrait.

Caesar's rise to power. After a successful military career in the Iberian peninsula, Julius Caesar joined with Pompey, another military hero, and Crassus, one of the wealthiest men in Rome. Their support made it possible for Caesar to become consul. In 60 B.C. the three men formed the First Triumvirate [trī um′və rāt′], a three-person governing body that was to rule the Roman state.

From 58 to 51 B.C., in the Gallic Wars, Caesar conquered Gaul and extended Roman borders northward to include most of modern France and Belgium. He also led his legions to invade Britain. These accomplishments made Caesar popular with the Roman masses. The jealous Senate, fearing his growing power, ordered him to return to Rome without his army. Caesar knew that to obey meant imprisonment or death. Crassus had died fighting a battle, and Pompey, he knew, out of fear of Caesar, had conspired with the Senate to ruin him.

On January 10, 49 B.C., Caesar brought his army across the Rubicon River, the southern boundary of Caesar's province, into the northern part of the Italian peninsula. By defying the Senate's orders to come alone, Caesar had in effect declared war on his former ally Pompey and the Senate. Today the expression "crossing the Rubicon" means taking a step that commits a person to a set course of action. Caesar's set course of action was war.

Afraid of the legions who were friendly to Caesar, Pompey and most of the senators fled to Greece. Caesar followed and defeated them. When Caesar returned to Rome, he became dictator.

Caesar's rule as dictator. During his five years of rule, Caesar made moderate reforms. These reforms were generally made to strengthen both Rome and Caesar's own power. He weakened the power of the Senate, but at the same time increased its membership to 900 by allowing more representation of the provinces. Roman citizenship was extended to persons living outside Italy, an action that helped to unite the Roman territory. In the provinces taxes were adjusted and the administration worked to reduce corruption.

Caesar also reduced unemployment among the poor by creating public building projects. In addition, he introduced a new, more accurate calendar that was based on Egypt's ancient calendar. With minor changes, it is still in use today.

The Senate feared that Caesar meant to make himself king and establish a dynasty, a change in the government that would threaten the Senate's role in the selection of the ruler. A group of men including Marcus Brutus, one of his best friends, joined in a plot to murder Caesar. On March 15, 44 B.C., a day known to the Romans as the "Ides of March," the plotters surrounded Caesar on the floor of the Senate building and killed him.

Octavian became the first Roman emperor Augustus.

Before his death, Julius Caesar had made his grandnephew and adopted son, **Octavian**, his heir. (An heir has the right to receive a property or title after the death of its owner.) The 18-year-old Octavian joined with Mark Antony, Caesar's chief lieutenant, to restore order in Rome after Caesar's death and to punish the murderers. They attacked Brutus and his fellow conspirators, defeating them in the battle of Philippi, which took place in 42 B.C.

For the next ten years, Octavian and Antony shared absolute power in the republic. Octavian ruled Rome and the western part of the empire while Antony ruled Egypt and the eastern part. During the time that Octavian was shrewdly increasing his power in Rome, Antony had fallen in love with Cleopatra, the ambitious queen of Egypt. When word reached Rome that Antony had given Roman territory to Cleopatra and was plotting to seize the whole empire, Octavian persuaded the Romans to declare war on Egypt.

In 31 B.C., at Actium, a cape on the western coast of Greece, Octavian's fleet clashed with that of Antony and Cleopatra. When Cleopatra fled the battle, Antony deserted his men and followed her to Egypt. The following year, when Octavian landed in Egypt, both Antony and Cleopatra committed suicide after failing to rally support against Octavian. Soon Egypt became a Roman province.

Octavian returned to Rome and proclaimed that he would restore the government to a republic. Although he was careful to observe the forms of republican government, he still kept the final power in his own hands, largely through his control of the army. He was called *imperator* ("victorious general"), a term from which the word "emperor" comes. In 27 B.C. the Senate gave Octavian the honorary title of *Augustus*, a title previously reserved for the gods meaning "the Majestic." After a century of civil war, Rome at last had been united under one ruler. With the reign of Augustus, the Roman Empire began.

Section 2 Review

Identify Carthage, Punic Wars, Hannibal, Tiberius and Gaius Gracchus, Julius Caesar, Octavian

Main Ideas

1. Why was Carthage an effective rival for Rome? Why did the First Punic War center around Sicily?
2. How did the lives of the small Roman landowners change as Rome became a world power? How did their problems affect city life?
3. How was Julius Caesar able to secure enough power to become dictator? Why did the Senate fear him?
4. How did Octavian become supreme ruler?

Critical Thinking

Assessing Cause and Effect: Why do you think Rome's rapid expansion would result in a significant strengthening of the power of the Senate and a weakened role for the plebeians in the government?

<table>
<tr><td>3</td><td>The Roman Empire lasted for many centuries.</td></tr>
</table>

During the reign of Augustus, from 27 B.C. to A.D. 14, the Roman Empire extended east to the Euphrates River and west to the Atlantic Ocean, north to the Rhine and Danube rivers, and south across the Mediterranean to the sands of the Sa-

Augustus, whose youthful face graces the front side of this Roman coin, was a wise and powerful emperor.

3 Lesson Plan

Essential Learning Objectives

Students will learn to:
- evaluate the leadership of the Roman emperors.
- identify the economic and political problems that threatened Rome's greatness.

1 FOCUS AND MOTIVATE

Draw a long, horizontal time line at the top of the board placing the dates 27 B.C. and A.D. 14 near the left end of the line. Label this period *Rule of Augustus*. Ask how long he ruled. (41 years) Be sure that students understand that Jesus was born during this period. As the class discusses this section, select students to place the name and years of rule of each emperor on the time line. The time line should end at A.D. 395.

2 TEACH

- Below the time line, divide the chalkboard into two large sections titled *Strengths* and *Weaknesses*. List under the appropriate headings the accomplishments and qualities that characterized the Roman Empire. (Examples of strengths: civil service, professional army, *Pax Romana*. Examples of weaknesses: Judean policies, economic decline, political instability, despotism)

The Roman Empire, About A.D. 117

Legend:
- Roman Empire in A.D. 14
- Provinces added after A.D. 14
- Frontier Provinces
- X Battles

0 250 500 MILES
0 250 500 KILOMETERS

 MAP STUDY This map uses different colors to show changes over time. Note that the Romans gradually brought under their control all of the Mediterranean world. Which of the following provinces—Egypt, Dacia, Gaul, Thrace, Britain—were added after A.D. 14?

hara. By the 2nd century A.D., the empire included an estimated 100 million people of different cultures, faiths, and customs.

Augustus was the architect of the *Pax Romana*.

Generally, the first two centuries of the empire were peaceful and prosperous. This period, from 27 B.C. to A.D.180, is known as the **Pax Romana**, or "Roman Peace." Within the empire, business grew as conditions for trade improved. Bandits and pirates were hunted down, and roads and sea lanes were cleared for commerce.

Ostia, at the mouth of the Tiber River, served as a seaport for Rome. Egypt, North Africa, and Sicily furnished grain for the entire empire. Timber and various farm products came from Gaul and central Europe, and the Iberian peninsula supplied gold, silver, and lead. Outside the empire, Rome carried on a thriving trade with such distant lands as India and China.

Augustus proved to be a wise ruler. He improved the government that had grown corrupt during the later days of the republic, especially in the provinces. To do this, Augustus created a professional civil service, open to all classes and based on talent. In addition, he established a permanent, professional army that was loyal to the emperor and stationed away from the political arena out in the isolated frontier provinces. A census of citizens was taken and tax rates were adjusted. A program of public works was begun, and roads and bridges were built.

Augustus was not successful, however, in his at-

ANSWER TO MAP STUDY Dacia, Thrace, and Britain

tempts to restore the old ideas of Roman simplicity and home life. Laws were passed to encourage large families, to strengthen the bonds of marriage, and to limit luxurious living—but with little lasting effect. Augustus made the old religious rituals again a part of the affairs of state by rebuilding old temples and reviving religious festivals. In time, worship of the emperor began, and as the years went by, served as a unifying bond.

The Roman Empire maintained its strength despite its generally poor leaders.

When Augustus died in A.D. 14, the Senate voted the title of imperator to his stepson, Tiberius, who proved to be only an adequate ruler. It was during his reign, which lasted until A.D. 37, that Jesus was crucified in Judea. (See Chapter 10.) From the time of Tiberius to the end of the western empire in A.D. 476, Rome was ruled by more than 70 emperors, only a few of whom were very capable. (See the list of Roman rulers on pages 802–803.)

In spite of incompetent rulers, the empire held together until A.D. 395. Efficient administrators at many levels of responsibility kept justice and order, and commercial strength helped keep the empire stable. Only when economic decline and social unrest set in did the lack of good leadership at the top seriously weaken the empire.

Several of Rome's poor leaders were brutal tyrants who are remembered for their violent and irrational deeds. For instance, Caligula was a madman who killed many people, including his sister, and made his favorite horse a senator. Nero, judged the most wicked and worthless ruler ever to rule Rome, murdered his wife and his mother. He was also accused of persecuting Christians and setting fire to Rome in A.D. 64, a great nine-day catastrophe that destroyed half the city.

During the 2nd century A.D., however, the empire enjoyed the rule of several competent emperors. Trajan, a Spanish general who ruled from 98 to 117, was an ambitious military leader. Under his rule, the empire reached its greatest extent. His successor, Hadrian, ruled from 117 to 138. Hadrian made it his policy to strengthen the frontiers. Traveling throughout the empire, he supervised the building of many public works. One of the most famous projects was Hadrian's Wall in Britain,

BACKGROUND Legends have Nero fiddling madly as Rome burned. Nero may or may not have been responsible for the fire. He did, however, use the disaster as an excuse for terrible persecutions of the Christians, whom he blamed for the fire.

built as a protection against the Celtic tribes of Scotland. (See the map on page 102.)

Marcus Aurelius, who ruled from 161 to 180, was one of the few emperors to win the respect of his people. Although he was troubled by invading Germanic tribes, he preferred the quiet study of books to the blood and brutality of the battlefield. His volume of essays, called *Meditations*, remains one of the most powerful expressions of the Stoic philosophy, which promoted the view that virtue is the highest good and that passion should be restrained. (See Chapter 5.) Marcus Aurelius' advice was, "Blot out vain pomp; check impulse; quench appetite; keep reason under its own control."

Roman mismanagement led to the destruction of Judea.

It would be wrong to assume that all the inhabitants of the Roman Empire were happy under Ro-

This portrayal of the emperor Marcus Aurelius is the only bronze equestrian statue (depicting a rider on horseback) to have survived from Roman times.

• Discuss with students the meaning of despotism as experienced by Romans under the rules of Diocletian and Constantine. Elicit the reasons that businesses found it difficult to carry on trade under rigid regulations and point out how this caused further economic decline. Emphasize that the division of the Roman Empire was an obvious admission that no one ruler could control the entire area.

GUIDED PRACTICE
Have students write short essays explaining how Augustus' policies began the *Pax Romana*. Also for guided practice:

 Overhead Transparency 11

The arch of Titus, a detail of which is shown here, was built in commemoration of the Roman triumph over the Jewish rebellion. Roman soldiers carry off spoils of the victory, including the 7-branched menorah that stood in the Holy Temple.

man rule. One of the worst failures of Roman imperial administration was the mismanagement of Judea, the land of the Jews. (See map, page 102.) High taxes, harsh enforcement of the law, and interference in their religion led Jews to revolt between A.D. 66 and 70. The Romans brutally suppressed the Jews, destroyed their state, enslaved many, and removed large numbers to other parts of the empire.

In A.D. 135, after the Jews had made some progress toward returning Judea to its former prosperity, the emperor Hadrian tried to obliterate Jerusalem as a Jewish city and construct a temple to Jupiter on the site of the Holy Temple. This sparked a vast uprising in which at least half a million Jews were killed. Hadrian outlawed the Jewish religion and renamed Judea "Palestine," the Latin name for the Philistines who had once lived along the coast many centuries earlier. After this uprising was put down, the Jews became a minority in

their own country. The center of Jewish life gradually shifted to the **Diaspora**—communities outside Judea where many Jews already lived, such as Alexandria, Damascus, and Babylon.

Economic decline and political instability weakened the empire.

By the end of the 2nd century A.D., attacks on the frontiers of the Roman Empire came more and more often. To meet these threats, Roman leaders doubled the size of its army. The drain on the supply of troops and resources brought on an economic crisis that was made more severe by several other factors.

Economic decline. Poverty and unemployment were on the rise. In addition, imports (goods brought into the empire from foreign lands for sale or use) began to exceed exports (goods sent out of the empire for sale or use elsewhere), creating an unfavorable balance of trade. In an attempt to save

BACKGROUND Before the Jewish Revolt, an estimated 10 percent of the population of the Roman Empire was Jewish. Many Jews lived outside Judea.

BACKGROUND The Jewish dream of an independent country remained strong for almost 19 centuries; it was finally realized when the United Nations recognized the independent state of Israel in 1948.

some of the valuable metals that were leaving the empire as money, the emperors reduced the gold and silver content of the money in circulation.

The replacement of these metals with lead served to devalue, or decrease the value, of the coins. Because money was worth less, people charged higher prices. This in turn led to **inflation**—a sharp increase in prices caused by a great expansion of the money supply. The inflation experienced throughout the empire caused yet more hardship and poverty.

Political instability. Business was hurt by crime of all kinds which, in turn, was caused by political instability. Meetings of the Senate and the popular assembly had become mere formalities. These two groups were no longer effective in governing the state since the political power was held by the emperor, who himself was often at the mercy of the army. Peaceful succession to the throne was rare, and the death of an emperor signaled a free-for-all struggle. Of the 29 emperors who ruled between A.D. 180 and 284, only four died of natural causes. The others were murdered.

The soldiers had the real power to select the new emperor. As a result, emperors often followed the cynical advice of Emperor Septimius Severus, who is said to have told his sons, "Make the soldiers rich and don't trouble about the rest." To keep the legions at full strength, members of Germanic tribes were recruited and war captives were forced to enlist. These new legionnaires cared for the empire only so long as they were paid. However, the empire was still strong and had lasted a very long time. In A.D. 248 Emperor Philip celebrated the 1,000th anniversary of Rome's legendary founding on April 21, 753 B.C.

Two emperors tried despotism to save Rome.

After a century of decline and civil disorder, two emperors were able to halt for a while the disintegration of the empire. The first was Diocletian [dī-ə klē′shən], who reigned from A.D. 284 to 305. He set up a full-fledged **despotism**, which is a government ruled by someone with unlimited power. Harsh laws controlled all business.

Constantine was the next emperor, and he enforced even more despotic control over his sub-jects. He also moved the capital of the empire from Rome to Byzantium, which he then renamed Constantinople after himself. (See map, page 102.)

Diocletian and Constantine halted civil war and economic decline for a time. Yet, as a cure, despotism proved worse than the ills from which the empire suffered. State regulation of business killed individual initiative. A secret police force choked off reform. Trade came to a standstill in many places, and the amount of wealth available for taxation decreased. After the death of Constantine in 337, rivals for the throne butchered one another. The last ruler of a united Roman Empire was Theodosius I. At his death in 395, the empire was divided between his two sons. In effect, the period of Roman dominance and greatness was over.

Section 3 Review

Identify *Pax Romana*, Diaspora, inflation, despotism

Main Ideas
1. How did Augustus improve the government during the *Pax Romana*?
2. Why was the empire able to survive during periods when there were bad rulers?
3. How did the Romans mistreat the Jews?
4. What problems weakened the empire between A.D. 180 and 284? Who held the real political power?
5. How did the despotism of Diocletian and Constantine affect Rome?

Critical Thinking
Predicting Effects: What do you think might have happened if Rome had been ruled by effective leaders at the beginning of its economic problems?

---

  4 | *The Romans developed a lasting Greco-Roman culture.*

Most roots of Western civilization can be traced to the blend of Greek and Roman culture, known as **classical culture**, that flourished during the *Pax Romana*. The Romans admired Hellenistic culture and borrowed widely from the Greeks. In the process, certain elements of Roman culture were

Write the following on the board:
Latin: *unus, duo, tres*
Italian: *uno, due, tre*
French: *un, deux, trois*
Spanish: *uno, dos, tres*
Elicit from students that these are the words for *one, two,* and *three.* Guide students to recognize that the similarities between these languages are the results of Roman rule. Tell students that many other aspects of Roman culture still are in use today.

2 TEACH

- Explain to students that Greco-Roman culture refers to the blend of Greek and Roman ideas and styles that were spread throughout the empire by the Romans. Point out that we call this culture "classical," because these ideas still serve as standards for us today.

- Roman law and the Latin language in particular left a lasting contribution to Western civilization. Elicit from students that law and language were important in ruling and communicating with the various peoples of the empire. Point out the areas where law codes based on Roman principles still are used. Also point out that many present-day structures show evidence of Roman engineering and architectural forms (arches, vaults, domes) and materials (cement, concrete, stucco).

- List the authors named in this section and add the titles and short descriptions of their works. Point out that Roman writers often dealt with factual subjects. (Caesar wrote of his wars in Gaul. Vergil praised Roman rule.)

changed. For example, Roman sculpture became even more lifelike than the Greek; Roman architecture, more elaborate and more secular, or nonreligious, in function. In addition, the Romans made many contributions of their own, such as an outstanding legal system.

Roman law and the Latin language contributed to Western civilization.

A common set of laws and a common language served to unify the diverse peoples of the Roman Empire. In addition, both Roman law and Latin, the language of the Romans, had a great influence on the development of modern civilizations.

Roman law. In modern-day Italy, France, Spain, and Latin America, law codes based on Roman legal principles are still in use. Law in modern English-speaking countries was also greatly influenced by Roman law. In fact, along with the Latin language, the system of law devised by the Romans is probably their most lasting contribution.

Written Roman law developed from the Law of the Twelve Tables—those written laws won by the plebeians so that they would know how they were being ruled. As Rome expanded, laws governing noncitizens were added. The legal interpretations, or decisions, of magistrates in the provinces were kept, and these served as precedents, or examples,

to help other judges decide similar cases in court.

Sometimes, the existing laws of a conquered place influenced the magistrate's decision. In this way, local rules and customs became a part of the larger body of Roman law. Roman laws became international, particularly the laws dealing with commerce. When Augustus was emperor, professional law schools were established to teach the law. Later, in the 6th century A.D., Justinian, emperor of the Eastern empire, had this huge body of laws codified, meaning that the laws were organized into a system that could more easily be used.

Latin language. Latin is one of the Indo-European languages, as are English, German, Slavic, Greek, Persian, and Sanskrit. The Romans did not develop writing until the 7th century B.C., when they adopted the Greek-style alphabet used by the Etruscans, which was based on the Phoenician alphabet. (See Chapter 3.)

Latin was the official language of business, religion, education, government, and the arts throughout the empire. During the Roman years, two forms of Latin developed. One was literary Latin, the form used in writing. It was highly admired for its logic and exactness. The second form was the vernacular [vər nak′yə lər], or informal spoken language used in people's everyday dealings. From this form of Latin developed the modern Romance

DAILY LIFE

Roman artwork, books, artifacts, and buildings have revealed much about the lives and times of these people. This collection shows how a wealthy young Roman girl may have spent her days. The painting (near right) shows her with a pen and book, studying. The room (left) was a bedroom, and the comb (far right), carved from wood. Note that the leather shoe is quite modern in its styling.

Latin Words in English

Latin is the source of many English words. Of course, the English language did not exist in Roman times, but ever since the Middle Ages, when English began to take shape as a separate language, new words with Latin roots have entered the English vocabulary.

audio	mobile
demonstrate	noble
erase	peace
face	puerile
graduate	question
homicide	radius
index	salary
journey	salmon
kitchen	tuba
labor	umbrella

languages, which include Spanish, French, Italian, Portuguese, and Romanian.

All of these languages are written in the Roman alphabet, as are English, German, Dutch, Polish, Czech, Hungarian, Finnish, Swedish, and Turkish. Although English is a Germanic language, it includes thousands of words with Latin origins. Literary Latin was preserved for centuries after the end of the western Roman Empire because it was the official language of the Roman Catholic Church. Many American high-school students have continued to study Latin in the 20th century.

The Romans were inventive engineers and architects.

A network of roads knit together the Roman realm. They were built to help speed the movement of armies and military supplies, but the roads were open to the public for travel and commerce. Built of several layers of stone, the Roman roads were superior to any highways constructed in Europe until the 1800s. Roman engineering skill was used throughout the empire in the construction of numerous dams, bridges, drainage systems, and **aqueducts**, which are bridgelike structures that hold water pipes.

In the early years, the Romans had learned from the Etruscans how to build arched constructions

• Have students identify the conflict between Aristarchus' sun-centered and Ptolemy's earth-centered theories. Emphasize that Ptolemy's writings were accepted as fact by most people until the 17th century. Point out the practical ways in which the Romans used Greek knowledge. (hospitals, school of medicine, surgical procedures)

GUIDED PRACTICE
Have students identify the types of structures built by the Romans. (roads, dams, bridges, aqueducts, vaulted and domed buildings, amphitheaters) Use illustrations in Chapters 4, 5, and 6 to point out the similarities and differences in styles.

This aqueduct at Segovia, Spain, demonstrates the building skills of the Romans.
Water ran through the pipes at the top, which were situated at a slight downward tilt.
Huge stone arches helped support the pipes and even out the flow of water.

called vaults. Little by little, the Romans improved vault forms so that large interior spaces could be enclosed. They also invented domes to roof over huge structures.

To make their structures solid and lasting, Roman architects used cement and concrete as basic materials. Exteriors were faced with marble or stucco, a plaster that sets with a hard, stonelike coat, and decorated with sculpture. The Romans preferred ornate decoration to the simplicity of earlier Greek architecture. Also in contrast to the Greeks, whose greatest architectural achievements were usually reserved to honor their gods, the Romans' finest buildings were used for judicial or other public functions.

Roman public buildings were both magnificent and practical. The public baths were multileveled structures that included steam rooms, bathing and swimming pools, gardens, gyms, and libraries. The Roman baths, which were like modern athletic clubs, served as popular meeting places. Entry to the baths was frequently paid for by political candidates seeking votes.

The Roman Colosseum, a huge amphitheater, was a main feature of a special welfare system used by Roman politicians to keep the plebeians happy and under control. This welfare system, known as "bread and circuses," provided free grain (the "bread") and free entertainment (the "circuses"). The Colosseum, where much of the free entertainment took place, was the scene of mock naval battles and bloody gladiator fights, in which war prisoners and condemned criminals fought fiercely to the death for the amusement of the crowds. At the Circus Maximus, a stadium in Rome, thrilling chariot races were held.

The Romans are justly famous for city planning. Provincial cities and towns were usually built around a forum, a public square that would be close to the crossing of two main roads. The main civic buildings and the marketplace were centrally located in the forum area, and building codes were enforced to keep architectural styles uniform.

The logical planning in the provinces was in strong contrast to the capital city of the empire. Rome had narrow, winding streets, a poor drainage system, and was overcrowded. In the 2nd century A.D., the city's population of more than a million persons was jammed into 9 square miles. Augustus claimed that he had found Rome brick and had left it marble. However, the splendid public buildings were often flanked by dark and flimsy tenement houses. During the lifetime of the empire, Rome was a sprawling, bustling city of both magnificence and squalor.

The Romans used Greek models for literature.

Throughout the history of Rome, Greek literature remained the most important influence on Latin literary works. An educated Roman was expected to know Greek. Wealthy families often owned Greek slaves who served as tutors for the children of the household. With Greek models to imitate, the Romans developed a literature of the first rank.

Although it was the Greek genius to speculate brilliantly about destiny and the universe, the Ro-

The Colosseum, which you will read more about on page 113, was a marvel of Roman engineering. Removable awnings gave shelter from sun and rain.

3 | ASSESS AND CLOSE

ASSESS
1. Which group, Greek or Roman, was most concerned with practical uses of scientific knowledge? (Romans)
2. Name the Roman writer whose work was modeled on Homer's *Iliad* and the *Odyssey*. (Vergil)

OPTIONAL RETEACHING
On the board write these topics: Roman law, Latin language, Engineering, Architecture, Literature, Science. Select students to add specific examples under each.

Students also may be assigned Activities reteaching page 33.

OPTIONAL ENRICHMENT
1. Have students compare maps of the Roman Empire and of present-day Europe, Africa, and Asia to identify cities which have survived from Roman times. (average)
2. Ask students to create a scale model of a section of an aqueduct or a vaulted arch or dome using small clay "bricks." (challenging)
3. Students also may be assigned Activities enrichment page 34.
4. Also for enrichment:

 Overhead Transparency 12

 Source Reading 6B

INDEPENDENT PRACTICE/ HOMEWORK
Assign the Section Review, the Chapter Review items, Activities page 32, or Workbook page 22.

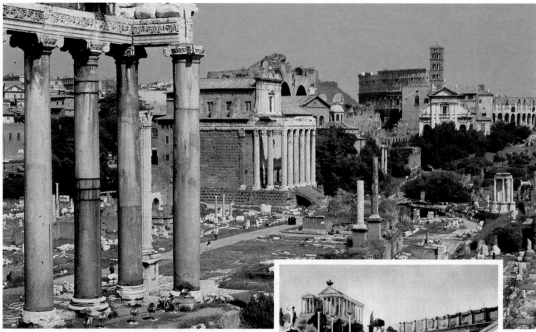

The Roman Forum, shown both in ruins today and how it might have looked in Roman times (inset), grew from a market place to the center of civic life.

mans had a gift for describing less abstract ideas, using literature to point out important ethical concepts of right and wrong. Further, just as the Greeks are noted for their philosophical original thinking, the Romans are known for being practical and for adapting the ideas of others.

The wealth and leisure resulting from Roman conquests provided a growing audience for literature. From about 100 B.C. to A.D. 14, Latin literature was at its height. This period has been called the Golden Age of Latin literature.

One of the leading writers of the Golden Age was the master statesman and polished orator, Cicero [sis′ə rō′]. His speeches, letters, and essays showed a wide-ranging intellect and noble character. The respect he commanded as spokesman for the Senate made Mark Antony jealous, and, in 43 B.C., Antony had Cicero put to death.

Another famous statesman, Julius Caesar, also contributed to Latin literature. His military history, *Commentaries on the Gallic Wars*, is famous for its careful descriptions and vigorous style. Caesar's contribution to literature also served the political purpose of keeping the name of the ambitious general in the public eye. Later, in 47 B.C., Caesar gained lasting fame with a brief but meaningful message sent to the Roman Senate after a victory in battle. Since then, the message, containing only the words *Veni, vidi, vici* [wā′nē wē′dē wē′kē] meaning "I came, I saw, I conquered," has been studied by generations of American students.

The greatest poet of the Golden Age was **Vergil** [vèr′jəl]. He has been called the "Homer of Rome" because the *Iliad* and the *Odyssey* served as models for his epic, the *Aeneid* [i nē′id]. The chief character in Vergil's work was Aeneas, the legend-

BACKGROUND Ptolemy's work on astronomy is known as *Ho megas astronomos* ("The Great Astronomer"), later shortened to *Almagest. Almagest* is the only comprehensive treatise of Greek astronomy to come down to us today.

GEOGRAPHY

A Key to History

THE WORLD OF CLAUDIUS PTOLEMY

"We shall only report what was rigorously proved by the ancients, perfecting as far as we can what was not fully proved or not proved as well as possible. A view, therefore, of the general relation of the whole earth to the whole of the heavens will begin this composition of ours."

With these words, Claudius Ptolemy (tol′ə mē) confidently began his review and summary of everything that had been described up until that time by all the astronomers of the ancient world. Ptolemy's review filled thirteen books! Ptolemy was a Greek mathematician, astronomer, and geographer who lived in the A.D. 100s at Alexandria, Egypt, the foremost center of learning in the Roman world.

Ptolemy also found time to write five books on optics (the study of the properties of wavelengths, including light), and eight books on geography.

Below is Ptolemy's world map as interpreted in the 1400s.

He contributed much valuable information in each field. For example, he calculated a value for pi—the symbol showing the relationship between the circumference of a circle and its diameter—at 3.1416, a value commonly used today.

Ptolemy's books, however, also perpetuated serious errors. For example, Ptolemy argued that the earth's position was constant at the center of the universe. As one means of proof, he had observed that objects fall toward the center of the earth. Arguing that all bodies fall toward the center of the universe, he concluded that the earth must be at the center of the universe. A second proof, he believed, was his observation that an object thrown straight up in the air fell back to the same spot. If the earth were turning in space, he reasoned, the object should fall to a different place.

Ptolemy applied his observations to the making of maps. His maps used a grid system—a network of lines showing latitude and longitude, so that any place on the earth can be pinpointed in relation to other places. However, because travelers through "their love of boasting . . . magnify distances"—and because instruments for measuring exact east-west distances took centuries to perfect— maps locating places as precisely as Ptolemy had wished were not made for many centuries after his death.

REVIEW

1. List some of Claudius Ptolemy's accomplishments. What were some of his mistakes?
2. In view of his accomplishments, do you think Ptolemy's mistakes should be ignored? Why or why not?

Answers to Section 4 Review

Identify

Key Terms, People, and Places are defined on pages indicated in parentheses. Also see the Glossary and Biographical Dictionary.
classical culture (105), aqueduct (107), Vergil (110), Ptolemy (112)

Main Ideas

1. Roman law still can be found in its original or in modified forms in Italy, France, Spain and Latin America. It also has greatly influenced the legal systems of English-speaking countries. From Latin developed the Romance languages, such as French, Spanish, and Italian. Many English words come from Latin roots.
2. Roman roads and the aqueducts. Roman architecture was more ornate and secular than Greek and had new forms, such as vaults and domes.
3. Greek literature had the greatest influence on Roman literature. Some writers were Julius Caesar (*Commentaries on the Gallic Wars*), Vergil (the *Aeneid*), Livy (*From the Founding of the City*), Tacitus (*Germania*).
4. Ptolemy was the first to draw the earth as round. Galen discovered that human arteries contained blood.

Critical Thinking

Greeks valued religion, simplicity of form, and originality. Romans valued practicality, law and government, and ornate decoration.

ary Trojan hero who overcame many obstacles before founding the city of Rome. The most outstanding aspect of the *Aeneid* is Vergil's patriotism; the glories of Rome were praised in poetry, such as in the following excerpt.

> Others, doubtless, will mould lifelike bronze with greater delicacy, will win from marble the look of life, will plead cases better, chart the motions of the sky with the rod and foretell the risings of the stars. You, O Roman, remember to rule the nations with might. This will be your genius—to impose the way of peace, to spare the conquered and crush the proud.

Another patriotic writer was Livy [liv′ē], whose history of Rome was called *From the Founding of the City*. By picturing the past greatness of Rome in glowing terms, he hoped to convince his readers to return to the simple ways of their ancestors.

The Roman historian Tacitus [tas′ə təs] is best known for *Germania*, his study of the German tribes who lived north of the imperial frontiers. Like Livy, Tacitus urged a return to traditional Roman values. His work contrasts the strength and simplicity of the Germans with the weakness and immorality of upper-class life in Rome.

Another important writer was the Greek biographer Plutarch [plü′tärk]. His masterpiece, *Parallel Lives*, paired 46 biographies of Greek and Roman statesmen, orators, or warriors whose careers and talents were similar. Plutarch did not flatter the Greeks at the expense of the Romans; his accounts were well balanced and his judgments of character sound. His descriptions of people and events are so colorful that *Parallel Lives* proved to be an invaluable source for later writers. The famous English playwright William Shakespeare drew heavily on Plutarch's biographies when writing *Julius Caesar* and *Antony and Cleopatra*.

Greeks in the empire made important scientific discoveries.

During Roman times most of the noted men of science were Greeks. The center for research and experimentation was Alexandria, Egypt. One famous Greek scholar was the astronomer **Ptolemy** [tol′ə-mē]. Between A.D. 127 and 151, he brought together in one book all that was then known about astronomy. For 1,500 years Ptolemy's views were generally accepted by educated people and were widely taught.

Unlike the Greek scientist Aristarchus before him, who believed that the earth revolved around the sun, Ptolemy believed that the sun revolved around the earth. Also a mapmaker, Ptolemy was the first to draw the earth as round, although Greek astronomers had known that it was round since the 3rd century B.C. In his map, Ptolemy exaggerated the size of Asia. This exaggeration later led the explorer Christopher Columbus to believe that the Atlantic Ocean was smaller than it is and to set sail from Spain in search of Asia.

The Greek physician Galen [gā′lən], who lived in the 2nd century A.D., also studied in Alexandria. Next to Hippocrates, the famous Greek who encouraged the study of medicine and disease, Galen was the most famous doctor of ancient times. He discovered that arteries contain blood, and not air, as had been previously believed. Although the Romans themselves made few contributions to scientific knowledge, they were skillful in applying Greek findings in medicine and public health. The Romans built the first hospitals. About A.D. 14 the first school of medicine was begun in Rome. It was there that Celsus [kel′səs], a well-known Roman-born physician, wrote and taught. One of his books describes surgical procedures for removing tonsils and cataracts.

Section 4 Review

Identify classical culture, aqueduct, Vergil, Ptolemy

Main Ideas

1. In what ways did Roman law and the Latin language continue to be used after the end of the empire?
2. What are two examples of the Romans' skill in engineering? How was Roman architecture different from that of the Greeks?
3. What was the greatest influence on Roman literature? Name two of the writers of the Golden Age and list at least one of their works.
4. What were two important scientific discoveries made by Greeks during Roman times?

Critical Thinking

Recognizing Values: Consider the different approaches and functions of Greek and Roman architecture. What do you think are some of the underlying values of each society?

HIGHLIGHTS OF CIVILIZATION

Roman Engineering

Ingenious builders, the Romans created monuments that are marvels of architecture and engineering. Their mastery of concrete and the arch enabled the Romans to cover enormous buildings with arched roofs of stone, brick, and mortar. Arches are capable of bearing the weight of the material above an opening, such as a door or window. Arched roofs, in the form of vaults or domes, permit the building of vast interior spaces without the use of columns. (See diagrams, below right.)

One familiar Roman monument, the Colosseum, is a huge stadium four stories high. (See page 109.) Tiers of 80 arches each form the first three stories. Flooded with water pipes beneath the floor, the Colosseum could become a lake for mock naval battles.

Another famous structure, almost perfectly preserved from Roman times, is the Pantheon (below left), a temple dedicated to the gods associated with the major planets. The Pantheon was built in 27 B.C. by the Roman general and consul Marcus Agrippa. Destroyed by fire, it was rebuilt a hundred years later during the Emperor Hadrian's reign. Later still, the Pantheon became a Christian church.

At the center of its soaring dome, a 28-foot-wide opening, called the oculus ("eye" in Latin) provides the Pantheon's only source of light. Bronze molding and gilded bronze tiles once decorated its dome inside and out. These treasures have since been stripped from the Pantheon, but the perfect harmony of its proportions remains.

Natural light fills the Pantheon.

Arch

Vault

Dome

Domed building

Answers to Test Yourself

Key Terms, People, and Places
The key terms, people, and places tested here were introduced in the chapter sections and reviewed in the Section Reviews. For definitions see the page references at the appropriate Section Reviews. Also see the Glossary and Biographical Dictionary.

Main Ideas
The main ideas tested here were introduced in the sections of this chapter and reviewed in the Section Reviews. For answers to these questions, see the appropriate Section Reviews.

Critical Thinking
1. Students should make a decision based on information contained in the chapter or from outside sources, and then write an answer that uses factual material for support.
2. The Romans were a very practical people who valued the accomplishments and skills of others. They could honor the original thinking of others by adapting things to fit their own needs and circumstances.

CHAPTER 6 REVIEW

Section Summaries

Section 1
The Roman Republic arose on the Italian peninsula.
Conquered by the Etruscans in the 7th century B.C., the Romans overthrew their king in 509 B.C. and set up a republic that lasted for almost 500 years. This republic was governed by consuls and the Senate, with some plebeian participation. On the foreign front, the strong Roman military led the state's expansion, and by 270 B.C., the Italian peninsula was conquered.

Section 2
The republic became a far-flung empire.
Rome continued to experience military success. Rome battled and finally defeated Carthage in the Punic Wars. Although conquest brought wealth to Rome, it also created serious political and economic problems for the republic. After unsuccessful attempts at reform, a civil war broke out. Following this, Rome's rulers included Julius Caesar, a popular general, and Octavian (later known as Augustus), whose reign marked the beginning of the Roman Empire.

Section 3
The Roman Empire lasted for many centuries.
The first 250 years of the empire were peaceful and prosperous, and the *Pax Romana* was extended by military success. By the 3rd century A.D., however, the Roman Empire had begun to show signs of decay. Poverty increased, business activity declined, and the central government weakened. Diocletian and Constantine chose despotism to strengthen the government, but civil wars followed their reigns.

Section 4
The Romans developed a lasting Greco-Roman culture.
The Romans' codified legal system and Latin language served to hold together the many different peoples and cultures of the empire. Engineers and architects built excellent roads, bridges, aqueducts, and massive public buildings. Literature flourished, particularly during the last century of the republic and the reign of Augustus.

Test Yourself

Key Terms and People
Identify the significance of each of the following:

Section 1
a. Rome
b. patricians
c. plebeians

d. republic
e. pyrrhic victory

Section 2
a. Carthage
b. Punic Wars
c. Hannibal

d. Tiberius and Gaius Gracchus
e. Julius Caesar
f. Octavian (Augustus)

Section 3
a. *Pax Romana*
b. Diaspora

c. inflation
d. despotism

Review Dates

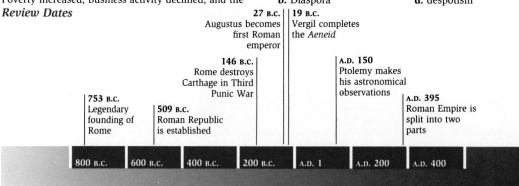

753 B.C.
Legendary founding of Rome

509 B.C.
Roman Republic is established

146 B.C.
Rome destroys Carthage in Third Punic War

27 B.C.
Augustus becomes first Roman emperor

19 B.C.
Vergil completes the *Aeneid*

A.D. 150
Ptolemy makes his astronomical observations

A.D. 395
Roman Empire is split into two parts

| 800 B.C. | 600 B.C. | 400 B.C. | 200 B.C. | A.D. 1 | A.D. 200 | A.D. 400 |

Section 4
a. classical culture   **c.** Vergil
b. aqueduct   **d.** Ptolemy

Main Ideas

Section 1
1. What skills or practices did the Romans learn from the Etruscans?
2. Who were the rulers of the Roman Republic?
3. In what region did Rome's early expansion occur? In what defensive alliance did Rome first enroll?
4. What advantages did Rome's military efforts enjoy?
5. Why were the plebeians successful in demanding equal rights in the Roman government? What are two examples of their success?

Section 2
1. What were the strengths of Rome's rival Carthage?
2. What were the effects of Rome's expansion on the small landowners? On city life?
3. Where did Julius Caesar get the power to become dictator of Rome? Why was he murdered?
4. How did Octavian become Augustus?

Section 3
1. What were two or three of the positive effects of Augustus's rule during the *Pax Romana*?
2. How was the empire able to maintain its strength despite having many poor and ineffective rulers?
3. In what ways did the Romans mistreat the Jews? What was the effect on the Jewish population?
4. How was the empire weakened between A.D. 180 and 284? Who was in control?
5. What were the intentions and effects of the rules of Diocletian and Constantine?

Section 4
1. In what ways have Roman law and the Latin language had lasting effects?
2. In what two areas of engineering did the Romans excel? In what ways did Roman architecture differ from that of the Greeks?
3. What was a major influence on Roman literature? Give two or three examples of Roman writers.
4. Name two Greek scientists, working during Roman times, and their achievements.

Critical Thinking
1. **Evaluating Sources of Information** Consider the opinions of the writers quoted in the introduction on page 90. With whom do you agree? Why?
2. **Recognizing Values** The Romans borrowed and modified many techniques and practices from such peoples as the Etruscans and the Greeks. What values do you suppose the Romans held that allowed them to borrow so heavily?

Chapter Skills and Activities

Practicing Study and Research Skills
Using an Index
If you want to know what a book is about, the easiest place to look is the Table of Contents. If you want to find specific information, however, look in the index. An index is a detailed alphabetical guide to a book's contents that often appears at the end of the book. By using a book's index properly, you can save yourself hours of fruitless hunting for information. Instead of taking out a stack of library books and reading them all, you can pick out only those books that have the best information on the topic you are studying.

Use the index at the back of this book to find the page(s) on which each of the following appears:
1. Roman law
2. the *Aeneid* by Vergil
3. the rise to power of Julius Caesar
4. the Punic Wars
5. the Latin League

Linking Past and Present
As you learned on page 107, many English words come from Latin root words. Using a dictionary, make a list of ten additional English words that come from Latin words. Note that a word's entry in the dictionary often ends with a phrase describing its origins.

Learning History Through Maps
Use the map on page 102 to name at least five cities studied in previous chapters that were part of the Roman Empire by A.D. 117.

CRITICAL THINKING QUESTION LEVEL 1. easy; 2. average

Chapter

7 The Flowering of Civilization in India

OVERVIEW

The chapter describes the development of a culture rich in ideas and art that spread outward from the once geographically isolated subcontinent of India.

PLANNING CHART

Section	Text Pages	Key Concept	Suggested Teaching Time
1 Geography shaped history in India.	117–119	High mountains, temperature extremes, and seasonal monsoons shaped the history of the Indian subcontinent.	One day **Less time?** Assign Section 1 to be read before class and teach it with Section 2. Use *Overhead Transparency 13.*
2 Many features of Indian life date from ancient times.	121–125	Invaders coming through mountain passes mixed with India's native Dravidians to produce a unique civilization.	One day **More time?** Use *Source Reading 7A.*
3 Strong rulers built empires in India.	125–128	As strong leaders built Indian empires, new religious ideas and forms of art developed and spread throughout Southeast Asia.	One day **More time?** Use *Overhead Transparency 14* or *Source Reading 7B.*
4 Gupta rule launched a golden age.	129–130	Indians prospered, and learning, literature, and art flourished under a long line of Gupta emperors.	One day **More time?** Use *Source Reading 7B.*

ANCILLARIES

Materials that may be used with this chapter to reinforce, reteach, enrich, and assess learning are pictured on the following pages.

Teacher's Resource File

ACTIVITIES

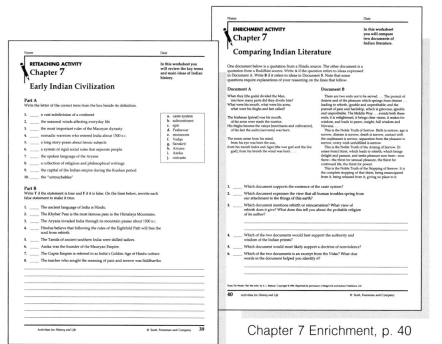

Section 1 Activity, p. 35

Section 2 Activity, p. 36

Section 3 Activity, p. 37

Section 4 Activity, p. 38

Chapter 7 Reteaching, p. 39

Chapter 7 Enrichment, p. 40

Teacher's Resource File

GEOGRAPHY SKILLS

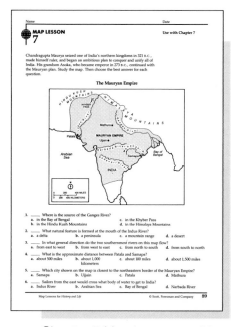

Chapter 7 Geography

Chapter 7 Map Lesson, p. 89

Worksheet/Map, pp. 15–16

TESTS

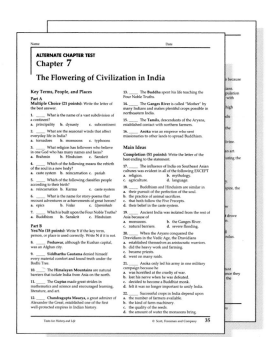

Chapter Test, pp. 33–34

Alternate Chapter Test, pp. 35–36

Other Optional Ancillaries

WORKBOOK

Section 1 Worksheet, p. 23

Section 2 Worksheet, p. 24

Section 3 Worksheet, p. 25

Section 4 Worksheet, p. 26

SOURCE READINGS

Source Reading 7A
Source Reading 7B

OVERHEAD TRANSPARENCIES

Overhead Transparency 13
Overhead Transparency 14

TEST GENERATOR

40 multiple-choice questions for Chapter 7

Chapter

7

CHAPTER INTRODUCTION
Ask students to tell what similarities they see between India in the 4th century B.C., as described here, and various present-day nations, such as, for example, the United States or the Soviet Union.

LOCATOR GLOBE
Call students' attention to the globe, which indicates the general area of the world discussed in this chapter. (A detailed map appears on page 118.)

TIME LINE
Call students' attention to the time line and have them calculate about how many years ago the Buddha was born. (more than 2,500 years ago)

The Flowering of Civilization in India

1500 B.C. – A.D. 500

1600 B.C.	
1500 B.C.	Aryans invade India
563 B.C.	The Buddha is born
A.D. 320	Gupta Empire is established
A.D. 400	
A.D. 500	

In the 4th century B.C., the mighty Mauryan Empire [mä′ûr yən], named after its first ruler, Chandragupta Maurya [chun′drə gup′tə- mä′ûr yə], extended from the Ganges River Valley in northeastern India to beyond the Khyber Pass in the northwest. Locate this region on the map on page 118.

Chandragupta was the very model of a fairy-tale king with all of the splendors of royalty. At Pataliputra, his capital city, Chandragupta built a great palace with gold and silver vines covering the pillars. He maintained a company of armed women as his personal bodyguards, and he himself was an excellent charioteer. Once a year in a special ceremony, he had his hair washed in public as a symbol of his readiness to stand before the gods for his people. On special holidays he often toured Pataliputra, displaying his great wealth to the world. A Greek visiting the city in 302 B.C. saw just such a procession and described its color and majesty. First came the monarch, riding high above the crowd on a huge elephant.

> Then came a great host of attendants in holiday dress, with golden vessels such as huge basins and goblets six feet broad; tables, chairs of state, drinking and washing vessels, all of Indian copper, and many of them set with jewels such as emeralds, beryls, and Indian garnets. Others wore robes embroidered in gold thread and led wild beasts such as buffaloes, leopards and tame lions, and rare birds in cages.

This visitor was favorably impressed by the prosperity of the empire. Famine was almost unknown because farmers used irrigation and crop rotation to increase their yield. Since all land already belonged to the state, a tax on farm products was the chief source of government income. Trade and craft industries thrived. Goods from China, Mesopotamia, and Asia Minor were sold in the markets of Pataliputra and in other cities of the empire.

BACKGROUND The Mauryan army, with 600,000 infantrymen and 30,000 cavalry, used some 9,000 war elephants in much the same way that modern armies use tanks.

Indian civilization has been shared and unified to a large degree by Hinduism. This Hindu god Shiva holds emblems of both creation and destruction.

Although the Mauryan dynasty lasted only 150 years, they were years of relative peace as the kingdoms of northern India were united.

Reading Preview

In this chapter you will read how various cultures shaped India's unique civilization.

1. *Geography shaped history in India.*
2. *Many features of Indian life date from ancient times.*
3. *Strong rulers built empires in India.*
4. *Gupta rule launched a golden age in India.*

BACKGROUND Excellent roads, with milestones showing distances, connected the many Mauryan villages and towns. One road, between Pataliputra and the provincial city of Taxila, was

Geography shaped history in India.

India's geography is a picture of contrasts. On the one hand there are fertile river valleys and heavy rainfall, on the other, immense deserts and areas of permanent snow. The highest mountains in the world rest on immense, flat plains. Note too that one of the world's longest coastlines offers few useful harbors. The Indian landscape is varied and productive, but the climate is often quite difficult, even harsh.

Natural barriers isolated ancient India.

India is commonly called a **subcontinent**, that is,

1,200 miles long. Locate these two cities on the map on page 118.

1 *Lesson Plan*

Essential Learning Objective

Students will learn to describe the effects India's geography and climate have had on its culture and its development.

1 FOCUS AND MOTIVATE

Without reference to any maps, ask students to tell where India is located and what countries and bodies of water border it. List students' responses on the chalkboard. Next, have students turn to the Atlas map of Asia on page 795 to check the accuracy of what is listed on the chalkboard.

2 TEACH

- Direct students to draw on a piece of paper a triangle representing the shape of India. Have them put the information from the chalkboard on this "map" and then add the names of other geographical features described in this section that border India. Students should understand that these natural barriers have isolated India by allowing people to enter only through mountain passes or by sea.

- Using the information from the Geography essay on page 120, make two lists on the board to clarify details of the differences between the summer and winter monsoon seasons. Check to be sure students grasp the importance of the monsoons in bringing water for crops and the fact that too much or too little rain can be equally disastrous.

Have students draw two additional "triangle maps." Label one "Summer Monsoons" and the other "Winter Monsoons." Students can use colored arrows to indicate the direction of the winds. Indicate the correct months for each season. Also for guided practice:

 Overhead Transparency 13

3 ASSESS AND CLOSE

ASSESS

What mountains border India in the northwest? (Hindu Kush) How were people able to cross this barrier? (through the Khyber Pass and other passes)

OPTIONAL RETEACHING

Use the outline map of Asia in the Geography Skills book. Moving in a clockwise direction, have students name the geographical barriers that surround India. Draw an arrow representing winds going from southwest to northeast and ask what these winds carry. (cool, dry air)

OPTIONAL ENRICHMENT

1. Have students find out the heights of the major peaks of the Himalayas. These might be shown on a poster to illustrate their various heights. (average)
2. Have students research the most recent summer monsoon season in India to find out if the rains came on time and how India's crop production was affected. (challenging)

INDEPENDENT PRACTICE/ HOMEWORK

Assign the Section Review, Activities page 35, or Workbook page 23.

Ancient India

 MAP STUDY   The map above of ancient India shows the major mountain ranges that isolate India. What two mountain ranges lie to the north of India?

a vast subdivision of a continent, not only because it is so large, but also because it is relatively isolated from the rest of Asia by natural barriers. Shaped like a triangle, the Indian subcontinent extends south into the Indian Ocean, with the Arabian Sea off its west coast and the Bay of Bengal to the east. Notice that India's third side on the north is an immense wall formed by the Hindu Kush and **Himalayan** [him′ə lā′ən] **mountains**. You can see on the map above how isolated India is.

Ancient India once included all that is now India, Pakistan, and Bangladesh. See the Atlas map of Asia on page 794.

Mountain passes and rivers controlled access and settlement patterns.

The Himalayas make up the largest part of the mountain barrier that walls India off from the rest of Asia. These huge mountains prevented people from the Asian steppes from easily entering the

ANSWER TO MAP STUDY the Hindu Kush and Himalaya mountains

BACKGROUND The total area of Ancient India was about 2 million square miles, or half the size of the United States.

country. In the northwest, however, there are passes in the Hindu Kush Mountains that invaders used for 4,000 years as gateways into India. The best known of these gateways is the Khyber Pass [kī'bər], shown on the map on page 118.

India's history is a story of succeeding invasions of people through the passes. Faced by the forbidding mountains, small bands of people drifted through the gateways, gradually mingling with the people who had come before. The peoples of India eventually became so intermixed that it is difficult in modern times to distinguish their varied origins.

Two major river systems that cross India have also been important to decisions regarding human habitation. In the northwest is the Indus River, where, as you learned in Chapter 2, one of the world's first civilizations began. Settled life in the arid northwest would not be possible even today without the Indus. The **Ganges River** [gan'jez'], running from the Himalayas southeast to the Bay of Bengal, is sacred to many Indians, who call it "Mother." The Ganges has often made the difference between food and famine. Locate the Indus and Ganges rivers on the map on page 118.

Climate constitutes a special challenge in India.

Climate, as well as geology, has helped shape the lives of the Indian people. In general, India is an extremely hot land. In the south where it is warm year-round, the average monthly temperature never falls below 65°F. In the northern plains, temperatures are more extreme. Summer highs of 125°F. have been recorded, and winter temperatures may drop well below freezing. Unlike much of North America, where winter means cold and summer hot, in India rain, not temperature, distinguishes one season from another. Summer is the wet season, and winter, the dry.

The most important aspect of India's climate is the impact the seasonal winds, called **monsoons**, have on everyday life. The monsoon pattern, described in 'Geography: A Key to History' on page 120, is a normal, fairly dependable feature of the Indian year.

Because of variation in the monsoons, however, a need has always existed to control water supplies. For instance, ancient Indians created thousands of cisterns, or covered reservoirs, around the country so that rainfall could be saved for use during the dry season. Dikes, channels, and dams were also built to help control flooding during India's wet season.

The Ganges River has always been important to the Indians who depend upon its water for their food and drink. Here, people bathe in the Ganges' waters.

Section 1 Review

Identify subcontinent, Himalayan Mountains, Ganges River, monsoons

Main Ideas
1. What natural barriers isolated the Indian subcontinent?
2. How did mountain passes control access to India? What contribution did the Indus and the Ganges river systems make to developing Indian settlements?
3. What makes India's climate particularly challenging?

Critical Thinking

Making Hypotheses: Why do you think that some invaders might be attracted to India, despite its difficult climate?

CLOSURE

Tell students that India is a subcontinent cut off from neighboring lands by high mountains and large bodies of water. Throughout its history, however, groups of people have been able to enter India through passes in the mountains or across the Arabian Sea. The monsoon winds that are so important in crop production also enabled trade between India, the Arabian peninsula, and Africa.

Answers to Section 1 Review

Identify

Key Terms, People, and Places are defined on pages indicated in parentheses. Also see the Glossary and Biographical Dictionary. subcontinent (117), Himalayan Mountains (118), Ganges River (119), monsoons (119)

Main Ideas
1. Himalayan and Hindu Kush mountains on the north, Arabian Sea and Bay of Bengal along the east and west coasts
2. Invaders were forced to enter India in small numbers over a period of time; without the two river systems, northeastern and northwestern India could not support a settled population.
3. generally hot, areas with extreme temperatures, only rain comes with seasonal monsoons, which do not always bring right amount

Critical Thinking

Invaders pushed by population pressures or curiosity would find that India had vast areas of good land, water, and people unable to resist invasion.

GEOGRAPHY

A Key to History

MONSOON WINDS AND INDIAN HISTORY

Like other parts of southern Asia, India has been greatly affected by the seasonal winds called monsoons. The winds are mainly caused by seasonal changes in air pressure. During the summer, hot air accumulates above the Asian landmass, forming a low-pressure area. From June through September, moist air from the Indian Ocean sweeps across India, blowing from the southwest into this low-pressure area.

The moist air brings heavy rains, especially where mountains or hills force the air to rise. As many as 35 inches of rain have fallen within a 24-hour period in the northeast corner of the subcontinent as the Himalayas force the winds upward and cause the clouds to drop their moisture. These rainwaters often flood the Ganges River Valley.

India gets about 90 percent of its yearly rainfall from the summer monsoons. The people rejoice at the sight of the first great drops of rain. Without the rains, crops wither and die, and the people may starve.

During the winter the monsoons reverse direction. The interior of Asia becomes an icebox with an attendant high-pressure area. The monsoon then blows across India from the northeast as cool, dry air flows from the interior to the Indian Ocean.

The monsoons have affected transportation and trade too. During the 1st century A.D., a sea captain named Hippalus discovered that the winds in the Indian Ocean regularly blew in certain directions. By using the summer winds, ships could sail directly across the Indian Ocean from the Red Sea or Africa, rather than following the coast. This route cut the sailing time from twelve months to two. The winter monsoons enabled ships to make a rapid return journey. With this discovery, sea trade between India and Africa increased.

Which arrows show the winds that bring the most rainfall to the Ganges River Valley?

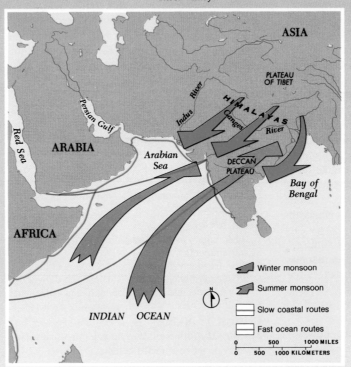

REVIEW

1. How do the summer and winter monsoon winds in India differ?
2. Explain why ships from India often waited several months along the coast of Africa during the winter before returning home.
3. With the growth of trade across the Indian Ocean after the 1st century A.D., where would you expect to find the chief ports of India? Why?

2 Many features of Indian life date from ancient times.

During the centuries between 1500 and 500 B.C., the Indian people developed a unique civilization that involved certain strict rules of social behavior. People began following customs that even today influence how many Indians make a living, worship, dress, and eat. Two important religions, Hinduism and Buddhism, were established, and an important literature was born.

Aryan nomads invaded in the Vedic Age (1500–500 B.C.).

About 1500 B.C. tribes of invaders began pouring through the mountain passes into northwest India. See the map on page 118. These people were Aryans, members of a larger group known as Indo-Europeans who may have come originally from Central Asia. In ancient times one branch of this group moved westward into Greece, Italy, and western Europe. Another branch pushed into Asia Minor and the Middle East. The third group, the Aryans, crossed the Hindu Kush Mountains into India.

The Aryans [er'ē ənz] were nomad warriors, people who wandered with their herds, fighting and feasting as they went. The richest families were those who had the most cattle. In fact, the Aryan word for war meant "a desire for more cows." The richest man in a tribe was its ruler, or rajah [rä'jə].

When the Aryans came into India, they found Dravidians [drə vid'ē ənz] already living there. Some historians believe that the Dravidians were descended from the people of the Indus Valley civilization and achieved a cultural level to rival the Sumerians and Egyptians. Whether or not they were as successful as that hypothesis implies, the Dravidians were a strong, well-organized people. They built several large cities, especially in the south, and from these centers Dravidian merchants regularly traded westward with Babylon and the cities of the Fertile Crescent.

Slowly, however, over several generations, the Aryans moved east along the river valleys of northern India, conquering the more civilized Dravidians and establishing themselves as aristocratic warriors who preferred raiding to farming. With

the Dravidians to do the heavy work, the Aryans herded cattle, sheep, and goats between raids, tanned leather, worked metals, and wove cloth. They built no cities, settling instead into fortlike villages. The western trade the Dravidians had developed with the Middle East died from neglect. Besides fighting and feasting, the Aryans loved music, dancing, and gambling.

The first Aryan-influenced civilization in India lasted some 1,000 years, a period called the Vedic Age [vā'dik]. The word Vedic comes from *Veda*, which means "knowledge." The *Vedas* are a collection of writings on religion, philosophy, and magic that were composed and passed down orally between 1500 and 500 B.C. The writings also contain a great deal of information about the kind of life the Aryans lived, much as the books of the Old Testament describe the life of the ancient Israelites.

During the Vedic Age, most people lived in villages. Early Indian village life followed a pattern similar to the life lived in modern Indian villages. The village leader either inherited the post or was elected. This person was assisted by an elected council of villagers who distributed land and collected taxes. The villagers, who could be farmers or craftworkers or both, lived in mud-wall houses with thatched roofs. Both men and women wore a garment made from a single piece of cloth wound around the body. The sari, a garment made of silk or cotton that many Indian women still wear, is modeled on this ancient dress.

The family was the center of all religious and social life. Marriage, for example, was a very serious business since it joined families and their property. As sons brought their wives home to live, they created small family units within the larger home. In modern India several parts of a family may still live under the same roof. One result of this close lifestyle was a strong concern for the group. To this day, the welfare of the Indian family is often more important than the wishes of the individual.

Hinduism teaches that God is one, but has many names and faces.

Although some aspects of **Hinduism**, the dominant Indian religion, probably date back to the Indus Valley people, formal Hinduism had its origins in the Vedic Age. Like the Israelites, the early

BACKGROUND Indian society has been based on three factors: the independent village, the joint family, and the caste system. The rajah's government was maninly concerned with

collecting taxes from the villages. The joint-family system was important in maintaining a secure society.

Essential Learning Objectives

Students will learn to:
- describe the formation of Indian culture.
- give examples of similarities between Indo-European languages.
- explain the basic principles of Hinduism and Buddhism.

1 FOCUS AND MOTIVATE

Use the Atlas world map on pages 784–785 to have students trace the routes of the Indo-Europeans from central Asia into the Middle East, Greece, Italy, western Europe, and India. Clarify that the Aryans invaded India about the same time that the Latins were moving onto the Italian peninsula, about 1500 B.C. Check to see that students recall that invaders entered India through passes in the mountains, such as the Khyber Pass.

2 TEACH

- Describe the cultural differences between the Aryan invaders of India and the established Dravidians. Explain that many aspects of life in India developed from the contacts and conflicts between the two groups. Examples are the village leadership systems, family structures, and the caste system.

- Draw a long horizontal time line on the chalkboard to teach the writings of the Vedic Age. List the *Vedas, Upanishads,* and *Rig Veda* under 1500–900 B.C. Under the *Later Vedic Age,* 900–500 B.C., list the epic poems—the *Mahabharata,* the *Bhagavad-Gita* and the *Ramayana.* Have students identify the subject matter of each of these works as you list them on the chalkboard. Clarify the use of Sanskrit for the writings and emphasize the importance of this alphabet in tracing the relationship of prehistoric peoples of Europe and western Asia through Sanskrit-based words.

- List the basic principles of Hinduism identifying the role of the various divinities. Discuss the concept of reincarnation, pointing out the differences between Western and Hindu attitudes toward rebirth. Clarify the origin of Buddhism as a reform movement. Use the excerpts provided to encourage students to identify the values and major principles of Buddhism.

GUIDED PRACTICE
On blank outline maps from the Geography Skills book, have students label the countries in which words similar to the Sanskrit word *mata* are used. Students could also use foreign language dictionaries to find similar forms of the word "mother" in other languages. The form used in each country should be printed under the name. Have students title their maps appropriately.

Aryans sacrificed animals to heaven, but unlike the Israelites, they prayed to many gods. They brought with them into India a number of gods from their Central Asian homeland. Among them were the mighty Indra, warrior god of thunder and battle, and the twin gods, Mitra and Varuna.

In time, the followers of Hinduism moved to a belief that everything in the universe is God, or Brahman, the Principle of Truth. The many gods with their individual names are merely different faces of Brahman, the single, supreme, unifying Power. During the Vedic Age, three divinities were worshiped as specific expressions of Brahman: Brahma the Creator, Vishnu the Preserver, and Shiva the Destroyer.

One of the essential beliefs in Hinduism is the Law of Karma. Simply stated, one's future life depends on one's present behavior. Each person will be born as many times as is necessary to perfect the soul, and the circumstances in which a person's life is lived is a direct result of the effort made in the life just before it. Hindus long for the happiness that comes when the soul can escape these cycles of rebirth, or **reincarnation** ("to be put again into a body"), and is taken into the "world soul," or Brahman.

Western people who have heard about reincarnation tend to imagine that it is a wonderful thing to live again and again. For Hindus, however, earthly life exists for only one reason: so that the soul can learn the difference between illusion and truth. Hindus believe that what we call the "real world" is actually just an illusion, a dream. The only reality is Brahman. Reincarnation is a kind of classroom in which the soul studies until it learns the difference between the dream and reality. Just as students need more than one year to complete their whole education, so most souls need more than one lifetime to learn this truth.

Hindus actually see little difference between life and death. The following lines from one of their epic poems, the *Bhagavad-Gita* [bäg′ə vəd gē′tə], God's Song, celebrates the continuity of existence:

All that doth live, lives always! To man's frame
As there come infancy and youth and age,
So come there raisings-up and layings-down
Of others and of other life-abodes
Which the wise know and fear not.

These ideas continue to have a profound effect on people's lives today. Because Hinduism promotes a deep appreciation for all forms of art and beauty, the religion has made serious contributions to world culture. Because it recognizes many paths to truth, Hinduism encourages religious toleration, that is, the freedom to follow one's own beliefs. Finally, because it supports labor and scholarship, Hinduism encourages civic responsibility.

The Aryans created a caste system.

At the time of their first invasions, some Aryans married Dravidians. Soon, however, the invaders began to see that it would take only a few generations before an Aryan would be indistinguishable from a Dravidian. Moreover, the Dravidians might attempt to claim a right to the high government

This figure of the four-headed Brahma the Creator from southern India dates from a later period in Indian history—the 10th or 11th century A.D.

BACKGROUND The groupings that developed into the caste system were: (1) *Brahmins,* the priestly families; (2) *Kshatriyas,* the warrior and ruler families; (3) *Vaishas,* merchants, skilled craftworkers, and farmers; (4) *Shudras,* serfs and laborers; and (5) *Pariahs,* the so-called Untouchables.

positions that the Aryans wanted. To prevent this, the Aryans developed a system of rigid social rules that barred the Dravidians from marrying Aryans or even from associating with them too closely.

For some time the system was just a simple division between the two peoples. Gradually, however, five distinct groups appeared. The four highest groups came to believe that the touch, even the shadow, of the lowest group, the pariahs, or untouchables, would contaminate them.

From this beginning evolved an even more rigid and complex social organization called the **caste** [kast] **system**. The members of each caste could be identified by skin color, politics, social status, work, wealth, and religion. The caste controlled not only marriage choice, but every aspect of life including work options and religious rites. A person was born into a particular caste, and nothing could change this fate. The pariahs were especially despised because they were considered to be beyond the caste system, in other words, "outcastes." From this idea comes our English word "outcast" for someone barred from the group.

The orderly growth and maturing of Hindu culture owes a great deal to the priestly caste, the Brahmins. Set apart as they were from the concerns of the world, they were able to devote themselves to preserving the sacred texts and to perfecting the ceremonies and rules of conduct in Hinduism. They were often called upon to settle legal disputes and to provide counsel to rulers. Eventually the Brahmins were not only priests, but also the teachers, judges, and lawgivers.

The Later Vedic Age produced the Sanskrit alphabet (900–500 B.C.).

For 600 years the Aryans gradually pushed east to the valley of the Ganges River and then south. As settlements were made on the banks of the rivers of central India, the last 400 years of the Vedic Age began, a period known both as the Later Vedic Age and the Epic Age. Our knowledge of this period comes from **epics**, the long story-poems on heroic subjects that many peoples have composed to preserve their prehistory.

The two important poems of India's Epic Age were the *Mahabharata* [mä hä′bə rä′tə] and the *Ramayana* [rä′mä yä′nə]. Unlike the *Vedas,* which

A Hindu temple-hanging illustrates a scene from the *Ramayana,* the longest and most popular of the Indian epics.

were specifically religious writings, the epics tell of the adventures of ancient heroes and offer moral and ethical instruction. The *Mahabharata* is the tale of an important war and includes the famous *Bhagavad-Gita,* excerpted on page 122. In the *Gita,* as it is usually called, there are verses referring to reincarnation and descriptions of caste virtues. The *Gita* also emphasizes the importance of doing one's duty and not fearing death. In the *Ramayana,* a hero wanders abroad, often with his wife, having fantastic adventures with the gods.

Between 1500 and 500 B.C., the Aryans invented an alphabet for their spoken *Sanskrit* [san′skrit] language. Original Sanskrit became a sacred language for the Hindus, used primarily as a tool for writing down the *Vedas* and the *Upanishads,*

BACKGROUND Modern Indian leaders have often based their actions on the *Bhagavad-Gita.* Some have used it to justify war; others have used its ideals in developing the political techniques of non-violence and passive resistance. The *Mahabharata* and *Ramayana* are still chanted by holy men to crowds of listeners at feasts and other ceremonies.

ASSESS

1. What kind of government structure developed in Indian villages during the Vedic Age? (a village leader, either elected or hereditary, assisted by elected councils)
2. True or false? Both Hindus and Buddhists believe in reincarnation. (True)

OPTIONAL RETEACHING

Ask students to suggest aspects of life for people in a typical Indian village in 1000 B.C. Write responses on the chalkboard. (occupation, amount of education, and choice of marriage partner defined by caste; Hindu religion; Sanskrit language spoken by all, but written only by priests and poets; large extended families with wives living with husbands' parents)

OPTIONAL ENRICHMENT

1. Have students research Indian religious art to find out the ways in which the various Hindu gods are depicted. Written descriptions or drawings may be presented. (average)
2. Assign students to research and give oral reports on the present status of the caste system in India. (challenging)
3. Also for enrichment:

Source Reading 7A

INDEPENDENT PRACTICE/ HOMEWORK

Assign the Section Review, Activities page 36, or Workbook page 24.

CLOSURE

Summarize the lesson by telling students that traditional Indian culture resulted from the Aryan conquest of the Dravidians and the interrelationships that developed over many years. Two major world religions originated in India that have contributed many high ideals to civilization.

which is a commentary by scholars on the *Vedas*. By 300 B.C. the spoken language had diverged so sharply from the written Sanskrit used by priests and poets that it had begun to develop into the various modern Indian languages of today. Like the Latin of western Europe, Sanskrit preserved the religious literature of the Hindus but became in effect a dead language.

In the 18th century A.D., Europeans discovered Sanskrit. This discovery had an enormous impact on our knowledge of both the spread of prehistoric peoples throughout Europe and western Asia and the origins of languages. Since Sanskrit preserves the oldest Aryan recorded material, it became the basis for a comparative study of the whole Indo-European family of languages, a group that includes Greek, Latin, English, Persian, and German as well as many other languages. Comparative linguistics, as this study is called, can now trace the relationship of common words through languages that seldom seem similar. The Sanskrit word *mata*, for example, became *ma* in Hindi, *mater* in Latin, *matka* in Polish, *madre* in Spanish, *mütter* in German, and *mother* in English. In addition, the English words *brother, sister, daughter*, and *son* are related to

An ancient stone carving shows a young Prince Siddhartha, who later became the Buddha, and his companions on their way to school in a chariot.

bhrata, svasis, duhita, and *sunu* in Sanskrit.

The oldest work in Sanskrit literature is the sacred *Rig-Veda*, the "Hymns of Knowledge," composed during the Early Vedic Age (before 900 B.C.). Passed by word of mouth from one generation to the next, the hymns, written in praise of the many Hindu gods, number more than 1,000. In "The Hymn to the Dawn," one of the songs of the *Rig-Veda*, the poet calls to the sleeping world:

> Arise! the breath, the life has reached us. Darkness has gone away and light is coming. She leaves a pathway for the sun to travel: We have arrived where men prolong existence.

By the beginning of the Later Vedic Age, the Aryans, influenced perhaps by their Greek cousins, had also begun to experiment with the city-state form of government. Each city was ruled by a petty king who held the title of Rajah, an echo of the ancient cattle lord. The rajah kept an army, collected taxes, and made war on his neighboring city-state, just like the Greeks did.

As some city people became rich through trade, they began to form a middle class between the villagers and the nobles. This new class needed some kind of money to make it easier to trade, and as a result, copper coins came into use. By the end of the Vedic Age, around 500 B.C., the Indians had also established a banking and credit system.

Buddhism accepted some parts of Hinduism, but rejected others.

In time, some thoughtful Indians began to criticize their society's caste system and the elaborate rituals that Hinduism had acquired. One such critic was **Siddhartha Gautama** [sid′är′thə gô′tə mə], who lived from 563 to 483 B.C. Gautama was the son of a king whose land lay close to the Himalayas. When he was 29, he suddenly left his wife and child and the life of a prince to search for an answer to the question, Why do people suffer pain and sorrow? He lived with holy men, fasted, and denied himself every material comfort. This denial freed him for meditation on spiritual things. Then one day, as he sat meditating under the sacred Bodhi Tree, he knew that the truth had come to him.

Thereafter he was known as the Buddha [bü′də], a title meaning "The Enlightened One."

From the Archives

The Noble Eightfold Path

The Buddha summarized in bare outline some of his basic teachings in his first sermon, preached in the Deer Park at Varanasi, India, in the company of five monks. In the sermon the Buddha taught the existence of suffering, the cause of suffering, and the escape from suffering through following the Middle Way and the Noble Eightfold Path.

And what, monks, is that middle path which giveth vision [and leads to Nirvana]? Verily, it is this Ariyan [supremely human] eightfold way, to wit: Right view, right aim, right speech, right action, right living, right effort, right mindfulness, right concentration. This, monks is that middle path which giveth vision, which giveth knowledge, which causeth calm, special knowledge, enlightenment, [Nirvana].

The Buddha believed that following the rules of the Eightfold Path would finally free the soul from the bondage of rebirth. For the rest of his life, he taught the Four Noble Truths, later the foundation of **Buddhism**, the religion of the Buddha. Learn about the Buddha's Eightfold Path, the last of the Noble Truths, in the 'From the Archives' box above.

The Buddha, as a reformer of the Hinduism of his time, preached against the teachings of the priests and broke with their rules of caste by treating all people alike. He also attacked the extremes practiced by some holy men who tortured their bodies in order to deny their physical nature and heighten spiritual awareness. Instead, the Buddha taught the Middle Way, or moderation in all things. He left some of the noblest as well as simplest rules for human conduct in The Five Precepts:

Harm no living thing.
Take nothing that is not given.
Speak no untruth.
Live chastely.
Ingest nothing that clouds the mind.

During his lifetime the Buddha founded several communities of monks and nuns whose monasteries became centers of great learning. Soon his teachings had spread throughout India.

The Buddha died in 483 B.C., the victim of food poisoning. One of his followers, knowing how much he liked mushrooms, unwittingly gathered some of the poisonous variety and prepared them for his master. As the holy man lay dying, his disciple wept bitterly for his stupidity. "Never mind, good friend," the gentle Buddha said, wanting to comfort him, "the dish was truly delicious."

Section 2 Review

Identify Hinduism, reincarnation, caste system, epics, Siddhartha Gautama, Buddhism

Main Ideas

1. In what ways were the Aryan invaders different from the Dravidians already living in India?
2. What are some of the names of God in Hinduism? What are some of God's special qualities?
3. Why did the Aryans create the caste system?
4. What did the Later Vedic Age Indians do with their new Sanskrit alphabet? Why are modern scholars of language interested in Sanskrit?
5. What Hindu practices did the Buddha attack? What beliefs and practices of his own did he introduce?

Critical Thinking

Analyzing Comparisons: Many people think that the Buddha's Five Precepts are a short way of saying the Ten Commandments. Decide which Commandments, which can be found in Chapter 3, look like Precepts. Explain why any Commandments do not seem to fit a Precept.

FROM THE ARCHIVES The excerpt from the Buddha's sermon is from *Buddhism*, edited by Richard A. Gard (New York: George Braziller, 1961), p. 128. Ask students if they are familiar

with other creeds or codes similar to the Eightfold Path. (Similarities may be noted to the Scout creeds.)

Critical Thinking

The Buddha's five precepts can be compared with the Ten Commandments as follows: The first precept—the 6th commandment (Thou shalt not kill.); 2nd precept—the 8th and 10th commandments (Thou shalt not steal, and Thou shalt not covet thy neighbor's house....); 3rd precept—the 9th commandment (Thou shalt not bear false witness against thy neighbor.); 4th precept—the 7th commandment (Thou shalt not commit adultery.) fits clearly, but others, including the 3rd, 4th, and 5th commandments seem to follow in the same vein of thought (Thou shalt not take the name of the Lord thy God in vain. Remember the sabbath day, to keep it holy. Honor thy father and thy mother.) The 5th precept seems to have no parallel in the commandments, and the 1st and 2nd commandments seem to have no parallels in the precepts.

3 | Strong rulers built empires in India.

Shortly after the end of the Vedic Age, India was threatened by a new attack from the northwest. This time the invasion was led by the Macedonian

3 Lesson Plan

Essential Learning Objectives

Students will learn to:
- evaluate the contributions of Indian and foreign rulers in India.
- discuss trade relationships between India and the Roman Empire.

1 **FOCUS AND MOTIVATE**

Write the Five Precepts of Buddhism (listed on page 125) on the chalkboard. Ask students how a ruler who was a devout Buddhist might be affected by these principles. (Rule would be tolerant, marked by generosity and caring.)

2 **TEACH**

Draw a long time line on the chalkboard. Divide it into three sections titled: Mauryan rule 321–184 B.C., Greek rule 183–130 B.C., and Kushan rule A.D. 78–200. Under Mauryan rule list Buddhist influences on Asoka's policies and describe his efforts to spread the religion. Under Greek rule list and explain efforts to unite Greek and Indian culture. Under Kushan rule list and describe Gandharan art and trade with Rome through Tamil ports.

GUIDED PRACTICE

On an outline map of the world from the Geography Skills book, have students show trade routes between India and China and Rome. Label routes to indicate the items carried.

general Alexander the Great. In 328 B.C. Alexander defeated the Persian Empire and two years later, hoping to conquer the rest of Asia, he crossed the Indus River into India. Alexander battled various Indian armies until his men, weary of foreign campaigns, forced him to return to their homeland.

After one battle, Asoka held the Mauryan Empire in peace (321–184 B.C.).

One young Indian influenced by Alexander was **Chandragupta Maurya**, the young king whose rule of splendor you read about in the chapter introduction. In 321 B.C. he seized one of India's northern kingdoms and, from Pataliputra, the capital city, he declared himself ruler. As his power grew in the years following, he married the daughter of one of Alexander's generals, extended his

This lion pillar, built by Asoka, is modern India's national symbol. The wheel beneath the lions is the Wheel of Law, which represents Buddhist teaching.

rule to include all of northern India, and established the Mauryan Empire. Although he was the father of the Mauryan dynasty, Chandragupta was not its most important member. That role was left to **Asoka** [ə sō′kə], his famous grandson.

Asoka, who became emperor in 273 B.C., continued with the Mauryan plan to unify India. After leading his army in his first military campaign, however, Asoka experienced such horror at the cruelty of war that he never fought again. His sorrow for his victory is clear in the words he had carved on a rock wall for all to see:

> Kalinga was conquered by his Sacred and gracious Majesty [Asoka] when he had been consecrated eight years. 150,000 persons were thence carried away captive, 100,000 were slain [in battle], and many times that many died [of their wounds]. . . . Thus arose [Asoka's] remorse for having conquered the Kalingans because the conquest of a country previously unconquered involves the slaughter, death and carrying away captive of the people.

At about this time Asoka became a Buddhist. His new religion may well have been the reason he refused to make war and would have supported him in his determination to maintain peace in the empire. On stone pillars 30 to 40 feet high that survive to this day, you can still see the rules of conduct Asoka had carved to remind his people to live virtuous lives. Because he believed that all life should be honored, he forbade animal sacrifices in the temples. By encouraging his nobles to travel to Buddhist and other shrines on pilgrimages, he hoped to discourage one of their favorite pastimes, the hunt. He himself never ate meat, and he encouraged others to be vegetarians.

Although Asoka was a devout Buddhist, he nevertheless tolerated other religions in his empire. At the same time, he sent missionaries out to teach the world about the Buddha—north to the Himalayan lands, south to the tip of India, east to Burma, and west across Syria to North Africa. Follow the course of Buddhism's spread on the map on page 127. As a result of such missionary efforts, Buddhism became very well known in the Eastern Hemisphere. The religion spread also to the Western Hemisphere by way of Asian immigrants in the 19th and 20th centuries.

ASIA

MONGOLIA

KOREA

JAPAN

Peshawar
AFGHANISTAN

Huang River

CHINA

PAKISTAN

TIBET

NEPAL

Chang (Yangtze) River

INDIA

Indus River

Ganges R.

Kapilavastu
Birthplace of
the Buddha

BURMA

ARABIAN
SEA

Bay of
Bengal

SOUTHEAST
ASIA

SOUTH
CHINA
SEA

PACIFIC
OCEAN

SRI LANKA

MALAYSIA

INDIAN OCEAN

BORNEO

EQUATOR

SUMATRA

BALI

JAVA

Tigris River

Euphrates River

Nile River

AFRICA

**The Spread of Buddhism,
500 B.C.–A.D. 1250**

→ Spread of
Buddhism

▨ Kushan Empire,
about A.D. 100

▨ Area under Hindu influence,
about A.D. 1250

0   1000 MILES
0   1000 KILOMETERS

N

 MAP STUDY
The map above shows how Buddhism spread outward from India. Through which countries did Buddhism travel on its way to Japan? Below are five Buddhist symbols that are frequently encountered in Asian art, along with the qualities that they represent.

Wheel—
Buddha's
teachings

Lotus—
purity and
truth

Endless knot—
eternal
happiness

Pair of fish—
salvation

Conch shell—
Buddha's voice;
prayer

Asoka was one of the great rulers of history. He gave India unity and peace as well as responsible government. Soon after his death in 232 B.C., however, his empire began to crumble. Weak kings ruled until 184 B.C., when the last Mauryan emperor was assassinated. Following that event, a series of invasions brought northern India once more under foreign rule.

Foreign rulers introduced new ideas into India (183 B.C.–A.D. 200).

During the next period of Indian history, many foreign groups invaded the country and took com-

mand. Some of these foreign rulers included the Greeks and the Kushans.

Greek rule (183–130 B.C.). The eastern part of Alexander's Greek empire, the kingdom of Bactria, bordered on India. Its king, Demetrius, conquered much of northern India, taking the capital city of Pataliputra in 183 B.C. Demetrius, following Alexander's lead, believed in joining East and West in an equal society. For example, coins minted during his rule had Greek writing on one side and Indian on the other.

In 130 B.C. Bactria, with its majority population Indian and its ruling class Greek, was itself at-

ANSWER TO MAP STUDY From India, Buddhism traveled through China and Korea before reaching Japan.

127

4 Lesson Plan

Essential Learning Objectives

Students will learn to:
- describe the achievements and far-reaching influence of Gupta rulers and scholars.
- evaluate the causes of India's decline in the 7th century.

1 FOCUS AND MOTIVATE

Discuss with students the meaning of the term "Golden Age." Students

---

BACKGROUND Although the Buddha never claimed to be divine, some of his followers believed that he was. The Kushans strongly supported this view. They developed the Mahayana

tacked by nomads from Central Asia. As a result, Greek rule in India ended. Greek influence persisted, however, especially in the arts.

Kushan rule (A.D. 78–200). An unsettled period of many wars and various rulers followed the fall of Bactria. By the 1st century A.D., however, the Kushans proved to be the most important of the invaders. Their kings expanded their rule of northwestern India to include what is now Afghanistan. Then, like the ancient Aryans before them, they pushed south into central India. The Kushan capital was no longer Pataliputra but **Peshawar** [pə shä′wər], today a city in Pakistan.

The Kushan kings were Buddhists who promoted a style of religious art called Gandharan [gandhär′ən]. Before this time, artists, faithful to the teachings of the Buddha that had forbidden idol worship, had never shown him in human form. In Gandharan art, which owes much to the Greeks, the Buddha is shown in beautiful flowing robes; his face is always serene, his attitude prayerful.

As the Kushans flourished, so did Gandharan art. In the secluded Bamian Valley in Afghanistan, huge carvings can still be seen on the face of a rock cliff. One image of the Buddha towers 170 feet. A person standing on this Buddha's shoulder is about as tall as its ear. Around the statues, caves in which monks lived and prayed were carved out of the solid rock.

India traded with the Roman Empire.

During the Kushan period, trade with the western world was revived. A large volume of goods was exchanged between the Kushan and Roman empires, with most of the traffic passing through the ports of southern India.

The people of southern India, the **Tamils** [tam′əlz], were descendants of the ancient Dravidians. The Tamils, especially those at the southmost tip of India, were skilled sailors. Their ships regularly traveled the treacherous sea lanes of the Arabian and Red seas, following the monsoon wind patterns to the African coast and back.

The Tamils built lighthouses to guide ships safely into their harbors and offered convenient wharves and well-equipped warehouses. After the Romans discovered the trick of sailing with the seasonal monsoons, they brought gold, wine,

BACKGROUND Excavations have uncovered many Roman coins in southern India, as well as pieces of pottery inscribed with the names of Italian craftsmen. An ivory statue of an Indian goddess was found in the ruins of Pompeii.

---

branch of Buddhism, which worshiped the Buddha as a divine being and as a savior of humanity.

glass, and pottery to the southern India ports. Always short of grain, the Roman captains took back rice and the silks and pearls.

The spices of India—pepper, ginger, and cinnamon—were a highly valued commodity, as important to the Romans as they would be to many other peoples around the world, even to this day. For the Romans and others throughout history, food spoiled fast in the days before refrigeration, and strong spices were used both to preserve foods and to mask the bad taste of spoiling meat.

Section 3 Review

Identify Chandragupta Maurya, Asoka, Peshawar, Tamils

Main Ideas
1. Why was Asoka's first military campaign also his last? How did he encourage Buddhism?
2. How did the Kushan ideas about the Buddha change Buddhism?
3. What goods were traded between the Indians and the Romans?

Critical Thinking
Assessing Cause and Effect: What were some of the effects of foreign contact on Indian religion, art, and culture in general? Give examples of how the Indian culture changed because of contact with foreign civilizations.

This cave Buddha, located in China, was carved in the Gandharan style of art. It dates from the 4th or 5th century A.D.

4 Gupta rule launched a golden age in India.

After the fall of the Kushans about A.D. 200, northern India broke up into many small states. In the 4th century, following this period of instability, a new line of kings, the **Guptas** [gup′təs], came to power. Their reign is called the Golden Age of Hindu culture.

People prospered during the Gupta Empire (A.D. 320–500).

The Gupta emperors ruled strongly and fairly. Their income came from port duties, from royal land and mine holdings, and from a tax on farm produce. Trade and manufacturing flourished, making life very prosperous.

Buddhism, however, was no longer one of the chief religions of India. Indian Buddhism had become so much like Hinduism that it was looked upon as merely a sect of Hinduism. Since people could not perceive much difference, they began to believe that Hinduism was a more truly Indian religion. As a result, Buddhism experienced a steady decline. Moreover, Gupta rulers enhanced the prestige of Hinduism by supporting its priests.

Indian learning flourished during the Golden Age.

The Guptas encouraged the development of learning, literature, and art during their rule. They were especially accomplished in the areas of mathematics and science.

The contributions of Indian mathematicians to world civilization are among the greatest of any people. They developed the number symbols that served as a basis for our own numerals. (We call these numerals Arabic and not Indian because Arab traders adopted them and carried them westward to Europe.) Gupta scholars also invented the decimal system and were among the first—along with the Maya of the Yucatán Peninsula—to use the zero. In addition, Indian mathematicians computed the value of pi (π) to four places (3.1416).

The Guptas excelled in other areas of scientific learning as well. In astronomy they knew about the rotation and spherical shape of the earth and cal-

culated the size of the moon. In addition, they wrote on the subject of gravitation. In chemistry Indians found new uses for the science in the area of manufacturing, and their steel was the best in the world. They were the first to make cashmere and such cotton fabrics as calico and chintz. In the field of medicine, Gupta doctors were among the finest doctors of the time. The Guptas established medical schools where physicians learned to clean wounds, perform surgery, and treat diseases.

In literature the Guptas are famous for their fairy tales and fables. The most famous storybook of the time is the *Panchatantra* [pan′chə tan′trə], a collection of stories written between A.D. 300 and 500. Other Indian writings include the world-famous story of Sinbad, which later found its way into *The Arabian Nights*. Some Indian fables were translated into European languages and adapted by such authors as Geoffrey Chaucer, the brothers Grimm, and Rudyard Kipling. Much excellent poetry and drama were also written during the Gupta period.

Indian culture influenced much of Southeast Asia.

From about the 2nd to the 10th centuries A.D., Indian settlers, traders, and armies carried their way of life to many distant places. The influences were gradual, but they eventually reached as far west as Madagascar and as far east as Taiwan.

Indian influence was strongest in Sri Lanka, Burma, and central Thailand. The culture in those areas became almost Indian. In more distant places such as Java, Cambodia (Kampuchea), and Vietnam, Indian influence was weaker, and Indian culture blended with local customs.

Indian art, however, made a strong impression on all of Southeast Asia. It influenced a Buddhist dynasty in central Java to build the world's largest Buddhist shrine at Borobudur in the 8th or 9th century. At about the same time, Hindus in Cambodia (Kampuchea) began to construct one of the most impressive religious buildings in the world, the temple of Angkor Wat.

Indian culture spread so widely throughout Southeast Asia, particularly between 650 and 1250, that scholars call the phenomenon "the Indianization of Southeast Asia." On the Malay Peninsula, and in Sumatra, Java, and Borneo, local rulers

should compare India's Golden Age with what they learned about the golden ages of Greece and Rome.

2 TEACH

- Call attention to the sources of revenue that brought prosperity to the Gupta empire. Clarify that trade and manufacturing were important sources of this prosperity.

- Identify Indian accomplishments under the headings: mathematics, science, medicine, literature, art.

- Compare the factors that brought prosperity with those that caused India's decline after the death of Chandragupta II.

GUIDED PRACTICE
Have small groups of students prepare lists of specific uses that might have been made of the scientific accomplishments of Indian scholars.

3 ASSESS AND CLOSE

ASSESS
What achievements of Indian mathematicians are used in our society? (number system, zero, decimals)

OPTIONAL RETEACHING
Guide students to grasp the relationships between scientific advances and inventions and the creation of occupations that result in growth in the society.

Students also may be assigned Activities reteaching page 39.

OPTIONAL ENRICHMENT
1. Ask students to find works of European authors that were based on Indian fables. (challenging)

BACKGROUND During the Gupta period, Indian painters and sculptors freed themselves from Greek influences to create a distinctly Indian art, inspired chiefly by Hinduism.

Answers to Section 4 Review

Identify
Key Terms, People, and Places are
defined on pages indicated in parentheses. Also see the Glossary
and Biographical Dictionary.
Guptas (129)

Main Ideas
1. Trade and manufacturing flourished, leading to a time of prosperity.
2. achievements in mathematics relating to the Arabic number system
and pi; in science relating to astronomy, chemistry, and medicine; in
literature, fairy tales and fables
3. Indian influence strongest in Sri
Lanka, Burma, and central Thailand;
influence can be seen in religion, art,
language, and mythology.
4. an attitude of disinterest and self-
imposed isolation

Critical Thinking
India, with its enormous population,
may have been better suited to play
the role of a world leader today had
their period of scientific and literary
achievement not gone into decline.

Chronology of Early India

2500–1500 B.C. Harappan Age
The cities of Mohenjo-Daro and
Harappa were sites of highly developed
cultures.

1500–500 B.C. Vedic Age
Indo-Aryan invaders swept into India
about 1500 B.C. This period is called
the Vedic Age from the *Vedas*, Indo-
Aryan books of sacred knowledge.

900–500 B.C. Epic Age (Later Vedic Age)
The name comes from the two epics
written in this period (the *Mahabharata*
and the *Ramayana*) in which the ideas
of the Hindu religion are presented in
heroic stories.

563–483 B.C.
Life of the Buddha

327–325 B.C.
Invasion of Alexander the Great

321–184 B.C. Mauryan Empire

183 B.C.–A.D. 320
Period of invasions and petty kingdoms.
During the Kushan period (A.D. 78–200)
Buddhism spread.

A.D. 320–500 Gupta Empire
The golden age of Hindu culture

A.D. 606–647 Harsha's Empire

A.D. 650–1250
The Indianization of Southeast Asia

---

adopted the Sanskrit language and script, along
with Indian mythology. The Indian religions of Hinduism and Buddhism made a lasting impact on
Southeast Asia. Buddhism was especially important
since it emphasized the value of popular education.
Buddhist missionaries helped bring education to the
common people and taught many kings and local
rulers the value of good and humane government.

BACKGROUND Students from all over Asia attended India's
university at Nalanda. Founded in the fifth century A.D., it had
an enrollment of 10,000 students.

Centuries of disunity followed the Gupta decline.

Gupta power began to decline after Chandragupta
II died in A.D. 413. India once again faced invasion,
this time from the northeast. The Huns, a fierce
people from the central Asian plains, crossed into
India near the end of the 5th century, and by the
middle of the 500s, the Gupta Empire was finished.

Not only did strong government disappear, but
other areas of life also suffered. For example, no
longer were foreign guests and merchants with
their foreign cultures welcome to establish themselves in Indian cities. Literature and science were
allowed to stagnate. The Hindus were satisfied
with what they had become. A 10th century visitor
to India wrote:

> The Hindus believe that there is no country but
> theirs, no nation like theirs, no religion like theirs,
> no sciences like theirs. . . . If they traveled and
> mixed with other nations they would soon change
> their mind, for their ancestors were not so narrow-
> minded as the present generation.

This attitude not only halted progress in India, it
also weakened the country. Self-imposed isolation
kept Indians from learning new methods of warfare, an ignorance that prevented them from successfully defending themselves against their next
invaders, the Muslims in the 11th century.

Section 4 Review

Identify Guptas
Main Ideas
1. What economic conditions allowed the Indians to
prosper during the Gupta Empire?
2. What contributions did Gupta scholars make in
mathematics, science, and literature?
3. Where in Southeast Asia was Indian influence
strongest? What effects are visible in these other
cultures?
4. What attitude weakened India after the Guptas?
Critical Thinking
Predicting Effects: Predict what you think might
have happened in India and in neighboring areas if the
power of the Guptas had not declined in the 5th
century. What role do you think India might play in the
world today?

Gupta Temple Architecture

This gold asoka with its clustered blooms
Is like a bride with many ornaments.

The poet and playwright Kalidasa, writing in the 5th century A.D., thus gracefully described the blossoming asoka tree in a royal garden, a setting for one of his plays. In Kalidasa's time, worshipers brought the golden branches of this showy tree to decorate their temples, as they do even today.

The temple pictured here, Bodh Gaya [bùd gə yä′], can also be seen as "a bride with many ornaments." Clusters of carvings embellish its massive tower, repeating the same details over and over again like some ornate floral arrangement or lavish wedding cake.

Earlier Gupta temples were rather small, square buildings with flat roofs. During the golden age of the Gupta period, architects emphasized the importance of the small sacred space within by creating an imposing superstructure outside.

Although Gupta rulers had returned to Hinduism, many people remained Buddhist. Architects of the Gupta period designed both Hindu and Buddhist temples.

Bodh Gaya is a Buddhist shrine built at the place of the Buddha's enlightenment in northeastern India. The site is considered holy by Hindus as well. In fact, one Hindu sect worships Buddha as an incarnation of the Hindu god Vishnu.

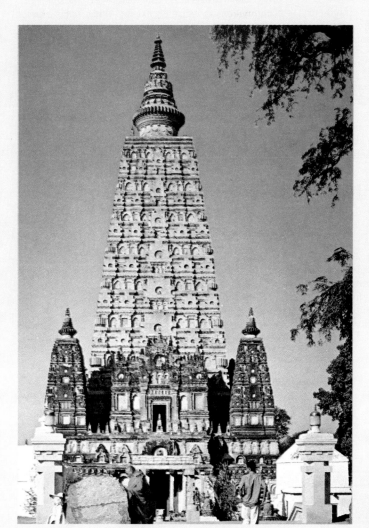

A Buddhist monk in orange-yellow robes at Bodh Gaya, one of the holiest places of Buddhism. The temple was built in the 600s and embellished over many centuries. The Buddha is said to have attained enlightenment as he sat under a Bodhi tree at this site.

Ask students to compare the Gupta temple with the Parthenon in the "Highlights of Civilization" feature for Chapter 4. What similarities and differences do they notice? (Similarities include carved-stone construction, the use of columns, and the buildings' purpose as a center for pilgrimages or processions; differences include the simplicity of style and human scale of the Parthenon as compared with the massive ornateness of the Bodh Gaya. Students may note also that the pillars of the Parthenon are freestanding and that those of the Bodh Gaya are mostly attached.)

Answers to Test Yourself

Key Terms, People, and Places
The key terms, people, and places tested here were introduced in the chapter sections and reviewed in the Section Reviews. For definitions see the page references at the appropriate Section Reviews. Also see the Glossary and Biographical Dictionary.

Main Ideas
The main ideas tested here were introduced in the sections of this chapter and reviewed in the Section Reviews. For answers to these questions, see the appropriate Section Reviews.

Critical Thinking
1. Nomads move their herds to forage. As permanent settlers the Aryans could only use the land they lived on, which might limit the size of their herds and reduce their food supply. This could force the Aryans to supplement their diet with grains and vegetables, which they would be able to raise as permanent settlers.
2. The speaker assumes that the Guptas were not advanced enough to have developed these skills on their own. The speaker assumes that other groups of people made these achievements in astronomy and medicine.

CHAPTER 7 REVIEW

Section Summaries

Section 1
Geography shaped history in India.
The Indian subcontinent was isolated from the rest of Asia in ancient times. Mountain passes, however, allowed small bands of invaders to enter the northern plains and settle there. In addition, two great river systems provided fertile soil for the development of civilization.

Section 2
Many features of Indian life date from ancient times.
Aryans invaded India from the northwest in about 1500 B.C., defeating the more civilized Dravidians and establishing a civilization that would last some 1,000 years. Hinduism, based on the belief of a single supreme power with many faces, spread and became the dominant religion of India. To preserve their power, the Aryans established a rigid caste system. Eventually, Siddhartha Gautama rejected the rigidity of Hinduism and as the Buddha, preached the religion of the Middle Way, which became known as Buddhism.

Section 3
Strong rulers built empires in India.
Chandragupta Maurya united northern India under the Mauryan dynasty. His grandson, Emperor Asoka, brought peace and encouraged Buddhism in the Mauryan Empire. Following the decline of the Mauryans, a series of invaders took command in India and introduced new ideas.

Section 4
Gupta rule launched a golden age.
The Gupta Empire supported a prosperous India. Gupta contributions to civilization include the numerals used in many modern cultures, the decimal system, and advances in chemistry, astronomy, and medicine. Writers and artists also made their own important contributions to Indian civilization. Under the Guptas Indian culture spread throughout Southeast Asia. Eventually invasion by the Huns brought an end to the Gupta Empire, and progress in India slowed to a halt.

Test Yourself

Key Terms, People, and Places
Identify the significance of each of the following:

Section 1
a. subcontinent
b. Himalayan Mountains
c. Ganges River
d. monsoons

Section 2
a. Hinduism
b. reincarnation
c. caste system
d. epics
e. Siddhartha Gautama
f. Buddhism

Section 3
a. Chandragupta Maurya
b. Asoka
c. Peshawar
d. Tamils

Section 4
a. Guptas

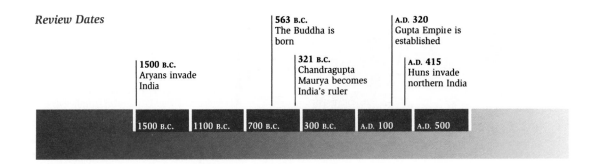

Review Dates

| | 563 B.C.
The Buddha is born | A.D. 320
Gupta Empire is established |
| 1500 B.C.
Aryans invade India | 321 B.C.
Chandragupta Maurya becomes India's ruler | A.D. 415
Huns invade northern India |

| 1500 B.C. | 1100 B.C. | 700 B.C. | 300 B.C. | A.D. 100 | A.D. 500 |

Main Ideas

Section 1
1. List the geographical barriers that separated India from its neighbors.
2. What part did the passes of the Himalaya and Hindu Kush mountains play in the invasions of India? How did river valleys affect the settlement of India?
3. What are the special problems of India's climate?

Section 2
1. How did the lifestyle of the Aryans clash with the lifestyle of the native Dravidians?
2. By what names do Hindus refer to God? Identify some of God's characteristics.
3. What drove the Aryans to develop the caste system?
4. How did the Aryans make use of the Sanskrit alphabet? What importance does Sanskrit have today?
5. What Hindu practices did the Buddha believe clashed with the spirit of the Middle Way? With what did the Buddha replace these objectionable practices?

Section 3
1. Why did Asoka encourage peace in his empire? How did Buddhism affect the way Asoka reigned?
2. In what way did the Kushans influence change in Buddhist worship?
3. What goods did the Romans trade to India? What Indian goods did the Romans receive in exchange?

Section 4
1. What factors made India strong and prosperous under the Guptas?
2. In what fields did the Guptas make significant achievements? List some of their accomplishments.
3. What Asian countries were the most influenced by Indian culture? How did Indian influence affect these other cultures?
4. How did India contribute to its own decline after the Gupta dynasty disappeared?

Critical Thinking

1. Predicting Effects What change in diet might the nomadic Aryans, who raised cattle, have been forced to make upon their becoming permanent settlers in India's river valleys?

2. Identifying Assumptions What assumptions might this speaker be making in the following statement: "I'm amazed that the Guptas knew so much about astronomy and medicine."

Chapter Skills and Activities

Practicing Study and Research Skills

Translating Information from One Medium to Another
Study the map on page 127 entitled "The Spread of Buddhism." Using the information provided in the map, write a paragraph that describes the spread of Buddhism throughout Asia. Your paragraph should include the following:
1. the dates for which the map shows the spread of Buddhism
2. the point from which the spread of Buddhism began
3. the directions and paths of Buddhism's spread
4. the countries that Buddhism reached

Linking Past and Present
Both Hinduism, believed to be the oldest world religion, and Buddhism still have very large followings, including the young Buddhist monk above. Consult a current almanac or encyclopedia to find out how many people in the modern world are Hindu and how many people are Buddhist.

Learning History Through Maps
Referring to the map of India on page 118, locate Pataliputra, the center of the Mauryan Empire. Why was this a good location for a capital city?

CRITICAL THINKING QUESTION LEVEL 1. easy; 2. average

Answers to Chapter Skills and Activities

Practicing Study and Research Skills
Sample answer: Buddhism spread throughout much of Asia between 500 B.C. and A.D. 1250. From Kapilavastu, the birthplace of the Buddha, the religion fanned outward in all directions. West from this point, Buddhism reached through Nepal and northern India into Afghanistan and Pakistan. From Peshawar near the Indus River, the religion crossed through Asia north of India and stretched northeast into Mongolia. Joining with an eastern path from Kapilavastu, this path from Peshawar continued into China, Korea, and Japan. From Kapilavastu Buddhism spread northeast into Tibet and south through southern India and Sri Lanka. A southeastern movement from Kapilavastu brought Buddhism through Burma into Southeast Asia, Malaysia, Sumatra, Borneo, Java, and Bali.

Linking Past and Present
Students should look under "Religion" in an encyclopedia or world almanac to find the current population figures of Hindus and Buddhists. In the late 1980s the Hindu population was estimated to be about 647 million; the Buddhist population was estimated to be about 307 million.

Learning History Through Maps
Sample answer: Patiliputra was located at the junction of three major rivers: the Ganges, the Gogra, and the Jumna. These rivers provided good routes to much of northern India and to the Bay of Bengal, making trade convenient. The fertile river valleys were good places for the Mauryans to raise crops, since they provided rich soil and water.

Chapter

8 China Reaches a Golden Age

OVERVIEW

This chapter focuses on the achievements of four great dynasties in expanding Chinese territory, developing a unique culture, and reaching a golden age.

PLANNING CHART

Section	Text Pages	Key Concept	Suggested Teaching Time
1 Geography helps explain China's early development.	135–138	Chinese civilization developed from three distinct river valley cultures that were isolated by natural barriers from the outer world.	One day **More time?** Use *Overhead Transparency 15.* **Less time?** Teach Section 1 combined with Section 2. For homework the night before beginning the chapter, have students make outline maps of China on which they label external and internal geographic barriers.
2 The Zhou dynasty ruled longest in China.	138–142	China's longest-ruling dynasty was so marked by frequent clashes between nobles that, to ensure stability, a system of choosing officials by their ability began.	One day **More time?** Use *Source Reading 8A.*
3 The Qin and Han dynasties united China.	142–144	Strong governments expanded Chinese territory and reached out to trade with Rome and India.	One day **More time?** Use *Overhead Transparency 16.*
4 The Tang dynasty gave China a golden age.	144–146	Wise leaders encouraged education and literature in China's golden age.	One day **More time?** Use *Source Reading 8B.*

ANCILLARIES

Materials that may be used with this chapter to reinforce, reteach, enrich, and assess learning are pictured on the following pages.

Teacher's Resource File

ACTIVITIES

GENERAL WORKSHEET
Chapter 8, Section 1

In this worksheet you will review the ways in which China's geography influenced its history.

The Influence of China's Geography

Part A
Use information from the text to complete each of the following sentences.

1. Outside cultures had little influence on the development of Chinese civilization **because**

2. The Chinese called their country the Middle Kingdom **because**

3. The Great Wall was built in the northern part of the country **because**

4. The people of southern China were more likely to be traders **because**

Part B
Only three of the four terms in each group are related in some way. Circle the term that does not belong and explain in a sentence how the other terms are related.

1. Himalayas · plateau of Tibet · Xi River · salt marshes

2. loess · Huang River · wheat · deserts

3. harbor · South China Sea · dikes · Xi River

4. jungles · Mongolia · nomads · invaders

Section 1 Activity, p. 41

GENERAL WORKSHEET
Chapter 8, Section 2

In this worksheet you will review the many achievements of the Zhou period.

The Zhou Dynasty

For each statement below, write two or three sentences that support or provide details for that statement.

1. The power of the Zhou rulers weakened as the feudal system in China began to disintegrate.

2. A wide disparity developed during the Zhou period between the rich nobles and the common people.

3. One legacy of the Zhou dynasty was the Chinese civil service system.

4. Increased trade during the Zhou dynasty led to the growth of towns and advances in art.

5. The turmoil of the Zhou period gave rise to two major schools of philosophy that greatly influenced Chinese society.

Section 2 Activity, p. 42

GENERAL WORKSHEET
Chapter 8, Section 3

In this worksheet you will review the achievements of the Qin and Han dynasties.

The Qin and Han Dynasties

Part A
Write Q if the statement refers to an event that occurred during the Qin dynasty; write H if it refers to an event during the Han dynasty.

1. ___ the establishment of the caravan trading route known as the Silk Road
2. ___ the construction of a vast network of roads connecting the different regions of China
3. ___ the invention of paper
4. ___ the introduction of Buddhism into China
5. ___ the completion of the Great Wall of China
6. ___ the invention of the yoke for draft animals
7. ___ a decree ordering the destruction of the writings of Confucius
8. ___ the compilation of a comprehensive Chinese history

Part B
Write the letter of each effect next to its cause.

Causes
1. ___ completion of the Great Wall
2. ___ construction of extensive road network
3. ___ contact with Kushan Empire in India
4. ___ establishment of Silk Road
5. ___ invention of yoke
6. ___ order to destroy Confucian writings

Effects
a. alienation of the educated class
b. alienation of the working class
c. introduction of Buddhism
d. expansion in trade outside the empire
e. increase in trade inside the empire
f. more efficient farming

Section 3 Activity, p. 43

GENERAL WORKSHEET
Chapter 8, Section 4

In this worksheet you will review the achievements of China's Golden Age.

China's Golden Age

Write T if the statement is true and F if it is false. On the lines below, rewrite each false statement to make it true.

1. ___ Although he expanded Chinese territory to the south, the emperor Taizong was never able to push back nomad invaders from the north.
2. ___ Taizong believed that reducing expenses, lowering taxes, and employing honest officials were the best ways to stop crime.
3. ___ Like other emperors before him, Taizong respected the ideas of the Mandate of Heaven.
4. ___ Only wealthy candidates could afford to participate in civil service examinations.
5. ___ The civil service examinations were structured to allow people to advance to higher government posts.
6. ___ Because of the content of Chinese civil service examinations, Chinese officials had difficulty adjusting to changing technology and new ideas.
7. ___ Although the Chinese invented block printing, they used it only to make paper money and printed playing cards.
8. ___ Chinese poetry of the Tang period had wide appeal because of its precise rhyming scheme.

Section 4 Activity, p. 44

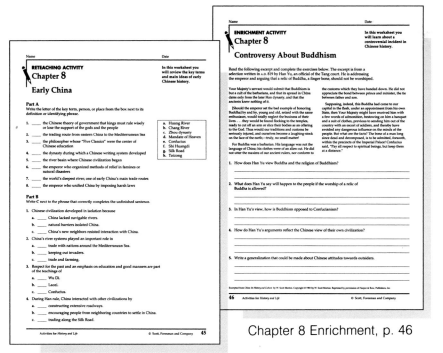

RETEACHING ACTIVITY
Chapter 8

In this worksheet you will review the key terms and main ideas of early Chinese history.

Early China

Part A
Write the letter of the key term, person, or place from the box next to its definition or identifying phrase.

1. ___ the Chinese theory of government that kings must rule wisely or lose the support of the gods and the people
2. ___ the trading route from eastern China to the Mediterranean Sea
3. ___ the philosopher whose "Five Classics" were the center of Chinese education
4. ___ the dynasty during which a Chinese writing system developed
5. ___ the river basin where Chinese civilization began
6. ___ the emperor who organized methods of relief in famines or natural disasters
7. ___ the world's deepest river; one of early China's main trade routes
8. ___ the emperor who unified China by imposing harsh laws

a. Huang River
b. Chang River
c. Zhou dynasty
d. Mandate of Heaven
e. Confucius
f. Shi Huangdi
g. Silk Road
h. Taizong

Part B
Write C next to the phrase that correctly completes the unfinished sentence.

1. Chinese civilization developed in isolation because
   a. ___ China lacked navigable rivers.
   b. ___ natural barriers isolated China.
   c. ___ China's new neighbors resisted interaction with China.
2. China's river systems played an important role in
   a. ___ trade with nations around the Mediterranean Sea.
   b. ___ keeping out invaders.
   c. ___ trade and farming.
3. Respect for the past and an emphasis on education and good manners are part of the teachings of
   a. ___ Wu Di.
   b. ___ Laozi.
   c. ___ Confucius.
4. During Han rule, China interacted with other civilizations by
   a. ___ constructing extensive roadways.
   b. ___ encouraging people from neighboring countries to settle in China.
   c. ___ trading along the Silk Road.

Chapter 8 Reteaching, p. 45

ENRICHMENT ACTIVITY
Chapter 8

In this worksheet you will learn about a controversial incident in Chinese history.

Controversy About Buddhism

Read the following excerpt and complete the exercises below. The excerpt is from a selection written in A.D. 819 by Han Yu, an official of the Tang court. He is addressing the emperor and arguing that a relic of Buddha, a finger bone, should not be worshiped.

Your Majesty's servant would submit that Buddhism is but a cult of the barbarians, and that its spread in China dates only from the later Han dynasty, and that the ancients knew nothing of it.

[Should the emperor set the bad example of honoring Buddha] by and by, young and old, seized with the same enthusiasm, would totally neglect the business of their lives. . . . they would be found flocking to the temples, ready to cut off an arm or slice their bodies as an offering to the God. Thus would our traditions and customs be seriously injured, and ourselves become a laughing-stock on the face of the earth;—truly, no small matter!

For Buddha was a barbarian. His language was not the language of China; his clothes were of an alien cut. He did not utter the maxims of our ancient rulers, nor conform to the customs which they have handed down. He did not appreciate the bond between prince and minister, the tie between father and son.

Supposing, indeed, that this Buddha had come to our capital in the flesh, under an appointment from his own State, then Your Majesty might have received him with a few words of admonition, bestowing on him a banquet and a suit of clothes, previous to sending him out of the country with an escort of soldiers, and thereby have avoided any dangerous influence on the minds of the people. But what are the facts? The bone of a man long since dead and decomposed, is to be admitted, forsooth, within the precincts of the Imperial Palace! Confucius said, "Pay all respect to spiritual beings, but keep them at a distance."

1. How does Han Yu view Buddha and the religion of Buddhism?

2. What does Han Yu say will happen to the people if the worship of a relic of Buddha is allowed?

3. In Han Yu's view, how is Buddhism opposed to Confucianism?

4. How do Han Yu's arguments reflect the Chinese view of their own civilization?

5. Write a generalization that could be made about Chinese attitudes towards outsiders.

Chapter 8 Enrichment, p. 46

Teacher's Resource File

GEOGRAPHY SKILLS

Chapter 8 Geography
Worksheet/Map, pp. 17–18

Chapter 8 Map Lesson, p. 90

TESTS

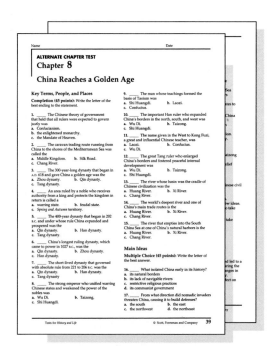

Chapter Test, pp. 37–38

Alternate Chapter Test, pp. 39–40

Other Optional Ancillaries

WORKBOOK

Section 1 Worksheet, p. 27

Section 2 Worksheet, p. 28

Section 3 Worksheet, p. 29

Section 4 Worksheet, p. 30

SOURCE READINGS

Source Reading 8A
Source Reading 8B

TEST GENERATOR

40 multiple-choice questions for Chapter 8

OVERHEAD TRANSPARENCIES

Overhead Transparency 15
Overhead Transparency 16

8

China Reaches a Golden Age

1027 B.C. – A.D. 907

1100 B.C.

1027 B.C.   Zhou dynasty is established

551 B.C.   Confucius is born

202 B.C   Hans begin 400-year reign

100 B.C.

A.D. 100

Astronauts orbiting Earth can easily see many of the planet's natural features. With the unaided eye, however, they can recognize only a few humanmade features. One humanmade feature astronauts might see from space is the Great Wall of China. Extending for about 1,500 miles, the Great Wall of China is the longest wall in the world. The Chinese began building the Wall in the 3rd century B.C., raising it as a defensive barrier. They were most concerned about warlike nomads, related to the Huns, who periodically attacked China's northern borders.

Building the Wall was a cruel task. Hundreds of thousands of men and women were forced to labor, cutting and moving blocks of stone, hoisting them into place, and fitting them into the Wall. So many people died during the construction that the Chinese say that every block cost a human life. When complete, the Wall was 40 to 50 feet high and its base measured 15 to 30 feet thick. In some places it consisted of three different walls, built one behind the other for better defense. Every few hundred yards were tall watch towers where guards could look across the countryside for signs of invaders.

The Wall helped ensure China's safety from invasion. Over the centuries, various rulers have ordered repairs or improvements to maintain the Wall, a restoration project that continues to this day. Now, however, the Wall is not being rebuilt as a defense, but instead as a symbol of China's strength. The Great Wall also represents China's uniqueness as a culture, set apart from all other cultures of the world.

The course of Chinese history described in this chapter covers about 2,000 years. During this long period, Chinese culture developed and took its distinctive shape. To this day its essential character remains. Over the centuries, China produced thought-provoking philosophies, great poetry, and beautiful paintings. The

Visitors make their way toward a watch tower of the Great Wall of China. The Wall, begun in the 3rd century B.C., remains a popular attraction both for the Chinese people and for visitors from around the world.

Chinese developed the first civil service system in the world, and their country was the birthplace of a number of advanced technologies, such as printing and papermaking, which were not introduced in the West until thousands of years later.

Reading Preview

In this chapter you will read how the interplay between geography and history led to the development of China's unique culture.

1. *Geography helps explain China's early development.*
2. *The Zhou dynasty ruled longest in China.*
3. *The Qin and Han dynasties united China.*
4. *The Tang dynasty gave China a golden age.*

BACKGROUND Following are the Pinyin names in this chapter and, in parentheses, the same names with the Wade-Giles spelling that students may occasionally encounter: Shi Huangdi (Shi Huang-ti), Qin Ling Mountains (Tsinling Mountains), Huang River (Hwang Ho), Chang River (Yangtze River), Xi River (Hsi River), Zhou dynasty (Chou dynasty), Laozi (Lao-tse), Qin dynasty (Ch'in dynasty), Wu Di (Wu Ti), Taizong (T'ai Tsung), Li Bo (Li Po).

 Geography helps explain China's early development.

In every country, geography influences how people live. You read in Chapter 2 that the valley of the Huang River (also called the Yellow River) was the cradle of Chinese civilization. As with many of the world's early civilizations, development was spurred by the ready supply of water, the rich farmland, and the transportation routes provided by a major river. However, China was unlike the other early civilizations in that its natural borders and vast distance from other centers of culture allowed it to develop essentially in isolation for thousands of years.

Natural borders isolated China.

China's borders of seawater, jungles, mountains,

135

1 *Lesson Plan*
Essential Learning Objectives
Students will learn to:
- discuss why China chose to increase its natural isolation from its neighbors.
- describe the societies that developed along China's three major river systems.

1 FOCUS AND MOTIVATE

Help students familiarize themselves with China's location in Asia by directing them to compare the map on page 136 of this section with the Atlas maps of Asia on pages 794–795. Have students identify the natural barriers that form political borders between China and its neighbors today.

2 TEACH

- Remind students that India also was invaded by Hun tribes around the end of the 5th century and that a period of self-imposed isolation there brought about decline. Discuss the reaction of the Chinese to these similar invasions. (Chinese culture flourished, producing significant achievements in art, literature, philosophy, and technology.)

- List on the chalkboard details of the geography, climate, agriculture, and trade in each river valley. Discuss how ways of living might have varied in the three areas.

GUIDED PRACTICE

Have students use the map of China on page 136 to write descriptions of the geographical areas through which China's three major rivers flow. Students should use the scale of miles to determine approximate distances from the source to the mouth of each river. Also for guided practice:

 Overhead Transparency 15

Ancient China

🌐 **MAP STUDY** Into what seas do the Huang, Chang, and Xi rivers flow? What direction are these seas from the rivers? Through which coastal cities do the Chang and the Xi rivers pass to get to the sea?

and deserts are natural barriers that have isolated China and hampered invaders from other parts of the world. Until the 19th century, the wide salt marshes on the seacoast and the lack of natural harbors stopped invaders from the east. To the south, the thick jungles and steep mountains of Southeast Asia also made a natural border that was difficult to penetrate. To the west, the towering Himalayas and the rugged plateau of Tibet, more than 10,000 feet above sea level, protected China from invasion. Use the map above to locate the major land features that form China's borders.

The isolation of China led the Chinese to think of their country as the center of the world. Referring to themselves as inhabitants of the Middle Kingdom, they considered the nomadic people who lived in the dry lands to the north and west of China to be barbarians. Find these lands, including

Manchuria, Mongolia, and Xinjiang [shin′jyäng′] on the map. The Chinese scornfully named these vast neighboring regions the Outer Kingdoms.

China built defenses along its northern border.

For many thousands of years, the nomadic tribes of the Outer Kingdoms were the only people ever successful at invading China's self-contained world. In fact, the Chinese built the Great Wall exclusively to thwart these invaders. These tribes, who were directly related to the Huns who overran Europe around the 5th century A.D., roamed the deserts and dry grasslands northwest of China. In these dry regions, there was little farming. The nomads moved their settlements each season as their herds grazed on the tough grasses that grew in scattered patches throughout the region. In dry years when

ANSWER TO MAP STUDY Yellow Sea, East China Sea, and South China Sea; Northeast, east, and southeast; Shanghai and Guangzhou [Canton]

little grass was available for the herds, the tribes would begin to push south into the fertile valleys.

As you have learned, the Chinese thought of themselves as superior to their neighbors to the north. They considered the nomads to be backward because they did not farm or build cities. However, because these outsiders posed such an obvious threat, China developed a guarded culture that was focused inward, with a distinct perception that all other cultures were on the outside. This inward focus allowed China to flourish for thousands of years, producing monumental achievements in literature, art, philosophy, and technology.

Chinese civilization developed in three river valleys.

Within China natural features isolated different parts of the country from each other. The rough, hilly land made it difficult to build roads across China. Mountain ranges such as the Qin Ling [chin-ling'] naturally separate China into parts. North of the Qin Ling Mountains is the **Huang River** basin, the birthplace of China's civilization, and south of the Qin Ling Mountains are the **Chang** (or Yangtze) **River** basin and the **Xi** [shē] **River** basin. Find these river basins on the map on page 136. Each of these regions has played an important role in China's early development.

Huang River. As you learned in Chapter 2, the Huang River meanders through the loess-filled plains of northern China. The fine, dusty, yellow loess, which the river deposits along its flood plain, makes good soil for farming. Because the region is fairly cool and dry, millet and wheat are the most important crops.

Irrigation is important in the Huang River basin, as is control for periodic floods. A centralized government developed early in this region, partly because of the need to maintain canals for irrigation and dikes for the prevention of floods. The river is shallow and unsuitable for navigation by large boats, and at its mouth are salt marshes. As a result, this river never developed as a trade route.

Chang River. The Chang River flows through the rough, hilly land of southern China. This region is relatively wet, because monsoon winds from the Pacific Ocean bring large amounts of rain. During the wet season, the numerous bodies of water that make up the lake plains expand. These lakes, streams, and marshes ultimately flow into the Chang, making it a river that varies greatly in width. The Chang is also the world's deepest river. It is navigable for 600 miles inland, and early on it became one of China's main trade routes.

Because of the warm, wet climate and the extensive seasonal flooding, the Chang River basin became an important rice-growing region. The Chinese developed elaborate irrigation systems to channel the flood waters into their rice paddies.

Xi River. In the southernmost part of China is the Xi Valley. It is isolated from the rest of China by rough hills. Like the Chang River basin, the Xi River basin has a warm, wet climate suitable for rice farming. However, the Xi basin is warmer than the Chang basin and thus is arable year-round. The point where the Xi River empties into the South China Sea is one of the few natural harbors in China. Early in China's history, the villages near the river's mouth developed as trading centers.

The Huang is the second longest river in China—after the Chang. The Chinese ship above, called a junk, is sailing on the Huang River.

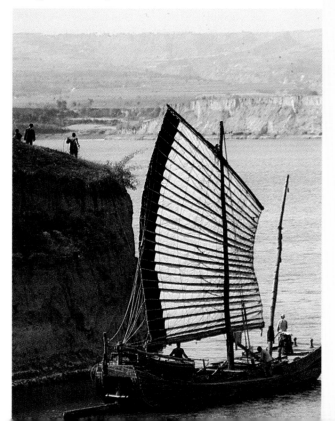

ASSESS
What prevented invaders from entering China by sea? (salt marshes and the lack of harbors)

OPTIONAL RETEACHING
Have students list in one column factors that have isolated the Chinese from external contact with other nations. In a second column, list those internal features that have separated different parts of China. Students should grasp that different ways of life also can set up barriers between people.

OPTIONAL ENRICHMENT
1. Have students do research to find out what grains are grown in China's three river valleys today. (average)
2. Assign groups of students to compare the populations of the three areas of China today. Names of the major cities and descriptions of their geographical locations and major industries should be included. (challenging)

INDEPENDENT PRACTICE/ HOMEWORK
Assign the Section Review, Activities page 41, or Workbook page 27.

CLOSURE
Summarize the lesson by telling students that much of China's cultural development and its relationships with other nations can be traced to its geography. Isolated from contact with foreigners by natural barriers, China's leaders built the Great Wall to further ensure its security from invasion.

Identify

Key Terms, People, and Places are defined on pages indicated in parentheses. Also see the Glossary and Biographical Dictionary. Huang River (137), Chang River (137), Xi River (137)

Main Ideas

1. salt marshes on the sea coast, steep mountains to the west and to the south, thick jungles to the south
2. China had no natural defense along its northern border. The Chinese considered the nomads to be barbarians.
3. Huang River region is good for growing wheat and millet. Because irrigation and flood control were necessary, government developed here. Chang River region is wet, warm, and good for growing rice. Chang was one of China's early trade routes. Xi River region is wet, warm, and arable year-round. At the river's mouth is one of China's few natural harbors.

Critical Thinking

The nomads might have considered the Chinese to be very isolated and provincial. They also might have felt superior to them in military matters. Most Chinese probably viewed the nomads as ignorant barbarians.

2 Lesson Plan

Essential Learning Objective

Students will learn to give examples of important social structures, lasting achievements, and philosophies that developed during Zhou rule.

Section 1 Review

Identify Huang River, Chang River, Xi River

Main Ideas
1. Describe the natural borders that isolated China.
2. Why did the Chinese build defenses along their northern border?
3. Contrast the three rivers that have been important in the history of China.

Critical Thinking

Recognizing Values: The nomadic tribes who lived north and west of China were fierce warriors. Mounted on horseback, they could easily outmaneuver the Chinese soldiers who rode in chariots. They also had trading contacts with people as far away as Greece and present-day Iran. How do you think these nomads and the Chinese felt about each other? Support your answer with evidence.

---

2 The Zhou dynasty ruled longest in China.

As you learned in Chapter 2, the Shang dynasty arose about 1500 B.C., centered in the Huang River basin on the North China Plain. Although the early Shang kings had ruled justly and wisely, the later kings were corrupt. This weakened Shang rule, and the Shangs were eventually conquered by a group of people called the **Zhou** [jō]. The Zhou originally were a seminomadic people who settled in the Wei River Valley and adopted Chinese ways. In 1027 B.C. the Zhou overran the Shang capital and laid claim to the kingdom.

Many changes took place during the Zhou period (1027–256 B.C.)

The Zhou dynasty lasted for almost 800 years. This period was characterized by many political, military, and social changes.

Political changes. During the first 250 years or so of the Zhou dynasty, the kingdom was made up of more than 1,000 feudal [fyü′dl] states. A **feudal state** is an area ruled by a noble who gets his authority from the king. In return, the noble owes the king allegiance and must raise armies to help

BACKGROUND In 771 B.C. some dissatisfied nobles joined together and assassinated the Zhou king. Although they put a new Zhou king on the throne, the nobles allowed the king little power. In effect, the king's role was reduced to that of a high

---

keep order and to protect the kingdom. At first, the nobles were loyal to the Zhou king. Toward the end of this period, however, the nobles began using their soldiers to fight among themselves and to compete with the king for power. The disintegration of feudal allegiances was the beginning of the downfall of the Zhou rule.

The period from 771 B.C. to 456 B.C. is called the *Spring and Autumn* period, named after a document that chronicles the history of these times. During this period the Chinese conquered the Chang River basin. Partly as a result of this expansion, strong nobles continued to consolidate their power. In doing so they took control over the lands of the weaker nobles. Thus, the number of feudal states decreased, but those that survived increased in power. The Zhou king was less and less able to keep the peace.

Military changes. From 456 B.C. to 256 B.C., the nobles were constantly battling with one another. In this period, sometimes called the Era of Warring States, there were advances in military techniques and technologies. The Chinese invented catapults to break down the walls of enemy towns. They adopted tactics developed by their nomadic neighbors, such as employing small groups of archers to stage surprise attacks.

Around this time the Chinese also began to make weapons of cast iron. These new iron weapons were stronger and held their cutting edge longer than the older weapons, which were made of bronze. The new military techniques made warfare extremely fierce and further weakened the Zhou's control over China.

Social changes. The political and military changes that occurred during the Zhou dynasty spurred changes throughout Chinese society. A wide disparity developed between the rich nobles and the common people, a group that included the Chinese peasants and laborers. The rich lived in large, glorious homes with courtyards and gardens. They held huge banquets that were feasts of the five flavors—sweet, sour, salty, spicy, and bitter—and spent their leisure time hunting, fencing, and participating in archery contests.

The poor, in contrast, lived in mud huts with thatched roofs and subsisted on rice or millet, a small, nutritious seed, depending upon where they

priest who performed state religious rituals similar to those performed by the Shang kings.

lived. Many farmers found it hard to make a living, and their farms were often too small to produce crop surpluses for use when the harvests were bad. Because the family unit was very important in Chinese culture, family members stayed together. As the population grew during the Zhou period, more and more people had to be supported from the harvests of farms that were too small.

When the farmers were not working their own small plots of land, they were often forced to labor on projects for the local nobles or on government building projects. These projects included the building of dikes, the digging of irrigation canals, or the construction of walls and forts for defense.

The Zhou period was characterized by lasting achievements.

The 800 years of the Zhou rule are sometimes considered the most important in Chinese history in terms of cultural development. This era is often called the classical period because many basic elements of Chinese civilization developed during that time. Important developments occurred in the areas of government, trade, and the arts.

Government. During the Zhou era, the Chinese combined some very old theories of government with newer ideas. The Chinese, like the Egyptians, had always believed that their rulers were divine. Unlike the Egyptians, however, the Chinese limited the power of their kings. According to the Chinese theory of government, called the **Mandate of Heaven**, all rulers were expected to govern justly and to look after the well-being of the people. If a king did not do this, he would no longer have the support and favor of the gods and could be overthrown by the people.

When the Zhous came to power, they invoked the Mandate of Heaven, claiming that they had the right to take over because the Shangs had not ruled justly and thus had lost the support of the gods. Throughout Chinese history, the Mandate of Heaven has been a key concept. It is the basis of the belief that revolution, the violent overthrow of a government, is sometimes necessary and right.

Fierce competition among strong nobles led to an important innovation in the Chinese government. This innovation was the idea of choosing government officials based on their intelligence and

This bronze wine vessel, with its complicated designs of animal forms, dates from the Zhou dynasty and illustrates the exquisite detail in Chinese art.

ability to make wise decisions rather than on their social status. In time, this led to a Chinese civil service system that lasted into the 20th century.

Trade. Trade grew during the Zhou dynasty, especially within the kingdom itself. The goods traded included jade ornaments, bronze mirrors and vessels, iron tools, silks, furs, and furniture.

Along with increased trade, towns grew in size and number. Many people who settled in the growing urban areas became merchants or artisans. Skilled workers who practiced the same craft organized guilds, or associations, to help each other and to set standards of quality. Some of their finest works have survived to this day, and are prized as works of art throughout the world.

Art. The advanced state of craftwork during the Zhou dynasty led the Chinese to produce some of the world's finest art. Their achievements include handsome bronze vases, intricate lacquerware, and beautiful pieces of carved jade—a semiprecious

Remind students that under the first dynasty, the Shangs, the king was a religious leader who held political control over only a small area. Strong nobles ruled their own lands and fought among themselves. Direct students to look for changes in these ways under Zhou rule.

2 TEACH

- On the chalkboard, identify the three periods of Zhou rule, emphasizing political, military, and social changes. Students should grasp that increased power meant greater wealth for the strongest nobles while growing numbers of poor were in ever worsening conditions.

- Discuss the achievements of the classical period in government, art, and writing. Point out that extensive internal trade supplied goods for the nobles and enabled the growth of towns as crafts and trade centers.

- Clarify the similarities and differences between the teachings of Confucius and Laozi, emphasizing the importance of each in reflecting the values of Chinese culture.

GUIDED PRACTICE

Ask students to suggest reasons why selecting government officials according to their abilities was a good idea. (better government and increased political stability) stone that varies in color from pure white to emerald green with all shades and streaks of color in between. The important Chinese philosopher Confucius, whom you will read more about later in this section, was once asked why the Chinese liked jade so much. His reply follows:

> It is because, ever since the olden days, wise men have seen in jade all the different virtues. It is soft, smooth, and shining, like kindness; it is hard, fine, and strong, like intelligence; its edges seem sharp but do not cut, like justice; . . . the stains in it, which are not hidden and which add to its beauty, are like truthfulness.

The present Chinese writing system was developed during the Zhou period.

Chinese is believed to be the oldest living language in the world. It is called a tonal language, because words may be differentiated not only by consonant and vowel sounds, but also by their intonation patterns. For example, the sound *fu* means "rich," "store up," or "not" depending on whether the speaker uses a rising, falling, or level tone.

A writing system has been in use in China for more than 3,500 years. The first Chinese writing system, like the Egyptian hieroglyphs, developed from picture writing. However, unlike the Egyp-

Chinese Writing

Calligraphy is the art of beautiful handwriting. In Chinese calligraphy a brush is used. Shown above is the character for *yung,* which means "forever" or "eternity." This character is considered a good test of the calligrapher's art because it makes use of the basic calligraphic strokes. The separate strokes are shown below. This writing cannot be done by left-handed people, so all Chinese are trained to write with their right hands.

tians, who eventually adopted a true alphabet, the Chinese continued to used one symbol for each word or idea. By the end of the Zhou rule, the Chinese writing system was so well developed that it has survived into the present with few changes.

Two important teachers developed influential schools of philosophy.

The Zhou period was a time of great turmoil in China. Many different schools of philosophy arose, each proposing a different solution for ending the chaos. The two most important of these schools, Confucianism, founded by Confucius, and Taoism, founded by Laozi, were founded during this time. These philosophies are a mainstay of Chinese culture, influencing people to this day.

The ideas of Confucius. Kong Fuzi, better known in the West as **Confucius** [kən fyü′shəs], was born in 551 B.C., a few years after the Buddha. Although his goal was to hold high political office, Confucius never reached this goal. However, he did become a great teacher and is revered as one of the most influential figures in all of Chinese history. Unlike the Buddha, Confucius did not seek to escape from the world. Instead, he wanted to find a way for people to be happy in this life on earth.

Confucius taught that human nature is good, not bad, and he believed that if people would think and act properly, most of the world's evils would disappear. His teachings also held that individuals should be tolerant and kind and have respect for older people. In government, he believed that the ruler was like the father in a family. As a father is responsible for the well-being of the family, Confucius taught that a ruler is responsible for the welfare of the people. Confucius also stressed education, good manners, and respect for the past.

His teachings about how people should act toward one another led to a code of politeness. This social code is still the standard of behavior today for people in China and Chinese-influenced societies, such as Korea and Vietnam. The following sayings of Confucius, from a collection called the *Analects*, show his wisdom and understanding of human nature.

A man who has committed a mistake and doesn't correct it is committing another mistake.

He was asked, "What do you think of repaying evil with kindness?" Confucius replied, "Then

FROM THE ARCHIVES The excerpts from *The Analects* are from *Masterpieces of the Orient*, edited by G. L. Anderson (New York: W. W. Norton), pp. 394–399.
Ask students whether or not they think Confucius' sayings

From the Archives

The Analects of Confucius

Confucius (identified here as "the Master") gave the following advice to students and to teachers 2,500 years ago.

The Master said, Learn as if you were following someone whom you could not catch up, as though it were someone you were frightened of losing. (VIII, 17)

The Master said, Respect the young. How do you know that they will not one day be all that you are now? But if a man has reached 40 or 50 and nothing has been heard of him, then I grant there is no need to respect him. (IX, 22)

what are you going to repay kindness with? Repay kindness with kindness, but repay evil with justice."

Confucius did not think of himself primarily as an inventor of new ideas. Instead, he considered his most important role to be to preserve and pass on the ideas of others. Confucius assembled some of the finest Chinese literature from ancient times into a collection of writings known as the "Five Classics." This collection formed the core of Chinese education for more than 2,000 years.

After Confucius's death, his followers combined his teachings with religious ideas about ancestor worship to make a religion called Confucianism [kən fyü′shə niz′əm]. The religion, which is still followed today, places its emphasis on how to have a happy, well-balanced life. Confucianism also instills an admiration for learning and has influenced the Chinese to accord the highest respect to scholars and philosophers.

The ideas of Laozi. Zhou China produced another influential teacher, **Laozi** [lou′dzu′]. Laozi lived around the same time as Confucius. Little is known about him as a person, but Laozi's teachings have formed the basis of a religion known as Taoism [dou′iz′əm]. The word Tao means "way." Taoists believe that those people who follow the way as set out by Laozi will learn the meaning of

apply to students and teachers today and to give their reasons. (Students will probably find the sayings remarkably modern.)

ASSESS

1. What military advances helped warring Chinese nobles? (catapults, archers, iron weapons)
2. How is Chinese writing different from writing using an alphabet? (Chinese has a separate symbol for each word or idea.)

OPTIONAL RETEACHING

Ask students to identify and categorize, from highest to lowest, the status of people in Chinese society during the Zhou period. (the emperor, stronger nobles, weaker nobles, government officials, teachers and philosophers, merchants, artisans, farmers and laborers)

OPTIONAL ENRICHMENT

1. Assign students to find examples of art from the Zhou period. Drawings or tracings accompanied by short descriptions of the art should be prepared. (average)
2. Have students research additional examples of the teachings of Confucius or Laozi. Selections may be presented orally with students giving their interpretation of the meaning of each teaching. (challenging)
3. Also for enrichment:

 Source Reading 8A

INDEPENDENT PRACTICE/ HOMEWORK

Assign the Section Review, Activities page 42, or Workbook page 28.

CLOSURE

Summarize the lesson by telling students that the 800-year rule of the Zhou dynasty, the longest in China's history, was also the period when important aspects of Chinese culture began. The philosophies of Confucius and Laozi had long-lasting influence.

the universe through the secrets of nature.

The religion holds that people should be kind, free from pride, humble, thrifty, and should return an injury with a kindness. In contrast to Confucius, who had stressed the importance of good government, Laozi believed that the less people were governed, the better off they would be.

Over the centuries, Taoism became buried under a blanket of superstition and magic. Many Taoist teachers claimed they had supernatural powers, and sorcery, fortune-telling, and charm-selling came to be important aspects of Taoism. Early Taoists, however, because of their stress on a simple life, nature, and inner peace, made important contributions to Chinese thought. Taoism provided a philosophy that greatly strengthened the Chinese social order. It gave people a sense of internal peace during the Zhou period and during other tumultuous eras of China's long history.

Taoist Symbols

The figure on the left is the basic symbol of Taoism. It is meant to represent the dualism of yin-yang; this is the harmony of male and female, light and dark, active and passive, positive and negative. These opposites were believed by the Chinese to balance one another. The jade ornament on the right shows the Taoist symbol circled by eight trigrams. The meaning of each trigram is explained below. Each trigram is composed of broken lines, representing yin, and/or unbroken lines, representing yang.

heaven	☰	water	☵
earth	☷	fire	☲
thunder	☳	mountain	☶
wind	☴	body of water	☱

BACKGROUND Other sayings of Confucius: A man who brags without shame will find great difficulty in living up to this bragging. A gentleman blames himself, while a common man blames others.

Section 2 Review

Identify Zhou dynasty, feudal state, Mandate of Heaven, Confucius, Laozi

Main Ideas

1. Describe a political, military, and social change that took place during the Zhou period.
2. What were some of the lasting achievements in government, trade, and art from the Zhou period?
3. Describe the Chinese language and the development of the Chinese writing system.
4. What were the main ideas of the Chinese philosophers Confucius and Laozi?

Critical Thinking

Making Hypotheses: Confucius, in stressing the importance of good behavior and concern for the rights of others, once spoke the following words: "We don't know yet how to serve men, how can we know about serving the spirits?" Do you agree or disagree with Confucius' words? Why? How is this statement true in our modern society today? Support your answer.

---

3 The Qin and Han dynasties united China.

As you have read, in the last years of the Zhou dynasty, many of the feudal states were at war with one another. In 256 B.C. the Zhou dynasty fell, and a long power struggle ensued between the kings of several feudal states. The king of the state of Qin [chin] emerged as the most powerful military ruler. He seized control of China in 221 B.C. and began a new dynasty that eventually gave China its name.

The Qin emperor centralized and strengthened China (221–206 B.C.).

Qin rule was short-lived, lasting only until 206 B.C., but during this brief period, the government had absolute control over the people. Only a very able, strong ruler could have brought about such a state of affairs. This ruler called himself **Shi Huangdi** [shėr′hwäng′dē′], a name that means "first supreme emperor."

Shi Huangdi subdued and unified the warring Chinese states by enforcing a single set of harsh laws throughout the new empire. His strict leader-

BACKGROUND The Hans ruled for more than 400 years—from 202 B.C. to A.D. 220. During Han rule, China grew as large and prosperous as the Roman Empire of the same

period. The Han rule was so outstanding that some Chinese today still call themselves "sons of Han."

ship strengthened the central government and weakened the power of the nobles.

Shi Huangdi extended China's boundaries southward, as you can see on the map on page 144. He also connected the different regions of China by building an extensive network of roads throughout the country. To protect the northern and western border areas from the frequent invasions of nomadic tribes, Shi Huangdi added to and joined together several protective walls to make the Great Wall of China. These massive building projects required almost one million laborers and almost half as many soldiers to oversee the construction and keep the laborers from fleeing. The harsh work requirements made many Chinese people chafe under Qin rule.

Shi Huangdi not only alienated the laborers and farmers, he also alienated China's educated class. He considered Confucianism and other moral philosophies of the Zhou period dangerous. Because Confucian literature promoted ideas that weakened the absolute control of the emperor, such as justice, education, and family loyalty, Shi Huangdi ordered that these writings be destroyed. Most Chinese continued to value Confucius' teachings however. Many of these books were hidden away during this time, so that this important body of literature has been preserved.

The Han dynasty extended the boundaries of China (202 B.C.–A.D. 220).

Shortly after the death of Shi Huangdi in 210 B.C., civil war broke out in China. Political intrigue, including the murder of Shi Huangdi's heir, and general discontentment with Qin rule prevented the dynasty from continuing. After eight years of fighting, the ruler of a new dynasty gained control of China. The ruler took the family name of Han because he had once led an army on the Han River.

The most important Han ruler was **Wu Di** [wü′-dē′], who reigned between 140 and 87 B.C. He was a tough leader who drove his soldiers relentlessly. Under Wu Di, the Chinese pushed the encroaching nomads back from the Great Wall and took over part of Korea. Wu Di extended the empire south to Vietnam and west to Central Asia. After making these conquests, he brought an era of peace to most of Asia under Chinese rule. Study the map

BACKGROUND The emperor further eroded nobles' power by dividing China into 36 military provinces, each governed by an official named by the central government. This basic form of government lasted for about 2,000 years until 1912.

The Chinese earthquake detecting device above was invented in A.D. 132. At the slightest tremor, one of the dragons drops a ball to sound a unique alarm.

on page 144 to learn about the growth of China during the Han dynasty.

During Han rule, the Chinese made a number of cultural advances. For example, they invented the yoke, or shoulder collar, for draft animals around 100 B.C. This invention made it possible for farm animals to pull heavier loads. Europeans did not adopt a similar device for another 1,000 years.

By A.D. 100 the Chinese had also invented paper. Around this time they also wrote one of the world's first dictionaries. Finally, during the Han dynasty Chinese scholars compiled a complete history of their civilization. This source is outstanding because it attempts to differentiate between legend and documented facts. Scholars of Chinese history still refer to this text today.

3 *Lesson Plan*

Essential Learning Objectives

Students will learn to:
- evaluate the Qin and Han dynasties.
- discuss the effect of foreign contact on Chinese culture.

1 FOCUS AND MOTIVATE

Ask students to give examples of problems that existed in China at the end of Zhou rule. Guide students to recognize how constant warfare between nobles disrupted society.

2 TEACH

- Under Qin Dynasty (221–206 B.C.) on the chalkboard, list details of the unified China established by Emperor Shi Huangdi. Ask students to tell why many Chinese opposed his policies.

- Under Han Dynasty (202 B.C.–A.D. 220), list details about lands added to China's territory, and its advances in culture and in foreign trade.

GUIDED PRACTICE

On a blank outline map of Asia from the Geography Skills book, have students label and indicate by colors the areas ruled by Rome and by the Hans around A.D. 100. Add the route of the Silk Road. Also for guided practice:

 Overhead Transparency 16

3 ASSESS AND CLOSE

ASSESS

Which dynasty ruled the longest, the Qin or the Han? (Han) How long did each dynasty have power? (Qin, 15 years; Han, 422 years)

OPTIONAL RETEACHING

Ask students to list advances made during Han rule. (yoke, paper, dictionary, factual history) Students should then rank the advances in order of their importance to society.

OPTIONAL ENRICHMENT

Assign a group to research and prepare three parallel time lines illustrating the years of the dynasties that ruled in China and in India at the same time as various leaders ruled in the Roman Empire. Indicate the years during which contact occurred among any of the three. (average)

INDEPENDENT PRACTICE/ HOMEWORK

Assign the Section Review, Activities page 43, or Workbook page 29.

CLOSURE

Tell students that the Qin and Han dynasties made important contributions to Chinese culture. Although his dynasty ended with his death, the system of government established by Shi Huangdi persisted for 2,000 years. Han rule greatly expanded China's borders and trade with other cultures.

Answers to Section 3 Review

Identify

Key Terms, People, and Places are defined on pages indicated in parentheses. Also see the Glossary and Biographical Dictionary.
Shi Huangdi (142), Wu Di (143), Silk Road (144)

Main Ideas

1. It unified China by enforcing laws throughout the empire. Shi Huangdi built an extensive system of roads and extended existing walls to form the Great Wall.

China had contact with other civilizations through trade along the Silk Road.

Growth during Han rule brought China into contact with other peoples. Trade expanded with the boundaries of the empire, and a caravan trading route known as the **Silk Road** was established. This route ran along the Great Wall of China, past the deserts and mountains of Central Asia, all the way to the shores of the Mediterranean Sea. Trace the Silk Road on the map on page 136.

Few caravans completed the entire route. Instead, caravans from China met those from India and the West somewhere near the middle of the route. There they exchanged goods through commercial middlemen from Central Asia and the Middle East. The Chinese traded silks, spices, and exotic furs for wool, gold, and silver from the Roman Empire.

The two groups exchanged not only goods, but also ideas and information. People of the West learned about such fruits as peaches, apricots, and rhubarb from the Chinese. From Central Asian peoples, the Chinese learned about alfalfa, a nutritious horse feed, and grapes. Contact with traders from the Kushan Empire, which you read about in Chapter 7, led to the introduction of Buddhism in China. From the 1st century A.D. onward, this religion spread rapidly in China. Buddhist symbols, such as the lotus flower, became increasingly common in Chinese art.

Section 3 Review

Identify Shi Huangdi, Wu Di, Silk Road

Main Ideas

1. How did the Qin dynasty strengthen the Chinese government?
2. What were some important accomplishments of the Han dynasty?
3. Why was the Silk Road important to Chinese development?

Critical Thinking

Assessing Cause and Effect: As you learned in this chapter, the Han dynasty rulers lifted the Qin dynasty ban on Confucian texts and teachings. What effects did this act likely have? Support your answer with evidence. What assumptions are you making in responding this way?

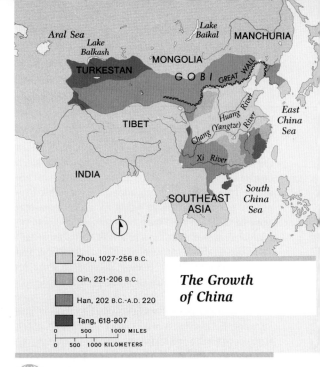

The Growth of China

Zhou, 1027–256 B.C.
Qin, 221–206 B.C.
Han, 202 B.C.–A.D. 220
Tang, 618–907

0   500   1000 MILES
0   500   1000 KILOMETERS

 MAP STUDY Which dynasty was the first to extend China's boundaries north of the Great Wall? Which region did the Tangs acquire to extend its rule westward?

4 The Tang dynasty gave China a golden age.

The glory of the Hans faded in the 3rd century A.D. when strong nobles seized parts of the empire and overthrew the last of the Hans. China was then broken up into little warring kingdoms. Nomad invaders broke through the Great Wall and took control of northern China, forcing many Chinese to flee south to the Chang River basin. China, like India and Europe at the same time, went through a period of great confusion. Science, art, literature, and trade underwent serious decline.

Chinese recovery began in 618, when the **Tang** [täng] **dynasty** came to power. For almost 300 years, the Tangs gave China a golden age in which peace reigned and literature and art flourished. Early Tang rulers repaired the Great Wall of China to help prevent foreign invasion. As a result, a

ANSWER TO MAP STUDY Han dynasty; Turkestan

more stable government developed and trade was allowed to increase. Strong leadership in government, an expanded educational system, and the development of printing all helped cultivate the Chinese golden age under the Tangs.

A strong Tang emperor governed wisely.

A Tang ruler, **Taizong** [tī′dzŭng′], became emperor in 627, when he was only 21 years old. Before becoming the emperor, Taizong had been an able general who united warring factions in China and consolidated the empire under the rule of his father, the first Tang emperor. In his first years on the throne, Taizong pushed back invaders and enlarged the borders of China until it stretched from northern Korea to present-day Afghanistan—about the same distance as that from New York to San Francisco. Use the map on page 144 to study the Chinese expansion during the Tang dynasty.

Taizong also concentrated on the peaceful internal development of China. He worked to set up a strong central government that was both efficient and fair. He established storehouses for grain to provide food during periods of famine, and in regions beset by natural disasters, such as earthquakes and floods, Taizong instituted tax relief.

Taizong did not believe harsh laws were the way to stop crime. He explained that "diminish[ing] expenses, lighten[ing] the taxes, and employ[ing] only honest officials . . . will do more to abolish robbery than the employment of the severest punishments." Like other Chinese rulers, Taizong believed that he ruled with the Mandate from Heaven as long as he governed justly and wisely.

Education strengthened the Chinese government.

Taizong strengthened the Chinese government by improving the country's educational system. From the time of Confucius on, education had an important place in Chinese culture. In fact, government officials were often chosen based on their mastery of classical Chinese texts. Civil service examinations were expanded under the early Tang rulers.

Under Taizong, many schools organized especially to train students for the civil service examinations were established throughout China. Good students were sent from local schools to the colleges of their provinces. In addition, the best students went to the imperial school in the capital to prepare for the civil service examinations.

The examinations were written tests that were given once every three years. They covered current events, Confucian classics, creative writing, Chinese law, and mathematics. While taking the test, each candidate sat in a small, separate room that was somewhat like a telephone booth. In some towns acres of these booths sat in long rows. The test lasted three days, during which time food was brought in by servants and officials watched from high towers to see that no one cheated.

Major Chinese Dynasties, 1500 B.C.–A.D. 907

Shang Dynasty c. 1500–1027 B.C.
bronze culture • writing system invented • wheeled chariots

Zhou Dynasty 1027–256 B.C.
classical period • iron used • Laozi (604–529 B.C.) • Confucius (551–479 B.C.) • towns grew • farming improved • coins used • art and literature flourished

Qin Dynasty 221–206 B.C.
Great Wall built • China unified • weights and measures standardized • Confucian literature burned

Han Dynasty 202 B.C.–A.D. 220
borders expanded • trade with India and Rome • Buddhism introduced • yoke and paper invented

Tang Dynasty A.D. 618–907
further expansion into Central Asia • civil service exam system made universal • printing invented • great age of poetry

c. means *circa*, or approximate date

---

4 Lesson Plan

Essential Learning Objective
Students will learn to identify the factors that created a golden age of peace and creativity under the Tangs.

1 FOCUS AND MOTIVATE

Ask students to predict the conditions that followed the end of the Han dynasty. Students should recognize the cyclical nature of Chinese history as periods of strong government followed by decline and conflict.

2 TEACH

- Ask: What preparation for leadership did Taizong have that might explain his wise policies? (father founded the dynasty; as a general, Taizong helped unite nobles; he understood the past 400 years of war)
- Discuss what values and social goals were fostered by allowing poor, young Chinese men to take the civil service exam. (value of education for all

---

Candidates who did not pass the test the first time could take it again and again. In addition, bright young men from very poor families were allowed to take the easiest form of the test. If successful, they could enter the lowest civil service rank. With more study and experience, they might be promoted to the highest posts. In this way, the Chinese civil service examination created a sense of opportunity and mobility in Chinese government. This belief was similar to the "log cabin to White House" idea, which stresses that a person from any walk of life could become president, that is found today in the United States.

This selective system produced in China intelligent, well-trained, and well-respected government officials. These officials collected taxes, kept order, punished criminals, managed the postal service, and conducted the tests for government service. The high quality of Chinese schools led other Asian countries to send their young men to China to be educated. As a result, Chinese influence spread well beyond its borders.

The Chinese system of selecting government workers by public examination lasted until the early 1900s. Although the civil service system was more advanced than any other such system in the world, it did have a serious fault. Although the candidates were tested on current events, most of the exam focused on the old classics. Therefore, little emphasis was placed on new ideas among officials in the Chinese government. In modern times, when new ideas and technologies led to rapid changes in all aspects of life, this weakness became very serious for China. It has at times prevented China from meeting many of the challenges of a world in constant flux.

The Tang developed printing and encouraged literature.

One of the technologies that both spurred the expansion of the educational system and led eventually to the development of literature during the early years of the Tang dynasty was the invention of block printing in about the year 600.

To print a Chinese text, the printer carved raised characters on a block of wood, wet the raised surface of the block with ink, and pressed sheets of paper against the block. Most early Chinese books were printed on rolls of paper. Gradually, however, the Chinese developed books with pages and covers. They also invented paper money and printed playing cards.

The invention of printing, the stable government, and the expansion of education all contributed to a flowering of literary culture. Poetry, the most popular form of writing, was the subject of a saying of the time, "Whoever was a man was a poet." One of the most significant of the Tang poets was Li Bo [lē′ bô′], one of whose poems is translated as follows:

> One evening, on the bank of the river, as I breathed the perfume of the flowers, the wind brought me the sound of a distant flute. That I might answer it, I cut a willow branch and the song of my flute trilled out into the enchanted night.
> Since that evening, every day at the hour when the country goes to sleep, the little birds hear two unknown birds calling to each other. They do not know who the singers are, but nevertheless, they understand the song.

Note that this poem is graceful and direct. It embodies the reverence for nature and the awe for the mysteries of life that give Chinese poetry a worldwide appeal.

Section 4 Review

Identify Tang dynasty, Taizong
Main Ideas
1. What are some reasons Taizong is considered a great emperor and wise ruler?
2. How did the expansion of the educational system under Tang rule lead to a stronger government?
3. How did the invention of printing influence literature during the Tang dynasty?

Critical Thinking
Analyzing Comparisons: Do you think that the comparison between Chinese and American society made in this section concerning the "log cabin to the White House" idea is valid? Explain your reasons. What factors do you think might have limited the ability of people to move up within the society of Tang China? What factors might limit or facilitate social mobility in the United States today? Give reasons.

HIGHLIGHTS OF CIVILIZATION

Tang Dynasty Pottery

In ancient China when an emperor died, court attendants and animals were sacrificed and buried in the same tomb, to attend the spirit of the ruler in the afterlife. Later, pottery figurines replaced the human and animal victims. Today, Tang dynasty grave figures, such as those shown

A Tang dynasty camel with musicians (below, top) and women polo players (bottom).

below are among the priceless art treasures of the world.

Pottery has always assumed much importance in China. Chinese potters began making large urns as early as 2000 B.C. By the 3rd century B.C., they were applying glass paint and firing their pots to achieve shiny glazes in several different colors. During the Tang dynasty, potters produced thousands of dazzling objects demonstrating brilliant innovative techniques. In addition to the grave figures for which they are justly noted, Tang potters created elegant jars, vases, and other vessels of every shape and size. Their glazes included a whole rainbow of colors— dark reds and blues, greens, oranges, yellows, and browns. Sometimes long burial made the colors iridescent—that is, changing in color when the object is turned.

As might be expected, grave figures usually present a somber appearance. The men and women here, however, appear lively and cheerful. Even the camel seems to be enjoying the music.

147

Answers to Test Yourself

Key Terms, People, and Places

The key terms, people, and places tested here were introduced in the chapter sections and reviewed in the Section Reviews. For definitions see the page references at the appropriate Section Reviews. Also see the Glossary and Biographical Dictionary.

Main Ideas

The main ideas tested here were introduced in the sections of this chapter and reviewed in the Section Reviews. For answers to these questions, see the appropriate Section Reviews.

Critical Thinking

1. Accept either answer as long as it is well supported. Upheaval might produce more cultural advances, because people work to solve problems and find ways to end chaos. Stability might produce cultural advances because people have the freedom from cares and worries and the leisure to spend time pursuing creative interests, such as painting, writing, and music.

2. Three assumptions might include that history is cyclical, that the cycles can be predicted, and that empires inevitably fall. Accept students' opinions about the validity of these assumptions.

CHAPTER 8 REVIEW

Section Summaries

Section 1

Geography helps explain China's early development. Natural barriers isolated China from other civilizations and lent the country an inward focus that allowed its culture to flourish. Over time Chinese civilization developed in three separate river basins. The Huang River was the cradle of Chinese civilization. The Chang River provided a main trade route and a basin for growing rice. The Xi River promoted year-round farming, and trading centers developed at its mouth.

Section 2

The Zhou dynasty ruled longest in China. The Zhou period, from 1027 B.C. to 256 B.C., is often called classical because many basic elements of Chinese civilization developed at that time. Long-lasting traditions in government, trade, and art, and the Chinese writing system became well established. Two influential philosophies, Confucianism and Taoism, developed during Zhou rule.

Section 3

The Qin and Han dynasties united China. After the fall of the Zhou dynasty, the Qin dynasty united the warring feudal states in 221 B.C. Shi Huangdi established a strong central government and built much of the Great Wall. After the death of Shi Huangdi, Qin

Rule weakened, the Han dynasty began its 400-year rule in 202 B.C. Under Han rulers the Chinese empire expanded and significant cultural advances were made.

Section 4

The Tang dynasty gave China a golden age. The end to Han rule divided China into warring kingdoms, and turmoil ensued. In 618 the Tang dynasty came to power and reunited China. Under Taizong, the greatest Tang ruler, China's borders expanded and the country enjoyed peace.

Test Yourself

Key Terms, People, and Places

Identify the significance of each of the following:

Section 1
a. Huang River   c. Xi River
b. Chang River

Section 2
a. Zhou dynasty   d. Confucius
b. feudal state   e. Laozi
c. Mandate of Heaven

Section 3
a. Shi Huangdi   c. Silk Road
b. Wu Di

Review Dates

	551 B.C. Confucius is born			**A.D. 600** Block printing is invented	
1027 B.C. Zhou dynasty is established		**221 B.C.** Qin rule unites China			
		202 B.C. The Hans begin 400-year reign		**A.D. 618** Tang dynasty comes to power	
1100 B.C.	700 B.C.	300 B.C.	A.D. 100	A.D. 500	A.D. 900

Section 4
a. Tang dynasty   **b.** Taizong

Main Ideas

Section 1
1. How did natural barriers isolate China?
2. Why did the Chinese build the Great Wall?
3. Describe the importance of each of China's three main rivers.

Section 2
1. Describe the major political, military, and social changes of the Zhou period.
2. What cultural developments in government, trade, and art were achieved during Zhou rule?
3. How did the Chinese writing system develop?
4. Describe the philosophies of Confucius and Laozi.

Section 3
1. In what ways did Qin rule increase the power of the Chinese government?
2. How did China change politically and culturally during Han rule?
3. What goods and ideas were exchanged along the Silk Road?

Section 4
1. What accomplishments gave Taizong a reputation as a wise ruler?
2. How did Chinese government benefit from an expanded educational system?
3. What are some reasons literature flourished under the Tang dynasty?

Critical Thinking

1. Making Hypotheses The Zhou dynasty was a period of great upheaval and the Tang dynasty was a period of relative stability. Yet both periods produced important cultural advances. Do you think upheaval or stability is more important for cultural development? Explain your answer.

2. Identifying Assumptions An early Tang emperor once said, "By using a mirror of brass, you may . . . adjust your cap; by using antiquity as a mirror you may . . . foresee the rise and fall of empires." Identify three assumptions the Tang emperor must have made to hold this view of history. Do you agree with these assumptions? Why or why not?

Chapter Skills and Activities

Practicing Study and Research Skills

Applying Economics to History
The economic decline of Rome stemmed in part from Rome's huge importation of silk from China. The resulting unfavorable balance of trade drained Rome's economy and hastened the fall of the Roman Empire. With Rome no longer able to buy silk, China's economy, in turn, seriously declined. What do you think the Roman or Chinese rulers could have done to prevent this economic decline? How might such actions have affected the economic and political experiences of both empires?

Linking Past and Present
The Chinese had a monopoly on silk for thousands of years. Use an encyclopedia or other reference to find out how knowledge of silk production spread to the West and what countries of the world are the major silk producers today. Write several paragraphs about what you learn.

Learning History Through Maps
You have read that the Chinese established an overland trading route with the West by way of the Silk Road. A sea route was also established for trade starting in the 2nd century A.D. Turn to the political map of Asia on page 794. Trace the sea route ships would have taken from Aden on the Arabian peninsula to the southern coast of China. List the present-day countries passed on the route.

CRITICAL THINKING QUESTION LEVEL 1. average; 2. challenging

---

9 Africa and the Americas in the Classical Age

OVERVIEW

This chapter focuses on how people in Sub-Saharan Africa and in North America formed distinctive civilizations as they learned how to survive challenging environments.

PLANNING CHART

Section	Text Pages	Key Concept	Suggested Teaching Time
1 Africa's varied geography produced a variety of cultures.	152–155	Cultural development in Africa responded to the geography and climates of four main ecological regions.	Two days **More time?** Use *Overhead Transparency 17.*
2 Ancient Africans developed distinctive societies.	155–161	The people of the African savanna and forest developed political and social structures that helped foster community order.	Two days **Less time?** Combine Sections 1 and 2 by summarizing the four major regions and teaching Section 2 as part of the material on the savanna and forest. **More time?** Use *Source Reading 9A.*
3 Native American cultures developed over many centuries.	162–163	Many different groups populated the North American continent and learned to use its resources in many different ways.	One day
4 The Maya achieved a most complex civilization.	164–166	The Maya in Central America possessed highly advanced skills and knowledge.	One day **More time?** Use *Overhead Transparency 18* or *Source Reading 9B.*

ANCILLARIES

Materials that may be used with this chapter to reinforce, reteach, enrich, and assess learning are pictured on the following pages.

Teacher's Resource File

ACTIVITIES

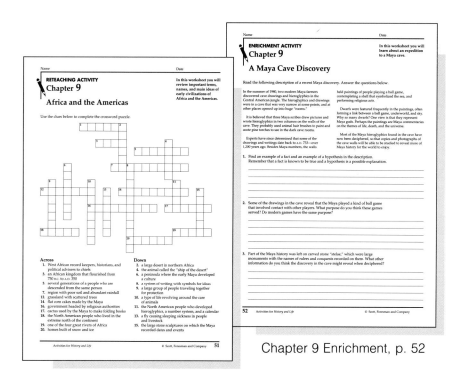

Section 1 Activity, p. 47

Section 2 Activity, p. 48

Section 3 Activity, p. 49

Section 4 Activity, p. 50

Chapter 9 Reteaching, p. 51

Chapter 9 Enrichment, p. 52

149b

Teacher's Resource File

GEOGRAPHY SKILLS

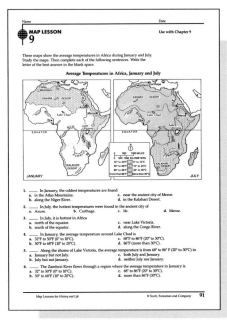

Chapter 9 Geography
Worksheet/Map, pp. 19–20

Chapter 9 Map Lesson, p. 91

TESTS

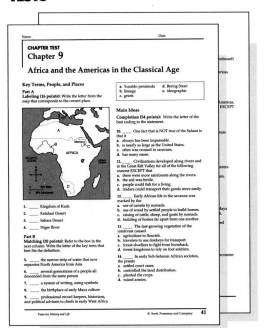

Chapter Test, pp. 41–42

Alternate Chapter Test, pp. 43–44

Other Optional Ancillaries

WORKBOOK

WORKSHEET
Chapter 9, Section 1

In this worksheet you will review Africa's major natural vegetation regions and the lifestyles of the people who inhabited them.

African Lifestyles

Part A
Only three of the four terms in each group are related in some way. Circle the term that does not belong and explain how the remaining three terms are related.

1. desert | forest | irrigation | savanna

2. Ice Age | climate change | dry land | oasis

3. cave paintings | camel caravans | oases | traders and travelers

4. thatched straw roofs | wooden buildings | farming villages | compound

5. poor, infertile soil | hot, wet climate | donkeys | tsetse fly

Part B
For each set of statements write M before the main idea and S before any statements that support or help to explain the main idea. One statement in each set is not related to the main idea. Put X next to this statement.

Set 1
___ Towns, farms, and markets dotted the valleys formed by Africa's four great rivers.
___ Farmers settled near rivers because flooding produced rich soil.
___ The rivers provided fish for food and were routes for traders.
___ African civilization grew along the Great Rift Valley.

Set 2
___ Traders used donkeys to carry goods in the savanna.
___ The people moved their homes in response to the needs of their livestock.
___ One lifestyle in the savanna was that of nomadic herder.
___ Nomadic herders established useful relationships with the farmers.

Worksheets for History and Life | © Scott, Foresman and Company | **31**

Section 1 Worksheet, p. 31

WORKSHEET
Chapter 9, Section 2

In this worksheet you will review important events in African history.

Early African History

Part A
Write the letter of the event from the box next to the approximate time it took place.

1. ___ 3000 B.C.
2. ___ 2000 B.C.
3. ___ 800 B.C.
4. ___ 750 B.C.
5. ___ 630 B.C.
6. ___ 500 B.C.
7. ___ A.D. 350
8. ___ A.D. 100–1000

a. Kushite power declined.
b. Kushites invaded and conquered Egypt.
c. East Africans became herders.
d. Africans began to grow rice along the Niger.
e. Forest people learned to grow yams; ironworking began in central Nigeria.
f. West Africans migrated into central and southern Africa.
g. Kushites were driven from Egypt back to their own land.
h. Ironworking became common in Egypt.

Part B
Select the word from the box that best completes each statement.

1. The kingdom of ___ flourished from 750 B.C. to A.D. 350.
2. By the first century B.C., Kush was carrying on a thriving ___ trade with Egypt, Arabia, and India, as well as with other parts of Africa.
3. Scholars have not yet deciphered Kush ___.
4. Several generations of a people all descended from the same person make up a ___.
5. A lineage took care of its own members and assumed the responsibility for punishing its ___.
6. Kings, queens, chiefs, and ___ often had to come from certain lineages.
7. Among some of the West Africans, ___ gained influence and power.
8. The ___ of the community were not written down but were known by everyone.
9. In the absence of written records, many families had their own ___ who memorized the family history.

laws	Kush	elders
griots	iron	criminals
priests	hieroglyphics	lineage

32 Worksheets for History and Life | © Scott, Foresman and Company

Section 2 Worksheet, p. 32

WORKSHEET
Chapter 9, Section 3

In this worksheet you will review Native American cultures.

Native American Cultures

Part A
Write the letter of the phrase that best completes each statement.

1. ___ Scientists believe that at one time exposed land formed a pathway across the Bering Strait. From this belief, scientists have concluded that
   a. the first Americans arrived in Alaska about 10,000 years ago.
   b. the first Americans were the Inuit.
   c. the first Americans were migrants from northeastern Asia.

2. ___ Scientists learn about ancient American cultures from
   a. studying artifacts.
   b. reading books and other writings found in ancient temples.
   c. researching connections between cultures in the Americas and the Old World.

3. ___ Scholars believe that the presence of similar inventions in the Eastern and Western hemispheres indicates that
   a. early people crossed the Pacific Ocean or Atlantic Ocean.
   b. early people brought new ideas to the Americas from Europe and Asia.
   c. people had similar ideas when they faced similar problems.

4. ___ It is reasonable to believe that hundreds of distinct groups developed in North America over the centuries as a result of
   a. varied types of government.
   b. varied climate and geography.
   c. varied reasons for coming to the Americas.

Part B
Write a cause for each effect.

1. Our knowledge of 16th-century American cultures is sketchy.

2. Unlike many other Native American cultures, the Inuit did not develop an agricultural economy.

3. The Inuit did not develop a centralized form of government.

4. Hundreds of distinct Native American groups developed in North America.

Worksheets for History and Life | © Scott, Foresman and Company | **33**

Section 3 worksheet, p. 33

WORKSHEET
Chapter 9, Section 4

In this worksheet you will review the achievements of the Maya civilization.

Maya Civilization

Part A
Use information from the text to complete each of the following statements about the Maya.

1. Archaeologists think that the cultures of Central America and South America progressed more quickly than those in the north **because**

2. The Maya probably built "stelae," or large stone sculptures, **in order to**

3. Scholars have guessed that the Maya began to abandon their cultural centers in the 800s **because**

4. Some historians regard mathematics as the Maya's area of greatest achievement **because**

Part B
Study the explanation of the Maya number system in your text. Express each Arabic numeral in Maya fashion.

| 1. 80 | 3. 320 |
| 2. 16 | 4. 11 |

34 Worksheets for History and Life | © Scott, Foresman and Company

Section 4 Worksheet, p. 34

SOURCE READINGS

Source Reading 9A
Source Reading 9B

TEST GENERATOR

40 multiple-choice questions for Chapter 9

OVERHEAD TRANSPARENCIES

Overhead Transparency 17
Overhead Transparency 18

Africa and the Americas in the Classical Age

3000 B.C.–A.D. 500

4000 B.C.

⇩

3000 B.C.   Corn is first used in Mexico and millet in West Africa

750 B.C.   Kush begins to flourish

500 B.C.   Maya civilization develops

A.D. 100

A.D. 500

Deep in the Yucatán jungles of Guatemala, a complex of pyramids and temples sits, surrounded by silence, their ancient symbols still not completely deciphered by scholars. On a hill overlooking Axum, an ancient capital of Ethiopia, towers a single carved stele, a royal burial monument, the last of several dozens that once displayed the glory of the Ethiopian kings. In a museum in Nigeria, 2,000-year-old terra cotta (earthenware) heads, mouths open, eyes hollow, stare from their display posts. The purpose of these heads, only recently discovered by tin miners, remains unclear.

At the same time as various civilizations were rising and falling in the Mediterranean and Asian worlds, important civilizations in Africa and the Americas were taking shape. However, unlike the Greeks, Romans, Indians, or Chinese, these early civilizations of Africa and the Americas have scant evidence of their presence still in existence.

Today archaeologists trying to piece together the clues left by the early Africans and Americans can only observe fragments of these cultures. Very few artifacts or written documents exist to reveal how these early people lived, dressed, or communicated.

In Africa the harsh extremes of climate, which you will learn about in this chapter, have contributed to the destruction of documents, buildings, clothing, and artwork. Historical disruptions and invasions have also affected our knowledge of early Africa. Although many Africans passed along the collected history of their people—the births, the deaths, the celebrations, the wars, the achievements—in an oral form, many of these oral histories were lost as societies were weakened or ceased to exist.

European conquest of both Africa and the Americas during the 16th and 17th centuries also distorted our record of these civilizations. These European invaders raided or destroyed significant

Ruins left by the Maya evoke the many mysteries that still exist concerning early Africa and the Americas. Here an ocelot slinks in the shadows of the Maya ruins.

stores of surviving artifacts, monuments, and records, and they suppressed native cultures. In addition, many of the writings of the Native Americans that have survived to this day have yet to be studied or deciphered.

It is precisely our lack of knowledge that makes Africa and the Americas seem remote and mysterious, intriguing and compelling. Yet scholars are discovering more about these civilizations every year. We are now learning that, confronted with the difficulties of survival in the ancient world, early Africans and Americans came up with their own unique and successful solutions.

Reading Preview

In this chapter you will read how African and American civilizations developed.

1. *Africa's varied geography produced a variety of cultures.*

2. *Ancient Africans developed distinctive societies.*

3. *Native American cultures developed over many centuries.*

4. *The Maya achieved a most complex civilization.*

The desert was both a barrier and a bridge for early Africans.

After Asia, Africa is the second largest continent in the world. It has four major ecological regions—coast, desert, savanna, and forest. As you can see from the map at left, two narrow regions of fertile coast lie at the very north and south of the African continent. These small areas receive sufficient rainfall for productive farming, especially with irrigation. A relatively short distance inland, these areas give way to deserts—the huge **Sahara** in the north and the **Kalahari** in the south.

Early life on the Sahara. The Sahara was not always dry and barren of plants. Until about 2000 B.C., regular rainfall made it possible for plants, animals, and people to live there easily. Paintings in caves and on rocky sides of mountains show what life must have been like between 6000 and 1500 B.C. In these Mesolithic paintings, horses pulled carts and hunters gave chase to giraffes and elephants. People also gathered wild grain. Musicians played for women who wore elaborate hair styles and long robes and capes.

What happened to the nameless people whose artists decorated the Sahara caves? Scientists believe that as the Ice Age ended in Europe, about 2000 B.C., the climatic conditions of the Sahara also changed and the land became dry. Over the years rainfall gradually stopped, and the people died or moved to more fertile areas. Some moved to the Nile Valley, some to the northern African coast, and some south to the savanna.

Travel across the Sahara. Although most of the Sahara was no longer habitable, travel across it never stopped. It has always been a link between the Mediterranean world and the parts of Africa that are to the south. Through the ages travelers followed trails across the Sahara, carrying goods, moving armies, and exchanging ideas. Many oases [ō ā'sēz'] helped keep the trails open. An oasis is a place in the desert where an underground spring comes close to the surface. People kept the oases habitable by digging wells and irrigating nearby land. Traders and travelers regularly stopped at oases to rest and water their animals.

Just as the Sahara was sometimes called an ocean of sand, so the camel was called the "ship of the desert." Beginning about A.D. 100, people

Africa: Natural Vegetation Regions

Broadleaf forest—rainforest

Broadleaf forest—deciduous

Broadleaf forest—other

Grassland

Desert—little or no vegetation

Desert—scrub with grassy patches

High mountains (vegetation varies with elevation)

MAP STUDY What type of natural vegetation region dominates northern Africa? Where are the rainforests?

1 Africa's varied geography produced a variety of cultures.

In Africa there are many different climates and landforms, each region with its own distinct assortment of plants and animals. Over the centuries the many different peoples of Africa have learned to adapt their ways of living to the climate, landforms, soils, vegetation, and animal life available in their own region.

1 Lesson Plan

Essential Learning Objectives

Students will learn to:

- name the ecological regions of Africa and describe their features.
- tell how early African civilizations adapted to environmental conditions.

used camels to cross the Sahara. Camels were much better suited to the hot, dry climate than were donkeys or horses. They could travel fully loaded in the desert for four days without water.

To guard against becoming lost and as protection against bandits, people crossed the Sahara in large groups, called caravans. Long lines of camels, sometimes as many as 10,000, carried the heavy goods, including leather bags of water. Caravans journeyed from Morocco or Tunisia in the north to large trading cities along the **Niger River** [nī′jər], such as Timbuktu. The journey usually took two months under the leadership of a skilled guide.

Despite the dangers and hardships of the desert, caravans made large profits by guiding passengers across the Sahara and by selling the caravan's goods. Salt, copper, and cloth from North Africa brought good prices in the cities on the Niger River. In exchange, such items as gold, ivory, and hides from the savanna and forests were prized in Mediterranean markets.

Large populations flourished in the savanna.

Savannas lie along the borders of the deserts. If you think of typical African wildlife films, you can picture a savanna. Lions stalk zebras and antelope

As in the past, the oases of the Sahara still bring water and life to the dry lands. This settlement, which was formed around an oasis, is ringed by palm trees.

through tall grass, and giraffes reach high to nip the leaves off the isolated acacia trees.

The African savanna has traditionally supported large populations of people. In fact, most Africans lived on the savanna. On the savanna, there were two types of lifestyle—settled and nomadic.

Settled life on the savanna. For the past 2,000 years, farming villages and some large cities and towns have been scattered throughout the grasslands. People raised livestock and grew crops such as millet, which produces very small, nutritious seeds, and rice.

Because few trees grew in the savanna, wooden buildings were uncommon. People of the savanna used all available wood to support the roofs of their houses and to make fires, tools, and weapons. For the walls of their buildings, they used a strong plaster made of a mixture of mud and straw. At times the mud and straw mixture was baked into bricks.

On the savanna, there were two main building styles. In the cities and towns, people built multi-storied, square houses that were located close together for protection. The houses were usually separated by narrow streets.

In rural villages, however, people built one-room round houses and topped them with thatched straw roofs. The straw roofs and thick mud walls of the houses protected the home's interior from the heat of the sun. The air inside was usually quite cool. Several of these one-room houses formed a circle, and a wall or fence around the houses provided protection and privacy. The many buildings that were clustered inside the barrier formed a larger living area called a compound. As you can see from the diagram on page 154, in the center of the compound, a courtyard provided space for cooking and visiting. In some areas of the savanna, people continue to build houses as their ancestors have done for the past 2,000 years.

Nomadic life on the savanna. Some people in the savanna were nomadic herders who raised cattle, sheep, and goats. Unlike the savanna's villagers and city-dwellers, they moved their homes whenever their livestock needed new places to graze and drink. These two groups, however, often established useful relationships with one another. The herders' animals provided milk, meat, and leather for the farmers of the savanna, and the farmers in turn sold grains to the herders.

The donkey was an important domesticated animal in the grasslands. Although camels were vital for crossing the desert, they were not well suited to the savanna because their soft hooves rotted in the wetter climate. Therefore, when a caravan reached the southern edge of the Sahara, the camels were unloaded, and donkeys were used for the trip across the grasslands.

The forest affected African lifestyles and governments.

Some people believe that Africa is covered with wild, overgrown "jungles" teeming with tangled vines and exotic flora. In fact, forests and rainforests cover only about 20 percent of the African continent. They have, however, played a significant role in African history.

The African forests support a wide variety of plant species under an elegant canopy of tall, leafy trees. The leaves filter out the sun's hot rays, creating an open and lightly vegetated area below where only a few shade-loving plants can grow.

The forests of tropical Africa are thus not the dense, impassable jungles portrayed in so many novels and movies. The jungles, with their dense, entangled underbrush, appear only along the edges of rivers, or where the tall trees of the rainforest have been cleared by nature or by people.

Life in the African forest. The forest has always presented many challenges to the peoples who developed civilizations within their boundaries. Surprisingly, the soil of even the lushest, greenest rainforest is quite poor and infertile. The hot, wet climate of the forest prevents the accumulation of nutritious soil, and the heavy rains leach many of the minerals from the soil.

As a result, forest-dwellers had to acquire special skills to overcome the difficulties of life in the rainforest. They worked hard to build their villages, clear fields, and cultivate small farm plots. They found that some crops that could not grow in the drier savanna, such as plantains [plan′tənz] (a very nutritious type of banana) and yams (a kind of sweet potato), could be grown in the forests. They also learned to take advantage of the many kinds of fruit that grew in the forests.

The layout of a compound house similar to this one in Namibia, an arrangement of small thatched-roof buildings, is shown in the diagram.

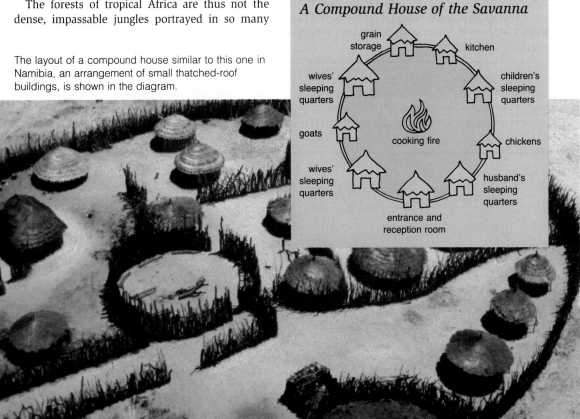

A Compound House of the Savanna

grain storage · kitchen · children's sleeping quarters · chickens · husband's sleeping quarters · entrance and reception room · wives' sleeping quarters · goats · wives' sleeping quarters · cooking fire

Another challenge to life in the forest was the tsetse [tset′sē] fly. This insect causes sleeping sickness in people and a similar disease in cattle, horses, and other livestock. The tsetse fly probably has been present in the African forests for thousands of years, thriving in the trees and shrubs. Because of the tsetse fly danger, forest-dwellers could not keep herds of cattle. As a result, they found meat for their diets in other places, such as hunting wild game or raising fowl. The tsetse fly also affected transportation in the forests. Because donkeys and horses fell victim to African sleeping sickness, they could not be used to carry heavy loads. Therefore, in forest regions, goods were carried by people.

Government in the African forest. In the forest, large roads quickly became overgrown with vegetation. This meant that many small groups of people in the forest were isolated from each other. Villages were seldom visited by travelers, traders, or even tribute collectors.

However, large kingdoms were able to repair roads and make large clearings in the forest for their towns. The forest provided wood to build strong houses, furniture, and tools, and the regular rainfall yielded good crops. As a result, many Africans lived in the forest, and powerful kingdoms such as Asante [ə sän′tē] and Benin [bə nēn′] developed there.

The difficult conditions of the forest affected how these forest kingdoms engaged both in combat and in communication. Because of the tsetse fly, the Africans had no cavalry. Instead, the forest kingdoms relied on foot soldiers in times of war. The soldiers fought hand-to-hand combat among the trees and across the rivers with spears, machetes, and bows and arrows. They were highly disciplined and ready to react in case of any sudden change in the battle.

Civilizations developed along rivers and in the Great Rift Valley.

Four great rivers, the Niger, the Congo, the Zambezi [zam bē′zē], and the Nile, flow through the savanna and forest regions. Find them on the physical map of Africa on page 797. Towns, farms, and markets dot each of these river valleys. Farmers settled near rivers because the yearly flooding

renewed the fertility of the soil. People used the rivers to fish, and traders used them for traveling.

In addition to forming in these river valleys, African civilization also gained a foothold in a region of East Africa known as the Great Rift Valley. Locate the Great Rift Valley on the map on page 797. Throughout the valley the soil is very fertile and the climate is pleasant. The large lakes provide both a ready source of water and good fishing.

Section 1 Review

Identify Sahara, Kalahari, Niger River
Main Ideas
1. How did the Sahara both divide and link early African peoples?
2. How did settled and nomadic life differ on the savanna?
3. Describe some of the challenges that African forest-dwellers faced in their daily lives and government.
4. Why did African peoples settle along rivers and in the Great Rift Valley?

Critical Thinking
Evaluating Sources of Information: Think of a book that you have read or a movie that you've seen that presents an image of the African rainforest. After reading this section, would you say that the portrayal was accurate? Why or why not?

---

2 Ancient Africans developed distinctive societies.

As you learned earlier in this chapter, some of the peoples of the Sahara moved south into the savanna when the conditions of the desert began to change. In the savanna they developed farming techniques and other skills that responded to the many challenges of their natural environment.

African farmers and herders adapted to different physical conditions.

In Africa farming and herding were both important means of supporting early populations. Neither occupation, however, was easy, given the extremes of the African continent. Farming, which probably

caravans crossed the desert carrying goods and ideas between people near the Mediterranean and those who lived south of the Sahara.
2. Settled farmers—as well as village- and city-dwellers—lived in permanent homes set in communal groupings; nomadic peoples moved their homes frequently as they raised cattle, sheep, and goats.
3. Forest-dwellers faced the rainforest's infertile soil and the dangers of the tsetse fly. Governments faced difficult conditions in combat and in communication.
4. because the rivers were an important source of fresh water and fish, as well as a route for travel and trade; Great Rift Valley provided fertile soil, fresh water, and a good climate.

Critical Thinking
The students' responses will depend upon what book or movie they discuss, but should display an understanding of the environment and cultures of African rainforests.

---

2 *Lesson Plan*

Essential Learning Objectives

Students will learn to:
- describe the importance of farming, herding, and ironworking in African civilizations.
- explain the bases of power in early African societies.

A MYSTERY IN HISTORY

Ask students to find Ethiopia and Israel in the Atlas of their text. Ask: Approximately how many miles would the Queen of Sheba have traveled to reach Israel? (approximately 1,350 miles) What route would her camel caravan have probably taken? (along the western coast of the Red Sea and across the Sinai peninsula)

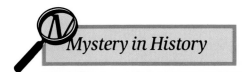

Mystery in History

WHO WAS THE QUEEN OF SHEBA?

Now when the Queen of Sheba heard of the fame of Solomon concerning the name of the Lord, she came to test him with hard questions.

I Kings 10:1

Thus begins the Bible story of a famous Old Testament encounter—the meeting of King Solomon and the Queen of Sheba. Solomon, the second son of David and Bathsheba, ruled Israel in the 900s B.C. when the kingdom was at its height. The great temple at Jerusalem was built during Solomon's reign. He was also known as the wisest person of his time.

The story of their visit has been familiar to Jews, Christians, and Muslims for thousands of years, but many details about the queen remain a mystery. Where was the land of Sheba? Did the Queen of Sheba really visit Solomon to ask him riddles, or did she have other purposes in mind?

The record in the Scriptures provides clues to some of the answers. The queen came with a "very great retinue" of people, with "camels bearing spices, and very much gold, and precious stones." She and Solomon were said to have exchanged riddles. At the end, she was impressed not only by his wisdom, but also by "the house he had built, the food of his table, the seating of his officials, and the attendance of his servants, their clothing, his cupbearers, and his burnt offerings which he offered at the house of the Lord." The queen praised Solomon and his God, and Solomon gave her many gifts. She then returned to her own land.

The reference to camels suggests that Sheba was a center of a land-based trading empire, probably on the Arabian Peninsula. Camels also help date the account because they were first used for long-distance trade about 1000 B.C. Assyrian records mention Sheba as a commercial center about this time. Many modern scholars believe that Sheba was such a center in southwestern Arabia and may well have had outposts for trade in Africa.

However, Ethiopian documents dating from the 4th century A.D. tell the story of Solomon and the queen almost as the Bible does. They say that the queen, named Makeda [mə-kā'də], was from Ethiopia and that while she was in Jerusalem, Solomon fell in love with her. When she later returned to her own country, she gave birth to a son of Solomon. This son, the Ethiopians claim, was their first king, called Menelik I [me'nə lik]. When he grew up, he is said to have ruled justly and to have introduced Judaism into Ethiopia.

Could the story be true? Could the Queen of Sheba have come from Ethiopia? Historians may never know, but many Ethiopians have been convinced of it for centuries.

A modern Ethiopian manuscript depicts Solomon and Sheba telling riddles.

began in Africa in the Nile Valley, was difficult throughout much of the continent. Herding likewise presented challenges to those Africans who depended upon it.

Farming. Outside of the Nile Valley, which you learned about in Chapter 2, farmers learned that wheat and barley, which were good crops along the Nile, did not grow well in the savanna. As a result, the savanna people of the Niger River Valley had to experiment to find plants they could cultivate. Beginning about 3000 B.C., they grew African rice, a variety that does not need large amounts of water, and they grew millet.

None of these crops, however, grew well in the forest. By 500 B.C., however, the forest peoples had learned to grow yams. About the same time, Indian sailors landed small boats in East Africa, bringing with them bananas, which adapted easily to Africa. These new foods added more nutrition to the diet and made it possible for larger numbers of people to live in Africa.

Although simple, the farming methods of these early farmers were quite successful. As you learned earlier in this chapter, the soil in the savanna and forests of Africa was often not very fertile because the rain and sun removed many of the nutrients that helped plants grow. African farmers observed this phenomenon and learned to let the land lie fallow, or uncultivated for a certain period of time, to regain the nutrients needed for another good crop. In addition, African farmers were continually developing new crops.

African farmers also learned to adapt their tools to the soils. Most farms were cultivated by hoes, which are tools with a thin blade set across the end of a long handle. Farming with a hoe required much more work than did a plow. However, plows were not suitable for the poor African soils because they cut too deeply, turning up infertile soil and increased erosion.

Herding. Cattle, sheep, and goats were not native to Africa, but they became the foundation for a very important segment of the African population. These animals were imported from Mesopotamia first to northern Egypt and then south along the Nile River. By 2000 B.C. the people in East Africa had become herders, and some societies that developed were based entirely on herding and rais-

On the edge of the Great Rift Valley, a Pokot couple today turn soil with hoes that are similar to the iron-bladed tools that came into use after 500 B.C.

ing cattle. The life of people in such a society was pastoral, that is, it revolved around the care of the cattle.

Pastoral children learned at an early age to watch and tend cattle. They knew every animal in their family's herd by name. The children sang songs to the animals, much as cowboys of the American West sang songs to quiet their herds.

Adults in pastoral societies measured their wealth by how many cattle they owned. Cattle were important for their milk and blood, which were the major items in the pastoralists' diet.

Kush was an important ironworking center (750 B.C.–A.D. 350).

About 800 B.C. ironworking became common in Egypt, where it had first been introduced by the Hittites. Around the same time, Africans further south were also working with iron. Historians are not certain how Africans far away from Egypt

Select students to share with the class a bit of their family history, relating events that happened as long ago as possible. Ask that they explain their sources of information. Discuss the difficulties involved in remembering all the important events in one's history. Point out that African cultures relied on oral rather than written records.

- Identify the food crops grown in savanna and forest regions, clarifying farming methods, including the use of hoes rather than plows for the shallow soils. Check to be sure students grasp the importance of herds in pastoral societies and why animals would seldom be butchered. (The size of the herd represented wealth.)

- Emphasize the changes that the use of iron brought about in Kush. (It made Kush militarily stronger, enabled an increase in food supplies, and led to population growth and expansion.)

- Discuss the interrelationships of the lineage systems, emphasizing how a lineage provided for all members of the family and maintained order.

- Discuss the roles of griots and artists in preserving the community's history. Elicit the kinds of information that could be passed on through these methods. (stories about powerful rulers, wars, religious events, disasters)

GUIDED PRACTICE

Divide students into small groups and have them, one by one, each relate a fact from this section. One student can serve as recorder so facts will not be repeated.

learned to make iron, but many now believe that the skill of ironmaking developed independently in West Africa about the same time that the Egyptians learned about it. The knowledge of ironmaking might also have spread from Egypt along ancient trade routes. Archaeologists have found ironworking sites in central Nigeria that date from about 500 B.C.

Vast iron ore deposits, from which iron is made, were located south of Egypt on the Nile River in what is today Sudan. Here the African kingdom of **Kush** developed and flourished from about 750 B.C. to A.D. 350. Locate Kush on the map on page 160. The Kushites had been Egyptian subjects, but about 750 B.C. they invaded and conquered Egypt. The Kushite kings then made themselves the 25th Dynasty of the pharaohs of Egypt. By about 630 B.C., however, the Kushites were no longer able to defend Egypt against outside attacks and were driven back to their own land.

There they continued to rule independently from their capital at Meroe [mə rō′]. By the 1st century B.C., Meroe was carrying on a thriving iron trade with Egypt, Arabia, India, what is now Ethiopia, and portions of Africa farther south. Around A.D. 350, however, the power of Kush declined.

Historians believe that Kush fell when armies from the African kingdom of Axum destroyed Meroe. Locate Axum on the map on page 160.

Today Meroe is uninhabited. However, the extensive heaps of iron refuse and ruins of brick palaces, pyramids, temples, and homes attest to Kush's former splendor. Exquisite jewelry and iron utensils and chairs have been found in the ruins. In addition, iron weapons and artifacts have been discovered buried with Kush kings and queens.

Kush had its own hieroglyphics, which modern-day scholars are unable to read. Because the records of Kush have yet to be deciphered, historians do not know exactly what happened during the centuries of rule from Meroe and what brought this kingdom to an end. However, Kush's importance as a trade, ironworking, and cultural center is certain from its archaeological remains.

The use of iron caused major changes in Africa. Iron tools were stronger and longer-lasting than stone or wood ones. These stronger tools made it possible to grow more food and feed more people. Better hunting weapons meant more meat for the community. Strong weapons meant that people were not as afraid to venture into strange lands, because they could protect themselves.

As early as 3100 B.C., Kush nobles visited Egypt. The wall paintings of Pharoah Seti I show a parade of Egyptians and Kushites at Seti's funeral.

The pyramids at Meroe, shown above in their present ruined state, serve as vivid reminders of the Kushite city's former grandeur.

Between A.D. 100 and 1000, the people of western Africa made large migrations into central and southern Africa as their populations expanded. The route of the migrations is shown on the map on page 160. These large movements of people are called the Bantu migrations, from the name of the group of languages that most of these people spoke. Much of central and southern Africa became settled by Bantu-speaking peoples as a result of these migrations.

Governments developed as societies became more complex.

The increasing use of iron and the advances in tools, farming techniques, food plants, and trade laid the foundation for African civilizations throughout the centuries. In Africa, as in other parts of the world, improved farming meant more food. Everyone in the community then did not need to work at getting food and some people could pursue other occupations. These societal changes challenged the existing power structures of African communities, and modifications in government took place.

Lineage. Government in most African societies was a matter of custom based on family relationships. Persons in an ethnic group belonged to subsections, called lineages [lin′ē ə jəz]. A **lineage** is several generations of a people who are all descended from the same person. Most people in Africa belonged to the lineage of their father, although in some societies, people belonged to the lineage of their mother. It was through a person's lineage that he or she had a place in the society.

A lineage took care of its own members, giving food and money to those who were in trouble. If a person committed a crime, the lineage took responsibility for the fine and made certain that the criminal was punished. Widows, orphans, the old, and the sick were also taken care of by their lineage. Individuals knew their own status in the lineage and treated older members with respect. Communities recognized a few of the oldest members, called elders, as their leaders. The kings, queen mothers (important women who were usually the mother of the heir apparent to the king), chiefs, and elders, however, often had to come from certain lineages.

ASSESS

1. What crops were grown in forest areas? (yams and bananas that had been brought from India)
2. Why were griots so well taken care of by their families? (Griots assured that families would be remembered; they also provided entertainment.)

OPTIONAL RETEACHING

Direct students to write a paragraph explaining why ironmaking caused major changes in Africa.

OPTIONAL ENRICHMENT

1. Ask a group of students to research and prepare a large map of Africa indicating the age, location, and type of ancient and traditional art found on the continent. (average)
2. Have students design a chart depicting the lineage of an imaginary African king and his descendants. (challenging)
3. Also for enrichment:

 Source Reading 9A

INDEPENDENT PRACTICE/ HOMEWORK

Assign the Section Review, Activities page 48, or Workbook page 32.

CLOSURE

Summarize the lesson by telling students that the communities of early sub-Saharan Africa prospered despite climatic or geographical hardships. Lineage systems ensured that care was provided for all members of the group. Oral historians and artists preserved important aspects of the culture.

African Kingdoms, Before A.D. 1000

ATLANTIC OCEAN

MOROCCO

TUNISIA

Mediterranean Sea

EGYPT

Nile R.

Red Sea

ARABIAN PENINSULA

GHANA • Kumbi-Saleh

KANEM

Meroe •

• Axum

GONJA

Ife •

• Benin

Lake Chad

Lake Victoria

NYAMWEZI

INDIAN OCEAN

→ Bantu migrations, A.D. 100-1000

▢ Kush, 750 B.C.-A.D. 300

▢ Nok, 500 B.C.-A.D. 200

▢ Axum, 500 B.C.-A.D. 650

▢ Ghana, A.D. 400-1235

▢ Kanem, A.D. 800-1400

0   700   1400 MILES
0   700   1400 KILOMETERS

N

MAP STUDY Find Kush on the map of African kingdoms above. What is the major city of Kush? Between what years did Kush flourish?

Religion. As Sub-Saharan African societies increased in size and skills from the 1st century A.D. on, the need for political organization, accepted rules of behavior, and an official religion increased. Among some peoples, such as the early Gonja in West Africa, certain priests gained influence. Gradually the priests who prayed for rain and good crops came to control the distribution of land within the community. They set the proper time for planting crops and even decided which crops should be planted.

Politics. In other communities, such as the many Nyamwezi [nī′am wē′zē] groups who lived

in what is now Tanzania, a chief with political duties was more important than the priests. The chief's power came from such activities as raising armies, collecting taxes, and settling court cases. Disputes about taxes and trade were common.

Although the laws of the community were not written down, everyone knew the laws and agreed to them. These laws were remembered, and much care was taken to pass them on from generation to generation. A chief, although very powerful, had to conform to the laws of the community. Eloquent debating in court cases was a skill practiced by many young Africans who wanted to be leaders.

Early Africans recorded their histories through words and artwork.

Knowledge of events and laws of the past became more important over time. Kings wanted to know who their ancestors had been and what brave deeds they had accomplished. Other people wanted to know how land had been divided and how taxes had been paid so they would not be cheated. In most of Africa, however, local languages were not written.

In West Africa a special group of men called **griots** [grē′ōz] were the professional record keepers, historians, and political advisers to chiefs. Griots were living libraries of information about their society's past.

Having a griot attached to one's family ensured that the family's name and deeds would be remembered. In addition, the griot entertained the family with poems and stories of their ethnic group's history. If a noble family fell on hard times, the members often would sell their horses and all their belongings before they would dismiss their griot.

Through griots, history has been passed on from generation to generation for at least the last eight centuries. Some griots today know the brave deeds of kings from 700 years ago and can remember detailed family histories that go back more than 200 years.

The most common forms of African artwork were sculpture and wood carvings depicting people and animals. Although some pieces were very realistic, others were done in a more imaginative style, showing people with exaggerated faces and

BACKGROUND Alex Haley, author of the book *Roots*, in which he traces his family background, traveled to a small village in Africa where he met a griot who provided information about his ancestors who were slaves brought to America from Africa.

From the Archives

**An Oral History
of King Sundiata**

In the 1950s D. T. Niane, a professional griot, recorded an oral history of Mali that had been handed down from generation to generation, perhaps from the 1200s. His account tells how Sundiata established the kingdom of old Mali after destroying the rival city-state of Sosso in 1235. In the excerpt below, Sundiata and his warriors prepare to attack Sosso, a city noted for its skilled ironworkers.

Sosso was a magnificent city. In the open plain her triple rampart with awe-inspiring towers reached into the sky. The city [was guarded by] 188 fortresses and the palace of [its ruler] loomed above the whole city like a gigantic tower. Sosso had but one gate; colossal and made of iron, the work of the sons of fire. . . .

The sun was beginning to set when [Sundiata] appeared before Sosso. . . . From the top of a hill, [Sundiata and his warriors] gazed upon the fearsome city of the sorcerer-king. The army encamped in the plain opposite the great gate of the city and fires were lit in the camp. [Sundiata] resolved to take Sosso in the course of a morning. He fed his men a double ration and the tam-tams beat all night.

been found near the town of Nok, Nigeria, dating from as early as 500 B.C. Terra cotta is a kind of hard, often unglazed, brownish-red earthenware. The heads are those of human beings, and the style is somewhat realistic. These Nok sculptures were probably made for religious purposes.

Section 2 Review

Identify Kush, lineage, griots

Main Ideas

1. How did African farmers learn to survive in Africa's climate?
2. How did iron contribute to the strength of Kush?
3. Describe the three sources of power within the changing African society.
4. How were the griots and artists of early African communities allowed the time to practice their arts?

Critical Thinking

Making Hypotheses: What problems might a society have that has no written language? How might it overcome those problems?

This terra-cotta head, made by Nok farmers in the 300s B.C., was probably used to help ensure a new field's fertility.

bodies. Statues of kings and queens were sometimes covered with symbols of their reign. This practice was especially common in the area of central Africa now the country of Zaire.

The Africans used both wood and clay to make their sculptures and carvings, sometimes using ivory for decoration. Unfortunately, wood does not last long in the African climate. As a result, the oldest wood carvings that have been found were made only 400 years ago. Clay, on the other hand, lasts much longer. As you read in the chapter introduction, some terra cotta sculptured heads have

FROM THE ARCHIVES The excerpt is from *Sundiata: An Epic of Old Mali,* by D. T. Niane, translated by G. D. Pickett (London: Longmans, Green, 1969). Ask students how oral histories differ from written histories. (Oral histories are spoken,

rather than written, and may vary in details according to the mood of the speaker and the occasion.)

Essential Learning Objective

Students will learn to describe the origin of the earliest people of North America.

1 FOCUS AND MOTIVATE

Ask students how Native Americans came to be called *Indians*. Have a volunteer point out on a world map the Indies that Columbus believed he had reached when he landed in the New World.

2 TEACH

On a map of the world, have students locate the Bering Strait area where nomads are thought to have first crossed from Asia to North America. Remind students that these were Stone Age hunters and gatherers, who did not begin to farm until 7000 B.C.

GUIDED PRACTICE

Have students outline the ways in which the Inuit were able to use their harsh environment to satisfy their basic needs.

3 ASSESS AND CLOSE

ASSESS

What crop was most important in the Western Hemisphere after 3000 B.C.? (corn)

OPTIONAL RETEACHING

Have students list developments in the Americas from the time of the first crossings from Asia to about 3000 B.C.

3 Native American cultures developed over many centuries.

When Christopher Columbus reached the Caribbean islands at the end of the 15th century, he was under the impression that he had landed in the Indies in Asia. As a result, he mistakenly called the people he met "Indians." The lands and people he reached, however, were not a part of the "Old World," as Columbus had expected. Instead, Columbus had landed in a "New World" that had experienced a long and complex history of its own.

As you read in the chapter introduction, we know very little of this history because most of the Native American cultures were destroyed or greatly weakened by contact with Europeans. For example, Spanish conquerors killed many of the Indian leaders, tore down their temples, and burned their books because they were convinced that the idols and writings of the Indians were works of the devil.

As a result, very few Indian writings survived. From these few remaining texts and from the often sketchy accounts of Indian life written by European conquerors has come much of our knowledge of 16th-century American cultures. For the earlier periods, archaeologists are limited to studying the many artifacts left by early cultures. Of course, archaeologists, in their continuing study of the region, are still uncovering previously unknown artifacts. In the process our knowledge of ancient American cultures is constantly being expanded and revised.

The first North Americans probably came from Asia.

Most scientists now believe the Americas were peopled by nomads who crossed a land bridge between Alaska and northeastern Asia between 40,000 and 20,000 years ago. These people followed the migrations of herds of wild animals.

At that time the Ice Age had caused much of the earth's water to be locked up in glaciers. As a result, waters had receded from the **Bering Strait**—the narrow strip of water that now separates North America from Asia near the Arctic Ocean. The land beneath the waters of the Bering Strait was ex-posed above water, providing a pathway for travel. Throughout the next thousands of years, many separate migrations of peoples are believed to have crossed over the strait into the Americas.

The prehistoric people of the Americas had a paleolithic culture. They used stone tools, wore skin clothing, and hunted with domesticated dogs. Most of these early Americans lived simply as hunters or gatherers. During the centuries before the coming of the Europeans, descendants of these people settled all throughout the Americas, from the Alaskan peninsula in the north to the tip of South America.

Most evidence indicates that the American Indians were isolated from the civilizations of the Old World. A few researchers believe that some daring seafarers crossed the Pacific or Atlantic oceans to reach America centuries before the Vikings or Columbus. Most scholars believe, however, that the Indians developed their cultures independently. They maintain that the presence of similar inventions in the Eastern and Western hemispheres indicate only that peoples often hit upon similar ideas when they face the same problems.

The development of farming changed North American life.

Perhaps as early as 7000 B.C., some Americans learned to grow crops. As time passed, the people developed new varieties of plant life. The most important of these new crops was corn, which was developed about 3000 B.C. in Mexico. Corn became as important in the Western Hemisphere as wheat was in the Eastern Hemisphere.

The development of farming allowed people in the Americas, as it had in the Middle East, to settle in communities, to develop such skills as weaving and pottery making, and to set up a division of labor. These skills spread slowly throughout the Americas.

As people all around the world have done, the people of North America learned to live with the conditions of their natural environment. Since the climate and geography of the huge North American continent are so varied, people in different parts of the continent developed different cultures. Hundreds of distinct groups developed over the centuries, with different physical characteristics, different languages, and different customs. The way of life a group followed depended heavily on the land and other available resources, such as food, water, and shelter.

One group, the Inuit [in'ü it], is an example of a people living in an extremely cold environment. As you can see from the map on page 341, the Inuit lived in the frozen lands of the extreme north. The short growing season in this northern region prevented the Inuit from growing crops. Instead, the people fished and hunted for food, particularly walrus, whales, seals, small fish, and caribou. They used the bone and ivory of some of these animals to make tools such as needles, knives, fishhooks, and harpoons, and with the skins they made clothing and tents.

The Inuit also built houses, called igloos, out of snow and ice. They lived in small family groups since the resources of the extreme north were not great enough to support a large, centralized population. As a result, the Inuit never needed to develop a form of central government.

Section 3 Review

Identify Bering Strait

Main Ideas

1. How do most scientists believe that the first Americans reached this continent?
2. How did the lives of the Indians change with the development of farming? What was the Indians' most important crop?

Critical Thinking

Recognizing Values: Reread the chapter introduction. Why do you think the Europeans who came to Africa and the Americas failed to respect the native cultures?

The Inuit built snow houses (at right) for the harsh Arctic winters, and they used a bow drill (at left) to cut holes in tough materials such as walrus ivory.

Essential Learning Objectives

Students will learn to:

- compare the two time periods of Maya civilization.
- discuss Maya accomplishments in architecture, mathematics, writing, and science.

Ask students to recall the factors which indicate civilization. (cities, organized governments, specialization of labor, writing, number systems, and the construction of large structures) Tell students to look for ways in which the Maya met these criteria.

- Write the time periods of the Classic and Post-Classic periods on the chalkboard. List the major events of each period under its heading. Clarify those aspects of Maya culture influenced by the Olmecs and Toltecs.

- Discuss the features of Maya cities as primarily religious centers where priests performed ceremonies and engaged in scientific and mathematical learning. Point out that the common people lived in outlying villages and only entered the cities on feast days or for markets.

GUIDED PRACTICE

Have students give specific examples of Maya achievements that indicate a high degree of civilization.

The Maya achieved a most complex civilization.

At about the same time that the Romans and the Hans of China were building their empires, the Indians in Mexico and in Central and South America began to develop complex civilizations. The Maya [mī′ə, mä′yə] in the Yucatán [yü′kə tan′], the Aztecs of central Mexico, and the Incas in Peru had civilizations that in some respects rivaled those of Egypt and Mesopotamia. (You will read about the Aztecs and Incas in Chapter 18.)

Archaeologists believe that these cultures of the south developed further than those of the north because the southern Indians had learned earlier how to raise corn. As a result, they had lived in one place for longer periods than the northern Indians. This stability allowed for more time to develop various crafts and other skills.

Maya culture had two main periods: Classic and Post-Classic.

Beginning about 500 B.C., the **Maya** developed a culture located chiefly in the **Yucatán peninsula** (present-day southeastern Mexico, Guatemala, and Belize). (See map, page 336.) Over the next 500 years, the Maya, influenced by a neighboring Indian group named the Olmec, developed hieroglyphic writing, a system of numbers, and a very accurate calendar. Like the Olmec, the Maya began to build pyramids and carve stone monuments.

Classic period. By A.D. 300 the Maya had established a distinctive civilization in Honduras, northern Guatemala, and nearby areas of Mexico. The early phase of this civilization, which lasted until about 900, is called the Classic period, or Old Empire. During this time, the Maya experienced the greatest achievements of the civilization. They built several cities, such as Piedras Negras [pē-ā′drəs nā′grəs] and Tikal [ti käl′], where they perfected their arts, science, and learning. Some of their most distinctive legacies are large stone sculptures known as "stelae," on which the Maya recorded important dates and events.

In the 800s the Maya began to abandon their cultural centers. Why they left remains a mystery. Some scholars have guessed that the population

grew too large for the food supply or that the people were defeated by disease or crop failure. Others have suggested that invasion of other groups into the Maya area or revolts by farmers may have caused the civilization to topple.

Post-Classic period. After the Old Empire crumbled, large numbers of the Maya evidently moved northward and built new cities in the northern tip of the Yucatán peninsula. This later phase of Maya civilization, usually called the Post-Classic period or the New Empire, flourished from about 900 to 1200. Around the new Maya centers, which included the cities of Chichén Itzá [chē-chen′ ēt zä′] and Mayapán, developed city-states similar to those of other early peoples.

This Post-Classic period was characterized by new cultural influences, in particular stemming from contact with an invading group of Indians from the central highlands of Mexico known as the Toltec. Toltec warriors conquered the Mayas of the Yucatán around 950, and remained in control for about 200 years. During that time the Toltec introduced the Maya to the worship of a feathered-serpent god named Kukulcán and influenced the Maya's art and architecture. The giant stone structures of Chichén Itzá, built between 1000 and 1200 under Toltec direction, are evidence of the Toltec influence on the Maya.

After this time the Maya city-states seem to have gone into a long period of decline. Certainly, their cities were not as well built or as elaborately decorated as they had been in earlier times. Some scholars, however, think that the Maya were simply focusing their attention on economic activities such as trade rather than on religious affairs.

Maya cities were trade and religious centers.

Maya cities were chiefly religious centers filled with huge stone pyramids, astronomical observatories, temples, and monuments. Each city had its own government, thought to be a theocracy, that controlled the surrounding area. A theocracy, you

---

A Maya nobleman prepares for a ball game, discussed on page 166. His elaborate costume includes a necklace of jaguar claws and a jaguar pelt.

BACKGROUND The Maya constructed all their buildings and temples with Stone Age technology. They had no metals, no wheels, and no pulleys. They cut and quarried stones with flint tools, transported the stones on log rollers, and pulled up the stones with ropes along log inclines.

ASSESS

1. During which period of Maya history were its greatest achievements? (Classic period)

2. Name three major Maya achievements. (accurate calendar, system of mathematics including zero, writing, and carvings)

OPTIONAL RETEACHING

Have students review the text to identify ways in which the Maya had specialized labor systems. Direct students to categorize workers into a class structure.

Students also may be assigned Activities reteaching page 51.

OPTIONAL ENRICHMENT

1. Have students prepare a research report on the art and artifacts left by the Maya. Tell students to include specific finds and the age and location of sites where artifacts were found. (average)

2. Ask students to research and prepare a chart indicating the major time divisions of the Maya calendar. (challenging)

3. Students also may be assigned Activities enrichment page 52.

4. Also for enrichment:

 Overhead Transparency 18

 Source Reading 9B

INDEPENDENT PRACTICE/ HOMEWORK

Assign the Section Review, the Chapter Review items, Activities page 50, or Workbook page 34.

Tell students that the Maya built one of the earliest and most impressive American civilizations. They had advanced mathematical and astronomical skills, an accurate calendar, and monumental stone structures decorated with detailed carvings and hieroglyphics.

Answers to Section 4 Review

Identify

Key Terms, People, and Places are defined on pages indicated in parentheses. Also see the Glossary and Biographical Dictionary. Maya (164), Yucatán peninsula (164), ideographic (166)

Main Ideas

1. During the Classic period the Maya built several cities in northern Guatemala and nearby areas of Mexico where they perfected their arts, science, and learning. The Post-Classic period, in contrast, took place in the northern areas of the Yucatán peninsula and was a time of conquest by the Toltec Indians.
2. religious and trade centers
3. architecture, sculpture, writing, astronomy, and mathematics. Examples of their skill are pyramids with carved stone figures, their writing system, their calendar, and the concept of zero.

Critical Thinking

Their writing system has not been completely deciphered. In addition, many books and other writings were destroyed by the Spanish when they conquered the area.

---

remember, is a government headed by religious authorities. A few of the larger cities may have controlled some smaller cities as well, but no centralized government is believed to have existed.

The Maya people generally did not live in these cities. Most Maya were corn farmers who lived in thatched huts on the outskirts of the cities. When a religious ceremony was to be held, the people would come from the nearby farm villages and gather in the large stone buildings. Here priests, often dressed in headdresses decorated with brightly colored feathers, would conduct ceremonies honoring or appeasing one of the many gods and goddesses worshiped by the Maya. The worship of these gods, who were seen as both helpful and harmful, was a central part of daily life.

Each city usually had a market square that drew the farmers from the villages. There merchants and shoppers carried on their business of buying and selling items such as foodstuffs, cotton cloth, and pottery. Traders set up booths to display carved jade, jewelry made of shells, and brilliant feather headdresses to be used for special ceremonies. Women ran restaurant stalls where they sold beans and hot tortillas [tôr tē′yəs], which are flat corn cakes. These foods are still an important part of the diet of the Mexican and Guatemalan people today.

Maya cities also had large game courts. In these courts, a serious game was played by two teams. Players hit a large rubber ball with their elbows, hips, or knees and tried to get it through vertical stone or wooden rings about 20 feet above the ground. Some scholars believe the ball represented the sun and that the two teams fought a symbolic struggle between the forces of light and darkness, or life and death. Some evidence exists that the losing team was offered up as a sacrifice to the Maya gods.

The Maya excelled in many different fields.

In the field of the arts, Maya architecture and sculpture were outstanding. The most dramatic type of building looked like a flat-topped pyramid. The structure was faced with limestone and held at its top a temple. Carved stone figures covered the outsides of these pyramids, and brightly colored murals, depicting lifelike figures participating in festivals or battles, decorated the interiors.

The Maya developed an **ideographic** system of writing in which symbols stood for ideas. Scholars are just beginning to learn to read the writing, except for some of the symbols that stand for gods, stars, and dates. To record their writing, the Maya produced paper from bark or tough fibers of the maguey [mag′wā] cactus and used it to make folding books.

Perhaps the most significant accomplishment of the Maya was their calendar. Maya astronomers discovered that the year was slightly less than 365¼ days long, and they divided the year into 18 months of 20 days each. The five days left at the end of the year were considered unlucky and were used by the Maya to fast and make sacrifices to the gods.

The Maya were also very skilled in mathematics. They worked out a system of numbers that included the idea of zero, a concept that was new at this time. The Maya zeros looked like this: ◉ Numbers up to nineteen were made by adding ones and fives. For example:

•	•••	—	••	••••
1	3	5	7	19

The number system was based on the number 20. That is, zero at the end of a number meant 20 times the number before it.

| ◉ | or | 1
×20
20 | Two
hundred
is | ◉ | or | 10
×20
200 |

Section 4 Review

Identify Maya, Yucatán peninsula, ideographic

Main Ideas

1. What are some differences between the Classic and Post-Classic periods of Maya civilization?
2. What were the two major functions of Maya cities?
3. What were two areas in which the Maya excelled? Give examples.

Critical Thinking

Making Hypotheses: Why do you suppose that scientists and historians have difficulty discovering why the Maya abandoned their cities in the 800s?

HIGHLIGHTS OF CIVILIZATION

Maya Architecture

Lofty pyramids crowned with temples, many-columned palaces, and monumental pillars of carved stone rise from the flat plain of the Yucatán and dot the nearby highland regions. These remains of what were once enormous ceremonial centers bear testimony to the skill of Maya architects and artisans.

The principle of the arch was unknown to Maya architects. Instead, they built walls close enough to span them with a single beam or slab of stone, or they used the corbeled, or false, arch. (See diagram.) In essence, the corbeled arch consists

The Temple of the Warriors is at Chichén Itzá, in Yucatán, Mexico.

of sloping walls that converge, or come together. Massive walls are needed to support this type of arch. Consequently, rooms are narrow, usually only 10 or 12 feet across.

These dark, narrow chambers were brightened inside and out with stucco, a hard, stonelike coating of plaster. Then artisans embellished the walls, which were usually white, with brilliantly colored murals. The Temple of the Warriors at Chichén Itzá is pictured below. A reclining ceremonial figure guards the entrance to this temple. The figure, known as Chac Mool was derived from the Toltecs and holds a bowl on its stomach to receive sacrificial offerings.

HIGHLIGHTS OF CIVILIZATION

Explain that the corbeled arch is relatively weak and that buildings such as those of the Maya require enormous amounts of material and labor to enclose relatively small spaces. Ask students to consider why the Maya, who made such astonishing advances in astronomy, would not have discovered the advantages of the true arch in construction. (Students might conjecture that the Maya hierarchy was conservative and unwilling to experiment; that they were more interested in understanding and manipulating the forces that governed their fate; also that the mild climate permitted people to live in simple huts, with the temples and palaces serving primarily ceremonial functions.)

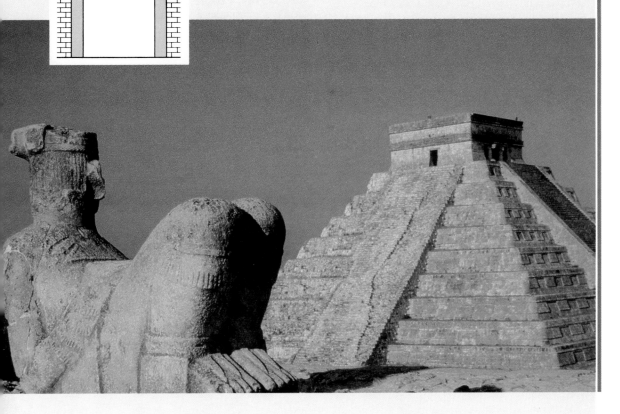

Answers to Test Yourself

Key Terms, People, and Places
The key terms, people, and places tested here were introduced in the chapter sections and reviewed in the Section Reviews. For definitions see the page references at the appropriate Section Reviews. Also see the Glossary and Biographical Dictionary.

Main Ideas
The main ideas tested here were introduced in the sections of this chapter and reviewed in the Section Reviews. For answers to these questions, see the appropriate Section Reviews.

Critical Thinking

1. our inability to completely decipher a writing system; also lack of writing, geographical isolation, choice of materials used to record events, and invasions caused differences in success

2. Students might mention types of occupations such as hunters or gatherers, types of building materials, housing patterns and styles, crops grown, types of agriculture, and inventions.

CHAPTER 9 REVIEW

Section Summaries

Section 1
Africa's varied geography produced a variety of cultures.
The continent of Africa has several different geographical regions. In the north and south are narrow regions of fertile coast, and farther inland are large deserts. These deserts merge into large regions of savanna where populations prospered. Rivers connected the villages and cities of the valleys. In East Africa people lived in the Rift Valley.

Section 2
Ancient Africans developed distinctive societies.
Useful farming methods and ironworking helped Africans grow more food and control their environment. Migrations of Bantu peoples populated central and southern Africa. One of the earliest ironworking sites in Africa developed in Kush. Ethnic groups and lineages formed the basis of African societies. Later, priests became important in some groups, but in other groups political chiefs became powerful. Law and history were memorized.

Section 3
Native American cultures developed over many centuries.
The first Americans probably came from Asia and spread out gradually. There were many different Native American cultures, each reflecting the way people learned to live with their environment. These groups included the Inuit in the extreme north.

Section 4
The Maya achieved a most complex civilization.
In the Maya Old Empire, located on the Yucatán peninsula, writing was developed, a system of numbers came into use, and a very accurate calendar was invented. Several cities were centers of learning and commerce. In the New Empire, priests ruled, until they were conquered by the Toltec.

Test Yourself

Key Terms, People, and Places
Identify the significance of each of the following:

Section 1
a. Sahara   c. Niger River
b. Kalahari

Section 2
a. Kush   c. griots
b. lineage

Section 3
a. Bering Strait

Section 4
a. Maya   c. ideographic
b. Yucatán peninsula

Review Dates

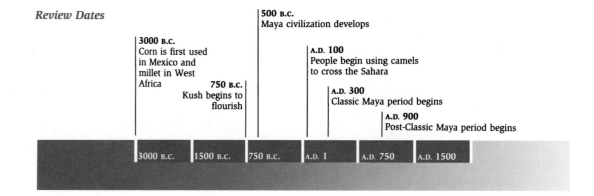

3000 B.C.
Corn is first used in Mexico and millet in West Africa

750 B.C.
Kush begins to flourish

500 B.C.
Maya civilization develops

A.D. 100
People begin using camels to cross the Sahara

A.D. 300
Classic Maya period begins

A.D. 900
Post-Classic Maya period begins

| 3000 B.C. | 1500 B.C. | 750 B.C. | A.D. 1 | A.D. 750 | A.D. 1500 |

Main Ideas

Section 1
1. In what ways did the Sahara both link early African peoples to other civilizations and divide them from one another?

2. Compare how settled and nomadic life differed on the African savanna.

3. What were some challenges faced by forest-dwellers in their daily lives and government?

4. Describe why African peoples settled along rivers and in the Great Rift Valley.

Section 2
1. How did African farmers adapt to the particular challenges of their climate?

2. In what ways did the production of iron strengthen Kush?

3. Identify the three sources of power within the changing African society.

4. What conditions of society allowed the griots and artists of early African communities the time to practice their arts?

Section 3
1. According to most scientists, how did the first Americans reach this continent?

2. In what ways did the lives of Indians change with the development of farming? What was the Indians' most significant crop?

Section 4
1. How were the Classic and Post-Classic periods of Maya civilization different?

2. What were the two major functions of the Maya cities?

3. Describe two areas of science or culture in which the Mayas excelled.

Critical Thinking
1. Making Hypotheses Why do you think that historians have been more successful in gathering information about the history and culture of some societies rather than others? Why would some historical societies attract more attention?

2. Assessing Cause and Effect How does the geography of an area encourage people to develop special skills? Give specific examples from African history.

Chapter Skills and Activities

Practicing Study and Research Skills
Making an Outline

Making an outline is a good way to organize a large amount of information. An outline can be used either as preparation to write an essay or as a study guide for a test. Either way, the outline will give you a framework on which to fit your ideas and facts.

An outline is usually composed of complete sentences organized with numbers and letters, with the most important ideas coming after a Roman numeral. Below the main idea, there should be sub-points—at least two—that are listed with capital letters. In turn, these sub-points can be further broken down using Arabic numerals. For example, this outline organizes the first main idea section of Chapter 9. Turn to pages 152–153.

I. The desert was both a barrier and a bridge for early Africans.

  A. Early life on the Sahara was different from life there today.

    1. There was more rainfall.

    2. People were hunters and gatherers.

  B. Travel across the Sahara allowed the exchange of ideas and goods.

    1. Travelers could rest at oases.

    2. People traveled in caravans on camels.

    3. Caravans were led by skilled guides.

Use this form of outline to organize the main idea section that follows the one above. Begin your outline with the following line: **II.** Large populations flourished in the savanna.

Linking Past and Present
In studying about Africa in this chapter, what differences do you see with Africa today? From what you know about Africa today, which period would you prefer to live in?

Learning History Through Maps
Examine the World physical map on pages 784–785. Compare the lands where the early Americans lived with the lands of the early Africans. What similarities and differences can you find?

CRITICAL THINKING QUESTION LEVEL 1. easy; 2. average

Answers to Test Yourself

Key Terms and People
1. e
2. f
3. c
4. d
5. b
6. a

Key Dates
D, H, B, G, F, A, E, C

Key Places
C—Rome, E—Himalayan Mountains, D—Athens, A—Yucatán peninsula, B—Sahara

Main Ideas
1. a
2. a
3. b
4. c
5. b

Critical Thinking
1. Possible answers should consider peace, strong governments, adequate food supply, fair leaders, level of participation in government, and the justice system.
2. Possible answers should consider the extent of the civilization, government, education, culture, and scientific progress.

Summarizing the Unit

Chapter 4
The Rise of Greek Civilization
Ideas developed in the city-states of Greece were essential to the development of Western civilization. The Greeks inspired other peoples to think about the ideals of freedom, equality before the laws, and civic involvement.

Chapter 5
The Greek Achievement
The most significant impact of the ancient Greeks on Western civilization has been in the realm of ideas—in philosophy, politics, science, literature, drama, and religion.

Chapter 6
The Roman Legacy
The Roman Empire, which began in central Italy, preserved and expanded Greek culture. Rome's military strength, legal system, and governmental genius served as models for later European rulers.

Chapter 7
The Flowering of Civilization in India
During India's classical times, two important religions developed that continue to shape life in India and around the world—Hinduism and Buddhism.

Chapter 8
China Reaches a Golden Age
In its classical period, China became a vast empire. The philosophies of Confucianism and Taoism developed in China during this period.

Chapter 9
Africa and the Americas in the Classical Age
Although there is scant evidence today of early civilizations in Africa and the Americas, people such as the Kushites of East Africa and the Maya of the Yucatán developed complex civilizations.

Using Writing Skills

In Unit 1 you began your writing experience with a freewriting activity. Other elements of prewriting include choosing a topic and developing ideas. Just how thorough do you have to be while getting and fleshing out ideas? One tool that many writers use for inspiration is the photograph. Pictures often offer a rich visual image from which to draw both creative ideas and factual detail.

   Activity. Select a photograph that interests you from within Unit 2. What thoughts does the photograph stir? What can you learn about the culture of the society portrayed in the image? Use the freewriting techniques you've learned to help you develop ideas from the photograph for a writing experience. Make a list of several ideas or themes from which you could later write an essay or story.

Test Yourself

Key Terms and People
Match each term or person with the correct definition.
1. Athenian statesman and military commander
2. Greek philosopher who wrote about different kinds of government
3. military leader who became dictator of Rome
4. Indian philosopher who taught moderation
5. professional African historian
6. Chinese philosopher who helped people to be happy in this life on earth
a. Confucius
b. griot
c. Julius Caesar
d. the Buddha
e. Pericles
f. Aristotle

Key Dates

Match the letters on the time line with the events for which they stand:

2000 B.C.	1600 B.C.	1200 B.C.	800 B.C.	400 B.C.	A.D. 1	A.D. 400

A   B   C DEFG   H

____ The Buddha is born.
____ The Gupta Empire is established.
____ The Zhou dynasty begins.
____ The "Age of Pericles" begins.
____ The Maya civilization develops.
____ The Mycenaeans invade Greece.
____ The Roman Republic is established.
____ Kush begins to flourish.

Key Places

Match the letters on the map with the places described below:

____ leading central Italian city
____ isolated India from the rest of the continent
____ home of the Parthenon
____ location of the Maya civilization
____ called an "ocean of sand"

Main Ideas

1. Alexander the Great was best known for ____
a. trying to create "one world."
b. treating conquered people inhumanely.
c. his inability to keep his troops' loyalty.
d. his destruction of culture in conquered lands.
2. Carthage had an advantage over Rome because ____
a. it had a strong navy.
b. its people spoke the same language.
c. its army had better supply lines.
d. it had a stronger government.
3. One of the major beliefs of Hinduism is that ____
a. one has no control over one's own destiny.
b. future life depends on present behavior.
c. there is no afterlife.
d. it is important to die in a religious war.
4. The civilization that provided for the greatest social mobility through education was the ____
a. Roman.
b. Maya.
c. Chinese.
d. Indian.
5. The development of farming around 3000 B.C. changed North American life because ____
a. people began to keep records.
b. people began to establish settled communities.
c. new crops introduced unfamiliar diseases.
d. people began to move around more.

Critical Thinking

1. Making Hypotheses After examining the civilizations described in this unit, what do you think was the most important reason for their successes?
2. Making Comparisons Which civilization would you consider to be the most advanced? Athens under Pericles; Rome under Augustus; India under the Guptas; China under the Tangs?

PART TWO

Civilizations Connecting

A.D. 500–1500

In Part One you read how each of the classical age civilizations developed distinctive religions, social systems, political organizations, artistic styles, and economies. In Part Two, which covers the period from 500 to 1500, we enter a time when rich and powerful centers of civilization came into existence not only in Europe and Asia, but in Africa and the Americas as well. No one of them was able to dominate the others. That is one of the chief characteristics of this 1,000-year-period in world history. Another is that in each civilization there was a pattern of widening connections until each became regional in scope. In the case of Islam, the connecting links reached all the way from North Africa to the Philippines.

Throughout this period the widening regional connections came mainly through religion and trade. In the next 500 years, we will see the Europeans using these same techniques, along with superior technology, on a global scale. As you read through Part Two, consider how civilizations in geographic regions such as East Asia, the Middle East, Europe, West Africa, and the Americas were influenced by particular religions, cultures, and trade patterns.

500 Kingdom of Ghana develops	622 Muhammad journeys from Mecca to Medina

500	600	700

Sacred Mosque, Mecca, 600s

ARCTIC OCEAN

NORTH AMERICA

AZTEC EMPIRE

PACIFIC OCEAN

SOUT AMERI

INCA EMPIRE

Regional Civilizations, to 1500

- Christian world
- Byzantine Empire in 1100
- Islamic world in 1500
- Ottoman Empire
- Delhi Sultanate
- Swahili city-states

172

800	960	1066	1215	1325	1453
Charlemagne is crowned head of Holy Roman Empire	Song dynasty begins	Normans conquer England	King John signs Magna Carta	Tenochtitlán is built by Aztecs	Ottoman Turks conquer Constantinople

800	900	1000	1100	1200	1300	1400	1500

Emperor Taizu, founder of Song dynasty

Norman conquest of England, Bayeux Tapestry, c. 1080

Aztec serpent pendant, of turquoise and shell

ARCTIC OCEAN

EUROPE

BYZANTINE EMPIRE

ASIA

OTTOMAN EMPIRE

DELHI SULTANATE

MING CHINA

ATLANTIC OCEAN

GHANA/MALI/ SONGHAI

KANEM-BORNU

ETHIOPIA

BENIN

AFRICA

KONGO

SWAHILI CITY-STATES

ZIMBABWE

INDIAN OCEAN

PACIFIC OCEAN

AUSTRALIA

Other African states and empires to 1500

Ming China

Aztec Empire

Inca Empire

N

0	2000 Miles
0	2000 Kilometers

The Era of Regional Civilizations: Christendom and Islam

ADDITIONAL TEACHING AIDS FOR UNIT THREE

OVERVIEW

This unit covers the rise of Christendom and Islam and the growth of European feudal societies into national monarchies.

Literature for the Teacher

Arjomand, Said Amir. *Turban for the Crown: The Islamic Revolution in Iran.* New York: Oxford University Press, 1988.

Boardman, John, Jasper Griffin, Oswyn Murray. *The Oxford History of the Classical World.* Oxford University Press, 1986.

Bradford, Ernest. *The Sword and the Scimitar— Saga of the Crusades.* G. P. Putnam & Sons, 1974.

Claster, Jill N. *The Medieval Experience 300– 1400.* New York: New York University Press, 1982.

Cottrell, Alvin J. editor. *Persian Gulf States: A General Survey.* Johns Hopkins University Press, 1980.

Gabrieli, F. R. and E. J. Costello translators. *Arab Historians of the Crusades.* Berkeley: University of California Press, 1984.

Hibbert, Christopher. *Rome: The Biography of a City.* New York: W. W. Norton & Co., 1985.

Payne, Robert. *The Dream and the Tomb: History of the Crusades.* New York: Stein & Day, 1984.

Scherman, Katharine. *Birth of France— Warriors, Bishops, Kings.* Random House, 1987.

Seaman, L. C. B. *A New History of England 410–1975.* Sussex: Harvester Press, 1982.

Literature for the Student

Bridge, Anthony. *The Crusades.* New York: Franklin Watts, 1982. (challenging)

Brooks, Polly S. *Queen Eleanor: Independent Spirit of the Medieval World.* Harper Row, 1983 (average)

Campbell, James Graham. *The Vikings,* British Museum Press, 1980. (easy)

Davies, Nigel. *Voyagers to the New World.* New York: Wm. Morrow & Co., 1979. (challenging)

Morrison, Karl F. *Europe's Middle Ages.* Glenview: Scott, Foresman and Co., 1970. (challenging)

Simpson, Jacqueline. *The Viking World.* New York, St. Martins Press, 1988. (average)

Strayer, Joseph R. *Western Europe in the Middle Ages: A Short History* (Third Edition). Glenview: Scott, Foresman and Co., 1982. (challenging)

Winston, Clara & Richard. *Daily Life in the Middle Ages.* American Heritage, 1975. (easy)

Audio-Visual Materials*

The Christians. Film, 13 titles, about 42 minutes each, color, [McGraw-Hill], 1976. Considers the origin and spread of Christianity, the decline of Rome and of the papacy, the Reformation, missionaries in Britain and Africa, Vatican II, and more

England in the Middle Ages. Video or film, 30 minutes, color, [EB], 1982. Describes the main historical features and developments between 1066 and 1453

The Glory That Remains: Invaders and Converts. Film, 28 minutes, color, [Time-Life], 1969. Mongul invasions and the legend of Islamic art

Liberty: The Legacy of the Magna Carta. Video, 10 minutes, color, [PBS Video], 1986. Brief examination of this historic document and its importance to Western civilization

The Middle Ages. Video, 5 programs, 20 minutes each, color, [Films, Inc.], 1987. "Peasants' Revolt," "The Castle," "The Church," "The Town," and "The Traders." Re-creation of 13th–14th century medieval life

The Rise of Nations in Europe (revised). Film, 13 minutes, color, [Cornerstone or University of Illinois], 1977. Follows the changes that occurred in western Europe during the transition from feudal states to central governments ruled by powerful monarchs

The Torchbearers: Bridging the Dark Ages. Video or film, 25 minutes, color, [EB], 1984. Shows how Islam helped bridge the 800-year gap between the fall of Rome and the onset of the European Renaissance in the early 14th century

* For a complete listing of sources of audio-visual materials see page T30.

The Triumph of the West. Video, 4 titles, 50 minutes each, color, [Films, Inc.], 1987. "A New Direction"—Greco-Roman and Judaic roots. "The Heart of the West"—The Fall and Rise of Christianity. "The World's Debate"—Interaction with Islam. "East of Europe"—Russia and the East

The Tudors. Video, 7 programs, 20 minutes each, color, [Films, Inc.], 1987. "Ships and Seaman," "The Great House," "Vicars of Aessle," "The Beggars Are Coming," "Mary, Queen of Scots," "Search for the Mary Rose," and "Secrets of the Mary Rose." Detailed and historically accurate picture of the Tudor period in British history

OPTIONAL WRITING ASSIGNMENTS

1. You are an art critic for a Roman newspaper. Write a review of Michelangelo's recently completed work on the ceiling of the Sistine Chapel.

2. You are a realtor for Feudal Farms Realty. Write an advertisement offering a manor for sale. Be sure to point out the many fine features of the manor to attract the attention of potential purchasers. A drawing of the manor should accompany your ad.

3. As a reporter for your local newspaper in Russia, you have been asked to write the obituary of your late ruler, Ivan the Terrible. While you have been instructed to center your attention on his accomplishments, you are free to explain why he became known as Ivan the Terrible.

4. As an adviser to a leader of a German tribe, write a letter to your leader encouraging attacks on the Roman Empire. Your letter must explain why the attacks should be undertaken.

5. You are a teenager living in Constantinople in the year 1200. Write a letter to a cousin in a small village in another part of the Islamic Empire. Your letter should describe what you do and do not like about living in Constantinople.

UNIT TESTS
IN THE TEACHER'S RESOURCE FILE

Unit Test, pp. 73–74

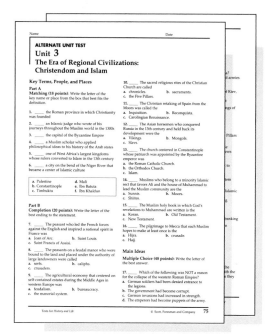

Alternate Unit Test, pp. 75–76

FINE ART IN UNIT THREE

Fine art forms an integral part of the historical record of events portrayed in this textbook. A listing of the paintings, drawings, sculpture, historic photographs, architecture, and other works of fine art selected to illustrate this unit follows. Students may be asked to research the artists and their works and report their findings to the entire class. Students also may be asked to write one or more paragraphs describing what they see upon a detailed study of a work of art and what the artist was attempting to communicate.

The Era of Regional Civilizations: Christendom and Islam

Themes and Patterns   The age of classical civilizations ended in the late 6th century. By then the Han, Gupta, and Roman empires had all collapsed, and a variety of nomadic invaders had plunged Europe and Asia into turmoil. Out of this chaos several civilizations emerged, whose influence reached beyond political boundaries. Two of these regional civilizations, Christendom and Islam, were shaped largely by religion. Both originated in the Mediterranean area and became international in their reach.

Christianity united almost all the peoples of Europe. Although people of other faiths also lived in this area, Christian laws and customs governed the way of life. Christendom was divided into two parts. Western Christendom looked to the head of the Church in Rome for leadership, and Latin was the language of religion and governments. Eastern Christendom looked to Constantinople, and the official language was Greek.

The civilization of Islam arose in the 7th century when nomadic Arabs adopted the Muslim faith and conquered a powerful empire that stretched from Spain to India. Muslim civilization was held together by a common religion and the Arabic language and further united by widespread trade.

This manuscript is from the Book of Kells, a masterwork made by Irish monks around A.D. 800. Note the small figures concealed with the Greek letters X and R. The intricate interlacing is derived from traditional Celtic and Anglo-Saxon styles.

Chapters in This Unit

10 Rome and the Rise of Christendom

OVERVIEW

This chapter covers the rise of the Christian Church from its early beginnings in Rome through the Christianization of western Europe.

PLANNING CHART

Section	Text Pages	Key Concept	Suggested Teaching Time
1 Christianity became a strong religion in the Roman world.	177–181	Christianity established itself as a strong, well-organized religion in Rome as a result of its appealing creed and the decline of the Roman Empire.	One day **More time?** Use *Source Reading 10A.*
2 The Roman Empire collapsed under attacks from Germanic tribes.	182–184	As the Christian Church was growing stronger, mass migration of Germanic tribes occurred throughout Europe and led to invasions by Germans and to the collapse of the Roman Empire.	One day **More time?** Use *Overhead Transparency 19.*
3 The Church became a force in preserving civilization.	185–186	As the government of the Rome Empire ceased to function, the Christian Church provided protection, order, and government as it spread beyond the boundaries of the empire.	One day **More time?** Use *Overhead Transparency 20.* **Less time?** Assign Section 3 to be read before class and teach it together with Section 4.
4 An alliance of popes and Franks helped western Christendom grow and prosper.	186–188	The Roman Catholic Church became the major political, cultural, and religious power in western Europe as a result of an alliance between popes and Frankish rulers.	One day **More time?** Use *Source Reading 10B.*

ANCILLARIES

Materials that may be used with this chapter to reinforce, reteach, enrich, and assess learning are pictured on the following pages.

Teacher's Resource File

ACTIVITIES

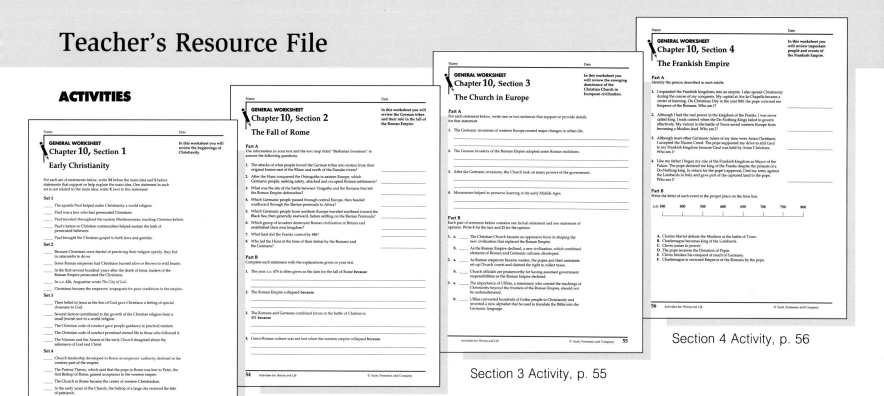

GENERAL WORKSHEET
Chapter 10, Section 1

Early Christianity

In this worksheet you will review the beginnings of Christianity.

For each set of statements below, write **M** before the main idea and **S** before statements that support or help explain the main idea. One statement in each set is not related to the main idea; write **X** next to this statement.

Set 1
____ The apostle Paul helped make Christianity a world religion.
____ Paul was a Jew who had persecuted Christians.
____ Paul traveled throughout the eastern Mediterranean, teaching Christian beliefs.
____ Paul's letters to Christian communities helped sustain the faith of persecuted believers.
____ Paul brought the Christian gospel to both Jews and gentiles.

Set 2
____ Because Christians were fearful of practicing their religion openly, they hid in catacombs to do so.
____ Some Roman emperors had Christians burned alive or thrown to wild beasts.
____ In the first several hundred years after the death of Jesus, leaders of the Roman Empire persecuted the Christians.
____ In A.D. 426, Augustine wrote *The City of God*.
____ Christians became the emperors' scapegoats for poor conditions in the empire.

Set 3
____ Their belief in Jesus as the Son of God gave Christians a feeling of special closeness to God.
____ Several factors contributed to the growth of the Christian religion from a small Jewish sect to a world religion.
____ The Christian code of conduct gave people guidance in practical matters.
____ The Christian code of conduct promised eternal life to those who followed it.
____ The Nicenes and the Arians of the early Church disagreed about the substance of God and Christ.

Set 4
____ Church leadership developed in Rome as emperors' authority declined in the western part of the empire.
____ The Petrine Theory, which said that the pope in Rome was heir to Peter, the first Bishop of Rome, gained acceptance in the western empire.
____ The Church in Rome became the center of western Christendom.
____ In the early years of the Church, the bishop of a large city received the title of patriarch.

Section 1 Activity, p. 53

GENERAL WORKSHEET
Chapter 10, Section 2

The Fall of Rome

In this worksheet you will review the German tribes and their role in the fall of the Roman Empire.

Part A
Use information in your text and the text map titled "Barbarian Invasions" to answer the following questions.

1. The attacks of what people forced the German tribes into motion from their original homes east of the Rhine and north of the Danube rivers?
2. After the Huns conquered the Ostrogoths in eastern Europe, which Germanic people, seeking safety, attacked and occupied Roman settlements?
3. What was the site of the battle between Visigoths and the Romans that left the Roman Empire defenseless?
4. Which Germanic people passed through central Europe, then headed southward through the Iberian peninsula to Africa?
5. Which Germanic people from northern Europe traveled southeast toward the Black Sea, then generally eastward, before settling on the Iberian Peninsula?
6. Which group of invaders destroyed Roman civilization in Britain and established their own kingdom?
7. What land did the Franks control by 486?
8. Who led the Huns at the time of their defeat by the Romans and the Germans?

Part B
Complete each statement with the explanations given in your text.

1. The year A.D. 476 is often given as the date for the fall of Rome **because**
2. The Roman Empire collapsed **because**
3. The Romans and Germans combined forces in the battle of Chalons in 451 **because**
4. Greco-Roman culture was not lost when the western empire collapsed **because**

Section 2 Activity, p. 54

GENERAL WORKSHEET
Chapter 10, Section 3

The Church in Europe

In this worksheet you will review the emerging dominance of the Christian Church in European civilization.

Part A
For each statement below, write one or two sentences that support or provide details for that statement.

1. The Germanic invasions of western Europe created major changes in urban life.
2. The German invaders of the Roman Empire adopted some Roman traditions.
3. After the Germanic invasions, the Church took on many powers of the government.
4. Monasteries helped to preserve learning in the early Middle Ages.

Part B
Each pair of sentences below contains one factual statement and one statement of opinion. Write **F** for the fact and **O** for the opinion.

1. a. ____ The Christian Church became an oppressive force in shaping the new civilization that replaced the Roman Empire.
   b. ____ As the Roman Empire declined, a new civilization, which combined elements of Roman and Germanic cultures, developed.
2. a. ____ As Roman emperors became weaker, the popes and their assistants set up Church courts and claimed the right to collect taxes.
   b. ____ Church officials are praiseworthy for having assumed government responsibilities as the Roman Empire declined.
3. a. ____ The importance of Ulfilas, a missionary who carried the teachings of Christianity beyond the frontiers of the Roman Empire, should not be underestimated.
   b. ____ Ulfilas converted hundreds of Gothic people to Christianity and invented a new alphabet that he used to translate the Bible into the Germanic language.

Section 3 Activity, p. 55

GENERAL WORKSHEET
Chapter 10, Section 4

The Frankish Empire

In this worksheet you will review important people and events of the Frankish Empire.

Part A
Identify the person described in each riddle.

1. I expanded the Frankish kingdoms into an empire. I also spread Christianity during the course of my conquests. My capital at Aix-la-Chapelle became a center of learning. On Christmas Day in the year 800, the pope crowned me Emperor of the Romans. Who am I?
2. Although I had the real power in the kingdom of the Franks, I was never called king. I took control when the Do-Nothing Kings failed to govern effectively. My victory in the battle of Tours saved western Europe from becoming a Muslim land. Who am I?
3. Although most other Germanic rulers of my time were Arian Christians, I accepted the Nicene Creed. The pope supported my drive to add Gaul to my Frankish kingdom because Gaul was held by Arian Christians. Who am I?
4. Like my father I began my rule of the Frankish kingdom as Mayor of the Palace. The pope declared me king of the Franks despite the protests of a Do-Nothing king. In return for the pope's approval, I led my army against the Lombards in Italy and gave part of the captured land to the pope. Who am I?

Part B
Write the letter of each event at the proper place on the time line.

A.D. 450   500   550   600   650   700   750   800

A. Charles Martel defeats the Muslims at the battle of Tours.
B. Charlemagne becomes king of the Lombards.
C. Clovis comes to power.
D. The pope receives the Donation of Pepin.
E. Clovis finishes his conquest of much of Germany.
F. Charlemagne is crowned Emperor of the Romans by the pope.

Section 4 Activity, p. 56

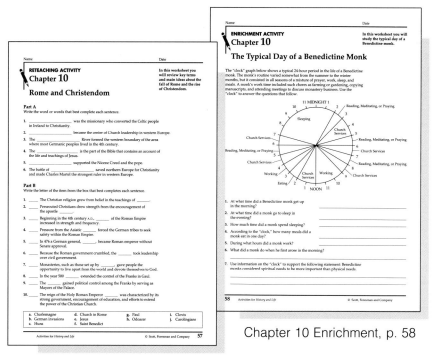

RETEACHING ACTIVITY
Chapter 10

Rome and Christendom

In this worksheet you will review key terms and main ideas about the fall of Rome and the rise of Christendom.

Part A
Write the word or words that best complete each sentence.

1. _____ was the missionary who converted the Celtic people in Ireland to Christianity.
2. _____ became the center of Church leadership in western Europe.
3. The _____ River formed the western boundary of the area where most Germanic peoples lived in the 4th century.
4. The _____ is the part of the Bible that contains an account of the life and teachings of Jesus.
5. _____ supported the Nicene Creed and the pope.
6. The battle of _____ saved northern Europe for Christianity and made Charles Martel the strongest ruler in western Europe.

Part B
Write the letter of the item from the box that best completes each sentence.

1. ____ The Christian religion grew from belief in the teachings of ____.
2. ____ Persecuted Christians drew strength from the encouragement of the apostle ____.
3. ____ Beginning in the 4th century A.D., ____ of the Roman Empire increased in strength and frequency.
4. ____ Pressure from the Asiatic ____ forced the German tribes to seek safety within the Roman Empire.
5. ____ In 476 a German general, ____, became Roman emperor without Senate approval.
6. ____ Because the Roman government crumbled, the ____ took leadership over civil government.
7. ____ Monasteries, such as those set up by ____, gave people the opportunity to live apart from the world and devote themselves to God.
8. ____ In the year 500 ____ extended the control of the Franks in Gaul.
9. ____ The ____ gained political control among the Franks by serving as Mayors of the Palace.
10. ____ The reign of the Holy Roman Emperor ____ was characterized by its strong government, encouragement of education, and efforts to extend the power of the Christian Church.

a. Charlemagne	d. Church in Rome	g. Paul	i. Clovis
b. German invasions	e. Jesus	h. Odoacer	j. Carolingians
c. Huns	f. Saint Benedict		

Chapter 10 Reteaching, p. 57

ENRICHMENT ACTIVITY
Chapter 10

The Typical Day of a Benedictine Monk

In this worksheet you will study the typical day of a Benedictine monk.

The "clock" graph below shows a typical 24-hour period in the life of a Benedictine monk. The monk's routine varied somewhat from the summer to the winter months, but it consisted of a mixture of prayer, work, sleep, and meals. A monk's work time included such chores as farming or gardening, copying manuscripts, and attending meetings to discuss monastery business. Use the "clock" to answer the questions that follow.

1. At what time did a Benedictine monk get up in the morning?
2. At what time did a monk go to sleep in the evening?
3. How much time did a monk spend sleeping?
4. According to the "clock," how many meals did a monk eat in one day?
5. During what hours did a monk work?
6. What did a monk do when he first arose in the morning?
7. Use information on the "clock" to support the following statement: Benedictine monks considered spiritual needs to be more important than physical needs.

Chapter 10 Enrichment, p. 58

Teacher's Resource File

GEOGRAPHY SKILLS

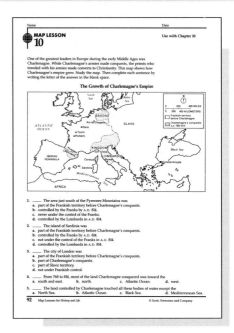

Chapter 10 Geography
Worksheet/Map, pp. 21–22

Chapter 10 Map Lesson, p. 92

TESTS

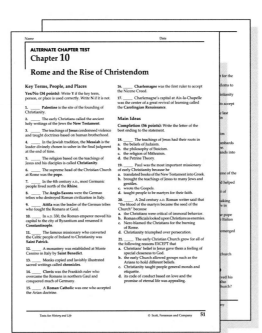

Chapter Test, pp. 49–50

Alternate Chapter Test, pp. 51–52

Other Optional Ancillaries

WORKBOOK

Section 1 Worksheet, p. 35

Section 2 Worksheet, p. 36

Section 3 Worksheet, p. 37

Section 4 Worksheet, p. 38

SOURCE READINGS

Source Reading 10A
Source REading 10B

TEST GENERATOR

40 multiple-choice questions for Chapter 10

OVERHEAD TRANSPARENCIES

Overhead Transparency 19
Overhead Transparency 20

10

Rome and the Rise of Christendom

A.D. 1–800

A.D. 300

A.D. 395	Christianity becomes official religion of the Roman Empire
A.D. 476	Rome "falls"
A.D. 800	Pope crowns Charlemagne emperor

A.D. 900

A.D. 1000

The decline of a great empire and the rise of a great religion happen slowly. The decline of the Roman Empire and the growth of Christianity both took centuries.

There are many reasons for the decline of the Roman Empire. Corruption and immorality among the Romans themselves weakened the empire. Powerful German tribes threatened to overrun the empire and drained Roman military resources.

As early as the 1st century A.D., the Roman historian Tacitus [tas'ə təs] sensed what might happen. An admirer of the republican form of government, Tacitus was extremely critical of the decline in Roman moral standards. To show how these were weakening the empire, he wrote a book called *Germania* that described the German tribes to the north. Almost as a warning to Rome, he noted the German drive for constant military action:

> If their native state sinks into the sloth of prolonged peace and repose, many of its noble youths voluntarily seek those tribes which are waging some war, both because inaction is odious [hateful] to their race, and because they win renown [fame] more readily in the midst of peril, and cannot maintain a numerous following except by violence and war. . . . Nor are they as easily persuaded to plow the earth and to wait for the year's produce as to challenge an enemy and earn the honor of wounds. Nay, they actually think it tame and stupid to acquire by the sweat of toil what they might win by their blood.

The Roman Empire survived for another 300 years. However, Tacitus's description of the Germans helps us understand why those northern people were eventually able to conquer Rome.

In the year 800, a Germanic king named Charlemagne was proclaimed emperor of a new Roman Empire. He established a strong central government in much of Europe and represented the forces that would reshape western Christendom.

This elaborate 6th-century portrait of Jesus is a mosaic, a picture made from small glass tiles. It is one of the masterpieces of Christian art in the Church of St. Vitale in Ravenna, Italy.

Reading Preview

In this chapter you will read about the rise of Christianity and the decline of Rome.

1. *Christianity became a strong religion in the Roman world.*
2. *The Roman Empire collapsed under attacks from Germanic tribes.*
3. *The Church became a force in preserving civilization.*
4. *An alliance of popes and Franks helped western Christendom grow and prosper.*

 Christianity became a strong religion in the Roman world.

By the middle of the 4th century, the once-powerful and prosperous Roman Empire showed unmistakable signs of decay. The government was riddled with corruption. Barbarian tribes broke through the imperial frontiers time after time. Heavy taxes burdened the citizens. City mobs shouted for bread as food production continued to drop off. Confronted with these severe problems, many Romans lost confidence in the ability of mere humans to deal with life. Certainly they lost

1 *Lesson Plan*

Essential Learning Objectives

Students will learn to:
- explain the reasons for the spread of Christianity in the Roman Empire.
- analyze the organization of the Christian Church.

1 FOCUS AND MOTIVATE

Have students give examples of decay in the Roman Empire from the first through the third century A.D. (more than 70 emperors, many of whom were inept, corrupt, or brutal; harsh treatment of Roman colonies; revolts in colonies; increase in crime; hardships in Rome; mercenary rather than citizen army) Ask students to name present-day societies that may, in their opinion, be decaying.

177

- Discuss the effect of decay in Roman society on the general population. Ask students their opinions on why Romans turned to religion rather than to a search for political and economic solutions to their problems. Have students make suggestions for possible reforms that might have resulted in the continuation of the empire.

- Compare the teachings of Jesus to the code of ethics set forth in the Ten Commandments, studied in Chapter 3. Emphasize that Jesus' teachings are an outgrowth of that code. Have students give examples of how some of the standards of Judeo-Christian ethics for human behavior are reflected in today's laws in Western civilizations.

- Discuss the spread of Christianity in the Roman Empire. Have students cite the causes and effects of persecution by Roman emperors. Ask them for their opinions on (1) why the Roman population tolerated the inhuman treatment of Christians, and (2) why the Christians did not revolt.

- Draw a triangular, hierarchical chart ranking the leaders of the Christian Church according to power. Have students describe the duties of each type of leader. Discuss the division of early Christendom into the eastern and western Christian Churches.

GUIDED PRACTICE

List the following on the board: Old Testament, New Testament, Epistles, Vulgate Bible, *The City of God*. Have students evaluate their importance in the spread of Christianity.

The Spread of Christianity to A.D. 1100

Legend:
- To A.D. 200
- A.D. 200–400
- A.D. 400–800
- A.D. 800–1100
- --- Journeys of St. Paul

MAP STUDY Saint Paul brought Christianity to many different peoples between A.D. 37 and 67. To which regions did he make his journeys?

faith in their human leaders. The Romans turned more and more to religion, though some turned to philosophy—particularly Stoicism. This Greek philosophy taught that people should accept their fate with quiet courage.

In the search for solace and divine support, many Romans called upon their old gods—Mars, Jupiter, and Minerva—for help. However, people began to doubt these gods also, given the terrible conditions of the times. Thousands began to look at other Middle Eastern religions, such as Judaism and Christianity.

The interest in Christianity was of major significance in the history of Western civilization. Christianity was a religion that had been founded in **Palestine**, then a Roman province, in the 1st century A.D. This faith was based on the teachings of a Jew named Jesus.

Christianity began with Jesus.

Most of what is known about Jesus comes from the Gospels, the first four books of the New Testament. The **New Testament** is the part of the Bible that contains the life and teachings of Jesus. The Gospels—named Matthew, Mark, Luke, and John—were written in Greek many years after Jesus lived. According to the Gospels, **Jesus** was born in Bethlehem, a town in Judea, and reared in

What's In a Name?

BETHLEHEM Bethlehem, the birthplace of Jesus, is located a few miles south of Jerusalem. It is one of the world's most famous towns. The name comes from the Hebrew words *bet lechem*, which mean "house of bread."

ANSWER TO MAP STUDY Palestine, Asia Minor, Greece, and Italy the village of Nazareth in the Galilee, a district to the north. Around the age of 30, Jesus stopped working as a carpenter and began to travel throughout Palestine, preaching his doctrines. (See the map, page 178.)

The teachings of Jesus had their roots in Judaism. In keeping with Judaism, Jesus condemned violence and selfishness and taught doctrines based on human brotherhood. His teachings, his personal examples of love and caring, and his sacrificial death on the Cross provided the foundations of the Christian faith. Jesus and his followers declared him the **Messiah**, or "anointed one." (Messiah is a Hebrew word; in Greek the same word is Christ.) Most Jews, however, did not accept Jesus' claim that he was the Messiah—the leader divinely chosen to usher in the final judgment at the end of time.

The Gospels report that Jesus developed a group of faithful followers and attracted crowds of people wherever he went. Both Roman rulers and Jewish leaders reacted against Jesus' preaching. To the Romans, who feared political turmoil in Palestine, Jesus seemed to be encouraging overthrow of the government. To Jewish leaders, proclaiming oneself the Messiah was blasphemy [blas′fə mē], or contempt for sacred teachings.

Historians differ as to exactly what happened in the later years of Jesus' life. However, around A.D. 33 Jesus was put to death by crucifixion on the order of Pontius Pilate [pon′shəs pī′lət], the Roman governor of Judea.

The New Testament relates how Jesus reappeared to his disciples following the Crucifixion and confirmed his teachings of eternal life. The disciples, as missionaries of the new faith, spread the news of the Resurrection and the teaching that Jesus was the Son of God, sent to earth to show the way to eternal life through faith and Christian living. Followers of these teachings called themselves "brethren," brothers of "the way." Later, believers in "the way" were called Christians and their faith became known as **Christianity**.

Paul spread the teachings of Jesus.

The most important missionary or apostle [ə pos′-əl], was Paul, a well-educated Jew from Tarsus in Asia Minor. (See map, page 178.) As a young man,

From the Archives

The Letter of Paul to the Romans

The letters, or epistles, of the Apostle Paul are the earliest Christian writings in existence today. In his epistle to the Romans, Paul's view of the Christian life reaches its classic expression.

Owe no one anything, except to love one another; for he who loves his neighbor has fulfilled the law. The commandments, "You shall not commit adultery, You shall not kill, You shall not steal, You shall not covet," and any other commandment, are summed up in this sentence, "You shall love your neighbor as yourself." Love does no wrong to a neighbor; therefore love is the fulfilling of the law.

Romans 13:8–10

Paul believed that Christian teachings went against Judaism, and he took part in the persecutions of Christians. According to the Acts of the Apostles (9:1–5) in the New Testament, Paul was on his way to arrest any men or women whom he found to be followers of "the way," when he was suddenly surrounded by "a light from heaven." After this experience, Paul became dedicated to Christianity.

Immediately, Paul set out to bring Jesus' teachings to as many people as possible—to Jews and gentiles (non-Jews) alike. He became the "Apostle" to the gentiles. From about A.D. 37 until his death in the year 67, Paul journeyed to many cities around the eastern Mediterranean, spreading the Christian gospel. (Note Paul's journeys on the map on page 178.)

Paul's letters to the small Christian communities he visited strengthened Christian beliefs among the persecuted believers. To this day, the letters of this apostle are considered fundamental doctrines of the Christian faith. Paul's life and teachings helped Christianity grow from a small Jewish sect in Palestine to a world religion.

Christianity triumphed over persecution.

Officials of the Roman government generally al-

FROM THE ARCHIVES Suggest that students review the Ten Commandments (From the Archives, Chapter 3) and decide to what degree each commandment involves an individual's rela-tionships with his or her neighbors. If everyone loved his or her neighbors as Paul suggests, would laws be necessary?

ASSESS

1. Why was the Council of Nicaea called? (to resolve whether God and Christ were of the same substance)
2. Who organized the theology of the Christian Church? (a group of men known as the Church Fathers)

OPTIONAL RETEACHING

Divide students into several groups and have each group list the reasons for the spread of Christianity in the Roman world. Next, have them compile the reasons on both lists into one master list.

OPTIONAL ENRICHMENT

1. Assign students to research and write a description of the way of life of early Christians in Rome. (average)
2. Students who are interested in philosophy could research Stoicism and compare the beliefs of Stoics to those of Christians. Have students present the comparison in chart form. (challenging)
3. Also for enrichment:

 Source Reading 10A

INDEPENDENT PRACTICE/ HOMEWORK

Assign the Section Review, Activities page 53, or Workbook page 35.

CLOSURE

Summarize the lesson by telling students that Christianity spread in the Roman Empire because its inhabitants rejected the fatalism of their old religion for the Christian God who holds individuals responsible for their actions through exercise of free will. The concept of the equality and dignity of each individual has been one of the most important legacies of the Christian Church to Western society.

BACKGROUND One of the reasons for the growth of Christianity was its appeal to many frightened and restless people during the difficult days of Rome's decline. Many exotic cults arose at this time, but they did not fulfill a strong need. Christianity taught the brotherhood of all and the sure reward of immortality.

lowed various religions to exist in the empire as long as the people accepted government authority. The Christians, however, were critical of the immoral behavior so widespread in the Roman world. Moreover, they refused to obey many of the Roman laws—particularly that of emperor worship. Roman officials, therefore, looked upon Christians as enemies of the state.

As you learned in Chapter 6, the Roman emperor Nero blamed the Christians for the burning of Rome in A.D. 64 and persecuted them severely. He and other emperors, seeking excuses for bad conditions during their reigns, used the Christians as scapegoats. These emperors crucified Christians, threw them to wild beasts in crowded arenas, or had them burned alive.

The first widespread persecution of the Christians was carried on between A.D. 249 and 251. The last mass persecution was ordered in 303 and ended in 313. During these years Christians lived a hunted existence and were forced to practice their religion hidden in catacombs, which were underground rooms where tombs were placed.

Still, even with all the suffering, the religion could not be wiped out. In fact, the courage with which Christians met death inspired a Roman writer of the 2nd century to say that "the blood of the martyrs became the seed of the Church."

In 311 Christianity was made a legal religion in the eastern Roman Empire. About two years later, in the western empire, the Emperor Constantine issued the Edict of Milan, which legalized Christianity throughout the empire. In 395, as you read earlier in Chapter 6, the Emperor Theodosius made Christianity the official religion.

Christianity was strengthened by its appealing creed.

There are several reasons for the successful growth of the early Christian Church. First, Christianity had the Bible, which was regarded as the Word of God. Second, Christians believed that Jesus was the Son of God, which gave believers a special closeness to God. Third, Christianity taught an appealing code of conduct based on love and held out the promise of eternal life for those who followed that code. Fourth, in addition to teaching general morals, the code also guided people in very practical ways—such as how to behave toward equals and superiors. Finally, Christianity gave people spiritual comfort in a troubled world filled with inequality and injustice.

Early Christians held different views of the substance of God and Christ. To resolve this conflict, the Emperor Constantine called the Council of Nicaea [nī sē'ə] in the year 325. This body put together a creed that said God and Christ were of the same substance.

All members of the council agreed to the Nicene [nī sēn'] Creed except for a priest named Arius and a few of his followers. This group, called Arians, believed that God and Christ were of different substances. The Arians were therefore banished from the Church as heretics [her'ə tiks], or persons who hold a belief different from the accepted view. However, many people continued to cling to Arian beliefs. As the years passed, the Nicenes and the Arians struggled for leadership in the Church. The Nicenes were finally victorious.

In addition to the Nicene Creed, the early Church developed an official book of sacred writings. The holy writings of the Jews, which the early Christians called the Old Testament, were combined with religious writings collected after

This enameled dove is a symbol of the Holy Ghost, the spirit of God. It contained wafers for communion, a holy rite of the Church.

BACKGROUND Later edicts by Theodosius practically extinguished all religions except Christianity within the empire.

the death of Jesus. Twenty-seven of these collections, or books, were selected to make up what became the New Testament.

The letters of advice and encouragement that Paul wrote to Christians in various cities were also included in this book. In fact, these letters, or epistles, make up some of the most important books of the New Testament.

The official teaching, or theology, of the Christian Church was organized by a group of men known as the Church Fathers. Saint Jerome, one of the most famous of the Church Fathers, lived from about 340 to 420. From the Hebrew original, he made a Latin translation of the Bible called the Vulgate. Including both the Old and New Testaments, the Vulgate Bible is still the official version used in the Roman Catholic Church.

In 426 another Church Father, Saint Augustine [ô gəs′tən], finished a work called *The City of God.* This book provided much of the foundation of Christian theology.

The Christian Church became very well organized.

At first, Christians met in small groups, often in their homes. As time went by and more people became Christians, a tighter organization developed, based on Roman governmental units.

Presbyters [prez′bə tərz], later known as priests, were ordained, or officially consecrated, to conduct both services and the business of village churches. Several villages in a region made up a diocese [dī′ə sēs′], which was placed under the direction of a bishop. Bishops were priests who administered the religious affairs of a church district.

A number of dioceses made up a province, which was placed under the authority of an archbishop. A group of provinces in turn made up a patriarchate. The title of patriarch [pā′trē ärk] was given to the bishop of a large city, such as Rome, Constantinople, or Alexandria. Gradually, in the western Roman world the Bishop of Rome assumed leadership as **pope,** from a Greek word meaning "father."

Church leadership in the West developed in Rome partly because Rome was the capital of the empire. As the emperors' authority declined in the western part of the empire, Roman bishops per-

Pope John Paul is the first Polish pope in the 2,000-year history of the Church.

formed more and more governmental duties. Eventually the popes claimed supremacy of the Christian Church on the basis of the Petrine Theory. This theory said that the pope in Rome was the heir to Peter, the first Bishop of Rome.

Acceptance of the Petrine Theory contributed greatly to making the Church in Rome the center of western Christendom. By 600 Rome was in fact the capital of the western Church and the pope its head. The eastern Christian Church, however, rejected the Petrine Theory and refused to recognize the pope as its leader.

Section 1 Review

Identify Palestine, New Testament, Jesus, Messiah, Christianity, pope

Main Ideas
1. Why did the Roman rulers and Jewish authorities in Jerusalem disapprove of Jesus' teachings?
2. How did Paul the Apostle help spread the Christian religion?
3. Why were Christians persecuted more than followers of some other religions?
4. Name three reasons for the strength of the early Christian church.
5. Why did Rome become the capital city of western Christianity?

Critical Thinking

Assessing Cause and Effect: Consider the following statement: Conditions in the Roman world helped strengthen Christianity. List reasons why you agree or disagree with this statement.

BACKGROUND The Petrine Theory grew from the Gospel of St. Matthew in which Jesus gave his leading disciple, who was known as Simon in Hebrew, the name Peter. In Greek, Peter means "rock." Bestowing this name on the leader of his

disciples, Jesus said, "Thou art Peter and upon this rock I will build my church."

181

Lesson Plan

Essential Learning Objectives

Students will learn to:

- describe the Germanic invasions of the Roman Empire.
- explain the factors that helped the eastern Roman Empire remain strong.

1 FOCUS AND MOTIVATE

Call students' attention again to Tacitus' description of the German warrior in the chapter introduction. Ask students to describe Tacitus' view of the German warrior and speculate on whether his description is based on personal observation or on hearsay. (personal observation)

2 TEACH

- On an outline map of Europe and Asia from the Geography Skills book, have students indicate the approximate places where these Germanic tribes originally lived: East Goths, West Goths, Vandals, Lombards, Alemanni, Burgundians, Franks, Jutes, Angles, Saxons.

- Discuss the way of life, religion, and government of the Germanic peoples. Have students compare the behavior of the Romans as victors to the behavior of victorious Germanic peoples. Ask students to speculate on why Germanic warriors did not enslave people they conquered.

- Using the map on page 182, have students deduce which migrations of German tribes resulted because of the threat of an invasion by the Huns and which might have been caused

Germanic Invasions, A.D. 150–568

🌐 **MAP STUDY** The map shows the path of the major Germanic invasions that destroyed the western Roman Empire. It also shows the route of the Huns, a people from Central Asia. What country is the farthest west the Huns reached?

---

2 The Roman Empire collapsed under attacks from Germanic tribes.

While the Church was growing stronger, the once mighty government of the Caesars was crumbling. Internal problems of the Roman Empire, such as corruption and disunity, made it easier for external forces to destroy it. Then came the final crushing blows—attacks by Germanic tribes.

German tribes pressed against the Roman frontier.

In the 4th century A.D., most Germanic peoples in Europe lived east of the **Rhine** and north of the **Danube** rivers. To the west and north of the Black Sea were Gothic peoples, that is, the East Goths—Ostrogoths—and the West Goths—Visigoths. To the west of these tribes and extending over a large

area east of the Rhine, were the Vandals, Lombards, Alemanni, Burgundians, and Franks. In and near present-day Denmark lived the Jutes, Angles, and Saxons. (Study the map above to locate the places and peoples discussed in this section.)

These Germanic groups were seminomads, that is, they both herded their cattle and farmed for a living. They were energetic and vigorous, and as a people prized strength and courage in battle. They worshiped many gods, including Tiw [tē′ü], the god of war; Wotan, the chief of the gods; Thor, the god of thunder; and Freya [frā′ə], the goddess of fertility. (The names of these gods live on today in the English words Tuesday, Wednesday, Thursday, and Friday.)

The Germanic peoples governed themselves through tribal assemblies made up of voting freemen. Their laws were based on long-established customs. These political practices, especially the use of assemblies, had a strong influence later in

ANSWER TO MAP STUDY Gaul—present-day France

medieval England, where they laid a foundation for parliamentary government and English common law.

For hundreds of years, Romans and Germans had fought each other on the borders of the Roman Empire. Still, there were long periods of war and long periods of peace. During the peaceful periods, Roman and Germanic peoples mixed with one another. Some Germans entered the Roman Empire and settled on vacant lands. Others, captured in war, became slaves on Roman estates, and still others became soldiers in the legions. If this process had been allowed to continue, the Germans might have been gradually absorbed into the empire. However, the German tribes, under attack by other tribes and aware of the decay and weakness of the Roman Empire, took advantage of the opportunity. They turned the gradual mixing into an overwhelming invasion.

German tribes forced their way into all parts of the western Roman Empire.

The German tribes were forced into motion by a group of people called the Huns, whom you read about in Chapter 8. During the 4th century, the Huns moved out of their territory in Central Asia into China, India, and Europe. (See the map, page 182.) Mounted on swift horses, they attacked with lightning ferocity. Crossing the Dnieper [nē′pər] River, they conquered the Ostrogoths in eastern Europe. The Visigoths in the path of the Huns, fearing attack also, sought safety by attacking and occupying Roman settlements.

In 378 the Roman emperor Valens led a large army against the Visigoths at Adrianople in present-day Bulgaria. Surprisingly, the Visigoths won the battle of Adrianople, scattered the Roman forces, and killed the emperor. This battle is considered one of the most decisive in history because it left the Roman Empire defenseless. It was the first major battle that Rome had lost in hundreds of years. German tribes outside the empire began to round up their cattle, mobilize their fighting men, and move toward the Roman borders.

Thirty-two years after the battle of Adrianople, in 410 the Visigothic general, Alaric, led the Visigoths to Rome itself, which they sacked and looted. By that time, other German tribes—the

Franks, Vandals, and Burgundians—were also moving into the empire. About 450, German tribes from northwest Europe—the Angles, Saxons, and Jutes—sailed to Britain, where they killed or enslaved some of the Britons and forced others to retreat into Wales and Scotland. (See the map, page 182.) The Romans, who had previously occupied Britain, had withdrawn their troops earlier to protect the empire nearer Italy.

The **Anglo-Saxon** invaders destroyed Roman civilization in Britain and set up rival kingdoms. For the next 600 years, Anglo-Saxon England had a weak central government. However, the people did develop a strong tradition of participation in local government, which was a seed for later democratic government in the area, that is, a government run by the common people.

To add to the violence and confusion, the Huns, led by **Attila** [at′l ə], also invaded the empire, threatening to enslave or destroy both Romans and Germans. So, forgetting their own differences for a while, the Romans and Germans united against their common enemy, the Huns. Romans and Ger-

The Anglo-Saxons made elaborate jewelry, such as the gold purse lid (right) and the silver and enamel brooch (below). Both pieces were found in England.

by other factors, such as population increases, scarcity of arable land, harsh climate, or ambitious leaders.

- Draw a time line extending from A.D. 300–600 and add the following dates at the top: A.D. 378, A.D. 410, A.D. 451, A.D. 453, A.D. 476. Have students name and describe the event that occurred on each date.

GUIDED PRACTICE
Have students write several sentences on why the eastern part of the Roman Empire endured and was not invaded. Also for guided practice:

 Overhead Transparency 19

3 | ASSESS AND CLOSE

ASSESS
1. Who was the feared leader of the Huns? (Attila)
2. What tribe was the victor at the battle of Adrianople? (Visigoths)

OPTIONAL RETEACHING
Have students write summary statements on the Germanic invasions of the western part of the Roman Empire.

OPTIONAL ENRICHMENT
1. Have students research and write a summary of the famous battle in the Teutoburg Forest in A.D. 9 during which Arminius, a Cheruscan prince, defeated Varus, a provincial Roman governor. (average)
2. Assign students to research and write a short paper on the revival of learning and literature under Theodoric, including the contributions of the scholars Boethius and Cassiodorus. (challenging)

Answers to Section 2 Review

Identify
Key Terms, People, and Places are defined on pages indicated in parentheses. Also see the Glossary and Biographical Dictionary.
Rhine (182), Danube (182), Anglo-Saxons (183), Attila (183), Constantinople (184)

Main Ideas
1. They fought along the borders of the Roman Empire but also mixed with each other during times of peace.
2. The Huns from Central Asia conquered the Ostrogoths and threatened the Visigoths, pushing them into Roman territory where they attacked the Romans, defeating them at the Battle of Adrianople. Germanic tribes then spread through the empire.
3. In that year Odoacer, a German leader, deposed the Roman emperor.

Critical Thinking
Statement erroneously assumes that because the Germans conquered a highly civilized people—the Romans—they were wandering barbarians with little valuable culture of their own.

mans stood together against the Huns in Gaul (present-day France) and defeated Attila at the battle of Chalons [shä lōn'] in 451.

The western empire collapsed in 476.

Meanwhile, the emperors in Rome had become so weak that they were mere puppets of the army. Many Roman soldiers were of German birth, and one, Odoacer [ō'dō ā'sər], became a commander of the Roman armies. In 476 he deposed the last of the puppet Roman emperors, a German boy named Romulus Augustulus.

Odoacer was the first German ruler of Rome not officially approved by the Senate. Thus the date 476 is often given as the date for the "fall" of Rome. In a strict sense, however, there was no "fall." The decline of Roman imperial power had been slow and complicated. Weak emperors, corrupt officials, and the admission of German soldiers into the legions had all played a part.

Since the early decades of the 4th century, several emperors at Rome had sensed the growing weakness of the western empire. As you learned in Chapter 6, in 330 Emperor Constantine had moved his capital to the city of Byzantium, which he then renamed **Constantinople**, in the eastern part of the empire. By the end of the century, the Roman Empire had become permanently divided. One emperor ruled in the west and another in the east. Still, the two sections of the empire, although separated, continued to be thought of as one.

In fact, the western part of the empire was breaking up. By the year 476, when Odoacer became the Roman ruler, German kingdoms had been established in many former Roman provinces. The Anglo-Saxons were in England. The Visigoths ruled Spain. In North Africa, the Vandals had established a kingdom, and by 486, the Franks controlled Gaul. Italy was the scene of much warfare, and in 493 it fell to the Ostrogoths. Then it was ravaged by civil war and further invasions. Italy, which had been the center of the mighty Roman Empire, would not be united again under one government until the 19th century.

The eastern part of the empire, however, did not collapse or give way to internal decay and invasions. With its capital at Constantinople, the Byzantine Empire endured, ruled by emperors, for

Highlights of Germanic Conquests

The German tribes originally lived north of the Danube and east of the Rhine, but Huns from Central Asia pushed them into the Roman Empire. There they carved the empire into separate kingdoms, listed below.

Visigoths (378) defeated Romans at Adrianople; (410) sacked Rome; (c. 480) controlled southern Gaul and Spain

Angles, Saxons, and Jutes (449) began invasions of Britain

Vandals (429) invaded North Africa from Spain; (455) sacked Rome from North Africa

Ostrogoths (453) moved into Roman Empire; (493) Theodoric established kingdom in Italy

Franks (481) Clovis became king and expanded Frankish kingdom; (507) Franks controlled all Gaul

another thousand years. During all that time, it preserved much of Greco-Roman culture and served as a buffer for western Europe against invasions from the Middle East.

Section 2 Review

Identify Rhine, Danube, Anglo-Saxons, Attila, Constantinople

Main Ideas
1. What was the relationship between German tribes and Romans in the 4th century A.D.?
2. What happened in the 4th century to the relationship between German tribes and Romans?
3. Why is 476 called the year of the "fall" of Rome?

Critical Thinking
Identifying Assumptions: Consider the following statement: The Germanic tribes were barbarians compared to the Romans and offered nothing except violence and destruction to the people they conquered. What assumptions are being made in this statement?

3 The Church became a force in preserving civilization.

As the Roman Empire declined, a new civilization developed in its place. This civilization combined elements of the old Roman culture with the vigor and energy of the conquering Germanic tribes. The Christian Church became the main force in shaping this new civilization.

The Church provided protection and order.

During the Germanic invasions, the Roman government gradually stopped providing the services needed to carry on daily urban life. City populations shrank as commerce declined and people turned to farming for survival. Living as farmers in rural areas, people found security by working for powerful local landowners. However, as the farmers fell behind in rent payments, Roman law bound them to the land to work off their debt.

Such changes were slow and occurred over hundreds of years. Most people were unaware that more and more people were becoming the property, or serfs, of their lords.

In many regions the Germans moved in and outnumbered the old inhabitants. The newcomers soon took on Roman customs and continued the blending of peoples that had been going on before the invasions. The Germans adopted many of the old Roman practices and kept Latin as the official language. They also converted to Christianity and supported the Church.

In Rome, as the emperors became weaker, the popes and their assistants took on some of the powers of the government. Church officials set up Church courts and claimed the right to collect taxes. The governmental power of the Church was especially evident from 590 to 604, when Gregory the Great was pope. He supervised the police, directed the generals of the army, coined money, and kept the all-important aqueducts, or water carriers, in repair.

Missionaries spread Christianity.

As early as the 3rd century, fearless missionaries had carried the teachings of Christianity beyond the frontiers of the Roman Empire. One of the most important of these missionaries was Ulfilas [ul'fi ləs]. An Arian Christian, Ulfilas preached among the Gothic peoples and converted them to Christianity. Ulfilas invented a Gothic alphabet, which he used to translate the Bible into the Germanic language.

Another famous missionary, **Saint Patrick**, was born in Britain about 389. He journeyed to Ireland to convert the Celtic peoples to the faith and founded many monasteries that became famous as centers of learning. (See the map, page 178.) In 596 Pope Gregory sent a Roman monk, Augustine, as missionary to England. Augustine converted Ethelbert, King of Kent, to Christianity and later became the first Archbishop of Canterbury.

Monks and nuns helped preserve culture.

During the years of the Roman persecutions, a few Christians went into the wilderness, giving up worldly interests and living alone. Others lived in groups, dedicating themselves to the service of God. Christian monasteries and convents were places where groups of monks or nuns lived apart from the world. They were first set up in Egypt in the 4th century and soon spread to other parts of the Roman Empire.

When men and women went out to live a holy life alone, they were often very hard on themselves. The earliest of these people withdrew from the world to live alone in deserts or in the wilderness. Some hermits, as they were called, tormented themselves by prolonged fasting, rolling in

Runes

| k | ng | d | a | y | o |

Runes are the letters of an alphabet used by German tribes between A.D. 200 and 1200. The word *rune* [rün] means "secret," and only a few persons, mainly priests, knew how to read them. When the German tribes converted to Christianity, the use of runes was discontinued. Runic writing may have been adapted from the Etruscan alphabet.

3 Lesson Plan

Essential Learning Objective

Students will learn to evaluate the contributions of the early Church.

1 FOCUS AND MOTIVATE

Have students name and list positive Roman, Christian, and Germanic attributes and predict how these attributes might blend and what kind of civilization might result.

2 TEACH

Discuss the changing role of the government and of the Church in the Roman Empire during the invasions. List and discuss the various ways in which the Christian Church helped provide law and order, took on powers of the government, spread Christianity, and preserved culture.

GUIDED PRACTICE

Ask students to explain why they agree or disagree with this statement: The invasions of Rome strengthened Christian culture.

3 ASSESS AND CLOSE

ASSESS

What Germanic tribe had the first Bible in their language? (Goths)

OPTIONAL RETEACHING

Have one team of students list the Church's contributions in preserving the old civilization and another list its contributions in shaping the new.

thorns, or living in snake-infested swamps. One hermit, St. Simeon Stylites, built a pillar 60 feet high and spent the last 30 years of his life on top of it. These hermits were driven by extreme spiritual feelings. They believed that by suffering or depriving themselves they could purify their souls.

Such practices were not typical of most Christians of the time. The less extreme monks and nuns concluded that the solitary life of the hermit was not the proper way to practice Christianity. Instead, these Christians chose to live together in communities. They did not engage in prolonged fasting but did farming and other productive work and spent many hours of the day and night in meditation, or silent spiritual thinking.

Monasteries and convents gave these people a way to live apart from society and dedicate their lives to God, yet live productively. About the year 520, **Saint Benedict** set up a monastery at Monte Cassino in Italy and drew up rules for the monks to live by. Saint Benedict's rules required obedience and poverty, daily prayers, and at least six hours of useful work each day. The rules of the Benedictine order were widely adopted by other monasteries and are still followed today.

In German lands beyond the old frontiers, where life remained crude and isolated, monks not only spread the teachings of Christianity but also advanced civilization. In wild and forested regions, monks often cleared forests, drained swamps, and introduced new crops. The few schools that existed in Europe during the early Middle Ages were set up and run by monks. Some monasteries also served as hospitals and as inns for travelers.

At a time when libraries were neglected and precious manuscripts were destroyed or lost in looting, monks wrote out the Scriptures and other works and preserved them in monasteries. Nearly every important monastery had a writing room where monks copied manuscripts by hand. These manuscripts were lavishly illustrated, or illuminated, with brilliantly colored designs and intricate letters. Inks were made of gold and rare minerals.

The monks also kept historical records, called **chronicles.** One of these chronicles, The *Ecclesiastical History of the English Nation,* written by Saint Bede in the early 700s, is the best account available of 200 years of early English history.

Section 3 Review

Identify Saint Patrick, Saint Benedict, chronicles

Main Ideas

1. Why were Church officials able to take over Roman governmental power?
2. What did the early Church missionaries accomplish?
3. Name one major contribution of the monks who founded the early monasteries. Explain its importance.

Critical Thinking

Assessing Cause and Effect: Is it fair to say that monastic communities thrived during the medieval period because they offered people calm and security in a world of turmoil? Give reasons for your answers.

---

 4 *An alliance of popes and Franks helped western Christendom grow and prosper.*

In the late 5th century, the Franks, a German tribe, began to develop a powerful empire in Gaul. The modern-day country of France is named after this German tribe. The Frankish Empire became the largest empire in Europe during early medieval times.

Clovis united the Franks and extended the power of the Church.

In 481 **Clovis** began his remarkable career as the ruler of a small Frankish kingdom located on the Rhine River in present-day Germany. Within 20 years, Clovis had overcome the last remnants of Roman authority in northern Gaul and conquered much of Germany.

Clovis became one of the most powerful rulers in western Europe. He was the first important Germanic king to become a **Roman Catholic**, that is, to accept the Nicene Creed upheld by the pope in Rome. All of the other Germanic rulers and their subjects—except those in England—were Arian Christians.

The pope considered all Arians to be heretics. This gave Clovis an excuse to attack his Arian neighbors. He declared, "I cannot endure that

186

Charlemagne's Empire, Around A.D. 814

North Sea

Baltic Sea

ATLANTIC OCEAN

• Aix-la-Chapelle

KINGDOM OF THE FRANKS
about 750

• Tours

GAUL

Conquered by Charlemagne after 774

IBERIAN PENINSULA

Conquered by Charlemagne after 774

Mediterranean Sea

BYZANTINE EMPIRE

PAPAL STATES
• Rome

Black Sea

• Constantinople

0   200   400 MILES
0   200   400 KILOMETERS

N

MAP STUDY Charlemagne's empire reached as far east as modern Romania and as far south as modern Spain. Did his empire extend into present-day Yugoslavia? Refer to the map on page 792 to find out.

those Arians should possess any part of Gaul. With God's aid we will go against them and conquer their lands." He defeated the Arians, extending his lands and the pope's authority at the same time.

Clovis died in 511, but his successors were generally incompetent. These weak, immoral rulers are known as the Do-Nothing Kings.

The Carolingian family won control of the Franks.

Because the Frankish kings did not perform their duties, the office of Mayor of the Palace became politically important in the Frankish kingdom. One mayor, Charles Martel, took total control of the kingdom and became sole ruler, although he never took the title of king. In 732 he defeated Muslim invaders at the battle of Tours. This victory saved northern Europe for Christianity and made Charles a Christian hero and the strongest ruler in western Europe.

When Charles Martel's son, Pepin, became Mayor of the Palace, he asked the pope to decide whether Pepin or a Do-Nothing King should be

considered the legal ruler of the Franks. Pepin held the real power but the incompetent Frankish ruler still held official authority. The pope decided in favor of Pepin and declared him king.

In return for the pope's approval, Pepin successfully led an army against the Lombards, who were threatening the papacy, that is, the office and government of the pope. In 756 Pepin turned over to the pope a part of the territory in Italy that the Lombards had controlled. This became known as the Donation of Pepin and the land involved became the Papal States, a region that covered about a quarter of the Italian peninsula.

Charlemagne built an empire that preserved Roman culture.

Thus began the Carolingian [kar′ə lin′jē ən] line of kings. The line was called Carolingian after Charles Martel, whose Latin name was *Carolus.* In 771 Pepin's son Charles inherited the throne. Called Charles the Great, or **Charlemagne,** he expanded the Frankish lands into a large empire. (See the map above.)

ANSWER TO MAP STUDY yes

BACKGROUND Other names for Charlemagne included Karl der Grosse and Carolus Magnus.

---

4 Lesson Plan

Essential Learning Objective

Students will learn to describe how the Frankish kings, Clovis, and Charlemagne spread Christianity and preserved culture.

1 FOCUS AND MOTIVATE

Have students cite the one major difference in belief between Arian and Roman Christians. (Arians rejected belief that God and Jesus were of the same substance.) Lead students to predict possible conflicts between the Goths and other Arian tribes and Christian tribes.

2 TEACH

- Discuss factors that led the Roman Catholic Church in western Europe to gain power. Have students describe Clovis', Martel's, Pepin's and Charlemagne's relationships with the Church and ask students' opinions on whether a church has the right to participate in or interfere with a government. Elicit reasons that the United States Constitution provides for separation of church and state.
- Discuss the blending of western European cultures in the areas of government, art, and education. Have students cite examples of how Christianity began to rule people's lives.

GUIDED PRACTICE

Have students list five factors that helped the Church become the major power in western Europe.

Charlemagne also extended the bounds of Christianity. Priests commonly traveled with Charlemagne's armies. While the armies made conquests for Charlemagne, the priests made converts for the Church, sometimes peacefully, sometimes with force.

Charlemagne modeled his capital at Aix-la-Chapelle [äks' lä shä pel'] on Roman cities. He imported statues and marble from the Italian peninsula to beautify his capital city. Aix-la-Chapelle, which is located in present-day Aachen, West Germany, was also famous as the center of a great revival of learning, the **Carolingian Renaissance**. The word Renaissance [ren'ə säns'] means "rebirth" or "revival."

Charlemagne urged priests to study and improve their education. He also sponsored a refinement of the system of handwriting then in use and generously supported Church schools. One of his reforms was the invention of small letters, which did not exist in the Roman alphabet up to that time. In the Church schools, boys were taught Christian doctrine, arithmetic, grammar, and singing. The rebirth of learning during Charlemagne's rule helped to preserve Greco-Roman culture and ideas in western Christendom.

Charlemagne was crowned emperor by both the Church and the state.

In the year 800, Charlemagne traveled to Rome. On Christmas Day, while Charlemagne was attending church services, the pope placed a crown on the king's head and declared, "To Charles Augustus crowned of God, great and pacific Emperor of the Romans, long life and victory."

Whether the pope planned this action with Charlemagne's knowledge is unknown. However, the crowning of Charlemagne as Emperor of the Romans showed that the idea of the Roman Empire was still alive and that there was a strong desire to bring back its political unity.

The coronation also illustrated another great theme of medieval history: the struggle for power between Church and state. By the act of crowning Charlemagne, the pope claimed that it was he, the pope, who made emperors. Kings and queens who held power not connected with the Church soon came to resent this view. From that time on, popes and rulers both claimed to have the highest authority, and major political conflicts arose over this issue.

Christendom emerged as a civilization.

Most important of all, the crowning of Charlemagne by the pope completed the blending of two major ideas after a period of some 400 years. One of these ideas was the concept of political unity, an idea that had been represented by the Roman Empire. The other was the idea of religious unity, represented by the Christian Church. The mixture of the two ideas resulted in a civilization best described as Christendom.

In the world of Christendom, Christianity was the single most powerful force in a person's life. Throughout Europe, Christian beliefs influenced the way people behaved and what they valued.

As members of the Christian faith, people celebrated the same holidays, such as Christmas and Easter, and attended services that followed the same rituals everywhere. People who lived in this world thought of themselves as Christians, not Romans. The religious unity of western Christendom was to last for more than 700 years.

Section 4 Review

Identify Clovis, Roman Catholic, Charlemagne, Carolingian Renaissance

Main Ideas

1. Why did Clovis's victories have religious importance?
2. How did Pepin become the first Carolingian king? Why did the pope support Pepin?
3. How did Charlemagne preserve Roman culture in western Europe?
4. What did Charlemagne's coronation signify for Christendom?
5. What two elements combined to create the civilization called Christendom?

Critical Thinking

Making Hypotheses: Bestowing an emperor's crown on a leader as powerful as Charlemagne could be a dangerous thing to do because the pope could have set up a rival to challenge his authority. Why do you think the pope took this action? Form a hypothesis for your answer.

Illuminated Manuscripts

Printing was not known in Europe until the mid-1400s. Before that time, all books were handwritten.

Scribes in ancient Egypt, Israel, Greece, and Rome had produced tens of thousands of books. These books took the shape of scrolls until the 2nd century A.D., when the codex, or bound book, appeared. Many valuable libraries were lost, however, with the ruin of the Roman Empire.

The Rule of Benedict, adopted in A.D. 529, required monks to read four hours a day, thus encouraging new interest in handwritten books. During the 8th and 9th centuries, the monks created manuscripts in which capital letters and other decorative details became exquisite jewellike miniatures. In their zeal for the sacred texts they were copying, the monks embellished their work with gold or silver so that each page seemed to be filled with light, or illuminated. They worked on thinned, whitened sheets of parchment made from the skin of such animals as sheep or goats.

Byzantine influence is apparent in many of the manuscripts. Favorite motifs included brightly colored birds of paradise, fish, and other lively animals, real or imaginary.

Another frequently used motif from the eastern Mediterranean is a cross with the Greek letters *alpha* and *omega* hanging from the arms. These are the first and last letters of the Greek alphabet. Their significance as "the beginning and the end" reflects Christian symbolism.

Early Christians also used the image of the fish as a symbol, or the Greek word for fish, which is *ichthys*. The Greek letters that form this word are an acrostic, a connected group of words whose first, middle, or last letters have a special meaning. In this case, the composition formed from the initials of the words *Iesous Christos, theou hyios soter,* stands for "Jesus Christ Son of God Savior."

An 8th-century Frankish manuscript depicts fish beneath the arms of the cross forming symbolic Greek letters.

parentheses. Also see the Glossary and Biographical Dictionary. Clovis (186), Roman Catholic (186), Charlemagne (187), Carolingian Renaissance (188)

Main Ideas

1. He became a Roman Catholic, conquering lands for the Church.
2. Pepin asked the pope to decide between him and the Frankish king, and the pope chose Pepin because he needed Pepin to defend him against the Lombards.
3. He modeled his capital on Rome and supported a rebirth of learning that included Roman culture.
4. His coronation by the pope established a bond between church and state.
5. political unity represented by the Roman Empire and religious unity represented by the Christian Church

Critical Thinking

The pope took this action mainly *because* Charlemagne was so powerful as a secular ruler. It was the pope's way of becoming a superior power over the emperor.

HIGHLIGHTS OF CIVILIZATION

Encourage students to visit museum exhibits of illuminated manuscripts from the period before printing was known. Artistically inclined students may want to make an illuminated manuscript page of their own design.

Main Ideas
The main ideas tested here were introduced in the sections of this chapter and reviewed in the Section Reviews. For answers to these questions, see the appropriate Section Reviews.

Critical Thinking
1. Reasons for accuracy: Tacitus lived during the period about which he wrote and perhaps had firsthand knowledge of the German tribes. Reasons for inaccuracy: Tacitus could have been overstating the German military traits in order to impress Roman leaders of impending danger and move them to action.
2. Charlemagne valued a well-rounded life and a culture that included not only military might and political power but also learning, the arts, and a sense of obligation to preserve the best of civilization for future generations.

CHAPTER 10 REVIEW

Section Summaries

Section 1
Christianity became a strong religion in the Roman world.
The Christian religion grew from the teachings of Jesus. With an appealing creed and well-planned organization, the Church gradually spread throughout the empire and eventually became the official religion.

Section 2
The Roman Empire collapsed under attacks from Germanic tribes.
German invasions, which had begun as early as the 2nd century B.C., increased in strength and frequency during the 4th century A.D. In 476 a German general, Odoacer, became Roman emperor. German kingdoms soon sprang up in many former Roman provinces.

Section 3
The Church became a force in preserving civilization.
As the western part of the Roman Empire crumbled, the Church in Rome took leadership over the civil government. Missionaries carried Christianity and many features of Roman culture to the German frontiers and beyond. Monasteries and convents helped preserve major elements of civilization.

Section 4
An alliance of popes and Franks helped western Christendom grow and prosper.
In Gaul, about the year 500, the Frankish king Clovis grew powerful and extended his lands in the name of his new religion, Christianity. The greatest Frankish ruler was Charlemagne. Charlemagne's coronation by the pope fostered the concept of Christendom, a Europe united by political and religious unity.

Test Yourself

Key Terms, People, and Places
Identify the significance of each of the following:

Section 1
a. Palestine
b. New Testament
c. Jesus
d. Messiah
e. Christianity
f. pope

Section 2
a. Rhine
b. Danube
c. Anglo-Saxons
d. Attila
e. Constantinople

Section 3
a. Saint Patrick
b. Saint Benedict
c. chronicles

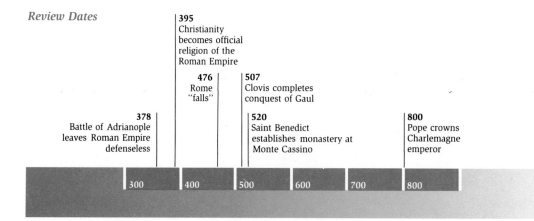

Review Dates

395 Christianity becomes official religion of the Roman Empire

476 Rome "falls"

507 Clovis completes conquest of Gaul

378 Battle of Adrianople leaves Roman Empire defenseless

520 Saint Benedict establishes monastery at Monte Cassino

800 Pope crowns Charlemagne emperor

300 400 500 600 700 800

Section 4
a. Clovis **c.** Charlemagne
b. Roman Catholic **d.** Carolingian Renaissance

Main Ideas

Section 1
1. How did Jesus' teachings conflict with both Roman rulers and Jewish authorities in Jerusalem?
2. Why was Paul the Apostle important to Christianity?
3. Give two main reasons why Christians were persecuted more than followers of other religions.
4. What did the Christian religion offer its followers?
5. Why was Rome a center for Christianity?

Section 2
1. Describe the interaction between German tribes and Romans in the 4th century A.D.
2. Why did the rather peaceful relationship between German tribes and Romans change in the 4th century?
3. What significant event in 476 made that year the date for the "fall" of Rome?

Section 3
1. How did the Church become the governing power in the Roman world?
2. How did missionaries strengthen the Church?
3. What was one major task of monks in the early monasteries? Why was that task important?

Section 4
1. Why was Clovis important to the Christian Church?
2. How was the pope involved in making Pepin the first Carolingian king? How did the pope benefit?
3. How did Charlemagne help preserve Roman culture?
4. How did Charlemagne's coronation affect the western Christian world?
5. What two major ideas blended together in the civilization called Christendom?

Critical Thinking

1. Evaluating Sources of Information Study the quotation from Tacitus in the chapter introduction on page 176. Do you think this source of information is accurate? Why or why not?
2. Recognizing Values Charlemagne conquered and governed an empire. He also set up centers of learning to preserve Roman culture. What does this tell you about the values Charlemagne held?

Chapter Skills and Activities

Practicing Study and Research Skills
Working with Special Purpose Maps
A map that focuses on one topic, such as a historical movement, is called a special purpose map. Such maps show only what relates to the topic. Refer to the map showing the spread of Christianity on page 178. This map presents change over time by using different colors for time periods. Maps like this one are generalizations. Not everyone in each area became a Christian during the time period shown. Also, the boundaries between different colors are approximations. Use the map to answer the following questions.
1. What city on the Greek peninsula served as a center for the spread of Christianity? On the Italian peninsula?
2. Where was Christianity established first, in Ireland or Germany? In Spain or Norway? In Finland or Russia?
3. During which time period did Christianity spread over the largest area?

Linking Past and Present
Today in countries that still have monarchies the kings or queens are often more symbolic than actual rulers. An example is Britain, where Queen Elizabeth II is the reigning monarch. She was crowned by the head of the Church of England in 1953. On her death her son Charles, shown top right on the postage stamp above, will be crowned in the same way. How does this modern tradition link with the coronation of Charlemagne in 800?

Learning History Through Maps
Refer to the map on page 182. Write five sentences describing the Germanic and other invasions using only information given on the map.

CRITICAL THINKING QUESTION LEVEL 1. easy;
2. average

11 The Formation of Europe

OVERVIEW

This chapter describes the social, economic, and religious forces that molded the lives of people during the Middle Ages.

PLANNING CHART

Section	Text Pages	Key Concept	Suggested Teaching Time
1 Feudalism developed in Western Christendom.	193–196	The inheritance of Charlemagne's Empire by weak successors led to the rise of secular and ecclesiastical lords resulting in decentralization of government and in feudalism.	One day **More Time?** Use *Overhead Transparency 21*.
2 The feudal manor was the center of economic life.	196–199	The economy of the Middle Ages was based mainly on the manorial system, in which lords owned the lands and peasants labored on them in return for safety and provisions.	One day **More time?** Use *Overhead Transparency 22*.
3 The Church unified western Christendom.	199–202	The Church was a unifying force in the Middle Ages, establishing rules to live by, punishing wrongdoers, taking over secular powers from weak rulers, and urging crusades against Muslims.	One day **More time?** Use *Source Reading 11A*.
4 Town life revived in the later Middle Ages.	202–207	Increase in trade, use of money, and improved technology created new towns and a revival of cities and led to the establishment of a middle class.	One day
5 Education, learning, and the arts advanced.	207–210	Universities developed where scholars studied mathematics, science, and technology, and literature and the arts contributed to religious and everyday life.	One day **Less time?** Assign Section 5 to be read before class and teach it together with Section 4. **More time?** Use *Source Reading 11B*.

ANCILLARIES

Materials that may be used with this chapter to reinforce, reteach, enrich, and assess learning are pictured on the following pages.

Teacher's Resource File

ACTIVITIES

Section 1 Activity, p. 59

Section 2 Activity, p. 60

Section 3 Activity, p. 61

Section 4 Activity, p. 62

Section 5 Activity, p. 53

Chapter 11 Reteaching, p. 64

Chapter 11 Enrichment, p. 65

Teacher's Resource File

GEOGRAPHY SKILLS

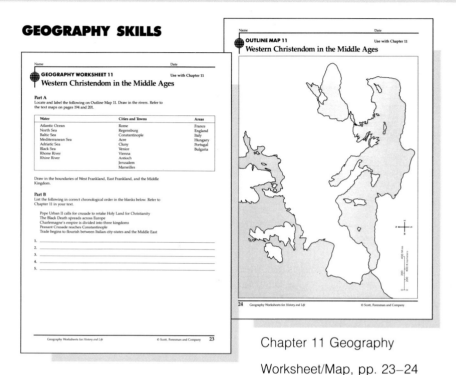

Chapter 11 Geography
Worksheet/Map, pp. 23–24

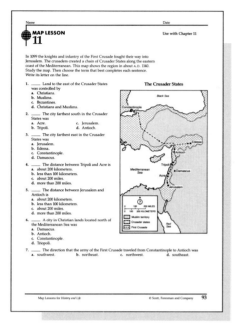

Chapter 11 Map Lesson, p. 93

TESTS

Chapter Test, pp. 53–54

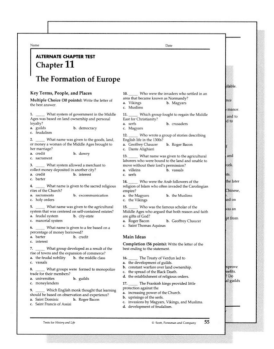

Alternate Chapter Test, pp. 55–56

Other Optional Ancillaries

WORKBOOK

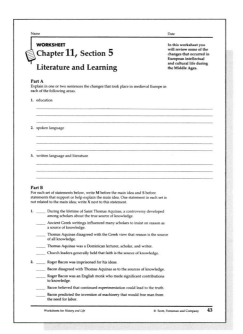

Section 1 Worksheet, p. 39

Section 2 Worksheet, p. 40

Section 3 Worksheet, p. 41

Section 4 Worksheet, p. 42

Section 5 Worksheet, p. 43

SOURCE READINGS

Source Reading 11A
Source Reading 11B

OVERHEAD TRANSPARENCIES

Overhead Transparency 21
Overhead Transparency 22

TEST GENERATOR

40 multiple-choice questions for Chapter 11

11

CHAPTER INTRODUCTION

Point out the use of the term *Middle Ages* in the chapter introduction. Have students speculate about the reason for this name for the period between A.D. 800–1500. (period between ancient and modern times)

LOCATOR GLOBE

Call students' attention to the globe, which indicates the general area of the world discussed in this chapter. (A detailed map appears on page 201.)

TIME LINE

Have students use the time line to figure out why the signers of the Treaty of Verdun could not have joined the First Crusade. (because 252 years elapsed between the two events)

The Formation of Europe

800–1400

800	
843	Treaty of Verdun divides the Carolingian Empire
1095	Crusades begin
1348	Black Death breaks out in Europe
1400	
1500	

"In the name of God, Saint Michael, and Saint George, I dub thee knight. Be valiant." To an English nobleman in the Middle Ages, these words, along with the tap of a sword blade on his neck or shoulder, meant that he had become a knight. To receive this honor, a person had to own a horse and be able to supply armor and weapons. In return for military service to his lord, a knight was granted landholdings. Knights usually developed their land into farming estates, called manors, and built fortified castles to live in and for protection from enemies.

Knighthood reached its greatest importance in western Europe between 800 and 1200, when central governments were weak and the real power was in the hands of local lords or nobles. The lords owned most of the land and ruled by means of a system called feudalism.

The great unifying force in western Christendom during the Middle Ages was the Church. The Christian Church held vast areas of land, and Church clergy were involved in feudal rivalries.

In the early Middle Ages, most people lived and worked on manors in the countryside. However, in the 11th century, trade gradually expanded beyond the local villages that were tied to the manor, and town life began to revive. A middle class of merchants, artisans, and shopkeepers developed in the towns. Some of these towns have since become the great cities of modern Europe—London and Paris, for example.

Some members of the middle class grew so wealthy and powerful that they became rivals of the feudal lords. Many people of this middle class used their wealth to advance education, learning, and the arts. Thus, by the late Middle Ages—around 1200—the civilization of western Europe had greatly advanced from the low levels that followed the breakup of the western Roman Empire in the 400s.

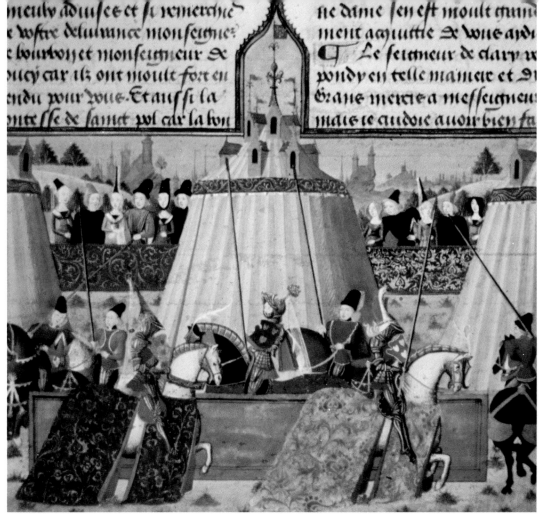

ncuils admi fee et fi remerche / e voltre delumance monfeigne: / e bourtoyet monfeigneur de / uicy car ils ont moult fort en / dii pour vous. Et auffi la / ntreffe de famt pol car la bon

ne dame fen eft moult emi / ment aquitte Se vous apdi / Le feigneur de clary re / pondy en telle maniere et S / Grane mertie a meffeigneur / mate te audoie auoir bien fa

French knights in a 14th-century tournament test their skill at jousting, a form of combat using lances. These contests followed strict rules laid down by the code of chivalry.

Reading Preview

In this chapter you will read about feudalism, the Church, and the revival of towns in medieval Europe.

1. Feudalism developed in western Christendom.

2. The feudal manor was the center of economic life.

3. The Church unified western Christendom.

4. Town life revived in the later Middle Ages.

5. Education, learning, and the arts advanced.

1 *Feudalism developed in western Christendom.*

The Carolingian kings who followed Charlemagne could not hold the reins of power. Strong and ambitious nobles forced Charlemagne's weak successors to grant them special rights. As a result, centralized government gradually disappeared, and local rule again became important.

The Carolingian empire declined.

There were many reasons for the breakup of Charlemagne's empire. Lack of an effective tax system

1 **Lesson Plan**

Essential Learning Objective

Students will learn to describe the feudal system of the Middle Ages.

1 **FOCUS AND MOTIVATE**

Point out to students that in his empire, Charlemagne held the power over the secular functions of government as well as over the clergy. Ask students to speculate about how weak heirs might dissipate this power.

193

- Discuss the division of the Carolingian Empire into kingdoms. Have students cite three reasons for the breakup of the empire and decentralization of power.

- Define *feudalism*. Ask students to describe the feudal system. List the classes of feudal people according to status on the chalkboard. Have students describe the feudal contracts between people of different rank, including rights and obligations.

GUIDED PRACTICE

Ask students to defend or refute this statement: No one person or group in feudal society held all the power, but all had the power to resist and bargain. Also for guided practice:

 Overhead Transparency 21

ANSWER TO MAP STUDY France, part of Spain; West Germany, part of East Germany, Czechoslovakia, Austria, Yugoslavia, Switzerland

The Division of Charlemagne's Empire, A.D. 843

West Frankland to Charles the Bald
The middle of kingdom to Lothair
East Frankland to Louis the German
Present-day boundaries and countries

North Sea
NETH.
EAST GERMANY
BELG.
Rhine R.
WEST GERMANY
CZECH.
Verdun
LUX.
ATLANTIC OCEAN
FRANCE
AUSTRIA
SWITZ.
Rhône R.
Adriatic Sea
ITALY
SPAIN
Mediterranean Sea
300 MILES
300 KILOMETERS

MAP STUDY Which present-day countries or portions of countries were once part of West Frankland? East Frankland?

left the central government constantly short of money. Poor means of communication made it difficult to enforce laws and unify the kingdom. Most important, the German practice of dividing landholdings among all surviving sons when a king died led to quarrels and constant small wars that weakened the kingdom.

In 843 Charlemagne's grandsons signed the Treaty of Verdun, which divided the empire into three parts. Refer to the map above. Charles the Bald received lands west of the Rhone River, called West Frankland. This land later became France. Louis the German received lands east of the Rhine, called East Frankland, which later became modern

BACKGROUND Emphasize that it was hundreds of years before these divisions of Charlemagne's empire became modern nations.

BACKGROUND The Vikings also sailed as far as North America.

Germany. A narrow strip of land between these two kingdoms was given to the eldest grandson, Lothair. Ever since, disputes over the ownership and government of Lothair's land have led to many wars between Germany and France.

The three kingdoms were still considered parts of one great empire, but none of the three brothers was strong enough to rule with any real authority. Government was actually in the hands of hundreds of local counts, dukes, and other nobles.

Vikings, Magyars, and Muslims attacked the empire.

During and after Charlemagne's rule, the empire was invaded by bands of Scandinavian pirates and warriors. These brigands were called Norsemen, or **Vikings**. Sailing from their homelands in what is now Sweden, Norway, and Denmark, the Vikings raided Russia, England, and coastal cities in western Europe and the Mediterranean. They burned towns and carried off movable wealth.

Some Vikings repeatedly raided the coast of West Frankland. To stop these attacks, the Frankish king, in the year 911, granted the invaders a territory in West Frankland on the condition that the newcomers accept Christianity. Those Vikings were known as Normans, and the area they settled became known as Normandy. Eventually, the Normans developed a well-governed, Christian state.

At the end of the 9th century, another group of invaders, the nomadic Magyars from the region west of the Ural Mountains attacked central Europe. By the late 10th century, they had settled down, adopted Christianity, and built a new state known as Hungary.

Meanwhile, a very powerful group was building an empire to the south. This group was the Arab **Muslims**, followers of the religion of Islam. (See Chapter 14.) From their bases in Spain and North Africa, the Muslims pushed into southern Italy and the southern coast of West Frankland where they sacked towns and sold their captives in the slave markets of North Africa. With bases on islands throughout the Mediterranean, Muslim warships drove Christian commerce from the sea.

During these invasions, the Carolingian kings provided little protection to their people. No central government worthy of the name existed.

Feudalism, a new form of government, emerged.

As the Carolingian kings lost power, a new system of government based on land ownership and personal loyalty developed. This system is known as **feudalism** [fyü′dl iz′əm]. Under feudalism, ruling power is held by private lords. During the Middle Ages, these lords were landowners, and the people they ruled were dependent on them for livelihood.

Feudalism began during the rule of the Roman Empire. In the 3rd and 4th centuries, when agricultural production declined sharply, the Roman government bound many agricultural laborers to the land as **serfs**. The word serf comes from the Latin word *servus*, meaning slave. Like slaves, these serfs were placed under the authority of owners of large estates. This system was a large step towards feudalism.

A German tribal custom also contributed to the development of feudalism. German chiefs divided the spoils of war among their warriors in return for pledges of loyalty and military service. The warriors thus became lords. In turn, these lords granted lands to followers for the same pledges.

The person who received land from a lord was called a vassal and the parcel of land granted, whether large or small, was called a fief [fēf] or a feud [fyüd]. A feudal contract between the lord and the vassal laid out rights and duties of each. For example, the lord agreed to protect the vassal and his family by defending them against enemy attacks and providing justice in a court. The vassal agreed to provide military service, pay taxes, and give shelter, entertainment, and food to the lord.

Fiefs and vassal services were not supposed to be hereditary, that is, passed on at the death of the person holding them. However, it soon became customary for the son of a vassal who had died to take over his father's land and obligations. Over time, ownership of fiefs did become hereditary.

Feudalism was an awkward system of governing because it divided western Europe into thousands of small, local political territories. Loyalties and lines of authority were complicated and often overlapped. For example, one lord might be the vassal of several other lords. Even a king, with many vassals of his own, might become the vassal of another king. For example, King John of England, who held lands in France, was a vassal of the French king, Philip.

The Church entered into feudal contracts.

Grants of land to the Church often carried feudal obligations. As a result, a clergyman holding a fief was both a servant of the pope and the vassal of a lord. The clergy sometimes were in conflict as to whom they owed first loyalty—the Church or the lord who owned the fief. When a Church official died, the Church still held the land granted to that official. In this way, Church landholdings expanded until the Church controlled much of the land in western Europe.

From the Archives

The Wife's Lament

The following song by an unknown Anglo-Saxon woman dates from about A.D. 900. Much poetry of this type was written during the early Middle Ages expressing the grief people felt when forced to leave their homes during long periods of exile.

I make this song sadly about myself,
about my life. I a woman say
I've been unhappy since I grew up,
yet no old pain like now
for now I know dark exile.
First my lord left his people,
went over the rolling waves. I had dawn
    sorrow,
wondering in what land my lord was.
Then I went out into friendless exile
to remedy my grief. . . .
My love sits
under a stone slope rimed with storms,
a lord weary in mind, soaked with water
in a dreary room. My lord endures
much mind-sadness. Often he remembers
a joyful floor. Grief for them
who wait longing for love.

FROM THE ARCHIVES The excerpt is from "The Wife's Lament," translated by Willis Barnstone and Elene Kolb, in *A Book of Women Poets from Antiquity to Now*, edited by Aliki Barnstone and Willis Barnstone (New York: Schocken Books, 1980), p. 432–433. Ask students to list the words that express sorrow or discomfort and then explain why the wife is sad. She is alone, isolated from her husband, friends, and family in an unfriendly, distant land.

ASSESS
What two groups of invaders settled in the Carolingian Empire? (Norsemen or Normans, Magyars)

OPTIONAL RETEACHING
Have students describe the contractual relationship between king and lord and between lord and vassal.

OPTIONAL ENRICHMENT
1. Assign students to research and report orally on the culture of the Vikings. (average)
2. Ask interested students to research the daily life of lords and present the material in story form written in the first person. (challenging)

INDEPENDENT PRACTICE/ HOMEWORK
Assign the Section Review, Activities page 59, or Workbook page 39.

CLOSURE
In summarizing the lesson tell students that none of the kings who signed the Treaty of Verdun was truly sovereign. Each became enmeshed in the feudal system, with obligations to and agreements with lords and clergy. The lords and clergy, in turn, had agreements with vassals who received lands for services.

Medieval society had fixed classes: nobility, clergy, and peasants.

The nobility was made up of nobles—kings, vassals, and lesser lords. The status of nobles was inherited—that is, automatically passed on to children at birth.

Clergy, or church officials, were generally the only group educated in subjects other than warfare. Bishops and high-ranking clergy lived much like wealthy lords. Village priests usually came from the lower classes and often had little education.

Peasants were at the bottom of the social scale and were by far the largest group. Nearly all peasants were serfs. As serfs, they did not own their land but were allowed to live off some of the harvest. The land worked by serfs belonged to a lord, and most of the crops went to that lord.

By law, serfs had to work the land on which they were born and could not move away without their lord's permission. A serf could never become a noble, although a person from the peasant class might become a priest and rise within the Church.

A very small group of people, called villeins [vil′ənz], worked the land and had a status slightly higher than serfs but much lower than nobility. These people rented land from the lord. Villeins could hire someone to work the land for them and they could also leave to work elsewhere if they found a tenant to replace them.

Section 1 Review

Identify Vikings, Muslims, feudalism, serfs
Main Ideas
1. How did the Treaty of Verdun lead to lasting divisions in Europe?
2. How did the Frankish kings react to invasions by Vikings, Magyars, and Muslims?
3. Describe typical duties of a feudal lord and a vassal.
4. How did the Church fit into the feudal form of government?
5. Describe the classes of feudal society.

Critical Thinking
Making Hypotheses: If the Frankish kings after Charlemagne had been stronger rulers, medieval society in western Europe might have been very different than it was. How might medieval society have been different? Form a hypothesis for your answer.

BACKGROUND The size of a manor varied from about 350 acres, containing perhaps a dozen families, to 5000 acres, supporting fifty families.

2 The feudal manor was the center of economic life.

In western Europe during the Middle Ages, the economy depended on the **manorial system**. This was an agricultural system that was centered on self-contained estates called manors. Almost all goods and services were produced on the manors, which were run by the nobles. As you will see, the farmlands were organized in long strips and worked cooperatively by the peasants.

The manorial system developed at a time when towns in Europe were becoming smaller and fewer in number. The Germanic invasions had destroyed trade, and the fall of the Roman Empire led to a lack of government services. As a result, throughout western Europe, most people lived on manors as serfs.

The manorial system was based on farming.

Each manor was the center of the social and economic life of the people who lived in it. Travel between manors was almost nonexistent. The peasants depended on the lord for protection and provisions, and the lord depended on the labor of the peasants who worked his estates.

The heart of the manor was the manor house, which was often a fortified castle. The land on which it stood was the lord's demesne [də mān′]. Also located on the demesne were various buildings, such as the lord's barns, stables, mill, bakehouse, and cookhouse. Near the manor house were the church, the priest's house, and the village where peasants' huts lined a narrow street. The lord allotted meadows and woodlands as he pleased, but made a pasture available to everyone.

The entire population of the manor shared in the division of farmland. The lord usually took the best portion for his demesne and granted the remainder to the peasants. A three-field planting system kept the land from being overworked. The land was divided into three portions: the spring planting ground, the autumn planting ground, and the fallow (unplanted) ground. (See the diagram on the facing page.) The fields were rotated each year so that the land remained fertile.

BACKGROUND Neither Charles Martel nor Charlemagne had standing armies. They raised armies by giving land to mounted knights in return for their services in war. This practice helped the growth of a powerful class of nobles.

The three fields were further divided into long narrow strips that were allotted to various people: the lord, the lord's officials, the priest, and the serfs. Each person had strips within the three fields in order to share in different kinds of land. Because their holdings were scattered, the peasants worked the land cooperatively, usually sharing ownership of the plow and the oxen.

Because a lord with many estates could live on only one of them at a time and was often away fighting wars, the day-to-day running of the manor was left to certain officials. In England, they were known as the steward, the bailiff, and the reeve.

The steward had the highest rank. He was a legal adviser to the lord and traveled from one manor to another, checking on conditions. He reviewed accounts and held court on the manors.

The bailiff supervised the peasants and farm work. This official was responsible for getting crops harvested and collecting rents, dues, and fines owed by the peasants.

The reeve helped the bailiff supervise the work of the manor. A large manor might need many

reeves just as a large factory today needs many supervisors. The reeves oversaw the growing and storage of hay, the care of the bees and the herds of cattle and sheep, and the harvesting of crops. The reeve told the lord of any complaints that peasants had about manor officials.

Before working their own land, the serfs had to work the land that belonged to the lord. In addition, serfs had to repair bridges, cut wood, and do other tasks demanded by the lord. Most of the flour, bread, and wine produced by serfs in the manor's mill, oven, or wine press was given to the lord. Serfs could not leave the manor of their own free will, and they were considered to be property not much above the level of cattle.

Women worked hard on the manor.

Peasant women in the Middle Ages took care of the home, raised large families, and worked on the estate. These women did every kind of farm work except heavy plowing. They planted and harvested grain, sheared sheep, milked cows, and even thatched roofs.

Diagram of a Medieval Manor

A self-contained economic unit, the medieval manor operated on a system of rights and obligations based on custom. The peasants worked on the lord's land in return for protection, strips of farmland, and the right to use common land. The lord, various officials, and the parish priest had strips of farmland, which the peasants cultivated. Crops were rotated each year to keep the land fertile.

Forest

Common Pasture

Forest

Common Pasture

Mill

Pond

Oven

Graveyard

Lord's Manor House

Barn

Church

Gallows

Forest

Peasant Village

SPRING PLANTING

Blacksmith

FALL PLANTING

Common Pasture

Orchard

Vineyard

FALLOW FIELD

Forest

☐ A single peasant family's holdings
☐ Lord's strips
☐ Parish priest's strips
☐ Other peasants' or officials' strips

---

2 *Lesson Plan*

Essential Learning Objective

Students will learn to describe the medieval manor and analyze the manorial class system of the Middle Ages.

1 FOCUS AND MOTIVATE

Have them compare and contrast the relationship between medieval lords and their serfs and between Romans and their slaves.

2 TEACH

- Discuss the reasons for the development of the manorial system. Ask students to cite possible economic and political factors that caused manors to become self-sufficient. Have them give reasons why money would be of little use in such a system.

- Ask students to identify the buildings that make up a manor and describe the living conditions in the manor house. Have students cite evidence that defense against attack was an important aspect of manorial life.

- List the various roles and responsibilities of people who worked on a manor. Discuss the division of the manor lands and the division of labor between men and women. Guide students to see that women were important as workers, managers, and caretakers of children and the sick.

GUIDED PRACTICE

Have students write a paragraph comparing the lives of serfs with the lives of slaves on 19th-century plantations in the United States. Also for guided practice:

 Overhead Transparency 22

ASSESS

1. What was the purpose of a dowry? (to provide property for a woman to take to a marriage)

2. Why were travelers and wandering musicians welcome at castles? (passed on gossip and news and provided entertainment)

OPTIONAL RETEACHING

Ask students to work in teams. Have one team describe the duties and responsibilities of a person on a manorial estate and the other team guess the identity of the person. The team which guesses correctly describes next.

OPTIONAL ENRICHMENT

1. Have students research and show in a drawing the locations and functions of the various buildings of a manorial estate. (average)

2. Ask students to research and report orally on methods used to attack and defend castles. (challenging)

INDEPENDENT PRACTICE/ HOMEWORK

Assign the Section Review, Activities page 60, or Workbook page 40.

CLOSURE

In summarizing the lesson tell students that the manorial system arose out of the peasants' need for safety and food and out of the lords' need for services. All members of a manor were expected to cooperate for the common good.

Coats of Arms

A coat of arms is a shield, or drawing of a shield, bearing designs symbolic of family history, used especially by noble families in Europe. Coats of arms, worn on shields and garments placed over armor, were originally a means of identifying warriors on the medieval battlefield. Heraldry is the science or art dealing with coats of arms. *Below left* is a diagram of the areas of a shield. "Dexter" means right; "sinister" means left, seen from behind the shield. *Below right* is the coat of arms of the Washington family in England, George Washington's ancestors. *Above* is an English coat of arms embellished with animal crests, a motto, and various designs.

Women of the nobility could inherit land and hold offices. In the absence of the lord, the lady of the manor managed the estate. Sometimes, women had to oversee the defense of the manor during an enemy attack. If a lord was taken prisoner, his wife was expected to raise the ransom to save him. Noblewomen also performed medical services on the manor, as there were few doctors in those times.

Women of all classes married young, often by the time they were 14 years old. Fathers usually arranged the marriages, sometimes while the daughters were still infants. Among the upper classes, every father tried to provide a **dowry** for his daughter—that is, some amount of money,

BACKGROUND The iron grating that protected the castle entrance is called a *portcullis.* The name comes from 2 French words meaning "sliding gate."

land, or goods, that she took to her marriage. Without a dowry, it was almost impossible for a girl to marry. Letters and diaries of the time indicate that arranged marriages in the Middle Ages often turned out well.

Living conditions in the castle were crude.

The lord's manor house or castle was built to live in, but it was also a defense against enemies. The great stone tower, or keep, provided a safe shelter during a siege. Stables and food storage buildings were located near the keep.

A high wall, often several feet thick, surrounded the buildings. During a battle defenders could stand on walkways near the top of the wall. From there they could pour burning oil or drop heavy rocks on the enemy below. A moat [mōt], or ditch filled with water, ran around the outside of the wall. Entrance to the castle was controlled by a drawbridge that was lowered across the water from inside a gate in the wall. A heavy iron grating could be dropped to close the drawbridge gate.

By modern standards a castle had few comforts. Rooms were dark, cold, and musty. In winter hearth fires warmed only small areas of a room. Because chimneys did not come into use until the 14th century, rooms were often full of smoke.

At meals in the great hall, nobles usually sat at tables made of boards placed on sawhorses. Sometimes food scraps were simply dropped on the floor for the dogs to eat. Straw spread over the floor to lessen the cold became filthy and foul smelling from the garbage that collected in it. Carpets were not used until late in medieval times.

The huge, heavy beds used by the noble family were usually built on platforms. The beds had canopies on top and heavy curtains around the sides for privacy and protection from drafts. It was not uncommon for falcons, dogs, and even farm animals to sleep in the same room as the family.

During the evenings jesters and clowns entertained the nobles and their guests. Travelers were welcome, because they brought news and gossip from places beyond the manor. Wandering musicians who moved from one castle to another were also welcome as they entertained with songs and poems that told of heroic deeds, romantic love, and great adventures.

BACKGROUND Remind students that cities of India's Epic Age were fortified with walls and moats, just as medieval manors were in Europe.

Section 2 Review

Identify manorial system, dowry

Main Ideas

1. What was the main occupation on the manor? Which class of people did most of the work?
2. Name three major responsibilities of peasant women and three of women of the nobility.
3. What kind of living conditions did a medieval castle provide?

Critical Thinking

Analyzing Comparisons: Consider the following statement: "The responsibilities of women in the Middle Ages were similar to those of women in modernized nations of the world today." Is this comparison valid? Why or why not?

Medieval peasants gather the harvest, using simple tools and back-breaking labor. Compare the tools used with those in the Egyptian harvest shown on page 26. Medieval tools had not improved much.

3 The Church unified western Christendom.

The Church was the unifying force in the Middle Ages. As Christians, most Europeans believed that only the Church could give eternal salvation. Church influence was so strong that Europe was referred to as Christendom. In areas where rulers were weak, government services were provided by the Church, and its laws crossed political borders.

The Church had grown very wealthy with income that amounted to more than that of many kings and princes. Every Christian was expected to give a tithe, or tenth part of income, to the Church. Also, the Church frequently received large gifts of land from lords and kings.

People looked to the Church for salvation.

The Church had developed a body of beliefs and **sacraments** that all Christians accepted. Most important were the seven sacraments: (1) baptism, (2) confirmation, (3) penance, (4) the Holy Eucharist, (5) extreme unction, (6) matrimony, and (7) holy orders. People looked to the Church for salvation, and the sacraments were believed necessary for salvation.

In baptism, a person—usually an infant—became a Christian. In confirmation, the individual passed from childhood to become an adult member of the Church. In penance, the individual confessed sins to a priest, atoned for the sins, and was forgiven. In the Holy Eucharist, a priest reenacted Jesus' Last Supper with his disciples and offered the congregation consecrated bread and wine. Extreme unction was given to a dying person by a priest.

All Church members received these five sacraments. Only some received the other two sacraments. Matrimony was the marriage ceremony, and holy orders were for men who became priests.

The Church enforced its rules.

The Church had courts to help protect the weak and to punish those who did wrong. Church courts also tried clergy and others for religious offenses. People on trial in these courts were judged by canon law—the law of the Church.

believed it had the right to say who was to be emperor.) Help students understand the power struggle this act signified. (Kings and popes both wanted the highest authority.)

- Describe the role the Church played in the lives of medieval people. List the seven sacraments on the chalkboard. Have students explain how each sacrament was carried out.

- Discuss the reasons for the growth in power of the Church. Have students explain why the monks at Cluny deemed a reform program necessary. Ask students to give their opinions on why Innocent III was able to usurp the power of kings. Point out that by lowering the status of kings to vassals, the pope established the papacy as the highest power.

Describe the events preceding and during each of the Crusades to the Holy Land. Ask students to suggest what might have motivated people to join the Crusades. Guide students to conclude that the following were important motives: religious fervor, spirit of adventure, love of fighting, desire to plunder, desire for land, loyalty to the pope. Have students suggest reasons that the Crusades failed.

GUIDED PRACTICE

Have students make two lists, one of the positive and one of the negative results of the Crusades.

BACKGROUND Another weapon used by the Church was the interdict, which stopped Church services (except Baptism and Extreme Unction) on a disobedient noble's land to cause

Heresy, the holding of religious opinions contrary to established Church doctrines, was considered the worst of all crimes, a crime against God. The Church actively looked for and punished heretics, or people suspected of heresy. One of the most terrible weapons used against heretics was excommunication. A person who was excommunicated was no longer a member of the Church, could not receive the sacraments, and therefore could never be saved. The Church usually tried to persuade heretics to give up their beliefs. If heretics refused, they could be burned at the stake.

The Church became stronger and more independent.

During the 10th century, while the papacy was growing in power, it depended upon a strong German king for protection against feudal abuses, unruly Italian nobles, and Roman mobs. This arrangement led later German kings to interfere in Church affairs, even in the election of popes.

In the 11th century, a great religious reform movement was begun by the monks at Cluny [klü′nē] in present-day France. The monks spoke out against kings and nobles who interfered in Church affairs. The reform program called for removing all civil control over the pope, forbidding the sale of positions in the Church and, particularly, preventing kings and nobles from choosing bishops. In 1059 the College of Cardinals was created to elect a successor to the pope as the choice of the Church, not of a king or group of nobles.

The power of the Church grew under the reign of Pope Innocent III, who became supreme overlord of Europe during his reign from 1198 to 1216. Pope Innocent III claimed that his authority was above that of any other ruler and that the word of the Church was final. With this claim, the pope forced King John to give all of England to the papacy and then take England back as a fief. This action, which made John a vassal of the pope, was also taken against the rulers of Denmark, Portugal, Poland, Hungary, and Aragon.

During the 12th and 13th centuries, two influential religious orders were founded—the Franciscans and the Dominicans. **Saint Francis of Assisi** founded the Franciscan order, which stressed vows of poverty and gentleness to all creatures.

BACKGROUND The Church did not punish people itself. People such as heretics were handed over to secular authorities to carry out sentence.

the noble's subjects to protest and make the noble obey Church law.

The Dominicans, founded by **Saint Dominic**, also took vows of poverty and stressed missionary work among the common people.

Monks in both orders preached in the towns and countryside to spread the gospel and fight heresy. The monks often became university teachers and were influential at a time when many people criticized the Church for being too interested in power and wealth.

The Church urged crusaders to regain the Holy Land for Christians.

Arab Muslims had conquered the Holy Land in 638, but Christians were still allowed to visit places associated with the life of Jesus. However,

The deadly confidence of the crusading knights is dramatized by this bronze container made during the period of the crusades.

The Crusades

(map labels)

North Sea

Baltic Sea

ENGLAND

ATLANTIC OCEAN

POLAND

HOLY   Regensburg
Cluny   ROMAN   Vienna
FRANCE
Clermont•   EMPIRE   HUNGARY
Lyons   Venice
Genoa   Canossa   Zara
Marseilles
BULGARIA   Black Sea
PORTUGAL
SPANISH KINGDOMS
Rome   BYZANTINE   Constantinople
Bari   SELJUK TURKS
MUSLIM   Brindisi   EMPIRE
STATES   KINGDOM
OF   Antioch
SICILY
Mediterranean Sea   •Damascus
•Acre
CRUSADER•Jerusalem
STATES

N

0   200   400 MILES
0   200   400 KILOMETERS

- - - - First 1096-1099
– ·– · Second 1147-1149
——— Third 1189-1192
· · · · Fourth 1202-1204
· · · · Political boundaries, 1140 A.D.

 MAP STUDY   This map greatly simplifies the history of the crusades. On which crusade did Europeans go by land from Constantinople to Jerusalem? When was this crusade?

in the 11th century, Seljuk Turks, who were also Muslim, swept into the Middle East. By 1089 they had gained control of **Jerusalem** and were threatening to conquer Constantinople, the capital of the Byzantine Empire. The Byzantine emperor asked the pope for help in fighting Muslim domination.

In 1095 Pope Urban II called a meeting of Christian nobles in the French city of Clermont to organize support for the Byzantine emperor against the Turks. The pope urged thousands of lords and knights to become **crusaders**, a word that means "marked with the cross." As crusaders, these Christians would fight the Muslims and regain the Middle East for Christianity.

Pope Urban promised the crusaders forgiveness for their sins, freedom from their debts, and a choice of fiefs in the lands to be conquered. This last promise was especially important for second sons of the nobility who could not inherit landholdings in Europe. (At that time, only first sons inherited property from their fathers.)

While the knights began to organize an army, preachers wandered through France and Germany urging peasants to join the crusade. Aroused by fiery preaching, mobs of peasants started on the long road to Jerusalem. These undisciplined people frequently killed and pillaged during what became known as the "Peasant Crusade."

Many of the victims of these "crusaders" were Jews, who were singled out as people who did not believe in Christianity. When the crusade reached Constantinople in 1096, the mob burned and

3 | ASSESS AND CLOSE

ASSESS

For what was the Church criticized during the 12th and 13th centuries? (its interest in power and wealth)

OPTIONAL RETEACHING

Draw a horizontal time line on the board, extending from 600 to 1300. Above it write the dates: 638, 1089, 1096, 1099, 1144, 1147, 1189, 1202, 1204, 1261. Have students name the events that took place during these years. (Arab Muslims conquered Holy Land, Seljuk Turks conquered Jerusalem, Peasant Crusade, First Crusade, Muslims captured Edessa, Second Crusade, Third Crusade, Fourth Crusade, Crusaders sacked Constantinople, Byzantine Empire restored)

OPTIONAL ENRICHMENT

1. Have students research the Children's Crusade of 1212 and summarize their findings in a paragraph. (average)
2. Ask interested students to find information about the Arabic-Islamic technology, architecture, scientific knowledge, philosophy, and literature that influenced the crusaders. (challenging)
3. Also for enrichment:

 Source Reading 11A

INDEPENDENT PRACTICE/ HOMEWORK

Assign the Section Review, Activities page 61, or Workbook page 41.

In summarizing the lesson tell students that the Church became wealthy during the Middle Ages, usurped the power of the kings, and unified western Christendom. The Church and the papacy became so powerful, they led the peoples of Europe into a series of military expeditions to the Holy Land.

Answers to Section 3 Review

Identify

Key Terms, People, and Places are defined on pages indicated in parentheses. Also see the Glossary and Biographical Dictionary.
sacraments (199), Saint Francis of Assisi (200), Saint Dominic (200), Jerusalem (201), crusaders (201)

Main Ideas

1. Christians believed the sacraments were necessary for salvation.
2. If excommunicated, a person was no longer a member of the Church and could not go to heaven.
3. The Franciscans and Dominicans lived lives of poverty and preaching and overcame some of the criticism of the Church's wealth and power.
4. Church leaders and other Christians felt it their duty to fight the Muslims in the Middle East and secure those lands for Christianity.

Critical Thinking

It is assumed that crusaders went to war for the good of the Church and to protect Christian beliefs when in fact many crusaders went to war to gain land and honor for themselves. Much of the Crusade movement acted against Christian beliefs by bringing violence and death.

looted the city. After leaving Constantinople, the crusaders were attacked by the Turks and massacred. Few ever reached Jerusalem.

Unlike the Peasant Crusade, the First Crusade was undertaken by an organized, disciplined army. Led by Frankish princes and nobles, this crusade included 3,000 knights on horseback and 12,000 infantry, or foot soldiers. In 1099 this army fought its way from Constantinople into Jerusalem and mercilessly slaughtered Muslim, Jewish, and even Christian residents.

The crusaders seized the Holy Land and created a chain of Crusader States along the eastern Mediterranean coast. The ruins of their fortresses can be seen today in Israel, Lebanon, Syria, and Jordan. Nearly 50 years later, Muslims attacked the Crusader States and in 1144 recaptured the crusader kingdom of Edessa in Armenia.

In 1147 a Second Crusade was begun to stem the Muslim resurgence, but it was unsuccessful. In 1187 Jerusalem was taken by a Muslim army led by Saladin. This event led to the Third Crusade in 1189, which also failed. With this crusade, Christians won the right to visit Jerusalem, although Saladin had long been willing to grant Christians this privilege even without the crusade.

In 1202 a Fourth Crusade began. However, instead of fighting the Muslims, the crusaders captured and sacked Constantinople in 1204 and set up their own government. In 1261 the Byzantine Empire was restored, but it never wholly recovered from the blow dealt by the Fourth Crusade. Thirty years later, Acre, the last crusader stronghold, was reconquered by the Muslims. This defeat marked the end of the crusades.

The violence of the crusades caused unforeseen negative results. Before the crusader wars, Muslims had been tolerant of Christians. After the slaughter and destruction of the wars, however, many Muslims viewed Christians as uncivilized enemies. In Europe, a tragic result was the unleashing of extreme religious persecution against nonconformists.

On the positive side, new products and ideas were introduced into Europe by the returning crusaders. Perfumes, spices, sugar, silk, and many other items not common in the west were in demand by European nobility. Thus the crusades

stimulated east-west trade in the Mediterranean region and spurred the growth of cities, especially in Italy. The expansion of trade also encouraged development of banking and a money economy in Europe. Exposure to the intellectual achievements of the Middle East enriched the languages and learning of the West.

Section 3 Review

Identify sacraments, Saint Francis of Assisi, Saint Dominic, Jerusalem, crusaders

Main Ideas

1. Why were the Church sacraments so important to Christians?
2. Why was excommunication such a powerful weapon of the Church?
3. Give one reason why the Franciscans and Dominicans were important during this period.
4. What was the main religious reason for the crusades?

Critical Thinking

Identifying Assumptions: "The crusaders went forth to save the Church and Christian beliefs from being destroyed by Muslims." What assumptions are being made in this statement?

 Town life revived in the later Middle Ages.

During the 10th and 11th centuries, new towns developed in western Europe and older cities that had survived the fall of the Roman Empire began to revive. Gradually, new classes of people grew in wealth and power, and cities became centers for education, literature, and the arts.

Many factors caused the growth of towns and cities.

Cities expanded rapidly during the 13th century mainly because of three developments. These were (1) an increase in trade, (2) the use of money, and (3) improved technology.

Increase in trade. In 1204, after the end of the Fourth Crusade, trade flourished between the Middle East and Italian city-states such as Venice and

Details about life in medieval France can be learned from manuscript illustrations like this painting of a 13th-century town. From left to right are tailors, furriers, a barber, and a grocer.

Genoa. People in western Europe, especially the nobility, wanted to buy spices and silks that Arab merchants brought back from India and China.

Large fleets of Italian ships sailed through the Mediterranean Sea and along the coast of France bringing luxury goods to England and northern Europe. As international trade increased, towns grew, and as towns grew, international trade increased even more.

Use of money. During the early Middle Ages, barter, that is trade by exchanging goods or services without the use of money, was a common way to do business. Local markets were held each week in the open squares near castles or churches. At these markets, peasants bartered homemade goods for farm products—perhaps a wooden spoon was exchanged for eggs or meat.

As trade spread beyond local areas, feudal lords set up annual fairs. These fairs became meeting places for merchants from all over Europe. In time, people began to use money at these fairs, but many people brought different types of money depending on where they lived. To solve this problem, money changers set up booths and, for a small fee, exchanged foreign coins for local currency. This was an early form of banking.

As money came more into use, merchants found that it was safe to leave large sums with money changers. The money changers, in turn, lent money to borrowers and charged **interest**, which

BACKGROUND Both goods and ideas were exchanged at the fairs. People met and discussed new methods of industry, agriculture, and transportation.

4 *Lesson Plan*

Essential Learning Objective

Students will learn to describe the causes and effects of the growth of towns, the Black Death, and the persecution of European Jews.

1 FOCUS AND MOTIVATE

Ask students to identify elements in a manor that might be found in a town. Have them speculate about whether manors might ever develop into towns.

2 TEACH

- Discuss how the exposure of crusaders to Middle Eastern goods created a market for luxury items in western Europe. Describe the expansion of trade from local to international markets. Have students explain how the use of money and a banking system stimulated the growth of cities.

- List and discuss the technological developments and their effects on crop production, land usage, the standard of living, and population size. Relate the resulting labor shortage to the improvements in the lives of peasants. Ask students to cite reasons why serfs left manors for towns.

- Discuss the development of a middle class and of guilds. Have students compare today's labor unions with guilds and cite their similarities and differences.

- Trace and discuss the history of Jews in medieval society. Describe the role of the Church in the persecution of Jews. Have students cite the Jews' contributions to European society.

GUIDED PRACTICE

Have students describe the causes and effects of the bubonic plague.

GEOGRAPHY

A Key to History

EUROPE'S AGRICULTURAL REVOLUTION

Europe is divided into two geographic regions by the Alps and other mountains. The region south of the Alps has a Mediterranean climate characterized by hot, dry summers and mild, moist winters. The climate and the soil were both well suited to early agriculture.

The region north of the mountains has a marine west coast climate with rainfall throughout the year. Dense forests and heavy, rain-sodden soils restricted agriculture to a few favored locations until new techniques of farming were developed between 500 and 1200.

At first, the Romans who came to northern Europe attempted to plow the heavy northern soils by adding wheels to their simple plows. Even with this improvement, however, the Roman plows were inadequate.

The heavy plow and horsecollar worked an agricultural miracle (left). Find the areas on the map where the heavy plow was used. What climate predominates there?

Later, the Germanic tribes introduced a heavier plow reinforced with iron. To pull this heavy plow required as many as six or eight oxen, more than any one peasant could afford. As a result, the German peasants cooperated so that each contributed an ox and several peasants shared a plow. Our measurement of an acre is the amount of land a team could plow between sunrise and sunset.

Gradually, horses replaced the oxen because horses could work far more quickly. Their speed, however, was offset by extremely inefficient methods of working horses. For example, horseshoes were not generally used, so horses damaged their hooves. Even worse, the clumsy harnesses pressed into a horse's windpipe when it began to pull a load, choking the poor beast.

Eventually, peasants adopted horseshoes, a rigid horsecollar, and the tandem harness—a new method of harnessing horses one behind the other instead of side by side as shown at the top left. Using these innovations and feeding the horses more nutritious oats, as well as hay, increased their productivity.

Together, these innovations transformed the large forests of the North European Plain into productive farmland. More and better food made it possible for more children to survive. In time, this population growth strengthened the political power of Europe north of the Alps.

REVIEW

1. Why were horses better than oxen for farm work?
2. Explain three agricultural improvements that increased the political power of northern Europe.

Dry climates
- Steppe

Mild climates
- Marine west coast
- Humid subtropical
- Mediterranean

Continental climates
- Humid continental, warm summer
- Humid continental, cool summer

High altitudes
- Highlands

- Southern boundary of areas where heavy plow was widely used
- Boundaries, 1140

0   500 MILES
0   500 KILOMETERS

BACKGROUND The English word *bank* comes from the Italian word *banca*, meaning "bench," upon which the money lenders sat.

is a fee based on a percentage of money borrowed. A merchant could also deposit money in one city, get a receipt, and collect the money in another city. This system of **credit** was a safer way to handle money than carrying it when traveling.

The use of money instead of barter made it easier for merchants to develop businesses and interact financially with people in other cities. This led to the growth of cities as centers for banking and all kinds of commerce.

Improved technology. Changes in technology had a marked effect on town growth. Three inventions—the tandem harness, the horse collar, and horseshoes—led to improved farming and transportation of products. New farming methods yielded bigger crops, provided better living standards, and led to an increase in population. Higher farm production and better transportation made food available in cities for people who could not grow their own food. With improved technology, more land became available for farming as forests were cleared, swamps drained, and land reclaimed from the sea. The Middle Ages was thus the great pioneering era of western Europe.

The lords who developed these wilderness lands needed workers to build dikes, cut timber, and cultivate the new land. To attract and keep workers, many lords promised serfs freedom and the right to rent land at fixed fees. Thus a growing number of peasants could choose either to remain on the manor or move to the town.

Gradually, towns gained independence from the manors and developed political stability. City living became increasingly desirable, and serfs continued to leave the manors to earn a living as laborers and craftsmen and craftswomen. Such workers were needed to fill the increasing number of jobs available in cities. This exodus from manor to town lasted for hundreds of years and was one of the great social and economic revolutions in Western history.

The Black Death devastated Europe.

In the early stages of growth, towns were rural in character and relatively uncrowded. However, as more and more people left the manors, the towns became congested, unhealthy, and even unsafe. Sanitation was poor, and plagues—dangerous diseases that spread through the population—were common. Wooden houses in which open fires provided heat and light were a constant cause of large city fires.

Nevertheless, opportunities to make money and gain personal freedom in the cities were more important than the danger of plagues and fire. In the 1200s and 1300s, as cities grew larger, public health and safety laws appeared. Some cities started paving streets and requiring fireproof roofing. In 1388 England forbade people to throw waste into ditches and rivers.

Still, very few cities had underground sewers, and none provided for garbage collection. Refuse was usually thrown into the streets to be washed away by rain or eaten by the pigs and dogs that roamed everywhere.

In 1347 an epidemic of bubonic plague began in southeastern Europe near the Black Sea and spread to Constantinople. This disease was caused by fleas that lived on black rats. In 1348 and 1349, the plague spread throughout Europe and Asia, carried along trade routes by travelers and caravans coming from infected areas. People called this disease the **Black Death** because corpses of the victims turned a dark color.

The hideous plague struck Europe again and again. It is believed that one-fourth to one-half of the entire population of Europe died of the Black Death between 1348 and 1370. The disease struck hardest in cities such as Florence, Italy, where the population dropped from 114,000 to 50,000 in five years. The plague had other severe effects. Food became scarce because in many places there were few people left to plant or harvest crops. Education, commerce, and crafts declined for lack of people to do the necessary work.

Although the Black Death caused untold suffering and grief, it did help end serfdom. Since laborers were scarce, those who survived could command higher wages and gain independence from the manors.

A new class of town dwellers arose.

As the Black Death waned, cities slowly recovered. Populations throughout western Europe began to increase. By the middle 1400s, Brussels had a population of 35,000 and London had a population of

BACKGROUND In town, the former serf could become a wealthy craftsman or merchant, completely changing his or her way of life. Many serfs ran away from the manor to the more inviting towns.

3 ASSESS AND CLOSE

ASSESS
1. What is barter? (trade by exchanging goods and services)
2. What two Italian city-states were important medieval trading centers? (Venice, Genoa)

OPTIONAL RETEACHING
List the steps that led to the development of a banking system. Ask students to explain how each step benefited the merchants and consumers.

OPTIONAL ENRICHMENT
1. Have students research and prepare a list of the various goods for which a demand developed after the Crusades. (average)
2. Have students research what cities were founded in medieval Europe. Have them draw a map showing locations of the new cities and of older cities that revived. (challenging)

INDEPENDENT PRACTICE/ HOMEWORK
Assign the Section Review, Activities page 62, or Workbook page 42.

CLOSURE
Tell students that increase in trade, use of money, and improved technology led to the founding and expansion of towns and cities in medieval times. These three factors led to an increase in food production, specialization among workers, the development of a middle class, the freeing of serfs, and a higher standard of living.

Answers to Section 4 Review

Identify
Key Terms, People, and Places are defined on pages indicated in parentheses. Also see the Glossary and Biographical Dictionary.
interest (203), credit (205), Black Death (205), Paris (206), middle class (206), guilds (206)

Main Ideas
1. increase of trade, use of money, improved farming methods and transportation, increased need for workers both on manors and in towns that helped serfs earn freedom to leave manors.
2. plagues and fires; the Black Death killed almost one-half of Europe's population, caused food production, education, and commerce to decline because of the lack of people to do the necessary work.
3. the middle class or bourgeoisie; guilds
4. The persecution against nonconformists during the Crusades made Jews a target for hatred and intolerance; devastation of the Black Death was blamed on Jews.

Critical Thinking
Disagree. Cities grew because of increased trade, growth of banking systems, improved farming methods that led to greater food production and less need for serfs, and better living conditions in cities.

40,000. **Paris,** the largest city in western Europe, had grown to 300,000.

With the rise of towns and the expansion of commerce, a powerful new class of people developed in western Europe. This "middle" class, which gained wealth through business rather than farming and war, ranked lower than the feudal nobility and higher than the serfs. The people in this class were called burghers [bėr′gərz], or the bourgeoisie [bùr′zhwä zē′], meaning "people of the town" (burg). The bourgeoisie, or **middle class**, had its origin in medieval towns.

The feudal nobility looked down upon the bourgeoisie. However, the burghers continued to prosper and gradually established a kind of nobility of their own. In turn, the bourgeoisie came to look down on those below them on the social scale, such as skilled craftsmen and unskilled workers. Gradually, class differences developed along lines of wealth rather than of birth.

The economic life of the towns was regulated by organizations called **guilds**. Merchants and artisans had separate guilds—there were bankers' guilds, carpenters' guilds, weavers' guilds, and so on. The main purpose of guilds was to monopolize trade for members and to prevent competition. (A monopoly is the exclusive control of a product or service.) Guild courts settled disputes among members and regulated conduct according to guild rules. Guilds also helped needy members, built homes for the poor, and held banquets and other social events.

The crusades promoted violence against Jews.

By the late 11th century, many towns in western Europe had small Jewish populations. These people were descendants of slaves captured in the Jewish revolts against Rome or Jews who had migrated from Mediterranean cities during and after the end of the Roman Empire.

Although the wealthier Jews were mainly merchants, most Jews were artisans, such as wool and silk weavers, dyers, goldsmiths, and glassmakers. These skills were greatly needed in feudal Europe. Consequently, Charlemagne and other Christian kings and lords welcomed Jewish settlers and granted them town charters and freedom to follow their faith. Jews had the status of royal serfs under direct control of the king.

The walled city of Carcassonne in southern France is a spectacular remnant from medieval times. The walls were built between 1240 and 1285.

Jews considered it their religious duty to educate their sons to study the Bible and the Talmud (commentaries and interpretations of the Bible). Their daughters often received a rudimentary education as well. Thus the Jews were generally literate in an age when most Europeans, even some kings, could not read or write.

The crusades unleashed a strong religious reaction against Jews, as they did against all noncomformists and heretics. The atmosphere of hatred was heightened by the Black Death, which some communities blamed on the Jews. As a result, the Jewish people of western Europe were attacked, barred from guilds, and banned from most crafts.

Increasingly Jews were forced to turn to moneylending, which the Church condemned as a sin and forbade to Christians (until the rise of banking made moneylending more respectable). The intolerance reached its height in the 13th and 14th centuries when anti-Jewish laws were passed by the Church. This was followed by violent attacks on Jewish communities, and the expulsion of all Jews from England, France, and parts of Germany.

Despite the violence and persecutions, Italy, the Netherlands, and other areas welcomed Jewish settlers. Poland especially encouraged Jewish immigration and gradually became the great center of European Jewry.

Section 4 Review

Identify interest, credit, Black Death, Paris, middle class, guilds

Main Ideas
1. What major factors led to the growth of towns and cities in western Europe?
2. Name two hazards faced by early city dwellers. Briefly describe the effects of the Black Death.
3. What new class of people arose in medieval towns? Name one major institution of this class.
4. What caused a change in the European attitude toward Jews?

Critical Thinking
Assessing Cause and Effect: "The main cause for the growth of cities in the Middle Ages was the rebellion of serfs against their masters on the manors." Do you agree with this statement? Why or why not?

5 Education, learning, and the arts advanced.

By the year 600, formal education had almost come to an end in western Christendom. The few schools that did exist were run by the Church to train people to become priests or monks. This situation lasted for nearly 500 years. Then, as times changed, new conditions created a need for special kinds of training and education.

Universities developed in Christendom.

During the 1100s three factors encouraged the growth of learning in Christendom: (1) the rise of cities and a wealthy middle class, (2) Church reforms, and (3) contact with Muslim learning. Also, as life became more complex, both the Church and civil governments needed specially trained people to work in scholarly fields such as law and government. To meet these needs, teachers and students formed groups called **universities**. One university, begun at Bologna [bə lō′nyə], Italy, about 1158, was well known for teaching law. Another university, started at Paris about 1200, became a noted school of theology.

The earliest universities had no set courses of study, no permanent buildings, and few rules. Students were granted freedom from military service and from the control of town officials. Often students set up their own university administration, hired teachers, and made rules for the school.

Classrooms in the early universities were usually uncomfortable. In cold climates, students wore heavy gowns and hoods and sat on floors covered with straw for warmth. Each student went to one or two classes a day, each class being several hours long. Once darkness fell, studying ceased, because candles were expensive and there was no other form of lighting.

One of the most famous scholars of the Middle Ages was **Saint Thomas Aquinas** [ə kwī′nəs], who lived from about 1225 to 1274. Saint Thomas joined the Dominican order as a youth and became a brilliant lecturer and writer. During his lifetime, a controversy developed among scholars about the true source of knowledge. Ancient Greek writings were widely read, and, exposed to those sources,

5 Lesson Plan
Essential Learning Objectives
Students will learn to:
- identify the factors that aided in the growth of learning during the Middle Ages.
- describe the origins and development of modern language and literature.

1 FOCUS AND MOTIVATE

Ask students to name the kinds of activities of medieval people that required manual labor, skill, or intellectual studies. Have them give reasons why few of the activities required a formal education.

2 TEACH

- Discuss the establishment of universities during the Middle Ages. Compare early universities with those today.

- List the areas of knowledge European scholars studied. Ask students to speculate about why each area was important to people of the Middle Ages. Have them explain why Aquinas' contribution was important to theology and Bacon's, to science.

- Describe the origin and development of the Romance and Germanic languages. Have students explain why many words in the sciences today are still Latin or Latin-based.

● List on the chalkboard the various forms of literature of the Middle Ages. Ask students to identify those that served as entertainment and those that served to educate people in the religious beliefs of the Church.

GUIDED PRACTICE

Have students compare the beliefs of Thomas Aquinas and Roger Bacon on knowledge and faith and write a paragraph explaining how their beliefs are similar.

many scholars insisted on reason as a source of knowledge rather than faith.

Saint Thomas argued that both reason and faith are gifts of God and cannot contradict each other. He believed that certain truths can be understood by reasoning, but other truths can be understood only by faith. So convincing were Saint Thomas' arguments that his work *Summa Theologia* (Summation of Theological Knowledge) is still an authority for the Roman Catholic Church.

Scientific knowledge made some progress in the later Middle Ages.

Greek and Arab scientific works flowed into Christendom after 1100, especially from Muslim Spain and Sicily. Euclid's *Geometry* and Arab works on algebra, geometry, and trigonometry added to the scope and accuracy of mathematics.

In the 1100s the compass, invented by the Chinese, was introduced into Europe. About 1300 an improved rudder for large ships was developed. During the 1300s the introduction of the blast furnace led to progress in iron working. Greek, Persian, and Arab writings on biology became available to doctors and helped advance medicine.

Roger Bacon, an English monk of the 1200s, contributed significantly to scientific knowledge. Bacon felt that learning should be based on observation and experience, not just on faith or pure reason. He argued that experimentation could lead to the invention of machinery that would do most things better than human and animal labor.

As a result of his work, Bacon was attacked by many of the learned men of his day. Toward the end of his life, Bacon was imprisoned for 15 years, and his works were condemned. However, it was Roger Bacon who predicted the coming of power-driven ships, cars, and flying machines.

Popular languages replaced Latin.

All through the early Middle Ages, Latin was an international means of communication among educated people. Almost all writings of the Church, governments, and schools were in Latin. However, most people in western Europe could not speak or understand the language, even though they came in contact with Latin in the Church. In everyday life people spoke their own local, or vernacular, languages such as French, German, and English.

Most local languages developed after the fall of the Roman Empire as a result of changes in Latin. The changes varied from area to area. Latin-based languages evolved in Italy, France, Spain, and Portugal during the early Middle Ages. These languages are known as Romance languages because they are based on Roman Latin. Several hundred Germanic words also became part of the Romance languages during and after the Germanic invasions. Contact with the Middle East also added Greek, Persian, Turkish, and Arabic words.

DAILY LIFE

Simple pleasures sometimes interrupted the round of planting, growing, and harvesting that set the pattern of medieval life. In these scenes from the 14th and 15th centuries, men, women, and young people engage in a snowball fight (left), prepare the lord's dogs for the hunt (right), and play with balls and bat (far right).

Persian, Turkish, Arabic Words in English

admiral	gazelle	lilac	spinach
candy	ghoul	magic	tariff
cipher	hazard	orange	tulip
crimson	horde	sofa	zenith

English, Dutch, modern German and the Scandinavian languages are Germanic languages. However, through contact with the Roman world, hundreds of Latin words entered the Germanic languages. That is why English shares much of its vocabulary with Romance languages like Italian, French, and Spanish. The Latin original and its variations can be seen clearly in the English words "study," "letter," and "city":

Latin	Italian	French	Spanish
studiare	studiare	étudier	estudiar
littera	lettera	lettre	letra
civitas	citta	cité	ciudad

Literature developed in the Middle Ages.

Latin was used in serious works and in the lively poetry written by university students. Traveling students, in exchange for food and housing, sometimes entertained their hosts with happy, irreverent verses about the joys of wine, love, and song.

The earliest form of native literature was the epic, a long poem that told of adventures of great heroes. *Beowulf*, written in the Anglo-Saxon language (Old English) in the 8th century, is an example of an early epic.

With the increase in city life and the growth of a middle class that could read and write, a short story form became popular. These stories were comical, often scandalous. Also popular were animal stories, such as *Reynard the Fox*, and ballads, such as those about Robin Hood.

Dante Alighieri [dän′tä ä′lē gyer′ē] was an Italian poet and philosopher who was born in Florence in 1265. Dante wrote a poem that later admirers called the *Divine Comedy*. Written in Italian, this work reflects the religious spirit of the times, telling of a mythical journey through hell, purgatory, and paradise. Dante was one of the first Italian poets to write in both Latin and Italian.

Geoffrey Chaucer, the son of a wine merchant, was born about 1340 in London. Chaucer's best-known work is *The Canterbury Tales*, which tells the story of 30 pilgrims on their way to Canterbury cathedral in England. This group of stories offers a vivid, earthy picture of English life in the 1300s. The Midland dialect Chaucer used in writing was the base from which modern English developed.

3 | ASSESS AND CLOSE

ASSESS

1. From what art form did morality plays develop? (stories)
2. What was the purpose of medieval statues and paintings? (to educate people in beliefs of Christianity)

OPTIONAL RETEACHING

List on the chalkboard the three factors that encouraged the growth of learning in Christendom. Have students give examples of the kinds of learning to which each factor led.

Students also may be assigned Activities reteaching page 64.

OPTIONAL ENRICHMENT

1. Have students find information and give an oral report on the teachings of Roger Bacon. (average)
2. Have students read one of the following pieces of medieval literature: *Beowulf*, *The Gestes of Arthur* by Wace, *The Song of the Nibelungen*, or *The Voyage of Bran*. Have students write a brief report stating what insights the piece provided about the beliefs and customs of people of the Middle Ages. (challenging)
3. Students also may be assigned Activities enrichment page 65, or:

📖 *Source Reading 11B*

INDEPENDENT PRACTICE/ HOMEWORK

Assign the Section Review, the Chapter Review items, Activities page 63, or Workbook page 43.

CLOSURE

In summarizing the lesson tell students that as life became more complex in the Middle Ages, universities arose as places to acquire theoretical and practical knowledge. Latin remained the language of the Church while local Latin-based or Germanic languages were spoken by most Europeans and were used in native literature. Medieval art and literature either served the Church to teach its beliefs or were used for enjoyment and entertainment.

Answers to Section 5 Review

Identify
Key Terms, People, and Places are defined on pages indicated in parentheses. Also see the Glossary and Biographical Dictionary.
universities (207), Saint Thomas Aquinas (207), Roger Bacon (208), Geoffrey Chaucer (209)

Main Ideas
1. The Church and governments needed people with special skills and knowledge, such as theology and law.
2. Greek and Arab scientific works were studied; scientists, such as Roger Bacon, encouraged learning by observation and experimentation.
3. After the fall of the Roman Empire, changes in Latin occurred locally. Germanic invasions caused Germanic words to mix with Latin. Contact with the Middle East introduced Arabic, Persian, Turkish, and Greek words.
4. a long poem that tells of adventures of great heroes; *Beowulf*
5. religion

Critical Thinking
Such sources are not reliable by themselves because the purpose of literature is not historical accuracy. Used with other factual documents, however, literature gives insight into the thinking and customs of the times.

This medieval manuscript illustration of English travelers shows how the pilgrims in Chaucer's *Canterbury Tales* might have looked.

The arts served the needs of the Church.

Most music in the Middle Ages was written for Church services and was sung or chanted. Musicians played instruments such as organs, violins, dulcimers, and lutes.

Dramatizations of Bible stories and religious teachings were performed in the churches. At first, these stories were sung by the choir; later, they developed into plays. In time, plays were performed in local languages and in public places outside of church buildings. However, the plays kept their religious character, and most were known as morality plays.

Artists of the day were hired to decorate churches and cathedrals. Both outside and inside walls were covered with statues and paintings showing events in the lives of Jesus and the saints and scenes from Bible stories. These were used to instruct the people, who were illiterate, in the beliefs of Christianity. The construction of stained-glass windows, which dated from ancient times, became a fine art in the medieval period.

Section 5 Review

Identify universities, Saint Thomas Aquinas, Roger Bacon, Geoffrey Chaucer

Main Ideas
1. Why did universities develop in the Middle Ages?
2. How did scientific knowledge advance in the later Middle Ages?
3. How did local languages evolve in western Europe?
4. What is an epic? Give one example of an epic.
5. What was the main theme of art in the Middle Ages?

Critical Thinking
Evaluating Sources of Information: Epics and other literature from the Middle Ages give us descriptions of people and ways of life of the times. Do you consider such sources reliable as historical documents? Why or why not?

HIGHLIGHTS OF CIVILIZATION

Gothic Cathedrals

Between 1050 and 1200, churches in western Europe were built in the Romanesque style with thick walls, small windows, and low ceilings. In the mid-1100s, French builders developed the Gothic style. With supports called flying buttresses taking the weight off the walls, it became possible to build huge, airy buildings.

Towns began to compete with each other to build the tallest cathedral. The cathedral at Bourges [bûrzh], in a small town in central France, rises 122 feet in height at the entrance. The cathedral at Amiens [am yan´], north of Paris and the largest church in France, is 144 feet in height. Constructing the cathedrals, said the 19th-century American writer Henry Adams, was like "building up a skeleton of stone ribs and vertebrae, on which every pound of weight is adjusted, divided, and carried down from level to level till it touches ground at a distance as a bird would alight."

Chartres Cathedral frames its famous Rose Window (top left). Note the flying buttresses at Bourges (below) which support the walls, making large expanses of stained glass possible.

HIGHLIGHTS OF CIVILIZATION

The cathedral at Bourges was built between the 12th and 14th centuries and partially reconstructed in the 16th when the north tower collapsed.

Ask students why they think so many Gothic cathedrals were built in France. (Wealth was concentrated there. People had time and money to support cathedral building and to develop the skills involved—architecture, stonemasonry, sculptural decoration, and the creation of stained glass.) What do students think Henry Adams meant when he said the framework of the cathedral "touches ground at a distance as a bird would alight"? (Its immense weight is so distributed that the structure touches the ground lightly and gracefully.)

CHAPTER 11 REVIEW

Section Summaries

Section 1
Feudalism developed in western Christendom.
With the decline of central government, local lords with large landholdings became rulers throughout Europe. Feudalism developed as a form of government with fixed relationships among the nobility, peasants, and the Church.

Section 2
The feudal manor was the center of economic life.
Most of the people in Europe lived on self-sufficient manors. Nobles and officials managed the manors; serfs and other peasants did the farm work.

Section 3
The Church unified western Christendom.
The Church grew strong and independent of civil authority. Trade between Europe and the Middle East increased gradually.

Section 4
Town life revived in the later Middle Ages.
As a result of increased trade, use of money, and improved technology, towns began to prosper. Banking and commerce developed. After the devastation of the Black Death, a new class of people called the bourgeoisie, or middle class, developed in cities.

Section 5
Education, learning, and the arts advanced.
During the Middle Ages, universities developed to teach special skills and knowledge. University scholars made advances in mathematics, science, and technology. Literature was written in local dialects, and the arts enhanced religion and everyday life.

Test Yourself

Key Terms, People, and Places
Identify the significance of each of the following:

Section 1
a. Vikings   c. feudalism
b. Muslims   d. serfs

Section 2
a. manorial system   b. dowry

Section 3
a. sacraments   d. Jerusalem
b. Saint Francis of Assisi   e. crusaders
c. Saint Dominic

Section 4
a. interest   d. Paris
b. credit   e. middle class
c. Black Death   f. guilds

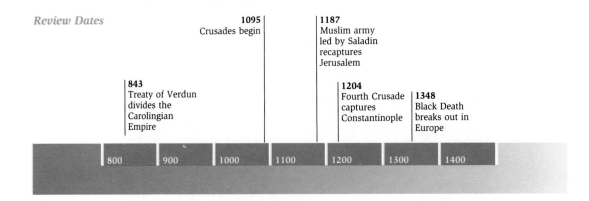

Review Dates

	1095 Crusades begin	1187 Muslim army led by Saladin recaptures Jerusalem

843 Treaty of Verdun divides the Carolingian Empire

1204 Fourth Crusade captures Constantinople

1348 Black Death breaks out in Europe

| 800 | 900 | 1000 | 1100 | 1200 | 1300 | 1400 |

Section 5

a. universities   **c.** Roger Bacon
b. Saint Thomas Aquinas   **d.** Geoffrey Chaucer

Main Ideas

Section 1

1. What was the effect of the Treaty of Verdun?
2. Explain the Frankish kings' reaction to invasions from Vikings, Magyars, and Muslims.
3. What were the duties of lord and vassal?
4. What was the relationship of the Church and feudalism?
5. Describe each class in feudal society.

Section 2

1. What was the basis of the manorial system? Who did most of the work on manors?
2. Describe the responsibilities of peasant women and noble women on medieval manors.
3. Describe living conditions in a medieval castle.

Section 3

1. Explain the significance of the Church sacraments for Christians.
2. What was the punishment of excommunication?
3. Why were the Franciscans and Dominicans important in the medieval period?
4. Explain one major reason for the crusades.

Section 4

1. Why did towns and cities develop rapidly during the later Middle Ages?
2. Describe two of the most serious problems faced by city dwellers. How did the Black Death affect Europe?
3. Name the new social class that arose in medieval towns. What institution was important to this class?
4. Why did persecution against the Jews take hold in medieval Europe?

Section 5

1. What need of society led to the development of universities?
2. What factors contributed to the advancement of scientific knowledge in the later Middle Ages?
3. Describe the development of local languages in western Europe.
4. Explain what an epic is and give an example of one.
5. What was the subject of most medieval art?

Critical Thinking

1. **Recognizing Values** As a young man, Saint Francis of Assisi gave up a life of comfort and security for vows of poverty. He founded a monastic order devoted to caring for God's creatures. What values are expressed in the life of Saint Francis?
2. **Making Decisions** Suppose that you were a serf working on a manor during the time when towns and cities were expanding. You have the opportunity to stay on the manor or leave and start an independent life in the town. What would you decide? Why?

Chapter Skills and Activities

Practicing Study and Research Skills

Making a Time Line

As you learned in Chapter 1, a time line shows events in the order that they occurred. Study the time line at the beginning of this chapter and in the Chapter Review. Draw a time line of the period of the crusades, starting with the Peasant Crusade and ending with the Fourth Crusade. Fill in dates for main events in each crusade. Work out a scale for the time line related to the total number of years you will show. How many years did the period of the crusades last?

Linking Past and Present

In the Middle Ages, universities developed to meet the needs of a changing world. Lawyers, doctors, philosphers, and mathematicians had to be trained in special skills. In what ways do modern universities and other schools carry out the same functions?

Learning History Through Maps

Refer to the map on page 201 showing the crusades. Information on this type of historical map is simplified because showing every detail would make the map cluttered and unreadable. Use the map to answer the following questions.

1. Political boundaries shown are probably most accurate for which crusade? Why?
2. In which crusade did a major army sail from England?

CRITICAL THINKING QUESTION LEVEL 1. average; 2. easy

12 The Growth of National Monarchies

OVERVIEW

This chapter covers the disintegration of the feudal system and the development of nations in Europe.

PLANNING CHART

Section	Text Pages	Key Concept	Suggested Teaching Time
1 Feudalism did not meet the needs of growing nations.	215–217	A number of factors including expansion in trade, a desire for law and order, and unhappiness with feudal obligations, led the middle class to support monarchs who were striving to strengthen their power.	One day **Less time?** Assign Section 1 before class and teach it together with Section 2.
2 England became a nation.	217–222	English monarchs strengthened their power, governmental structure, and laws and in the process united the English as a nation with pride in their monarch and country.	One day **More time?** Use *Overhead Transparency 23* or *Source Reading 12A*.
3 French kings built a national state.	222–224	Although the French monarchs also established a centralized government and built a national state, it was Joan of Arc who ignited the national spirit in France.	One day **More time?** Use *Overhead Transparency 24* or the One-Day Play, *The Trial of Joan of Arc*.
4 Spain, Portugal, and other nations formed in Europe.	224–226	The Portuguese and Spanish, as well as other Europeans, began to build nations while England and France were becoming stronger; however, Germany and Italy did not unify until the 1800s.	One day **More time?** Use *Source Reading 12B*.

ANCILLARIES

Materials that may be used with this chapter to reinforce, reteach, enrich, and assess learning are pictured on the following pages.

Teacher's Resource File

ACTIVITIES

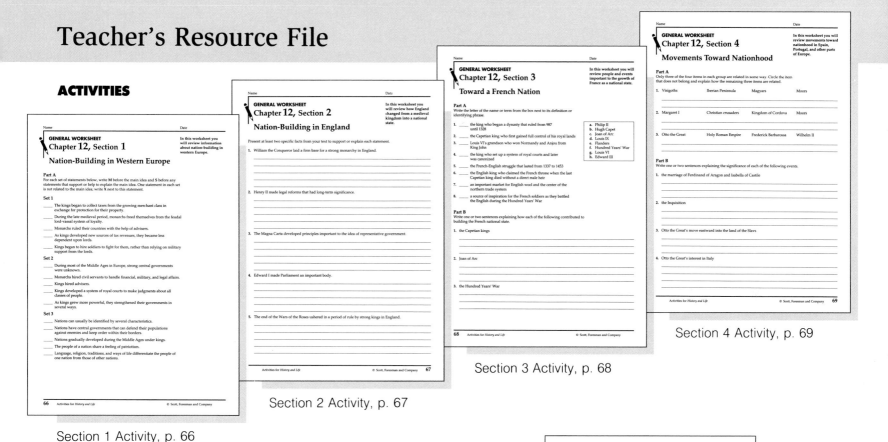

GENERAL WORKSHEET
Chapter 12, Section 1

Nation-Building in Western Europe

In this worksheet you will review information about nation-building in western Europe.

Part A
For each set of statements below, write **M** before the main idea and **S** before any statements that support or help to explain the main idea. One statement in each set is not related to the main idea; write **X** next to this statement.

Set 1
_____ The kings began to collect taxes from the growing merchant class in exchange for protection for their property.
_____ During the late medieval period, monarchs freed themselves from the feudal lord-vassal system of loyalty.
_____ Monarchs ruled their countries with the help of advisers.
_____ As kings developed new sources of tax revenues, they became less dependent upon lords.
_____ Kings began to hire soldiers to fight for them, rather than relying on military support from the lords.

Set 2
_____ During most of the Middle Ages in Europe, strong central governments were unknown.
_____ Monarchs hired civil servants to handle financial, military, and legal affairs.
_____ Kings hired advisers.
_____ Kings developed a system of royal courts to make judgments about all classes of people.
_____ As kings grew more powerful, they strengthened their governments in several ways.

Set 3
_____ Nations can usually be identified by several characteristics.
_____ Nations have central governments that can defend their populations against enemies and keep order within their borders.
_____ Nations gradually developed during the Middle Ages under kings.
_____ The people of a nation share a feeling of patriotism.
_____ Language, religion, traditions, and ways of life differentiate the people of one nation from those of other nations.

Section 1 Activity, p. 66

GENERAL WORKSHEET
Chapter 12, Section 2

Nation-Building in England

In this worksheet you will review how England changed from a medieval kingdom into a national state.

Present at least two specific facts from your text to support or explain each statement.

1. William the Conqueror laid a firm base for a strong monarchy in England.

2. Henry II made legal reforms that had long-term significance.

3. The Magna Carta developed principles important to the idea of representative government.

4. Edward I made Parliament an important body.

5. The end of the Wars of the Roses ushered in a period of rule by strong kings in England.

Section 2 Activity, p. 67

GENERAL WORKSHEET
Chapter 12, Section 3

Toward a French Nation

In this worksheet you will review people and events important to the growth of France as a national state.

Part A
Write the letter of the name or term from the box next to its definition or identifying phrase.

1. _____ the king who began a dynasty that ruled from 987 until 1328
2. _____ the Capetian king who first gained full control of his royal lands
3. _____ Louis VI's grandson who won Normandy and Anjou from King John
4. _____ the king who set up a system of royal courts and later was canonized
5. _____ the French-English struggle that lasted from 1337 to 1453
6. _____ the English king who claimed the French throne when the last Capetian king died without a direct male heir
7. _____ an important market for English wool and the center of the northern trade system
8. _____ a source of inspiration for the French soldiers as they battled the English during the Hundred Years' War

a. Philip II
b. Hugh Capet
c. Joan of Arc
d. Louis IX
e. Flanders
f. Hundred Years' War
g. Louis VI
h. Edward III

Part B
Write one or two sentences explaining how each of the following contributed to building the French national state.

1. the Capetian kings

2. Joan of Arc

3. the Hundred Years' War

Section 3 Activity, p. 68

GENERAL WORKSHEET
Chapter 12, Section 4

Movements Toward Nationhood

In this worksheet you will review movements toward nationhood in Spain, Portugal, and other parts of Europe.

Part A
Only three of the four items in each group are related in some way. Circle the item that does not belong and explain how the remaining three items are related.

1. Visigoths   Iberian Peninsula   Magyars   Moors

2. Margaret I   Christian crusaders   Kingdom of Cordova   Moors

3. Otto the Great   Holy Roman Empire   Frederick Barbarossa   Wilhelm II

Part B
Write one or two sentences explaining the significance of each of the following events.

1. the marriage of Ferdinand of Aragon and Isabella of Castile

2. the Inquisition

3. Otto the Great's move eastward into the land of the Slavs

4. Otto the Great's interest in Italy

Section 4 Activity, p. 69

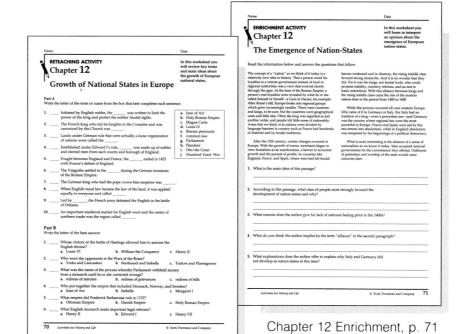

RETEACHING ACTIVITY
Chapter 12

Growth of National States in Europe

In this worksheet you will review key terms and main ideas about the growth of European national states.

Part A
Write the letter of the term or name from the box that best completes each sentence.

1. _____ Initiated by English nobles, the _____ was written to limit the power of the king and protect the nobles' feudal rights.
2. _____ The French king who led his knights in the Crusades and was canonized by the Church was _____.
3. _____ Lands under German rule that were actually a loose organization of nations were called the _____.
4. _____ Established under Edward I's rule, _____ was made up of nobles and elected men from each county and borough of England.
5. _____ Fought between England and France, the _____ ended in 1453 with France's defeat of England.
6. _____ The Visigoths settled in the _____ during the German invasions of the Roman Empire.
7. _____ The German king who had the pope crown him emperor was _____.
8. _____ When English royal law became the law of the land, it was applied equally to everyone and called _____.
9. _____ Led by _____, the French army defeated the English in the battle of Orleans.
10. _____ An important medieval market for English wool and the center of northern trade was the region called _____.

a. Joan of Arc
b. Holy Roman Empire
c. Magna Carta
d. Louis IX
e. Iberian peninsula
f. common law
g. Parliament
h. Flanders
i. Otto the Great
j. Hundred Years' War

Part B
Write the letter of the best answer.

1. _____ Whose victory at the battle of Hastings allowed him to assume the English throne?
   a. Louis VI   b. William the Conqueror   c. Henry II
2. _____ Who were the opponents in the Wars of the Roses?
   a. Yorks and Lancasters   b. Ferdinand and Isabella   c. Tudors and Plantagenets
3. _____ What was the name of the process whereby Parliament withheld money from a monarch until he or she corrected wrongs?
   a. redress of statutes   b. redress of grievances   c. redress of bills
4. _____ Who put together the empire that included Denmark, Norway, and Sweden?
   a. Joan of Arc   b. Isabella   c. Margaret I
5. _____ What empire did Frederick Barbarossa rule in 1152?
   a. Ottoman Empire   b. Danish Empire   c. Holy Roman Empire
6. _____ What English monarch made important legal reforms?
   a. Henry II   b. Edward I   c. Henry VII

Chapter 12 Reteaching, p. 70

ENRICHMENT ACTIVITY
Chapter 12

The Emergence of Nation-States

In this worksheet you will learn to interpret an opinion about the emergence of European nation-states.

Read the information below and answer the questions that follow.

The concept of a "nation" as we think of it today is a relatively new idea in history. That a person owed his loyalties to a remote government instead of local or regional authorities was a view that evolved slowly through the ages. At the time of the Roman Empire, a person's real loyalties were revealed by what he or she called himself or herself—a Gaul or Dacian, for example. After Rome's fall, Europe broke into regional groups which grew increasingly smaller. There were countries and kings, to be sure, but the countries were geographical units and little else. Often the king was regarded as just another noble, and people felt little sense of nationality. Areas that we think of as nations were divided by language barriers (a country such as France had hundreds of dialects) and by feudal traditions.

After the 12th century, certain changes occurred in Europe. With the growth of towns, merchants began to view feudalism as an anachronism, a barrier to economic growth and the pursuit of profits. In countries like England, France, and Spain, where wars had left feudal barons weakened and in disarray, the rising middle class favored strong monarchs. And it is no wonder that they did. For it was the kings, not feudal lords, who could promise stability, currency reforms, and an end to trade restrictions. With this alliance between kings and the rising middle class came the rise of the modern nation-state in the period from 1400 to 1600.

While this process occurred all over western Europe, little came of it in Germany or Italy. For Italy had no tradition of a king—even a powerless one—and Germany was the country where regional ties were the most powerful in Europe. France and Spain were led by this movement into absolutism, while in England absolutism was tempered by the beginnings of a political democracy.

What is most interesting is the absence of a sense of nationalism as we know it today. Men accepted national governments for the convenience they offered. Outbursts of patriotism and worship of the state would come centuries later.

1. What is the main idea of this passage?

2. According to this passage, what class of people most strongly favored the development of nation-states and why?

3. What reasons does the author give for lack of national feeling prior to the 1400s?

4. What do you think the author implies by the term "alliance" in the second paragraph?

5. What explanations does the author offer to explain why Italy and Germany did not develop as nation-states at this time?

Chapter 12 Enrichment, p. 71

213b

Teacher's Resource File

GEOGRAPHY SKILLS

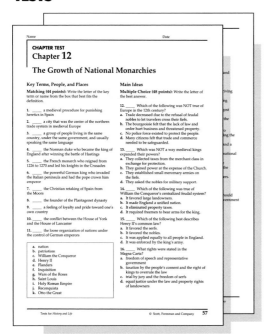

Chapter 12 Geography

Worksheet/Map, pp. 25–26

Chapter 12 Map Lesson, p. 94

TESTS

Chapter Test, pp. 57–58

Alternate Chapter Test, pp. 59–60

ONE-DAY PLAYS

The Trial of Joan of Arc

Other Optional Ancillaries

WORKBOOK

WORKSHEET
Chapter 12, Section 1

In this worksheet you will review factors that led to the growth of nations.

The Growth of Nations

Part A
Each pair of sentences below contains one factual statement and one statement of opinion. Write F for the fact and O for the opinion.

1. a. _____ All the people within a nation are loyal to and proud of their national group.
   b. _____ A nation is a group of people occupying the same country, living under the same government, and usually speaking the same language.
2. a. _____ The bourgeoisie occupied a social status lower than that of the nobles who owned land but higher than that of the peasants who farmed the nobles' land.
   b. _____ The bourgeoisie was the most important class of the late medieval period.
3. a. _____ In the late medieval period, trade within and between states expanded.
   b. _____ Since the expansion of trade increased a state's wealth, kings should have provided free protection for commerce.
4. a. _____ Strong kings were a blessing for all the people of Europe.
   b. _____ The development of strong national governments followed the pattern of freeing the monarch from the old feudal lord-vassal patterns.

Part B
Each pair of sentences establishes a relationship of cause and effect. Identify which sentence states the cause and which states the effect by writing C for cause and E for effect.

1. a. _____ The bourgeoisie grew richer and more influential than some of the noble class.
   b. _____ During the late medieval period, trade between nearby and more distant regions grew rapidly.
2. a. _____ Feudal nobles controlled the highways that passed through their fiefs.
   b. _____ Citizens became unhappy with the high tolls charged for the use of roads.
3. a. _____ Monarchs could free themselves from the feudal system by paying their own soldiers to take the place of the armies of feudal lords.
   b. _____ The monarchs found new sources of income by taxing the bourgeoisie.
4. a. _____ The systems and applications of law became more uniform.
   b. _____ Monarchs forced local nobles to turn over their courts to the king.

44   Worksheets for History and Life   © Scott, Foresman and Company

Section 1 Worksheet, p. 44

WORKSHEET
Chapter 12, Section 2

In this worksheet you will review England's change from a medieval kingdom into a national state.

Toward an English Nation

Part A
Write T if the statement is true and F if it is false. On the lines below, rewrite each false statement to make it true.

1. _____ William the Conqueror gained the name "Conqueror" because he defeated Harold at the battle of Hastings in 1066.
2. _____ The rule of the Tudor kings began with the ascendancy of Henry II to the English throne.
3. _____ Among the important reforms made by Henry II was the establishment of Parliament as a legislative body.
4. _____ Thomas à Becket, archbishop of Canterbury, may have been murdered by Henry II's knights because he had quarreled with Henry.
5. _____ The Magna Carta, developed by King John's nobles, increased the power of the English monarchy.
6. _____ Parliament began to refuse to grant money to a ruler until a ruler corrected wrongs, or addressed grievances.

Part B
Write the letter of each event at its approximate place on the time line.

1050 1100 1150 1200 1250 1300 1350 1400 1450 1500 1550 1600 1650

A. King John agrees to the Magna Carta.
B. The Wars of the Roses begin.
C. William defeats Harold in the battle of Hastings.
D. Henry Tudor (Henry VII) wins the throne.
E. Henry II's reign begins.
F. The Tudor dynasty ends.
G. Edward I conquers Wales.
H. Edward I calls together the Model Parliament.

Worksheets for History and Life   © Scott, Foresman and Company   45

Section 2 Worksheet, p. 45

WORKSHEET
Chapter 12, Section 3

In this worksheet you will review the growth of France as a national state.

Nation-Building in France

Part A
Number the events in the order in which they happened.

_____ The centralized government collapsed.
_____ Louis VI gained full control of royal lands.
_____ Charlemagne centralized the Frankish government.
_____ Hugh Capet was elected king of France by the nobles.
_____ Edward III claimed the French throne.
_____ Joan of Arc led the French army to victory at Orleans.
_____ Louis IX set up a system of royal courts.
_____ The Hundred Years' War ended.

Part B
Write C next to each phrase that correctly completes the unfinished sentence. (Each incomplete sentence may have more than one correct ending.)

1. The Capetian kings strengthened the French government by
   _____ putting down the barons who threatened their power.
   _____ encouraging private wars and trial by combat.
   _____ winning Normandy, Anjou, and other English holdings.
   _____ setting up a system of royal courts.
   _____ developing a strong parliament.
2. The Hundred Years' War resulted from
   _____ a dynastic quarrel between France and England.
   _____ English possession of lands in France.
   _____ the last Capetian king leaving a war-loving young son to reign.
   _____ English and French conflict over the control of Flanders.
   _____ France's desire to have William the Conqueror as its king.
3. Joan of Arc was successful in rallying the French during the Hundred Years' War because
   _____ she was the long-lost daughter of the French king,
   _____ the French soldiers accepted her as a heaven-sent leader.
   _____ the French soldiers were exhausted from the long siege of Orleans.
   _____ she gave the French soldiers a nearly mystical confidence in themselves.
   _____ she bewitched the English soldiers.

46   Worksheets for History and Life   © Scott, Foresman and Company

Section 3 Worksheet, p. 46

WORKSHEET
Chapter 12, Section 4

In this worksheet you will review the growth of national states in Spain, Portugal, and other areas of Europe.

The Growth of National States

Part A
Number the events in each set in the order in which they happened.

Set 1
_____ The Moors conquered the kingdom of the Visigoths on the Iberian peninsula.
_____ Ferdinand of Aragon married Isabella of Castile.
_____ Ferdinand and Isabella conquered Moorish Granada and united Spain.
_____ Portugal became an independent kingdom.
_____ Christians began a crusade to regain Spain for Christendom.

Set 2
_____ German kings began to bring their country under a strong central government.
_____ Otto the Great was crowned emperor by the pope, effectively beginning the Holy Roman Empire.
_____ Frederick Barbarossa warred against the Italian city-states.
_____ Henry the Fowler forced his nobles to pledge their loyalty to him.
_____ Both Italy and Germany were unified.

Set 3
_____ Polish tribes were united under one king; the Czechs of Bohemia and Moravia were joined under the king of Bohemia.
_____ Norway broke away from Denmark.
_____ Sweden revolted and broke away from the Danish empire.
_____ Magyar tribes formed the kingdom of Hungary.
_____ Danish queen Margaret I forged Denmark, Norway, and Sweden into an empire.

Part B
Use information from your text to complete each of the following sentences.

1. The _____ is the modern-day home of Spain and Portugal.
2. The breakup of the kingdom of the _____ inspired Christians to regain Spain for Christendom.
3. The reconquest of Spain by the Christians is known as the _____.
4. Since Ferdinand and Isabella believed that national unity required religious conformity, they revived the _____, a medieval procedure for punishing heretics, and expelled the _____ from Spain.
5. _____ was the first ruler of the Holy Roman Empire.

Worksheets for History and Life   © Scott, Foresman and Company   47

Section 4 Worksheet, p. 47

SOURCE READINGS

Source Reading 12A
Source Reading 12B

TEST GENERATOR

40 multiple-choice questions for Chapter 12

OVERHEAD TRANSPARENCIES

Overhead Transparency 23
Overhead Transparency 24

Chapter

12

The Growth of National Monarchies

1000–1600

1200

1215	King John signs the Magna Carta
1453	Hundred Years' War ends
1492	Ferdinand and Isabella unite Spain

1500

1600

On the afternoon of August 26, 1346, a large army of rain-soaked French knights rode across a muddy field near the village of Crecy [krā sē'], France. Before them stood a small English army of foot soldiers, archers with longbows, and knights without horses.

The rain showers ended. The French knights charged toward the outnumbered English. Suddenly, the English archers bent their longbows, and the arrows flew. One observer said, "It was like snow." The heavy armor of the charging knights could not stop the deadly arrows. Many French fell, killed or wounded, yet the army charged again and again. By midnight, more than a thousand French knights lay dead. The English had lost only about 50 men.

This battle was only one of many between the English and French in the Hundred Years' War, which lasted from 1337 to 1453. Although the war seesawed between English victories and French victories, the real victor was the new spirit that emerged in both countries—the spirit of nationalism.

By 1453, the English and French were becoming more than groups of people from a certain village or followers of a specific noble. People were becoming loyal to their country. With their love of country, a common language and customs, and with growing central power, the English and French were becoming nations.

New weapons and a loyal population helped change the way lands and governments were organized. The government of a national monarchy had much more power than its feudal predecessor. Its king ruled over more land and people than did the government of any local prince. The move toward strong national monarchies, which started in western Europe, lasted into the 18th century. The movement spread through eastern Europe as well and gave rise to the strong central governments and national spirits of today.

The Bayeux tapestry shows the Norman conquest of England in 1066. Note the stirrups on the horses. This new invention gave the Normans stability in the saddle.

Reading Preview

In this chapter you will read how national monarchies developed in western and parts of eastern Europe.

1. *Feudalism did not meet the needs of growing nations.*
2. *England became a nation.*
3. *French kings built a national state.*
4. *Spain, Portugal, and other nations formed in Europe.*

 Feudalism did not meet the needs of growing nations.

During most of the Middle Ages in Europe, strong national governments were unknown. In France, for example, at least 10,000 pieces of land were in some way separate countries. France had a king who in theory ruled over his nobles, but those nobles often did just as they pleased. In contrast, a **nation** is a group of people occupying the same country, under the same government, and usually

215

and personal ownership of highways were harmful to trade and commerce.

- List the steps strong kings took to establish a central government. Have students explain how the merchants indirectly helped free monarchs from the old lord-vassal patterns. Discuss how people's lives improved under strong monarchs.

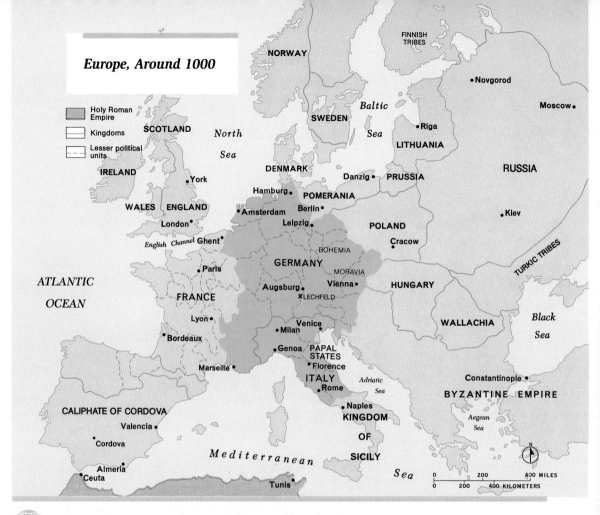

Europe, Around 1000

MAP STUDY   This map gives a simplified view of European countries 1,000 years ago. Were England, Scotland, and Wales separate countries at that time? Were Germany and Italy unified countries?

speaking the same language. Until France and other countries were united under a strong central government, they could not be called "nations."

As you read this chapter, keep in mind the view that nations usually have the following three characteristics: First, a nation has a central government that can defend itself against enemies and can keep order within its borders. Second, a nation's people are set off from neighboring groups by language, religion, traditions, and ways of life. Third, the people within a nation are loyal to and proud of their group. This feeling is called **nationalism** or **patriotism**.

Wider trade within and between states required improved government.

By the year 1100, cities had begun to grow rather rapidly. Trade between nearby and more distant regions had expanded, and the population of Europe had grown.

The bourgeoisie—or middle class—disliked the lack of law and order because it hurt business and threatened property. Citizens were becoming unhappy with the feudal obligations of land taxes and military service. In addition, the many separate legal systems of rival nobles, the monarchy, and the Church upset them. Each noble had his own court, as did the monarch and the Church. Church courts tried not only churchmen, but also students, crusaders, and churchmen's servants.

Many people also felt that trade and commerce needed to be safeguarded. A feudal noble alone could decide whether a highway that passed through his fief, that is, his land or estate, would be kept in good repair. The noble often charged high tolls for use of a road or a river that went through his land. Worse, people had no reliable police force to protect them. The rocky, muddy roads were filled with bandits who attacked travelers.

Strong kings extended their powers.

Almost all nations that established central national governments during this period followed a similar pattern. First, the king gained power at the expense of the Church and the nobles. Then, the king began to collect taxes from the growing merchant class in exchange for protecting their property. This new source of wealth helped the king to become more independent of the nobles. At the same time the king gained a new source of support—the merchants whose property he protected.

In earlier times the king had been completely dependent upon lords and their vassals for military support. Because vassals owed first allegiance to a local lord, the lord could decide whether or not a king would get help. However, as the king developed new sources of taxation, he was freed from total dependence upon lords. With more tax money, the king could pay mercenaries—professional soldiers and officers—to fight for him. Any strong fighter—even a peasant—could become a soldier for the king. Almost all countries that developed strong central governments during this time followed the pattern of freeing the monarch from the old feudal lord-vassal patterns.

As kings gained power, they strengthened their governments. They hired civil servants—that is, government workers who handled money matters, military affairs, and legal problems. Advisers were hired to help kings rule their countries. The kings

freed people in towns from some feudal obligations, such as certain tolls, and they provided greater protection for travelers. Instead of allowing each noble to set his own laws, kings began to develop a system of royal courts that would make judgments about all classes of people. These courts tried to apply the same laws to everyone. Gradually, kings built the larger, stronger units we call nations.

Section 1 Review

Identify nation, nationalism, patriotism
Main Ideas
1. Why did feudalism no longer meet the needs of citizens by the 15th century?
2. How did kings strengthen and expand their powers?
3. What are the characteristics of a nation?
Critical Thinking
Analyzing Comparisons: In what ways does the United States today have or not have the features of a nation as described in Section 1?

England became a nation.

England began to build a strong centralized government as early as the 11th century. When the king of England died in 1066, William, duke of the French region of Normandy, stated his right to be king. William based his claim on a weak hereditary right and on the promise from an earlier king that William could become the ruler of England in the future. However, the throne was given instead to Harold, the powerful earl of Wessex. William then crossed the English Channel with an army of Norman soldiers, whom he promised to reward with lands. In England he defeated Harold at the battle of Hastings. William, who earned the name "Conqueror," thus became king of England.

William the Conqueror established a strong monarchy.

As king, **William the Conqueror** was too strong to let his nobles challenge his power. He used and

2 Lesson Plan

Essential Learning Objectives

Students will learn to:
• describe how English kings strengthened their monarchies.
• describe the evolution of England's governmental structure.

Students might be surprised to learn that parts of Sherwood Forest still remain near Mansfield and Rotherham, boroughs in north central England.

Ask students to compare the reality of existence for a peasant in the 1200s and 1300s, as described in the text, with what they know about Robin Hood and his followers. Why would the legend of Robin Hood appeal to the peasants? (Students will probably picture Robin Hood as a gallant, merry, and handsome hero, known for his skill with a bow and arrow, who managed to live well with his friends deep within a beautiful forest. The peasants' lives, on the other hand, were filled with hard, repetitious work; they lived in surroundings that were often dark and cold, and they rarely had enough to eat.) Ask students if they can think of any present-day Robin Hoods. (Possible answer: Many people today believe that the government, through taxation or by encouraging private charity, should take a portion of the income of the rich to help support poor, homeless, or otherwise needy people.)

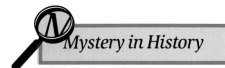

Mystery in History

DID ROBIN HOOD REALLY EXIST?

Lithe and lysten, gentylmen,
*   That be of frebore blode:*
I shall you tell of a good yeman.
*   His name was Robyn Hode.*

Countless old songs and stories describe this courteous outlaw and his merry band of followers who lived in Sherwood Forest, an ancient royal woodland in central England. The outlaws, according to legend, stole from the rich and gave to the poor.

No one knows for certain whether Robin Hood was a real person and, if he did exist, where and when he carried on his struggles for the poor and downtrodden. A chronicler suggested, probably in the 16th century, that Robin Hood was a noble who had fallen on hard times. This theory persists, and today most stories and films about Robin Hood describe him as a knight who has lost his wealth. Historians reject this view, however, as out of keeping with the more authentic 14th-century ballads.

Several 19th-century historians tried to prove that the real Robin Hood was not a noble but a freeborn peasant named Robert Hood, who bought a plot of land in 1316. On investigation, this dating seemed too late because a charter of 1322 referred to Robin Hood as a legendary figure of what was then the distant past.

Even the location of Robin Hood's exploits has been questioned. A part of the medieval forest of Sherwood associated with his name remains to this day in Nottinghamshire. Furthermore, Robin Hood's archenemy was the ruthless sheriff of Nottingham. Yet evidence in the early ballads indicates that Yorkshire, not Nottinghamshire, was the scene of the action.

Although historians may never identify the real Robin Hood, his legend remains important because it shows the resentment of the poor and landless against landowners and corrupt officials. Robin Hood has always represented the noble hero who would fight to win justice and protect the weak and helpless.

Robin Hood and his companions make a surprise attack from behind an ancient, gnarled beech in this famous painting by N. C. Wyeth.

changed the old Anglo-Saxon system of government that had existed in England. More important, he introduced centralized feudalism into England. With this system, William required all nobles to become his vassals and to swear an oath of allegiance directly to him. He also broke up the largest feudal holdings of the nobles and distributed the land to his vassals. William further increased his power by requiring all freemen of England to bear arms for the king so that he did not have to rely on his nobles' armies. If a noble revolted against the king, William had his own army to crush the rebellion.

William also added to his sources of money. He ordered a census, an official count, of all the taxable wealth in his kingdom. Census facts were gathered into the *Domesday Book,* a listing of all property owned by English people, which today gives an excellent picture of 11th-century England.

England was not a unified nation in 1066, and William did not make it one. Yet, William did lay a firm base for a strong monarchy in that country.

Henry II improved the legal system.

William and the three kings who ruled after him are called the Norman kings because of the region in northwest France from which William had come. (For a complete list of rulers, see page 802 in the Reference Section at the back of this book.) After the Norman kings, England came under the rule of **Henry II**, the founder of the Plantagenet [plan taj′ə nit] dynasty. Henry II was the son of William's granddaughter, Matilda, who had married Geoffrey Plantagenet, the count of Anjou in France. Thus continued the link between the English royal house and France.

The reign of Henry II (1154–1189) was one of the most important in English history. Henry was determined to unite all of England under his rule. He wanted all the people to look to him and to their national government for justice and protection. To do so he made three major reforms that had lasting importance for our own legal system.

Common law. Henry II made his royal law the law of the land. Because royal law was the same for everyone, it was fairer than the many different kinds of law in use during this period. Over time,

the royal law became known as **common law** because it was applied equally to all people throughout the country. Common law was based on custom and court decisions and is the basis for the law used today in most of the United States and in other nations that were once English colonies.

Circuit courts. Henry II followed an old custom of sending judges on regular tours all over the country. These traveling judges combined local legal customs with legal opinions from the king's court to form their decisions. These decisions, in turn, formed the basis of the common law. Judges who went from place to place were strangers in each district, so they were not open to bribes, threats, or feelings about friends. As a result, the law became fairer and the quality of judicial decisions improved. In addition, the king—as the dispenser of justice—became more powerful.

These traveling courts became known as circuit courts because each judge followed a regular circuit, or route. An important part of the English judicial system today, this practice was also the basis of the U.S. circuit court system.

The jury system. The first juries were men who came before a royal judge to accuse someone of breaking a law. The accusers only brought charges, they did not decide whether the person was guilty. From this early jury came the grand jury of today. The grand jury decides whether enough evidence has been presented against the accused to permit holding that person for trial. About a century after Henry's time, another kind of jury came into use. It heard evidence and decided on the guilt of the accused. This kind of jury is called a petit jury or trial jury. The word petit comes from the French for "little."

Henry II was an able ruler who contributed greatly to the growth of a strong monarchy and the law. However, his success in making his royal courts stronger than those of the nobles was not equaled by his attempts to make his courts more powerful than those of the Church.

The Church fought Henry's moves because it resented his interference with the system of Church courts. Henry believed that Church courts were often too easy on offenders, and he wanted all his subjects to be ruled under one system of justice. His stand led to a famous quarrel with the Church.

1 FOCUS AND MOTIVATE

Ask students to name the groups who made their own laws under the feudal system. Have them cite reasons why justice cannot exist in a society that has no uniform code of law.

2 TEACH

- Discuss William the Conqueror's ascendancy to the throne. Have students describe the changes he instituted to take away the powers of the lords. Ask students to explain what William's purpose was for taking a census.

- Have students describe the major reforms Henry II brought about in England. Outline and discuss the benefits of common law, the circuit courts, and the jury system. Ask students to describe the power struggle with the Church over the courts and its results.

- Discuss the importance of the Magna Carta. Have students explain how its principles safeguarded against royal tyranny. Point out that because the king could not levy new taxes without consent, he could not increase his army, ensuring a balance of power.

- Describe the development of Parliament. Ask students in what way these changes in government laid the foundation for representative democracy in the United States.

- Discuss the lineage of the Tudor family. Ask students to describe how the government functioned under the Tudors. Have them name elements that united the English people and gave rise to an English nationality.

GUIDED PRACTICE

Have students list the steps by which Parliament became a legislative body.

Thomas à Becket, archbishop of Canterbury, opposed Henry. As a result, some of Henry's knights murdered Becket.

Although there is no proof that Henry actually ordered the murder of Becket, Henry's enemies believed that he approved and perhaps arranged the murder. Henry's role in Becket's death remains one of history's great mysteries. As a result of Becket's death, nobles and the Church were greatly angered and Henry's cause was hurt. His dream of one system of justice was not realized until after the Middle Ages.

The Magna Carta stated some basic rights.

Henry II's youngest son, John, became king in 1199. John was an unreasonable, cruel ruler, who was described by a modern historian as "a paunchy little man, five feet, five inches tall, with erect head, staring eyes, flaring nostrils and lips set in a cruel pout." In 1215 King John's nobles rebelled against his unjust rule and forced him to agree to the **Magna Carta** [mag′nə kär′tə], or Great Charter. The document limited John's power and protected the nobles' feudal rights.

Despite the myth that has developed over the meaning of this document, the Magna Carta did not, at the time, guarantee representative government. Taxation by the people's consent and trial by jury were not written into it. However, these principles later developed from the rights that the Magna Carta did state.

The importance of the Magna Carta lies in three principles: first, the law is above the king; second, the king can be forced to obey the law; and third, there is equal justice under the law. The Magna Carta forced the king to make this promise: "To no one shall we sell, deny, or delay right or justice." John also promised to stop taking his vassals' property and to stop forcing them to give him more money than feudal custom determined. The king could collect no more money than that allowed by the old laws of feudalism except "by the common consent of our kingdom."

Later King John's words came to mean that the king could not raise any new taxes unless the people agreed through their representatives. American colonists used this principle in objecting to "taxa-

tion without representation." Another clause of the Magna Carta declared:

> No free man shall be taken or imprisoned . . . nor shall we pass sentence on him except by the legal judgment of his peers or by the law of the land.

These words were later interpreted to mean that all freemen had a right to trial by jury. Most English people were still serfs, but as more of them became free, they also gained the rights promised to freemen in 1215.

Parliament became important under Edward I.

Edward I (1239–1307) tried to bring the island of Great Britain—shared by England, Scotland, and Wales—under one rule. In 1284 he took over Wales. To show respect to the Welsh, Edward gave his oldest son the title "Prince of Wales," as English monarchs still do today. Edward also tried to conquer Scotland, but he could not defeat the Scottish troops. These wars were costly and Edward needed more money, so he collected extra taxes. The taxes were approved by the people's representatives in a council.

English kings had long been advised by a council, or group made up of churchmen and nobles. In 1295 Edward I called these great nobles and churchmen to meet with him. He also ordered the sheriffs, the local officers of the law, to hold elections in their shires, or counties. Freemen chose two knights from each county to serve in the national council called **Parliament** [pär′lə mənt]. The word comes from the French word *parler*, meaning "to speak." From each chartered town, they chose two burgesses, or citizens. This group came to be known as the Model Parliament because later Parliaments were modeled on it.

In time, the Church withdrew from Parliament. The great nobles, or lords, made up what became the House of Lords. Elected knights and townsmen made up what later became the House of Commons. This second group was a representative body; that is, each member spoke for many people and voted in their interests.

Early kings asked Parliament to meet mainly to get money. However, Parliament began to have other thoughts. Its members began to refuse to

This illustration is the oldest known view of Parliament, which was called together by Edward I around 1279. The dignitaries on the outer benches are nobles and church officials. In the center are judges seated on wool sacks. The wool sacks symbolize the importance of the wool trade to England's economy at that time. Below the judges are representatives from the towns and shires.

grant money until a ruler corrected wrongs. This process was called redress of grievances. Parliament drew up statements of demands, called bills. After the ruler signed them, they became laws, called acts or statutes. As a result of Parliament's role in making demands that the king met, it became a lawmaking, or legislative, body. In many countries the word "parliament" has come to mean the highest lawmaking body. Thus England has earned the name "mother of parliaments."

The Wars of the Roses brought a new line of strong kings.

In 1455 two branches of the English royal family, the House of York and the House of Lancaster, began to fight over the throne. These wars lasted for 30 years. They were called the **Wars of the Roses** because the York emblem was a white rose and the Lancaster emblem was a red rose. During these wars, many noble families of England were destroyed. In 1485 Henry Tudor of the House of Lancaster won the throne. As Henry VII, he united the families by marrying a York heiress and began the

Tudor dynasty, which ruled England until 1603. (The Tudor kings and queens are named in the list of rulers on page 802 in the Reference Section at back of this text. The two most notable were Henry VIII and Elizabeth I.)

The reign of the Tudor family was a period of strong royal power. Parliament was comparatively weak, and the nobles had been subdued. the king's or queen's judges enforced the common law, and an efficient group of civil servants helped govern the kingdom. England under the Tudors gained increasing leadership in European affairs and enjoyed a great flowering of culture. The reign of Elizabeth I was especially important in establishing England as a major sea power.

By 1600 the English nation had become firmly established. All the people lived under the common law, and a national government ruled in all parts of the realm. The once separate Norman and Saxon customs and languages had merged into something new—English nationality. The people felt united by a common pride in their monarch and their country.

Identify

Key Terms, People, and Places are defined on pages indicated in parentheses. Also see the Glossary and Biographical Dictionary.
William the Conqueror (217), Henry II (219), common law (219), Magna Carta (220), Parliament (220), Wars of the Roses (221)

Main Ideas

1. He made nobles become his vassals, broke up large feudal holdings, had all men bear arms and conducted a census of taxable wealth.
2. He made royal law the law of the land, thereby establishing a system of laws for everyone (common law), sent judges on circuits (which made them more impartial) and had accusers of wrongdoers come before a royal judge.
3. equal justice under law, no taxation without representation, and the right to trial by jury.
4. He called together representatives of the people to approve added taxation.
5. wars between two branches of the English royal family; wars ended with victory of Henry Tudor of the House of Lancaster

Critical Thinking

The lowest classes and women probably were little affected by the changes of this period.

3 *Lesson Plan*

Essential Learning Objectives

Students will learn to:
- describe the development of the French state.
- give reasons for the Hundred Years' War and France's victory.

Section 2 Review

Identify William the Conqueror, Henry II, common law, Magna Carta, Parliament, Wars of the Roses

Main Ideas

1. In what ways did William the Conqueror change the feudal system to support his desire for a strong monarchy?
2. How did Henry II improve the legal system?
3. What rights did the Magna Carta protect?
4. How did Parliament develop under Edward I?
5. What were the Wars of the Roses? What was their outcome?

Critical Thinking

Making Hypotheses: William the Conqueror, Henry II, John, and Edward I expanded the rights of English people far beyond those of earlier periods. From what you have read, do you think that the poorest men and women also had more rights? Why or why not?

---

3 | French kings built a national state.

Across the English Channel, France lagged far behind England in developing unity. During Charlemagne's reign as emperor (800–814), a centralized government had ruled the land, but it collapsed after his death. After 814 feudal governments grew up in its place, and by the late 900s, the name "France" referred only to a small region around Paris. What was vaguely thought of as a kingdom was really just a group of feudal states. As a result, the French kings' task of uniting their nation was harder than that of their royal neighbors in England.

In 987 the French nobles elected Hugh Capet [kə-pā′], Count of Paris, as king. Many of his feudal nobles were much more powerful than he, but the Capetian [kə pē′shən] family grew strong through wars and pacts with powerful nobles. The Capetian dynasty ruled until 1328.

The Capetian kings strengthened the French Government.

The Capetian kings first had to show that they were stronger than the nobles. The first of the

---

kings able to do that was Louis [lü′ē] VI, Louis the Fat, who ruled from 1108 to 1137. Louis VI gained full control over his royal lands, called the Île de France [ēl də frans′], and put down the barons who threatened his power. His grandson, Philip II, won Normandy, Anjou, and other English holdings in France from King John. Year by year, the Capetian kings pushed out from their capital at Paris to make the region under their rule larger and larger.

Like the monarchs in England, the French kings gave the people better government than had the feudal lords. Louis IX set up a system of royal courts. He also outlawed private wars and trial by combat. In addition, he told the people to ask his officials for help if the nobles wronged them. In this way he let all French people know that their government was sensitive to their well-being. The French, however, did not develop a strong parliament. The king, for example, did not have to ask a French representative council for approval of new taxes.

Louis IX, who reigned from 1226 to 1270, led his knights in the crusades and, when held as a prisoner of the Muslims, remained brave and dignified. Peace and justice seemed far more important to him than military conquests. Later, in 1297, he was canonized, that is, made a saint, by the Church and thereafter called **Saint Louis.**

France and England fought the Hundred Years' War (1337–1453).

French kings not only had worries at home but also often faced possible trouble with England as well. Some French lands still lay in English hands. William the Conqueror, who had come from the French region of Normandy, had not given up his French lands when he conquered England. William's successors gained even more land through inheritance and marriage. Therefore, English kings such as Henry II, whose land holdings in France were large, were both English kings and vassals of the French kings. The English believed themselves the equals of their French lords and did not want to be seen as servants of the French crown. As a result, from the mid-1100s to the mid-1400s, the English and the French were often at war with each other.

In 1328 the last Capetian king died without leav-

HIGHLIGHTS OF CIVILIZATION

The Magna Carta

On June 15, 1215, in a meadow called Runnymede beside the Thames River outside of London, one of the most significant events in history was enacted. Under threat from rebellious nobles, King John sealed the Magna Carta. This agreement made all the freemen of the kingdom equal under the law— the king, the nobles, and commoners alike— and marked the change from judgments and convictions based on the absolute authority of the king to rule by law.

The Magna Carta has been and still is part of the law of England and of many other countries. The clause "that no man shall be taken or imprisoned . . . except by the legal judgment of his peers" is embodied in the 5th Amendment of the U.S. Constitution.

Another clause provided that "common pleas shall not follow our Court, but shall be held in some certain place." This provision led to the establishment of an independent judiciary. Before the Magna Carta, the judges moved about with the king, and subjects could only get justice where the king happened to be.

Other ideas and even phrases from the U.S. Constitution can be traced directly to the Magna Carta. Its principles have been the basis for the development of democratic government in many countries throughout the world.

In 1215, at the peaceful meadow of Runnymede (below), King John placed his Great Seal (left) on the Magna Carta. At far left is one of the four originals of the Magna Carta.

227

Main Ideas

1. Alphonso I of Portugal declared Portugal independent of Spain in 1129. Ferdinand and Isabella's marriage united much of Spain and the conquest of Granada completed its unification.
2. regions that became Sweden, Norway, Denmark, Hungary, Poland, and Bohemia
3. While Otto the Great tried to conquer Italy, German nobles regained power. Frederick Barbarossa wanted to unite Germany and Italy but was defeated by the Italian cities.

Critical Thinking

Students might advise the kings to spend more time trying to build strong national states rather than attempting to resurrect the Roman Empire.

HIGHLIGHTS OF CIVILIZATION

The text of the Magna Carta may be found in the *Micropedia, Encyclopaedia Britannica,* 1988 edition, and slightly abridged in *The Development of Civilization,* by Harry J. Carroll, et al. (Glenview, Illinois: Scott, Foresman, 1969). If possible, obtain a copy of this key document and have students search for ideas and phrases in the U.S. Constitution directly traceable to the Magna Carta.

Explain that the Magna Carta was written in Latin on parchment and that it was not signed but rather sealed by the King. Unlike other early documents which granted liberties to monasteries or barons, this charter granted liberties "to all free men of our kingdom."

CHAPTER 12 REVIEW

Section Summaries

Section 1
Feudalism did not meet the needs of growing nations.
As the Middle Ages advanced, national governments began to replace some of the feudal governments that had existed in earlier years. Kings began to control money, laws, and military affairs directly.

Section 2
England became a nation.
William, duke of Normandy, conquered England in 1066 and established a strong centralized government. Under Henry II, royal courts spread equal justice among England's citizens and the jury system developed. In 1215 King John was forced to sign the Magna Carta, guaranteeing certain feudal rights to the nobles. This document set the precedent for many of the rights we take for granted as part of representative government. During the reign of Edward I, Parliament became a lawmaking body.

Section 3
French kings built a national state.
The French Capetian kings who ruled from 987 to 1328 strengthened the French monarchy. The Hundred Years' War between England and France (1337–1453) led to England's loss of all French territories except Calais.

Section 4
Spain, Portugal and other nations formed in Europe.
The marriage of Ferdinand of Aragon and Isabella of Castile in the 15th century united Spain. In eastern Europe, Magyars moved into Hungary, and Poland and Bohemia became nations. Despite German unification efforts, Germany and Italy did not establish strong central governments, and internal divisions lasted in those countries until the 19th century.

Test Yourself

Key Terms, Places, and People
Identify the significance of each of the following:

Section 1
a. nation
b. nationalism
c. patriotism

Section 2
a. William the Conqueror
b. Henry II
c. common law
d. Magna Carta
e. Parliament
f. Wars of the Roses

Section 3
a. Saint Louis
b. Flanders
c. Hundred Years' War
d. Joan of Arc

Section 4
a. Iberian peninsula
b. Reconquista
c. Inquisition
d. Otto the Great
e. Holy Roman Empire

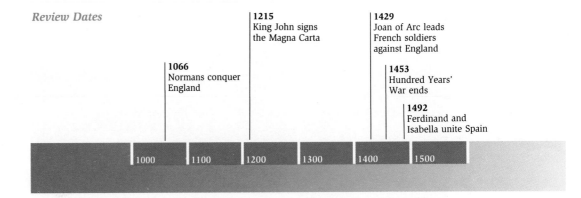

Review Dates

1066 Normans conquer England

1215 King John signs the Magna Carta

1429 Joan of Arc leads French soldiers against England

1453 Hundred Years' War ends

1492 Ferdinand and Isabella unite Spain

1000   1100   1200   1300   1400   1500

Main Ideas

Section 1
1. In what ways were 15th century citizens no longer satisfied with feudalism?
2. What were some impacts of the strengthened central power of monarchies during the Middle Ages?

Section 2
1. How did William the Conqueror change feudalism?
2. What actions did Henry II take to make England's legal system fairer?
3. What provisions did the Magna Carta include?
4. What impact did Edward I have on Parliament?
5. What were the cause and outcome of the Wars of the Roses?

Section 3
1. How did the Capetian kings strengthen the French government?
2. What was the basis of English claims to French territory? How did the English and French settle these claims?
3. What role did Joan of Arc play in French history?

Section 4
1. Why are Alphonso I of Portugal and Ferdinand and Isabella of Spain important in their nations' histories?
2. In what other countries did strong central governments begin to develop between 900 and 1600?
3. Why did Germany and Italy fail to develop strong central governments during the Middle Ages?

Critical Thinking

1. Analyzing Comparisons England, France, Spain, and Portugal developed a spirit of nationalism during the Middle Ages. Other countries, including Germany and Italy, did not. List some characteristics of the countries in which nationalism was found and contrast these with countries where local nobles and city-states remained strong.
2. Assessing Cause and Effect Law and government in the United States are based on the English model. Although the Magna Carta actually reaffirmed the feudal rights of nobles, the Magna Carta is considered the source of many of our freedoms. Review the rights described in the Magna Carta and describe the impact of these rights on those of United States citizens today.

CRITICAL THINKING QUESTION LEVEL 1. average; 2. challenging

Chapter Skills and Activities

Practicing Study and Research Skills

Recognizing Historians' Interpretations
Many historical events and personalities are judged by writers, years or centuries after the event took place. Even when there are contemporary accounts, historians have their own ideas, or interpretations, of what the events meant and how important they were, or how a person behaved and why the individual acted in certain ways.

Read the following paragraph about King John of England. Then read the description of King John in Section 2 of this chapter. Upon what evidence might the authors of this textbook have based their comments about King John's character?

Matthew Paris wrote, "Foul as it is, hell itself is defiled by the presence of King John," and this pretty well sums up John's reputation—until 1944, that is. For in that year, Professor V. H. Galbraith demonstrated . . . that the chief chronicle source for the reign of John was utterly unreliable. Since then bad King John has been getting better and better.

Linking Past and Present
Compare and contrast the purpose of the *Domesday Book* as described on page 219 with the U.S. census, made every ten years. The purpose of the census is stated in the U.S. Constitution in Article 1, Section 2, Clause 3. You can find a copy of the Constitution in many reference books in your library.

Learning History Through Maps
The map on page 216 gives a simplified political picture of Europe as it was around A.D. 1000. Some of the most important borders in Europe are shown by red lines and dashes. Red lines show boundaries between kingdoms and other large states. Red dashes show dukedoms and other, smaller political units.
1. Judging from this map, were Lithuania, Poland, and Hungary kingdoms or smaller states in A.D. 1000?
2. How are the boundaries of the Holy Roman Empire indicated on this map? Judging from the text, is it an important political unit, or not?

Chapter

13 The Byzantine Empire and the Formation of Russia

OVERVIEW

This chapter describes the rise and decline of the Byzantine Empire and the formation of Russia.

PLANNING CHART

Section	Text Pages	Key Concept	Suggested Teaching Time
1 The Eastern Empire survived the fall of Rome.	231–235	The Byzantine Empire, Roman in foundation, law, and heritage, thrived for more than a thousand years before it fell to the Turks.	One day **More time?** Use *Overhead Transparency 25* or *Source Reading 13A.*
2 The Byzantines created a magnificent civilization.	235–239	A lasting partnership between the Orthodox Church and stable rulers enabled Byzantine culture to excel in art, architecture, recording of history, and theology.	One day **More time?** Use *Overhead Transparency 26.*
3 Kiev became the first Russian state.	239–242	Early Russians created city-states and adopted Byzantine culture through their conversion to Orthodox Christianity.	One day **More time?** Use *Source Reading 13B.*
4 Autocrats ruled Russia after the Mongols.	242–244	Mongols brought terror and destruction to Russia, delayed its development, and created social conditions that enabled autocratic rulers to come to power.	One day **Less time?** Assign Section 4 to be read before class and teach it together with Section 3.

ANCILLARIES

Materials that may be used with this chapter to reinforce, reteach, enrich, and assess learning are pictured on the following pages.

Teacher's Resource File

ACTIVITIES

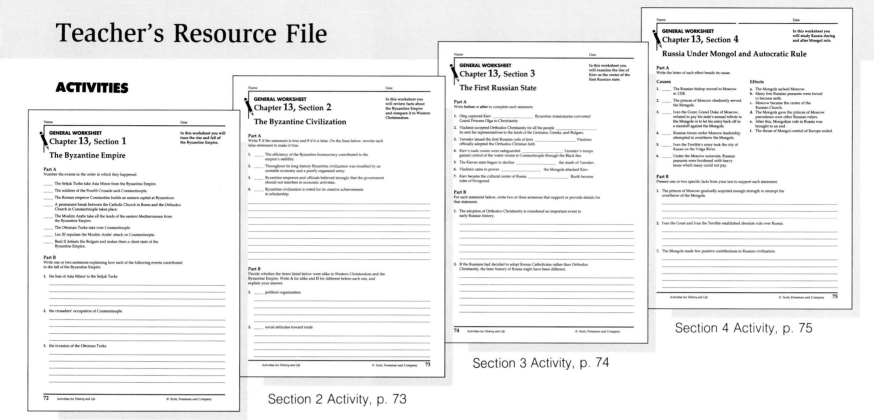

GENERAL WORKSHEET

Chapter 13, Section 1

In this worksheet you will trace the rise and fall of the Byzantine Empire.

The Byzantine Empire

Part A
Number the events in the order in which they happened.

_____ The Seljuk Turks take Asia Minor from the Byzantine Empire.
_____ The soldiers of the Fourth Crusade sack Constantinople.
_____ The Roman emperor Constantine builds an eastern capital at Byzantium.
_____ A permanent break between the Catholic Church in Rome and the Orthodox Church in Constantinople takes place.
_____ The Muslim Arabs take all the lands of the eastern Mediterranean from the Byzantine Empire.
_____ The Ottoman Turks take over Constantinople.
_____ Leo III repulses the Muslim Arabs' attack on Constantinople.
_____ Basil II defeats the Bulgars and makes them a client state of the Byzantine Empire.

Part B
Write one or two sentences explaining how each of the following events contributed to the fall of the Byzantine Empire.

1. the loss of Asia Minor to the Seljuk Turks

2. the crusaders' occupation of Constantinople

3. the invasion of the Ottoman Turks

Section 1 Activity, p. 72

GENERAL WORKSHEET

Chapter 13, Section 2

The Byzantine Civilization

Section 2 Activity, p. 73

GENERAL WORKSHEET

Chapter 13, Section 3

The First Russian State

Section 3 Activity, p. 74

GENERAL WORKSHEET

Chapter 13, Section 4

Russia Under Mongol and Autocratic Rule

Section 4 Activity, p. 75

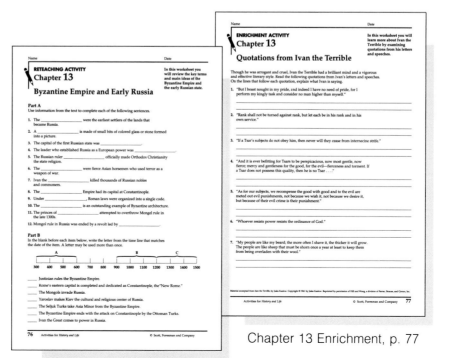

RETEACHING ACTIVITY

Chapter 13

Byzantine Empire and Early Russia

Chapter 13 Reteaching, p. 76

ENRICHMENT ACTIVITY

Chapter 13

Quotations from Ivan the Terrible

Chapter 13 Enrichment, p. 77

Teacher's Resource File

GEOGRAPHY SKILLS

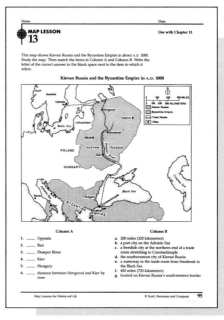

Chapter 13 Geography
Worksheet/Map, pp. 27–28

Chapter 13 Map Lesson, p. 95

TESTS

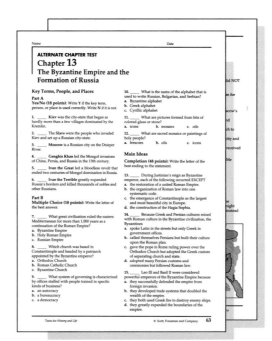

Chapter Test, pp. 61–62

Alternate Chapter Test, pp. 63–64

Other Optional Ancillaries

WORKBOOK

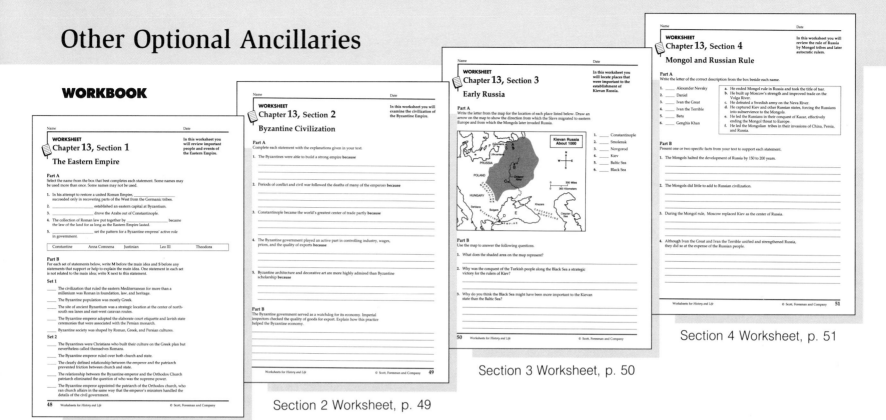

Section 1 Worksheet, p. 48

Section 2 Worksheet, p. 49

Section 3 Worksheet, p. 50

Section 4 Worksheet, p. 51

SOURCE READINGS

Source Reading 13A
Source Reading 13B

TEST GENERATOR

40 multiple-choice questions for Chapter 13

OVERHEAD TRANSPARENCIES

Overhead Transparency 25
Overhead Transparency 26

The Byzantine Empire and the Formation of Russia

A.D. 330–1584

300

330 — Constantine establishes capital at Constantinople

1453 — Ottoman Turks conquer Constantinople

1480 — Ivan the Great frees Russia from Mongol rule

1500

1600

Although civilization in western Europe declined after the fall of Rome, eastern civilization flourished in the lands of the Byzantine [biz′n tēn′] Empire. Constantinople, its splendid capital, attracted many visitors who admired its immense wealth and unique culture. One such visitor was Rabbi Benjamin of Tudela, a Jew from northern Spain, who traveled through the Middle East between the Second and Third Crusades. Around 1170 he reached Constantinople of which he wrote:

> [Merchants] come to it from every country by sea or land, and there is none like it in the world except Baghdad, the great city of Islam. . . . The Greek inhabitants are very rich in gold and precious stones and they go clothed in garments of silk with gold embroidery, and they ride horses and look like princes.
>
> Wealth like that of Constantinople is not to be found in the whole world. Here also are men learned in all the books of the Greeks, and they eat and drink, every man under his vine and his fig-tree.

A continuation of the Roman Empire, the Byzantine Empire lasted for more than 1,000 years. Over time, Byzantine influence spread beyond the empire's borders, especially north to the Slavs living beyond the Black Sea.

Unlike Byzantium, early Russia was just a grouping of city-states under the leadership of Kiev, a city on the Dnieper [nē′-pər] River. Through Kiev the Byzantine form of Christianity spread into Russia. The Mongols conquered Kiev in the 13th century, but the princes of Moscow eventually rallied to form a new Russia. Russia then became the most autocratic state in all of Europe. After Constantinople fell to the Ottoman Turks in 1453, the Russians claimed direct descent from the Byzantines, calling their new empire the Third Rome.

Byzantine emperors Justinian (left) and Constantine I (right) offer gifts to the Virgin Mary in this mosaic from Hagia Sophia in Istanbul, Turkey.

Reading Preview

In this chapter you will learn about the Byzantine Empire and the early history of Russia.

1. The Eastern Empire survived the fall of Rome.

2. The Byzantines created a magnificent civilization.

3. Kiev became the first Russian state.

4. Autocrats ruled Russia after the Mongols.

1 The Eastern Empire survived the fall of Rome.

Strictly speaking, no such entity as a "Byzantine Empire" ever existed. The magnificent civilization that ruled the eastern Mediterranean for more than a millennium was Roman in foundation, law, and heritage. The label **Byzantine Empire**, used by modern historians for this civilization, comes from an ancient trading center named Byzantium.

When the Roman emperor Constantine built an eastern capital at Byzantium, his choice of site was

1 Lesson Plan

Essential Learning Objectives

Students will learn to:

- identify factors that contributed to the development of the Byzantine civilization and describe its outstanding aspects.
- list the causes of the decline and destruction of the Byzantine Empire.

1 FOCUS AND MOTIVATE

Have students recall what they have learned about the division of the Roman Empire into eastern and western parts, and the collapse of the western part.

- Have students identify geographic and cultural factors that contributed to the development of the Byzantine civilization. List the groups of peoples who made up the Byzantine culture, and have students describe how they affected it. Point out how Alexander the Great's dream of mixing cultures was realized in the Eastern Empire.

- Have students cite accomplishments under Emperor Justinian and describe their significance. Tell students that the body of Roman law was huge and that by organizing it into a system, Justinian made it considerably easier to use.

- Chart and discuss the similarities and differences of the Catholic Church in the West and the Orthodox Church in the East. Ask students to speculate how history might have been different if a division between church and state had existed in the West. Have students also compare the division between church and state in the United States with that in the Byzantine Empire.

GUIDED PRACTICE

List the attacks on the Byzantine Empire between the 7th and 15th centuries. Have students describe their outcomes, the reasons for the outcomes, and, when appropriate, the long-term effects. Emphasize that the crusaders' attack was most devastating because it ruined the economy, which led to rebellion, invasion by the Turks, and the end of the Byzantine Empire. Also for guided practice:

 Overhead Transparency 25

Justinian's Empire, A.D. 527–565

 MAP STUDY   This map shows the Byzantine Empire at its height under Justinian. Its capital, Constantinople, was located near which sea?

influenced by its strategic location at the center of north-south sea lanes and east-west caravan routes. In 330 the completed city was dedicated as Constantinople, the "New Rome." A thriving metropolis from the beginning, the city was soon the envy of the world, not only for its prosperity, but also as a symbol of what an imperial city should be. While Germanic tribes carved up the West, a series of strong emperors held Byzantium steady, an eastern bulwark against the barbarians.

Many accomplishments adorned Justinian's reign.

The several capable emperors who ruled after Constantine had to battle continual pressure from invading nomad tribes as well as Rome's old enemy, Persia. A peace treaty with the Persians in 387 protected the empire's eastern front, and for the next century, Byzantium fought to maintain itself against the Visigoths, Huns, and Ostrogoths, who beat against its northern frontiers.

Justinian, who ruled from 527 to 565, was probably the Byzantine Empire's greatest ruler. He was a general, a builder, a statesman, and an impressive administrator. During his 37-year reign, Justinian attempted to restore a united Roman Empire, but succeeded only in recovering, at immense cost, some parts of the crumbling West from the Germanic tribes.

Although he considered this recovery the main goal of his reign, Justinian's most important contribution to Western civilization was the organization of Roman law into one systematic code. Known now as the Justinian Code, it remained the law of the land throughout the history of the Byzantine Empire. Roman law, which might otherwise have been forgotten, was thus preserved.

Justinian lavished money on Constantinople, which he crowned by the building of a church called Hagia Sophia [ī′yə sō fē′yə], a triumph of engineering and architectural design. The name means Church of the Holy Wisdom. Throwing

ANSWER TO MAP STUDY Black Sea

BACKGROUND One of the most important roles of the Byzantine empire was to act as a barrier in protecting Europe from the Turks and other attackers.

modesty to the winds during its dedication ceremony in 537, the emperor raised his hands and cried, "Glory to God, Who has judged me worthy to perform this great work! O Solomon, I have surpassed you!"

Theodora, Justinian's wife, set the pattern for Byzantine empresses. She held her own court, received ambassadors, rewarded office-seekers, and advised the emperor. Many Byzantine empresses were similarly active in affairs of state.

At his death Justinian left a realm dangerously weakened by the combination of foreign wars and costly building projects. Not only was the treasury empty, but the western borderlands were overextended and hard to defend. Moreover, in battling to reclaim them, Justinian had neglected his eastern provinces. Slavs, Bulgars, Persians, and others were quick to note this neglect and promptly moved their troops against the empire's frontiers.

Orthodox Byzantium mixed Greek, Persian, and Roman cultures.

After Justinian's death, the Western Empire was sliced away by more Germanic conquests. The idea of a united Roman Empire was not forgotten, but it was never again achieved. Moreover, by the 8th century, the Eastern Empire had developed a culture that was definitely more Greek and Middle Eastern than Roman and European.

The Byzantine population was largely Greek, although Slavs, Jews, Syrians, and other peoples were also citizens of the empire. Everyone spoke Greek in the streets and, until the 700s, Latin in government offices. For the most part, the Byzantines were Christians who called themselves Romans but built their culture on the Greek plan.

Eventually, however, customs of Persia mingled with those of Greece to replace Roman influence on Byzantium. The elaborate court etiquette and lavish state ceremonies associated with the demigod status of the Persian monarch were adopted by the Byzantine emperor. Rome still shaped the law courts and the political power of the ruler, but the outward trappings were eastern. For example, before anyone approached the emperor, he or she would touch forehead to the floor three times.

Slowly the **Orthodox Church** in Constantinople became distinct from the Catholic Church in Rome. In the West the rising power of the Church was strengthened by the loss of centralized government when Rome fell because bishops assumed certain civil powers. In the East the relationship between church and state was quite different. The Byzantine emperor ruled over both church and

Cast around 300 B.C., these magnificent bronze horses were stolen from Constantinople by Venetian crusaders.

ASSESS

1. How did Justinian's wife contribute to her husband's reign? (She was active in the affairs of state.)

2. In what major way does the Orthodox Church differ from the Catholic Church in Rome? (The Orthodox Church rejects the pope as the highest religious authority.)

Divide students into three groups. Assign each group to compile a list on one of the following topics: the outstanding accomplishments of the Byzantine civilization, the groups of peoples who attacked Byzantium, the major events and conditions that led to the decline and destruction of the empire. Have each group present their lists and give reasons why the items on the list merited inclusion.

1. Assign a small group of students to compile a bibliography listing readily available books on Byzantine culture, art and architecture, Russian history, and Mongol culture. Have the group provide a copy of the list to each class member for reference. Ask for volunteers to research and give reports on each of the topics. (average)
2. Have students trace a map that includes Europe, Asia, and northern Africa and show the location of and label the Byzantine Empire and the lands of the peoples that attacked and invaded the empire. Textbook maps and a historical atlas could be used as sources. (challenging)
3. Also for enrichment:

 Source Reading 13A

Assign the Section Review, Activities page 72, or Workbook page 48.

During its existence the Byzantine Empire attracted traders, who increased its wealth; visitors, who spread word of its magnificence; and invaders, who wanted to possess it for reasons of their own. Byzantine culture was Roman in the beginning but eventually became a mixture of Greek and Middle Eastern culture.

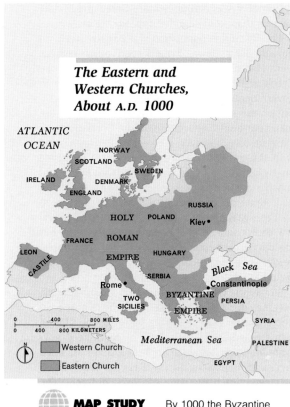

The Eastern and Western Churches, About A.D. 1000

MAP STUDY By 1000 the Byzantine Empire had declined considerably. Which Church did the empire support? Which Church did Russia support?

state. He appointed the patriarch, the head of the Orthodox Church, but let the patriarch run church affairs, just as he left the details of civil government to his ministers. This arrangement was usually successful.

As early as 381, Constantinople rejected the pope as the highest religious authority on earth. Later, arguments over dogma (belief) and ritual (ceremony) added to the bitterness of the quarrel. A complete break came in 1054, when the pope and the patriarch excommunicated each other, creating a permanent schism, or division, in Christianity. Various ecumenical or world councils have discussed reuniting these two parts of Christianity, but so far none has been successful.

Powerful emperors periodically restored the empire.

Between 330 and 1453, periods of imperial strength and prosperity alternated with periods of instability and economic decline. For ten centuries, Constantinople fought off numerous attempts to destroy it, but the 150 years after Justinian's death were particularly difficult. In the 7th century, Emperor Heraclius [her′ə klī əs] once more battled the Persians and took back Syria, Palestine, and Egypt. However, a new power—the Muslim Arabs—soon replaced the Persians as the perennial enemy, and Heraclius' gains were lost again.

By the end of the 7th century, the Arabs had swept across North Africa and conquered most of the eastern Mediterranean. Turning their eyes toward the richest prize of all, they unsuccessfully attacked Constantinople in the winter of 717–718. They were forced to retreat because of Byzantium's weapon, Greek fire, a liquid made from a secret formula that set fire to enemy ships.

From the 8th to the 11th centuries, two emperors stood out as powerful, effective rulers. Leo III (717–741) routed the Arabs from Constantinople and strengthened the defenses of Asia Minor. He expanded the empire's armies by granting land to farmers in exchange for military service.

Basil II (976–1025) followed several able emperors who worked to rebuild the power and prosperity of the empire after another long period of decline. For his ruthless conquest of the Bulgars, Basil was called the "Bulgar Slayer."

In the 7th century, the Bulgars, a nomadic people from Central Asia, attacked the northern Balkans. Find the Balkans on the map on page 232. They enslaved the populace and settled into what is now Bulgaria, establishing a powerful state on the Byzantine Empire's doorstep.

Over the centuries, relations between the two peoples were far from cordial. Finally, after winning a fiercely fought battle, Basil had 15,000 Bulgar soldiers blinded, leaving only a handful with a single eye each to guide the rest home. The Bulgarian king is said to have died of shock when this sightless multitude returned. Once the enemy surrendered, however, Basil made the Bulgars a client state of the empire, freeing future emperors from that particular menace.

The destruction of the Byzantine Empire followed centuries of invasions.

Byzantine fortunes fell again after Basil's death. The city-state of Venice and other emerging merchant powers offered serious competition to Byzantine trade in the eastern Mediterranean. Further, the Seljuk Turks—a foe more powerful than any the Byzantines had yet faced—appeared from Central Asia to threaten Constantinople. In 1071 the empire lost the whole of Asia Minor to the Turks after a humiliating defeat.

The loss of Asia Minor was a serious blow. Not only had it served as a buffer against surprise attack by eastern invaders, it also supplied the empire with food and recruits for the army. If the loss of Asia Minor was unfortunate, however, the sack of Constantinople was catastrophic.

In 1204 the soldiers of the Fourth Crusade descended on Constantinople, supposedly to await transport to Jerusalem. Instead, at the instigation of an envious Venice, the army swarmed through Constantinople, burning, killing, and looting the treasure house of the empire. Some of the treasure was irrevocably lost; some of it was shipped west. Today, four bronze horses from Constantine's Hippodrome (racetrack) can be found in Saint Mark's Cathedral in Venice, where Venetian lords sent them in 1204. These are shown in the photograph on page 233.

After three days of rioting, a Roman Catholic king sat on the throne of Byzantium. The pope was appalled when he heard the reports, but took advantage of events to appoint Roman Catholic bishops to the Orthodox churches. Fifty-seven years later, in 1261, the Byzantines threw the crusaders out.

The Byzantine Empire never recovered from the sack of Constantinople. Even after the crusaders were ejected, the empire knew little peace. Civil war broke out as various princes fought for the throne, and religious quarrels divided people.

In 1354 the Ottoman Turks, former subjects of the Seljuk Turks, bypassed Constantinople, crossing the Bosporus further south. They quickly spread out into the countryside, beginning a state that would become the Ottoman Empire. By 1445 all that remained of the once-mighty Byzantine Empire was the city of Constantinople.

BACKGROUND The Italian city-states such as Venice were among the first to revive in the later Middle Ages. Some historians suggest it was merchants from these city-states who incited the people of the Fourth Crusade to attack Constantinople.

The end of the Byzantine Empire finally came in 1453 when barely 8,000 defenders were left to face the besieging Turkish army of 160,000 troops. After eight heroic weeks, the city fell. As the Turks stormed the walls, the emperor rushed to meet them, crying out as he was cut down, "God forbid that I should live an Emperor without an Empire! As my city falls, I fall with it."

Section 1 Review

Identify Byzantine Empire, Justinian, Orthodox Church

Main Ideas
1. Describe three of Justinian's accomplishments.
2. How did Byzantine civilization mix Greek, Persian, and Roman elements?
3. Why were Leo III and Basil II considered powerful emperors?
4. What major invasions weakened the empire and led to its final collapse in 1453?

Critical Thinking
Predicting Effects: Do you think the same kind of civilization would have flourished if Constantine had chosen Ravenna, Italy, instead of Byzantium as the site for his New Rome? Explain your answer.

---

2 ## The Byzantines created a magnificent civilization.

Byzantine civilization was more advanced than any in western Europe. Not until the 1300s were Byzantine standards of art and scholarship equaled by the West. Two factors accounted for this amazing strength and endurance.

First, the Byzantines had a centralized government with a well-trained **bureaucracy**. A bureaucracy is a system of governing by means of government offices staffed with people trained in specific kinds of business, such as tax collection. Byzantine bureaucracy was adapted from the Persians and worked well through most of its history.

Second, the empire's social institutions were healthy. It had an efficient army and navy, a stable and effective religious leadership in the Orthodox Church, and a strong economy to support a high standard of living.

2 ## *Lesson Plan*
Essential Learning Objective

Students will learn to compare and contrast the government, the role of the Church, and the economy of the Byzantine Empire with that of medieval western Europe.

1 FOCUS AND MOTIVATE

Have students recall the characteristics of feudal government in Europe during the Middle Ages. Have them speculate as to what factors led to the development of the magnificent civilization of the Byzantine Empire while European culture regressed.

2 TEACH

- Compare and contrast in broad terms the structure of government in the Byzantine Empire and in western Europe during the Middle Ages. Have students contrast the power of the medieval kings with that of strong Byzantine emperors and cite reasons for the differences. Have them identify other differences in the governments of both societies, including the role of the Church, and explain how these differences affected the development of culture.

- Discuss how the lack of a clear legal system of succession to the throne caused a variety of problems in imperial Rome as well as in Byzantium.

- Describe how Byzantine civilization spread in eastern Europe. Have students contrast its spread to that of Roman civilization.

- Outline and discuss the economy in Byzantium, including details pertaining to currency, trade, social status, and the role of government in relation to wages, prices, quality control, and farming. Have students compare and contrast the various aspects of the Byzantine economy with those of the medieval European economy.

- Describe the similar roles of monasteries as centers for scholarship in the West and in Byzantine society. Have students explain how the roles of

Byzantine success reflected a unique partnership of imperial power.

Unlike the feudal system of western Europe, the Byzantine state was centralized. In theory the emperor had absolute authority, but in reality custom and tradition limited his power. The most effective emperors worked in a unique partnership with the Church, the army, and the bureaucracy. Weak emperors might be dominated by strong ministers, but strong rulers sought advice, support, and cooperation from them. An army of civil servants was responsible for the actual workings of government. Despite some corruption and bribery, these officials were usually conscientious and efficient.

However, as in imperial Rome, the lack of a clear, legal system of succession to the throne marred the peace of the empire. Any upstart could attempt to become emperor, and many succeeded. The story of the rise and fall of Byzantine emperors is a record of intrigue, violence, and death. Of the 88 emperors who ruled between A.D. 395 and 1453, 29 died violent deaths.

Constantinople's excitable population added to the hazards of government. Uprisings like the Nika Revolt in 532 often broke out. Named for its rallying cry *nika*, meaning "victory," the rebellion lasted for seven days during the reign of Justinian. Before it was over, some 30,000 people lay dead. According to the historian Procopius [prō kō′pē-əs], the Empress Theodora inspired her husband to stay and crush the rebels, saying:

> If . . . it is your wish to save yourself, O Emperor, there is no difficulty. For we have much money, and there is the sea, here the boats . . . as for myself, I approve a certain ancient saying that the purple makes a good burial-shroud.

Byzantine civilization spread throughout eastern Europe, especially to the Slavic peoples of Russia and the Balkans, who were the most deeply influenced by it. Because missionaries carried Christianity to these peoples in the 9th century, today the Orthodox faith is the major religion of Russia, Yugoslavia, and Bulgaria as well as Greece. The **Cyrillic alphabet** [si ril′ik] used to write Russian, Bulgarian and Serbian, is named for the monk Cyril who, with his brother, Methodius, converted the Slavs to Orthodox Christianity. The two monks left these new Christians a modified form of the Greek alphabet to use in writing their own languages,

In this mosaic from the Church of St. Vitale in Ravenna, Italy, Empress Theodora is shown with her court attendants. Built during the reign of Justinian, the church contains the finest examples of Byzantine mosaics.

which explains why much early Russian literature, especially the lives of the saints, is Byzantine in origin.

Byzantium's economy supported a prosperous society.

Built astride the crossroads of Europe and Asia, Constantinople was the world's greatest center of trade for nearly 1,000 years. A stable currency based on gold successfully supported the empire's strong economic position. In fact, Byzantine gold coins served as international currency throughout the medieval world where other coins were scarce or worthless.

Unlike western Europe where trade was tolerated but considered a demeaning activity, the Byzantines approved of ambitious merchants rising in life. Important court offices were legally sold to the highest bidder and titles of nobility were regularly bought by wealthy commoners. On the other hand, the loss of a fortune reduced a family's social status.

Because economic activity was so important to the health of the empire, the government was a stern watchdog over the economy. Industry was rigidly controlled; and wages, prices, and working conditions were fixed. Imperial inspectors monitored manufacturing, and the quality of exports was strictly regulated. Articles made by skilled artisans—jeweled ornaments, magnificent tapestries, carved ivory, and exquisite leather work—were the pride of Constantinople. Clothmaking soon became its chief industry.

Until A.D. 550 silk cloth was a luxury item imported at great expense from China, the only known source. The Chinese forbade the export of the silk-making process, threatening with execution anyone caught selling or stealing this knowledge. Around 550 two Greek monks packed silkworm eggs into hollow canes and, smuggling them out of China, headed for Constantinople. There the emperor rewarded them for their precious secret. The silk industry became a profitable state monopoly, and splendid silk fabrics were available for the richly ornamented clothing the Byzantines loved.

There was the usual gap between the wealth of the court and the rest of the people in Byzantium, but strong emperors took pains to help the small

FROM THE ARCHIVES This passage is included in the collection of source materials compiled by Deno J. Geanakoplos, *Byzantium: Church, Society and Civilization Seen through Contemporary Eyes*, (Chicago: University of Chicago Press, 1984),

From the Archives
A Mother Who Ruled Byzantium

Alexius Comnenus reigned as the Byzantine emperor between 1081 and 1118. Comnenus not only held his mother, Anna Dalassena, in high regard, he also entrusted to her much of the responsibility for ruling the empire. This account is from the writings of Anna Comnena, daughter of Comnenus and granddaughter of Anna Dalassena.

[My] father accorded his mother such high honor in these matters and . . . deferred to her in all respects, as if he were turning over the reins of the empire to her and running alongside her while she drove the imperial chariot, contenting himself simply with the title of emperor. . . . He took upon himself the wars against the barbarians . . . while he entrusted to his mother the complete management of [civil] affairs: the selection of civil magistrates, the collection of incoming revenues and the expenses of the government. . . . [My] grandmother was . . . so highly skilled in controlling and running the government, that she was not only able to manage the Roman empire but could have handled every empire under the sun. She had a vast amount of experience and understood the internal workings of many things: she knew how each affair began and to what result it might lead, which actions were destructive and which rather were beneficial.

farmers. Since the Byzantine economy was relatively stable, government supervision of the large estates improved the daily life of the farmers.

Monasteries and scholars preserved classical learning.

Byzantium inherited the intellectual treasures of both Greece and Rome, with the works of Plato

p. 303. Was it a good idea to divide the responsibilities of ruling an empire into defense and foreign relations on one hand and internal affairs on the other? (Large institutions always need a division of responsibilities.)

nuns differed. Elicit reasons why there were women scholars in Byzantium but not in medieval European society.

GUIDED PRACTICE

Have students examine the pictures in this chapter of Byzantine art and architecture. Ask students what theme or themes they detect in the pictures and tell them to write one or more sentences describing what they perceive. (A religious theme is apparent.)

3 ASSESS AND CLOSE

ASSESS

1. What Byzantine industry was a profitable state monopoly? (silk)
2. On which alphabet is the Cyrillic alphabet based? (Greek alphabet)

OPTIONAL RETEACHING

Assign students to make charts comparing either the government, the role of the Church, or the economy in the Byzantine Empire and in western Europe during the Middle Ages. Encourage students to review appropriate sections of Chapter 11.

OPTIONAL ENRICHMENT

1. Assign students to work together to research and construct collages on the daily life of the Byzantine people, their public works, or their art and architecture. (average)
2. Have students make two parallel vertical time lines extending from 300 to 1500. On one have them indicate important dates and events that took place in western Europe; on the other have them indicate important dates and events in the Byzantine Empire. Students should supplement information given in this textbook with research. (challenging)
3. Also for enrichment:

 Overhead Transparency 26

237

Hagia Sophia was built by Justinian in the 530s. The minarets—the
four tall towers—were added by the Turks 1,000 years later. At left is
an interior view of the church.

and Aristotle especially revered. Credit for the preservation of the classics must be shared between ordinary scholars and the monasteries that were an important part of the Byzantine world.

Monasticism, a system in which people live a community life devoted to spiritual things, was an important part of Byzantine civilization. Like the monasteries of the West, Byzantine religious houses became famous as centers of scholarship. In these quiet, well-ordered places, monks and nuns copied manuscripts, translated ancient thought, and taught the wisdom of the classical world. Lay scholars, those who were not members of the religious orders, contributed in the fields of philosophy, history, and literature.

Most Byzantine scholarship was dull and lacked originality, however. Only in history and theology did the empire produce works of real excellence. For example, Anna Comnena [kom nē ′nə], daughter of an 11th-century emperor, wrote an important work on the life and times of her father. The best-known historian, however, is Procopius. His notorious *Secret History* is a biased but fascinating account of Justinian's reign, filled with backstairs court gossip and stories about the scandalous behavior of the aristocracy.

The libraries of the empire were rich in their collections of masterpieces in classical philosophy and literature. Although numbers of priceless manuscripts were lost in the various plunders of Constantinople, the works that did survive helped revive Western culture.

Byzantine ingenuity created magnificent works of art.

The creativity of the empire in architecture and decorative art contrasts sharply with its lack of originality in scholarship. In the Hagia Sophia, Byzantine genius came to full flower. Justinian's magnificent church, wrote Procopius, "soars to a height to match the sky, and, like a ship riding at anchor . . . it looks down upon the remainder of the city."

Built in the shape of a Greek cross, which is nearly square, the church was topped by a huge dome suspended 180 feet above the floor. Crowning a square space with a circular dome was a specialty of Byzantine engineers and became a hall-

BACKGROUND The works of Plato and Aristotle were regarded as pagan by the Church in the West at this time.

mark of Byzantine architecture. The triumph of Hagia Sophia is apparent even today, 1,400 years after its dedication. It dominates the skyline of modern Istanbul, a visual link between the Byzantine Empire and the 20th century.

In decorative art, the Byzantines are best known for their use of **mosaics**—small bits of colored glass or stone formed into pictures. When particles of gold were set into the mosaic, the whole picture sparkled with light. Another trick was to set the tiles at slightly uneven angles. The scene then appeared to ripple in a wave movement as the viewer passed. Mosaics were usually placed on the walls and ceilings of churches and homes, either displaying designs of religious importance, or simply decorative scenes of daily life. Wall paintings and icons added richness to building interiors.

Icons are mosaics or paintings of holy people, usually of Jesus, but also of Mary and other saints. Icons are considered sacred by Orthodox Christians, who treat them with great reverence. Copies of famous icons are often seen in Orthodox homes, but modern artists rarely attempt to produce original icons since their creation is governed by extremely precise rules.

Secular or worldly art was also created on a dazzling scale for royal palaces. Along with mosaics were polished marbles, inlaid bronzes, rich fabrics, gold and silver dishes, and jeweled ornaments—all representative of the Byzantine genius.

Section 2 Review

Identify bureaucracy, Cyrillic alphabet, mosaics, icons
Main Ideas
1. How did the relationship between the emperor, and the Church, the army, and the bureaucracy help the Byzantine Empire succeed?
2. What made the Byzantine Empire prosperous?
3. How did monasteries preserve classical learning?
4. Name three outstanding kinds of Byzantine architecture and art.

Critical Thinking

Identifying Assumptions: Historians say that Greek monks risked their lives to bring silkworm eggs from China to Byzantium to establish a Byzantine silk industry. With this information, what assumptions can you make about monks and the silk industry?

3 Kiev became the first Russian state.

The original homeland of the **Slavs** is unknown, but they were probably one of many peoples who migrated from Central Asia long before the Christian era. By the early 700s, the eastern Slavs had settled between the Baltic and Black seas, farming, hunting, fishing, and trading. The Slavs did not have central government but were organized into city-states ruled by wealthy merchants.

The first Russian state was founded on the Dnieper.

The Viking raiders of the coasts and inland waterways of Europe in the 800s also reached Slavic lands. (See Chapter 11.) According to tradition, in 862 a Viking chief named Rurik, probably a Danish feudal lord, became ruler of Novgorod [nôv′gə-rot′], an important city in northwest Russia.

One of Rurik's chieftains, Oleg, captured **Kiev** [kē′ef], a city on the Dnieper River. When Oleg took another city, Smolensk, he formed the first Russian state, making Kiev its capital. The Vikings and Slavs intermarried, merging their two cultures into one civilization later known as Russian.

Over the next century, the Grand Princes of Kiev crushed their enemies, the Khazars in the south and the Bulgars to the east. By the 10th century, Kievan Russia had the strongest ruler in eastern Europe, though it remained a loose confederation of city-states. Its site on the Dnieper River made it a major stop on the trade route with the Byzantines.

Russia adopted Byzantium's Orthodox Christianity.

In the mid-10th century, Byzantine missionaries converted to Christianity Olga, Grand Princess of Kiev and the first female ruler in Russia. Olga did not try to convert the rest of Russia herself, leaving that to her grandson Vladimir [vlad′i-mir]. Before deciding which faith to choose, however, Vladimir sent out teams to observe the Muslim Bulgarians, the Catholic Germans, and the Orthodox Byzantines. On their return they reported:

We journeyed among the Bulgarians . . . there is no happiness among them, but instead only sor-

Byzantines and carried on extensive trade linking China, Slavic lands, and the Arab Empire.

239

GEOGRAPHY

A Key to History

STRATEGIC STRAITS

A body of water can divide people. On the other hand, if it can be easily navigated, a body of water can also help bring people together. The straits and small sea that separate Asia from Europe are the latter kind. These strategically located bodies of water—the Bosporus, the Sea of

What bodies of water shown on the map connect the Black Sea with the Mediterranean? Which of these are straits?

Marmara, and the Dardanelles—have helped human contact more than they have been a barrier. These bodies of water do indeed separate Europe from Asia. However, they also link the Black Sea to the Mediterranean.

For several thousand years, some important city has controlled one or the other of the straits. Troy once controlled the Dardanelles. Later Byzantium controlled the Bosporus.

When Constantine chose his' capital, he selected Byzantium, which was renamed Constantinople in A.D. 330. Constantinople occupied the most easily defended site in the area, a promontory, or high point of land, overlooking a natural harbor called the Golden Horn.

During the Middle Ages, Constantinople was the most important trading center between Europe and Asia. Its wealth was a magnet for the envious and greedy. Arabs, Russians, Italians, and Turks—all attacked Constantinople between the 7th and 16th centuries. In 1453 Constantinople fell to the Turks, and the Byzantine Empire came to an end. The Turks, who renamed the city Istanbul, have controlled the straits since that time. Today, however, treaties keep the straits open to vessels of all nations.

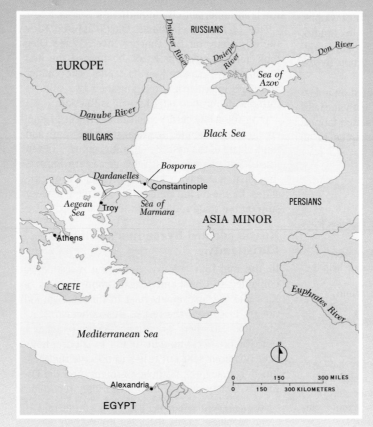

REVIEW
1. Why did Constantine choose Byzantium as the site for his capital city? What advantages did this site have?
2. What rivers shown on the map drain into the Black Sea?
3. How do you think these rivers would affect trade moving through the Bosporus, the Sea of Marmara, and the Dardanelles?

Early Russia, Around 1000

MAP STUDY The Russian state shown here was conquered by the Mongols in 1240. River travel was important in early Russia. Its capital, Kiev, was located on which river? Why did the Russians want to control the land of the Pechenegs?

row and a dreadful stench. . . . Then we went among the Germans . . . but we beheld no glory there. Then we went on to Greece . . . to the buildings where they worship their God, and we knew not whether we were in heaven or on earth. For on earth there is no such splendor or such beauty.

Vladimir officially adopted the Orthodox faith for all his people, although it was several hundred years before Christianity was accepted by most of the Russians.

The adoption of Orthodox Christianity was the single most important event in Russia's early history. Through the Church, Byzantine culture influenced the literature, art, laws, and customs of Kievan Russia and helped unify the people in a common faith. By accepting Orthodox Christianity, however, Russia was not, by definition, part of the Roman Catholic Church. This choice started Russia toward eventual isolation from the Latin civilization of western Europe.

ANSWER TO MAP STUDY Dnieper; for access by river to trade with Constantinople

Yaroslav established Russia as a European power.

Kievan Russia reached the height of its power during the rule of Vladimir's grandson, **Yaroslav** [yu-ru slaf'] the Wise, who reigned from 1019 to 1054. During his long reign, Kiev became the religious and cultural center of Russia, as well as one of the wealthiest and most civilized cities in all of Europe. The reigning kings of Hungary, Poland, and France welcomed Yaroslav's daughters as queens, and his son claimed a Byzantine princess as his wife. Yaroslav founded schools and libraries to support scholars and artists, and he issued the first Russian code of laws. With the help of Byzantine architects, he had a copy of the cathedral of Hagia Sophia built in Kiev. The Byzantine patriarch then sent a bishop to head the Kievan Church.

Yaroslav extended his domain by defeating his Slavic neighbors to the north and west. When he had subdued the Pechenegs, a Turkic people living along the Black Sea, Kiev was able to control its

3 | ASSESS AND CLOSE

ASSESS

What two cultures merged in Russia through intermarriage of peoples? (Viking and Slavic cultures)

OPTIONAL RETEACHING

Have students write a paragraph citing evidence that Yaroslav embraced the Byzantine culture. Choose students to read their paragraphs aloud.

OPTIONAL ENRICHMENT

1. Divide students into two groups. Have one group list the ways in which Russian culture might have been different in the 11th century if Islam had been adopted and the other, if Catholicism had been chosen. (average)
2. Also for enrichment:

 Source Reading 13B

INDEPENDENT PRACTICE/ HOMEWORK

Assign the Section Review, Activities page 74, or Workbook page 50.

CLOSURE

Tell students that the adoption of Orthodox Christianity was the most important event in early Russian history, marking the beginning of Russia's move toward isolation from the Latin civilization of western Europe.

241

The Virgin of Vladimir is Russia's most revered icon. It was probably painted in the 12th century.

water access to Constantinople, safeguarding this vital trade route.

Because of his accomplishments, Yaroslav is known as the New Charlemagne and, like his Frankish counterpart, was a beloved ruler. Like the empire of Charlemagne also, the Kievan state declined after the death of Yaroslav as Russian unity disintegrated into civil war among his heirs.

Kievan Russia revived briefly in the 1100s. It then subsided again into a fragmented shadow of its former glory, prey to the marauding armies of yet another Central Asian invader, the Mongols.

Section 3 Review

Identify Slavs, Kiev, Yaroslav

Main Ideas
1. Briefly describe the origins of the first Russian state.
2. By adopting Orthodox Christianity, what barrier did Russia create?
3. How did Yaroslav make Russia a successful European power?

Critical Thinking
Evaluating Sources of Information: The Old Chronicle, kept by monks of a later era, says that the Slavs invited Rurik and his Vikings to rule Novgorod because the people there were quarreling among themselves. Why should one be suspicious of the truth of such an assertion?

4 Autocrats ruled Russia after the Mongols.

From the time of the Huns in the 5th century, periodic waves of invaders from Central Asia swept into Europe. The Russians held off these invasions, but in the 13th century a far more serious threat appeared. Led by **Genghis Khan** [jeng′gis kän′], Mongol invaders overran parts of China, Persia, and Russia. (See page 302, Geography—A Key to History.) In 1240 Genghis Khan's grandson, Batu, captured Kiev and other Russian states, forcing the Russians into subservience to Mongol overlords.

Mongol tribes ruled Russia for two centuries.

The **Mongols** were fierce horse riders who used terror as a weapon of war. Showing no mercy as they rampaged over the countryside, they massacred most of the men they found and took the women and children into slavery. Their savagery is graphically related in the Old Chronicle's description of Batu's capture of a city three years before he sacked Kiev:

> They came to the Cathedral . . . and they cut to pieces the Great Princess Agrippina, her daughters-in-law, and other princesses. They burned to death the bishops and the priests and put the torch to the holy church. And they cut down many people, including women and children. Still others were drowned in the river. . . . And not one man remained alive in the city. All were dead. . . . And there was not even anyone to mourn the dead.

So widespread was the destruction and so large was the tribute the Mongols required that some historians believe the Mongols held back the development of Russia by 150 or 200 years. Tribute is the money, goods, and services a conquered people are required to pay their conquerors on a regular basis.

Cut off by the Mongols from trade with Constantinople, and with no other markets for their honey and furs, the Russians were devastated by the tribute payments. In addition the Mongols kept them in nearly complete isolation from western Christendom for 200 years.

The Mongols made very few positive contributions to Russian civilization. As Muslims in a Christian land, they were alien to the culture and this, together with their conviction that they were far superior to the rest of the world, kept them apart from the Russians. Although they did not interfere with the Orthodox Church, they did force the clergy to support their rule. The Mongols deserve credit for introducing a postal system and a census to Russia, but they added nothing to the culture of the Russians.

Russian princes recovered political and trade initiatives.

Russia's national hero during the early years of Mongol rule was Prince Alexander of Novgorod. Known as Alexander Nevsky for his defeat of a Swedish army on the Neva River in 1240, he also fought attacks in 1242 by the Teutonic Knights, a German group of crusaders. Nevsky never dared challenge the Mongols, however. From his capital at Vladimir, he led the Russians with Mongol permission. Daniel, Alexander Nevsky's youngest son, inherited the city-state of **Moscow**, hardly more than a few villages dominated by the Kremlin, a walled, wooden fortress. Daniel and his successors built up Moscow's strength and gained control of

the rivers, which improved their trade on the Volga River. Moscow became the new center of the Russian Church when the head of the Church moved there in 1328.

The princes of Moscow were obedient and reliable servants of the Mongols. As a reward they were given precedence over other Russian rulers, thus increasing their opportunities to strengthen their position. As Mongol power began to disintegrate in the late 1300s, Russian forces under Moscow's leadership attempted to overthrow Mongol rule. In retaliation, the Mongols sacked Moscow and once again forced the Russians to pay regular tribute. Not until the 15th century were the Mongols finally beaten, allowing Moscow to take over leadership of Russian lands.

Two Russian rulers established autocratic government.

The beginnings of a Russian nation can be traced to two harsh but able rulers, both named Ivan. The first was Ivan III, called **Ivan the Great**. The second was his grandson, Ivan IV, known as **Ivan the Terrible**. Both were ambitious and both took advantage of special conditions in Russia to increase their power. Unlike medieval Europe, for example, Russia had no parliament or Magna Carta to limit

effects of Mongol rule and suggest reasons why the Mongols gave the princes of Moscow power over other Russian rulers. Ask why these princes never dared challenge the Mongols.

● Discuss the rules of both Ivan III and Ivan IV. Compare autocratic government to dictatorship and contrast it with parliamentary government.

Have students write summary statements on the positive contributions of the Mongols, the accomplishments of Ivan the Great, and the inhumanity of Ivan the Terrible.

3 ASSESS AND CLOSE

ASSESS

What city became the center of the Russian Church in 1328? (Moscow)

OPTIONAL RETEACHING

Have students outline the long- and short-term effects of Mongol rule on Russia under these headings: Trade, Economy, Government, Culture.

Students also may be assigned Activities reteaching page 76.

OPTIONAL ENRICHMENT

Have students find information on Ivan the Great and write a short biography of the ruler. (average)

Students also may be assigned Activities enrichment page 77.

INDEPENDENT PRACTICE/ HOMEWORK

Assign the Section Review, the Chapter Review items, Activities page 75, or Workbook page 51.

DAILY LIFE

The Mongols who ruled Russia between 1240 and 1480 led a life of constant movement, always searching for fresh grazing grounds for their herds. Boys learned to ride ponies at age three, and women were expert riders as well. As they moved from place to place, the Mongols often carried their felt tents on large wagons drawn by many oxen (far left). The nomadic herders who inhabit Mongolia today live in similar tents called yurts (left).

The Russian soldiers shown in this engraving are encased in heavy padded clothing to protect them from the cold.

the power of its rulers. Towns had no special privileges, and the Church usually favored the crown. Russian nobles maintained no armies of their own. Nothing stood between a determined leader and total power.

Ivan the Great, the Grand Duke of Moscow, ruled from 1462 to 1505. Slowly, under the very noses of the Mongols, Ivan acquired one small state after another until he ruled most of the Russian people. After 20 years of increasingly successful resistance, Ivan challenged the Mongols by refusing to pay the annual tribute. For weeks his army faced the Mongols across a small river, but both armies eventually withdrew without battle. Ivan's bloodless revolt in 1480 ended 240 years of Mongol rule in Russia.

Ivan the Great was Russia's first independent ruler since the time of Kievan Russia. He began the style of leadership in Russia that produced the absolute ruler or autocrat. Because of his marriage to Zoë, niece of the last Byzantine emperor, he and his descendants claimed to be successors of the Byzantine emperors. Before Ivan's death in 1505, a Russian monk prophesied: "Two Romes have fallen; a third now is. A fourth will never be."

Ivan the Terrible was three years old when his father died. When he was 14, he took over the gov-

ernment. He imagined that he was descended from the Roman emperor Augustus, so in 1547, he had himself crowned first tsar of Russia. The word tsar is the Russian equivalent of caesar, or emperor. Under Ivan the Terrible, the Russians pushed far into the eastern steppes. (See the map on page 604.) They took Kazan, chief city of the Mongols on the Volga River, ending the Mongols' power.

Ivan the Terrible had been badly treated as a child by the boyars, the warrior nobles of Moscow. Long years spent in the company of these cruel and often savage men may have fostered a growing emotional instability in the young prince. In any event, he earned his nickname "the Terrible" by killing thousands of nobles and other Russians, by having friends and courtiers mutilated on a whim, and finally, by striking his son and heir so hard with his walking staff that the young man died of the blow.

The Russian people paid a terrible price for the growing power of the Moscow autocrats. The few towns that had been self-governing, like Novgorod, lost their freedom. Loyal nobles received new lands, but heavier taxes forced free Russian peasants into slave-like serfdom at the very time serfdom had died in western Europe. By the year of Ivan the Terrible's death in 1584, Russia was tearing itself apart in another civil war. It was an era known as the "Time of Troubles."

Section 4 Review

Identify Genghis Khan, Mongols, Moscow, Ivan the Great, Ivan the Terrible

Main Ideas
1. How did the Mongols rule Russia?
2. What did Alexander Nevsky do to strengthen Russia during the Mongol rule? How did his son Daniel improve trade?
3. Which two Russian rulers developed an autocratic style of government? What did they accomplish?

Critical Thinking

Analyzing Comparisons: Both Ivan the Great and Ivan the Terrible have been called autocratic rulers. What autocratic actions did each perform? Based on the evidence of their actions, can you say that an autocrat is automatically a good or bad ruler?

HIGHLIGHTS OF CIVILIZATION

Byzantine Religious Art

Gold, gems, and jewellike bits of brilliantly colored enamel form this icon of St. Michael, leader of the heavenly army. Byzantine icon-makers chose their most precious materials to create these holy images.

The Greek word "icon" simply means image, but the word holds a religious meaning as well as an artistic one. The Byzantines believed that a special relationship existed between the image they were making, the person looking at that image, and the holy person whom the image represented. According to Byzantine theologians, the icon shown here was actually created by St. Michael himself, in much the same way that an object creates its own shadow. What is more, the people for whom the icon was made believed that the image could transfer some of St. Michael's holy powers to anyone looking upon it. In other words, the icon opened a direct pathway to St. Michael, and both icon and viewer shared in his sanctity.

The strict rules that govern icon making dictate that the main figure is shown full-face. Thus, the eyes stare toward the viewer, creating a powerful bond between icon and onlooker.

Byzantine artisans bent and curved thin strips of gold into elaborate patterns to make the icon shown here. Powdered enamel laid within these tiny golden walls was then fused at a high temperature, forming a shimmering, jewel-colored surface. Golden light reflects through the semitransparent enamel from the precious metal beneath.

The sheet of gold and silver from which the icon was made was worked from the back with a hammer and other tools, to create the raised design in a technique known as repoussé [rə pü sā']. The figure of St. Michael at left projects from its golden background, face forward, striding toward eternity. Only the eyes recede, dark windows that draw the beholder into a world of profound faith.

This icon of St. Michael was made in Constantinople about 1100. The crusaders who looted Constantinople in 1204 carried it to Venice.

CHAPTER 13 REVIEW

Section Summaries

Section 1
The Eastern Empire survived the fall of Rome.
The eastern Roman Empire survived the fall of Rome to become the Byzantine Empire. It inherited its territory and much of its political tradition from Rome, and drew its cultural traditions from Greece and Persia. The break between the Roman (Latin) Catholic Church and the Eastern (Greek) Orthodox Church completed the cultural separation between the Byzantines and western Europe. The Byzantines withstood many invaders, but finally fell to the Turks in 1453.

Section 2
The Byzantines created a magnificent civilization.
Constantinople, the strategically placed Byzantine capital, was a prosperous city that kept the best of Greco-Roman culture. Rulers maintained a strong central government that acted as a stern watchdog over all parts of the economy. Byzantine scholars tended to be imitative rather than creative, but artists and architects created magnificent domes, mosaics, and paintings.

Section 3
Kiev became the first Russian state.
In the mid-800s, the eastern Slavs and their Viking rulers created the foundation of a new state—Russia. For three centuries, Kiev was the capital of a loose confederation of city-states. Vladimir's choice of Orthodox Christianity was the most critical event in Russia's early history because it separated Russians from their Roman Catholic neighbors. Yaroslav the Wise, who ruled from 1019 to 1054, brought Kievan Russia to the peak of its power. After his death, civil war destroyed the unity that he had created.

Section 4
Autocrats ruled Russia after the Mongols.
In the 13th century, the Mongols brought terror and destruction to Russia, along with demands for tribute and heavy taxes. Mongol rule seriously delayed Russia's development. Alexander Nevsky, Russia's national hero, recovered western Russian lands but bowed to Mongol power. The principality of Moscow slowly grew in strength. In 1480 Ivan the Great ended tribute payments to the Mongols. Social conditions permitted Ivan the Great and other ambitious rulers to become absolute or autocratic rulers. Ivan the Terrible, the first tsar of Russia, expanded the empire his grandfather had begun, but his policies were extremely harsh, and the country suffered a devastating civil war soon after his death.

Test Yourself

Key Terms, People, and Places
Identify the significance of each of the following:

Review Dates

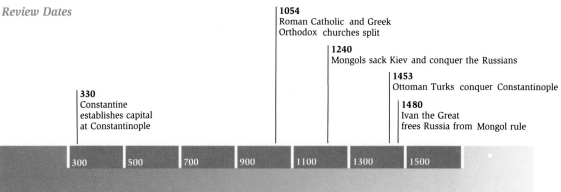

330
Constantine establishes capital at Constantinople

1054
Roman Catholic and Greek Orthodox churches split

1240
Mongols sack Kiev and conquer the Russians

1453
Ottoman Turks conquer Constantinople

1480
Ivan the Great frees Russia from Mongol rule

| 300 | 500 | 700 | 900 | 1100 | 1300 | 1500 |

Section 1
a. Byzantine Empire   **c.** Orthodox Church
b. Justinian

Section 2
a. Cyrillic alphabet   **c.** mosaics
b. bureaucracy   **d.** icons

Section 3
a. Slavs   **c.** Yaroslav
b. Kiev

Section 4
a. Genghis Khan   **d.** Ivan the Great
b. Mongols   **e.** Ivan the Terrible
c. Moscow

Main Ideas

Section 1
1. Which of Justinian's accomplishments is he best remembered for?
2. How were Greek, Persian, and Roman influences represented in Byzantine culture?
3. How did Leo III and Basil II help strengthen the Byzantine Empire?
4. Which invaders were responsible for major conquests of Byzantine territory that weakened the empire and led to its final collapse?

Section 2
1. Describe the relationship between the emperor, the Church, the army, and the bureaucracy that helped the Byzantine Empire succeed for many centuries.
2. What elements made the Byzantine economy prosperous?
3. What did the monasteries do to preserve classical learning?
4. For which particular examples of architecture and decorative art are the Byzantines known?

Section 3
1. How did the first Russian state begin?
2. How did the choice of Orthodox Christianity later isolate Russia?
3. In what ways did Yaroslav create a successful European power?

Section 4
1. What form did the Mongol rule of Russia take?
2. What did the two princes, Alexander Nevsky and Daniel, contribute to the strengthening of Russia?

3. Which Russian rulers developed an autocratic style of government? How did they help the country develop?

Critical Thinking

1. Predicting Effects The Byzantines allowed rich commoners to buy titles of nobility that could be inherited by their children. What effect might this practice have on a civilization?

2. Analyzing Comparisons In many ways Kievan Russia mirrored the Byzantine civilization. What elements are the most obviously similar? How do they differ?

Chapter Skills and Activities

Practicing Study and Research Skills

Using an Encyclopedia
Ivan IV was cruel, but no more brutal than many contemporary rulers in other countries. "Terrible" is a mistranslation of the Russian word for "awe-inspiring." Look up Ivan the Terrible in an encyclopedia and write down some of the accomplishments that made him an outstanding ruler.

Linking Past and Present
In 1975 Western European countries, the United States, the Soviet Union, and Turkey signed treaties pledging to keep the Bosporus, the Sea of Marmara, and the Dardenelles open to vessels of all nations. How does this action compare to the use and control of these straits in the past?

Learning History Through Maps
It has been stated that Constantinople was built astride the "crossroads of Europe and Asia." Look at the physical maps of Europe and Asia on pages 793 and 795 and answer these questions:
1. How did Constantinople's location enable it to become a crossroads between Europe and Asia?
2. What mountains separated Europe and Asia in other regions?

CRITICAL THINKING QUESTION LEVEL 1. easy;
2. average

Chapter

14 The Rise and Expansion of Islam

OVERVIEW

This chapter covers 900 years of Islamic history from 622 to 1526—its founding by Muhammad, its beliefs and practices, its divisions, and its conquests.

PLANNING CHART

Section	Text Pages	Key Concept	Suggested Teaching Time
1 The Prophet Muhammad founded Islam.	250–253	Islam was founded in Arabia by Muhammad through revelations received from Allah, the one God.	One day **More time?** Use *Overhead Transparency 27* or *Source Reading 14A.*
2 Muslim Arabs conquered a huge empire.	253–256	In the 100 years between Muhammad's return to Mecca in 632 and the Muslim defeat at Tours in 732, Islam spread from Spain to western India.	One day
3 Disputes over leadership troubled Islam.	257–259	Islam, like Christianity, was shaken by internal conflict and division.	One day **More time?** Use *Overhead Transparency 28.*
4 Turks and Mongols dominated the Muslim world.	260–263	Arab domination of the Islamic world gave way to Turko-Mongol control in the 11th , 12th, and 13th centuries.	One day **Less time?** Teach Section 4 and Section 5 together, using the maps on pages 261 and 264. **More time?** Use *Source Reading 14B.*
5 Muslims controlled India for centuries.	263–266	Between 1000 and the mid-18th century, India was largely under often harsh Afghan and Turko-Muslim control.	One day

ANCILLARIES

Materials that may be used with this chapter to reinforce, reteach, enrich, and assess learning are pictured on the following pages.

Teacher's Resource File

ACTIVITIES

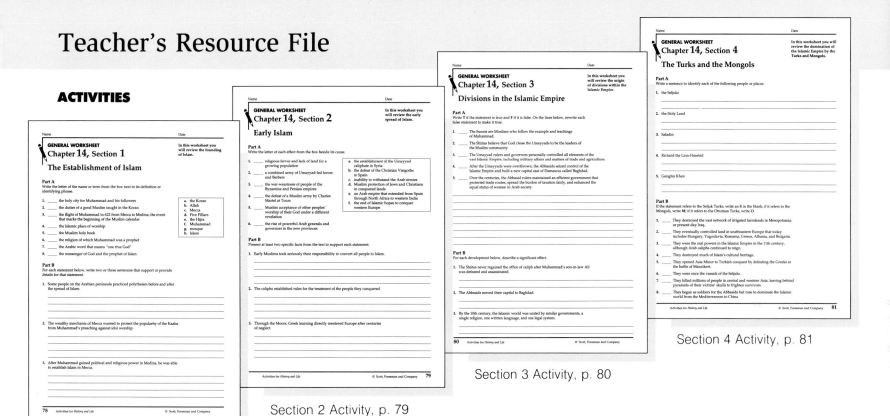

Part A
Write the letter of the name or term from the box next to its definition or identifying phrase.

1. _____ the holy city for Muhammad and his followers
2. _____ the duties of a good Muslim taught in the Koran
3. _____ the flight of Muhammad in 622 from Mecca to Medina; the event that marks the beginning of the Muslim calendar
4. _____ the Islamic place of worship
5. _____ the Muslim holy book
6. _____ the religion of which Muhammad was a prophet
7. _____ the Arabic word that means "one true God"
8. _____ the messenger of God and the prophet of Islam

a. the Koran
b. Allah
c. Mecca
d. Five Pillars
e. the Hijra
f. Muhammad
g. mosque
h. Islam

Part B
For each statement below, write two or three sentences that support or provide details for that statement.

1. Some people on the Arabian peninsula practiced polytheism before and after the spread of Islam.

2. The wealthy merchants of Mecca wanted to protect the popularity of the Kaaba from Muhammad's preaching against idol worship.

3. After Muhammad gained political and religious power in Medina, he was able to establish Islam in Mecca.

Section 1 Activity, p. 78

Part A
Write the letter of each effect from the box beside its cause.

1. _____ religious fervor and lack of land for a growing population
2. _____ a combined army of Umayyad-led forces and Berbers
3. _____ the war-weariness of people of the Byzantine and Persian empires
4. _____ the defeat of a Muslim army by Charles Martel at Tours
5. _____ Muslim acceptance of other peoples' worship of their God under a different revelation
6. _____ the rise of powerful Arab generals and governors in the new provinces

a. the establishment of the Umayyad caliphate in Syria
b. the defeat of the Christian Visigoths in Spain
c. inability to withstand the Arab armies
d. Muslim protection of Jews and Christians in conquered lands
e. an Arab empire that extended from Spain through North Africa to western India
f. the end of Islamic hopes to conquer western Europe

Part B
Present at least two specific facts from the text to support each statement.

1. Early Muslims took seriously their responsibility to convert all people to Islam.

2. The caliphs established rules for the treatment of the people they conquered.

3. Through the Moors, Greek learning directly reentered Europe after centuries of neglect.

Section 2 Activity, p. 79

GENERAL WORKSHEET
Chapter 14, Section 3
Divisions in the Islamic Empire
In this worksheet you will review the origin of divisions within the Islamic Empire.

Part A
Write T if the statement is true and F if it is false. On the lines below, rewrite each false statement to make it true.

1. _____ The Sunnis are Muslims who follow the example and teachings of Muhammad.
2. _____ The Shiites believe that God chose the Umayyads to be the leaders of the Muslim community.
3. _____ The Umayyad rulers and governors personally controlled all elements of the vast Islamic Empire, including military affairs and matters of trade and agriculture.
4. _____ After the Umayyads were overthrown, the Abbasids seized control of the Islamic Empire and built a new capital east of Damascus called Baghdad.
5. _____ Over the centuries, the Abbasid rulers maintained an efficient government that protected trade routes, spread the burden of taxation fairly, and enhanced the equal status of women in Arab society.

Part B
For each development below, describe a significant effect.

1. The Shiites never regained the office of caliph after Muhammad's son-in-law Ali was defeated and assassinated.

2. The Abbasids moved their capital to Baghdad.

3. By the 10th century, the Islamic world was united by similar governments, a single religion, one written language, and one legal system.

Section 3 Activity, p. 80

GENERAL WORKSHEET
Chapter 14, Section 4
The Turks and the Mongols
In this worksheet you will review the domination of the Islamic Empire by the Turks and Mongols.

Part A
Write a sentence to identify each of the following people or places.

1. the Seljuks

2. the Holy Land

3. Saladin

4. Richard the Lion-Hearted

5. Genghis Khan

Part B
If the statement refers to the Seljuk Turks, write an S in the blank; if it refers to the Mongols, write M; if it refers to the Ottoman Turks, write O.

1. _____ They destroyed the vast network of irrigated farmlands in Mesopotamia, or present-day Iraq.
2. _____ They eventually controlled land in southeastern Europe that today includes Hungary, Yugoslavia, Romania, Greece, Albania, and Bulgaria.
3. _____ They were the real powers in the Islamic Empire in the 11th century, although Arab caliphs continued to reign.
4. _____ They destroyed much of Islam's cultural heritage.
5. _____ They opened Asia Minor to Turkish conquest by defeating the Greeks at the battle of Manzikert.
6. _____ They were once the vassals of the Seljuks.
7. _____ They killed millions of people in central and western Asia, leaving behind pyramids of their victims' skulls to frighten survivors.
8. _____ They began as soldiers for the Abbasids but rose to dominate the Islamic world from the Mediterranean to China.

Section 4 Activity, p. 81

Part A
Use information from the text to complete each of the following sentences.

1. After being kept to the edge of the Indian subcontinent for 300 years, the Muslims began to invade India **because**

2. The Muslim invaders believed it was their duty to conquer and plunder India **because**

3. Although the Hindus had always managed to absorb those who had conquered them, they never absorbed the Muslim invaders **because**

4. Despite their harsh policies toward the Hindus, the Muslim rulers were not overthrown **because**

Part B
For each statement below, write two or three sentences that support or provide details for that statement.

1. The Muslims tried hard to convert the Hindus to Islam.

2. Several factors contributed to the Muslims' victory over the Hindus.

3. Tamerlane was one of history's cruelest conquerors.

Section 5 Activity, p. 82

RETEACHING ACTIVITY
Chapter 14
The Rise and Spread of Islam
In this worksheet you will review the key terms and main ideas of the rise and spread of Islam.

Part A
Write the letter of the name from the box next to its identifying phrase.

1. _____ Arabian city near the Red Sea where Muhammad was born
2. _____ the brutal Turko-Mongol invader who ravaged India
3. _____ the name of the caliphs of Islam who built their capital at Baghdad
4. _____ people of mixed Arab and Berber ancestry whose name describes a Muslim civilization in Spain
5. _____ the dynasty, based in Damascus, under which the Islamic Empire was born
6. _____ the Muslims who followed the Sunnah, the example and teachings of Muhammad
7. _____ the principal minister of the Seljuk sultan who took the throne for himself when the last Fatimid ruler died
8. _____ the city from which Muslims governed northern India and part of the Deccan region

a. Moors
b. Umayyad dynasty
c. Tamerlane
d. Sunnis
e. Mecca
f. Saladin
g. Abbasid dynasty
h. Delhi

Part B
Write T if the statement is true and F if it is false. On the lines below, rewrite each false statement to make it true.

1. _____ Islam is a monotheistic religion of which Muhammad was the prophet.
2. _____ The Arabs' need for land, the jihad, and the weakness of the neighboring Byzantine and Persian empires contributed to the early spread of Islam.
3. _____ After the Abbasids seized control of the Islamic Empire, they continued the Umayyad policy of treating non-Arab Muslims as second-class citizens.
4. _____ The later Abbasid rulers restored to Muslim women freedoms that had been lost under the Umayyad dynasty.
5. _____ The Mongols' destructive invasion of the Middle East was so extensive that parts of the region have not recovered to this day.
6. _____ The Muslim warrior tribes proved to be benevolent rulers of India and gradually were absorbed by the Hindu culture.

Chapter 14 Reteaching, p. 83

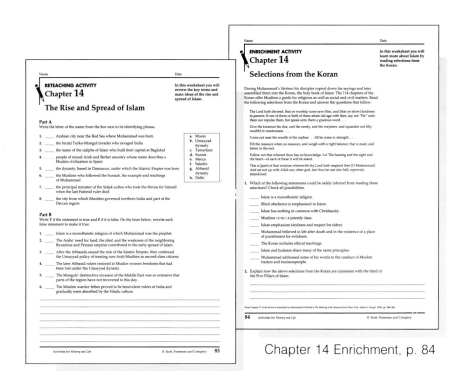

ENRICHMENT ACTIVITY
Chapter 14
Selections from the Koran
In this worksheet you will learn more about Islam by reading selections from the Koran.

During Muhammad's lifetime his disciples copied down his sayings and later assembled them into the Koran, the holy book of Islam. The 114 chapters of the Koran offer Muslims a guide for religious as well as social and civil matters. Read the following selections from the Koran and answer the questions that follow.

The Lord hath decreed, that ye worship none save Him, and [that ye show] kindness to parents. If one of them or both of them attain old age with thee, say not "Fie" unto them nor repulse them, but speak unto them a gracious word. . . .

Give the kinsman his due, and the needy, and the wayfarer, and squander not [thy wealth] in wantonness. . . .

Come not near the wealth of the orphan . . . till he come to strength. . . .

Fill the measure when ye measure, and weigh with a right balance; that is meet, and better in the end.

Follow not that whereof thou has no knowledge. Lo! The hearing and the sight and the heart—of each of these it will be asked.

This is [part] of that wisdom wherewith thy Lord hath inspired thee [O Muhammad]. And set not up with Allah any other god, lest thou be cast into hell, reproved, abandoned.

1. Which of the following statements could be safely inferred from reading these selections? Check all possibilities.
_____ Islam is a monotheistic religion.
_____ Blind obedience is emphasized in Islam.
_____ Islam has nothing in common with Christianity.
_____ Muslims revere a priestly class.
_____ Islam emphasizes kindness and respect for elders.
_____ Muhammad believed in life after death and in the existence of a place of punishment for evildoers.
_____ The Koran includes ethical teachings.
_____ Islam and Judaism share many of the same principles.
_____ Muhammad addressed some of his words to the conduct of Muslim traders and businesspeople.

2. Explain how the above selections from the Koran are consistent with the third of the Five Pillars of Islam.

Chapter 14 Enrichment, p. 84

Teacher's Resource File

GEOGRAPHY SKILLS

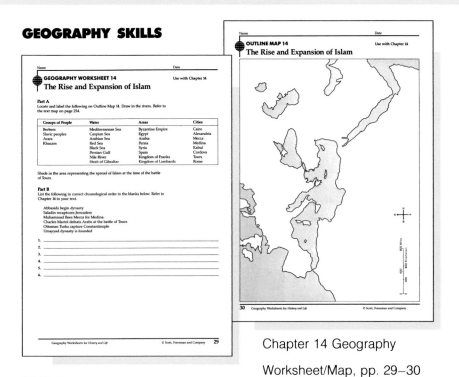

Chapter 14 Geography
Worksheet/Map, pp. 29–30

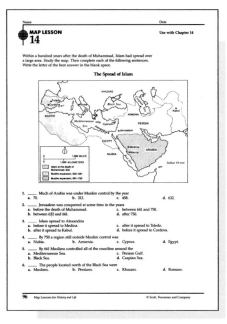

Chapter 14 Map Lesson, p. 96

TESTS

Chapter Test, pp. 65–66

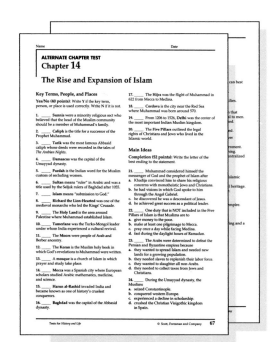

Alternate Chapter Test, pp. 67–68

Other Optional Ancillaries

WORKBOOK

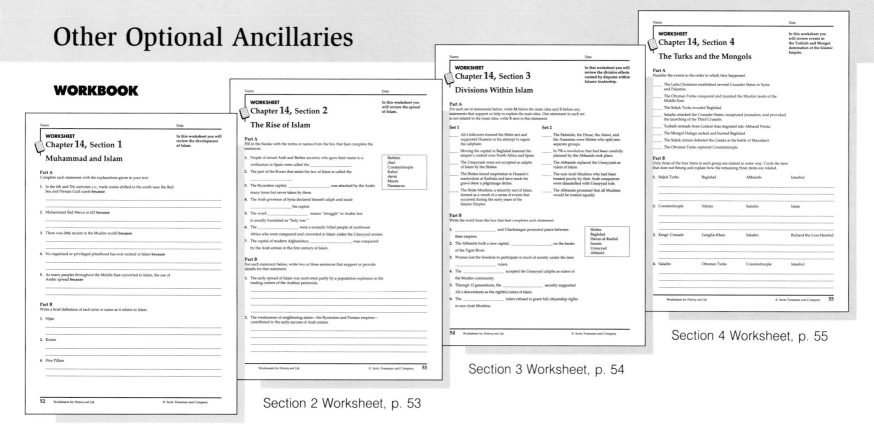

Section 1 Worksheet, p. 52

Section 2 Worksheet, p. 53

Section 3 Worksheet, p. 54

Section 4 Worksheet, p. 55

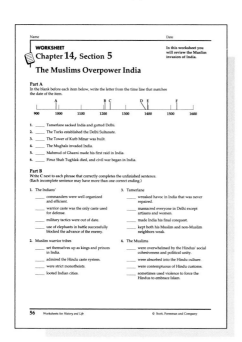

Section 5 Worksheet, p. 56

SOURCE READINGS

Source Reading 14A
Source Reading 14B

OVERHEAD TRANSPARENCIES

Overhead Transparency 27
Overhead Transparency 28

TEST GENERATOR

40 multiple-choice questions for Chapter 14

The Rise and Expansion of Islam

622–1526

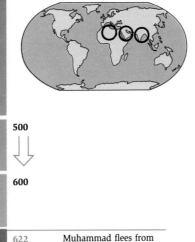

500	
600	
622	Muhammad flees from Mecca to Medina
1453	Ottoman Turks conquer Constantinople
1500	
1600	

A busy spider spun her silver web across the mouth of a cave that hid three men. When the captain of the pursuing war party neared the arch, he saw the web and called to his men. "No one has entered here. The web is as good as a seal. Search elsewhere." As their enemies rode away, Muhammad ibn Abdullah, his friend, Abu Bakr, and their guide wiped the sweat from their faces and said a prayer of thanksgiving for their tiny savior. Only when they were certain the men had gone did they lead their camels out. Although the city of Medina [mə dē′nə] was their destination, they rode off in the opposite direction, winding through the hot Arabian desert to throw the hunters off the trail. Ten days later the three tired men rode into Medina, their journey safely ended.

The year was 622, and the journey was the Hijra [hi′jər ə], the flight of the prophet of a new religion called Islam from his home in Mecca to Medina, 250 miles to the north. Islam spread quickly after that journey, first into the Arabian peninsula, then in all directions. Among the religions of the world today, only Christianity has more followers.

After Muhammad's death in 632, his Arab followers conquered huge territories beyond Arabia, including the great empire of Persia and parts of Byzantium, converting many people to Islam. The empire they established is known as the Islamic Empire. At its height, the Islamic Empire was larger than either the Byzantine or Roman empires had ever been. Within a hundred years of the Hijra, the empire included peoples of such diverse backgrounds as Egyptians, Persians, Turks, and Berbers.

Since there was no clear plan of succession to follow when the Prophet died, his close companions elected his friend Abu Bakr to be caliph [kā′lif], leader of the Muslims. Most of the community agreed with this choice, becoming known as Sunnis [sü nēz], those who follow the teachings of the Prophet. Some Muslims

وكـاد يـرع الـجمـال الـشمـر وانشـد
ما الحج يـزل ناوينا ولايا ولا لعـيا نـل اجمـا لا اجدلا

The joyful procession shown in this manuscript painting is the caravan of a wealthy woman who is making a pilgrimage to Mecca.

preferred to have Muhammad's son-in-law, Ali, as caliph. These dissenters formed a minority Islamic sect that opposed the new government and were called Shiites [shē īts], people who favor the house of the Prophet.

After the first four caliphs, the succession became hereditary. The early Arab rulers eventually gave way to Turks who had become Muslims. In some areas Turkish rule lasted for 900 years, from the 1100s to 1923. In addition, Muslim Turks and Afghans invaded India and ruled there for many centuries.

Reading Preview

In this chapter you will learn how Islamic civilization grew and spread.

1. *The Prophet Muhammad founded Islam.*

2. *Muslim Arabs conquered a huge empire.*

3. *Disputes over leadership troubled Islam.*

4. *Turks and Mongols dominated the Muslim world.*

5. *Muslims controlled India for centuries.*

249

Lesson Plan

Essential Learning Objectives

Students will learn to:
- locate selected Middle Eastern landforms and places.
- state basic Islamic beliefs and practices.

Have students turn to the maps of Asia on pages 794–795. On these contemporary maps, have students locate the Middle Eastern nations of Saudi Arabia and Iran (once Persia). Also have them locate the Red Sea, the Persian Gulf, and Mecca. Have students note that Saudi Arabia is on a huge peninsula—land that is surrounded by water on all sides but one. Ask why Europeans refer to this area as the Middle East. (From a European's point of view, it is not as distant as the Far East.)

2 TEACH

Review the story of how Muhammad became the prophet of Islam. Explain that Islam (meaning "submission to God") is the name of the religion and that a Muslim is a follower of Islam. Although Muhammad was regarded as an imposter and even the devil by many medieval Europeans, he may more properly be regarded as a reformer.

GUIDED PRACTICE

Write the following analytical categories on the board: 1. Name of religion; 2. Founder and date; 3. Holy book; 4. Monotheistic or polytheistic; 5. Basic tenets (Five Pillars); 6. Proscriptions (Don'ts); 7. Heaven and Hell; 8. Marriage; 9. Priesthood; 10. Worship (place and frequency);

---

1 *The Prophet Muhammad founded Islam.*

In early times tribes of Arab nomads called Bedouins, from the Arabic word for "desert dwellers," lived in the deserts of the Arabian peninsula. Their principal social unit was the clan, groups of related families, and their principal occupation was herding. They worshiped spirits that they believed lived in trees and rocks.

In the 6th and 7th centuries A.D., constant warfare between the Persians and Byzantines had interrupted commerce in the eastern Mediterranean. Trade routes shifted to the south, to prosperous trading cities near the Red Sea and Persian Gulf

---

Historic Calendars

A calendar is a system for keeping track of time. There are three main kinds—lunar, solar, and lunisolar. Lunar calendars are based on the 29½-day lunar month; 12 lunar months equal 354 days. A solar year is 365¼ days. Lunisolar calendars mark both lunar months and solar years. Special days and months are needed to keep all calendars accurate. Here are several historic calendars. Some have been in use for thousands of years.

Muslim This calendar is lunar, and days begin at sunset. Years are dated from Muhammad's Hijra. According to the Muslim calendar, we are now in the early 15th century. Since this calendar is lunar, the year is 354 days long, and New Year's Day moves back in time each year.

Gregorian This is the world's newest calendar, and the most widely used. It is now accepted almost everywhere for nonreligious purposes. A solar calendar, it is named for Pope Gregory XIII, who reformed the Julian calendar in 1582. Names of months are taken from the Julian calendar, and events are dated from the birth of Jesus.

Julian This calendar is based on the one devised by the Egyptians in 4236 B.C. (See Chapter 2). It is named for Julius Caesar, who introduced it into Rome. In the Middle Ages, the birth of Jesus was gradually established as the Year One. Russia used this calendar until 1918. By that date it was 13 days behind the Gregorian calendar, which is why the Soviet Union celebrates its "Great October Revolution" in November.

Jewish This lunisolar calendar was adapted from the Babylonians and is one of the world's oldest calendars still in use. The Jews were the first to establish the 7-day week with the Sabbath as a day of rest. Days begin at sunset, and events are dated from a day once calculated as being the day of Creation. The New Year—Rosh Hashanah—celebrates the birthday of the world. According to this calendar, we are in the mid-58th century.

Ancient Egyptian For thousands of years Egyptians used a lunar calendar, but they switched to a solar calendar in 4236 B.C. This date was Year One, so if we had continued the counting system begun by the Egyptians, this would be the 62nd century.

Chinese The Chinese and other Asians celebrate the New Year based on the traditional Chinese calendar. This lunisolar calendar dates from 2637 B.C. It follows a 60-year cycle, and each year is named after one of 12 animals: Rat, Ox, Tiger, Hare, Dragon, Snake, Horse, Sheep, Monkey, Fowl, Dog, and Pig.

Maya The Mayas were gifted astronomers (see Chapter 9) and developed one of the world's most accurate calendars. The solar year was divided into 18 months of 20 days each, with 5 "unlucky" days added at the end of each year to make 365. The Mayas also used a sacred calendar of 260 days to mark sacred events and ceremonies.

coasts. (See map, page 254.) Caravans traveling the trade routes that connected India and China with the Byzantine Empire, stopped at cities like **Mecca**, near the Red Sea. It was in Mecca that Muhammad was born around 570, and it was to Mecca that he returned triumphant in 630. Mecca became a holy city for **Muhammad**, the prophet of Islam, and for his followers.

Muhammad became the messenger of God and the prophet of Islam.

Muhammad's father died before he was born, and his mother died when he was six. Raised by his uncle, a respected Meccan merchant, the young Muhammad went to work for a wealthy widow named Khadija [kä dē′jə], who owned several caravans. Muhammad traveled with the caravans, seeing to the affairs of his employer. He met many people in his work, among them monotheistic Jews and Christians with whom he spoke about the concern of his heart, the oneness of God.

Khadija's respect and love for Muhammad grew until one day she asked him to marry her. She was 40 years old and Muhammad was 25. They were very happy together, eventually becoming the parents of four children. His marriage freed Muhammad from financial worries, but more important, it gave him the time he needed for meditation.

When Muhammad was about 40, he had visions in which God spoke to him through the Angel Gabriel. Muhammad was called to be the messenger or prophet of the one true God, named Allah in the Arabic language. According to his vision, although God had sent many messengers into the world, from Adam to Abraham to Moses to Jesus, Muhammad would be the last of them, the prophet of **Islam**, preaching submission to God. "Islam" means "submission to God."

As Muhammad's teachings became more widely known, the wealthy merchants who dominated Mecca feared that his preaching against idol worship would drive pilgrims away from the Kaaba. The Kaaba, a cube-shaped building in the middle of Mecca, housed a sacred black stone and the idols of several hundred tribal gods. Every year thousands of Arabs made pilgrimages to the Kaaba, contributing enormously to the income of local merchants. Suspicious that Muhammad was

BACKGROUND Arabic-speaking Christians and Jews also call God Allah.

Above is the Sacred Mosque of Mecca. Within its courtyard is the Kaaba, Islam's holiest shrine.

also trying to become ruler of Mecca, the Meccans began to persecute him and his few followers.

In 622, at the urging of the city of Medina, Muhammad left Mecca for the safety of Medina. (See map, page 254.) This journey, the **Hijra**, is so important to Muslims that it marks the beginning of the Muslim calendar, just as the birth of Jesus signals the beginning of the Christian calendar.

Muhammad was both political and religious leader in Medina. With converts from the surrounding Bedouin tribes, he formed an army and launched a successful campaign against his enemies. In 630 he returned to Mecca in triumph, purging the Kaaba of its idols and dedicating it to God. Before his death in 632, Muhammad saw Islam spread to most of Arabia.

Muhammad taught the Five Pillars of Islam.

The essence of Islam is contained in a single statement, "There is no God but God, and Muhammad is the messenger of God." Islam is a monotheistic religion like Judaism and Christianity and shares many of the same principles. Parts of the Old and New Testaments are revered by Muslims, and Christians and Jews are called "the Peoples of the Book," meaning they also have received a revelation from God.

God's revelations to Muhammad were written down in the **Koran**, the Muslim holy book. Because the Koran contains the inspired word of God, spoken to Muhammad in Arabic, Muslims insist that only the Arabic words of the Koran be used for the formal prayers of worship. Use of Arabic in prayer accounts for its spread to many areas of the Middle East.

11. Slavery; 12. Racism; 13. Status of women; 14. War. Working individually or in pairs, give students 15 minutes to take notes that address each category. Discussion should follow.

3 | ASSESS AND CLOSE

ASSESS

What are the Five Pillars? (Make the testimony of faith; pray five times daily; give money to the poor; fast during daylight hours of Ramadan, the holy month; and make a pilgrimage to Mecca at least once in a lifetime if able.)

OPTIONAL RETEACHING

An understanding of the section requires an understanding of key terms. Give students the following descriptive phrases and see how many they can identify with the appropriate term: 1. the holy city for Muslims (Mecca); 2. the prophet of Islam (Muhammad); 3. means "submission to God" (Islam); 4. Muhammad's flight from Mecca to Medina (Hijra); 5. the Muslim holy book (Koran); 6. the duties of a good Muslim (Five Pillars); 7. the churches of Islam (mosques).

OPTIONAL ENRICHMENT

1. Ask students to make a poster or bulletin board display comparing Buddha, Jesus, and Muhammad. Data could be gathered on the following: a. Birthplace; b. Birth date (estimates acceptable); c. Parents; d. Occupation before preaching; e. Basic teachings; f. Date and circumstances of death. (average)
2. Encourage enterprising students to conduct research on the life of Muhammad. Who was Muhammad? Was he well liked by those who knew him? What kind of person was he purported to be? (challenging)

3. Also for enrichment:

 Overhead Transparency 27

 Source Reading 14A

INDEPENDENT PRACTICE/ HOMEWORK

Assign the Section Review, Activities page 78, or Workbook page 52.

CLOSURE

Like Christianity before it, Islam did not arrive in a land that was without religion. It had to compete with other faiths—local polytheistic religions as well as Judaism and Christianity. As the next section describes, this competition led to conquest.

From the Archives

Allah the Creator

The Holy Koran, the sacred book of the Muslims, was revealed to Muhammad over a period of 22 years. It has 114 chapters, called surahs. The following verses describe the power of Allah as the creator of heaven and earth.

Allah is He Who raised the heavens without any pillars that you see, and He is firm in power and He made the sun and the moon subservient [to you]; each one pursues its course to an appointed time; He regulates the affair, making clear the signs that you may be certain of meeting your Lord.

And He it is Who spread the earth and made in it firm mountains and rivers, and of all fruits He has made in it two kinds; He makes the night cover the day; most surely there are signs in this for a people who reflect.

In a high garden
Where they hear no idle speech,
Wherein is a gushing spring,
Wherein are couches raised
And goblets set at hand
And cushions ranged
And silken carpets spread.

According to the Koran, those in hell will be:

Toiling, weary,
Scorched by burning fire,
Drinking from a boiling spring.
No food for them save the bitter thorn-fruit
Which doth not nourish nor release from hunger.

Islam unified various peoples into one civilization.

Because Muhammad taught that every believer is equal to every other believer, there was little racism in the Muslim world. Arab, African, Asian, and European converts mingled freely in the mosques and marketplaces. Christians and Jews who lived in Islamic communities paid a special tax and at times were forbidden to hold public office. However, at other times they might wield the power of adviser to the caliph, depending on his mood. The ancient Arab custom of slavery continued, with polytheists—those who worshiped many gods—the ones most frequently enslaved. One Muslim could not enslave another, however, and it was considered virtuous to free a slave. In practice, however, Arab rulers depended on large numbers of slaves.

Muslim women were equal to men in the sight of God, but within the social context of Arabia, it was a man's world. Muhammad limited men to four wives, an improvement over pre-Islamic times when there was no limit. Although Arab customs dictated that women's activities be restricted to the home, many Arab women were extremely influential in their communities. It was only necessary that a woman arrange for a man to act as her agent in public business. According to Islamic law, any property a woman inherited was hers to use or dispose of as she pleased. Moreover, a woman was absolute mistress of her home; a husband considered himself a guest in his wife's house.

No organized or privileged priesthood as such has ever existed in Islam, because Islam teaches

The Koran teaches the five duties of a good Muslim. These duties are called Islam's **Five Pillars**. The first and most important duty or pillar is to make the testimony of faith. To say, "There is no God but God, and Muhammad is the messenger of God," makes one a Muslim. The second duty is to pray five times daily, facing toward Mecca. Giving money to the poor is the third, and fasting during the daylight hours of Ramadan, the holy month, is the fourth duty. The fifth duty is to make a pilgrimage to Mecca at least once in one's lifetime if one is able. For those who cannot make the pilgrimage, it is enough to want to go.

In addition to describing what good Muslims ought to do, the Koran prohibits certain actions. Worshiping idols, eating pork, drinking liquor, and gambling are all strictly forbidden.

The Koran teaches about life after death. The faithful will be rewarded with the eternal joys of heaven, but the wicked are condemned to the fires of hell. The Koran says that believers will be:

FROM THE ARCHIVES The excerpt is from the Holy Qur'an (Flushing, New York: Tahrike Tarsile Quran), Surah XIII, verses 2–4, p. 227. The last line of this passage makes it emphatic that believers are to look for signs in the text. In this context, what are some synonyms for the word "signs"? (symbols, Divine manifestations, prophecies, omens, forewarnings, clues, signals, lessons, examples, etc.)

that no human can intervene between God and another person. There are learned teachers, called ulema [ü′lə mä], who explain religious doctrines and an imam [i mäm′], who leads group prayer, but there are no priests.

Saying the noon prayer together in the **mosque** [mosk] on Fridays, the holy day of Islam, is especially desirable. Mosques are the churches of Islam, a place of prayer and study. Some mosques are simple circles of stones, but others are immense open spaces within a walled enclosure, furnished with fountains and beautiful tiled walls. Most mosques have a minaret, a tower from which a muezzin [myü ez′n] makes the call to prayer five times a day. Today minarets have loudspeakers, but the call to prayer is still the same chant it was 1400 years ago:

> God is most great!
> I testify there is no God but God.
> I testify that Muhammad is the Messenger of God.
> Come to prayer;
> Come to salvation;
> God is most great!
> There is no God but God.

Section 1 Review

Identify Mecca, Muhammad, Islam, Hijra, Koran, Five Pillars, mosque

Main Ideas
1. How did Muhammad become the messenger of God? What was Muhammad's mission?
2. What are the Five Pillars of Islam?
3. What customs distinguish Islam from other religions?

Critical Thinking
Analyzing Comparisons: Compare and contrast the lives and teachings of the Buddha, Jesus, and Muhammad.

At right is Cairo's Mosque of Ibn Tulun, built around 876. The tower is a minaret from which the faithful are called to prayer five times a day. In the courtyard of the mosque is an enclosed fountain (far right) where Muslims cleanse themselves before prayer.

2 Muslim Arabs conquered a huge empire.

Muhammad was both a religious and political ruler of Medina, Mecca, and much of the Arabian peninsula. In this theocratic state, he governed according to the laws and values that became the *sharia*, the law of Islam. The *sharia* deals with all areas of life, including trade, inheritance, taxation, and such military matters as war plunder and prisoners. The Prophet controlled an army, negotiated

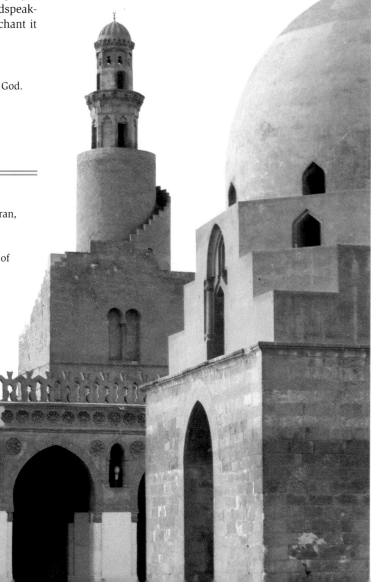

Briefly review these types of government: aristocracy, monarchy, oligarchy, plutocracy, democracy, theocracy. Emphasize that Muhammad did more than found a religion; he founded an Islamic-based theocracy. Muhammad was much more political than Jesus or Buddha.

- Before his death Muhammad commanded the spread of Islam. Ask students to turn to the map on page 254. Explain that Islam spread from Arabia to Spain in only 118 years. With the exception of Spain and Portugal, this territory remains heavily Islamic to this day. Ask students to use the Atlas to name as many modern nations as they can that were embraced by this Islamic revolution. (About 25 modern nations lie within this area.)

- Review the terms *sharia* and *jihad*. Elicit from the class that the *sharia* provided the legal framework for the Islamic Empire and was taken directly from the Koran. The *jihad* was the commandment from Muhammad himself to forcibly spread Islam among "pagans" and non-believers. Point out that in doing this Muslims were turning their backs on centuries of Arabic religious beliefs and practices.

Ask two map "experts" to step up to a wall map of the Middle East. Ask other volunteers to name places referred to in this section. The map experts should use the text map on page 254 to locate the places that they then point out on the wall map.

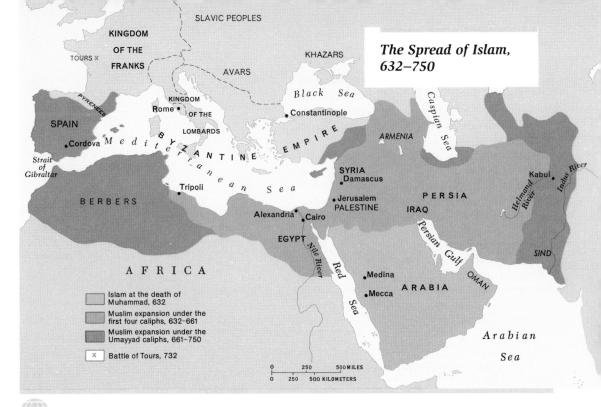

The Spread of Islam, 632–750

Legend:
- Islam at the death of Muhammad, 632
- Muslim expansion under the first four caliphs, 632–661
- Muslim expansion under the Umayyad caliphs, 661–750
- × Battle of Tours, 732

MAP STUDY This map shows the rapid spread of Islam from Arabia westward to Spain and eastward to India. How far did Islam extend at the time of Muhammad's death in 632?

peace treaties with surrounding peoples, and judged disputes according to the law of Islam.

In response to Muhammad's command to spread the faith, his successors led Arab armies in a series of conquests after his death. A growing population's need for new lands to settle spurred the Muslims on. Within 100 years of the Prophet's death, most of the peoples from Spain through North Africa to western India were living under Arab Muslim rule. The map on this page shows the rapid expansion of Islam.

The Arabs ruled many kinds of peoples.

When Muhammad died, Abu Bakr, his companion on the Hijra, was elected **caliph** [kā′lif], which means successor of the Prophet. Muslims swore obedience to the caliph because he upheld the Koran and the *sunna*, the teachings of the prophet. In continuing Muhammad's work of spreading the

faith, the caliphs pushed out into the areas surrounding Arabia.

The spread of Islam has been linked with *jihad*, an Arabic word which means "struggle," but which is usually translated "holy war." The early Muslims took very seriously their responsibility to convert everyone to Islam and considered the struggle to convert people a "holy war" against polytheists and those who had no faith at all. In modern times *jihad* has been distorted by certain Muslims who tend to call any religious or political movement a "holy war."

Religious fervor was only one reason for Arab expansion. Another reason was a population explosion. The Arabian deserts could not support large numbers of people, and when the prosperity of the caravan trade and the Meccan markets generated a population increase, an intolerable strain was put on the land's resources. New areas were

ANSWER TO MAP STUDY Arabia

needed for settlements and new peoples waited for the message of Islam. The Arabs turned to their immediate neighbors.

The weaknesses of their neighboring states—the Byzantine and Persian empires—contributed to the early success of Arab armies. The Byzantines and Persians had been fighting each other for centuries, and the conquered peoples in these two empires were tired of the warfare and heavy taxes. They put up little resistance to the Arabs, even welcoming them for the better government and treatment that was becoming the hallmark of Muslim rule.

One of the first places the Arabs attacked was Syria, at that time an important part of the Byzantine Empire. (See the map on the facing page.) Damascus, its capital, was easily conquered in 635, and from Syria the Arabs moved southward into Palestine and Egypt. From bases in the Nile River Valley they spread into North Africa, claiming the land for Islam. Trace their route on the map on the facing page.

Other Muslim armies moved northeast into the Persian Empire and conquered Iraq. They repeatedly defeated the Persian army, and within 10 years of Muhammad's death, they had destroyed the Persian Empire altogether.

The caliphs soon needed to establish rules for the treatment of conquered peoples. Those who fought back were treated more harshly than those who surrendered without bloodshed. Non-Arab polytheists were usually killed and their children enslaved because nothing was worse to a Muslim than the worship of many gods. Jews and Christians were given the choice of either becoming Muslims or paying special taxes. Muslims considered Jews and Christians misguided but protected them because they worshiped the same God under a different revelation. Muslim cities had large Jewish and Christian populations who paid their separate tax and who had to obey certain restrictions. As time passed, many Jews and Christians converted to Islam, even though non-Arabs were treated as second-class citizens. After the first 100 years of the empire, however, non-Arab Muslims assumed the same status as Arab Muslims when Muhammad's teaching of equality was gradually extended to all believers.

The Umayyad dynasty increased Arab lands.

The first four caliphs elected by the Muslims in Mecca had all been close companions of Muhammad. The expansion of Muslim territory, however, yielded a new kind of ruler. The Arab generals and governors of the new provinces had become more powerful than the caliphs in Mecca. In 661 the Arab governor of Syria declared himself caliph and made **Damascus** his capital. The new caliph founded the **Umayyad dynasty** [ū mī′yad] and a caliphate which lasted until 750. Under the Umayyad caliphs, the Islamic Empire was born.

As you read the following paragraphs, follow the action on the map on the facing page. Along the northwest coast of Africa, in modern Morocco, Algeria, and Tunisia, lived the Berbers, nomadic tribal peoples. Under Umayyad leadership, Arab armies moved into this area, conquered the Berbers, and converted them to Islam. Then, in 711 a combined army of Arabs and Berbers, led by the able Berber commander, **Tarik,** crossed the Strait of Gibraltar into Spain and crushed the Christian Visigothic kingdom there, establishing Muslim rule. The next step took the Muslim army across the Pyrenees [pir′ə nēz] Mountains that form the border between modern Spain and France.

The southwest area of France was a Christian land whose people feared a Muslim conquest. The Muslims pushed hard into their country, marching far into central France. In 732 the Frankish general Charles Martel, grandfather of Charlemagne, defeated the Muslims at Tours in a decisive victory. (Check the map to see how far north into Europe the Muslims went.) The battle of Tours is a landmark event, marking the end of Islamic hopes to conquer western Europe. Muslim rule in Spain, however, continued for more than 700 years.

The people of mixed Arab and Berber ancestry known as **Moors** gave their name to the Moorish civilization of Spain. During the late Middle Ages, Moorish Spain was an important influence on Christian scholarship.

During the golden age of Muslim culture, from 900 to 1100, European scholars went to the great cities of **Cordova** and Salamanca to learn Arabic mathematics, medicine, and science. There, too, they studied Arabic translations of Plato, Aristotle,

BACKGROUND Be sure students understand that Muslim and Arab are not interchangeable terms. Muslim refers to the followers of the Islamic religion. These followers live in all parts of the world today and come from all ethnic groups. Arab refers to a member of a Semitic people now widely scattered over northern Africa and southwestern and southern Asia. Some Arabs are Muslims; others are not. Also some Muslims are Arabs, and others are not.

ASSESS

1. What is a caliph? (a successor of the Prophet)
2. What battle marked the end of Islamic hopes to conquer western Europe? (Tours)

OPTIONAL RETEACHING

1. Review why it was possible for Islam to expand so far so fast. (simultaneous weakness of the Byzantine and Persian empires) Might there be other explanations? (Islam provided justification for conquest.)
2. Ask students to write the name of the modern country that they associate with each of the following:
1. Mecca; 2. Tours; 3. Moors;
4. Baghdad; 5. Constantinople;
6. Damascus.

OPTIONAL ENRICHMENT

1. Arabic calligraphy is among the most beautiful in the world. Ask interested students to photocopy or trace examples of this writing and show them to the class. Students should describe the Arabic lettering and its arrangement of consonants and vowels. (average)
2. Modern astronomy is a testimonial to the influence of Arabic astronomers during the centuries that followed Muhammad. Ask interested students to research this influence, with special attention to the many Arabic star names used in the Western world today. For example: Deneb, Aldebaran, Betelgeuse, Algol, Rigel. (challenging)

INDEPENDENT PRACTICE/ HOMEWORK

Assign the Section Review, Activities page 79, or Workbook page 53.

The speed with which Islam spread throughout the Middle East and North Africa was remarkable. As often happens in history, however, the growth of an empire would lead to problems of control and disputes over rule. These will be the focus of the next section.

Answers to Section 2 Review

Identify
Key Terms, People, and Places are defined on pages indicated in parentheses. Also see the Glossary and Biographical Dictionary.
caliph (254), Damascus (255), Umayyad dynasty (255), Tarik (255), Moors (255), Cordova (255)

Main Ideas
1. Religious fervor, population explosion, weak neighboring states; they were treated harshly if they resisted but benignly if they capitulated.
2. Charles Martel decisively defeated the Moors at the battle of Tours in 732.

Critical Thinking
Jews and Christians share with the Muslims the same God. Polytheism was highly objectionable to the monotheistic Muslims. Anyone resisting the armies of Islam was impeding the spread of the faith and should be punished.

---

and other classical Greek authors whose writings the Arabs had preserved. Through the Moors, Greek learning directly reentered Europe after centuries of neglect. Islamic influences, especially in art, architecture, and music, are still strong in modern-day Spain.

The farthest east the Islamic Empire extended was the region of Sind in present-day Pakistan. In the first century of Islam, Arab armies conquered Kabul, capital of modern Afghanistan, and then captured Sind. By 724 Arab governors ruled these regions directly as the caliph's representatives. The people were converted to Islam and remain Muslims to this day.

The Arabs repeatedly attacked Byzantium's capital, Constantinople. In the famous siege of 717–718, Constantinople successfully held off the Arab navy by stretching a huge chain across the narrow entrance to the harbor, the Golden Horn, as well as by using their deadly Greek fire, an inflammable liquid made from a secret formula. The Umayyads were never able to conquer the city.

For many centuries, the Pyrenees Mountains in the west and Constantinople in the east formed boundaries between Islam and Christendom. The Indus Valley separated the Islamic and Hindu worlds. By the end of Islam's first century, the Islamic Empire extended over vast numbers of peoples who represented many cultures, languages, and religions.

What's in a Name?

GIBRALTAR The Arabic word for mountain is *jebal*, which makes the towering rock at the southern tip of Spain *Jebal al-Tarik*, or Gibraltar, Tarik's mountain.

Section 2 Review

Identify caliph, Damascus, Ummayad dynasty, Tarik, Moors, Cordova

Main Ideas
1. Why did the Arabs expand their rule into Syria, Palestine, North Africa, and Persia? How did the Arabs treat conquered peoples?
2. Under the Umayyads, the Moors nearly conquered France. What prevented them from doing so?

Critical Thinking
Recognizing Values: Even when Jews and Christians refused to convert to Islam, the Muslims did not kill or enslave them, in contrast to their treatment of polytheists or those who resisted their armies. What factors might explain this different treatment?

A forest of columns (below) supports horseshoe arches, a characteristic of Muslim architecture, in the Great Mosque at Cordova, Spain. The silver coin (right) was minted by the first caliph of Spain.

3. Disputes over leadership troubled Islam.

Most Muslims accepted the Umayyad caliphs as rulers of the Islamic community and empire. As you learned earlier, these Muslims were called **Sunnis**, those who followed the *Sunna*, the example and teachings of Muhammad. Today 90 percent of the world's Muslims are Sunnis. In Iran and part of Iraq, however, **Shiites** are a majority. This division dates to the early days of Islam.

Shiites are a minority sect who follow Ali.

When the Umayyads became caliphs in Damascus, some Muslims refused to accept their rule. They believed that the ruler should be a member of Muhammad's family. The Umayyads had won power by claiming that the fourth caliph, Muhammad's son-in-law Ali, was a poor leader and defeating him in battle. Ali was assassinated, but his followers persisted, forming the Shiites.

The Shiites believe that God chose the Prophet's family to be the leaders of the Muslim community. This family included Ali, the son-in-law of Muhammad, his wife Fatima [fə tē′mə], Muhammad's daughter, and their two sons. After Ali's death the Shiites gathered around Ali's son, Hussein, and declared him their caliph. In 680, at the battle of Karbala [kar′bə lə] in present-day Iraq, the Umayyad caliphs defeated the rebels. Hussein was killed, and his severed head was sent to Damascus as a sign of victory.

Although defeated, the Shiites found inspiration in Hussein's martyrdom. They still mourn his death in passion plays that reenact Karbala, and at his grave there is a pilgrimage shrine.

Because Shiites never regained the office of caliph, Shia Islam attracted political dissidents who felt oppressed by the government. Shiites supported Ali's descendants secretly through 12 generations, and when the 12th Shia caliph, or imam, disappeared one day during prayers, they said he was deliberately hiding. Shiites believe he will return to this world when needed to lead his followers to victory.

Shiites believed other things that were at odds with mainstream Islam. For instance, they thought that Ali's descendants had divine power to guide people and interpret the Koran. As time went on, not all Shiites agreed with each other on these interpretations, nor on who were the rightful descendants of Ali. Thus the Shiites themselves split into several groups. The Fatimids, the Druse, the Alawi, and the Assassins are some of the best known. Their beliefs and ritual were often kept secret so that they could not easily be persecuted.

The Abbasids replaced the Umayyad rulers of Islam.

The vast Islamic Empire that the Umayyads conquered was difficult to rule. The Umayyad rulers and governors occupied themselves with military affairs, leaving matters of trade and agriculture to local officials. When Arab expansion ended, the armies became less important. What was needed then was a government that promoted trade and agriculture.

The people themselves were also ready for new rulers. The non-Arab Muslims who had been treated as second-class citizens by their Arab conquerors were profoundly dissatisfied. Many had adopted Islam in the hopes of being received as partners by their rulers, but the Umayyads maintained full control of every part of government.

A carefully orchestrated revolution took place in 750. After months of secret planning, protests, and even terrorist activities, the Umayyads were overthrown. New rulers called the Abbasids [ab′ə sidz] seized the empire and began the **Abbasid dynasty**. Like the Umayyads, the Abbasids were Sunni Muslim Arabs, but the Abbasids promised that all Muslims—Arabs and non-Arabs alike—would be treated as equals. Many non-Arabs were appointed to office in the new government.

The most famous Abbasid caliph was the 8th-century ruler **Harun al-Rashid** [hä run′ al ra-shēd′]. His deeds were recorded in the tales of *The Arabian Nights*, narrated by the slave Scheherazade. According to legend, she had to tell stories to a certain prince for a thousand and one nights or else lose her life. The tales included the popular "Aladdin and His Lamp" and "Ali Baba and the Forty Thieves."

Harun al-Rashid was a contemporary of Charlemagne and carried on a lively correspondence with

Essential Learning Objectives

Students will learn to:
- explain the difference between Sunni and Shiite Muslims.
- diagram the divisions of Islam.

1 FOCUS AND MOTIVATE

Using a wall map of the Middle East, point to Iran and Iraq. Explain that the most calamitous war of the 1980s (1980–1988) was waged between these two Islamic countries. Iran, for example, lost more men, and boys, than the United States lost in World War II. One factor in this dispute was the fact that Iran is about 93% Shiite and is a Shiite theocracy. Iraq, despite having a Shiite majority (55%), has Sunni leadership. Today's lesson examines some of these divisions within Islam.

2 TEACH

- Remind students that the Christian religion is not a single religion. Over the centuries it has split (Catholic and Protestant) and resplit (Protestant sects). Islam has undergone a similar transformation. Two major "splittings" are described in this section.

- Discuss the first split of Islam, the division into Sunni and Shiite sects. Emphasize the text explanation that this split occurred almost immediately after Muhammad's death and was the result of differing views about who should succeed Muhammad. The story of Hussein's martyrdom is to this day at the very heart of Shiite religious intensity. Note briefly that the Shiites have experienced further subsplits.

- Focus next on the Sunnis. In 661 the Sunnis organized under the Umayyad dynasty that lasted for 89 years. This dynasty was then driven west and replaced by another Sunni dynasty, the Abbasids. Explain to students that under Abbasid rule non-Arab Muslims were treated equally, a new capital was built in Baghdad, and over time Muslim women lost freedom of movement and were expected to wear the veil. Point out to students that in early Islam, women were not as secluded.

- Finally, have students refer to the map on page 259 to see how by around 1000 three Islamic groups—the Sunni Abbasids, the Sunni Umayyads, and the Shiite Fatimids—had divided power.

Finally, have students refer to the map on page 259

GUIDED PRACTICE

Ask students to create an "Islamic Religion Tree" with Muhammad at the trunk and branches that include: Sunni, Shiite, Umayyads, Abbasids, Druse, Fatimids, Alawi, and Assassins. Volunteers can put their diagrams on the chalkboard. Also for guided practice:

 Overhead Transparency 28

3 ASSESS AND CLOSE

ASSESS

1. What is the fundamental difference between Shiites and Sunnis? (Shiites follow Ali and Sunnis follow the *Sunnah,* the example and teachings of Muhammad.)
2. To what division of Islam did both Umayyads and Abbasids belong? (Sunni)

OPTIONAL RETEACHING

Write the following pairs of items on the chalkboard and ask students to state the relationship. 1. Muhammad and Ali; 2. Fatima and Ali; 3. Fatima

the Christian emperor. The two exchanged gifts to encourage peace between them. The emperor sent the caliph illuminated manuscripts and bales of furs. Harun al-Rashid sent Charlemagne fabrics, perfumes, and an elephant named Abu-Lababah, meaning "father of intelligence."

The Abbasids built a new capital east of Damascus called **Baghdad**. (See map, facing page.) Many trade routes crossed at Baghdad and fertile farmland surrounded the new capital, making it a desirable site. More than 100,000 workers labored more than four years on the banks of the Tigris River to create the great circular city and its glorious palace in the center.

The Abbasid rulers surrounded themselves with luxury, pomp, and a culture with strong Persian overtones. For the next 500 years, Baghdad would be an important world center of ideas, trade, and government.

The Abbasids gradually lost power.

Over the centuries, the Abbasid government slowly became corrupt as the luxury of their palaces and the indolence of riches distracted the caliphs from the business of the empire. Court standards of morality declined as many rulers concentrated exclusively on leading lives of pleasure. Throughout the empire, taxes rose to support the caliph's lavish court, but these taxes were not collected fairly. The caliphs did little to protect the trade routes from bandits or to ensure farmers a fair price for their produce. In short, they did not govern as rulers should.

The Abbasids were also responsible for a change in the status of women. During Umayyad rule and the early years of Abbasid rule, traditional Arab practices were followed. Women moved freely about their business and many upper-class women had political influence. Some were highly educated and respected for their poetry, musical talent, and storytelling. Others were accomplished artists and horsewomen. Women led armies and ruled over countries. Under the later Abbasids, however, the Persian custom of veiling women gradually became common. In the cities women were secluded in harems—rooms set aside for the exclusive use of women. These customs never took hold in the villages because there everyone was needed to

DAILY LIFE

Daily life in the Islamic Empire centered about Islam, as revealed in the Koran. For that reason, learning took place in mosque schools under Muslim religious teachers (far left). There students memorized verses and prayers from the Koran and learned Arabic, the language in which the Koran is written. Note the boy pulling a ceiling fan. The riders (near left) are pilgrims about to celebrate with feasting and gift-giving the end of the Hajj, or yearly pilgrimage to Mecca. "There is no God but Allah," their banners proclaim.

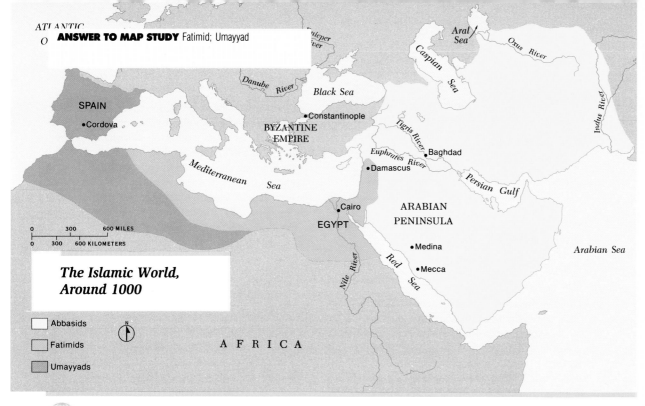

The Islamic World, Around 1000

- Abbasids
- Fatimids
- Umayyads

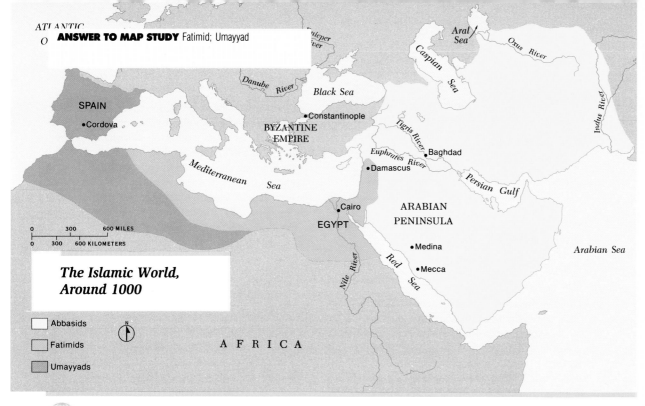

MAP STUDY In the year 1000, the Islamic world had cultural but not political unity. By that date the Abbasids had lost control of Syria, Palestine, and North Africa. Which dynasty ruled Egypt? Which ruled Spain?

work in the fields. No one could afford to keep half the able-bodied workers out of sight.

Moving the capital to Baghdad lessened the empire's control over North Africa and Spain. From 756 Umayyad descendants asserted their independence, especially in Spain, and in the early 900s, resistance movements began all over the Islamic Empire. The major unrest was in North Africa, where rulers called the Fatimids [fä′tə midz], who claimed descent from Muhammad's daughter, Fatima, drew Egypt and Tunisia away from direct allegiance to the Abbasids.

Refer now to the map above. You can see that by the 10th century, 300 years after its beginning, the world of Islam had experienced many political and religious divisions. Nevertheless, from Spain to Egypt, from Syria to India, people had essentially similar governments, a single religion—Islam, one written language—Arabic, and one legal

system. Despite periods of insecurity, important advances in culture, trade, and farming occurred under the Umayyad and Abbasid caliphates.

Section 3 Review

Identify Sunnis, Shiites, Abbasid dynasty, Harun al-Rashid, Baghdad

Main Ideas
1. What caused the split between the Sunnis and the Shiites?
2. Why did the Umayyads lose power? How did the role of women then change in Muslim society?
3. Why did the Abbasids gradually lose power?

Critical Thinking
Making Hypotheses: What important role did the Byzantine Empire play in Muslim efforts to conquer more Christian lands? (Review Chapter 13, for ideas.)

259

---

and Hussein; 4. Druse and Fatimids; 5. Sunni and Shiite; 6. Damascus and Baghdad; 7. al-Rashid and Charlemagne; 8. Spain and India (western and eastern extremes of Islamic Empire).

1. Ask interested students to peruse several stories in *The Arabian Nights* and read aloud a selection to the class. (average)
2. Ask volunteers to investigate the status of women today in Saudi Arabia. A good beginning is *National Geographic,* October, 1987. (challenging)

Assign the Section Review, Activities page 80, or Workbook page 54.

While a fact of Islamic history is its political and religious divisions, it is crucial to remember its unifying characteristics—a legal system based on the *sharia,* a common language (Arabic), and a commitment to the Five Pillars of Islam.

Answers to Section 3 Review

Identify
Key Terms, People, and Places are defined on pages indicated in parentheses. Also see the Glossary and Biographical Dictionary.
Sunnis (257), Shiites (257), Abbasid dynasty (257), Harun al-Rashid (257), Baghdad (258)

Main Ideas
1. The Shiites wanted Muhammad's descendants to be caliph.

2. Non-Arabs revolted to gain power; introduction of veiling and seclusion kept women from public life.
3. Their government became corrupted by luxury and indolence. They abused taxation, neglected the work of ruling, allowed banditry, and failed to protect the food supply.

Critical Thinking

It shielded eastern Europe from Islamic invasions for more than 700 years.

4 *Lesson Plan*

Essential Learning Objective

Students will learn to describe the contributions and the devastation brought to the Islamic Empire by the Turks, Christian Crusaders, and Mongols between A.D. 1000 and 1400.

1 FOCUS AND MOTIVATE

Write the words *Turks* and *Mongols* on the board. Ask students who these people were and where they came from. The Turks were not originally from the land we now call Turkey. Like the Mongols, they were a nomadic horse-raising people from Central Asia who lived, among other places, in Mongolia. In fact, some scholars believe that the Mongols once spoke Turkish. What is remarkable is that these two nomadic groups conquered much of the Islamic world, with the Mongols eventually terrorizing more than half of the known world.

2 TEACH

• Acknowledge to students that this period of Islamic history can be confusing. An image that may help is to

4 Turks and Mongols dominated the Muslim world.

About the year 1000, Turkish nomads from Central Asia migrated into Abbasid Persia. Seljuk, one of their chieftains who converted to Islam, led the tribes that became known as the Seljuk Turks. They served as soldiers for the Abbasids and were so powerful that before the end of the century they dominated the world of Islam from the Mediterranean to China.

Seljuk Turks ruled the empire during the crusades.

In 1055 the Seljuk Turks invaded Baghdad. At first they were only interested in warfare. However, the Seljuks appreciated the high level of Abbasid civilization, and under their patronage, Baghdad continued to be the center of eastern Muslim culture for another 200 years. The Seljuk rulers did not depose the Abbasid caliphs. Instead they took the title **sultan**, meaning "ruler" in Arabic. Although the caliphs continued to reign, the sultans were the real powers in the empire.

The Seljuk armies attacked Byzantine holdings in Asia Minor, dealing the Greeks a major defeat in 1071 at the battle of Manzikert. As a result, all of Asia Minor was opened to Turkish conquest. These Seljuk advances prompted the First Crusade. As you will recall from Chapter 11, both religious and economic reasons fueled the crusades. Christendom watched with dismay when Seljuk governors harassed pilgrims to the **Holy Land**, the parts of Palestine where Jesus lived and died. When Seljuk armies swept into the Byzantine Empire, the Byzantine emperor begged the pope and princes of western Christendom for help in recovering both the Holy Land and his lost provinces, promising to share with them the riches of Constantinople if the Crusader's Cross were not reward enough. He never dreamed that 200 years later crusaders would indeed "share" his city's wealth in their murderous sack of Constantinople.

The First Crusade was the most successful because the Seljuks were taken by surprise. By 1100 Latin Christians had established several Crusader States in Syria and Palestine.

Muslims were shocked by the barbaric conduct of the Christian conquerors, all of whom they called Franks since so many came from France. They watched the crusaders slaughter not only Muslims, but Jews and Arab Christians as well. Unable to understand Arabic, and convinced that everyone in sight was an enemy of Christ, the crusaders killed friend along with foe. The crusaders' eating habits, bathing customs, and medical practices especially disgusted the civilized Muslims. Over time some crusaders acquired some scientific and technological skills from Islam, as well as some food and clothing preferences. Eventually, they carried these discoveries back to Europe where they improved European culture.

By 1150, just as Islam began to rally against the invaders, the Seljuks fell to quarreling among themselves. The sultan's principal minister, known to the West as **Saladin** [säl'ə dən], waited through the dying days of the last Fatimid ruler, then seized the throne. One historian says that he "kept the sultan fully uninformed, that the wastrel might die in peace!" From his power base in Egypt, Saladin, one of history's most competent rulers, prepared to recover his land from the Europeans.

In 1187 Saladin attacked the Crusader States and recaptured Jerusalem. The stunned West then launched the Third Crusade, called the Kings' Crusade after the three famous medieval monarchs who led it: Frederick Barbarossa of Germany, **Richard the Lion-Hearted** of England, and Philip Augustus of France. Frederick drowned swimming a river in Asia Minor without ever setting foot in the Holy Land. Philip, furious that Richard refused to yield him the leadership of their combined forces, went home. Only Richard of England was left to uphold the honor of Christendom.

Saladin and Richard eventually signed a ten-year truce allowing pilgrims safe access to Jerusalem, a concession Saladin had been prepared to grant from the first, before all the bloodshed. By the time of his death in 1193 Saladin had nearly destroyed the Crusader States in the East.

Mongol invaders devastate the Islamic Empire.

In the mid-1200s, the Mongol Genghis Khan stormed into the Middle East, devastating lands

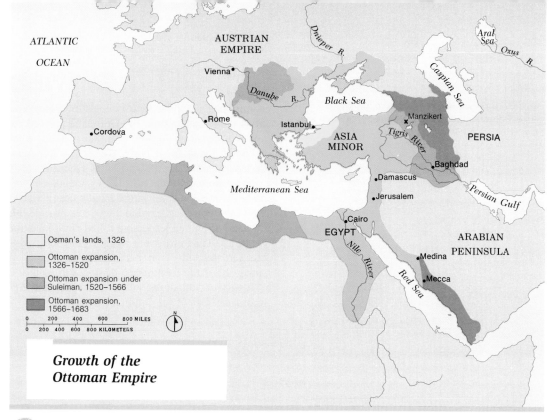

Growth of the Ottoman Empire

Osman's lands, 1326

Ottoman expansion, 1326–1520

Ottoman expansion under Suleiman, 1520–1566

Ottoman expansion, 1566–1683

0   200   400   600   800 MILES
0   200   400   600   800 KILOMETERS

MAP STUDY The Ottoman Empire grew from the lands controlled by Osman in 1326. What lands did Osman control in 1326? During which years did the Ottoman Empire make its greatest territorial gains?

think of the Islamic Empire in A.D. 1000 as a large and varied culture of reinforced sand castles surrounded by a vast sea. Periodically, that sea would well up, and waters would rush across Islam, settling in its valleys and towns. Some of its political structures, language, art forms, libraries and social customs would be eroded and smoothed, but eventually the waters would sink into the sand or evaporate and the fundamentals of Islamic culture would remain.

- In order, discuss the following ''waves'' that washed over the Islamic world: 1. the Seljuk Turks; 2. the European Christians of the First Crusade; 3. Saladin; 4. the Mongols. Ask students to give opinions on which had the most hurtful impact on the Islamic people and which had the most positive impact. Emphasize the barbarity of the First Crusaders who indiscriminately killed Muslims, Jews, and Christians when they conquered Jerusalem. Further emphasize that the horrors brought by the Mongols were even greater and extended fully across the Islamic Empire from India to eastern Europe. Just as important, Saladin is perhaps the greatest of all Muslim heroes. He is remembered both for his commitment to the faith and for his wisdom and kindness to all people, even Crusaders.

GUIDED PRACTICE

Write *Islam* on the board and ask students to free-associate words that come to mind as they contemplate the term. Write these on the board. Then underline factual terms, circle pejorative terms, and star complimentary words. What kind of picture emerges? Ask students if that picture is more or less positive than it would have been before beginning the chapter.

that have not recovered to this day. When Genghis Khan's grandson, Hulagu, sacked and burned Baghdad in 1258, more than 100,000 citizens and their caliph were massacred. The Muslim world was shattered. With the end of the Abbasid dynasty, there would never again be an Arab caliph.

Millions of people in central and western Asia were killed during the Mongol invasions, and pyramids of their victims' skulls were left behind to frighten those who survived. The Mongols destroyed mosques and libraries. They also destroyed the vast network of irrigated farmlands that had fed the population of Mesopotamia since the dawn of history. This region, present-day Iraq, only began to revive in this century.

When the Mongols rampaged through the Muslim world, much of Islam's cultural heritage was lost. A powerful mercenary army in Egypt, called the Mamluks, stopped the Mongols from advancing westward but they then turned back eastward to terrorize Iraq and Persia for many decades. Gradually, descendants of the Mongols became Muslims and were assimilated into the populations of Southwest Asia.

Ottoman Turks champion Islamic civilization.

The Muslim Turks in Egypt, Syria, and Asia Minor conserved many cultural achievements of the Islamic world. Once the vassals of the Seljuks, around 1300 the Ottoman Turks conquered lands in Asia Minor on the edge of the weakened Byzantine Empire. After repeated attacks, the Ottomans gained control of much of Asia Minor.

ANSWER TO MAP STUDY a small part of Asia Minor; between 1326 and 1520

ASSESS

1. Who was Saladin? (Seljuk leader responsible for nearly destroying the Crusader States in the East.)
2. From where did Turks originally come? (Central Asia)

OPTIONAL RETEACHING

Have the class create a time line on the chalkboard extending from 1000 to 1500, using events and dates mentioned in this section.

OPTIONAL ENRICHMENT

1. Do the Mongols deserve the reputation they have? Ask for volunteers to bring in descriptions of Mongol conduct during their years of conquest. (average)
2. Ask interested students to explore further why both Europeans and Muslims had high regard for Saladin. (challenging)
3. Also for enrichment:

 Source Reading 14B

INDEPENDENT PRACTICE/ HOMEWORK

Assign the Section Review, Activities page 81, or Workbook page 55.

CLOSURE

Islam withstood many blows between 1000 and 1400. Some were administered by Muslims themselves; others were inflicted by non-Islamic invaders. And yet, through it all, Islam survived.

The Ottoman Turks continued the artistic traditions of the regions they controlled. The manuscript below, which dates from the 1400s, shows Persian influence. It is an illustration from a Koran depicting a wedding procession. At bottom are two mosques built in Istanbul in the 1500s. Both use architectural forms developed by the Byzantines with the addition of the minarets.

In 1453 the Ottoman Turks did what the Arabs had tried to do for 750 years: they captured Constantinople. Stopping long enough to change the city's name to Istanbul, the Ottomans pressed on into southeastern Europe, eventually taking what is known today as Hungary, Yugoslavia, Romania, Greece, Albania, and Bulgaria.

The Ottomans then turned to conquer and reunite the Muslim lands of the Middle East. By 1500 they were poised to provide the Islamic world with the kind of unified leadership it had not known for centuries. They also were ready to threaten western Christendom as it had not been threatened since the Arab conquests of the 7th century. You will read about the military, political, and cultural successes of the Ottomans in Chapter 23.

Section 4 Review

Identify sultan, Holy Land, Saladin, Richard the Lion-Hearted

Main Ideas
1. What role did the Seljuk Turks play in defeating the crusades?
2. Describe the devastation of the Middle East at the hands of the Mongols.
3. How did the Ottoman Turks become the new champions of Islam after the destruction of the Abbasids?

Critical Thinking
Analyzing Comparisons: How was the Mongol invasion of the Middle East different from the invasion of the Seljuk Turks?

5 Muslims controlled India for centuries.

During the first century of the expansion of Islam, Arab Muslims reached as far east as the Indus Valley. The rulers of India stopped them in A.D. 711, holding them at the edge of the subcontinent for 300 years. Then, stimulated by the Turkish successes in the Middle East, Muslim forces renewed their attacks on India. About 1200 the Turks established the Delhi [del′ē] Sultanate, the most important power in India until the Mughal [mug′əl] invasion in 1526.

Muslim invaders entered India from Central Asia.

During the 10th, 11th, and 12th centuries, Muslim warrior tribes from present-day Afghanistan streamed through the passes of the Hindu Kush and invaded India. Some of the tribes were Afghans. Others were Turks from Central Asia.

Strict monotheists, these Muslim warriors were contemptuous of the Hindus, considering them idol worshipers and infidels, or unbelievers. Moreover, Muslim misunderstanding of the Hindu caste system was profound. Since Islam taught that all people were equal in the eyes of God, the apparent inequities of the caste system struck Muslims as

immoral. They believed that it was their duty to conquer India and plunder it as punishment for Indian arrogance.

At first the invaders came as thieves to loot the Indian cities and destroy Hindu temples and shrines. **Mahmud of Ghazni**, who made his first raid into India in 986, believed implicitly in his duty to kill Indians and his right to their treasure. He usually left his cool mountain country in the fall of the year, returning home with his plunder as the winter monsoons ended. In all, Mahmud made 17 raids in which he attacked many cities, fought terrible battles, massacred populations, and defeated Hindu armies.

Several factors led to the invaders' victories. First, Hindu military tactics were considerably out of date. Second, although the Hindus had huge armies, jealous commanders sabotaged each other's efforts to plan strategy and carry out a consistent defense. Third, the many elephants used by the Hindus usually bolted in panic once the fighting began, causing chaos and injury to Hindu and Muslim alike. Finally, the Hindus used only one warrior caste for defense. In Muslim society every man was a potential soldier.

Once it was clear how rich and weak India really was, Muslim leaders began setting themselves up as kings and princes. Between the years 1000 and 1500, they established many sultanates, that is, independent Muslim kingdoms in India.

The Delhi Sultanate was India's most powerful state.

The most important Muslim kingdom centered around the city of **Delhi**. From 1206 to 1526 much of northern India and part of the Deccan region were governed from Delhi. (See map, next page.)

The history of the Delhi Sultanate is not a pleasant one. Its rulers were an amazing mixture of opposite qualities—cruelty and harshness, but also generosity and a keen interest in learning and art. One sultan obtained his throne by murdering his father and killing the close relatives whom he regarded as rivals. It was said that at his door one could always see either some poor person on the way to wealth or on the way to execution.

Firuz Shah Tughlak [fē rüz′ shä′ təg lak′], was the most able Delhi sultan. He stopped the torture

- Briefly review the section, emphasizing that India was under varying degrees of foreign Muslim control from 1000 until the mid-1700s. This began in earnest with the first raid of Mahmud of Ghazni in 986.

- Divide the class into groups of four. Explain that each group will get an identical list of four statements. Their job is to understand each statement and discuss whether or not they agree with it. Students should make notes on their statement sheets. Full class discussion will follow. The statements are:

1. India must share the blame for Islam occupation. Weakness is as great a sin as bullying and conquest.

2. It's clear why the Hindus lost to the Muslims—elephants and caste.

3. Islam was theologically restrictive; Hinduism was socially restrictive. Neither would have been acceptable to anyone concerned with basic human freedom.

4. History books are like newspapers—they often give more coverage to the bad than to the good. Firuz Shah Tughlak, a good leader, gets only a few lines, and Mahmud of Ghazni and Tamerlane, two cruel leaders, get many more lines. This coverage should be reversed.

GUIDED PRACTICE

Have students cite reasons why the Muslim invaders were not absorbed into the Hindu culture.

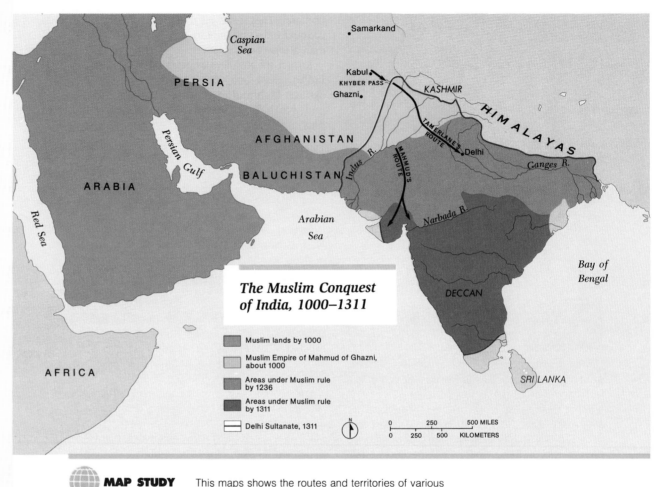

The Muslim Conquest of India, 1000–1311

- Muslim lands by 1000
- Muslim Empire of Mahmud of Ghazni, about 1000
- Areas under Muslim rule by 1236
- Areas under Muslim rule by 1311
- Delhi Sultanate, 1311

0   250   500 MILES
0   250   500   KILOMETERS

MAP STUDY This maps shows the routes and territories of various Muslim conquerors of India. Which empire controlled the most territory?

of criminals and built towns, dams, bridges, and hospitals. Although he had little use for Hinduism and destroyed some of its temples, his reign was prosperous and fairly peaceful. With his death in 1388 came civil war.

Ten years later the Turko-Mongol leader Timur, or **Tamerlane**, one of history's cruelest conquerors, invaded India. Although a Muslim, Tamerlane's general policy was to keep both his Muslim and non-Muslim neighbors weak compared to his own strong Central Asian empire. After destroying

all the territories and cities within a 500-mile radius of his Samarkand capital, Tamerlane turned toward Delhi.

In 1398 Tamerlane sacked and gutted Delhi, massacring everyone except the artisans and women who were carried off to Samarkand as slaves. It was said that "for two whole months not a bird moved a wing in the city." Tamerlane left India in 1399 and went on to ravage Turkey, Syria, and Iraq. The Delhi Sultanate slowly revived but regained little power.

ANSWER TO MAP STUDY the Delhi Sultanate

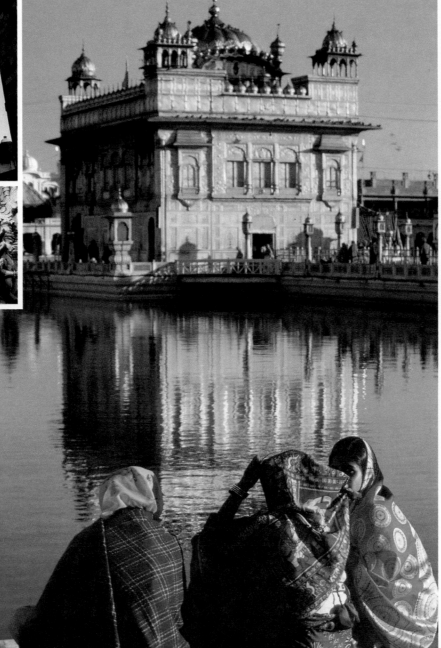

The tower (top left) is the minaret of the Kutb Minar, built in Delhi around 1200. Despite Muslim conquests, India still remains a land of varied religions. The many-armed god (bottom left) guards a Hindu temple. The Golden Temple (below) is the central shrine of the Sikh religion. Sikhism was founded in the 1400s by Guru Nanak to reform what he saw as problems in Hinduism. The Sikh religion is monotheistic, combining Hindu and Muslim elements.

3 | ASSESS AND CLOSE

ASSESS

1. Who was Tamerlane? (the Turko-Mongol leader who was one of history's cruelest conquerors)
2. Were the Muslims who conquered India after 1000, Arabs, Afghans, Turks, or Mongols? (all *except* Arabs)

OPTIONAL RETEACHING

Ask students to judge Muslim rule in India between 1000 and 1500. In terms of the well-being of the Indian people, was it positive or negative? Ask students to support positions with evidence from the text.

Students also may be assigned Activities reteaching page 83.

OPTIONAL ENRICHMENT

1. Has history been too harsh on Tamerlane? Ask interested students to investigate this Turko-Mongol ruler with an eye out for the positive side. (Note: Some sources may call him *Timur.*) (average)
2. The Islamic practice of purdah is found in Islamic nations today. For example, in northern Nigeria it is not unusual for a 14-year-old Muslim girl to get married and enter 20 or more years of virtual social seclusion in the compound of her husband. Invite interested students to research purdah as it is practiced in the Islamic world today. (challenging)
Students also may be assigned Activities enrichment page 84.

INDEPENDENT PRACTICE/ HOMEWORK

Assign the Section Review, the Chapter Review items, Activities page 82, or Workbook page 56.

Afghan and Turko-Mongol nomads carried Islam to the center of India during the century that followed Muhammad's death. Although the religion dominated India for 500 years, it was not embraced by most Indians.

Answers to Section 5 Review

Identify

Key Terms, People, and Places are defined on pages indicated in parentheses. Also see the Glossary and Biographical Dictionary. Mahmud of Ghazni (263), Delhi (263), Tamerlane (264), purdah (266)

Main Ideas

1. Muslim monotheists believed Hindu polytheists were infidels, who also should be punished for their caste system, a system contrary to Muhammad's teaching about human equality. Indian defenses were out of date and disorganized.
2. cruel, harsh, generous, art-loving. Tamerlane destroyed Delhi and the Delhi Sultanate.
3. They opposed the Hindu caste system and polytheism. Failing to convert the Hindus, the Muslims often treated them harshly.

Critical Thinking

Muslims perceived the caste system as essentially unfair because it started with the premise that everyone was not born equal. Hindus did not believe that equality was as important as escaping rebirth by fulfilling the duties of the caste into which one was born.

A Muslim minority harshly ruled the Hindu majority.

Until the Muslim invasions, the Hindus, like the Chinese, had always absorbed their invaders, who then took on an Indian aspect. During the Delhi Sultanate, however, there was very little mixing between the two peoples. The Muslims thought of themselves as superior human beings, and this attitude, together with the seclusion of Muslim women, forestalled any chance for alliances. Moreover, the Muslims ate meat, which disgusted the vegetarian Hindus. All in all, the Muslims created much bitterness with their brutal methods of conquest and their contempt for Hindu customs.

There was some contact between the two peoples, however. Some Hindus were employed as officials in the Muslim government, and others converted to Islam. Marriages between Muslim men and Hindu women, though not common, did take place. Various habits of living were exchanged. Some Hindus adopted the Muslim custom of secluding women, which they called **purdah** [per′də] in their own language, and copied Muslim dress styles. Nevertheless, since most Muslims lived in cities, their rule had little effect on village life. Hindu villagers continued the customs and ways of their ancestors in spite of the Muslims, a governing minority in a foreign land.

This dilemma of a minority head and a majority body continued to haunt the Muslims. The Koran clearly stated that it was the duty of a ruler to convert the infidel. The sultans in India, therefore, used violence, social pressure, and missionaries to force Hindus to embrace Islam, all without much success. Strict Muslims believed that Hindus who refused to convert should be killed, but the Muslim sultans knew that most of the taxes and all of the tribute paid to the government came from Hindu pockets. To have killed all the Hindus would have bankrupted the country.

How then, should India be governed? In the early 14th century, a sultan consulted a Muslim scholar. This good man suggested that the Hindus should be taught to revere their Muslim masters so deeply that they would eagerly offer their gold to their lords. The sultan replied:

Oh, doctor, thou art a learned man, but thou hast no experience; I am an unlettered man, but I have seen a great deal; be assured then that the Hindus will never become submissive and obedient till they are reduced to poverty [and so have no gold left to give up].

Many sultans followed this harsh policy. They were able to do so because they had strong armies and the Hindus were fragmented, with no political unity.

Not all the Muslim sultans in India were cruel and brutal. Some were just and able governors. A few were even considered the most effective of all Muslim rulers. Others were strong supporters of art, literature, and architecture. While they were in India, the Muslims created many beautiful buildings that blended both Indian and Islamic features. The arch, dome, and minaret were especially featured. One can see many fine examples of this cultural combination in India today. A famous minaret at Delhi, the Tower of Kutb Minar that dates from around 1230, is decorated with beautiful carvings and stands unrivaled anywhere in the Muslim world.

By 1500 the rulers of the Delhi Sultanate had become weak and divided. The havoc wreaked by Tamerlane was never repaired, and the new invaders that arrived in 1526—a group of Muslim Turks called Mughals—caught the ripe fruit that was India just as it was falling. The empire they would establish would be larger and more glorious than the Delhi Sultanate had ever been, even at its best.

Section 5 Review

Identify Mahmud of Ghazni, Delhi, Tamerlane, purdah

Main Ideas

1. How did the Muslims justify invading India? Why was it weak?
2. Name some of the qualities of the Delhi sultans. How did Tamerlane affect the Delhi Sultanate?
3. Why did the Muslim rulers treat the Hindus harshly?

Critical Thinking

Recognizing Values: The Muslim invaders of India thought the Hindu caste system defied the Islamic concept that everyone is equal before God. Review the caste system in Chapter 7. Explain how Muslims and Hindus could both be "right" on this sensitive issue.

HIGHLIGHTS OF CIVILIZATION

Islamic Calligraphy

To Muslims, the Koran is the word of God, as revealed to the Prophet Muhammad. Thus, Arabic, the language in which the Koran is written, is considered sacred. In the earliest days of Islamic civilization, there arose an honored tradition of copying inscriptions from the Koran. From this tradition came the art of

Islamic calligraphy—literally "beautiful writing."

Two distinct styles of script developed during different periods of Islamic history. The angular Kufic script was the earlier style, used from the 8th to the 11th century. The manuscript in the photograph, an excerpt from the Koran, was written in Kufic. A cursive script called thuluth [thü'ləth] was developed in the 13th century. In most parts of the Arabic world today, variations of the thuluth script are used for everyday writing.

Although each of these scripts has a vastly different feel to it, they both demonstrate a harmony between vertical and horizontal lines. Arabic writing lacks capital letters and has strict rules about which letters can be joined. These attributes produce a pleasing balance between curves and open space in each of the two scripts.

Islamic calligraphy ultimately became a form of art. Because Muhammad is said to have frowned upon representational art, writing became an important decorative element in painting, textiles, and architecture. As ornamentation, the Kufic script became so stylized that only a practiced eye could read many inscriptions. However, even when executed in stone, Islamic calligraphy had a graceful, flowing quality that influenced decorative arts from northern Europe to East Asia.

A rare copy of the Koran on colored vellum, or parchment (left), was made in North Africa about 900. Shown above are the inks and lettering tools used to create the elegant calligraphic styles.

HIGHLIGHTS OF CIVILIZATION

Calligraphic inscriptions were instructional as well as beautiful. For example, the phrase "Only Allah is the most powerful," was inscribed at the entrance to a spectacular palace. Ask students to infer the purpose of this inscription. (to remind the most powerful rulers that Allah was the true source of power in the world) Let them discuss whether such inscriptions would be effective.

Ask if any students have learned how to do calligraphy. Encourage such students to bring in samples of different scripts for the class to discuss techniques and aesthetics for different styles of calligraphy.

Answers to Test Yourself

Key Terms, People, and Places
The key terms, people, and places tested here were introduced in the chapter sections and reviewed in the Section Reviews. For definitions see the page references at the appropriate Section Reviews. Also see the Glossary and Biographical Dictionary.

Main Ideas
The main ideas tested here were introduced in the sections of this chapter and reviewed in the Section Reviews. For answers to these questions, see the appropriate Section Reviews.

Critical Thinking
1. The Damascene court probably became more ornate than the Meccan court. Lavish ceremonies would replace simple rituals. Bureaucratic government might become a possiblity. Heavily ornamented and jeweled clothing, preferably silk, would replace simple wool robes. Rich living would become a standard. The lives of upper-class women would be restricted.

2. Western Europe might well have fallen to Muslim rule, a Christian majority with a Muslim minority government, anticipating the Indian problem; as People of the Book, Christians would be better treated than the Hindus; more intermarriage, interaction, respect; the map of Europe would look very different, might not have countries as we know them, perhaps provinces of an Islamic Empire; no Crusades, no sack of Constantinople, no fall of Constantinople.

Section Summaries

Section 1
The Prophet Muhammad founded Islam.
During the 7th century A.D., an Arab named Muhammad founded the religion of Islam. In 622 Muhammad left Mecca for Medina in a journey known as the Hijra. He became the political and religious leader of Medina and conquered most of the Arabian peninsula. Muhammad's teachings were written down in the Koran, the Muslim revelation, which describes the religious duties of a good Muslim.

Section 2
Muslim Arabs conquered a huge empire.
Muhammad established a theocracy, using his revelation as the basis for all laws in the Muslim state. The caliphs who came after him continued to rule as heads of both the religion and the government. By 750 Muslim rule extended from Spain to India.

Section 3
Disputes over leadership troubled Islam.
Some Muslims, refusing to accept the Umayyads as caliphs, formed a splinter group called Shiites. In 750 another group, the Abbasids, overthrew the Umayyads. Although split by dissension and schisms, the Muslim world continued to be united by one religion, one written language, and one legal system.

Section 4
Turks and Mongols dominated the Muslim world.
In 1055 Seljuk Turks took over Baghdad and ruled as sultans, allowing Abbasid caliphs to continue in title only. The Mongols destroyed Baghdad in 1258, finishing the Abbasids. Ottoman Turks took over from their former lords, the Seljuks, and began to build an empire. In 1453 the Ottomans conquered Constantinople, ending the Byzantine Empire.

Section 5
Muslims controlled India for centuries.
Many Muslim invaders came into India in the 10th, 11th, and 12th centuries. Of the kingdoms they established in northern India, the Delhi Sultanate was the most powerful. In 1398 Tamerlane's army captured Delhi, killing most of the population. The sultanate was rebuilt, but its power was diminished. The Mughals destroyed the Delhi Sultanate in 1526.

Test Yourself

Key Terms, People, and Places
Identify the significance of each of the following:

Section 1
a. Mecca
b. Muhammad
c. Islam
d. Hijra
e. Koran
f. Five Pillars
g. mosque

Review Dates

622
Muhammad journeys from Mecca to Medina

750
Abbasids gain power

1192
Saladin defeats the soldiers of the Third Crusade

1258
Genghis Khan sacks Baghdad

1453
Ottoman Turks conquer Constantinople

600   800   1000   1200   1400   1600

Practicing Study and Research Skills

1. Gregorian
2. (a) Gregorian and Chinese
   (b) Gregorian and Muslim
   (c) Gregorian and Jewish
   (d) Gregorian
3. Muslim and Jewish

Linking Past and Present

Such stories are lively and imaginative and treat universal themes.

Learning History Through Maps

Appropriate outline maps in the Geography Skills book can be photocopied for use by students. Students' maps should reflect accurate knowledge of their selected countries.

Section 2
a. caliph
b. Damascus
c. Umayyad dynasty
d. Tarik
e. Moors
f. Cordova

Section 3
a. Sunnis
b. Shiites
c. Abbasid dynasty
d. Harun al-Rashid
e. Baghdad

Section 4
a. sultan
b. Holy Land
c. Saladin
d. Richard the Lion-Hearted

Section 5
a. Mahmud of Ghazni
b. Delhi
c. Tamerlane
d. purdah

Main Ideas

Section 1
1. What was Muhammad's mission?
2. What are the five major duties of a Muslim?
3. What are some specific customs pertaining to Islam?

Section 2
1. Why did the Arabs conquer Syria, Palestine, North Africa, and Persia?
2. Why did the Moors fail to conquer France?

Section 3
1. What caused the Shiite split from mainstream Islam?
2. Why did the Abbasids take over from the Umayyads? How did the Abbasids affect the lives of women?
3. Why did the Abbasids become weak?

Section 4
1. How did the West lose the Crusader States?
2. What did the Mongols do in the Middle East?
3. How did Ottoman Turks become a major power?

Section 5
1. How did the Muslims defend their invasions of India? List four weaknesses that led to India's defeat.
2. What were some of the contradictory characteristics of the Delhi sultans? How did Tamerlane treat Delhi?
3. How did the Muslim rulers treat the Hindus?

Critical Thinking

1. **Predicting Effects** Persian influence seems to have had the same effect on Islam that it had on Byzantium. Basing your answer on your knowledge of the changes in Byzantine ways after exposure to Persia, what can you predict about changes in Arab ways?

2. **Making Hypotheses** The Muslims attacked France at one of the few moments during the early Middle Ages when the Europeans had the ability to repulse them. Suppose Charles Martel had not been able to defeat the Muslims at Tours in 732. What difference might that have made to the history of western Europe?

Chapter Skills and Activities

Practicing Study and Research Skills

Analyzing Information

Many interesting facts can be learned through careful reading. For example, look at the Historic Calendars chart on page 250. This chart gives a great deal of information in a fairly small space. Read the chart and then answer the following questions:

1. Which calendar is used today almost everywhere for nonreligious purposes?
2. Which calendars would you expect to find in common use in (a) China, (b) Egypt (c) Israel (d) France?
3. For which two calendars does the day begin at sunset?

Linking Past and Present

Why have stories like "Aladdin and His Lamp" and "Ali Baba and the Forty Thieves" continued to be popular among children and adults more than 1,200 years after the rule of Harun al-Rashid?

Learning History Through Maps

Pick a country mentioned in this chapter, either by its ancient name or its modern one, for example, either Asia Minor or Turkey, and look for maps showing it at about 200-year intervals, beginning around 600 and ending in the present. Ask your teacher or librarian for an outline map of the area that includes your chosen country and make 8 copies. Trace the boundaries of your country at each period onto one of the outline maps. Make one for the present. Include any name changes. You will have a map history of one country, showing its changing boundaries for about 1,400 years.

CRITICAL THINKING QUESTION LEVEL 1. average; 2. challenging

Chapter

15 Islamic Civilization

OVERVIEW

Because of the impetus of the Islamic faith and the interconnections established and maintained by Muslim traders, Islamic civilization became one of history's largest and most influential empires.

PLANNING CHART

Section	Text Pages	Key Concept	Suggested Teaching Time
1 Religion and government encouraged prosperity.	271–274	Through the unifying effects of the Hajj and the Arabic language, Islamic rule spread and prosperity followed.	One day **More time?** Use *Source Reading 15A*. **Less time?** Sections 1 and 4 can be read aloud and highlighted in one session.
2 Vigorous trade spread Islamic culture.	274–277	During the 600 years of empire, traders did much to spread Islam and knit the empire together.	One day **More time?** Use *Overhead Transparency 29*.
3 Science and the arts flourished.	277–282	For nearly five centuries Islamic civilization was in the vanguard in the field of medicine, chemistry, physics, math, astronomy, literature, and the arts.	Two days **More time?** Use *Source Reading 15B*.
4 Islam spread to West Africa through trade.	283–284	West Africa and the Islamic world strongly influenced one another.	One day **More time?** Use *Overhead Transparency 30*.

ANCILLARIES

Materials that may be used with this chapter to reinforce, reteach, enrich, and assess learning are pictured on the following pages.

Teacher's Resource File

ACTIVITIES

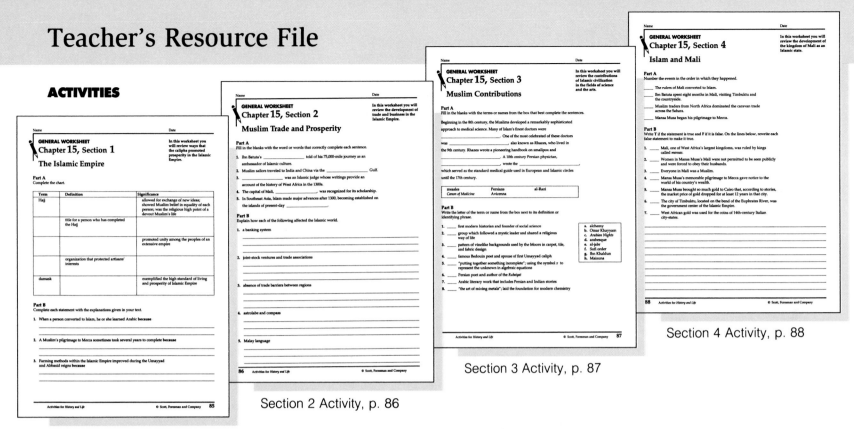

Section 1 Activity, p. 85

Section 2 Activity, p. 86

Section 3 Activity, p. 87

Section 4 Activity, p. 88

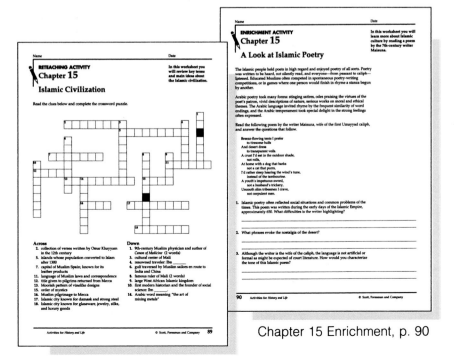

Chapter 15 Reteaching, p. 89

Chapter 15 Enrichment, p. 90

Teacher's Resource File

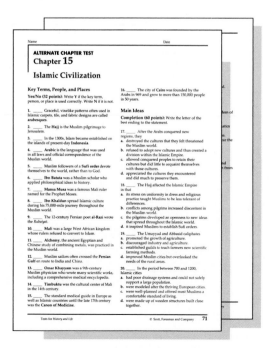

Chapter 15 Geography
Worksheet/Map, pp. 31–32

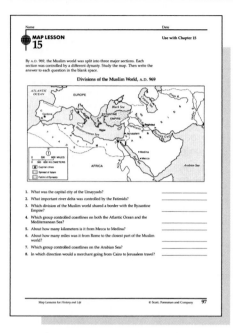

Chapter 15 Map Lesson, p. 97

TESTS

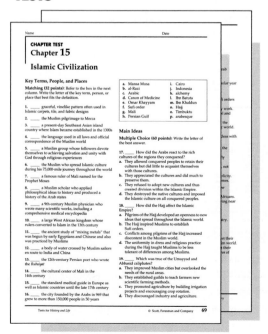

Chapter Test, pp. 69–70

Alternate Chapter Test, pp. 71–72

Other Optional Ancillaries

WORKBOOK

WORKSHEET

Chapter 15, Section 1

The Islamic Empire

In this worksheet you will review some aspects of life in the Islamic Empire.

Part A
Write a cause for each effect.

1. Arabic became the vernacular throughout the Middle East and North Africa.

2. Occasionally, kings gave up their rule after performing the Hajj.

3. The Hajj became an enormous school for the pilgrims.

4. In general, Muslims were a literate people.

5. Persian and Byzantine culture did not disappear upon conquest by the Arab armies.

Part B
Support each statement with examples from your text.

1. Most of the major cities of the Islamic Empire specialized in the manufacture of particular products.

2. People in the cities of the Islamic Empire enjoyed a standard of living higher than that of the Europeans of the same time period.

Worksheets for History and Life   © Scott, Foresman and Company   **57**

Section 1 Worksheet, p. 57

WORKSHEET

Chapter 15, Section 2

The Economy of the Islamic Empire

In this worksheet you will review the conditions that encouraged the growth of trade in the Islamic empire.

Part A
Complete each statement with the explanations given in your text.

1. Muslim joint-stock ventures encouraged the growth of business **because**

2. The spread of Islam to Southeast Asia suffered a major setback in 1571 **because**

3. Ibn Batuta's *Travels* may be regarded as an important historical source **because**

4. Ibn Batuta was able to find work wherever he went during his 75,000-mile journey **because**

5. During the 1300s Muslim merchants and navigators were important in spreading Islam **because**

Part B
Write C next to each phrase that correctly completes the unfinished sentence. (Each incomplete sentence may have more than one correct ending.)

1. Practices that encouraged the growth of trade in the Islamic Empire included
    ____ the absence of tariffs or import duties.
    ____ reliance on barter.
    ____ the formation of joint-stock ventures.
    ____ the development of a banking system.

2. Muslim sailors
    ____ sailed to India and China hundreds of years before Western Europeans.
    ____ used the compass and the astrolabe.
    ____ were unable to help the advance of Islam in Indonesia.
    ____ avoided the Persian Gulf and the Indian Ocean.

58   Worksheets for History and Life   © Scott, Foresman and Company

Section 2 Worksheet, p. 58

WORKSHEET

Chapter 15, Section 3

Muslim Science and Arts

In this worksheet you will review the contributions of Islamic civilization in the fields of science and literature.

Part A
Only three of the four items in each set are related in some way. Circle the one that does not belong and explain how the remaining three items are related.

1. Averroes   Maimonides   Aristotle   Avicenna

2. minarets   horseshoe arch   Ionic columns   arcade

3. Cordova   Baghdad   Damascus   Ibn Khaldun

4. arabesques   geometric patterns floral designs portraits

Part B
Give at least one example of a Muslim achievement in each of the following areas.

1. chemistry

2. optics

3. astronomy

4. literature

Worksheets for History and Life   © Scott, Foresman and Company   **59**

Section 3 Worksheet, p. 59

WORKSHEET

Chapter 15, Section 4

Islam and West Africa

In this worksheet you will review the impact of Islam on West Africa, particularly the kingdom of Mali.

Part A
Place the letter of the effect from the box next to its cause.

1. ____ existence of large gold deposits in West Africa
2. ____ 13th-century conversion of mansas to Islam
3. ____ Mansa Musa's pilgrimage to Mecca in 1324
4. ____ Mansa Musa's attempt to convert people to Islam by force

a. the threat of a strike by Mali miners
b. world notice of the wealth of Mali
c. the development of caravan trade routes across the Sahara
d. transformation of Mali into the center of Islamic culture in West Africa

Part B
Describe Mali life in the 14th century in each of the following areas.

1. role of women

2. laws and legal code

3. scholarship and education

60   Worksheets for History and Life   © Scott, Foresman and Company

Section 4 Worksheet, p. 60

SOURCE READINGS

Source Reading 15A
Source Reading 15B

TEST GENERATOR

40 multiple-choice questions for Chapter 15

OVERHEAD TRANSPARENCIES

Overhead Transparency 29
Overhead Transparency 30

Chapter

15

Islamic Civilization

700–1500

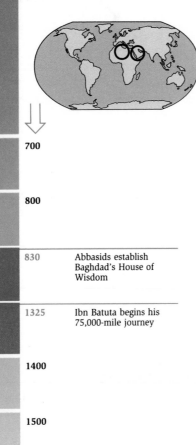

CHAPTER INTRODUCTION

Historians generally agree that the golden age of Islam was between A.D. 900 and 1100. The respect for learning shown by Harun al-Rashid in the story from the *Arabian Nights* is the same respect that helped the Islamic Empire to flourish.

LOCATOR GLOBE

Call students' attention to the globe, which indicates the general area of the world discussed in this chapter. (A detailed map appears on page 275.)

TIME LINE

How many years elapsed between the establishment of the House of Wisdom and Batuta's trip? (495 years) How does this compare with the years that have elapsed since Columbus first landed in the New World? (about the same number of years)

700

800

830   Abbasids establish Baghdad's House of Wisdom

1325   Ibn Batuta begins his 75,000-mile journey

1400

1500

There is a story in the *Arabian Nights* about a woman named Towaddud. She was the slave of a good, but very poor, master, Abdullah. In order to solve the problem of their poverty, Towaddud suggested that Abdullah sell her to the caliph, Harun al-Rashid, for 100,000 pieces of gold. Her master sadly agreed and together they went to the palace. Harun al-Rashid was amused by their suggestion. He asked why they thought she was worth such an enormous price. Towaddud replied that she could prove herself to be as wise and knowledgeable as all the caliph's most intelligent advisers. Her boast intrigued Harun al-Rashid, who promptly sent for the most learned scientists, teachers, and scholars of the land.

For days Towaddud was questioned by the learned men about every subject under the sun. They asked her first about the Koran, and then about grammar, poetry, history, mathematics, philosophy, astronomy, geography, law, and medicine. All were amazed to find that she could answer anything they asked. In addition, she was a talented musician and poet. She even defeated the chess master of the empire three times.

Impressed by her many talents, the caliph agreed to pay Towaddud's price. When he offered to grant her any favor she wished, she replied she wanted only to be restored to Abdullah. So Harun al-Rashid made him an official at the palace, and Towaddud and her master lived happily ever after.

The story of Towaddud's knowledge is obviously an exaggeration, but it was not unusual even for slave girls and boys to receive some education when the Islamic Empire was at the height of its culture, from 900 to 1100. Those 200 years are often called the golden age of Muslim learning. Throughout the Muslim world, scholars and artists made outstanding contributions in their many fields.

270

This gold-embroidered robe, worn by a Norman king of Sicily at his coronation in 1103, was made at a textile works established during Muslim rule.

Reading Preview

In this chapter you will learn about the brilliant legacy of Islamic culture.

1. *Religion and government encouraged prosperity.*
2. *Vigorous trade spread Islamic culture.*
3. *Science and the arts flourished.*
4. *Islam spread to West Africa through trade.*

 Religion and government encouraged prosperity.

The Islamic Empire lasted from the mid-600s to the mid-1200s, reaching its height between 900 and 1100. Religion and government in this empire were inseparable. During its early years the caliph was the head of both religion and government, and the Koran, the holy book, gave rules for both areas. The pilgrimage and various government activities brought many different people together to learn from each other. With the caliph's support, agriculture and industry grew, making the empire one of the most prosperous in history.

Arabs preserved the cultures of the peoples they conquered.

Often the Arab armies conquered regions where the armies and governments were weak but the peoples had rich cultures. For example, the Arabs conquered some of Persia and Byzantium's richest lands. These empires had well-planned towns with thriving markets, highly developed crafts, and productive farms. The Arabs, who had been desert-dwelling Bedouins before becoming conquerors, appreciated the cultures they encountered and did much to preserve them. As Arab civilization became more urbane, the Arabs translated many Greco-Roman classics into Arabic. They also trans-

 Lesson Plan

Essential Learning Objective

Students will learn to describe key attributes of Islamic culture during the prosperous years of the 10th and 11th centuries.

1 FOCUS AND MOTIVATE

Write the names of the following cities on the board: Denver, Miami, Seattle, Cleveland, Washington, Dallas, New Orleans, Phoenix. Ask students what they all have in common. (They all have smaller populations, not counting surrounding suburbs, than did Baghdad in A.D. 1000. Indeed, the largest, and perhaps most spectacular city in the world at this time was Baghdad, the hub of the Islamic Empire.)

2 TEACH

Divide students into pairs. Explain that many of the main points of Section 1 are included in 15 phrases, each drawn from the section. (See the list below. These phrases can be written on the board or typed on a handout.) Give the student pairs 15 minutes to write a sentence or two that explains the meaning or significance of each phrase. Discussion should follow.

1. ". . . [the] caliph was the head of both religion and government."
2. ". . . Arabs translated many Greco-Roman classics."
3. "Arabic was quickly adopted . . . as the vernacular."
4. "Cultural exchanges worked both ways."
5. ". . . the Hajj was the high point of a devout life."

271

6. ". . . king or farmer could hardly be distinguished for those ten days."
7. "They became known as Hajji . . ."
8. "The Hajj thus became an enormous school . . ."
9. ". . . ones of peace . . ."
10. "irrigation . . . crop rotation . . . fertilizer."
11. "ship of the desert"
12. "tempered steel and damask"
13. "860 licensed doctors"
14. "polo, chess . . . backgammon [and] frying pans."
15. "1,500 public baths"

GUIDED PRACTICE

After discussing the 15 phrases, ask students to take an analytical step back and, individually, write one or two sentences that generalize about Islamic culture in the 10th century. Share some of these statements. Next, ask if reading this section altered any stereotypes students had about the Islamic world.

lated the Persian and Indian classics, making them available to a much broader audience.

All the laws and official correspondence of the Muslim world were in **Arabic**, the language of the Arabs, even in areas where most of the people spoke Persian or Greek. Moreover, when a person converted to Islam, he or she learned Arabic in order to say the prayers and read the Koran. As a result of this exposure, Arabic was quickly adopted by peoples all over North Africa and the Middle East as the vernacular, or everyday language.

The spread of the Arabic language was one of the Arabs' most important contributions to the development of a high culture in the Muslim world. The curvilinear Arabic alphabet was also adopted by Persians, Turks, and some Sub-Saharan Africans for writing their own languages (for example, Hausa and Swahili).

Cultural exchanges worked both ways. A wide variety of people contributed to Islamic civilization, including many non-Arabs and non-Muslims.

According to Muslim belief, the Archangel Asrafil will sound the last trumpet on the Day of Judgment. This painting was probably made in Iraq around 1370.

Egyptians, Persians, Turks, Jews, Syrians, Christians, Greeks, Armenians, Indians, Berbers and other Africans—each group brought its special ideas, customs, and crafts to the Islamic world.

The pilgrimage encouraged the exchange of ideas.

Each Muslim tried to make the **Hajj**, the pilgrimage to Mecca, at least once in a lifetime. For a sincere Muslim, the Hajj was the high point of a devout life. When pilgrims set out from their homes, elaborate celebrations gave them a festive send-off. In those days such a journey to Mecca could take several years as pilgrims traveled over land and sea, on camels, donkeys, in tiny boats, or on foot. Some travelers never returned home. They either died on the way from the hardships of the journey, or they took up residence in the holy city to prepare for death. Muslims arrived in Mecca during the week set aside for the Hajj, the first ten days of the last month of the Muslim calendar. During that week Mecca was filled with hundreds of thousands of believers from all over the world. All the pilgrims, both men and women, were dressed exactly the same—in a seamless white cloth. Rich or poor, king or farmer could hardly be distinguished for those ten days. Everyone prayed at the same time and performed the rituals of the Hajj together. The modern pilgrim's experience is almost exactly like that of his or her ancestors.

The Hajj often inspired Muslims to reform their lives. Chiefs and kings were known to give up their rule after performing the Hajj, and even ordinary Muslims acknowledged the profound impression the Hajj made on them. Upon return from Mecca, Muslims received a special title of respect. They became known as Hajji [hä′jē], that is "Pilgrim," to all who knew them.

In the early days of Islam, Muslims exchanged ideas and compared differences and similarities with the people they met in Mecca. Pilgrims acquired a tolerance for these differences and developed an openness to new ideas that other people often lacked. These attitudes of acceptance became strengths in the Islamic world. When pilgrims returned home with new ideas and information, people in their communities listened because the Hajji spoke with the authority of one who had seen the

BACKGROUND The Arabic language and the Mecca pilgrimage were important factors in unifying peoples of different cultures.

Islamic artists made such items as the Persian vase (far left), the Turkish fabric (center), and the Egyptian pendant (above).

3 | ASSESS AND CLOSE

ASSESS

1. His name is Hajji Ali Danbatta. What do you know about him? (He had performed the Hajj.)
2. Would it be in the world's best interest if English became the vernacular for everyone? (Have students explain their opinions.)

OPTIONAL RETEACHING

Have students explain some of the agricultural or technological advances made under Islam. Suggested topics: Irrigation Systems, Crop Rotation, Steel Tempering, Glass-making.

OPTIONAL ENRICHMENT

1. Games similar to backgammon have a 5,000 year history. Encourage students new to the game to learn it. Classmates who know the game might assist. An after-school backgammon tournament might be held. (average)
2. Carpet weaving is one of the most fascinating and time-consuming crafts. Carpet makers can spend many years working on a single piece. Encourage interested students to research carpet-making techniques used in the Middle East and report back to the class. (challenging)
3. Also for enrichment:

 Source Reading 15A

INDEPENDENT PRACTICE/ HOMEWORK

Assign the Section Review, Activities page 85, or Workbook page 57.

CLOSURE

While Europe was passing through its Dark Ages, the Islamic Empire was in its fullest glory. In many ways, Islam carried the torch for world civilization during this period.

world. Moreover, after listening, people learned to integrate the new ideas into their own ways of thinking and doing. The Hajj thus became an enormous school through which general information was exchanged and disseminated throughout the Islamic Empire.

The caliphs improved farming methods and encouraged industry.

The centuries of the Umayyad and Abbasid reigns were generally ones of peace within the Islamic Empire. This peace allowed agriculture and trade to expand without disruption.

The caliphs built vast irrigation projects. They extended the canals of ancient Egypt, Mesopotamia, and Persia, and encouraged scientific farming methods such as crop rotation and the use of fertilizer. Wheat and other grains grew in the Nile Valley. Cotton, flax, and sugar cane were cultivated in North Africa; fruits, olives, and fine wines were produced in Spain. The arid regions of the Middle East and North Africa blossomed.

Stock breeding flourished in Asia Minor, Persia, and Syria. New varieties of sheep furnished raw material for fine woolen cloth. Arabian horses were bred for their speed and endurance. The camel, the "ship of the desert," became the chief means of land travel across the Sahara.

Industry centered around the major cities of the Islamic Empire, most of which specialized in the manufacture of particular products. Baghdad was noted for glassware, jewelry, silks, and luxury goods, and Cordova for its leather products. Damascus was likewise known for strong, tempered steel and damask—linen, silk, or cotton fabric that is decorated with a woven design that stands out from the surface.

Using the wool of sheep raised in Asia Minor, Persia, and Syria, workers made the beautiful, durable, hand-woven carpets known today as "Oriental" carpets. Arab and Persian artisans learned some of the secrets of Byzantine metalworking in gold, silver, and bronze. Papermaking was brought from China. Throughout the empire, Muslim workers, like their Christian counterparts, formed guilds. Within the guilds, members protected their interests, supervised the training of new artisans, and controlled the production and sale of goods.

273

Identify

Key Terms, People, and Places are defined on pages indicated in parentheses. Also see the Glossary and Biographical Dictionary. Arabic (272), Hajj (272), Cairo (274)

Main Ideas

1. The Arabs absorbed and preserved these cultures.
2. unification of the Islamic Empire and tolerance of new ideas
3. He encouraged irrigation, crop rotation, fertilization.
4. good planning; amenities such as fountains, libraries, markets, sewers, licensed doctors, bakeries, colleges, baths, fresh foods, new inventions

Critical Thinking

Arab culture, oriented to a desert world, was relatively simple and unsophisticated. The Arabs wanted the more complex elements of the lives of Persians, Byzantines, and southern Europeans—their urban sophistication, bureaucratic government, and engineering and architectural products. By willingly absorbing these elements, the Arabs achieved their own advanced civilization.

2 Lesson Plan

Essential Learning Objectives

Students will learn to:
- indicate on a map the area of the Islamic Empire.
- explain the role of coins, money changing, money lending, and checks in facilitating trade.

1 FOCUS AND MOTIVATE

Have students study the map on page 275. Give each student an outline

---

Cities enjoyed a high standard of living.

City life in the Islamic Empire in the period between 700 and 1200 was far more developed than in western Europe at that time. The heavily populated and well-planned Muslim towns had fountains, libraries, teeming markets, and efficient drainage systems, some of which still function today. In the year 1000, Baghdad, the capital of the empire, had a population of more than 1 million. **Cairo**, founded by the Arabs in 969, grew to more than 150,000 people in 50 years. These and other cities flourished in sharp contrast to the smaller, less healthy wooden towns and crude, cold stone castles surrounded by serfs' and peasants' huts in Europe at that time. In the year 1000, the European manorial economy could not support large urban centers, and only three or four European towns had reached a population of even 25,000.

The Islamic Empire's prosperous economy contributed directly to the good health of its citizens. As a result of extensive agriculture and irrigation projects, people could choose from a large variety of fruits and vegetables for their tables. The common people as well as the aristocracy enjoyed some leisure time. They often spent it listening to lute players or poetry recitations. Public coffeehouses and restaurants for men and special hours at the public baths for women were opportunities for meeting friends. At a time when many Europeans did not bathe once in a whole year, the city of Baghdad had 1,500 public baths.

Section 1 Review

Identify Arabic, Hajj, Cairo

Main Ideas

1. How did the conquering Arabs react to the more advanced cultures they met?
2. What was the result of exchanging ideas among the pilgrims of the Hajj?
3. What farming methods did the caliph improve?
4. What conditions contributed to the high standard of living in the cities?

Critical Thinking

Recognizing Values: Instead of destroying the cultures of conquered peoples, the Arabs accepted and preserved them. What value did the Arabs see in the civilizations they conquered?

BACKGROUND Point out to students that the trade routes to Italy concentrated on the prosperous northern Italian cities of Venice and Genoa and bypassed the less productive south. Students can find these routes on the map on p. 275.

---

2 Vigorous trade spread Islamic culture.

Unlike many Christians in western Europe in the Middle Ages, Muslims considered trading to be an honorable profession. Throughout the Islamic Empire, commerce was a bigger business than either industry or agriculture.

Many factors encouraged the business of trade.

Within the empire no trade barriers, such as taxes or import duties, existed between regions. In contrast to Europe, where most people depended on barter, in Islamic lands gold and silver coins were used in trade, and every market had its money-changer or moneylender. Business terms such as tariff, traffic, check, bazaar, and caravan came into the English language from Arabic.

A complex banking system developed in the Islamic world three centuries before it did in western Europe. Central banks were formed with branches in distant cities of the empire. The Muslims, as well as Greeks, Jews, Armenians, and other non-Muslims, used a variety of business and banking practices. Receipts, checks, and letters of credit were commonly employed in commercial transactions. A merchant who placed money in the care of a banker in Baghdad could therefore draw on that money from the banker's relative or employee when he arrived in Damascus or some other city far from his home bank.

Merchants and traders also developed joint-stock ventures and formed trade associations, early forms of modern capitalism. By using these devices, it became possible for several persons to pool their money and finance large trading expeditions. Since an expedition might take several years to send goods to markets in a distant country and return with the profits, no single member of the association would have been able to afford such a large, long-term expense alone.

Muslim trade spread culture to foreign lands.

Trade flourished far beyond the borders of the empire. China, India, Europe, Russia, and West, Cen-

Muslim Trade Routes, Around 1000

Areas of Muslim Influence
⊙ Leading Trade Centers
• Other Important Cities
━━ Chief Trade Routes
━━ Other Trade Routes

0   300   600 MILES
0   300   600 KILOMETERS

MAP STUDY Muslim overland routes extended as far east as China and as far southwest as Mali. How did traders reach East Africa and Southeast Asia?

tral, and East Africa were all trading partners with the Islamic Empire. To see this, study the map above. While daring traders opened up new overland routes to East Asia, Muslim sailors undertook sea voyages to India and China by way of the Red Sea, the **Persian Gulf**, and the Indian Ocean centuries before Western navigators discovered the Atlantic route around Africa to the East. Inventions such as the compass and the astrolabe, an instrument to identify latitude, helped sailors find their way.

Along with their goods, Muslim merchants carried their religion, spreading Islam to parts of East and West Africa, India, China, and Southeast Asia. In Southeast Asia Islam made major advances after 1300, becoming established on the islands of present-day **Indonesia**. Find Indonesia on the Atlas map of Asia on page 794. From the islands of Indonesia, traders carried the faith to the Philippines. This advance was halted, however, when the Span-

ish seized Manila in 1571 and introduced Christianity. The Malay language, written in Arabic script, came to be one of the most important vehicles for spreading Islamic literature and philosophy in Southeast Asia.

Ibn Batuta traveled throughout the Muslim world.

Perhaps no single person saw as much of the Muslim world as did **Ibn Batuta** [ib′ən bä tü′tä], whose travels were a symbol of the cultural unity of Islamic civilization. Ibn Batuta was born in Morocco, North Africa. (See the map above.) In 1325, when he was 21, he set out on the pilgrimage to Mecca. He was already well educated, having been trained as a judge in Islamic law, but by the time he reached Egypt, Ibn Batuta knew that he wanted to learn more about the peoples and places of the world. He was determined to travel, setting himself

ANSWER TO MAP STUDY They used sea routes.

map from the Geography Skills book on which to attempt to color by memory the area encompassed by the Islamic Empire in about A.D. 1000. The map should include areas in North Africa, southern Europe, and in the Middle East to the Indian border.

2 | TEACH

- Have students turn again to page 275 and compare their maps with the text map. Have students adjust their maps.

- Write these terms on the board: Coins, Moneychanger, Moneylender, and Check. Explain to students that each of these played an important role in the growth of trade in the Islamic Empire. Ask students to explain the function of each. Explanations might be as follows: *Coins:* Trading for money was a big improvement over barter. Coins were more portable, durable, and exchangable than, say, goats or cloth. *Moneychanger:* An exchanger of currencies. Coins in one currency can be bought with coins of another currency making foreign trade easier. *Moneylender:* One who lends money for a fee (interest). In 9th–13th century Europe, the Catholic Church declared usury—charging interest on loaned money—to be illegal. The commercial revolution and the trading success of the Islamic world soon changed the Church's thinking. Interest provided the incentive to make money available for business enterprises and trade. *Checks:* A way to buy something without barter or money, requiring a banking network in Islamic cities. Checks are a strong indicator of how interconnected the Islamic Empire had become.

GUIDED PRACTICE

Have students take out a sheet of blank paper. Using pencil, ask them to do a freehand map of the Islamic Empire in about A.D. 1000. Again have students compare their map with the text map on page 275, making any needed corrections. Also for guided practice:

 Overhead Transparency 29

3 ASSESS AND CLOSE

ASSESS
How did moneychanging boost Islamic trade? (permitted trade with other regions)

OPTIONAL RETEACHING
Review the travels of Ibn Batuta. Emphasize the extent of these travels. Finally, on their just-completed maps, have students use the text to draw in Batuta's travels. Their starting point can be Tangier.

OPTIONAL ENRICHMENT
1. Have an interested student demonstrate to the class how an astrolabe works, and why it was crucial to sailing on the open sea. (average)
2. Indonesia was the farthest eastern extension of Islam. Today it is about 90 percent Muslim. Encourage students to research how Islam was successfully carried more then 6,000 miles to Indonesia. (challenging)

INDEPENDENT PRACTICE/ HOMEWORK
Assign the Section Review, Activities page 86, or Workbook page 58.

CLOSURE
As of A.D. 1200, it is accurate to say that no civilization on earth, including the Roman or Chinese, had spread as far as Islam. Islam was carried largely on the backs, and in the hearts, of traders.

The Arabs were far-ranging sea traders, and the merchant-explorers who traveled eastward added to the store of geographic knowledge in the West. One of the oldest-known descriptions in the West of China is an Arab merchant's eyewitness account of his travels there in the mid-800s.

the rule "never to travel any road a second time."

Ibn Batuta journeyed through Egypt, Syria, Arabia, Iraq, and Persia. Locate these places on the map on page 275. Then he went down the East African coast, along southern Arabia, northward to the Black Sea, and finally to Central Asia and India. In Delhi he worked for several years as a judge for a Muslim sultan. In 1342 the sultan sent Ibn Batuta on an official mission to China. Travel was dangerous in those days, and it took Ibn Batuta several years to reach China. Robbery and shipwreck dogged his journey, pirates attacked his ship in the Indian Ocean, and all his notes and diaries were lost. Eventually, he arrived in China and discharged his mission for the sultan.

Ibn Batuta returned home to Morocco, but he was not yet content since he had not fulfilled his dream to visit every Muslim country in the world. He went next to Spain, then back to North Africa, journeying south across the Sahara to the Muslim country of Mali in 1352. His account of Mali, describing everything from the scholarship of the capital, Timbuktu, to the curious hippopotamuses in the Niger River, is one of the most valuable sources for the history of West Africa at that time. After traveling in West Africa, Ibn Batuta returned to Morocco to settle down and write his book *Travels.* Altogether he covered about 75,000 miles.

Ibn Batuta was able to travel so far because the Islamic world at that time was far-flung and peaceful. He could stop and work as a judge wherever he went because Islamic law was in use in most of the places he visited. Because he was considered a wise and religious man, he was received with respect. As he traveled, he both learned from others and taught them, too. In his journeys from China in the east to Mali in the west, Ibn Batuta served as an ambassador of Islamic culture.

Section 2 Review

Identify Persian Gulf, Indonesia, Ibn Batuta

Main Ideas

1. Which factors were especially encouraging to trade? Name three or more business practices that helped trade in the Islamic world trade.
2. Where did trade spread the Muslim religion and culture?
3. Why was Ibn Batuta able to travel so far and to find work wherever he went?

Critical Thinking

Making Hypotheses: Suppose a European scholar had traveled through Europe in 1300 the way Ibn Batuta traveled through the Muslim world. What obstacles would he or she probably meet?

| **3** | *Science and the arts flourished.* |

Before the time of Muhammad, the Arabs had little knowledge of the physical and natural sciences. Their desire for trade and their extensive travel, however, promoted a need for more understanding of mathematics and astronomy. The Umayyad and Abbasid rulers who followed the early Arabs were tolerant of new ideas. Early Abbasid caliphs encouraged scholarship and paid for the systematic translation of books. Scholars eagerly studied the science and philosophy of the Greeks, and the works of Aristotle, Euclid, Ptolemy, Archimedes, and Galen were translated into Arabic. Later, the people of Europe would rediscover these Greek classics in Muslim Spain and, during the crusades, in Syria and Palestine. In addition to preserving Greek knowledge, Arab and Persian scientists also contributed many discoveries and theories of their own. In medicine, mathematics, astronomy, chemistry, and physics, Muslim achievements were particularly noteworthy.

Muslim medical practices were the most advanced of the time.

Islamic medicine is perhaps the best known of the Muslim achievements. In fact, it was only a century ago that Western schools of medicine stopped including Islamic medical practices and textbooks as part of their requirements.

Well-equipped hospitals, usually associated with medical schools, were located in principal cities throughout the Islamic Empire. Much of the medical knowledge obtained from Greek works was transmitted by conquered Byzantine and Persian Christians. Some of the empire's finest doctors were Persians. Jews were also famed for their medical knowledge, and the brilliant Jewish philosopher and scientist, Moses Maimonides [mī mon′ə-dēs], was Saladin's personal physician.

At a time when superstition still hampered the practice of medicine in Europe, Muslim physicians throughout Spain, North Africa, and the Middle East developed cures based on careful observation of the patient, the symptoms, and the effects of treatment. Licensed physicians treated illnesses and performed delicate surgery. Pharmacies were common, and druggists had to pass an examination in order to practice.

Muhammad's directive that Muslims care for the poor and underprivileged inspired caliphs to provide medical services to rural areas. Caliphs also supported the licensing system that made medicine and health care so highly developed in the Muslim world. In the 8th century, Harun al-Rashid established a large hospital in Baghdad. The 12th-century Spanish traveler, Rabbi Benjamin of Tudela, described it in his journal:

> Here there are about 60 physicians' stores which are provided from the Caliph's house with drugs and whatever else may be required. Every sick man who comes is maintained at the Caliph's expense and is medically treated. . . . Money is given to those who have stayed in the hospices on their return to their homes. . . . All this the Caliph does out of charity to those who come to the city of Baghdad, whether they be sick or insane. The Caliph is a righteous man, and all his actions are for good.

Probably the greatest of all Muslim physicians was the 9th-century Persian, **al-Razi**, known in the West as Rhazes [rā′zēz]. He was the author of many scientific works, including a comprehensive medical encyclopedia and a pioneering handbook on smallpox and measles. Other Muslim doctors each is associated. (in order: chemistry, astronomy, architecture/art/weaving, math, philosophy, religion, literature)

Divide the class into five groups. Assign each group to a different area of Islamic/Arabic culture. These areas are:

1. Medicine
2. Science and Math
3. Arts and Literature
4. Philosophy
5. Architecture, City Planning, and Interior Design.

Explain to the students that they will have about 5 minutes to reread material in the section that relates to their subject. Then they will have an additional 15–20 minutes to prepare a 3–5 minute presentation for the class that includes:

1. A framework outline of their subject area that can easily be written on the board.
2. A summary of key ideas to be delivered orally and that follow the framework outline.
3. A closing comment that begins, "If you remember nothing else about (medicine), remember . . ."
4. Three objective quiz questions related to their presentation that can be answered with a word or phrase. This will be given directly to the teacher and not shared with the class.

If necessary, review with students a simple Roman numeral outline format. Encourage clarity, enthusiasm, and attention to both the significant and the interesting.

Islamic scholarship did much to increase medical knowledge. At left is a page showing surgical instruments from a medical text written around 1000. The pages with plants (below) are from a 14th-century pharmaceutical text translated from Greek. The diagram of the eye (bottom), from a 9th-century text, is the earliest-known work on the eye and its diseases.

advanced the treatment of eye diseases and developed an early method of vaccinating against smallpox. A 10th-century Persian physician, Avicenna [av'ə sen'ə], wrote the huge *Canon of Medicine*, which was the standard guide in European as well as Islamic medical circles until the late 17th century.

Muslim physicists founded the science of optics, the study of light. Al-Hazen [al hä'zen], a Persian who lived from 965 to 1039, challenged the Greek view that the eye sends rays to the object it sees. Al-Hazen said, correctly, that it was the other way around: one sees because the object sends rays of light to the eye.

Related to the field of medicine was the field of **alchemy** [al'kə mē], an Arabic word that means "the art of mixing metals." Alchemy was an ancient study that went back to early Egypt and early China. Alchemists worked with combining different metals to make stronger or more beautiful materials.

Muslim alchemists searched for a way to change less valuable metals such as lead into more precious ones such as gold. Although they were not successful, their experiments succeeded in perfecting ways of analyzing materials that became the basis of modern chemistry. For example, alchemists invented various methods of distillation and crystallization, which include melting, boiling, evaporating, and filtering. They also discovered new substances such as alum, borax, nitric and sulfuric acids, carbonate of soda, cream of tartar, antimony, and arsenic. The English words alcohol, borax, and alkali, for example, are derived from the Arabic *al-kuhl, buraq,* and *al-qili.*

Astronomy, mathematics, and literature advanced.

Because Muslims needed to know exactly what time it was in order to say the daily prayers and to begin and end the fast of Ramadan they developed a concern for accurate timekeeping. Pilgrims, traders, and sailors also needed good ways of finding directions. Arab travelers like Ibn Batuta provided geographers and mapmakers with a wealth of information. Building on the work of Ptolemy and other Greek scientists, Arab astronomers made more accurate measurements of the length of the solar year, calculated eclipses, and made atlases of the night sky. Today, we still use Arabic names for some of the brighter stars, such as Altair ("the Eagle") and Algol ("the Demon").

Calculations for determining the positions of the planets, distances across land, and complex calendars, as well as the requirements for an advanced Muslim banking system, gave rise to the need for better mathematics. Arab mathematicians improved upon Gupta Indian numerals and the decimal system, combined it with their knowledge of arithmetic, and launched modern mathematics.

The Arabs were the first people to use the symbol x to represent the unknown in solving algebraic equations. Arab mathematicians developed algebra, from Arabic *al-jabr* meaning "putting together something incomplete," establishing it as a major field of mathematics. Important advances were also made by Arab scholars in analytical geometry and trigonometry.

Throughout history, scholars, philosophers, and poets have found it difficult to earn a living from their work. Today, such people often teach to earn money and can only do their own work in their spare time. This was also true in past times, but often rulers or wealthy nobles and merchants who enjoyed music, books, and works of art provided scholars and artists with enough support that they could concentrate on their work. Those who give such financial support are called patrons.

The Umayyad caliphs were generous patrons of the arts and scholarship. They supported literature and poetry, and they encouraged people to write down the early nomadic poetry that was only an oral tradition until then. In 830 an Abbasid caliph established a House of Wisdom in Baghdad for the translation of the Greek, Persian, Hebrew, and Indian classics. Here also was housed a research library, a museum, and an academy where scholars taught students.

In pre-Islamic days, the poets of the nomadic Arab desert tribes had held positions of respect. They had been entertainers, historians, and mental record-keepers of political and judicial events. As a result, they often had major political influence.

During the early days of the Islamic Empire, Arab poets began to write down their poems, which sometimes reflected social situations and

GUIDED PRACTICE
Have student groups give their presentations. Their short outline frameworks can be put on the board before or during each presentation. Monitor time. At their desks, students should take notes, eventually building a complete outline of the section. Remember to collect quiz questions.

From the Archives

A Muslim Prayer

Rabiah al-Adawiyya, a saintly Muslim of the 9th century from Basra (now in Iraq), devoted her life to performing good works and writing prose and poetry in praise of Allah. The following poem shows the purity and depth of her religious commitment.

Stars are shining
the eyes of men are closed
kings have shut their doors
and every lover is alone with his beloved

and here am
I
my Lord
alone with Thee

---

problems. For example, Maisuna, a famous Bedouin poet who married the first Umayyad caliph, expressed what many of the Arabs must have felt after they left their life in the desert to settle and govern in Damascus:

A tent with rustling breezes cool
Delights me more than palace high,
And more the cloak of simple wool
Than robes in which I learned to sigh.

The people of the Muslim world enjoyed hearing poetry recited for much the same reason that Americans enjoy watching a movie—because it was good entertainment. The verses told a story and were often accompanied by music. People who could compose good poems and recite them well were famous and popular.

By the time of the Abbasid caliphs, Arabic poetry and literature were strongly influenced by Persian sources. The *Arabian Nights*, written in Arabic, includes many Persian and Indian stories. One of the most famous Persian poets was **Omar Khayyam** [ō′mär kī yäm′], who wrote the *Rubaiyat* [rü bī ät′] in the 12th century. Omar Khayyam's poems reflected the rich imagery found in much Islamic literature, as these lines from two verses in the *Rubaiyat* show:

A Book of Verses underneath the Bough,
A Jug of Wine, a Loaf of Bread—and Thou
   Beside me singing in the Wilderness—
Oh, Wilderness were Paradise enow!

The Moving Finger writes; and, having writ,
Moves on: nor all your Piety nor Wit
   Shall lure it back to cancel half a Line,
Nor all your Tears wash out a Word of it.

Sufi orders complemented philosophic scholarship.

With their interest in religious matters, Muslims considered it necessary for every scholar to know philosophy. Islamic thinkers like the physician Avicenna valued the works of Plato, Aristotle, and other Greek philosophers and compared their ideas to the teachings of Muhammad.

A century before Saint Thomas Aquinas attempted the reconciliation of the teachings of Aristotle with those of Christianity, Averroes [ə-ver′ō ēz′] brought the principles of Aristotle and the faith of Islam together. Averroes lived in Cordova, in Moorish Spain in the 12th century. He was the personal doctor of the caliph. His books on Aristotle's works were read in Arabic throughout Christendom long before the original Greek texts were available. Another important interpreter of Aristotle in the Islamic world was the 12th-century Jewish philosopher-scientist Moses Maimonides, whom you read about earlier. His most famous work, *Guide to the Perplexed,* written in Arabic, influenced Jewish, Christian, and Muslim thinkers in the centuries that followed.

Muslim scholars also wrote excellent histories and biographies. **Ibn Khaldun** [ib′ən kal dün′] of Tunis applied philosophical ideas to history. He produced a lengthy history of the Arab states, emphasizing Spain and North Africa. In this work he showed history as an evolutionary process in which societies and institutions change continually. Historical development depends on a number of things, according to Ibn Khaldun, including geography, climate, economics, and personalities, as well as moral and spiritual forces. Such ideas are not new today, but in Ibn Khaldun's time they

---

3   ASSESS AND CLOSE

ASSESS

1. What is the Arabic word for algebra? *(al-jabr)*
2. What was the House of Wisdom? (a place for translating Greek, Persian, Indian, and Hebrew classics, with a library, museum, and academy)

OPTIONAL RETEACHING

1. Following is a list of cultural achievements. Dictate these items to students and ask them to star those that existed in the Islamic Empire between A.D. 750 and 1500:
a. medical schools
b. licensed physicians
c. socialized medicine in Baghdad
d. alcohol
e. ability to accurately predict eclipses
f. alchemical success in changing lead to gold

were. Because of this attempt to see history in this broad, evolutionary way, Ibn Khaldun is often said to be the first modern historian and the founder of social science.

As learning, philosophy, and theology developed during the era of the Abbasids, some Muslims began to feel a need for a more personal and individual relationship with God. Rather than studying about God, they sought to bind themselves in union with God through mystical experiences. One of the earliest mystics was a woman, Rabiah [rä-bē′ə], who wrote exquisite poetry about the soul's desire for God. Rabiah so loved God that she wanted to throw fire into Paradise and water into Hell so that the distinctions between the two would disappear and it would be clear who worshiped God only from love, not out of fear of Hell or hope for Paradise.

Often such mystics renounced everyday life and withdrew into remote places much like monasteries. They wore rough wool clothing called *suf*, and when a group of followers gathered around a particularly inspiring teacher the religious way of life they shared became a **Sufi order**. Hundreds of Sufi orders have been formed throughout the Muslim world since the 9th century, and new ones still appear even today. Sufis devote themselves to achieving salvation and unity with God through religious experiences brought on by prayers, fasting, singing, and the practice of rituals unique to a particular order. One of the orders best known to Westerners uses a whirling dance full of symbolic gestures in its ritual. This order originated in Turkey under the leadership of a famous Sufi named Rumi and is called The Whirling Dervishes. The member of a Sufi order is called a *dervish* if the order has Turkish connections, and a *fakir* [fä-kēr′], if it is Arab-centered. Both words mean "very poor person" or "beggar," the state every Sufi should be in before God.

The charming balcony shown here is part of a Moorish-style house in Cordova, one of the most attractive cities of Muslim Spain. Note the lavish use of tiles, a style that the Spanish adapted from the Moors.

g. vaccination for smallpox
h. knowledge of trigonometry
i. knowledge of calculus
j. Arabic translations of Aristotle
k. Arabic translations of Thomas Jefferson
l. yogurt
m. charcoal cooking
n. government financial support for poets
o. whirling dervishes
(All of these could be found in the Islamic Empire *except* letters f, i, and k.)

2. Administer a 10- to 15-item quiz using the questions from the student presentations.

OPTIONAL ENRICHMENT

1. Encourage interested students to create a True/False/Insufficient Evidence quiz based upon material in the text. Ask them to write clear, concise statements that are based on main ideas. (average)

2. Encourage other students to prepare a 10- to 25-item multiple choice test. This test is more difficult to write because the test writer must create credible foils. As above, urge students to avoid trivia and ambiguity. (challenging)

3. Also for enrichment:

 Source Reading 15B

INDEPENDENT PRACTICE/ HOMEWORK

Assign the Section Review, Activities page 87, or Workbook page 59.

CLOSURE

It has been the tendency of Western nations to understate their debt to Islamic culture. Indeed, from our numbering system to our chemistry, and from our medicine to our business successes, we owe a tremendous debt to the Islamic world.

Architecture, planning, and engineering produced beautiful Muslim cities.

Although there were many large cities throughout the Islamic world, the majority of Arabs had originally lived in tents in the desert. As they conquered lands, they moved into houses, and they built mosques wherever they went. In the Byzantine territories they often built on the sites of Christian churches.

In time a distinctive Muslim style developed. This style used domes that had been used in Byzantine churches and added minarets from which the faithful were called to prayer. The arcade, the horseshoe arch, and the extensive use of colored tiles are other features of Muslim architecture.

Soon the caliphs and wealthy Muslim citizens began to build beautiful palaces and homes for themselves. Much care was taken to make whole cities attractive and convenient for everyone. Damascus, for example, had a city water supply that is still in use today. Baghdad, constructed in a perfect circle with the caliph's palace in the center, led the Muslim world in beauty, wealth, and public services.

Second only to Baghdad in splendor and comfort was Cordova, the capital of Muslim Spain. (See the map on page 275.) In the 11th century, Cordova had paved streets with street lights, hot and cold running water in some homes, 80,000 shops and perhaps as many as 3,000 mosques. It had 113,000 homes, many suburbs surrounding the city, and a population of around 500,000. There were schools and a university with a huge library. A bridge with 15 arches spanned the river that ran through town. The royal palace, with quarters for thousands of slaves and guards, was surrounded by gardens with rare fruit trees, shade trees, fountains, and flowers. Other lush gardens were located throughout the city.

An ordinary home in Cordova was located on a narrow, clean street. The wooden doors and windows of the house were usually shut to keep out street noise. Inside, a long archway led into a sunlit central courtyard. All the rooms of the house opened onto it. The tile floor was easy to keep clean. In the center, surrounded by lemon trees and flowers, was a large clay pot filled with cool water, with a pottery cup hanging from a thong tied to its handle.

In the far corner of the first floor was the kitchen. Bread baking in brick ovens and meat cooking over charcoal fires sent waves of delicious odors into the garden. A cooler room stored fruits, vegetables, milk, and yogurt. Colorful plates and dishes stood on pantry shelves. Upstairs, sleeping rooms opened onto a balcony overlooking the courtyard. Scattered about the floors of the bedrooms were feather mattresses made up with linen sheets, pillows, and intricately embroidered wool coverlets. Even today, many Arab Muslims prefer to sleep on mattresses on the floor rather than on bedsteads.

The Moors of Muslim Spain enjoyed rooms decorated with luxurious furnishings and elaborate patterns. Intricate geometric and floral designs and decorative Arabic script covered the surfaces of tiled mosaic walls and floors, giving homes a gardenlike feeling. The graceful vinelike patterns that often provide the background for larger motifs are called **arabesques** [ar′ ə besks′], a word that the French coined to mean "Arablike" because they are so universally used in carpet, tile, and fabric designs in the Islamic world. Many of these designs originated among the Turks and Persians. Various handicrafts, such as rug weaving, pottery making, and metalwork, showed exquisite workmanship, and these products also adorned the interiors of quite ordinary Moorish homes.

Section 3 Review

Identify al-Razi, alchemy, Omar Khayyam, Ibn Kaldun, Sufi order, arabesque

Main Ideas

1. List three or more practices that show the advanced level of Muslim medicine.
2. What advances did Muslims make in astronomy and mathematics?
3. How did philosophers in the Islamic world contribute to general knowledge? What qualities did the Sufis bring to balance philosophic scholarship?
4. How did the Muslims implement architecture, planning, and engineering in their cities?

Assessing Cause and Effect: What conditions hampered the spread of knowledge in western Europe but not in the Islamic world? (See page 196.)

MAP STUDY This Spanish map, made in 1347, shows Mansa Musa, the king of Mali, awaiting the arrival of an Arab trader. The Atlas Mountains are depicted as a rock wall.

1 | FOCUS AND MOTIVATE

Isaac Newton's laws of gravity state that two bodies exert a mutual gravitational pull on each other. Two cultures may also attract one another. This was certainly true between the Islamic world and Mansa Musa's Mali Empire.

2 | TEACH

Review the text material on Mansa Musa and elaborate on his pilgrimage to Mecca in the 1320s. Included in Musa's entourage were 60,000 people, 12,000 of whom were Musa's personal slaves. Musa was immediately preceded by 500 slaves each carrying a six-pound golden staff. (Note: Today the gold in one staff would bring about $40,000. Musa also had 80 camels each bearing 300 pounds of gold, a cargo worth about $2 million today.)

GUIDED PRACTICE

To say that two cultures have a kind of gravitational pull on each other is to say that they are interconnected. Several examples of these interconnections appear in the section. Ask students to state the interconnection of cultures with regard to:

1. Mansa Musa's name
2. Wangara (West African) gold and the Italian Renaissance
3. Wangara gold and Egyptian inflation
4. Mansa Musa and Ibn Batuta's trip to Mali 20 years after Musa's death.
Also for guided practice:

 Overhead Transparency 30

4 Islam spread to West Africa through trade.

In the early days of the Arab conquests, the Sahara was a huge barrier that even the conquering armies of Islam did not venture to cross. As Islam settled into a more peaceful era, however, traders and merchants traveled where soldiers had failed to go. Muslim traders were drawn south of the Sahara to West Africa by the large quantity of gold produced in West African mines. (See Chapter 18.) By the year 1000, West African markets were full of goods from the Islamic Empire and West African households were full of ideas about Islam, both spread by the Muslim merchants.

Traders buying gold from Mali brought Islam to the African kingdom.

Muslim traders from North Africa began to dominate the caravan trade across the Sahara in the 8th and 9th centuries. Attracted by Middle Eastern wares such as steel knives, bronze vessels, and luxury fabrics, West Africans eagerly traded their gold, ivory, and slaves for the foreign goods. Gradually, the Muslim traders began to convert the people to Islam, especially those who lived near the market towns. By the 11th century, these con-

ASSESS

1. When, where, and what did Mansa Musa rule? (14th century; Mali; a vast empire spread across West Africa)
2. Why is Timbuktu famous? (cultural center of Mali)

OPTIONAL RETEACHING

Tell students they have ten minutes to write one or two paragraphs about Timbuktu. Include information about location, administrative importance, glory years, women, law and order, and libraries.

Students also may be assigned Activities reteaching page 89.

OPTIONAL ENRICHMENT

Timbuktu today is a different place than it was 650 years ago. Ask an enterprising student to research the current population and economic health of the city and report back to the class. (average)

Students also may be assigned Activities enrichment page 90.

INDEPENDENT PRACTICE/ HOMEWORK

Assign the Section Review, the Chapter Review items, Activities page 88, or Workbook page 60.

CLOSURE

Emphasize to students that Islam is presently the fastest growing religion in the world, a fact that may well have widespread ramifications for a number of presently non-Islamic cultures.

Answers to Section 4 Review

Identify
Key Terms, People, and Places are defined on pages indicated in

verted West Africans began to demand that their own governments reflect Islamic law and values.

In the 13th century, the rulers of **Mali**, one of West Africa's largest kingdoms, converted to Islam. The kings of Mali were called *mansas*. **Mansa Musa**, one of Mali's most famous rulers, was named for the Prophet Moses, *Musa* in Arabic. His domain was a vast empire that spread across West Africa from the Gambia River to the great bend of the Niger River. Mali soon became a center of Islamic learning and culture in West Africa.

Not everyone in Mali was a Muslim. Side by side with Islamic elements, sturdy strains of non-Islamic culture existed in such spheres as architecture and literature. Most of the common people of Mali, especially those in the rural areas, remained attached to their non-Islamic religions and customs. The record shows that Mali gold miners once threatened to strike when Mansa Musa attempted to convert them to Islam by force. Since most of the townspeople and merchants were Muslim, however, the mansas of Mali tried to incorporate at least some Islamic law into their rule.

Mansa Musa's kingdom was immensely rich because it controlled some of the richest gold mines then known at the time. Mali supplied gold to the Islamic cities of the Middle East and North Africa. It also supplied gold to Europe, though many Europeans did not know that the gold was coming from Mali. Conveyed from trader to merchant to customer, its origins were obscured. We know now that West African gold was used in the 14th century for the coins of the Italian Renaissance city-states and principalities.

In 1324 Mansa Musa set out on his pilgrimage to Mecca. It was an amazing journey. Records tell of thousands of servants, gifts of gold and ivory, and a cavalcade of camels, horses, and slaves. When this caravan reached Cairo in Egypt, it brought so much gold, spent so much of it, and gave so much to the poor that the market price of gold in Cairo dropped for at least 12 years.

Timbuktu became a center of Islamic culture.

The city of **Timbuktu**, located on the bend of the Niger River, was the cultural center of Mali. Conversion to Islam had introduced Mali's kings to Ar-

abic, and large collections of Arabic literature were stored in a huge library in Timbuktu. When Mansa Musa's pilgrimage served notice to the world of the wealth of his country, many learned Muslims and just curious travelers flocked to Timbuktu to see for themselves the wonders of Mali. Students from all over the Muslim world came to study with the scholars of Timbuktu.

The globe-trotting Ibn Batuta spent eight months in Mali during 1352, visiting Timbuktu and the countryside. He found a people with a strong sense of justice. Wrongdoers were quickly punished, and both the city streets and the countryside were safer than they were in any other place he had noted in his wide travels. He also wrote about the women of Mali. Unlike most countries in the Muslim world, women in Mali were not kept out of public sight and were not required to obey their husbands. Some of the women he met were very well educated. Ibn Batuta was impressed by the scholarship, wealth, comfortable living, and amount of trade he saw in Mali.

Mali is an important example of how far the influence and culture of Islam was spread through the world by peaceful means—through trade, learning, and gradual conversion rather than by conquest. Nor is Islam's appeal limited to past centuries. The religion of the Prophet Muhammad is today the fastest growing of the world's major religions, with most of its new converts living in Africa and Asia.

Section 4 Review

Identify Mali, Mansa Musa, Timbuktu

Main Ideas
1. How did trade become the means of converting the people of Mali to Islam?
2. What event best advertised Timbuktu's importance as a center of Islamic culture? When Ibn Batuta visited Timbuktu, what did he notice about this center of Islamic culture?

Critical Thinking
Making Decisions: Mansa Musa decided to display his immense wealth to the world when he went to Mecca on pilgrimage. If you had been the mansa, would you have advertised your country in this way?

HIGHLIGHTS OF CIVILIZATION

Islamic Architecture

"In their genius for ornamentation," wrote one Arab historian, "the architects and craftsmen of Islam had no peers in the medieval world." The mosque depicted below shows you why. Islamic buildings were usually covered with geometric designs, floral patterns, and calligraphy, giving them a dazzling richness.

However, the motifs in Islamic architecture are not only decorative but have a religious meaning. These motifs represent the idea that there is order in the universe, order which can be understood through God's laws. The diagram shows how complex patterns can be formed from circles, which symbolize the link between infinite diversity and divine unity. By combining beautiful patterns and forms with religious symbolism, Islamic architects created art that was both pleasing and inspiring to the followers of Islam.

Designs on Moorish buildings in Spain were even more intricate. The outer facades were decorated with colorful mosaics. The inner walls and ceilings were covered with lacy webs and honeycombs of carved and painted plaster. One Muslim poet wrote of the Alhambra [al ham'brə], a splendid palace in Granada, Spain, "all other cupolas [domed roofs] vanish and disappear."

Decorative stalactites known as muqarnas support the ceiling above the entrance to the mosque built about 1003 in what is now Isfahan, Iran (left). The diagram (below) shows how the highly ornate patterns are obtained.

parentheses. Also see the Glossary and Biographical Dictionary.
Mali (284), Mansa Musa (284), Timbuktu (284)

Main Ideas

1. Muslim traders persuaded foreign buyers to accept Islam.
2. Mansa Musa's gold-plated pilgrimage to Mecca; safe streets, women not secluded, wealth, quality of life, impressive trade

Critical Thinking

Possible answers: Yes, I would like to attract visitors to Mali—more visitors mean more trade, and more trade equals more wealth. No, I do not want to attract hostile invaders who would try to seize my kingdom's wealth.

HIGHLIGHTS OF CIVILIZATION

You may wish to show the students photographs of the inside of the Alhambra. Other stunning examples of Moorish art and architecture can be found in "When the Moors Ruled Spain," in *National Geographic,* July, 1988, pages 86–119.

Ask students where they have seen designs similar to those in Islamic buildings. (Students may be aware of stain-glass designs, Byzantine mosaics, and Indian temples that use geometric designs.)

You may wish to point out that most of the abstract Islamic designs are optical illusions. Sometimes the light-colored figures seem to come forward; other times the dark-colored figures seem to come forward. Encourage students to block out the diagram with a piece of paper, so that only the black and white patterns show to see this effect.

CHAPTER 15 REVIEW

Answers to Test Yourself

Key Terms, People, and Places
The key terms, people, and places tested here were introduced in the chapter sections and reviewed in the Section Reviews. For definitions see the page references at the appropriate Section Reviews. Also see the Glossary and Biographical Dictionary.

Main Ideas
The main ideas tested here were introduced in the sections of this chapter and reviewed in the Section Reviews. For answers to these questions, see the appropriate Section Reviews.

Critical Thinking
1. Chances are very good that the two men met in Mecca. Although Batuta left several months later than Musa, Musa traveled much more slowly than Batuta because of his huge entourage. They probably arrived in Mecca at about the same time. If Batuta had met Musa he probably would have been encouraged to visit Mali much earlier than he did (1352).
2. Muslims were unified under one legal system, one major religion that had a tolerance for minority beliefs, one language for legal and administrative use, usually one civil government at a time, and a common cultural heritage influenced by local traditions. All of the above ties apply to the United States.

Section Summaries

Section 1
Religion and government encouraged prosperity.
The large empire that the Arabs conquered in the 7th century soon became the foundation of a creative and prosperous civilization. The religion of Islam, the central government provided by caliphs, and the Arabic language gave unity to the many varied peoples of the Islamic Empire.

Section 2
Vigorous trade spread Islamic culture.
Trade was an honorable profession in the Muslim world, and many factors encouraged its growth. Lack of taxes between regions helped its activity, coins and banking practices eased the way, and joint stock companies made complex trade ventures possible. Through trade Islam gradually spread to parts of East and West Africa, India, China, and Southeast Asia.

Section 3
Science and the arts flourished.
Scholars throughout the Islamic Empire preserved and studied ancient works and added their own ideas and observations. Al-Razi, Avicenna, and others made important discoveries in medicine, chemistry, and mathematics. Islamic rulers were patrons of poets,

scholars, and artists. Throughout the Islamic Empire, ordinary people enjoyed a high standard of living.

Section 4
Islam spread to West Africa through trade.
Muslim traders were drawn to West Africa by the gold mined there. They also converted many West Africans to Islam, especially those in cities. The rulers of the West African empire of Mali became Muslim, and their most famous king, Mansa Musa, made a memorable pilgrimage to Mecca.

Test Yourself

Key Terms, People, and Places
Identify the significance of each of the following.

Section 1
a. Arabic   c. Cairo
b. Hajj

Section 2
a. Persian Gulf   c. Ibn Batuta
b. Indonesia

Section 3
a. al-Razi   d. Ibn Khaldun
b. alchemy   e. Sufi order
c. Omar Khayyam   f. arabesque

Review Dates

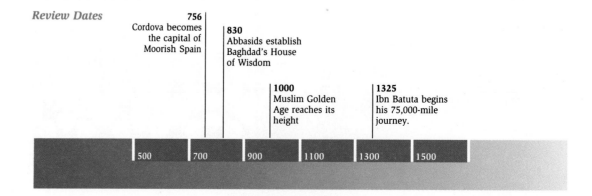

756 Cordova becomes the capital of Moorish Spain

830 Abbasids establish Baghdad's House of Wisdom

1000 Muslim Golden Age reaches its height

1325 Ibn Batuta begins his 75,000-mile journey.

500   700   900   1100   1300   1500

Section 4

a. Mali   **c.** Timbuku

b. Mansa Musa

Main Ideas

Section 1

1. What was the Arab response to the cultures of the peoples they conquered?

2. How did the exchange of ideas among the Hajj pilgrims affect the Islamic Empire as a whole?

3. How did the caliphs contribute to improved farming methods?

4. What amenities contributed to the high standard of living enjoyed in the cities of the Islamic Empire?

Section 2

1. How did the Islamic Empire encourage trade?

2. To which areas of the world did Islam spread its culture and religion?

3. Why was Ibn Batuta able to accomplish his goal of visiting every Muslim country in the world?

Section 3

1. What practices show that Muslim medicine was fairly advanced?

2. What were some of the advances Muslims made in astronomy and mathematics?

3. What advances in general knowledge did scholars in the Islamic world make?

Section 4

1. What part did traders play in the conversion of people in Mali to Islam?

2. What event made the Muslim world notice Mali? Describe Mali through the eyes of Ibn Batuta.

Critical Thinking

1. Making Hypotheses Ibn Batuta and Mansa Musa began their pilgrimage journeys within a year of each other, one starting from Mali in 1324 and one from Morocco in 1325. Given the time it took to travel any distance, what do you think the chances are that the two men met in Mecca? What difference might such a meeting have made to Ibn Batuta?

2. Recognizing Values Describe the ties that unified the Muslim world in the period around 1300. How do similar ties bind the people of the United States today? Give specific examples.

CRITICAL THINKING QUESTION LEVEL 1. average; 2. easy

Chapter Skills and Activities

Practicing Study and Research Skills
Observing for Detail

A history text like this one contains thousands of generalizations and supporting details. Because so much information is covered, it is easy to miss many details that are given in the book. For example, on page 277 the text states that Muslim medical practices were the most advanced of the time. Find ten examples in the text of Muslim medical practices that support this generalization.

Linking Past and Present

Above is a photograph of Egyptian students at Cairo University. Education was important in the early Muslim world and remains so today. Use your library to find out about educational trends in Muslim countries today.

Learning History Through Maps

In 1325, Ibn Batuta traveled from Morocco to Mecca. Later he made journeys to Persia, East Africa, the Black Sea, India, and Timbuktu. Do you think that he carved new trails or that he followed existing routes? Use the map on page 275 to help answer this question.

Key Terms and People
1. c
2. a
3. b
4. e
5. d

Key Dates
B, G, A, F, C, D, E

Key Places
E—Mecca; C—Constantinople; A—Iberian peninsula; B—Kiev; D—Timbuktu

Main Ideas
1. b
2. a
3. c
4. a
5. d

Critical Thinking
1. Students should consider the contributions of these civilizations in the areas of law, science, architecture, medicine, and religion.
2. Students' answers should consider religion, type of government, and economy.

UNIT THREE

REVIEW

Summarizing the Unit

Chapter 10
Rome and the Rise of Christendom
Christianity began in Palestine in the 1st century A.D. and spread throughout the Roman Empire. Around 400 the declining western Roman Empire was destroyed by Germanic invasions. Around 800 the civilization called Christendom came under the control of the Frankish king Charlemagne, who helped revive learning in western Europe.

Chapter 11
The Formation of Europe
During the Middle Ages, the great unifying force in western Europe was the Christian Church. Central governments were weak, and the real power lay in the hands of hundreds of local feudal lords. The crusades and the revival of towns brought enormous changes to western Europe.

Chapter 12
The Growth of National Monarchies
A sense of national identity had emerged in many parts of Europe by the mid-1400s. In England, France, Spain, and other countries, feudalism declined and a central government headed by a monarch gained the loyalty of the people.

Chapter 13
The Byzantine Empire and the Formation of Russia
After the fall of Rome in 476, the eastern Roman Empire flourished, and became known as the Byzantine Empire. Early Russia began as a grouping of city-states on the Dnieper River. Conquered by the Mongols in 1240, Russia emerged again in 1480 under Ivan the Great.

Chapter 14
The Rise and Expansion of Islam
After the death of Muhammad in 632, his Arab followers established an Islamic Empire, larger than either the Byzantine or Roman empires had been. Muslim conquerers also extended Islam into India.

Chapter 15
Islamic Civilization
Throughout the Muslim world, scholars and artists made outstanding contributions in medicine, mathematics, astronomy, and other fields, an outgrowth of their belief in the importance of education. Muslim traders spread Islam to Africa and Southeast Asia.

Using Writing Skills

The step that follows prewriting is the actual writing stage, when you put the ideas you've learned from your prewriting activities on paper. In actual practice, the stages of writing are not completely separate. Once you begin to write, you may find yourself going back to do some more prewriting. You might realize that you need some more information or a different way to approach your reader. That's why the process of writing is a continuous activity.

Activity. Imagine that you're living in the period covered in this unit (500–1500). You might be Joan of Arc defending her beloved France, or a peasant farmer or a feudal lord, a Muslim on a pilgrimage to Mecca, or a soldier in a Muslim army of conquest. Begin a journal in which you can describe how you would feel as this person in history. Write journal entries for at least three days, detailing what your daily activities might be, and how you might dress and eat.

Test Yourself

Key Terms and People
Match each term or person with the correct definition.
1. leader who created the Frankish Empire
2. system of government based on land ownership and personal loyalty
3. period of religious persecution in Spain
4. leader who codified Roman law
5. majority of the world's Muslims
a. feudalism   d. Sunnis
b. Inquisition   e. Justinian
c. Charlemagne

Key Dates

Match the letters on the time line with the events for which they stand:

300	500	700	900	1100	1300	1500

A   B   C   D   E   F   G

____ Muhammad journeys from Mecca to Medina.
____ Ivan the Great frees Russia from Mongol rule.
____ Christianity becomes the official religion of the Roman Empire.
____ The Black Death breaks out in Europe.
____ The pope crowns Charlemagne emperor.
____ The crusades begin.
____ King John signs the Magna Carta.

Key Places

Match the letters on the map with the places described below:

____ Islam's holiest city
____ capital of the Byzantine Empire
____ area in Europe the Moors conquered
____ first capital of Russia
____ cultural center of Mali

Main Ideas

1. By crowning Charlemagne emperor, the pope ____
a. gave up his control of western Europe.
b. declared that his authority was higher than that of the kings.
c. increased the importance of the feudal lords.
d. protected himself from the Byzantine threat.
2. A side effect of the Black Death was ____
a. a shortage of farm labor.
b. a shortage of drinkable water.
c. a rise in the number of soldiers.
d. a rise in the number of feudal lords.
3. Jews differed from many other Europeans in the Middle Ages because ____
a. they were permitted only to farm.
b. they were forced out of European countries.
c. they were generally literate.
d. they were permitted only in Catholic countries.
4. Muslims were similar to Jews and the Christians because ____
a. they believed in one God.
b. their religions all began in the same century.
c. the birthplace of their religions was Europe.
d. they expanded into northern Europe.
5. Cities in the Islamic Empire between 700 and 1100 ____
a. relied on barter for trade.
b. had no advanced form of medicine.
c. were constantly under siege from non-Muslims.
d. were more advanced than those in Europe.

Critical Thinking

1. Recognizing Values In what ways did the Byzantines and the Muslims contribute to the advance of Western civilization?
2. Analyzing Comparisons How and why did the development of early Russia, from the 9th to the 14th centuries, differ from that of western Europe?

CRITICAL THINKING QUESTION LEVEL 1. average;
2. challenging

The Era of Regional Civilizations: Asia, Africa, and the Americas

OVERVIEW

This unit covers regional civilizations that flourished in Asia, Africa, and the Americas from about 500 to 1500.

ADDITIONAL TEACHING AIDS FOR UNIT FOUR

Literature for the Teacher

Connah, Graham. *African Civilizations.* Cambridge University Press, 1987.

Farb, Peter. *Man's Rise to Civilization: Cultural Ascent of Indians of North America.* E. P. Dutton, 1978.

Umesao, Tadao. *Seventy-Seven Keys to Civilization of Japan.* Union City: Heian International Inc., 1985.

Wu, K. C. *The Chinese Heritage.* Crown Publishing, 1982.

Yuan-Tsang Chen. *The Dragon's Village.* Pantheon, 1981.

Literature for the Student

Ching, Frank. *Ancestors: 900 Years in the Life of a Chinese Family.* Princeton University, 1988. (challenging)

Focus on Korea: Korean History. Seoul International Publishing House, 1986. (easy)

Lum, Peter. *Six Centuries in East Asia.* New York: S. G. Phillips, 1973. (average)

Morton, W. Scott. *China: Its History and Culture.* New York: Lippincott & Crowell, 1980. (challenging)

Rossabi, Morris. *Kublai Khan: His Life and Time.* Berkeley: University of California Press, 1988. (challenging)

Spry-Leverton, Peter, and Peter Kornicki. *Japan.* New York: Facts on File Publishing, 1987. (easy)

Treasures of the World (series): The African Kings. Silver Burdett, 1983. (average)

Audio-Visual Materials*

China: The Age of Maturity (film 8 in the Chinese History Series). Film, 22 minutes, color [Indiana University], 1976. Recalls the invasions, rebellion, and disunity that characterized the five regimes that preceded the Sung Dynasty

China Under the Mongols (film 9 in the Chinese History Series). Film, 19 minutes, color. [Indiana University], 1976. Shows Kublai Kahn eliminating Sung Dynasty and bringing all of China under foreign domination for the first time in history

The Story of the Aztecs. Video, 20 minutes, color, [Films, Inc.], 1975. Traces the history and past glories of the Aztec Empire

The Tribal Eye: Sweat of the Sun. Film, 53 minutes, color, [Time-Life], 1975. The gold of the Aztecs and the legend of El Dorado in their historical context and setting

Tropical Africa. Film, 29 minutes, color. [International Film Foundation], 1961. Surveys the 3,000-year history of Africa and examines the continent's outlook for the future

* For a complete listing of sources of audio-visual materials see page T30.

OPTIONAL WRITING ASSIGNMENTS

1. Write a short five-minute script for a Public Broadcasting System radio program comparing life in China during the Song Dynasty with life in your community today.

2. You are traveling with Marco Polo to Asia. Write six to ten diary entries describing your most memorable days.

3. As a visitor in 794 to Japan from China, write a letter to a friend describing aspects of Japanese life that you find very familiar and aspects that you find very different.

4. You work at a trading post along the Niger River in 10th-century Sudan. Prepare a brochure that promotes your area as a site for trade. Your brochure should contain drawings of the area and its activities as well as written descriptions encouraging traders to use your facilities.

5. You are a travel reporter for *World Exploration* travel magazine in 1400. You have been assigned to write an article describing the splendors of modern (1400) Zimbabwe. Prepare an article describing Zimbabwe and explaining to potential tourists why they should consider it as a possible destination.

UNIT TESTS
IN THE TEACHER'S RESOURCE FILE

Unit Test, pp. 89–90

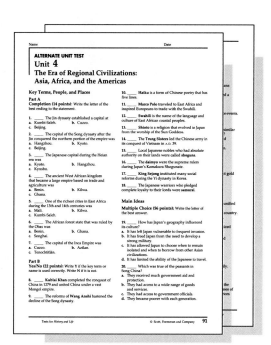

Alternate Unit Test, pp. 91–92

FINE ART IN UNIT FOUR

Fine art forms an integral part of the historical record of events portrayed in this textbook. A listing of the paintings, drawings, sculpture, historic photographs, architecture, and other works of fine art selected to illustrate this unit follows. Students may be asked to research the artists and their works and report their findings to the entire class. Students also may be asked to write one or more paragraphs describing what they see upon a detailed study of a work of art and what the artist was attempting to communicate.

p. 343, Benin Empress's head, bronze, c. 17th century, University Museum, Philadelphia
p. 343, Benin rooster, bronze, c. 17th century, The Menil Collection, Houston

UNIT FOUR

The Era of Regional Civilizations: Asia, Africa, and the Americas

Themes and Patterns As you learned in Unit 3, the civilizations of Christendom and Islam were shaped by religions. Civilizations in Asia, Africa, and the Americas, however, took different forms.

During the 1,000 years between A.D. 500 and 1500, the overwhelming reality in Asia was the existence of a single powerful state, China. Its influence strongly affected Korea to the northeast, Japan to the east, and Vietnam to the south. The cultures of all these countries absorbed elements of Chinese civilization.

For about a century and a half, China itself was forcibly included in an even larger regional grouping forged by the Mongols. In the 1200s and 1300s, the Mongols ruled from the coast of China to the borders of Poland, creating the largest land empire in history.

On a smaller territorial scale, regional cultures and civilizations also emerged during this period in Sub-Saharan Africa and the Americas. From the 9th century on, Muslim traders and travelers came into contact with the West African kingdoms of Mali and Songhai, and the East African city-states. In the Americas the Aztecs of Mexico and the Incas of Peru each developed impressive regional civilizations.

The regional civilizations of this 1,000-year period were still mostly separated from one another. The era ended, however, in the late 15th and 16th centuries when one of these civilizations, Christendom, found ways to make contact with all the others. Thus began the early modern era and the creation of a worldwide network of communication and transportation.

A five-toed dragon, for centuries reserved as the symbol of the Chinese emperor, today graces a wall in Beijing's imperial Forbidden City.

Chapters in this Unit

16 China's Predominance in Asia

OVERVIEW

This chapter describes two basic themes of Chinese history: the dynastic cycle and the continuity of Chinese culture.

PLANNING CHART

Section	Text Pages	Key Concept	Suggested Teaching Time
1 Chinese civilization continued to flourish under the Songs.	293–296	Song rulers brought good government and advanced learning but lost control of the north.	One day
2 Daily life changed during the Song era.	296–300	Social divisions were emphasized as technology brought population growth.	One day **Less time?** Combine the material in Section 2 on daily life and social structures with the material on Chinese cultural advances in Section 1. Discuss the themes of dynastic cycles and continuity as an introduction to Section 3.
3 The Mongols ruled in China under the Khans.	300–301	Mongol rule began a new dynastic cycle and fostered Chinese culture as it encouraged cross-cultural contacts.	One day **More time?** Use *Overhead Transparency 31* or *Source Reading 16A.*
4 Chinese culture influenced Vietnam and Korea.	303–304	Vietnam and Korea struggled to maintain political independence while adopting Chinese customs.	One day **More time?** Use *Overhead Transparency 32* or *Source Reading 16B.*

ANCILLARIES

Materials that may be used with this chapter to reinforce, reteach, enrich, and assess learning are pictured on the following pages.

Teacher's Resource File

ACTIVITIES

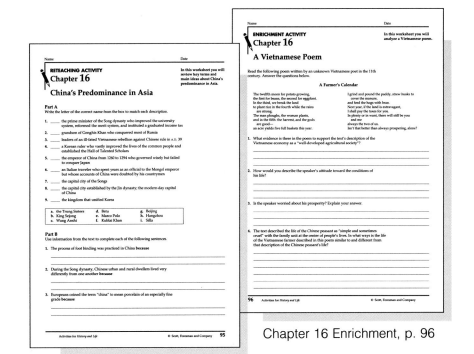

Section 1 Activity, p. 91

Section 2 Activity, p. 92

Section 3 Activity, p. 93

Section 4 Activity, p. 94

Chapter 16 Reteaching, p. 95

Chapter 16 Enrichment, p. 96

Teacher's Resource File

GEOGRAPHY SKILLS

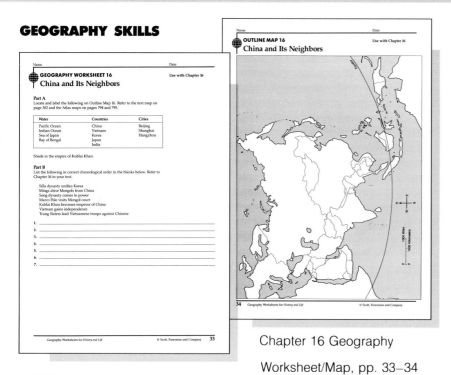

GEOGRAPHY WORKSHEET 16   Use with Chapter 16
China and Its Neighbors

Part A
Locate and label the following on Outline Map 16. Refer to the text map on page 302 and the Atlas maps on pages 794 and 795.

Water	Countries	Cities
Pacific Ocean	China	Beijing
Indian Ocean	Vietnam	Shanghai
Sea of Japan	Korea	Hangzhou
Bay of Bengal	Japan	
	India	

Shade in the empire of Kublai Khan.

Part B
List the following in correct chronological order in the blanks below. Refer to Chapter 16 in your text.

Silla dynasty unifies Korea
Mings drive Mongols from China
Song dynasty comes to power
Marco Polo visits Mongol court
Kublai Khan becomes emperor of China
Vietnam gains independence
Trung Sisters lead Vietnamese troops against Chinese

1. _____
2. _____
3. _____
4. _____
5. _____
6. _____
7. _____

Geography Worksheets for History and Life   © Scott, Foresman and Company   **33**

OUTLINE MAP 16   Use with Chapter 16
China and Its Neighbors

34   Geography Worksheets for History and Life   © Scott, Foresman and Company

Chapter 16 Geography
Worksheet/Map, pp. 33–34

MAP LESSON 16   Use with Chapter 16

In the 1200s and 1300s, the Mongols controlled much of Asia. Study this map. Then complete each of the statements by writing the best answer in the blank space.

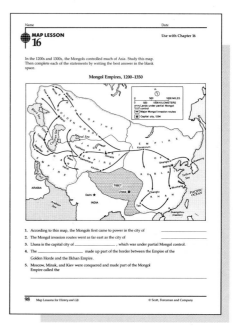

Mongol Empires, 1200–1350

1. According to this map, the Mongols first came to power in the city of _____
2. The Mongol invasion routes went as far east as the city of _____
3. Lhasa is the capital city of _____, which was under partial Mongol control.
4. The _____ made up part of the border between the Empire of the Golden Horde and the Ilkhan Empire.
5. Moscow, Minsk, and Kiev were conquered and made part of the Mongol Empire called the _____

98   Map Lessons for History and Life   © Scott, Foresman and Company

Chapter 16 Map Lesson, p. 98

TESTS

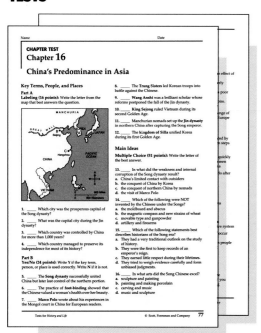

CHAPTER TEST
Chapter 16

China's Predominance in Asia

Key Terms, People, and Places
Part A
Labeling (16 points): Write the letter from the map that best answers the question.

1. _____ Which city was the prosperous capital of the Song dynasty?
2. _____ What was the capital city during the Jin dynasty?
3. _____ Which country was controlled by China for more than 1,000 years?
4. _____ Which country managed to preserve its independence for most of its history?

Part B
Yes/No (24 points): Write Y if the key term, person, or place is used correctly. Write N if it is not.

5. _____ The **Song dynasty** successfully united China but later lost control of the northern portion.
6. _____ The practice of **foot-binding** showed that the Chinese valued a woman's health over her beauty.
7. _____ **Marco Polo** wrote about his experiences in the Mongol court in China for European readers.

8. _____ The **Trung Sisters** led Korean troops into battle against the Chinese.
9. _____ **Wang Anshi** was a brilliant scholar whose reforms postponed the fall of the Jin dynasty.
10. _____ **King Sejong** ruled Vietnam during its second Golden Age.
11. _____ Manchurian nomads set up the **Jin dynasty** in northern China after capturing the Song emperor.
12. _____ The **kingdom of Silla** unified Korea during its first Golden Age.

Main Ideas
Multiple Choice (51 points): Write the letter of the best answer.

13. _____ In what did the weakness and internal corruption of the Song dynasty result?
a. China's limited contact with outsiders
b. the conquest of China by Korea
c. the conquest of northern China by nomads
d. the visit of Marco Polo

14. _____ Which of the following were NOT invented by the Chinese under the Songs?
a. the moldboard and abacus
b. the magnetic compass and new strains of wheat
c. movable type and gunpowder
d. artillery and firearms

15. _____ Which of the following statements best describes historians of the Song era?
a. They had a very traditional outlook on the study of history.
b. They were the first to keep records of history.
c. They earned little respect during their lifetimes.
d. They tried to weigh evidence carefully and form unbiased judgments.

16. _____ In what arts did the Song Chinese excel?
a. sculpture and painting
b. painting and making porcelain
c. carving and music
d. music and sculpture

Tests for History and Life   © Scott, Foresman and Company   **77**

Chapter Test, pp. 77–78

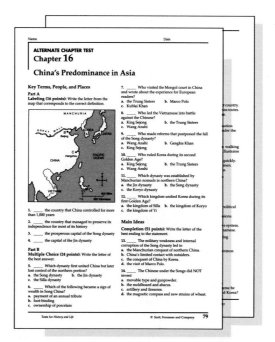

ALTERNATE CHAPTER TEST
Chapter 16

China's Predominance in Asia

Key Terms, People, and Places
Part A
Labeling (16 points): Write the letter from the map that corresponds to the correct definition.

1. _____ the country that China controlled for more than 1,000 years
2. _____ the country that managed to preserve its independence for most of its history
3. _____ the prosperous capital of the Song dynasty
4. _____ the capital of the Jin dynasty

Part B
Multiple Choice (24 points): Write the letter of the best answer.

5. _____ Which dynasty first united China but later lost control of the northern portion.
a. the Song dynasty   b. the Jin dynasty
c. the Silla dynasty

6. _____ Which of the following became a sign of wealth in Song China?
a. payment of an annual tribute
b. foot-binding
c. ownership of porcelain

7. _____ Who visited the Mongol court in China and wrote about the experience for European readers?
a. the Trung Sisters   b. Marco Polo
c. Kublai Khan

8. _____ Who led the Vietnamese into battle against the Chinese?
a. King Sejong   b. the Trung Sisters
c. Wang Anshi

9. _____ Who made reforms that postponed the fall of the Song dynasty?
a. Wang Anshi   b. Genghis Khan
c. King Sejong

10. _____ Who ruled Korea during its second Golden Age?
a. King Sejong   b. the Trung Sisters
c. Wang Anshi

11. _____ Which dynasty was established by Manchurian nomads in northern China?
a. the Jin dynasty   b. the Song dynasty
c. the Koryo dynasty

12. _____ Which kingdom unified Korea during its first Golden Age?
a. the kingdom of Silla   b. the kingdom of Koryo
c. the kingdom of Yi

Main Ideas
Completion (51 points): Write the letter of the best ending to the statement.

13. _____ The military weakness and internal corruption of the Song dynasty led to
a. the Manchurian conquest of northern China.
b. China's limited contact with outsiders.
c. the conquest of China by Korea.
d. the visit of Marco Polo.

14. _____ The Chinese under the Songs did NOT invent
a. movable type and gunpowder.
b. the moldboard and abacus.
c. artillery and firearms.
d. the magnetic compass and new strains of wheat.

Tests for History and Life   © Scott, Foresman and Company   **79**

Alternate Chapter Test, pp. 79–80

Other Optional Ancillaries

WORKBOOK

Name _____ Date _____

WORKSHEET
Chapter 16, Section 1
Song Achievements

In this worksheet you will review the major achievements of the Song dynasty.

Part A
Use information from your text to complete the chart.

Advances of the Song Era

Category	Advances	Significance
Farming		led to increased crop production and growth in population and trade
Industry	tools for spinning and weaving	
		advanced printing and scholarship
Trade		allowed merchants to conduct transactions more quickly
	magnetic compass, ships propelled by paddle wheels	

Part B
Define each theme and explain how it is illustrated by Song China.

1. dynastic cycle
definition:

in Song China:

2. continuity of Chinese culture
definition:

in Song China:

Worksheets for History and Life   © Scott, Foresman and Company   **61**

Section 1 Worksheet, p. 61

Name _____ Date _____

WORKSHEET
Chapter 16, Section 2
Life and Values in Song China

In this worksheet you will support generalizations about life and values in the Song era.

For each statement write at least one sentence that supports or provides details for that statement.

1. Women were subordinate to men.

2. Marriages were arranged for practical reasons.

3. Among the upper classes, a woman's beauty was considered more important than her health.

4. The Chinese family had an authoritarian structure.

5. Families assumed some duties that the police or judicial systems take care of in many countries.

6. Wang Anshi tried to improve the management of Chinese government.

7. Advances in farming technologies meant that Song China could support a larger population.

62 Worksheets for History and Life   © Scott, Foresman and Company

Section 2 Worksheet, p. 62

Name _____ Date _____

WORKSHEET
Chapter 16, Section 3
The Mongols

In this worksheet you will distinguish between statements of fact and of opinion about the Mongols.

Part A
For each set of statements below, write F for fact and O for opinion.

1. a. ___ Kublai Khan moved his capital city to Beijing and adopted Chinese ways.
   b. ___ If Mongols had kept to their own traditions, the Chinese would have hated them less.
2. a. ___ Kublai Khan's naval expeditions against Japan were doomed to failure.
   b. ___ Kublai Khan's ships were destroyed off Japan's coast by typhoons.
3. a. ___ People in Italy did not believe Marco Polo's accounts of the wealth and size of China.
   b. ___ Europeans probably would not have visited China for many centuries without Marco Polo's trip to arouse their interest.
4. a. ___ Europeans learned about printing and the use of gunpowder from the Chinese.
   b. ___ Eventually, Europeans themselves would have invented gunpowder and printing.
5. a. ___ The Mongols ruled an empire that spanned most of Eurasia.
   b. ___ The Mongols were the most despicable barbarians who ever lived.
6. a. ___ During the Mongol period, Chinese inventions were transmitted across Eurasia to other civilizations.
   b. ___ During the Mongol period, the Chinese progressed as a result of contact with the rest of Eurasia.

Part B
What do you see as the effects of Mongolian rule on China? Support your answer.

Worksheets for History and Life   © Scott, Foresman and Company   **63**

Section 3 Worksheet, p. 63

Name _____ Date _____

WORKSHEET
Chapter 16, Section 4
Korean and Vietnamese Milestones

In this worksheet you will review important events in Vietnamese and Korean history.

Using the numbers 1 through 8, arrange the events in chronological order. On the lines after each event, tell why it was an important happening.

a. ___ The Chinese seized control of Vietnam.

b. ___ Vietnam was wracked by civil war.

c. ___ Many Chinese moved into northern Korea.

d. ___ The Vietnamese defeated Kublai Khan.

e. ___ The Kingdom of Silla unified Korea.

f. ___ The Koryo took over from the Silla.

g. ___ King Sejong reigned in Korea.

64 Worksheets for History and Life   © Scott, Foresman and Company

Section 4 Worksheet, p. 64

SOURCE READINGS

Source Reading 16A
Source Reading 16B

TEST GENERATOR

40 multiple-choice questions for Chapter 16

OVERHEAD TRANSPARENCIES

Overhead Transparency 31
Overhead Transparency 32

CHAPTER INTRODUCTION

Emphasize to students the dominant cultural influence China had over many areas of Asia. Make students aware of the pattern of foreign invasion and the eventual assimilation of their conquerors into Chinese culture. Ask the students why they think such a pattern existed.

LOCATOR GLOBE

Call students' attention to the globe, which indicates the general area of the world discussed in this chapter. (A detailed map appears on page 302.)

TIME LINE

Have the students determine how many years elapsed between Marco Polo's visit to China and the defeat of the Mongols. (93 years)

China's Predominance in Asia

960 – 1368

900	
960	Song dynasty begins
1275	Marco Polo visits the Mongol court
1368	Mings oust the Mongols
1400	
1500	

Throughout history Chinese civilization has been the single greatest influence on many of its neighboring cultures, including Japan, Korea, and Vietnam. As you learned in Chapter 8, the Chinese developed a highly advanced culture that had its beginnings about 1000 B.C. For thousands of years, Chinese literature, philosophy, religion, and art affected the thinking of peoples throughout East Asia. The philosophies of Confucius and Laozi, introduced during China's Zhou dynasty, shaped the lives of many people throughout East Asia. In addition, Chinese goods were traded widely across the entire Asian continent.

In the Middle Ages, China's fame spread to Europe. A 13th-century European named Marco Polo returned to his home in Italy after nearly 20 years in China. He wrote a travel book that gave a vivid picture of China, but the experiences and objects he described seemed so unusual that Europeans refused to believe him. For example, he wrote of coal—which was commonly used in China but practically unknown in Europe. He described coal as pieces of black stone that burned like logs. "These stones," he said, "keep a fire going better than wood." For writing such descriptions, Marco Polo was called the "prince of liars" when he returned home.

The use of coal presents only one example of China's technological, scientific, and cultural advancement over Europe. For more than 1,000 years, no other nation in Asia could match the high cultural and scientific achievements of Chinese civilization. Even when the Chinese empire became politically or militarily weak and was invaded by foreigners, the invaders adopted Chinese culture and were absorbed into the Chinese population. As a result, China's way of life has remained distinctive and unique for almost 3,000 years, making it the oldest continuous civilization in the world.

The painters of Song China excelled in their craft. Here a painter captures the tragic story of the Chinese poet Lady Wen-chi (in the dress at right), who was kidnaped during the Han dynasty and taken to Mongolia.

Reading Preview

In this chapter you will learn how Chinese culture advanced between 960 and 1368.

1. *Chinese civilization continued to flourish under the Songs.*
2. *Daily life changed during the Song era.*
3. *The Mongols ruled in China under the Khans.*
4. *Chinese culture influenced Vietnam and Korea.*

BACKGROUND The Pinyin system for spelling Chinese names is used in this text, but to do library research, your students may need to know the Wade-Giles spelling system. Following are the names used in this chapter followed by the

Chinese civilization continued to flourish under the Songs.

Weakened by warfare along its borders and political corruption within the empire, the Tang dynasty came to an end in 907. Five weak dynasties followed until 960, when a strong, new government, the **Song dynasty**, came to power. Although nomadic tribes beyond the Great Wall presented a constant danger, there were many important achievements during this time.

Wade-Giles spelling in parentheses: Song dynasty (Sung dynasty), Jin dynasty (Chin dynasty), Beijing (Peking), Hangzhou (Hangchow), Wang Anshi (Wang An Shih), Hong Wu (Hung Wu), Qian Long (Ch'ien Lung).

293

1 *Lesson Plan*

Essential Learning Objectives

Students will learn to:

- explain how Song rule was typical of China's political history.
- identify ways Chinese culture progressed under the Songs.

1 FOCUS AND MOTIVATE

Tell students that this section discusses the sixth major Chinese dynasty since Shang rule began in 1500 B.C. Ask students to suggest factors that might bring about the end of a government. (foreign invasion, civil war) Point out that even though China's government changed periodically, the way of living of the people remained essentially the same.

2 TEACH

- Point out the years of Song rule (960–1279), emphasizing the strengths of their government. Clarify the reasons for the division of China and the dates of Jin rule in the north (1127–1234).

- Write the following words that describe the dynastic cycle in China's history across the chalkboard: Strong Rulers, Weak Rulers, Rebellion or Invasion, Overthrow of the Government. Elicit from students the cause and effect relationships of these cycles. Discuss China's assimilation of other cultures.

GUIDED PRACTICE

List advances of Song China, selecting students to describe the particular significance of each.

China is first united and then divided under Song rule (960–1279).

The first Song emperors were excellent rulers. They held firm control of the central government and gained cooperation from rival military leaders throughout China. They also reestablished order by enforcing fair and consistent laws, by appointing wise, well-educated government advisers, and by curbing excessive taxes.

However, the Songs were never as strong militarily as previous Chinese dynasties. Soon after the Song dynasty was established, a nomadic group from Manchuria soon controlled the region north of China. The Chinese reached a settlement with the new kingdom, agreeing to pay annual tribute. This settlement kept the peace for about 100 years.

The Songs then decided to join forces with a second group of Manchurian nomads, the Jin [chin], in an attempt to overthrow the northern kingdom. Their combined efforts were successful, but soon the Jin turned against their Chinese allies. China, weakened by internal corruption, was unable to hold the Jin behind the Great Wall. Within a few decades, the Jin overran China and captured the Song emperor. They set up the **Jin dynasty** in northern China, establishing their capital at **Beijing** [bā′jing′], a city that is today the modern-day capital of China.

The son of the captured Song emperor fled south to the Chang River basin. The Jin, who fought on horseback, were unable to penetrate this marshy land. The Songs set up a new capital at **Hangzhou** [häng′jō′], which is on the map on page 302. By 1127 there were two Chinese empires—the Jin in the north and the Song in the south.

Two themes of Chinese history are illustrated by the Song dynasty.

The fall of the Songs in the north illustrates two recurring themes in Chinese history: the dynastic cycle and the continuity of Chinese culture. Most of the dynasties that ruled China have been characterized by the following cyclic pattern.

At the beginning of the dynasty, the rulers are strong and wise and China prospers. However, in time the rulers become weak or selfish, and government officials become lazy and corrupt. The country is soon plagued by internal rebellion or threatened by invasion. The dynasty becomes weaker and is finally overthrown. A new, strong dynasty eventually gains power, and the dynastic cycle begins again. The rise and fall of the Song dynasty in northern China exemplifies this cycle.

The second theme of Chinese history, the continuity of Chinese culture, is also illustrated by what happened after the fall of the Songs in the north. In spite of the conquest of northern China by the Jin nomads, Chinese culture—including its language, literature, civil service, and agricultural way of life—continued to predominate in the region. In fact, within several generations many of the Jin leaders had also adopted Chinese culture.

In China this assimilation [ə sim′ə lā′shən]—absorption—of other cultures took place again and again. There is a saying that "China is a sea that salts all rivers that flow into it." This saying illustrates the continuity of China's culture and its pervasive influence on all the Asian cultures with which it came into contact.

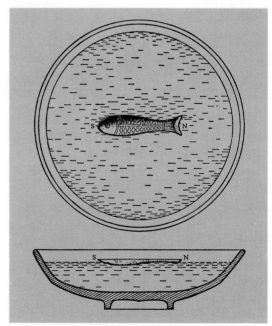

An early form of the magnetic compass, which was invented by the Chinese, relies upon a floating, fish-shaped iron leaf to indicate direction.

This Chinese contraption includes an astronomical observatory, from which scientists viewed the stars, and a water-powered clock in the area below.

Chinese culture advanced under the Songs.

Throughout the Song era, Chinese culture flourished. The Chinese made significant developments in technology, scholarship, and the arts.

Technology. During the Song dynasty, the Chinese invented more efficient farm implements, such as the moldboard, a curved plate at the end of the plow that overturns the soil. In addition, the introduction of new strains of rice from Southeast Asia further increased production. These improved farming methods led to tremendous growth in population and to healthy increases in trade.

Other inventions, made in China and elsewhere, also spurred trade and industry during the Song era. Silk and cotton production increased with the use of tools that made spinning and weaving more efficient. The use of the abacus, a device that aids calculation through the manipulation of rows of beads, allowed merchants to conduct transactions more quickly. In addition, sea trade expanded with the Chinese invention of the magnetic compass, which aided navigation, and with the development of fast ships propelled by huge paddle wheels turned by human power. Another Chinese inven-

tion, that of movable type in 1045, about 400 years before it was developed in Europe, advanced both printing and scholarship.

Chinese advances in military technology also spurred China's development. They invented gunpowder around the year 1000, at first using it only for firework displays. Later, however, the Chinese used gunpowder in warfare.

Scholarship. During the Song era, Chinese philosophers proposed that investigating natural phenomena was the best way for people to improve themselves morally. This philosophy led to major advances in all of the sciences and in mathematics.

The Chinese were also very interested in history. They believed that history was not just a record of the past, but also something that could serve as a guide from which people could learn. Since the Han dynasty, the government had written an official history of each emperor's reign. However, during the Song era, interest in history blossomed, and a number of scholars wrote about Chinese history. They based their writings on documents they studied, such as government records and biographies. They tried to weigh evidence carefully and tried not to make biased judgments. In these ways the Chinese had a very modern outlook on the study of history.

Arts. Although the Tang age had been a time of outstanding poets, the Song era was one of accomplished artists. Chinese painting reached a level of perfection never again achieved.

Throughout Chinese history, writing was considered a fine art. It was often done by painting on silk. Chinese written characters are complex, some

The abacus, also used by the ancient Egyptians, Greeks, and Romans, is a system of beads on which to perform a variety of arithmetic functions.

3 | ASSESS AND CLOSE

ASSESS

1. Where did the Jin invaders come from? (Manchuria)
2. Name Chinese inventions that led to an increase in trade. (abacus magnetic compass, paddle wheel)

OPTIONAL RETEACHING

Direct students to identify the ways in which Song rule was typical of the dynastic cycle theme. Using the headings on the chalkboard, write the actual event under the correct heading.

OPTIONAL ENRICHMENT

1. Ask students to report on one of the inventions of Song China, including pictures or models and descriptions of each. (average)
2. Have students choose one artist of the Song period to research. Tell students to study five of the artist's works and include their opinion of them in the completed report. (challenging)

INDEPENDENT PRACTICE/ HOMEWORK

Assign the Section Review, Activities page 91, or Workbook page 61.

CLOSURE

Summarize the lesson by telling students that although the leaders of the Song dynasty lost control of the north to the Jin for a time, the economy and culture of the south made many important advances.

Answers to Section 1 Review

Identify

Key Terms, People, and Places are defined on pages indicated in parentheses. Also see the Glossary and Biographical Dictionary.
Song dynasty (293), Jin dynasty (294), Beijing (294), Hangzhou (294) porcelain (296)

Main Ideas

1. In 907 the Song rulers gained cooperation of rival military leaders, and in 960 they took control of the central government. Later, the Songs lost control of the northern part of China to the Jin.
2. One theme is the dynastic cycle in which rulers are strong and China prospers, but then rulers become weak or selfish, leading to rebellion or invasion. A second theme is the continuity of Chinese culture no matter how often the government changes.
3. Technology: new farm implements, new strains of rice, new spinning and weaving tools, the abacus, the compass, paddle wheels, gunpowder, and movable type. Scholarship: increased study of science, mathematics, and history. Arts: a refined painting style and the development of porcelain.

Critical Thinking

Example: People could make their lives better by adopting Chinese culture. The Manchurians might have been attracted to the continuity between the past, present, and future in Chinese culture.

requiring more than 25 separate strokes. As a result, painting on silk meant that the artists had to be sure of every line, for they could not erase any marks. Through this careful, delicate method of writing, a distinctive style of painting arose.

This style was based on the special quality of lines made by the brush. Chinese painters using this style did not try to show exactly what the eye sees but instead tried to show the spirit of what they pictured. They might spend days simply thinking and looking at a scene until they grasped its singular meaning. However, they would not look at the scene while they painted. Following is the advice one Chinese master gave to guide students in this style of painting:

> Understand the character of what you paint. Look at the pine tree; it is like a wise scholar, dignified and stern; it is strong and constant and lives a long time. The willow, on the other hand, is like a beautiful woman, all grace and gentleness. The bamboo combs the hair of the wind and sweeps the moon, it is so bold that its shoots can break the hard ground as they push their way up; it is so gentle that it sways before every breeze. It is like wisdom itself. Keep the character of these things in your mind as you paint them.

Another art in which the Song Chinese excelled was the making of **porcelain**. This type of pottery was made from a special white clay that had been mixed with powdered rock, moistened, and made into a smooth paste. The potter shaped the porcelain in a mold or on a potter's wheel and fired it in a kiln. The Chinese discovered unusual glazes and used them to give the surfaces of porcelain

soft, rich color. One piece of green-glazed porcelain was described as being "like curling disks of thinnest ice, filled with green clouds."

The Chinese made porcelain plates, cups, bowls, candlesticks, and other objects. A small number of Chinese porcelain pieces were traded to Europeans by overland or sea trade routes. These objects were prized by Europeans, but the Europeans did not discover the secret of making porcelain for hundreds of years. Because the Chinese had exclusive knowledge of and techniques for making porcelain, Europeans coined the term "china" to mean porcelain of an especially fine grade. The pottery of China is discussed in more detail in the "Highlights of Civilization" feature on page 305.

Section 1 Review

Identify Song dynasty, Jin dynasty, Beijing, Hangzhou, porcelain

Main Ideas

1. How was China first united and then divided during the Song era?
2. Describe the two basic themes of Chinese history.
3. What were some of China's cultural achievements in technology, scholarship, and the arts during the Song era?

Critical Thinking

Making Hypotheses: Why do you think Chinese culture was adopted by many of the peoples who came in contact with China? What aspects of Chinese culture do you think would have been appealing to the Manchurians?

The porcelain bowl above, from the Song dynasty, glows with the soft, translucent, gray-green color of its celadon glaze.

<table>
<tr><td>2</td><td>Daily life changed during the Song era.</td></tr>
</table>

In the 12th century, Song China was the most advanced country in the world. Economically, the empire was prosperous. Towns and cities were centers of artistic and scholarly activity, although the cultural advancements of the city hardly influenced the simple and sometimes cruel lives of the peasants. In both town and country, the family unit was at the center of people's lives.

FROM THE ARCHIVES The essay describing the dragon boat race is from *Chinese Civilization and Society*, edited by Patricia Buckley Ebrey (New York: The Free Press, and London: Collier Macmillan, 1981), p. 133. Ask students how long the dragon boat race course was in miles? (about 3⅓ miles)

Advances in farming and increased foreign trade supported a large population.

Advances in farming technologies, such as the moldboard and new strains of rice, meant that Song China could support a large population. Partly as a result of the increased productivity of the land, the Chinese population grew from 60 million to 115 million between 960 and 1279, the years of the Song dynasty.

Improvements in transportation and advances in the arts spurred the growth of trade. Within China, urban areas grew and so did the bustling, open-air markets that facilitated the exchange of goods from regions near and far. Foreign trade was no longer carried out along overland caravan routes as it had been during the Han and Tang eras. In Song times the oceans became increasingly important as the main highways of commerce. Many large ships, with crews of several hundred persons, carried cargos to Korea, Japan, and Southeast Asia. Chinese ships also sailed to the Persian Gulf and to the east coast of Africa. Chinese exports included silks, art objects, and porcelains.

Tremendous contrasts between urban and rural ways of life existed in Song China.

As you have read, the cities in Song China were advanced cultural centers. In these urban areas, the people generally led pleasant lives and had access to a wide range of goods and services. However, in rural areas, the people lived differently.

City life. The prosperity of Song life is best seen in its urban centers, especially the capital, Hangzhou. This splendid city had a population of more than 1 million—much larger than any of the cities of Europe at that time. Hangzhou, a coastal city, was the trading center for China's rice belt and for its most important silk-producing region.

Hangzhou was laid out on a grid pattern with paved streets. One very wide central street led to the emperor's magnificent palace. Scattered here and there were other large buildings and palaces, and numerous shops and trading centers. In addition, a good system of garbage collection kept Hangzhou neat and clean. Although the number of poor city-dwellers steadily rose during the Song dynasty, for the most part these cities served as a showcase for China's wealth.

BACKGROUND The prosperous economic times led to the development of well-defined social classes. The five main classes were the peasants, the merchants, the soldiers, the artisans, and the scholars. Since Confucius' times during the

From the Archives

The Dragon Boat Race

The annual dragon boat race held in Hunan province in central China was not a simple sporting event but an elaborate festival held to ward off evil during the coming year. The race was centuries old by the time of the Song dynasty (960–1279). This account is by Yang Szu-ch'ang (1588–1641), a native of the region. The word "li" refers to a Chinese unit of measure equal to one-third of a mile.

On the day of the festival, flagmen and drummers on boats going to and fro make a deafening noise heard for about 50 li. The race course runs for about 10 li. . . . The southern shore is covered with grass, forests, and snowy white sands. On the northern shore are high buildings with beautifully painted balconies and old city walls. The spectators gather there . . . .

At the end of the race, the boats carry sacrificial animals, wine, and paper coins and row straight downstream, where the animals and wine are cast into the water, the paper coins are burned, and spells are recited. The purpose of these acts is to make pestilence [disease] and premature death flow away with the water.

Peasant life. The luxury of the capital and other cities stopped at their walls. Beyond the urban areas were the villages where peasants worked from dawn to dusk. Because inherited plots of land were continually divided through the generations, the peasants' plots became smaller and smaller. By the Song era, most plots were so tiny that they produced barely enough food to support a family.

All farm work was done by hand by the members of the peasant family. Adults did the heavy work—digging, planting, hoeing, and harvesting. Children looked after the pigs and chickens, gathered firewood, and brought water from the river or the well. A few feast days and festivals gave peasant families their only fun and relaxation.

Zhou dynasty, scholars had always been the most respected of the social classes. Unlike Europe, Chinese merchants and soldiers never achieved a very high social position.

2 *Lesson Plan*

Essential Learning Objectives

Students will learn to:
- identify the causes and consequences of population growth in China.
- describe reform policies instituted under a Song emperor.

1 FOCUS AND MOTIVATE

Remind students that China's population is the largest in the world today (more than 1 billion). Ask students to name factors that would lead to great increases in a nation's population. (ample food supplies, large families, good health, few wars, little emigration) Direct students to look for conditions in Song China that would have influenced population growth.

2 TEACH

- Clarify the elements of China's class structure by making a chart on the chalkboard to show the status and ways of life of city dwellers and peasants. Emphasize the self-sufficiency of the villagers and their isolation from government. Be sure that students grasp that peasant families needed many children to help raise food.

- Discuss Wang Anshi's reforms and remind students that China's civil service exams traditionally had emphasized memorization of Confucian classics rather than a more useful application of them. Stress the significance of tax structure changes.

GUIDED PRACTICE

Direct students to analyze the effects of Wang Anshi's reforms by identifying the groups that would have been helped or hurt by them.

This Song dynasty silk painting shows women preparing newly woven silk. The artist may have copied a Tang dynasty painting since the women's dress is Tang.

Very little contact existed between the peasants and the government. Officials collected taxes. They also picked several men from each village and forced them to work on government projects, such as building and repairing roads. Except for these obligations, the government left the peasants alone. The day-to-day life of the peasants in Song China was not much different from that of peasants in feudal Europe. The lives of Chinese farmers, however, remained almost unchanged well into the 1900s.

The family was always important in all classes of Chinese society.

The Chinese family was a tightly knit organization that included three or four generations. In the typical Chinese family, the older generations held authority over the younger generations, and males held authority over females. The structure of the family and the status of women affected Chinese society at all levels.

The structure of the family. The oldest male in the family, either the father or the grandfather, had the final word in all family matters. However, the eldest son had authority over younger brothers and all sisters. The grandmother had authority over her daughters, daughters-in-law, and granddaughters. The Chinese family took on duties that the police or judicial systems take care of in many countries. When conflicts arose between members of different families, the families involved tried to settle the problem themselves.

All marriages were arranged by heads of families to benefit the wealth or social position of each family involved. It could happen that a man and a woman engaged to be married might see each other for the first time at the wedding ceremony. However, the idea of romantic love was not absent from Chinese thought, and touching love stories abound in Chinese literature. Yet, romantic love usually had little to do with the practical aspects of selecting a mate and maintaining a marriage.

The status of women. In the society of Song China, women were considered subordinate to the men. The reality of this male-dominated hierarchy is evident in this saying by a famous Chinese philosopher: "I am happy because I am a human and not an animal; a male and not a female; a Chinese and not a barbarian." The belief that females were inferior to males influenced many Chinese social customs. For example, when a woman appeared in public with her husband, she was expected to walk ten steps behind him.

Among the upper classes, the status of women depended mainly upon their ornamental qualities, or "beauty." The Chinese valued a woman's "beauty" far above her health and mobility. In China, women who had tiny feet were considered beautiful and their feet were bound to make them small. When a girl was about four years old, she began the process of **foot-binding**. Her feet were tightly wrapped and gradually bent until the arch was broken and the toes were pushed under.

The foot-binding process made the girl's feet very small, but it also permanently crippled her, and she never could walk normally again. Because girls of the lower classes were needed to help their families by working, usually on a farm, bound feet became a sign of wealth for those women who did not have to dirty themselves with physical work. The practice of foot-binding, which literally limited a woman's mobility, was finally outlawed in the 20th century.

The Song government made reforms to try to stave off decline.

About 100 years after the Songs came to power, the government began to undergo serious decline. Corrupt officials took charge of many important government posts. Merchants who had become wealthy from increased foreign trade found ways to avoid paying taxes. Saddled with increasing taxes, the peasants began to rebel. To stem this disastrous tide, in 1069 the Song emperor made a minor official named **Wang Anshi** [wäng' än'shẽr'] his prime minister. Wang Anshi was a brilliant scholar who had studied the histories of earlier Chinese governments.

He made broad reforms in government and financial policy. To improve the management of the Chinese government, Wang Anshi tried to get honest, intelligent officials by improving the university system. He made the civil service examinations more practical and reformed the merit system to reduce corruption among government officials.

BACKGROUND The idea of a graduated income tax may need to be clarified. Help students to understand the difference between a graduated tax and a flat rate tax.

Wang Anshi used tax reform to improve the government's financial position. He instituted a graduated income tax, that is, a tax that requires wealthy people to pay a greater percentage of their income than poorer people pay. This new form of taxation relieved the peasants of their enormous taxes and increased government revenues. The extra tax money was used to hire workers for government projects, thus abolishing the forced labor system. The earlier system, in which peasants had to perform work for the government, was seen as unfair to the peasants.

After the death of Wang Anshi in 1086, his reforms were eventually scrapped and forgotten. The Song empire continued to decline until it met its end—the completion of this dynastic cycle—in 1279, when it was conquered by the Mongols.

Chinese Dynasties, 960–1911

Song Dynasty 960–1279
Jin in north 1127–1234
Song in south 1127–1279
great age of scholarship, landscape painting, and porcelains • sea trade • paper money • footbinding begun • compass invented

Mongol Dynasty 1279–1368
new capital Beijing • Marco Polo's visit

Ming Dynasty 1368–1644
flowering of culture • great sea trade • stable, prosperous era • Forbidden City built • foreigners banned

Manchu Dynasty 1644–1911
borders expanded • prosperity, then falling standard of living • Western missionaries and foreign trade • China forced to accept treaty ports • Republican revolution (1911)

3 ASSESS AND CLOSE

ASSESS

1. How were Chinese peasants affected by government policies? (Except for taxation and labor projects, there was little contact. Wang Anshi brought improvements but only during his term.)
2. What enabled China's population to increase during Song rule? (Peasants increased food production by using better tools, new types of rice.)

OPTIONAL RETEACHING

Direct students to make a chart illustrating the class structure and functions of each level of society in Song China.

OPTIONAL ENRICHMENT

1. Have students create a time line of the Song period including the dates of Jin rule, inventions, and Wang Anshi's term in office. (average)
2. Assign a research paper on the reforms of Wang Anshi's new policies. Instruct students to include specific improvements, their results, and the amount of opposition each met. (challenging)

INDEPENDENT PRACTICE/ HOMEWORK

Assign the Section Review, Activities page 92, or Workbook page 62.

CLOSURE

Summarize the lesson by telling students that the advanced culture of Song China brought prosperity to the upper classes and enabled peasants to increase food production. The tax reforms of Wang Anshi helped peasants, but the reforms were short-lived as conservatives brought about a return to more traditional policies.

Answers to Section 2 Review

Identify

Key Terms, People, and Places are defined on pages indicated in parentheses. Also see the Glossary and Biographical Dictionary. foot-binding (299), Wang Anshi (299)

Main Ideas

1. Increased farm productivity caused population growth. Increased foreign trade brought economic growth and social classes.
2. Cities were prosperous, but peasants had barely enough food.
3. The family was a tightly organized unit that established order and settled conflicts in Chinese society.
4. He instituted educational and financial reforms, employed honest officials, instituted merit promotions and a graduated income tax, and abolished forced labor.

Critical Thinking

No, the graduated tax was simply to raise revenue; the head tax also punished "non-believers."

Not only were the Mongols skilled riders, as the warrior at left illustrates, but their chief weapon, an improved bow, was so strong that it could shoot an arrow with deadly force for an eighth of a mile.

3 Lesson Plan

Essential Learning Objective

Students will learn to discuss effects of Mongol rule and the importance of contacts between China and Eurasia.

1 FOCUS AND MOTIVATE

Ask students how an advanced culture, such as Song China, could be conquered by a less civilized people.

Section 2 Review

Identify foot-binding, Wang Anshi

Main Ideas

1. How did the growth of farming and trade affect Song China?
2. How did city life differ from peasant life in Song China?
3. In what ways was the family important in Chinese society?
4. How did Wang Anshi try to prevent the decline of the Song government?

Critical Thinking

Analyzing Comparisons: Can you make a comparison between the graduated tax the Chinese adopted and the tax imposed in the Arab Empire, which you learned about in Chapter 14? How were the goals of these taxes similar and different?

---

3 The Mongols ruled in China under the Khans.

Throughout Chinese history nomadic groups from the north had been breaking through the Great Wall. In the 1200s the Mongols, under Genghis

Khan, whom you studied in Chapters 13 and 14, conquered Jin China. The Chinese thus became part of a vast Mongol empire.

Kublai Khan became Mongol emperor of China (1260–1294).

After Genghis Khan's death in 1227, the Mongols continued their conquests. In 1234 Genghis' successor brought the Jin dynasty to an end and established a Mongol dynasty in northern China. In addition, as you read earlier, Genghis Khan's grandson Batu conquered most of Russia, and his grandson Hulagu conquered much of the Middle East. (See map, page 302.)

The most powerful of Genghis Khan's grandsons, however, was **Kublai Khan** [kü′blī kän′], who became Mongol emperor in 1260. He completed the conquest of China in 1279.

China was now part of a huge Mongol empire that sprawled across most of Eurasia. The only areas of Eurasia not conquered by the Mongols were western Europe, India, and Southeast Asia. To rule this vast territory, the Mongols divided the empire into four khanates, or kingdoms.

Although the Mongols in all the other khanates adopted the Islamic faith, Kublai Khan moved his capital from the Mongolian city of Karakorum to

BACKGROUND According to Rashid al-Din, a 14th century Persian historian, Genghis Khan said that "Man's highest joy is in victory: to conquer one's enemies, to pursue them, to deprive them of their possessions, to make their beloved weep, to ride on their horses, and to embrace their daughters and wives."

Beijing and adopted Chinese ways. He was more interested in being the emperor of China than in being the emperor of the Mongol empire. However, he was just as ambitious as his grandfather had been in conquering new territories.

To this end he brought Korea and parts of Indochina under his control. Kublai Khan even sent naval expeditions against the island of Java in the south and against Japan in the east, but the results were disastrous in both areas. As you will read in Chapter 17, when Kublai Khan tried to invade Japan, typhoons destroyed his navy.

Kublai Khan enjoyed more success within China, where he showed outstanding ability in governing the country. He ruled as the Chinese emperor until his death in 1294. During his rule he built roads, filled granaries with wheat for use in times of famine, and gave state aid to orphans and the sick. He also built elaborate palaces for himself and his government in Beijing.

Kublai Khan understood the importance of commerce and therefore encouraged trade by inviting foreign merchants to visit China. Many were Muslims who came from Central Asia, India, and Persia. Some, however, were Christians who came from Europe.

Marco Polo visited the Mongol court (1274–1292).

The best-known of the European visitors were the Polos, an Italian merchant family. They became famous because of a book written by one of them entitled *The Travels of Marco Polo*. The book provides historians with a vast amount of information about Kublai Khan's empire. **Marco Polo** was 17 years old when he left his home town of Venice in 1271 to travel with his father and uncle to the court of Kublai Khan. The journey through Central Asia and across the terrible Gobi to China took four years.

Marco Polo stayed in China until he was 34. During that time he became a favorite of the Mongol emperor and served as a valuable official of the government. He returned to Venice in 1295, where he had trouble convincing his fellow Italians of the truth of what he had seen. As you read in the chapter introduction, they thought his stories exaggerated the size of the population and wealth of

China, and they called him "Marco Millions" as well as the "prince of liars." However, other Europeans—missionaries and merchants—followed Polo's route to distant China and confirmed his reports. These early descriptions of China's wealth inspired Europeans in the following century to search for sea routes that would lead them to the rich East Asian empires.

Mongol rule permitted important exchanges.

Historically the Mongol empire lasted only from the mid-13th to the mid-14th century. During its brief existence, however, trade and travel across Eurasia was safer than ever before. As a result, ideas and inventions were transmitted from one end of the continent to the other. It was during this period that Chinese inventions such as gunpowder and printing became known first to Muslims and then to Europeans.

Ideas from the rest of Eurasia were also brought to China. Kublai Khan, for example, welcomed to his court representatives from practically every known religion. The Chinese, however, reacted in a very different fashion. They hated their conquerers, and once they drove out the Mongols in 1368, the new rulers of China, the Mings, limited contacts with outsiders. They did all they could to keep China free from any more invasions.

Section 3 Review

Identify Kublai Khan, Marco Polo

Main Ideas

1. How did the Mongol emperor Kublai Khan's rule help China?
2. In what way was Marco Polo important in world history?
3. What conditions allowed for cultural exchanges between China and other civilizations during the time of the Mongol Empire?

Critical Thinking

Evaluating Sources of Information: If you were an Italian living at the time of Marco Polo, how would you decide whether or not to believe his tales of faraway China? What criteria might you use in making your decision? How might you be able to verify Marco Polo's information?

2. Marco Polo introduced Chinese culture to Europe and also introduced medieval Europe to the Chinese.

3. safe conditions for trade and travel across Eurasia

Critical Thinking
Example: Person should consider how reliable the source is—whether that source is likely to be accurate and unbiased. Also one should consider any objects from China or other travelers corroborating reports.

GEOGRAPHY:
A KEY TO HISTORY

Ask students how the Mongols were able to create such a large empire. (Genghis Khan organized their armies into the most efficient fighting force in the world.)

Answers to REVIEW

1. provided grass for their animals and a corridor to the settled areas
2. Possible answers: fostered trade and the spread of ideas throughout a large expanse of land, reduced the threat of raids, unified the Mongols

Answer to MAP QUESTION

Opinion. The short grasses of the steppe were suited for nomadic herding. However, the nomads needed some of the products of the settled communities that could be obtained through trade or by banding together and raiding communities outside the steppe region.

GEOGRAPHY

A Key to History

THE STEPPE AND THE MONGOLS

Stretching across west central Asia north of the Black, Caspian, and Aral seas is a wide band of grassland, the steppe. The northeastern steppe reaches into Mongolia, a vast plateau that straddles the borders of modern China. Throughout history, the steppe has provided a corridor through which people moved across Asia.

The steppe never attracted farmers because rainfall was unreliable. Instead, about 800 B.C. migratory, horse-riding people began occupying the steppe, grazing cattle, sheep, and ponies on the natural grasses.

Locate the steppe region on the map. How would the steppe have fostered contacts among the Mongols and promoted trade?

The Mongol Empire, About 1290

Steppes

Venice
RUSSIA
SIBERIA

Black Sea
•Sarai
Karakorum
Mediterranean Sea
Aral Sea
MONGOLIA
KOREA
Tabriz•
Caspian Sea
Beijing•
Samarkand
CHINA
Hangzhou•
TIBET
Red Sea
ARABIA
INDIA
INDOCHINA
Arabian Sea
N
AFRICA
Bay of Bengal
South China Sea

0   1000 MILES
0   1000 KILOMETERS

Life on the steppe was a hard struggle against a harsh environment. Raiding and looting was an accepted way to make a living. The most admired leaders were those who conducted successful wars of plunder.

All the ancient civilizations, from China in the east to the Roman Empire in the west, suffered from massive raids by these migrating steppe peoples. The most devastating attacks of all, however, were launched by the Mongols in the early 13th century under the leadership of Genghis Khan.

Genghis Khan's supreme achievement was in uniting all the rival Mongol groups—all the "dwellers in felt-walled tents." He then conquered most of the steppe by organizing the Mongol army into the most efficient fighting force of its time.

From his capital at Karakorum, Genghis Khan raided China. Under his sons and grandsons, the Mongols created the largest land empire in history, spreading east into China, north into Russia, and west into the Islamic world. (See map.)

Too large to endure for long, the Mongol empire fell apart after about 100 years. After its collapse in the mid-14th century, the migratory peoples of the steppes never again seriously threatened the settled civilizations. A new weapon—firearms—decisively changed the balance of power against the bows and arrows of the steppe raiders.

REVIEW

1. In what ways was the steppe environment helpful to the Mongols?
2. What benefits might have resulted from Genghis Khan's conquests?

4 Chinese culture influenced Vietnam and Korea.

As the dominant civilization in East Asia, China had an impact well beyond its borders. That impact was particularly strong on two neighboring countries, **Vietnam** to the south and **Korea** to the northeast. Yet the Vietnamese and Koreans maintained their own national identities, which spurred each of them to fight for independence from China, not once, but several times. Locate Vietnam and Korea on the map on page 794.

Vietnam was under Chinese rule for more than 1,000 years(100 B.C.–A.D. 900).

Early Vietnamese culture was a mixture of the cultures from many different regions of Southeast Asia and the nearby Indonesian islands. By 200 B.C. the Vietnamese had a well-developed agricultural society. However, the Vietnamese did not have the military might to match the expanding Chinese empire. In 100 B.C., during the early years of the Han dynasty, the Chinese seized control of Vietnam. During the next 1,000 years, China had a tremendous influence over Vietnam's cultural development. The Vietnamese imitated Chinese art and literature and adopted Confucian social and religious ideas. They also took on the Chinese administrative system.

Even though the Vietnamese made many advances because of Chinese influence, they resented and rebelled against harsh Chinese rule. The most famous rebellion occurred in A.D. 39 and was headed by two noblewomen, known as the **Trung Sisters**. They led Vietnamese troops into battle against a more powerful Chinese army. Although they were defeated, the Trung sisters showed such spirit and courage that modern Vietnamese look upon them as national heroes.

Vietnam gained independence in A.D. 939.

The Vietnamese finally liberated themselves from Chinese rule at the beginning of the 10th century. For the next 800 years, however, they continually had to fight off attempts by China to reimpose its control. During this time the Vietnamese gained impressive military strength. In fact, in the 1200s they defeated Kublai Khan, preventing the Mongols from overrunning Southeast Asia.

In time the Vietnamese, who were concentrated in the north, began to expand southward. After a brief struggle against the Ming Chinese, who took control of Vietnam for about 20 years in the early 1400s, Vietnam conquered large areas of Southeast Asia. The Vietnamese set up a well-run empire with an advanced legal code, a liberal land distribution policy, and a vibrant culture. However, in the 16th and 17th centuries, Vietnam was wracked by civil war, which made the country an easy target for European colonial powers a century later.

The Koreans were able to maintain a distinct culture in spite of turmoil.

Like Vietnam, Korea was long influenced by China but unlike Vietnam, Korea preserved a distinct political and cultural identity. The country, on China's northeastern border, was an important link in many of China's trade routes to the east. Korea was also important to China as a buffer state between China, Russia, and Japan. As a result, China used its strength to preserve Korea's independence. In return, the Koreans paid tribute to the Chinese government.

Although the Chinese remained clear of Korea for most of its history, in the 2nd century B.C., when China was under the Han dynasty, many Chinese moved into northern Korea. During this time the Koreans adopted and modified many Chinese agricultural techniques and their system of writing.

The strong resistance of the Koreans eventually drove the Chinese away in A.D. 313. However, dissension among three rival Korean kingdoms kept the peninsula in turmoil for more than 300 years.

The Silla dynasty (668–935). In 668 one of these kingdoms, the kingdom of **Silla** [shē′lə], gained control over the entire peninsula and unified the country. From 668 to 935, the unified Silla period, Korea experienced a Golden Age in which it enjoyed peace and grew prosperous. The flowering of Chinese civilization under the Tang dynasty benefited Korea, as the Koreans absorbed Chinese art and literature and made them part of their own culture. Buddhism, imported from China, became increasingly influential.

4 Lesson Plan

Essential Learning Objectives

Students will learn to:
- evaluate the extent of Chinese influence on Vietnamese culture.
- discuss how Korea preserved some independence and culture.

1 FOCUS AND MOTIVATE

Ask students to suggest problems that countries on China's borders might have experienced in living near such a dominant culture.

2 TEACH

- Clarify the chronology of Vietnam's relationship with China. Point out aspects of Chinese culture and government adopted by the Vietnamese.
- Stress Korea's significance to China as a trade link and buffer state. Referring to the map on page 302, clarify Korea's strategic location.

GUIDED PRACTICE

Direct students to make lists of ways in which Vietnamese and Korean culture reflected Chinese influences.

3 ASSESS AND CLOSE

ASSESS

1. What democratized learning in Korea? (the invention of a Korean alphabet in the 15th century)

OPTIONAL RETEACHING

Select students to prepare parallel time lines on the chalkboard to compare events in Vietnam and Korea.

Students also may be assigned Activities reteaching page 95.

The intricate Korean royal gold and jade crown above dates from the 5th or 6th century A.D. It was worn by a king of the Silla dynasty.

Eventually, however, the Silla dynasty grew decadent and slowly weakened. In A.D. 935 the king of Silla peacefully surrendered to the rival dynasty known as the Koryo. Modern Korea gets its name from the Koryo dynasty, which lasted until 1392.

The Koryo dynasty (935–1392). Under the Koryo many reforms were undertaken. A civil service system was revived, land was universally distributed, and education became available to all. In addition, the introduction of movable metal type spurred the printing of many books, including an important collection of Buddhist texts.

Near the end of the Koryo dynasty, Korea faced both a growing decadence in the government and increasing attacks from the Mongols and Japanese raiders. Eventually the Koryo dynasty was overthrown, and in 1392 the Yi dynasty began.

The Yi dynasty (1392–1910). For the early part of this dynasty, which was founded upon the principles of Confucianism, Korea experienced a second Golden Age. During this period of flourishing art and scholarship, **King Sejong** reigned from 1419 to 1451. He instituted many social reforms, making significant improvements in the daily lives of the common people.

King Sejong also established the Hall of Talented Scholars, a group of scholars that is credited with the invention of a practical new Korean alphabet. This alphabet eventually replaced the cumbersome Chinese word-characters and democratized learning. Today this alphabet, known as *han'gul,* is so revered that its anniversary, October 9, is a national holiday.

The second Golden Age came to an end in the early 1600s when Korea was subjected to repeated foreign invasions. The Japanese were the first of these foreign powers to try to conquer Korea, laying the country to waste. Although the Japanese were unsuccessful in their invasion attempt, in its weakened state, Korea could not ward off the second wave of invaders, the Chinese, who overran the country and exacted large tribute payments.

As a result of these frequent invasions, Korea adopted a policy of isolation similar to that of Ming China. It became a "hermit nation" for the next 250 years. No foreigners were allowed to enter the land, and only a few Koreans could leave, usually on missions to China. By the late 1800s, Korea's government had become weak and corrupt, ripe for exploitation by European and Asian powers.

Section 4 Review

Identify Vietnam, Korea, Trung Sisters, Silla, King Sejong

Main Ideas
1. How did China influence Vietnam during its 1,000-year rule?
2. How did the Vietnamese regain control of their culture from the 10th century to the 16th century?
3. How was Korea able to maintain its distinct culture throughout centuries of internal and external turmoil?

Critical Thinking
Making Decisions: Do you think that national isolation was a wise policy for Vietnam and Korea? Give reasons for your decision.

Blue-and-White Chinese Porcelain

Chinese porcelain has always been highly prized within China and abroad for its beauty, its strength, and its translucence, or partial transparency. Vases and wine jars and even porcelain pillows were created for the use of emperors in their royal palaces during the Song dynasty (960–1279). At that time, Chinese potters began to paint their ware with designs—usually brown or black—under the influence of Islamic pottery from Persia.

The fish on the Mongol dynasty jar (below right) denotes wealth and harmony. The other porcelains were found in Syria.

During the Mongol dynasty (1279–1368), decorations in a rich, cobalt blue were first applied to translucent white porcelain. This blue-and-white porcelain became immensely popular during the Ming dynasty (1368–1644), which you will read about in Chapter 24. It has influenced pottery making in other parts of the world ever since.

Seventeenth-century Dutch trading ships brought huge quantities of blue-and-white porcelain to Europe. The potters of Delft, in the Netherlands, eventually learned to make their own blue-and-white Delftware. In the late 1700s, Josiah Spode, a British potter, began copying Chinese designs that featured a large blue willow tree by a little blue bridge. This Willowware pattern is still popular today.

During the Mongol and Ming dynasties, Chinese potters produced as many as 100,000 pieces of porcelain in a single year. Most of the blue-and-white ware was exported. Fragments of such porcelain have been found in Egypt, East Africa, Sri Lanka, Java, and the Philippines.

The highest price to date paid at auction for a piece of blue-and-white Ming porcelain has been $ 1 million. (An underglaze red vase sold for more than $ 2 million.) Blue-and-white porcelain was made in enormous quantities, mostly for export—as many as 100,000 pieces a year or more. As a result, prices for Yuan and Ming dynasty porcelains vary widely, from a few hundred dollars or less to a few hundred thousand dollars. A fairly standard but rare piece would command $1,000 to $1,500.

Ask students to generalize about trade during the Mongol and Ming dynasties on the basis of the objects pictured in the feature. (Possible answer: Chinese porcelain was traded throughout the known world.) What other generalizations can students make about the Chinese porcelain from this period? (Possible answer: The porcelain pieces must have been strong as well as highly prized by their owners to have survived so long.) For extra credit, students might check an encyclopedia or books on East Asian art for a picture of a porcelain pillow—actually a neck support that was reputedly quite comfortable.

CHAPTER 16 REVIEW

Section Summaries

Section 1

Chinese civilization continued to flourish under the Songs.

After the fall of the Tang rulers, China lost much territory. In 960 the Song dynasty came to power, but was militarily weak, and soon the Chinese empire became divided. A nomadic tribe from Manchuria, the Jin, seized control of the north and drove a Song emperor to set up a new capital in the south. Under the Songs many advances in technology, scholarship, and art took place.

Section 2

Daily life changed during the Song era.

Advances in farming technologies supported a large increase in population. Foreign trade brought great wealth to the cities, where rich culture thrived. However, country life was little affected by the wealth and prosperity of the cities. Peasants led hard lives. However, the family was important in all classes of Chinese society, dictating social organization and many social customs.

Section 3

The Mongols ruled in China under the Khans.

As the Mongol emperor of China, Kublai Khan encouraged trade, promoted economic development, and invited foreigners to his court. One of the most important foreign visitors was Marco Polo, who stayed in China for 17 years and wrote a book about his experiences.

Section 4

Chinese culture influenced Vietnam and Korea.

During the Han dynasty, China invaded parts of Vietnam and Korea. As a result, these areas were strongly influenced by Chinese culture. Although Vietnam and Korea both eventually broke away from Chinese rule and developed distinctive identities, China left its mark on the art, literature, government, and customs of each country.

Test Yourself

Key Terms, People, and Places
Identify the significance of each of the following:

Section 1
a. Song dynasty
b. Jin dynasty
c. Beijing
d. Hangzhou
e. porcelain

Section 2
a. footbinding
b. Wang Anshi

Section 3
a. Kublai Khan
b. Marco Polo

Review Dates

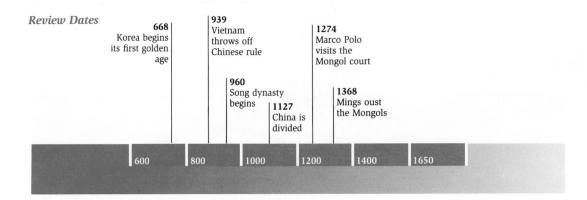

668 Korea begins its first golden age

939 Vietnam throws off Chinese rule

960 Song dynasty begins

1127 China is divided

1274 Marco Polo visits the Mongol court

1368 Mings oust the Mongols

600 800 1000 1200 1400 1650

Section 4

a. Vietnam   **d.** Silla

b. Korea   **e.** King Sejong

c. Trung Sisters

Main Ideas

Section 1

1. Outline the history of China during the Song dynasty.

2. What two themes have been central to Chinese history?

3. Describe some of China's accomplishments in technology, scholarship, and art during the Song dynasty.

Section 2

1. How did advances in farming and trade change Chinese life under the Songs?

2. How did Chinese city-dwellers live differently from the peasants during the Song era?

3. What was the significance of the family in Chinese society?

4. Describe Wang Anshi's reforms of the Song government.

Section 3

1. How was Kublai Khan's rule beneficial to China?

2. Why was Marco Polo's visit significant in European and Chinese history?

3. Why were cultural exchanges so common during the rule of the Mongols?

Section 4

1. What were the effects on Vietnam of Chinese influence between 100 B.C. and A.D. 900?

2. What happened to Vietnamese culture after the Chinese were ousted?

3. How was a distinctive Korean culture preserved throughout its history?

Critical Thinking

1. Identifying Assumptions Why do you think Europeans refused to believe Marco Polo when he returned from China? What assumptions do you think they were making about their own civilization that they would discount Polo's descriptions?

2. Recognizing Values Reread the directions of the Chinese painter on page 296 of this chapter. Using this artist's way of looking at nature, choose a tree, flower, or other living object to study. Write a paragraph about what you feel is the character or spirit of your subject. Keep in mind the values of the Chinese painter.

Chapter Skills and Activities

Practicing Study and Research Skills
Synthesizing Information

To synthesize information means to combine different parts of something, making it a complex whole. To bring together what you've learned about China in this chapter and about Europe in the last unit, choose a partner and role-play a conversation between a Mongol emperor and a European merchant in a Chinese court. The two people should be trying to establish trade relations between their two countries.

Linking Past and Present

Chinese porcelain, about which you learned in this chapter, is still quite popular today. Find a modern example of Chinese porcelain in a book or magazine such as this tea cup and lid, and discuss its similarities with or differences from ancient Chinese pottery.

Learning History Through Maps

Compare the map of the Mongol empire on page 302 with the physical map of Asia on page 795. What physical features do you think might have prevented the Mongols from taking over India and Indochina? Why do you think the Mongol empire did not spread into the northern part of Asia? What other lands do you think the Mongols might have conquered if they had developed a navy?

CRITICAL THINKING QUESTION LEVEL 1. easy;
2. challenging

Chapter

17 The Emergence of Japan

OVERVIEW

This chapter focuses on the development of Japanese history and culture from the prehistoric period to the first European contact in the 16th century.

PLANNING CHART

Section	Text Pages	Key Concept	Suggested Teaching Time
1 Japan's geography influenced its history and its culture.	309–311	The history and culture of Japan reflects its position as an island-nation and its rugged environment.	One day **Less time?** Combine the material on daily life in Section 4 with the treatment in Section 1 of Japanese culture. Discuss the material on women's status in Section 4 with Section 2.
2 Early Japanese civilization borrowed from China.	311–316	Japan's rulers chose useful aspects of China's civilization and adapted them to their own needs.	One day **More time?** Use *Overhead Transparency 33.*
3 Feudalism and a samurai warrior-class developed.	316–319	In Japanese feudal society, highly disciplined warriors became important, and artists and scholars created masterpieces in the arts and architecture.	One day **More time?** Use *Overhead Transparency 34* or *Source Reading 17A.*
4 The Japanese created distinctive home and family customs.	319–320	Japanese daily life was unique.	One day **More time?** Use *Source Reading 17B.*

ANCILLARIES

Materials that may be used with this chapter to reinforce, reteach, enrich, and assess learning are pictured on the following pages.

Teacher's Resource File

ACTIVITIES

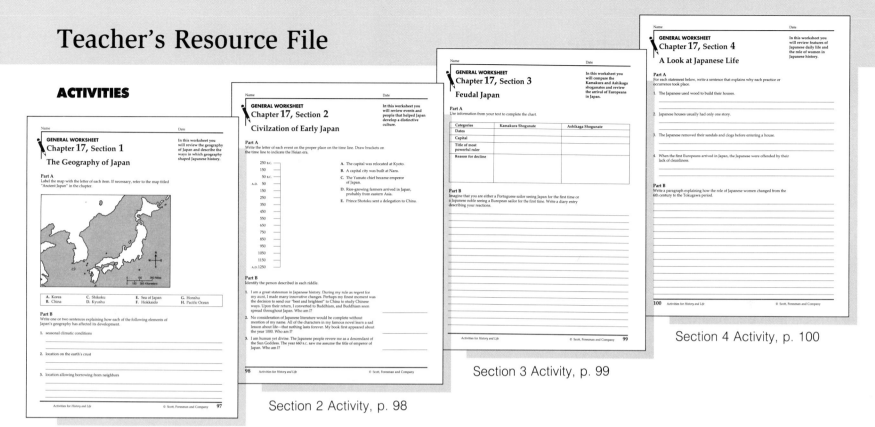

Section 1 Activity, p. 97

GENERAL WORKSHEET
Chapter 17, Section 1
The Geography of Japan

In this worksheet you will review the geography of Japan and describe the ways in which geography shaped Japanese history.

Part A
Label the map with the letter of each item. If necessary, refer to the map titled "Ancient Japan" in the chapter.

| A. Korea | C. Shikoku | E. Sea of Japan | G. Honshu |
| B. China | D. Kyushu | F. Hokkaido | H. Pacific Ocean |

Part B
Write one or two sentences explaining how each of the following elements of Japan's geography has affected its development.

1. seasonal climatic conditions
2. location on the earth's crust
3. location allowing borrowing from neighbors

Section 2 Activity, p. 98

GENERAL WORKSHEET
Chapter 17, Section 2
Civilzation of Early Japan

In this worksheet you will review events and people that helped Japan develop a distinctive culture.

Part A
Write the letter of each event on the proper place on the time line. Draw brackets on the time line to indicate the Heian era.

A. The capital was relocated at Kyoto.
B. A capital city was built at Nara.
C. The Yamato chief became emperor of Japan.
D. Rice-growing farmers arrived in Japan, probably from eastern Asia.
E. Prince Shotoku sent a delegation to China.

Part B
Identify the person described in each riddle.

Section 3 Activity, p. 99

GENERAL WORKSHEET
Chapter 17, Section 3
Feudal Japan

In this worksheet you will compare the Kamakura and Ashikaga shogunates and review the arrival of Europeans in Japan.

Part A
Use information from your text to complete the chart.

Categories	Kamakura Shogunate	Ashikaga Shogunate
Dates		
Capital		
Title of most powerful ruler		
Reason for decline		

Part B
Imagine that you are either a Portuguese sailor seeing Japan for the first time or a Japanese noble seeing a European sailor for the first time. Write a diary entry describing your reactions.

Section 4 Activity, p. 100

GENERAL WORKSHEET
Chapter 17, Section 4
A Look at Japanese Life

In this worksheet you will review features of Japanese daily life and the role of women in Japanese history.

Part A
For each statement below, write a sentence that explains why each practice or occurrence took place.

1. The Japanese used wood to build their houses.
2. Japanese houses usually had only one story.
3. The Japanese removed their sandals and clogs before entering a house.
4. When the first Europeans arrived in Japan, the Japanese were offended by their lack of cleanliness.

Part B
Write a paragraph explaining how the role of Japanese women changed from the 6th century to the Tokugawa period.

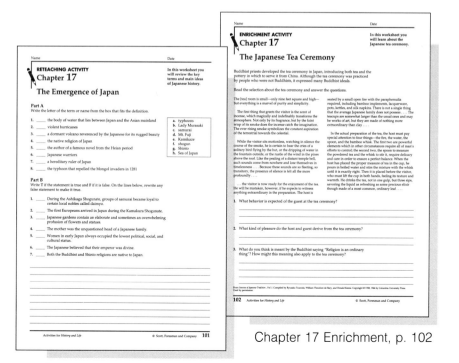

Chapter 17 Reteaching, p. 101

RETEACHING ACTIVITY
Chapter 17
The Emergence of Japan

In this worksheet you will review the key terms and main ideas of Japanese history.

Part A
Write the letter of the term or name from the box that fits the definition.

Chapter 17 Enrichment, p. 102

ENRICHMENT ACTIVITY
Chapter 17
The Japanese Tea Ceremony

In this worksheet you will learn about the Japanese tea ceremony.

Teacher's Resource File

GEOGRAPHY SKILLS

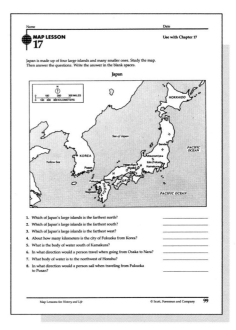

Chapter 17 Geography
Worksheet/Map, pp. 35–36

Chapter 17 Map Lesson, p. 99

TESTS

Chapter Test, pp. 81–82

Alternate Chapter Test, pp. 83–84

Other Optional Ancillaries

WORKBOOK

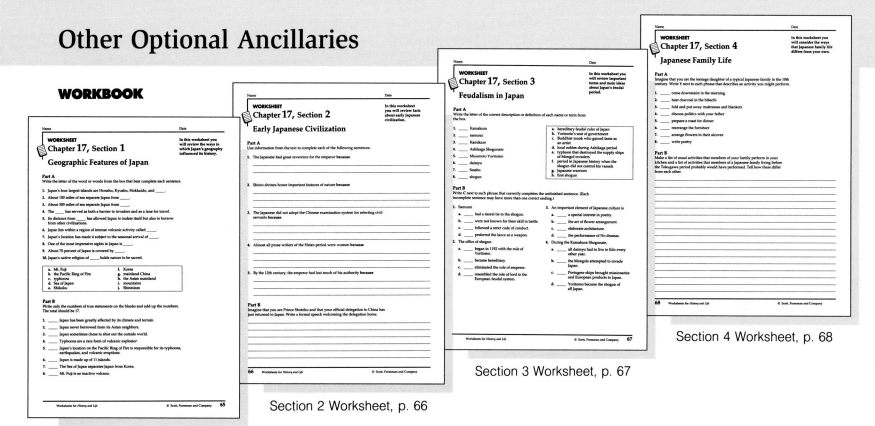

Section 1 Worksheet, p. 65

Section 2 Worksheet, p. 66

Section 3 Worksheet, p. 67

Section 4 Worksheet, p. 68

SOURCE READINGS

Source Reading 17A

Source Reading 17B

TEST GENERATOR

40 multiple-choice questions for Chapter 17

OVERHEAD TRANSPARENCIES

Overhead Transparency 33

Overhead Transparency 34

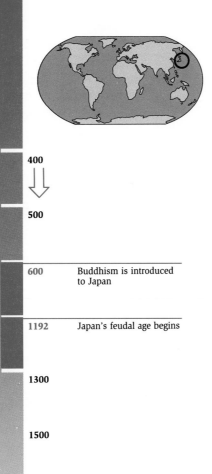

The Emergence of Japan

500 – 1603

400

500

600   Buddhism is introduced to Japan

1192   Japan's feudal age begins

1300

1500

Many Japanese say that their greatest literary work is *The Tale of Genji,* a novel written around the year 1000 by Lady Murasaki, a noble at the court of a Heian emperor. (See page 314.) Some think that *The Tale of Genji* reflects a uniquely Japanese attitude toward living. The novel's characters, they say, show a special sensitivity to beauty in all its forms. In addition, the characters all learn the sad lesson that love and beauty are always transient, that nothing lasts forever.

The hero of the novel is young prince Genji, a son of the emperor. In the passage below, Genji wanders through his garden, mourning his wife's early death:

> Whatever he did and wherever he went, he felt that a light was gone out of his life and he was very despondent.
>
> Among the withered undergrowth in the garden Genji found to his delight a few gentians still blossoming . . . he plucked some and bade the wet nurse Saiso give them to [Genji's] child's grandmother, together with the verse: "The gentian flower that lingered amid the withered grasses of the hedge I send you in remembrance of the autumn that is passed." "To you," he added, "it will seem a poor thing in contrast to the flowers that are gone."
>
> The Princess looked at her grandson's innocent smiling face and thought that in beauty he was not far behind the child she had lost. Already her tears were pouring faster than a stormy wind shakes down the dry leaves from a tree, and when she read Genji's message, they flowed faster still. This was her answer: "New tears, but tears of joy it brings—this blossom from a meadow that is now laid waste."

The Tale of Genji focuses on court life in Heian Japan. The novel does not deal with the condition of the lower classes at that time, nor does it say much about contemporary politics. Yet the constant struggle among aristocratic families for wealth, position, and power was indeed a force that helped shape the Japanese political tradition.

Fragrant cherry blossoms frame the distant Mt. Fuji, located on Japan's island of Honshu. Mount Fuji is the country's highest mountain.

Reading Preview

In this chapter you will read how a distinctive civilization developed in Japan.

1. *Japan's geography influenced its history and its culture.*
2. *Early Japanese civilization borrowed from China.*
3. *Feudalism and a samurai warrior-class developed.*
4. *The Japanese created distinctive home and family customs.*

 Japan's geography influenced its history and its culture.

Japan is a nation of islands—four large islands, called Hokkaido [hō kī′dō], Honshu [hon′shü], Kyushu [kyü′shü], and Shikoku [shi kō′kü], and more than 3,000 small ones. In total land area, the country is about the same size as California.

The geography of Japan has helped shape its people and history.

Japan's location, along with its climate and terrain, played an important role in the country's develop-

What is the predominant geographical feature of Japan? (The four major islands are 70% mountains.)

OPTIONAL RETEACHING
Write Islands, Mountains, and Forests on the chalkboard. Ask students to name aspects of daily life that have been influenced by these features.

OPTIONAL ENRICHMENT
1. Assign a research report on volcanism in Japan. (average)
2. Assign small groups of students to research the native vegetation, animal life, and natural resources of Japan. (challenging)

INDEPENDENT PRACTICE/ HOMEWORK
Assign the Section Review, Activities page 97, or Workbook page 65.

CLOSURE
Summarize the lesson by telling students that Japanese culture developed in response to geographical and climatic influences. Protected from invasion by the Sea of Japan, the Japanese were yet able to learn from China and Korea. A close spiritual relationship between the people and nature is reflected in Japan's religion, literature, and arts.

Ancient Japan

MAP STUDY Japan is a nation of islands. What are the four major islands of Japan? Which of the major islands is the farthest north? Which is the farthest south?

ment. Japan has been far enough away from other countries to discourage invasion and to remain isolated when it chose to shut out the outside world. At the same time, the country has been near enough to the Asian mainland to be able to borrow from other Asian civilizations, especially the Chinese, whenever the Japanese felt it desirable to do so. In fact, about 100 miles of water separate Japan from Korea, and 500 miles of sea stand between Japan and mainland China. These waters have contributed to Japan's unique relationship with the sea.

The Japanese islands are places of rugged natural beauty. Mountains cover about 70 percent of the country, and thick forests are common. The **Sea of Japan**, which lies between Japan and the Asian mainland, has served both as a barrier to invaders and as a lane for travel. The Japanese could choose to travel either between their own islands or beyond. The sea also served as a source for food (fish and other seafood) for the Japanese society.

Throughout its history, Japan, like much of Asia, has experienced the seasonal arrivals of **typhoons**, which are violent hurricanes, and monsoons. The winter monsoons generally bring cold air and snow to the northern islands, and the summer monsoons bring hot, humid weather to central and southern Japan. In addition to the monsoons, Japan has often felt the destructive power of tidal waves, earthquakes, and volcanic eruptions that are the result of its location on a very unstable part of the earth's crust. Japan lies within a region of intense volcanic activity that encircles the Pacific Ocean, often called the Pacific Ring of Fire.

Japanese culture reflects a reverence for nature.

Nature also has had a strong influence on Japanese life. Japan is a rugged, mountainous land noted for its picturesque scenery. One of the most impressive sights is **Mount Fuji**, a dormant volcano more than 12,000 feet high on the island of Honshu. In winter, Mount Fuji is covered with snow and skiiers, and in spring, its lower slopes are decorated with fragrant cherry blossoms. For such wonders of nature, the Japanese have developed a deep appreciation that is reflected in all aspects of their culture.

Japan's native religion of Shintoism holds nature to be sacred, and Shinto shrines have been built in many beautiful places throughout the country. The Japanese love of simple, natural beauty is also seen in their arts—in their style of architecture, sculpture, painting, and literature.

Japanese poetry especially reflects this style. The following poem, which uses one of the Japa-

What's in a Name?

JAPAN The Chinese told Marco Polo of the island kingdom which they called Zipangu, meaning "sun-origin kingdom." This is how Europeans first learned it. Later, Zipangu became Japan, the "land of the rising sun."

ANSWER TO MAP STUDY The four main islands are Hokkaido, Honshu, Shikoku, and Kyushu. Hokkaido is the farthest north. Kyushu is the farthest south.

BACKGROUND Only about 10–15% of the land in Japan is arable.

nese names for their country, Yamato [yä′mä tō], expresses the poet's feelings for Japan.

> If one should ask you
>   What is the heart
> of Island Yamato—
> It is the mountain cherry blossom
>   Which shines brightly in the
> morning sun.

Section 1 Review

Identify Japan, Sea of Japan, typhoons, Mt. Fuji
Main Ideas
1. How has Japan's location influenced the country's culture?
2. In what ways does Japanese culture reflect an appreciation for nature?

Critical Thinking
Making Hypotheses: Consider Japan's identity as a mountainous island nation. How do you think its geography might affect Japan's relationships with other nations?

2 | Early Japanese civilization borrowed from China.

According to Japanese mythology, the islands were created and settled by a sea god and sun goddess. Drops of water falling from the Sea God's silver spear are said to have formed the islands. A divine grandson of the Sun Goddess was chosen to be the ruler of these islands, and in 660 B.C. one of his human descendants, Jimmu Tenno, was said to become the first Japanese emperor.

The Japanese belief in the divine origin of the emperor has played an important role in Japanese thinking. To this day, the Japanese consider themselves to be unique in their heritage. As one Japanese historian wrote:

> Great Yamato [Japan] is a divine country. It is only our land whose foundations were first laid by the Divine Ancestor. It alone has been transmitted by the Sun Goddess to a long line of her descendants. There is nothing of this kind in foreign countries.

Archaeology has revealed Japan's ancient past.

Archaeological digging since the 1950s has done much to fill in gaps of knowledge that have existed about Japan's ancient history. People have lived in the Japanese islands for many thousands of years, probably from as early as 30,000 B.C. These early people are known to have hunted and fished and maintained a stone-age culture.

Around 250 B.C. a new people came to Japan, probably from eastern Asia. These people were farmers who knew how to grow rice in flooded fields, using a farming method common in southern China. Iron axes, knives, and hoes and bronze swords, spears, mirrors, and other things that were found through archaeological research have led scientists to believe that these people also knew how to weave cloth and use metals.

A new emperor spread the worship of the Sun Goddess.

Japanese contact with the Asian mainland, and with Korea in particular, was strong from the 3rd through the 6th centuries A.D. Large groups of immigrants, each of whom brought new skills and ideas, continued to move onto the islands of Japan. Among these immigrants were people with a strong warrior-tradition who were skilled at fighting on horseback. These warrior people rapidly populated the islands.

By the A.D. 400s, one of these warrior chiefs, who ruled a small inland plain called Yamato, extended his rule over much of Japan and became recognized as the country's emperor. The Yamato chief claimed descent from the Sun Goddess. His tokens of power—an iron sword, a curved jewel, and a bronze mirror representing the Sun Goddess—remain the symbols of the Japanese imperial family today.

As the Yamato chief and his descendants extended their rule, they spread the worship of the Sun Goddess. This faith, which later came to be called **Shinto** or "the way of the gods," held that nature had to be understood and reverenced. Many shrines were built during this early period in Japanese history to honor important features of nature, such as waterfalls, impressive groves of trees, and massive pieces of rock.

2 | Lesson Plan

Essential Learning Objectives
Students will learn to:
- describe the origins of many aspects of early Japanese culture.
- identify the ways in which Japanese political traditions differed from China's.

1 | FOCUS AND MOTIVATE

Discuss with students ways in which cultures borrow from each other. Ask students to describe aspects of

American life that have been borrowed by other nations as well as
things that we have adopted from others. (Most obvious examples are
foods, clothing styles, and automobiles. Remind students that our system of laws and government have
been adopted by many nations.)

- Draw a time line on the chalkboard to
illustrate the chronological development of early Japan from 30,000 B.C.
to A.D. 1250. Indicate the dates and
contributions of the groups that entered Japan.

- Point out that the Japanese emperor
sent delegations to China to learn
certain features of Chinese civilization. Stress that some features were
rejected, such as having civil service
exams open to all and the revolutionary tradition of the Mandate of
Heaven.

- Describe court life at Kyoto in the
Heian era pointing out the difference
between the lives of courtiers and
peasants.

- Describe how the gaining of tax-free
estates weakened the power of the
emperor.

GUIDED PRACTICE

Have students write tanka or haiku following the pattern described. The 5
lines of tanka should have 5, 7, 5, 7,
7 syllables respectively. The first three
lines standing alone would be haiku.

A torii, the symbol of Shinto, stands at the entrance of this shrine in Kyoto. Its posts
represent pillars that support the sky, and its crossbars symbolize the earth.

Japan borrowed its writing, religion, and other cultural elements from China.

When the Yamato rulers became emperors, Japan had no written language and little architecture or art of any importance. The central government had little real power. In contrast, however, China had been developing a rich civilization for centuries.

Writing. In the 6th century A.D., large numbers of Korean immigrants began crossing from the mainland. Possibly as early as the 5th century, educated Koreans brought with them, in addition to their arts and crafts, the Chinese writing with its character script. Chinese characters continue to play an important role in Japanese language today.

Religion. Under the guidance of a great statesman, Prince Shotoku (574–622), Chinese ways were systematically copied. Prince Shotoku [shō-tō′kü] ruled as regent for his aunt, Empress Suiko. In A.D. 600 he sent a large official delegation to China. In this delegation were a number of promising young men eager to study mainland civilization. Many returned home as converts to the Chinese religion of Buddhism and champions of Chinese arts and institutions.

Prince Shotoku accepted Buddhism, as did the royal court. Buddhism gradually gained broad appeal throughout Japan, but Shintoism continued to be widely supported. Many Japanese chose to practice both faiths simultaneously.

Other cultural ties. In addition to their writing and Buddhism, Japan borrowed many other useful styles and technologies from the Chinese. These included the calendar, ways of dress and cooking, and temple architecture. In addition, Chinese became the written language of the ruling class and scholars, who, with their command of the Chinese characters, were able to read the Chinese literary classics.

The Japanese tried to copy the efficient government of the Chinese as well. A law code similar to the Chinese code was drawn up, and strong efforts were made to extend the Japanese central government's power into the countryside as the Chinese had done. The Japanese rulers, however, were never wholly successful in this extension of power. In addition, Japan's rulers also made all land the property of the central government and established a taxing system throughout the country.

FROM THE ARCHIVES The excerpt is from *Sources of Japanese History*, Vol. I, by David John Lu (New York: McGraw-Hill, 1974). Ask students if they think government officials today would benefit from accepting the principles of official behavior

From the Archives

Japan's First "Constitution"

In A.D. 604 Prince Shotoku issued a series of instructions for the Japanese people called the Seventeen Article Constitution. These statements were not laws but moral teachings gathered from Buddhist, Confucian, Taoist, and other sources. The following excerpt deals with the way officials should behave.

I. Harmony is to be cherished, and opposition for opposition's sake must be avoided as a matter of principle. Men are often influenced by partisan feelings, except a few sagacious [wise] ones. Hence there are some who disobey their lords and fathers, or who dispute with their neighboring villages. If those above are harmonious and those below are cordial, their discussion will be guided by a spirit of conciliation, and reason shall naturally prevail. There will be nothing that cannot be accomplished.

Following the Chinese example, Japanese leaders decided to build a capital. Until this time, Japan had had no important political center. In 710, however, a capital city was built at Nara. Like the Chinese capital of the Tangs, it had fine palaces and temples.

In effect, however, the Japanese did not adopt all Chinese ways. The Chinese examination system for selecting civil servants was not used because the Japanese believed that government officials should be chosen on the basis of birth and social rank. In addition, unlike the Chinese, who believed that people could overthrow a bad ruler under the Mandate of Heaven, the Japanese maintained that their divine emperor should never be overthrown. Thus, although powerful families might gain actual political control in Japan, they always ruled behind the scenes. The emperor always remained honored in name as supreme ruler of Japan.

outlined in the excerpt. Have students explain their reasons.

ASSESS

1. What aspects of China's government were adopted by Japan? (law codes, central government system) Which were not? (civil service exams, right to overthrow bad rulers)

2. What writing system was used by Japanese women? (the kana alphabetic system, as they were not taught the Chinese characters)

OPTIONAL RETEACHING

Have students list aspects of Japanese culture learned from immigrants from Korea or through delegations sent to China. Discuss ways in which Japan's culture was similar to and yet different from China's.

OPTIONAL ENRICHMENT

1. Have students research events in China at the time of the Japanese delegations to find out the achievements that were developing in China at that time. (average)

2. Have students find and bring to class selections of Japanese poetry in the form of tanka or haiku. Students should describe their reactions to specific poems. (challenging)

3. Also for enrichment:

 Overhead Transparency 33

INDEPENDENT PRACTICE/ HOMEWORK

Assign the Section Review, Activities page 98, or Workbook page 66.

CLOSURE

Tell students that Japan learned about and adopted many cultural features from immigrants from Korea and from study groups sent to China. Life at the Heian court was luxurious and refined, unlike that of the peasants who labored under warrior-landlords in rural Japan.

The Shinto goddess of poetry and music plays on the biwa, a guitar-like instrument. This religious print dates from the 9th to 12th centuries.

A distinctive Japanese culture developed during the Heian Era (794–1192).

In 784 Nara ceased to be the emperor's court. After two moves, the capital was located in 794 at Heian-kyo, which was later renamed **Kyoto**.

The founding of this new capital began what is known as the Heian [hā′än] period. During this time Japan began to create its own kind of culture and separate itself from China. Japan sent its last major embassy to Tang China in 838, and by the early 900s, a distinct Japanese civilization was being created in painting, architecture, and literature.

This flowering of cultural life was fostered by the emperor and his court in Heian-kyo. These nobles lived a sheltered life and hardly ever left the capital except to visit Buddhist temples and Shinto shrines. They spent their days in ceremonies and festivities connected with court life and in endless pursuits of taste and culture.

Some of Japan's earliest prose literature was produced during this fertile time, written almost

BACKGROUND The tankas and haiku below have been translated from Japanese and may therefore not match the syllabic format in English.

entirely by women. One reason that women were the prose writers of this time was that Japanese women were not taught to write by using the complicated and cumbersome characters of Chinese, as the men of the court were. Instead, they wrote in their native language using kana. Kana was actually a kind of alphabetic representation of the 47 syllables of the Japanese language that was developed in the 9th century.

Using kana, court women wrote diaries, letters, essays, and novels in abundance. One of the most famous works of the Heian period is *The Tale of Genji*, a selection of which you read in the introduction on page 308, by **Lady Murasaki**. This novel—one of the first in any language—tells the story of Prince Genji, the "Shining Prince," and his many romances. It is a literary classic that is still read and studied today.

Another important and popular form of writing at this time was poetry. The form used was the tanka, a poem that could only be five lines long and had to include a total of 31 syllables. The tanka was to remain the poetic model for more than 1,000 years, and is still a favorite form. Here are two early examples:

> When spring comes
> the melting snow
> leaves no trace
> Would that your heart too
> melted thus toward me.

and:

> I will think of you, love
> On evenings when the grey mist
> Rises above the rushes,
> And chill sounds the voice
> Of the wild ducks crying.

In a later period, the tanka became even more refined and compressed to three lines and 17 syllables. It was then called the **haiku** [hī′kü]. Here is an example:

> To the moon, a handle
> add—a good
> fan indeed.

While the aristocrats in Heian-kyo were living lives of ease and comfort, Japanese outside the capital had rough and hard lives. Most were serfs,

BACKGROUND Matsuo Bashō (1644–1694) is considered the greatest of all writers of haiku. Most of his poems are simple descriptions of real scenes and events.

GEOGRAPHY

A Key to History

EAST ASIA'S BRIDGELAND

Although Chinese culture strongly influenced the Japanese, Japan's island location made travel between the two lands difficult. Furthermore, no major ocean current flows from Japan to China, and the dangerous reefs dotting the Yellow Sea hampered navigation. Thus, travel by sea from Japan or Korea to China was difficult until the 19th century, when steam power made it possible for large

The Korean peninsula is mostly mountainous. The shortest distance between Korea and Japan at the Korea Strait is 129 miles.

MONGOLIA
Pyongyang
KOREA
Sea of Japan
JAPAN
Hwang Ho
Yellow Sea
Pusan
Korea Strait
CHINA
Yangtze R.
East China Sea
TAIWAN
PACIFIC OCEAN
Currents
Sandbars
South China Sea
PHILIPPINES
N
0   250   500 MILES
0   250   500 KILOMETERS

ships to move against the current and the wind.

The Korean peninsula does, however, serve as a bridge between Japan and China. In fact, some scholars believe that the Japanese people are a blend of three different groups: the Ainu [ī′nü], whose ancestors may have been the first people to inhabit Japan; Malaysians, who came by sea from Southeast Asia; and Mongolians, who came by way of Korea.

Chinese influences entered Korea by contacts over both land and sea. Buddhism and Confucianism spread to Korea during the Han dynasty (202 B.C.–A.D. 220). The Koreans may have adopted rice cultivation at an earlier date. Later, the Koreans in turn brought Buddhism and its related art forms to the Japanese.

East Asia's bridgeland has attracted many invaders. Despite this, Korea has been able to maintain its own identity, borrowing from neighbors only what it liked. Although Korea has at times been subject to China or Japan, for most of its history, Korea has maintained its independence.

REVIEW

1. In what two ways has Korea served as a bridgeland between Japan and the Asian mainland?
2. Do you think it would be easier for China to influence Japan or for Japan to influence China? Why?

Be sure that students realize that Korea is bounded on three sides by seas: the Yellow Sea to the west, the Sea of Japan to the east, and the East China Sea to the south. Then explain that the Tsushima Current sends steady streams of warm water from the tropics into all three seas. This current is similar to the Gulf Stream. The trade winds blowing from the east push tropical water against the Chinese coast where it is turned northward. In the winter, monsoon winds move against the current and enable ships to sail from Japan to China. In the summer both the winds and the current move from China to Japan.

A key resource for teachers interested in Korea is the special issue of *Social Studies* for July/August, 1988.

Answers to REVIEW

1. Korea has served as a bridgeland between China and Japan for both people and ideas. Early people migrated to Japan from Asia by way of Korea. Later, religion, art, and culture followed the same route.
2. Most students will conclude that it was easier for China to influence Japan because the former was much larger and more powerful. The current also encouraged travel from the mainland to Japan. The opposite view, however, should be respected, especially in the light of twentieth century developments.

Identify

Key Terms, People, and Places are defined on pages indicated in parentheses. Also see the Glossary and Biographical Dictionary.
Shinto (311), Kyoto (Heian-kyo) (314), Lady Murasaki (314), haiku (314)

Main Ideas

1. Archaeologists have learned that the first inhabitants of the Japanese islands probably arrived as early as 30,000 B.C. These stone-age people are believed to have hunted and fished.
2. Shinto, too, was based on nature.
3. The Chinese language was brought to Japan by way of Korean immigrants, and Buddhism was carried to Japan by a delegation of young Japanese men that had travelled to China in A.D. 600.
4. During the Heian era, the emperor and his court led a very sheltered life and spent their time encouraging and seeking out the finest in art and literature.

Critical Thinking

Students' answers should reflect the element of choice—that a country would likely assume those customs that appealed to or aided them in some way.

3 | Lesson Plan

Essential Learning Objectives

Students will learn to:
- describe the political power systems of feudal Japan.
- discuss artistic achievements that began during the feudal periods.

BACKGROUND In the 12th century, land was increasingly held privately, which meant it was not taxed. Income to support the emperor declined.

people who worked a bare existence out of the land and had to give a large share of their crops to their local warrior-landlords. These landlords in turn had to pay heavy taxes to the tax collectors from the emperor's court to support the central government. The system gradually weakened when powerful court families and important local people got tax-free estates. As the taxing ability of the government declined, so did its power. By the middle of the 12th century, the emperor had authority in name only.

Section 2 Review

Identify Shinto, Kyoto (Heian-kyo), Lady Murasaki, haiku

Main Ideas

1. What have archaeologists learned about Japan's earliest inhabitants?
2. How did Shinto develop and spread from the worship of the Sun Goddess?
3. How were the Chinese language and Buddhism spread to Japan?
4. What political circumstances encouraged the development of Japanese arts and literature?

Critical Thinking

Making Hypotheses: How do you think the Japanese, or other nation, might decide which elements of a foreign culture to adopt and which to reject? Support your answer with evidence.

---

3 | Feudalism and a samurai warrior-class developed.

In 1156 outright civil war burst out between two powerful provincial, landowning families. Each family had its own loyal following of warriors, called **samurai** [sam′ù rī′], who pledged complete loyalty to their lord. This allegiance was similar to the lord-vassal system of feudalism that grew up in Europe following the fall of Rome.

The Kamakura Shogunate ruled during Japan's first feudal period (1192–1333).

During the fighting, palaces were burned and people were massacred. A leader named Minamoto

---

Yoritomo [mē nä mō′tō yō rē tō′mō] won, and to protect his victory, he was ruthless. He had his rivals killed, including his own brother. Yoritomo became the undisputed ruler of Japan, and in 1192 he had the emperor name him the **shogun** [shō′gun] the supreme general of the entire country. This office became hereditary, that is, it passed down from father to son. Yoritomo's seat of government was Kamakura, a small coastal town. The emperor, in far-off Kyoto, ruled in name only.

Under Yoritomo, Japan entered its feudal age, which lasted nearly 700 years. The feudal age was divided into three major periods: the Kamakura Shogunate [kä mä kù′rä], the Ashikaga Shogunate [ä shē kä′gä], and the Tokugawa Shogunate [tō kù gä′wä]. During this feudal period, the samurai warriors were the most important class of people.

The loyalty of this samurai class was the key to the military and political power of the shoguns. Unlike European feudalism, the loyalty of the sa-

A samurai warrior, dressed in elaborate military garb, prepares for battle. During Japan's feudal period, the warriors held the highest place in society.

murai knights was not a legal, contractual obligation but was instead a moral tie. The samurai developed a code of conduct that came to be called Bushido [bü'shē dō], "the way of the warrior," which stressed unswerving loyalty and a kind of spartan spirit of indifference to pain and hardship. Seppuku, or hara-kiri, a form of suicide committed by ripping open one's abdomen with a knife, was considered preferable to dishonor or surrender because it was a way of saving one's "face" or dignity. The spirit of this code of honor has survived to modern times in Japan, with the Japanese people determined to maintain their dignity.

The samurai were very agile on the battlefield, wearing light armor that weighed no more than 25 pounds. Their most important weapon was a sword, the perfection of which led to many stories. Tales are told of swords that could split a hair floating in space or slice through a stack of coins without leaving a scratch on the blade.

A Kamikaze wind saved Japan from Mongol invasion.

Although the Kamakura shoguns created order in Japan with samurai rule, their greatest test came from overseas. The Mongol ruler of China, Kublai Khan, sent two invasions to conquer his island neighbor. The final attempt was made in 1281 when 150,000 soldiers carried in a great fleet were sent to conquer Japan. The Mongols were able to force a landing, and the samurai fought desperately. However, to the joy of the Japanese, a powerful typhoon blew in and destroyed many of the Mongol supply ships. Kublai's invaders were forced to withdraw, thus losing many of their ships and soldiers. The Japanese gratefully called the typhoon the **Kamikaze** [kä'mē kä'zē], or "the Divine Wind." The name "kamikaze" was revived during World War II to recognize Japanese suicide pilots. These pilots were often assigned to dive an airplane loaded with explosives into a target, usually a naval vessel.

The Kamakura victory over the Mongols was its last great effort. Much treasure and strength had been spent defending the country. By the end of the 13th century, the power of the Kamakura shoguns was rapidly declining, and the country eventually was broken up among various feudal

BACKGROUND Zen Buddhism came to Japan from China during the 10th–13th centuries. It was characterized by meditation, sword mastery, discipline, and learning. It appealed to shogun and samurai alike.

Feudal Japan

Emperor
Had little political power.

The Warrior Class

Shogun
Supreme general who held reins of power.

Daimyo
Local landowning nobles who for a time had more power than the shogun.

Samurai
Vassal warriors loyal to shogun or daimyo.

Farmers, Serfs
8 out of 10 Japanese

Artisans

Merchants

groups. In 1333 Kamakura rule ended, and a new military group soon seized power. This latest group established the Ashikaga Shogunate.

Nobles struggled for power during the Ashikaga Shogunate (1335–1573).

In the Kamakura period of Japanese feudalism, the shoguns ruled through their vassals, the samurai knights. In this second period, however, the shoguns did not control their vassals, of whom there were now too many. The power of the shogun was limited and hardly extended outside the capital, which was now back at Kyoto. Instead, groups of samurai came to follow certain local nobles who were called **daimyo** [dī'myō], which meant "great name." The daimyo became absolute rulers on their lands, setting and enforcing their own laws. This system of regional rule was very similar to the

317

ASSESS

1. What happened to the position of the Japanese emperor during the shogunates? (The office survived—the emperors lived in Kyoto but had no real power.)
2. What Europeans were the first to enter Japan? (Portuguese sailors)

OPTIONAL RETEACHING

Have students list the characteristics that made the samurai warriors a formidable opponent. (Bushido code, finely crafted swords, armor, religion that stressed an honorable death through sacrifice)

OPTIONAL ENRICHMENT

1. Have students research the reactions of the Jesuit missionary Francis Xavier to the Japanese. Have them include an account of the early successes of attempts to convert the Japanese. (average)
2. Also for enrichment:

 Overhead Transparency 34

📖 *Source Reading 17A*

INDEPENDENT PRACTICE/ HOMEWORK

Assign the Section Review, Activities page 99, or Workbook page 67.

CLOSURE

Tell students that as the power of the emperor declined, rival families fought for control. Samurai warriors supported the shoguns and fought off two attempts at invasion by the Mongols. Later the shoguns' power fell to local daimyo lords. In 1543 Portuguese ships reached Japan and brought guns, new plants, and Christian missionaries to the islands.

type of feudal government that existed in Europe during the early Middle Ages.

During the period of the Ashikaga Shogunate, no effective central government existed in Japan. The daimyo struggled with one another for more power and territory. As a result, local rivalries and wars raged over the countryside of Japan.

The Ashikaga Shogunate was known for its art and the arrival of Europeans.

Despite the turmoil, the country enjoyed one of its most productive eras in the arts. The Ashikaga period, like the Heian period long before it, was a golden age for Japanese culture. Brilliant achievements took place in architecture, literature, and drama.

The No drama developed at this time. This theatrical art was performed by two main characters in splendid costume and featured poetic passages chanted by a chorus. The No plays are still performed today. (See the Chapter 24 "Highlights of Civilization" for more detail on the costumes of the Japanese theater.)

Another glory of the Ashikaga age was the painting. Stunning landscapes and action-packed scenes of battle were popular subjects, and humorous drawings of people and animals were common as well. The most famous artist of this time was a Buddhist monk named Sesshu (1419–1506) who painted landscapes in the tradition of Chinese silk drawing. He is most famous for his masterpiece—a long painted scroll of Chinese river scenery.

The Ashikaga era is also important for its perfection of three distinctly Japanese arts. The first was flower arrangement, an art that began as floral offerings to Buddhist deities and later developed special rules and skills for placing blossoms and branches. The second art was the tea ceremony, held in a simple setting, such as a tea house adjoining a garden. The tea was served in a ceremonious way amid quiet and thoughtful conversation. Special rules and customs guided each participant's actions.

The third art was landscape gardening, greatly influenced by Buddhism. Here the goal was to create the illusion of a vast landscape, even in a small garden, by the artful placement of rocks, trees, shrubs, pools, and running water. A famous tem-

ple garden in Kyoto has no plants but only 15 rocks arranged on a bed of raked white sand, suggesting islands in a tranquil ocean. (See the "Highlights of Civilization" on page 321 for more detail on these Japanese gardens.)

The Ashikaga period is noted for another important event as well—the arrival of Europeans in Japan. In 1543 a group of Portuguese sailors landed on a Japanese island, and within a few years, ships were making frequent stops. At first, the newcomers were welcomed. Foreign trade increased, and economic growth occurred as the handicraft industry advanced, farm production increased, and towns developed. The Japanese experienced a craze for all kinds of European gadgets, especially firearms. New plants, including tobacco and the potato, were introduced. Some Portuguese words—such as *pan* meaning "bread"—even found their way into the Japanese language.

To most Japanese, however, the European newcomers were not so welcome and indeed appeared to be quite strange. The Europeans' coloring, of hair and skin, was lighter than that to which the Japanese were accustomed. Red hair was considered a particular oddity to the black-haired Japanese. In addition, the European sailors were scorned for being dirty and "evil smelling" by the fastidious Japanese.

The painting below, done by the accomplished Buddhist monk Sesshu, is an autumn landscape skillfully painted with India ink on paper.

Highlights of Japanese History

Early period 30,000 B.C.–A.D. 600
settlement of Japanese islands • inflow of culture from Korea and China • Yamato chief recognized as emperor • Shinto worship spread

Nara period 600–784
Buddhism promoted • Chinese became written language of nobles and scholars • power centralized

Heian period 794–1192
kana letters developed • great age of prose (*The Tale of Genji*) and poetry (tanka)

Kamakura Shogunate 1192–1333
feudal era began • *Bushido* code developed • victory over Mongols (1281)

Ashikaga Shogunate 1335–1573
central government weak • constant civil wars • great age of painting and drama (No plays) • flower arrangement, tea ceremony, and landscape gardening developed • Europeans brought trade and Christianity

Tokugawa Shogunate 1603–1868
central government strong • foreign contacts banned • Christianity outlawed • growth of cities • rise of merchant class • flowering of culture • decline of samurai

Modern era 1868–present
contact with the West • period of modernization and expansion • World War II • rise of democracy

The Europeans were also known for introducing Christianity into Japan. The Jesuit Saint Francis Xavier first began preaching in the islands soon after the arrival of the first Europeans. His preaching and attempts to convert the Japanese to Christianity soon provoked suspicion and anger among Japanese feudal rulers who saw the new religion as a threat to their power.

During the end of the Ashikaga period in the late 1500s, fierce fighting continued between various noble groups. However, the larger and more powerful daimyo gradually began to win control over their weaker rivals. Eventually, two powerful rival groups dominated the islands. In 1600 the battle of Sekigahara was fought between the two, and Ieyasu [ē ye yä′sü], of the Tokugawas, was declared the victor three years later. You will read more about the Tokugawas in Chapter 24.

Section 3 Review

Identify samurai, shogun, Kamikaze, daimyo

Main Ideas
1. How were the samurai important to the Kamakura Shogunate's rule during the feudal period?
2. What effect did the Kamikaze have on Japan's battle with Kublai Khan's invading fleet?
3. Who held political power during the Ashikaga Shogunate?
4. What were three of the most important Japanese arts developed during the Ashikaga Shogunate?

Critical Thinking

Analyzing Comparisons: In this section, the vassals of Japanese feudalism are compared to those of European feudalism. In what other ways can the two systems be compared? Use what you have learned in this chapter and in Chapter 11 to explain what similarities and differences existed.

4 *The Japanese created distinctive home and family customs.*

During their long history, the Japanese developed a unique way of life. In their homes and family lives, customs became quite different from those in other parts of the world.

Japanese houses were simple centers of family life.

Houses were made of wood, since there was an abundance of wood. Homes usually had only one

GUIDED PRACTICE

Ask students to suggest what may have led to the lessening of women's position in Japanese society. (increasing importance of warrior role)

ASSESS

What important positions did women hold in early Japan? (They had been empresses and famous writers.)

OPTIONAL RETEACHING

Have students list objects found in Japanese homes and the materials to make each item. Point out the extent to which Japan was self-sufficient.

Students also may be assigned Activities reteaching page 101.

OPTIONAL ENRICHMENT

1. Ask students to obtain and explain a menu from a Japanese restaurant or cookbook. (average)
2. Assign a research report on one period of residential architecture in Japan before 1600. (challenging)
3. Students also may be assigned Activities enrichment page 102, or:

 Source Reading 17B

INDEPENDENT PRACTICE/ HOMEWORK

Assign the Section Review, the Chapter Review items, Activities page 100, or Workbook page 68.

CLOSURE

Tell students that Japanese daily life and customs illustrated the people's traditional values of simplicity, order, and closeness to nature.

The woodblock print shown above, made in the 1600s, illustrates a traditional Japanese street scene. Note the simple construction and decoration.

story in order to withstand the earthquakes that frequently occurred in Japan. Sliding panels made of heavy paper on wooden frames separated the rooms. These panels could be moved easily to make a room larger or smaller or to open it to the garden.

The homes had very little furniture—no chairs, beds, or sofas. Usually, the only piece of furniture was a low table for serving food, around which people sat crosslegged on cushions. Meals consisted mostly of rice, fish, and vegetables, with a little seaweed and fruit. Very little meat was eaten.

Floors were covered with straw mats. These mats were protected by the custom of taking off sandals and clogs before entering a house. At night, mattresses and blankets, which were kept hidden in cupboards during the day, were spread out on the floor for sleeping. Most rooms had no decoration except for a nook or alcove in which flowers could be placed. On the wall of these alcoves might have hung a single painting on paper or silk.

Heat for the house came from a large earthware pot, the **hibachi** [hi bä′chē], that burned charcoal. Japanese houses generally had large tubs that could hold very hot water for bathing. Bathing was an important part of the Japanese day. Whether rich or poor, everyone bathed daily, washing themselves thoroughly before entering the bath. Besides cleaning, the baths were also used for relaxation. With this strong tradition of cleanliness, one can understand how upset the Japanese were at meeting

European sailors who had been out at sea for months on end.

The family in Japan, as in India and China, was the basic social unit. It was generally made up of a father and mother, their eldest son, his wife, and their children. The power of the father was unquestioned, and children were drilled in parental obedience. The head of the family represented the group at all meetings and to some degree was responsible for the actions of its members.

The status of women changed throughout Japanese history.

During the earliest period of Japanese history, some women enjoyed high political, social, and cultural status. In fact, from the end of the 6th century to the late 8th century, Japan had six empresses as rulers. At that time, women were the leaders in literary circles, and for 100 years, all important authors were women. Laws protected the right of women to inherit and keep property. In addition, during the Kamakura feudal days, samurai women were expected to have spartan virtues, and young girls were taught the use of weapons.

However, Japanese society gradually moved toward complete male supremacy and women eventually lost their inheritance rights. By the Tokugawa period, which you will read more about in Chapter 24, women had become socially and legally inferior to men. Women were taught to serve men, and boys were valued more than girls. A wife did not share in her husband's social activities. This situation continued with little change well into the 20th century.

Section 4 Review

Identify hibachi
Main Ideas
1. In what ways were Japanese family homes simple?
2. How did the status of women change throughout Japanese history?

Critical Thinking
Recognizing Values: Considering what you have learned in this chapter about the Japanese religious and cultural heritage, what do you think might be some common Japanese values?

BACKGROUND Very poor Japanese usually did not have bathtubs in their homes and used public bath houses instead.

HIGHLIGHTS OF CIVILIZATION

Japanese Gardens

One who has trodden this garden path cannot fail to remember how his spirit, as he walked in the twilight of evergreens over the regular irregularities of the stepping stones . . . became uplifted above ordinary thoughts.

This comment by a noted Japanese art historian reflects the importance the Japanese place on having a private space separated from the densely populated outside world—even in the midst of a city, as pictured at the bottom left. It reflects also the serenity esteemed as part of Japan's Buddhist heritage.

Geography, too, exerts a powerful influence on the design of Japanese gardens. Japan consists of many mountainous islands covered with luxurious forests. Thus, mountains and the sea relate to the main types of gardens: hill gardens and flat gardens. The hill garden seeks to remind viewers of the beauty of Mount Fuji, an almost perfect volcanic cone. The flat garden represents the sea with its rocky shore.

Within the garden, boulders and smaller stones are painstakingly arranged. Reverence for nature is part of Japan's cultural tradition, and numerous shrines provide settings for stones as objects of meditation. Water and vegetation are other important garden elements. In a small garden, water may drip from a bamboo stalk onto a rock below. Evergreens, flowering cherries, or maples bring cool emerald light and splashes of color. The soft touch of moss may symbolize a forest. Carefully shaped shrubs may suggest hills or clouds.

A centuries-old inscription beside a plum tree in a Japanese monastery expresses the feeling of the Japanese for natural beauty. It reads: "Whoever cuts a single branch of this tree shall forfeit a finger therefor."

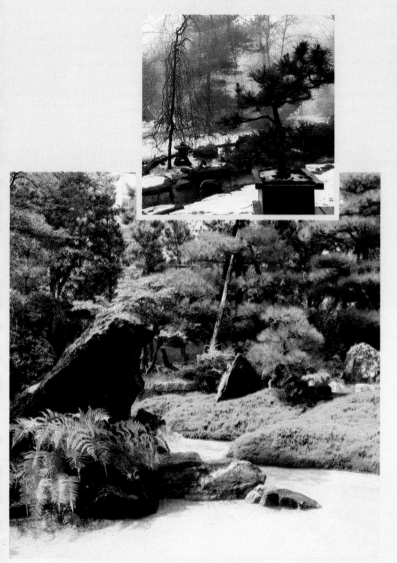

A Japanese garden in winter (inset, top left) and a private garden viewed from a home in Japan (bottom left) show the Japanese reverence for nature.

Answers to Test Yourself

Key Terms, People, and Places
The key terms, people, and places tested here were introduced in the chapter sections and reviewed in the Section Reviews. For definitions see the page references at the appropriate Section Reviews. Also see the Glossary and Biographical Dictionary.

Main Ideas
The main ideas tested here were introduced in the sections of this chapter and reviewed in the Section Reviews. For answers to these questions, see the appropriate Section Reviews.

Critical Thinking
1. Possible answers should consider modern transportation, communications, construction techniques, weather, and fishing.
2. Possible answers: a respect for beauty, desire to honor nature, imitation of other societies, for religious purposes.

Section Summaries

Section 1
Japan's geography influenced its history and its culture.
The story of Japan has been greatly influenced by geography and climate. Beautiful rugged mountains, forested slopes, and varied landscapes created a strong love for nature among Japan's people. In addition, the country's separation from the Asian mainland gave it protection from invasion but still allowed selective borrowing to take place.

Section 2
Early Japanese civilization borrowed from China.
In the early stages of its history, Japan borrowed heavily from China, mainly in the areas of language, religion, government, and art. By the 9th century, however, when Japanese emperors had established their capital in Heian-kyo (modern-day Kyoto), Japan had begun to create its own special style of civilization, with distinct forms of prose, poetry, and painting.

Section 3
Feudalism and a samurai warrior-class developed.
From the 12th through the mid-19th centuries, Japan's system of government was feudalism. There were three periods of feudal government—the Kamakura, Ashikaga, and Tokugawa—when the real ruler was the shogun. Emperors were mere figureheads but were respected because the Japanese thought them to be of divine descent. During the early periods of feudal government, there was much discord and fighting between powerful noble families and their followers, the samurai. Finally this civil war ended by the advent of the Tokugawa Shogunate in 1603.

Section 4
The Japanese created distinctive home and family customs.
During their long history, the Japanese people developed their own distinctive way of life. Japanese homes and furnishings were simple, and family life revolved around the father. The place of women in society changed over the years. From the Tokugawa period on, women had a lower status than men.

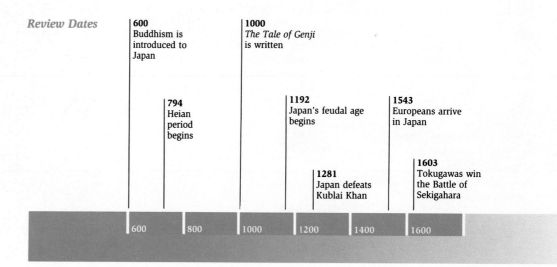

Review Dates

600 Buddhism is introduced to Japan

1000 *The Tale of Genji* is written

794 Heian period begins

1192 Japan's feudal age begins

1543 Europeans arrive in Japan

1281 Japan defeats Kublai Khan

1603 Tokugawas win the Battle of Sekigahara

600 800 1000 1200 1400 1600

Test Yourself

Key Terms, People, and Places

Identify the significance of each of the following:

Section 1
a. Japan
b. Sea of Japan
c. typhoons
d. Mount Fuji

Section 2
a. Shinto
b. Kyoto (Heian-kyo)
c. Lady Murasaki
d. haiku

Section 3
a. samurai
b. shogun
c. Kamikaze
d. daimyo

Section 4
a. hibachi

Main Ideas

Section 1
1. In what way has Japan's geography shaped her people and history?
2. How does Japanese culture show a respect for nature?

Section 2
1. What has evidence uncovered by archaeologists told us about Japan's earliest inhabitants?
2. How did the worship of the Sun Goddess lead to the development of a new Japanese religion?
3. What impact did the Chinese have on the development of language and religion in Japan?
4. In what ways did the political environment encourage the development of Japanese culture?

Section 3
1. What influence did the samurai have on the Kamakura Shogunate's rule during the feudal period?
2. How did the Kamikaze help the Japanese in their battle with Kublai Khan?
3. How did political power change during the Ashikaga Shogunate?
4. In what ways did the arts develop in Japan during the Ashikaga Shogunate?

Section 4
1. Describe the simplicity in the design and decor of Japanese family homes.

2. What changes occurred to the role of women throughout Japanese history?

Critical Thinking

1. **Making Hypotheses** Considering the importance of geography to early Japanese history, do you think it has the same effect on modern Japan? Support your answer with evidence.
2. **Recognizing Values** Considering what you have learned about the cultural development of Japan, why do you think the arts have had such importance? Support your answer with evidence.

Chapter Skills and Activities

Practicing Study and Research Skills

Locating and Gathering Information

A resource that is particularly useful when gathering information on a current topic is the *Readers' Guide to Periodical Literature*. The *Readers' Guide* is published every month in paperback. Each issue lists magazine articles organized by subject and author, and fiction by title and author. Each issue of the *Readers' Guide* lists articles from more than 150 magazines, along with a translation of the special abbreviations used in the entries. Here is an example of an entry: A yen for fun. E. Paris. il *Forbes* 142:38–9 J1 11 '88. This entry means that an article entitled "A Yen for Fun," written by E. Paris, can be found, with illustrations, in the July 11, 1988 issue of *Forbes*, Volume 142, pages 38–39. Using the *Readers' Guide*, find out about Japanese family life today. Compare it to the home life described in the chapter. How has it changed or stayed the same?

Linking Past and Present

The Japanese first developed relations with Europeans during the Ashikaga Shogunate. What similarities or dissimilarities do you see compared to our relations with the Japanese today?

Learning History Through Maps

Compare the map of China on page 136 and the map of East Asia's Bridgeland on page 315 with the map of Japan on page 310. What conditions do you see that made contact between Japan and China difficult?

CRITICAL THINKING QUESTION LEVEL 1. average;
2. challenging

18 Empires in Africa and the Americas

OVERVIEW

A number of well-established empires existed in Africa, Central America, and South America before the coming of the Europeans. These included Ghana, Mali, Songhai, and Zimbabwe in Africa; the Aztec in Mexico; and the Inca in South America. A rich variety of cultures also existed in North America.

PLANNING CHART

Section	Text Pages	Key Concept	Suggested Teaching Time
1 Famous empires grew in the West African savanna.	325–329	Control of the salt and gold trade led to the great West African empires of Ghana, Mali, and Songhai.	Two days **More time?** Use *Source Reading 18A.*
2 City-states and kingdoms flourished in East Africa.	329–333	Control of the ivory and gold trade led to the prosperity of the East African city-states.	One day **Less time?** Teach Sections 2 and 3 together.
3 The forest states developed strong governments.	333–335	The forest state of Benin prospered long before the coming of the European and the decimating effect of the Atlantic slave trade.	One day **More time?** Use *Overhead Transparency 35.*
4 The Aztecs and Incas created strong empires	335–339	The Aztecs of Mexico and the Incas of the Andes were the two most powerful peoples in the two Americas at the time of European arrival.	One day **More time?** Use *Source Reading 18B.*
5 North America supported a variety of cultures.	341–342	The Indians of North America offered a remarkable cultural variety.	One day **More time?** Use *Overhead Transparency 36.*

ANCILLARIES

Materials that may be used with this chapter to reinforce, reteach, enrich, and assess learning are pictured on the following pages.

Teacher's Resource File

ACTIVITIES

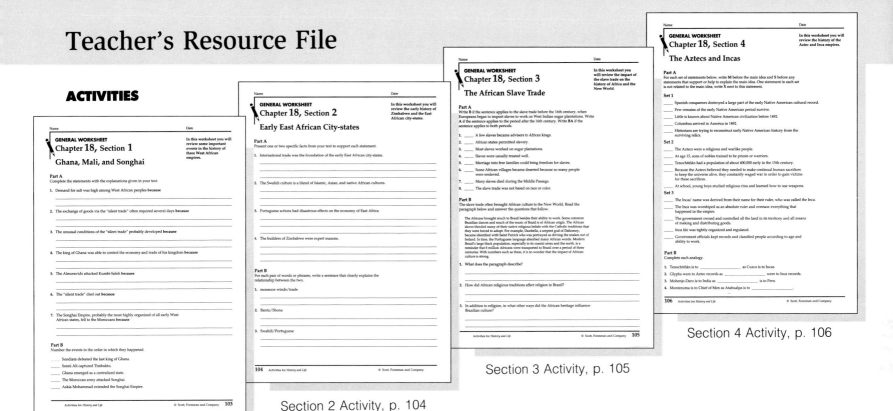

GENERAL WORKSHEET
Chapter 18, Section 1

Ghana, Mali, and Songhai

In this worksheet you will review some important events in the history of three West African empires.

Part A
Complete the statements with the explanations given in your text.

1. Demand for salt was high among West African peoples **because**

2. The exchange of goods via the "silent trade" often required several days **because**

3. The unusual conditions of the "silent trade" probably developed **because**

4. The king of Ghana was able to control the economy and trade of his kingdom **because**

5. The Almoravids attacked Kumbi-Saleh **because**

6. The "silent trade" died out **because**

7. The Songhai Empire, probably the most highly organized of all early West African states, fell to the Moroccans **because**

Part B
Number the events in the order in which they happened.

_____ Sundiata defeated the last king of Ghana.
_____ Sonni Ali captured Timbuktu.
_____ Ghana emerged as a centralized state.
_____ The Moroccan army attacked Songhai.
_____ Askia Mohammad extended the Songhai Empire.

Section 1 Activity, p. 103

GENERAL WORKSHEET
Chapter 18, Section 2

Early East African City-states

In this worksheet you will review the early history of Zimbabwe and the East African city-states.

Part A
Present one or two specific facts from your text to support each statement.

1. International trade was the foundation of the early East African city-states.

2. The Swahili culture is a blend of Islamic, Asian, and native African cultures.

3. Portuguese actions had disastrous effects on the economy of East Africa.

4. The builders of Zimbabwe were expert masons.

Part B
For each pair of words or phrases, write a sentence that clearly explains the relationship between the two.

1. monsoon winds/trade

2. Bantu/Shona

3. Swahili/Portuguese

Section 2 Activity, p. 104

GENERAL WORKSHEET
Chapter 18, Section 3

The African Slave Trade

In this worksheet you will review the impact of the slave trade on the history of Africa and the New World.

Part A
Write B if the sentence applies to the slave trade before the 16th century, when Europeans began to import slaves to work on West Indian sugar plantations. Write A if the sentence applies to the period after the 16th century. Write BA if the sentence applies to both periods.

1. _____ A few slaves became advisers to African kings.
2. _____ African states permitted slavery.
3. _____ Most slaves worked on sugar plantations.
4. _____ Slaves were usually treated well.
5. _____ Marriage into free families could bring freedom for slaves.
6. _____ Some African villages became deserted because so many people were enslaved.
7. _____ Many slaves died during the Middle Passage.
8. _____ The slave trade was not based on race or color.

Part B
The slave trade often brought African culture to the New World. Read the paragraph below and answer the questions that follow.

The Africans brought much to Brazil besides their ability to work. Some common Brazilian dances and much of the music of Brazil is of African origin. The African slaves blended many of their native religious beliefs with the Catholic traditions that they were forced to adopt. For example, Danbela, a serpent god of Dahomey, became identified with Saint Patrick who was portrayed as driving the snakes out of Ireland. In time, the Portuguese language absorbed many African words. Modern Brazil's large black population, especially in its coastal areas and the north, is a reminder that 5 million Africans were transported to Brazil over a period of three centuries. With numbers such as these, it is no wonder that the impact of African culture is strong.

1. What does the paragraph describe?

2. How did African religious traditions affect religion in Brazil?

3. In addition to religion, in what other ways did the African heritage influence Brazilian culture?

Section 3 Activity, p. 105

GENERAL WORKSHEET
Chapter 18, Section 4

The Aztecs and Incas

In this worksheet you will review the history of the Aztec and Inca empires.

Part A
For each set of statements below, write M before the main idea and S before any statements that support or help to explain the main idea. One statement in each set is not related to the main idea; write X next to this statement.

Set 1
_____ Spanish conquerors destroyed a large part of the early Native American cultural record.
_____ Few remains of the early Native American period survive.
_____ Little is known about Native American civilization before 1492.
_____ Columbus arrived in America in 1492.
_____ Historians are trying to reconstruct early Native American history from the surviving relics.

Set 2
_____ The Aztecs were a religious and warlike people.
_____ At age 15, sons of nobles trained to be priests or warriors.
_____ Tenochtitlán had a population of about 400,000 early in the 15th century.
_____ The Aztecs believed they needed to make continual human sacrifices to keep the universe alive; they constantly waged war in order to gain victims for these sacrifices.
_____ At school, young boys studied religious rites and learned how to use weapons.

Set 3
_____ The Incas' name was derived from their name for their ruler, who was called the Inca.
_____ The Inca was worshiped as an absolute ruler and oversaw everything that happened in the empire.
_____ The government owned and controlled all the land in its territory and all means of making and distributing goods.
_____ Inca life was tightly organized and regulated.
_____ Government officials kept records and classified people according to age and ability to work.

Part B
Complete each analogy.

1. Tenochtitlán is to _____ as Cuzco is to Incas.
2. Glyphs were to Aztec records as _____ were to Inca records.
3. Mohenjo-Daro is to India as _____ is to Peru.
4. Montezuma is to Chief of Men as Atahualpa is to _____.

Section 4 Activity, p. 106

GENERAL WORKSHEET
Chapter 18, Section 5

Indians of North America

In this worksheet you will review the cultures of several North American Indian groups.

Part A
Write T if the statement is true and F if it is false. On the lines below, rewrite each false statement to make it true.

1. _____ The North Pacific Coast Indians hunted, fished, and gathered wild berries.
2. _____ The Woodland Indians were farmers who developed a system of irrigation canals.
3. _____ The Sioux and Cheyenne were buffalo hunters prior to the arrival of the Spanish in America.
4. _____ The Pueblo believed that people should live in harmony with nature.
5. _____ Native American literature consists of poetry, myths, and legends passed on by word of mouth from generation to generation.
6. _____ The most important contributions of the early peoples of the Americas made to Europeans were in the fields of science and technology.

Part B
Use information from your text to complete the chart.

Indian Item or Practice	Culture	Description	Purpose
		festive ceremony during which the family gave away prized possessions	to celebrate a family event; to emphasize the values of generosity and harmony
		long, dome-shaped house made out of poles covered with bark and skins	
adobe		sun-dried clay used to make several-storied houses	to keep cool in the intense heat
		a political organization of five Iroquois groups	

Section 5 Activity, p. 107

RETEACHING ACTIVITY
Chapter 18

Early African and American Cultures

In this worksheet you will review key terms and main ideas about early cultures in Africa and the Americas.

Part A
Write the correct name on the blank next to its clue.

1. He was the first ruler of the Mali Empire.
2. The center of this people's culture was Tenochtitlán.
3. It was one of the richest cities in East Africa, controlling most of the gold trade.
4. These Native Americans formed the Five Nations.
5. It became a powerful empire by controlling the gold trade.
6. Women played an important part in this West African forest state.
7. This people settled in the valley of the Andes around the 11th century.
8. This North American people used adobe for dwellings.

Part B
Place the letter of each effect beside its cause.

Causes
1. _____ Aztec custom of human sacrifice
2. _____ Almoravid attack (1076)
3. _____ Sundiata's attack (1235)
4. _____ demand for plantation labor in New World
5. _____ interchange between African, Indian, and Arab traders in East African port cities
6. _____ conflict between Morocco and a West African state
7. _____ arrival of Portuguese in Africa
8. _____ the Middle Passage

Effects
a. increase in slave traffic between African merchants and European traders
b. evolution of Swahili culture
c. decline of kingdom of Ghana
d. creation of Mali Empire
e. decline of Songhai Empire
f. deaths of millions of Africans enroute to the New World
g. introduction of the gun to Africans
h. constant warfare with adjoining Indian peoples

Chapter 18 Reteaching, p. 108

ENRICHMENT ACTIVITY
Chapter 18

The African Slave Trade

In this worksheet you will learn more about the African slave trade.

Read the following information about the slave trade and answer the questions that follow. The description of the trade's effect on Africa is based on the research of the historian Basil Davidson.

Between the 15th and 19th centuries, the "single largest forced migration in the history of mankind" transformed the history of West Africa, Europe, and the Americas. For almost four centuries, the civilized world carried on a large-scale trade in human cargo, and few voices were raised in protest. No one knows exactly how many Africans were transported to the New World, but several historians have made estimates that as many as 50 million Africans migrated.

Because Europe had a limited need for laborers, the number of slaves taken from Africa before the year 1500 did not exceed 10,000. After the discovery of the New World, the slave trade changed to become a solution to one of the most difficult problems in the New World—the need for a reliable source of plantation labor.

At the height of the slave trade, England controlled over half of the traffic and attempted to satisfy not only the growing demand of its own colonies for slaves, but also that of other countries' colonies. Originally a byproduct of African warfare, the slave trade became a big business. Africans had to engage in the ruthless manhunt or to sell themselves as slaves. African chieftains increasingly became trapped in a muskets-for-slaves cycle. Possession of firearms became necessary for survival, and slaves had to be traded in order to obtain firearms.

It was not until the end of the 18th century that the liberal ideas of the Enlightenment had some effect on the ending of the slave trade. In 1717 England became the first to abolish the trade, followed by the United States in 1808. But the trade persisted long after 1808, not until Lincoln empowered the British Navy to board and search suspicious American vessels (on the high seas) did it effectively stop.

1. Explain the dilemma facing most West African chieftains during the 15th to 17th centuries.

2. How did the discovery of the New World change the nature of the slave trade?

3. How did England play a major role in both the slave trade and its abolition?

Chapter 18 Enrichment, p. 109

323b

Teacher's Resource File

GEOGRAPHY SKILLS

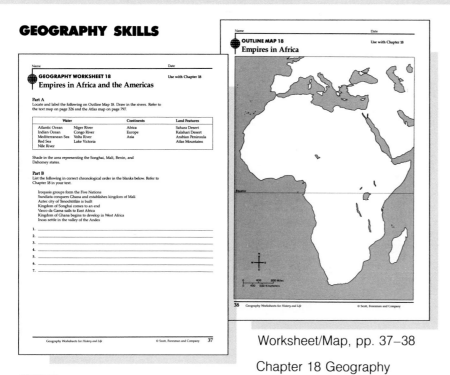

Worksheet/Map, pp. 37–38

Chapter 18 Geography

Chapter 18 Map Lesson, p. 100

TESTS

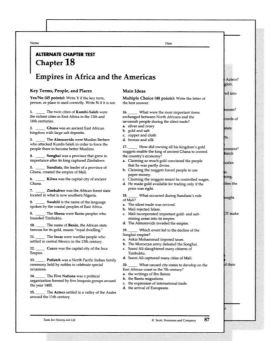

Chapter Test, pp. 85–86

Alternate Chapter Test, pp. 87–88

Other Optional Ancillaries

WORKBOOK

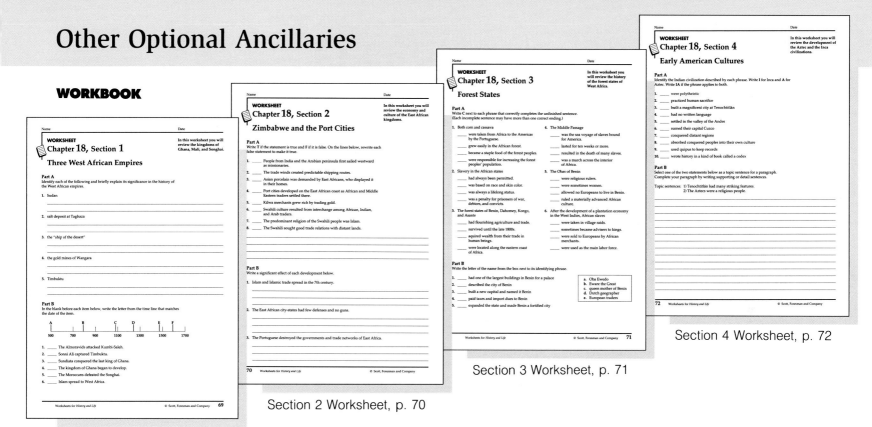

Section 1 Worksheet, p. 69

WORKSHEET
Chapter 18, Section 1

In this worksheet you will review the kingdoms of Ghana, Mali, and Songhai.

Three West African Empires

Part A
Identify each of the following and briefly explain its significance in the history of the West African empires.

1. Sudan
2. salt deposit at Taghaza
3. the "ship of the desert"
4. the gold mines of Wangara
5. Timbuktu

Part B
In the blank before each item below, write the letter from the time line that matches the date of the item.

500 700 900 1100 1300 1500 1700

1. _____ The Almoravids attacked Kumbi-Saleh.
2. _____ Sonni Ali captured Timbuktu.
3. _____ Sundiata conquered the last king of Ghana.
4. _____ The kingdom of Ghana began to develop.
5. _____ The Moroccans defeated the Songhai.
6. _____ Islam spread to West Africa.

Worksheets for History and Life © Scott, Foresman and Company 69

Section 2 Worksheet, p. 70

WORKSHEET
Chapter 18, Section 2

In this worksheet you will review the economy and culture of the East African kingdoms.

Zimbabwe and the Port Cities

Part A
Write T if the statement is true and F if it is false. On the lines below, rewrite each false statement to make it true.

1. _____ People from India and the Arabian peninsula first sailed westward as missionaries.
2. _____ The trade winds created predictable shipping routes.
3. _____ Asian porcelain was demanded by East Africans, who displayed it in their homes.
4. _____ Port cities developed on the East African coast as African and Middle Eastern traders settled there.
5. _____ Kilwa merchants grew rich by trading gold.
6. _____ Swahili culture resulted from interchange among African, Indian, and Arab traders.
7. _____ The predominant religion of the Swahili people was Islam.
8. _____ The Swahili sought good trade relations with distant lands.

Part B
Write a significant effect of each development below.

1. Islam and Islamic trade spread in the 7th century.
2. The East African city-states had few defenses and no guns.
3. The Portuguese destroyed the governments and trade networks of East Africa.

Worksheets for History and Life © Scott, Foresman and Company 70

Section 3 Worksheet, p. 71

WORKSHEET
Chapter 18, Section 3

In this worksheet you will review the history of the forest states of West Africa.

Forest States

Part A
Write C next to each phrase that correctly completes the unfinished sentence. (Each incomplete sentence may have more than one correct ending.)

1. Both corn and cassava
   _____ were taken from Africa to the Americas by the Portuguese.
   _____ grew easily in the African forest.
   _____ became a staple food of the forest peoples.
   _____ were responsible for increasing the forest peoples' population.

2. Slavery in the African states
   _____ had always been permitted.
   _____ was based on race and skin color.
   _____ was always a lifelong status.
   _____ was a penalty for prisoners of war, debtors, and convicts.

3. The forest states of Benin, Dahomey, Kongo, and Asante
   _____ had flourishing agriculture and trade.
   _____ survived until the late 1800s.
   _____ acquired wealth from their trade in human beings.
   _____ were located along the eastern coast of Africa.

4. The Middle Passage
   _____ was the sea voyage of slaves bound for America.
   _____ lasted for ten weeks or more.
   _____ resulted in the death of many slaves.
   _____ was a march across the interior of Africa.

5. The Obas of Benin
   _____ were religious rulers.
   _____ were sometimes women.
   _____ allowed no Europeans to live in Benin.
   _____ ruled a materially advanced African culture.

6. After the development of a plantation economy in the West Indies, African slaves
   _____ were taken in village raids.
   _____ sometimes became advisers to kings.
   _____ were sold to Europeans by African merchants.
   _____ were used as the main labor force.

Part B
Write the letter of the name from the box next to its identifying phrase.

1. _____ had one of the largest buildings in Benin for a palace
2. _____ described the city of Benin
3. _____ built a new capital and named it Benin
4. _____ paid taxes and import dues to Benin
5. _____ expanded the state and made Benin a fortified city

a. Oba Ewedo
b. Ewure the Great
c. queen mother of Benin
d. Dutch geographer
e. European traders

Worksheets for History and Life © Scott, Foresman and Company 71

Section 4 Worksheet, p. 72

WORKSHEET
Chapter 18, Section 4

In this worksheet you will review the development of the Aztec and the Inca civilizations.

Early American Cultures

Part A
Identify the Indian civilization described by each phrase. Write I for Inca and A for Aztec. Write IA if the phrase applies to both.

1. _____ were polytheistic
2. _____ practiced human sacrifice
3. _____ built a magnificent city at Tenochtitlán
4. _____ had no written language
5. _____ settled in the valley of the Andes
6. _____ named their capital Cuzco
7. _____ conquered distant regions
8. _____ absorbed conquered peoples into their own culture
9. _____ used quipus to keep records
10. _____ wrote history in a kind of book called a codex

Part B
Select one of the two statements below as a topic sentence for a paragraph. Complete your paragraph by writing supporting or detail sentences.

Topic sentences: 1) Tenochtitlán had many striking features.
2) The Aztecs were a religious people.

72 *Worksheets for History and Life* © Scott, Foresman and Company

Section 5 Worksheet, p. 73

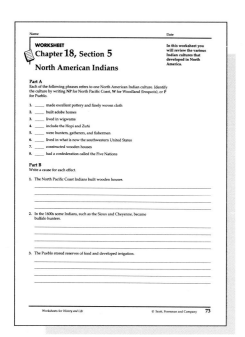

WORKSHEET
Chapter 18, Section 5

In this worksheet you will review the various Indian cultures that developed in North America.

North American Indians

Part A
Each of the following phrases refers to one North American Indian culture. Identify the culture by writing NP for North Pacific Coast, W for Woodland (Iroquois), or P for Pueblo.

1. _____ made excellent pottery and finely woven cloth
2. _____ built adobe homes
3. _____ lived in wigwams
4. _____ include the Hopi and Zuñi
5. _____ were hunters, gatherers, and fishermen
6. _____ lived in what is now the southwestern United States
7. _____ constructed wooden houses
8. _____ had a confederation called the Five Nations

Part B
Write a cause for each effect.

1. The North Pacific Coast Indians built wooden houses.
2. In the 1600s some Indians, such as the Sioux and Cheyenne, became buffalo hunters.
3. The Pueblo stored reserves of food and developed irrigation.

Worksheets for History and Life © Scott, Foresman and Company 73

SOURCE READINGS

Source Reading 18A
Source Reading 18B

OVERHEAD TRANSPARENCIES

Overhead Transparency 35
Overhead Transparency 36

TEST GENERATOR

40 multiple-choice questions for Chapter 18

18

Empires in Africa and the Americas

500–1590

CHAPTER INTRODUCTION

A variety of economic, geographic, and cultural factors led to the rise and decline of many civilizations in Africa and America before European domination of these areas.

LOCATOR GLOBE

Call students' attention to the globe, which indicates the general areas of the world discussed in this chapter. (Detailed maps appear throughout this chapter.)

TIME LINE

How many years elapsed between the development of the Kingdom of Ghana and the building of Tenochtitlán? (825)

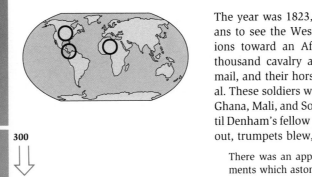

300	
400	
500	Kingdom of Ghana develops
1325	Tenochtitlán is built
1400	
1500	

The year was 1823, and Dixon Denham—one of the first Europeans to see the West African interior—rode ahead of his companions toward an African city in the savanna. Suddenly, several thousand cavalry appeared. The soldiers were dressed in chain mail, and their horses were decorated with quilted cloth and metal. These soldiers were the descendants of the ancient kingdoms of Ghana, Mali, and Songhai. The African cavalry remained steady until Denham's fellow travelers caught up with him. Then a shout rang out, trumpets blew, and the cavalry charged to welcome them:

> There was an appearance of tact and management in their movements which astonished me: Three separate small bodies . . . kept charging rapidly towards us, to within a few feet of our horses' heads . . . . These parties . . . [were] mounted on small very perfect horses who stopped and wheeled from their utmost speed with great precision and expertness, shaking their spears over their heads, exclaiming "Barka! Barka!" [that is] . . . Blessing, Blessing!

Denham was surprised to find so powerful a cavalry and such a well-administered state in Africa. European explorers were equally surprised to discover large, well-run empires in the Americas. After the time of the Maya, whom you learned about in Chapter 9, came the Aztecs and the Incas. As a reminder of one of these empires, the impressive Inca city of Machu Picchu stands high in the Andes Mountains in Peru. The city, which you can see on page 453, was only first viewed by Europeans in 1911.

Beyond the awareness of the Europeans, large empires had been rising and falling in Africa and the Americas for centuries. These empires had rich trade, effective governments, good roads, large cities, and productive and innovative farming. Thriving trade led to the development of powerful governments in Africa, including Ghana, which benefited from the gold trade, and Zimbabwe, which flourished along the East African coast.

The Golden Stool, this low wooden seat covered with gold, was the state symbol for the Asante, a later West African people who united many small clans around 1670.

Reading Preview

In this chapter you will learn about the civilizations that developed in Africa and the Americas between 500 and 1590.

1. Famous empires grew in the West African savanna.

2. City-states and kingdoms flourished in East Africa.

3. The forest states developed strong governments.

4. The Aztecs and Incas created strong empires.

5. North America supported a variety of cultures.

 Famous empires grew in the West African savanna.

The Sahara can be compared to an ocean, crossed by the "ship of the desert," the camel. Just as cities grew up on ocean coasts, cities grew up on the edge of the desert. The towns in the Sudan (a name for the northern savanna of Africa, not to be confused with the modern nation of that name) were much like port cities. For more than eight centuries, they took turns as capitals for three powerful empires: Ghana, Mali, and Songhai.

Gold and salt were traded in West Africa.

A rich gold-mining area lay in West Africa in a forest region called Wangara [wäng gä′rə], which is

Lesson Plan

Essential Learning Objectives

Students will learn to:
- explain the connection between control of commerce and empire building.
- describe the significance of ancient Ghana, Mali, and Songhai.

1 FOCUS AND MOTIVATE

Ask students to refer to the West Africa map on page 326. Have them note that West Africa is about the size of the continental United Sates. Emphasize the distances traveled by

325

traders, and the area held by the three great empires described in this section. Next have students find Wangara, ancient Mali, and Songhai. Find ancient Ghana on the map on page 160.

2 | TEACH

- Discuss the significance of Wangara and barter trade. Point out the exchanges: gold for salt, copper, or cloth.

- Review the growth and decline of Ghana, Mali, and Songhai. Underline that the key to power was—and still is—the control of the trade routes.

- Discuss the connection between control of commerce and empire building. Provide an example of nations exchanging gold for salt. If these goods could not be exchanged or sold, both nations would weaken. Control of the trade center made collecting taxes easy. This money was used to support an army which also controlled the country.

GUIDED PRACTICE

Have the students write a short essay explaining the rise and decline of the Songhai Empire.

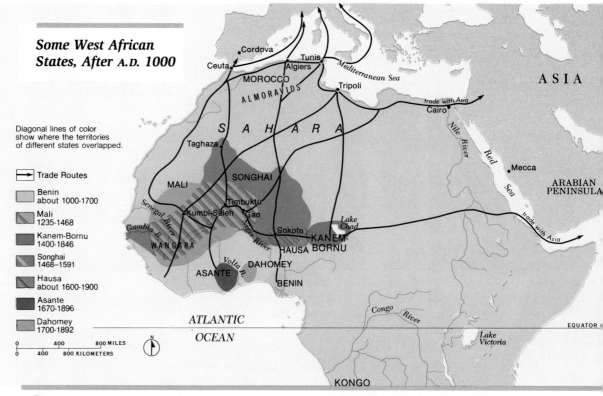

Some West African States, After A.D. 1000

Diagonal lines of color show where the territories of different states overlapped.

⇨ Trade Routes

Benin about 1000-1700

Mali 1235-1468

Kanem-Bornu 1400-1846

Songhai 1468–1591

Hausa about 1600-1900

Asante 1670-1896

Dahomey 1700-1892

MAP STUDY In the map above, the cartographer has indicated change over time with alternating strips of colors. Name three cities that were controlled by both Mali and Songhai at different points in time.

shown on the map above. Gold from Wangara—prized by many nations—was the basis for profitable trade as far back as Roman times.

Traders brought the gold through the forests to the savanna. There, they met other traders from the cities of the North African coast, who exchanged goods for the gold and carried it across the Sahara to cities on the Mediterranean Sea. From there, much of the gold was shipped for sale in Europe and Asia.

One important item the West Africans needed was salt, which is essential to people's diets. Because they lived in a hot climate, the West Africans needed even more salt than those people who lived in cooler places. However, very few salt deposits existed in West Africa. When a place named Taghaza [tə gä′zə] developed near a salt deposit in the Sahara, it became a major stop on the trade routes. Even today, caravans of camels and jeeps come to Taghaza to buy salt for the people in the savanna.

The 10th-century Arab geographer al-Masudi described what has come to be called the "**silent trade**." He said that traders from the north crossed the desert and came to a place in the Sudan, possibly on the Niger River. At this same place every year, they laid their goods—salt, cloth, and copper—on the ground. Then, they beat their drums to let people of the savanna know the market was ready and withdrew a half-day's journey away.

BACKGROUND Scholars disagree on whether this is an accurate description of silent trade. It may have been a story Sudanese told to keep Saharan and North African traders out of their business.

BACKGROUND Examples of the silent trade have been cited from all over the world in ancient times. Remind students that even today some U.S. companies keep production and design secrets by prohibiting visitors in certain parts of their facilities.

Next, the savanna people came and placed piles of gold beside the goods in as large a quantity as they thought them worth. Then, they too went a half-day's journey away, beating drums to signal to the merchants from the north.

The North Africans returned, and, if they thought the price was right, they took the gold and left. If not, they withdrew again to wait for the savanna traders to put down more gold. The exchange went on for several days until both groups were satisfied with the price. Neither group ever saw or spoke with the other. The conditions of this trade probably developed because the Africans wanted to keep the source of their own valuable goods a secret from outsiders. Thus, they prevented foreigners from learning about their country or even learning their language.

Ancient Ghana controlled the gold trade (500–1235).

About the year 500, the kingdom of **Ghana** [gä′nə] began to develop in West Africa. (See the map on page 160. It should not be confused with the modern country of the same name, which is far to the south of this ancient kingdom.) Ancient Ghana grew near the marketplace of the gold traders, and its power came from its location. By the end of the 7th century, the spread of Islam brought people of the Muslim world to West Africa, and these new arrivals began to write about Ghana.

The king. From the writings of Arab geographers, we know that by this time Ghana was a large empire based on trade and agriculture. Its strong central government was ruled by a king, who appointed the different officers of the kingdom and who was the final judge of all court cases. Ghana's ruler was believed to be partly divine and able to communicate with the gods for the good of the empire.

Whenever the king appeared in public, he was surrounded by servants carrying gold swords. The princes and advisers of the empire, in splendid dress, accompanied him. Horses with gold cloth blankets and dogs with gold and silver collars were also part of his parade.

The king claimed to own all the gold nuggets that came from the mines of Wangara. Other people could trade only in gold dust. With this right,

the king of Ghana could control the economy by holding back gold nuggets from trade if the price were not right. In addition to owning all the gold nuggets, the empire taxed all goods entering and leaving Ghana, including salt and gold.

The kingdom. The twin cities of **Kumbi-Saleh** [kum′bē sä′lə] made up the capital of ancient Ghana. The king and his officers lived in one town, and merchants and visitors lived in the other. The towns, located on the edge of the Sahara, were about six miles apart. Between the two towns were small mud houses for the people who grew food to support the inhabitants of the capital.

The king's town was built like a fortress. A powerful army, consisting of 200,000 warriors, protected the kingdom and helped the king control the large variety of peoples within its boundaries. The traders' town included two-story stone houses and public squares. After the 7th century A.D.,

The gold trade brought riches to West Africa. In the photograph below, a modern leader of the Asante people wears a regal gold ring and bracelet.

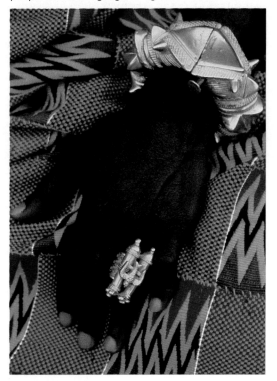

ASSESS

1. What is a savanna? (grasslands)
2. Who was Askia Muhammad? (Emperor of Songhai)

OPTIONAL RETEACHING

Ask students to write a sentence explaining the relationship between the following places: savanna, Sudan; Askia, Sanni Ali; Timbuktu, Gao.

OPTIONAL ENRICHMENT

1. Ask interested students to list ten famous people who were contemporaries of Askia Muhammad. (average)
2. Ask students to research why gold has historically been regarded as so valuable. What characteristics make it so? (challenging)
3. Also for enrichment:

📖 *Source Reading 18A*

INDEPENDENT PRACTICE/ HOMEWORK

Assign the Section Review, Activities page 103, or Workbook page 69.

CLOSURE

Tell students that between 500 and 1600 three empires dominated West Africa. The Ghana, Mali, and Songhai empires encouraged trade and education. Large cities developed and culture flourished. Yet each empire declined because of foreign invasion.

mosques were built there because many of the traders were Muslim. The kings and farmers of Ghana, however, kept their old religious customs.

The decline. In the 11th century, a group of Muslim Berbers, the Almoravids [al′mə rä′vidz] lived north of Ghana. The Almoravids believed in living a very strict religious life. They also believed it was their mission to stamp out wickedness and convert people to Islam. In 1076 they attacked Kumbi-Saleh in order to force the people there to be better Muslims. The Almoravids occupied the capital for about ten years, until the people of Ghana won it back.

Ghana never recovered from the Almoravid occupation, and the many provinces of Ghana no longer obeyed the weakened government. Many merchants moved to other trading towns on the edge of the desert. Within 50 years an army from one of the provinces conquered Ghana, and a new empire emerged that became larger and wealthier than Ghana had ever been.

Trade and learning flourished in Mali and Songhai (1235–1590).

Sundiata [sun′dē ä′tə] was the leader of a province of Ghana called **Mali** [mä′lē]. The king of Ghana had 11 of Sundiata's brothers murdered so that the province would not be a threat to Ghana. These measures did not stop Mali's ambitions, however. In 1235 Sundiata led his people to victory over the last king of Ghana.

The Mali Empire. During his rule, Sundiata conquered vast territories and created the empire of Mali. He also brought under his control important gold- and salt-mining areas. Traders now penetrated deep into both of these regions, and, as commerce flourished, the silent trade died out. As the founder of a nation, Sundiata became a hero to his people, much as George Washington is to the people of the United States.

Sundiata's successors converted to Islam and worked hard to make Mali a Muslim state. As you read in Chapter 15, Mali's kings and its capital city, Timbuktu, became famous throughout the Muslim world for their wealth and learning. Most of the city dwellers and merchants converted to Islam, but most of the farmers, herders, and workers remained devoted to their African ancestral religions. Gradually the rulers of Mali lost control of their empire.

The Songhai Empire. Other provinces struggled to seize power. One was **Songhai** [song′hī], whose capital Gao [gow] was located not far from Timbuktu. In 1468 Sonni Ali [son′ē ä lē′], the king

Birds (left) perch on the pinnacle of a clay mosque that is similar in style to this modern-day mosque (below) in Mali.

of Songhai, attacked and captured Timbuktu. He then went on to capture many other cities of Mali.

Sonni Ali ruled for 35 years—a time of persecution and warfare. Sonni Ali had been a man of the countryside, and he had failed to understand or help the people of the towns. He had judged their dissatisfaction as disloyalty and had been brutal in his treatment of them. His reaction to a revolt in Timbuktu had been such widespread slaughter that he gained a permanent reputation as a ruthless tyrant. Upon Sonni Ali's death in 1493, one of his generals became head of the empire. This successor reversed this harsh policy.

Sonni Ali's successor, Askia [äs kē′yə] Muhammad, reigned for 35 years, during which time the Songhai Empire grew to include most of the grasslands of West Africa. It reached from the Atlantic Ocean halfway across Africa to Lake Chad, and from what is today the southern border of Algeria south to the edge of the rainforest. (Find Songhai on the map on page 326.) Askia Muhammad was an able administrator who gave the empire an improved system of government.

Askia Muhammad understood that the wealth of the empire depended on commerce. He set up a fair method of taxation and a good system of communication with the provinces. He also encouraged the Muslim religion, which was practiced by most of the townspeople, especially the traders. Under Askia Muhammad's leadership, Timbuktu reached new heights as a center for scholarship. A visitor in the early 1500s wrote this description:

> The rich king of Timbuktu has many plates and sceptres of gold, some whereof weigh 1300 pounds; and he keeps a magnificent and well-furnished court . . . Here are a great store of doctors, judges, priests and other learned men, that are bountifully maintained at the king's cost and charges. And hither are brought divers manuscripts of written books out of Barbary [North Africa] which are sold for more money than any other merchandise.

Songhai's decline. Songhai was probably the most highly organized and efficient of all the early West African states. Its wealth and power aroused the jealousy of the king of Morocco in North Africa, who sent an army of about 5,000 men to cross the Sahara and attack Songhai in 1590.

Only about 1,000 Moroccan soldiers survived the crossing, but these warriors had guns and gunpowder, weapons that were superior to the swords and spears of the Songhai army. The Moroccans eventually beat the Songhai, whose rulers had lost power since the time of Askia Muhammad. However, they were not able to hold the empire together. During the years that followed, many provinces, cities, and small groups broke away and began to govern themselves. This large and powerful West African empire—the Songhai—thus came to an end.

Section 1 Review

Identify silent trade, Ghana (ancient), Kumbi-Saleh, Sundiata, Mali, Songhai

Main Ideas
1. What two important resources were traded across the Sahara? Why were these important?
2. How did ancient Ghana control the gold trade?
3. What were the two major empires in West Africa during this period? What did their kings accomplish?

Critical Thinking

Identifying Assumptions: How do these descriptions of the powerful African empires compare with ideas you've had about Africa?

 2 *City-states and kingdoms flourished in East Africa.*

More than 2,000 years ago, people from India and the Arabian peninsula sailed westward looking for new sources of trade. The monsoon winds, or trade winds, of the Indian Ocean blew steadily toward East Africa for months and then steadily back toward India for months, giving sailors a safe, direct route. By about A.D. 120, a guidebook published in Egypt told where ports could be found along the East African coast.

The 7th-century expansion of Islamic trade caused the East African and Indian Ocean trade to boom. The expansion of trade in turn stimulated the rise of kingdoms such as Zimbabwe in the interior of East Africa.

2 *Lesson Plan*

Essential Learning Objectives

Students will learn to:
- identify the key city-states and kingdoms of East Africa and the reasons for their prosperity.
- describe the Portuguese role in destroying this prosperity.

Have students name words that have come to English from other languages. List them on the chalkboard. Then point out that the East African language developed as a result of the influences of many cultures. This language is Swahili, made up of sounds and words from Arab, African, and Indian sources.

2 TEACH

• Discuss the interaction between African, Arab, and Indian cultures and the interweaving of these three groups into the Swahili culture.

• Identify the key factors that led to the establishment of Zimbabwe. Point out the impact of gold on its economy and the reasons for its decline.

GUIDED PRACTICE

Direct the students to name as many occupations in East Africa as they can identify after reading the section. (engineers, gold miners, traders)

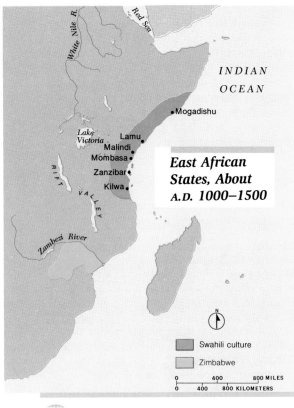

East African States, About A.D. 1000–1500

Swahili culture

Zimbabwe

| 0 | 400 | 800 MILES |
| 0 | 400 | 800 KILOMETERS |

MAP STUDY Compare the map above with the map on page 796. The Swahili culture was present in parts of which three modern-day nations?

International trade helped East African ports grow into city-states.

As in West Africa, there were large supplies of gold in East Africa. Ivory, which came from the tusks of the African elephant, was another valuable trade item. It was strong but soft enough to be carved into objects that were both beautiful and useful. Ivory was in much demand in the Islamic Empire, India, and China. A third item of export was iron, carried to the markets of Asia, where it was made into strong, sharp weapons.

Asian and Arab traders brought cotton cloth and porcelain utensils to sell in East Africa. Song and

Ming dynasty Chinese porcelain was so especially prized that East Africans built niches in the walls of their homes to display the finer pieces. Along the coasts of modern-day Kenya and Tanzania, broken pieces of old Chinese cups, saucers, and vases still lie in the sand, evidence of the trade that took place many centuries ago.

In response to the centuries-old trade, coastal marketplaces developed into large cities. Traders from Africa and the Middle East built homes and settled in the port cities to act as agents for distant traders. One of the richest cities was **Kilwa**. South of most of the other ports, Kilwa was closer to the gold fields of the kingdom of **Zimbabwe** [zim-bä′bwā], which means the "royal dwelling." Present-day Zimbabwe includes the area of the historic Zimbabwe kingdom.

The merchants of Kilwa controlled much of the gold trade and grew wealthy by imposing taxes on its sale. Ibn Batuta, the Muslim traveler about whom you read in Chapter 15, visited Kilwa in 1331 and wrote that it was one of the most beautiful and well-constructed towns he had seen. Today, impressive stone ruins of large palaces, mansions, mosques, arched walkways, town squares, and public fountains hint at Kilwa's glorious past. Coral and wood were once used to make carved arches, doors, and windows. The main palace of Kilwa stood on the very edge of a cliff overlooking the ocean. It had more than 100 rooms, as well as an eight-sided bathing pool in one of its many courtyards.

Kilwa was only one of several important trading towns. Each had its own ruler, government, laws, taxes, and small police force. The influence of each of these city-states spread a certain distance from the city itself, sometimes all along a trade route to the interior. Each city-state was in fierce competition with the others.

Swahili culture thrived in the city-states until the Portuguese arrived.

The African, Indian, and Arab traders who settled in the port cities intermarried and had large families. Eventually a way of living developed—called Swahili culture—that was a distinctive blend of Islamic, Asian, and African cultures and languages. **Swahili** [swä hē′lē] is the name of the language

ANSWER TO MAP STUDY Somalia, Kenya, and Tanzania

From the Archives

A Strong Ruler

Zara Yaqob (1434–1468) was a powerful king of Ethiopia during a period when that country was a strong and wealthy nation in East Africa. His lavish coronation, described in the following excerpt from an early chronicle, took place in the ancient capital of Ethiopia and marked the beginning of a long and peaceful rule.

All of the inhabitants, as well as the priests, went to meet him and welcomed him with a great rejoicing. . . . When he entered within the gates of the town, the king had on his right hand and on his left the governor of Tigre [an Ethiopian province) and the administrator of Axum who carried and waved according to custom, olive branches. . . . After arriving within the walls of Axum, the king had brought to him much gold which he scattered as far as the city gate on the carpets which were spread along his route. . . .

During the reign of our king Zara Yaqob, there was in the whole land of Ethiopia a great peace and a great tranquility, for the king taught justice and faith.

---

the coastal peoples spoke. It is an African language with many Indian and Arabic words mixed in. The Swahili people wrote poetry and stories in Swahili with Arabic script.

Life in the city-states was comfortable, and people were free to follow the religion of their choice. Although the Arab influence caused some people to convert to Islam, most of the Swahili continued to practice their own religions.

Swahili peoples kept in touch with distant lands and sought good trade relations. A famous Chinese painting (shown on page 443) pictures a giraffe sent to the emperor of China in 1414 by the people

of Malindi [mä lin′dē], one of the smaller city-states. Writing on this painting describes the Chinese emperor's pleasure with the gift. He sent a fleet of ships and thousands of Chinese sailors, carrying numerous gifts, to accompany the Malindi traders back to Africa.

The Portuguese also made contact with the Swahili people in the early 1500s. As you will learn in Chapter 20, the Portuguese first saw the East African coast when Vasco da Gama sailed around the tip of Africa in 1498.

The Portuguese were eager for gold and wealth and were delighted to find thriving city-states in East Africa. Descriptions by early Portuguese explorers give a picture of life in Kilwa as even more prosperous than when Ibn Batuta visited in the 1300s. The common Swahili people dressed in imported cottons and silks, and the wealthy wore gold, silver, and jeweled ornaments. Surrounding the towns were freshwater streams, orchards, and fruit gardens.

The Portuguese wanted to trade for these African riches, but the Swahili scorned them. The Swahili thought the Portuguese had bad manners, unclean habits, and cheap trading goods. The Portuguese, however, had guns—something few Swahili had. Most Indian Ocean trade was fairly peaceful at that time, and the East African city-states had few defenses.

Armed with their muskets and cannons, the Portuguese began a campaign of piracy and looting. An expedition ordered by the king of Portugal burned Kilwa in 1505. After capturing the town of Mombasa, which was further to the north, the Portuguese sailors broke into houses, swinging axes, and killed anyone who had not escaped before the attack. A Swahili poet later wrote of the ruin of his city: "Where once the porcelain stood in the wall niches, Now wild birds nestle their fledglings."

The Portuguese built their own trade fort at Mombasa. Still, just as the Moroccans failed to hold the Songhai Empire together, the Portuguese could not replace the governments and trade networks of East Africa. Although the destruction caused by the Portuguese led to a decline in trade, Swahili culture survived. Today, Swahili language and poetry play an important part in the modern-day countries of Tanzania and Kenya.

FROM THE ARCHIVES The source is translated in Basil Davidson, *The African Past* (Boston: Little, Brown and Co., 1964), pp. 118–119. Ask students to list some of the symbols that appear in this text. (olive branches for peace, laying out carpets to welcome an honored guest, gold as a display of wealth) Note how these symbols are still used today.

This huge stone fortification, constructed of local granite, dominates the ruins of ancient Zimbabwe.

The kingdom of Zimbabwe developed in the interior.

In 1868 a European hunter stumbled across the massive stone ruins of a group of palaces, fortresses, and houses in the interior of southeastern Africa near the Zambezi River. The impressive stone buildings of Zimbabwe had been built by expert masons from the 10th through the 18th centuries. The buildings, made from oblong slabs of granite, had walls 10 feet thick and 30 feet high. These elaborately patterned walls were not held together by mortar, but were instead built with stone that had been shaped to fit together exactly.

The founders of Zimbabwe. The builders of Zimbabwe were descended from the Bantu peoples who probably migrated from the Congo forest. By the 11th century, some Bantu peoples, called the **Shona** [shō′nə], had crossed the Zambezi River and pushed back or conquered any hunting and gathering peoples that lived there.

The Shona found gold deposits near Zimbabwe, which they mined and traded with the Swahili city-states. They also imported such Asian goods as cotton, brass, and porcelain. By the 1400s Zimbabwe was a strong state with a large population, much wealth, and a centralized government.

The ruler and city of Zimbabwe. Zimbabwe was ruled by a king who was believed to be semidivine. The king made the necessary decisions, but only his closest advisers were allowed to see him. If the king ever became ill, he was supposed to commit suicide so that a healthy king could take his place, keeping the country strong.

One of the major stone buildings at Zimbabwe is thought to have been the palace where the king lived with his royal wives, advisers, and officers. About 1,000 people lived in the palace at one time. Cooks, servants, farmers, and soldiers lived with their families in smaller stone buildings surrounding the palace. Ruined buildings of this type have been found not only at the capital but all over the region. The larger sites were probably the homes of provincial chiefs.

Many of the common people were involved in gold mining. The mines were pits dug into the earth, some being as much as 50 feet deep. Men and women both worked in the gold mines and along the streams, where even more gold washed out of the ground.

The decline of Zimbabwe. In the early 1500s, the Portuguese tried to gain control of the gold regions, but the rulers of Zimbabwe prevented them from even reaching the capital. The Zimbabwe kings also dictated to the Portuguese all rules concerning trade and taxes. Still, Zimbabwe's trade with the East African coast gradually dropped off as a result of the destructive Portuguese actions there.

Internal quarrels among brothers who all wanted to be Zimbabwe's king further weakened the kingdom. Zimbabwe survived until 1830, when it was attacked by Ndebele peoples from the south who were seeking land on which to settle. The large stone buildings were abandoned, and hoards of gold were left to be found later and carried off by European prospectors in the 19th century.

Section 2 Review

Identify Kilwa, Zimbabwe, Swahili, Shona

Main Ideas

1. How did trade help East African ports develop?
2. What cultures made up the Swahili culture?
3. How did the kingdom of Zimbabwe develop?

Critical Thinking

Making Hypotheses: Why were East Africans, Arabs, and Indians able to blend so harmoniously?

---

3 The forest states developed strong governments.

The forest states of Benin, Dahomey, Kongo, and Asante flourished on agriculture and trade. The trade in human beings, especially, became an important source of wealth for these states. As the demand for cheap labor on the plantations of the West Indies increased, slave raids in Africa took an enormous toll on the population. Eventually, the slave trade was stopped and efficient governments kept the forest states strong until the European conquests of the late 1800s.

Strong kings helped Benin grow wealthy and powerful.

The forest state of **Benin** [bə nēn′], located in what is now southern Nigeria, had kings known as **Obas**. The first Oba [ō′bə] lived some time in the 11th century. Oba Ewedo [ə wā′dō], who ruled in the 14th century, strengthened his position by weakening the power of the council of elders that helped him rule. Ewedo built a new capital, which he called Benin.

A 15th-century Oba, Eware [ə wä′rē] the Great, increased the strength of the Benin army. According to oral history, he then expanded the state by conquering 201 villages and states in the area. He also fortified the city of Benin by building high wooden walls.

The Obas of Benin were religious rulers. They were responsible for all religious ceremonies and prayed to the gods for Benin's welfare. Women played an important part in Benin's government.

At least two early Obas were women, and women had their own councils and held their own religious ceremonies. The queen mother of Benin had her own palace, which was one of the largest buildings in Benin city.

The government of Benin was described by visitors as just and fair. The brass and ivory carvings displayed in many houses were evidence of a comfortable leisure class of people and a skilled work force. A Dutch geographer wrote the following description of the city of Benin:

> The town is composed of thirty main streets, very straight and 120 feet wide, apart from an infinity of small intersecting streets. The houses are close to one another, arranged in good order; they have roofs, verandahs and balustrades [railings] . . . they wash and scrub their houses so well that they are polished and shining like a looking-glass . . . They are people who have good laws and a well organized police.

Hundreds of bronze wall plaques, such as the one below, were made in the forest state of Benin. This plaque depicts a king and two attendants.

Identify

Key Terms, People, and Places are defined on pages indicated in parentheses. Also see the Glossary and Biographical Dictionary. Kilwa (330), Zimbabwe (330), Swahili (330), Shona (332)

Main Ideas

1. Traders from Africa and the Middle East built homes and settled near the ports. Coastal marketplaces attracted people and thus developed into large cities as the trade grew.
2. It was a blend of African, Indian, and Arabic cultures.
3. Bantu peoples called Shona migrated from the Congo and found gold deposits. They traded with the Swahili city-states and became a strong state by the 1400s.

Critical Thinking

They were living in a wealthy area where there was plenty for everyone, which limited competition for resources.

3 Lesson Plan

Essential Learning Objectives

Students will learn to:

- discuss the history of Benin.
- describe the slave trade.

1 FOCUS AND MOTIVATE

Discuss with the students what they know about slavery. Write the responses on the chalkboard. Ask the students to formulate questions based on each response. (Slaves were imported to America—when and why were slaves imported to America?)

- Discuss Benin, pointing out the fairness that was observed by visitors, the role of women, the neatness of Benin City. Then discuss the first years of European contact, including Portuguese contributions.

- Write the following phrases on the chalkboard: pre-European slave practices in West Africa; what led Europeans to use slaves; the participants in the trade. Have students develop each statement by locating information in their texts.

GUIDED PRACTICE

Distribute blank outline maps of the world from the Geography Skills book. Direct students to indicate how most slaves were moved from Africa to America. Have them label key political and geographical features. Also for guided practice:

 Overhead Transparency 35

ASSESS

1. Where was the Benin Empire located? (southern Nigeria)
2. How were Africans involved in the Atlantic slave trade? (selling captives from the interior of Africa)

OPTIONAL RETEACHING

Have the students write paragraphs on the collection of slaves in Africa and on conditions on slave ships.

OPTIONAL ENRICHMENT

Have students research the extent of the slave trade in East Africa. (average)

INDEPENDENT PRACTICE/ HOMEWORK

Assign the Section Review, Activities page 105, or Workbook page 71.

The reigns of the Obas were recorded on cast bronze plaques that were hung on the palace walls. Many of these plaques have been preserved, and they give historians details about Benin's past. Benin is one of the best examples of a strong, just, and materially advanced African culture that developed in the absence of European or Middle Eastern influence.

Europeans arrived in West Africa.

In the late 1400s, sailors from Portugal came to the coast of West Africa, looking for places to trade their country's manufactured goods. They took muskets and metal utensils to exchange for gold and spices. The first visit of a Portuguese ship to Benin was in 1472.

By 1500 the English, French, and Dutch were also trading with Benin, which closely regulated trade with the Europeans. The foreign traders had to pay port taxes and import duties, and they

This 16th-century map shows the location of Portuguese forts along the West African coast. The Portuguese did not explore the interior at this time.

could only trade with chosen representatives of the Oba. Europeans were not allowed to live in Benin. They could visit for a short time, but they had to live on their ships anchored off the coast.

The Portuguese brought corn and cassava (a plant also known as manioc, from which tapioca is made) from their colonies in the Americas. These foods grew so well in the African forest that within 50 years they had become staple items in the forest people's diet. As a result, the population increased.

The slave trade brought wealth to the cities and terror to the countryside.

The African states had always permitted slavery. Prisoners of war, debtors, and convicts could be made into slaves. Some international trade in slaves also existed in the Muslim cities. However, this slave trade was not based on race since both light- and dark-skinned people were sold in slave markets. Slaves were rarely for plantation labor and were usually treated well, though they were sometimes underfed. Some slaves were able to gain freedom through hard work and marriage into free families. A few even became advisers to kings.

By the early 16th century, the Europeans had begun to operate sugar plantations in the West Indies and needed many slaves to work the plantations. These slaves, many of whom were bought from West African markets, were treated very cruelly and had almost no chance of gaining their freedom.

Many West African states, such as Benin, Dahomey [də hō′mē], and Asante, kept strict control over the slave trade. They made certain the Europeans did not leave the coast and capture slaves for themselves. These West African states grew very rich by selling captives from the interior of the continent. African merchants raided isolated villages, where people did not have centralized governments to protect them, and kidnaped anyone they could find. Villages responded by posting children in trees to act as lookouts for the approach of slave raiders. Firsthand accounts tell of the widespread horrors of these raids. In some places, such as the Kongo, so many people were enslaved and taken to the Americas that the area became almost deserted.

The double-headed serpent, a symbol of the Aztec rain god Tlaloc, adorns a pendant worn by a high priest. The pendant was made of turquoise and shell.

The worst part of the slave trade occurred, however, after the slaves were put on ships bound for America. The **Middle Passage**, as the sea voyage was known, lasted a grueling ten weeks or more. Slaves, often held in chains, were packed in large numbers below the deck of the ship and fed mostly thin porridge. More slaves died from illness, suicide, and unclean conditions on the Middle Passage than from capture in Africa or hard labor in America. Not until early in the 19th century was antislavery sentiment in America and Europe strong enough to finally end the slave trade.

Section 3 Review

Identify Benin, Obas, Middle Passage

Main Ideas
1. How was the government of Benin strengthened in the 14th and 15th centuries?
2. What were the Europeans looking for when they came to West Africa?
3. How did the slave trade affect the forest states? What happened in the countryside?

Critical Thinking

Making Hypotheses: Why do you suppose it took so long to do away with slavery even though it caused so much misery?

BACKGROUND The slave trade was made illegal in the United States and in Britain's colonies in 1807. Slavery was abolished in Britain's colonies in 1833, in the United States in 1865, and in Brazil by 1888.

| 4 | *The Aztecs and Incas created strong empires.* |

As you learned in Chapter 9, our knowledge of Native American civilization before the arrival of Columbus in 1492 is limited. Spanish conquerors had little time for collecting information about American history and destroyed much of the American cultural record. Only a few artifacts, paintings, writings, and buildings have survived. From these, archaeologists and historians are reconstructing the history of some of the larger pre-Columbian American cultures, including the Aztecs and the Incas.

The Aztecs created a capital in central Mexico.

In the 13th century, a warlike people swept into central Mexico from the northwest. They called themselves **Aztecs**, which probably refers to their original name, Aztlan, meaning "White Land." Scholars think the name Aztlan may refer to the land that is now southern Utah or northern Arizona. Since the Aztecs also called themselves the Mexica people, the lands they conquered eventually came to be known as Mexico. Aztec power reached its height during the 15th and early 16th centuries. (Find the Aztec Empire on the map on page 336.)

Have the students turn to maps of Mexico and South America in the Atlas and list the geographical features of both Mexico and Peru. Ask students to predict what kind of impact such features had on the establishment of pre-Columbian empires in those areas.

2 TEACH

Have students work in small groups to locate and record information to complete a chart comparing the Aztec and Inca empires. Have them compare the following: population of empire (in 1500), capital city, population of capital, ruler at time of Spanish conquest, economic base, form of money, use of water, marriage practices, evidence of government strength, system for keeping records, and human sacrifice. Discuss their completed charts.

GUIDED PRACTICE

Hand out an outline map of North and South America from the Geography Skills book. Have students draw the boundaries of both the Aztec and Inca empires.

The city. The center of the Aztec Empire was their city of Tenochtitlán [tā nŏch′tē tlän′], which was probably built about 1325. According to legend, the Aztecs decided to locate their capital on the spot where they saw a heaven-sent eagle, with a snake in its beak, sitting on a cactus that was growing from a rock in a lake. This scene is pictured on the flag of modern-day Mexico, and Mexico City now stands on the ancient site of Tenochtitlán and the vanished lake.

Tenochtitlán prospered and probably had a population of about 400,000 by the early 15th century. The setting of this city was magnificent. It sat out in the water, on islands and land reclaimed from the shallow lake. Canals existed between the islands. A visitor could enter the heart of the city either by canoe or by walking over one of the long stone causeways that connected the central city to the mainland.

Striking features of Tenochtitlán were the large temples and pyramids that stood in the city square. Near the temples were ball courts, where the Aztecs played a game of religious significance similar to that of the Maya. Most of the people lived in houses made of adobe [ə dō′bē], or sun-dried clay, which they painted white and then trimmed with bright colors.

Several lively marketplaces existed in Tenochtitl′an. In one section, merchants sold fruits and vegetables, and in another, cloth and ready-to-wear clothing. People also sold delicate jewelry made of jade, shell, and turquoise. Customers either traded items by barter or paid for them with cacao [kə kā′ō] beans—the source of chocolate—which were used as money.

The government. The Aztecs did not destroy or absorb the tribes they conquered. Instead, they ruled over them and forced them to pay tribute in the form of cacao beans, deer hides, conch shells, and bolts of cotton cloth. A form of writing that used pictures, called glyphs, was used to record these payments. By 1500 the city of Tenochtitlán was the center of an empire that included at least 5 million people, most of whom were farmers.

The head of the Aztec government was called the Chief of Men. When the Spanish arrived, the Aztec leader was Montezuma [mon′tə zü′mə]. Although the Chief of Men was looked upon almost

The Maya, Aztec, and Inca Empires

- Maya Empire Around A.D. 900
- Aztec Empire Around A.D. 1500
- Inca Empire Around A.D. 1500
- Present-day boundaries

© SF

MAP STUDY Use the maps on pages 788 and 790 to name the countries in which the Aztec and Inca empires once reigned.

as a god, many nobles, merchants, and leaders held nearly as much power.

Young people were formally educated to prepare them for their futures.

At the age of 15, the sons of nobles and rich merchants began to study at the "house of youth." They trained to become warriors or priests, the two most important professions in Aztec life. At these schools they studied religious rites and duties, learned Aztec history, practiced using weapons, and trained in arts and crafts. Aztec history was written on long strips of paper that were folded like a fan to make a book, called a codex. Priests also taught the boys Aztec rules of good conduct, such as "never tell lies," and "console the poor and unfortunate."

ANSWER TO MAP STUDY Aztec—Mexico; Inca—Peru, Chile, Argentina, Bolivia, Ecuador, and a bit of Colombia

Although barred from the top of society, even boys from poor Aztec families had a chance through education to become army officers, land-holders, or government officials. Some young women, too, were trained to become priests and to take part in temple ceremonies. Others took charge of booths in the markets, watched over the production and sale of crops, or ran households. Aztec mothers taught their girls to be respectful daughters and faithful wives. One Aztec mother advised her daughter to "take care that your garments are decent and proper; and . . . do not adorn yourself with much finery, since this is a mark of vanity and folly."

Aztec girls married at 16 and the boys at 20. Parents arranged the marriages, and at the time of the ceremony a feast was held. The celebration included the giving of many presents and much drinking and dancing.

Religion and war dominated Aztec life.

The Aztecs had many gods. Huitzilopochtli [wēt'zēl ō potch'tlē], the god of the sun and war, was one. Other important gods were Tlaloc [tlä'lok], the rain god, and Quetzalcoatl [ket'säl-kō'ə tl], represented in the form of a feathered snake. The Aztecs believed the world had been created and destroyed four times. The fifth and present creation of the world was the result of Quetzalcoatl's sacrifice of his own blood. The Aztecs believed that to keep the universe alive, they needed to make continual human sacrifices.

The Aztecs required massive numbers of prisoners for these sacrifices. Therefore, they were almost always at war with other groups of people. The subject peoples were deeply bitter because the Aztecs constantly demanded victims to be sacrificed on the temple-pyramids of Tenochtitlán. By the time a small band of Spaniards landed in Mexico in 1519 in search of gold, many conquered peoples were ready to turn against the Aztecs.

The Incas unified an extensive empire.

Far to the south of the Aztecs, in South America, various peoples lived in the Andes Mountains and along the Pacific Coast. By A.D. 500 some of them had developed complex cultures. The Tiahuanaco culture was one of these.

High in the Andes, near the shores of Lake Titicaca [tit'i kä'kä], lies a mass of gigantic stones—the ruins of Tiahuanaco [tē'ə wä nä'kō]. Like Mohenjo-Daro in India, the name of this site, which is believed to be a religious center, means "the place of the dead." Little is known about the people who lived in the Tiahuanaco region, but they were clearly skillful builders. Some of these skills were evidently passed on to later peoples of the area such as the **Incas**.

A few centuries after the decline of Tiahuanaco, a people of the Peruvian mountains began to develop a distinctive way of life. The ruler of these people was known as the Inca. The term has since been applied to the entire group.

Around the 11th century, the Incas settled in a valley of the Andes. They eventually conquered the people there and set up a capital city called **Cuzco** [küs'kō]. The Incas soon expanded their rule to neighboring mountain valleys. By 1400—like the Aztecs of Mexico—the Incas conquered distant regions. By the 1500s the Incas ruled an empire of more than 12 million people who spoke 20 different languages and belonged to more than 100 different ethnic groups. (Find the Inca Empire on the map on page 336.)

Unlike the Aztecs, the Incas absorbed the peoples they conquered into their own culture. They brought the sons of conquered chiefs to Cuzco and

This Inca wooden drinking cup took the shape of a puma, resembling one of the Inca feline gods. It is adorned with a silver neckband and whiskers.

ASSESS

1. What was Tenochtitlán? (the main city of the Aztec Empire)
2. Who were the "Chosen Women"? (Inca women trained in religion, weaving, and cooking)

OPTIONAL RETEACHING

Have the students write a short paragraph contrasting how the Aztecs and Incas got along with neighboring states. Have them decide which group was more successful.

OPTIONAL ENRICHMENT

1. Ask interested students to research why Inca buildings were so unique, using pictures to support the research. (challenging)
2. Also for enrichment:

 Source Reading 18B

INDEPENDENT PRACTICE/ HOMEWORK

Assign the Section Review, Activities page 106, or Workbook page 72.

CLOSURE

Summarize the lesson by telling the students that the Aztec and Inca cultures were remarkable for their size, their architecture, and their political organization. The Aztecs enslaved other nations around them, but the Incas absorbed the people they conquered.

educated them in the Inca ways. In addition, they sent colonies of loyal subjects to live in conquered areas, where they showed the new subjects the Inca way of life.

The Incas held their empire together with highly organized systems of government, communication, and transportation. An Inca road ran from one end of the empire to the other along the Pacific Coast, and another ran along the crest of the Andes Mountains. Many sections of the roads were paved, and suspension bridges hung over gorges and rivers. These bridges were marvels of engineering for the age in which they were built. Over these roads and bridges, relays of Inca runners rushed messages from one part of the empire to another.

Inca life was carefully regulated.

At the head of the Inca government was the emperor, or Inca. He claimed to be a descendant of the sun god, and during his lifetime, he was worshiped as an absolute ruler. As the Inca ruler Atahualpa [ä′tə wäl′pä] said to the Spanish conqueror Francisco Pizarro [pi zär′ō] "In my kingdom no bird flies, no leaf quivers if I do not will it."

Inca government. The Inca government owned and controlled all the land in its territory and all means of making and distributing goods. In addi-

tion, government officials in Cuzco kept records of the number of people in every area of the empire. All persons were classified according to their age and ability to work. Most men had to serve in the army and were forced to spend a certain amount of time working on government projects.

The government also regulated the private lives of individuals. If a young man was unmarried by a certain age, he had to choose a wife or take one selected by lot. Every so often, all engaged couples were married at huge state ceremonies held in the name of the Inca.

Unlike the Maya and Aztecs, the Incas had no written language. They kept records on knotted strings called quipus [kē′püz]. Using various kinds and colors of knots, they recorded crop production and other data needed by the Inca government. Only specially trained people could interpret the quipus. Inca history and legends were learned by heart, and then passed down from generation to generation. Most of our information about the Incas comes from this memorized poetry, which was later written down in Spanish. The languages of the Incas, Quechua, and Aymará are still spoken in Peru and Bolivia.

Inca people. Most Incas were farmers. In the mountainous Andean landscape, they learned to raise crops on terraced hillside plots. They built

DAILY LIFE

The Inca took advantage of the many resources around them. Their textiles (left) were usually covered with geometric designs and small figures. Gold objects, such as these cups (near right) used for religious ceremonies, were reserved for the families of Inca nobles. Modern-day woven boats are still a mode of travel on Lake Titicaca, high in the Andes Mountains between Peru and Bolivia.

low stone walls that kept the dirt from slipping and constructed complex irrigation systems to water their crops. The Inca farmers used the llama [lä′mə], a member of the camel family, as a beast of burden. Their chief food crops were corn, white and sweet potatoes, and peanuts. For meat, they raised guinea pigs and ducks. In addition, fishing was important along the coast.

Some Incas were artists who wove fine cloth or made excellent pottery. Incas also worked as miners, digging for gold, silver, and copper. They smelted the ore and designed jewelry for priests and noble families and decorations for temples. The Incas had specially trained surgeons who knew how to set broken bones, perform amputations, and even do brain surgery. For an anesthetic, or pain killer, the surgeons probably gave their patients coca [kō′kə], a plant from which cocaine is made.

The Incas had no formal schools, but they did train young men of the noble class in warfare and religion. Some were taught the skill of building in the tradition of the people of Tiahuanaco. Some of their temples still stand, despite centuries of devastating earthquakes.

A small number of young women were selected to be Acllacuna [äk′lä kü′nä], or "Chosen Women." They were particularly well trained in religion, weaving, and cooking. Some of the women became wives of nobles, and others served in the temples.

Like the Aztecs and various other peoples of the Americas, the Incas practiced human sacrifice. However, they limited it to special occasions—for example, when a new emperor was installed or in times of serious crisis such as plague or military defeat.

Section 4 Review

Identify Aztecs, Incas, Cuzco

Main Ideas

1. Where was the capital of the Aztec Empire? When did the empire reach its height of power?
2. For what sorts of careers were Aztec young people prepared?
3. What was the connection between religion and war in Aztec life?
4. How did the Incas hold their empire together?
5. How were people's lives controlled by the Inca government?

Critical Thinking

Analyzing Comparisons: The Aztec and Inca empires were similar in some ways and different in others. Name three of the differences.

A MYSTERY IN HISTORY

In 1983 Phyllis Pitluga spent the Thanksgiving weekend in Peru. She was an astronomer from the Adler Planetarium in Chicago who had been asked to help with research on the lines. Five years later she commented on the Thanksgiving trip that changed her life:

"I spent the next three weeks measuring the direction of the lines of that figure (of the spider) and determining which stars would have set visually beyond the ends of those lines 2000 years ago. I came up with such a stunning, persuasive result that it held my fascination. I've been going back ever since."

This newspaper feature was called "Decisive Moment" and carried a quotation as a heading: "I was so intrigued by Nasca, I had to learn more." Warn students that their encounter with world history might change their lives as well, but probably not in such a dramatic "decisive moment"!

Mystery in History

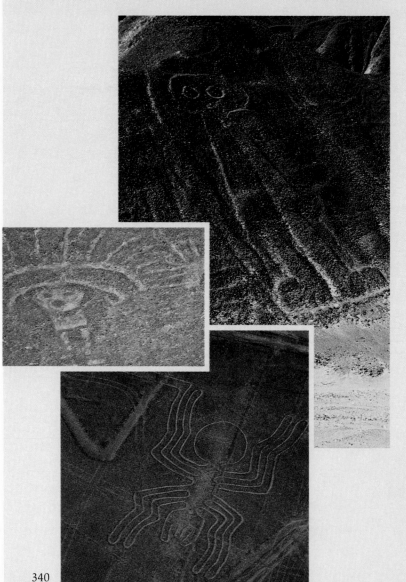

WHAT DO THE NAZCA LINES MEAN?

An amateur pilot was flying over an arid plateau in southwestern Peru in the late 1920s when he made a startling discovery. There below, on the flat surface of the desert, he saw a giant field of bold lines radiating out in every direction for a distance of 30 miles. Some of the lines took the shape of giant spiders, monkeys, fish, birds, plants, and strange-looking human forms. Other lines were straight, varying in width from two to several hundred feet. Scholars named these strange markings the Nazca [näs′kə] lines after the site of an early South American culture in that region.

For what purposes were the Nazca lines created? Scientists and historians hold differing views but generally agree that the lines are between 1,000 to 1,700 years old.

The lines were relatively easy to construct, but the precise location of the lines indicates that the people who made them had considerable technical skill. The white, sandy soil of the desert is covered with a thin layer of dark rocks, each about the size of a potato. To create a line, people picked up the rocks and piled them along the edge so as to outline a strip of white sand, usually about three to six feet wide. Because this region is arid and flat, erosion has hardly disturbed these ancient patterns.

In the 1940s Paul Kosok, a historian, became convinced that the Nazca lines were used as an observatory for sighting heavenly bodies at different times of year and thus creating a sort of calendar. Other scholars believe that the lines may have pointed to sacred mountains or to water sources, or that they may have been used as roads for religious pilgrimages or ceremonies.

Scholars will continue to search for answers. Someday their search may yield new keys to understanding a complex and many-sided early civilization.

From the air the Nazca lines seem like the doodling of a prehistoric giant. The designs include crude figures, some with headdresses, and an enormous spider.

340

5 North America supported a variety of cultures.

As you learned in Chapter 9, the peoples of North America were a diverse mix of cultures and lifestyles. By the 15th century, Indian groups dominated the coasts, woodlands, and plains.

Indians adapted their lives to their resources.

In a heavily forested area that reached from southern Alaska to the present state of Washington lived the North Pacific Coast Indians. They hunted and fished for food, gathering wild berries from the forest as well. These Indians lived in villages and used the plentiful resources of their forested territory to build wooden houses.

The people of the North Pacific groups were divided into nobles, common people, and slaves, whom they captured from other groups. One important custom of the nobles, the people of the highest status, was a ceremony called "**potlatch**." On special occasions, particularly those marking events in their children's lives—such as the day a daughter gathered her first berries—noble families would hold a potlatch. This ceremony would include an elaborate feast put on by the family. At the feast, the family would give away its most prized and beautiful possessions because these Indians considered giving to be a greater virtue than receiving.

In the eastern part of the continent, in the northeast woodlands, the Indians were not only hunters but also farmers. These Woodland Indians lived in villages and built long, dome-shaped houses called wigwams, which were made out of poles covered with bark and skins. Around the year 1400, five Iroquois groups joined together to form a confederation called the **Five Nations**. Through this political organization, the five groups acted together on matters of common interest. Rivalry among the groups was strong and frequently erupted in war, but the union remained quite powerful into the 1700s. Some historians believe that this league may have influenced the political design of the confederation of states that later became the United States of America.

BACKGROUND The introduction of the horse—a form of more advanced technology—led to the reversal of the common pattern of hunters becoming farmers.

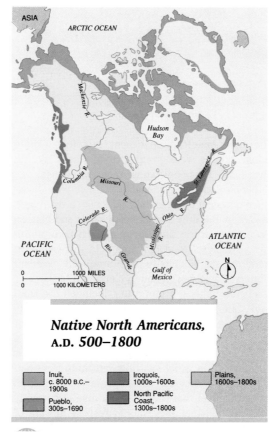

Native North Americans, A.D. 500–1800

Legend:
- Inuit, c. 8000 B.C.–1900s
- Pueblo, 300s–1690
- Iroquois, 1000s–1600s
- North Pacific Coast, 1300s–1800s
- Plains, 1600s–1800s

MAP STUDY Which two groups shown on the map above lived in what is now the central United States? In what is now Oregon and Washington State?

In the river valleys of central North America, most of the Indians were farmers until the 1600s. At this time, when the Spanish brought horses to America, some Indians, such as the Sioux and the Cheyenne, became buffalo hunters.

Pueblo Indians were peaceful farmers.

One of the oldest and most complex cultures north of the Rio Grande was that of the Pueblo, an Indian group that lived in what is now the southwestern United States. The Pueblo used adobe to build several-storied houses that have been called

ANSWER TO MAP STUDY Pueblo and Plains; Pacific Northwest Coast

341

5 Lesson Plan

Essential Learning Objectives

Students will learn to:
- identify Indian contributions to modern American culture.
- discuss the relationship between the environment and materials used by Indians for food, shelter, and clothing.

1 FOCUS AND MOTIVATE

Ask students what they know about Indians that lived in their state in the 15th century. Ask them to point out differences in the way Indians lived in other regions of North America. Now contrast those cultures with the Inca and Aztec empires.

2 TEACH

- Describe the culture of the Iroquois, the Pueblo, and two Pueblo subgroups—the Hopi and Zuni. Stress the relationship between climate and culture for each group.

- In discussing the Kwakiutl, the Iroquois, and the Pueblo give special attention to the relation between the environment and food and shelter.

GUIDED PRACTICE

Have the students write a paragraph describing the differences between Iroquois and Pueblo culture.

3 ASSESS AND CLOSE

ASSESS

1. What is a "potlatch"? (Indian celebration in which a family gives away its most prized possessions.)
2. What materials did the Pueblo use for building? (adobe)

The Hopewell culture, which flourished in Ohio from 100 B.C. to A.D. 600., produced this copper falcon.

the first American apartment buildings. These adobe houses were grouped into villages. Within the village, the people chose their own chiefs.

Pueblo Indians were master farmers who developed a system of irrigation canals. Their main crop was corn, but they also gathered seeds and berries. As a safeguard against drought, each family built up a supply of food that was held in reserve. In addition, the Pueblo Indians produced excellent pottery, finely woven cotton cloth, and baskets.

Pueblo Indians, a group that included the Hopi and Zuñi, were peaceful people. They rarely fought wars, and then only when necessary for survival. An example of their peaceful nature is a long cleansing ritual, intended to get rid of their "madness," in which warriors returning from battle had to participate. The religion of the Pueblo Indians taught that people should live in harmony with nature, that they should respect the life of others and the traditions of the past, and that they should do things in moderation.

Native Americans made many enduring contributions.

All Native American peoples, even those without writing, had literature. It was passed on by word of mouth from generation to generation. Most of the literature took the form of poetry and often expressed religious ideas or group traditions.

In arts and crafts, Indians produced beautiful baskets, weaving, embroidery, metalwork, painting, sculpture, and architecture. Indians also made fine pottery, especially in what is now the southwestern United States.

Indians also are credited with many inventions and discoveries still in use today. They invented the snowshoe, toboggan, and canoe. In medicine, they first used quinine, cocaine, and the bulb syringe. They first discovered the properties of rub-

ber, developed adobe for building, and invented the game of lacrosse. Indian ingenuity also provided such technical contributions as cochineal [koch'ə nēl'] dye, a red dye made from the dried bodies of an insect, and henequen [hen'ə kin], a fiber from the leaves of a desert plant used for making rope.

The most important contributions of the early peoples of the Americas, however, were in the field of agriculture. Although most of the early Europeans who conquered the Indians had eyes only for the gold and silver they could carry home, it was the humble farm products they took back that made the most lasting impression on world civilization. The Indians were the first to grow corn, potatoes, tomatoes, squash, pumpkins, avocados, and several kinds of beans. From them other peoples of the world also learned about pineapples, strawberries, vanilla, cinnamon, tapioca, and chocolate. Indians were also the first to make maple sugar and to develop chicle [chik'əl], the main ingredient in chewing gum.

All these products greatly increased the quantity and variety of the food supply in Europe and Africa. In Ireland and much of northern Europe, for example, the white potato became a major food crop. (See the "Mystery in History" in Chapter 22 for more details.) When Europeans began settling in the New World, it was these foods, as well as the farming techniques that the Indians taught them, that made it possible for the European colonists to survive and flourish.

Section 5 Review

Identify potlatch, Five Nations

Main Ideas

1. Give two examples of Indians adapting their lives to available resources.
2. What was distinctive about the Pueblo Indians?
3. Name two or more contributions Indians made to world civilization.

Critical Thinking

Predicting Effects: Consider the Pueblo's ritual for warriors returning from battle. What is the group saying in this ritual? How might this practice help soldiers returning from war in our culture today? How might it help our culture?

Benin Bronzes

Anybody who sees beauty and does not look at it will soon be poor.

These lines from a Yoruba (Nigeria) poem might well be applied to the bronze head of a queen mother in her curving, conical crown depicted below left. Notice the high collar, symbolic of her royal status. This sculpture was made in Benin, between 1550 and 1680. Elegant portraits such as this with their elaborate headdresses and highly polished surfaces were kept on royal altars as memorials.

The artists of Benin first began to cast bronze in the late 14th century. Benin artists made their bronze sculptures using the lost-wax process. First, the artist made a model in wax of the sculpture. Because the wax was soft, it could be sculpted with delicacy and precision. The wax model was then covered with clay and heated. As the wax melted, it ran out of small holes left in the mold and was thus "lost." Then, molten bronze was poured into the space left vacant by the wax inside the clay form. When the bronze cooled, the clay was washed away, revealing an exact bronze copy of the wax original.

All artwork was done by specialized guilds in Benin. Only royalty could possess the bronze sculptures. The portraits of those of lesser rank were carved from wood or sculpted in terracotta, a reddish earthenware.

In the 16th century, trade with the Portuguese made bronze more plentiful in Benin. According to a chronicle from 1668, numerous bronze plaques decorated the wooden pillars of the royal palace at that time. The plaques were carried off by the British when they occupied the capital city in 1897.

The magnificent bronze head (far left) and the cock (top left) date from the 16th century or later. The hunter bearing an antelope is of unknown date.

and Cheyenne hunted buffalo with horses introduced by the Spanish.
2. They lived in several-storied adobe houses grouped in villages, were master farmers, and fought wars only rarely.
3. arts and crafts, important food products

Critical Thinking
The implication is that war taints those who fight so that they need to be cleansed to be peaceful. Such a practice might help present-day soldiers re-enter civilian life, perhaps creating a less stressful culture.

HIGHLIGHTS OF CIVILIZATION
Students will enjoy *Black Images: The Art of West Africa,* by Penelope Naylor with photographs by Lisa Little (New York: Doubleday, 1973), from which the introductory verse is taken (page 95).

Explain that early people often found gold, silver, and copper in their pure state and molded them into ornaments. Bronze, which is usually made from copper and tin, is extremely durable, melts easily, and, probably for these reasons, is the oldest alloy known.

Have students turn ahead in their text to the "Geography: A Key to History" feature in Chapter 37. Ask students: In what part of Africa could the people of Benin have found copper? (south-central Africa) Where could they have found tin? (West Africa, inland from the mouth of the Niger River) How might the presence of mineral resources have influenced early Africans' skills in metalworking? (An abundance of minerals undoubtedly contributed to the development of such skills. In addition to their bronzes, early African cultures are noted for their craftsmanship in gold and iron.)

Key Terms, People, and Places
The key terms, people, and places tested here were introduced in the chapter sections and reviewed in the Section Reviews. For definitions see the page references at the appropriate Section Reviews. Also see the Glossary and Biographical Dictionary.

Main Ideas
The main ideas tested here were introduced in the sections of this chapter and reviewed in the Section Reviews. For answers to these questions, see the appropriate Section Reviews.

Critical Thinking
1. Possible answers: the attitude that non-Christians were sinners; general ignorance among Europeans; a feeling of revulsion about human sacrifice; greed for gold outweighed admiration
2. Possible answers: collect taxes, give better deals to countries that gave me good deals on their resources, give better deals to countries that had things that I really needed, only trade with countries that had good policies on human rights

CHAPTER 18 REVIEW

Section Summaries

Section 1
Famous empires grew in the West African savanna.
Towns grew up near the edge of the Sahara desert. The gold and salt in the area became the basis for active trade. Around A.D. 500 the kingdom of Ghana grew into a great empire and controlled the gold trade. When Ghana was weakened in the 1200s, the kingdoms of Mali and Songhai took over the area.

Section 2
City-states and kingdoms flourished in East Africa.
The East African coastal trading centers developed into large cities. Swahili culture developed from the blend of African, Indian, and Arab traders. Portuguese activity after 1498, however, weakened trade and culture.

Section 3
The forest states developed strong governments.
Powerful forest states such as Benin became increasingly rich. The Europeans, who were settling new lands in the Americas, needed slaves to work on their plantations and looked to West Africa to supply them. The African merchants profited, but the slaves faced a terrible fate.

Section 4
The Aztecs and Incas created strong empires.
The Aztecs built their empire in central Mexico, with a magnificent capital. The young people received strict, formal education. The Incas, centered in Peru, had a well-organized, highly regulated life, which held their vast empire together.

Section 5
North America supported a variety of cultures.
Native Americans developed distinctive lifestyles and customs that were well adapted to their environments. The Pueblo Indians of the southwestern United States had one of the oldest and most complex cultures.

Test Yourself

Key Terms and People
Identify the significance of each of the following:

Section 1
a. silent trade
b. Ghana (ancient)
c. Kumbi-Saleh
d. Mali
e. Sundiata
f. Songhai

Review Dates

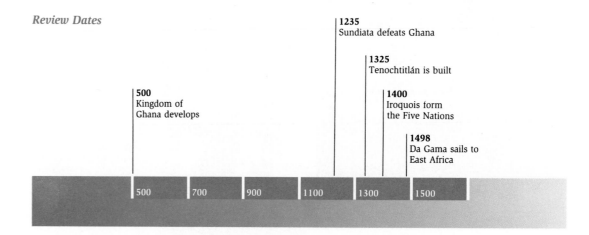

500
Kingdom of
Ghana develops

1235
Sundiata defeats Ghana

1325
Tenochtitlán is built

1400
Iroquois form
the Five Nations

1498
Da Gama sails to
East Africa

500   700   900   1100   1300   1500

Section 2
a. Kilwa   **c.** Swahili
b. Zimbabwe   **d.** Shona

Section 3
a. Benin   **b.** Obas   **c.** Middle Passage

Section 4
a. Aztecs   **c.** Cuzco
b. Incas

Section 5
a. potlatch   **b.** Five Nations

Main Ideas

Section 1
1. What were two major West African resources?
2. How was the gold trade controlled by Ghana?
3. Name two major West African empires. How did their kings make them powerful?

Section 2
1. How did trade affect East African ports?
2. What three cultures merged into Swahili culture?
3. How did Zimbabwe grow into a powerful kingdom?

Section 3
1. How did the Obas strengthen Benin?
2. Why did the Europeans go to West Africa?
3. What effect did the slave trade have on the forest states? What was the effect in the country?

Section 4
1. Where was the center of the Aztec Empire?
2. What careers were available to Aztec youths?
3. How were war and religion connected for Aztecs?
4. How was the Inca Empire held together?
5. How did the Inca Empire control its subjects?

Section 5
1. How did Indians use their natural resources?
2. Discuss the lives of the Pueblos.
3. What were some Indian cultural contributions?

Critical Thinking

1. Making Hypotheses Why do you think Europeans were unable to appreciate the high level of culture they found in the Americas?
2. Making Decisions If you controlled an important resource that many other countries needed, what rules would you make for trade?

Chapter Skills and Activities

Practicing Study and Research Skills
Comparing Sources of Information
Few written records exist from early African and American cultures. Still, sources for learning about them exist, such as this Cahokia mother and child from a prehistoric site in southern Illinois. List five. Is any one source better than the others? Why?

Linking Past and Present
The Africans carefully regulated trade with the Europeans. Name two ways that the United States regulates trade today.

Learning History Through Maps
Using the map on page 326, find:
1. the cities controlled by both Mali and Songhai
2. two bodies of water mentioned in this chapter

CRITICAL THINKING QUESTION LEVEL 1. average; 2. challenging

Answers to Test Yourself

Key Terms and People
1. b
2. c
3. d
4. e
5. a

Key Dates
E, F, A, D, C, B, G

Key Places
D—Hangzhou; E—Sea of Japan; C—Kilwa; B—Kumbi-Saleh; A—Cuzco

Main Ideas
1. b
2. a
3. c
4. d
5. d

Critical Thinking
1. People develop similar answers to similar situations. Some groups may have the same origins.
2. Students should note the spread of Americn clothing styles, especially blue jeans and the business suit, fast-food restaurants, music, movies, and other business activities around the globe. They may predict that there will be an increasingly global society in years to come, perhaps with the United States taking the lead. The students may think this is a positive trend or a negative one, meaning the loss or weakening of the many unique cultures around the world. Signs of other cultures in the United States include international in-fluences in such areas as food, mu-sic, clothing, and architecture.

UNIT FOUR

REVIEW

Summarizing the Unit

Chapter 16
China's Predominance in Asia
In 960 the Song dynasty came to power in China. Under the Songs many advances in technology, scholarship, and art took place. In 1279 Kublai Khan conquered the Songs and ruled as Mongol emperor of China. Throughout its history China has been the single greatest influence on many of its neighboring cultures, including Japan, Korea, and Vietnam. For thousands of years, Chinese literature, philosophy, religion, and art affected the thinking of peoples throughout East Asia. In addition, Chinese goods were traded widely across the entire Asian continent.

Chapter 17
The Emergence of Japan
Japan has been greatly influenced by its geography and climate. The country's separation from the Asian mainland gave it protection from invasion but still allowed selective borrowing to take place. Early in its history, Japan borrowed heavily from China, but eventually the Japanese civilization developed its own style. After 1192 Japan had a feudal government.

Chapter 18
Empires in Africa and the Americas
Regional cultures and civilizations developed from 500 to 1590 in Africa and the Americas. In West Africa the kingdoms of Ghana and Mali grew around the gold trade. In East Africa trading centers developed along the coast. In the Americas the Aztecs and Incas built strong empires, and other peoples developed a variety of cultures.

Using Writing Skills

When working on the second or actual writing stage of the complete process of writing, your main goal is to get your ideas down on paper. These ideas should have been generated and organized during the prewriting stage, so that you are ready when you sit down to begin writing.

When writing, stick to a determined plan. If you are writing an essay, the first paragraph should introduce your main idea. Then, each paragraph should begin with its own topic statement, that sentence that puts into writing the most important and central idea of the paragraph. The rest of the paragraph then must support that topic statement, offering arguments, details, or examples. When you're writing your first draft of a paper, that is, your first attempt, remember that the most important thing is to get your ideas on paper. Don't be concerned about spelling or grammatical errors.

Activity. Imagine that you were a traveler like Marco Polo. Select one of the civilizations that you have studied in this unit, and write a description of your impressions. Consider that the readers of your essay will not have heard much about this culture and possibly may not understand some of the customs or beliefs.

Test Yourself

Key Terms and People
Match each term or person with the correct definition.
1. language that is a blend of African, Arabic, and Indian
2. political leadership that unified the Korean peninsula
3. faith that held that nature had to be understood and revered
4. Iroquois political organization
5. Chinese political leadership of the 1100s
a. Song dynasty
b. Swahili
c. Silla dynasty
d. Shinto
e. Five Nations

Key Dates

Match the letters on the time line with the events for which they stand:

A B C D E F G

____ Marco Polo visits the Mongol court.
____ Tenochtitlán is built.
____ The kingdom of Ghana develops.
____ Japan's feudal age begins.
____ The Song dynasty begins.
____ Buddhism is introduced to Japan.
____ The Iroquois form the Five Nations.

Key Places

Match the letters on the map with the places described below:

____ trading center for the rice belt
____ both a barrier and a lane for travel
____ rich city near the gold mines of Zimbabwe
____ capital of ancient Ghana
____ capital of the Inca Empire

Main Ideas

1. During the Mongol control of China, ____
a. the Chinese became more isolated from foreigners.
b. trade and travel across Eurasia became safer.
c. there was continuous famine.
d. there was a climate of religious intolerance.
2. Korea's Yi dynasty was important because ____
a. King Sejong made many social reforms.
b. Buddhism became increasingly important.
c. Korea took its name from this dynasty's leaders.
d. Korea's first Golden Age took place.
3. Japan borrowed much of its culture from ____
a. Burma.
b. Vietnam.
c. China.
d. Mongolia.
4. The empires of West Africa ____
a. were famous for their silk-making.
b. were isolated from each other.
c. fought hard against the export of slaves.
d. traded between themselves and with foreigners.
5. The Incas differed from the Aztecs because ____
a. the Incas did not practice sacrifice on a large scale.
b. the Incas did not build large cities.
c. the Incas did not support education.
d. the Incas absorbed the peoples they conquered.

Critical Thinking

1. **Making Hypotheses** Why do you think that different groups of people in various parts of the world, isolated from one another, often invent similar tools and develop similar ideas? What accounts for the development?

2. **Predicting Effects** Just as China has influenced the cultures of its East Asian neighbors for centuries, the United States is now influencing cultures around the world with its economic policies and social customs. Give examples of how American culture is evident in other countries around the world today. What do you think the effects of this enormous spread of American culture will be? Do you see the influences of other cultures in that of the United States? Give examples.

CRITICAL THINKING QUESTION LEVEL 1. easy;
2. challenging

PART THREE

Civilizations Interacting

| **1492** | **1552** |
| Columbus reaches the Americas | Ivan the Terrible begins Russian expansion to the east |

| 1500 | 1550 | 16 |

Magellan's route around world, 1519–1522

1500–Present

In Part Two you read how Christianity and Islam helped shape regional civilizations in Europe and the Middle East, how Chinese culture influenced East and Southeast Asia, and how the expansion of commerce created links between all these civilizations, as well as with those that developed in Africa and the Americas.

Part Three covers the last 500 years of world history, a time of increasing communication between civilizations. First ships, then railroads and airplanes tied the globe together in a vast network for transporting goods and people, transmitting ideas and technology, and extending military power and political control. The growing interaction between civilizations is one of the main themes of the last five centuries.

As the period opened, the major civilizations of the world were more or less in balance. Three centuries later, Europe had grown so powerful that it dominated the globe. Western dominance brought about a global economy and an interdependent world, which is another key theme of this period. As you read through Part Three, consider how the West gained its position of world dominance and how that contributed to an interdependent world.

ARCTIC OCEAN

NORTH AMERICA

PACIFIC OCEAN

SOUTH AMERIC

Global Interdependence Today

—— Major air routes

▬▬ Major shipping lanes

△ Major transportation centers

348

1687	1776	1837	1914	1969
Isaac Newton publishes the law of universal gravitation	United States declares independence	Victoria begins her 63-year reign as Britain's queen	World War I begins	United States sends astronauts to moon

1650	1700	1750	1800	1850	1900	1950	2000

Silver inkstand, used to sign Declaration of Independence

Queen Victoria, as a young ruler

First landing on the moon, 1969

The Early Modern Era: Europe's Transformation and Expansion

OVERVIEW

This unit describes Europe from the Renaissance and the Reformation through the building of overseas empires and the Scientific Revolution.

ADDITIONAL TEACHING AIDS FOR UNIT FIVE

Literature for the Teacher

The Age of the Renaissance, edited by Denys Hay. London: Thames & Hudson, 1986.

Calder, Angus. *Revolutionary Empire—The rise of the English-Speaking Empires.* New York: E. P. Dutton, 1981.

Derry, T. K. *History of Scandinavia.* University of Minnesota Press, 1979.

Erlanger, Rachel. *The Unarmed Prophet: Savonarola in Florence.* New York: McGraw-Hill, 1988.

Goetzmann, William. *New Lands, New Man.* Viking Press, 1986.

Rosenblum, Mort. *Mission to Civilize: The French Way.* Harcourt Brace Jovanovich, 1986.

Literature for the Student

Caselli, Giovanni. *History of Everyday Things: The Renaissance and the New World.* New York: Peter Bedrick, 1986. (easy)

Morison, Samuel. *The Great Explorers.* Oxford University Press, 1978. (challenging)

O'Brien, Maire and Conor Cruise. *History of Ireland.* New York: Beckman House, 1972 (easy)

Udall, Stewart. *To the Inland Empire: Coronado and Spanish Legacy.* Doubleday, 1987. (average)

Audio-Visual Materials*

Dissolution of the Monasteries. Video, 27 minutes, color, [EB], 1986. Looks at the campaign to destroy the monastic system in England

Elizabeth: The Queen Who Shaped an Age. Video or film, 27 minutes, color, [Learning Corporation of America], 1970. A dramatization of the reign of Elizabeth I of England and a study of political power used for noble ends

European Expansion: Its Influence on Man. Film, 19 minutes, color, [McGraw-Hill], 1970. Suggests answers to the question: Why did expansion originate in Europe and not elsewhere?

* For a complete listing of sources of audio-visual materials see page T30.

The Reformation (revised). Video or film, 14 minutes, color, [Cornerstone], 1979. Summarizes the significant causes, events, personalities, and consequences of the Reformation

The Reformation: Age of Revolt. Video or film, 24 minutes, color, [EB], 1973. Shows how Martin Luther's grievances against the Church in the 16th century produced a chain of events that left an impact on the modern world, particularly in the areas of religion and politics

The Renaissance (revised). Film, 13 minutes, color, [Cornerstone], 1978. Describes the outstanding characteristics of the Renaissance period: art, science, technology, exploration, and the new sense of the importance and potential of human beings

Spirit of the Renaissance. Video or film, 31 minutes, color, [EB], 1970. Illustrates the intellectual and artistic climate of Florence during the 14th and 15th centuries by observing the daily life of a contemporary Florentine

Towards a Modern Europe. Film, 30 minutes, color, [International Film Foundation], 1974. Maps, artwork, and photography used to outline the movements and conditions that prepared Europe for modernity

The Triumph of the West: New Worlds. Video, 50 minutes, color, [Films, Inc.]. Explores how Europe shaped the Americas and European impact on the indigenous and black-slave populations

OPTIONAL WRITING ASSIGNMENTS

1. As a news correspondent for the British Broadcasting System in 1436, you have been assigned to Florence, Italy. Write a script for a radio broadcast describing life in Florence. Be sure also to describe the dedication of Santo Mario del Fiore.

2. You write book reviews for a Florence, Italy, newspaper. Write a review of a recently published book, *The Prince,* by Niccolo Machiavelli.

3. You are a Catholic priest in Wittenberg, Germany, who observes Martin Luther's posting of his document on the door of the Castle Church. Write a letter to a friend describing your reactions to what you have seen and to his document.

4. You are an adviser to Peter the Great. Write a letter offering him ideas which you feel would make Russia an even greater country. Be sure to make specific policy recommendations and to support your recommendations.

5. You are a reporter for a newspaper in the Bahamas, and you observe the landing of Christopher Columbus on one of the islands. Write an article describing the landing and the reactions of the Spaniards and the Bahamians.

UNIT TESTS
IN THE TEACHER'S RESOURCE FILE

Unit Test, pp. 117–118

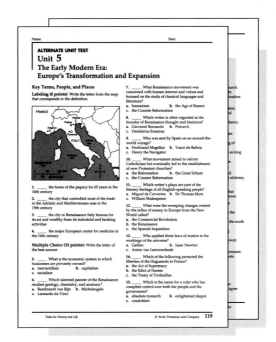

Alternate Unit Test, pp. 119–120

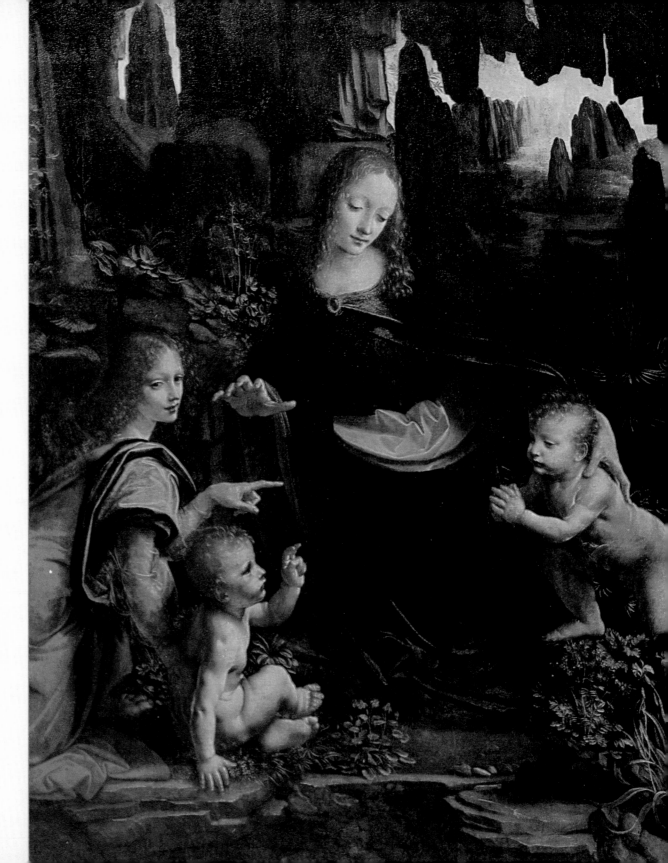

FINE ART IN UNIT FIVE

Fine art forms an integral part of the historical record of events portrayed in this textbook. A listing of the paintings, drawings, sculpture, historic photographs, architecture, and other works of fine art selected to illustrate this unit follows. Students may be asked to research the artists and their works and report their findings to the entire class. Students also may be asked to write one or more paragraphs describing what they see upon a detailed study of a work of art and what the artist was attempting to communicate.

The Early Modern Era: Europe's Transformation and Expansion

Themes and Patterns We like to think of ourselves as living in modern times. What does the term "modern times" mean and when did they begin? Historians say that modern times began about 500 years ago when the era of regional civilizations gave way to increasing communication among all the world's peoples. Eventually, intercommunication led to the emergence of an interdependent world, the kind we all live in today.

How did this movement toward intercommunication get started? In Units 5 and 6, we will answer this question by looking at what was happening in the major regional civilizations between 1500 and 1800. Historians usually call this period the early modern era, a time when a small number of civilizations controlled most of Eurasia. These civilizations included Western Europe, China, Japan, India, Russia, and the Ottoman Empire.

Between them, these six centers ruled 75 to 80 percent of the world's population. In 1500 this population was probably about 430 million. By 1800 it had almost doubled to 900 million. For most of the early modern era, despite wide differences in culture, the six major centers of civilization and population were roughly at the same level of economic development, political organization, and military development. During this period, however, Europe experienced a particularly remarkable internal transformation and expansion.

The Italian Leonardo da Vinci personified the quest for knowledge that distinguished Europe in the early modern era. His *Virgin of the Rocks* hangs today in Paris.

Chapters in This Unit

p. 365, Rembrandt van Rijn, *Titus at his Desk,* c. 1655, Museum Boymans-van Beuningen, Rotterdam

p. 371, Holbein, Hans the Younger, *The Ambassadors* (detail), 1533, The National Gallery, London

p. 372, Portuguese carracks painting, The National Maritime Museum, London

p. 372, Astrolabe, 16th century, The Adler Planetarium, Chicago

p. 383, Maria Sibylla Merian, botanical plates, Surinam 1719, The National Museum of Women in the Arts

p. 387, Queen Elizabeth I, *Armada Portrait,* (artist unknown) c. 1588, Private collection

p. 390, Cranach, Lucas, *John Frederick the Magnanimous,* 1530, Toledo Museum of Art, Toledo, Ohio

p. 392, Holbein, Hans the Younger, *Henry VIII,* c. 1537, National Gallery, Rome

p. 397, *Defeat of the Spanish Armada,* National Maritime Museum, Greenwich, England

p. 399, Michelin, Jean, *The Baker's Cart,* 1656, Metropolitan Museum of Art

p. 402, Tsar's jeweled crown, Russia c. 1628, Tretyakov Gallery, Moscow

p. 404, Borovikovsky, Vladimir, *Catherine the Great at Tsarskoe Selo,* 1794, Tretyakov Gallery, Moscow

p. 405, De Carmontell, *Mozart at the Piano,* The National Gallery, London

p. 409, Hannah, Robert, *William Harvey Demonstrating Experiments to King Charles I,* Royal College of Physicians, London

p. 414, Van Gogh, Vincent, *The Potato Eaters,* 1885

p. 415, West, Benjamin, *Benjamin Franklin Drawing Electricity from the Sky,* c. 1805, The Philadelphia Museum of Art

19 The European Renaissance

OVERVIEW

This chapter covers the origins and flowering of the Renaissance in northern Italy and northern Europe.

PLANNING CHART

Section	Text Pages	Key Concept	Suggested Teaching Time
1 The Renaissance began in Italy.	353–357	Important ideas and practices, including international trade, capitalism, individualism, republican government, and despotism, had their roots in the northern Italian Renaissance.	Two days
2 Humanism flourished in the Renaissance.	357–360	Humanism in northern Italy was grounded in the belief that life in *this* world is important and that the works of artists and writers can elevate the human experience.	One day **Less time?** Assign Sections 2 and 3 to be read together and concentrate on the Guided Practice exercise in Section 2 and the Teach exercises in Section 3. **More time?** Use *Source Reading 19A.*
3 Italians created art masterpieces.	360–363	Renaissance artists, such as Giotto, Michelangelo, and Donatello, developed new techniques to produce some of the finest art the world has ever known.	One day **More time?** Use *Overhead Transparency 37* and *Source Reading 19B.*
4 The Renaissance spread to other countries.	363–366	Boosted by the introduction of the printing press and influenced by the work of northern Italians, the Renaissance spread to flourish in northern Europe.	One day **More time?** Use *Overhead Transparency 38.*

ANCILLARIES

Materials that may be used with this chapter to reinforce, reteach, enrich, and assess learning are pictured on the following pages.

Teacher's Resource File

ACTIVITIES

Section 1 Activity, p. 110

Section 2 Activity, p. 111

Section 3 Activity, p. 112

Section 4 Activity, p. 113

Chapter 19 Reteaching, p. 114

Chapter 19 Enrichment, p. 115

Teacher's Resource File

GEOGRAPHY SKILLS

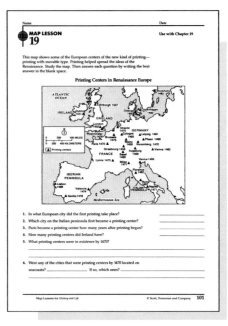

Chapter 19 Geography
Worksheet/Map, pp. 39–40

Chapter 19 Map Lesson, p. 101

TESTS

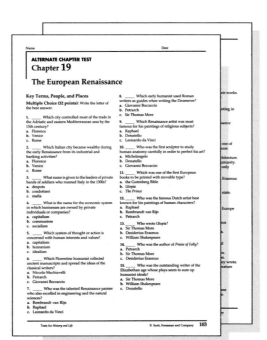

Chapter Test, pp. 101–102

Alternate Chapter Test, pp. 103–104

Other Optional Ancillaries

WORKBOOK

Section 1 Worksheet, p. 74

Section 2 Worksheet, p. 75

Section 3 Worksheet, p. 76

Section 4 Worksheet, p. 77

SOURCE READINGS

Source Reading 19A
Source Reading 19B

TEST GENERATOR

40 multiple-choice questions for Chapter 19

OVERHEAD TRANSPARENCIES

Overhead Transparency 37
Overhead Transparency 38

Chapter

19

The European Renaissance

1300–1600

CHAPTER INTRODUCTION

Use the map of Renaissance Europe on page 354 to locate Florence, in northern Italy. Geographically, why were Florence and other northern Italian cities in a better position than, say, Paris, London, or Prague, to be leaders of a rebirth in Europe?

LOCATOR GLOBE

Call students' attention to the globe, which indicates the general area of the world discussed in this chapter. (A detailed map appears on page 354.)

TIME LINE

Have students examine the time line. What generalizations can they make about the Renaissance, based on the events shown there? (Sixteenth century art and literature were important components of the Renaissance.)

1400	
c. 1505	Leonardo da Vinci paints the *Mona Lisa*
1508	Michelangelo begins painting the Sistine Chapel
1532	Machiavelli's *The Prince* is published
1600	c. means *circa*, or approximate date
1700	

On March 25, 1436, the people of Florence held a joyous festival. They were dedicating a cathedral, begun in the late 1200s and just finished. Church officials, state leaders, artists, writers, musicians, and other well-known people of the time were there. They had journeyed to the proud city to see the cathedral christened Santa Maria del Fiore—Saint Mary of the Flower.

A long parade moved through the banner-lined streets. A person who was there wrote that a great band of musicians led the parade. "[Each carried] his instrument in hand and [was dressed] in gorgeous cloth of gold garments." Following them were choirs. They "sang at times with such mighty harmonies that the songs seemed to the listeners to be coming from the angels themselves." Then came the pope, wearing white robes and a crown. Seven cardinals in bright red and 37 bishops and archbishops in purple came next, followed by city officials and heads of guilds.

The citizens of Florence, rich and poor alike, filled the streets and crowded into the cathedral. Their eyes and thoughts were on its grand dome that crowned the cathedral, the new symbol of the city's prestige. Florentines felt pride in their glorious city.

In many ways Florence was indeed splendid, but so were other cities in Italy. Based on trade and industry, the number and size of cities had grown rapidly in northern Italy. Florence and other rich urban centers dominated northern Italy in the 1400s. The wealth of these cities supported much creative activity. From it came some of the finest art, architecture, and literature the world has known. Many people began to think more critically about the world they lived in. Indeed, a whole new culture was born in the Italian cities of the 14th and 15th centuries.

This new cultural style was known as the Renaissance [ren'ə-säns'], a French word that means "rebirth." The word also names the time during which these changes took place. Ideas that grew

BACKGROUND Unlike many terms now used to describe historical periods, the term "Renaissance" was actually used by the people of that era. The people of those years sensed that there was something different or unusual about their own time.

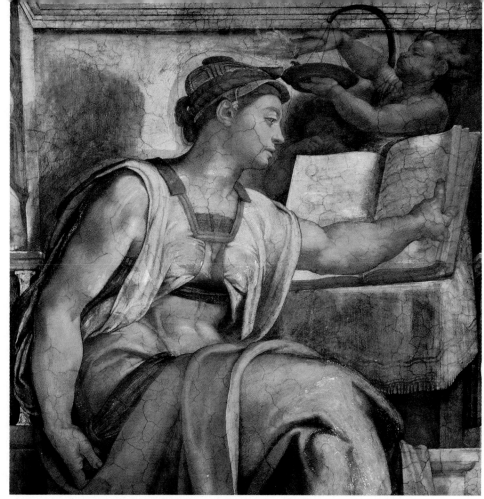

Michelangelo (1475–1564), one of the finest Renaissance artists, labored for years painting the ceiling of the Vatican's Sistine Chapel, a section of which is shown.

up in Renaissance Italy spread to most other European countries and, in this way, the western world began moving from medieval to modern times.

Reading Preview

In this chapter you will learn how the Renaissance transformed European culture.

1. The Renaissance began in Italy.

2. Humanism flourished in the Renaissance.

3. Italians created art masterpieces.

4. The Renaissance spread to other countries.

 The Renaissance began in Italy.

The Renaissance was mostly a secular movement, that is, its major interests lay outside the sphere of religion. People in this era were interested in the literature, art, and ideas of classical—Roman and Greek—culture, which emphasized the importance of individual human beings and life on earth. These ideas appealed to the city dwellers who first cultivated Renaissance culture.

People came to believe that individual human beings could perfect themselves through study and, thereby, could form perfect societies if they

1 Lesson Plan

Essential Learning Objective

Students will learn to define and explain the historical connections which link these key ideas: Renaissance, capitalism, individualism, republic, despotism, Machiavellian.

1 FOCUS AND MOTIVATE

Have students read the chapter opener. Write the Latin word *nasci* on the board and ask students what it means. (to be born) Then write the Latin prefix *re-* in front of *nasci* and ask for its meaning. (again) Ask students what people or things today might experience some kind of rebirth, or renaissance (Examples: a political party, a type of art). Finally, ask students to speculate on what might cause an area such as northern Italy in the 1400s to be reborn. When was Italy first born?

2 TEACH

Write the six key ideas listed in the Learning Objective on the chalkboard. Explain to students that this is a concept-rich section in which each idea could be a lesson or a course unto itself. Their purpose is to develop a basic understanding of the terms. Discuss the six ideas, listing key attributes under each term.

353

Divide the class into small groups. Direct each group to discuss and prepare to explain to the class how any two of the six terms listed on the chalkboard are related to each other. (Example: Capitalism encourages individualism by allowing private ownership of businesses.)

wished. In an age of troubles, when Italy was torn by war and plagues such as the Black Death struck from time to time, this optimistic idea attracted many people, not the least of whom were the monarchs of countries and rulers of cities in Europe.

Growing trade brought new wealth to the Italian cities.

As you have learned, the Renaissance style was born in the cities of Italy during the middle of the 14th century. There are several reasons—some economic and some political—that this culture emerged at this particular time and in this particular place. One of the most important reasons was the growing trade conducted by Europeans and the wealth it brought to the cities. That wealth supported art and learning from east to west.

Italy was supremely situated to take advantage of the growing trade with the East. Most of the trade routes from the East met at the eastern end of the Mediterranean Sea. Italian merchants purchased goods sold there and brought the goods back to ports in northern Italy. From that point, the goods were carried overland across the Alps into northern Europe or by ship to western Europe. Some valuable commodities coming into Europe at that time were spices—pepper, ginger, cloves, and cinnamon—and jewels.

The political structure of northern Italy also contributed to the spread of the riches of the trade. The region was divided into a number of independent city-states, each with its own territory and sovereign government. Growing trade brought vast riches to these cities, the most important of which were Venice, Florence, Milan, and Genoa.

Of these four cities, **Venice**, the "Queen of the Adriatic," was the most powerful. Find Venice on the map at right. Well situated at the center of East-West trade routes, the city's power and wealth came from the sea. By the 15th century, Venetian merchants had built up a fleet of 3,000 ships, and the city controlled most of the trade in the Adriatic and eastern Mediterranean.

Florence, famous for its art, became wealthy from its industrial and banking activities. Find Florence on the map above. In 1500 it was the fifth largest city in Europe, with a population of some 130,000. Many of them—perhaps 30,000—worked

Renaissance Europe, About 1490

MAP STUDY The Renaissance began in Italy, mostly in the cities. Identify the Italian city-state that spanned the northeastern coast of the Adriatic Sea.

in Florence's fabric industry, whose products were traded all over Europe.

Capitalism emerged as an important economic system.

The new wealth that was accumulating in the Italian cities was the key to the development of Renaissance culture. Money came into these cities as the result of new business methods, and it was here that modern capitalism was born. **Capitalism** is an economic system in which private individuals

ANSWER TO MAP STUDY Venice

or companies, not the government, own businesses. The goal of capitalists is to make as much profit as possible and to reinvest money in business in order to make even more profits.

Banking was one new capitalist enterprise. As European merchants grew rich, they looked for ways to protect, invest, and borrow money. Many turned to the Italians, who had been among Europe's first bankers, and banking became a major Italian industry in the 1300s and 1400s. Bills of exchange—receipts for payment of goods in one city that were exchanged for similar goods in another city—came into widespread use. Florentine banking houses such as the Medici [med′ə chē′] loaned money to other merchants, nobles, and kings at high interest rates, thus accumulating large amounts of money, or capital.

The typical company of 1400 was a family affair. A small group of merchants and their relatives would create a company that invested capital in some enterprise. Their interest might be in trade, banking, or managing small factories that made the goods they traded. The powerful Medici family of Florence, for instance, ran silk and woolen cloth factories, managed papal moneys, and operated the largest banking system in Europe. They also ruled Florence during its golden age of Renaissance art. From these early beginnings, capitalism developed into Europe's main economic system.

New political ideas emerged from the Italian city-states.

As you learned earlier, Italy's political situation provided another base for the Renaissance. During the Middle Ages, German monarchs had wanted to rejoin Italy and Germany together as the Holy Roman Empire, as Charlemagne had done. The popes, however, fearing a loss of political power, strongly opposed the idea.

However, neither the emperors nor the popes had the strength to conquer the Italian city-states, so each tried to make allies among them. The city-states received special privileges, such as the right to elect their own officials, make their own laws, and raise their own taxes. As a result, a republican form of government arose in most cities.

Republican government meant that many citizens participated fully in the lives of the cities and,

Florence, a center for Renaissance culture, was alive with activity of all kinds, as depicted in these 15th-century woodcuts. Florentine bankers, top, were among the leaders of their industry. Other Florentine activities, shown above, included painting (top left), metalworking (center left), and sculpting (bottom left).

ASSESS

1. Erase the chalkboard and then ask students to name five key ideas that are associated with the Renaissance in northern Italy.
2. Why might a city-state getting rich from trade want a despot for a leader?

OPTIONAL RETEACHING

Ask for student volunteers to ask and answer questions using the key ideas they have just learned. (Example, Student #1: Could an American President be a despot? Student #2: Despotism isn't really possible under our present Constitution.)

as such, citizens were less willing to accept the authority of either the pope or emperor. In such an atmosphere, the old medieval idea that the individual human being was less important than society as a whole was turned upside down.

During the beginnings of the Renaissance, the individual became more important. Old restrictions against freedom of thought and deed broke down as people began to express their own ideas about life and art. They started to speak out against long-held customs and beliefs, and they found new glory in their own strengths. These new political ideas, arising in the cities of Italy, formed part of the groundwork of the Renaissance.

Despots came into power in the Italian city-states.

There was a negative side to the independent spirit of the city-states. Since no central government existed in Italy, each city maintained its own laws— or lack of laws. Within cities quarrels often broke out between groups of wealthy merchants, and noble families sometimes joined in the feuds. The

The power of Venice rested in the doge, the elected leader of the aristocratic merchants. Leonardo Loredano (c. 1500) was one of the wisest doges.

opening scene of William Shakespeare's play, *Romeo and Juliet,* written in the 1590s, showed how such a feud was carried out—in a street brawl. Indeed, the whole tragedy of that play, two young people unable to marry, comes about because of the conflict between their families.

Because most people wanted law and order, leaders called "despots" arose in the 1300s. Sometimes these daring men gained power by force and trickery, but others were invited by leading citizens to take control of a city. On the whole, most of the despots were interested in keeping their people satisfied. Therefore, they provided well-run governments, helped business, maintained defense, and added to the glory of their cities with splendid buildings and arts. Some despots, such as those of the Medici family of Florence, had been bankers and merchants. Others, such as the Sforzas of Milan, began as **condottieri** [kon′dôt-tye′rē], that is, leaders of private bands of soldiers.

Italian despots came to power because they were strong, clever, and able. Once in power, however, they needed to use their talents to stay there. A ruler had to keep constant watch for plots to overturn him because life in Renaissance Italy was dangerous. People were well trained in the use of daggers, poisoned drinks, and timely "accidents."

Machiavelli excused the use of force and trickery in politics.

No one is more closely identified with the treacherous politics of Renaissance Italy than the writer, diplomat, and scholar **Niccolo Machiavelli** [mak′-ē ə vel′ē]. *The Prince,* a small book published in 1532, five years after the author's death, seems to be a guide for the ways that a ruler should act.

In the Middle Ages, writings on government were rare. Mostly well meaning and dull, these works only described rulers as good, moral people. *The Prince,* however, was quite different from these medieval guides. Condemned by many as immoral and followed by political leaders ever since, it quickly became one of the best-known works ever written.

Machiavelli was born in Florence in 1469, to an impoverished noble family. A man with bright, shrewd eyes, Machiavelli served his city as a diplomat and government officer, where he met the

From the Archives

Love or Fear?

In the following excerpt from The Prince, *Machiavelli considers whether it is better for a ruler to be loved or feared.*

I don't doubt that every prince would like to be both; but since it is hard to accommodate these qualities, if you have to make a choice, to be feared is much safer than to be loved. For it is a good general rule about men, that they are ungrateful, fickle, liars, and deceivers, fearful of danger and greedy for gain. . . . [Love] is a link of obligation which men, because they are rotten, will break any time they think doing so serves their advantage; but fear involves dread of punishment, from which they can never escape.

most powerful leaders in Italy and observed how they retained their power.

The Prince, of which you can read an excerpt in the "From the Archives" box above, was essentially a set of rules by which a strong ruler could create and hold a state. *The Prince* described political affairs as they really were, controlled by ruthless men who sought power above all else. Machiavelli stated that to get power and stay in power, a ruler had to forget ideals and use every possible means to get and keep power. *The Prince* stressed that every political act had only one means of measure—success. Lying, cheating, and murder were acceptable if a ruler needed them to gain his ends.

Since it was published, *The Prince* has been closely studied and hotly debated. For some, Machiavelli was a clever judge of why people behaved as they did, seeing what others missed. To others, he was immoral, since he seemed to pay no attention to religion or ethical standards of human behavior. In actual fact, Machiavelli did not approve of this behavior, but insisted that this was the way successful rulers behaved. In Machiavelli's opinion

FROM THE ARCHIVES The excerpt is from *The Prince,* by Niccolo Machiavelli, translated and edited by Robert M. Adams (New York: W. W. Norton, 1977), pp. 47–48. Ask students whether or not they would vote for Machiavelli's Prince if he

the state must be stable at all costs, an idea that became a blueprint for many rulers who built strong, united nations. To this day the term "Machiavellian ruler" is common.

Section 1 Review

Identify Venice, Florence, capitalism, condottieri, Niccolo Machiavelli

Main Ideas
1. How did riches accumulated from a growing trade affect Italian cities?
2. What factors led to the development of capitalism in Italy?
3. In what ways did the Italian city-states gain from the political wranglings between the Holy Roman emperors and the popes?
4. What was the appeal of despots to the Italian people?
5. What is the basic advice to rulers in Machiavelli's *The Prince*?

Critical Thinking
Recognizing Values: What is your opinion of Machiavelli's advice to the rulers of Renaissance Europe? What do you think should be the standards of behavior for a government official? A business person? A member of the clergy? A high-school student?

2 *Humanism flourished in the Renaissance.*

One of the chief elements of the Italian Renaissance was a new movement called **humanism**. Humanism, which is a system of thought or action concerned with human interests and values, had a major effect on Italy.

Humanism focused attention on the individual.

Humanism meant several things in the age of the Renaissance and through the rest of European history. At first, humanism meant the study of ancient classical literature and languages. Partly because ancient Romans were ancestors of 14th-century Italians, humanists looked to ancient

were running for office today. (Opinion: Most people disapprove of strong, unprincipled leaders, but ruthless politicians sometimes win elections. You might point out that Machiavelli did not really want to see a ruler like the Prince assume power.)

rich and powerful centers of culture and population.
2. As they became rich from international trade, the merchants of Europe needed ways to protect, invest, and borrow money. Italian bankers provided their services, thus accumulating large amounts of money, or capital, from the profits they made.
3. The Italian city-states, which were sought out as allies by both the Holy Roman Emperors and the popes, benefited from the special privileges granted them by both sides. The people had more rights, and a republican form of government emerged.
4. The despots responded to the people's fear of anarchy and their desire for security and law and order.
5. Machiavelli advised rulers to forget their ideals and to do whatever it took, however immoral, to achieve success and power.

Critical Thinking
Students' responses should demonstrate an understanding of Machiavelli's idea that the security of the state was of utmost importance and should be maintained at all cost.

2 ## Lesson Plan

Essential Learning Objectives
Students will learn to:
- describe some of the beliefs and values of a Renaissance humanist.
- identify four Italian humanists—Petrarch, Boccaccio, Castiglione, and Da Vinci—and explain some contributions of each.

Divide the class into four groups—the Petrarchs, the Boccaccios, the Castigliones, and the Da Vincis. First, have each group reread the material pertaining to their humanist. Second, have each group make a list of the beliefs, achievements, or qualities that define that person as a humanist. (Example: Petrarch—loved the classics, acquired a library of classical works, believed in the importance of life in this world, wrote love sonnets, was interested in history, language, and ethics.) Have a spokesperson for each group give a report to the class.

GUIDED PRACTICE

Castiglione discusses the ideal traits of a "Renaissance man." Individually or in pairs, have students make a list of up to ten attributes of the ideal all-around person in today's world. Ask for volunteers to write their lists on the chalkboard. Discuss: How different are these traits from those of Castiglione's Renaissance man?

Greece and Rome as models for many aspects of life, including literature.

In particular, humanism reflected the philosophy that human beings were noble creatures, alone among all others endowed with dignity and the intelligence to understand the world about them. Humanists believed that men and women could change the world and make it a better place for all. This optimistic attitude contrasted with a 14th- and 15th-century world ridden with disease and war. Perhaps for that reason, humanist ideas spread throughout Europe during these centuries.

Petrarch and Boccaccio were early humanists.

If Renaissance thought and literature had a founder, that person was Francesco Petrarca, commonly known as **Petrarch** [pē'trärk] (1304–1374). A Florentine, Petrarch was one of the most important writers of his age. Born to a family in the legal profession, the young Francesco resented his father's desire to have him become a lawyer. For comfort, he began to read the Roman writers Cicero and Vergil. One story tells us that Petrarch's father became so frustrated with his son's stubbornness that he once threw the boy's books into the fire. The youth cried so much, though, that his father grabbed the books back.

As a devoted son, Petrarch chose to study law at a university. After his father's death in 1326, however, Petrarch devoted his life to studying classical writers and from this course came a new approach to life. From reading ancient literature, he found that the Romans had believed that this world on earth was indeed important for people.

Petrarch collected as many works of ancient literature as he could. His ideas about these classical works became popular and before long, scholars and princes alike scrambled to collect ancient manuscripts. They spent huge amounts of money and time trying to find old manuscripts. Monasteries were searched for prized pieces of parchment, and libraries everywhere were ransacked. In addition, humanists sent agents to Constantinople to buy whatever they could. Here Greek manuscripts became more plentiful after 1453, when the Turks conquered Constantinople. At that time, many Greek scholars were able to escape to Italy.

Petrarch and his beloved Laura, the subject of much of his poetry, illustrate a page from the first printed edition of his book *Canzoniere* (1470).

In his early years, Petrarch wrote poetry in his native Italian tongue. These sonnets, inspired by his love for a woman named Laura, made him one of the most famous lyric poets of all time. Of his love for her he wrote:

> If this should not be Love, O God, what
>   shakes me?
> If Love it is, what strange, what rich delight?

Although Petrarch believed deeply in the teaching of Christianity, he also thought that the Church was wrong to ignore the real world in which people lived. The educated person, said Petrarch, should do as the ancient Romans did and study humankind. They should thus study history, languages, literature, and ethics.

Giovanni Boccaccio [bō kä'chē ō], a friend of Petrarch, was another noted humanist who wrote both poetry and prose. Boccaccio used the Black Death as the setting for one of the most famous works of European literature, the *Decameron*. In it, seven young women and three young men escaped the plague by living in a lonely country house. To pass the time, they told the tales that make up the book. Many of the stories mirrored the spirit of the times by making fun of feudal customs and even the Church. Some of the stories, though, are deeply religious.

What makes the *Decameron* so important is that it is a collection of short stories. Based on Roman writers, these tales have clear beginnings, middle parts, and endings. Like much else in Renaissance culture, Boccaccio's work strongly influenced all European writing to this day.

Education created the "Renaissance man."

In medieval times, education had two chief uses—to train priests for preaching and scholars for debating. During the Renaissance, however, following Petrarch's lead, people decided that education had more uses. Its goal became that of making people well rounded, meaning that they were exposed to many aspects of learning and experience.

The ideal Renaissance man was an aristocrat or member of the moneyed class, well-mannered, and witty. He had learned enough to understand good literature, painting, and music. The so-called Renaissance man was well formed in body and good at sports. In the arts of war, he was a brave and able soldier. In *The Courtier*, Baldassare Castiglione [käs′tē lyô′ne] outlined this all-around man, and he also had similar ideals for women. He wrote the following words:

> If you examine ancient histories . . . you will find that worth has constantly prevailed among women as among men . . . and that there have always been women who have . . . governed kingdoms with the greatest prudence and justice, and done all that men have done.

To reach the goals of Renaissance education, Italian schools taught less theology and more literature. The humanists, who taught classical language and literature, gained such respect that people journeyed far to hear their lectures. Rich families and rulers took humanists into their homes to teach their sons and daughters.

Renaissance people used many talents.

Renaissance ideas about the individual gave people faith in their own powers. A new spirit of questioning, of searching for knowledge, spread through Europe. From searching for new continents to inquiring into the secrets of nature, people sought new knowledge. Many began to question Church authority.

Leonardo da Vinci, a Renaissance man, left a wide body of work that included the *Mona Lisa* (c. 1503) and these sketches of a helicopter and flower.

3 Lesson Plan

Essential Learning Objectives
Students will learn to:
- describe and identify important characteristics and techniques of Italian Renaissance painting.
- name important Italian Renaissance artists.

Of all the brilliant people of the time none could match **Leonardo da Vinci** [lē′ə när′dō də vin′chē] (1452–1519). Leonardo was one of world history's true geniuses, perhaps the best example of a many-sided person. Besides being one of the most talented painters of all time, he also studied geology, chemistry, and anatomy and designed items as diverse as buildings, canals, and weapons.

Leonardo da Vinci left more than 5,000 pages of notes and drawings in his notebooks. As the keenest observer of nature and humankind, he dissected human corpses to discover muscle structure and studied plants and other animals in minute detail. Leonardo sketched these things and many more—cannons, engines, flying machines, and hundreds of other devices. Some of his inventions were perfected only centuries later. His most lasting fame, however, came as the painter of such masterpieces as the *Mona Lisa*, *The Last Supper*, and two versions of *The Madonna of the Rocks*.

Some Renaissance people went too far in claiming that the individual was the center of the world. For example, Benvenuto Cellini [chə lē′nē], a brilliant sculptor and goldsmith, turned away from society, caring not at all for laws or morals. According to Cellini and others of his viewpoint, anything a person was able to get away with seemed to be all right.

Section 2 Review

Identify humanism, Petrarch, Giovanni Boccaccio, Leonardo da Vinci

Main Ideas
1. Why might humanism have gained popularity during the Italian Renaissance?
2. How were Petrarch and Boccaccio influenced by classical Romans and Greeks?
3. How did the goals of education change during the Renaissance?
4. How is Leonardo da Vinci an example of a Renaissance man?

Critical Thinking
Analyzing Comparisons: Compare the purposes of education during the Renaissance and the present. Should a person aim to be well-rounded today? Define your terms and give reasons to support your judgment.

 Italians created art masterpieces.

The most impressive achievements of the Renaissance were in the fine arts, that is, painting, sculpture, and architecture. Major changes in the arts took place for two main reasons. First, people became interested in the arts of the classical age. Second, the new wealthy merchants and princes of the Italian cities supported artists.

As bankers and merchants grew rich from trade, their new wealth allowed them to enjoy free time for study and appreciation of art. Spurred by humanist ideas, they served as patrons to artists and philosophers, supporting them with approval and money. Many patrons also invited artists and philosophers to live and work in their palaces. The rulers of Italian cities, together with merchants, led the way in supporting artists and writers. The reward was glory, not only for rulers' families but also for their cities.

Renaissance painters depicted real-life figures.

During the Renaissance, painting underwent a major change from the religion-dominated art of the Middle Ages. Renaissance artists wanted to show how people and nature really were in life, and they began to re-create the natural world in their works. By the 15th century, painters and sculptors learned to depict human figures that seemed real and studied anatomy to perfect the real-life qualities of their work.

Florence led the way to changes in the art of painting beginning early in the 1300s, led by Giotto [jot′ō] di Bondone (1266–1336). He was the first European artist since classical times to make figures appear to move, to be alive. So important were Giotto's works that later painters looked upon him as a founder of their art. In the years after Giotto's death, Florence became the art center of Europe.

Florentine artists learned to draw human figures accurately. They tried to make feelings and ideas show in the face and body through the use of light and shadow. Using materials such as oils, they mixed new colors to enhance this technique. Pos-

Raphael's *The School of Athens* (1511) expresses the Renaissance admiration for the ancient Greeks. The two main figures are Aristotle and Plato, in the center.

- Write three terms on the chalkboard: Perspective, Anatomical Realism, and Chiaroscuro (a technique which uses light and shadow to give realistic form to people and objects). Discuss the meaning of each term. Ask students to study the paintings in this chapter of their text and grade each painting from 1 (low) through 3 (high) on each of the techniques. Ask volunteers to explain their ratings.

- Ask for volunteers to come to the chalkboard to demonstrate how perspective can be achieved by using a vanishing point in a composition. (A vanishing point is that spot where the principle lines of a composition converge, as can be illustrated by the converging rails of a railroad as they become more distant.)

GUIDED PRACTICE

Examine all of the Renaissance paintings included in Chapter 19 and ask students to say how much they like each and why. Encourage students to discuss the quality of the paintings in terms of the techniques you have been discussing. You might mention that one reason the *Mona Lisa* has a mysterious aura about her is that Da Vinci created two vanishing points. Can students find them?

sibly most important, they figured out ways to make viewers feel as if they were looking into a painting instead of at it. Just as in the real world, distant things appeared to be smaller and near things larger. This art of illustrating objects on a flat surface so as to give the appearance of depth or distance is called perspective. Artists have used this technique ever since.

Of all painters of religious subjects, none was more famous than **Raphael** [raf′ē əl] (1483–1520). A handsome and friendly man, Raphael, like many other major artists of the Renaissance, achieved fame in his early years. Raphael's lasting reputation as a painter is based in part on his pictures of Madonnas, of Mary, the mother of Jesus. Raphael became the favorite artist of two popes— Julius II and Leo X.

Florence may have been the first major center for the arts, but Venice eventually became its rival. The citizens of Venice wanted to adorn their city with art treasures, among them many paintings. By the early 1500s, Venetian painters had begun their own traditions. Among these were paintings done in oils on canvas rather than on walls because Venice, which was located on the sea, was so damp that wall paintings tended to peel. Venetian painters also became famous for their use of rich, glowing colors.

Two important Venetian painters of this time were Giovanni Bellini [be lē′nē], born about 1430, and his most famous student Titian [tish′ən]. Bellini painted in a style that was soft and gentle with vibrant colors. Titian's landscapes were masterpieces of art, but his most important triumphs were his portraits. These precisely detailed paintings are treasured to this day for the way that Titian captured the spirit of his famous subjects.

During the Renaissance, a few women also became well-known painters. Sofonisba Anguisciola [sō′fō nēz′bä äng gwē′shō lä] (1532–1625) was famous for her work as a painter of portraits. She spent 10 years as a noted artist at the court of Philip II of Spain.

Sculpture and architecture flourished.

Sculpture followed much the same pattern as painting. By the 15th century, statues cut from stone or cast in bronze were naturalistic portraits of human beings and the world. The outstanding sculptor of the early 1400s was the Florentine Donato Bardi, best known as **Donatello** [don′ə tel′ō] (1386–1466). After studying ancient Roman sculpture, he decided that he could sculpt human beings only after he completely understood how the human body moved. Therefore, he was the first sculptor of this time to carefully study human anatomy in order to perfect his art. One of Donatello's best-known works is his grand statue of the Venetian general Gattemelata, the first large-sized figure on horseback since Roman times. In the general's face, Donatello caught the spirit of the Italian despot—proud, powerful, and cruel.

Italian Renaissance architects used Greek and Roman models for their buildings. However, these uses of buildings and the needs of churches and palaces were different from those of classical times. Different treatments of Greek and Roman pillars and domes were needed, so Renaissance architects adapted the classical models to suit their own times. As a result, their work was new and had lasting beauty. Many buildings constructed in the United States during the late 19th and early 20th centuries are based on Renaissance models.

Michelangelo was the most important Renaissance artist.

Some of the most important figures in the history of Western art lived during the Italian Renaissance. One, **Michelangelo** [mī′kə lan′jə lō] (1475–1564),

At left is Donatello's colossal bronze statue of Gattemelata. Above, Titian's portrait of a prominent Venetian reveals the artist's skill with detail.

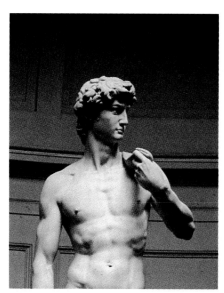

Michelangelo's marble statue (1504) of David, the king of ancient Israel around 1000 B.C., now stands in Florence.

is thought by many to have been the most outstanding of them all. He did everything well, including sculpting, painting, and architecture. He was even a fine poet. Michelangelo came from a noble but poor family who lived near Florence. At 13, Michelangelo became a helper to a painter and learned to make frescoes. For a number of years, Lorenzo de' Medici, ruler of Florence, helped Michelangelo carry on his studies.

Michelangelo's fame came from both painting and sculpture. Many of his painted figures have the solid feeling of statues. He often said, "It is only well with me when I have a chisel in my hand." People, however, always wanted him to paint. Pope Julius II asked Michelangelo to paint frescoes on the walls and ceiling of the Sistine Chapel in the Vatican. He painted lying on his back on a high scaffold most of the time. The huge task of picturing the Bible story of Genesis from the Creation to the Flood took four years. When finished, the painting covered some 10,000 square feet divided into nine massive panels. It remains one of the world's most admired paintings.

Michelangelo lived only for his art and had little interest in money or comfort. Hard work and lack

of decent food seem to have led to depression, for Michelangelo was often plagued by fears of sudden death. His will to work was so strong, however, that he drove himself without mercy. The grueling work on the Sistine Chapel left him with a crippled, hunched back for the rest of his life.

As a sculptor, as well, Michelangelo was in a class by himself. Talented as he was with brush and paint, he was even more so with chisel and stone. His statues are massive, naturalistic, and filled with real human expressions. Most famous are the *Pietà* [pyā tä'], *Moses,* and *David,* but he created many other brilliant pieces. Michelangelo also carved exquisite and powerful figures for the Medici chapel and for the tomb of Pope Julius.

Section 3 Review

Identify Raphael, Donatello, Michelangelo

Main Ideas

1. In what ways was Renaissance painting changed from art in the Middle Ages?
2. How did the sculpture and architecture of the Renaissance reflect the humanist philosophy?
3. What were some of the talents that made Michelangelo an outstanding Renaissance artist?

Critical Thinking

Analyzing Comparisons: Consider the role of the artist both in the Renaissance society and in our modern society. How do you think it has changed or stayed the same? What do you think is the best role? Why?

4 The Renaissance spread to other countries.

Beginning in the middle of the 15th century, the Renaissance spread northward through Europe. Humanism was carried across the Alps by the many scholars, merchants, and diplomats who spent time in Italy. The Renaissance style took root in the cities of Europe, just as it had in Italy and for many of the same reasons. However, in northern Europe humanists tended to be more religiously inclined than many of the Italians.

The printing press was a great accomplishment of the Renaissance in northern Europe. To dramatize its importance, give students this problem: Hannah Riis, a shopkeeper in Amsterdam in 1425, determines to give each of her four children a hand-written parchment copy of the Bible on their sixteenth birthdays. Hannah can neatly write 10 words a minute with her quill pen. The Bible has approximately 1,000 pages and 900 words per page. Working by candlelight at night, Hannah has time to devote 20 hours a week to her project. How long will it take her to copy four Bibles?

- Ask students to hypothesize effects the printing press might have had on the following: literacy, growth of democracy, business, scientific invention, power of the Catholic Church.

- Two humanist writers who benefited from the press were Erasmus and More. What ideas of Erasmus might a present-day supporter of democracy cite? What ideas of More might a supporter of communism cite?

- Have students examine the paintings of Dürer, Brueghel, and Rembrandt. Is there evidence of perspective, knowledge of anatomy, use of light and shading?

GUIDED PRACTICE

Ask students to write a paragraph describing the qualities of the Renaissance figures described in this section that caused them to be known as *humanists*. Also for guided practice:

 Overhead Transparency 38

The invention of printing helped spread literacy and the Renaissance spirit.

Printing helped spread the Renaissance throughout the rest of Europe. Two important developments led to the invention of printing. One was paper, and the other was movable type. In the 1100s, Europeans learned about paper from the Moors, who knew about it from their Arab neighbors. They, in turn, had learned of it from the Chinese, who made it from a pulp of wood and rags.

At the time books were written by hand, and therefore expensive. For example, when the Medici family of Florence wanted 200 books for their library, 45 skilled copyists worked for two years to make them. Under such conditions, even large libraries had only a few hundred books. Many people never saw a book, much less owned one.

As you learned in Chapter 16, the Chinese invented movable type, but whether the invention came directly to Europe from China is not known. Credit for the first use of movable type in Europe is generally given to a German, Johann Gutenberg [güt′n bėrg′], sometime before 1450. Perhaps Gutenberg invented movable type, but the printing press design came from that of the old European wine press.

Possibly the first European book printed with movable type was the **Gutenberg Bible**, finished about 1455. By the end of the 1400s, 18 countries had printing presses with movable type, and by the early 1500s, European presses had printed 8 million books. Prices for books plummeted to less than 20 percent of their former levels.

The invention of movable type had important results. Books could be made rapidly and in great quantities, and the cost was much less than that of hand copying. The new books were far more accurate as well. Before printing, two exact copies of a book could not be made because copyists often made mistakes. More important, printing made books cheaper and thus available to more people. Even peasants now owned some books, and literacy spread throughout Europe.

Printing also helped spread the Renaissance spirit. Books, pamphlets, and broadsheets could be printed and spread rapidly. In this way, new ideas circulated very quickly through Europe, including humanist writing. The new movement in the rest of Europe was called the Northern Renaissance. It changed as each country added some ideas of its own.

Humanists of the Northern Renaissance were concerned with religion and ethics.

Northern humanists looked at social and religious problems. Most humanists in northern Europe were deeply involved in the religious, political, and social issues of their time. In general, they favored reform in many areas, especially the education of the young. Religion and ethics, questions of right and wrong, played an important part in their thinking.

The best example of Northern Humanist thought is found in the writings of **Desiderius Erasmus** [i raz′məs] (1466?–1536). Erasmus came from the Netherlands where, in cities such as his native Rotterdam, people had been interested in education for a long time. A priest, he spent much time studying Greek and Latin writings. Erasmus was also himself a prolific writer of books and letters, all in Latin. In his various works, he said that men and women were misled by ignorance and superstition, but that through education people could overcome all the injustices of the world and create more perfect societies.

Erasmus' most famous work was *Praise of Folly* (1511), which satirized human ignorance, intolerance, and greed. Erasmus attacked superstition, warlike princes, and false priests. He also took to task scholars who wasted time with silly problems.

All his life, Erasmus fought against ignorance, stupidity, and vice. He kept up a huge correspondence with learned people around Europe and in that way, he helped spread humanistic ideals. When he died in 1536, he left behind a large number of writings that later thinkers could study. Most important, Erasmus always spoke for social and religious reform and, especially, for peace.

Erasmus was one of many humanists who appeared in all the regions of Europe. One of his friends, Sir **Thomas More** (1478–1535), became England's leading humanist. He carried on a lifelong correspondence with Erasmus, who visited him in England several times. More became a lawyer and served in many government posts under England's King Henry VIII. Like many other hu-

BACKGROUND Copies of the Gutenberg Bible are still in existence today and can be seen in museums such as the Henry E. Huntington Library and Art Gallery at San Marino, near Pasadena, California.

More than the Italians, the artists of the Northern Renaissance painted everyday life. Above, the Flemish painter Pieter Brueghel, in *The Fall of Icarus,* shows how ordinary peasant life was more important to him than classical Greek culture. Among other everyday subjects, the Dutch artist Rembrandt van Rijn painted his son, Titus (1655), near right, and the German Albrecht Dürer, this *Young Hare* (1502), far right.

3 | **ASSESS AND CLOSE**

ASSESS

1. Why was the introduction of the printing press so significant?
2. What important ideas were promoted by Erasmus? By More?

OPTIONAL RETEACHING

Have students close their texts and write down the names of all the northern European Renaissance figures they can remember who are mentioned in this section. (Gutenberg, Erasmus, More, Van Eyck, Dürer, Brueghel, Rembrandt, Shakespeare, Cervantes) Call on volunteers to recount the contributions of each person.

Students also may be assigned Activities reteaching page 114.

OPTIONAL ENRICHMENT

1. Select one of the people covered in this section. Using at least one source beyond the text, write a 150-word obituary for the "Gutenberg Times" that celebrates the deceased's most important accomplishments. (average)
2. One of Pieter Brueghel's most famous paintings is *Children's Games.* It shows more than 50 games played in Flanders in the 16th century, many of which have lasted into this century. Research the painting and its contents and report back to the class. Research hint: See *Sports Illustrated,* Jan. 11, 1971. (challenging)

Students also may be assigned Activities enrichment page 115.

INDEPENDENT PRACTICE/ HOMEWORK

Assign the Section Review, the Chapter Review items, Activities page 113, or Workbook page 77.

manists, he wanted to reform society and create a better world for humankind.

To this end, More laid out a program in his most famous work, *Utopia.* "Utopia" is Greek for "nowhere," a place More invented as the perfect state. In Utopia all property was held in common, thus eliminating the need for greed or warfare. In this world, as well, all people were to be well educated and, therefore, tolerant, wise, and just. Although Utopia was not real, readers could compare it with their own society. This backdoor attack on society's evils led to laws that helped the poor.

Renaissance art flourished in northern Europe.

Painters in the Low Countries—now Belgium and the Netherlands—began early to break away from medieval ways. They started painting in new ways, such as experimenting in oils, even before Italian Renaissance art reached northern Europe. In fact, this school of painting, called Flemish, is one of the most important in European history.

Among the first of the painters using this Flemish style was Jan van Eyck [van īk] (1385–1440). Van Eyck portraits are realistic but they also show the spiritual side of his subjects. He painted realistic landscapes, carefully showing trees, grass, and flowers as they appeared in nature. At the same time, Van Eyck's paintings were filled with religious symbols.

The skill of Italian painters impressed artists throughout northern Europe. Even more, they admired the Italians' use of perspective and their mastery of anatomy. A German, Albrecht Dürer [dүʹrər] (1471–1528), was one of the best-known artists to study in Italy. On his first visit to Italy about 1494, Dürer noted the artists' high social status. He noted with amazement that "Here I am a

Remind students that the Renaissance in northern Italy and northern Europe launched the world into the modern era. The Catholic Church remained powerful, but artists and writers increasingly focused on the description, celebration, and improvement of life in this world, not the hereafter.

Answers to Section 4 Review

Identify

Key Terms, People, and Places are defined on pages indicated in parentheses. Also see the Glossary and Biographical Dictionary. Gutenberg Bible (364), Desiderius Erasmus (364), Sir Thomas More (364), Rembrandt van Rijn (366), William Shakespeare (366), Miguel de Cervantes (366)

Main Ideas

1. the spread of literacy, with an increase in the number of books in circulation and the spread of Renaissance ideas
2. Northern European humanists were more concerned with religion than were Italian humanists. They were also concerned with reform and ethics.
3. new techniques, such as oil painting, and for the Flemish school of painting
4. Both wrote about the full range of human emotions and deeds, both good and bad, and treated humans as existing within the sphere of the natural world.

Critical Thinking

Students should be aware that "angel" reflects spiritual values and "dust" symbolizes the body. The conflict here could be between heaven and earth, or the Church and humanism.

---

lord, at home a parasite." Dürer's most widely known works are the number of woodcuts and engravings that illustrated the new printed books.

Intense interest in the natural world is seen in artist Pieter Brueghel the Elder [broi′gəl] (1525–1569). He was Flemish, that is, a native of Flanders in the Low Countries. He spent his life painting country landscapes and hearty scenes of peasant life. Although these paintings were of ordinary people, Brueghel's subjects were mostly religious and humanist.

The Low Countries remained a significant center for painting into the 17th century. One of the outstanding artists of the 1600s was the Dutch painter **Rembrandt van Rijn** [rem′brant vän rīn′] (1606–1669). Like the other Low Country painters, Rembrandt was interested in nature and his landscapes are beautiful and accurate etchings. His main interests, however, were the human characters that he painted so well. Rembrandt's influence on artists after him was profound, even to this day.

Shakespeare and Cervantes were important writers.

Literature in England excelled during this period. Queen Elizabeth I, like many rulers of the time, helped and inspired writers. The outstanding writer in the Elizabethan age, and indeed one of the finest in world literature, was the English playwright **William Shakespeare** (1564–1616).

Shakespeare's plays are part of the literary heritage of all English-speaking people. He had a deep understanding of human beings, and he expressed the whole range of human emotions in his plays. Some of the characters that he brought to life were Lady Macbeth, Hamlet, Portia, Julius Caesar, and Falstaff. Hundreds of sayings have come from his rich writing into everyday English speech, as you will learn in the "Highlights of Civilization" feature on page 367.

Shakespeare was not only a genius, but his plays also seem to sum up humanist ideals. Hamlet, in the play of the same name, says this:

> What a piece of work is a man! How noble in reason . . . in action how like an angel! in apprehension [understanding] how like a god! the beauty of the world! the paragon of animals! And, yet, to me, what is this quintessence of dust?

BACKGROUND Part 1 of *Don Quixote* was published in 1605 when Cervantes was 58 years old. Part II was published in 1615, the year before the author's death.

To Shakespeare, human beings, since they were created in God's image, had the intelligence to be like angels and gods, the best of all the animal world. And yet, said Shakespeare, humans are part of the natural world, merely dust.

In France and Spain, humanists wrote about the evils of their day. The most significant Spanish author was the Spaniard **Miguel de Cervantes** [sər van′tēz] (1547–1616). A nobleman who served in the military, he wrote the novel *Don Quixote* [kē hō′tē] upon his retirement.

Toward the end of the 1500s, when Cervantes wrote *Don Quixote*, feudalism and knighthood had gone out of fashion. However, the codes of chivalry still appealed to many people in Spain. Cervantes' hero, Don Quixote, was a poor but proud Spanish gentleman who loved to read knightly romances. At the age of 50, he made a suit of armor and set off with his old horse to seek adventures. His comic servant Sancho Panza went with him, often commenting on his master's silly antics. Cervantes' novel is a Renaissance work in two ways. First, it clearly shows Spanish life at the time. Second, it laughs at the ideals of knighthood chivalry in the funny adventures of Don Quixote. His deeds were absurd, but Cervantes admired his hero's ideals of bravery and goodness. However, Cervantes seems to have felt that these ideals were no longer respected in the world as he knew it.

Section 4 Review

Identify Gutenberg Bible, Desiderius Erasmus, Thomas More, Rembrandt van Rijn, William Shakespeare, Miguel de Cervantes

Main Ideas

1. What were two results of the invention of movable type?
2. What were some of the typical concerns of northern European humanists?
3. For what were the painters of the Northern Renaissance famous?
4. In what ways were Shakespeare and Cervantes major Renaissance writers?

Critical Thinking

Making Hypotheses: Consider Hamlet's speech at left. Do you see any contradictions—between "angel" and "dust"? What might account for the conflict?

Shakespeare's Influence on English

"All's well that ends well."
"Sweets to the sweet."
"The course of true love never did run smooth."
"Love is blind."

Have you ever used any of these expressions? If so, you were quoting William Shakespeare, perhaps without realizing it.

Shakespeare shaped and molded English as no other writer has. His influence is second only to that of the King James Version of the Bible, which dates from 1611 and is also widely admired for the grace and beauty of its language.

Shakespeare wrote his plays for the Globe Playhouse in London. People of all sorts came to the theater six days a week for afternoon entertainment. In fact, the mayor of London tried to limit the number of performances so that working people would not lose time from their jobs. The owners of the theater simply moved to a new site outside the city walls, beyond the control of the puritanical city officials.

Although Shakespeare's plays were enthusiastically received when seen in performance, the printed texts were appreciated as well. All 38 of Shakespeare's plays were in print within a short time after his death, and people have enjoyed reading them ever since.

Before printing was available, many English-speaking people had only a limited command of their language. Shakespeare's works became a major factor in broadening people's vocabularies and establishing models for grammar.

Shakespeare's heroine Helena tries to prove herself worthy of Bertram, a countess' son, in All's Well That Ends Well.

Tell students that Sir Francis Bacon, Shakespeare's contemporary, wrote in Latin as well as English because he assumed that Latin would continue to be understood and read by educated people in the form he wrote it. After Shakespeare, however, scholars and authors had complete confidence in the permanence and acceptance of English.

You might want to explain that Shakespeare's use of language also reflects the strong influence of the Bible, although probably in a popular translation made 50 years before the King James Version.

Ask students to look in a book of quotations for other familiar phrases that Shakespeare wrote. Choose a collection organized by author rather than subject, for example *John Bartlett's Familiar Quotations* or *The Oxford Dictionary of Quotations*. If time permits, small groups could choose a brief passage from Shakespeare for one student to read aloud while others in the group pantomime appropriate actions.

CHAPTER 19 REVIEW

Section Summaries

Section 1
The Renaissance began in Italy.
Italian city-states were well placed on the trade routes between East and West. New wealth from trade allowed merchants and rulers to help artists and writers. Out of this new wealth came the Renaissance.

Section 2
Humanism flourished in the Renaissance.
One of the important new ideas that grew up in Renaissance Italy was called humanism. Humanists, such as Petrarch and Boccaccio, raised much interest in the classical writings of Greece and Rome. Leonardo da Vinci was an important Renaissance man.

Section 3
Italians created art masterpieces.
The most glorious showing of the Renaissance spirit took place in art, especially painting and sculpture. Well-known Italian artists of the time are Giotto, Raphael, Michelangelo, and Titian. The Italians also made important strides in architecture during this time.

Section 4
The Renaissance spread to other countries.
People, together with books printed from movable type, spread the ideas of the Renaissance. The writings of Italian humanists influenced two major European scholars, Erasmus and Sir Thomas More. Northern European humanists were particularly impressed with the problems of society. Northern painting and writing also gained from the Italian Renaissance. Among northern artists were Van Eyck, Dürer, Brueghel, and Rembrandt van Rijn. Shakespeare and Cervantes were important writers.

Test Yourself

Key Terms, People, and Places
Identify the significance of each of the following:

Section 1
a. Venice
b. Florence
c. capitalism
d. condottieri
e. Niccolo Machiavelli

Section 2
a. humanism
b. Petrarch
c. Giovanni Boccaccio
d. Leonardo da Vinci

Section 3
a. Raphael
b. Donatello
c. Michelangelo

Section 4
a. Gutenberg Bible
b. Desiderius Erasmus
c. Thomas More
d. Rembrandt van Rijn
e. William Shakespeare
f. Miguel de Cervantes

Review Dates

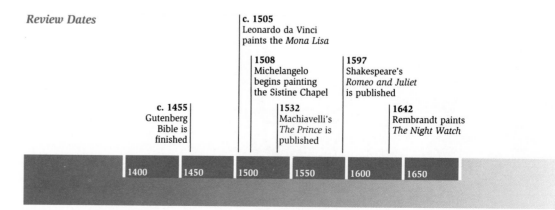

c. 1505
Leonardo da Vinci paints the *Mona Lisa*

1508
Michelangelo begins painting the Sistine Chapel

1597
Shakespeare's *Romeo and Juliet* is published

c. 1455
Gutenberg Bible is finished

1532
Machiavelli's *The Prince* is published

1642
Rembrandt paints *The Night Watch*

| 1400 | 1450 | 1500 | 1550 | 1600 | 1650 |

Main Ideas

Section 1

1. Describe how riches that accumulated from a growing trade affected the Italian cities.
2. What caused the development of capitalism in Italy?
3. How did the Italian city-states gain from the political wranglings between the Holy Roman emperors and the popes?
4. Why did the despots appeal to the Italian people?
5. How did Machiavelli advise rulers to behave in *The Prince?*

Section 2

1. For what reasons might humanism have gained popularity during the Italian Renaissance?
2. In what ways were Petrarch and Boccaccio influenced by classical Romans and Greeks?
3. What changes in the goals of education occurred during the Renaissance?
4. Why is Leonardo da Vinci an example of a Renaissance man?

Section 3

1. How did Renaissance painting differ from art in the Middle Ages?
2. In what ways did the sculpture and architecture of the Renaissance reflect the humanist philosophy?
3. Describe some of the talents that made Michelangelo an outstanding Renaissance artist.

Section 4

1. Identify two results of the invention of movable type.
2. Describe some of the typical concerns of northern European humanists.
3. Why were the painters of the Northern Renaissance famous?
4. For what reasons were Shakespeare and Cervantes considered to be major Renaissance writers?

Critical Thinking

1. **Recognizing Values** How was the Renaissance a break with the past? Do you think humanist ideals are out of date? Support your opinion with evidence.
2. **Analyzing Comparisons** Why were both Leonardo da Vinci and Michelangelo considered to be Renaissance men? Support your answer with evidence and examples.

Chapter Skills and Activities

Practicing Study and Research Skills

Identifying Primary and Secondary Sources

All historical information falls into two basic categories—primary sources or secondary sources. Primary sources are firsthand, direct descriptions of people, places, and events. They are written or recorded when and where the people lived or the event happened. Secondary sources are based on the study of one or more primary sources. They are written after the people lived or the event occurred. Identify each of the following as a primary or a secondary source:

a. Machiavelli's *The Prince*
b. an encyclopedia article on Machiavelli
c. Leonardo da Vinci's notebooks
d. a biography of Michelangelo
e. the Gutenberg Bible

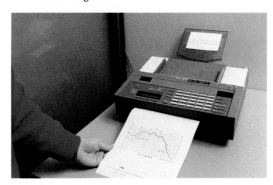

Linking Past and Present

The use of the printing press revolutionized the Renaissance period. What communications developments, such as the fax machine above, have revolutionized today's society? How?

Learning History Through Maps

During the Renaissance, the Italian peninsula became divided into many small states, most of them centered around a city. Both the state and the leading city usually had the same name. Look at the map on page 354 and identify the Italian city-states whose capital city is the same name as the state.

CRITICAL THINKING QUESTION LEVEL 1. challenging; 2. average

20 The Age of Exploration

OVERVIEW

This chapter covers 250 years of exploration and empire building between 1450 and 1700—its causes, its discoveries, and its consequences.

PLANNING CHART

Section	Text Pages	Key Concept	Suggested Teaching Time
1 Europeans found lands and trade routes previously unknown to them.	371–374	A desire for Asian goods prompted first Portugal, then Spain, to take the lead in finding new routes to the East.	One day **More time?** Use *Source Reading 20A.* **Less time?** Eliminate the outlining exercise in Section 1 and substitute with discussion. Combine Sections 1 and 2
2 Europeans explored the New World.	375–376	England, France, and the Netherlands were quick to join Spain and Portugal in exploration and settlement of the New World.	One day Use *Overhead Transparency 39.*
3 Europeans built overseas empires.	377–379	European empire building was not confined to the Americas, but extended to Africa and Asia as well.	One day **More Time?** Use *Source Reading 20B.*
4 The new discoveries brought many changes to Europe and the Americas.	379–382	New discoveries led to a revolution in commerce, the development of new business practices, and mercantilism.	Two days **More time?** Use *Overhead Transparency 40.*

ANCILLARIES

Materials that may be used with this chapter to reinforce, reteach, enrich, and assess learning are pictured on the following pages.

Teacher's Resource File

ACTIVITIES

Section 1 Activity, p. 116

Section 2 Activity, p. 117

Section 3 Activity, p. 118

Section 4 Activity, p. 119

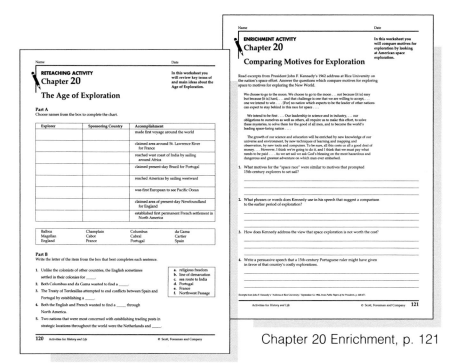

Chapter 20 Reteaching, p. 120

Chapter 20 Enrichment, p. 121

Teacher's Resource File

GEOGRAPHY SKILLS

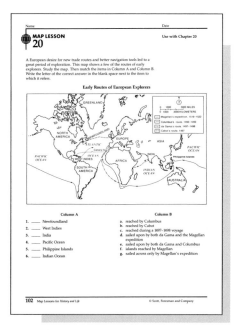

Chapter 20 Geography
Worksheet/Map, pp. 41–42

Chapter 20 Map Lesson, p. 102

TESTS

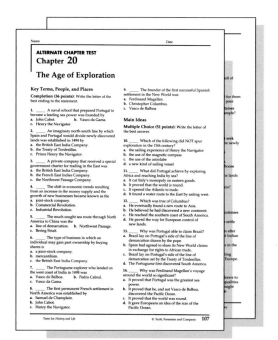

Chapter Test, pp. 105–106

Alternate Chapter Test, pp. 107–108

Other Optional Ancillaries

WORKBOOK

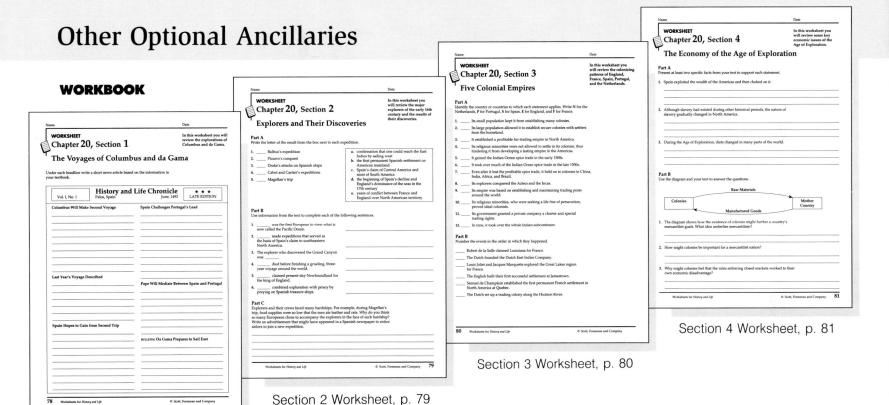

Section 1 Worksheet, p. 78

Section 2 Worksheet, p. 79

Section 3 Worksheet, p. 80

Section 4 Worksheet, p. 81

SOURCE READINGS

Source Reading 20A
Source Reading 20B

TEST GENERATOR

40 multiple-choice questions for Chapter 20

OVERHEAD TRANSPARENCIES

Overhead Transparency 39
Overhead Transparency 40

20

The Age of Exploration

1400–1700

CHAPTER INTRODUCTION

Discuss with students what was needed to carry out exploratory expeditions. In students' opinions, were most expeditions successful in accomplishing their goals?

LOCATOR GLOBE

Call students' attention to the globe, which indicates the general area of the world discussed in this chapter. (A detailed map appears on page 378.)

TIME LINE

Have students examine the time line and ask them whether the Renaissance and the Age of Exploration overlapped. (yes)

1300	
1400	
1415	The first Portuguese ships explore Africa
1492	Columbus reaches the Americas
1500	
1600	

The crews of the three small ships were worried. After two months of sailing west across unknown seas, they did not know where they were. The ocean seemed endless, and some sailors wanted to turn back for their homes in Europe. The admiral, however, insisted that they sail on. Finally, late on the night of October 11th:

> The Admiral . . . saw a light, though it was so uncertain that he could not [be sure] it was land. He called Pero Gutierrez . . . and said that there seemed to be a light, and that he should look at it. He did so, and saw it. . . . It seemed . . . to be an indication of land; but the Admiral [wanted to make] certain that land was close. . . . At two hours after midnight . . . land was sighted [by a sailor named Rodrigo de Triana] at a distance of two leagues [six miles]. . . . The vessels were hove to [stopped], waiting for daylight; and on Friday [October 12th] they arrived at a small island. . . . Presently they saw naked people.

You may have figured out that the admiral mentioned in the excerpt above was Christopher Columbus. The description came from the journal he kept during the voyage of 1492. Columbus' successful landing on the small island, which is in the present-day Bahamas, marked the beginning of one of the most important periods in history.

As one of the early events in what has come to be known as "the Age of Exploration," Columbus' voyage opened the way for Europeans to discover a new world that they never had dreamed existed. The Age of Exploration lasted from about 1400 to about 1700. It led to the building of colonies and a great increase in world trade. Europe's discovery of new lands and new trade routes led to economic and cultural changes that revolutionized the lives not only of Europeans but of Americans, Africans, and Asians as well.

New inventions and techniques aided bcth exploration and cultural exchange, as shown in this painting by Hans Holbein the Younger, *The Ambassadors* (1533).

Reading Preview

In this chapter you will learn how the Europeans explored and settled lands in the New World.

1. *Europeans found lands and trade routes previously unknown to them.*
2. *Europeans explored the New World.*
3. *Europeans built overseas empires.*
4. *The new discoveries brought many changes to Europe and the Americas.*

---

1 | Europeans found lands and trade routes previously unknown to them.

There were two basic reasons why Christopher Columbus and other Europeans sailed out into the uncharted oceans: to expand trade routes and to spread Christianity to the non-Christian world. However, the explorers did not act on their own. Their expeditions were sponsored by competing European governments that jealously guarded

BACKGROUND Be sure students realize that Europeans were not actually finding areas that were new to all peoples, since most often these "new lands" were already inhabited by others.

371

statements in what they believe is the most logical order. Discuss several arrangements.

Begin an outline on the chalkboard with Roman numeral headings for the subsections in the text. Ask students to record a minimum of two subtopics under each Roman numeral heading and one question they would like answered. A completed outline might look like this:

I. New technology spurring exploration
   A. Different sails
   B. Compass and astrolabe
   C. Improved shipbuilding
   Question: How does an astrolabe work?
II. Portuguese explorations
   A. Prince Henry the Navigator, northwest coast of Africa
   B. Bartolomeu Dias, tip of Africa
   C. Vasco da Gama, west coast of India
   Question: Do compasses work in the Southern Hemisphere?
III. Spanish explorations
   A. 1492: Columbus' grand mistake
   B. Amerigo Vespucci's deduction
   Question: Would it not be more appropriate for our country to be called the United States of Columbus?
IV. Portugal and Spain in conflict
   A. Papal decrees
   B. Treaty of Tordesillas
   Question: Why did Portugal agree to the treaty?

GUIDED PRACTICE

Ask students to share their questions with the class. Have the class discuss possible answers.

Two developments in sailing technology were in ship and sail design (above) and the astrolabe (left), used to measure the altitude of the sun or stars.

their expanding knowledge of new horizons. The high value Europeans placed on goods from India and China helps explain why people were willing to risk long voyages in small, leaky ships through unknown waters.

Improvements in technology spurred exploration.

Before they could make the long voyages required to search for new trade routes, the Europeans needed to develop ships capable of such voyages. These ships had to be able to sail efficiently both with and against the winds. These capabilities were essential so that the explorers and their crews could return to Europe from distant regions.

By using two square sails, characteristic of northern European ships, and one triangular sail, characteristic of southern European ships, shipbuilders of the 1300s developed vessels both powerful and maneuverable in winds. The square sails helped the ship sail speedily with the wind. The triangular sail allowed the ship to sail against the wind.

The adoption of better navigational devices, such as the compass and the astrolabe, also helped build the confidence of those curious to venture into unknown seas. Although even in the 14th century some sailors feared the "magical" properties of the magnetized compass needle, most thought its direction-finding abilities well outweighed any risk of "black magic." Europeans had been familiar with the compass probably since the 12th century, and by the 1300s it was standard equipment on all long voyages.

Additional refinements in shipbuilding and advances in navigational sciences resulted from the opening of a naval school in Portugal. At the beginning of the 15th century, a son of the Portuguese royal family, Prince Henry, gathered the most knowledgeable sailors, the most skilled shipbuilders, the most precise mapmakers, and the best scientists from all over Europe. In doing so, the young prince prepared his country to become a leading sea power. Although Prince Henry never set sail himself, he became known as **Henry the Navigator** because of his guidance and direction.

Portugal explored Africa and found a sea route to India.

A small country with a long sea coast, Portugal had always looked to the sea as a source of livelihood. As world trade became a key to the wealth and power of European countries, the Portuguese were eager to take advantage of their nautical knowledge and their prime location on the southwest edge of Europe. They sought to make contact with the gold-rich kingdoms of Africa and to find an all-water route to the Indies.

Beginning in 1415, Prince Henry the Navigator sponsored yearly voyages of exploration around the northwest coast of Africa. Before that time, sailors had refused to travel far in the uncharted south Atlantic, afraid that they would never find their way back to Europe. However, the well-built Portuguese ships and increased knowledge of navigation gave the sailors confidence. By the year of Henry's death in 1460, Portugal had explored and laid claim to the Azores, the Madeira Islands, and the Cape Verde Islands. The Portuguese had also sailed around the western edge of Africa, claiming the land all the way to the Gold Coast.

During the next 40 years, successive Portuguese kings continued sponsoring the yearly sailing voyages begun by Prince Henry. Portugal explored the entire western coast of Africa. In 1488 the Portuguese explorer Bartolomeu Dias rounded the tip of the continent. Because he was blown around this large jut of land by a storm, Dias named the southern end of Africa the "Cape of Storms." The success of Dias' expedition hinted that a sea route to the East did indeed exist. This news so pleased the king of Portugal, that he renamed the "Cape of Storms," the "Cape of Good Hope."

Dias' voyage was a boon for the Portuguese. In the next ten years, the Portuguese made significant inroads in their trade with Africa. However, their most noted success came when **Vasco da Gama** reached the west coast of India in 1498. Although the Muslims held tight control of the Indian spice trade, da Gama managed to obtain cinnamon and pepper. Fleeing for his life from the Muslim traders who planned to have him killed, da Gama left India with his small cargo. When he returned home to Portugal in 1499, he was hailed as a hero. By cutting Italy's monopoly on goods from the East, Portugal was fast becoming the world's most powerful trading nation.

Spain sent Columbus sailing west to find an all-water route to the East.

While the Portuguese had been systematically exploring the coast of Africa in search of a passage to India, a tall, red-haired Italian sea captain named **Christopher Columbus** had been working. He had been gathering evidence for the idea that a water route to India could be found by sailing not east but west. With charts from famous mapmakers and arguments resting on the work of ancient classical scholars, Columbus traveled from Spain to Portugal and back again, trying to convince one of the Iberian monarchs to fund a voyage westward across the Atlantic.

Although the young Italian cut an impressive figure and spoke passionately about his ideas, for years no one heeded him. Finally, Spain, jealous of Portugal's continued success in sea exploration took the gamble in 1492. On August 2, 1492, Columbus set out to cross the Atlantic with three ships—the Niña, the Pinta, and the Santa Maria.

As you have read, Columbus reached land in October, 1492. Sure that he had reached islands on the east coast of Asia, Columbus named the islands the "Indies" and their inhabitants, "Indians." He claimed these lands for Spain and returned to Europe triumphant. After this first voyage, Columbus was able to sail three more times, in 1493, 1498, and 1502. On these expeditions he found many more islands and even landed on the northern coast of South America. However, he never found the rich kingdoms of Asia he was so sure he would find, nor did he ever realize that he had discovered lands previously unknown to Europeans.

Other Europeans deduced what Columbus himself failed to realize. One of the first people to deduce that Columbus' newly discovered lands were not part of Asia was Amerigo Vespucci [vespü′chē]. Although Vespucci claimed to have made

3 | ASSESS AND CLOSE

ASSESS

What triggered the European Age of Exploration? (desire to expand trade routes and to spread Christianity)

OPTIONAL RETEACHING

Ask students to write brief explanations of how each of the technological improvements described in the text helped explorers sail longer distances.

OPTIONAL ENRICHMENT

1. Amerigo Vespucci has lent his name to numerous places, songs, and book titles. Ask interested students to make a list of the name changes that might have resulted if our country had been named after Columbus. (average)
2. Some scholars feel that Columbus received too much credit for his New World discovery. Have interested students investigate other discovery claims such as Norsemen, Irish monks, Lost Tribe of Israel, Siberian hunters, and so on. (challenging)
3. Also for enrichment:

 Source Reading 20A

INDEPENDENT PRACTICE/ HOMEWORK

Assign the Section Review, Activities page 116, or Workbook page 78.

CLOSURE

Summarize by explaining that the discoveries made by the Portuguese and Columbus opened up a world greater in size than most Europeans had ever imagined. (Columbus had estimated the distance from West Africa to Japan to be about 2,400 miles, 8,200 miles too short.) Europe and the world would never be the same.

From the Archives

A Reward for Columbus

Christopher Columbus did not approach the risks and dangers of his great voyage of discovery without hope of reward and honors. His demands for a noble title and authority to rule any lands discovered in the name of the king and queen were so excessive that Ferdinand and Isabella at first refused to sponsor the voyage. Eventually, they relented and issued the following letter of appointment.

[You,] Christopher Columbus, are going by our command, with some of our vessels and men, to discover and subdue some Islands and Continent in the ocean, and it is hoped that by God's assistance, some of the said Islands and Continent in the ocean will be discovered and conquered by your means and conduct, therefore it is but just and reasonable, that since you expose yourself to such danger to serve us, you should be rewarded for it. . . . [Our] will is, That you . . . shall be our Admiral of the said Islands and Continent you shall so discover and conquer; and that you be our Admiral, Vice-Roy, and Governor in them . . . and that your sons and successors in the said employment, may call themselves Dons, Admirals, Vice-Roys, and Governors of them.

a number of voyages to the "New World," as he called it, many historians doubt that he ever left Europe. These historians believe that Vespucci merely collected and publicized stories told by explorers. A German mapmaker, hearing of the New World from Vespucci's stories, used Vespucci's first name to label the new continent.

Thus, Columbus was never honored by the naming of the new continents he found. Yet he goes down in history as one of the world's most important figures because, in effect, Columbus paved the way for Europe's domination of vast new lands.

FROM THE ARCHIVES Henry Steele Commager, ed., *Documents of American History* 9th ed., (Englewood Cliffs, New Jersey: Prentice-Hall, 1973), I, p. 1. This document presents Columbus in another light. Ask students to articulate the images

The pope divided new lands between Spain and Portugal.

Along with being early leaders in exploration, Portugal and Spain were also fierce rivals. The two countries soon came into conflict over claims for land in the newly discovered parts of the world. Three papal decrees in the 1450s gave Portugal a monopoly on African exploration and trade. In 1493 Spain asked the pope to give Spain rights to all newly discovered land across the Atlantic. After consulting his scientists and mapmakers, the pope drew an imaginary north-south line, about 250 miles west of the Azores. He decreed that all newly discovered lands east of the line were to go to Portugal and those west of the line to Spain. However, Portugal would not agree to the papal line of demarcation. Therefore, representatives from both countries met in 1494 and drew up the **Treaty of Tordesillas**, which moved the line of demarcation about 700 miles farther west.

Neither nation knew the extent of the land they were bargaining for. In the next 50 years, however, Portugal would stake its claim to Brazil, and Spain would stake its claim to the rest of South America as well as to Central America and North America on the basis of this treaty.

Section 1 Review

Identify Henry the Navigator, Vasco da Gama, Christopher Columbus, Treaty of Tordesillas

Main Ideas
1. Describe two improvements in sailing technology that aided exploration.
2. How did Portuguese exploration lead to increased trade from Africa and India?
3. What were the lasting results of Columbus' voyage?
4. How did Spain and Portugal seek to settle disputes about rights to newly discovered lands?

Critical Thinking
Making Decisions: Until Prince Henry's explorations led to rich trade with Africa, many people claimed the voyages he sponsored were a waste of Portugal's money. If you were the Portuguese monarch, what criteria would you use to decide whether or not to fund Prince Henry's navigational research? How would your criteria be different from those you might use to determine whether to fund the space program today?

they have of Columbus as an explorer, adventurer, or scientist. How does this document fit these images? (It adds a dimension of Columbus as an ambitious social climber with a good business sense.)

2 Europeans explored the New World.

The sudden realization that unknown expanses of land lay across the Atlantic led to a flurry of exploration in the early 16th century. Early explorers faced disease and starvation, risking death on the chance that they might discover and seize untold wealth for themselves and for their country.

The Spanish and Portuguese laid claim to the Americas.

In 1500 Pedro Cabral sailed to the east coast of South America, claiming for Portugal all the land east of the line set by the Treaty of Tordesillas. This region came to be called Brazil. Meanwhile, Spain sent numerous expeditions to Central America and tried to establish permanent settlements there. **Vasco de Balboa** began the first successful Spanish settlement on the American mainland on the east coast of the Isthmus of Panama in 1510. Three years later, having waded through treacherous swamps, crossed steaming jungles, and climbed rugged mountains, Balboa became the first European to gaze at what he called the South Sea, later renamed the Pacific Ocean.

Balboa had crossed the Isthmus of Panama to try to reach an empire, rich in gold, which natives had told him lay to the southwest. However, Balboa never completed his quest. He was arrested by Francisco Pizarro, an agent of the new governor of Spain's American colonies. He was then dragged back across the Isthmus, falsely accused of treason, and beheaded. With Balboa out of the way, Pizarro discovered and conquered the rich Inca empire of Peru, claiming most of South America for Spain.

The huge amounts of gold and silver Pizarro plundered from Central and South America inspired other Spanish adventurers to search for treasure. In the early 1500s, Juan Ponce de León explored the Bahama Islands in search of the fabled Fountain of Youth—a spring which supposedly restored the youth of those who bathed in its waters. During this search Ponce de León discovered and explored the coast of Florida. Although he never found the mythical fountain, his expedi-

tions were the basis of Spain's claim to the southeastern corner of North America.

Another Spanish explorer, Hernando de Soto, continued the exploration of the southeastern part of North America. Between 1539 and 1542, de Soto led an expedition of almost 600 men from the present-day states of Florida to Oklahoma. They never came across any riches, but they were the first Europeans to see the Mississippi River.

The southwestern regions of North America were explored by another Spaniard, Francisco de Coronado. In 1540 Coronado was sent on an exploratory mission by the Spanish colonial ruler of Mexico. Traveling north in search of seven legendary cities of gold, Coronado spent several years exploring what is now the southwestern United States. He discovered the Grand Canyon and marveled at the immense herds of buffalo roaming the plains. However, Coronado, like de Soto, never found the riches of which he dreamed.

The Spanish sent Magellan to find a new sea route to the East.

Balboa's discovery of the Pacific Ocean gave Spain renewed hope of fulfilling Columbus' original mission—finding an all-water route to the East by sailing west. Spain sent **Ferdinand Magellan**

The fanciful map below shows the route of Magellan's ships in his first round-the-world voyage, 1519–1522.

375

investigate the fate of New World explorers, specifically Henry Hudson, Jacques Marquette, Panfilo de Narvaez, Etienne Brule, or Robert La Salle. (average)

INDEPENDENT PRACTICE/ HOMEWORK

Assign the Section Review, Activities page 117, or Workbook page 79.

CLOSURE

Summarize by explaining that early European exploration of the New World was marked by about equal parts of excitement, hardship, brutality, hope, and disappointment.

Answers to Section 2 Review

Identify

Key Terms, People, and Places are defined on pages indicated in parentheses. Also see the Glossary and Biographical Dictionary. Vasco de Balboa (375), Ferdinand Magellan (375), Northwest Passage (376)

Main Ideas

1. Pedro Cabral claimed Brazil for Portugal. In 1510 Vasco de Balboa began the first successful Spanish settlement on the American continent. Francisco Pizarro conquered the Incas of Peru for Spain. The Spanish explorer, Juan Ponce de León, reached the Bahama Islands and the coast of Florida. Hernando de Soto and his group were the first Europeans to see the Mississippi River. Francisco de Coronado explored the American southwest in 1540, claiming the region for Spain.
2. went around the world in search of an all-water route from Europe west to the Indies. His voyage

---

on a voyage around the world in 1519, to find this western passage and to claim any lands he discovered for Spain. From the beginning Magellan's voyage was a rough one.

Before he even reached the coast of South America, he had to placate his disgruntled crew. On the perilous trip around the tip of South America, one of Magellan's ships deserted him and sailed back to Spain. With ice stiffening the rigging and gale winds tearing into the ships, Magellan forced the frightened sailors onward.

Crossing the Pacific, Magellan sailed for three months without sighting land. Stores of food and water were low, and the crew suffered terribly from disease and hunger. In March, 1521, Magellan reached some islands, which he named the Philippines in honor of King Philip of Spain. After making a treaty with one of the local rulers, Magellan became involved in a war against another rival native group, in which he and several crew members died. The surviving members of Magellan's crew continued their westward voyage. Only one of Magellan's five original ships actually made it to the East Indies. They loaded the ship with a rich cargo of spices, crossed the Indian Ocean, rounded Africa, and finally came to port at Seville, Spain, in September, 1522. After three years and 12 days, with only 18 out of 243 sailors left, the first ship to go around the world had returned. Magellan's arduous journey was important because it was Europe's first indication of the wide expanse of the Pacific Ocean.

The English and French searched for the Northwest Passage.

While Spain sent Magellan to find a sea route to the East around South America, England and France sent expeditions to North America to find the **Northwest Passage** to China. The first such voyage set off in 1497. An Italian, known by the English version of his name, John Cabot, was commissioned by King Henry VII of England and charged to "sail to all parts, regions, and coasts of the eastern, western, and northern sea . . . to find, discover and investigate whatsoever islands . . . which before this time were unknown to all Christians." Cabot landed on the coast of present-day Nova Scotia or Newfoundland, and claimed the

---

area for the king of England. Although he was unsuccessful, Cabot continued his search for the Northwest Passage. He died while on his second voyage in 1498.

About 35 years after Cabot explored North America, France sent the explorer Jacques Cartier [zhäk′ kär tyā′] in search of the passage. Sailing up the broad St. Lawrence River, Cartier got as far as modern-day Montreal, claiming the land for France. Although neither Cabot nor Cartier found a passage through North America, their claims to North America for their respective countries led to years of conflict as both powers fought for control of the continent.

Because the search for the Northwest Passage along the east coast of North America seemed to have failed, in 1577 England's Queen Elizabeth I sent Sir Francis Drake to look for the outlet to the passage on America's west coast. Combining exploration with piracy, Drake preyed on Spanish treasure ships in the Atlantic and the Pacific. Drake's voyage, though not successful in its hunt for the Northwest Passage, was the beginning of eventual English domination of the seas in the 17th century.

Section 2 Review

Identify Vasco de Balboa, Ferdinand Magellan, Northwest Passage

Main Ideas

1. List the Portuguese and Spanish explorers who laid claim to the Americas and tell what each did.
2. Describe the voyage of Ferdinand Magellan and discuss its significance.
3. In what ways did the expeditions in search of the Northwest Passage influence the later history of England and France?

Critical Thinking

Recognizing Values: For many of the voyages of discovery discussed in this section, the crew members who went on the expeditions were not given information about the destination or purpose of the voyage. Also, records of the voyage were regarded as secret government documents. What do you think was the purpose of keeping such information a secret? Why would leaks of such information to another country have been perceived as being against national interests?

3 Europeans built overseas empires.

After their first discoveries, the Europeans began to take control over many of the areas they claimed. Their superior weapons, such as cannons and guns, and their ease in covering distances with their ships and their horses, helped enable a small number of Europeans to conquer large numbers of native peoples. Once in control of an area, Europeans thought of it as their colony. European nations soon came to see these colonies as crucial to their power and prestige.

Portugal established a far-flung trade empire.

Because Portugal did not have a large population, its overseas empire was based mainly on establishing and maintaining trading posts in strategic locations throughout the world. Early in the 16th century, the king of Portugal appointed Afonso de Albuquerque to crush the Muslim monopoly over the spice trade and establish Portuguese control. Under his leadership Portugal established control over the Indian Ocean and the spice trade in the early 1500s. The Portuguese also sailed to the coast of China, and in 1557 were granted a trading colony along the Chinese coast at Macao.

This engraving (1634) by the French artist Theodore de Bry portrays English settlers offering beads and knives to the people they met in Virginia.

However, the Portuguese monopoly of the spice trade was not to endure for long. Portugal became weak politically, and in 1580 the Spaniards took over the Portuguese government. The Dutch, through the work of spies, gained control of the Portuguese spice trade. Nonetheless, Portugal held on to colonies in China, India, Africa, and Brazil.

Spain established many settlements in the New World.

Spain, like Portugal, started establishing colonies by military conquest. Spanish adventurers succeeded in conquering two advanced empires—the Aztecs in Mexico and the Incas in South America.

Although the Spanish were bold and ruthless, their main advantage against the Aztecs and Incas was not military but biological. The Spanish unwittingly brought with them disease germs for scarlet fever, influenza, measles, smallpox, chicken pox, and the plague. The native peoples of the Americas had never been exposed to these diseases and had no resistance to them. Thus, these diseases swept through the Americas with deadly thoroughness. For example, the population of the Aztec Empire dropped from 10 million before 1517 to about 1 million by 1600.

Because Spain had a much larger population than Portugal, it was able to establish more secure colonies. Most settlers came from the poorer regions of Spain. They hoped to make their fortunes by establishing plantations on large land holdings.

England set up colonies in North America and achieved control over India.

The English built their first successful settlement on the American mainland at Jamestown, Virginia, in 1607. King James I of England charged the colonists to "digg, mine, and searche for all manner of mines of goulde [gold], silver, and copper."

However, these English colonists had all they could do to survive. Searching for riches was out of the question. Nevertheless, by 1640 about 60,000 English people had moved to the New World. Some were poor farmers who had gone into debt and been driven off their land. Others, such as the Puritans and Quakers, held religious views that made them subject to persecution in England. These people were looking to build a

BACKGROUND The European rulers were able to lay claim to as much land as their armies were able to defend. As Christians they felt they had the right to take the land of the pagan peoples they conquered.

showed such a route to be impractical.

3. caused both to claim overlapping regions of North America, leading to years of conflict

Main Ideas

If information about the route and purpose of voyages leaked out, other countries might use the information to get ahead of the country sponsoring the voyage.

3 Lesson Plan

Essential Learning Objective

Students will learn to identify some motives behind colonial expansion.

1 FOCUS AND MOTIVATE

Review with students the meanings of the words *colony* and *empire*. Have students make up sentences that use the words appropriately.

2 TEACH

List on the chalkboard the colonies held by England, France, Spain, Portugal, and the Netherlands, as you discuss this section.

GUIDED PRACTICE

Have students add names of the colonial regions on the world outline maps they used in Section 2. Ask volunteers to state the motives for colonizing each region.

Which nations colonized North America? (Spain, England, France, Netherlands)

OPTIONAL RETEACHING

Have each student write four questions about the main ideas of this section. Have them trade papers and answer each other's questions.

OPTIONAL ENRICHMENT

1. One hundred years ago people said that "the sun never set on the British Empire." Have students explain the meaning of this statement. (average)

2. Also for enrichment:

 Source Reading 20B

INDEPENDENT PRACTICE/ HOMEWORK

Assign the Section Review, Activities page 118, or Workbook page 80.

CLOSURE

Summarize by pointing out that by 1700 the political map of the world had changed dramatically. Europe, comprising only seven percent of the land mass of the earth, was well on its way to dominating the world.

Answers to Section 3 Review

Identify

Key Terms, People, and Places are defined on pages indicated in parentheses. Also see the Glossary and Biographical Dictionary.
British East India Company (378), Samuel de Champlain (378)

Main Ideas

1. It established trading posts in strategic locations throughout the

Empires and Trading Posts, Around 1700

Legend: British, Dutch, French, Spanish, Portuguese, European trading posts

 MAP STUDY The map above shows the empires of the world in 1700, along with their trading posts and territorial claims. Which European power claimed most of Latin America? Which two powers split control of North America?

new way of life for themselves based on their religious beliefs. Their spirit and determination made them ideal colonists. England became interested in the East, too, particularly as the power of Portugal declined. Through the enterprising efforts of the **British East India Company**, set up in 1600 as a private business with a special English government charter, England later gained control of wealthy trading posts in India. In time the English government took over the whole Indian subcontinent.

France built a fur-trading empire.

Jacques Cartier's voyage down the St. Lawrence River inspired France to build a New World empire. In 1608 the explorer **Samuel de Champlain** established the first permanent French settlement in North America at Quebec.

Furs were to France what gold was to Spain. Seeking new regions to trap and trade, the French

were among the first Europeans to explore the Great Lakes region. In 1673 Louis Joliet and Jacques Marquette paddled canoes from the Great Lakes into the Mississippi, and in 1682 Robert de la Salle traveled down the Mississippi to its mouth. De la Salle claimed for France all the land drained by the Mississippi river system, naming the territory Louisiana in honor of King Louis XIV.

However, the French dream of an American empire never came to pass. Unlike England, France did not allow its religious minorities to settle in the colonies. Few French Catholics had any incentive to leave their comfortable homes to settle in the cold northern regions of North America. Some French people did settle in the warmer lands of Louisiana and in the Caribbean colonies of Martinique, Guadeloupe, Tortuga, and Haiti, but never in the numbers that settled in the Spanish and the English colonies in the Americas.

ANSWER TO MAP STUDY Spain; Britain and France

BACKGROUND Joliet and Marquette traveled as far south on the Mississippi as the mouth of the Arkansas River at which point they were convinced that the Mississippi did indeed flow into the Gulf.

The Netherlands took control of Portugal's colonies.

The Netherlands, like Portugal, was a small country that looked to the sea for its livelihood. The Netherlands built itself up as one of the strongest trading nations in Europe. Although they were dominated by Spain during the 16th and early 17th centuries, the Dutch expanded their overseas commercial empire.

The Dutch took over much of the Portuguese East Indian spice trade and founded the Dutch East Indies Company in 1602. The Dutch East Indies Company was similar to that of the British, a private company with a charter and special trading rights granted by the Dutch government. The Dutch dominated this lucrative trade until the end of the 18th century.

In the New World the Dutch settled islands in the West Indies, such as Curaçao, as well as Dutch Guiana on the coast of South America. In North America the Dutch bought the island of Manhattan from a group of Native Americans in 1626 and set up a small trading colony that extended along the Hudson River from its mouth to present-day Albany. Like Portugal, the population of the Netherlands was too small to allow heavy settlement in their new colonies.

Section 3 Review

Identify British East India Company, Samuel de Champlain

Main Ideas
1. How did Portugal establish its empire?
2. Why was Spain more successful than Portugal in holding on to its colonies?
3. What made the English settlers in North America good colonists?
4. Why did France's colonies in North America fail to develop?
5. How did the Dutch trading colonies in the East and the West fare?

Critical Thinking
Making Hypotheses: Why do you think the Dutch had to rely more on the organization of native peoples for the success of their empires than the British or Spanish did?

4 The new discoveries brought many changes to Europe and the Americas.

Through their discoveries, Europeans encountered lands and peoples different from their own. They learned about new farm products and practices and about the true geography of the world. Contact among peoples led to staggering changes both for good and bad. The introduction of new foods led to rapid population increases in the Old World, but European diseases killed huge numbers of the New World's peoples. World trade grew rapidly, but the slave trade also greatly expanded.

As a result of conquests, Europeans acquired large amounts of gold and silver, which they shipped back to Europe from the colonies. This influx of money led to a **Commercial Revolution** that brought great changes in the European economy, including the growth of modern capitalism. However, these economic changes pushed many in the lower classes into deep poverty.

World trade expanded.

The discovery of new trade routes ended the monopoly long enjoyed by the Italians. Trade centers moved from Italy's Mediterranean ports to the north Atlantic ports of London, Amsterdam, and Antwerp.

Increased goods. From Asia and the Middle East came large shipments of spices, gems, paper, ivory, porcelain, textiles, and items new to Europe, including tea and coffee. Central and South America shipped gold and silver and introduced such agricultural products as tobacco, cocoa, vanilla, and corn to European markets. North America exported codfish, furs, wood, and turpentine. The West Indies produced sugar, molasses, rum, and indigo for trade. Africa sent hardwoods, ivory, gold, and ostrich feathers. The increased volume of goods led to booming business in the north Atlantic ports. From there the goods stimulated increased trade and industry throughout Europe.

Slavery. The slave trade became an increasingly important part of European commerce. Slavery had existed throughout the world for thousands of years, but with the European colonization of Africa

world, especially in the East.

2. Spain, unlike Portugal, had a large enough population to send many colonists to the New World.

3. Many English colonists had suffered religious persecution. They were determined to build a better life for themselves in North America, based on their spiritual beliefs.

4. France did not allow its religious minorities to settle in New France, and very few French Catholics wanted to leave France.

5. The Dutch took over Portugal's spice trade in the East. In the New World, the Dutch established colonies, but did not have the population for heavy settlement of North America.

Critical Thinking
Because the Dutch could not send large numbers of colonists, they had to rely on native peoples' interest in making profits to keep a hold on the spice monopoly. The British were able to set up successful colonies in both the East and the West because they had larger populations.

4 Lesson Plan

Essential Learning Objective
Students will learn to evaluate the significance of the Commercial Revolution.

1 FOCUS AND MOTIVATE

Suggest to students that most movements in history have their bright and dark sides. Explain that they will examine one of history's most important revolutions, the Commercial Revolution, to evaluate whether the benefits outweighed the costs.

A Key to History

TRADE, EXPLORATION, AND THE SPREAD OF DISEASE

What does each set of colored arrows show? Where and when did the Black Death first occur? Where and when is it last shown?

Throughout history, trade and exploration have not only been responsible for social and economic advances but also for the spread of disease. One of the most famous trade routes in all history, the Silk Road, brought contagious diseases from both the East and the West that devastated communities along its path. (See map.)

Certain diseases caused only minor illnesses in places where people, through repeated exposure, had developed an immunity. Sometimes, however, these same illnesses had a disastrous impact on a population that was exposed for the first time.

The most feared pestilence in European history was the Black Death, bubonic plague. As you read in Chapter 11, in 1347 the bubonic plague entered Europe from the Crimean Peninsula, carried on shipboard by infected rats from India and China. Because of widespread illness and death, trade declined. In the 14th and 15th centuries, as the Renaissance brought a revival of trade, successive waves of diseases swept through Europe.

The most extensive devastation from disease in the Western Hemisphere occurred when Europeans reached the Americas in the late 1400s. Before 1492 the Indians of the Americas had been almost completely isolated from European diseases. These Indians were extremely vulnerable to Old World germs, viruses, and parasites. As a consequence, whole areas were entirely depopulated by epidemics of such European diseases as smallpox and measles introduced by the explorers, fishermen, and sailors.

Diseases of the American Indians —polio, venereal syphilis, hepatitis, and yaws (a skin disease)—also spread to Europe. Some of these diseases were quickly carried by sailors throughout the rest of the world as part of this mutual transfer of killing disease.

REVIEW

1. What is the relationship between trade and the spread of disease?
2. Why did the discovery of North and South America lead to a decline in New World populations?

and the New World, the nature of slavery gradually changed.

The slave trade began to increase in the mid-1400s, when the Portuguese established extensive trade relations with Africa. At this time some Africans began selling their prisoners, usually taken in war from other African groups, to Europeans. Because of the colonization of the Americas, the European market for slaves expanded. Europeans who went to the New World needed help with the hard physical labor required to build new homes, clear and farm plantations, or mine ore.

Between the 17th and 19th centuries, about 20 million Africans were shipped to the Americas. The slaves traveled in filthy, crowded ships under conditions so bad that at least one-fourth of the slaves died on the voyages. In addition, the survivors often suffered excessive cruelty at the hands of their white owners. Such inhumane treatment was a result of a growing belief that slavery was not a temporary legal condition, as had formerly been the case, but a permanent status based on African birth or heritage. This attitude became the basis for the racial prejudice that developed in the United States and in certain European countries.

Capitalism grew in Europe and caused the Commercial Revolution.

Increased trade led to changes in the economic systems of Europe. You learned in Chapter 19 that the accumulation of wealth in Italy stimulated the growth of capitalism there. Likewise, as the centers of trade shifted to Spain and Portugal, and then to northern Europe, the influx of money led to more private investment. This shift in economic trends, based on the establishment of many new businesses, is called the Commercial Revolution. The Commercial Revolution resulted from an increase in Europe's money supply. It led to new business practices and new methods of producing goods.

Soon after the Spanish colonization of the New World, huge quantities of gold and silver were sent back to Spain. Because Spain spent this tremendous wealth on everything from Asian luxury goods to European manufactured cloth, the gold and silver, which was minted as coins, circulated throughout Europe. The huge influx of money stimulated capitalism and led to the introduction

BACKGROUND Remind students that Italians learned of many of these new business practices from the Muslims with whom they did business.

and refinement of new industries, such as banking and insurance.

One new business practice that developed during the Commercial Revolution was the **joint-stock company**. A person could gain part ownership in this type of company by buying one or more shares of its stock. If the company made a profit, each stockholder received a dividend. If there were no profits, the value of the shares went down. Because they often attracted many investors, joint-stock companies made it possible to gather together much larger amounts of money than any single merchant could amass alone. The Dutch East India Company and the British East India Company were both joint-stock companies.

The increased competition that developed among new manufacturing businesses led to changes in how goods were produced. During the Middle Ages, guilds controlled manufacturing and limited the quantities of goods produced. This kept the supply of goods low and ensured that all guild members would make a profit. With the increased money supply, markets grew, and new companies could increase their profits by producing goods on a larger scale. In addition, any labor-saving machines led to an increase in profits.

European countries followed mercantilist policies.

The growth of trade in Europe led the emerging nations to develop a new set of economic and political policies toward one another. This set of policies, followed by most of Europe between 1600 and 1700, became known as **mercantilism**. The foundation of mercantilism was the idea that to be strong, a country had to export more than it imported. Under these conditions, more gold and silver would flow into the country than out of it, producing a favorable balance of trade. To maintain such a trade balance, each country would try to sell as much as it could to other countries, buying as little as possible in return.

To stimulate foreign trade, a mercantilist government might aid export and shipping companies with loans or tax breaks. This would reduce the cost of selling goods abroad. The government might also help set up new local industries to manufacture products that formerly had been bought

2 TEACH

Underscore the mercantilist belief that it is better to export than import, and that wealth and power result from keeping gold and silver in the country. Explain that this idea has some weaknesses: inflation can hurt the value of gold and silver, making it wiser to store wealth in the form of factories and machinery; it may not be smart to manufacture at home what could more cheaply be bought abroad; and mercantilism limits economic freedom at home and in the colonies. Point out that a nearly opposite idea, free trade, is supported by many economists today.

GUIDED PRACTICE

On students' outline maps of the world, have them identify each country and their colonial empire using one color. Label products delivered to each colonial power. Repeat for all major colonial nations.

3 ASSESS AND CLOSE

ASSESS

What were two benefits and two costs of the Commercial Revolution? (benefits: end of Italian monopoly, increased goods; costs: slave trade, inflation)

OPTIONAL RETEACHING

Write *Nobles, Merchants,* and *Farmers* on the chalkboard. Ask the students how inflation affected each group. Students also may be assigned Activities reteaching page 120.

OPTIONAL ENRICHMENT

1. Students may be assigned Activities enrichment page 121.
2. Also for enrichment:

 Overhead Transparency 40

Assign the Section Review, the
Chapter Review items, Activities
page 119, or Workbook page 81.

CLOSURE

Tell students that the Commercial Revolution changed the lives of nobles, merchants, and farmers. It also provided the financial basis for the Age of Exploration. However, it created economic and political problems for future generations.

Answers to Section 4 Review

Identify

Key Terms, People, and Places are defined on pages indicated in parentheses. Also see the Glossary and Biographical Dictionary. Commercial Revolution (379), joint-stock company (381), mercantilism (381)

Main Ideas

1. spices, gems, paper, ivory, porcelain, textiles, coffee, tea, gold, silver, tobacco, cocoa, vanilla, corn, codfish, furs, wood, turpentine, sugar, molasses, rum, indigo, hardwoods, ostrich feathers

2. The influx of money led to an increase in private investments, which led to an increase in the new businesses spearheading the Commercial Revolution. New industries included banking and insurance. New production methods concentrated on producing goods on a larger scale.

3. The main goal of mercantilism was for a country to export more than it imported. The colonies contributed raw materials and were developed as closed markets for the mother country's goods.

4. A large influx of gold and silver from the New World caused inflation, a growing disparity between rich

from other countries. Colonies were important sources of raw materials for mercantilist nations. In addition, the colonies were developed as closed markets by the mother country. This meant that only the mother country could sell manufactured goods in its colonies, and colonists were not allowed to produce anything that the mother country exported even if it were cheaper to produce such goods in the colonies.

Inflation led to social unrest in many parts of Europe and ruined Spain.

Long-term inflation beset Europe in the 16th and 17th centuries. The original source of this inflation was the influx of gold and silver from the New World by way of Spain. As you have read, this increased the money in circulation, stimulated the economy, and induced Europeans to buy more goods. However, goods could not be produced fast enough to keep up with the demand. This low supply and high demand caused steady inflation in most countries in Europe.

This long-run inflation hurt some people and helped others. Merchants in the towns became richer because the goods they owned increased in price. As prices rose, people at the bottom of the economic heap became poorer and poorer. The growing disparity between the rich and the poor led to serious social tensions. Many poor farmers were thrown off their land, and so they came to cities in search of work or charity. Riots against high food prices became a common occurrence all over Europe.

Of all the European nations, Spain suffered the most harm in this age of inflation. It is an irony of history that Spain exploited the wealth of the Americas and then choked on it. Inflation means not only rising prices, but a decline in the value of money. Therefore, the coins minted from the gold and silver that arrived in Spain became worth less as time went on. As the amount of precious metals from the colonies began to decline in the 1600s, Spanish influence fell dramatically and the nation became a second-rate power in Europe.

A revolution in world ecology took place.

The sailing ships of the Age of Exploration tied all parts of the world together for the first time in human history. They carried not only people, but also plants, animals, and disease germs from one part of the world to another. This brought about the most significant change in ecology—the distribution of living things—in recorded history.

One result of the direct or indirect contact between people of different continents was the introduction of new food crops to all parts of the world. New World crops, including potatoes, corn, sweet potatoes, and manioc—a plant with a starchy root—became new staples in certain parts of Europe, Africa, and Asia. Tomatoes, peppers, beans, squash, pumpkins, vanilla, and cacao also came from the New World.

The European colonists also introduced such staples as wheat, rye, oats, and rice to the Americas. They brought with them from Europe many kinds of domesticated animals, including the donkey and the mule to carry heavy loads, the ox to pull the plow, cattle for meat and milk, as well as the pig, the goat, the horse, wool-bearing sheep, and barnyard chickens.

Section 4 Review

Identify Commercial Revolution, joint-stock company, mercantilism

Main Ideas

1. What were some of the goods exchanged between Europe and its colonies?
2. Tell how the increased money supply led to the Commercial Revolution in Europe. Describe some of the new industries and the new ways of producing goods that occurred.
3. What was the main goal of mercantilism? How did colonies contribute to this goal?
4. State the cause of inflation in Europe between 1550 and 1650. Describe some of its effects.
5. How did world ecology change as a result of the Age of Exploration?

Critical Thinking

Predicting Effects: Certain policies of the Spanish government seem to have worsened Spain's economic problems in the 16th and 17th centuries. For example, during this time Spain distributed vast amounts of tax-free land to rich nobles who converted farm fields to pasture for sheep. Predict at least two possible harmful effects that could result from such a policy.

HIGHLIGHTS OF CIVILIZATION

New Species in the New World

The explorers who discovered the Americas introduced Europeans to a whole new world of plants and animals. These explorers brought back exotic plants and reports of unusual insects and animals that excited the curiosity of nature lovers back home. In the late 1600s and early 1700s, people began to travel to the New World to learn more about these new species.

One of the most talented of these natural historians was a Dutch woman named Maria Sybilla Merian (1617–1717). Her first published work was a two-volume book of hand-colored engravings of the insects of Europe. This book included pictures of the metamorphosis of caterpillars into butterflies. Merian was among the first to publish studies of this process.

At age 51 Merian and her daughter traveled to the South American colony of Surinam (now spelled Suriname). Here she made detailed studies of the insects and plants that she observed in their natural habitats. Her lifelike paintings, which were later engraved and hand colored, were first published in 1705. They gave Europeans realistic images of America's tropical plants and insects. They were also among the first such paintings made from direct observation. The style of clear, accurate nature painting that Merian helped develop led to important advances in both science and art.

The development of a butterfly was recorded by Maria Sybilla Merian from egg to caterpillar to chrysalis to final, perfect form.

and poor, and the downfall of Spain as a world power.
5. Plants and animals were introduced into new areas.

Critical Thinking

Possible answers: an increase in food prices because of the reduced production of grain; the need for Spain to import food; unemployment and poverty among small farmers; growth of the cities, as farmers migrate to find jobs

HIGHLIGHTS OF CIVILIZATION

You may wish to obtain a copy of *The Art of Natural History: Animal Illustrators and Their Work* by S. Peter Dance, (The Overlook Press, 1978) or *The Book of Flowers* by Alice M. Coats, (Phaidon Press, 1973). Show the students some of the pictures from these books. Encourage students to discuss what a naturalist might learn from examining such pictures. Students may be curious to learn that before Merian and others like her began painting realistically, many artists who painted plants and animals did not study plants and animals in their own habitats and did not necessarily try to paint realistically. Often these painters relied on stories or legends about the animals instead of observation and produced paintings of animals more imaginary than real. You might show the work of Louis Renard, or samples of pictures from books called "bestiaries." Let students evaluate which type of work might be more useful to naturalists and why.

Ask students if they think that Merian was an unusual woman for her time. Encourage them to give reasons for their opinions. (Many students will realize that Merian was unusually independent for her time in traveling to Surinam on her own.

Answers to Test Yourself

Key Terms, People, and Places
The key terms, people, and places tested here were introduced in the chapter sections and reviewed in the Section Reviews. For definitions see the page references at the appropriate Section Reviews. Also see the Glossary and Biographical Dictionary.

Main Ideas
The main ideas tested here were introduced in the sections of this chapter and reviewed in the Section Reviews. For answers to these questions, see the appropriate Section Reviews.

Critical Thinking
1. More money would be changing hands for increased shipments of goods, and people would have had physical difficulty transporting large volumes of gold and silver to pay for the goods over long distances. In addition, because of the increase in trade, there would be an increase in investments. Credit could, therefore, have developed not only as a convenience, but as an investment tool as well.

2. Students might perceive that these explorers sought out wealth and fame, as well as glory for their countries. Many explorers also may have valued the vast amounts of knowledge the European world was gaining.

CHAPTER 20 REVIEW

Section Summaries

Section 1
Europeans found lands and trade routes previously unknown to them.
At the beginning of the 1400s, Europeans were mainly interested in finding new trade routes to the East. Improvements in navigation aided their search.

Section 2
Europeans explored the New World.
Magellan's ships reached the East by going west, discovering the vastness of the Pacific Ocean. The Portuguese explored Brazil, and the Spanish fanned out through the Americas. The English, French, and Dutch looked for a Northwest Passage to China.

Section 3
Europeans built overseas empires.
Portugal came to dominate the spice trade during the 1500s, and the Spanish established settlements in the Americas. England sponsored colonies in North America and built a trading empire in Asia. The French gained dominance for a time in the fur trade.

Section 4
The new discoveries brought many changes to Europe and the Americas.
The discovery of new trade routes to the East and of valuable resources in the New World led to a significant increase in world trade. The African slave trade also grew. Increased trade led to the growth of capitalism and the Commercial Revolution.

Test Yourself

Key Terms, People, and Places
Identify the significance of each of the following:

Section 1
a. Henry the Navigator
b. Vasco da Gama
c. Christopher Columbus
d. Treaty of Tordesillas

Section 2
a. Vasco de Balboa
b. Ferdinand Magellan
c. Northwest Passage

Section 3
a. British East India Company
b. Samuel de Champlain

Section 4
a. Commercial Revolution
b. joint-stock company
c. mercantilism

Main Ideas
Section 1
1. What were two improvements in sailing technology that aided exploration?

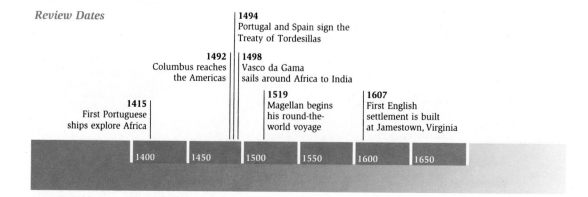

Review Dates

1415
First Portuguese ships explore Africa

1492
Columbus reaches the Americas

1494
Portugal and Spain sign the Treaty of Tordesillas

1498
Vasco da Gama sails around Africa to India

1519
Magellan begins his round-the-world voyage

1607
First English settlement is built at Jamestown, Virginia

1400 1450 1500 1550 1600 1650

2. How did Portugal's exploration of Africa lead to increased trade?

3. How did Columbus' mission affect Europe and the Americas?

4. In what way did Spain and Portugal try to resolve disputes over claims to newly discovered lands?

Section 2

1. Who were the Portuguese and Spanish explorers who came to the Americas and what did each of them accomplish?

2. What was Magellan's course as he sailed around the world, and why was this journey significant?

3. Discuss how the expeditions in search of the Northwest Passage would later influence the history of England and France.

Section 3

1. Describe how the Portuguese established their overseas empire.

2. In contrast with Portugal, why was Spain better able to hold on to its colonies?

3. Why were the English colonies in North America successful?

4. Why did the French colonies in North America fail to thrive?

5. What happened to the Dutch colonies both in the East and in the Americas?

Section 4

1. Name some of the goods exchanged between Europe and its colonies.

2. How did the increased money supply lead to the Commercial Revolution in Europe?

3. State the main goal of mercantilism and tell how the colonies contributed to this goal.

4. What was the cause of inflation in Europe between 1550 and 1650? What were some of the effects?

5. Tell how world ecology changed as a result of the Age of Exploration.

Critical Thinking

1. Assessing Cause and Effect Europe in the 16th century saw a great increase in the use of credit systems, bills of exchange, and the issuing of checks in business transactions. How do you think the increase in world trade might have caused these business practices to develop?

2. Recognizing Values During the Age of Exploration, many people set off to find new territory and trade routes for their countries. What values do you see supporting the quest for more knowledge and land? Support your answer with evidence.

Chapter Skills and Activities

Practicing Study and Research Skills
Organizing and Expressing Ideas in Written Form
A well-written paragraph begins with a strong, clear topic sentence. The rest of the paragraph serves to explain or detail that topic statement. Every sentence that follows should be related and supportive of the main topic presented. Any unnecessary ideas or facts should be omitted. Begin with the following topic statement: "The desire of modern nations to explore the moon and the planets of our solar system make our time similar to the Age of Exploration." Write a well-organized paragraph that develops this idea.

Linking Past and Present
Plan typical menus for breakfast, lunch, and dinner. List all of the ingredients found in each item on your menu, then research the continent where each ingredient originated.

Learning History Through Maps
By 1700 European countries had established trading colonies in port cities of Mughal India and Manchu China. Which empire had interests in each of the following: Bombay, Goa, Calcutta, Macao, and Cochin?

CRITICAL THINKING QUESTION LEVEL 1. average; 2. easy

21 The Reformation and National Power

OVERVIEW

This chapter covers the impact of the Protestant Reformation on Europe, including the loss of power by the Catholic Church, religious and political warfare, and the emergence of absolute monarchies.

PLANNING CHART

Section	Text Pages	Key Concept	Suggested Teaching Time
1 The Catholic Church lost power.	387–388	The Great Schism, a new secularism, and corruption caused the decline of the Catholic Church.	One day **Less time?** Summarize Section 1 for students and move directly to Section 2.
2 The Reformation divided Europe.	389–394	The challenge of Martin Luther, aimed at the Catholic Church, led to other religious protests and the division of Christendom into several parts.	Two days **More time?** Use *Source Reading 21A.*
3 Religious differences mixed with political conflicts.	394–397	Challenges to Catholic authority caused political leaders to take sides. War often resulted.	One day **More time?** Use *Overhead Transparency 41.*
4 France became Europe's leading power.	398–400	Religious and political turmoil brought a yearning for order and the rise of absolutism in France.	One day
5 Absolutist monarchies arose in central and eastern Europe.	400–404	Absolutism in the 17th and 18th centuries spread east to Austria, Prussia, and Russia.	Two days **More time?** Use *Overhead Transparency 42* and *Source Reading 21B.*

ANCILLARIES

Materials that may be used with this chapter to reinforce, reteach, enrich, and assess learning are pictured on the following pages.

Teacher's Resource File

ACTIVITIES

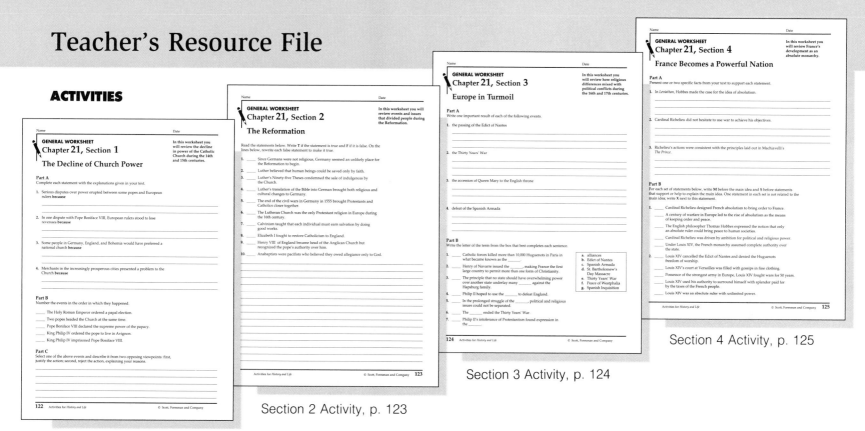

Section 2 Activity, p. 123

Section 3 Activity, p. 124

Section 4 Activity, p. 125

Section 1 Activity, p. 122

Section 5 Activity, p. 126

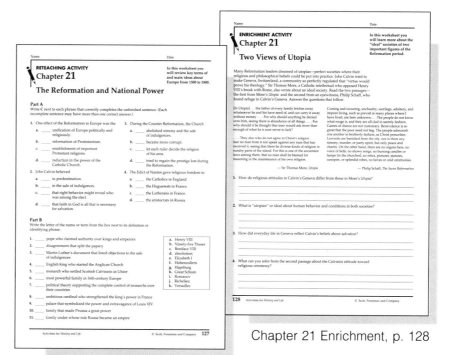

Chapter 21 Reteaching, p. 127

Chapter 21 Enrichment, p. 128

Teacher's Resource File

GEOGRAPHY SKILLS

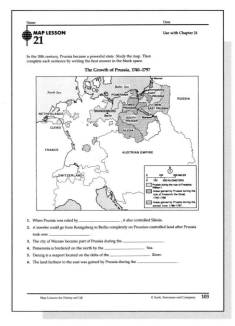

Chapter 21 Geography
Worksheet/Map, pp. 43–44

Chapter 21 Map Lesson, p. 103

TESTS

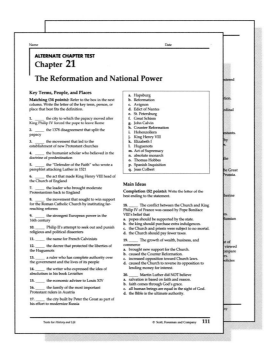

Chapter Test, pp. 109–110

Alternate Chapter Test, pp. 111–112

Other Optional Ancillaries

WORKBOOK

WORKSHEET
Chapter 21, Section 1

The Church Loses Power

In this worksheet you will review terms dealing with what you have learned about the Catholic Church.

Read the clues below and complete the crossword puzzle.

Across
1. the traditional home of the papacy
4. businessmen; a class that challenged Church power
8. papal city in 1309
8. the kind of ideas fostered by the rise of cities
10. the method of choosing one pope that was demanded by the Holy Roman Emperor
11. church document said to free sinners from punishment after death
12. name given to the 1378 division in the Church (two words)
13. supreme Church authority whose status had fallen by 1417

Down
2. a period of cultural rebirth in the Italian cities
3. age when the Church reached the height of its power
5. churchmen claimed by Boniface to be above royal law
6. an urban business group whose activities were forbidden by the medieval Church
7. the kind of power Boniface claimed for the pope
7. the kind of church that people in England and Germany began to want
9. the arrogant pope who declared the pope's absolute power; _____ VIII

Section 1 Worksheet, p. 82

WORKSHEET
Chapter 21, Section 2

Reformation Leaders

In this worksheet you will review important Reformation leaders and their beliefs.

Part A
Identify the Protestant religious leader most likely to make each statement by writing L for Luther or C for Calvin.
1. _____ Those who would be saved were "elected" or "predestined" by God.
2. _____ Salvation is based on faith alone, and faith comes through God's grace.
3. _____ All believers are priests in their own right.
4. _____ Correct behavior might produce clues as to who is among the elect.
5. _____ Indulgences have no value since sins can be forgiven only by faith.
6. _____ The Bible is the ultimate religious authority, and people can interpret it themselves.
7. _____ All people deserve punishment in hell.

Part B
Only three of the four items in each group are related in some way. Circle the item that does not belong and explain how the remaining three items are related.

1. Luther   Calvin   King Henry VIII   Pope Leo X

2. church services   pilgrimages   epistles   indulgences

3. Bible   simony   printing press   Ninety-five Theses

4. Counter Reformation   Council of Trent   Ignatius Loyola   Anglican Church

Section 2 Worksheet, p. 83

WORKSHEET
Chapter 21, Section 3

Religious and Political Conflict

In this worksheet you will review 16th- and 17th-century European conflicts that were both political and religious.

Part A
Read the statements below. Write T if the statement is true and F if it is false. On the lines below, rewrite each false statement to make it true.
1. _____ Philip II used the Inquisition to destroy Protestantism.
2. _____ The Hapsburg family was the strongest power in Europe during the 16th century.
3. _____ The Holy Roman Emperor Charles V had absolute control of the rulers of Germany during the Reformation period.
4. _____ Queen Mary advanced Protestantism, and Elizabeth I promoted Catholicism in England.

Part B
Read the following excerpts from the Edict of Nantes and complete the exercises.

VI. We permit those of the so-called Reformed Religion to live and abide in all the towns and districts of this our Realm . . . free from inquisition, molestation or compulsion to do anything in the way of religion, against their conscience . . . .

XVIII. We forbid all our subjects . . . to take children of this religion, by force or persuasion to be baptized or confirmed in the Catholic Apostolic and Roman Church.

XXVII. Members of this religion are capable of holding any office or position in this Realm.

1. Identify the "Reformed Religion" mentioned in the Edict.

2. What is one action that the Edict specifically forbade?

3. What do you think the Edict means by the phrase "free from inquisition"?

5. Henry IV of France reportedly remarked after converting to Catholicism that "Paris is worth a Mass." What do you think he meant?

Section 3 Worksheet, p. 84

WORKSHEET
Chapter 21, Section 4

Absolute Monarchy in France

In this worksheet you will review the development of France as an absolute monarchy and the leading nation in Europe.

Part A
Complete each statement with the explanations given in your text.
1. Absolutism appealed to Europeans in the 17th century **because**

2. In *Leviathan*, Hobbes claimed that human beings needed absolutism **because**

3. Louis XIII allowed Cardinal Richelieu to act with almost absolute power over France **because**

4. France fought the Thirty Years' War **because**

5. At the end of Louis XIV's reign, France was left with an empty treasury **because**

6. Louis XIV took away freedom of worship from the Huguenots **because**

Part B
Number the events in the order in which they happened.
_____ Richelieu became chief minister of France.
_____ Henry IV died.
_____ Louis XIV cancelled Edict of Nantes.
_____ Cardinal Mazarin died.
_____ *Leviathan* was published.

Section 4 Worksheet, p. 85

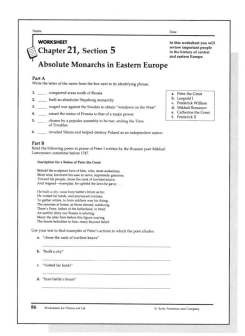

WORKSHEET
Chapter 21, Section 5

Absolute Monarchs in Eastern Europe

In this worksheet you will review important people in the history of central and eastern Europe.

Part A
Write the letter of the name from the box next to its identifying phrase.

1. _____ conquered areas south of Russia
2. _____ built an absolutist Hapsburg monarchy
3. _____ waged war against the Swedes to obtain "windows on the West"
4. _____ raised the status of Prussia to that of a major power
5. _____ chosen by a popular assembly to be tsar, ending the Time of Troubles
6. _____ invaded Silesia and helped destroy Poland as an independent nation

a. Peter the Great
b. Leopold I
c. Frederick William
d. Mikhail Romanov
e. Catherine the Great
f. Frederick II

Part B
Read the following poem in praise of Peter I written by the Russian poet Mikhail Lomonosov sometime before 1747.

Inscription for a Statue of Peter the Great

Behold the sculpture here of him, who, most audacious,
Most wise, forewent his ease to serve, supremely gracious,
Toward his people: chose the rank of lowliest knave,
And reigned—exemplar, he upheld the laws he gave; . . .

He built a city, oose bore battle's brunt as he;
He visited far lands, and journeyed overseas;
To gather artists, to train soldiers was his doing,
The enemies at home, as those abroad, subduing;
There's Peter, father of the fatherland, in brief;
An earthly deity our Russia is adoring,
Many the altar fires before this figure soaring,
The hearts beholden to him, many beyond belief.

Use your text to find examples of Peter's actions to which the poet alludes.

a. "chose the rank of lowliest knave"

b. "built a city"

c. "visited far lands"

d. "bore battle's brunt"

Section 5 Worksheet, p. 86

SOURCE READINGS

Source Reading 21A
Source Reading 21B

OVERHEAD TRANSPARENCIES

Overhead Transparency 41
Overhead Transparency 42

TEST GENERATOR

40 multiple-choice questions for Chapter 21

Chapter

21

The Reformation and National Power

1500–1800

1500	
1517	Reformation begins with Luther's protest
1598	Edict of Nantes is signed
1648	Thirty Years' War ends
1700	
1800	

On October 31, 1517, Martin Luther, a German priest, is said to have nailed a document to the door of the Castle Church of Wittenberg. It was a custom of the time to announce debates in this way. Written in Latin, the document attacked the Church practice of selling indulgences—documents freeing sinners from punishment after death if they paid the Church. Luther's protest began an important movement called the Reformation.

Historians disagree about the significance of the Reformation for Europe and for world history. They do agree that one result was to spread intense religious feelings among the peoples of Europe. Not everyone, however, had the same religious beliefs. As a consequence, the Reformation split the world of western Christendom in two ways. First, it created a deep and lasting division between Catholics and Protestants. Second, it led to the rise of national churches, both Catholic and Protestant, controlled by secular rulers. Whether caused by religion or not, power shifted from church to state—another step in the rise of the modern nation-state.

The Reformation had two basic phases: the Protestant Reformation and the Catholic Counter Reformation. In both phases leaders tried to bring Christian practices closer to Christian ideals. Catholics believed that reforms had to take place within the Church, but they did not support changes in church law. Protestants believed that there could be no reforms without major changes in church law. So the Protestants set up their own churches. They also rejected the authority of the pope and his right to interpret the Bible for all Christians.

The events of the Reformation were closely tied to political and social conflict. Kings and queens used religious differences to gain political ends, and religious leaders looked to rulers for support of their religious movements.

386

Elizabeth I, the queen of England from 1558 to 1603, strengthened Protestantism in her country at a time when religious change was occurring throughout Europe.

Lesson Plan

Essential Learning Objective

Students will learn to explain reasons for the decline of the Catholic Church.

1 FOCUS AND MOTIVATE

Write the word *catholic* on the board. Ask students what the word means. (universal) Explain that with few exceptions all Christians in western Europe before 1517 were members of the Catholic Church.

2 TEACH

Mention reasons for the decline of the Catholic Church. Clarify corruption and outside reform. Explain power politics, secularism, and the schism.

GUIDED PRACTICE

Have the students write a short essay explaining how secularism led to a decline in the influence of the Church.

Reading Preview

In this chapter you will learn how the Reformation brought religious and political changes to Europe.

1. The Catholic Church lost power.

2. The Reformation divided Europe.

3. Religious differences mixed with political conflicts.

4. France became Europe's leading power.

5. Absolutist monarchies arose in central and eastern Europe.

1 *The Catholic Church lost power.*

The medieval period had been truly an age of faith, a time when the Catholic Church, led by the papacy, reached the height of its political power. Paradoxically, at the height of its authority, people began to question the Church. The Church's decline came about for several reasons: power politics, the rise of cities and secular ideas, corruption in the Church, and calls for reform in many parts of Europe.

387

Answers to Section 1 Review

Identify

Key Terms, People, and Places are defined on pages indicated in parentheses. Also see the Glossary and Biographical Dictionary. Boniface VIII (388), Avignon (388), Great Schism (388)

Main Ideas

1. whether the churches should have to pay taxes; whether the priests were subject to royal law
2. growth of wealth, business, and

Power politics affected the Church.

The Church became involved in the politics of nations, and some popes saw themselves as having greater power than any king or emperor. None displayed more arrogance than **Pope Boniface VIII** (1294–1303), who once said that people who were healthy, rich, and lucky were already in paradise. Boniface got into serious disputes with several rulers over whether churches should pay taxes and whether priests had to obey royal law like any other citizen. He declared that the Church and priests were subject to no mortal and that the pope had absolute power over everything and everyone on earth.

King Philip IV of France (1285-1314) became so angry at this that he sent armed men to capture the pope in his palace in Rome. Boniface was thrown into prison, but the people of Rome rescued him a few days later. Boniface, in his eighties, died a few weeks later. Philip then forced the next pope to leave Rome and live in **Avignon** [à vē nyôn'], France, in 1309. During its 65 years at Avignon, the papacy became very unpopular, and many people saw it as corrupt and greedy. Also, many Europeans thought that the popes were puppets of the French kings and, therefore, just part of international politics.

In 1378 a disagreement that came to be called the **Great Schism** actually split the papacy. When the papacy attempted to return to Rome, the French popes objected. As a result, Italian cardinals elected an Italian pope, who ruled at Rome, and French cardinals chose a French pope, who remained at Avignon. Each pope claimed to be the only true head of the Church. Each enjoyed the support of several European rulers, but many faithful believers in Christianity held them in contempt. The dispute finally ended when the Holy Roman Emperor intervened and demanded the election of one single pope in 1417. By that time, however, the long conflict had significantly lowered the status of the papacy.

New forces challenged the Church.

The people of the increasingly wealthy cities of Europe often opposed the Church on several grounds. For one thing, as the merchants of the Italian cities became wealthier, they often became more interested in material possessions than in spiritual concerns. We have already seen the new culture of the Italian cities, called the Renaissance. Church leaders also became part of this Renaissance culture and became just as secular in their ways. Their behavior undermined basic Church doctrines.

The growth of business and commerce also presented a problem for the Church. During the Middle Ages, the Church had looked upon some business activities, such as lending money for interest, as sinful. The rising merchant class did not like Church laws that forbade such activities. What especially angered many people, though, was that many Church leaders were greedy moneylenders themselves. They broke Church laws rather than observing them and thus acquired much wealth.

To many people the Church was simply another secular state, one interested only in power politics and material wealth. Furthermore, the growing wealth of the Church led to greed and corruption from within. The sale of **indulgences,** documents that were said to free sinners from punishment after death, angered many lay people throughout Europe. Worse still for many Europeans, most of the money they gave the Church was sent to Rome. Some people in countries such as Germany, England, and Bohemia began to think it might be better to have a national church, run by members of their own communities.

Section 1 Review

Identify Boniface VIII, Avignon, Great Schism, indulgences

Main Ideas

1. What political issues did the Church become involved in?
2. What forces challenged Church power in the 15th century?

Critical Thinking

Assessing Cause and Effect: How did most people during the Middle Ages regard the Church? How might the changes described, such as the schism and money lending, have affected your devotion to the Church during the 14th century? How might secular activities undermine basic Church doctrines in general?

2 The Reformation divided Europe.

Historians usually say that Germany was the natural place for the Reformation to begin for two reasons. First, since the 14th century, Germany was a center for deep and serious religious feelings. Many new religious groups sprang up that taught people how best to understand the Bible and the word of God. Everywhere religious symbols, such as public crucifixes, abounded. Many devout people thought that the Church had been corrupted and had to be purified.

Second, Germany contained hundreds of independent states that resisted outside control. The pope in Rome, located so far away from Germany, had difficulty keeping these states under papal jurisdiction and collecting money from them. These religious and political conditions made Germany ripe for revolt against the universal Church. Only a spark was needed, and an obscure monk named **Martin Luther** supplied it.

Luther led the Reformation and started his own church.

Martin Luther was born in 1483 to an affluent German family in the mining business. Although young Luther studied law at a university, he became deeply religious and decided to become a monk. A brilliant man, Luther became a professor of religion at the University of Wittenberg in Saxony. During his years in a monastery and as a teacher, he studied the problem of salvation, or how to save one's soul from hell. Luther felt himself filled with evil thoughts and worried that human beings could never be saved from corruption. How could God, he thought, the all-powerful stern judge, ever forgive a wicked humanity?

Luther's ideas. Luther soon saw the way out of the problem. A close reading of St. Paul's epistles led Luther to the idea that salvation was based on faith alone, an idea called justification by faith. Because human beings were so weak, he said, their faith had to be granted by God through a miracle. Therefore, according to Luther, salvation was a matter directly between an individual and God. It did not require the help of priests or church ritual.

True believers might even sin and still be saved. As Luther once said, "Sin bravely and believe more strongly."

Luther's ideas are the basis of all Protestant thought. Three basic ideas lie at the heart of Lutheranism. The first idea is that salvation is by faith alone, and faith comes through God's grace. Therefore, every individual has a direct relationship with God. Second, Lutherans believe that the Bible is the ultimate authority, and people can interpret it for themselves. Third, they believe that all human beings are equal in the sight of God, and therefore, all believers are priests in their own right. This is called the priesthood of all believers.

Luther's views brought him into direct conflict with the Church. Catholic doctrine held that people's souls were saved only through the Church. Luther thought that rituals such as going to church services and going on pilgrimages could not bring salvation. Luther objected strongly, too, to the sale of indulgences, especially when Pope Leo X sent an agent to Wittenberg to raise money. The agent, a monk named Johann Tetzel, was an expert salesman. His little jingle has become famous, "So soon

Martin Luther's objections to the practices of the Catholic Church led him to post his Ninety-five Theses on these church doors in Wittenberg, Germany.

commerce from outside, and corruption from within

Critical Thinking

People looked to the Church for both spiritual and political leadership. Problems and divisions in the Church might lower respect for and devotion to it, and weaken basic Church doctrines.

2 Lesson Plan

Essential Learning Objectives

Students will learn to:
- distinguish between the teachings of Martin Luther and John Calvin.
- state the meaning of the Counter Reformation.

Provide a framework for the lesson by clarifying with students the fundamental differences between Catholicism (belief in Jesus as the son of God and the pope as the head of the Church); and Protestantism (belief in Jesus as the son of God but independence from the pope as head of the Church). Explain that the split in the 1500s between Catholics and Protestants is the focus of this lesson.

- Divide the chalkboard vertically into four sections. Write *Lutheran* in the first section, *Calvinist* in the second, *Anglican* in the third, and *Anabaptist* in the fourth. Elicit the beliefs of each group from students and record them under the correct heading. Some of the concepts students should include are salvation by faith, interpretation of the Bible, and predestination.

- Discuss the Catholic Counter Reformation and the contribution of Ignatius Loyola. Explain that there were Catholics sincere about reforming the Catholic Church from within. Point out that Loyola and his followers established schools throughout the world.

GUIDED PRACTICE

Have students copy the following pairs of terms and write a sentence that states the difference *or* the relationship between the two items: Reformation and Counter Reformation; indulgences and grace; Protestant and Lutheran; Huguenots and Puritans; Act of Supremacy and Anglican Church.

the coin in the basin rings, then right to heaven the soul springs." Luther declared that Tetzel was "an ignorant and impudent" monk and, besides, indulgences had no value since sins could be forgiven only by faith in Christ's sacrifice.

In 1517, as you read in the chapter introduction, Luther nailed up a list of his arguments against the sale of indulgences. These Ninety-five Theses, as they were called, caused a great stir. Instantly translated into German and printed on printing presses, the Theses spread rapidly throughout Germany. Luther then publicly burned indulgences in the main square of Wittenberg. These two events ignited the fires of the Reformation in Europe. The **Reformation**, a movement originally aimed at re-

Luther (left) enjoyed the protection of John Frederick the Magnanimous, elector of Saxony (center). This painting (1530) includes some associates of Luther.

form within the Roman Catholic Church, led to the establishment of new Protestant churches.

Luther's new church. Luther finally declared in 1520 that no clergy of any kind could aid in salvation. In God's eyes, said Luther, all human beings were equal—priest, pope, or lay people. The Bible alone was the key to salvation, and through faith in its teaching, people might find God's grace. By this time at least 30,000 copies of Luther's writings were in print. In 1521 the Holy Roman Emperor summoned Luther to a meeting. Told to retract his statements, Luther said that he could not because it was "neither safe nor right to go against conscience." Shortly afterward, the pope excommunicated him.

Luther's life was soon endangered by Catholic forces, but several German princes came to his aid. Protected by the powerful ruler of Saxony, Luther began to organize a new church. His translation of the Bible into German was especially important because it allowed lay people to read and interpret it for themselves. This translation also became the basis for the modern German language.

The spread of Luther's ideas. A number of princes of the independent German states became Lutheran. Some used the new religion to gain political independence from the Holy Roman Emperor, in name the head of the German states, but most converted on grounds of conscience. All, however, seized Church lands and drove out Catholic priests. The emperor, Charles V, and other Germans remained Catholic. When they tried to restrict Lutheranism, several of the Lutheran princes protested. This expression gave rise to the word Protestant.

Disputes between the two religious groups quickly led to civil wars. People fought on religious grounds as well as political ones. After much bloodshed the leaders of both sides reached an agreement in 1555. It said that each prince could choose between Catholicism and Lutheranism. Their subjects would then follow that choice. In this way the divisions between Protestants and Catholics became hardened for several centuries.

Luther's ideas spread to many other parts of Europe, particularly Scandinavia. There Protestantism gained the support of the governments of Sweden and Denmark, which included Norway at that time. Not all Protestants agreed completely with Luther's ideas however. During the 16th century, three other major Protestant groups—Calvinists, Anabaptists, and Anglicans—came into existence. Each played an important role in European and world history.

Calvin started a new branch of Protestantism.

Born in 1509, **John Calvin** was a French lawyer and humanist scholar. Having had a sudden conversion to Protestantism, Calvin became a minister but fled from persecution in France, where Catholicism remained strong. In 1536 he visited the Protestant city of Geneva—in present-day Switzerland. Settling down, Calvin quickly became the outstanding pastor in the city. By 1541, when the people of Geneva asked him to lead the church and state, he did so.

Calvin's ideas. Although Calvin had been inspired by Luther, he disagreed with him—especially on the matter of salvation. To Calvin, God was so powerful, so remote, that human beings could never understand God's purposes. Humanity, said Calvin, was so completely corrupted by sin that no good works could bring salvation. He believed that all people deserved eternal punishment in hell.

Still, Calvin believed that God chose some select souls to be saved while the rest of humanity suffered in hell. This doctrine, called predestination, is the core of Calvin's ideas about God and humanity. Since God had already decided who was to be saved and who was to be damned, a person could do nothing to change this decision. Because nobody knew how God had decided in each case, a person's purpose in life, therefore, was not to seek salvation but to honor God. Anyone destined for salvation could be expected to behave righteously. Thus, correct behavior might be a clue as to who was among the elect. Calvinists therefore strongly emphasized right behavior.

Calvin's church. At Geneva, Calvin set up a government that strictly controlled not only church affairs, but also politics, education, amusement, and family life. Calvinism taught that one's work was actually part of one's religious life. Christian virtues included hard work, moral living,

This classroom sketch of John Calvin, done by one of his students, is one of the few likenesses that exist. Calvin thought of art with contempt and suspicion.

and thrift. According to Calvin, his followers had certain obligations in the world—among them the obligation to teach God's word and laws. These ideas are still very much a part of Protestantism.

Only members of Calvin's church participated in the government, but all believers had a voice in their church and government. The people chose their own church ministers who, together with secular leaders, formed a council that ran the state. Strong communities in which everyone knew their place and worked to honor God are the hallmarks of the Calvinist communities. All communities had constitutions and were somewhat democratic—ideas that became very important for the future.

The spread of Calvin's ideas. Calvinism spread rapidly among the middle classes of Europe. City people and smaller landowners liked the order that Calvinism gave to the world. They saw that their hard work was really part of God's plan, and they warmly embraced Calvin's ideas. Calvinism also appealed to many in the working classes who objected to their poor living and working conditions. Strengthened by Calvinist ideas, such people rebelled during the 16th and 17th centuries.

Other new churches were soon set up, based on the Calvinist model. The Dutch Reformed Church and the Presbyterian Church, begun by John Knox in Scotland, were two examples. In France, Calvinists were known as Huguenots [hü′gə notz] and, as we shall see, almost took political control of that country in the 1500s. Probably the most famous Calvinists went to the English colonies in America. These Calvinists, the Puritans, founded most of the New England colonies and governed them according to Calvin's rules. These colonies were living models of the ideas of constitutional government.

A third branch of the Reformation arose.

A group of religious sects loosely grouped under the name Anabaptists formed the third branch of the Reformation. The name comes from a belief that only adults should receive baptism, not children. Baptism is a ceremony in which sin is symbolically washed away and Christianity accepted. Catholics, Lutherans, and Calvinists alike baptized children, because they worried that the souls of infants who died would not get to heaven. Anabaptists, or "re-baptizers," thought that baptism implied faith in God through Jesus Christ, and only an adult could be capable of that faith. This belief and many others distinguished Anabaptists.

For the most part, Anabaptists were peasants and poor townsfolk, largely uneducated, who saw the existing church as corrupt because it did not obey God's word as set down in the Bible. For the most part, Anabaptists believed in the priesthood of all believers. Also, church and state were separate in Anabaptist thinking. For that reason and because they lived strictly by the Bible, Anabaptists took no oaths to any state, refused to perform public service, and were pacifists, refusing to fight wars or kill other people. They lived in small communities in which everyone shared goods and land.

Regarded as threats to society by Catholics and Protestants alike, Anabaptists were persecuted. Tens of thousands were tortured and killed for their beliefs. Driven out of much of Germany, Anabaptists fled to the Netherlands, England, and Bohemia. From there many went to the English colonies in the 17th century. German and Dutch Mennonites and English Quakers are among the best known Anabaptist groups to emigrate to the New World. Their ideas became very important in English and American history, especially their concepts of voluntary groups and democratic values.

Henry VIII, famous for establishing the English monarch as head of the Church of England, sat for this portrait by Hans Holbein the Younger about 1537.

England broke with Rome.

The fourth branch of the Protestant Reformation arose in England. During the early years of the Reformation, most of England remained loyal to the Catholic Church. **King Henry VIII,** who ruled from 1509 to 1547, even wrote a pamphlet in 1521 attacking Luther. For this the pope rewarded Henry VIII with the title "Defender of the Faith," a title that still appears on English coinage to this day.

Henry's quarrel with the pope. Soon afterward, however, Henry wanted the pope to dissolve his marriage to Catherine of Aragon because their only child was a daughter, Mary. The king declared that he needed a male heir to the throne of England. When the pope refused the English monarch's request, Henry chose a new archbishop of Canterbury who, in 1533, ruled that Catherine was not Henry's lawful wife. Henry was now free to marry Anne Boleyn, who he hoped would produce a male heir. However, Anne also gave birth to a daughter, Elizabeth.

3 | ASSESS AND CLOSE

ASSESS

1. What is the chief difference between Lutherans and Calvinists? (Lutherans believe in salvation by faith, but Calvinists stress predestination.)
2. What distinguished a supporter of the Reformation from a supporter of

Henry's acts against the pope in Rome had widespread support among the English clergy, who, like the Germans, resented Rome's influence in English church affairs. In this way, the English break with Rome was nationalistic in much the same way as the German break.

Henry's breach with Rome widened, and in 1534 he had Parliament issue the **Act of Supremacy**. This act made Henry VIII head of the Church in England. He then abolished monasteries and took much of the Catholic Church's property. One of the few changes he made in the religion was to use English instead of Latin in the services.

The Anglican Church and the Puritans. Edward VI was the son of Henry VIII and his third wife, Jane Seymour. A sickly child, Edward died at age 16, and Henry's daughter Mary became queen in 1553. As you will learn in the next section, Mary was a loyal Catholic who severely persecuted English Protestants, leading people to call her "Bloody Mary." **Elizabeth I**, who succeeded Mary, brought back moderate Protestantism. Parliament then passed laws that began a national church of England. To this day the head of this Anglican Church of England, as it is called, is the king or queen of England, not the pope.

Most English people were happy with the Anglican Church, but others objected because certain Catholic symbols and rituals were still used. Basing their ideas on Calvinism, these English reformers wanted the Church of England to be so pure that they were called Puritans. Unhappy in England, many of them went to the colonies in America. Puritans who remained at home rebelled against the royal government, overthrew it, and ruled England for more than 15 years.

The Anglican Church and the Irish. Even more unhappy were the Irish, whom the English had partly conquered in the 12th century. England never fully controlled Ireland—in part because the Irish continually fought against English rule. Relations grew worse when Henry VIII established a Protestant "Church of Ireland" in the 1530s. Because most of the Irish remained Catholic, the seeds of bitter religious conflict were now added to the Irish-English struggle.

During the reign of Elizabeth I, the Irish rebelled three times. Each time they were brutally defeated.

Much later, after 1690, the English settled Scottish Calvinists in the six northern counties of Ireland called Ulster. Bitter conflict between Protestants and Catholics still remains a feature of life in Northern Ireland today.

The effects of the Reformation spread.

The time of the Reformation was an era when religious feeling and expression gained a new momentum in Europe. After years in which secular ideas had begun to dominate people's minds, religion came to the fore.

The Counter Reformation. The Renaissance spirit of free inquiry had led to questions about religion. Erasmus, the acclaimed Dutch scholar, criticized religious hypocrisy and the worship of images, but he felt that the Catholic Church could reform itself from within. Partly in response to this kind of thinking and partly in response to the spread of Protestantism, the Roman Catholic Church sought to win people back with far-reaching reforms, a movement that became known as the **Counter Reformation**.

One reform was the founding of new groups to strengthen the Church through teaching and missionary work. Most famous was the Jesuit Order, made an official part of the Church in 1541. Ignatius Loyola [ig nā′shəs loi ō′lə] (1491–1556), a native of Spain and the founder of this movement, had been a professional soldier fighting in the service of Spain when he was severely wounded. While recovering in a hospital, Loyola decided to dedicate his life to God and Church. The Jesuit Order became known for its schools and its missions, with which it won many people to the Church.

In 1542 Pope Paul III (1534–1549) called the Council of Trent to deal with Church problems and suggest reforms. Delegates, meeting from 1545 to 1563, upheld all existing Roman Catholic doctrine. Specifically, the Council upheld the doctrine that final religious authority stemmed from both the Bible and Church traditions. For Catholics, good works as defined by the Church remained the route to salvation. However, the Council ended such things as simony—the selling of Church positions—and the abuse of indulgences. It also improved Church administration and education and reformed life in the monasteries.

The Catholic Counter Reformation, especially the work of the Jesuits, was very successful. By the 17th century, the Roman Catholic Church had stopped the spread of Protestantism in France. It won back Hungary and Poland and kept Catholicism strong in Bavaria, Austria, Ireland, and the southern Netherlands.

Widespread effects. The Reformation spread the ideas of democracy and representative government. The importance of lay people in church government increased, particularly among Calvinists, and this idea of self-government carried over into politics. Calvinism also glorified work, thrift, and profits, beliefs that led to the middle class gaining new dignity and power.

In addition, the Reformation encouraged education. Although religious intolerance, wars, and persecution of unpopular religions accompanied this era, in the long run, the Reformation aided religious tolerance and freedom. However, the 1,000-year-old unity of western Christendom had split. Protestants and Catholics were all Christians, but they were no longer joined in the same church. Northern Europe became mostly Protestant, and southern Europe remained mostly Catholic. That same division still exists today.

Section 2 Review

Identify Reformation, Martin Luther, John Calvin, King Henry VIII, Act of Supremacy, Elizabeth I, Counter Reformation

Main Ideas
1. What ideas of Martin Luther led to the Reformation?
2. Describe the main beliefs of Calvinism.
3. What distinguished the Anabaptists from other Protestants?
4. Why did England break with Rome?
5. What were some of the religious and secular effects of the Reformation?

Critical Thinking
Assessing Cause and Effect: Consider the following statement: "The Reformation probably would not have occurred were it not for the Renaissance and the Age of Exploration." Do you agree or disagree with this statement? Support your answer with evidence.

3 Religious differences mixed with political conflicts.

During the 16th century and into the 17th, Europe was in turmoil. Economic systems changed rapidly. Money from the New World poured into Europe causing severe inflation, and the poor grew ever poorer—often unable to buy food or find decent housing. Old patterns of farming and manufacturing broke down, leaving people uncertain about how to live. When the Reformation occurred, it fanned the flames of religious hatreds. Finally, political struggles grew more severe, because they often had religious tones.

Spanish power threatened Europe.

In the 16th century, the **Hapsburg** family was the strongest power in Europe. They ruled central Europe, Spain, southern Italy, French Burgundy, and the Netherlands. From 1516 to 1556, one ruler held all these lands plus large tracts of the New World. Charles V, grandson of Ferdinand and Isabella of Spain, not only held all these lands but, at age 19, was elected Holy Roman Emperor. By 1519 his power, in theory, stretched across Europe. The Holy Roman Emperor ruled in name only, however, for Charles could not control the independent rulers of Germany.

To counteract the power of Charles V, several states banded together against him. Although not a new idea, the principle underlying the alliances came to be called "the balance of power," which meant that no one country should have overwhelming power over the others.

In 1556 Charles gave up his throne and retired to a monastery on the coast of Spain. He was in failing health and had grown tired of trying to hold his vast empire together. Austria went to his brother Ferdinand I, who became Holy Roman Emperor in 1558. Spain and the rest of the lands went to his son Philip II.

Philip II, who ruled from 1556 to 1598, was an ardent defender of the Catholic faith and was obsessed with a wish to crush Protestantism. He administered his vast territories personally from his palace in Madrid. Philip thought that those who did not agree with his religious policies should be

Protestant–Catholic Europe, Around 1600

NORWAY
SWEDEN
Baltic Sea
SCOTLAND
North Sea
DENMARK
IRELAND
ENGLAND
•London
NETHERLANDS
GERMAN STATES
•Wittenberg
SAXONY
POLAND
WESTPHALIA
BOHEMIA
English Channel
HOLY ROMAN
ATLANTIC OCEAN
•Nantes
FRANCE
Augsburg•
BAVARIA
AUSTRIA
EMPIRE
HUNGARY
SWITZERLAND
Geneva•
•Trent
Black Sea
•Avignon
ITALY
PORTUGAL
NAVARRE
Rome•
SPAIN
LIMITS OF WESTERN CHRISTIAN FAITHS

Mediterranean Sea

Protestant Areas
Areas with Protestant Minorities
Catholic Areas
Areas with Catholic Minorities

0   150   300 MILES
0   150   300 KILOMETERS
N

MAP STUDY The map above illustrates the division throughout Europe between Protestants and Catholics. Which major countries remained Catholic? In which part of Europe—northern or southern—were these countries?

imprisoned or killed. He used the Inquisition—a procedure for punishing heretics—to root out both religious and political dissenters. The Spanish Inquisition became infamous in Europe for persecution and terror.

During Philip's reign Spain became the strongest military power in Europe. Spain's armies dominated Europe and its navy protected shipping. With these forces Philip tried to spread Catholic control into Protestant Europe. The policy failed.

Elizabeth I led England in its defeat of Spain.

After the death of young Edward VI in England, Henry VIII's eldest daughter Mary became queen.

She had been raised a Catholic but promised not to overthrow the new Anglican Church. However, Mary's advisers persuaded her to marry the young King Philip of Spain and to place England in the hands of the Catholic Church. Soon after this diplomatic marriage, however, Philip left England. Under Mary's rule, a bloody purge of Protestants took place, with some 400 clergy being executed, before Mary herself died of cancer in 1558. Then England turned to Mary's Protestant half-sister, Elizabeth.

Once Elizabeth became queen, Philip saw Protestant England as a chief enemy. Although Elizabeth considered a marriage to Philip for political reasons for a while, she eventually rejected the idea and remained hostile to Spain. She allowed

ANSWER TO MAP STUDY Portugal, Spain, Italy, and most of France; southern Europe

3 ***Lesson Plan***

Essential Learning Objective

Students will learn to identify the political and military effects of the Reformation.

1 FOCUS AND MOTIVATE

Have students examine the map of Protestant-Catholic Europe (1600) on page 395. Be sure that students see the potential for international religious warfare where borders are not clearly defined. Ask the students how border disputes might arise and how they can lead to major conflicts between nations.

2 TEACH

- On the chalkboard list the political goals of both Phillip II and Elizabeth I. Point out that religious differences, conflicts over the Netherlands, and the issue of piracy all led to political and military conflict between England and Spain.

- Identify the religious and political conflicts in France during 1500–1600. Point out how the Edict of Nantes helped the Huguenots.

- Identify the political, religious, and social results of the Thirty Years' War.

GUIDED PRACTICE

Direct students to name three major military conflicts that resulted from religious friction. (defeat of the Armada, civil war in France, Thirty Years' War)

ASSESS

1. What was the significance of the defeat of the Spanish Armada? (England became a major sea power.)
2. Why is the Edict of Nantes famous? (gave Huguenots political, religious, and economic freedom)

OPTIONAL RETEACHING

Hand out to each student an outline map of Europe from the Geography Skills book. Have students use the map on page 401 to draw in the boundaries of nations after the Peace of Westphalia. Have them compare this map to the political map of Europe in about 1600 on page 395.

OPTIONAL ENRICHMENT

1. Have students report on how the English were able to defeat the Spanish Armada. (average)
2. Have students investigate recent underwater archaeological discoveries of the Spanish Armada in the Irish Sea. (challenging)
3. Also for enrichment:

 Overhead Transparency 41

INDEPENDENT PRACTICE/ HOMEWORK

Assign the Section Review, Activities page 124, or Workbook page 84

CLOSURE

To summarize, point out that the Reformation resulted in major political and military conflict throughout Europe. During this period, Spain declined politically, while England became a major sea power. France began to dominate Western Europe, while Germany remained weak and divided between Catholic and Protestant areas.

From the Archives

The Golden Speech

In 1601, near the end of her reign, Queen Elizabeth I looked back on the period of triumph, prosperity, and cultural attainment through which she had guided England. She expressed her gratitude to Parliament and the English people in a speech, often called her "Golden Speech," from which the following excerpt is taken.

There is no jewel, be it of never so rich a prize, which I prefer before this jewel, I mean your love, for I do more esteem it than any treasure or riches. . . . And though God has raised me high, yet this I count the glory of my crown, that I have reigned with your loves. . . . I do not so much rejoice that God hath made me to be a queen as to be a queen over so thankful a people. . . .

To be a king and wear a crown is more glorious to them that see it than it is pleasure to them that bear it. For myself, I was never so much enticed with . . . the royal authority of a queen as delighted that God hath made me this instrument to maintain His truth and glory, and to defend this kingdom . . . from peril, dishonor, tyranny, and oppression. There will never [a] queen sit in my seat with more zeal to my country or care to my subjects, and that will sooner with willingness yield and venture her life for your good and safety than myself.

English sea captains to pirate Spanish treasure ships. In addition, she helped the Protestant rebels in the Netherlands.

In 1588 Philip decided to rid himself of this rival for power. He sent out the **Spanish Armada**, a fleet of more than 130 large ships, to attack England and prepare the way for an invasion. However, the ships of the English navy were smaller and faster, and they were expertly sailed by such

FROM THE ARCHIVES From George P. Rice, Jr., *The Public Speaking of Queen Elizabeth* (New York: AMS Press, 1966), pp. 106, 109.
Why would people call this Queen Elizabeth's "Golden

---

bold captains as Sir Francis Drake, John Hawkins, and Martin Frobisher. Part of the Armada was destroyed in the English Channel. Most of the fleet sailed into the North Sea, where storms drove the ships away.

Elizabeth gained two important results from her victory over Spain. England remained free and Protestant. It also emerged as a formidable sea power. From this point England developed into the most important naval power in Europe.

Civil war broke out in France.

Meanwhile, in France, a civil war broke out between French Calvinists, called **Huguenots**, and Roman Catholics. By the 1550s about 10 percent of France had become Calvinist, mainly the middle classes and peasants of southern France. Always well organized and dedicated, these Huguenots ran their part of the country almost as an independent state. The royal family was Catholic and defended the Church. The powerful Bourbon family from southern France led the Protestants. What began as a religious fight eventually developed into the issue of which group would control the throne.

From 1559 through 1589, France was ruled by weak kings, all brothers. The real power in France was their mother, Catherine de' Medici, who served as regent—a person who rules until the rightful ruler is able to. Catherine hated Protestants so intensely that she agreed to the mass murder of all Huguenots.

Catholic forces planned a general uprising against their Protestant enemies for August 24, 1572. That night Huguenots were to celebrate the marriage of their leader, Henry of Navarre—a member of the Bourbon family, in Paris. At midnight the mass murder began. Mobs attacked and killed anyone they thought might be Protestant. At least 10,000 Huguenots died in the bloody St. Bartholomew's Day Massacre. Protestantism, however, was not stamped out.

In 1589 Henry of Navarre, who had barely escaped the Massacre, was next in line for the throne. Most French people, now weary of warfare and fearing that a Spaniard might become king, supported Henry. He converted to Catholicism in order to become King Henry IV, but he did not forget the Huguenots. After signing a peace treaty

Speech"? (There are many answers, but note that she was in her "golden years" when she delivered it and England was then in a "golden age." Moreover, the words expressed golden qualities of humility, generosity, service, loyalty, and love.

with Spain in 1598, he issued the **Edict of Nantes**, which protected the liberties of the Huguenots and allowed them to hold public office. France thus became the first large country to permit more than one form of Christianity.

The Thirty Years' War raged from 1618 to 1648.

Of all the areas in Europe, the German states of the Holy Roman Empire were most sharply divided between Catholics and Protestants. These states fought each other and their neighbors between 1618 and 1648 in a bitter struggle known as the Thirty Years' War. The war lasted so long because power politics became mixed up with religion.

The fighting began when a staunchly Catholic Hapsburg prince, Ferdinand II, was chosen king of Bohemia in 1618. Many Bohemians were Protestant and, fearing Catholic rule, they revolted. Ferdinand attacked Bohemia, defeated the Protestants, and returned the country to Catholicism.

After a number of similar victories, it looked as if Ferdinand II and his allies might defeat all the German Protestant states. Fearing Catholic and Hapsburg power, other Protestant nations declared war. Germany now became a battleground.

When Ferdinand's armies defeated Denmark, the first to join the war, Protestant Sweden became alarmed and entered the war. Gustavus Adolphus, Sweden's king, was a military genius who not only stopped the advance of the Hapsburgs but crushed the enemy armies in two decisive battles. The Hapsburgs were only saved by the Swedish king's death in battle in 1632.

The war dragged on, tearing Germany to pieces. France entered the war in 1635 and, together with Sweden, waged unrelenting war on the Hapsburgs. The war ended in 1648 with the Peace of Westphalia. What had begun as a religious struggle in 1618 ended as a war to stop the Hapsburgs from dominating Europe.

The Thirty Years' War had many important results. First, Germany remained divided between Protestants in the north and Catholics in the south. Second, hundreds of small German states retained their independence. Germany thus remained politically disunited for more than two centuries. Finally, perhaps a third of the German population died in the war, and much of the economy fell apart because of the country's devastation. The hatred and bitterness remained for generations.

Section 3 Review

Identify Hapsburgs, Spanish Armada, Huguenots, Edict of Nantes

Main Ideas
1. How did Spanish power threaten Europe?
2. How did England defeat Spain?
3. What caused the civil war in 16th-century France?
4. How was the Thirty Years' War a religious struggle as well as a political one?

Critical Thinking
Making Hypotheses: Why did religious and political issues become intermixed in Europe during the 16th and 17th centuries? Could it happen again?

The Spanish Armada, sent out by Philip II to invade England, is shown here facing its defeat. The Armada was outwitted by the smaller and faster English fleet in 1588.

Lesson Plan

Essential Learning Objectives

Students will learn to:

- assess advantages and disadvantages of absolutism.
- explain Louis XIV's justification for the extravagances of Versailles.

1 FOCUS AND MOTIVATE

Different centuries have been associated with the domination of different western nations. On the chalkboard write the six centuries from the 15th through the 20th century. Ask students to name those nations they believe dominated each century. Possible responses: 15th, Italian city states; 16th, Spain; 17th, France; 18th, France, then England; 19th, England; 20th, United States.

2 TEACH

- Discuss absolutism. To better judge the advantages and disadvantages of absolutism, write the following objectives on the board: (1) crime prevention; (2) economic strength; (3) national security; (4) smooth transition from one leader to another; (5) quickness of response in an emergency; (6) encouragement of the arts; (7) moral behavior of citizenry; (8) happiness of the citizenry. Discuss whether democracy or absolutism would best assure reaching each objective.

- Briefly review the roles of the two Cardinals, Richelieu and Mazarin, in building French power.

- Discuss an absolute monarch. Ask the students why Louis XIV built Versailles. Did its building have anything to do with absolute monarchy? (The

4 France became Europe's leading power.

The long years of warfare in Europe between 1550 and 1650 brought many changes in European society and politics and led to a new political system in Europe's nations. It was called absolutism, and it meant that monarchs had, in theory, complete control over their nations. This system gave strength to the **absolute monarch**, a ruler who has complete authority over the government and the lives of its people. Control of all the laws and courts and the ability to collect and spend taxes all rested on royal control of large standing armies. To Europeans sickened by a century of brutal warfare and an age when undisciplined bands of soldiers ravaged Europe, absolutism seemed the best way to keep the peace.

One writer, an Englishman named **Thomas Hobbes**, best expressed the idea of absolutism. His classic book, *Leviathan*, was published in 1651. Hobbes thought that human beings were basically selfish and greedy and, unless some stronger power controlled them, they would constantly be at war. Before societies arose to exert such control, said Hobbes, people existed in a state of war, and their lives were "nasty, brutish, and short."

The only way for humans to live in peace was therefore to have a ruler govern them absolutely. Even if the ruler was a tyrant, Hobbes declared, that was better than continual turmoil. Hobbes' ideas have left a lasting impression.

Two cardinals helped make France strong.

Henry IV, the first Bourbon king, set France on the road to recovery from its wars of religion and to international power. He died in 1610, leaving behind a wife, Marie de' Medici, and an infant son. Marie became regent for their young son, but she mismanaged the country. The treasury was depleted, and the Huguenots seemed ready to rebel.

Eventually, in 1624, an ambitious churchman named Richelieu [rish′ə lü] surfaced as the leading minister of state. This ambitious man became the architect of French absolutism. Born to a minor noble family, the future cardinal saw the Church as an excellent path upward. By age 22 Richelieu

became a bishop and talked his way into the confidence of the queen. In 1622 he was made a cardinal in the Catholic Church, and by 1624 **Cardinal Richelieu** was the chief minister of France. When Henry's son Louis XIII was old enough to reign, he found he could not get along without Cardinal Richelieu. Louis allowed him almost absolute control over France.

Cardinal Richelieu followed principles stated by Machiavelli in *The Prince*. Among these principles was the idea that the state needed absolute power so that it could create order in the world. Leaders could use any means to bring about this result. Cardinal Richelieu had several major aims. The first was to strengthen the power of the French king within France, which meant subduing the nobility and Huguenots. The second, to make France supreme in Europe, meant breaking Hapsburg power in Europe. Last, the cardinal promised to make the French king, Louis XIII, famous throughout the world.

To accomplish the first goal, Cardinal Richelieu took political rights away from the Huguenots and power away from the nobles. When the Huguenots resisted, the cardinal declared war on them and personally led the royal armies. The eventual Protestant surrender gave the state total control over these people. To reach the second goal, Cardinal Richelieu took France into the Thirty Years' War and victory over the Hapsburgs. Cardinal Richelieu was harsh and made the common people pay heavy taxes to support the army. When he died in 1642, the people rejoiced.

Louis XIII died a year later, leaving his four-year-old son Louis XIV as king. Cardinal Richelieu had already trained Jules Mazarin [zhül mȧ zȧ raN′], an Italian-born cardinal, to be his successor. Cardinal Mazarin ran the government until Louis XIV was 22 years old. Although Cardinal Mazarin followed Richelieu's policies, things did not go well at first. The nobility and many common people hated the new royal authority that Richelieu had imposed on the country, and they rebelled against the young king and Cardinal Mazarin. Between 1648 and 1653, the turmoil in France was so intense that the king had to hide out in the countryside. Eventually, Cardinal Mazarin subdued all rebellious forces and brought peace to France.

Louis XIV was one of the most powerful French kings.

Ruler of France from Mazarin's death in 1661 until 1715, **Louis XIV** may be the perfect example of an absolute ruler with unlimited power. His motto was "L'État, c'est moi" (I am the state), meaning that he alone held all authority. Louis believed in the divine right of kings—that is, the right of kings to rule, supposedly given by God. By this theory, all citizens should offer obedience as a kind of religious duty. Louis XIV set an example for other rulers who claimed to rule by divine right.

Louis XIV was not brilliant, nor well educated, but he had good common sense and worked hard at being king. His capable economic adviser, **Jean Colbert** [kôl ber′], helped France by strengthening France's overseas colonies in the West Indies and Canada. Colbert also improved the quality of French goods so that more people would buy them. Louis XIV strengthened the country by adding to the powers of the intendants, appointed officials who carried out his orders in the country. Finally, the government reorganized the French army and strengthened the navy.

Although Louis XIV was a capable ruler, he was not always wise. A strong believer in Catholicism, he feared that non-Catholics would be disloyal and would weaken France. In 1685 Louis canceled the Edict of Nantes and took away freedom of worship from the Huguenots. Thousands of Huguenots fled to Prussia, England, and America.

In other areas, too, Louis' policies were unwise. "Le Roi Soleil," or Sun King, as Louis XIV was often called, demanded luxury as well as power. He built a lavish palace at Versailles, a village about 12 miles outside Paris. There he surrounded himself with nobles who did nothing but serve and amuse him. Louis made the nobles dependent on him and thus controlled them. Elaborate court rituals, sumptuous feasts, infinite attention to fine clothing, and an endless round of petty court gossip kept the nobility too occupied to plan revolts.

The luxury and waste of Versailles cost the French taxpayers dearly. In addition, by living at Versailles, Louis cut himself and his successors off from contact with the people. Although this isolation had serious results for the kings who came after him, Louis XIV gave France more unity and a stronger central government than ever before.

Louis XIV's wars weakened France.

As the absolute monarch of Europe's greatest state, Louis XIV followed Richelieu's old promises to make France the most powerful country on the continent. He was already the most famous and glorious king on earth, so he thought. Louis had

DAILY LIFE

Enormous contrasts existed in 17th- and 18th-century French life, which were highlighted in Louis XIV's Versailles palace. The formal gardens (near left) show the exquisite perfection of the grounds. However, the Versailles work force (far left) presents a view behind the scenes—of the dignified poverty of the French peasants. This oil painting, *The Baker's Court*, was done in 1656 by Jean Michelin.

was strengthened by expanding overseas colonies, better production methods at home, and the largest army in Europe.

Answers to Section 4 Review

Identify
Key Terms, People, and Places are defined on pages indicated in parentheses. Also see the Glossary and Biographical Dictionary.
absolute monarch (398), Thomas Hobbes (398), Cardinal Richelieu (398), Louis XIV (399), Jean Colbert (399)

Main Ideas
1. Cardinals Richelieu and Mazarin tightly controlled the French government and army with absolute power, superseding the king.
2. strengths—developed overseas colonies, began French East India Company, improved quality of French goods, strengthened army; weaknesses—took freedom of religion from Huguenots and forced them to flee; lavish, wasteful, and isolated life at Versailles; imposed heavy tax burden
3. Wars cost a significant loss in men and money.

Critical Thinking
Students should consider that many people have a love or need for power, and this greed propels them to take over land, people, or political offices.

Lesson Plan

Essential Learning Objectives
Students will learn to:
• describe the political and economic problems faced by eastern

---

the strongest army in Europe, and with it he fought four long wars in the course of nearly 50 years. None met with success. Louis XIV's wars and life of luxury left France with an empty treasury and a large debt. As he grew older, Louis doubted the wisdom of his many military adventures. On his deathbed in 1715, he warned his heir: "Try to preserve peace with your neighbors. I have been too fond of war."

Section 4 Review

Identify absolute monarch, Thomas Hobbes, Cardinal Richelieu, Louis XIV, Jean Colbert

Main Ideas
1. How did the cardinals Richelieu and Mazarin make France strong?
2. What made Louis XIV one of the most powerful French kings? What weakened him?
3. How did Louis XIV's wars weaken France?

Critical Thinking
Identifying Assumptions: Imagine that you were an absolute monarch at the time of Louis XIV and Cardinal Richelieu. Why do you think you might want absolute control of the government? What do you think drives people, then and now, to want to take over large countries, blocks of land or political offices?

---

5 Absolutist monarchies arose in central and eastern Europe.

The same ideas about government that circulated through western Europe also affected the rulers of central and eastern Europe. Still, many differences existed between these main regions. Their economies, for example, differed dramatically. During the later Middle Ages in western Europe, serfdom gradually died out, and commerce and cities became increasingly important. The middle classes grew in importance economically and politically, and money became the key to success.

In eastern Europe nothing like that happened. The old medieval system of controlling land and labor was still the major source of power. In Hungary, Poland, Bohemia, Prussia, and Russia, most

---

peasants remained bound to the land as serfs. Few cities with large middle-class populations existed. Furthermore, the Church owned large amounts of land, and none could be taxed.

Nevertheless, modern ideas about government swept eastern Europe in the 17th century. Monarchs wanted to build centralized, even absolutist, states. In part this desire stemmed from the constant warfare. A number of German princes, including the Hapsburgs who ruled large sections of eastern Europe, had fought in the Thirty Years' War and knew just what it took to build modern armies. However, most of them did not have the economic or political power to do it. With few money-producing cities, with nobles and clerics they could not control, and with a peasantry sunk in poverty, most rulers found it impossible to build strong central governments. However, a few rulers did succeed.

The Hapsburgs retained power in central Europe.

The area called central Europe was centered in German-speaking Austria, composed of Hapsburg family lands. From the 15th century on, Hapsburgs had been Holy Roman Emperors here, but the area had been only a collection of independent states and free cities.

One of the Hapsburgs, Emperor Leopold I (1658–1705), constructed a more compact state that included Hungary, Bohemia, and Austria, with its capital at Vienna. Leopold managed to build an absolutist monarchy, but one that was quite different from that of France. The Hapsburg monarchy was challenged by demands from the many different ethnic groups who lived on their lands and wanted local independence. The nobility, who controlled large feudal estates, also wanted a good share of power. Still, the Hapsburg lands were rich enough to support a central monarchy to oversee the area, and to build a large army. On this basis, the Hapsburgs were one of Europe's main powers into the 19th century.

Prussia rose to power.

During the late Middle Ages, a new state began to take shape in northeastern Europe. This state, later called **Prussia**, owed its rise to the **Hohenzollern**

Europe, 1721

MAP STUDY In the map above, a dark black line surrounds the area that was the Holy Roman Empire in 1721. What modern-day countries does it cover? (See page 792.)

[hō′ən zol′ərn] family, who were rulers of the small, poor country of Brandenburg with a capital at Berlin. The Hohenzollerns obtained both land and power through clever diplomacy. Although devastated by the Thirty Years' War, the Hohenzollerns quickly became the most important Protestant rulers in the German states. By 1701 they were kings of Prussia.

Frederick William (1640–1688), called the Great Elector, and his son decided that such disasters as their defeat in the war would never happen again. Only a powerful army could defend the small state, and Frederick William therefore built one. By offering his troops as mercenary soldiers during various wars, Frederick William became wealthy enough to be the strongest power in Germany. Using military force, the Great Elector crushed opposition from the junkers [yůng′kərz]—powerful landowning aristocrats—and the townspeople. From the 1680s both groups served in the army and served the state. In return, the townspeople could engage in trade, and the junkers held control of their estates and the serfs who worked them.

Frederick William's descendants built their state into a major power. His great-grandson, Frederick II (1740–1786), had many interests other than war. He enjoyed history, poetry, music, and the ideals of the Enlightenment. He abolished torture in

ANSWER TO MAP STUDY Belgium, the Netherlands, West Germany, East Germany, Austria, and parts of Poland, Czechoslovakia, and Yugoslavia

European nations between 1650 and 1750.

- provide examples of absolute monarchy in eastern Europe.

1 FOCUS AND MOTIVATE

Explain to students that the 17th and 18th centuries in Europe are important, partly because these were the years of the development of modern nations and governments. Discuss what factors make a nation today. (cultural activities, language, political beliefs, and common economic system) Show how these factors existed 200 years ago also.

2 TEACH

- On the chalkboard list the limitations of Hapsburg political control in eastern and central Europe. Stress ethnic problems and power of the nobility.

- Identify the stages that allowed Prussia to become the most important Protestant nation. Make certain students understand how Prussia was able to take territory from Austria and Poland.

- On the chalkboard, list the characteristics of Russian westernization during the reign of Peter the Great and Catherine the Great. Give examples of how both rulers extended Russian boundaries at the expense of Turkey and Poland.

GUIDED PRACTICE

Have student volunteers point out on a wall map of Europe how Peter the Great was able to gain "windows on the west."

401

criminal cases and reformed the civil courts. Like his great-grandfather, the Great Elector, Frederick II allowed all religions to practice in Prussia. He also worked hard to improve the government, industry, education, and living conditions of his people.

Although Frederick II was a moral and intelligent ruler, he took strong military actions. He felt that the king served the state, and what was best for the state was best for all its citizens. Shortly after he became king in 1740, he invaded, and ultimately conquered, the Austrian territory of Silesia, an area rich in farmland and industries. At the time, Austria was led by a young princess named Maria Theresa.

After his victory over Austria, in which Prussia acquired Silesia, Frederick—who was now known as "**Frederick the Great**"—still wanted more land. His chance came in 1772. Prussia, Russia, and Austria each forced a weak Poland to give up land. Poland suffered further dismemberment in the 1790s, sliced up twice more by these greedy neighbors. Poland then disappeared as an independent nation until after World War I.

New leaders ended the Russian Time of Troubles.

At the end of the 16th century, Russia was swept by great unrest. As you learned in Chapter 13, a period followed the death of Tsar Ivan the Terrible known as the Time of Troubles, in which all government broke down. The old ruling family did not have a male heir, and the peasants rose up in rebellion. Armies from Poland and Sweden took advantage of Russia's weakness and, for a short time, Poles ruled Moscow. The Time of Troubles ended

This crown belonged to the Russian tsar Mikhail Romanov and dates from 1627–1628. It is made of gold, jewels, and a band of fur.

in 1613 when a popular assembly chose a young nobleman named Mikhail Romanov [mē kə ēl′ rō′mə nôf] as tsar. The Romanovs eventually built Russia into a great empire and ruled until 1917.

Mikhail's grandson was Peter I—usually called **Peter the Great**—who came to the throne in 1682 determined to make Russia a strong, modern state. Russia was easily the most backward country in Europe, and the Russian Orthodox Church and the tsars attempted to keep out all foreign influences. The most conservative religious group, the powerful Old Believers, wore long black coats and long beards to symbolize their ancient ways. Wholly uneducated and with little hope of changing their condition, the peasants lived under a yoke of serfdom so oppressive that it resembled slavery.

Peter the Great westernized Russia.

To make Russia strong, Peter felt he needed the advanced technology of the European countries that lay to the west. In 1697 the tsar left Russia to see for himself what the west was like. As he traveled through Germany, the Netherlands, and England, he inspected workshops and factories, and even worked for a while as a carpenter in a Dutch shipyard. When he returned home, he brought with him many European craftworkers, engineers, and scholars. They helped Peter start new industries, set up scientific institutions, and reform the calendar and alphabet. Peter also ordered young men of Russia's noble families to go abroad, at their own expense, to learn technical skills such as navigation and fortification.

Like all other absolutists, Peter saw a strong military as the key to national power. He created a small navy and newly modernized army. Army ranks were filled with conscripts and heavy taxes on everything—even beards—paid for it. In his desire to change old for new, Peter decided to build a new capital city, **St. Petersburg**, which is now called Leningrad. Like the other absolutist monarchs, Peter wanted a new splendid setting.

Peter also removed all traces of local self-government, put the Russian Orthodox Church completely under his control, and made all Russians serve the state. The peasants, who had to pay heavy taxes and were already reduced to virtual slavery, suffered the most. Now serfs could be

GEOGRAPHY

A Key to History

RUSSIA AND ICE-FREE PORTS

Explain why Russia, with its long coastline, had only a few good seaports. Where were the most important ports located?

Throughout history, a nation with good seaports has had an advantage in carrying on trade and conducting wars. In general, trade by water has been easier, cheaper, and often faster than trade by land.

Russia has the longest seacoast of any country in the world, yet it has had few usable seaports. Waters along most of Russia's Arctic coast are frozen over for nine to ten months a year. Murmansk is the only Arctic port that is ice-free the year-round. Its usefulness is limited, however, because the seas joining it to the Atlantic Ocean are treacherous.

The Russian desire for ice-free ports led to a series of wars. In particular, Russian leaders wanted ports on the Baltic Sea because it offers an open route to the Atlantic Ocean and Western Europe.

One important Baltic port was Riga, near the mouth of the Western Dvina [də vē′nä] River. From 1557 to 1582, Tsar Ivan IV (the Terrible) tried unsuccessfully to conquer Riga and Narva, another Baltic port.

Peter the Great made further attempts to win control of Baltic ports.

In 1703, hoping to open a new avenue to the West, he began building St. Petersburg on the Gulf of Finland. As a result of the Great Northern War with Sweden (1707–1721), Peter became master of the eastern shore of the Baltic.

Russian leaders also looked for outlets to the sea in the east and in the south. Russian adventurers pushed eastward across Siberia, eventually reaching the Pacific Ocean. The port of Okhotsk [ō kätsk′] was established in 1648 on the Pacific Ocean, but it was not until 200 years later that Russia acquired Vladivostok, an ice-free port in the east. Russia also pushed to get an ice-free port on the Black Sea by way of the straits. (See page 240.) It achieved this goal in 1794 when the port of Odessa was founded.

REVIEW

1. Why do the long rivers flowing across Siberia to the Arctic Ocean not have large port cities at their mouths?
2. How do you think the lack of seaports has affected Russia's history?

GEOGRAPHY: A KEY TO HISTORY

A basic chronology of the founding of Russia's major outlets to world oceans will tie this feature directly to the historical narrative. Note that Archangel on the White Sea was established in 1583 as Russia's window to the outside world, but its harbor is frozen for six months of the year. Okhotsk dates from 1648, just 22 years after the Dutch purchased Manhattan from the Indians and founded New Amsterdam. Odessa (1794) was founded during the period of the French Revolution. Murmansk was hurriedly built in 1915 to provide a source for war materials during World War I.

Teachers who wish to expand and update this feature into a general discussion will profit from James Long, "The Harsh Realities of Soviet Geography: Some Notes for Teachers," *Social Studies* (September-October, 1985), 228–230.

Answers to REVIEW

1. because the Arctic Ocean in these regions remains frozen for nine or ten months of the year
2. Opinion. The lack of seaports has contributed to several wars and has hampered the development of Russia's economy.

Answers to MAP QUESTIONS

Ice blocks most of the coast in the northwest, north, and northeast; in the west through central Europe and into Russia. It brought occasional moments of security for some but years of war and virtual slavery for many.

A portrait of Catherine the Great places her on a walk in the Tsarskoe Selo park. The painting was done by Vladimir Borovikovsky in 1794.

bought and sold at will. Peter had made this compromise with the nobility in order to keep their allegiance. Many peasant uprisings occurred.

Peter and Catherine extended Russian boundaries.

Peter the Great and later Russian rulers had a major goal in foreign affairs—to obtain "windows on the West." These ice-free seaports on the Black Sea or Baltic Sea would enable Russia to trade with western Europe by water. To gain such "windows," Peter waged war against the Swedes, who controlled much of the Baltic region. Russia was at war during most of Peter's rule. To learn more about these efforts to gain ice-free ports, see the "Geography: A Key to History" on page 403.

Peter's Great Northern War against Sweden, for which he allied with Poland, Saxony, and Denmark, was especially successful. When the Great Northern War ended in 1721, Sweden had lost nearly all of its land along the eastern Baltic. Russia had gained its Baltic "window" and had also become the dominant power in northern Europe.

Several weak rulers followed Peter the Great. Then came Catherine II, usually called **Catherine the Great**. A German princess, she seized the throne after her mentally unfit husband, Peter III, was murdered in 1762. Catherine the Great was gifted and well educated. She liked to think of herself as enlightened, but in reality, she was a despot. She improved schools and modernized laws, but the condition of the peasantry became worse. Catherine made serfs of more than one million peasants who lived in the newly conquered areas in the south of Russia. Her territorial conquests earned her the name "Catherine the Great."

As with other absolutists, the cost of complete power was high. In the 1770s, while Catherine's armies were away fighting the Turks, a peasant rebellion broke out in southwestern Russia. Led by a Cossack trooper named Emelyan Pugachev [pügə′chóf′], thousands of serfs, poor soldiers, and religious people joined in his call for the end of serfdom and for equal distribution of land. Pugachev's ragged armies ran free through the south, causing panic in the capital itself. Finally, Pugachev was betrayed by a friend, captured, tortured, and executed. His name lived on as a symbol of resistance to an oppressive government. As a French writer said of Louis XIV, "the prince's grandeur always brings his subjects misery."

Section 5 Review

Identify Prussia, Hohenzollerns, Frederick the Great, Peter the Great, St. Petersburg, Catherine the Great

Main Ideas
1. How did the Hapsburgs' absolutist state in central Europe differ from that of France?
2. How did Frederick William raise Prussia to power?
3. What problems were left after the Time of Troubles?
4. Why did Peter the Great try to westernize Russia?
5. At what cost were Russian borders extended?

Critical Thinking
Analyzing Comparisons: What did the absolutist states of central Europe, Prussia, and Russia have in common? How did they treat their ordinary people? Why did they so treat them?

Master Composers of the 18th Century

"Great works contain the thoughts of a generation, and the ideas of many generations," wrote a famous music critic in discussing the composer Wolfgang Amadeus Mozart (1756–1791). Mozart studied the works of the masters of music of the early 18th century—George Handel, Johann Sebastian Bach, and the opera-writer Georg Philipp Telemann. Acknowledging his debt to these composers and to his contemporary —Josef Haydn—who also inspired him, Mozart gave the world a body of work so original, expressive and varied that people today still marvel at his genius. Mozart's work brought to its culmination the Classical period of music, known for its grace, melody, and emotion.

Even before he was six years old, Mozart showed considerable musical ability. In 1762 Mozart's father, who was music director for the Archbishop of Salzburg, Austria, took young Wolfgang and his sister on a tour of Europe to show off their talents. Over the next ten years, the Mozart children became famous, and Wolfgang's abilities in music continued to grow.

However, the early flowering of Mozart's career did not lead him to success in later life. Although Mozart enjoyed recognition for certain operas, concertos, and symphonies, he made enemies in the music world in part because his contemporaries were jealous of his talents. Mozart died penniless at age 35.

Soon after his death, however, Mozart became a legend. His works profoundly influenced the great 19th-century composers Beethoven, Schubert, and Brahms. His musical ideas still thrill and inspire us today.

The young Mozart is shown at the piano (left) with his father and sister. He wrote the "Minuet in G Major" (below) at age six.

CHAPTER 21 Review

Section Summaries

Section 1
The Catholic Church lost power.
The Protestant Reformation that swept Europe in the 16th and 17th centuries greatly reduced the power of the Catholic Church. Corruption had weakened the Church from within, and many Europeans began to resent papal control.

Section 2
The Reformation divided Europe.
The Reformation shattered the religious and political unity of western Europe and led to the establishment of three major branches of Protestantism. New Protestant religions included Lutherans, Calvinists, Anabaptists, and Anglicans. As Protestantism grew, the Catholic Church tried to regain lost ground with the Counter Reformation.

Section 3
Religious differences mixed with political conflicts.
European countries fought several wars between 1550 and 1650. Spain enjoyed its greatest glory, and jealous nations tried to check it to keep a balance of power. That balance shifted when England defeated the Spanish Armada in 1588. Civil war between Protestants and Catholics weakened France, but the Edict of Nantes gave Protestants some religious freedom. Religious fighting reached its peak in the Thirty Years' War.

Section 4
France became Europe's leading power.
Cardinals Richelieu and Mazarin started France on the path to greatness. Louis XIV then unified France and made it Europe's leader. However, he weakened France with his excessive spending and wars.

Section 5
Absolutist monarchies arose in central and eastern Europe.
Prussia became a strong military state. Frederick the Great, in most areas an enlightened ruler, wanted to increase Prussia's size. Peter the Great used his absolute power to modernize Russia and expand its territory. Catherine the Great also expanded Russia.

Test Yourself

Key Terms, People, and Places
Identify the significance of each of the following:

Section 1
a. Boniface VIII
b. Avignon
c. Great Schism
d. indulgences

Section 2
a. Reformation
b. Martin Luther
c. John Calvin
d. King Henry VIII
e. Act of Supremacy
f. Elizabeth I
g. Counter Reformation

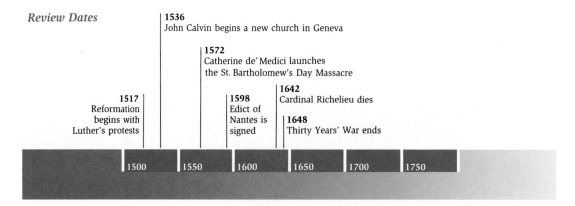

Review Dates

1536 John Calvin begins a new church in Geneva

1572 Catherine de' Medici launches the St. Bartholomew's Day Massacre

1517 Reformation begins with Luther's protests

1598 Edict of Nantes is signed

1642 Cardinal Richelieu dies

1648 Thirty Years' War ends

1500   1550   1600   1650   1700   1750

Section 3
a. Hapsburgs
b. Spanish Armada
c. Huguenots
d. Edict of Nantes

Section 4
a. absolute monarch
b. Thomas Hobbes
c. Cardinal Richelieu
d. Louis XIV
e. Jean Colbert

Section 5
a. Prussia
b. Hohenzollerns
c. Frederick the Great
d. Peter the Great
e. St. Petersburg
f. Catherine the Great

Main Ideas

Section 1
1. Name two political issues the Church faced.
2. Which forces inside and outside the Church challenged it?

Section 2
1. Which of Martin Luther's ideas led to the Reformation?
2. What main ideas was Calvinism based on?
3. How were the Anabaptists different from other Protestants?
4. Why and how did England break with Rome?
5. Name some changes that came with the Reformation.

Section 3
1. Why were the Spanish rulers a threat to Europe?
2. How was England able to defeat Spain?
3. Why was a civil war fought in 16th-century France?
4. How was the Thirty Years' War both religious and political?

Section 4
1. In what ways did Cardinals Richelieu and Mazarin strengthen France?
2. How was Louis XIV strong? How was he weak?
3. In what ways did Louis XIV's wars weaken France?

Section 5
1. How did absolutist France and central Europe differ?
2. How did Prussia grow under Frederick William?
3. What was Russia like after the Time of Troubles?
4. Why did Peter the Great want to westernize Russia?
5. What was the cost of Peter's and Catherine's wars?

Critical Thinking
1. Making Hypotheses Many important leaders in this period were women—Elizabeth I, Catherine de' Medici, and Catherine the Great. Why do you think they had so much power so long before our modern ideas of feminism developed? Is there a lesson to be learned from this period in history?
2. Assessing Cause and Effect Why do you think that many societies throughout history have become divided by the issue of religion? Support your answer with evidence. Consider situations either in the past or the present—Northern Ireland or the Middle East—where disputes over religious beliefs or authority have erupted into violence.

Chapter Skills and Activities

Practicing Study and Research Skills
Analyzing Historians' Interpretations
History is made up of certain verifiable facts—for example, that Peter the Great came to the throne in 1682. Still, as you learned in the Chapter 12 Review, different historians interpret these facts in different ways. For instance, two historians writing about Peter the Great could paint entirely different pictures of this Russian ruler's motivations and significance in world history. Consider the verifiable facts about Peter, and give two examples of possible interpretations of his rule. How do you think the author of this textbook has interpreted it?

Linking Past and Present
People throughout history have complained about paying taxes. In many U.S. presidential elections, the issue of raising taxes is hotly debated. What complaints about taxation might a middle-class person in the 17th century and a middle-class person today share?

Learning History Through Maps
Using the map on page 401 called Europe, 1721, find
1. The country where the Hohenzollerns originated.
2. The place where Martin Luther built his new church.
3. The place where Peter's luxurious palace was.
4. The place where Louis XIV built his great palace.

CRITICAL THINKING QUESTION LEVEL 1. challenging; 2. average

Chapter

22 The Scientific Revolution

OVERVIEW

This chapter covers scientific inquiry in astronomy, mathematics, chemistry, physics, and medicine, emphasizing the importance of scientific method and reason.

PLANNING CHART

Section	Text Pages	Key Concept	Suggested Teaching Time
1 Scientists worked out new theories about the universe.	409–411	The scientific community moved from a geocentric to a heliocentric understanding of the universe.	One day **More time?** Use *Overhead Transparency 43* or *Source Reading 22A.*
2 Several branches of science moved forward.	411–415	Driven by new findings in astronomy and aided by new tools in math, scientific discovery escalated in the 17th and 18th centuries.	One day **Less time?** Combine Sections 2 and 3 using a time line to show approximate times of and people involved in scientific progress.
3 Medical knowledge grew.	416	The scientific method produced major breakthroughs in disease theory and in the study of anatomy.	One day **More time?** Use *Overhead Transparency 44* or *Source Reading 22B.*

ANCILLARIES

Materials that may be used with this chapter to reinforce, reteach, enrich, and assess learning are pictured on the following pages.

Teacher's Resource File

ACTIVITIES

Section 1 Activity, p. 129

Section 2 Activity, p. 130

Section 3 Activity, p. 131

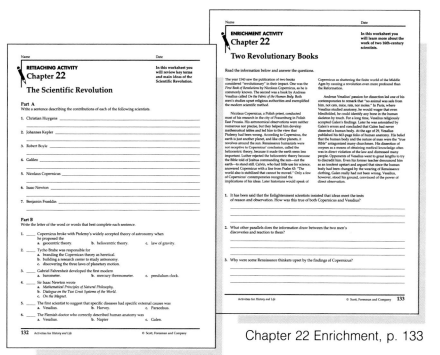

Chapter 22 Reteaching, p. 132

Chapter 22 Enrichment, p. 133

Teacher's Resource File

GEOGRAPHY SKILLS

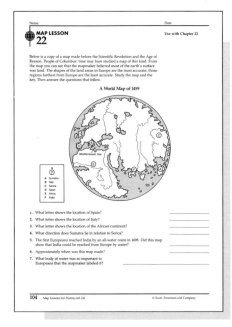

Chapter 22 Geography
Worksheet/Map, pp. 45–46

Chapter 22 Map Lesson, p. 104

TESTS

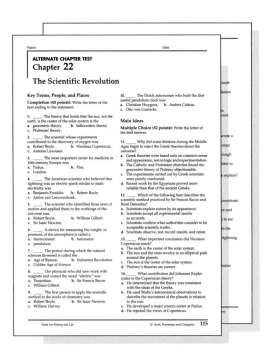

Chapter Test, pp. 113–114   Alternate Chapter Test, pp. 115–116

Other Optional Ancillaries

WORKBOOK

Section 1 Worksheet, p. 87

Name _____ Date _____

WORKSHEET
Chapter 22, Section 1

In this worksheet you will review the ideas and methods of certain important scientists.

Scientists and the Scientific Method

Part A
Read each description below. Underline any factual errors you find and correct them on the lines below.

1. Sir Francis Bacon supported the scientific method: experiment, observe carefully, and record the results. In his view, once an experiment was completed, the experiment did not have to be repeated.

2. Réne Descartes was a mathematician who believed in truth based on logical thinking and experimentation. His ideas had an enormous influence on European thinkers of his time and form the basis of modern science.

3. Copernicus believed that the earth circled the sun. This was in direct contradiction to Ptolemy's belief, which was supported by the churches. However, the Copernican theory gained quick acceptance, because it was based on common sense.

4. Galileo's discoveries formed the basis for modern geology. By experimentation, Galileo discovered that mathematics can be used to explain the movement of objects through space and time.

Part B
Write the letter of the term from the box next to its identifying phrase.

1. _____ Leonardo da Vinci's description of the experiment
2. _____ Galileo's description of his own and Copernicus' theories
3. _____ Copernicus' theory that the sun is the center of the solar system and the earth and planets move around it
4. _____ the oval path followed by the planets
5. _____ Ptolemy's belief that the earth was fixed and the heavenly bodies moved around it
6. _____ Kepler's scheme of the solar system

a. ellipse
b. *Dialogue on the Two Great Systems of the World*
c. heliocentric theory
d. "the mother of certainty"
e. geocentric theory
f. three laws of planetary motion

Worksheets for History and Life © Scott, Foresman and Company **87**

Section 2 Worksheet, p. 88

Name _____ Date _____

WORKSHEET
Chapter 22, Section 2

In this worksheet you will review developments in mathematics, astronomy, chemistry, and physics.

Scientists and Their Discoveries

Choose words from the box to complete the chart.

Scientist	Accomplishment	Importance of Accomplishment
John Napier		allowed mathematicians to calculate large numbers quickly
Gabriel Fahrenheit		made accurate measurement of termperature possible
Otto von Guericke		
Christian Huygens		
Sir Isaac Newton		
Robert Boyle		
William Gilbert		contributed to the understanding of electricity
Benjamin Franklin		contributed to the understanding of electricity

first used the scientific method in chemistry
invented first air pump capable of creating a vacuum
explained why planets do not fly off into space
led to development of the steam engine
invented pendulum clock
invented the first modern mercury thermometer
invented logarithms
allowed scientists correctly to measure small units of time
transformed alchemy into the scientific study of chemistry
invented first lightning rod
developed theory of gravity
used sulfur and glass to create static electricity

88 *Worksheets for History and Life* © Scott, Foresman and Company

Section 3 Worksheet, p. 89

Name _____ Date _____

WORKSHEET
Chapter 22, Section 3

In this worksheet you will review the impact of the Age of Reason on the study of medicine.

The New Medicine

Part A
For each set of statements below, write M before the main idea and S before any statements that support or help to explain the main idea. One statement in each set is not related to the main idea; write X next to this statement.

Set 1
_____ Paracelsus suggested treatment of diseases with medicines derived from minerals.
_____ Paracelsus believed that poisons caused most diseases.
_____ Paracelsus disagreed with the medical thought of his day.
_____ Paracelsus was born in Switzerland in 1493.
_____ Paracelsus stated that the causes of most diseases could be discovered by observation.

Set 2
_____ Vesalius' methods of learning anatomy soon became the standard for modern medical studies.
_____ Vesalius sometimes robbed the gallows for dead bodies.
_____ Vesalius was able to describe the human body correctly.
_____ Vesalius challenged Galen's theories about anatomy.
_____ Vesalius became a pioneer in anatomy.

Set 3
_____ By using the microscope, physicians learned about the body and the causes of disease.
_____ Leeuwenhoek's descriptions led to the belief that germs cause disease.
_____ The microscope might have been invented by an eyeglass maker.
_____ The discovery of the microscope led to many discoveries in medicine.
_____ The microscope allowed scientists to examine tiny organisms.

Set 4
_____ The discoveries of the Age of Reason were based on the scientific and intellectual advances of the 17th century.
_____ The natural sciences flourished during the Age of Reason.
_____ The scientific method enabled people to make discoveries about the universe.
_____ The ancient Greeks were the first to set forth scientific theories.
_____ During the Age of Reason, scientists' discoveries showed that the universe was a well-ordered machine, working according to the laws of nature.

Part B
Number the events in the order in which they happened.
_____ Vesalius published *On the Fabric of the Human Body.*
_____ Harvey explained how the heart works.
_____ Leeuwenhoek worked with microscopes.
_____ The Age of Reason reached its height.
_____ Paracelsus broke with the ideas of the Greeks.
_____ Galen developed his theories about anatomy.

Worksheets for History and Life © Scott, Foresman and Company **89**

SOURCE READINGS

Source Reading 22A
Source Reading 22B

OVERHEAD TRANSPARENCIES

Overhead Transparency 43
Overhead Transparency 44

TEST GENERATOR

40 multiple-choice questions for Chapter 22

The Scientific Revolution

1500–1800

1400	
1500	
1543	Copernicus sets forth his sun-centered theory of the structure of the universe
1752	Benjamin Franklin discovers electricity
1800	
1900	

In 1676 Thomas Shadwell produced a popular comedy called *The Virtuoso* about Sir Nicholas Gimcrack, who thinks he is a great scientist. He carried on such experiments as transfusing sheep blood into a human being to produce human wool and watching soldiers fight battles on the moon through his telescope. In the play, a skeptic visits Sir Nicholas and finds him lying on a table, moving as if he were swimming.

> Skeptic: Do you intend to practice in the water, Sir?
> Gimcrack: Never, Sir. I hate the water . . . .
> Skeptic: Then there will be no use of swimming.
> Gimcrack: I content myself with the speculative . . . . I seldom bring anything to use . . . . Knowledge is my ultimate end.

The audience of 1676 understood the comedy well—a nonsensical nobleman playing at being a scientist, not interested in any practical application of what he studied. A century before, no audience would have understood the humor in this play, much less what a scientist was. Something happened in the 17th century, a revolution in the way that people saw the world.

In 1500 the printing press had just been invented, and Columbus had just reached America. Within the next four centuries, every area of life changed, as did the ways people thought about themselves and the universe in which they lived. Perhaps nothing changed those ideas more than the advances in science that began in the Western world toward the end of the 15th century.

The scientific revolution resulted from both new information about nature and a new way of gathering that information that was based on experiment and reasoning. Together, these discoveries affected every area of thought and experience. This fundamental shift in attitude distinguished Europe's scientific revolution and made it quite significant in world history.

William Harvey, an English doctor who was among those scientists fostering Europe's scientific revolution, demonstrates his animal experiments.

1 *Lesson Plan*

Essential Learning Objectives

Students will learn to:
- define the geocentric and heliocentric theories of the universe.
- explain the scientific method.

1 FOCUS AND MOTIVATE

Before class draw a top hat on the board making certain that its height and width are identical. Ask students if the hat is taller than it is wide. Explain that this top hat represents the world view of people in 1500. For centuries people simply believed what their eyes told them, without experimenting or measuring. Have a student volunteer to measure the hat. The scientific revolution has begun.

2 TEACH

- Ask students how the Renaissance, the Age of Discovery, and the Reformation all set the scene for the scientific revolution. (Renaissance and Age of Discovery created interest in this world, not the next. Reformation weakened Church's stranglehold on truth.)

- What was the accepted model of the universe in 1500? Have a student draw Ptolemy's geocentric model on the chalkboard. Ask why the Catholic Church had such a stake in that model. (God's creation must be center of universe.) Have another student draw the heliocentric model of the universe. Ask how Copernicus came up with this model. (He relied heavily on mathematical calculations.)

- Underscore the contributions of Bacon and Descartes by discussing the basic steps of the scientific method. What made it so revolutionary?

Reading Preview

In this chapter, you will learn how scientific research changed the way we see the world.

1. *Scientists worked out new theories about the universe.*
2. *Several branches of science moved forward.*
3. *Medical knowledge grew.*

1 Scientists worked out new theories about the universe.

Most ancient Greeks had tried to explain nature by its appearance rather than by experimenting and carefully watching what happened. As a result, these pioneers in the study of nature sometimes made mistakes. For example, Greek astronomers

409

such as Ptolemy believed that the earth was a round, unmoving ball.

Their belief was based on simple common sense—the earth did not seem to move to anyone living on it. What did seem to move were the sun, moon, stars, and planets. As a result, Ptolemy thought that the heavenly bodies were embedded in crystal spheres forever circling the earth. For more than 1,000 years, most people in Europe accepted Ptolemy's view, called the geocentric, or earth-centered, theory.

A scientific method began to develop.

By the end of the Middle Ages, however, some thinkers began to doubt Ptolemy's theory and methods. As early as the 15th century, Leonardo da Vinci wrote: "Those sciences are vain and full of errors which are not born of experiment, the mother of certainty."

Two philosophers gave spark to the new science—the English **Sir Francis Bacon** (1561–1626) and the French **René Descartes** [rə nā′ dā-kärt′] (1596–1650). Bacon urged that all scientists experiment, carefully observe, and then write down what happened in the experiment. Information gathered this way would lead to explanations that could be tested by repeating the experiments or devising new ones. Human progress might come from the knowledge gained this way.

Descartes, a mathematician, had even more of an impact on European ideas. Based on work in geometry and algebra, Descartes declared that there were basic truths about nature that could be understood by clear mathematical formulas. His method went like this: First one doubts; then one finds the truth based on logical thinking and experiment. Today, the scientific method expressed by Bacon and Descartes is the basis of all science.

Copernicus questioned an old belief.

Modern science may have begun with the Polish scientist **Nicolaus Copernicus** (1473–1543), who died before either Descartes or Bacon was born. Living in a small town in northern Poland, Copernicus developed his own ideas about the way the sun and the planets moved. In his view, the sun was the center of the solar system, and the earth and planets moved around it. He believed that the earth turned on its axis each day as it made its yearly trip around the sun.

Copernicus developed this theory—the sun-centered, or **heliocentric system**—and rejected Ptolemy's ancient theories. He could not see the heavenly bodies, so he worked from mathematical tables. Although urged to publish his work, Copernicus was not anxious to do so. He knew that his theory would upset the Catholic and Protestant churches, both of whom supported the work of Ptolemy. The Copernican theory really got little attention at first. Even astronomers found it hard to accept because the theory contradicted common-sense observation. The system was branded as heretical, godless, and fanatical.

Brahe and Kepler improved the Copernican theory.

Tycho Brahe [brä] (1546–1601), a Dane, never accepted Copernicus' heliocentric thesis, but he did

Tycho Brahe's observatory, shown in this 16th-century drawing, was a model of exquisite detail.

realize the importance of collecting precise data. Brahe built a major research center, the first of its kind in Europe, dedicated to astronomy. From there Brahe compiled many astronomical observations, the most accurate up to his time. These, he left to his student, Johannes Kepler.

A German, **Johannes Kepler** (1571–1630) was the first professional astronomer to agree openly with Copernicus' views. After years of trying to prove Copernicus wrong with Brahe's calculations, Kepler became convinced that the earth and other planets did in fact revolve around the sun.

His three laws of planetary motion—in which he described the oval path, called an ellipse, that the planets follow—put an end to Greek ideas of astronomy. His scheme of the solar system has been followed ever since.

Galileo made important discoveries.

The heliocentric theory received more help from the Italian astronomer **Galileo** [gal'ə lā′ō] (1564–1642), who lived at the same time as Kepler. Born in Pisa, Italy, Galileo became a professor of mathematics, as well as a brilliant instrument maker.

None of the astronomers before Galileo had ever used a telescope to observe the heavens because none knew about this instrument. In 1609 Galileo heard about the telescope, which had been developed in the Netherlands around 1600, and set about making one.

Galileo's discoveries formed some of the bases for modern physics. He was interested in finding out how the planets and stars moved. Ancient Greek theory held that heavy bodies fall faster than light bodies. Galileo experimented in his laboratory by rolling weights down an inclined plane. He demonstrated that bodies of different weights fall at the same speed. By this and other experiments, Galileo discovered that forces exist that move objects through space, and that the movement of objects through space and time can be described by mathematics.

Galileo did not publish his theories because in 1616 the Church had told him not to teach or defend the heliocentric theory. In 1632, however, in his *Dialogue on the Two Great Systems of the World,* he seemed to agree with the Copernican theory. As he had feared, the Church called him to

BACKGROUND On January 7, 1610, Galileo discovered four satellites of Jupiter. Later that year, he moved to Florence and became philosopher and mathematician to Cosimo II de' Medici.

Galileo published these star charts in a 1610 collection—a group of stars known as the Pleiades (left), and the belt and sword of Orion (right).

court in 1633 and closely questioned him. Finally Galileo, almost 70 years old and exhausted by his questioners, agreed to say that the earth does not move around the sun. Legend says, however, that after he publicly denied that the earth moves, he whispered to himself, "But it does move!"

Section 1 Review

Identify Francis Bacon, René Descartes, Nicolaus Copernicus, heliocentric system, Johannes Kepler, Galileo

Main Ideas
1. What principles made up the new scientific method?
2. Which old belief did Copernicus question?
3. What did Brahe and Kepler contribute to science?
4. Why were Galileo's discoveries so important?

Critical Thinking
Making Decisions: If you were Galileo or Copernicus, would you have fought for your beliefs, even at the risk of being executed or jailed?

Several branches of science moved forward.

By the mid-17th century, wide public interest in the work of scientists developed. In part this new attention came from writers who saw the potential benefits that scientific findings could bring. Popu-

411

For some students it is surprising that mathematics had to be invented. To demonstrate the importance of math inventions write this problem on the board: CXLVII × CCXIV. Before the invention of Arabic numerals, solving this problem was nearly impossible. People had to invent "0," and new ways of writing and manipulating numbers.

Announce to students that an unexpected guest from the past is present. His name is Salius, and he is reputed to have been Europe's top scientist in 1590, having studied as a lad in Poland with Copernicus. (A student or colleague can play Salius.) Say that you have rigged a simple quiz to test the man's credentials. Salius enters the room (if possible, in long gown and flowing white beard) and starts lauding the heliocentric model of the universe. You reveal these terms, written on the chalkboard: telescope, Fahrenheit scale, Celsius scale, gravity, oxygen, thermometer, electricity, Newton's laws. You say, "Salius, with all due respect, prove to us that you are no imposter by explaining these terms." Salius is perplexed. He knows not one term. Whirl to your students and say, "Aha! Have we not found him out?" (No. These were discoveries after Salius' time.)

GUIDED PRACTICE

Ask students to explain the terms to Salius by naming the discoverer and giving an explanation of each term.

Twelve Important Scientists, 1500–1800

Nicolaus Copernicus 1473–1543	In 1543 published his heliocentric (sun-centered) theory of the solar system.
Andreas Vesalius 1514–1564	Studied anatomy by dissecting corpses; in 1543 published the first scientific work on human anatomy.
William Gilbert 1544–1603	Studied magnetism and electricity; explained how a compass needle works.
Galileo Galilei 1564–1642	Brilliant experimental astronomer and physicist who observed the sun, moon, and planets and defended Copernicus' theory.
Johannes Kepler 1571–1630	Around 1600 devised three laws of planetary motion that supported Copernicus' theory.
William Harvey 1578–1657	Published book in 1628 on the circulation of the blood.
René Descartes 1596–1650	Developed analytic geometry; made other contributions to mathematics, and to optics, physiology, psychology, and philosophy.
Robert Boyle 1627–1691	First to use scientific method in chemistry; discovered difference between elements and compounds; formulated Boyle's law of gases under pressure.
Christian Huygens 1629–1695	Physicist, astronomer, and mathematician who built the first useful pendulum clock; made improved telescopes and discovered the rings of Saturn.
Anton van Leeuwenhoek 1632–1723	The "father of microbiology"; discovered bacteria, protozoa, blood corpuscles, and other tiny objects never before seen by the human eye.
Isaac Newton 1642–1727	Invented calculus, found that light is made up of the colors of the spectrum, and discovered the laws of gravity.
Antoine Lavoisier 1743–1794	One of the founders of modern chemistry; demonstrated the role of oxygen in combustion; developed a classification system for elements and compounds.

lar enthusiasm led to increased support for research and ever more discoveries.

Improved mathematics and new tools helped scientists.

Collecting accurate information and testing it are keys to the scientific method. Scientists need tools, which include both mathematics and instruments. Modern mathematics began after the year 1000, when merchants and scholars started to use Arabic numerals. The decimal system was introduced, and math symbols, such as +, −, ×, and = came into use.

Astronomers such as Copernicus, Brahe, and Kepler all used mathematics in their calculations, but new methods made things easier. Early in the 17th century, John Napier, a Scot, invented logarithms, a short way of doing calculations with very large numbers. The Scottish mathematician also perfected the decimal system by suggesting the use of the decimal point. Meanwhile, in France, René Descartes developed analytic geometry.

By the 17th century, new and more accurate tools for measuring and observing also became available. As you read, Galileo made revolutionary discoveries with the newly invented telescope. In 1668 Sir **Isaac Newton** (1642–1727), an English scientist, made a better telescope more powerful than Galileo's, with less distortion. Wider areas of the heavens now opened to European scientists.

A German physicist named Otto von Guericke [gā′ri kə] (1602–1686) invented the first air pump capable of creating a vacuum. Guericke also showed that the pressure of air could drive a piston along a cylinder. This discovery eventually led to the development of the steam engine, which would revolutionize transportation and manufacturing.

Temperature was another quantity that interested researchers. A German physicist, Gabriel Fahrenheit [far'ən hīt] (1686–1736), invented the first modern mercury thermometer. It showed freezing at 32° and boiling at 212°. A Swedish astronomer, Anders Celsius [sel'sē əs] (1701–1744), used another scale that read 0° at freezing and 100° at boiling.

To study physics, scientists needed to be able to measure time accurately. Clocks based on gears appeared in Europe during the 14th century, but they were not very accurate. Galileo, however, discovered the principle of the pendulum, which would one day lead to more precise timekeeping. A Dutch astronomer, **Christian Huygens** [hī'gənz] (1629–1695), built the first useful pendulum clock in 1656. Scientists could then measure small units of time in complex physics experiments.

Newton brought together scientific knowledge.

In the 17th century, some brilliant researchers gained public attention and fame through their work. Isaac Newton was just such a person, one of the most accomplished scientists the world has ever known.

Newton was born in 1642, the year that Galileo died. He came from a family of poor illiterate farmers, but encouraged by a local minister, he went to Cambridge University, where he worked his way through school. Newton was so brilliant that he became a professor of mathematics. While still in his twenties, he worked out the system of advanced mathematical figuring called calculus.

Using his newly perfected telescope, experiments with balls rolled on inclines, and mathematics, Newton worked out a revolutionary theory called the law of universal gravitation. In *Mathematical Principles of Natural Philosophy* (1687), one of the most important scientific books ever written, he explained his findings.

Basically, said Newton, the laws of nature were the same for everything from small to large. The universe was like a gigantic machine that could be described mathematically. Three main laws described all motion: first, an object in motion keeps

From the Archives

The First Rule of Science

Sir Isaac Newton once summarized the work of a scientist as a fourfold task: (1) discovering the way nature operates, (2) reducing these discoveries to general laws, (3) establishing the truth of these laws by experiments, and then (4) "deducing the causes and effects of things." In 1686 Newton set down several rules for scientific reasoning, the first of which follows.

RULE I
We are to admit no more causes of natural things than such as are both true and sufficient to explain their appearances.

To this purpose the philosophers say that Nature does nothing in vain, and more is in vain when less will serve; for Nature is pleased with simplicity and affects [uses] not the pomp of superfluous [more than necessary] causes.

moving in a straight line unless forced by outside pressure to change direction; second, an outside force acting on an object moves the object in the direction of the force; and third, for every action, there is an equal and opposite reaction.

Applying these laws to the universe, Newton found that all objects attract one another with a force called gravity. The more an object weighs, the stronger the pull. The closer together the objects, the greater the pull between them. The force of gravity, therefore, is what keeps planets in orbit.

Isaac Newton's own words may best describe his outlook:

I do not know what I may appear to the world; but to myself I seem to have been only like a boy playing on the seashore, and diverting myself in now and then finding a smoother pebble or a prettier shell than ordinary, whilst the great ocean of truth lay all undiscovered before me.

FROM THE ARCHIVES From H. S. Thayer, ed., *Newton's Philosophy of Nature: Selections from His Writings* (New York: Hafner, 1953), p. 3. Newton's first rule of reasoning in science held that the simplest explanation was best. Ask the students whether this rule could be extended to history as well. Is history "pleased with simplicity" and are human actions sometimes "in vain"? (Answers will vary, but will lead to a discussion of multiple causation in history and human behavior.)

413

A MYSTERY IN HISTORY

Another mystery concerning the potato is why it is called the Irish potato in the United States if it really came from Peru. This mystery may be easily solved. The Indians in North America did not know about the potato until the Spanish explorers brought some from Peru to the Caribbean region. The new food was then traded among Indian tribes and it seems to have spread rapidly. Francis Drake, after raiding the Spanish Main in 1568, stopped at Sir Walter Raleigh's colony on Roanoke Island and carried some potatoes, which the colonists had obtained from the Indians, home to England. They were then planted on Raleigh's estate in Ireland.

One of the first crops was given by Raleigh to Queen Elizabeth, but the potato remained an exotic plant raised mainly for its greens or its supposed medicinal qualities. It took at least a century before it was commonly raised for food. Then, about 1728 some farmers from Ireland immigrated to America and brought the new crop with them, which the Americans then called Irish potatoes.

The story of the potato in history is summarized in Claire Shaver Haughton, *Green Immigrants* (New York: Harcourt Brace Jovanovich, 1978), pp. 293–305, a volume students will find to be of great interest.

Vincent van Gogh painted *The Potato Eaters* in 1885. Ask students what this painting shows about the artist's understanding of peasants and laborers. (Opinion. Most students will probably consider the painting true to life and the figures sympathetically drawn. Support for this position can be found in *The Letters of Vincent van Gogh,* edited by Mark Roskill and published in New York by Atheneum in 1986.)

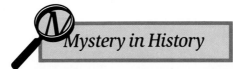

Mystery in History

DID THE POTATO CHANGE HISTORY?

For centuries, the population of Europe remained almost unchanged. Then in the 1750s, it began to grow so rapidly that by 1850 Europe's population had doubled. Historians call this sudden spurt a population explosion. This rapid growth changed people's lives in Europe and elsewhere as millions of Europeans sought new land and opportunities in other parts of the world.

Why did it happen? Historians are not sure. At first, they thought the population had increased because the death rate declined sharply in the 18th century. However, new research has shown that the death rate was not much lower in the 18th century than it had been. Life expectancy remained short, and disease continued to take a heavy toll. On the other hand, the evidence shows that between 1750 and 1850 the birthrate rose sharply among Europeans. More people were being born and stayed alive than ever before.

How was this possible? To feed so many more people, much more food was needed, more than Europeans had ever grown before. How did they get the extra food? That is at the heart of the mystery.

Could it be that Europeans found new kinds of food? Some historians think so. They say that Europeans learned to grow two new plants brought over from the New World— the potato and corn. Both foods are nutritious, easy to cultivate with hand tools (especially the potato), and can be grown in large quantities on a small piece of land.

The conquistadors had brought the potato to Europe from Peru in the 1530s. At first, however, the European peasants feared that potatoes were poisonous and refused to eat them. In the 1700s royalty, including Catherine the Great of Russia and Frederick William I of Prussia, encouraged their subjects to plant and eat potatoes. Soon, potatoes became the peasants' main food.

Besides being easy to grow, potatoes provided more food per acre than most grains. A single acre of potatoes could feed a family of six, plus one farm animal, for nearly a whole year. As a result, more children lived to become adults and have children themselves. Thus, the population grew. The potato may be the missing link that helps explain Europe's population explosion. It may well have changed history.

European Population Since A.D. 1000

Year	Population in millions
1000	36
1100	44
1200	58
1300	79
1400	60
1500	81
1600	100
1700	120
1800	180
1900	390
2000 Est.	800

According to the table, how much did Europe's population increase from 1600 to 1700? From 1700 to 1800? Vincent Van Gogh's The Potato Eaters *depicts Dutch peasants in 1885.*

Benjamin West, an American artist, painted this portrait of Benjamin Franklin drawing electricity from the sky in 1805.

Experiments began modern chemistry.

Long a mix of fact and magic, the study of chemistry had no scientific base until the middle of the 17th century. Medieval alchemists—people whose work combined science, magic, and philosophy—believed, as had the Greeks, that all matter was made of four elements—earth, air, fire, and water.

The first person to use the scientific method in chemistry was an Irishman, **Robert Boyle** (1627–1691). In *The Skeptical Chemist* (1661), Boyle transformed alchemy into chemistry by concluding that the Greeks' four elements were not mystical substances at all, but rather material ones. Neither were they elements, substances that could not be broken down by chemical means. A century later, the English scientist Henry Cavendish gave a final blow to the Greek notion when he proved that water was not an element because it was made up of hydrogen and oxygen.

Joseph Priestley (1733–1804), an English minister, identified several chemical substances, including ammonia and carbon monoxide. In 1774 he discovered an element he called "dephlogisticated air." **Antoine Lavoisier** [än twän′ lä vwä zyā′] (1743–1794), who worked about the same time in France, proved that a burning substance does not give off phlogiston [flō jis′tən], as had been previ-

ously believed. Instead, it combines with "dephlogisticated air," which he called oxygen.

Physicists studied magnetism and electricity.

One branch of physics, the study of magnetism and electricity, owes much to **William Gilbert** (1540–1603), an Englishman. Gilbert's book *On the Magnet* (1600) explained how a compass needle worked by describing the earth as a large magnet. Gilbert also knew that certain bodies behaved rather like magnets and attracted light objects.

Ever since the time of the Greeks, thinkers had been puzzled by the power of amber, which when rubbed picked up bits of feathers or paper—a demonstration of static electricity. Gilbert found that other substances, such as sulfur and glass, also behaved in the same way. For them, he coined the word electric—from the Greek word elektron, which means "amber."

Benjamin Franklin, the first important American scientist, believed that lightning was an electric spark, exactly like the static electricity Gilbert had described. In 1752 he tested his idea by flying a wire-tipped kite during a thunderstorm. Electricity went through the rain-soaked string and produced sparks in a key tied to it. When Franklin put his hand near the key, he felt a shock. The experiment was dangerous, but it proved his idea. He used this principle of attracting and conducting lightning through metal to invent the lightning rod, which is still used today to protect buildings.

Section 2 Review

Identify Isaac Newton, Christian Huygens, Robert Boyle, Antoine Lavoisier, William Gilbert, Benjamin Franklin

Main Ideas
1. Name some of the new tools and their inventors.
2. How did Newton bring together scientific knowledge?
3. How was modern chemistry different from alchemy?
4. Which scientists studied electricity?

Critical Thinking
Making Hypotheses: How did Isaac Newton's theories change the way that people viewed the universe?

Students will learn to describe the medical contributions of Paracelsus, Vesalius, Harvey, and Leeuwenhoek.

---

1 FOCUS AND MOTIVATE

Write the following list on the board: small pox, yellow fever, malaria, pneumonia, polio, measles, whooping cough, cholera, diphtheria, rabies, and bubonic plague. In 1600 catching these diseases often led to death.

---

2 TEACH

Review the contributions of Vesalius, Harvey, and Leeuwenhoek. Vesalius borrowed dead bodies to conduct anatomy studies. William Harvey experimented with live fish, frogs, and birds. Are such experiments justified?

GUIDED PRACTICE

Have students write suggestions for solving these 17th century medical problems:
1. Does blood carry disease?
2. Is the heart the source of emotion?

---

3 ASSESS AND CLOSE

ASSESS

What is the Age of Reason? (period when natural sciences flowered)

OPTIONAL RETEACHING

Students may be assigned Activities reteaching page 132.

OPTIONAL ENRICHMENT

1. Students may be assigned Activities enrichment page 133.
2. Also for enrichment:

 Overhead Transparency 44

 Source Reading 22B

---

3 Medical knowledge grew.

As some scientists explored the universe, others looked to the smaller worlds of the human body and microbes. In this way modern medicine and biology began.

Scientists studied the human body.

The first steps on the road to modern medicine were taken by a Swiss doctor known as **Paracelsus** [par′ə sel′səs] (1493–1541). In his time, doctors relied on ancient Greeks who said that illness came from imbalances within the body.

Paracelsus suggested instead that specific diseases had specific external causes, poisons mostly, which could be discovered by observation. Furthermore, diseases could be treated by new medicines derived from minerals.

By the 16th century, physicians and surgeons knew something about the body, but they hadn't systematically studied it. Instead, most medical people relied on the works of Galen, a 2nd-century Greek doctor, and his theories about anatomy and balances within the body.

Andreas Vesalius [və sā′lē əs], a Flemish doctor, changed that, however, and became the pioneer in anatomy. To learn anatomy, Vesalius gathered dead bodies, sometimes robbing the gallows. He occasionally got into trouble with the law for this, but he then moved to **Padua**, Italy, where authorities supported his studies. They even provided him with the corpses of executed criminals. Vesalius' work helped to make Padua the most important center for medicine in Europe.

After careful studies, in 1543 Vesalius published a book, *On the Fabric of the Human Body*. In this book, Vesalius correctly described the anatomy of the human body. Fellow teachers, jealous of Vesalius, bitterly attacked his ideas. Nevertheless, Vesalius' methods soon became the standard for all medical practice to this day.

Vesalius described all parts of the human body, but he did not know how they actually worked. **William Harvey** (1578–1657), an English doctor, set medicine on the road to the modern age. Harvey watched his patients closely and experimented with fish, frogs, and birds. He learned that the blood moves in a circulatory system with the heart as the central pump. In 1628 he wrote a book that explained for the first time how the heart really works.

The microscope led to important new discoveries.

Physicians learned more about the body and, much later, about the cause of disease by using the microscope. Historians are not sure who first invented this instrument for seeing small objects, but it may have been a Dutch eyeglass maker in about 1590.

No one really explored the world of tiny organisms, however, until **Anton van Leeuwenhoek** [lā-vən hük′] (1632–1723), a Dutch merchant. Leeuwenhoek never went to a university, but he became fascinated with microscopes and began to build them. Leeuwenhoek later saw and described many other tiny forms of life from bacteria to red blood corpuscles. Although he never knew how important these tiny creatures are in human health, he opened the way for the discovery of germ-caused diseases.

Scientists' discoveries showed that the physical universe was a well-ordered machine, working according to the laws of nature. This period in which the natural sciences flowered is called the **Age of Reason.** It had its roots in the scientific and intellectual advances of the 17th century, and it reached its highest point in the 18th century.

Section 3 Review

Identify Paracelsus, Andreas Vesalius, Padua, William Harvey, Anton van Leeuwenhoek, Age of Reason

Main Ideas
1. What did physicians discover from studying the human body?
2. What discoveries were made with the microscope?

Critical Thinking

Identifying Assumptions: Consider the following statement: "Galen was wrong about anatomy so his work is useless." True or false? Support your answer with evidence.

HIGHLIGHTS OF CIVILIZATION

The Telescope and the Microscope

What surpasses all wonders by far . . . is the discovery of four wandering stars not known or observed by any man before us.

The "stars" Galileo had just discovered were the moons of Jupiter, and the instrument with which he observed them was one of the world's first telescopes. Though no

Galileo looked through his telescope (below left) and drew what he saw (top left). Below are Leeuwenhoek's microscope and sketches of red corpuscles.

more powerful than a good set of binoculars, this crude instrument opened up vast new worlds to 17th-century scientists. The telescope made the moon's mountains and craters distinctly visible. It showed the Milky Way not to be a cloud of dust, but a dense cluster of individual stars. It allowed people to see thousands of stars previously invisible.

Just as Galileo's telescope suddenly brought the vast realms of distant space into focus, Anton van Leeuwenhoek's microscope brought the kingdoms of miniscule life forms into view. Scientists could see thousands of microorganisms teeming in a drop of water. In time, more powerful microscopes would reveal the workings of the living world, packed in the structure of the cell.

The telescope and the microscope enlarged the 17th-century world, bringing near the distant stars and making visible the invisible. Without these instruments, the scientific discoveries of later centuries could not have been made.

INDEPENDENT PRACTICE/ HOMEWORK

Assign the Section Review, the Chapter Review items, Activities page 131, or Workbook page 89.

CLOSURE

Medical breakthroughs discussed in this section can share much of the credit for the world's population increase from 500 million in the 1500s to almost 6 billion today.

Answers to Section 3 Review

Identify

Key Terms, People, and Places are defined on pages indicated in parentheses. Also see the Glossary and Biographical Dictionary. Paracelsus (416), Andreas Vesalius (416), Padua (416), William Harvey (416), Anton van Leeuwenhoek (416), Age of Reason (416)

Main Ideas

1. that disease came from outside the body rather than from imbalances within and that diseases could be treated with new medicines derived from minerals
2. organisms too tiny to be seen with the naked eye. This laid the groundwork for later discoveries of germ-caused disease.

Critical Thinking

Galen laid the groundwork for the study of the body. Each scientist built on the work of the ones before.

HIGHLIGHTS OF CIVILIZATION

Students may be interested in reading *Discoveries and Opinions of Galileo,* a translation of Galileo's writings translated by Stillman Drake (Doubleday Anchor Books, 1957).

Answers to Test Yourself

Key Terms, People, and Places
The key terms, people, and places tested here were introduced in the chapter sections and reviewed in the Section Reviews. For definitions see the page references at the appropriate Section Reviews. Also see the Glossary and Biographical Dictionary.

Main Ideas
The main ideas tested here were introduced in the sections of this chapter and reviewed in the Section Reviews. For answers to these questions, see the appropriate Section Reviews.

Critical Thinking
1. If people began to question one aspect of the Church belief system, they might question others. This questioning would weaken Church power and authority.
2. Students' ideas of the ideal will vary. Qualities listed might be: brilliant, disciplined, imaginative, creative, courageous enough to question age-old beliefs and to think that they themselves might be as good or better than those authorities who came before them, curious about what makes things work, anxious to see beyond what is easily visible.

Section Summaries

Section 1
Scientists worked out new theories about the universe.
A new era in Western thought began in the 16th century with the development of experimental science. One of the most important changes was a new view of the universe. Copernicus proposed a new heliocentric, or sun-centered, theory. His ideas received little attention at first, but scientists later improved on them. Kepler's laws of planetary motion aided the heliocentric theory, as did some of Galileo's discoveries. The so-called Copernican revolution climaxed with Newton. He brought together earlier discoveries in the laws of universal gravitation.

Section 2
Several branches of science moved forward.
By the mid-17th century, wide public interest in the work of scientists developed. This popular enthusiasm led to increased support for research and ever more discoveries and inventions. New mathematical tools (logarithms, analytic geometry, and calculus) and means of measurement (clocks and thermometers) were developed, aiding scientists. Chemistry became a science with the work of Boyle, Priestley, and Lavoisier. The field of physics owed much to the discoveries of Gilbert, Galileo, Newton, and Franklin.

Section 3
Medical knowledge grew.
As some scientists explored the universe, others looked to the smaller worlds of the human body and microbes. In this way modern medicine and biology began.

Test Yourself

Key Terms, People, and Places
Identify the significance of each of the following:

Section 1
a. Francis Bacon
b. René Descartes
c. Nicolaus Copernicus
d. heliocentric system
e. Johannes Kepler
f. Galileo

Review Dates

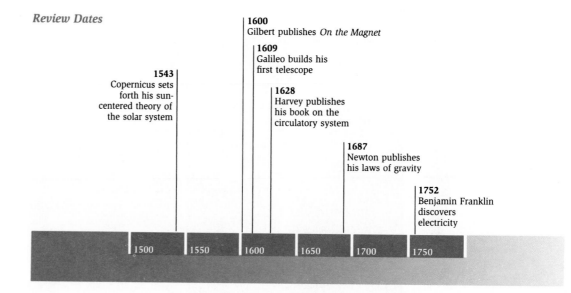

1543
Copernicus sets forth his sun-centered theory of the solar system

1600
Gilbert publishes *On the Magnet*

1609
Galileo builds his first telescope

1628
Harvey publishes his book on the circulatory system

1687
Newton publishes his laws of gravity

1752
Benjamin Franklin discovers electricity

1500   1550   1600   1650   1700   1750

Section 2

a. Isaac Newton
b. Christian Huygens
c. Robert Boyle
d. Antoine Lavoisier
e. William Gilbert
f. Benjamin Franklin

Section 3

a. Paracelsus
b. Andreas Vesalius
c. Padua
d. William Harvey
e. Anton van Leeuwenhoek
f. Age of Reason

Main Ideas

Section 1

1. What were the principles of the new scientific method?

2. What old beliefs did Copernicus challenge with his theories?

3. What contributions to science did Tycho Brahe and Johannes Kepler make?

4. Why were Galileo's scientific breakthroughs significant in history?

Section 2

1. What were some of the new tools invented in this period? Give the names of their inventors.

2. How did Newton's theories bring together the scientific knowledge of the past?

3. How did the modern chemists differ from the alchemists?

4. Name three important scientists who studied electricity.

Section 3

1. What new discoveries did physicians make from studying the human body?

2. What important discoveries did the use of the microscope lead to?

Critical Thinking

1. Making Hypotheses Why did the Church resist some of the scientific advances—particularly the heliocentric thesis—discussed in this chapter?

2. Analyzing Comparisons What qualities did all the scientists described in this chapter have in common? Use your observations about the scientists in the chapter to create an image of your ideal scientist. Describe this scientist, concentrating on such areas as skills, habits, talents, motivation, and achievements.

CRITICAL THINKING QUESTION LEVEL 1. average; 2. challenging

Chapter Skills and Activities

Practicing Study and Research Skills

Distinguishing Fact from Opinion

Throughout the scientific revolution, scientists were striving to discover and prove facts. A fact is a statement that expresses something that is known to be true or to have happened. A fact can be proved. An opinion, in contrast, is a statement that shows someone's judgment or way of thinking. An opinion cannot be proved. Identify these statements as fact or opinion.

a. Water boils at 212°F.
b. Isaac Newton is the greatest scientist ever.
c. Scientists should not cut up corpses for research.
d. The earth orbits around the sun.

Linking Past and Present

Major advances in science are often controversial because they change our way of thinking. These advances also often raise important ethical questions and come into conflict with traditional religious values—conflicts as explosive and troubling as those Copernicus and Galileo had with the Church. Give two examples of scientific advances that have raised such controversy today.

Learning History Through Maps

Using a blank outline map of Europe (ask your teacher for one), plot the places in which the scientific discoveries discussed in this chapter were taking place.

REVIEW

Summarizing the Unit

Chapter 19
The European Renaissance
The Renaissance was an intellectual movement that began in Italy in the 14th century, in which people believed that individual human beings could perfect themselves through study of secular rather than religious subjects. Literature, art, and classical culture underwent much development.

Chapter 20
The Age of Exploration
From about 1400 to about 1700, European governments sponsored exploration to expand trade routes and to spread Christianity around the world. The resulting increase in trade stimulated the development of capitalism.

Chapter 21
The Reformation and National Power
The Reformation, as sparked by Martin Luther's protests in 1517, resulted in increased religious feeling among the Europeans. Protestantism emerged, and it gave rise to national churches controlled by secular leaders.

Chapter 22
The Scientific Revolution
The scientific revolution resulted both from new information about nature and from a new way of gathering information that was based on experiment and reasoning. These discoveries affected every area of thought and experience.

Using Writing Skills

The biography can be a most interesting form of writing when done properly. This account of a person's life should describe the subject in such a way as to make him or her come alive—using personal descriptions, quotations from and about the subject, and unique experiences. A good biography is thus much more than a listing of the subject's accomplishments or birth and death dates.

   Activity. This unit deals with a revolution in ideas, led by some of the most intriguing individuals in history. Select one of the people in whom you have some interest. Some possibilities include Ferdinand Magellan, Catherine de' Medici, Martin Luther, Leonardo da Vinci, Elizabeth I, or Rembrandt van Rijn. Find a biography of that person in your library, perhaps in a larger book or encyclopedia. Read about your subject, and select one aspect of that person's life that you feel best represents his or her experience. It could be, for example, an event, an accomplishment, or a decision. Describe your selection in a paragraph, working to make your subject come alive for your readers.

Test Yourself

Key Terms and People
Match each term or person with the correct definition.
1. system of thought or action concerned with human interests and values
2. person who taught the idea of predestination
3. economic system in which private individuals or companies own businesses for profit
4. person considered to be the father of modern science
5. movement that led to the establishment of new Protestant churches
6. economic idea stating that a strong country must export more than it imports
a. capitalism
b. Nicolaus Copernicus
c. mercantilism
d. Reformation
e. John Calvin
f. humanism

Key Dates

Match the letters on the time line with the events for which they stand:

_____ Michelangelo begins painting the Sistine Chapel.
_____ Machiavelli's *The Prince* is published.
_____ The Edict of Nantes is signed.
_____ The Thirty Years' War ends.
_____ Leonardo da Vinci paints the *Mona Lisa.*
_____ Benjamin Franklin discovers electricity.
_____ The Reformation begins with Luther's protest.

Key Places

Match the letters on the map with the places described below:

_____ city known as the "Queen of the Adriatic"
_____ home of the pope in the 1300s
_____ state controlled by the Hohenzollern family
_____ new capital city built by Peter the Great
_____ Italian city famous for its Renaissance art

Main Ideas

1. During the Renaissance _____
a. people felt they could perfect themselves through study.
b. the study of religious studies increased.
c. people's lives were governed by strong central governments.
d. the study of art declined.
2. One of the main reasons the Spanish were able to conquer the Aztecs and the Incas was that _____
a. they had more people.
b. they brought unfamiliar diseases.
c. they were friendly to the Americans.
d. they converted the Americans to Christianity.
3. Prince Henry the Navigator was important during the Age of Exploration because _____
a. he sponsored Columbus' journey to the Americas.
b. he found the Northwest Passage.
c. he was the first to sail around the world.
d. he made Portugal a leading sea power.
4. The Catholic Church declined in power during the 14th and 15th centuries because _____
a. many people believed that the Church was only interested in politics and material wealth.
b. people felt religion did not protect them from the Black Death.
c. people could not read the Bible themselves.
d. people could not afford to pay tithes.
5. During the scientific revolution, Copernicus did not publish his works because _____
a. they were unfinished.
b. he was censored by the government.
c. they ran counter to established religious views.
d. he did not think it was important to do so.

Critical Thinking

1. Analyzing Comparisons In what ways did the Renaissance represent a break with medieval times? Support your answer with evidence.
2. Assessing Cause and Effect What factors led to the growth of strong secular states? What might have been the impact of this new political development on the people who lived in them? Support your answer with evidence.

CRITICAL THINKING QUESTION LEVEL 1. average; 2. challenging

The Early Modern Era: Asia, Africa, and the Americas

OVERVIEW

This unit covers Asia and the Americas from 1500 to 1800 including Muslim empires, Manchu China, Tokugawa Japan, and the formation of Latin America.

ADDITIONAL TEACHING AIDS FOR UNIT SIX

Literature for the Teacher

Bausani, Alessandro. *From Earliest Days to 20th Century: The Persians.* St. Martins Press, 1971.

Cespedes, A. Guillermo. *Latin America: The Early Years.* Alfred A. Knopf, 1974.

Hennessy, Alastair. *The Frontier in Latin American History.* University of New Mexico, 1978.

Lewis, Bernard. *The Muslim Discovery of Europe.* W. W. Norton & Co., 1982.

Patnaik, Naveen. *A Second Paradise: Indian Courtly Life 1590–1947.* New York: Doubleday & Co., 1985.

Stradling, R. A. *Europe and the Decline of Spain.* George Allan and Unwin, Ltd., 1981.

Zaki, Muhammad, *Arab Accounts of India During the Fourteenth Century.* South Asia Books, 1983.

Literature for the Student

Cooke, Jean and Ann Kramer, T. Rowland-Entwistle. *History's Timeline.* New York: Crescent Books, 1981. (easy)

Reischauer, Edwin. *Japan: Story of a Nation* (3rd edition). Alfred A. Knopf, 1981. (average)

Reischauer, Edwin. *The Japanese Today: Change and Continuity.* Cambridge: Harvard Press, 1988. (challenging)

Tames, Richard. *Servant of the Shogun.* New York: St. Martins Press, 1987. (average)

Audio-Visual Materials*

China: The Manchu Rule (film 11 in the Chinese History Series). Film, 19 minutes, color, [Indiana University], 1976. Depicts the Ch'ing regime

The Glory That Remains: The Great Moghuls. Film, 30 minutes, color, [Time-Life], 1969. Akbar, third and great of India's Moghul rulers builds the city of Fathepur-Sikri

Japan: A Historical Overview. Film, 14 minutes, color, [Cornerstone], 1964. Traces major events from 800 B.C. to today

Mexico: An Introduction. Video, 24 minutes, color, [University of Illinois Film Center], 1982. Describes the geographical and cultural diversity that helped shape the character and history of Mexico

The Puritan Experience. Video, 2 titles, 30 minutes, color, [Learning Corporation of America], 1975. "Forsaking England" and "Making a New World." Personalizes the experiences of the Puritans who went to the New World

Sentinels of Silence. Film, 19 minutes, color, [EB], 1971. Civilizations of pre-Columbian Mexico with Orson Welles' narrative speculating about the people responsible for those civilizations

* For a complete listing of sources of audio-visual materials see page T30.

OPTIONAL WRITING ASSIGNMENTS

1. You are an adviser to Firuz Shah Tughlak, one of the Delhi Sultans. He has asked you to submit, in writing, the proposals that you have discussed with him regarding suggested policies to govern the people in his territory. He especially wants you to review the policies of earlier rulers, to make suggested changes, and to give reasons for the changes.

2. You are a teenage peasant in 12th-century China. You are returning to your village from your first trip to Hangzhou. Write a letter to your parents explaining why you are thinking about leaving the family and the village to live in the large city.

3. Write a pamphlet for Samurai warriors during the Tokugawa Shogunate. Your pamphlet should inform all samurai about the code of conduct known as Bushido.

4. You are a Spanish soldier accompanying Cortés to his meeting with Montezuma. Write entries in your diary describing your landing and your meeting with and conquest of the Aztecs.

5. Write an editorial for your local newspaper in Mexico protesting the treatment of Indians under the encomienda system.

UNIT TESTS
IN THE TEACHER'S RESOURCE FILE

Unit Test, pp. 133–134

Alternate Unit Test, pp. 135–136

FINE ART IN UNIT SIX

Fine art forms an integral part of the historical record of events portrayed in this textbook. A listing of the paintings, drawings, sculpture, historic photographs, architecture, and other works of fine art selected to illustrate this unit follows. Students may be asked to research the artists and their works and report their findings to the entire class. Students also may be asked to write one or more paragraphs describing what they see upon a detailed study of a work of art and what the artist was attempting to communicate.

The Early Modern Era: Asia, Africa, and the Americas

Themes and Patterns When European voyagers began to explore the world, the Chinese, Japanese, and Muslims generally remained content to concentrate on their own cultures and had little admiration for any other. They had wealthy civilizations, and their outstanding rulers, such as Suleiman in Turkey, Akbar in India, and Kangxi in China, stood on a par with Charles V of the Holy Roman Empire and Louis XIV of France.

When Europeans in this period tried to deal with Japan, China, India, and the Middle East in order to benefit from their wealth, the technique they used was to establish trade relations. Each of the Asian powers was too strong for the Europeans to impose political control, especially at the beginning of the early modern era. Even trade became a difficult matter. The Tokugawa shoguns became so suspicious of the Europeans that they cut off all trade in the 17th century, except for one European ship a year. Although some of these powers expanded militarily, generally they also followed inward-looking policies. In the long run, these policies proved to be a serious mistake, for this was the very time that Europe was making great strides in science and technology.

With weaker civilizations, the story was different. European expeditions were able to overwhelm the Aztecs in Mexico, the Incas in Peru, and the varied peoples of the East Indies. In the Americas, the Europeans created empires of settlement and then transported millions of Africans to work as slaves in the mines and on the plantations. The blending of European, American Indian, and African cultures during the 300 years of the early modern era led to the formation of a new civilization, that of Latin America.

Nestled in a garden of trees and reflecting ponds is the Taj Mahal, a tomb built by Emperor Shah Jahan for his wife, Mumtaz Mahal. This white marble building is one of the glories of Mughal architecture.

Chapters in This Unit

23 Muslim Empires in Turkey, Persia, India, and Africa

OVERVIEW

In the 16th and 17th centuries, Islamic rule was established in eastern Europe and the Middle East by the Ottoman Turks, in Persia by the Safavids, in India by the Mughals, and in Kanem-Bornu by Idris Alooma.

PLANNING CHART

Section	Text Pages	Key Concept	Suggested Teaching Time
1 The Ottoman Turks dominated the Muslim world.	425–427	The Ottoman Turks built an Islamic empire that stretched from North Africa to Iraq and lasted 500 years.	One day **More time?** Use *Overhead Transparency 45* or *Source Reading 23A.*
2 The Safavid dynasty brought Shiism to Persia.	428–430	Persia held off the Ottomans and became a Shiite stronghold under the Safavids.	One day
3 The Mughals united and ruled most of India.	430–433	India enjoyed two of its most glorious centuries in the 1500s and 1600s under Mughal rule.	One day **More time?** Use *Overhead Transparency 46* or *Source Reading 23B.*
4 Islam shaped new states in West Africa.	435–436	Islam moved into the Lake Chad region of West Africa and was forcefully spread among the Hausa people in the 19th century.	One day **Less time?** Have students read Section 4 as homework. Briefly summarize in class.

ANCILLARIES

Materials that may be used with this chapter to reinforce, reteach, enrich, and assess learning are pictured on the following pages.

Teacher's Resource File

ACTIVITIES

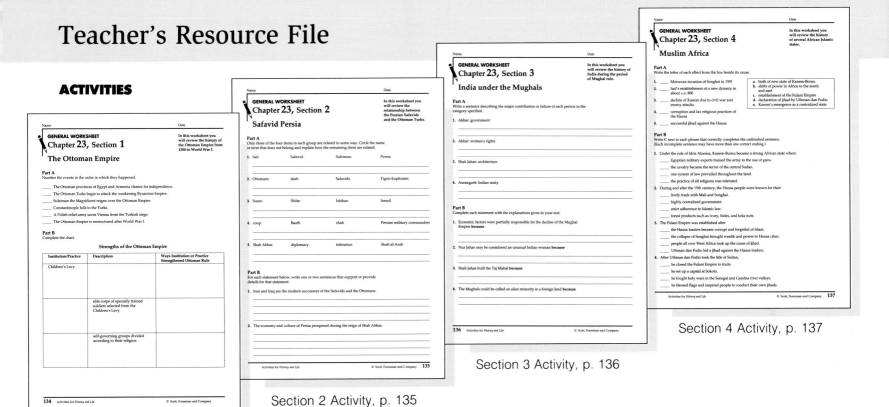

GENERAL WORKSHEET
Chapter 23, Section 1

The Ottoman Empire

In this worksheet you will review the history of the Ottoman Empire from 1300 to World War I.

Part A
Number the events in the order in which they happened.

___ The Ottoman provinces of Egypt and Armenia clamor for independence.
___ The Ottoman Turks begin to attack the weakening Byzantine Empire.
___ Suleiman the Magnificent reigns over the Ottoman Empire.
___ Constantinople falls to the Turks.
___ A Polish relief army saves Vienna from the Turkish siege.
___ The Ottoman Empire is restructured after World War I.

Part B
Complete the chart.

Strengths of the Ottoman Empire

Institution/Practice	Description	Ways Institution or Practice Strengthened Ottoman Rule
Children's Levy		
	elite corps of specially trained soldiers selected from the Children's Levy	
	self-governing groups divided according to their religion	

Section 1 Activity, p. 134

GENERAL WORKSHEET
Chapter 23, Section 2

Safavid Persia

In this worksheet you will review the relationship between the Persian Safavids and the Ottoman Turks.

Part A
Only three of the four items in each group are related in some way. Circle the name or term that does not belong and explain how the remaining three are related.

1. Safi / Safavid / Suleiman / Persia
2. Ottomans / shah / Safavids / Tigris-Euphrates
3. Sunni / Shiite / Isfahan / Ismail
4. coup / Baath / shah / Persian military commanders
5. Shah Abbas / diplomacy / toleration / Shatt-al-Arab

Part B
For each statement below, write one or two sentences that support or provide details for that statement.

1. Iran and Iraq are the modern successors of the Safavids and the Ottomans.

2. The economy and culture of Persia prospered during the reign of Shah Abbas.

Section 2 Activity, p. 135

GENERAL WORKSHEET
Chapter 23, Section 3

India under the Mughals

In this worksheet you will review the history of India during the period of Mughal rule.

Part A
Write a sentence describing the major contribution or failure of each person in the category specified.

1. Akbar: government
2. Akbar: women's rights
3. Shah Jahan: architecture
4. Aurangzeb: Indian unity

Part B
Complete each statement with the explanations given in your text.

1. Economic factors were partially responsible for the decline of the Mughal Empire **because**
2. Nur Jahan may be considered an unusual Indian woman **because**
3. Shah Jahan built the Taj Mahal **because**
4. The Mughals could be called an alien minority in a foreign land **because**

Section 3 Activity, p. 136

GENERAL WORKSHEET
Chapter 23, Section 4

Muslim Africa

In this worksheet you will review the history of several African Islamic states.

Part A
Write the letter of each effect from the box beside its cause.

1. ___ Moroccan invasion of Songhai in 1591
2. ___ Saif's establishment of a new dynasty in about A.D. 800
3. ___ decline of Kanem due to civil war and enemy attacks
4. ___ corruption and lax religious practices of the Hausa
5. ___ successful jihad against the Hausa

a. birth of new state of Kanem-Bornu
b. shifts of power in Africa to the south and east
c. establishment of the Fulani Empire
d. declaration of jihad by Uthman dan Fodio
e. Kanem's emergence as a centralized state

Part B
Write C next to each phrase that correctly completes the unfinished sentence. (Each incomplete sentence may have more than one correct ending.)

1. Under the rule of Idris Alooma, Kanem-Bornu became a strong African state where
   ___ Egyptian military experts trained the army in the use of guns.
   ___ the cavalry became the terror of the central Sudan.
   ___ one system of law prevailed throughout the land.
   ___ the practice of all religions was tolerated.

2. During and after the 15th century, the Hausa people were known for their
   ___ lively trade with Mali and Songhai.
   ___ highly centralized government.
   ___ strict adherence to Islamic law.
   ___ forest products such as ivory, hides, and kola nuts.

3. The Fulani Empire was established after
   ___ the Hausa leaders became corrupt and forgetful of Islam.
   ___ the collapse of Songhai brought wealth and power to Hausa cities.
   ___ people all over West Africa took up the cause of jihad.
   ___ Uthman dan Fodio led a jihad against the Hausa leaders.

4. After Uthman dan Fodio took the title of Sultan,
   ___ he closed the Fulani Empire to trade.
   ___ he set up a capital at Sokoto.
   ___ he fought holy wars in the Senegal and Gambia river valleys.
   ___ he blessed flags and inspired people to conduct their own jihads.

Section 4 Activity, p. 137

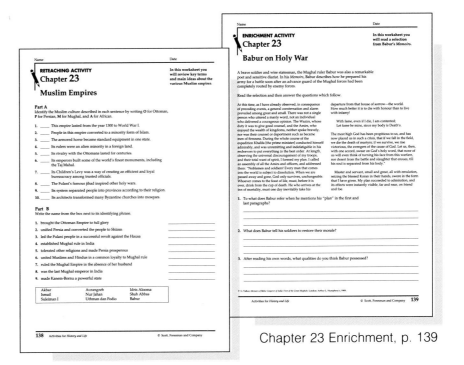

RETEACHING ACTIVITY
Chapter 23

Muslim Empires

In this worksheet you will review key terms and main ideas about the various Muslim empires.

Part A
Identify the Muslim culture described in each sentence by writing **O** for Ottoman, **P** for Persian, **M** for Mughal, and **A** for African.

1. ___ This empire lasted from the year 1300 to World War I.
2. ___ People in this empire converted to a minority form of Islam.
3. ___ The armored horse became standard equipment in one state.
4. ___ Its rulers were an alien minority in a foreign land.
5. ___ Its rivalry with the Ottomans lasted for centuries.
6. ___ Its emperors built some of the world's finest monuments, including the Taj Mahal.
7. ___ Its Children's Levy was a way of creating an efficient and loyal bureaucracy among trusted officials.
8. ___ The Fulani's famous jihad inspired other holy wars.
9. ___ Its system separated people into provinces according to their religion.
10. ___ Its architects transformed many Byzantine churches into mosques.

Part B
Write the name from the box next to its identifying phrase.

1. brought the Ottoman Empire to full glory ___
2. unified Persia and converted the people to Shiism ___
3. led the Fulani people in a successful revolt against the Hausa ___
4. established Mughal rule in India ___
5. tolerated other religions and made Persia prosperous ___
6. united Muslims and Hindus in a common loyalty to Mughal rule ___
7. ruled the Mughal Empire in the absence of her husband ___
8. was the last Mughal emperor in India ___
9. made Kanem-Bornu a powerful state ___

Akbar	Aurangzeb	Idris Alooma
Ismail	Nur Jahan	Shah Abbas
Suleiman I	Uthman dan Fodio	Babur

Chapter 23 Reteaching, p. 138

ENRICHMENT ACTIVITY
Chapter 23

Babur on Holy War

In this worksheet you will read a selection from Babur's Memoirs.

A brave soldier and wise statesman, the Mughal ruler Babur was also a remarkable poet and sensitive diarist. In his *Memoirs*, Babur describes how he prepared his army for a battle soon after an advance guard of the Mughal forces had been completely routed by enemy forces.

Read the selection and then answer the questions which follow.

At this time, as I have already observed, in consequence of preceding events, a general consternation and alarm prevailed among great and small. There was not a single person who uttered a manly word, not an individual who delivered a courageous opinion. The Wazirs, whose duty it was to give good counsel, and the Amirs, who enjoyed the wealth of kingdoms, neither spoke bravely, nor was their counsel or deportment such as became men of firmness. During the whole course of the expedition Khalifa [the prime minister] conducted himself admirably, and was unremitting and indefatigable in his endeavours to put everything in the best order. At length, observing the universal discouragement of my troops, and their total want of spirit, I formed my plan. I called an assembly of all the Amirs and officers, and addressed them: "Noblemen and soldiers! Every man that comes into the world is subject to dissolution. When we are passed away and gone, God only survives, unchangeable. Whoever comes to the feast of life, must, before it is over, drink from the cup of death. He who arrives at the inn of mortality, must one day inevitably take his

departure from that house of sorrow—the world. How much better it is to die with honour than to live with infamy!

With fame, even if I die, I am contented;
Let fame be mine, since my body is Death's.

The most high God has been propitious to us, and has now placed us in such a crisis, that if we fall in the field, we die the death of martyrs; if we survive, we rise victorious, the avengers of the cause of God. Let us, then, with one accord, swear on God's holy word, that none of us will even think of turning his face from this warfare, nor desert from the battle and slaughter that ensues, till his soul is separated from his body."

Master and servant, small and great, all with emulation, seizing the blessed Koran in their hands, swore in the form that I have given. My plan succeeded to admiration, and its effects were instantly visible, far and near, on friend and foe.

1. To what does Babur refer when he mentions his "plan" in the first and last paragraphs?

2. What does Babur tell his soldiers to restore their morale?

3. After reading his own words, what qualities do you think Babur possessed?

F. G. Talbot, Memoirs of Babur, Emperor of India; First of the Great Mughals. London: Arthur L. Humphreys's, 1909.

Chapter 23 Enrichment, p. 139

423b

Teacher's Resource File

GEOGRAPHY SKILLS

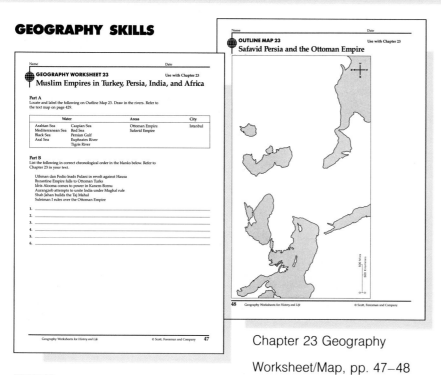

Chapter 23 Geography
Worksheet/Map, pp. 47–48

Chapter 23 Map Lesson, p. 105

TESTS

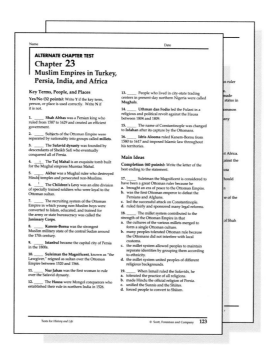

Chapter Test, pp. 121–122

Alternate Chapter Test, pp. 123–124

Other Optional Ancillaries

WORKBOOK

WORKSHEET
Chapter **23**, Section **1**

The Ottoman Turks

In this worksheet you will review the culture and history of the Ottoman Turks.

Part A
Fill in the blanks, using information given in your text.

The culture of the Ottoman Turks included a distinctive style of architecture and interior design. The Turks often turned churches into _____ and combined features of Islamic architecture with those of the peoples they conquered. For example, the Ottomans preserved and modified the most famous church in Constantinople, _____. A pattern developed in Ottoman architecture; a mosque or palace would have several small _____ surrounding a central _____, with four to six _____, or towers, at the building's edges. Inside, the walls and floors were covered with _____. Ottoman homes were also impressive, with costly carpets, intricately designed tables, and brass tea urns called _____. The style was simple, yet magnificent at the same time.

Part B
Write T if the statement is true and F if it is false. On the lines below, rewrite each false statement to make it true.

1. _____ The defeat of Constantinople in 1453 by the Ottoman Turks marked the fall of the Byzantine Empire.
2. _____ After the Turks conquered Constantinople, they renamed the city Byzantium.
3. _____ The Children's Levy gave the Ottoman Turks an efficient recruiting system for their army and state bureaucracy.
4. _____ Suleiman I is considered a great ruler because he united the Persians and Afghans.
5. _____ One of the strengths of the Ottoman Empire was the organization of its government.
6. _____ At its height the Ottoman Empire included parts of southern and eastern Europe, Asia Minor to the Caspian Sea, and much of the northern coast of Africa.

90 Worksheets for History and Life   © Scott, Foresman and Company

Section 1 Worksheet, p. 90

WORKSHEET
Chapter **23**, Section **2**

The Safavids in Persia

In this worksheet you will review the development of Persia under the Safavid dynasty.

Part A
The Safavid dynasty established a unified Persia. Indicate which of the following three Safavid rulers was responsible for each action or accomplishment listed below.

A. Sheikh Safi   B. Ismail   C. Shah Abbas

1. _____ set out to conquer the world as an orphaned 13-year-old
2. _____ built a capital city at Isfahan
3. _____ encouraged Shiites in Asia Minor to rebel against their Ottoman rulers
4. _____ founded a religious group in Persia and developed a militaristic following
5. _____ made Shiism the official religion of Persia
6. _____ created an efficient government that excluded the military
7. _____ encouraged free trade with the European powers and tolerated non-Muslim religions

Part B
Using the pair of words in each set, write a sentence describing Persia under the Safavids.

1. Sunni/Shiite

2. 200 years/Ottoman-Safavid conflict

3. military/shah

4. national unity/early Safavid rule

Worksheets for History and Life   © Scott, Foresman and Company   91

Section 2 Worksheet, p. 91

WORKSHEET
Chapter **23**, Section **3**

India Under Mughal Rule

In this worksheet you will review the Mughal rule of India.

Part A
Number the events in the order in which they happened.

_____ Nur Jahan is exiled to Lahore.
_____ Babur defeats the sultan at Delhi.
_____ Aurangzeb claims authority over all of India.
_____ Babur captures Kabul.
_____ Akbar becomes ruler of all northern India.
_____ Shah Jahan restores Islam as the state religion.

Part B
The following rulers were prominent in the rise and fall of the Mughal Empire. Write B for Babur, J for Jahangir, A for Akbar, or SJ for Shah Jahan to identify the ruler described by each phrase.

1. _____ tolerated the practice of religions other than Islam
2. _____ allowed his wife to rule in his absence
3. _____ was a descendant of Tamerlane and Genghis Khan
4. _____ built a magnificent *taj* to the memory of his dead wife
5. _____ built 52 palaces at Delhi
6. _____ ended the religious freedom allowed by his grandfather
7. _____ conquered Kabul and established Mughal rule in India
8. _____ ruled during the high point of Mughal power in India
9. _____ attempted to outlaw suttee

Part C
Write a paragraph contrasting the reigns of Akbar and Aurangzeb.

92 Worksheets for History and Life   © Scott, Foresman and Company

Section 3 Worksheet, p. 92

WORKSHEET
Chapter **23**, Section **4**

Islam in Africa

In this worksheet you will review the rise and fall of several Muslim states in West Africa.

Part A
Write the letter of the word or words from the box that best complete each sentence.

a. Islamic law
b. holy war
c. handicraft industries
d. Muslims
e. Fulani
f. city-states
g. Lake Chad
h. jihad
i. kola nut

1. _____ In the Sudan, the Fulani revolution was the largest and most famous _____.
2. _____ Uthman dan Fodio was a leader of the _____.
3. _____ The Hausa lived in independent _____.
4. _____ In addition to trading forest products, the Hausa developed _____.
5. _____ A jihad is best defined as a _____.
6. _____ The state of Kanem developed east of _____.
7. _____ Idris Alooma, ruler of Kanem-Bornu, imposed _____ throughout his territories.
8. _____ Until the late 1500s few of the common people of the Sudan were _____.
9. _____ The _____ is a product that, when chewed, enables one to go for long periods of time without food or water.

Part B
Write a cause for each effect.

1. During the 1600s the balance of trade and political power shifted to the south and east in Africa.

2. Ambassadors from the Ottoman Empire traveled to Kanem-Bornu.

3. The Fulani people rose up against the Hausa leaders.

Worksheets for History and Life   © Scott, Foresman and Company   93

Section 4 Worksheet, p. 93

SOURCE READINGS

Source Reading 23A
Source Reading 23B

TEST GENERATOR

40 multiple-choice questions for Chapter 23

OVERHEAD TRANSPARENCIES

Overhead Transparency 45
Overhead Transparency 46

Chapter

23

Muslim Empires In Turkey, Persia, India, and Africa

1450–1800

1400	
1500	
1501	Safavids conquer Persia
1648	Taj Mahal is built
1700	
1800	

It was May 29, 1453. The siege of Constantinople by the Ottoman armies had been going on for two months. All of the old Byzantine Empire's territories in Asia Minor to the east and most of its European holdings to the west had already fallen to the Ottoman Turks. Only Constantinople remained, defended by a few hundred Byzantine army regulars and a few thousand hired mercenaries. The Ottoman artillery began lobbing half-ton shells at the 100-foot high, 1,000-year-old walls. Among the Ottoman cannon was one so large it took 12 oxen to move it and took so long to load that it could only be fired seven times a day. The Byzantines did not possess even one cannon.

The Byzantine emperor, Constantine XI, 88th successor to Constantine I, founder of the city, took communion in the Hagia Sophia basilica and rejoined the battle. As the enemy breached the walls, the heir of the Romans threw himself into the worst of the fighting and died, the last emperor of the Eastern Roman Empire. The Byzantine Empire, a Christian bastion against every invader from Central Asia for a thousand years and Europe's defense against the might of Islam for more than 800 years, had fallen. The conquest of the city of Constantinople was only one of many victories claimed by Muslim armies during the 15th, 16th, and 17th centuries.

The Islamic world had begun to experience a great revival. Many of its converts set out to conquer new territories for their religion and to revitalize and reform older Islamic governments that had become weakened. The most successful of these new champions of Islam were the Ottomans in Turkey, the Safavids in Iran, the Mughals in India, and the Fulani in West Africa. The Muslims advanced further into Eastern Europe, Asia, and Africa than they ever had before. The governments established then still greatly influence these areas today.

424

Persian carpets became famous in the Safavid era. This carpet represents a formal Persian garden with flower beds and running water in which fish swim.

Reading Preview

In this chapter you will read about the Muslim governments that flourished in Turkey, Persia, India, and West Africa in the period 1450–1804.

1. *The Ottoman Turks dominated the Muslim world.*

2. *The Safavid dynasty brought Shiism to Persia.*

3. *The Mughals united and ruled most of India.*

4. *Islam shaped new states in West Africa.*

 ## The Ottoman Turks dominated the Muslim world.

During the 1200s the powerful Seljuks, the Turks whose armies had controlled most of the Islamic world for two centuries, began to quarrel among themselves. Another group, the Ottoman Turks, began to expand.

Ottoman Turks extended the boundaries of Islam.

Once vassals of the Seljuk Turks who ruled much of Asia Minor, the Ottoman Turks, led by their chieftain Osman, pushed steadily against the bor-

Essential Learning Objective

Students will learn to describe the long-lasting dominance of the Ottoman Empire.

1 FOCUS AND MOTIVATE

Explain that between the time of Muhammad's death in 632 and the end of World War I in 1918, the Middle East was dominated by two major groups, the Sunni Arabs until 1055 and then various Turko-Mongol groups for the next 850 years. Point out that all Turks and Mongols were originally from Mongolia. The Seljuk Turks dominated the Middle East from about 1050 to 1258; the Mongols under Genghis Khan swept into Baghdad in 1258, killed everyone, and headed back east; the Ottoman Turks took over and built one of the longest-lasting empires in history.

2 TEACH

- Write the following modern countries on the chalkboard and ask which were once part of the Ottoman Empire: Greece, Turkey, Italy, Syria, Israel, northern Libya, Spain, Iraq, Egypt, Hungary. (all except Italy and Spain) Refer to the Atlas maps of Europe and Asia.

- Write this question on the chalkboard: How did the Ottoman sultans successfully rule over such a large area for such a long time? Divide the class into groups. Have each group select a topic, such as the Children's Levy, Janissary Corps, and the millet system. Have groups determine how

425

each institution allowed the Ottoman sultans to have control over many different groups of people and large areas.

GUIDED PRACTICE

Have students write a paragraph that supports this statement: The Muslim reformers of the Middle East spread their ideas by force, but maintained their governments with statesmanship.

3 | ASSESS AND CLOSE

ASSESS

What was the Janissary Corps? (division of specially trained soldiers)

OPTIONAL RETEACHING

Write the following on the chalkboard and ask students to explain how each is related to the Ottoman Turks: Asia Minor, Seljuk Turks, Byzantine Empire, Istanbul, Vienna, child-gathering, four millets, and Hagia Sophia.

OPTIONAL ENRICHMENT

1. Ask interested students to determine the economic effect of the fall of Constantinople on the Italian city-states involved in the Middle East trade. (challenging)
2. Also for enrichment:

 Overhead Transparency 45

 Source Reading 23A

INDEPENDENT PRACTICE/ HOMEWORK

Assign the Section Review, Activities page 134, or Workbook page 90.

ders of the weakened Byzantine Empire. The main goal of the first Ottomans was to conquer new lands for Islam. This meant attacking the last remnants of the Byzantine Empire and moving westward into eastern Europe. Gradually, the Ottomans conquered most of Asia Minor and the part of eastern Europe that surrounded the Byzantine capital, Constantinople.

When the Ottomans captured Constantinople, they changed the city's name to **Istanbul**, and established Islam as its religion. From their new capital, the Muslims pressed deep into Europe, eventually taking Christian lands included in modern Greece, Bulgaria, Romania, Hungary, Albania, and Yugoslavia. As a result, there are large Muslim populations in some of these countries today.

With the wealth gained from their European conquests, the Ottomans went on to control the Islamic lands of Iraq, much of the Arabian peninsula, Egypt, and most of North Africa. Not since the Umayyads had this entire area been unified under one Muslim leader. By the 1500s the Ottoman sultans were proclaiming themselves the new caliphs of Islam. Only the Persians and the Afghans, controlled by a powerful rival dynasty called the Safavids, withstood the Ottoman ambition to unite the entire Islamic world.

Suleiman I brought the Ottoman Empire to full glory.

Between 1520 and 1566 the famous Suleiman I [sü'lā män'], known to Europeans as **Suleiman the Magnificent**, reigned as sultan over the Ottoman Empire. He was responsible for some of the Muslim conquests shown on the map on page 261. In 1529 he laid siege to Vienna but failed to take the city. He was then forced to withdraw his armies in the face of approaching winter. In the years to follow, Suleiman's attempts to conquer more lands in Europe and Asia met with varying degrees of success.

Among Muslims Suleiman is known as "the Lawgiver" because of the justice of his rule and the legal reforms he sponsored. Europeans called him "the Magnificent" for his splendid court, his military might, and his wisdom in diplomacy.

Although the sultan did indeed love magnificence, he still managed to maintain a certain sim-

The army of Suleiman the Magnificent besieged Vienna in 1529. The siege ended when winter set in, and his troops refused to remain in place.

plicity. For instance, it was the custom for Ottoman sultans to cultivate some kind of craft or handiwork. Suleiman was trained from boyhood as a jeweler. In later years he often turned to his workbench for relief from the pressures of state.

Special strengths supported the Ottoman Empire.

One of the strengths of the Ottoman Empire was the organization of its government. Every five years, thousands of young boys were chosen from among the conquered non-Muslim peoples of the empire in a drive called the **Children's Levy**. The boys were taken to Istanbul where they were converted to Islam, rigorously educated, and trained for either the army or the state bureaucracy. Only those boys who failed to show enough ability for an official appointment were actually treated as slaves. The most intelligent could hope to become generals, court officials, craft masters, even advisers to the sultan himself. Many a family bribed the child-gatherers to take their son because the opportunities open to him were so great. With this efficient recruiting system, the Ottomans forestalled the dangers of family loyalties among trusted officials since the chosen boys owed allegience to no one but the sultan.

One military group, called the **Janissary Corps**, was an elite division of specially trained soldiers who were selected from the Children's Levy. The Janissaries were patriotic in the extreme in their personal devotion to the sultan. Their special status allowed them many privileges, and letting the sultan know when they were annoyed was one of them. In that case they would upend the huge cooking kettles of the corps and beat on them with their swords. It was an ominous sound that no sultan ever wanted to hear.

Another strength of the Ottoman Empire lay in its system for ruling a vast population of diverse peoples. The Ottoman government chose to divide the population into groups according to their religion rather than by language or nationality. These groups were called **millets**, and originally there were four: Muslims, Jews, Greek Orthodox Christians, and Armenian Orthodox Christians. Each millet had its own religious head who was responsible for collecting taxes and administering justice. Each millet also had its own laws and courts.

Members of the four millets tended to live in separate "quarters" of a town, the word quarters itself deriving from the four groups: the Jewish Quarter, the Armenian Quarter, and so forth. Even today in Middle Eastern countries a distinct identity and a legal system based on religion instead of ethnicity or language testifies to the strength of the legacy of the millet system. Because the Ottomans did not interfere with local customs, many peoples tolerated their rule.

The Ottomans loved splendid buildings. When Sultan Mehmet II, the victor at the fall of Constantinople, came upon a soldier vandalizing a church, he struck the man with his sword saying: "For you the treasures and the prisoners are enough. The buildings are mine." The Ottomans turned many churches into mosques, including the great Hagia Sophia.

Wherever they ruled, the Ottomans also built new mosques and palaces. The pattern tended to be the same: four to six smaller domes surrounding one large central dome. Usually four, sometimes six, tall minarets were built at the outer edges of mosques. Inside, the walls and floors glowed with magnificent mosaics. The Ottomans filled their homes with luxurious carpets, comfortable embroidered cushions, intricately inlaid low wooden tables, and ornate *samovars*, the large brass tea urns that originated in Central Asia. In the literary arts the Ottomans composed lyrical Turkish poetry that they wrote in Arabic script.

In 1683 the Ottomans again laid siege to Vienna. The city held out for months and was on the verge of starvation, when a Polish relief army arrived and saved the city. To celebrate the failure of the Turkish siege, the bakers of Vienna shaped small rolls into crescents, the symbol of the Ottomans. The Viennese ate these *croissants*, or crescent rolls, as a sign that the power of the Ottomans was waning, as indeed it was. Their wars in the east with Safavid Persia were costly, weakening the empire accordingly.

In the 18th century, European states such as Austria and Russia grew strong enough to retaliate. At the same time Ottoman provinces such as Egypt and Armenia clamored for independence. Various attempts in the 19th and 20th centuries to reform the empire failed. At the end of World War I, the Ottoman was one of three empires restructured in the peace that followed.

Section 1 Review

Identify Istanbul, Suleiman the Magnificent, Children's Levy, Janissary Corps, millets

Main Ideas
1. What was the full extent of the Ottoman Empire?
2. Why did Muslims and Europeans call Suleiman I "the Lawgiver" or "the Magnificent"?
3. What special strength did the millet system give the Ottoman Empire?

Critical Thinking
Assessing Cause and Effect: What problems did the Ottomans avoid when they appointed only men taken from the ranks of the Children's Levy to the empire's highest offices?

Essential Learning Objective

Students will learn to describe the strengths and weaknesses of Safavid rule in Persia.

1 FOCUS AND MOTIVATE

Remind students of what they learned about the historic rift between Sunni and Shiite Moslems. Point out that since the Ottoman Turks were Sunni and the Persian Safavids were Shiite, it is not surprising that these two empires were in nearly constant conflict in the 1500s and 1600s.

2 TEACH

Discuss the origins of the Safavids, the role of Ismail, and the 200-year conflict between the Ottoman Sunnis and the Safavid Shiites. Use the map on page 429 to point out the Tigris and Euphrates delta where much of the conflict (both then and in the 1980s) took place.

GUIDED PRACTICE

Shah Abbas is remembered as a great Persian ruler. Elicit from students, and list on the chalkboard, Shah Abbas's contributions to Persia.

2 The Safavid dynasty brought Shiism to Persia.

In the 1500s Ottoman hopes of controlling all the Muslim world were blocked by a rising new dynasty in Persia (present-day Iran) called the Safavids [sä fä′vidz]. The Safavids followed Shiism, the Islam practiced by a minority of Muslims, in contrast to the Ottomans who followed the Islam of the Sunni majority. The two empires fought each other for several centuries, neither able to defeat the other, until they had worn each other out by the 18th century.

The Safavids began as a Shiite Sufi order.

The Safavids had their beginnings in the 1300s with a religious group founded in Persia by a Sufi sheikh [shāk], or leader, named Safi who developed a militaristic following. Descendants of Sheikh Safi formed the **Safavid dynasty** and eventually conquered all of Persia. A boy named Ismail [is mä ēl] was the first major Safavid ruler.

In 1501 the orphaned 13-year-old Ismail, leading his father's Safi warriors, set out to conquer the world. By his 16th birthday, he had taken all of northwest Persia and declared himself shah, or king. At his death in 1524 Ismail ruled over most of present-day Iran.

Ismail was devoted to Shiism. At the time of Ismail's conquests, most Persians were Sunni Muslims. Shiite Ismail forced people to convert to Shiism and executed anyone who refused. Before long Shiism was the official religion of Persia and remains so to this day.

Rivalry between the Safavids and Ottomans lasted for centuries.

Ismail tried to encourage Shiite Muslims in a province in Asia Minor to rebel against their Sunni rulers, the Ottomans. The Ottoman sultans put down these rebellions and attacked the Safavids in retaliation. The Ottomans soundly defeated the Safavids in 1514, but the exhausted Ottoman armies were unable to conquer any Persian territory. Withdrawing, the Ottomans turned westward for future conquests, and the Safavids turned eastward for their expansion.

Two hundred years of conflict between the Ottomans and the Safavids followed. Neither side was ever completely successful, though they continued to struggle with each other over their shared border, especially the Tigris and Euphrates river delta that controls access to the Persian Gulf. In the 1980s Iran and Iraq, the modern successors of the Safavids and the Ottomans, fought a destructive war over the same access to the Gulf, known today as the Shatt al-Arab.

Persian prosperity increased under Shah Abbas.

For many years following Ismail's death in 1524, military commanders on campaigns of conquest became nearly as powerful as the shahs. In the late 1500s some engineered a coup [kü], a military takeover, by executing all the Safavid princes in sight, including the heir and his mother. A younger brother, Abbas, escaped, and after many years in hiding, he was finally crowned shah in 1587.

This Persian miniature, painted around 1565, is a book illustration that depicts a romantic tale.

Safavid Persia, 1629

0 500 MILES	
0 500 KILOMETERS	

Safavid Empire, 1629

Boundary of Ottoman Empire, 1683

MAP STUDY Did the Safavid Empire ever include Baghdad? Did the Ottoman Empire ever reach the Caspian Sea?

Shah Abbas is remembered as one of Persia's greatest kings, ruling for many prosperous years until his death in 1629. One of his first decisions was to create an efficient government that did not depend on faithless generals. He executed the leaders of the coup who had killed his mother and brothers. He then created a new, smaller army, loyal only to himself, which he equipped with guns and artillery.

Throughout his reign the major enemy of Shah Abbas remained the Ottomans. In order to isolate them diplomatically, he encouraged good relations between Persia and the European powers. He allowed these countries to trade freely with Persia, welcomed Christian missionaries to his court, and established diplomatic embassies with European governments. Although a Shiite Muslim himself, Shah Abbas tolerated other religions in his kingdom and encouraged Christian as well as Muslim artisans to settle in his cities. Christians were allowed to own property and to ride horses, privileges no other shah had ever permitted them.

During the reign of Shah Abbas, the economy and culture of Persia prospered. He built a new capital city at **Isfahan** in west central Persia where even today the beauty of the blue-tiled and mosaic-covered mosques, markets, fountains, universities, and palaces hint at splendors of the past. Iranian children learn a rhyme that describes how Persians think of Isfahan: *Isfahan nisf-i-jehan;* "Isfahan is half the world."

Trade for Persian goods prospered during the reign of Shah Abbas. Bookbinding, carpet weaving, and silk production reached new heights of excellence. European ships began to sail the Persian Gulf on their way to India and China, trading cloth, foodstuffs, and manufactured goods for Persian carpets, silks, linens, and spices. European and Asian traders were encouraged to come overland by the ancient caravan routes and to stay in the caravanserai, the travelers' inns that Shah Abbas built in nearly every major town.

Very ordinary people enjoyed a comfortable life under the shah. Parks, bridges, baths, libraries, and tree-lined avenues for strolling were all common in Isfahan and other Persian cities. The popular pastimes of the day were coffee houses for men, women's day in the markets and the baths, puppet shows for the children, and traveling religious plays for all.

Despite weaknesses, the Safavids defined a Persian national identity.

Although a just and tolerant ruler of his people, Shah Abbas was not kind to his own family. He had two sons blinded, one executed, and his brothers imprisoned. This left Persia with a weakened succession that was further damaged by continuous wars with the Ottomans.

The Safavids ruled over Persia until the mid-1700s, but during their turbulent years, they were often overthrown or overshadowed by powerful military commanders. The Shia religious leaders were also a formidable factor in a shah's life as they fought to restrain deviations from strict Islamic traditions.

Despite the weaknesses of later rulers, the early Safavids, especially Shah Abbas, are remembered as strong leaders who united the varied peoples of Persia both politically and religiously. The Safavids presided over a period of rich cultural productivity and created a sense of national unity that Iranians, the Persians of today, still share.

ANSWER TO MAP STUDY yes; yes

Answers to Section 2 Review

Identify
Key Terms, People, and Places are defined on pages indicated in parentheses. Also see the Glossary and Biographical Dictionary.
Safavid dynasty (428), Shah Abbas (429), Isfahan (429)

Main Ideas
1. from a Sufi sheikh named Safi
2. They fought over the Tigris-Euphrates delta they shared, called the Shatt al-Arab today.
3. allowed foreign ships to dock in the Persian Gulf; traded carpets, silks, linens, and spices for cloth, foods, and manufactured goods; built caravanserais for merchants
4. It helped establish the Persian national identity.

Critical Thinking
It improved prosperity by encouraging foreign, non-Muslim trade, which increased Persian profits and contributed to everyone's well-being.

③ Lesson Plan

Essential Learning Objective

Students will learn to describe strengths and weaknesses of Mughal rule in India.

1 FOCUS AND MOTIVATE

Ask the students to name foreign influences on our culture. Write students' responses on the chalkboard. Point out that the Mughals, guided by their Islamic culture, introduced many similar social, political, and artistic changes in India.

Section 2 Review

Identify Safavid dynasty, Shah Abbas, Isfahan

Main Ideas
1. How did the Safavids get their name?
2. Give an example of the rivalry between the Ottomans and the Persians over boundaries.
3. How did Shah Abbas promote Persian prosperity?
4. What was the legacy of the Safavid dynasty?

Critical Thinking
Predicting Effects: Shah Abbas' policies for treating Christians and other non-Muslims made life more comfortable for these minority groups in Safavid Persia. What effect did it also have on the economy of the country? Give examples.

---

③ **The Mughals united and ruled most of India.**

In the early 1500s Islam also revived and expanded in India. By 1500, India's Muslim rulers, known as the Delhi Sultans, had grown weak. (See Chapter 14.) Then new Muslim conquerors, called Mughals, came through the mountain passes from Central Asia to establish their rule in northern India. The Mughals quickly expanded their control of India to include all but the southern tip. (See the map on page 433.)

Babur, descendant of the Mongols, established Mughal rule in India.

A young man named Babur [bä′bər] once ruled a small kingdom in Central Asia. An adventurer as well as a warrior, he was descended from the dreaded Mongol conquerors Tamerlane and Genghis Khan. In 1504 Babur reached out to capture the important city of Kabul [kä′bul], capital of modern Afghanistan.

The riches of India aroused Babur's interest. He periodically raided the country before completely defeating the weak Muslim sultan at Delhi in 1526. A group of hopeful Hindu princes gathered an army to regain control of northern India, but Babur defeated them also. The era of the **Mughals,**

Rulers of the Mughal Empire

Babur 1526–1530
Founded the Mughal Empire

Humayun 1530–1540, 1555–1556
Period of warfare; lost throne to an Afghan but later regained it

Akbar 1556–1605
Efficient, prosperous government; religious tolerance; implanted Persian culture in India

Jahangir 1605–1627
Period of warfare and expansion; Queen Nur Jahan ran the government

Shah Jahan 1628–1658
High taxes; religious intolerance; golden age of Mughal art and architecture

Aurangzeb 1658–1707
Outlawed Hinduism; destroyed temples; tried to conquer all India; Mughal Empire disintegrated after his death

---

from the Persian word for Mongol, had begun.

Since Babur died only five years after his conquest, he had little time to organize his government. Nevertheless, he is regarded as one of India's great leaders.

Akbar, Nur Jahan, and Shah Jahan were powerful Mughal rulers.

For more than 20 years after Babur's death, rival groups weakened Mughal control. At that time Babur's grandson, **Akbar**, became sultan at the age of 13. Over the next 40 years, Akbar added lands in every direction, and by 1595 he was undisputed ruler of all northern India.

Akbar divided the empire into a dozen provinces which he placed in the hands of efficient, well-paid civil servants. As a result, educated, capable bureaucrats from all over Central Asia flocked to his service. Throughout the country these bureaucrats formed a network that carried out the sultan's orders. In addition, Akbar stationed soldiers in the provinces and kept 12,000 horsemen ready for emergencies.

BACKGROUND At birth, her name was Mihr-un-nisa. When she married Jahangir, he gave her the honorary name of Nur Mahal, which means "Light of the Palace." This name was soon changed to Nur Jahan, which means "Light of the World."

Justice in Mughal India was administered fairly. In each village a headman kept law and order. In the cities special officials decided law cases. Akbar himself often acted as judge, since anyone under his rule had the right to appeal to him personally. He tried to outlaw the practice of suttee, the custom of burning a widow alive on her husband's funeral pyre, but did not achieve success. He also made it legal for widows to remarry and illegal to arrange child marriages.

Unlike the Delhi sultans, Akbar allowed the practice of other religions and tolerated Hinduism. In name a Muslim, his doubts about this faith caused him to search for one that all people in his empire could accept. Akbar enjoyed discussions about religion. Once he invited visiting Catholic priests to explain the doctrines of Christianity. Finally, he created his own religion, called the Divine Faith, a synthesis of several creeds. It never became popular, however.

As emperor, Akbar labored to unite all Muslims and Hindus in a common loyalty to Mughal rule. He accepted Hindu princes into his government and himself married several Hindu princesses, giving them an honored place in the royal household. He offered all his subjects justice, religious freedom, and relief from unfair taxes.

Akbar, one of the most effective rulers in history, had many talents and interests. He enjoyed both the sport of hunting and the excitement of battle. He could ride for hours without tiring. He loved architecture, paintings, and good books. When he died in 1605, his empire was one of the best governed and most prosperous in the world.

Akbar's successors, rulers like Jahangir and his wife **Nur Jahan**, continued the prosperity that he initiated. Nur Jahan made her place in history by ruling India at a time when wealthy women were kept behind veils and walls.

Intelligent, well-educated, brave, and ambitious, the Persian-born wife of Emperor Jahangir ran the Mughal Empire while her husband fought wars. She oversaw the daily administration of the government in his absence. Her authority was publically recognized in the coins struck in her name, and in public rituals. Nur Jahan appointed court officials, heard law cases, and twice put down revolts. When Emperor Jahangir was taken prisoner,

Court painters during the Mughal period did many beautiful studies of flowers, birds, and animals. Both the zebra and the wild birds were painted by Mansur, around 1620. The zebra was a gift to Emperor Jahangir, who believed that the animal was a rare mule.

BACKGROUND Nur Jahan built one of the world's most beautiful tombs for her father, Itimad-ud-daula, at Agra. From the top of this tomb one can look out across Agra and see the Taj Majal.

431

ASSESS

1. What two centuries are most associated with Mughal rule in India? (16th and 17th centuries)
2. What Mughal leader was most tolerant of Hindus? (Akbar)

OPTIONAL RETEACHING

Have students compare Akbar's rule to that of his successors—Jahangir, Shah Jahan, and Aurangzeb. (Students should conclude that no successor matched Akbar's intelligent leadership.)

OPTIONAL ENRICHMENT

1. Encourage interested students to research and report on the building of the Taj Mahal. (average)
2. Ask students to research and report on the Hindu practice of suttee during the Mughal and other periods in India. (challenging)
3. Also for enrichment:

 Source Reading 23B

INDEPENDENT PRACTICE/ HOMEWORK

Assign the Section Review, Activities page 136, or Workbook page 92.

CLOSURE

Point out that the Mughal Empire, launched by Babur and raised to greatness by Akbar, lasted about 200 years. It succeeded because Akbar accommodated his rule to the India that already existed. It fell from greatness when the culture of this existing India was not respected.

BACKGROUND Nur Jahan married her only child (by a previous marriage) to Jahangir's son Shahriyar, whom she hoped

From the Archives

The Realm Beyond Going

The poetry of medieval India remains popular today and none more so than that of Mirabai, who was born about 1550. A follower of the Hindu god Krishna, who is often referred to as the Dark Lord, Mirabai defied the conventions of her time and created in her poems an inner life that still provides for modern Indians a refuge from the burdens of existence.

Let us go to a realm beyond going,
Where death is afraid to go,
Where the high-flying birds alight and
    play,
Afloat in the full lake of love. . . .
Garbed in goodness—their ankle bells—
They dance the dance of content
And deck themselves with the sixteen
    signs
Of beauty, and a golden crown—
There where the love of the Dark One
    comes first
And everything else is last.

she voluntarily joined him, then formulated the plan that allowed them both to escape.

Jahangir died in 1627, the victim of opium addiction. His successor, Shah Jahan, exiled Nur Jahan to the city of Lahore, where she died 18 years later. Being deprived of power, she said, was like death itself.

The reign of Akbar's grandson, Shah Jahan, was the high point of Mughal power, a golden age for the Muslim rulers. Famous for the luxury of his court, Shah Jahan supported artists, musicians, and poets, and financed the building of magnificent palaces and monuments.

People did not live as well as they had under Akbar, however. For one thing, their taxes were heavier. Moreover, Shah Jahan ended the religious freedom permitted by his grandfather. Hindu temples were destroyed, and Islam was restored as the official state religion.

FROM THE ARCHIVES The excerpt is from *Sources of Indian Tradition*, 2d ed., Vol. I. From the Beginning to 1800, Edited and revised by Ainslee T. Embree (New York: Columbia University Press, 1988), p. 369. Ask a student to read the

---

would succeed Jahangir. This support led to a protracted battle between Nur Jahan and Shah Jahan, another of Jahangir's sons who eventually won out.

Aurangzeb tried uniting all of India.

Rivalries broke out among the aged Shah Jahan's heirs when he became too ill to rule. These ended in 1658, when his son Aurangzeb [ôr'əng zeb'], gained the throne after killing three brothers, one son, and a nephew. Aurangzeb also threw his father into prison, where his father soon died.

Aurangzeb's reign was the beginning of the end for Mughal rule in India. Once emperor, he proved to be a stern and devout Muslim with a will of iron. He raised the taxes of Hindus, removed Hindus from government office, and destroyed Hindu temples and schools. He thought of himself as the ruler of a Muslim nation, not the ruler of the people of India. He opposed most forms of recreation, dismissing the court musicians and artists.

Aurangzeb's main ambition was to unite India under Muslim rule, but his efforts were a disaster. He spent the last 26 years of his life trying to conquer the Hindu kingdoms in central and southern India. By 1690 Aurangzeb claimed that his authority extended from northern India to the very southern tip, but the conquest was never actually completed and revolts were continuous.

Aurangzeb, old and ill from directing his armies, left southern India in 1705 and died two years later. He was the last real Mughal emperor.

During the next 50 years, civil law broke down completely in India. Rival armies feuded incessantly, and local governors created independent kingdoms. The principal victims of this chaotic time were the peasants; no power protected them from soldiers and bandits.

The Mughals built some of the world's finest monuments.

During their peak years, the Mughal emperors lavishly promoted the arts. Painters, writers, and mu-

What's in a Name?

KABUL Travelers on major trade routes between east and west often stopped at a place just west of the Hindu Kush. The city that grew up was called Kabul, "warehouse" in Persian, because caravans stored huge quantities of goods there for later distribution.

verses aloud to the class. Discuss the mood of the poem and the symbolism. Ask students what the "realm beyond going" would be called in the language of Western Civilization. (heaven, paradise, Zion, life everlasting, eternity) sicians enjoyed royal favor, but architects were most in demand. Akbar was an avid builder of forts, tombs, and palaces. Within his capital city of Fatehpur Sikri [fät′ə per si′krē] he created dozens of beautiful buildings and mosques. When his empress Mumtaz Mahal died, the sorrowing Shah Jahan built an exquisite tomb, a *taj*, to her memory. It took more than 20 years, the labor of 20,000 workers, and much gold to build the **Taj Mahal** [täj′ mə häl′]. Tall minarets surround the central dome and a reflecting pool perfectly mirrors the shimmering marble. You can see a photograph of the Taj Mahal on page 422.

At Delhi, Shah Jahan built 52 new palaces. One famous hall had ceilings of gold and silver panels and contained the emperor's jewel-studded Peacock Throne. Painting was also promoted by the Mughals. Their artists developed an unusual style that combined Persian, Hindu, and European methods. (See the paintings on pages 431 and 437.) Mughal literature flourished in Persian, the official court language, recording valuable memoirs along with important poems and histories.

Unfortunately, the glories of Mughal India depended for their safety on the strength of the throne. In 1739 the shah of Persia invaded the weakened country, captured Delhi, and plundered the royal treasury. It was the end of Mughal power. The famous Peacock Throne and the crown jewels that were taken to Persia are on display today in a special vault built into the basement of a bank in Tehran, the capital of modern Iran.

Many reasons have been given for the fall of the Mughals. The old Mughal nobility, once so strong, had been wiped out in the bloody wars of succession. Further, the Mughals were really an alien minority in a foreign land. Only Akbar's policies to promote unity between Muslim and Hindu addressed this weakness. There were economic reasons for the decline also, such as the corruption of tax officials, the oppression of the farmers, and wasteful wars.

In 1750 the emperor still had his title, but India was fragmented and vulnerable to conquest. This time the invaders did not come through the mountain passes. Instead they came across the oceans, from a country called Britain. You will read about the British conquest of India in Chapter 30.

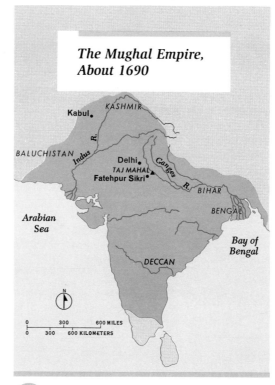

The Mughal Empire, About 1690

Kabul

KASHMIR

BALUCHISTAN

Indus R.

Delhi
TAJ MAHAL
Fatehpur Sikri

Ganges R.

BIHAR

BENGAL

Arabian Sea

Bay of Bengal

DECCAN

N

0   300   600 MILES
0   300   600 KILOMETERS

 MAP STUDY The Mughal Empire included almost all of India. Did it include both the Indus and Ganges rivers?

Section 3 Review

Identify Mughals, Akbar, Nur Jahan, Taj Mahal

Main Ideas

1. What role did Babur play in Indian history?
2. What kind of organization did Akbar create for ruling India? What measures did he take for uniting India?
3. How did Aurangzeb destroy Akbar's progress toward unity?
4. What were some of the artistic achievements of the Mughals?

Critical Thinking

Recognizing Values: What essential difference between the Mughals and the Ottomans caused one to decline while the other endured for many centuries?

433

GEOGRAPHY

A Key to History

A GLOBAL PERSPECTIVE AND SYNCHRONIC THINKING

One of geography's most important gifts to history is the global perspective, a view of the world as a whole and the attempt to think in worldwide terms. However, a sense of time is needed as well as a sense of space.

In other words, there is a synchronic dimension to world history as well as a global perspective. Synchronic means "occurring at the same time." This dimension involves keeping in mind the fact that things are happening all over the world at the same time.

A number of maps in the text show synchronic thinking—the maps opening each of the three main parts of the text (pages xxiv–1, 172–173, and 348–349) as well as the historical maps on pages 800–801 of the Atlas. You can also learn about synchronic thinking from the map below, which depicts events that occurred within the short time period from 1492 to 1550.

By 1492 Islam had spread to many parts of Asia and Africa. At the same time that Europeans were first venturing across the Atlantic, Indian,

Where were the major points of contact between the Christian and the Islamic worlds between 1492 and 1550?

and Pacific oceans, three strong Muslim empires were emerging across the Afro-Eurasian landmass.

About 1500 the Ottoman Empire stretched from the Danube River Valley to the Persian Gulf. In 1501 Ismail I (1487–1524) established himself as shah of the Safavid Empire centered in Persia. A bit later, in 1526, Babur won a crucial battle that led to the establishment of the Mughal Empire in India.

In the centuries following 1492, as the European discoveries revealed the true size of the world and the true outline of the world map, the Islamic empires were also reaching their height. If we keep these facts in mind, we will add synchronic thinking to our global perspective.

REVIEW

1. What is a global perspective?
2. What does synchronic mean?
3. Which synchronic events on the map show the development of Islamic empires?
4. What are some major synchronic events occurring in Asia, Africa, and North America at the present time?

4 Islam shaped new states in West Africa.

By the 1500s, several Muslim states had risen in West Africa. The strongest and largest of these, Songhai, was invaded in 1591 by a Moroccan army from across the Sahara. (See Chapter 18.) Strong enough to destroy Songhai power but too weak to establish a new government, the Moroccans disturbed the balance of trade and political power enough to shift it south and east. For a while the Muslim state of **Kanem-Bornu** [kä′nem bor′nü] became the strongest military state of the central Sudan. (See map, page 326.) Later, fierce religious wars converted the people of the Hausa states to Islam. Religious warfare continued in West Africa until the early 1800s.

Idris Alooma was the most famous ruler in Kanem-Bornu's long history.

The rich empires of Ghana, Mali, and Songhai overshadowed the lesser states of the Sudan before 1600. Some of these lesser states did, however, become important. Around A.D. 800 a centralized state with a king emerged in Kanem east of Lake Chad. Kanem's first king, Saif, [sef], was the founder of a dynasty that ruled for a thousand years.

In 1085 the king of Kanem was converted to Islam. As the kingdom grew stronger, Islam took firm root in the lives of its rulers though most of the agricultural population continued to observe the traditional religions. Like other states of the Sudan, Kanem traded with the communities north of the Sahara, exchanging cloth and leather goods for salt.

By the 15th century, civil war and enemy attacks from the east had weakened Kanem. The king moved his court to Bornu, the land west of Lake Chad, and the new state of Kanem-Bornu was born.

When Songhai fell in 1591, Kanem-Bornu became the strongest state in the central Sudan. Its most famous ruler, **Idris Alooma** controlled Kanem-Bornu from 1580 to 1617. Perhaps inspired by the Islamic revival in Ottoman territories, Idris Alooma set out to make the people in his state better Muslims. He imposed Islamic law throughout

This engraving was made from a drawing by a British explorer around 1827. It depicts a bodyguard of the ruler of Kanem-Bornu.

his territories and forced the common people to become Muslims, something which had not happened in Ghana, Mali, or Songhai.

Idris Alooma built up the cavalry of Kanem-Bornu until it was the terror of the central Sudan. Both riders and horses wore chain mail over padded coverings, like the knights and horses of western Christendom. Military experts from Egypt and Asia Minor trained the army in the use of guns imported from North Africa, but Idris Alooma himself led the cavalry into battle.

Rulers of smaller states soon began to imitate Kanem-Bornu's cavalry, and in no time the armored horse became standard equipment for every aspiring king in the Sudan. So important did Kanem-Bornu become that ambassadors from the Ottoman Empire arrived to confirm that the state was part of the Muslim world and to cement good relations between their emperor and its king.

As often happens, the rulers who followed Idris

4 Lesson Plan

Essential Learning Objective

Students will learn to describe Muslim states that arose in the 1500s in West Africa.

1 FOCUS AND MOTIVATE

Ask students with which culture they associate knights and horses covered with chain mail. (They will probably name one or more European cultures.) Tell students that in the late 1500s Kanem-Bornu in the central Sudan in Africa had such a cavalry.

2 TEACH

- Discuss the achievements of Idris Alooma and Uthman dan Fodio. Place Alooma (c.1600) in time by asking students to name any of his contemporaries from other nations. Contemporaries include Akbar, Queen Elizabeth I, Shakespeare, and Galileo. Dan Fodio lived 200 years later (1754–1817).

- Write the word *jihad* on the chalkboard. Ask the students how Uthman dan Fodio used a jihad against the Hausa rulers. Ask how is a jihad similar to a political revolution? How is it different? (Students should understand the religious dimensions of a jihad.)

GUIDED PRACTICE

Have the students prepare a list of economic products from each region in West Africa. Ask the students how these products influenced political power.

ASSESS

1. What is a jihad? (a holy war)
2. What is the connection between Uthman dan Fodio and the Hausa people? (He led the Fulani in a revolution against the Hausa.)

OPTIONAL RETEACHING

Ask a volunteer to draw a large outline map of West Africa on the chalkboard. Then have other students draw in the following: Mediterranean Sea, Atlantic Ocean, Lake Chad, Kanem-Bornu, Hausa territory, Sokoto, and Timbuktu.

Students also may be assigned Activities reteaching page 138.

OPTIONAL ENRICHMENT

Have students look up and report on a modern jihad, perhaps examining the wars in Afghanistan or between Iran and Iraq. (average)

Students also may be assigned Activities enrichment page 139.

INDEPENDENT PRACTICE/ HOMEWORK

Assign the Section Review, the Chapter Review items, Activities page 137, or Workbook page 93.

CLOSURE

Summarize by saying that during the 17th, 18th, and 19th centuries, Islam solidified its hold on the sub-Saharan peoples of West Africa through religious war. Islam continues to have great influence in these areas today.

Answers to Section 4 Review

Identify

Key Terms, People, and Places are defined on pages indicated in

---

Alooma were not as able as he was. The state gradually weakened until finally the last king was killed in 1846 in a religious war.

Trade flourished in the Hausa states.

A people called the **Hausa** [hou′sə] lived in city-state trading centers in what is now northern Nigeria. The Hausa cities were not united, remaining individual states, each with its own government, laws, and taxes.

The Hausa city-states were relatively insignificant until the 15th century, when Islam was introduced. After that, these cities enjoyed a lively trade with Mali and later Songhai, as well as with the lesser states of Central Africa.

The Hausa were traders and manufacturers. From the forest they collected ivory, hides, and kola nuts to trade with North Africa. Kola nuts contain caffeine, which not only keeps one awake, but also helps one go long periods of time without food or water. The kola nut was popular with the Muslims, who chewed it like gum. Today's cola drinks are also derived from kola nuts.

In addition to trading forest products, the Hausa developed many handicraft industries, including the manufacture of leather goods and cloth.

Uthman dan Fodio preached revolt against the Hausa.

Living in the Sudan and the Hausa cities were a people called the Fulani [fü lä′nē]. Following the collapse of Songhai in the 1600s, the Hausa cities became more wealthy and powerful. The leaders of the Hausa, however, became increasingly lax, corrupt, and forgetful of Islam. The Fulani began to resent the control the Hausa had over them, and after more than a hundred years of discontent and minor uprisings, a leader finally arose. Between 1804 and 1809, **Uthman dan Fodio** led the Fulani in a religious and political revolution against the Hausa.

Uthman dan Fodio believed that God spoke to him in visions. Told to "take up the sword of truth," and attack the Hausa rulers who were no longer good Muslims, Uthman began to preach and soon had a large following. His writings and speeches severely criticized the lax religious practices of the Hausa, as well as their high taxes, mil-

itary conscription, and neglect of the rural peoples under their control. Like many another sincere reformer, Uthman dan Fodio measured religious and political practices against the perfection of their possibilities and ended by declaring jihad, or holy war, against the Hausa rulers. He claimed his jihad was a revolution fought to please God and reform the Islam of the Hausa Muslims.

Uthman dan Fodio's revolution was successful. By the time of his death in 1817, he had established the Fulani Empire over the fragmented Hausa city-states. In imitation of Muslim rulers of large territories all over the Islamic world, the new ruler took the title Sultan. He reigned from the capital at Sokoto and set up trade and diplomatic exchanges with the Ottoman Empire.

The jihad against the Hausa was not the only holy war fought in the Sudan. Earlier religious wars in the Senegal and Gambia river valleys had produced several new Muslim states. Uthman dan Fodio's revolution, however, was the largest and most famous jihad. People from all over West Africa journeyed to receive a flag blessed by him, which they then carried back to their own lands as a rallying point for their own jihad. Hundreds of thousands of people converted to Islam during these jihads, and those who were already Muslims became more devout. Islam continues to gain converts in Africa today though the means used are now peaceful.

Section 4 Review

Identify Kanem-Bornu, Idris Alooma, Hausa, Uthman dan Fodio

Main Ideas

1. What made Idris Alooma famous?
2. Name five items traded by the Hausa.
3. What were Uthman dan Fodio's reasons for rebelling against the Hausa? How did he help spread Islam in West Africa?

Critical Thinking

Making Hypotheses: According to some statistics, Islam is making more converts in Africa today than either Christianity or Buddhism, the other two major missionary religions of the world. If you were a religious leader, how might you go about encouraging converts?

Mughal Painting

The Mughal rulers were steeped in the arts. Most employed Persian masters to head up a large department of official court painters. The resulting paintings—scenes of court life, historic works, and studies of plants and animals—were noted for their color and fine detail.

The Mughal artists worked in teams. A master designer usually laid out the composition, outlining it on blank paper. The rough drawing was covered with a translucent white wash that allowed the sketch to show through. Portrait specialists would then add details to the faces. Other painters might concentrate on the intricate patterns of mosaics.

After the drawing was fully worked out, a colorist would apply the paint. Many of the paints were derived from vegetable dyes. Some, however, were made from rare and costly minerals. For example, the semiprecious stone lapis lazuli [lap'is laz'yə lī] was used to make a bright blue paint, and the highly valued mineral malachite [mal'ə kīt] was used to make a brilliant green. Copper, silver, and gold powders were applied for highlights. After brushing on several thin layers of paint, the colorist would burnish, or polish, the surface. This gave the painting a smooth, delicate sheen.

Among the most famous of the Mughal paintings were illustrations from a biography of Muhammad's uncle Hamzeh. Note the complex tilework on the buildings, details styled after Persian paintings. Hindu art, on the other hand, was the source of inspiration for the expressive animal faces. In other works the Mughal painters showed Byzantine influence in their portrayal of religious figures. Thus, the Mughal painters combined art styles of three strikingly different civilizations in a stunningly beautiful way.

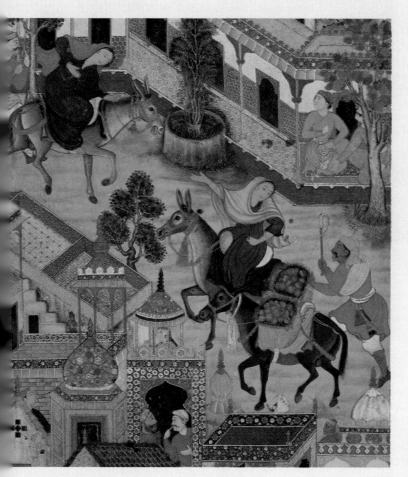

The powerful dramatic sense of Mughal painting is evident in this illustration from the life of the early Muslim hero Hamzeh. Akbar commissioned the work in 1562. It grew to include 1,400 illustrations.

parentheses. Also see the Glossary and Biographical Dictionary. Kanem-Bornu (435), Idris Alooma (435), Hausa (437), Uthman dan Fodio (437)

Main Ideas
1. He forcibly spread Islam, created armored cavalry, and had diplomatic relations with Ottoman Empire.
2. ivory, hides, kola nuts, leather goods, cloth
3. Hausa were lax Muslims, poor rulers, had high taxes, and a conscripted army. Dan Fodio preached, wrote, and sent blessed flags around with converts as rallying points for new revolts.

Critical Thinking
word of mouth, good example by friends or neighbors, preaching by Muslims, door-to-door missionaries, reading

HIGHLIGHTS OF CIVILIZATION

Tell students that Mughal paintings were usually book illustrations or miniatures. Remind students that most Islamic art does not contain human figures or lifelike depictions of animals. This was because Muhammad is believed to have opposed representational art. However Mughal art was inspired by Persian art, and the Persians did not follow this prohibition.

Ask students how the subject matter of Mughal painting differs from that of art that might be found in mosques. (Students should realize that most of the illustrations were not religious in nature, but historic, scientific, or political.)

Section Summaries

Section 1

The Ottoman Turks dominated the Muslim world.
The Ottoman Turks took over from their former overlords, the Seljuks, and over the next 200 years established a huge empire. Ottoman rule reached its peak under Suleiman the Magnificent. The Ottoman Empire lasted until after World War I.

Section 2

The Safavid dynasty brought Shiism to Persia.
In 1501 Ismail, the founder of the Safavid dynasty, declared himself shah and forced the people to convert to Shia Islam. The Safavids were rivals of the Ottomans and fought many battles with them. After Shah Abbas, the Safavid rulers were weaker, but the Persian identity that the Safavids had fostered remained.

Section 3

The Mughals united and ruled most of India.
After Babur's conquests, the most important Mughal ruler was Akbar. He provided efficient government, uniform administration of justice, and religious toleration. Later, Aurangzeb made enemies of his Hindu subjects, and revolts were frequent. After his death, the Mughal Empire began to collapse, and by 1750 it had disintegrated.

Section 4

Islam shaped new states in West Africa.
Islam was a major influence in West Africa as well as in the Middle East. The rulers of Mali, Songhai, and Kanem-Bornu were Muslims. In the 17th and 18th centuries, waves of Muslim reform movements spread over West Africa. Uthman dan Fodio united the Hausa states in a holy war in 1804–1809 and established the Fulani Empire. Large numbers of people were converted to Islam, and more Islamic states were formed.

Review Dates

1501
Safavids conquer Persia

1520
Suleiman I begins his rule of the Ottoman Empire

1526
Babur establishes the Mughal Empire

1648
Taj Mahal is built

1804
Uthman dan Fodio leads revolt against the Hausa

| 1400 | 1500 | 1600 | 1700 | 1800 | 1900 |

Test Yourself

Key Terms, People, and Places
Identify the significance of each of the following:

Section 1

a. Istanbul   d. Janissary Corps

b. Suleiman the Magnificent   e. millets

c. Children's Levy

Section 2

a. Safavid dynasty   c. Isfahan

b. Shah Abbas

Section 3

a. Mughals   c. Nur Jahan

b. Akbar   d. Taj Mahal

Section 4

a. Kanem-Bornu   c. Hausa

b. Idris Alooma   d. Uthman dan Fodio

Main Ideas

Section 1

1. How far did the Ottoman Empire at its peak extend?
2. Why did Muslims and Europeans admire Suleiman I?
3. Why was the millet system a strength of the empire?

Section 2

1. Who were the Safavids?
2. How did the Safavids and the Ottomans express their rivalry?
3. How did Shah Abbas further Persian prosperity?
4. What was the legacy of the Safavid dynasty?

Section 3

1. Describe Babur's role in Indian history.
2. How was Akbar's empire ruled?
3. Which of Aurangzeb's efforts damaged unity?
4. What were some Mughal artistic achievements?

Section 4

1. Why was Idris Alooma the most famous ruler in Kanem-Bornu?
2. What products did the Hausa trade?
3. Why did Uthman dan Fodio lead a revolt against the Hausa? What means did he use to spread Islam?

Critical Thinking

1. **Recognizing Values** What do the Persians mean when they say "Isfahan is half the world"?

2. **Making Hypotheses** Nur Jahan ruled with her husband Jahangir. Could she have inherited the Mughal throne in her own right?

Chapter Skills and Activities

Practicing Study and Research Skills
Drawing Conclusions
Information comes from many sources, not all of which are obvious. Sometimes we can derive information from evidence that was not especially designed to give it. The painting on page 437 comes from the Golden Age of Mughal rule and represents one aspect of daily life in India during the 16th century. You will be able to draw certain conclusions about this period by looking closely at the pictures.

1. Both women are riding while their male companions walk. What might this indicate about the status of the women in this picture?
2. Look at the faces of the two women. Judging from this painting, do you think that the Mughals probably required women to veil their faces from men in public places?
3. Study the buildings shown in the street scene. How would you describe these buildings?

Linking Past and Present
Competition for the Shatt al-Arab, the part of the Tigris-Euphrates delta shared today by Iran and Iraq, began when the Safavids and the Ottomans quarreled over the same piece of geography. What would be a practical solution to this ancient problem?

Learning History Through Maps
Using the maps on pages 261 and 429 as your sources, draw a simple map that shows the Ottoman Empire and the Safavid Empire. Locate and label Istanbul and Isfahan. Be sure to include a scale of miles on your map. Approximately how far is it between Istanbul and Isfahan? Are Isfahan and Istanbul both still capitals of countries? If they are not, find out what the capitals now are.

Chapter

24 China and Japan in Seclusion

OVERVIEW

This chapter tells how an isolated China became the most advanced nation in the world during the Ming and Manchu dynasties, and how Tokugawa Japan flourished under similar isolation.

PLANNING CHART

Section	Text Pages	Key Concept	Suggested Teaching Time
1 The Mings began to limit outside contacts.	441–443	The Ming were world trade leaders in the early 1400s. By 1500 they were intensely isolationist.	One day **More time?** Use *Overhead Transparency 47*. **Less time?** Compress Sections 1 and 2 and teach in 1 day.
2 The Manchu dynasty maintained Chinese culture.	443–445	The Manchus, who followed the Ming, achieved peace and prosperity but continued isolationism.	One day **More time?** Use *Source Reading 24A*.
3 Tokugawa shoguns restricted foreign influences.	445–448	Peace, unity, isolationism were the central themes in Japan during the Tokugawa period.	One day **More time?** Use *Overhead Transparency 48* or *Source Reading 24B*.

ANCILLARIES

Materials that may be used with this chapter to reinforce, reteach, enrich, and assess learning are pictured on the following pages.

Teacher's Resource File

ACTIVITIES

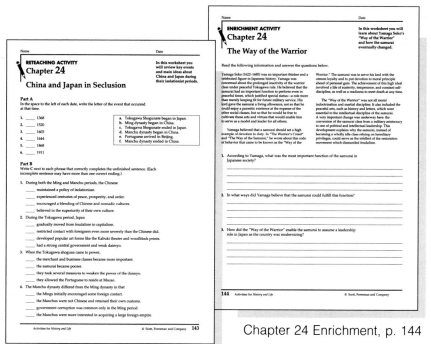

Section 1 Activity, p. 140

Section 2 Activity, p. 141

Section 3 Activity, p. 142

Chapter 24 Reteaching, p. 143

Chapter 24 Enrichment, p. 144

Teacher's Resource File

GEOGRAPHY SKILLS

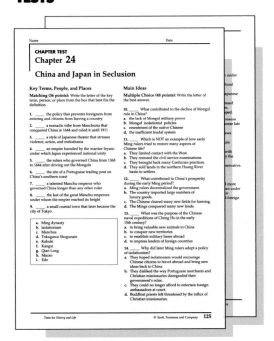

Chapter 24 Geography

Worksheet/Map, pp. 49–50

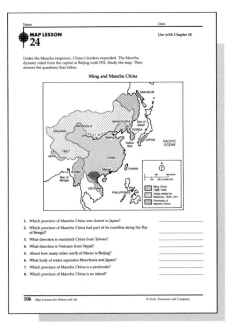

Chapter 24 Map Lesson, p. 106

TESTS

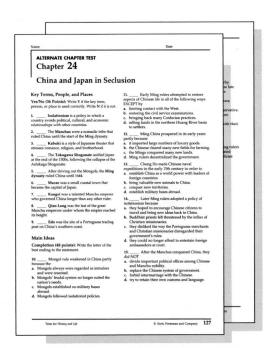

Chapter Test, pp. 125–126

Alternate Chapter Test, pp. 127–128

439c

Other Optional Ancillaries

WORKBOOK

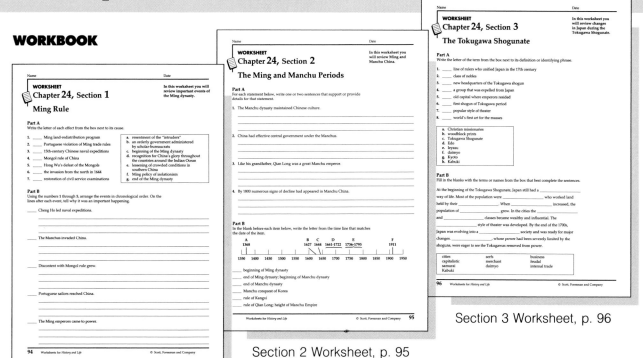

Section 1 Worksheet, p. 94

Section 2 Worksheet, p. 95

Section 3 Worksheet, p. 96

SOURCE READINGS

Source Reading 24A
Source Reading 24B

TEST GENERATOR

40 multiple-choice questions for Chapter 24

OVERHEAD TRANSPARENCIES

Overhead Transparency 47
Overhead Transparency 48

China and Japan in Seclusion

1368–1800

1300

1368   Ming dynasty begins in China

1603   Tokugawa Shogunate begins in Japan

1644   Manchu dynasty begins in China

1700

1800

In 1661, the year that King Louis XIV gained control in France, a Manchu emperor named Kangxi [käng′shē′] came to power in China. Although the two rulers were widely separated by geography and culture, they were the most successful leaders of their time. Kangxi in particular was a shrewd, intelligent emperor who knew the importance of keeping an open mind and was always eager to learn new things. The following quotation from Kangxi's writings offers advice as sound today as when it was written 300 years ago:

> Too many people claim to know things when, in fact, they know nothing about them. Since my childhood I have always tried to find things out for myself and not to pretend knowledge when I was ignorant. Whenever I met older people, I would ask them about the experiences they have had and remember what they said.
>
> Keep an open mind and you'll learn things; you will miss other people's good qualities if you just concentrate on your own abilities. It's my nature to enjoy asking questions, and the crudest or simplest people have something of value to say, something one can check through to the source and remember.

The Manchu dynasty, which came to power in 1644, built upon the achievements of the Ming dynasty, which had ruled China since 1368. Throughout the 600 years of the Ming and Manchu dynasties, emperors based their rule on Chinese traditions. In those years, as China enjoyed a high level of prosperity, peace, and order, its rulers saw no reason to change the Chinese way of life. Thus, China became a self-centered civilization, largely secluded from the outside world.

However, after 1800 the policy of following old traditions and maintaining seclusion from the world worked against China. As the nations of Western Europe and the United States embarked upon an industrial revolution, China was left far behind.

This carving made in the 1600s shows women weighing jade (left) and a servant bringing food to her mistress (right). Note the clothing styles and architecture.

In Japan, too, the Tokugawa Shogunate, which had come to power in 1603, inaugurated a long period of peace that lasted into the mid-19th century. As Japan flourished, the shoguns restricted contact with Europeans even more severely than the Chinese emperors did. By the 1850s Japan's policy of national isolation had disastrous consequences for the Tokugawa Shogunate.

Reading Preview

In this chapter you will read about cultural and political trends in China and Japan from the 1300s to the 1800s.

1. The Mings began to limit outside contacts.

2. The Manchu dynasty maintained Chinese culture.

3. Tokugawa shoguns restricted foreign influences.

BACKGROUND One of the first concerns of the Mings was to prevent new invasions from the Mongol steppe regions of Asia. To protect against invasions, Ming emperors made vast repairs on the Great Wall, which had been severely damaged.

1 The Mings began to limit outside contacts.

As you learned in Chapter 16, after 1279 the Mongols ruled all of China. Although Mongol rule lasted almost 100 years and the Mongols made great efforts to adapt to Chinese life, they were always regarded as intruders.

The Ming dynasty prospered.

As discontent under the Mongols grew, rebellions broke out. One of the rebel leaders was a former Buddhist monk, Hong Wu, who gathered an army, captured the Mongol capital of Beijing, and, in 1368, drove out the Mongol rulers. Under the leadership of Hong Wu, China returned to Chinese rule. Hong Wu founded his own dynasty called Ming, which in Chinese means "brilliant and illustrious." The **Ming dynasty** ruled until 1644.

(Most sections of the Great Wall standing today date from the Ming era.) The Ming emperors also brought back many Confucian practices, and China once more became a well-governed country run by Confucian scholar-bureaucrats.

441

1 *Lesson Plan*

Essential Learning Objective

Students will learn to identify and evaluate the accomplishments of the Ming dynasty.

1 FOCUS AND MOTIVATE

Before reading the chapter opener, help students identify the reasons why countries change political leadership. Ask them to cite instances where internal and external conflicts bring change. Such changes brought new governments, called dynasties, to China.

2 TEACH

• Discuss how China prospered under the Ming emperors. Point to early 15th-century naval expeditions as an example of economic expansion.

• Discuss how the Ming became isolated after 1433 and point out the results. (a loss of trade and financial problems)

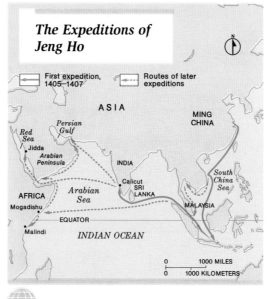

The Expeditions of Jeng Ho

First expedition, 1405–1407

Routes of later expeditions

ASIA

MING CHINA

Red Sea
Persian Gulf
Jidda
Arabian Peninsula
INDIA
Calicut
SRI LANKA
South China Sea
AFRICA
Arabian Sea
Mogadishu
MALAYSIA
EQUATOR
Malindi
INDIAN OCEAN

0   1000 MILES
0   1000 KILOMETERS

MAP STUDY Jeng Ho led an expedition from China to Africa. According to the map, what African cities did he reach?

Under a strong, efficient centralized government, Ming China, with a population of 100 million, enjoyed nearly 300 years of peaceful prosperity. In those years the Chinese cleared new fields for farming and planted vast new crops of mulberry trees to provide food for silkworms. During the early years of the dynasty, trade with distant countries increased, and luxury goods such as silk and porcelain were exported in large numbers.

In the early 15th century, China had a large, seaworthy merchant fleet that carried more export products than any other country in the world. The ships in this fleet were much larger than any ships built before that time. The ships carried crews of 1,000 men and had watertight compartments—the earliest recorded use of such a safety device.

Chinese naval expeditions sailed through the South China Sea and across the Indian Ocean. The most important expeditions were led by a court official named Jeng Ho, who commanded seven expeditions between 1405 and 1433. Refer to the map above. Jeng Ho's first expedition, with 62 ships and about 28,000 sailors, completed a two-year voyage that reached Malaysia, Sri Lanka, and southwest India. On the other six voyages, fleets sailed as far westward as the east coast of Africa.

Jeng Ho visited more than 50 countries and returned to China with a huge variety of items given in tribute. Some of these items, such as giraffes, ostriches, lions, and zebras, the Chinese had never seen before. The expeditions took place 100 years before the Portuguese created a naval empire in the Indian Ocean. It is interesting to note that the Ming emperors had ships, sailors, guns, and navigational skills to create their own naval empire before the Europeans came on the scene. However, the purpose of the voyages was not to create an empire but to establish China as a force in the world and to spread knowledge about its power and its products.

After 1433 the Ming emperors ceased all expeditions, halted construction of large ocean-going ships, and made it a crime for any Chinese to leave the country by sea. As a result, Chinese trade declined, and Chinese ships no longer sailed the Indian Ocean. This complete reversal in policy was caused in part by Confucian court officials who disliked Jeng Ho and plotted against him. Another cause was that naval expeditions were very expensive. The court thought it more important to use the money to strengthen China's northern land defenses where, even in the mid-1400s, the Mongols were still a menace.

The Mings limited contact with the West.

In the early 1500s, European powers were eager for trade with the East. Portuguese sailors reached China first, when representatives of Portugal arrived in Beijing in 1520. This early contact did not work out well because the Portuguese disregarded the strict Chinese trade laws. Portuguese traders set up smuggling operations along China's coast and resorted to plundering, kidnaping, and killing. The Chinese reacted with horror at this brutality and called the Portuguese "ocean devils."

As a result of conflicts with the Portuguese, the emperor's government tried to ban foreigners from China altogether. However, with the Portuguese at their door and other Western nations close behind, China could not remain completely isolated. In

BACKGROUND Ming rulers restored the civil service exams. The exams were given every three years at the provincial level and took a week to write. The best students went on to take the national exams offered at Beijing, exams also offered once every three years. The pressure must have been extreme.

BACKGROUND The Ming emperors made the capital of Beijing into one of the finest cities in the world. With its many palaces, temples, and walls, Beijing was actually four cities in one. In the center was an area called the Forbidden city, in which only members of the royal family were allowed to live.

1557 the Ming emperor allowed the Portuguese to establish a trading post at **Macao** (mə kou′), a city on China's southern coast. The emperor also allowed a few Christian missionaries to enter China, but they, like the sailors and merchants, did not always respect the rules of the Chinese government. Thus, for the most part, foreigners became unwelcome in Ming China.

The Ming rulers not only tried to keep foreigners out of China; they also tried to keep Chinese citizens from leaving the country. In 1619 the Ming emperor wrote to the tsar of Russia: "O Tsar, I neither leave my own kingdom nor allow my ambassadors or merchants to do so." This **isolationism** seriously interfered with trade, causing Ming China increasing financial troubles. Discontent grew within the country, and invaders from the north again threatened. In 1644 the Ming dynasty fell to nomad invaders called the Manchus.

Pictured below is the first giraffe ever seen in China. Jeng Ho's expedition sent it to the Chinese emperor around 1414.

Section 1 Review

Identify Ming dynasty, Macao, isolationism

Main Ideas
1. How did early Ming rulers help China prosper?
2. Why did later Ming emperors limit Chinese contact with other cultures? What were the effects of this policy on China?

Critical Thinking
Predicting Effects: The Ming emperors often behaved abusively toward the government officials who advised them. What effects do you think this might have had on the quality of the Chinese government during the Ming era?

---

2   *The Manchu dynasty maintained Chinese culture.*

The Ming dynasty gave China 300 years of stable government. That era was a period of great wealth and artistic achievement in China. To this day, Ming palaces, tombs, statues, and porcelain are admired for their beauty and craftsmanship. However, in the early 1600s, the Ming policy of isolation, combined with government corruption, weakened the empire. High taxes caused several peasant uprisings that the Ming emperors were unable to put down. Invasions from the north further disrupted Chinese life.

The Manchus invaded and conquered China.

Gradually, a nomadic northern tribe from Manchuria, the **Manchus**, expanded their territory. The Manchus rejected claims of Chinese domination and started a kingdom of their own.

Meanwhile, discontent grew within China. In addition to peasant rebellions, bands of Chinese robbers roamed the countryside, stealing land and livestock from local farmers. One powerful robber chief seized a large territory, and in 1644 threatened to attack the capital at Beijing.

Chinese military leaders called on the Manchus to help defend the capital. The Manchus responded by defeating the robber chief, taking Beij-

The Manchus made a point of separating themselves from the Chinese people they ruled. Have the students identify how the Manchu rulers were able to accomplish this separation. Discuss how Kangxi and Qian Long made China a major military power, and how their rule expanded the social and cultural well-being of China.

GUIDED PRACTICE

Have the students write down five words that identify the successes and failures of the Manchu dynasty.

ASSESS

What was the Manchu's biggest mistake? (their policy of isolationism)

OPTIONAL RETEACHING

Ask students to explain the significance or meaning of each of the following: inward-looking Chinese population, a nomadic northern tribe, queues as a sign of separateness, no need for the products of foreign barbarians, 5,000 volumes.

OPTIONAL ENRICHMENT

1. Have students estimate the number of square miles controlled by the Manchus at the height of their power. (about 5 million square miles) (challenging)

2. Also for enrichment:

 Source Reading 24A

INDEPENDENT PRACTICE/ HOMEWORK

Assign the Section Review, Activities page 141, or Workbook page 95.

CLOSURE

Summarize by explaining that the Manchu dynasty reached its zenith

ing for themselves, and making their own prince emperor of China. This new dynasty, the Manchu, ruled China until 1911.

The Manchu empire was huge. As you can see from the map on the facing page, land under Manchu influence included all of China, Korea, Manchuria, Mongolia, Nepal, Tibet, Xinjiang (East Turkestan), and much of Southeast Asia. The Manchus kept the Chinese system of government and divided important political offices among Chinese and Manchu nobility. However, to keep control the Manchus held most major offices.

Unlike the Mongols, the Manchus tried to retain their own customs and language rather than adapting to Chinese ways. Intermarriage with the Chinese was forbidden and many other strict rules kept the two groups separate. For example, the Manchus required Chinese men to wear queues [kyüz], or pigtails, as a sign of separateness and even inferiority.

During the first 150 years of Manchu rule, China was well governed and became a major military power. Beyond China's traditional borders, the Manchu emperors conquered vast new territories. (See the map on the facing page.) Within the empire, the government provided law and order, built roads and canals, stored grain for use in times of famine, assisted farmers in clearing land, and developed some industry. This period became one of

This richly embroidered robe belonged to a Manchu empress. It is decorated with her emblem, the phoenix, a Chinese symbol of peace and happiness.

the most progressive in Chinese history.

Two emperors in particular deserve much of the credit for China's growth during that time. One of those emperors was **Kangxi**, mentioned in the chapter introduction. The other outstanding emperor was Kangxi's grandson, **Qian Long** [chyen′ lung′]. Adding their two reigns together, these emperors ruled for 120 years.

Kangxi was on the throne for 61 years (1661–1722), the longest reign in Chinese history. He was a person of many talents—an excellent military leader, a strong administrator, a scholar, and a patron of the arts. He issued sound laws for his subjects, reduced taxes whenever possible, and governed with fairness. Kangxi sponsored major scholarly works, such as a massive encyclopedia of 5,000 volumes that was printed in 1728.

Qian Long reigned for 59 years (1736–1795) and was the last of the great Manchu emperors. Like his grandfather, Qian Long attended to government duties very earnestly. He took an interest in schools and improved the educational system throughout China. Qian Long was an efficient ruler who has been favorably compared to outstanding European rulers of the time, such as Catherine the Great of Russia and Frederick the Great of Prussia.

Isolation was a weakness of Manchu policy.

The Manchu Empire reached its height during the reign of Qian Long. However, signs of decline began to appear even with the peace and prosperity maintained by the Manchus. Stable conditions in China contributed to a sharp increase in population. In 1710 the population was 115 million, but by 1793, it had doubled.

Rapid population growth was not matched by advances in agriculture or industry. In fact, by 1800 almost all land available for farming was occupied. Thus, the constantly growing population had to be fed by intensive farming of land already being cultivated. This caused food shortages and gradually lowered the standard of living.

At the same time, the quality of government declined. Corruption became common in the emperor's court, among government officials in general, and in the military. To make matters worse, the Manchu policy of isolation from the rest of the

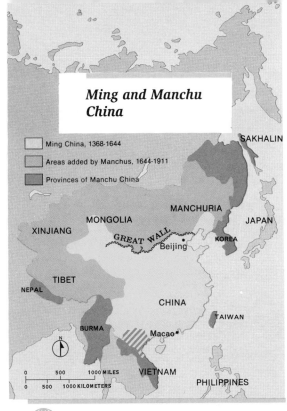

Ming and Manchu China

☐ Ming China, 1368-1644

☐ Areas added by Manchus, 1644-1911

☐ Provinces of Manchu China

SAKHALIN

MANCHURIA

MONGOLIA

JAPAN

XINJIANG

GREAT WALL

Beijing

KOREA

TIBET

NEPAL

CHINA

TAIWAN

BURMA

Macao

0   500   1000 MILES

VIETNAM

0   500   1000 KILOMETERS

PHILIPPINES

🌐 **MAP STUDY** Which regions did the Manchus add to China? Which regions became provinces under Manchu domination?

world kept out of China new inventions and ideas developed in other countries. The Manchus had little knowledge of the important advances in industry and science taking place in Europe and the United States. The inward-looking Chinese civilization still saw itself as the center of the universe, superior to all others on the outside.

An example of this attitude was expressed by an English traveler who visited Beijing in the 1790s. The Englishman was seeking trade privileges for English merchants, but the emperor Qian Long refused to grant the privileges. Qian Long explained his actions in a letter to the English king:

> The stores of goods in the Celestial Empire are extremely plentiful. There is nothing We do not possess, so that there is really no need for the products of the foreign barbarians in order to balance supply and demand.

However, the tea, silk, and porcelain produced

ANSWER TO MAP STUDY Manchuria, Mongolia, Xinjiang, Tibet; Sakhalin, Korea, Taiwan, Vietnam, Burma, Nepal

by the Celestial Empire are indispensable to the different states of Europe and to your kingdom. For this reason, We have, in Our grace and pity, established Our official trading companies. . . . It has been Our wish that all your daily needs be properly supplied and that everyone share in Our overly abundant riches.

Although there were some reasons for the Chinese to believe in the superiority of their culture—for more than 1,000 years no other nation in Asia could match China—the emperor's reply illustrates a naive attitude toward progress and the rest of the world. This lack of understanding would cause China to suffer much grief in the 19th century.

Section 2 Review

Identify Manchus, Kangxi, Qian Long

Main Ideas

1. Give examples of positive effects of Manchu rule on China.
2. How did the Manchu policy of isolation weaken China?

Critical Thinking

Assessing Cause and Effect: "The isolationist policy of the Manchus was the main reason for China's great political stability during the Manchu era." Tell why you agree or disagree with this statement.

---

3 | *Tokugawa shoguns restricted foreign influences.*

Like China, Japan gained political unity and centralized government in the 17th and 18th centuries. Also like China, Japan followed a policy of isolation. These developments took place under the Tokugawa Shogunate, which fought its way to power at the end of the 1500s.

The Tokugawa Shogunate unified Japan and adopted an isolationist policy.

As you learned in Chapter 17, in 1603 a strong and vigorous warrior named Ieyasu [ē ye yä′sü]

under Kangxi and Qian Long. After that, isolationism broken by the Western world that would not stay away and overpopulation combined to bring China's peace and prosperity to an end.

3 | *Lesson Plan*

Essential Learning Objectives

Students will learn to:

- describe the techniques used by the Tokugawa Shogunate to unify Japan.
- assess the positive and negative effects of isolationism on Japan.

445

A MYSTERY IN HISTORY

In spite of Westernization and the remarkable economic development of contemporary Japan, women still play a subordinate role in Japanese society. Some observers think this will change as Japan continues its economic growth and becomes more like Western societies. Others believe that Japanese economic power will encourage it to hold on to many of its distinctive cultural traits. A good class discussion may be provoked by explaining both lines of reasoning and asking "What will the future hold for the role of women in Japan?"

Additional material on women in Japan in the 1980s can be found in magazine articles, such as "Women: A Separate Sphere," in the *Time Magazine* special issue on Japan (August 1, 1983), pp. 68–69. The article points out that, although women received the right to vote in the 1947 revision of the Japanese constitution (dictated by American occupation forces), "extreme deference to the harmony of the group" made individual efforts toward full equality of the sexes difficult. The article quotes Yumiko Yansson, a Japanese feminist: "'Resignation is the first lesson of life,' the saying goes. In Japan, rebellion means being an outsider."

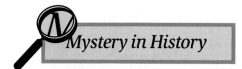

Mystery in History

WHY DID WOMEN'S ROLES CHANGE IN TOKUGAWA JAPAN?

The outward manner and temper of women is rooted in the negative (yin) power, and so temperamentally women are apt to be sensitive, petty, narrow, and jaundiced [unhealthy or discontented]. As they live confined to their homes day in and day out, theirs is a very private life and their vision is quite limited.

This view of women in the early Tokugawa period expressed by the Japanese philosopher Nakae Toju (1608–1648), stands in sharp contrast to the high political and social status women enjoyed in Heian Japan, as you read in Chapter 17. Folk tales make it clear that women in ancient Japan proposed marriage and newly married couples lived in the house of the bride's parents. Up to about 600, women even became emperors.

Changes in the status of women, however, apparently began when Confucian ideas reached Japan from China. Confucianism stressed the yin-yang principle that everything in the universe was organized around two poles: light/dark, active/passive, male/female. The century of warfare ending in 1603 also affected the position of women since sons became more valued as soldiers than daughters.

Tokugawa rule brought peace to Japan by dividing the people into classes and imposing rigid controls. Women fared the worst, losing all property rights. A wife had to obey her husband as lord and master.

Why did Japan turn away from its traditional society that honored women to adopt a system that treated women as inferior? Many scholars believe that the main factor may have been the introduction of Confucian ideas that denied equality to women. However, women themselves seem to have accepted the inferior role. Why they did so remains one of the mysteries of history.

The women of Kyoto watch a samurai parade from their homes in a screen painted by Fujiwara Mitsutaka in 1750.

BACKGROUND For nearly three hundred years Japan experienced an armed peace. A tax-collecting, sword-carrying class of some 2,000,000 warriors, all pledged to unquestioned obedience, enabled the Tokugawa shoguns to maintain the old feudal structure well into the 19th century.

founded the **Tokugawa Shogunate**. In that year Ieyasu became shogun and master of a unified Japan (although the emperors continued an unimportant existence in the old capital of Kyoto). The new shogun achieved his goals of national unity in several ways. For example, he made all daimyo, or nobles, sign a written oath of loyalty to the central government. From his headquarters in **Edo**, a small coastal town that later became the huge city of Tokyo, Ieyasu exercised supreme authority over all military forces in the country.

The shogun required the daimyo to attend court at Edo and spend every other year in the capital. Even when the daimyo left for their provincial homes, they had to leave their wives and children behind as hostages. Ieyasu successfully weakened the power of the daimyo in every way he could. Thus, during the period of Ieyasu's control, the central government became dominant.

Ieyasu's successor, the second Tokugawa shogun, initiated a policy of isolating Japan from foreign influence. When this shogun learned that Christian missionaries were intervening in Japanese political and military affairs, all foreign missionaries were expelled from the country or executed. Thousands of Japanese who had become Christians were also killed. As a result, by 1638 Christianity had become virtually extinct in Japan.

There were other effects of the Tokugawa isolationist policy. No Japanese were permitted to leave the homeland, and those who had left to study or live abroad were not allowed to return. Although not completely stopped, foreign trade was also very restricted. Finally, all Portuguese traders were driven out of Japan in 1638, but the shogun's government did allow one Dutch ship to trade in the port city of Nagasaki once each year.

Altogether, the Tokugawa Shogunate created a conservative system of rule. That system brought peace to Japan for more than 250 years but kept the country out of touch with the rest of the world—particularly that part of the world that was modernizing and growing in military power.

A merchant class and large cities developed in Japan.

Gradually, however, feudal ways of life were challenged. Under the Tokugawas, internal trade increased and several cities grew in population. For example, by the end of the 1700s, the population of Edo was more than a million. In the larger cities, merchant and business classes became wealthy and gained influence. One family, the Mitsui, developed a chain of stores with branches in several cities. The Mitsui chain of stores is still a leading company in modern Japan.

DAILY LIFE

Wiping dishes, paring vegetables, ladling soup, and tending the stove were everyday kitchen tasks in 18th-century Japan and elsewhere, then as today. Kitagawa Utamaro (1753–1806) raised the depiction of such homely tasks to the level of high art. Utamaro was a master of the woodblock print form *Ukiyo-e*, translated as "pictures of the floating world." Utamaro's works, shown in Paris in 1889, helped awaken the Western world to Japanese art.

1. Ask interested students to locate examples of woodblock prints showing daily life in Tokugawa Japan. (average)

2. Have students enact part of a Kabuki play. Refer to Faubion Bower's *Japanese Theatre* (1952) for English translations of three Kabuki plays. (challenging)

3. Students also may be assigned Activities enrichment page 144, or:

 Overhead Transparency 48

 Source Reading 24B

INDEPENDENT PRACTICE/ HOMEWORK

Assign the Section Review, the Chapter Review items, Activities page 142, or Workbook page 96.

CLOSURE

Explain that, like China, Japan bought peace by becoming isolationist. The price was that in the 19th century Japan would find itself politically and economically behind the West.

Answers to Section 3 Review

Identify

Key Terms, People, and Places are defined on pages indicated in parentheses. Also see the Glossary and Biographical Dictionary. Tokugawa Shogunate (447), Edo (Tokyo) (447), Kabuki (448)

Main Ideas

1. made the daimyo sign an oath of loyalty, exercised supreme authority over military forces, required the daimyo to spend every other year at court and held families as hostages; isolationism

2. Japan changed from a feudal, agricultural society to a more urban

---

From the Archives

A Lesson in Business

During the Tokugawa Peace in Japan, the merchant class grew rich and powerful. One of these merchants, Mitsui Takahira Hachirouemon (1655–1737) the founder of a large department store, wrote a book on merchandising for the instruction of his son. The following extract provides a lesson about business and politics.

[Some] merchants take on building for the government or other speculative ventures and make a fortune at one mighty bound, but they only go to prove the common adage that "he who lives by the river drowns in the river." . . .

[There] was a man in Edo called Fushimiya Shirobei [whose] father was a timber merchant. . . . Shirobei sought permission for an exchange of goods at Nagasaki. . . . His request was granted on payment of a contribution, and he proceeded down to Nagasaki for two years. He distributed large sums to the people of that place and to the local temples and shrines. . . . However, just when he was astonishing everyone with his luxury, a petition was put in by Takagi Hikoemon, a town elder of Nagasaki, offering a bigger contribution than that paid by Fushimiya. As a result, Fushimiya had his license revoked, and Takagi got the concession. Shirobei's position was therefore hopeless, and after 20 years he eventually ran out of food and died of starvation.

The wealthy business class did much to finance a new type of culture. Art and amusements were developed to please city people, who could afford to pay for such luxuries. The **Kabuki** style of theater became popular. Unlike the dignified No plays, Kabuki theater stressed violence and melodrama. Its heroes and villains from stormy feudal days captivated audiences then and still do today.

FROM THE ARCHIVES Reprinted from David John Lu, *Sources of Japanese History* (New York: McGraw-Hill, 1974) I, 225. Note how the purpose of the story is made clearer by knowing something about the person who wrote it and the oc-

---

Many city people wanted art for their homes but could not afford costly paintings. To meet this demand, woodblock prints were produced. These colorful, inexpensive prints pictured beautiful women, actors, and scenes from everyday life. They featured life in the streets of cities and villages, in eating houses, and in markets. Japanese woodblock art reached its highest point in the 1700s and has been called "the world's first art for the masses."

By the end of the 1700s, Japan was ready for major changes. The nation was becoming capitalistic. Most daimyo were in debt to the business class, and there was increasing discontent among the poorer samurai who had been severely limited in freedom of action by the Tokugawa shoguns.

There were also powerful clans, particularly in western Japan, that were weary of Tokugawa control and eager to see the Tokugawas removed from power. The young samurai in these clans became restless when they learned about other ways to rule a country than the way of the Tokugawas. Thousands of Japanese students obtained translations of books published in Europe and the United States and learned about Western culture.

The old Japanese feudal system was fading because it no longer met the nation's needs. Under these conditions it is not surprising that Japanese feudalism was swept away by the middle of the 19th century. You will read about these changes in Chapter 30.

Section 3 Review

Identify Tokugawa Shogunate, Edo (Tokyo), Kabuki

Main Ideas

1. How did the first Tokugawa shogun ensure unity and loyalty from the daimyo? What was the Tokugawa policy towards other countries?

2. How did Japanese society change under the Tokugawas?

Critical Thinking

Identifying Assumptions: "The Tokugawa rulers were wrong to maintain a policy of isolationism because the Western nations could have improved the government, economics, and daily life of Japan." What assumptions are being made in this statement?

casion of its writing. What is the moral of the story? (It is better to build a business by hard work and good service than on the favor of a government contract.)

HIGHLIGHTS OF CIVILIZATION

Japan's No Theater

The long period of war and civil strife that marked the collapse of Japan's feudal society between 1100 and 1600 established the somber, formal style of the No theater, Japan's oldest traditional dramatic form. The word *no* in Japanese means "talent," and the earliest No performances may have been a display of virtuosic acrobatic stunts and juggling feats. The No drama later turned to the portrayal of the actions of dramatic personages. Performances consisted of dancing and mime accompanied by chanting to tell the story. Male actors performed all the roles.

The early forms of the No drama were transformed in the 15th century by a famous No master, Zeami Motokiyo (1364?–1443). Under Zeami's influence, the No became a symbolic theater where the important actions were suggested, not represented. The actors attempted to convey emotion and create an intense atmosphere through the use of masks rather than through actions and words. Movements became frozen and stylized.

In Zeami's plays the central character was often a ghost, who would return in the second part of the play in his former appearance. Between the first and second parts of the play, musicians performed discordant music and uttered incomprehensible cries to suggest the actor's passage from the world of the dead. The final part of the play was a dance, symbolizing the resolution of the actor's suffering.

Yugen—a Japanese term that has been loosely defined as "mystery" — underlies the No theater, and Zeami wrote at length on how *yugen* [yü'gen] might be attained. Beauty, gentleness, tranquillity, and elegant costuming all served to help impart *yugen*.

When an actor conveyed *yugen*, the audience was aware of experiencing something beyond what was merely represented, something eternal. Zeami described the perfect expression of *yugen* as "silence beyond the form," and used as a metaphor for this stillness, snow piling up in a silver bowl.

The No actor dons a magnificent robe (far left) and superbly carved mask (left). Before making an entrance, he is said to gaze at his masked reflection in a mirror and "become" this reflected image.

one with a strong business class. New arts developed in cities. The daimyos and samurai became discontented with Tokugawa rule.

Critical Thinking
The Western cultures were superior to Japan.

HIGHLIGHTS OF CIVILIZATION

The concept of *yugen* is explained in *In Praise of Shadows*, by Jyunichiro Tanizaki (New Haven: Leete's Island, 1977). Donald Keene, in *Nō: The Classical Theatre of Japan* (Tokyo: Kodansha International Ltd., 1966), p. 11, makes an interesting comparison between the No and Greek drama. Similarities include the use of masks, a chorus, song, stately dances, and poetry. Differences include the intended audience—a large, general audience in the case of Greek drama and a small, aristocratic group of courtiers in the case of No. Characterization and action are also completely different. Keene states: "Contrary to all the predictions made to me in 1953, when I first saw Nō performed, Nō thrives today as never before, and the audiences consist increasingly of young people. . . ." Ask students to consider why such a slow-paced, remote, and symbolic art form would attract a younger generation accustomed to films and TV. (Opinion: Keene suggests that young audiences are "perhaps driven to Nō by dissatisfaction with entertainments supposedly devised for their pleasure.")

Answers to Test Yourself

Key Terms, People, and Places
The key terms, people, and places tested here were introduced in the chapter sections and reviewed in the Section Reviews. For definitions see the page references at the appropriate Section Reviews. Also see the Glossary and Biographical Dictionary.

Main Ideas
The main ideas tested here were introduced in the sections of this chapter and reviewed in the Section Reviews. For answers to these questions, see the appropriate Section Reviews.

Critical Thinking
1. The comparison is valid because both countries became isolationist to avoid contamination of their cultures by Westerners and to maintain internal political and cultural unity.
2. Sample answer: China would have had interchange with progressive Western nations through trade, social life, and politics and might have incorporated many of the scientific and industrial innovations of the West into China's very creative and adaptive civilization. This might have made China one of the world's economic leaders today instead of a nation that is lagging behind other world powers economically.

CHAPTER 24 REVIEW

Section Summaries

Section 1
The Mings began to limit outside contacts.
After ending Mongol rule, the new Ming dynasty expanded Chinese agriculture and foreign trade. With a strong, centralized government, China prospered. Chinese ships led by Jeng Ho sailed as far as Africa in the early 1400s. Later, Ming emperors halted the voyages because of political intrigue and pressing need for defense on land. The Mings adopted an isolationist policy after disastrous experiences with Europeans.

Section 2
The Manchu dynasty maintained Chinese culture.
In the mid-1600s, invading Manchus overthrew the Ming dynasty. For the first half of Manchu rule, China prospered and was well-governed, especially during the reigns of emperors Kangxi and Qian Long. However, China's problems grew as the population increased rapidly, causing food shortages and a lower standard of living. Believing China to be superior, the Manchus followed an isolationist policy that prevented new ideas and technologies from entering the country and severely restricted trade with other nations.

Section 3
Tokugawa shoguns restricted foreign influences.
In Japan the Tokugawa shoguns fought their way to power in 1603. The Tokugawas controlled the daimyo and established a strong, centralized government. However, an isolationist policy shut Japan off from outside contact for more than 250 years. By the mid-1800s, a new merchant class had developed and cities were expanding. The old feudal system became outdated, and many Japanese became open to new ideas and ready for sweeping changes.

Test Yourself

Key Terms, People, and Places
Identify the significance of each of the following:

Section 1
a. Ming dynasty   **c.** isolationism
b. Macao

Section 2
a. Manchus   **c.** Qian Long
b. Kangxi

Review Dates

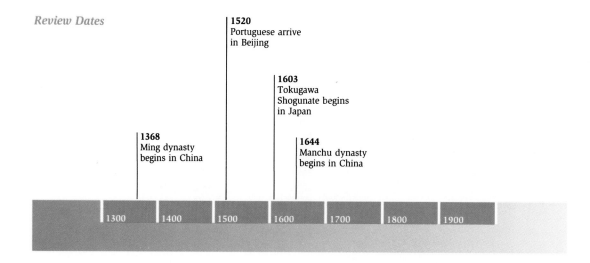

1520
Portuguese arrive in Beijing

1603
Tokugawa Shogunate begins in Japan

1368
Ming dynasty begins in China

1644
Manchu dynasty begins in China

| 1300 | 1400 | 1500 | 1600 | 1700 | 1800 | 1900 |

Section 3
a. Tokugawa Shogunate   **c.** Kabuki
b. Edo (Tokyo)

Main Ideas

Section 1
1. What actions taken by the Mings caused China to prosper during that dynasty?
2. Why was an isolationist policy followed by the Mings? What were the disadvantages of this policy for China?

Section 2
1. Name at least three positive results of Manchu rule in China.
2. How was the Manchu isolationism harmful to China?

Section 3
1. What steps did the first Tokugawa shogun take to control the daimyo? How would you describe the foreign policy of the Tokugawa Shogunate?
2. Explain the major changes in Japanese society during the rule of the Tokugawas.

Critical Thinking

1. Analyzing Comparisons   Consider the following statement: "The reasons for the Chinese policy of isolationism are similar to the reasons that Japan enforced the same policy." Is this comparison valid? Why or why not?
2. Predicting Effects   What do you think might have happened if the Manchu emperor had agreed to give trading privileges to the British as requested?

Chapter Skills and Activities

Practicing Study and Research Skills

Using a Specialized Vocabulary
Sometimes special words must be learned to understand the history of a particular culture or country. The following list of words are important for understanding Chinese and Japanese history. Write an explanation or definition for each word and give its equivalent meaning, if possible, in Western culture. Use your textbook or a dictionary as your sources.

CRITICAL THINKING QUESTION LEVEL 1. challenging;
2. average

1. dynasty   **4.** daimyo
2. shogunate   **5.** samurai
3. emperor

Linking Past and Present
In 1949 Chinese Communists gained control of China. They tried to throw out Western influence and isolate the Chinese in order to establish a perfect society according to their own plan. For example, as the photograph above illustrates, in 1966 Chinese leader Mao Zedong organized the Red Guards to eliminate all foreign and noncommunist thought from China. Compare this policy with Chinese policies under the Mings and Manchus.

Learning History Through Maps
Refer to the map of Ming and Manchu China on page 445. This map shows the expansion of the Chinese empire under the Manchus. Use the map to answer the following questions.
1. What areas were added by the Manchus during their reign?
2. From what direction did the Manchus come when they invaded China?
3. What areas were provinces of China but not part of China itself?
4. About how many miles long was the Great Wall in this period?

25 The Formation of Latin America

OVERVIEW

Spain and Portugal conquered a continent, intentionally and unintentionally killed off eighty percent of its Indians, and imported 17 million African slaves, resulting in richly varied, divided societies.

PLANNING CHART

Section	Text Pages	Key Concept	Suggested Teaching Time
1 Europeans conquered and colonized the Americas.	453–456	Cortés and Pizarro led expeditions of conquest that delivered large sections of a continent to the Spanish crown.	Two days **More time?** Use *Source Reading 25A* or the One-Day Play, *The Trial of Atahualpa*.
2 Spain controlled a large empire.	458–459	Spanish Latin America had a definite government structure and a definite class hierarchy.	One day **Less time?** Have students read Sections 2 and 3 as homework and discuss them together.
3 Indians and Africans were the main source of labor.	460–462	Through the encomienda system of forced Indian labor supplemented by African slavery, Spain and Portugal ruled Latin America for three hundred years.	Two days **More time?** Use *Overhead Transparency 49* or *Source Reading 25B*.
4 A Latin American civilization arose.	462–464	Latin American culture is a blend of Indian, African, Spanish, and Portuguese.	One day **More time?** Use *Overhead Transparency 50*.

ANCILLARIES

Materials that may be used with this chapter to reinforce, reteach, enrich, and assess learning are pictured on the following pages.

Teacher's Resource File

ACTIVITIES

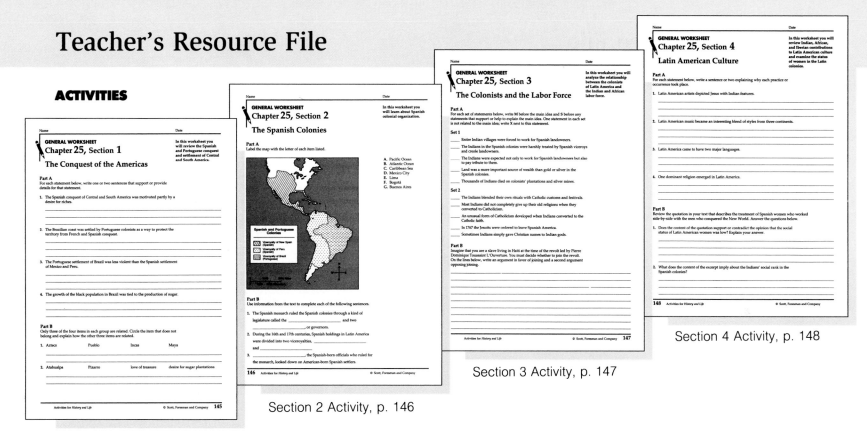

Section 1 Activity, p. 145

Section 2 Activity, p. 146

Section 3 Activity, p. 147

Section 4 Activity, p. 148

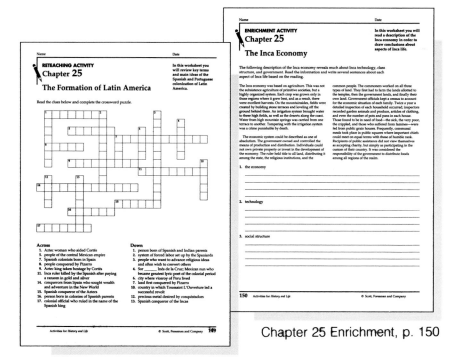

Chapter 25 Reteaching, p. 149

Chapter 25 Enrichment, p. 150

Teacher's Resource File

GEOGRAPHY SKILLS

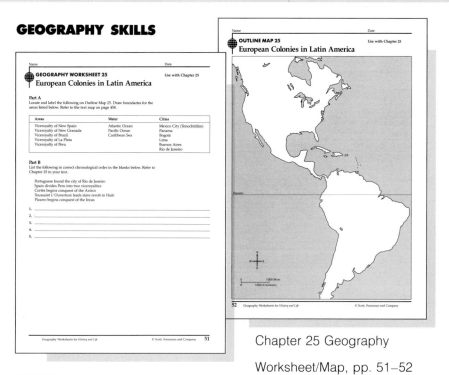

Chapter 25 Geography
Worksheet/Map, pp. 51–52

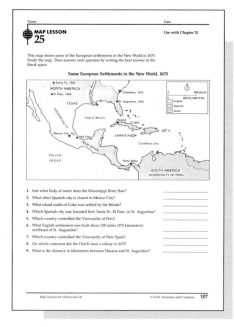

Chapter 25 Map Lesson, p. 107

TESTS

Chapter Test, pp. 129–130

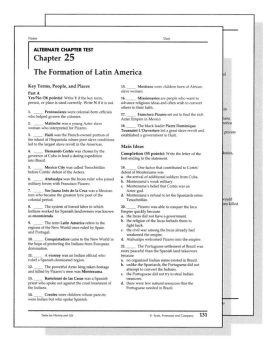

Alternate Chapter Test, pp. 131–132

ONE-DAY PLAYS

The Trial of Atahualpa

Other Optional Ancillaries

WORKBOOK

Section 1 Worksheet, p. 97

Section 2 Worksheet, p. 98

Section 3 Worksheet, p. 99

Section 4 Worksheet, p. 100

SOURCE READINGS

Source Reading 25a
Source Reading 25B

TEST GENERATOR

40 multiple-choice questions for Chapter 25

OVERHEAD TRANSPARENCIES

Overhead Transparency 49
Overhead Transparency 50

1400

1500

| 1519 | Cortés begins conquest of Mexico |

| 1531 | Pizarro begins conquest of Peru |

1600

1700

The Formation of Latin America

1492–1800

On November 8, 1519, a Spanish soldier of fortune named Hernando Cortés [kôr tez'] became the first European ever to come face to face with Montezuma, the king of the Aztecs, whom you read about in Chapter 18. The meeting between Cortés and Montezuma was described by a Spanish member of Cortés' party:

> Montezuma [left] his litter, and was borne in the arms of the princes . . . under a canopy of the richest materials, ornamented with green feathers, gold, and precious stones that hung in the manner of a fringe; he was most richly dressed and adorned, and wore buskins [half-boots] of pure gold ornamented with jewels. . . When Cortés was told that the great Montezuma approached, he dismounted from his horse and advanced toward him with much respect; Montezuma bid him welcome, and Cortés replied with a compliment.

That first friendly meeting between Montezuma and Cortés turned out to be one of the most important events in the history of the Americas. The meeting opened the way for Spain's conquest of Mexico, Central America, and the rich land of the Incas in Peru. Within a very short time, Spain ruled a huge colonial empire that stretched from Florida to Argentina. Meanwhile, Portugal took over Brazil.

The coming of Europeans to the Americas changed the course of history. Gold and silver from the Americas flowed into Europe, and new crops such as potatoes, corn and tomatoes were introduced into European diets.

Even more important was the fact that Europeans came to the New World to settle permanently. The culture they brought with them blended with the culture of the Indians. There was a further blending as millions of Africans were brought over to work as slaves. During a period of three centuries, the mix gave rise to a new civilization, which became known as Latin America.

Llamas graze on a hillside overlooking the ruins of Machu Picchu, a walled Incan city that once served as a refuge against the Spanish invaders.

Reading Preview

In this chapter you will read about the impact of European explorers and settlers on Latin America.

1. *Europeans conquered and colonized the Americas.*
2. *Spain controlled a large empire.*
3. *Indians and Africans were the main source of labor.*
4. *A Latin American civilization arose.*

 Europeans conquered and colonized the Americas.

On his second voyage across the Atlantic in 1493, Columbus brought more than 1,000 Spaniards to settle and explore the lands he had reached. These voyagers founded a settlement on the island of Hispaniola (now the Dominican Republic and Haiti). The settlement of Hispaniola in 1493 began the conquest of the Americas by Europeans and laid the basis for the countries of Latin America that we know today.

1 *Lesson Plan*

Essential Learning Objective

Students will learn to explain how Europeans conquered and colonized Latin America.

1 FOCUS AND MOTIVATE

Have students name as many Latin American countries as they can and list them on the chalkboard. Tell students that this chapter will deal with the history of many of these nations.

- Identify the steps in the Spanish conquest of Mexico. Discuss how Cortés used Indian alliances to overthrow Montezuma. Point out that Montezuma could easily have defeated Cortés, but he decided not to.

- Discuss Pizarro and his conquest of the Inca Empire. Compare the similarities with Cortés' military campaign in Mexico.

GUIDED PRACTICE

Pass out outline maps of Central and South America from the Geography Skills book. Have students draw and identify both Inca and Aztec Empires.

BACKGROUND Before the coming of the Spaniards, Cuba was inhabited by two Indian tribes: the Guanahuatebey and the more numerous Taino. These two had a combined population of about 50,000

Hernando Cortés conquered the Aztec Empire.

In 1494, more than 125 years before the Pilgrims landed at Plymouth Rock, the Spanish founded the city of Santo Domingo, now the capital of the Dominican Republic. By 1514 the Spanish had conquered the island of Cuba. Five years later, the Spanish governor of Cuba heard rumors of gold on the mainland. He chose 33-year-old **Hernando Cortés** to lead a daring expedition into Mexico.

Cortés was the son of well-to-do Spanish parents. He was one of the first of the **conquistadors** [kon kēs′tə dorz], or conquerors, who came to the New World in search of adventure and gold. He was bold, ambitious, and well-liked as a leader. With 11 ships, 16 horses, several small cannons, and about 600 troops, he set sail for the coast of Mexico in 1519. Since the Mexican Indians had never seen cannons or horses before, Cortés had an important advantage when fighting them.

Cortés also had good luck. Off the Mexican coast, he rescued a shipwrecked Spanish priest who had been the slave of a Maya chief. The priest had learned the Maya language and now joined Cortés as an interpreter.

The Maya chiefs, frightened by the cannons and the horses, gave Cortés a gift of 20 slaves. One of the slaves was a young Aztec woman named **Malinche** [mä lēn′chä] who spoke Maya and Nahuatl [nä′wä təl], the language of the Aztecs. The priest spoke to Malinche in Maya and also taught her Spanish. Through her, Cortés spoke directly to

The two paintings at left show Cortés and his army meeting Montezuma, the Aztec emperor. This peaceful scene contrasts sharply with the battle depicted below, an illustration from a 16th-century Aztec manuscript. The army of Cortés storms the main gate at Tenochtitlán, the Aztec capital.

BACKGROUND An estimated 1500 to 2000 languages existed in Latin America in 1500. Nearly 600 of these have been authenticated by linguists. Several hundred of these are now extinct. In addition, in Meso-America (Mexico to Panama) today, about 70 Indian languages are still spoken including Aztec, Yucatec, and Zapotec.

Aztec and Maya leaders. Malinche acted as a diplomat and informant and saved Cortés' life when she discovered an Indian plot to kill him.

Cortés sailed northwest from the Yucatán peninsula until he discovered a good harbor and then he founded the town of Vera Cruz. Cortés learned that the Aztecs ruled the various peoples of eastern Mexico and that these people were forced to send the Aztecs tribute and humans for sacrifices. The subject peoples hated their rulers, but warned Cortés that the Aztec king, **Montezuma**, was too powerful to be defeated. Some of Cortés' men wanted to return to Cuba to get more soldiers, but Cortés ordered all his ships burned. The men then had no choice but to march inland with him.

The coastal Indians and other subject peoples joined forces with Cortés as he moved inland and fought against various groups. Although Montezuma knew of Cortés' advance, he could not decide what to do. At first he sent Cortés presents of gold because he believed Cortés to be an ancient Aztec god who was supposed to return one day.

Montezuma had thousands of armed Aztec warriors at his command. He could have ordered them to attack Cortés' small force. Instead, he decided to welcome the Spaniards to Tenochtitlán, the Aztec capital. Once inside the city, Cortés took Montezuma hostage. A short time later, one of Cortés' captains invited Aztec nobles to a feast and murdered them. The Aztecs rose up in anger against the Spaniards and Montezuma was killed, but the Spaniards lost more than half their men getting out of Tenochtitlán.

Cortés soon obtained fresh supplies, cannons, and gunpowder from Cuba. Then he laid siege to Tenochtitlán for three months, cutting off the water supply. The Aztecs were further weakened by hundreds of thousands of deaths from smallpox, a dreadful disease that the Spaniards had unknowingly brought with them. In August, 1521, the Aztecs surrendered, and Tenochtitlán was renamed **Mexico City.**

Francisco Pizarro conquered the Inca Empire.

Ten years after the fall of the Aztecs, another conquistador made his mark. His name was **Francisco Pizarro** [pi zär′ō], and he set out to find the rich

BACKGROUND In Peru, Pizarro followed the Cortés formula of taking advantage of internal warfare among the Inca people. For the record, Pizarro was murdered in Peru by fellow Spaniards quarreling over who would rule.

Inca Empire he had heard existed in Peru. Late in 1530, Pizarro set sail from Panama with his brothers and a force of about 130 men.

Like Cortés, Pizarro also had some very good luck. As you learned in Chapter 18, the Inca Empire was tightly organized. However, in 1524 a civil war broke out, and two brothers, Huascar and Atahualpa, fought for the throne. **Atahualpa** [ä′tä wäl′pä] won, but the fight severely weakened his empire. In 1531 Pizarro met Atahualpa in battle in a city high in the Andes Mountains. Thousands of Incas were killed during the battle, and Atahualpa was taken prisoner. Not a single Spaniard was even badly wounded.

Atahualpa soon realized that the Spaniards were seeking gold. He offered to buy his freedom by filling a large room with gold, then filling another room twice with silver. However, after paying this ransom, probably worth 8 or 9 million dollars, Atahualpa was strangled by the Spaniards.

Pizarro, his brothers, and more than 100 Spanish soldiers divided the treasure. However, the men became greedy and began to fight among themselves. Although this in-fighting kept Peru in chaos, the rule of the Pizarro brothers lasted for 16 years. In 1547 a royal governor with Spanish troops took over.

The relationship between the Spaniards and the Indians, and the Spaniards' love of treasure, were described in a long letter written by an Inca noble, Huaman Poma, to King Philip III of Spain between 1567 and 1615:

> Your Majesty, in your great goodness you have always charged your Viceroyals . . . to look after our Indians and show favor to them, but once they disembark from their ships and set foot on land, they forget your commands and turn against us.

What's in a Name?

BRAZIL In Portuguese, "live coal" is *braza*. When Portuguese explorers landed on the eastern bulge of South America, they found a wood that produced a bright red dye. The wood was called brazil wood and the country that grew it, Brazil.

ASSESS

1. Over what people did Montezuma rule? (Aztecs)
2. What nation established fifteen armed towns along the coast of Brazil? (Portugal)

OPTIONAL RETEACHING

Ask students to compare Aztec and Inca empires. Have them identify differences and similarities in the areas of government, economics, religion. List information on the chalkboard.

OPTIONAL ENRICHMENT

1. Ask interested students to write a short biography of Hernando Cortés and have them report orally. (average)
2. Cortés sent five letters back to Spain while he was in Mexico. Assign a student to find *Hernando Cortés' Five Letters, 1519–1526,* translated by J. Bayard Morris (1926), read excerpts, and report back to the class. (challenging)

Answers to Section 1 Review

Identify

Key Terms, People, and Places are defined on pages indicated in parentheses. Also see the Glossary and Biographical Dictionary. Hernando Cortés (454), conquistadors (454), Malinche (454), Montezuma (455), Mexico City (455), Francisco Pizarro (455), Atahualpa (455)

Main Ideas

1. He welcomed Cortés as a god and was killed by the Spaniards.
2. He killed the Inca leader Atahualpa.
3. Central America, Ecuador, Chile, Colombia, and Argentina
4. Brazil.

Critical Thinking

Answers will vary but could include these ideas: both countries wanted to explore and dominate major land regions; the Spanish sought gold but the English sought land.

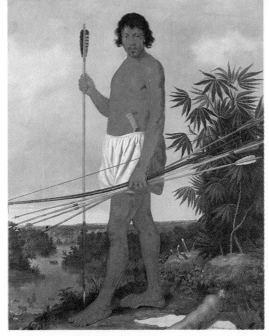

This portrait of a Tupi, one of the original inhabitants of Brazil, was painted in 1643 by Danish artist Albert Eckhout. It is one of the first realistic paintings made of a native Brazilian.

Our ancient idolatry [idol worship] and heresy was due only to ignorance of the true path. Our Indians . . . wept for their idols when these were broken up. . . . But it is the Christians who still adore property, gold and silver as their idols.

Spanish rule reached other areas.

Both Cortés and Pizarro later sent out small groups of Spanish troops to widen their control. Cortés' men pushed into Central America. Meanwhile, Pizarro moved into present-day Ecuador and Chile. The Indians in Chile fought hard, but they too, were weakened by smallpox and were no match for the Spanish.

One of Pizarro's men led a group into a rich valley in present-day Colombia, that was ruled by an Indian king named Bogotá [bō'gə tä']. There the Spaniards found houses decorated with gold and children playing marbles with uncut emeralds. The Spaniards quickly took control of the region as they had elsewhere.

In the mid-1530s, a rich Spanish noble led an expedition across the Atlantic at his own expense. He landed at the mouth of the Plata River, where the Spaniards founded a town named Buenos Aires [bwā'nəs er'ēz], now the capital of Argentina.

The Portuguese settled on Brazil's coast.

Although the Spaniards rapidly took over a huge area from Mexico to Chile, the Portuguese did very little with their claim to Brazil. They were much more interested in the large profits they were making from the spice trade with Asia. By the 1530s, however, the king of Portugal feared that Spain or France might try to take over the coast of Brazil. To prevent this from happening, he offered large grants of land to rich Portuguese nobles. In return the nobles had to set up and defend colonies at their own expense.

By the mid-1500s, there were 15 armed towns along the Brazilian coast. The king of Portugal sent out a governor general, colonists, and Jesuit missionaries to convert the Indians to Christianity. In 1565 the Portuguese founded the town of Rio de Janeiro [rē'ō dā zhə ner'ō].

Needing labor for their lands, the Portuguese raided Indian villages to capture slaves. Conflict, revolts, and disease sharply reduced the Indian population. The Portuguese began to import slaves from Africa to work on the sugar plantations. Sugar became Brazil's major export. By 1600, one-fourth of the 100,000 people in the Portuguese towns of Brazil were African slaves.

Section 1 Review

Identify Hernando Cortés, conquistadors, Malinche, Montezuma, Mexico City, Francisco Pizarro, Atahualpa

Main Ideas

1. What was Montezuma's first reaction to the coming of Cortés, and what finally happened to Montezuma?
2. How did Pizarro become ruler of Peru?
3. In addition to Mexico and Peru, what other regions and countries were conquered by the Spanish?
4. In what part of Latin America did the Portuguese establish a major colony?

Critical Thinking

Analyzing Comparisons: Read the following statement and explain why you agree or do not agree with it: "The Spanish reasons for exploring and settling Latin America were the same as the English reasons for exploring and settling North America."

GEOGRAPHY

A Key to History

CLIMATE AND POPULATION IN SOUTH AMERICA

The climate and vegetation of South America are influenced by the fact that much of the continent lies between the Equator and the Tropic of Capricorn. In general, the lowlands in the tropics are always hot because they get many hours of direct sunlight each day. In the highlands, however, the heat of the sun's rays is offset by the altitude. The higher the elevation, the cooler the air.

What areas of South America are probably lightly populated? Why?

EQUATOR

TROPIC OF CAPRICORN

- ■ Tropical rainforest
- ▨ Savanna
- ▨ Humid subtropical
- ▨ Mediterranean
- ▨ Marine west coast
- □ Desert
- ▨ Steppe
- ▨ Highlands

N

| 0 | 400 | 800 | 1200 | Kilometers |
| 0 | | 400 | 800 | Miles |

Before 1500 most South Americans lived in highland settlements. The highlands favored the development of agriculture, which is necessary for civilization and population growth.

The dominant highlands of South America, the Andes, parallel the Pacific Coast from north to south. Within the mountain ranges of the Andes are valleys, basins, and plateaus. In many of these areas, the combination of sun, rain, and temperature is well suited to the growing of staple crops.

By contrast, the lowlands are often less favorable for farming. The muggy rainforests of the Amazon River Basin occupy most of the northern third of the continent. Although covered with lush plant growth, the rainforest soils in most places will not support intensive agriculture.

When European colonists arrived, they settled along the Caribbean and the Atlantic coasts north and south of the rainforest. Beginning in 1531, the Portuguese imported large numbers of slaves from Africa. These slaves working under Portuguese and mestizo overseers turned the coastal regions into huge sugar plantations.

Later, in the 19th century, more than 8 million European immigrants came to these areas. Relatively few Europeans settled in the Andes Mountains or in the Amazon Basin. There, native Indian peoples and mestizos remained in the majority.

REVIEW
1. Why do you think civilization in South America developed in the highland areas?
2. How did the coming of Africans and Europeans affect population distribution?

GEOGRAPHY: A KEY TO HISTORY
The animal life of the rainforest has also been a major deterrent to dense human settlement. The small animals, insects in particular, often make life miserable. Mosquitoes and other insects are more than just pests, they also carry diseases such as malaria and yellow fever. In the absence of frosts, insects are always present.

Advanced students and teachers will find a lot of information on "Food, Population, and Dislocation in Latin America," in John P. Augelli's article in the *Journal of Geography,* (November-December, 1985), 274–281. Two excellent maps and several tables accompany the text.

Answers to REVIEW
1. Such areas are better suited to agriculture upon which civilization depends.
2. African slaves established sugar-cane plantations along the coastal regions north and south of the Equator, and Europeans also populated these and nearby temperate regions.

Answers to MAP QUESTION
the Andes and the Amazon Basin; High mountains and dense rainforest regions will not support intensive agriculture upon which large populatins depend.

Essential Learning Objective

Students will learn to diagram Spanish colonial government and social class hierarchies.

1 FOCUS AND MOTIVATE

To help students understand the difficulty in administering colonies, have students estimate these distances: Gibraltar—New York (3700 miles), Gibraltar—Vera Cruz (5700 miles), Gibraltar—Buenos Aires (6100 miles), Gibraltar—Lima (via Cape Horn) (10,600 miles). Discuss the administrative problems for Spain given such a far-flung empire.

2 TEACH

- Identify the key governmental positions in the Spanish colonies. Point to the dual Viceroy system and how the Spanish kings usually selected nobles and church officials born in Spain to administer the colonies.

- Discuss the social and class order in the Spanish colonies. Identify each group and point to their role.

GUIDED PRACTICE

Have students draw diagrams that show the government and social class structures of colonial Spain, for example, a simple pyramid with the king at the top, the Council of the Indies next, the viceroys third, and local administrators at the bottom.

3 ASSESS AND CLOSE

ASSESS

Name the vice-royalties in 18th-century Spanish Latin America. (New Spain, New Granada, Peru, and La Plata)

---

2 Spain controlled a large empire.

Spain's empire in America was different from most earlier empires in history. The empire lay far away from the home country, far across the Atlantic Ocean. It included islands as well as a huge area on the mainland. Cities and towns were sometimes thousands of miles apart, separated by mountains, deserts, and tropical rainforests. Travel from place to place was very difficult. Spain had to find a way to govern an empire that was many times larger than Spain itself.

The king ruled through a Council and Viceroys.

In 1524 Charles V set up a Council of the Indies to help him govern the colonies. The Council met in Spain but acted as a kind of legislature for the colonies. It drew up a code of laws to control colonial life for the benefit of the mother country. As time passed, new laws were added. By 1680 there was such confusion that all the laws had to be reorganized into a simpler code.

Spain's colonies in the New World. During the 16th and 17th centuries, Spanish holdings in Latin America were divided into two large viceroyalties, New Spain (which included Mexico, Central America, the Caribbean islands, and the north coast of South America) and Peru (which covered the rest of Spanish South America). A **viceroy**, or governor, ruled these Spanish-dominated regions in the king's name. The viceroy of New Spain lived in Mexico City, and the viceroy of Peru lived in Lima. In the 18th century, Spain divided Peru into three viceroyalties: New Granada, with its capital at Bogotá; Peru, with its capital at Lima; and La Plata, with its capital at Buenos Aires. Find the four Spanish viceroyalties of New Spain, New Granada, Peru, and La Plata on the map on this page.

Government in the colonies. The Council of the Indies chose nobles born in Spain, many of whom were relatives of the king, to serve as officials in the colonies. Church leaders, such as bishops and archbishops, were also from Spain. Many of these officials were corrupt and mistreated the local Indians by making them buy and sell from

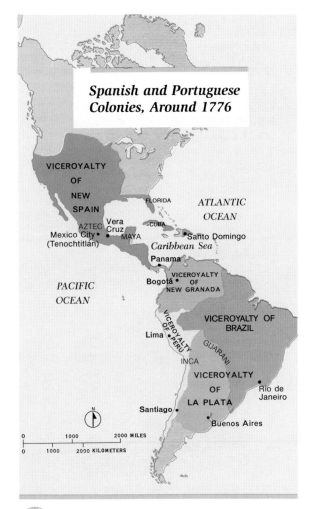

Spanish and Portuguese Colonies, Around 1776

MAP STUDY Portugal's colony, Brazil, is shown in purple. What were the names of Spain's four South American colonies?

---

the Spanish at unfair rates. The officials often returned to Spain far richer than when they had left. According to the Inca noble Huaman Poma:

> The so-called *corregidores* or royal administrators can usually count upon making [a large sum] in cash out of their term of office, and also upon retiring with an estate worth [a fortune]. It is their practice to collect Indians into groups and send

BACKGROUND Have students use dictionaries to determine the derivation of the word *viceroy*—*vice,* meaning "instead of" or "deputy"—and *roy* from the French *roi,* meaning "king." Thus, viceroy is literally "deputy king."

ANSWER TO MAP STUDY the viceroyalties of New Spain, New Grenada, Peru, and La Plata them to forced labour without wages, while they themselves receive the payment for the work. During their term of office the royal administrators make all sorts of contracts and deals, embezzle public funds . . . and raise loans from church funds. The Indian chiefs do not protest because they are accomplices. . . .

The royal administrators and the other Spaniards lord it over the Indians with absolute power. They can commit crimes with impunity [without punishment] because of the support which they can count on from higher authority.

Of course, administrators exist who commit no crimes and make no enemies, but even these virtuous ones invariably leave office with a well-filled purse.

Social differences grew in the Spanish colonies.

Spanish-born officials looked down on everyone else, even on very rich settlers who had been born in the New World. The permanent settlers hated

This 18th-century painting shows the wedding of an Inca noblewoman and a Spaniard. The Inca bride and the Spanish groom each wear their native garments.

this attitude of the **peninsulares** [pā nēn'sü-lä'rās], as they called the officials born in Spain. The American-born Spaniards were angry at being denied important jobs in government and could not understand why they were considered to be on a lower social plane when their backgrounds were almost the same as the peninsulares.

Another influence that shaped society in the Spanish colonies was religion. Spain permitted only Spanish Catholics to settle in the colonies. This was quite different from the policy followed in the English colonies of North America. There, people of almost any religion and nationality were allowed to settle.

Children whose parents were Spanish but who were born in the colonies were called **creoles** [krē'ōlz]. They had a lower social rank than their parents, even if their families were very rich. As time passed, the creole class included some people with Indian backgrounds as well, but the creole group was composed mainly of descendants of the conquistadors.

In the early years after the conquest, very few Spanish women came to Mexico or Peru. As a result, many Spanish soldiers married Indian women. The children born of these marriages were called **mestizos** [mə stē'zōs]. They had an even lower social standing than the creoles, and were not accepted by either the "higher," primarily Spanish-descended population or the "lower," mostly Indian population. The mestizos worked either as farmers on rented land or as shopkeepers, craftspeople, or soldiers. However, the mestizos were soon the largest group in colonial Latin America.

Section 2 Review

Identify viceroy, peninsulares, creoles, mestizos
Main Ideas
1. What structure did Spain establish for running its colonies?
2. Describe the social classes that developed in Spanish Latin America.

Critical Thinking
Making Hypotheses: Why do you think that Spain and England had different religious requirements for settlers in their colonies?

OPTIONAL RETEACHING
Ask volunteers to draw North and South America on the chalkboard and then shade in the three Spanish viceroyalties.

OPTIONAL ENRICHMENT
Encourage interested students to re-read the letter by the Inca noble Huaman Poma. Ask students to write a critique in which they consider such factors as the source from which the quote was taken, Poma's historical credibility, changes caused by translation and retranslation, and verifiability. (challenging)

INDEPENDENT PRACTICE/ HOMEWORK
Assign the Section Review, Activities page 146, or Workbook page 98.

CLOSURE
Say that on the surface Latin American government seemed simple. However, the interrelationship of many groups made Spanish Latin America a complex colonial society.

Answers to Section 2 Review

Identify
Key Terms, People, and Places are defined on pages indicated in parentheses. Also see the Glossary and Biographical Dictionary.
viceroy (458), peninsulares (459), creoles (459), mestizos (459)

Main Ideas
1. a Council of the Indies and appointed viceroys, or governors
2. peninsulares, creoles, mestizos, Indians

Critical Thinking
Possible answer: They wanted their colonies to follow their own religious practices.

Essential Learning Objective

Students will learn to describe Indian and African servitude in both the Spanish and Portuguese Latin American colonies.

1 FOCUS AND MOTIVATE

Ask students to estimate how many slaves were shipped from Africa to Spanish or Portuguese Latin America in the 1600s to work in the colonies. (11 million)

2 TEACH

- Discuss the system of forced labor known as the encomienda and underline the efforts of Las Casas to defend the Indians. Mention that Las Casas lived to 92, wrote widely on behalf of the Indian people whom he loved, and remains a hero to many in Latin America today.

- Discuss the slavery system in the West Indies, the working conditions of slaves, and loss of life on slave ships.

GUIDED PRACTICE

Ask the students to review the African slave trade by writing facts that are keys to understanding black servitude in the Spanish and Portuguese colonies. (The idea that should emerge is that while both Spanish and Portuguese slave practices were severe, slaves in Brazil had more rights than slaves had in the Caribbean or in English colonies to the north.)

3 Indians and Africans were the main source of labor.

The most important source of wealth in the Spanish colonies was the land itself, not the gold and other riches sought after by the early explorers. After the Aztecs and Incas were defeated, the conquistadors took away their land and divided it up among the Spanish soldiers. The children of these soldiers soon became the landed aristocracy. The Catholic Church also came to own very large amounts of land. Making the land produce crops took a great deal of manual work. As a result, finding a labor force became the biggest problem facing the Spanish colonists.

Indians were forced to work for the Spanish settlers.

At first, the Spanish colonists had the Indians cultivate the fields for them. The Indians also had to work in the rich silver mines of Mexico and what is now Bolivia. In the structure set up by the Spanish, entire villages of Indians were assigned to specific landowners. The Indians not only had to work in the landowners' fields, but also had to pay tribute to them. For their part, the landowners were supposed to protect the Indians and convert them to Catholicism. In practice, the landowners often treated the Indians like slaves.

This system of forced Indian labor was called the **encomienda** [en′kō mē en′də]. It was very much like the serfdom established in the early Middle Ages that you read about in Chapter 11. The Spanish government tried to reform the encomienda in the 1540s, but the viceroys and creole landowners at first resisted these reforms. As a result, Indians died by the hundreds of thousands on the plantations and in the silver mines.

Not only did the Indians receive very cruel treatment, they also suffered terribly from European diseases such as smallpox and measles. The effect of disease led to perhaps the greatest population disaster in recorded history. Before the Europeans came, about 15 to 25 million Indians are believed to have lived in Latin America. Within a single century, the population had plummeted to only about 4 million.

Slaves on Caribbean islands often worked under harsh conditions. This scene shows a sugar refinery on a plantation on Hispaniola.

The Church tried to protect the Indians and convert them to Christianity.

After Mexico and Peru had been conquered, many **missionaries** came to the New World to convert Indians to the Catholic religion. Missionaries are people who want to advance religious ideas and often wish to convert, or change, others to their faith. Catholic missionaries also set up schools, founded hospitals, and explored frontier areas. Some missionaries tried to protect the Indians against the creole landowners, but they did not have much success.

The most famous defender of the Indians was **Bartolomé de las Casas,** a Spanish priest who spoke out against the cruel treatment of the Indians. Las Casas said that the Indians were equal beings and deserved to be treated as humanely as the Spaniards. Because of his efforts, Charles V chose Las Casas to be "Protector of the Indians."

Charles V also supported other missionaries who tried to help the Indians. The efforts of the Church helped stop the creoles from working so many Indians to death. Although the encomienda system gradually disappeared from the Spanish lands, forced labor continued to be used for mining activities and estate work.

The most successful missionaries were members of a Catholic order named the Society of Jesus, or Jesuits. The Jesuits set up mission villages among the Guarani [gwä′rä nē′] Indians in what is now Paraguay. They taught the Guarani how to raise livestock and to grow grapes, oranges, olives, sugar cane, and corn. In addition, the Jesuits learned the Guarani language and taught the Indians how to write it. The Indians learned how to work printing presses and to print books in their own language. As a result, Guarani is still widely used in Paraguay.

However, Portuguese slave raiders from Brazil kept attacking the Jesuit missions. They kidnaped some 60,000 Guarani and sold them into slavery. Meanwhile, the Spanish government became suspicious of the Jesuit mission system as a state within a state. As a result, the Spanish government ended its support of the Jesuits, and in 1767, it ordered the Jesuits to leave Spanish America. The mission villages in Paraguay fell apart, and the landowners again used the Guarani for forced labor.

Although the Jesuits were forced out of Peru, other Catholic missionary groups remained. In addition, the Catholic Church and its priests worked among the Indians as well as serving the colonists. Through the missionaries, large numbers of Indians were baptized into the Catholic faith. Most, however, did not completely give up their old religions. They often blended their own rituals with Catholic customs and festivals. Sometimes, the Indians simply gave Christian names to Indian gods and built churches where the old temples had once stood.

In this way, Catholicism among the Indians of Spanish America developed an unusual form. Today in Peru, Ecuador, and Guatemala, Indians in Catholic churches use their own languages to say prayers that were used in the past for ancient gods.

African slaves were brought to Spanish America.

Large plantation owners in the West Indies and Brazil needed thousands of field hands to do difficult and unpleasant work. The great loss of the Indian population from European diseases and overwork led the Spanish government to import a new labor force in the form of slaves from Africa. More than 11 million people were shipped across the Atlantic Ocean to Spanish colonies. About 2 million of these captive people died on the way because of terrible conditions on the slave ships.

Most slaves worked on the sugar plantations of the Caribbean islands. By the mid-1600s, sugar cane had become the major crop of the islands. Slaves also worked on mainland plantations and on those where cacao, rice, cotton, and tobacco were grown. African slaves did the heavy labor in mines, too, and worked on the docks in the port cities. Some were used as personal servants.

Slavery on the Caribbean sugar plantations was brutal. Owners were interested only in profits and did not care how slaves were treated. The plantation owners often worked slaves to death and then bought new ones. This process was cheaper than treating the slaves better so they would live longer. Men and women, young and old, worked 18 hours a day during the sugar harvest. The work done by women was so heavy that very few of their babies were born alive. The babies who did live seldom survived to adulthood.

African slaves also worked on the sugar plantations along the Brazilian coast. Like the Spanish, the Portuguese government had encouraged the slave trade from Africa to make up for a shortage of forced Indian labor.

Although the African slaves in Brazil suffered from harsh working conditions, the Portuguese looked upon Africans as people with souls. Unlike the slaveholders on the Caribbean islands, the Portuguese in Brazil converted the slaves to Christianity. Brazilian slaves attended church and took part in religious ceremonies.

Some Brazilian slaves became skilled workers and craftspeople. A few were able to buy their freedom or were freed when their masters died. Children of Portuguese masters and African mothers were often given their freedom at birth or when they grew up. Some slaves were taught to read and write, and a few were sent to study at universities in Portugal. In contrast to the slaves on Caribbean islands, the slaves in Brazil also had a legal right to earn money and to inherit land.

Many slave rebellions broke out, although most were brutally put down. However, some slaves managed to escape to freedom. Runaway slaves in Cuba fled to the hills inland, where they lived for many generations.

ASSESS

1. What was the encomienda labor system? (a forced labor system based on serfdom)
2. How many slaves were shipped across the Atlantic? (11 million)

OPTIONAL RETEACHING

Ask students what these numbers mean in a discussion of Indians and slaves of the 16th and 17th centuries in Latin America: 15 to 25 million, 4 million, 11 million.

OPTIONAL ENRICHMENT

1. Have interested students research the life of Bartolomé de las Casas and give an oral report. (average)
2. Assign students to compare the encomienda system with the labor system used in feudal Europe and

---

Answers to Section 3 Review

Identify

Key Terms, People, and Places are defined on pages indicated in parentheses. Also see the Glossary and Biographical Dictionary. encomienda (460), missionaries (460), Bartolomé de las Casas (460), Haiti (462), Pierre Dominique Toussaint L'Ouverture (462)

Main Ideas

1. system of forced labor in which entire villages of Indians had to work on plantations and in mines
2. Missionaries converted Indians to their faith and spoke out against their mistreatment. Jesuits taught agriculture to the Guaranis and helped them preserve their language.
3. The death of millions of Indians from disease and overwork led to an immense labor shortage. The slaves were treated more harshly in the Caribbean.

Critical Thinking

Most Europeans considered Indians and Africans as labor to be exploited and as people without human rights.

Pierre Dominique Toussaint L'Ouverture led a major slave revolt in a struggle that led to Haitian independence in 1804.

On the French-owned island of **Haiti**, slave conditions were particularly bad. In 1791 Haitian slaves rose up in the largest and most successful slave revolt in the Americas. In 1804 Haiti became the first independent black nation in the Western Hemisphere.

Pierre Dominique Toussaint L'Ouverture [tü-saN′ lü ver tyr′], a great black leader, led the revolt and established a government in Haiti. He freed the slaves on the island and promoted good relations between blacks and whites. However, he defied the orders of the French dictator, Napoleon, and in 1802 he was captured and sent to prison in France. Toussaint died there in 1803, but he gave the world a symbol of black independence in the Americas.

Section 3 Review

Identify encomienda, missionaries, Bartolomé de las Casas, Haiti, Pierre Dominique Toussaint L'Ouverture

Main Ideas

1. What was the encomienda system?
2. What was the role of the Catholic Church in the development of Latin America?
3. Why were millions of people brought from Africa to work as slaves in Latin America? How did slavery on the Caribbean islands differ from that in Brazil?

Critical Thinking

Identifying Assumptions: What does the treatment of Indians and Africans tell you about the attitudes of Europeans toward these groups?

4 A Latin American civilization arose.

Spain and Portugal held on to their empires in the Americas for more than 300 years. During that period of colonial rule, three cultures—Indian, African, and Iberian—blended together. The mixture gave rise to a new civilization, **Latin America**. Latin America refers to the countries in the New World once ruled by Spain and Portugal, countries whose languages derive from Latin.

People intermarried in Latin America.

In spite of slavery and racial prejudice, whites, blacks, and Indians could mix and intermarry in the Spanish and Portuguese colonies. Today more than 50 million Latin Americans are descended from African slaves. In Mexico much of the population is a mixture of Spanish and Indian.

The greatest amount of mixing took place in Brazil. On Brazilian plantations slaveholders and slaves were still clearly divided, but black and white children played and received religious training together. Slaveholders and slaves took part together in religious services, and some slaves received an education. In Brazil color lines became less sharp than anywhere else in the Americas.

Indian and African influences were strong.

Both Indians and Africans made major contributions to music, painting, literature, politics, and cooking. In Latin America the Catholic faith was also greatly influenced by Indian and African religious ideas and customs.

For example, sculptures and wall paintings in Latin American churches were often done by native artists who showed Jesus with Indian features. Many churches and missions in the southwest United Stated blended Indian and European styles. Latin American music also became an interesting mix of styles from three continents. It combined Indian drums and pipes, African rhythms and dances, and Spanish and Portuguese folk songs and religious chants. Much Latin American music relied on various instruments—the marimba (similar to a xylophone) and maracas (gourd rattles)—that gave it a characteristic sound.

The dominant influence in Latin America was European.

Since Spain and Portugal were the conquerors, they forced their cultures upon everyone else. Spanish and Portuguese replaced hundreds of Indian languages, and Catholicism replaced many Indian beliefs. With only two major languages and one dominant religion from Mexico to Argentina, Latin America gained much cultural unity.

As you recall from Chapter 20, Europeans acquired many new foods and farming methods from the Indians, including corn and potatoes, which became major crops. European settlers also brought many different vegetables and animals to the Americas, and they introduced the plow, the potter's wheel, and the use of metals for tools. Just as important, the European settlers brought with them their legal systems, their form of government, and their ideas of private property.

Spanish aristocrats in the Americas lived mainly in the many newly founded towns and cities. Most cities were copied after cities in Spain, with a central plaza in front of a large Catholic church and streets in squares around the central plaza.

In 1620, when the Pilgrims were just landing at Plymouth Rock, there were already 4,000 stone houses in Lima, Peru. Spanish nobles lived in these mansions, which had balconies that looked out over the streets. Rich Peruvians (creoles) dressed in the latest European fashions and rode around Lima in fancy open carriages. The city obtained fresh water through an aqueduct that carried melted snow down from the mountains. Although the poor people still had a hard life, a visiting European scholar wrote that their lives were no worse than those of millions of poor peasants or city dwellers in Europe.

The Church controlled all levels of education in the colonies, just as it did in Spain and Portugal. Priests ran a few primary schools, but there were no high schools. Only about 10 percent of the people could read and write.

In the 1550s, however, two universities were started. One was at Mexico City and the other at Lima, Peru. Today these are the oldest universities in the New World. By the end of the 18th century, there were 25 colleges and universities in Spanish America.

The social status of women was low.

Universities and colleges were attended primarily by young men. For the most part, the Spaniards and Portuguese felt that women did not need higher education. From the time of the conquistadors, women were not considered equal to men. Here is a description of the treatment of the Span-

The mission church of San Francisco de Asis, built around 1710 near Taos, New Mexico, in the present-day United States, blends Indian and European styles.

463

Essential Learning Objective

Students will learn to describe colonial Latin American attitudes regarding intermarriage, language, status of women, literacy, and private property.

1 FOCUS AND MOTIVATE

Introduce the lesson by explaining that Africans, Indians, and Iberians intermixed and intermarried at a much higher rate than the English in North America did. As a result, most of Latin America is less color-conscious than its northern neighbors.

2 TEACH

- Discuss how different cultures mixed in Latin America. Point to examples in music, literature, and cooking.

- Describe how Catholicism replaced many Indian beliefs and Spanish and Portuguese replaced hundreds of Indian languages.

- Point out that though the social status of women was low, there were exceptions to this generalization.

GUIDED PRACTICE

Explain to students that historians often have to piece together a story from fragmentary evidence. Working individually or in pairs, ask students to reread the subsection, "The dominant influence in Latin America was European." From that data alone, have students hypothesize about the following questions: What kind of trade contact did the people of Lima have with Europe? How did they solve their water problems? Were there class divisions in Lima?

From the Archives

Self-Portrait

Sor Juana Inés de la Cruz (1651(?)–1695), a Mexican nun, is generally regarded as the finest Latin American writer of the 17th century. In the following excerpt from a sonnet, she criticizes her portrait with candor and humility.

What you see here is a colorful illusion,
an art bragging of its beauty and skill. . . .
[Here] where the flatteries of paint engage
to vitiate [destroy] the horrors of the
  years,
where a softening of harsh time appears
to triumph over oblivion and age
all is a vain, careful device of dress,
it is a slender flower in the gale,
it is a futile port for doom reserved,
it is futile labor that can only fail:
it is a wasting zeal and, well observed,
is corpse, is dust, is shade, is nothingness.

Sor Juana Inés de la Cruz was a noted Mexican poet.

ish women who worked side-by-side with the men who conquered the New World:

[The women] carried the firewood and the wounded on their backs. . . . They fired the crossbows and guns while the men lay down seeking a bit of shade in which to die. When the survivors of hunger and arrows reached the brigantines [ships], it was the women who hoisted the sails and set the course upriver, rowing and rowing without complaint. . . .

FROM THE ARCHIVES Translated in Gerald Flynn, *Sor Juana Inés De La Cruz* (New York: Twayne, 1971), pp. 93–94. This passage should be paraphrased before asking students to describe its attitude toward the passage of time. (Instead of

After twenty years Governor Irala has distributed Indians and lands in Asunción. Bartolomé García . . . mumbles his protests. Irala has given him only sixteen Indians, he who still carries an arrowhead in his arm. . . .

"What about me? If you're beefing, what shall *I* say?" cries Doña Isabel de Guevara.

She also had been there from the outset. She came from Spain to found Buenos Aires together with Mendoza and went with Irala up to Asunción. For being a woman, the governor has given her no Indians at all.

As in Europe, the Spanish and Portuguese in Latin America believed that a woman's main role was to have children. Poor women and slaves also had to do heavy work. Women whose husbands were landholders carried out the family's religious duties. A plantation owner respected his wife, but she was supposed to remain in the background. This attitude, which gave women an important role in the home but a much lesser one in public life, became part of Latin American culture.

Occasionally, a woman briefly managed to break through the rigid pattern in Latin America. One exception was **Sor Juana Inés de la Cruz** (1651–1695), a Mexican nun who became the greatest lyric poet of the colonial period. You can read an excerpt from one of her poems in the From the Archives box at left.

Section 4 Review

Identify Latin America, Juana Inés de la Cruz
Main Ideas
1. Briefly describe the features of Brazilian slavery that made it somewhat more humane than other slavery in Latin America.
2. How did Indian and African cultures influence Latin America?
3. Explain how European influences dominated Latin American culture and education.
4. What was the social status of women in Latin America?

Critical Thinking

Making Hypotheses: Using the information in this chapter, make a hypothesis that explains why there is still a large division in Latin America today between rich and poor and between people of European, Indian, and African ancestry.

The Blending of Cultures in Latin American Art

When the Europeans arrived in the New World, they found Indian artisans skilled at working with local materials and adept at intricate design. Eager to build churches and public buildings and to make their stamp on the land, the Europeans introduced the Indians to Europe's newest styles of art and taught them techniques for reproducing these styles.

As the Indians learned European techniques, the native art styles rapidly vanished. As one historian surmised, "[The Indian artisan] had to lay aside or forget his original source of inspiration, to hold his tongue, to conceal, to sharpen his talent for shrewdness. In time, he might conceivably smuggle in something that would recall his native land, its gods, and its myths."

The success of these Indian artisans in subtly preserving their native art styles can be seen in the details of 17th-century churches throughout Latin America. Many of the churches are richly adorned with gold leaf and intricate carvings. This fancy style of art and architecture, called Baroque [bə rōk′], was imported from Europe by the Spanish.

The main altar of the church of Santa María Tonantzintla [tō nan-tsint′la] in Puebla, Mexico, is an example of this imported Baroque style. Notice, however, the simple expressions of the cherubs in the plaster carvings. These carvings more closely reflect the native style of the Indians who made them. Indian symbols, such as corn and other fruits of the harvest, appear throughout the church. Such blending of Spanish, Indian, and African styles has led to unique, vital forms of art in Latin America.

Dazzling gold and brilliant color embellish the richly carved interior of Santa María Tonantzintla (left). Above is an Inca-style wooden beaker. Note the Indian official, Spanish trumpeter, and African drummer.

and the color lines were less sharp.
2. Cultures blended to create unique Latin American sculpture, music, painting, literature, politics, and cooking.
3. European languages, religion, farming techniques, legal and economic systems, and architecture dominated. Education was controlled by the Church; ten percent of the people could read and write; the oldest universities in the New World were founded in Mexico City and Lima, Peru.
4. Very low—women were expected to remain in the background.

Critical Thinking

Answers could include the idea that from the beginning of European conquest, the landowners were Europeans and the workers Indian or African. Thus, riches were divided according to race.

HIGHLIGHTS OF CIVILIZATION
Ask students why they think Indian artisans would have had to repress their original style when working on churches for the Spanish colonists. (Students should remember that the Indians came from a non-Christian culture; the Spanish might have been offended by non-Christian symbols in Indian art and they would have repressed such symbols in their new churches.)

Answers to Test Yourself

Key Terms, People, and Places
The key terms, people, and places tested here were introduced in the chapter sections and reviewed in the Section Reviews. For definitions see the page references at the appropriate Section Reviews. Also see the Glossary and Biographical Dictionary.

Main Ideas
The main ideas tested here were introduced in the sections of this chapter and reviewed in the Section Reviews. For answers to these questions, see the appropriate Section Reviews.

Critical Thinking
1. Most writers from this period were Catholic, male, and European or European-influenced.
2. Insurrections probably would have failed, but governments might have improved living conditions.

CHAPTER 25 REVIEW

Section Summaries

Section 1
Europeans conquered and colonized the Americas.
The formation of present-day Latin America began with the arrival of Spanish conquistadors in the early 1500s. Within a very short time, Spain took over most of the territory from Mexico to Argentina. The major exception was Brazil, which was claimed by Portugal.

Section 2
Spain controlled a large empire.
During the 16th century, Spain governed a huge territory in Central and South America and divided it into two regions, New Spain and Peru. Laws were created by a Council of the Indies and administered by viceroys, or governors. Social groups were divided by degree of Spanish heritage.

Section 3
Indians and Africans were the main source of labor.
The Spanish and Portuguese conquered native Indian peoples and forced them to work on plantations and in the mines. Because of disease and forced labor, the Indian population dropped from 15 or 25 million to about 4 million in a single century. About 11 million Africans were then forced to work in Latin America as slaves. African slaves lived mainly on the Caribbean islands and in Brazil.

Section 4
A Latin American civilization arose.
Latin American sculpture, painting, and music developed as a unique blend of cultures. However, European culture dominated in the areas of government and law, religion, language, and architecture. New foods, metal tools, and new methods of farming were also introduced into Latin America. Schools and universities were established in the regions. The status of women, however, remained low.

Test Yourself

Key Terms, People, and Places
Identify the significance of each of the following:

Section 1
a. Hernando Cortés
b. conquistadors
c. Malinche
d. Montezuma

e. Mexico City
f. Francisco Pizarro
g. Atahualpa

Section 2
a. viceroy
b. peninsulares

c. creoles
d. mestizos

Section 3
a. encomienda
b. missionaries
c. Bartolomé de las Casas

d. Haiti
e. Pierre Dominique
   Toussaint L'Ouverture

Review Dates

1493
Columbus brings first Spanish settlers to the New World

1519
Cortés begins conquest of Mexico

1530
Portugal begins settlement of Brazil

1531
Pizarro begins conquest of Peru

1791
Haitian slaves begin revolt against French rule

| 1400 | 1500 | 1600 | 1700 | 1800 | 1900 |

Section 4
a. Latin America   **b.** Juana Inés de la Cruz

Main Ideas

Section 1
1. How did Montezuma first react to the Spaniards?
2. How did Pizarro treat the Inca ruler of Peru?
3. The Spanish conquered Mexico, Peru, and a number of other regions and countries. Name these areas.
4. Portuguese colonial rule was established in what large Latin American region?

Section 2
1. Describe the way Spain governed its colonies.
2. What groups formed the social pyramid in Latin America?

Section 3
1. What was the system of forced labor in the Spanish colonies? How did the system operate?
2. How did Catholic missionaries and priests affect the native Indians in Latin America?
3. Why did African slavery take hold in Latin America? How did slavery in the Caribbean islands differ from that in Brazil?

Section 4
1. Describe the status of blacks in Brazil.
2. How does Latin American culture show the influence of Indian and African cultures?
3. What impact did European influences have in Latin America?
4. Describe the social status of women in colonial Latin America.

Critical Thinking
1. **Evaluating Sources of Information** As you read the quotation on page 455–456, were you able to spot any biases in Huaman Poma's opinions? What are they? In what ways would you expect writers about Latin America from the 16th through the 18th centuries to be biased?
2. **Making Hypotheses** The labor force in Latin America was made up mainly of Indians and, in some areas, African slaves. What might have happened if these two oppressed groups had joined and fought against their masters?

Chapter Skills and Activities

Practicing Study and Research Skills
Applying Economics to History
As you learned in Chapter 8, economics deals with the material welfare of people and the problems of money, labor, wages, prices, and taxes. Throughout history, the ownership and distribution of wealth have been major reasons why countries went to war and explored new lands. Based on your reading, answer these questions:
1. Why did the Spanish and Portuguese need to find new sources of cheap labor?
2. Why were African slaves imported to the Latin American colonies?
3. How did the need for labor affect the social class system and the culture of Latin America?

Linking Past and Present
Study the photograph above. It shows the blending of Indian and Spanish architectural features. Find examples of the mixing of two cultures in your neighborhood. How does mixing cultures enrich a civilization?

Learning History Through Maps
The map on page 458 shows Spanish and Portuguese colonies in the New World in the 18th century. Spain's colonies are shown in green and yellow; Portugal's are shown in purple. Refer to the map to answer these questions:
1. How many colonies did Spain have? How many did Portugal have?
2. The Guarani inhabited the border area between Brazil and which viceroyalty?
3. The major centers of Maya and Aztec civilization became part of which viceroyalty?

CRITICAL THINKING QUESTION LEVEL 1. challenging; 2. easy

Key Terms and People
1. d
2. c
3. a
4. f
5. b
6. e

Key Dates
B, G, A, E, F, C, D

Key Places
C—Istanbul; D—Isfahan; B—Kanem-Bornu; E—Macao; A—Haiti

Main Ideas
1. c
2. a
3. a
4. a
5. d

Critical Thinking
1. Students' answers should discuss the many centuries of opposition between the two religions and the hostility that has resulted. In Chapter 36 it will be pointed out that in 1947, when India became independent, Pakistan was created in the Muslim regions.
2. Answers should include a discussion of the ability of the leaders to govern, the allowance for new ideas, and the potential for peace within the empires.

UNIT SIX

REVIEW

Summarizing the Unit

Chapter 23
Muslim Empires in Turkey, Persia, India, and Africa
From 1450 to 1800, the Islamic world experienced a powerful revival. Many Muslim leaders set out to conquer new territories for their religion and to revitalize and reform older Islamic governments.

Chapter 24
China and Japan in Seclusion
Between 1400 and 1800, both China and Japan experienced periods of prosperity and peace. They became self-centered civilizations, largely secluded from the outside world.

Chapter 25
The Formation of Latin America
The coming of Europeans to the Americas in the 1500s changed the course of history. Riches and new crops from the Americas flowed into Europe, and at the same time, settlers from Europe came to the New World to find new permanent homes. The culture of the Europeans blended with that of the Indians and with that of the Africans, who were brought over to work as slaves.

Using Writing Skills

After prewriting and writing, on which you've worked in the last five unit reviews, the third step in the writing process is revising. This step involves many activities:

(1) Read and confer. First reread your rough draft and correct any obvious errors. Then, have a conference with one or more other students who read your writing and suggest ways to improve it.

(2) Make changes. Consider your classmates' suggestions and decide whether they are useful for your purposes. Then, make the necessary changes.

(3) Proofreading. Check for spelling, grammar, and content errors. Some common methods are reading aloud, following a checklist of questions, and checking a dictionary.

(4) Make a final copy. Make sure that all of your changes are made properly, and that your writing is as clear and interesting as possible.

Activity. Consider the following questions: What are the most important facts about China under the Mings and Manchus that you should know? Why should you know them? Jot down several ideas that might be useful if these questions were asked on a test. Next, share your ideas in a group of three or four students, narrowing the ideas to the one your group considers best. Then, write two or three paragraphs about it for a person who is not familiar with this period of Chinese history. Finally, follow the procedures listed to produce a final draft.

Test Yourself

Key Terms and People
Match each term or person with the correct definition.
1. Ottoman leader known for justice
2. non-Muslims who were converted to Islam and trained for the Ottoman army or bureaucracy
3. groups in the Ottoman Empire divided according to their religion
4. Manchu emperor with the longest reign in Chinese history
5. Spanish governor who ruled in the king's name
6. American-born people of Spanish descent
a. millets
b. viceroy
c. Children's Levy
d. Suleiman the Magnificent
e. creoles
f. Kangxi

Key Dates

Match the letters on the time line with the events for which they stand:

A   B C D   E   FG

____ The Safavids conquer Persia.
____ The Taj Mahal is built.
____ The Ming dynasty begins in China.
____ The Tokugawa Shogunate unifies Japan.
____ The Manchu dynasty begins in China.
____ Cortés starts his conquest of Mexico.
____ Pizarro begins his conquest of Peru.

Key Places

Match the letters on the map with the places described below:

____ city conquered and renamed by the Ottomans
____ capital built by Shah Abbas
____ Muslim military state in central Sudan
____ Portuguese trading port in China
____ first independent black nation in the Western Hemisphere

Main Ideas

1. The Ottoman Empire was successful in governing mainly because ____
a. it had the strongest army.
b. it defeated all neighboring rivals.
c. it devised a system for ruling diverse peoples.
d. it converted its citizens to Islam.
2. Mughal rule in India declined when ____
a. tolerance of Hindus ended.
b. the Black Death spread throughout India.
c. famine spread throughout the land.
d. the rulers spent too much money on luxury.
3. Initially, the Ming dynasty ____
a. established contact with Western countries.
b. stopped all contact with the West.
c. frequently was at war defending its borders.
d. discouraged the development of agriculture.
4. The daimyo changed the old feudal system in Japan in the mid-1800s mainly because ____
a. the Japanese feared invasion by Europeans.
b. there was a severe food shortage.
c. there was discontent among the business classes.
d. there was resentment toward isolationism.
5. Spain's empire in America was different from most earlier empires in history because ____
a. the land the Spanish governed was compact.
b. the Spanish permitted no contact between their citizens and the local peoples.
c. the Spanish used local people to govern.
d. the Spanish governed a land far away from home.

Critical Thinking

1. Analyzing Comparisons Why have the Muslims and the Hindus been unable to live together peacefully in India? How might this problem be solved? Consider other areas in which religious differences have not disrupted peaceful life.
2. Making Hypotheses How might the tolerance of other beliefs by ruling religious groups affect the development of empires? Support your answer with evidence from this and other units.

CRITICAL THINKING QUESTION LEVEL 1. average; 2. challenging

The Sweep of Revolutions in the West

ADDITIONAL TEACHING AIDS FOR UNIT SEVEN

OVERVIEW

This unit describes political and industrial revolutions in Western cultures that took place from 1500 to 1900.

Literature for the Teacher

Briggs, Asa. *A Social History of England*. New York: Viking Press, 1983.

Hibbert, Christopher. *The Days of the French Revolution*. Morrow, 1980.

Kenyon, J. P. *The Civil Wars of England*. New York: Alfred A. Knopf, 1988.

Lerner, Ralph. *The Thinking Revolutionary Principle and Practice in the New Republic*. Ithaca: Cornell University Press, 1987.

Smith, Page. *The Rise of Industrial America* (Volume 6). New York: McGraw-Hill, 1984.

Sulzberger, G. L. *The Fall of Eagles*. New York: Crown Publishing, 1977.

Wolff, Christopher. *Civilization in the West: Part 2—1600 to the Present* (fourth edition). Prentice Hall, 1981.

Literature for the Student

Egnal, Marc. *A Mighty Empire: Origins of the American Revolution*. Ithaca: Cornell University Press, 1988. (challenging)

Hawke, David. *Everyday Life in Early America*. New York: Harper & Row Publishing, 1988. (average)

Jackson, Donald Dale. *The Civil War: Twenty Million Yankees*. New York: Time-Life, 1985. (easy)

Knox, Diana. *The Industrial Revolution*. St. Paul: Greenhaven Press, 1980. (easy)

McDonough, James Lee, and J. Jones. *War So Terrible: Sherman and Atlanta*. New York: W. W. Norton, 1987. (average)

Mitchell, Reid. *Civil War Soldiers*. Viking Press, 1988. (average)

Symonds, Craig. *A Battlefield Atlas of the Civil War*. Nautical and Aviation Publications, 1983. (challenging)

---

*Audio-Visual Materials**

The Black West. Film, 28 minutes, color, [Beacon Films], 1981. Provides insights into the black experience on the American frontier

Bloody Schemes. Film, 17 minutes, color, [International Film Corporation], 1972. Presents slavery as one of the main forces of change in the history of three continents

The Civil War: A House Divided. Video or film, 25 minutes, color, [McGraw-Hill], 1968. Drawings, maps, paintings, and photographs outlining significant political, economic, and social factors and military operations of the Civil War

* For a complete listing of sources of audio-visual materials see page T30.

The Filibusters' War. Video, 28 minutes, color, [University of Illinois Film Center], 1982. Recreates the attempts to take over Nicaragua between 1855 and 1860 by mercenaries known as Filibusters

Grant and Lee on the Civil War. Film, 33 minutes, color, [Barr Films], 1984. Uses a game-show format in which the "host" interviews the two generals

History and Politics—German Style. Film, 20 minutes, color, [Journal]. Reviews Germany's history up to the turmoil of the 20th century, then presents the partitioning after World War II

Negro Slavery. Film, 26 minutes, color, [McGraw-Hill], 1968. Depicts the beginning and

development of slavery in the United States and describes the life of the American slave

The Triumph of the West: Age of Light. Video, 50 minutes, color, [Film, Inc.], 1987. Depicts Voltaire, Rousseau, and Jefferson as coexisting with slavery, superstition, and cruelty

The Triumph of the West: Monuments to Progress. Video, 50 minutes, color, [Films, Inc.], 1987. Shows that the Industrial Revolution sparked many significant changes

The Unification of Germany. Video, 33 minutes, color, [EB], 1986. The creation of a unified Germany in the 1860s as the single most important political development in 19th-century Europe

OPTIONAL WRITING ASSIGNMENTS

1. You are a member of England's Parliament during the reign of Charles I. You are also a supporter of Oliver Cromwell. Rumors are circulating through Parliament that you and other leaders of Parliament might be arrested by the king. Write a speech for delivery in Parliament in which you detail the reasons for your opposition to the king. You also should suggest what Parliament should do if attempts were made to arrest its leaders.

2. Write two newspaper reports of the growing unrest in England's colonies in America. Both articles should contain descriptions or information concerning specific events. However, each article should be written from different perspectives. One article should be written from the perspective of a reporter for a London newspaper and the other article from that of a Boston newspaper reporter.

3. You are a supporter of Napoleon Bonaparte. You served under him in Northern Italy and Egypt. He has told you of his ambitions and has asked for your help when he returns to France from Egypt. You are to design a one-page leaflet that will be given to people throughout France. The leaflet should glorify Napoleon's accomplishments and convince the reader that Napoleon is the leader that their country needs.

4. You are a French soldier in Napoleon's army in Russia. Write two letters to your family in Paris. The first letter should describe your thoughts, feelings, and experiences as you enter Russia in the summer of 1812. The second letter should describe your thoughts, feelings and experiences as you return from Russia during the winter.

5. You are a reporter for a London newspaper in 1850. You are going to interview a one-hundred-year-old person about changes that the person has seen during his or her long life. Prepare a list of questions to ask and then answer each as you think the person would. The answers should accurately reflect political, economic, and social changes.

UNIT TESTS
IN THE TEACHER'S RESOURCE FILE

Unit Test, pp. 153–154

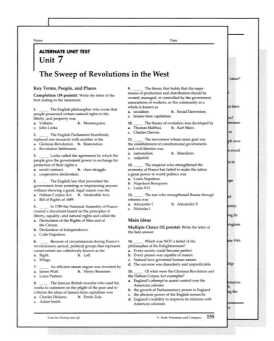

Alternate Unit Test, pp. 155–156

FINE ART IN UNIT SEVEN

Fine art forms an integral part of the historical record of events portrayed in this textbook. A listing of the paintings, drawings, sculpture, historic photographs, architecture, and other works of fine art selected to illustrate this unit follows. Students may be asked to research the artists and their works and report their findings to the entire class. Students also may be asked to write one or more paragraphs describing what they see upon a detailed study of a work of art and what the artist was attempting to communicate.

The Sweep of Revolutions in the West

All through the early modern era, western Europe had been undergoing a significant internal transformation, as you read in Unit 5. Between the mid-18th and mid-19th centuries, however, that strength was suddenly converted to overwhelming power by a series of revolutions that swept through most of the countries in the West.

The revolutions took various forms. One of these was political and resulted in dramatic upheavals, first in England and then in North America, France, and Latin America. The American and French revolutions in particular profoundly changed the role of the average person, from one of passive subject to one of participating citizen. Another form of revolution that took place was economic, and it occurred at the same time as the political revolutions. Called the Industrial Revolution, it changed human life so profoundly that historians rank it in importance with the agricultural revolution of 10,000 years ago.

The twin revolutions, political and economic, also gave rise to a set of ideals and doctrines that have continued to influence people around the world in our own times. The American and French revolutions both proclaimed the ideals of freedom, independence, and self-government and fostered the growth of nationalism. The Industrial Revolution in turn promoted the growth of capitalism and stimulated the rise of socialism as a response to the problems of an industrial society. Thus, from the perspective of world history, the sweep of revolutions that began some 200 years ago left an impact that changed the way we live today.

An 18th-century French poster proclaims the revolutionary program that changed Europe and influenced the Americas: liberty, equality, fraternity, and a united, indivisible republic.

Chapters in This Unit

Chapter

26 Democratic Revolutions in England and North America

OVERVIEW

This chapter covers the impact of the Enlightenment upon England and the United
States in the 17th and 18th centuries.

PLANNING CHART

Section	Text Pages	Key Concept	Suggested Teaching Time
1 Ideas about democracy began to develop	473–478	To Enlightenment philosophers who believed that human nature is both rational and perfectable, a belief in democracy was a logical next step.	Two days **Less time?** Give a full day to Section 1. Assign Sections 2 and 3 as homework and discuss in one class period.
2 Parliament triumphed in England.	479–483	Modern democracy had its beginnings in 17th-century England, where the power of the crown was limited by Parliament.	One day **More time:** Use *Overhead Transparency 51* or *Source Reading 26A*.
3 North American colonies fought for independence.	483–486	Modern democracy received its second boost when the 13 colonies won their independence and created a representative government.	One day **More time?** Use *Overhead Transparency 52* or *Source Reading 26B*.

ANCILLARIES

Materials that may be used with this chapter
to reinforce, reteach, enrich, and assess
learning are pictured on the following pages.

Teacher's Resource File

ACTIVITIES

Section 1 Activity, p. 151

Section 2 Activity, p. 152

Section 3 Activity, p. 153

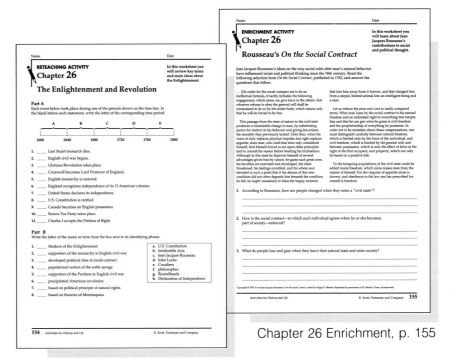

Chapter 26 Reteaching, p. 154

Chapter 26 Enrichment, p. 155

Teacher's Resource File

GEOGRAPHY SKILLS

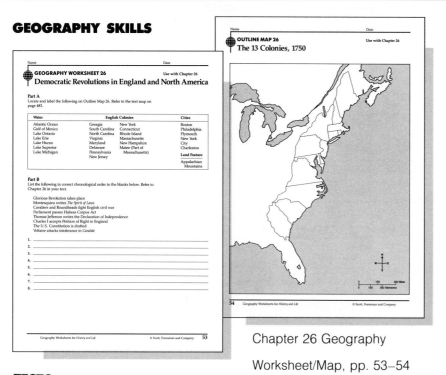

GEOGRAPHY WORKSHEET 26   Use with Chapter 26
Democratic Revolutions in England and North America

Part A
Locate and label the following on Outline Map 26. Refer to the text map on page 483.

Water	English Colonies		Cities
Atlantic Ocean	Georgia	New York	Boston
Gulf of Mexico	South Carolina	Connecticut	Philadelphia
Lake Ontario	North Carolina	Rhode Island	Plymouth
Lake Erie	Virginia	Massachusetts	New York
Lake Huron	Maryland	New Hampshire	City
Lake Superior	Delaware	Maine (Part of	Charleston
Lake Michigan	Pennsylvania	Massachusetts)	
	New Jersey		**Land Feature**
			Appalachian
			Mountains

Part B
List the following in correct chronological order in the blanks below. Refer to Chapter 26 in your text.

Glorious Revolution takes place
Montesquieu writes *The Spirit of Laws*
Cavaliers and Roundheads fight English civil war
Parliament passes Habeas Corpus Act
Thomas Jefferson writes the Declaration of Independence
Charles I accepts Petition of Right in England
The U.S. Constitution is drafted
Voltaire attacks intolerance in *Candide*

1. _____
2. _____
3. _____
4. _____
5. _____
6. _____
7. _____
8. _____

Geography Worksheets for History and Life   © Scott, Foresman and Company   53

OUTLINE MAP 26   Use with Chapter 26
The 13 Colonies, 1750

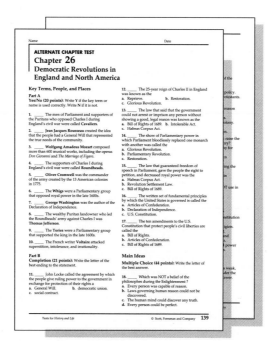

54   Geography Worksheets for History and Life   © Scott, Foresman and Company

Chapter 26 Geography

Worksheet/Map, pp. 53–54

MAP LESSON 26　Use with Chapter 26

In the Proclamation of 1763, the British government forbade American settlement in the land west of the Appalachians. The purpose of this measure was to avoid trouble with the Indians and to give the British time to develop plans for organizing the territory. The colonists, however, resisted the proclamation line. Study the map. Choose the term that best completes each sentence. Write its letter on the line.

The Proclamation Line of 1763

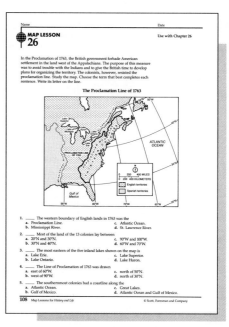

1. _____ The western boundary of English lands in 1763 was the
   a. Proclamation Line.   c. Atlantic Ocean.
   b. Mississippi River.   d. St. Lawrence River.
2. _____ Most of the land of the 13 colonies lay between
   a. 20°N and 30°N.   c. 90°W and 100°W.
   b. 30°N and 40°N.   d. 60°W and 70°W.
3. _____ The most eastern of the five inland lakes shown on the map is
   a. Lake Erie.   c. Lake Superior.
   b. Lake Ontario.   d. Lake Huron.
4. _____ The Line of Proclamation of 1763 was drawn
   a. east of 60°W.   c. north of 50°N.
   b. west of 90°W.   d. north of 30°N.
5. _____ The southernmost colonies had a coastline along the
   a. Atlantic Ocean.   c. Great Lakes.
   b. Gulf of Mexico.   d. Atlantic Ocean and Gulf of Mexico.

108   Map Lessons for History and Life   © Scott, Foresman and Company

Chapter 26 Map Lesson, p. 108

TESTS

CHAPTER TEST
Chapter 26
Democratic Revolutions in England and North America

Key Terms, People, and Places
Part A
Matching (20 points): Write the letter of the key name from the box that best fits the definition.

1. _____ the supporters of Charles I during England's civil war
2. _____ the French philosopher who created the idea that the people had a General Will
3. _____ the composer of more than 600 musical compositions, including the opera *Don Giovanni*
4. _____ the men of Parliament and supporters of the Puritans during England's civil war
5. _____ the wealthy Puritan landowner who led the Roundheads' army against Charles I
6. _____ a Parliamentary group that opposed royal power in the late 1600s
7. _____ the commander of the army created by the 13 American colonies in 1775
8. _____ the author of the Declaration of Independence
9. _____ a Parliamentary group that was loyal to the king in the late 1600s
10. _____ a French writer who attacked superstition, intolerance, and irrationality

a. George Washington	f. Roundheads
b. Thomas Jefferson	g. Cavaliers
c. Wolfgang Amadeus Mozart	h. Voltaire
d. Oliver Cromwell	i. Tories
e. Jean Jacques Rousseau	j. Whigs

Part B
Multiple Choice (21 points): Write the letter of the best answer.

11. _____ What did John Locke call the agreement by which the people give ruling power to the government in exchange for protection of their rights?
   a. social contract   b. democratic union
   c. General Will

12. _____ What was the 25-year reign of Charles II in England called?
   a. the Reprieve   b. the Restoration
   c. the Glorious Revolution
13. _____ Which English law said that the government could not arrest or imprison any person without showing a good, legal reason?
   a. the Bill of Rights of 1689
   b. the Habeas Corpus Act
   c. the Intolerable Act
14. _____ What name was given to the show of Parliamentary power in which Parliament bloodlessly replaced one monarch with another?
   a. the Restoration
   b. the Parliamentary Revolution
   c. the Glorious Revolution
15. _____ Which law guaranteed freedom of speech in Parliament, gave the people the right to petition, and decreased royal power?
   a. the Bill of Rights of 1689
   b. the Revolution Settlement Law
   c. the Habeas Corpus Act
16. _____ What is the written set of fundamental principles by which the United States is governed?
   a. the Articles of Confederation
   b. the U.S. Constitution
   c. the Declaration of Independence
17. _____ What are the ten amendments to the U.S. Constitution that guarantee people's civil liberties?
   a. the Bill of Rights
   b. the Bill of Rights of 1689
   c. the Articles of Confederation

Main Ideas

Completion (44 points): Write the letter of the best ending to the statement.

18. _____ The philosophies of the Enlightenment did NOT believe that
   a. it was impossible to discover the laws governing human nature.
   b. the human mind could discover any truth and achieve any ambition.
   c. every person was capable of reason.
   d. every person could be perfect.

Tests for History and Life   © Scott, Foresman and Company   137

Chapter Test, pp. 137–138

ALTERNATE CHAPTER TEST
Chapter 26
Democratic Revolutions in England and North America

Key Terms, People, and Places
Part A
Yes/No (20 points): Write Y if the key term or name is used correctly. Write N if it is not.

1. _____ The men of Parliament and supporters of the Puritans who opposed Charles I during England's civil war were called **Cavaliers.**
2. _____ **Jean Jacques Rousseau** created the idea that the people had a General Will that represented the true needs of the community.
3. _____ **Wolfgang Amadeus Mozart** composed more than 600 musical works, including the operas *Don Giovanni* and *The Marriage of Figaro*.
4. _____ The supporters of Charles I during England's civil war were called **Roundheads.**
5. _____ **Oliver Cromwell** was the commander of the army created by the 13 American colonies in 1775.
6. _____ The **Whigs** were a Parliamentary group that opposed royal power in the late 1600s.
7. _____ **George Washington** was the author of the Declaration of Independence.
8. _____ The wealthy Puritan landowner who led the Roundheads' army against Charles I was **Thomas Jefferson.**
9. _____ The **Tories** were a Parliamentary group that supported the king in the late 1600s.
10. _____ The French writer **Voltaire** attacked superstition, intolerance, and irrationality.

Part B
Completion (21 points): Write the letter of the best ending to the statement.

11. _____ John Locke called the agreement by which the people give ruling power to the government in exchange for protection of their rights a
   a. General Will.   b. democratic union.
   c. social contract.

12. _____ The 25-year reign of Charles II in England was known as the
   a. Reprieve.   b. Restoration.
   c. Glorious Revolution.
13. _____ The law that said that the government could not arrest or imprison any person without showing a good, legal reason was known as the
   a. Intolerable Act.   c. Habeas Corpus Act.
14. _____ The show of Parliamentary power in which Parliament bloodlessly replaced one monarch with another was called the
   a. Glorious Revolution.
   b. Parliamentary Revolution.
   c. Restoration.
15. _____ The law that guaranteed freedom of speech in Parliament, gave the people the right to petition, and decreased royal power was the
   a. Habeas Corpus Act.
   b. Revolution Settlement Law.
   c. Bill of Rights of 1689.
16. _____ The written set of fundamental principles by which the United States is governed is called the
   a. Articles of Confederation.
   b. Declaration of Independence.
   c. U.S. Constitution.
17. _____ The ten amendments to the U.S. Constitution that protect people's civil liberties are called the
   a. Bill of Rights.
   b. Articles of Confederation.
   c. Bill of Rights of 1689.

Main Ideas

Multiple Choice (44 points): Write the letter of the best answer.

18. _____ Which was NOT a belief of the philosophes during the Enlightenment?
   a. Every person was capable of reason.
   b. Laws governing human reason could not be discovered.
   c. The human mind could discover any truth.
   d. Every person could be perfect.

Tests for History and Life   © Scott, Foresman and Company   139

   Chapter Test, pp. 137–138   **Alternate Chapter Test, pp. 139–140**

Other Optional Ancillaries

WORKBOOK

Section 1 Worksheet, p. 101

Section 2 Worksheet, p. 102

Section 3 Worksheet, p. 103

SOURCE READINGS

Source Reading 26A
Source Reading 26B

TEST GENERATOR

40 multiple-choice questions for Chapter 26

OVERHEAD TRANSPARENCIES

Overhead Transparency 51
Overhead Transparency 52

Democratic Revolutions in England and North America

1600–1900

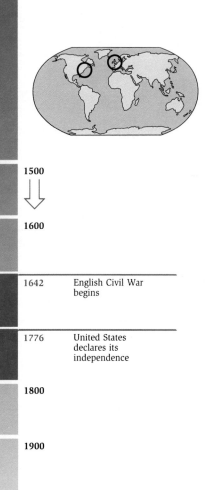

1500	
1600	
1642	English Civil War begins
1776	United States declares its independence
1800	
1900	

A modern historian has described the 1600s and early 1700s as "an age of kings." In no other period did European monarchs hold so much power, prestige, and glory, or face so little resistance from their people. For Louis XIV of France, being a king was simply "delightful."

Before the 18th century was over, however, the monarchies of Europe had grown much weaker. The powers of the king of England were greatly reduced by an increasingly assertive Parliament. The English colonies in North America declared their independence and then defeated the English army in a long and bloody revolutionary war. These events were soon followed by a violent revolution in France, during which the king was beheaded and France was declared a republic. By the early 1800s, the Spanish and Portuguese colonies in Latin America were also beginning to struggle for independence from their European rulers, and kings throughout Europe were fighting desperately to hold on to their thrones.

What then turned the age of kings into one of widespread revolutions? One reason was that Europe in the 17th and 18th centuries was experiencing a scientific revolution, as you learned in Chapter 22. At the same time, many thinkers in Europe were applying the new scientific method to questions about politics, economics, and social structures.

Near the end of his life, the American patriot John Adams, second president of the United States, summed up the period in the following way:

> We may say that the 18th century, notwithstanding all its errors and vices, has been, of all that are past, the most honorable to human nature. Knowledge and virtue were increased, and diffused; arts, sciences, useful to men, ameliorating their condition, were improved more than in any former equal period.

472

The ideas of the Enlightenment were discussed in such Parisian salons as the one above. Intelligent, fashionable women often presided over the salons.

The intellectual drive to understand and improve society, which Adams described, is called the Enlightenment, or the Age of Reason. Thinkers developed new ideas about liberty, democracy, and representative government, which helped bring about the end of the age of kings and the beginning of the age of democratic revolutions.

Reading Preview

In this chapter you will read how new democratic ideas helped bring new forms of government to England and North America.

1. Ideas about democracy began to develop.

2. Parliament triumphed in England.

3. North American colonies fought for independence.

1 | Ideas about democracy began to develop.

Scientific discoveries indicated that the physical universe was a well-ordered machine, working according to the laws of nature. Many thinkers believed that people also must be governed by natural laws. Therefore, they reasoned that the new scientific methods could be used to discover the laws pertaining to human nature and to improve society. In this vein, René Descartes declared:

> If we use the proper methods, we shall be able to outstrip our ancestors. The Golden Age is not behind us. Not only is progress possible, but there are no limits that can be assigned to it in advance.

The leading thinkers of the **Enlightenment** were known by the French *philosophes* [fē′lə zôfs].

473

- Explain that the Renaissance, the Commercial Revolution, and the Scientific Revolution developed into the Enlightenment, also known as the Age of Reason. By the 1700s western Europeans were quite convinced that they could make the world a better, more comfortable, more rational place in which to live because they had uncovered universal laws that govern all persons.

- Ask students to name the five philosophes featured in this section. (Locke, Montesquieu, Voltaire, Rousseau, and Diderot) Establish a short working definition of each political philosopher's contribution to government.

GUIDED PRACTICE

Have students list the names of the five featured philosophes, leaving several lines between each. Working individually or in pairs, tell students to write key words or phrases that are central to the thinking of each philosopher. Ask students which ideas they agree with and why.

Their ideas eventually gained much influence in their societies. The philosophes in western Europe and North America were an intellectual elite of journalists, social critics, and political scientists. Their ideas were published in books, pamphlets, and newspapers, and the message of the Enlightenment soon spread among the middle classes. Finally, most common people, even those who could not read, gained some notion of the ideas.

The philosophes had new views about human nature.

This period when many European thinkers looked at government, religion, and the arts in relation to natural law lasted more than a century. In the cities of France, England, and North America, thinkers debated political and philosophical issues with great gusto. They met in cafes and at salons— informal gatherings, often in the homes of wealthy patrons, where leading thinkers and the cream of society discussed the important ideas of the day. Women often participated in these discussions and usually ran the salons.

Despite constant debates and disagreements, the Enlightenment produced a basic set of ideas about human nature. These ideas grew out of Isaac Newton's view of the universe and nature as orderly and predictable, governed by eternal and unchanging natural laws. The philosophes believed that by observing human behavior, in history and in the present day, they could discover the laws that governed human nature and then use these laws to design a harmonious and orderly society.

In the philosophes' plan, the people would first be taught these newly found laws and trained in the use of reason. Next, educated people would meet in elected assemblies and decide, through open discussion, which laws were just, reasonable, and "natural." Through representative government and the legislative process, old institutions and practices that held back progress would be swept away, society would be rebuilt, and humanity would rise to new heights.

The philosophes believed that every person was capable of reason and that the human mind could discover any truth and achieve any ambition. Human beings, they said, were essentially good— every individual could be virtuous, and every so-

From the Archives

The Origin of Government

John Locke (1632–1704), the English philosopher and scientist, was also deeply interested in English politics. He supported the Glorious Revolution of 1688, and so in 1690 he wrote two books justifying this revolution. The first attacked the idea that kings ruled by divine right. In the Second Treatise of Government, *he explained the origin and purpose of government in the following terms.*

Men being, as has been said, by nature all free, equal, and independent, no one can be put out of this estate and subjected to the political power of another without his own consent, which is done by agreeing with other men, to join and unite into a community for their comfortable, safe, and peaceable living, one amongst another, in a secure enjoyment of their properties, and a greater security against any that are not of it. . . .

And thus every man, by consenting with others to make one body politic under one government, puts himself under an obligation to every one of that society to submit to the determination of the majority.

ciety could become perfect. Many Enlightenment thinkers also rejected traditional religion. They felt that a belief in mysteries, in miracles, or in the power of ritual or prayer could not stand up under the harsh light of reason.

Most philosophes, however, still stressed the ethics and values of Judaism and Christianity—human equality, individual dignity, and responsibility, but their view of the individual differed from that of the religious traditions. Both Jewish and Christian teachings said that people were born with imperfections, with a natural impulse to sin, so religion taught the importance of forgiving people's natural flaws. To the philosophes, however, every person could be perfect.

FROM THE ARCHIVES The quotation is from *Of Civil Government,* by John Locke (London: J. M. Dent & Sons, 1924). Discuss John Locke and his interest in politics. Ask: According to John Locke, how does a government come into being? (It is created when a group of people who are free by nature agree to establish a government to increase their peace, security and comfort.) Point out that Thomas Jefferson summarized Locke in the Declaration of Independence.

This belief in the possibility of human perfection did indeed lead to progress, but it also brought intolerance and cruelty. Modern thinking no longer left any room for the forgiveness of those people who disobeyed "reason" and "natural law." Thus, Enlightenment thinking made possible both the freest and the most oppressive of modern societies and governments.

The ideas of Locke and Montesquieu influenced government.

The person who perhaps most influenced the Enlightenment was **John Locke**, an English philosopher born in 1632. Locke believed that progress was certain if people would follow reason. He did not believe that a person was born good or evil, but instead as a "blank slate" on which virtue must be engraved through education.

In writing about government, Locke said that people possessed certain natural rights, chiefly the rights to life, liberty, and property. When the people set up a government, however, they gave it the power to protect these rights. Locke called this agreement between the people and the government a "**social contract**." If a government failed to protect their rights, Locke said, the people could set up a new government.

Locke's social-contract theory was eagerly studied in Europe and America. French and American philosophes built on his ideas, and in 1776 American revolutionaries used them to develop their Declaration of Independence and again, in 1787, in the U.S. Constitution.

Another thinker who used reason in the study of government was a French noble and judge, the Baron de **Montesquieu** [də mon′tə skyü]. In traveling abroad and reading widely about foreign peoples, he became an early critic of absolute monarchy and a defender of liberty against tyranny.

Montesquieu's most important work was *The Spirit of the Laws* (1748). This 20-year project was a study of laws and constitutions from ancient times to his own. Because of this book, Montesquieu is often called a founder of political science, which is the scientific study of government. From his studies, Montesquieu concluded that individual freedom must be protected from royal absolutism in several ways.

First, he believed, a rational society must contain many layers of social structures and governing bodies, from the individual at the bottom to the central government at the top. Montesquieu believed that local governments, guilds, courts, and social groups of many kinds all protected the citizen from the absolute power of a monarch.

Second, Montesquieu said that liberty required a separation and balance of powers in government, by which no one part of the government had more control than any other part. He thought that a good example of this principle was the political system of England, where the king and Parliament balanced each other and were in turn kept under control by an independent judiciary. Montesquieu's ideas on government had wide influence and guided the people who drew up the U.S. Constitution, in which there is a separation and balance of powers among various authorities.

Voltaire, Rousseau, and Diderot spread new ideas.

Voltaire on intolerance. François Arouet, born in Paris in 1694, later gave himself the name **Voltaire** [vol tar′]. A writer with a sharp and biting wit, Voltaire attacked what he saw as the follies of his time. For offending those in power, he was twice imprisoned in the Bastille in Paris and banished to England for three years. Like Montesquieu, Voltaire greatly admired England, and he used this opportunity to study and write about the English political system.

Voltaire wrote several books, hundreds of essays and pamphlets, and more than 50 plays. His best-known work is the satire *Candide* [kan dēd′] (1759), which makes fun of the idea that this is the "best of all possible worlds." Voltaire looked around him and saw a world full of superstition, intolerance, and irrationality.

Voltaire often bitterly attacked what he saw as the wrongs committed by the Catholic Church, but he also argued for tolerance of all religious beliefs. Because of his attacks upon the Church, Voltaire was often called an atheist, one who believes that there is no God. In actuality, he accepted a set of religious ideas known as deism.

To deists, the wonders of the natural order were proof of God's existence, just as the existence of a

BACKGROUND Among Voltaire's friends and correspondents were Catherine the Great of Russia, Frederick II of Prussia, and Lord Bolingbroke of England.

complicated clock meant that there had to have been a clock maker. Deists believed that God, the heavenly clockmaker, made the universe, set it up to work by natural laws, and then left it alone. They believed that God stayed out of people's daily lives and that praying for help was useless. Voltaire did, however, see a need for religious beliefs, since a belief in God often acted as "a brake" upon antisocial behavior. "If there were no God," he said, "it would be necessary to invent one."

Voltaire hated all forms of intolerance. He directly entered into several cases of religious persecution to gain justice. He is thought to have said: "I do not agree with a word you say, but I will defend to the death your right to say it."

Rousseau on freedom. The thinking of **Jean Jacques Rousseau** [zhäN zhäk rü sō′] was based more on emotion than on reason. He was born in 1712 in Switzerland and raised by relatives. Rousseau was apprenticed to a lawyer and then to an engraver, and then he ran away. For 20 years, he led a hand-to-mouth life as a servant, tutor, music teacher, and writer.

In 1750 Rousseau wrote an essay for a writing competition. The question asked whether the arts and sciences had helped to improve people's morals. Nearly everyone who entered the contest said that they had, but Rousseau's answer was different from the rest.

In this *Discourse on the Arts and Sciences*, he stated that people had been pure and good in the

Candide, Voltaire's most famous work, continues to be staged today. It is a satiric account of a young man's travels.

"state of nature" before they became civilized. Social organization—civilization—had spoiled them, and only by going back to nature could they become "noble savages" once again. Rousseau's entry won first prize, and he soon became a national celebrity. Rousseau's idea of honor in the simple life became very popular in France. The queen even had an artificial peasant village built, where she and her ladies played at being milkmaids.

One of Rousseau's most important books was the *Social Contract* (1762), which went beyond Locke's idea of an agreement between ruler and people. According to Rousseau, a community was based on an understanding among all the people. In Rousseau's community, all members felt that they were among people who shared common values and common attitudes. Rousseau called this feeling the "General Will." He said that it expressed the true desires of a people and held them together.

The General Will, however, was more than the decision of a majority vote. Rousseau believed that it represented the true needs of the community, regardless of what any individual or group thought. The General Will reflected what the community should do—what was really best for it—not what it wanted to do.

Rousseau never fully explained how the General Will worked or how it could be discovered for sure. Since his time, people have tried to figure this out, and Rousseau's ideas have been very influential. They have been read and repeated by many people who believed in democracy, for no one believed in the power of the people more than Rousseau did. Yet his ideas have also been used by harsh dictators, who claimed that they knew the true "General Will." Rousseau wrote that any citizen who refused to obey the General Will must be "forced to be free." Like much of philosophy, Rousseau's thinking has meant different things to different readers.

Diderot's encyclopedia. Denis Diderot [dē′də-rō′] decided to put all the new learning and ideas of his time into an encyclopedia. Science and philosophy had shown, he believed, that nature was orderly and was governed by laws, and that the same was true of society. The encyclopedia was meant to explain, clearly and precisely, the work-

Jean Jacques Rousseau's writings raised some of the most profound social and ethical questions of the Enlightenment.

ings of nature, of society, and of all the new machines and tools that people seemed to be inventing every day. Diderot wanted his books to give facts about all branches of learning and to speak for tolerance and against superstition and the unjust ways of the time.

Many important writers, such as Voltaire, Montesquieu, and Rousseau, sent articles to Diderot. He spent 30 years preparing the encyclopedia. The 35 large volumes, published between 1751 and 1772, spread the new ideas of the Enlightenment. (See sample entries, page 478.) Thousands of sets were printed in France, and editions appeared throughout Europe, even though the encyclopedia was banned in many countries for its attacks upon the Church and absolute monarchy.

Reformers wanted to improve human well-being.

The Enlightenment awakened concern for the well-being of all people. Religious liberty spread, and many improvements were made in public health and in the care of the sick and the insane.

Prisons also were reformed. They had always been dirty places governed by cruel laws. For example, in England, which had better prisons than most countries, jailers got no salaries. They depended for their living on money prisoners paid as "board," for food and housing.

Such conditions improved partly because of John Howard, a county sheriff who led a prison reform movement. His book, *The State of Prisons in England and Wales* (1777), pointed out the need for better prison administration. Prisons, Howard wrote, should not be used for punishment alone but should involve rehabilitation.

Reforms in education also occurred. The cruel discipline that had been common eased a little, and schools were opened for the lower classes. Rousseau's ideas about education became especially important. Rousseau believed that children should be allowed to progress in their own ways and learn through observation and example. Above all, children should be educated to become good citizens.

The arts were also affected by the Enlightenment.

Reason ruled not only scientists and scholars but also writers, painters, and musicians. Since "natural laws" were said to govern the universe and human society, many artists sought to find the "laws" that should be applied to their arts. Just as order and discipline were seen as the virtues of good citizens, they were also the qualities of this period's dominant artists. Many writers, painters, and architects admired the arts of ancient Greece and Rome, leading to a new style known as neoclassicism, in which classical culture was revived.

In architecture the grand baroque form seen in Louis XIV's palace at Versailles gave way to a more delicate form called rococo [rō kō′kō]. Both of these forms lost favor after 1750. The simple elegant neoclassicism that became popular in England and America can still be seen today.

The Enlightenment was noted for satire. The best-known poet of the time was Alexander Pope of England, whose elegant verses showed up the foolish ways of society. Jonathan Swift's book *Gulliver's Travels*, written in 1726, has the form of an adventure story. Children enjoy the tale, but to

3 | ASSESS AND CLOSE

ASSESS

1. What was John Locke's social contract theory? (A contract existed between the people and the government.)
2. What is separation of powers? (The branches of government are divided.)

OPTIONAL RETEACHING

Have students name the philosopher, author, or musician associated with each of the following: noble savage; The *Messiah*; "blank slate"; encyclopedia; "If there were no God, it would be necessary to invent one"; *Gulliver's Travels*; separation of powers.

OPTIONAL ENRICHMENT

1. Throughout the ages people have argued about the basic nature of humankind. Ask interested students to write a short essay in which they describe and choose between the Old Testament's doctrine of original sin, Locke's "blank slate," and Rousseau's noble savage. (average)
2. Ask interested students to research deism and write a short essay that explains deist beliefs. Have them include information about influential American deists. (challenging)

INDEPENDENT PRACTICE/ HOMEWORK

Assign the Section Review, Activities page 151, or Workbook page 101.

CLOSURE

Summarize the lesson by telling students that Enlightenment philosophers developed natural laws, or rules, which tried to clarify the relationship between the people and their government.

Answers to Section 1 Review

Identify

Key Terms, People, and Places are defined on pages indicated in parentheses. Also see the Glossary and Biographical Dictionary. Enlightenment (473), John Locke (475), social contract (475), Montesquieu (475), Voltaire (475), Jean Jacques Rousseau (476), Wolfgang Amadeus Mozart (478)

Main Ideas

1. Science said that the universe was orderly and ruled by "natural law." Philosophes applied this to human society.
2. Locke's social-contract theory became part of the American Declaration of Independence and the U.S. Constitution; Montesquieu's layers of government and separation and balance of powers guided those who drew up the U.S. Constitution.
3. Voltaire attacked superstition, intolerance, and irrationality; Rousseau was the ultimate democrat and created the idea that the people had a General Will that expressed what was best for the community; Diderot helped spread all the new ideas by compiling them in a 35-volume encyclopedia that was widely read.
4. more religious freedom; prison reform; education reform
5. Writers, painters, and musicians looked for the "laws" that should be applied to their arts. Order and discipline were the important values.

Critical Thinking

They saw the classical age as another Age of Reason, based on civic virtues of order, discipline, clarity, and rationality. Changing societies may look back in history for models of success—or failure—on which to build.

Diderot's *Encyclopedia* contained thousands of carefully rendered drawings such as this blast furnace (top) and the gardening tools (above). Each drawing was accompanied by witty and informative description.

adults it is a bitter satire on the meanness of human quarrels, wars, and vices.

Other kinds of writing benefited from the emphasis on reason, observation, common sense, and clarity. An early work in the novel form was Daniel Defoe's adventure story, *Robinson Crusoe*. Another early novel was Henry Fielding's *Tom Jones*, a fascinating picture of 18th-century England.

France had three important dramatic writers. Pierre Corneille [kôr nā'] and Jean Racine [zhäN ra sēn'] used stories from classical mythology in their tragedies. Molière [mō lyer'] wrote witty comedies that mocked affected manners, mostly among doctors, lawyers, and the newly rich.

Music in the 18th century, like literature, was balanced, controlled, and refined. The greatest musicians then came from Germany and Austria. Religion was important in the works of Johann Sebastian Bach [bäk] and George Frederick Handel, composer of the Messiah. The Austrian musician Franz Josef Haydn [hīd'n] wrote chamber music and a new form of music, the symphony. His gifted pupil, **Wolfgang Amadeus Mozart** [mōt'särt], wrote more than 600 musical compositions, among them such operas as *Don Giovanni* and *The Marriage of Figaro*.

Section 1 Review

Identify Enlightenment, John Locke, social contract, Montesquieu, Voltaire, Jean Jacques Rousseau, Wolfgang Amadeus Mozart

Main Ideas

1. How did the philosophes view human nature? How did the scientific revolution influence that view?
2. Which ideas of Locke and Montesquieu influenced government?
3. Briefly describe the contributions of Voltaire, Rousseau, and Diderot.
4. Name two reforms that improved human well-being during the Enlightenment.
5. How were the arts affected by Enlightenment?

Critical Thinking

Making Hypotheses: Why do you think the philosophes might have been particularly interested in the thought and arts of ancient Greece and Rome? How might an earlier culture be useful to a society in transition?

2 Parliament triumphed in England.

Even before the dawn of the Enlightenment, with its attacks upon royal absolutism, the kings of England were seldom as powerful as those of the European continent. As monarchs in France, Russia, and Prussia became increasingly strong, the powers of English rulers were balanced by the rights of Parliament and limited by an old, but unwritten, constitution. Without the consent of Parliament, the king could not make new laws, repeal old ones, or impose new taxes. This system of government was known as limited monarchy.

Before the 17th century, however, a strong English king with a dominating personality and an effective army could still hold a great deal of power. In the 1600s England had two revolutions, and the balance of power shifted into the hands of Parliament. England was still a monarchy, but now the Parliament truly controlled the government. This system was certainly not yet democracy, for Parliament was completely dominated by wealthy merchants and landowners. Yet England in the 17th century created a political system that protected individual rights and restricted royal power more than in any other European country.

James I raised new conflicts, and Charles I brought civil war.

The troubles of the 17th century began with the death of Elizabeth I in 1603. The queen never married or had children, so the English crown went to her cousin James Stuart, king of Scotland.

James I. The political system in Scotland differed from the English system, and James I had little understanding of the parliamentary tradition. He believed in the divine right of kings, and he felt that no one could stop him from ruling however he wanted. Because the English Parliament by tradition checked royal power, conflicts arose. These battles raised an important issue: Did the king or Parliament have supreme power?

Other forces complicated the conflict, too. Because of economic changes, two classes of people had become important in England during the previous century. One, the gentry, was made up of landowners who ranked just below the nobility. Merchants and manufacturers made up the other class. Through their representatives in Parliament in the House of Commons, both groups tried to gain more political power at the king's expense.

Religion raised other difficulties. Roman Catholics hoped to make England a Catholic country again, but Calvinist Protestants wanted to purify the Anglican Church of all remaining Catholic influences. These "Puritans" made up much of the gentry and middle class, so Parliament was increasingly dominated by Puritans as well.

Charles I. When James I died in 1625, his son took the throne as Charles I. Parliament distrusted Charles I as it had his father. Because of expensive wars against Spain and France, Charles I desperately needed funds, but Parliament refused to vote him the money he wanted. Charles I tried to save money by having soldiers stay in people's homes, and he raised more revenue by forcing subjects to give "loans" to the government. Rich men who refused to pay went to prison, and poor men went to the army.

The leaders of Parliament felt that these policies violated the constitutional liberties of the English. In 1628 Charles I was forced to accept a parliamentary petition that listed the "divers rights and liberties of the subjects." This Petition of Right of 1628 banned forced loans and the billeting of troops in people's homes, and it guaranteed the right of Parliament to control the government's money supply.

When Parliament continued to oppose the king's policies, Charles I dismissed it in 1629. He then ruled alone without allowing a single meeting of Parliament for the next 11 years. During this period, Charles I also ignored the Petition of Right of 1628. In 1640, however, his treasury was nearly empty, and he needed money to put down a rebellion in Scotland.

Charles I had no choice but to recall Parliament. Its members, however, refused to vote any money unless Charles agreed that Parliament must meet at least once every three years and that the king could not levy taxes without parliamentary consent. Charles did not want to give up any of his power. In 1642 he led a band of soldiers into the House of Commons and attempted to arrest five of

2 Lesson Plan

Essential Learning Objective

Students will learn to describe those events that led to the supremacy of parliamentary rule and human rights in England.

1 FOCUS AND MOTIVATE

Write "taxation without representation" on the chalkboard. Ask students who has the power to tax in the United States. List their answers on the chalkboard. Point out that the taxing policies of the English kings contributed to civil war and political reform.

2 TEACH

- Have students prepare a time line by drawing a vertical line down the middle of a sheet of paper and dividing it into ten-year increments from 1600 at the bottom to 1760 at the top. Have students title the time line "The Growth of Democracy in England, 1600–1760." Have students record the succession of monarchs beginning with Elizabeth I and ending with George II.

- Have students add and annotate these events on their time lines: Petition of Right, Civil War, Charles I beheaded, Cromwell dismisses Parliament, The Restoration, Habeus Corpus, Glorious Revolution, Bill of Rights.

GUIDED PRACTICE

Have students use their time lines and the text to write one or two paragraphs describing the growth of parliamentary power in England after 1600.

its leaders. When this power play failed, Charles fled from London to the north of England and asked all his loyal subjects to help him suppress the Parliament. Almost half the members of the House of Commons went to the king's aid, while the rest opposed him. Civil war began.

Charles I's wartime supporters, who were called **Cavaliers**, included most of the nobles and large landowners. The men of Parliament and supporters of the Puritans were called **Roundheads**, because they cut their hair short. Much of the population tried to remain neutral, but this became impossible as both armies began to draft soldiers.

The Roundheads' army was led by a member of Parliament named **Oliver Cromwell**, a wealthy Puritan landowner. Cromwell had little military experience, but he was nonetheless a military genius. He chose his troops for both military skill and religious enthusiasm, and never lost a battle. After four years of fighting, his parliamentary forces won the war, and the king surrendered. In 1649 Charles I was convicted of treason and beheaded.

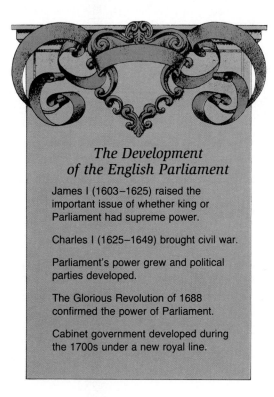

The Development of the English Parliament

James I (1603–1625) raised the important issue of whether king or Parliament had supreme power.

Charles I (1625–1649) brought civil war.

Parliament's power grew and political parties developed.

The Glorious Revolution of 1688 confirmed the power of Parliament.

Cabinet government developed during the 1700s under a new royal line.

Parliament's power grew, and political parties developed.

Parliament then voted to abolish the monarchy and declared England a Commonwealth and a "Protestant republic." Cromwell eventually took control of the government, and in 1653 he dismissed Parliament and took the title, "Lord Protector of England."

Many supporters of Parliament disliked the new system because it seemed little different from absolute monarchy. Also, many Puritans disliked Cromwell because he, though a devout Puritan, tolerated other religions more than they did. Many people also disliked the new high tax rates. Soon, Cromwell's only support came from the army, which he used to control political factions and any opposition. He became a military dictator.

When Cromwell died in 1658, he was succeeded by his son Richard. Richard soon lost the support of the army, however, and political chaos followed. No one was strong enough to take charge, and many people were tired of strict Puritanism and military rule. In 1660 Charles I's son, exiled in France, became king by agreeing to share power with Parliament.

Charles II was a clever, fun-loving king. His subjects called him the Merry Monarch. His 25-year reign was known as the **Restoration**, for that is when the monarchy was restored. Under Charles II, conflict between Parliament and the Crown continued. In 1679 Charles II's political opponents pushed the **Habeas Corpus Act** through Parliament. This law, still a cornerstone of individual freedom in both England and the United States, said that the government could not arrest or imprison any person without showing a good, legal reason.

Since Charles II had no legal heirs, his legitimate successor was his brother James, a devout Roman Catholic who believed in the divine right of kings. A group in Parliament called the **Whigs** tried to keep James off the throne. Whig supporters were the strongly Protestant middle class and merchants of London as well as the upper nobility. Opposing the Whigs were the **Tories**. Tory supporters were lower nobility and gentry who did not trust the London merchants and were loyal to the king. The Whigs and the Tories gradually developed, in the

Oliver Cromwell is shown both as Lord Protector (left) and as he dissolves Parliament in 1655 (right). To departing members, he ordered: "Be gone you rogues. You have sat long enough."

3 | ASSESS AND CLOSE

ASSESS
1. What was the Bill of Rights of 1689? (laws which protected members of Parliament and individuals in England)
2. Who was Oliver Cromwell? (Roundhead leader who became Lord Protector of England)

OPTIONAL RETEACHING
Ask students to explain the relationship between each of the following paired terms: Whig and Tory, Cavalier and Roundhead, Cromwell and Charles I, Irish Catholics and Scotch-Irish Protestants, absolute monarchy and limited monarchy.

OPTIONAL ENRICHMENT
1. Encourage enterprising students to convert their in-class time lines into large models for the bulletin board. (average)
2. Invite students to make photocopies of the English Bill of Rights and the U.S. Bill of Rights. Have students use yarn and different colors of highlighter to make a display that shows the similarities between the two documents. (challenging)
3. Also for enrichment:

 Overhead Transparency 51

 Source Reading 26A

INDEPENDENT PRACTICE/ HOMEWORK
Assign the Section Review, Activities page 152, or Workbook page 102.

following decades, into the first real political parties. When Charles II died in 1685, his brother became king as James II, despite the opposition.

The Glorious Revolution confirmed the power of Parliament.

James II wanted more authority for himself and for the Catholic Church. Thus, he soon angered almost everyone, including the Tories. In 1688 when the king's wife bore a son, both Tories and Whigs feared a long line of Catholic kings.

They invited James' Protestant daughter Mary and her husband, Prince William of Orange, the Dutch ruler, to help them save Protestantism in England. William invaded England, James II fled to France, and the Crown was offered jointly to William and Mary. This new show of parliamentary power, in which Parliament bloodlessly replaced one monarch with another whom it liked better, is called the **Glorious Revolution**.

When they took the throne, William and Mary agreed to several important measures passed by Parliament. These new laws are usually called the Revolution Settlement. Most important was the English **Bill of Rights of 1689**, which would later be very influential in the United States Constitution. (See excerpt, pages 506–507.)

The English Bill of Rights of 1689 guaranteed freedom of speech in Parliament, which would be required to meet more often. Further, the king could not interfere with the election of its members. The people gained the right to petition, or to ask the help of, the government. Excessive bail was not allowed, nor was cruel and unusual punishment of criminals. No army could be raised without Parliament's consent.

Why did Parliament triumph over royal authority in 17th-century England, while other European monarchies gained more absolute power? Historians have debated this question for the past three centuries, and no single correct answer exists. However, English conditions differed from those on the European continent in several ways.

Most important was England's parliamentary tradition. As you learned in Chapter 12, during the Middle Ages, English kings had made England a strongly united nation. French lords were often like little kings in their home areas, but no great

Summarize the lesson by telling students that England led the Western world in introducing democratic reforms in the 17th and 18th centuries. Point out that this occurred without removing the English monarchy.

Answers to Section 2 Review

Identify

Key Terms, People, and Places are defined on pages indicated in parentheses. Also see the Glossary and Biographical Dictionary. Cavaliers (480), Roundheads (480), Oliver Cromwell (480), Restoration (480), Habeas Corpus Act (480), Whigs (480), Tories (480), Glorious Revolution (481), Bill of Rights of 1689 (481)

Main Ideas

1. government finance, religion, and most important the question of whether supreme power belonged to Parliament or to the king
2. the passing of the Habeas Corpus Act under Charles II
3. Parliament now was able to peacefully replace a king it opposed, proving that Parliament held supreme political power.
4. A German king of England, who knew little about the country or its language, needed high-level advisers.

Critical Thinking

Possibly because kings want to hold on to their power. Evidence is that kings, beginning with John in 1215, have very reluctantly shared power with their subjects.

BACKGROUND Remind students that at the time of the Glorious Revolution property qualifications determined voting rights, and only men could vote.

noble of England was so powerful alone. Anyone who wanted to limit the king's power had to join with others. Parliament was where this joining together took place. When French kings like Louis XIV finally subdued their nobility, the nobility had no way to act in opposition; in England, however, Parliament grew increasingly strong.

Also, Parliament made it possible for different classes—nobles, gentry, and middle class—to work together against the king's power. Thus, when the 17th-century kings tried to increase their control, Parliament was able to resist.

Parliament triumphed in England before anywhere else, but it did not happen easily or smoothly. It took almost a full century, and it required a civil war, a military dictatorship, the beheading of one king, and the exile of another.

Cabinet government developed under a new line.

The last reigning Stuart monarch in Britain, Queen Anne, died in 1714, leaving no heirs. The law said that the monarch's closest Protestant relative would take the throne. Thus, a German second cousin became George I of England and began the Hanoverian dynasty. He spoke no English and spent most of his time in Germany.

Since he knew little about England, George I depended on a group called a cabinet to help him rule. These people were members of Parliament, mostly ministers in charge of government departments. During George I's reign, the cabinet began to make policy.

For half a century after 1714, the Whigs controlled the House of Commons. George I and George II, who ruled from 1727 to 1760, chose their ministers from the Whig party. Robert Walpole, head of the party from 1721 to 1742, was the principal minister—a position later called prime minister.

Walpole always chose his cabinet from the Whig party to be sure his policies would be supported in the House of Commons. When he lost support in Commons in 1742, he resigned as prime minister. Since then, English prime ministers and cabinets have come from the majority party in Parliament.

Queen Anne (right) had an enduring influence on styles, many of which still bear her name—such as the Queen Anne chair and the flower, Queen Anne's lace.

Section 2 Review

Identify Cavaliers, Roundheads, Oliver Cromwell, Restoration, Habeas Corpus Act, Whigs, Tories, Glorious Revolution, Bill of Rights of 1689

Main Ideas

1. What serious conflicts did James I and Charles I have with their subjects?
2. Give an example of growing parliamentary power in England.
3. How did the Glorious Revolution show Parliament's strength?
4. How did cabinet government develop?

Critical Thinking

Assessing Cause and Effect: Why do you think that the English kings and Parliament had so much difficulty getting along with each other? Support your answer with evidence from the chapter.

---

3 North American colonies fought for independence.

Many North American colonists had left Europe to escape religious persecution or debts or to find work. Settlers came from England, Scotland, Germany, the Netherlands, France, and Ireland.

Of course, not all immigrants to the colonies came willingly. During the 17th and 18th centuries, millions of Africans were forced on to ships and transported to North America as slaves.

Life in the colonies was different from life in Europe. Colonists were proud to be independent farmers, artisans, and merchants. They depended on themselves and on their own hard work and ambition. In the newly settled lands of North America, inherited privileges had little meaning.

The English tightened their control.

For many years England did little to regulate the North American colonies beyond appointing a royal governor. Both mother country and colonies prospered and profited from their relationship with each other. According to one historian, the English government treated the colonies with "immense ignorance and even vaster indifference."

BACKGROUND Some colonies had governors appointed by the English king, but each colony also had a legislature elected by those who owned land. Like Parliament in England, these representative assemblies controlled the money supply of the

The 13 Colonies, 1750

- New England Colonies
- Middle Colonies
- Southern Colonies

0   150   300 Miles
0   150   300 Kilometers

© SF

MAP STUDY The map above shows the American colonies in 1750. What were the three major colonial regions at that time?

By the early 18th century, the colonies had begun to expand westward. This expansion eventually brought them into conflict with French settlers, who were moving south from Canada along the Ohio River. France and England were bitter enemies throughout the 18th century.

colonial governments. Therefore, the legislatures usually dominated the royal governors, for they could hold back money from taxes until they got their way. Colonial assemblies even had the power to stop paying the governor's salary.

---

3 Lesson Plan

Essential Learning Objectives

Students will learn to:

- describe the chain of events that led to the American Revolutionary War.
- explain the basic differences between the Declaration of Independence, the Articles of Confederation, the U.S. Constitution, and the U.S. Bill of Rights.

1 FOCUS AND MOTIVATE

Write *civil war* and *revolutionary war* on the chalkboard. Ask students to define each. In what sense was the U.S. War for Independence both of these? (civil because, especially from the English and American Tory point of view, it was English against English)

2 TEACH

- Write a scrambled version of the following chronological list on the chalkboard and ask students to arrange the items in chronological order: westward expansion from the 13 colonies, collision with French territory, French-Indian War, English war debt, taxes imposed on the 13 colonies, taxation without representation, Intolerable Acts, Revolutionary War, American victory. Ask for a volunteer to use this list to tell the story of how revolution came to the American colonies.

- Four famous documents were products of the American Revolution: the Declaration of Independence, the Articles of Confederation, the Constitution of the United States, and the Bill of Rights. Ask students which of these is most famous for its weaknesses. (Articles) Which included a long list of

GEOGRAPHY

A Key to History

THE GULF STREAM

When Columbus landed in the West Indies in 1492, he immediately faced another problem: how to return home. The trade winds that had carried his ship westward across the Atlantic blew in the face of his homeward voyage. He correctly guessed that by sailing northward he would reach the broad band of westerly winds that blew in the right direction for a homeward voyage. The problem was that an area of calm, the doldrums, separated the trade winds from the westerlies.

About 25 years later, Spanish adventurers discovered a current that would take their ships north through the doldrums to the westerlies. As the trade winds blew steadily across the Atlantic, they piled up a huge quantity of warm water in the Gulf of Mexico. The sea level in the Gulf then became higher than in the Atlantic itself. This excess water eventually escaped through the narrows between Florida and Cuba in a broad flood across the Atlantic as the warm current called the Gulf Stream.

Much later, in 1768, officials of the British Empire complained about the long delays ships often met when sailing from London to North America. The Gulf Stream was usually the cause of these delays, pushing the boats eastward as they tried to sail westward. Benjamin Franklin, always alert to how science might be put to use in improving life, addressed the problem by publishing the first map of the Gulf Stream. He advised sea captains to get out of the Gulf Stream even if it meant sailing out of their way. As deputy postmaster general for the colonies, Franklin had copies of his Gulf Stream map printed and distributed to every boat carrying the mail. In this case, he turned to science to improve human life. Soon he would turn to politics and to revolution to pursue the same goals.

REVIEW

1. How do the trade winds help cause the Gulf Stream?
2. In what cases might the Gulf Stream prove helpful to sailors?

Benjamin Franklin charted the Gulf Stream in 1769 or 1770 after consulting his cousin Timothy Folger, a sea captain. Even today it remains a good summary of the Gulf Stream's path and width. In what directions does it flow?

484

In the 1750s, however, these powers fought a war for supremacy in North America. It eventually spread to Europe, where it is known as the Seven Years' War. In America the war is called the French and Indian War. In 1763 England defeated France, and Canada became an English possession.

The war in North America was won largely with English troops and ships and was paid for with English taxes. The English government thus had high expenses and large debts and decided that the increasingly prosperous colonies should share the costs of war and administration. England began to enforce old laws more strictly and to pass new laws to raise colonial taxes.

American colonists began to resist.

Between 1765 and 1774, the colonists opposed every effort to make them pay more taxes. They argued that only their colonial assemblies could levy taxes. Parliament had no such right because the colonists did not vote for its members. "No taxation without representation!" echoed throughout the colonies. The English tried to put a tax on the purchase of newspapers and then on sugar, tea, and other imported goods. The colonists resisted these new taxes by boycotting the taxed products. In 1773 a group of colonists boarded a ship in **Boston** harbor and threw a large shipment of English tea over the side so that the tax would never be paid.

This "Boston Tea Party," as it came to be known, was a serious crime. The colonists, disguised as Indians, had destroyed very valuable property. To the English it also seemed to be an

This unique earthenware teapot was made around 1765 with an inscription supporting the rebellion of the American colonists.

Robert Edge Pine's painting *Congress Voting Independence* (1788) is believed to be the most accurate representation of the event.

open act of rebellion, which demanded a harsh response. To teach the colonists a lesson, the English Parliament passed the so-called **Intolerable Acts**. These new laws closed Boston harbor to shipping, which meant economic ruin, and took back the charter of the Massachusetts colony, which ended local self-government. To the people of Massachusetts, and to many other colonists, these acts were tyranny. Revolution was now inevitable.

The colonies won their independence.

Fighting started in April 1775. The English government seemed unwilling to give in at all. The colonists also were growing less willing to compromise. Many now claimed that Parliament could not make any laws at all for the colonies. Increasingly, the colonies worked together, electing the Continental Congress and creating an army under the command of **George Washington**. American patriotism also grew. A group of colonists resisting the tyranny of a distant king was gradually being transformed into a new nation.

Finally, on July 4, 1776, the Continental Congress declared the 13 American colonies to be the independent **United States of America**. The Declaration of Independence claimed that the English king, George III, had harmed his American subjects in dozens of ways: "He has plundered our seas, ravaged our Coasts, burnt our towns, and destroyed the Lives of our people." (See excerpt, pages 506–507.) The declaration went on to state that any nation, when treated so unjustly, has the right to make itself free and to create a new government.

charges against George III? (Declaration) Which borrowed heavily from Montesquieu? (Constitution) Which added ten amendments to the Constitution? (Bill of Rights)

GUIDED PRACTICE
Ask students to use their texts to note facts that show that the new American republic was not a full democracy. Discuss their findings.

3 | ASSESS AND CLOSE

ASSESS
1. What is the difference between the Declaration of Independence and the U.S. Constitution? (Declaration established a new nation. Constitution created the basis for operating the U.S. government.)
2. What European nation provided critical assistance to the colonial war effort? (France)

OPTIONAL RETEACHING
Have students consider the English point of view and respond to these statements: (1) The 13 colonies were created by the English for England, and they have no right to separate. (2) The English government spent a great amount of money waging the French and Indian War and the colonists should help pay the war debt through taxation.

Students also may be assigned Activities reteaching page 154.

OPTIONAL ENRICHMENT
1. It is estimated that two thirds of the American colonists either opposed the revolutionary cause or were neutral. Ask students to imagine

they are colonists and write letters explaining their point of view. (average)

2. Ask students to research and report on allegations that King George III was mentally incompetent. (challenging)

3. Students also may be assigned Activities enrichment page 155.

4. Also for enrichment:

 Overhead Transparency 52

 Source Reading 26B

INDEPENDENT PRACTICE/ HOMEWORK

Assign the Section Review, the Chapter Review items, Activities page 153, or Workbook page 103.

CLOSURE

Tell students that the American Revolution resulted because colonists opposed new English taxes. After independence, Americans wrote a Constitution that incorporated many political beliefs of the Enlightenment.

Answers to Section 3 Review

Identify

Key Terms, People, and Places are defined on pages indicated in parentheses. Also see the Glossary and Biographical Dictionary. Boston (485), Intolerable Acts (485), George Washington (485), United States of America (485), Thomas Jefferson (486), U.S. Constitution (486), Bill of Rights (486)

Main Ideas

1. by raising taxes
2. refused to pay taxes, boycotted taxed goods, and finally declared independence
3. the ideas of John Locke—that all people have natural rights that no government may take away
4. It was a federal republic with power divided between the national

Thomas Jefferson, who wrote the Declaration, based the demand for independence on the ideas of John Locke, especially the idea that all people possessed natural rights that no government could take away. Although the ideas were not completely new, never before had a nation put them into practice on so grand a scale, or expressed them in such a clear way. Ever since, oppressed people in many countries have been inspired by Jefferson's words and followed the example of the American Revolution.

What had begun as an American fight for freedom soon became a worldwide conflict for empire among the European countries. France, Spain, and the Netherlands declared war against England to gain back territories lost in 1763 and earlier. The French fleet and 6,000 troops helped the new United States of America win the war. In 1783 a peace treaty was signed, and England recognized the 13 colonies as independent.

The United States set up a new government.

Early in the war, all 13 colonies passed new state constitutions because everyone agreed that a written constitution would help prevent government from becoming oppressive. It was more difficult, however, to create the framework for a national government, because none had ever existed before in America.

In 1777 the Congress passed a plan of government called the Articles of Confederation. The Articles created a very weak national government, leaving most political power in the hands of the states. The United States government was merely called a "league of friendship."

After the war ended, however, it became clear that the national government was too weak. Under the Articles of Confederation, the government could not regulate foreign trade or control the national economy. Thus, the new nation seemed weak in the eyes of the European powers. Gradually, more Americans became willing to accept the idea of a stronger central government. In 1787 a constitutional convention met, and in four months it drafted the **U.S. Constitution**, the written set of fundamental principles by which the United States is governed.

BACKGROUND The revolt of the 13 American colonies, and their success in creating a stable republican—and increasingly democratic—government, became an inspiration for people seeking freedom, especially in France and Latin America.

The convention created a federal republic, with power divided between the national and state governments. Political power of the federal government was to be balanced between the president, the two houses of Congress, and the courts. These "checks and balances," which limited the power of government and the strength of any person or group within the government, were based largely on the ideas of Montesquieu. The new Constitution was very controversial, and it was ratified only after a long and bitter political struggle.

To reassure those who feared a strong central government, the new Congress passed amendments to the Constitution that protected the people's civil liberties. Ten of these amendments were ratified by the states and are collectively known as the **Bill of Rights**. The Bill of Rights guarantees freedom of speech, religion, and the press; trial by jury; and the rights to life, liberty, and property.

The new American republic planted the seeds of democratic government, but it did not yet bring full democracy. Only men with property could vote. Women would not gain this right for more than a century. In addition, most black Americans were still enslaved, and they had no political or civil rights. Legally, they were not considered to be people. It took another 75 years and a bloody civil war before this injustice was corrected. Yet the American Revolution set in motion changes that made the spread of democracy inevitable.

Section 3 Review

Identify Boston, Intolerable Acts, George Washington, United States of America, Thomas Jefferson, U.S. Constitution, Bill of Rights

Main Ideas

1. How did England try to control the colonies?
2. How did the colonists resist English control?
3. What ideas fueled the colonists' fight for independence?
4. What was the new U.S. government like?

Critical Thinking

Assessing Cause and Effect: Thomas Jefferson used the ideas of John Locke in framing the Declaration of Independence. What happened to some of these ideas in the framing of the U.S. Constitution?

HIGHLIGHTS OF CIVILIZATION

Neoclassical Architecture

Architectural styles based on classical Greek and Roman models have swept in and out of fashion ever since the fall of Rome in the 4th century A.D. After 1660 a taste for simple, elegant classical buildings developed in reaction to the complex, highly decorated Baroque styles. According to a noted art historian, "What distinguishes this style from earlier classicisms is less its external appearance than its motivation; instead of merely reasserting the superior authority of the ancients, it claimed to satisfy the demands of reason, and thus to be more 'natural' than Baroque."

The greatest inspiration for 18th-century neoclassicism was the work of the Italian architect Andrea Palladio (1518–1580). Using the forms of the ancient Greeks and Romans—stately columns, semicircular arches, and round domes—Palladio created architectural designs of simple harmony and balanced proportion. Palladio's influence can be seen in the design of many English buildings.

Neoclassicism was also popular in 18th-century America. Thomas Jefferson's home, Monticello, was built in this style, with the classical columns, a round dome, and simple but elegant details. Also known in the United States as the Georgian style, neoclassicism is still popular. Its reliance on the pleasing proportions of the Greeks and Romans has allowed this style to endure.

Simplicy and restraint describe a London church, St. Stephen's, Walbrook, designed by Christopher Wren in the 1670s (left). Thomas Jefferson designed Monticello (below) between 1770 and 1808.

government and state governments. Power of the federal government was divided between the president, Congress, and the courts.

Critical Thinking

Not all of Locke's ideas were fully implemented. For example, government was based on the consent solely of white, male property owners.

HIGHLIGHTS OF CIVILIZATION

Encourage students to compare the photographs of neoclassical buildings with those of baroque buildings. Let students discuss which style they prefer.

Ask students to point out elements of classical architecture in buildings in your community or in famous buildings they may have seen pictured. (Answers will vary, but students may note that government buildings often have columns, domes, and semicircular arches.)

Explain that the dome is often considered a symbol of power. Point out that many government capitals have domes. Discuss why the dome might be used to symbolize power and authority.

487

Answers to Test Yourself

Key Terms, People, and Places
The key terms, people, and places tested here were introduced in the chapter sections and reviewed in the Section Reviews. For definitions see the page references at the appropriate Section Reviews. Also see the Glossary and Biographical Dictionary.

The main ideas tested here were introduced in the sections of this chapter and reviewed in the Section Reviews. For answers to these questions, see the appropriate Section Reviews.

1. Possible answers: Yes, they express the central values of the society and the time period. No, they only express the ideas of the intellectual elite. This gives a very limited picture of what was really going on.
2. possible answer: desire for military and economic security; belief that people have to take care of themselves and the government should not, desire for old-fashioned, traditional values surrounding home and family

Section Summaries

Section 1
Ideas about democracy began to develop.
John Locke, an Englishman, and the Baron de Montesquieu, a Frenchman, were two philosophes whose ideas of law and government had a lasting influence. Voltaire and Rousseau also expressed influential ideas about tolerance and freedom. Artists, too, applied the new ideas of the Enlightenment to their work.

Section 2
Parliament triumphed in England.
A conflict arose in England concerning who had the supreme power—the king or Parliament. During the reign of Charles I, the conflict grew into a civil war. Oliver Cromwell led the Roundheads, who triumphed over Charles I, and then took over the government. Order was not restored, however, until the king, Charles II, agreed to share power with Parliament.

Section 3
North American colonies fought for independence.
After enjoying a large degree of self-government, the 13 American colonies began to experience tightened English control following the French and Indian War. The colonists strongly opposed the English efforts and resisted by refusing to pay taxes, by boycotting taxed goods, and finally by declaring their independence. Helped by the French, the colonists won their war for independence and set up a new government in which the progress of democracy was ensured.

Test Yourself

Key Terms and People
Identify the significance of each of the following:

Section 1
a. Enlightenment
b. John Locke
c. social contract
d. Montesquieu
e. Voltaire
f. Jean Jacques Rousseau
g. Wolfgang Amadeus Mozart

Section 2
a. Cavaliers
b. Roundheads
c. Oliver Cromwell
d. Restoration
e. Habeas Corpus Act
f. Whigs
g. Tories
h. Glorious Revolution
i. Bill of Rights of 1689

Section 3
a. Boston
b. Intolerable Acts
c. George Washington
d. United States of America
e. Thomas Jefferson
f. U.S. Constitution
g. Bill of Rights

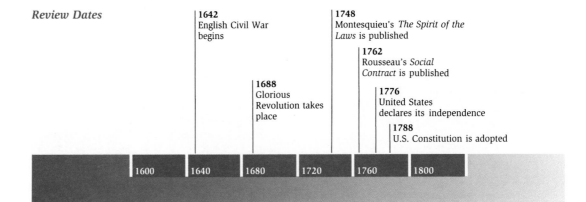

Review Dates

1642 English Civil War begins

1688 Glorious Revolution takes place

1748 Montesquieu's *The Spirit of the Laws* is published

1762 Rousseau's *Social Contract* is published

1776 United States declares its independence

1788 U.S. Constitution is adopted

| 1600 | 1640 | 1680 | 1720 | 1760 | 1800 |

Main Ideas

Section 1

1. Describe the philosophes' view of human nature. How was that view influenced by the scientific revolution?

2. How did Locke and Montesquieu's ideas influence government?

3. What were the major contributions of Voltaire, Rousseau, and Diderot?

4. How did reforms improve human well-being during the Enlightenment?

5. How did the Age of Reason affect the arts?

Section 2

1. On which serious matters did James I and Charles I clash with their subjects?

2. Name one way Parliament showed growing power.

3. What did the Glorious Revolution show about Parliament's power?

4. Why did George I begin cabinet government?

Section 3

1. What did England do to try to control its North American colonies?

2. Name three ways that the colonists resisted English control.

3. What philosophy was the basis for the colonial fight for independence?

4. Describe the U.S. government after the revolution.

Critical Thinking

1. Evaluating Sources of Information Do you think that the ideas of the philosophers are a good source for understanding this revolutionary time period in world history? Why?

2. Recognizing Values In keeping with Rousseau's idea, how might you describe the General Will of your country at the present time?

Chapter Skills and Activities

Practicing Study and Research Skills

Perceiving Cause-Effect Relationships

Much of the study of history is involved in looking at the causes and effects of events such as the French and American revolutions. A cause is something that produces an effect. An event, an action, or an idea may be a cause. An effect is the result of that event, action, or idea. For example, the American Revolution is the effect of a number of causes that included a desire among the colonists for independence, "taxation without representation," and the general thinking of the time. Name a possible effect of each of the following causes:

a. England tried to impose taxes on the 13 colonies.

b. John Howard wrote about prison conditions.

c. James I believed in the divine rights of kings.

d. The wife of James II bore a son.

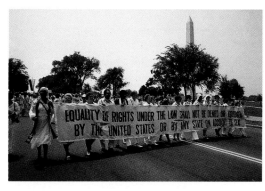

Linking Past and Present

Over the past 200 years, 26 amendments, or changes, to the U.S. Constitution have been adopted by the states of the union. However, more than 5,000 failed amendments have also been suggested. Research recent amendments that have either been adopted, such as that giving 18-year olds the right to vote, or simply suggested, such as the equal rights amendment. What might be some reasons people oppose changes to the Constitution?

Learning History Through Maps

Refer to the map of the 13 American colonies on page 483. In what ways is this map different from a map of the current northeastern United States, which shows 16 states? You can find a current political map of the United States in an atlas or encyclopedia in your classroom or library.

CRITICAL THINKING QUESTION LEVEL 1. average; 2. challenging

27 Revolutions in France and Latin America

OVERVIEW

The French Revolution and the Napoleonic era changed the political face of Europe and Latin America, and the legacy left by the American and French revolutions reshaped the entire world.

PLANNING CHART

Section	Text Pages	Key Concept	Suggested Teaching Time
1 The French Revolution changed society and government.	491–498	Class inequality and financial strain led France to suffer ten years of revolution.	Two days **More time?** Use *Overhead Transparency 53* or *Source Reading 27A.*
2 Napoleon became ruler of France.	498–502	Napoleon took advantage of France's desire for political stability—he seized power, extended reform, and led France to military glory followed by defeat.	One day **More time?** Use *Overhead Transparency 54.*
3 Latin American colonies became independent nations.	502–505	Spanish and Portuguese problems with Napoleon enabled Latin American nations to establish independence, but without liberal reform.	One day **More time?** Use *Source Reading 27B.*
4 The American and French revolutions had long-range effects.	505–508	The fallout from the American and French revolutions left rich soil for later democratic reform in Europe and throughout the world.	One day

ANCILLARIES

Materials that may be used with this chapter to reinforce, reteach, enrich, and assess learning are pictured on the following pages.

Teacher's Resource File

ACTIVITIES

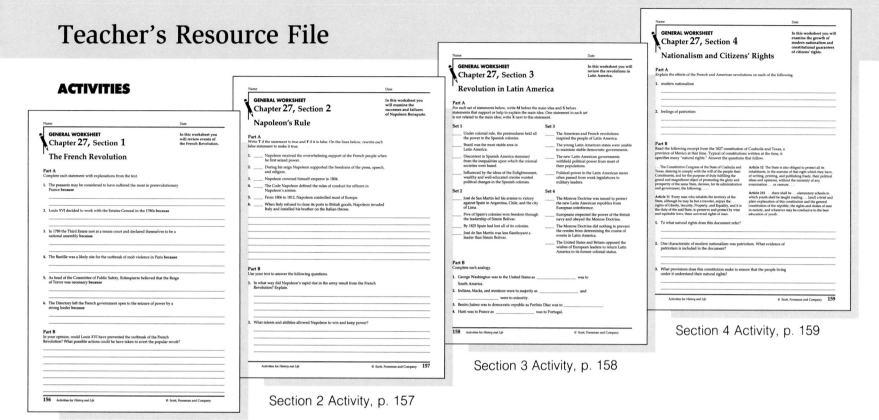

In this worksheet you will review events of the French Revolution.

Part A
Complete each statement with explanations from the text.

1. The peasants may be considered to have suffered the most in prerevolutionary France **because**

2. Louis XVI decided to work with the Estates-General in the 1780s **because**

3. In 1789 the Third Estate met at a tennis court and declared themselves to be a national assembly **because**

4. The Bastille was a likely site for the outbreak of mob violence in Paris **because**

5. As head of the Committee of Public Safety, Robespierre believed that the Reign of Terror was necessary **because**

6. The Directory left the French government open to the seizure of power by a strong leader **because**

Part B
In your opinion, could Louis XVI have prevented the outbreak of the French Revolution? What possible actions could he have taken to avert the popular revolt?

156 Activities for History and Life   © Scott, Foresman and Company

Section 1 Activity, p. 156

GENERAL WORKSHEET
Chapter 27, Section 2
Napoleon's Rule

In this worksheet you will examine the successes and failures of Napoleon Bonaparte.

Part A
Write **T** if the statement is true and **F** if it is false. On the lines below, rewrite each false statement to make it true.

1. _____ Napoleon received the overwhelming support of the French people when he first seized power.
2. _____ During his reign Napoleon supported the freedoms of the press, speech, and religion.
3. _____ Napoleon crowned himself emperor in 1804.
4. _____ The Code Napoleon defined the rules of conduct for officers in Napoleon's armies.
5. _____ From 1806 to 1812, Napoleon controlled most of Europe.
6. _____ When Italy refused to close its ports to British goods, Napoleon invaded Italy and installed his brother on the Italian throne.

Part B
Use your text to answer the following questions.

1. In what way did Napoleon's rapid rise in the army result from the French Revolution? Explain.

2. What talents and abilities allowed Napoleon to win and keep power?

Activities for History and Life   © Scott, Foresman and Company 157

Section 2 Activity, p. 157

GENERAL WORKSHEET
Chapter 27, Section 3
Revolution in Latin America

In this worksheet you will review the revolutions in Latin America.

Part A
For each set of statements below, write M before the main idea and S before statements that support or help to explain the main idea. One statement in each set is not related to the main idea; write X next to this statement.

Set 1
_____ Under colonial rule, the peninsulares held all the power in the Spanish colonies.
_____ Brazil was the most stable area in Latin America.
_____ Discontent in Spanish America stemmed from the inequalities upon which the colonial societies were based.
_____ Influenced by the ideas of the Enlightenment, wealthy and well-educated creoles wanted political changes in the Spanish colonies.

Set 2
_____ José de San Martín led his armies to victory against Spain in Argentina, Chile, and the city of Lima.
_____ Five of Spain's colonies won freedom through the leadership of Simón Bolívar.
_____ By 1825 Spain had lost all of its colonies.
_____ José de San Martín was less flamboyant a leader than Simón Bolívar.

Set 3
_____ The American and French revolutions inspired the people of Latin America.
_____ The young Latin American states were unable to maintain stable democratic governments.
_____ The new Latin American governments withheld political power from most of their populations.
_____ Political power in the Latin American states often passed from weak legislatures to military leaders.

Set 4
_____ The Monroe Doctrine was issued to protect the new Latin American republics from European interference.
_____ Europeans respected the power of the British navy and obeyed the Monroe Doctrine.
_____ The Monroe Doctrine did nothing to prevent the creoles from determining the course of events in Latin America.
_____ The United States and Britain opposed the wishes of European leaders to return Latin America to its former colonial status.

Part B
Complete each analogy.

1. George Washington was to the United States as _____ was to South America.
2. Indians, blacks, and mestizos were to majority as _____ and _____ were to minority.
3. Benito Juárez was to democratic republic as Porfirio Díaz was to _____.
4. Haiti was to France as _____ was to Portugal.

158 Activities for History and Life   © Scott, Foresman and Company

Section 3 Activity, p. 158

GENERAL WORKSHEET
Chapter 27, Section 4
Nationalism and Citizens' Rights

In this worksheet you will examine the growth of modern nationalism and constitutional guarantees of citizens' rights.

Part A
Explain the effects of the French and American revolutions on each of the following.

1. modern nationalism

2. feelings of patriotism

Part B
Read the following excerpt from the 1827 constitution of Coahuila and Texas, a province of Mexico at that time. Typical of constitutions written at the time, it specifies many "natural rights." Answer the questions that follow.

...The Constitutive Congress of the State of Coahuila and Texas, desiring to comply with the will of the people their Constituents, and for the purpose of duly fulfilling the grand and magnificent object of promoting the glory and prosperity of the same State, decrees, for its administration and government, the following: . . . .

Article 11 Every man who inhabits the territory of the State, although he may be but a traveler, enjoys the . . . rights of Liberty, Security, Property, and Equality, and it is the duty of the said State, to preserve and protect by wise and equitable laws, these universal rights of man.

Article 12 The State is also obliged to protect all its inhabitants, in the exercise of that right which they have, of writing, printing, and publishing freely, their political ideas and opinions, without the necessity of any examination . . . or censure . . . .

Article 215 . . . there shall be . . . elementary schools in which youth shall be taught reading . . . [and] a brief and plain explanation of this constitution and the general constitution of the republic, the rights and duties of men in society, and whatever may be conducive to the best education of youth.

1. To what natural rights does this document refer?

2. One characteristic of modern nationalism was patriotism. What evidence of patriotism is included in the document?

3. What provisions does this constitution make to ensure that the people living under it understand their natural rights?

Activities for History and Life   © Scott, Foresman and Company 159

Section 4 Activity, p. 159

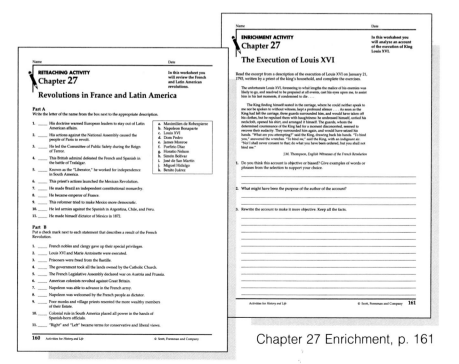

RETEACHING ACTIVITY
Chapter 27
Revolutions in France and Latin America

In this worksheet you will review the French and Latin American revolutions.

Part A
Write the letter of the name from the box next to the appropriate description.

1. _____ His doctrine warned European leaders to stay out of Latin American affairs.
2. _____ His actions against the National Assembly caused the people of Paris to revolt.
3. _____ He led the Committee of Public Safety during the Reign of Terror.
4. _____ This British admiral defeated the French and Spanish in the battle of Trafalgar.
5. _____ Known as the "Liberator," he worked for independence in South America.
6. _____ This priest's actions launched the Mexican Revolution.
7. _____ He made Brazil an independent constitutional monarchy.
8. _____ He became emperor of France.
9. _____ This reformer tried to make Mexico more democratic.
10. _____ He led armies against the Spanish in Argentina, Chile, and Peru.
11. _____ He made himself dictator of Mexico in 1872.

a. Maximilien de Robespierre
b. Napoleon Bonaparte
c. Louis XVI
d. Dom Pedro
e. James Monroe
f. Porfirio Díaz
g. Horatio Nelson
h. Simón Bolívar
i. José de San Martín
j. Miguel Hidalgo
k. Benito Juárez

Part B
Put a check mark next to each statement that describes a result of the French Revolution.

1. _____ French nobles and clergy gave up their special privileges.
2. _____ Louis XVI and Marie Antoinette were executed.
3. _____ Prisoners were freed from the Bastille.
4. _____ The government took all the lands owned by the Catholic Church.
5. _____ The French Legislative Assembly declared war on Austria and Prussia.
6. _____ American colonists revolted against Great Britain.
7. _____ Napoleon was able to advance in the French army.
8. _____ Napoleon was welcomed by the French people as dictator.
9. _____ Poor monks and village priests resented the more wealthy members of their Estate.
10. _____ Colonial rule in South America placed all power in the hands of Spanish-born officials.
11. _____ "Right" and "Left" became terms for conservative and liberal views.

160 Activities for History and Life   © Scott, Foresman and Company

Chapter 27 Reteaching, p. 160

ENRICHMENT ACTIVITY
Chapter 27
The Execution of Louis XVI

In this worksheet you will analyze an account of the execution of King Louis XVI.

Read the excerpt from a description of the execution of Louis XVI on January 21, 1793, written by a priest of the king's household, and complete the exercises.

The unfortunate Louis XVI, foreseeing to what lengths the malice of his enemies was likely to go, and resolved to be prepared at all events, cast his eyes upon me, to assist him in his last moments; he answered, if condemned to die . . . .

The King finding himself seated in the carriage, where he could neither speak to me nor be spoken to without witness, kept a profound silence . . . As soon as the King had left the carriage, three guards surrounded him, and would have taken off his clothes, but he repulsed them with haughtiness: he undressed himself, untied his neckcloth, opened his shirt, and arranged it himself. The guards, whom the determined countenance of the King had for a moment disconcerted, seemed to recover their audacity. They surrounded him again, and would have seized his hands. "What are you attempting?" said the King, drawing back his hands. "To bind you," answered the wretches. "To bind me," said the King, with an indignant air. "No! I shall never consent to that; do what you have been ordered, but you shall not bind me."

J.M. Thompson, *English Witnesses of the French Revolution*

1. Do you think this account is objective or biased? Give examples of words or phrases from the selection to support your choice.

2. What might have been the purpose of the author of the account?

3. Rewrite the account to make it more objective. Keep all the facts.

Activities for History and Life   © Scott, Foresman and Company 161

Chapter 27 Enrichment, p. 161

Teacher's Resource File

GEOGRAPHY SKILLS

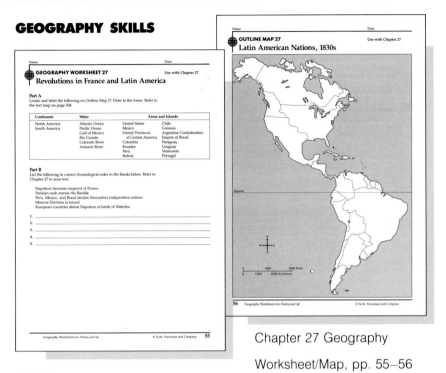

Chapter 27 Geography Worksheet/Map, pp. 55–56

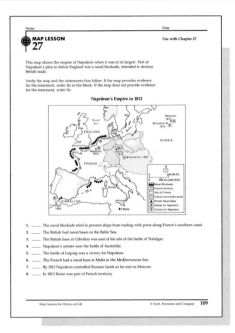

Chapter 27 Map Lesson, p. 109

TESTS

Chapter Test, pp. 141–142

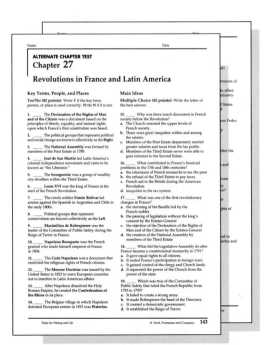

Alternate Chapter Test, pp. 143–144

Other Optional Ancillaries

WORKBOOK

WORKSHEET
Chapter 27, Section 1

Revolutionary Upheaval in France

In this worksheet you will trace events that caused the French Revolution or occurred during its upheaval.

Part A
Fill in the blanks with the words from the box that best complete the sentences.

Before the Revolution each French person belonged, by law, to one of three classes, or _____; the clergy belonged to the First Estate; the _____ belonged to the Second Estate; and everyone else belonged to the Third Estate. Growing discontent among and within these classes was one factor leading to _____ in France.

The government's _____ difficulty was another cause of the revolution. During the reign of Louis XVI, the French monarchy was close to _____, but laws exempted the First and Second estates from paying most _____. To address the crisis Louis XVI was forced to share his power with the _____, a legislative body. Since the Third Estate was not allowed to vote on an equal footing with the other two estates, the representatives from the Third Estate met separately and declared themselves to be a _____.

| bankruptcy | National Assembly | nobility | financial |
| estates | Estates-General | revolution | taxes |

Part B
Number the events in the order in which they happened.

_____ France becomes a constitutional monarchy.

_____ Louis XVI is sentenced to death by the National Constitutional Convention.

_____ Believing the Bastille to contain ammunition to be used against them, Parisian mobs storm that fort.

_____ France's Legislative Assembly, fearing an attempt by Austria and Prussia to restore the French monarchy, declares war on them.

_____ During rule by the Directory, political power resides in the upper middle class and former nobles.

_____ In response to the violent uprisings by the peasants throughout France, the nobility and clergy relinquish many privileges that they had held since the feudal era.

_____ Under Robespierre, the Committee of Public Safety embarks on the Reign of Terror.

Section 1 Worksheet, p. 104

WORKSHEET
Chapter 27, Section 2

Napoleon in Power

In this worksheet you will review the rise and fall of Napoleon Bonaparte.

Part A
Write C next to each phrase that correctly completes the unfinished sentence. (Each sentence may have more than one correct ending.)

1. Determined to rule all of Europe, Napoleon I
   _____ was defeated at the battle of Trafalgar by a superior British navy.
   _____ controlled most of the European continent by 1806.
   _____ was outmaneuvered by the British, who established an international economic boycott against France.
   _____ was defeated by the Confederation of the Rhine.

2. Napoleon enacted significant reforms that
   _____ awarded special privileges to certain groups.
   _____ increased the strength and efficiency of the central government.
   _____ denied freedom of religion but guaranteed that the government would refrain from controlling the French Catholic Church.
   _____ modernized French law.

Part B
Present at least two specific facts from your text to support each statement.

1. Napoleon attempted to discipline the Iberian peninsula because of the smuggling operations conducted there.

2. Napoleon brought many ideals from the French Revolution to the conquered countries of Europe.

3. The sentiments of people in other countries began to turn against Napoleon during his economic boycott of British goods.

4. Napoleon's invasion of Russia in 1812 eventually led to his downfall.

Section 2 Worksheet, p. 105

WORKSHEET
Chapter 27, Section 3

Latin American Revolutions

In this worksheet you will review people, events, and ideas of the revolutions of Latin America.

Part A
Write the correct name from the box that matches each description.

1. When he took control of Spain in 1808, Latin American colonists tried to break away from Spain.

2. After he was restored to the Spanish throne in 1814, he attempted to regain control of Spain's colonies.

3. Known as "the Liberator," he hoped to create a united states of Spanish America.

4. He was a creole soldier whose armies fought the Spanish in Argentina, Chile, and the city of Lima.

5. He launched the Mexican Revolution in 1810 by demanding independence from Spanish rule.

6. He was dictator of Mexico when it lost half of its territory to the United States in the Mexican War.

7. A mestizo army general, he set up a dictatorship that brought order and industry to Mexico.

8. In 1821 he became emperor of Brazil under a constitutional monarchy.

Santa Anna	Ferdinand VII	Dom Pedro
Miguel Hidalgo	Napoleon	Porfirio Díaz
José de San Martín	Simón Bolívar	

Part B
Write a paragraph in which you explain the circumstances that led to the issuing of the Monroe Doctrine. How did European leaders react to the Doctrine?

Section 3 Worksheet, p. 106

WORKSHEET
Chapter 27, Section 4

Influences of Two Revolutions

In this worksheet you will examine the impact of the American and French revolutions on the political and social ideas of other nations.

Part A
Write the name of the political concept from the box beside its example. (Not all names will be used.)

1. In the Pyrenees Mountains between France and Spain, a group of people known as the Basques work to create a separate nation for themselves. _____

2. In the United States, groups work to achieve the same rights enjoyed by other groups of citizens. _____

3. French and American revolutionary leaders claim that all people had the right to life, liberty, property, and the pursuit of happiness. _____

| equality | absolutism | natural rights |
| the Right | nationalism | male suffrage |

Part B
For each statement below, write two or three sentences that support or provide details for that statement.

1. The French Revolution introduced a system of labeling political groups that remains in use today.

2. The American and French revolutions provided precedents for peoples' right to overthrow repressive governments.

3. The American and French revolutions enhanced the idea of nationalism.

Section 4 Worksheet, p. 107

SOURCE READINGS

Source Reading 27A
Source Reading 27B

TEST GENERATOR

40 multiple-choice questions for Chapter 27

OVERHEAD TRANSPARENCIES

Overhead Transparency 53
Overhead Transparency 54

Revolutions in France and Latin America

1700–1900

CHAPTER INTRODUCTION

As the young Dutchman in the introduction observed, two powerful philosophies of government had just collided in the United States and France. Democracy survived the collision. Monarchy was quashed in the United States and badly crippled in France.

LOCATOR GLOBE

Call students' attention to the globe, which indicates the general areas of the world discussed in this chapter. (A detailed map appears on page 504.)

TIME LINE

How many years after the Declaration of the Rights of Man and of the Citizen was written did Mexico gain its independence? (32 years)

1700	
1789	Declaration of the Rights of Man and of the Citizen is written
1804	Napoleon is crowned French Emperor
1821	Mexico gains independence
1850	
1900	

In 1782 a 20-year-old Dutchman from Rotterdam came to the United States. He was not impressed. He did not believe the American system of government would last, and he did not think Europeans should adopt it. The Europeans paid little attention to him, and in less than ten years later he was forced to concede:

> Two great parties are forming in all nations. . . . For one, there is a right of government, to be exercised by one or several persons over the mass of people, of divine origin and to be supported by the church, which is protected by it. These principles are expressed in the formula, Church and State.
>
> To this is opposed the new system, which admits no right of government except that arising from the free consent of those who submit to it, and which maintains that all persons who take part in government are accountable for their actions. These principles go under the formula, Sovereignty of the People, or Democracy.

The new, democratic system that the Dutchman described was based on the ideas of the Enlightenment and on the revolutionary experiences of Britain and North America. By 1791 these ideas had been firmly planted in the soil of the European continent. A great revolution was taking place in France, a revolution which was to topple the French monarchy, bring years of war, and spread democratic ideas throughout Europe and to Latin America.

During the age of democratic revolutions, the predominant ideas of liberty and equality sparked many debates about political and social rights. Conflict arose over the definition of the concept of equality. Some moderates believed that political equality before the law was a sufficient reform. Other people, however, demanded a new kind of social equality and insisted that people's natural rights included not only life and liberty but also food, housing, and a job. Such political and social conflicts have continued in almost every country to this day.

Edouard Detaille painted the departure in July, 1792, of the first volunteers of the French Revolution, a war for democracy that would not end for 23 years.

Reading Preview

In this chapter you will read how democratic revolutions brought change to France and independence to Latin America.

1. *The French Revolution changed society and government.*

2. *Napoleon became ruler of France.*

3. *Latin American colonies became independent nations.*

4. *The American and French revolutions had long-range effects.*

BACKGROUND Remind students that France had not developed parliamentarian government as had England. Grievances in France were voiced by many people for a long time without the government hearing them.

 1 **The French Revolution changed society and government.**

In the years that followed the American Revolution, many French people felt encouraged to seek far-reaching changes in their own nation. In 1789 tentative attempts to increase political representation suddenly gathered speed and led to a sweeping revolution that changed the face of France and eventually of all of Europe. Although some change seemed unavoidable, the extent and the violence of the French Revolution came as a surprise to almost everyone. "Never," wrote a 19th-century

1 **Lesson Plan**
Essential Learning Objective
Students will learn to state the causes, chronology, and results of the French Revolution.

1 **FOCUS AND MOTIVATE**

Establish a working definition of *revolution* as a big change that occurs in a relatively short period of time. Explain that most revolutions involving a change of government have a predictable structure. First, there is a problem (P); second, there is some kind of action (A) taken to correct the problem by changing the government; third, there is often a reaction (R) to the change led by people who think things have gone too far. Tell students that since this is the typical structure, or pattern, it is *PAR* for the course. With this little mnemonic, they can structure the events of the French Revolution.

2 | TEACH

- Individually or in pairs, ask students to investigate the structure of the French Revolution. Specifically, their task is to list on a sheet of paper: (1.) the problems that led to revolution; (2.) the various actions that were taken at different stages to correct the problem; (3.) the reactions of those people who felt things had gone too far. Lists might include: *Problems*— class division, inequality between classes, inequality within each class, government debt, unfair taxes. *Actions*—convening of the Estates General, Third Estate declaring itself a National Assembly, oath in the tennis court, storming of the Bastille, peasant revolt, Declaration of the Rights of Man, Reign of Terror. *Reactions*—Louis XVI's placing 20,000 troops in Paris, war waged against France by nervous European monarchies, guillotining of Robespierre, and moderation under the Directory. (What is most important is that students understand these three structural categories, not that they get all of the possible problems, actions, and reactions listed.)

French historian, "was any such event so inevitable yet so completely unforeseen."

Inequality in French society bred discontent.

French society before the revolution, which came to be known as the Old Regime, was in many ways still a feudal society. By law, each person belonged to one of three political classes, or "estates." The First Estate included the clergy, the Second Estate included the nobility, and the Third Estate included everyone else, from the wealthy middle class to the poor. A person's social status, political rights, and economic privileges all depended upon his or her estate. Resentment developed both between and within these estates.

The First Estate. All members of the Roman Catholic clergy, from the humblest monks and vil-

Le tems passé

lage priests to the wealthiest and most powerful archbishops belonged to the First Estate. Since the Church was very strong in France, the clergy had much influence. The bishoprics and archbishoprics were positions of wealth, power, and prestige open only to men of noble birth. This restriction led to resentment among members of the lower clergy, creating friction within the First Estate.

The lay public, those people of the Church not belonging to the clergy, also resented the upper levels of the Church hierarchy. Every year French citizens were required to pay 10 percent of their income to the Roman Catholic Church. Usually this money went to Paris or to Rome, for the building of ornate cathedrals, the commission of expensive works of art, and for the payment of the salaries of Church officials. Although some people were proud of the displays of Church wealth, many people never traveled beyond their own villages and only saw their money drain away.

The Second Estate. The Second Estate—the nobility—included many different levels of wealth and power, from immensely rich landowners to poor farmers who owned little more than a small plot of land and the noble titles before their names. As with the First Estate, the disparity of wealth among members of the Second Estate created tension. Everyone resented the upper level nobility, who were legally entitled to the highest posts in the government, the courts, the army and the Church.

Resentment also developed among the lower nobility. To make money, many of the poorest nobles would sell their titles to members of the Third Estate, who were willing to pay large sums to gain entrance to the Second Estate. As the lower nobles saw their privileges erode, they became increasingly angry at losing what little power and prestige their titles conferred.

This satirical cartoon from 1789 shows, with irony, the French estate system. The aged, overworked peasant, representing the Third Estate, had to carry the weight of both the First and Second estates, symbolized here by the clergy and the nobility.

With its origins in the Middle Ages, the Estates-General was a governing body with obscure traditions and unclear rules and procedures. When the Estates-General had last assembled in 1614, each of the three estates had met and voted separately. Then all three estates convened and a representative from each reported on the voting for his estate.

The Third Estate.

The Third Estate, which included 99 percent of the population, had the most serious internal divisions. At its top stood wealthy city-dwellers. This group—the **bourgeoisie**—included lawyers, doctors, merchants, and manufacturers. The poorest of the bourgeoisie were barely better off than their workers. The richest, however, rivaled the nobility in wealth and power.

Below the bourgeoisie in social standing were skilled artisans, household servants, and laborers. Many of these workers lived in unsanitary and overcrowded housing. Unemployment was very high, and periodic food shortages brought many in the cities to the brink of starvation. When living conditions were at their worst, these workers could become an angry and violent mob.

The largest part of the Third Estate, and 80 percent of the French population, was made up of peasants. This group was also, by far, the poorest and the most oppressed. Peasants were burdened by high rents and high taxes. In addition, they were forced to pay dues, in the form of money, crops, and free labor, to the nobles and clergymen who were still their feudal lords. Many lived in the barest and crudest of dwellings.

In a society set up to be unequal, almost no group was fully satisfied with its position. Growing discontent among the three estates was one factor leading to revolution in France. The government's financial difficulty was another.

Weak kings brought France to the brink of bankruptcy.

France's financial problems began with the excessive spending of the French kings in the late 1600s and early 1700s. Because of inequities in the tax system, the financial situation worsened.

Inequities in the tax system. Of all the inequalities in French society, the most glaring was in the tax system. By law, the First and Second estates were excused from most taxes, and many of the richest members of the Third Estate were able to purchase exemption from taxes. The heaviest burden fell on the poorest members of the Third Estate, who, of course, had the least money.

This tax system caused difficult financial problems for the French government. Only a real tax reform—making the clergy and the nobility subject to taxation—could have brought in enough revenue to cover the government's expenses. Unfortunately, after Louis XIV, France produced no king with the political skill to push through the needed reforms.

Fiscal failures of the kings. Louis XV, who reigned from 1715 to 1774, was a weak monarch who had little interest in affairs of state. He saw the unrest among his people, and he knew of the growing financial problems, but his attempts at reform were half-hearted.

Louis XV was succeeded by **Louis XVI**, his grandson, who was only 20 when he took the throne in 1774. Louis XVI tried to rule effectively, but he lacked the forceful personality and strong will needed to stand up to the powerful and privileged classes who opposed reform.

During Louis XVI's reign, the French monarchy rapidly approached bankruptcy. French aid to the American Revolution was very costly, and between 1763 and 1789, the government's public debt more than doubled. In the 1770s and early 1780s, the French government sought to solve its financial crisis by imposing taxes on the wealthy classes. This tactic failed, however, because the nobility insisted that all new taxes required the approval of the Estates-General, a legislative body that included representatives from each of the three estates in French society.

Concessions of Louis XVI. With the nobles' demand for a meeting of the Estates-General, Louis XVI had to make an unhappy choice: to see his monarchy go bankrupt or share his power with the Estates-General. The king chose to work with the Estates-General.

Since the Estates-General had last met in 1614, disputes had arisen about the voting procedure. At that time, each estate cast one vote. The Third Estate was consistently outvoted, since the First and Second estates tended to vote in opposition to the Third Estate. Many people thought that voting should be not by estate but by person. Louis XVI added to the general chaos by decreeing that as many delegates could be elected to the Third Estate as to the First and Second estates combined. This confusion over rules and procedures was not resolved by the time the Estates-General met in May, 1789.

• When students finish their lists, discuss the particulars. It might be helpful to draw a social-class pyramid showing the three estates, with the broad, thick base reflecting the fact that the Third Estate contained 99% of the French people. Be sure to point out the complicating fact that wealthy members of the Third Estate were much better off and often had more power than lower members of the First and Second estates.

GUIDED PRACTICE

To understand the structure of the French Revolution, it is helpful to construct a time line of key events. This can be done individually, in pairs, or as a class. Time lines should extend from 1780 to 1800.

The *Fall of the Bastille: 14 July 1789,* painted by Claude Choat, one of the attackers, offers a unique perspective on the storming of this mighty fortress.

The meeting of the Estates-General led to revolutionary changes.

The confusion over voting procedures led to a power struggle among the three groups of the Estates-General. The clergy and the nobility insisted that the voting be done by estate, as it had been in the past. The commoners, however, felt that the three estates should meet together and vote by person. The debate went on for weeks.

Finally, Louis XVI, worried that the Third Estate was gaining support from the poor members of the clergy and some of the enlightened nobility, ordered his soldiers to lock the Third Estate out of their usual place of meeting. The Third Estate thus met at an indoor tennis court and declared themselves to be a **National Assembly.**

The National Assembly. The members of the National Assembly all took an oath in which they swore not to separate until they had written a constitution for France. Because the new National Assembly had no standing under the law, this declaration to change the government was an act of revolution. Yet this was but a modest revolutionary beginning. The National Assembly sought not to overthrow the king but simply to gain for the middle classes a modest share of political power.

Meanwhile, the peasants and the workers suffered from an economic depression and a very bad harvest. Food was scarce, prices were high, and unemployment was widespread. Faced with economic and political crisis, Louis XVI felt himself to be losing control. In early July, 1789, he moved almost 20,000 soldiers into the Paris area in an attempt to intimidate the National Assembly. The crowds in the city began to look for weapons to defend the Assembly. Violence increased culminating in the storming of the Bastille.

The storming of the Bastille. The Bastille [ba-stēl'] was a fortress built in the 1300s to protect the city walls around Paris. It had come to be used as a prison for people the French government felt were politically dangerous. Most prisoners locked in the Bastille had no rights and could only be released by order of the king. Although only seven people were imprisoned in the Bastille in July, 1789, the Third Estate had long considered the fortress a symbol of political oppression. A rumor was circulating that the Bastille contained barrels of ammunition, which the king might decide to use against the National Assembly and the violent Parisian mobs.

On July 14, a crowd that included members of the local militia stormed the Bastille, violently kill-

BACKGROUND The meeting of the Estates-General at Versailles was made up of 300 nobles, 300 clergy, and 600 commons. The voting dispute centered on whether to cast votes by each member individually, thus giving the commons control, or by group, thus giving the clergy and nobles control.

494

ing the prison guards and administrators and capturing the munitions. The rioters then marched on the City Hall, murdered the mayor of Paris, and set up a new city government, led by members of the middle classes. The king, awakened and given this news, was said to have asked, "Is this a rebellion?" "No," his aide told him, "it is a revolution." Finally realizing the seriousness of the situation, Louis XVI ordered his troops out of Paris and accepted the new government.

The meeting of the National Assembly and the storming of the Bastille were among the first acts of the French Revolution. In the two weeks after the fall of the Bastille, a wave of violence spread throughout France. Peasants refused to pay taxes and burned some nobles' manors to the ground. The spread of the rebellion showed that the revolution was now truly national, consuming not only Paris but also France's rural heartland.

The National Assembly set up a constitutional monarchy.

Alarmed by the spreading disorder, the National Assembly took its most dramatic action on the night of August 4. As a concession to the continuing peasant violence, the French nobles and clergymen, most of whom had by now joined the National Assembly, gave up their feudal dues, political privileges, and tax exemptions. In that one night, France's centuries-old feudal system was permanently dismantled.

The National Assembly then started to create a new kind of French government, beginning with the **Declaration of the Rights of Man and of the Citizen**, passed on August 26, 1789. This document was based on the ideas of the Enlightenment about natural law. As you can read on pages 506–507, the Declaration of the Rights of Man and of the Citizen proclaimed "inalienable rights" to liberty, property, security and resistance to oppression. It declared equality before the law for all French men, along with freedom of speech, religion, and the press. These principles of liberty, equality, and natural rights, were incorporated into France's new constitution, which the National Assembly labored over for the next two years.

France's first constitution. The new constitution abolished the privileged orders of the Old Re-

gime, as the estate system had come to be known, and handed political power to the general body of the wealthy, regardless of title or birth. The poorest one-third of the male population and all women were not given the vote, and only wealthy property owners could be elected to France's new governing body, the Legislative Assembly. The king retained many of his powers, but his veto power was weakened. The government gained control of the clergy and took over all lands owned by the Catholic Church, a policy that was to turn the Church and many religious Catholics against the Revolution.

Louis XVI did not like the new constitution, but he had no choice but to accept it. Thus, in 1791 France became a constitutional monarchy. However, the new government lasted less than a year, chiefly because of war with other countries.

Foreign wars. The French Revolution alarmed the monarchs of Europe, who thought that the ideas of liberty, equality, and natural rights would spread. This, they feared, might lead to revolutions and to a collapse of their rule. Also, the émigrés, those French nobles and army officers who had left France in 1789, persuaded the kings of Austria and Prussia that it was their duty to help restore the French monarchy. As a result of their activities, in 1792 France's Legislative Assembly declared war on Austria and Prussia.

As war fever rose in France, suspicion of the king mounted. In June of 1791, Louis XVI had tried to flee across the border, and many people believed that he had planned to lead foreign armies into France to destroy the Revolution. Furious citizens denounced the king, the Assembly's moderation, and the army's ineffectiveness. Surrounded by angry radicals, in August, 1792, the Legislative Assembly suspended the monarchy, put the royal family in prison, and agreed to disband. They then appointed a provisional government to form a new government for France.

With this suspension of the first French constitution, the revolution became more radical. Hostile armies at the borders and political chaos at home put the city of Paris in a panic. In September, 1792, the provisional government responded by ordering that nearly 2,000 royalists be executed as enemies of France.

3 | ASSESS AND CLOSE

ASSESS

1. What was the first act of violence in the French Revolution? (the storming of the Bastille)
2. Who was Robespierre? (leader of the Reign of Terror)

OPTIONAL RETEACHING

Another way for students to grasp an overview of the French Revolution is to draw a gently curved continuum on the board. Beneath the curved line write the label "French Revolution Human Rights Continuum." Also label the left end "No Rights" and the right end "Full Rights." Ask students to place entries from the time line they previously constructed on the continuum. (Students may disagree over exact placement, but should reach a general agreement over relative placement.)

France became a republic.

Beginning in September, 1792, France was ruled by the National Constitutional Convention, usually called the Convention. Elected by universal male suffrage, the Convention declared France a republic. The new government put the former king on trial. In January, 1793, Louis XVI was sentenced to death on the guillotine [gil'ə tēn'], the dreadful machine on which so many people were beheaded during the Revolution.

A time of war. Meanwhile, the Convention declared that France had been "called" to liberate the human race from tyrants, and vowed "to overthrow all thrones." Huge French armies swarmed across the borders into southern Germany and the area that is now Belgium. By 1793 France was at war with almost all of Europe. However, the war did not go well for France. In addition, wartime shortages caused hardship for the entire country. Food was scarce, causing already high prices to soar. In western France religious peasants rebelled against the revolutionary government, which had passed laws diminishing the power of the Catholic Church.

In the midst of these crises, the Convention voted to arrest its most moderate leaders in June 1793. The extreme radicals then took charge, instituting a reign of terror.

The Reign of Terror. The radicals put a 12-member committee, the Committee of Public Safety, in charge of the government, with a young lawyer named **Maximilien de Robespierre** [rōbz'pyer] at its head. The Committee created a violent dictatorship, declaring that "terror is the order of the day." During this Reign of Terror, anyone suspected of opposing those in power was arrested. According to Robespierre, this harsh policy was necessary in order to save the revolution and the Republic from enemies at home and abroad.

Between August, 1793, and July, 1794, more than 2,500 persons were executed as enemies of France. The former queen, Marie Antoinette, was among the first sent to the guillotine. The moderate political leaders soon followed. However, even people not involved in politics were put to death if they were suspected of criticizing the Revolution.

Meanwhile, France's war against her neighbors raged on. The Committee began a national draft

The French artist David's portrait of Marie Antoinette on her way to the guillotine catches the profound humbling of France's queen.

and mobilized the country in the production of food, uniforms, weapons, and other supplies for the army. These programs were the first attempts in modern times to bring together all the resources of a nation for war. They were remarkably successful. By the spring of 1794, France had the largest army in Europe. In addition, unlike the armies of its opponents, the French army was made up of citizens with strong feelings of patriotism.

By summer, 1794, this citizen army won several important battles. The army was led by young officers who had risen from the lower ranks because of the flight of high-ranking officers at the beginning of the Revolution. With France no longer in immediate danger, most people felt that the harsh rule of the Committee of Public Safety no longer had a purpose. As Robespierre sought to continue the Terror, other members of the Convention joined together and sent him and 20 of his followers to the guillotine.

Having consumed nearly all of its own leaders, the Reign of Terror was over. The more moderate members of the bourgeoisie once again came to power. They wrote a new constitution and established a new ruling body called the Directory in October, 1795.

The Directory. The Directory was not royalist, but neither was it democratic. The new govern-

BACKGROUND The guillotine is named for Joseph I. Guillotin (1738–1814), a French physician and advocate of its use.

496

BACKGROUND Robespierre was arrested by opponents within the Convention on July 27. He escaped but was seized later that day, summarily tried, and guillotined on July 28.

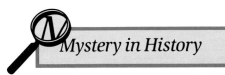

Mystery in History

WHAT IS THE REAL MEANING OF "LITTLE RED RIDING HOOD"?

Can "Little Red Riding Hood" tell us anything about the French Revolution? It can, in the opinion of Robert Darnton, a historian who believes he has established links between "Little Red Riding Hood" and other stories of 18th-century France and the world view of the French peasants at that time. The point is significant because peasants in the region known as the Vendée revolted against the revolutionary government in 1793–1796, the very government that was attempting to speak for the poor and downtrodden. Robespierre and other revolutionary leaders used the threat from the Vendée to justify their brutal Reign of Terror.

Because few peasants knew how to read or write, little direct evidence of their feelings exists. However, the peasants did tell the Mother Goose stories, and Darnton believes that the stories provide "points of entry" into 18th-century peasant thought and life.

"Little Red Riding Hood" is one example. In the French version, after the wolf killed Little Red Riding Hood's grandmother, he "poured her blood into a bottle, and sliced her flesh onto a platter. Then he got into her nightclothes and waited in bed."

When Red Riding Hood arrived at her grandmother's house, the wolf, in disguise, offered her this "meat and wine." After Little Red Riding Hood had eaten, she remarked,

"Oh, grandmother! What long nails you have!"

"It's for scratching myself better, my dear."

"Oh, grandmother! What big teeth you have!"

"It's for eating you better, my dear." And he ate her. So the story ends.

In Darnton's opinion, this grim tale shows that the peasants viewed 18th-century France as a world of nightmarish irrationality. The wolf reminded them of the Vendée nobility, who taxed the poor, driving them from the land. Thousands of ragged, starving people wandered the roads looking for work or something to eat. In some areas almost half the population died before the age of 10. To people as desperate as this, survival must be bought through any means including trickery.

Darnton believes that this is the real message of "Little Red Riding Hood" —that the French peasants' world was mean and hard and made up of clever wolves and their gullible victims.

Some historians disagree with Darnton. Who can say, they ask, what literary works "really mean"? Can the stories of bygone days help us recover the past? Such questions remain, part of the mystery of history.

A Gustave Doré engraving captures the nightmarish quality of the French peasants' "Little Red Riding Hood."

Identify

Key Terms, People, and Places are defined on pages indicated in parentheses. Also see the Glossary and Biographical Dictionary. bourgeoisie (493), Louis XVI (493), National Assembly (494), Declaration of the Rights of Man and of the Citizen (495), Maximilien de Robespierre (496)

Main Ideas

1. A person's social status, political rights, civil liberties, and economic privileges depended upon his or her estate, with most of the advantage going to the higher levels of the First and Second estates.

2. The First and Second estates were not taxed, and the upper levels of the Third Estate could get out of paying taxes by paying a lump sum. Therefore, the government was financed by the poorer members of the Third Estate, who had the least ability to pay.

3. The Third Estate, locked out of its regular meeting place, declared a National Assembly, the first act of revolution. The storming of the Bastille and the establishment of a new Paris city government followed this important meeting. Violence spread throughout France.

4. Events led to the establishment of a republic, September, 1792.

5. France became a republic; the committee of Public Safety took charge of the government; moderates established the Directory.

Critical Thinking

Students should recognize that Siéyès' assertions imply that a majority of the citizenry constitute a nation, not the privileged classes. His statement also implies that he values democratic ideals.

ment's leaders believed that France should be "governed by its best citizens, who are found among the property-owning class." Consequently, the Directory was headed by a council of five men called directors, who were chosen by a two-house legislature. The universal male suffrage of 1793 was rejected, and the vote was given only to men who paid taxes. Women and poor men, who did not own property, were thus deprived of a voice in the new government.

Political power was in the hands of the upper middle classes and former nobles, who had been pardoned and returned from exile. Since the Directory excluded much of the population and all people who had extreme political views, its base of power was shaky from the start. Repeatedly, directors had to violate the constitution, by removing royalist or radical legislators who had been legally elected, in order to hold on to power. The new government became corrupt and inefficient and was unable either to solve the country's problems or to achieve national unity. The time was ripe for a strong leader to seize power.

Section 1 Review

Identify bourgeoisie, Louis XVI, National Assembly, Declaration of the Rights of Man and of the Citizen, Maximilien de Robespierre

Main Ideas

1. How did inequalities in the estate system breed discontent?
2. How did the unfairness of taxes cause France financial problems?
3. How did the meeting of the Estates-General lead to revolutionary changes in France?
4. How were the events in France between August, 1789, and August, 1792, important?
5. Describe the changes in the French government between the fall of 1792 and 1795.

Critical Thinking

Recognizing Values: Emmanuel Siéyès, a liberal priest and leader of the Third Estate wrote, "the Third [Estate] . . . includes everything that belongs to the nation; and everything not of the Third cannot be regarded as of the nation. What is the Third? Everything." What values do Emmanuel Siéyès' assertions imply? Do you agree or disagree with his statements or values? Explain.

2 Napoleon became ruler of France.

A strong, new leader for France appeared in the person of **Napoleon Bonaparte** [nə pō′lē ən bō′nə pärt]. He came from a family of the lesser nobility on the Mediterranean island of Corsica.

Napoleon rose to power.

Because he lacked an important name and high connections in the royal army, Napoleon Bonaparte would have had little hope of advancing into the higher ranks of the officer corps before the Revolution. However, his fortune changed with the coming of the revolution, and the doors to power opened before him.

Military career. As you have read, many nobles fled France at the beginning of the Revolution, among them a large portion of the army leadership. As the French Republic rapidly built the largest army in French history, a shortage of skilled and experienced field officers arose. During this leadership crisis, many officers from the lower ranks, were able to advance to unexpected heights. For example, Napoleon Bonaparte advanced from the position of lieutenant in the artillery to full-fledged general.

By 1797 Napoleon was put in charge of the French army in northern Italy. After several victories there, he crushed the Austrians, who controlled Italy at that time, and became a hero. After this triumph Napoleon thought of a bold plan to reduce England's domination of India by taking control of the British trade route across Egypt. According to plan, he landed his army in Egypt in 1798. However, the British fleet destroyed the French supply ships, cutting off the army.

Napoleon was forced to desert his army in Egypt and return to France. Always a very skilled politician, he concealed the full extent of the Egyptian disaster from the French public. At the same time, the tide was again turning against France on the European war front. Many people saw Napoleon, with his previous victory against Austria and his false news of conquest in Egypt, as France's savior. Indeed, he timed his arrival to coincide with France's hour of need, when foreign enemies again gathered at the borders.

The military was not the only arm of the French government that was in trouble. After four years under a corrupt and unstable political system, the French people were becoming increasingly unsatisfied with the Directory. Napoleon, a man of limitless ambition, quickly moved to seize power. In November, 1799, he led a conspiracy to overthrow the Directory.

Establishment of the dictatorship. Napoleon had a deep knowledge of history and law, as well as of military science. People were dazzled by his sharp mind and tricked by his cunning. Although Napoleon used many of the phrases of liberal government, he had every intention of becoming a dictator. Soon after seizing power, he held a referendum in which all French men could vote to approve or disapprove of the new regime.

The people accepted Napoleon's seizure of power by a vote of 3 million to 1,500. With the solid support of the French people, he then moved

The French artist David succeeded in capturing on canvas the tremendous pride of Napoleon, as he led his famous march across the Alps in 1800.

to deprive them of virtually all political rights. Although the new constitution did include an elected legislature, as First Consul, Napoleon held all the real power. Claiming to represent the interests of the entire nation, he savagely crushed all opposition. He limited free speech, and severely censored the press. Even without political liberty and representative government, most French people liked Napoleon. After years of chaos, defeat, and disorder, he offered order, stability, efficiency, and above all, military victory.

The crowning of the emperor. By 1804 Napoleon's popularity was so immense that he was able to change France's form of government. After only 12 years as a republic, France became an Empire. General Napoleon Bonaparte, First Consul of the French Republic, crowned himself Napoleon I, Emperor of the French. The Republic was dead. Once again, the French people overwhelmingly approved this change in a national referendum.

Napoleon made important reforms.

Napoleon ruled France for 15 years—five years as First Consul and ten as emperor. During his reign, he carried out several important reforms and significantly increased the power and efficiency of the central government.

In many ways Napoleon finished the work of the revolution. No privileges were allowed, and the tax system was reformed. Promotion within the government or army was based on proven ability and achievement. In addition, Napoleon made an agreement with the pope. In it Napoleon confirmed the government's control over the Catholic Church, and, at the same time, ensured the Church's safety after a decade of turmoil and repression. Freedom of religion for all people was also established. However, Napoleon's best known work was the modernization of French law. The **Code Napoleon** set forth the principle of equality of all citizens before the law. This work remains the basis of French law today and has been adopted by other countries around the world.

Napoleon made himself master of Europe.

Although he was appreciated as a reformer, Napoleon was above all a warrior. Of his 15 years of rule, he spent 14 of those years at war. Driven by

Essential Learning Objectives

Students will learn to:
- describe Napoleon's rise to power.
- judge the degree to which Napoleon carried forward the French Revolution.

1 FOCUS AND MOTIVATE

Write the names of these three islands on the board: Corsica, Elba, and St. Helena. Ask students what is significant about them. Locate these islands for students on a wall map. These are the islands where Napoleon Bonaparte—the most famous European of the 19th century—was born, was temporarily exiled, and died as an exile.

2 TEACH

- Review Napoleon's rise to power during the last years of the 18th century and the first years of the 19th century. Key dates mentioned in the text are 1797, 1798, 1799, and 1804. Ask students the significance of each. (In order: victory over Austria in Italy, self-proclaimed victory over Britain in Egypt, seizure of power and title of First Consul, crowning self Emperor of France)

- Emphasize that Napoleon controlled more than half of Europe. His problem was that he bit off more than he could chew. Ask students what bites proved too big. (Spain, Britain, and especially, Russia)

GUIDED PRACTICE

Individually or in pairs, ask students to use their texts to evaluate whether or not Napoleon carried forward the reforms of the French Revolution. Have them work with two wide columns headed "Evidence that Napoleon extended the French Revolution" and "Evidence that Napoleon curtailed the French Revolution." Ask students to record evidence in both columns numbering each entry and documenting each entry with the page number on which it was found. (In the "extended" column answers may include: (1) Napoleon let people vote on his first seizure of power; (2) a referendum was held on Napoleon's self-coronation as Emperor. In addition, Napoleon (3) reformed tax system; (4) promoted by ability; (5) ended noble privilege; (6) modernized and equalized law for all people under Code Napoleon; (7) established freedom of religion, (8) abolished serfdom; (9) ended feudalism. In the "curtailed" column answers can include: (1) crowned self Emperor; (2) limited speech and censored press; (3) waged war to rule all of Europe.) Discuss the evidence. Did Napoleon carry the French Revolution forward?

Also for guided practice:

 Overhead Transparency 54

his ambition to rule all of Europe, he nearly succeeded. However, this obsession would eventually lead to his destruction.

Victory over Austria and Russia. When war broke out in 1803, Napoleon welcomed it as an opportunity. By 1805 a group of countries that included Britain, Austria, and Russia had allied against France. Of these countries, Napoleon defeated Austria and Russia with amazing speed.

In defeat, the Austrians were forced to give up control of the hundreds of German states that made up the Holy Roman Empire. Napoleon then dissolved the Holy Roman Empire, creating in its place the **Confederation of the Rhine**. This group of 38 states was placed under Napoleon's "protection," which really meant that they were under his domination. Nevertheless, in the Confederation and in every other country he conquered or dominated, Napoleon sought to impose modernizing reforms. His acts included the establishment of religious freedom, the abolition of serfdom and noble privilege, and the institution of the Napoleonic Code of law.

Defeat by Britain. After his victory over Austria and Russia, Napoleon next dreamed of invading Britain and conquering its empire. However, the British navy stubbornly resisted. In October, 1805, Lord Horatio Nelson, the British admiral who had defeated Napoleon in the Egyptian campaign of 1798, humiliated the combined French and Spanish fleets in the battle of Trafalgar. That victory proved British naval superiority and ensured Britain's safety from invasion.

From 1806 to 1812, Napoleon controlled most of the European continent, either directly, through puppet governments, or by imposing harsh and demeaning peace treaties. Since he could not defeat the British navy, he decided to try to wreck the country with economic warfare.

Economic warfare. In 1806 Napoleon instituted an economic boycott, closing all European markets to British goods. Even Russia, under threat of a French invasion, agreed to follow the plan. However, Napoleon's policy failed, partly because the British developed other markets, such as Latin America, and partly because successful smuggling operations were carried out all along the coast of western Europe.

One European country in particular, Portugal, refused to close its ports to British goods, and smuggling was rampant through Portugal's neighbor, Spain. To control the Iberian peninsula, Napoleon invaded Portugal, placed his brother Joseph on the Spanish throne, and stationed a large French army in Spain. The Spanish people fought back. Napoleon referred to the rebellion of the Spaniards as the "Spanish ulcer." It was the beginning of the downfall of his empire.

European powers joined forces to defeat Napoleon.

People in the other countries Napoleon had conquered were inspired by Spain's example. They were angered by Napoleon's demands for money and soldiers and resented the shortages of goods caused by his economic blockade. Most important, there was an upswelling of patriotic feeling that incited people to turn against the French. However, rebellion might never have broken out if Napoleon had not exposed his fatal weaknesses by trying to conquer Russia.

War with Russia. The loss of trade with Britain caused serious economic problems in Russia. Thus, in 1810 Tsar Alexander I revoked his agreement with Napoleon and resumed trade with the British. Napoleon, angry that Russia had blocked his plans to dominate all of continental Europe, decided that Russia must be crushed. He gathered a huge army of more than 500,000 men, many of whom came from countries conquered by France, and invaded Russia in the summer of 1812. Napoleon won several battles and advanced far into the Russian interior, but he could not destroy the Russian army. Even worse for Napoleon, many Russian landowners burned their crops as they fled. This "scorched earth" policy made it difficult for Napoleon to feed his soldiers.

In September, 1812, Napoleon and his armies reached Moscow, already evacuated by the Russians. The next night, a mysterious fire broke out and destroyed most of the city. With Moscow destroyed and winter approaching, Napoleon had neither adequate food or shelter for his vast armies. Within a few weeks, Napoleon ordered a retreat from the heartland of Russia. This was both a military defeat and a political humiliation. Dur-

Napoleon's Empire, 1810

Legend:
- Napoleon's Empire
- Subject to Napoleon
- Allied to Napoleon
- x Battles

MAP STUDY This map uses colors to symbolize political alliances in Europe. What color indicates the area that made up Napoleon's empire? What major Mediterranean island is shown as being a part of this empire? What areas on the map are allied to Napoleon?

ing the long march westward, the cruel Russian winter set in, and many soldiers died.

Napoleon's downfall. The Russian disaster was the final blow to Napoleon's power. Inspired by the Spanish and Russian examples, enemies struck from all directions, and all of Napoleon's conquered nations and unhappy allies turned against him. Napoleon's empire finally crumbled in 1814. Napoleon himself was banished to the island of Elba, which lay off the coast of Italy. He soon escaped, returned to France, and for 100 days claimed the role of emperor again. For a second time, the other countries of Europe united against Napoleon and defeated him in a battle at the Bel-

gian village of **Waterloo** in 1815. This time they then sent him to the distant and isolated South Atlantic island of St. Helena.

Leaders in Europe did not forget Napoleon or the many years of bloodshed that he had caused. A German noble wrote to Napoleon's jailer:

> Over and over again I have thought of that vast and solitary ocean and that interesting rock on which you are preserving the peace of Europe. Our safety depends on your watchfulness and your strength of character; once you relax your tight guard over the most cunning scoundrel in the world . . . our tranquility will be jeopardized and the honest people of Europe will be abandoned to their former fears.

ANSWER TO MAP STUDY yellow; Corsica; Norway and Denmark, Prussia, and the Austrian Empire

ASSESS

What was the Code Napoleon? (a legal work that made all French citizens equal before the law)

OPTIONAL RETEACHING

Write the following on the board: "Spanish ulcer," Waterloo, Russian winter, Trafalgar. Have students write sentences describing how each contributed to the defeat of Napoleon.

OPTIONAL ENRICHMENT

1. In late June, 1812, Napoleon Bonaparte's army of more than 500,000 men entered Russia. Six months later that same army had shrunk to a fighting force of 30,000. Have interested students research the Russian campaign to find out what went wrong. (average)

2. Two weeks after the defeat of the French army at Waterloo, Napoleon tried to sail to the United States. Napoleon was prevented from doing so by the British who then sent him into exile on St. Helena in the south Atlantic. Have interested students investigate the circumstances of the six years Napoleon spent on the island before his death. (challenging)

INDEPENDENT PRACTICE/ HOMEWORK

Assign the Section Review, Activities page 157, or Workbook page 105.

CLOSURE

Napoleon had let his ambition to become ruler of Europe override his interest in social reform. The result was his exile, and the return of monarchy to much of Europe.

Identify

Key Terms, People, and Places are defined on pages indicated in parentheses. Also see the Glossary and Biographical Dictionary. Napoleon Bonaparte (498), Code Napoleon (499), Confederation of the Rhine (500), Waterloo (501)

Main Ideas

1. Napoleon rose quickly through the military, because many royalist officers had fled at the start of the French Revolution. Napoleon overthrew the Directory and became a virtual dictator and then emperor.
2. He increased the power and efficiency of France's government. He also granted freedom of religion and created the Code Napoleon.
3. He was defeated in battle by Britain but planned an economic boycott to try to ruin that nation.
4. Positive effects included the abolition of feudalism and serfdom, the Napoleonic Code, freedom of religion, and tax reform.

Critical Thinking

peasants who gained equality under the law; the bourgeoisie who would have supported the increase in opportunity based upon achievement; peasants and middle class workers who benefited from the tax reforms

3 Lesson Plan

Essential Learning Objectives

Students will learn to:
- explain the connection between revolutions in the United States, France, and Latin America.
- evaluate how revolutionary Latin American revolutions were.

Napoleon's guards did their jobs, however, and Napoleon never was able to escape and return to Europe. He died at St. Helena in 1821.

Napoleon's far-reaching influence. Napoleon was a monarch and a dictator, but he always claimed to be fighting in the name of the common people. His soldiers and officials brought many of the principles of the revolution to the other countries of Europe. Everywhere the French army was victorious, new constitutions were drawn up. Feudalism and serfdom were wiped out. The Napoleonic Codes, which stressed equality before the law, were put into effect. Religious freedom became the law, and taxes were reformed. Even after Napoleon's downfall, although conservative monarchs returned to power, many of Napoleon's reforms remained in effect.

Section 2 Review

Identify Napoleon Bonaparte, Code Napoleon, Confederation of the Rhine, Waterloo

Main Ideas
1. How was Napoleon able to rise to power?
2. What reforms did Napoleon make as ruler of France?
3. How did Napoleon aim to destroy the British?
4. What were some positive effects of Napoleon's rule in Europe?

Critical Thinking
Making Hypotheses: Describe the groups in France that might have supported Napoleon's reforms. Explain why Napoleon would have earned the support of these groups.

---

3 Latin American colonies became independent nations.

The age of democratic revolutions also affected the Latin American colonies. In the 300 years that Spain and Portugal had ruled in Latin America, a new civilization had arisen there. However, as you learned in Chapter 25, it was a civilization fraught with injustice.

Discontent grew among Latin Americans.

At the root of the injustices in Latin America were economic and social inequalities. These led to great discontent among some groups of colonists. Colonial rule put all power in the hands of the peninsulares, those Spanish-born officials. The younger generation of creoles, wealthy and well-educated, had heard about the political ideas of Locke, Voltaire, Rousseau, and other Enlightenment thinkers. Many of the creoles believed that colonial governments should be more efficient, that the power of the Church should be reduced, and that real political changes should take place. After the American and French revolutions, creole demands grew still louder.

In the 1780s, encouraged by the North American example, colonists rebelled in Peru, Colombia, Ecuador, and Venezuela. Unlike the North Americans who had the help of France, Latin Americans fought their battles alone. The only successful uprising in the 18th century happened in the French colony of Haiti. There, as you learned in Chapter 25, Pierre Dominique Toussaint L'Ouverture, a freed black slave, led a rebellion in 1791. Although the Haitians won their independence in 1804, colonial rule continued in the Spanish and Portuguese dominions.

Tito Salas' painting of Simón Bolívar illustrates the tremendous influence Napoleon's dashing style had on other military leaders. (Compare to page 499).

From the Archives

Bolívar's Letter from Jamaica

Simón Bolívar (1783–1830), later called "the Liberator," was a leader in a whole cluster of revolutionary movements that brought independence to Latin America. In September, 1815, while in exile in Jamaica, he wrote a letter encouraging people throughout Spain's New World possessions to unite against Spain in the struggle for freedom.

It is harder, Montesquieu has written, to release a nation from servitude than to enslave a free nation. This truth is proven by the annals of all times, which reveal that most free nations have been put under the yoke, but very few enslaved nations have recovered their liberty. Despite the convictions of history, South Americans have made efforts to obtain liberal, even perfect institutions, doubtless out of that instinct to aspire to the greatest possible happiness, which, common to all men, is bound to follow in civil societies founded on the principles of justice, liberty, and equality.

Successful revolts freed South America.

Only a spark from distant Europe was needed to ignite the revolutionary flame in Latin America. When Napoleon took control of the Spanish government in 1808, the colonists saw their chance to break away from Spain. Revolts broke out all over the empire. However, with the fall of Napoleon, King Ferdinand VII regained his crown in 1814, determined to bring back Spanish control. He refused to make any concessions to demands that the governments be liberalized. The colonial independence movement gained support under the leadership of **Simón Bolívar**, who came to be known as "the Liberator."

Leadership of "the Liberator." Also known as "the George Washington of South America," Símon Bolívar was a wealthy, charming man, edu-

cated in Enlightenment philosophy and passionately committed to the struggle for independence. Born in 1783, he fought for more than 20 years to win freedom for Venezuela, Colombia, Panama, Bolivia, and Ecuador.

Another hero, **José de San Martín,** was a creole soldier who led armies against the Spanish in Argentina and Chile. Quieter and less flamboyant than Bolívar, San Martín was no less committed to his cause. In 1821 he entered Lima and declared the independence of Peru. He then met with Bolívar to decide how best to drive the Spanish from the rest of Peru. Bolívar resented having to share the glory of victory with another leader. When it was clear that Bolívar and San Martín could not work together, San Martín quietly and unselfishly turned his army over to Bolívar and left for France, where he died in 1850. For a time, San Martín was a forgotten figure, but today he is considered a national hero of Argentina.

By 1825 Spain was defeated in all of its American colonies. Inspired by the United States of North America, Bolívar dreamed of a kind of united states for all of Spanish America. For a time this seemed possible, as most of northern South America was united into the Republic of Gran Colombia, under Bolívar's leadership.

The Monroe Doctrine. Many European leaders who came to power after Napoleon's defeat were worried by the success of the Latin American rebel leaders. They wanted the colonies to return to the control of Spain or other European powers. However, the United States and Britain were against European interference in Latin American affairs. In 1823 the U.S. President, James Monroe, issued the **Monroe Doctrine**, which stated that the United States would not allow any European country to take over the emerging nations in the Western Hemisphere. Europe accepted this warning, knowing that the British navy would back it up. The Monroe Doctrine made the young republics of Mexico and Central and South America secure in their independence.

Failure of governments in South America. Despite the security the Monroe Doctrine afforded Central and South America, the new governments faced many difficulties. Bolívar's united republic of South America did not last long. By 1830 this im-

FROM THE ARCHIVES "The Jamaica Letter" is translated in *The Liberator: Simon Bolívar,* edited by David Bushnell (New York: Knopf, 1970), pp. 11 ff. Point out to the class that Bolívar is quoting a French political philosopher. Why did Montesquieu and Bolívar believe it was harder to release a nation from slavery than to enslave a free nation? (Enslaved nations do not know how to be free, therefore it is more difficult for them to achieve and maintain their freedom.)

Write these dates on the chalkboard and ask students how they are related: 1776, 1789, 1803, 1821. (These are the dates when independence was declared in the United States, France, Haiti, and Peru and Mexico.) Explain that the focus today will be to determine just how much change independence brought to the people of Latin America.

- Ask for a volunteer to explain, as concretely as possible, how the American and French revolutions triggered independence movements in Latin America. (The chain of events: (1) American Revolution excited revolutionary fervor in France. (2) France had its own revolution. (3) The French Revolution gave Napoleon the chance to become Emperor. (4) Napoleon invaded Spain and Portugal. (5) Revolutionaries used Spanish and Portuguese preoccupation with Napoleon to declare independence in Latin America.)

- Have students study the map on page 504 to see the extent of the independence movement in Latin America.

- It is a fact that most of Latin America was independent from Spanish and Portuguese rule by the year 1830. A question remains: How revolutionary were these Latin American revolutions? To answer this question prepare a debate. Give pro and con teams about 15 minutes to develop evidence that supports their side of the argument. Arguments should be organized by categories—political, economic, social, and religious.

GUIDED PRACTICE

After each group has prepared its arguments, draw straws to determine which pro and which con groups will debate in front of the class. Ask for introductory summary statements and then allow free challenge and response. The class should make judgments in a concluding open session.

3 | ASSESS AND CLOSE

ASSESS

1. Who was the George Washington of South America? (Simón Bolívar)
2. Did Brazilian independence from Portugal end slavery in that country? If not, why not? (No, the wealthy plantation owners still supported slavery.)

OPTIONAL RETEACHING

Ask students to state the relationship between each of the following: Haiti/ L'Ouverture, Napoleon/Spain/Bolívar, Peru/San Martín, Gran Columbia/Bolívar, Monroe Doctrine/Latin American Independence, Santa Anna/Juárez/ Díaz.

OPTIONAL ENRICHMENT

1. Venezuela means "little Venice." Ask interested students to research the story behind the names of other Latin American countries. (average)
2. Also for enrichment:

 Source Reading 27B

INDEPENDENT PRACTICE/ HOMEWORK

Assign the Section Review, Activities page 158, or Workbook page 106.

CLOSURE

Revolutions in the United States and France helped bring independence to Latin America. However, for most of the people—mestizo, Indian, and black—independence did not carry with it revolutionary change.

---

mense republic was collapsing. "In Latin America," wrote the disappointed Bolívar, "treaties are pieces of paper; . . . elections are combats; liberty is anarchy; and life is a torment."

One reason for South America's continual internal problems was that the creoles who had fought for the independence of South America were more interested in grabbing power for themselves than in making any real changes in the social or political systems. Although some creoles tried to institute representative governments, none attempted to create democracies that would address the needs of the entire population. Four-fifths of the people were poor, uneducated Indians, blacks and mestizos who were allowed almost no political power by the creoles and peninsulares.

Not long after new governments were established, the legislatures in many of the young republics collapsed. Military leaders then seized power with armed gangs. Thus, very few Latin American republics were able to maintain stable democratic governments during the 19th century.

Mexico fought for its independence.

Mexico fought long and hard for independence. The first leaders of the independence movement were poor priests who led Indians and mestizos in revolt against the harsh Spanish rule. Late on September 15, 1810, **Miguel Hidalgo** [ē däl′gō], a creole priest, launched the Mexican rebellion in a church in the town of Dolores. Here he read the *Grito de Dolores* (Cry of Dolores), in which he demanded independence from Spanish rule. Today, Mexicans celebrate September 16 as Independence Day. After Hidalgo's eventual capture and execution by the Spanish in 1811, Father José Morelos took charge. However, he too, soon became a martyr of the revolution. Nevertheless, the creoles took up the fight, and in 1821 Mexico gained its independence.

What's in a Name

 VENEZUELA *Venezuela* is Spanish for "little Venice." Venice, Italy, was first built on posts in a swamp. When Europeans first came to Venezuela, they found there an Indian village built on posts over the water.

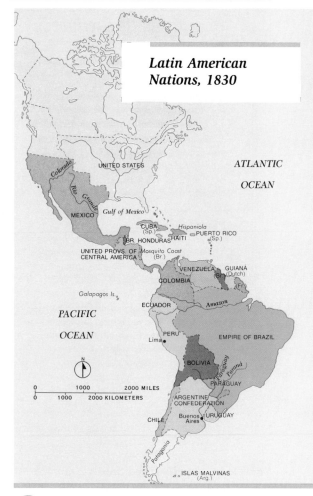

Latin American Nations, 1830

MAP STUDY The map above shows Latin America as it was in 1830. What was the largest nation in South America at that time?

In the years that followed, many people fought to rule Mexico. For many years, conservative creoles and military leaders maintained control. In 1834, however, Antonio López de Santa Anna declared himself dictator. While he ruled, Mexico lost half its land to the United States in the Mexican War (1846–1848). Santa Anna, a corrupt and pompous military man, was overthrown soon after this national humiliation.

BACKGROUND In 1836, Texas rose up in revolt and became independent of Mexico. In 1845, Texas was annexed to the United States, and this became a major cause of the Mexican War.

Mexicans who wanted reforms grew strong during the 1850s, and in 1861 their leader, Benito Juárez [hwär'es], an Indian, became president. He set out to create a more democratic republic. After Juárez died in 1872, Porfirio Díaz, a mestizo army general established a dictatorship. The dictatorship of Díaz, which lasted until 1911, brought order and industry to Mexico. However, liberal reforms were reversed, and the country was exploited by foreign investors.

Brazil gained its independence peacefully.

When Napoleon's troops entered Portugal in 1807, the Portuguese royal family fled to Brazil. Soon afterward the King João [zhwaù] VI made Brazil a self-governing dominion. When he returned to Portugal in 1821, his son Dom Pedro, stayed to rule Brazil. Dom Pedro declared the country an independent constitutional monarchy and was crowned emperor.

For many years Brazil was the most stable state in Latin America. Yet much inequality existed, including the clearest inequality—slavery. When the slaves were finally freed in 1888, the wealthy sugar plantation owners rebelled, aided by a number of conservative army officers. Although they could not bring back slavery, the rebels forced the emperor to step down. Then they set up a federal republic, which eventually came to be dominated by the army.

Section 3 Review

Identify Simón Bolívar, José de San Martín, Monroe Doctrine, Miguel Hidalgo

Main Ideas
1. What were the major causes of the Latin American revolutions?
2. What problem did the newly independent governments face?
3. What group of people led Mexico in its fight for independence?
4. Describe Brazil's rise to independence.

Critical Thinking
Analyzing Comparisons: Why do you think people compared Simón Bolívar with George Washington? Do you think this is a valid comparison? Why or why not?

 4 *The American and French revolutions had long-range effects.*

By the time the Spanish and Portuguese empires in the New World were destroyed, the age of democratic revolutions was coming to an end. Yet the revolutions of the 17th to 19th centuries in Britain, France, North America, and Latin America had long-lasting influences on Western culture. They led to permanent changes in the political and social structures of Europe and the Americas.

The democratic revolutions brought out new political issues.

Although France's first representative body, the Legislative Assembly, had members with widely different opinions, its members were divided into two main groups. The more conservative faction sat on the right side of the Assembly. This group generally supported the new constitution but felt that revolutionary changes had gone far enough. Across the aisle from the conservatives, on the left side of the Assembly chamber sat the more liberal faction. These members believed that the new French government should become more democratic, continuing revolutionary changes. As you have read, power bounced back and forth throughout the revolutionary period.

Ever since the French Revolution, the system of labeling political groups as belonging either to "the Right" or to "the Left" has been adopted throughout the world. These labels mean different things in every country and in every time period, but many of the basic political issues that divided the two sides were first set forth during the 18th-century revolutions. The **Right** represents conservatism, a belief that political and social structures work well the way they are and should generally be left alone. The **Left** usually represents political and social change, although the nature of the changes sought by the Left varies from country to country.

Another legacy of the democratic revolutions of North America and France is the belief that people have a right to rebel against an unfair government. When a government oppresses its people, said

Answers to Section 3 Review

Identify
Key Terms, People, and Places are defined on pages indicated in parentheses. Also see the Glossary and Biographical Dictionary.
Simón Bolívar (503), José de San Martín (503), Monroe Doctrine (503), Father Miguel Hidalgo (504)

Main Ideas
1. severe inequality within the Latin American class structure; economic inequalities
2. rebellion and the inability to maintain stable governments
3. At first leaders were poor priests; later, creoles
4. After Napoleon entered Portugal in 1807, the Portuguese royal family fled to Brazil. King João VI made Brazil self-governing and his son made the country an independent consitutional monarchy in 1821.

Critical Thinking
Yes, both started as military leaders in fights for independence and then became influential in government.

4 *Lesson Plan*

Essential Learning Objectives
Students will learn to:
- Describe the legacy of the American and French Revolutions.
- explain why *equality* and *liberty* have different meanings to different people.

1 FOCUS AND MOTIVATE

Write the word *equality* on the board. Ask students if they believe in equality for all people. As they think about it, students will see there is a definitional problem—equality of what? Opportunity? Treatment? Reward? And pushing it further, what exactly does *equal opportunity* mean?

Explain that the purpose of today's lesson is to look at the product, or legacy, of the American and French revolutions and investigate some of the problems that emerge with words such as *equality* and *liberty*. Have a volunteer write the legacy on the board as you uncover it with the class. Explain that the "Right" and "Left" political labeling that resulted from the revolution in France is part of the legacy. What is the next legacy students can find? In order, something approximating this list should emerge: Right and Left labeling; the right to rebel against an unjust government; the right of self-determination; concept of being citizens—not just subjects; feelings of patriotism; natural rights such as life, liberty, property ownership, and the pursuit of happiness; democratic practices such as elections and the right to vote (for males only); representative government; politically independent judges; equality before the law.

GUIDED PRACTICE

Write two questions on the board. (1.) Do you believe in equality? If so, what kind: equal opportunity? equal treatment? equal reward? (2.) Do you believe in liberty? If so, what limits, if any, would you place on it? First have students discuss the questions in groups. Then open the topics for full class discussion.

Foundations of Democracy

The following selections are excerpts from three of the most influential documents of our democratic tradition. The three documents are the English Bill of Rights, the U.S. Declaration of Independence, and the French Declaration of the Rights of Man and of the Citizen.

The English Bill of Rights (1689)

The Lords Spiritual and Temporal and Commons pursuant to their respective letters and elections, being now assembled in a full and free representative of this nation, . . . do . . . for the vindicating and asserting their ancient rights and liberties, declare

That the pretended power of suspending of laws or the execution of laws by regal authority without consent of Parliament is illegal.

That the pretended power of dispensing with laws or the execution of laws by regal authority, as it hath been assumed and exercised of late, is illegal. . . .

That levying money for or to the use of the crown by pretense of prerogative without grant of Parliament for longer time or in other manner than the same is or shall be granted is illegal.

That it is the right of the subjects to petition the king, and all commitments and prosecutions for such petitioning are illegal.

That the raising and keeping a standing army within the kingdom in time of peace unless it be with consent of Parliament is against law. . . .

That election of . . . Parliament ought to be free.

That the freedom of speech and debates or proceedings in Parliament ought not to be impeached or questioned in any court or place out of Parliament.

That excessive bail ought not to be required, nor excessive fines imposed, nor cruel and unusual punishments inflicted. . . .

And that for redress of all grievances and for the amending, strengthening, and preserving of the laws, Parliaments ought to be held frequently.

And they do claim, demand, and insist upon, all and singular, the premises as their undoubted rights and liberties and that no declarations, judgments, doings, or proceedings to the prejudice of the people in any of the said premises ought in any wise to be drawn hereafter into consequence or example.

The U.S. Declaration of Independence (1776)

When in the Course of human events, it becomes necessary for one people to dissolve the political bands which have connected them with another, and to assume among the Powers of the earth, the separate and equal station to which the Laws of Nature and of Nature's God entitle them, a decent respect to the opinions of mankind requires that they should declare the causes which impel them to the separation.

We hold these truths to be self-evident, that all men are created equal, that they are endowed by their Creator with certain inalienable Rights, that among these are Life, Liberty and the pursuit of Happiness. That to secure these rights, Governments are instituted among Men, deriving their just powers from the consent of the governed, That whenever any form of Government becomes destructive of these ends, it is the Right of the People to alter or to abolish it, and to institute new Government, laying its foundation on such principles and organizing its powers in such form, as to them shall seem most likely to effect their Safety and Happiness. Prudence, indeed, will dictate that Governments long established should not be changed for light and transient causes; and accordingly all experience hath shown, that mankind are more disposed to suffer, while evils are sufferable, than to right themselves by abolishing the forms to which they are accustomed. But when a long train of abuses and usurpations, pursuing invariably the same Object evinces a design to reduce them under absolute Despotism, it is their right, it is their duty, to throw off such Government, and to provide new Guards for their future security. Such has been the patient sufferance of these Colonies; and such is now the necessity which constrains them to alter their former Systems of Government. . . .

WE, THEREFORE, THE REPRESENTATIVES OF THE UNITED STATES OF AMERICA, in General Congress, Assembled, appealing to the Supreme Judge of the world for the rectitude of our intentions, do, in the Name, and by the authority of the good People of these Colonies, solemnly publish and declare, That these United Colonies are, and of Right ought to be FREE AND INDEPENDENT STATES; that they are Absolved from all Allegiance to the British Crown, and that all political connection between them and the State of Great Britain, is and ought to be totally dissolved. . . . And for the support of this Declaration, with a firm reliance on the protection of Divine Providence, we mutually pledge to each other our Lives, our Fortunes and our sacred Honor.

The Declaration of the Rights of Man and of the Citizen (1789)

The representatives of the people of France, formed into a National Assembly, considering that ignorance, neglect, or contempt of human rights, are the sole causes of public misfortunes and corruptions of Government, have resolved to set forth in a solemn declaration, these natural, imprescriptible, and inalienable rights: that this declaration being constantly present to the minds of the members of the body social, they may be for ever kept attentive to their rights and their duties; that the acts of the legislative and executive powers of government, being capable of being every moment compared with the end of political institutions, may be more respected; and also, that the future claims of the citizens, being directed by simple and incontestable principles, may always tend to the maintenance of the Constitution, and the general happiness.

For these reasons, the National Assembly doth recognize and declare, in the presence of the Supreme Being, and with the hope of his blessing and favour, the following *sacred* rights of men and of citizens:

I. Men are born, and always continue, free and equal in respect of their rights. Civil distinction, therefore, can be founded only on public utility.

II. The end of all political associations, is the preservation of the natural and imprescriptible rights of man; and these rights are liberty, property, security, and resistance of oppression.

III. The nation is essentially the source of all sovereignty; nor can any individual, or any body of men, be entitled to any authority which is not expressly derived from it.

IV. Political liberty consists in the power of doing whatever does not injure another. The exercise of the natural rights of every man, has no other limits than those which are necessary to secure to every *other* man the free exercise of the same rights; and these limits are determinable only by law.

V. The law ought to prohibit only actions hurtful to society. What is not prohibited by the law, should not be hindered; nor should any one be compelled to that which the law does not require.

VI. The law is an expression of the will of the community. All citizens have a right to concur, either personally, or by their representatives, in its formation. It should be the same to all, whether it protects or punishes; and all being equal in its sight, are equally eligible to all honours, places, and employments, according to their different abilities, without any other distinction than that created by their virtues and talents.

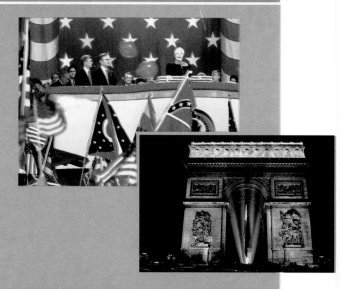

VII. No man should be accused, arrested, or held in confinement, except in cases determined by the law, and according to the forms which it has prescribed. . . .

VIII. The law ought to impose no other penalties but such as are absolutely and evidently necessary; and no one ought to be punished, but in virtue of a law promulgated before the offense, and legally applied.

IX. Every man being presumed innocent till he has been convicted, whenever his detention becomes indispensable, all rigour to him, more than is necessary to secure his person, ought to be provided against by the law.

X. No man ought to be molested on account of his opinions, not even on account of his *religious* opinions, provided his avowal of them does not disturb the public order established by the law.

XI. The unrestrained communication of thoughts and opinions being one of the most precious rights of man, every citizen may speak, write, and publish freely, provided he is responsible for the abuse of this liberty, in cases determined by the law. . . .

XVI. Every community in which a separation of powers and a security of rights is not provided for, wants a constitution.

XVII. The right to property being inviolable and sacred, no one ought to be deprived of it, except in cases of evident public necessity, legally ascertained, and on condition of a previous just indemnity.

3 ASSESS AND CLOSE

ASSESS

1. What is the meaning of the word "legacy"? (something handed down from those who went before)
2. Explain why "equality" is a controversial term. (because the kind of equality is arguable)

OPTIONAL RETEACHING

On a scale of one to four, have students judge the extent to which the United States today delivers on each of the following: (1) equal treatment before the law; (2) equal opportunity to make something of one's self in life; (3) equal reward for equally important work. Discuss students' responses.

Students also may be assigned Activities reteaching page 160.

OPTIONAL ENRICHMENT

1. Using the same scale and questions as above, ask interested students to poll fellow students, teachers, and family. Tally the results and compare to class responses. (average)
2. Do the same as above but include an "Anonymous Respondent Information Sheet" that asks poll-takers to identify their race, sex, religion, and age bracket. Tally results to see if responses differ by descriptive categories. (challenging)

Students also may be assigned Activities enrichment page 161.

INDEPENDENT PRACTICE/ HOMEWORK

Assign the Section Review, the Chapter Review items, Activities page 159, or Workbook page 107.

The legacy of the American and French revolutions is rich. These revolutions reshaped the Western world and seem still to have the momentum to continue that reshaping in other parts of the world for many years to come.

Answers to Section 4 Review

Identify
Key Terms, People, and Places are defined on pages indicated in parentheses. Also see the Glossary and Biographical Dictionary.
the Right (505), the Left (505)

Main Ideas
1. The terms "Right" and "Left" originated during the meetings of France's first Legislative Assembly.
2. The American Revolution spread the idea that each people had a right to form an independent nation. The French Revolution led to further nationalism.
3. New laws gave people more individual and political rights. Even in countries ruled by dictators, there was an effort to give the appearance of representative governments.

Critical Thinking
Students may say that the French and American revolutions did not result in full democracy because women, black Americans, and the landless poor were not granted the vote.

America's Declaration of Independence, "it is the right of the people to alter or to abolish it." France's Declaration of the Rights of Man and of the Citizen also stated that the right to resist against tyranny was a basic human right. People around the world have followed this revolutionary tradition, begun more than two centuries ago.

The revolutions led to the rise of modern nationalism.

Both the American and French revolutions contributed to the growth of modern nationalism. For example, the creation of the United States strengthened the idea that each people had a right to be an independent nation, treated as an equal by other nations. As you have seen, this idea was taken up quickly by Latin Americans. In America and in France, the revolutions also made people see themselves as members of a nation, as citizens, instead of just subjects of a king.

This shifting identity led to the growth of patriotic sentiments. France, during the Revolution, was consumed by an almost fanatical patriotism. It became a nation at arms, as almost all of the people's energy and the country's resources were directed toward the war effort. The Napoleonic wars brought a rise in patriotic feelings in most other European countries as well. People conquered by French armies began to feel that they were members of nations that had been humiliated. Many rulers, seeing the successes of France's huge national army, encouraged patriotism in the hope that it would help to strengthen their armies. These new feelings of nationalism were important causes of Napoleon's downfall.

The revolutions advanced individual rights and representative governments.

In transforming people from subjects to citizens, the democratic revolutions gave people new expectations of their governments. Both the American and French revolutions were based largely on ideas of the Enlightenment about natural laws—constant and unchanging rules that were said to govern the acts of individuals and of societies. Enlightenment thinkers had believed that government would be more just and more efficient if leaders would follow these natural laws.

The most important such laws concerned natural rights. In America and France, revolutionary leaders claimed that all people had the right to life, liberty, property, the pursuit of happiness. No government, they said, should have the power to take away these rights from any individual. Therefore, the rights of the citizens and the limitations on governments needed to be spelled out in a written constitution for all to see. A strong belief in the importance of written constitutions has been one of the enduring legacies of the American and French revolutions.

Revolutionary leaders also claimed that citizens naturally have a right to participate in their own government. Democratic institutions, such as elections, universal male suffrage, representative legislatures, and independent judges, which were adopted in America and France after the revolutions, helped citizens exercise their rights to participate in government.

Civil and political rights were granted slowly in most other countries. After the age of democratic revolutions, even dictators and monarchs had to pretend to respect the ideals of liberty, equality and self-government. Often they set up political structures, such as written constitutions, elections, and legislative assemblies, which gave their governments the appearance of being democratic. However, these structures were only a facade behind which lay an edifice of absolutism.

Section 4 Review

Identify the Right, the Left
Main Ideas
1. What were some of the political terms that originated during the age of revolutions?
2. How did American and French revolutions give rise to modern nationalism?
3. Explain how the revolutions advanced the causes of individual rights and representative governments.

Critical Thinking
Recognizing Values: To most people today, democracy promotes the rights of all people. Given this definition, do you think the French or the American revolutions resulted in full democracy? Provide evidence from the text and from your own experience.

The Influence of the U.S. Constitution

We the People of the United States, in Order to form a more perfect Union, establish Justice, insure domestic Tranquility, provide for the common defense, promote the general Welfare, and secure the Blessings of Liberty to ourselves and our Posterity, do ordain and establish this Constitution for the United States of America.

With these words, the framers of the U.S. Constitution outlined their ideas about the responsibilities of government. They agreed with a philosophy first put forth during the Enlightenment, that a government owed its existence to an implied compact between the governing and the governed. By writing the Constitution, they attempted to spell out the terms of this contract.

The framers of the U.S. Constitution were overwhelmingly successful in presenting acceptable and workable terms for their new government. At its 200th aniversary, in 1987, this document was the oldest surviving written constitution in the world. The writing of the Constitution of the United States inspired the French, who several years later revolutionized their government by adopting a written constitution. In the 1800s emerging Latin American nations also adopted constitutions similar to that of the United States. Since then the U.S. Constitution has inspired many other nations to define the powers of government by a constitution.

The Constitution divided power among the branches of government. Shortly after the Constitution was adopted, the Bill of Rights was added to delineate the rights of citizens. In both of these areas—dividing governmental power and guaranteeing individual rights—the U.S. Constitution has been a model for many other countries, setting standards for fair, just, and practical government throughout the world.

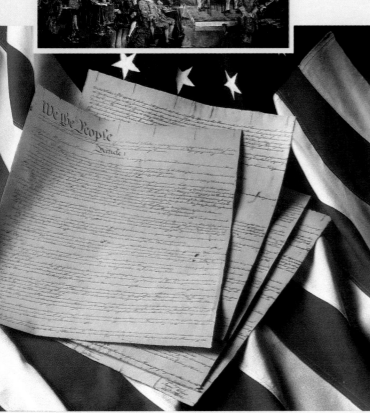

Delegates to the Constitutional Convention in 1787 unanimously selected George Washington to preside (top left). Together, they created the U.S. Constitution (left), "the supreme law of the land."

Read aloud the Bill of Rights (the first ten amendments to the Constitution) which was added in 1791. Encourage students to give opinions as to which of the rights mentioned are most important. (Students might mention the First Amendment freedoms, the right to bear arms to defend the State, freedom from unreasonable searches or seizures, the protections guaranteed in the Fifth Amendment for people accused of crimes, the right of trial by jury, and protection from excessive bail.)

The framers of the U.S. Constitution got many of their ideas from the Magna Carta and from the English Bill of Rights of 1689. You may wish to have students compare the U.S. Constitution to the English Bill of Rights and discuss what the two documents have in common.

CHAPTER 27 REVIEW

Section Summaries

Section 1
The French Revolution changed society and government.
In 18th-century France, anger grew over the inequalities of the class system and the unfair tax system. A meeting of the Estates-General in 1789 resulted in the adoption of a constitutional monarchy. However, foreign war led to a more radical government, the killing of the king, and a reign of terror in France.

Section 2
Napoleon became ruler of France.
A weak French government allowed Napoleon Bonaparte to take power—first as a dictator and, then, as emperor of France. He brought stability to the country and his military victories gave him control of most of Europe. By 1814, however, the people of Europe rose up against Napoleon.

Section 3
Latin American colonies became independent nations.
The overseas empires of Spain and Portugal were the oldest and largest of any European country. Although Spain ruled strictly, its New World colonies revolted and finally won their freedom. Brazil grew slowly and gained independence peacefully.

Section 4
The American and French revolutions had long-range effects.
Revolutionary politics in North America and France created political debate and a revolutionary tradition that has continued to this day. The revolutions spurred the growth of nationalism and spread ideas about natural rights, individual liberty, and representative government.

Test Yourself

Key Terms, People, and Places
Identify the significance of each of the following:

Section 1
a. bourgeoisie
b. Louis XVI
c. National Assembly
d. Declaration of the Rights of Man and of the Citizen
e. Maximilien de Robespierre

Section 2
a. Napoleon Bonaparte
b. Code Napoleon
c. Confederation of the Rhine
d. Waterloo

Review Dates

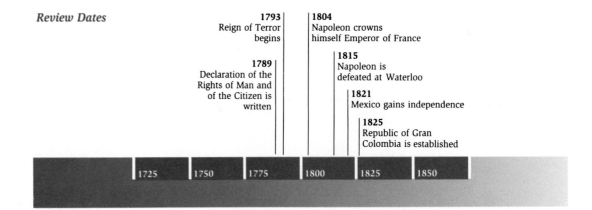

1793
Reign of Terror begins

1789
Declaration of the Rights of Man and of the Citizen is written

1804
Napoleon crowns himself Emperor of France

1815
Napoleon is defeated at Waterloo

1821
Mexico gains independence

1825
Republic of Gran Colombia is established

1725 1750 1775 1800 1825 1850

510

Main Ideas

Section 1
1. How did inequalities in the established estate system of French society lead to conflict in the country?
2. What were the causes of France's financial problems?
3. What were the events leading up to the French Revolution?
4. Explain the significance of French political history between 1789 and 1792.
5. What changes did the French government go through between 1792 and 1795?

Section 2
1. Describe how a soldier such as Napoleon was able to rise to power.
2. How did Napoleon reform French government?
3. How did Napoleon plan to defeat and conquer the British?
4. What were some of the positive effects that resulted from the rule of Napoleon?

Section 3
1. What forces led to rebellion in colonial Latin America?
2. What major problem did many emerging Latin American nations face?
3. What groups led the independence movement in Mexico?
4. Describe the manner in which Brazil gained its independence.

Section 4
1. Discuss some of the political terms that originated during the age of democratic revolutions that are still in wide use today.
2. Tell how the age of revolutions led to the rise of nationalism.
3. How were the causes of individual rights and representative government advanced during the age of democratic revolutions?

Critical Thinking

1. Evaluating Sources of Information In 1791 the British writer and politician Edmund Burke published his opinions on the French Revolution. Read the following excerpt from Burke's writing. Do you think Burke is sympathetic to the Revolution? Why or why not?

> I am unalterably persuaded that the attempt to oppress, degrade, impoverish, confiscate and extinguish the original gentlemen and landed property of a whole nation, cannot be justified under any form it may assume.

2. Making Hypotheses How were the ideas of Locke, Montesqueiu, Voltaire, and Rousseau, which you learned about in Chapter 26, important to the American, French, and Latin American revolutions?

Chapter Skills and Activities

Practicing Study and Research Skills
Analyzing Primary Source Material
Turn to pages 506–507 to reread three of the most influential documents of our democratic tradition: the English Bill of Rights (1689), the American Declaration of Independence (1776), and the French Declaration of the Rights of Man and of the Citizen (1789). Compare the language and ideas put forth in these three documents concerning the rights of individuals. What similarities do you see? What differences?

Linking Past and Present
July 14th, which is the anniversary of the storming of the Bastille, is France's most important national holiday. Use a book on holidays to find out how Bastille Day is celebrated in France and around the world.

Learning History Through Maps
Turn to the map of Napoleon's Empire on page 501. Study the coast of Europe. Why do you think Napoleon would have had a hard time enforcing the ban on British trade?

CRITICAL THINKING QUESTION LEVEL 1. average; 2. challenging

28 The Industrial Revolution

OVERVIEW

The Industrial Revolution gave rise to new products, to large cities, and to great problems that led to critics who brought reforms to the industrial world.

PLANNING CHART

Section	Text Pages	Key Concept	Suggested Teaching Time
1 The Industrial Revolution changed the Western world.	513–517	Driven by new industries, new production methods, and favorable conditions, the Industrial Revolution first took root in Britain.	One day **More time?** Use *Overhead Transparency 55* or *Source Reading 28A.*
2 A second Industrial Revolution took place.	518–521	A second Industrial Revolution centered around electricity, steel, and chemicals while breakthroughs came in science and medicine.	One day
3 Urbanism and industrialism created many social problems.	521–525	Industrialism produced problems, especially for workers living in cities, but laissez-faire capitalists argued the problems were unavoidable.	One day **Less time?** Briefly summarize the problems described in Section 3 and move on to Section 4.
4 Artists and thinkers responded to the problems of the Industrial Revolution.	525–529	Writers, artists, and political critics responded to the Industrial Revolution; one of the most influential writers was socialist Karl Marx.	Two days **More time?** Use *Overhead Transparency 56.*
5 An age of urban mass society and politics began.	529–532	Members of the new mass urban civilization pushed for reforms within the system.	One day **More time?** Use *Source Reading 28B.*

ANCILLARIES

Materials that may be used with this chapter to reinforce, reteach, enrich, and assess learning are pictured on the following pages.

Teacher's Resource File

ACTIVITIES

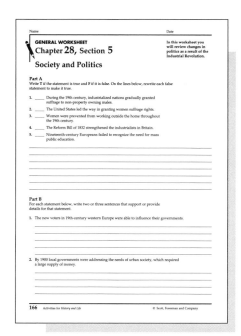

Section 1 Activity, p. 162

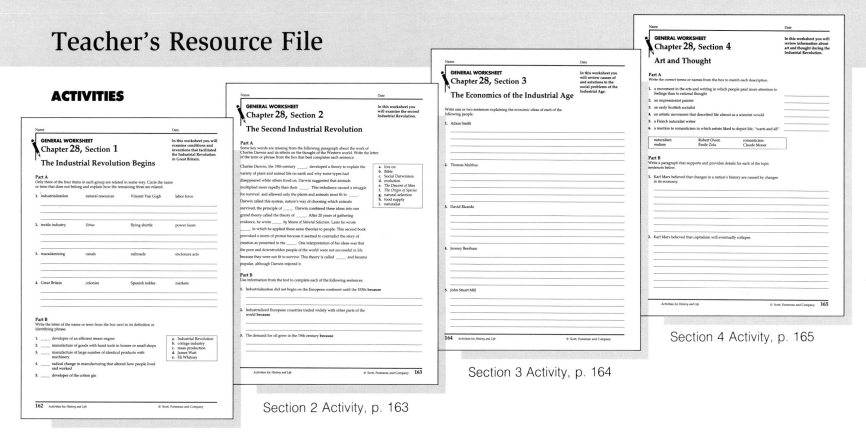

Section 2 Activity, p. 163

Section 3 Activity, p. 164

Section 4 Activity, p. 165

Section 5 Activity, p. 166

Chapter 28 Reteaching, p. 167

Chapter 28 Enrichment, p. 168

Teacher's Resource File

GEOGRAPHY SKILLS

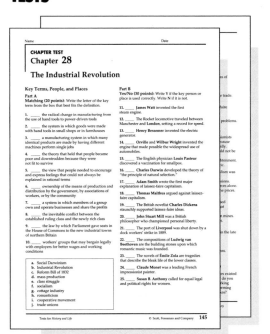

Chapter 28 Geography
Worksheet/Map, pp. 57–58

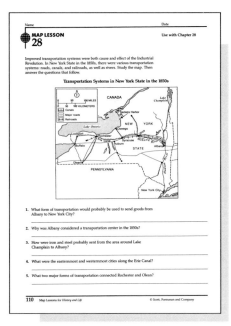

Chapter 28 Map Lesson, p. 110

TESTS

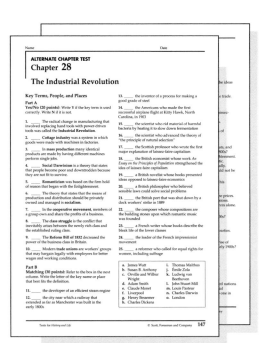

Chapter Test, pp. 145–146

Alternate Chapter Test, pp. 147–148

Other Optional Ancillaries

WORKBOOK

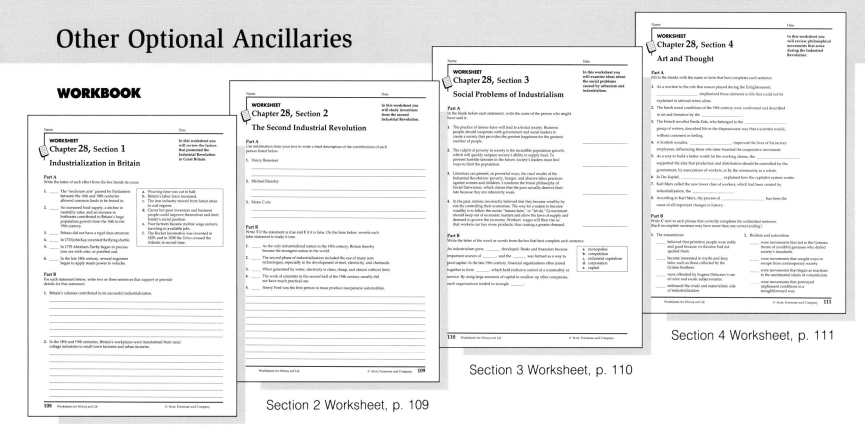

Section 1 Worksheet, p. 108

Section 2 Worksheet, p. 109

Section 3 Worksheet, p. 110

Section 4 Worksheet, p. 111

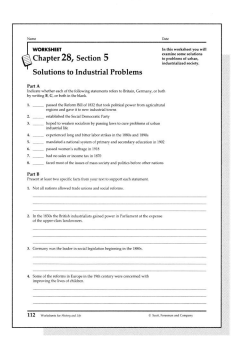

Section 5 Worksheet, p. 112

SOURCE READINGS

Source Reading 28A
Source Reading 28B

OVERHEAD TRANSPARENCIES

Overhead Transparency 55
Overhead Transparency 56

TEST GENERATOR

40 multiple-choice questions for Chapter 28

Chapter

28

The Industrial Revolution

1700–1900

1700

1800

1848   Karl Marx and Friedrich Engels write the *Communist Manifesto*

1903   Henry Ford begins mass producing automobiles

1910

1920

In November, 1774, a young inventor wrote to his father:

> The business I am here about has turned out rather successful, that is to say, the fire engine I have invented is now going and answers much better than any other that has yet been made.

James Watt, a Scottish instrument maker, wrote that letter. His "fire engine" was a steam engine that would transform the lives of people everywhere. When writing those words, Watt could not have known that he would become a leader in a movement that would quickly and dramatically change the course of human history—the Industrial Revolution.

Watt's involvement came about almost by accident. In 1763 a fellow teacher at the University of Glasgow asked him to repair a model steam engine (a primitive type that had been invented early in the century). Watt noticed that the engine wasted a great deal of fuel. He talked about the waste with several teachers at the university, but no one could think of any useful solution. For years he worked on perfecting his device and finally took out a patent on his improved steam engine.

Watts' steam engine eventually reduced or replaced old energy sources—horses, oxen, water, and people. By 1819, the year James Watt died, steam-powered machines were replacing hand tools in several British industries. During the 1800s the new industrial methods spread rapidly to the rest of western Europe and across the seas to the United States and Japan.

Industrialization sparked progress in other fields. New discoveries in science and medicine brought benefits as well as problems to humankind. They also changed people's ideas about the world and each other. Literature, art, music, and architecture also reflected the immense changes of the 1800s. The Industrial Revolution thus brought forth a new age of urban mass society.

In his *The Gun Foundry* (1866), the American John Ferguson Weir caught the intense drama of the Industrial Revolution in action.

Reading Preview

In this chapter you will learn how people adapted to a developing industrial society.

1. The Industrial Revolution changed the Western world.
2. A second Industrial Revolution took place.
3. Urbanism and industrialism created many social problems.
4. Artists and thinkers responded to the Industrial Revolution.
5. An age of urban mass society and politics began.

 The Industrial Revolution changed the Western world.

The word "revolution" means sudden, drastic change—usually implying violence in a political context—such as happened in the American or French revolutions. The word may also be applied to large-scale events in history that may not involve violence but that still produce upheaval and drastic change. The **Industrial Revolution** is one such event. It involved the change from hand tools to power-driven tools in manufacturing. This change radically altered the way goods were produced and, in turn, the way people lived.

513

- Review how the Industrial Revolution got launched in Britain. Write these topics on the chalkboard: Resources, Labor, Capital, Markets, Government, and Mobility. Ask questions about each: What basic resources in Britain fueled the Industrial Revolution? What groups does the text include within labor? (workers and inventors) Is capital only money? What markets did Britain have? What is a market? How did government boost the Industrial Revolution? What is the relationship between mobility and the incentive to work hard?

- Discuss inventions in the two bedrock industries—textiles and iron-making.

- Discuss power. What role did water and steam play in the Industrial Revolution?

GUIDED PRACTICE

Have students read the Geography: A Key to History feature on page 515. Note particularly the relation between city location, resource location, and water. Also for guided practice:

 Overhead Transparency 55

Conditions in Britain favored industrialization.

The Industrial Revolution got its start in Britain. Conditions there were ideal for making changes in the means of production for six major reasons.

First, Britain enjoyed plentiful natural resources. The country's land held rich deposits of coal and iron, and its short, swift rivers furnished the water power to keep water wheels moving. Britain also took advantage of the availability of natural resources from its colonies abroad. Wool and cotton from these colonies provided the raw materials for Britain's growing textile industry.

Second, and perhaps most important, Britain had a large labor force. In the 1700s new farming techniques significantly increased the country's food supply. New crops such as the potato appeared. These developments, along with a general decline in mortality rates and an increase in the birthrate, led to a huge growth in Britain's population. In addition, government policy encouraged the development of a mobile work force. Because of a series of "enclosure acts" passed by Parliament between 1500 and 1700, wealthy landowners were able to fence in open fields and common lands that had been used since medieval times by poor farmers. (See pages 196–197.) Most of these farmers then became wage earners who traveled to wherever there were jobs. Also, the British led the world in inventing machines and in training people to use them. As a result, Britain had more skilled and educated workers than other nations.

The third reason that Britain industrialized early was that its resources and labor force were combined by business people who had the capital—money, goods, or property used to start or carry on a business—to buy the new machines and build the new factories. For centuries the British had been building up capital from farming, handicrafts, and overseas trade. In addition, Britain had a well-developed banking system that granted loans at low interest rates.

Fourth, two large markets were waiting to buy finished goods, the rapidly growing British population and Britain's overseas colonies. To encourage the sale of British products, Parliament issued a series of laws, beginning in 1651, that forced colonists to buy British-manufactured goods. For all of these reasons, consumer demand—or consumers' desire for goods—boosted industrial production.

Fifth, the government of 18th-century Britain helped industrialism grow. The Parliament ensured that roads and canals were built, maintained, and protected, and it issued patents to protect inventors' work. The government lowered taxes on profits, and businesses became freer to do as they wished.

Finally, the sixth reason for Britain's superiority in industrialization was that the British had a rather mobile society. That is, a poor person who worked hard and saved money might one day become wealthy. The upper classes had long been in business, so the nobility did not look down on work, as did many French or Spanish nobles.

Machines for the textile industry helped build the factory system.

Most goods before the late 1700s were made with hand tools in small shops or in farmhouses. By that time about half Britain's textiles and other industrial products came from what became known as "**cottage industry**." Merchants handed out the raw materials to workers who spun the yarn and wove the cloth at home. This system was not efficient, though, because workers were spread over wide areas of the countryside.

In the early 1700s, new city dwellers and foreign markets wanted so much cotton cloth that workers could not meet the need. As a result, a series of inventions were developed that eventually improved the textile industry. In 1733 British weaver John Kay made a flying shuttle, which cut weaving time in half.

Now the problem became that the spinners could not supply enough yarn. By 1769 two other important inventions, the spinning jenny and the water-powered frame, met the challenge and provided yarn faster. Then, in 1779 Samuel Crompton put the best parts of the spinning jenny and the water frame together in one machine called a spinning mule, which made hundreds of fine threads at the same time. Finally, by 1800 Edmund Cartwright's power loom became available.

Cotton became the fiber most widely used for making cloth, but raw cotton came into the market slowly because of the time needed to clean seeds

BACKGROUND The spinning jenny was invented by James Hargreaves and named in honor of Hargreaves's wife.

BACKGROUND The name spinning mule was adopted because the machine is a hybrid of the water frame and spinning jenny much as the animal is a hybrid of a horse and a donkey.

GEOGRAPHY

A Key to History

RESOURCES AND INDUSTRIAL DEVELOPMENT

"One person's junk is another person's treasure." Paraphrased, this thought makes an important point about geography as a key to history: "One era's wastelands become another era's natural resources." If we define natural resources as "the things found in nature that a society uses and values," we can see that before people discover how to use certain resources, such resources have little economic worth. For example, before coal and petroleum became widely used as energy sources, these substances were regarded simply as nuisances. The key to making them valuable was the Industrial Revolution.

Britain's industrial development was aided by the presence of mineral resources. Britain had rich, well-placed coalfields and iron-ore deposits. Coal was used to convert iron ore into iron or steel and to provide steam power to run machines.

Steel mills and manufacturing plants were built near the coalfields and iron mines in and around Manchester, Sheffield, and Birmingham, which became major industrial cities. France and Germany also had deposits of coal and iron ore in the Ruhr and Saar valleys, which were linked by a network of rivers, canals, and railroads. As a consequence, these two countries became the industrial leaders of continental Europe. The northeastern United States had similar advantages.

Since the 1930s resources other than coal and iron ore have become increasingly important, for example, hydroelectric power, petroleum, natural gas, and uranium. Today, industrialization is taking place in areas, once considered unsuitable, that possess these new resources.

Industrialization in England, 1850

- Coal fields
- Iron ore deposits
- Industrial areas

Glasgow
Newcastle
Manchester
Liverpool
Sheffield
Birmingham
Thames R.
London
North Sea
Cardiff

0   75   150 MILES
0   75   150 KILOMETERS
N

Transportation in England, 1850

- Canals
- Railroads

Glasgow
Newcastle
Manchester
Liverpool
Sheffield
Birmingham
Thames R.
London
North Sea
Cardiff

0   75   150 MILES
0   75   150 KILOMETERS
N

Which industrial center shown on the map lacks coal and iron-ore deposits? What advantages of location might offset this deficiency?

REVIEW

1. Name at least three things that an area needs before industrial development can take place.
2. What are natural resources?
3. What three British cities became early industrial centers and why?

This feature makes several important points about natural resources before applying the concept to the Industrial Revolution. Note that (1) natural resources are determined by a culture as well as by technology. Seaweed is prized by one culture as a food, but rejected by others. Also note that (2) the economic value of a natural resource is set by the world economy. The value of iron ore, coal, petroleum and seaweed is really set by the price at which it is bought and sold on the world market. Thus trade makes it possible for nations that lack certain natural resources to develop into industrial powers.

A current example of a changing natural resource is the common rock called quartz. See the article by Bruce Hathaway, "Circuitry Wizards and New Agers Alike Can Get Good Vibes from Quartz," *Smithsonian,* 19:8 (November, 1988), 82–100.

Answers to REVIEW

1. People, raw materials, energy, and transportation facilities are referred to in the text. Capital and markets might be mentioned as well.
2. things found in nature that a society uses
3. Manchester, Sheffield, Birmingham
4. They had supplies of iron ore and coal as well as good transportation facilities.

Answer to MAP QUESTION

London; It is linked to the North Sea by railroads and by the Thames River and linked with outlying coalfields and iron-ore deposits by rail and water.

1. What is capital? (money, goods, or property used to start or carry on a business)
2. With what industry are Kay, Crompton, and Cartwright associated? (textiles)

OPTIONAL RETEACHING

Ask students to explain how each of the following contributed to the Industrial Revolution: enclosure acts, swift rivers, patent laws, cotton gin, canals.

OPTIONAL ENRICHMENT

1. Have interested students put together an illustrated presentation that explains how moving water was used in the textile industry. (average)
2. Encourage students to prepare a presentation that explains the steam engine and how it powered machinery. (challenging)
3. Also for enrichment:

📖 *Source Reading 28A*

INDEPENDENT PRACTICE/ HOMEWORK

Assign the Section Review, Activities page 162, or Workbook page 108.

CLOSURE

Most historians agree that no movement or revolution in human history did more than the Industrial Revolution to change the way we live. We spend much of our lives enjoying its benefits and doing battle with its less fortunate consequences.

from the cotton bolls. New Englander Eli Whitney learned of the problem in 1793 and in 10 days, he built a machine, the cotton gin, that could clean cotton as fast as 50 pairs of hands could.

To lower the costs of manufacturing, business owners located their new factories close to sources of power. Since water drove machines, small industrial towns sprang up on swift rivers. Now workers no longer had materials brought to their homes. Instead, they went to the factories, where they kept set hours and could not waste raw materials. When steam engines began to work machinery in the early 1800s, factories moved away from river towns and into cities.

The factory system, as it came to be known, permitted better control of quality and a steadier rate of production. Manufacturers could use new techniques such as **mass production**. That is, they could make a large number of identical products by having one type of machine rapidly do one small job, moving the product to another type of machine for another small job, and so on, until the product was finished. The factory system is still the core of industrial production today.

Coal and iron came into wide use.

Many new machines were made of iron, and thus, the need for iron increased. Most early iron was

Growth of the Railroads in the 19th Century

	France	Germany	Britain	U.S.A.
1840	300 miles*	300	1,500	2,800
1850	1,800	3,700	6,000	9,000
1860	5,700	7,200	9,000	30,600
1870	9,600	12,100	13,500	52,800
1880	14,300	21,000	15,500	93,400
1890	20,600	26,000	17,200	166,400
1900	23,600	31,900	18,600	192,900

*Mileage figures are rounded off to the nearest hundred.

The table at left shows the increase in miles of railroad track in four countries during the 19th century. Note the huge increase in track in the United States after 1860. The railroad train below was one of the first in use and ran between the British cities of London and Greenwich. Note that the passenger car resembles a horse-drawn carriage. Several decades passed before the cars became more comfortable.

made with charcoal, which was made from wood, a slow and costly process. Furthermore, Britain was undergoing a severe energy crisis in the late 17th and early 18th centuries. Almost all the forests had been cut down for fuel, building materials, and ship building—leaving less and less available wood for industry.

The energy problem in Britain was solved when coal, in rich supply in the country, came into wide use. In 1735 Abraham Darby began to make iron with coke, or purified coal. As a result, the iron industry moved from forest areas to coal regions.

In the 1780s Henry Cort, a contractor for the British navy, made two discoveries. By "puddling," or stirring, molten iron with long rods in a furnace, he could quickly burn off many impurities. Also, by passing hot iron through heavy rollers he could squeeze out further impurities and make iron sheets. By 1844 Britain produced 3 million tons of iron each year. Much cheaper now, iron became the building material for many products.

Transportation became faster and cheaper.

Moving about in the early 1700s was little different from getting around during the Middle Ages. Bad roads made traveling on horseback slow and uncomfortable. Moving goods overland was even slower and very expensive.

Early developments. Two Scottish engineers, Thomas Telford and John McAdam, set about improving roads after 1770. Both tried to improve drainage and to use layers of crushed rock to build roads. McAdam's money-saving plan, known as macadamizing, formed the base for all modern road building.

Waterways were also changed to accommodate new conditions. Rivers were made deeper to accept large ships, and in 1761 one of the first modern canals was dug. This seven-mile canal, built by the Duke of Bridgewater to link some of his coal mines with the city of Manchester, worked so well that the price of coal in Manchester dropped by 80 percent. After that, canal building began all over Britain. By 1830 the country had one of the best inland waterway systems in the Western world.

The steam engine. Steam provided the next boost to the transportation system. **James Watt**

developed a new engine, patented in 1769, that was much more efficient than the old ones. In 1781 Watt found a way to suit the engine to rotary motion, allowing it to be used to run machines.

From the 1780s on, several engineers worked to apply steam power to vehicles. When a group of business people decided to build a railway between **Liverpool** and Manchester, they offered a prize for the best locomotive. George Stephenson, a mining engineer, won the prize in 1829 with his Rocket. It pulled a train 31 miles at an average speed of 14 miles an hour.

Stephenson set off a railroad-building boom in Britain that reached its peak in the 1840s. By 1850 the most important routes were built, and freight trains ran steadily. Western Europe and the United States began building railroads in the mid-1800s. The massive effort needed to produce the iron and steel used to make bridges, railroad cars, and the thousands of miles of track spurred the rapid industrialization of the United States.

Until about 1880 most ships still used wind and sail. However, in 1838 a British ship, the *Sirius*, crossed from Liverpool to New York using steam power in 18 days. By 1850 ocean-going steamers ran at uniform times and did a good business in mail and passenger traffic. Only later did they take the place of sailing vessels for carrying cargo.

Section 1 Review

Identify Industrial Revolution, cottage industry, mass production, James Watt, Liverpool

Main Ideas
1. What six conditions favored industrialization in Britain?
2. Name three machines that helped start the factory system in the textile industry.
3. What developments helped make coal and iron more available?
4. What advances in transportation took place during the 1700s and 1800s?

Critical Thinking
Predicting Effects: Consider the enormous developments in technology that took place during the Industrial Revolution. How might your life today be different if these changes had not occurred? What modern technologies would you lack? Why?

entific discoveries were made, leading to the development of new industries and philosophies.

Industrialization spread to Europe and North America.

Industrialization did not begin on the European continent until the 1830s, largely because of poor transport systems, geographical trade barriers, and an unskilled population of workers. As in Britain, textile making provided the first phase of industrialization in continental Europe.

Two of the world's most talented inventors were the Americans Alexander Graham Bell and Thomas Alva Edison. Bell (far left) patented his invention of the telephone in 1876. Edison (near left) meanwhile patented 1,093 inventions in his lifetime, including the electric light and the phonograph, shown in this 1888 photograph.

Gradually, industrial knowledge spread through Europe. By the 1850s several European nations and the United States had well-established industries.

Between 1850 and 1870, for example, Germany increased coal production from 4 million to 24 million tons. European countries now traded widely with other parts of the world both to acquire the raw materials their new factories needed and to sell their finished products. By the 1870s these new industrial nations stood poised to challenge Britain's industrial supremacy.

New technologies began.

This second phase of industrialization included the development of many new technologies. Some of these involved steel, electricity, chemicals, and transportation.

2 A second Industrial Revolution took place.

The first Industrial Revolution encompassed only three key industries: textiles, iron making, and steam power. Much of Britain and Europe remained rural and followed the old patterns of farming and village life. All of that changed in the second Industrial Revolution, which began in the 1850s and built up momentum after the 1870s. First, several other nations of Europe and North America industrialized and challenged British supremacy. Then, a series of new inventions and sci-

Steel. Because steel is harder and more flexible than iron, it was adapted for many uses. However, until 1856 manufacturers found it difficult to make steel in large quantities. In that year a Briton, **Henry Bessemer,** invented a process for making a good grade of steel. When other scientists perfected Bessemer's process in the 1870s, the steel industry took off. Steel was used to build everything from skyscrapers to ships.

Electricity. This flexible form of energy can be sent over long distances to run machines of any size. When generated by water, electricity is clean, cheap, and almost without limit. Scientists experimented with electricity in the 18th century, but the principles of electrical generation were not established until the 1830s. Michael Faraday, a British scientist working on the connection between electricity and magnetism, showed how an electrical current could be made in 1831. The electric generator and the electric motor in use today are based on Faraday's principles. The first practical generators were built in the 1870s, and in the 1880s transformers that converted electrical energy for home use were introduced. With these inventions electricity became the primary energy source for both factories and homes.

Beginning in the 1870s, experimenters worked on electrical devices for public use. Some of these included the telegraph (1837), the telephone (1876), and the incandescent light bulb (1870s). By 1905, 10 million telephones were in use in the United States alone, and by 1900 some 2 million American buildings used electric lighting.

In 1885 Heinrich Hertz, a German, found and measured the speed of what were later called radio waves. An Italian, Guglielmo Marconi, used these discoveries to invent a wireless telegraph, or radio, which began service across the English Channel in 1898. Three years later, messages were able to cross the Atlantic.

Chemicals. Scientists working with chemicals made important strides during this period. Marie Curie, in particular, a French chemist and physicist, became famous for her research on radioactivity. In 1898 she and her husband Pierre discovered two new chemical elements, one of which was radium. During the 1800s chemists broke down nearly 70,000 chemical compounds. From this work came portland cement, vulcanized rubber, synthetic dyes, and petroleum products.

Up to the mid-19th century, petroleum, or oil, had not attracted much attention. Beginning in the 1860s, however, scientists began to build internal combustion engines, the more advanced of which used gasoline for fuel. The oil rush was on. In the last quarter of the 19th century, large oil companies began to supply the world's needs. By 1900 world industry largely transformed itself from steam-powered to oil- and electricity-powered.

Transportation. Electricity revolutionized public transportation. Building on the work of Faraday and others, inventors made electric generators that produced steady amounts of electricity cheaply. In cities, electricity powered trolley cars, elevated railways, subways, and trains.

An even more flexible means of transportation appeared with the internal combustion engine. Fueled by gasoline, these engines were lighter and could be made to power the automobile. In 1885 two German engineers, Gottlieb Daimler and Karl Benz devised the world's first automobiles, with Benz naming his car for his young daughter, Mercedes. Automobiles did not come into wide public use, however, until the American Henry Ford founded his company in 1903 and began

Important scientific advances were made in the late 1800s. Wilhelm Roentgen discovered X rays (below left), and Marie Curie (below right) discovered radium.

on the chalkboard. Then ask students to consider what their day would be like if there were no electricity. Tell students that they have the second Industrial Revolution to thank for electricity.

2 TEACH

- Ask students to explain the difference between the first Industrial Revolution and the second. List on the chalkboard industries and inventions that are associated with each.
- Explain that one of the most controversial developments of the 1800s involved a theory about the evolution of plants, animals, and human beings. Ask students to explain Charles Darwin's evolution theory. Why was it controversial? Why did it lead some social thinkers to the notion of Social Darwinism?

GUIDED PRACTICE

Following are a series of 20th-century institutions. Have students play the role of Social Darwinists and explain why they do or do not support the following: Food Stamps, the Humane Society, Social Security retirement pensions.

1. Who was Michael Faraday? (British scientist who showed how electrical current could be made)
2. What is natural selection? (nature's way of choosing which animals survive to reproduce)

OPTIONAL RETEACHING

Ask students to name a person whom we should thank for each of the following: an appendectomy free from infection (Lister), certainty about whether a finger is broken (Roentgen), music on the radio (Hertz or Marconi), New York to Los Angeles in four hours (the Wright brothers).

OPTIONAL ENRICHMENT

1. Ask students to make a collage of brand or corporate logos from inventors of the past. (e.g., Kodak, Listerine, Bell, Edison, Ford, Westinghouse, Oldsmobile, Singer) (average)
2. Ask students to prepare a two-paragraph section for an eighth-grade science book that explains how steel is made. (challenging)

INDEPENDENT PRACTICE/ HOMEWORK

Assign the Section Review, Activities page 163, or Workbook page 109.

CLOSURE

In many ways we are still living in the second Industrial Revolution. Recent technological breakthroughs have refined and improved steel production, electrical applications, and chemical products.

The 1913 photograph above shows one of the earliest automotive assembly lines developed by Henry Ford at Highland Park, Michigan. The workers at this plant produced Model T cars, such as the one at left.

making the inexpensive Model T using an assembly line mass production system.

Automobiles alone have changed the world's way of life, but the internal combustion engine had other uses as well. One was the long-sought dream of human flight. In 1903 a pair of Americans, **Orville and Wilbur Wright**, made the first successful airplane flight at Kitty Hawk, North Carolina, and another new industry was born.

Medical research advanced along with other sciences.

In the last half of the 19th century, almost everyone in the world recognized how important scientific research could be to their everyday lives.

When Wilhelm Roentgen [rent′gən], a German, discovered X rays—or rays that could pass through solids—in 1895, doctors quickly realized how useful they could be in diagnosing medical problems.

Edward Jenner, a British physician, also advanced modern medicine when he used a vaccination to protect against the often-deadly disease of smallpox. Jenner noticed that farm workers often got a mild form of pox called cowpox, but rarely got smallpox. In 1796 he inoculated a boy first with the virus of cowpox and later with smallpox. When the boy did not contract smallpox, Jenner knew he had made an important discovery.

It was French scientist **Louis Pasteur,** however, who used Jenner's discovery in the 1860s. Thinking that harmful bacteria caused disease, Pasteur tried heating material in order to slow down fermentation. Today almost all milk is treated by this process called pasteurization. In his work, Pasteur proved that microscopic organisms called germs cause infectious diseases. Pasteur also discovered several vaccines, including one for rabies.

Working with the new germ theory of disease, German scientist Robert Koch discovered the germs that cause 11 diseases, including tuberculosis and cholera. In the 1860s the British surgeon Joseph Lister found a chemical antiseptic that would destroy bacteria and make surgery safe. Lister's discoveries were said to have saved more lives than were lost in all the wars of the 1800s.

Biology changed society's ideas.

The growth of science and the new machine age brought many changes to people's ideas about the world. In the 19th century, the British naturalist **Charles Darwin** developed a theory to explain why there was such a variety of plant and animal types on earth, and why some had disappeared while others lived on.

Darwin suggested that because animals multiplied faster than their food supply, there is always a struggle to live. He concluded that those individuals with some kind of advantage would be more likely to survive and reproduce. Thus, their advantageous characteristics would be passed on to their offspring. Individuals with less advantageous traits would have relatively few descendants. This differential reproduction would produce future generations that were better suited to that environment, a process Darwin called the principle of natural selection. For more than 20 years, Darwin carefully gathered facts to support his theory. In 1859 his findings appeared in *The Origin of Species by Means of Natural Selection.*

In another book, *The Descent of Man* (1871), Darwin suggested that human beings and apes had the same ancestor. Just as 16th-century scientists had touched off a storm of protest when they said the earth was not the center of the universe, Darwin's ideas provoked arguments all over 19th-century Europe. Some devoutly religious people thought that Darwin's ideas contradicted the Bible's story of creation. Therefore, they said, Darwin was wrong and, worse, had offended God. In time, however, many persons, including some religious people, came to believe that science dealt with some parts of human life and religion with others. Therefore, many people could accept both Darwinism and Christianity.

Whatever the debates, Darwinism strongly influenced how people thought. Many people in the new age of capitalism believed that poor and downtrodden people became so because they were not fit to survive. Was not all life on earth subject to Darwin's laws, they argued. This theory is called **Social Darwinism** and, though Darwin himself rejected it, it became popular in the 19th and 20th centuries.

Section 2 Review

Identify Henry Bessemer, Orville and Wilbur Wright, Louis Pasteur, Charles Darwin, Social Darwinism

Main Ideas
1. Why did industrialization spread to Europe and North America later than to Britain?
2. Name three new technologies of this time.
3. What advances were made in medical knowledge?
4. What happened in biology to change ideas?

Critical Thinking
Assessing Cause and Effect: In your opinion, which of the discoveries discussed in this section had the greatest effect on modern life? Why?

 Urbanism and industrialism created many social problems.

The steam engine enabled cities to grow in the early 19th century. Using this power source, business owners built their factories in cities that had good transport systems and markets. Rural people flocked to the cities to find work, and, as a result, city populations rose. In Britain the percentage of people living in urban areas jumped from 17 percent in 1800 to 55 percent in 1890. Nothing like this huge, swift migration to cities had ever happened in European history.

Home building could not keep up with the large numbers of immigrants to cities, so landlords divided buildings into tiny apartments. Large families often lived in one small room. New houses for

Answers to Section 2 Review

Identify
Key Terms, People, and Places are defined on pages indicated in parentheses. Also see the Glossary and Biographical Dictionary.
Henry Bessemer (519), Orville and Wilbur Wright (520), Louis Pasteur (520), Charles Darwin (521), Social Darwinism (521)

Main Ideas
1. poor transportation, trade barriers, unskilled workers
2. making large quantities of steel, generating electricity, making petroleum products
3. X rays, smallpox vaccination, pasteurization
4. Darwin's theory of evolution said human beings and apes had the same ancestors; his survival of the fittest theory applied to social issues.

Critical Thinking
One possible answer is the automobile because it permits people to be more mobile and provides an industry that employs many workers. It also causes pollution, parking problems, and deaths and injuries from accidents.

3 ***Lesson Plan***
Essential Learning Objectives
Students will learn to:
- describe social conditions created by the Industrial Revolution.
- evaluate the effects of laissez-faire capitalism.

Explain to students that most big changes bring some problems. Moving to a new community, changing schools, changing classes, changing friends—all can have their difficult moments. Problems also are likely to occur with historical shifts. The Industrial Revolution was no exception.

2 TEACH

- Give students five minutes to skim through the section and list as many concrete facts as they can that describe living and working conditions in 19th-century European cities. Ask students what they found and write a composite list on the chalkboard.

- Also write the names Adam Smith, Thomas Malthus, and David Ricardo on the chalkboard. Under each write a few key phrases to distinguish them from each other and to highlight their contributions to laissez-faire capitalism. (Smith—first explanation of laissez-faire capitalism, supply and demand; Malthus—blamed population growth, predicted famine and death; Ricardo—industrial slant)

GUIDED PRACTICE

Ask students to write a list of arguments either supporting or challenging this statement: "Resolved: That government is best which governs least. Laissez-faire capitalism in Europe forever." After students have had adequate time, ask volunteers to read an item from their list.

workers were usually built in rows with only narrow alleys and little courtyards between. Little light ever entered these tiny homes, and sanitary conditions hardly ever existed since most of these row houses had no running water and no bathrooms. Filth and sewage could be found in every street. To make matters worse, such housing was located next to smoke-spewing factories and horribly polluted rivers.

Naturally, disease of every sort attacked the cities' poor, who were crammed into filthy, airless living quarters. Tuberculosis plagued 19th-century cities, as did typhus and cholera. Although governments began to clean up and rebuild cities after 1850, slums still blight cities today.

Workers labored under harsh conditions.

Working conditions in factories, mills, and mines were both unhealthy and dangerous. With few safety devices on machines, many accidents occurred. An injured worker almost never received compensation for the loss of a leg or an arm. Men, women, and children worked 12 to 15 hours a day.

Children who stood at machines every day for long hours at a stretch often developed physical deformities such as spinal curvature. In addition, these hard working children, generally uneducated, usually suffered from malnutrition. By the time the British Parliament passed laws in 1833 and 1842 controlling child labor, but not abolishing it, more than 50,000 children worked.

New social classes emerged in Europe.

Society in 19th-century Europe had three very distinct classes. Elites, made up of old aristocratic families and the wealthy capitalists, stood at the top of the social order. Below this upper class appeared a middle class made up of business people, factory owners, shopkeepers, and such professionals as physicians, lawyers, and teachers. The lowest 75 percent of the population included the urban workers.

The working class became the largest group in Europe's industrial age. Factory workers, mine hands, and day laborers replaced skilled artisans as the nucleus of the working class. Laborers needed no skills for the often tedious jobs provided by the new industries. Skilled jobs existed for people such as machinists, but these positions were not plentiful when compared with the vast number of unskilled jobs.

Most observers of the time noted the hard lives of the working people. Yet, people still poured into the cities, factory towns, and mines to make a better living than they could make on farms. One way to evaluate the quality of their lives is to look at

DAILY LIFE

Daily life in the late 1800s and early 1900s was often difficult for many children and families. Many young people worked in such industries as textiles (left) and coal mining (above right). They worked long hours and endured poor conditions. Many families were also forced to seek public assistance (right) in order to secure food and shelter.

real wages, or the amount of goods people can buy with their money.

Overall, real wages went up some 65 percent between 1800 and 1850. Mass production of goods brought prices down, and the cost of food declined. In general, then, working people had more and better food and clothing than they had before the Industrial Revolution began. Housing, though, became much worse in the rapidly growing cities and factory towns. Overall, the standard of living for the working class improved somewhat before 1850, but improved even more after that year.

Capitalism changed.

As industrialism grew, capitalism changed to suit the new kinds of businesses. This new form of capitalism is best described as industrial capitalism. Some industries, such as railroads, iron, and steel, needed huge amounts of capital to buy machines and tools. Since no one person had so much capital, some kind of joint firm was needed.

Thus, during the 1800s the corporation was born. The corporation could own property and bring and defend lawsuits, and it would continue even though shareholders and directors changed. Most corporations were managed not by their owners, but by salaried people who spent the money of others to do business. Banks and finan-

Stock certificates, such as the one reproduced here from the Seneca Oil Company of Connecticut, became common during the 1800s.

ciers became quite important because they were the sources of the large amounts of capital needed.

As corporations and financial organizations grew in the later 19th century, they often joined together to form monopolies. Monopolies held exclusive control of a commodity or service—from raw material through delivery of the finished product. A steel company, for example, might own coal and iron mines, rail lines, and steel mills. Using large amounts of capital to swallow up other companies, a monopoly tended to strangle competition, the very thing that had started the Industrial Revolution.

1. Which was the largest economic group in Europe's industrial age? (working class)
2. Who was Adam Smith? (explained laissez-faire capitalism)

OPTIONAL RETEACHING

Write the following terms on the chalkboard: class society, laissez-faire capitalism, corporation, monopoly, supply and demand. Have students write an explanation of each term.

OPTIONAL ENRICHMENT

1. Ask interested students to make a poster-size version of the world population graph on page 799. Present this chart to the class along with prepared comments on the predictions of Thomas Malthus. Was he correct? (average)
2. Encourage students to find and share passages in Charles Dickens' *Oliver Twist* or *Hard Times* that reveal his feelings about laissez-faire capitalism. (challenging)

INDEPENDENT PRACTICE/ HOMEWORK

Assign the Section Review, Activities page 164, or Workbook page 110.

CLOSURE

The bad conditions produced by the Industrial Revolution were explained away and even justified by many 19th-century writers and political leaders. However, critics were about to be joined by the revolutionary voice of Karl Marx.

Business leaders favored the laissez-faire system.

Many theories concerning how business should operate appeared with the rise of mass industries in the 19th century. One theory became popular among the bold middle-class men who owned the railroads, mines, and factories. They believed that government should leave business alone, and they favored the ideas of **laissez-faire capitalism**. *Laissez-faire* [les′ā fer′] is French for "let do." In business, the term came to mean "let them do as they please."

Adam Smith, a Scottish professor, wrote the first major explanation of laissez-faire capitalism. In *An Inquiry into the Nature and Causes of the Wealth of Nations* (1776), Smith stated that nations would gain wealth if they allowed free economic competition for their citizens. Governments should not, he said, regulate trade or business. In this environment, the laws of supply and demand would govern. If demand for a product rose, producers would automatically increase the supply by increasing production. On the other hand, if demand fell, they would cut back on supply by reducing production. Smith believed that workers' wages should also rise so that they could become consumers, thus creating demand.

More than 20 years later, **Thomas Malthus**, a British economist, added to the laissez-faire idea with *An Essay on the Principles of Population* (1798). Malthus placed the blame for poverty on the growing population. If the population continued to grow, he reasoned, the numbers of people would eventually outstrip the food supply. Malthus thus proposed that human populations should be limited to avoid the widespread famine and death that he predicted would occur. Malthus believed, too, that social reforms, such as better wages, simply led to larger populations.

Both Malthus and Smith wrote at a time when British society was still largely agricultural. In the early 1800s, British banker and economist David Ricardo combined Smith's free-trade ideas and Malthus' population theories and applied them to the new industrial society.

Ricardo believed that it was useless to try to improve workers' wages. When population grows, he reasoned, the labor supply also expands. As more workers would be competing for jobs, the jobs would go to those people willing to work for less. Workers in general would be poorer, and fewer of their children would survive to adulthood. The labor supply would eventually decline, and wages would rise. Furthermore, at the point when workers enjoy higher wages, they tend to have more children. As a result of higher wages, therefore, the labor market would once again become too full.

In effect, Ricardo's work suggested that any government efforts to improve the lot of factory workers were ineffective. Instead of interfering with the law of supply and demand, he advised that the government practice laissez-faire economics.

Members of the new industrial capitalist class eagerly accepted and strongly supported the concept of laissez-faire. They believed that supply and demand would control the production of goods and their selling prices. Consumers would then have fair wages and prices, as well as improved goods, and businesses could be sure of having good profits. Industrial capitalists cared little that laissez-faire did not always bring wages fit for living. For most of the 1800s, these ideas, together with Social Darwinism (survival of the fittest), were the accepted social philosophy of the growing middle class.

Some people objected to laissez-faire ideas.

Not all middle class people accepted these harsh views of society. Many writers and philosophers argued strenuously against them. In the mid-1800s, **Charles Dickens**, an outstanding British novelist, wrote powerful novels that showed the plight of the poor. *Oliver Twist* and *A Christmas Carol* are two famous examples. In *Hard Times*, Dickens not only showed the effects of poverty on people but also condemned the Social Darwinist attitude of rich factory owners.

Two British philosophers, Jeremy Bentham and **John Stuart Mill**, also argued for a more humane approach. Bentham popularized the phrase "the greatest happiness for the greatest number," which was one of his goals for society. Bentham's pupil, Mill, championed personal liberty. His essay "On Liberty" (1859) is a defense of individual freedom. Mill did not accept laissez-faire and believed, like

BACKGROUND John Stuart Mill worked together with his wife, Harriet Taylor Mill, to write *On Liberty*. Profoundly affected by his wife's death in 1858, Mill dedicated the work to her when it first was published the following year. Mill's ideas on reform and democratic change were in part due to the influence of his wife.

Bentham, that sensible social laws could solve human problems. Mill's ideas on liberty and his humane, practical ideas are still practiced.

Section 3 Review

Identify laissez-faire capitalism, Adam Smith, Thomas Malthus, Charles Dickens, John Stuart Mill

Main Ideas
1. What were common working conditions during the 19th century in Europe?
2. What was the new class structure during that time period?
3. How did capitalism change as industry developed?
4. Why did business leaders favor a laissez-faire approach to economics?
5. Why did some people object to the laissez-faire ideas?

Critical Thinking
Identifying Assumptions: What do the ideas of Smith, Malthus, and Ricardo assume about how society functions economically?

4 | *Artists and thinkers responded to the Industrial Revolution.*

Artists, writers, and philosophers expressed the thoughts and feelings that people had about this revolutionary new world. Some writers and artists firmly turned their backs on their own world in favor of fantasy, the exotic, or the past. Others described the forces that were changing society.

Romanticism dominated the early 1800s.

Toward the end of the 1700s, people began to turn against the firm hold of reason that had marked the Enlightenment. Several artists and thinkers took a different view, called **romanticism**.

Romanticists believed that people needed to pay attention to feelings they did not fully control. Feelings of love and the touch of beauty or religion, they said, could not be explained in rational terms alone. Romanticists believed above all that art should mirror the artist's self in the artist's own way. Romanticism was, in a sense, a turning away

The German Johann Wolfgang von Goethe [gėr'tə] was one of the leading Romantic writers. His masterpiece was *Faust,* a long dramatic poem.

from the ugly and materialistic side of the new industrial society.

In literature, writers let their imaginations run freely. Liberty was an important theme. A German movement known as *Sturm und Drang* (Storm and Stress) developed the theme of youthful geniuses who defied society's accepted standards. Among its members was Johann Friedrich von Schiller, whose drama *William Tell* (1804) dealt with the Swiss fight for freedom.

The romanticists thought, as did the French social philosopher Jean Jacques Rousseau, whom you read about in Chapter 26, that primitive people were noble and good because civilization had not spoiled them. Romanticists thus became quite interested in myths, fairy tales, and folk songs. Some collections of these stories and songs, such as the Grimm brothers' fairy tales, are treasures of the romantic movement.

Painting also mirrored romantic ideas. Frenchman Eugene Delacroix [də lä krwä'] (1799–1863), a master of color, painted both exotic scenes and subjects inspired by the revolts of the 1820s and 1830s. Landscape painters in Europe found inspiration in nature and often created scenes of turbulent natural phenomena such as storms and violent seas.

Romanticism in music, as in the other arts, meant a break with tradition. For example, the symphony became much longer and had more parts. The orchestra grew in size, and many instru-

Answers to Section 3 Review

Identify
Key Terms, People, and Places are defined on pages indicated in parentheses. Also see the Glossary and Biographical Dictionary.
laissez-faire capitalism (524), Adam Smith (524), Thomas Malthus (524), Charles Dickens (524), John Stuart Mill (524)

Main Ideas
1. unhealthy and dangerous work places, long workdays, child laborers abused
2. elite, middle class, and working class
3. It became industrial capitalism with corporations and monopolies developing.
4. It allowed them to run businesses as they liked, to pay low wages, and to make higher profits.
5. They objected to poverty and greed and believed social laws would help most people.

Critical Thinking
They assume society is ruled by natural laws; government regulation will only interfere with those laws.

4 | ***Lesson Plan***
Essential Learning Objectives
Students will learn to:
- define romanticism, realism, naturalism, impressionism, and socialism.
- explain the basic thinking of Karl Marx.

- Draw three vertical columns on the board headed romanticism, realism/naturalism, and impressionism. Beginning with column one, ask students to call out those words they associate with romanticism. Proceed to realism/naturalism and impressionism. Conclude by explaining that all of these schools, or "isms," were ways of seeing the world and expressing ideas and feelings.

- Erase the chalkboard and write four new terms: capitalism, socialism, communism, and Marxism. Ask students to use their texts to explain the key differences between capitalism and socialism. Next, have students define communism. Point out to students that when Karl Marx created his own brand of socialism, he insisted on complete community control. Thus, his version of socialism was called communism. Today, socialism is usually thought of as a middle ground between capitalism and communism.

GUIDED PRACTICE

Have students list these phrases associated with Marx and write a sentence about each: class struggle, workers' revolution, *Communist Manifesto*.

Claude Monet's *Impression, Sunrise* (far right), when displayed at an 1874 exhibit in Paris, introduced a dramatically new style of painting, one which a critic sarcastically dubbed "impressionist" after this painting. Auguste Renoir, a friend of Monet, was more interested in the human figure than his fellow impressionists, who were drawn to landscapes. His *Le Moulin de la galette* (near right) was painted in 1876. Following the lead of the impressionists in another direction was Vincent van Gogh, who painted *Irises* (below) in 1889 while in an asylum. The painting sold in 1988 for an incredible 49 million dollars.

ments were made easier to play. These changes appeared in the music of **Ludwig van Beethoven** (1770–1827). His grand symphonies and chamber music are building stones upon which romantic music was founded. Beethoven, a German, remains one of the world's most respected composers.

Later movements turned against romanticism.

In the mid-1800s, some very sentimental romantic art caused people to turn against its ideals. Some of the art had become stale and too sugary sweet for modern tastes.

A new style of art and literature—realism—emerged that appealed to people in the new industrial era. Realists, like the romanticists, saw the harsh social conditions of their times, but though romanticists tried to run from life, realists showed it as it was, "warts and all." Charles Dickens may be the most popular realist writer of all. His pic-

tures of poor and put-upon people called attention to needed reforms.

Another group of writers, the naturalists, tried to describe life as scientists would—without comment or feeling. From 1871 to 1893, a Frenchman, **Émile Zola**, wrote 20 novels that are almost like a doctor's case book of patients. These novels, among them *L'Assammoir* (The Slammer) and *Nana*, tell of the bleak life of the lower classes and are among literature's most powerful tragedies ever.

Painters also followed the path of naturalism. A school called impressionism experimented with new ways to portray light and color in paintings. These painters tried to present an impression of what a person sees at a single moment in time.

Claude Monet [mō nā′], the leader of the French impressionist movement, is known for catching the subtle effects of light in his paintings of outdoor subjects. His most famous paintings highlight the water lilies growing in his country garden in Giverny, France. Other talented impressionist artists included the French Edgar Degas, Auguste Renoir, and Georges Seurat, as well as the American Mary Cassatt. Although the impressionists were initially scorned, their paintings later achieved enormous popular and critical appeal.

Other artists, though, developed impressionism into something new. A Dutch artist, Vincent van

Gogh [*English* van gō′], may have been the most important post-impressionist. A tragic man who suffered from bouts of madness, Van Gogh used bright colors and bold outlines to show his inner impressions of people and places. In expressing a psychological reality, Van Gogh foreshadowed art of the 20th century.

Socialists asked for far-reaching changes.

In the face of the immense problems brought by the Industrial Revolution, philosophers turned their thoughts to finding solutions. Many of the period's thinkers took on the approaches of the novelists and artists of the time. That is to say, some were romantic, others realistic.

Among the people who proposed solutions, the socialists may be the most historically important. They proposed the theory of **socialism**, by which the major means of production and distribution are owned, managed, or controlled by the govern-

ment, by associations of workers, or by the community as a whole. These early socialists, generally known as utopian socialists, hoped to build a better world for all people, especially the working classes.

Robert Owen was one of the best known of the early socialists. He owned a textile mill in Scotland that had 2,000 workers, 500 of whom were children. In 1800 he began a program to improve the conditions for the workers. He raised wages and built schools and houses. No child younger than 11 years old was allowed to work in the mills. As life improved, crime and disease were almost wiped out. At the same time, Owen's mills continued to make a profit.

Owen's ideas eventually led to the founding of the **cooperative movement**. In 1844 a group of linen workers of Rochdale, England, gathered a sum equal to 140 dollars and started a store. Members of the cooperative purchased goods there for fair prices, and they shared the profits. Other co-

527

ASSESS

1. What caused some people to reject romanticism? (excesses of sentimentalism)

2. What is socialism? (government control of major means of production and distribution)

OPTIONAL RETEACHING

Ask students to identify the artistic or philosophical movement with which each of the following is associated: Ludwig van Beethoven (romanticism), Charles Dickens (realism), Émile Zola (naturalism), Claude Monet (impressionism), Robert Owen (socialism)

OPTIONAL ENRICHMENT

Encourage interested students to study impressionism by examining the paintings of Claude Monet. His haystacks series is a good example of momentary impressions. (average)

2. One of the best American examples of socialism in practice was at New Harmony, Indiana. Ask an interested student to do a report on this 1820s community founded by Robert Owen. (challenging)

3. Also for enrichment:

 Overhead Transparency 56

INDEPENDENT PRACTICE/ HOMEWORK

Assign the Section Review, Activities page 165, or Workbook page 111.

CLOSURE

Many political theorists do not really expect to change the course of events. Marx was different. He laid a philosophical foundation for the biggest political upheaval of the 20th century—the Russian Revolution.

BACKGROUND Point out that Marx lived at a time when working conditions were very harsh.

From the Archives

The Communist Platform

In 1847, at a convention in London, Karl Marx and Friedrich Engels were commissioned by the Communist League to write a declaration, or manifesto, of the group's principles. In Part III, the 1888 edition of the Communist Manifesto listed ten measures that would be put into effect when the workers gained control of a government.

1. Abolition of property in land and application of all rents of land to public purposes.
2. A heavy progressive or graduated income tax.
3. Abolition of all right of inheritance.
4. Confiscation of the property of all emigrants and rebels.
5. Centralization of credit in the hands of the State, by means of a national bank. . . .
6. Centralization of the means of communication and transport in the hands of the State.
7. Extension of factories and instruments of production owned by the State; the bringing into cultivation of wastelands, and the improvement of the soil generally in accordance with a common plan.
8. Equal liability of all to labor. Establishment of industrial armies, especially for agriculture.
9. Combination of agriculture with manufacturing industries. . . .
10. Free education for all children in public schools. Abolition of children's factory labor in its present form. . . . .

operative stores, or consumer co-ops, began to spring up elsewhere in Europe. Co-ops grew quite strong in Britain and in Scandinavia, where the co-ops owned and operated factories as well as retail stores. In the United States, storage and marketing co-ops became important.

FROM THE ARCHIVES The authorized English translation dates from 1888 and is reprinted in Robert C. Tucker, ed., *The Marx-Engels Reader* (New York: W. W. Norton, 1972), p. 352. The last point sees education as a great equalizer. Ask the class

Karl Marx taught that socialism was inevitable.

One of the most influential socialists of all time was **Karl Marx**. Marx (1818–1883) was born in Germany and attended school there, where he studied history, economics, and philosophy. He then took up a career as a journalist and went to France, where he met Friedrich Engels, who became his lifelong friend and colleague.

Together, Marx and Engels wrote the *Communist Manifesto* in 1848. This small pamphlet stated most of the ideas of Marxian socialism and set forth a whole plan for social revolution. The *Manifesto* drew little attention when it first appeared, but it eventually became one of the most important papers of modern history.

After participating in two failed revolts in France and Germany in 1848, Marx fled to London, where he spent the rest of his life. There he began *Das Kapital,* his major work. Both Marx and Engels were shocked by the treatment of workers in Europe. Thinking about how this economic system had grown, Marx posed two questions: (1) Why do changes take place in history? and (2) How does the capitalist system work?

Marx answered the first question by saying that changes in the economy are the cause of changes in history. He stated that those people who controlled the means of production—the ways goods were made and distributed—controlled the society. Therefore, the class that controlled a nation's economy also decided its laws, government, religion, and culture.

However, according to Marx, when new groups find new ways of making or distributing goods, they too become rich and powerful. They struggle against the older ruling class, and eventually, the new class wins. Marx called such conflict **class struggle** and said that all important changes in history have come about through this process.

Using the French Revolution to show how class struggle works, Marx showed how the capitalist class of merchants and bankers had overthrown the feudal landowners. The capitalist class had won the right to rule, but Marx believed that their rule would not last because industrialization had created a new lower class—the workers, whom Marx termed the proletariat. The laws of history

to apply this concern to present day issues in the United States. How does child labor contribute to inequality in a society? (Working children miss school time. Their lack of education keeps them from getting better jobs.)

BACKGROUND Marx went into exile in London in 1850 and spent the rest of his life there. He often did research at the British Museum. Much of Marx's life was spent in poverty.

dictated that a new class struggle would begin, and the workers would triumph over capitalism.

Marx based his belief in a coming workers' (socialist) revolution on his answer to the second question: How does the capitalist system work? In *Das Kapital,* Marx began to explain the answer with his labor theory of value. He stated that the value of any product depends on the amount of work needed to produce it. Because manufacturers sold goods at much higher prices than the cost of labor and materials, they made good profits. These profits, Marx reasoned, really belonged to the workers. Logically, in the existing system, the poor would become poorer and the rich richer as wealth settled into a few hands.

Meanwhile, goods would pile up because the workers would be too poor to buy them. As a result, businesses would fail, factories would close, and millions would lose jobs. Finally, after several depressions, capitalism would fall. The workers would take control and set up a socialist society.

Marx's predictions did not prove true.

Marx's ideas about changes in history taught many people that economic forces were important. In the late 1800s and early 1900s, wealth did settle into a few hands. Industry did grow ever larger, and several depressions did hurt business and workers.

Yet, events have shown that Marx was a poor prophet. Most historians believe that events do not happen because of economic forces alone. People act for other reasons as well—patriotism or religion, for example. Economists have shown, too, that Marx's labor theory of value is incorrect. The cost of making a product is not just in the labor needed to make it, but also in materials, equipment, repairs, storage, transportation, and much more. Then, too, economists noted that the general conditions of supply and demand help decide the price of a product. For example, an oversupply of an item can send the selling price below the cost of the work that went into it.

In the late 1800s, conditions for workers improved. Wages rose, and workers could buy the products made in the factories and mills. To be sure, some of the rich did become richer, but most of the poor did not become poorer. Instead, the general standard of living rose to new heights.

BACKGROUND Point out to students that Marx and Engels wrote the *Communist Manifesto* in the same year that revolts and revolutions—led mostly by workers—were taking place throughout Europe, but the *Manifesto* had no immediate effect.

Section 4 Review

Identify romanticism, Ludwig van Beethoven, Émile Zola, Claude Monet, socialism, cooperative movement, Karl Marx, class struggle

Main Ideas

1. Against what conditions or movements were the romanticists reacting?
2. What movements turned against romanticism? Why?
3. What kind of society did early socialists want?
4. Why did Marx think that socialism was inevitable?
5. What mistakes did Marx make in his predictions?

Critical Thinking

Analyzing Comparisons: Consider that romanticism, realism, and socialist ideas were all different responses to the same massive problems and changes of the time. In what ways are today's artists and musicians, especially those popular with high-school students, likewise responding to the rapid changes of our modern society? Give examples.

---

5 *An age of urban mass society and politics began.*

In the 19th century, Western civilization turned into an urban, industrialized society. Nothing like it had been seen before in all of human history. Mass politics were an important part of the new age, and remain so today.

Men gained new rights that women also wanted.

Beginning in the early 19th century, **suffrage**, or the right to vote, had become the chief symbol of democracy. People fought hard to acquire that right.

Male suffrage. For a long time, property-owning classes turned away every effort to give men without property the right to vote. After years of struggle, in 1871 France became the first country to allow all men to vote. Other countries followed, and by 1912 almost every country in western Europe had universal male suffrage.

The millions of new voters changed political parties into mass organizations. In the early 1800s, when only property owners could vote, only small

5 *Lesson Plan*

Essential Learning Objective

Students will learn to understand the workers' struggle for the new rights, benefits, and services that eventually improved living standards.

Emmeline Pankhurst, shown just right of center wearing a long white scarf, was one of the primary leaders in the British movement for women's rights.

Review with students the appalling conditions of workers in the mid-19th century. When Karl Marx wrote the *Communist Manifesto* in 1848, there was good reason to believe his predictions. Many industrial workers had nothing to lose by revolting. However, a communist workers' revolution never occurred in Western Europe or the United States. This lesson in part explains why.

- Write these three terms on the chalkboard and review their meaning: suffrage, trade union, progressive tax.

- Write this thesis on the board: "The Marxist workers' revolution never occurred in Western Europe and the United States because of reform *within* the Western capitalist nations." Give students 10–15 minutes to try to verify this thesis by listing reforms and civic improvements of the 19th and early 20th centuries. Ask them to list their reforms and improvements under these six categories: suffrage, women, workers, education, city services, taxes.

GUIDED PRACTICE

When students have completed their lists, write a composite list on the chalkboard. Circle individual items and ask volunteers to explain how that specific reform or improvement helped cool revolutionary feelings.

groups of upper-class men controlled political parties. Politicians did not need to ask for votes. In the late 1800s, though, when more men had voting rights, politicians had to court voters with expensive campaigns. To pay the bills, politicians needed large parties with dues-paying members. Today mass political parties and costly election campaigns are an expected part of political life in the West.

Women's rights. The general feeling toward women in the 1800s had two sides. Male-dominated society viewed women as inferior, but at the same time women were revered as the heart and strength of the home and family. Most men and many women feared that if women had a part in public business, they would not care for their families. The cornerstone of all civilized life, the home, would then fall apart. In most nations married women had few legal or economic rights.

However, women were needed in the growing workforce, and there was an increased demand for educated women. Florence Nightingale, a British nurse during the Crimean War (1854–1856), helped open nursing to women. Later, women entered some universities, especially in Italy and Switzerland. In the United States, where workers were needed most, large numbers of women became factory workers, teachers, and secretaries.

In the mid-1800s, reformers began to call for equal legal and political rights for women. Most of the leaders were middle-class women, such as the Americans **Susan B. Anthony** and Elizabeth Cady Stanton and the British Emmeline Pankhurst.

By the end of the 1800s, women in most Western countries had gained many rights—such as ownership of property—except for voting rights. In 1867 Australian women, with far more rights than women in other countries, were the first to gain the right to vote. Only after mass political movements did women win the vote in Britain (1918) and the United States (1920). Most European countries followed after that.

Governments made social reforms.

The reforms that western European governments made in the 19th and early 20th centuries demonstrated the influence of the new voters. Big towns and mechanized industry meant more voters in the industrial wage-earning classes. Because voters wanted government to become active in the social affairs of their nations, leaders of all European states paid more attention to social problems.

The Industrial Revolution's strongest critics saw many evils in the new society. They identified seven deadly sins: unhealthy, dangerous factories; impossibly long working hours; child labor; unjust

530

use of women; low wages; slums; and repeated loss of jobs. An angry public awakened to the terrible conditions, and a growing social consciousness called for something to be done about them. This force was felt strongly first in Britain.

In the **Reform Bill of 1832**, Parliament gave seats in the House of Commons to the new industrial towns of the north. Thus, it gave a share of political power to the new business class. Reformers then used this new power to end the evil of slavery around the British Empire in 1833. In 1835 their power helped reduce the upper-class landowners' hold on government and gain a hold for the industrialists.

Parliamentary groups were also set up to look into the awful conditions in the factories and mines. Between 1833 and 1847, these groups of legislators pushed through acts that regulated the use of children, prohibited the use of women and children in mines, and established a ten-hour work day. In the 1870s Parliament passed laws to govern housing and public health. In 1902 the Education Act mandated a national system of primary and secondary education.

Germany, however, was the leader in social legislation beginning in the 1880s. The German government hoped to weaken socialism by passing laws to cure the three big problems of urban industrial life—sickness, accident, and old age. Workers received free medical and hospital care. Factory codes and child labor laws came in 1914.

Many other countries followed the actions of Britain and Germany. By 1914 nearly every European country except Russia and the Balkan countries had rather good factory codes and labor laws. Minimum standards for building houses and streets and for the public preparation of food and drink also had been set.

Workers formed trade unions and political parties.

In the 1800s workers found a new tool with which to improve their work situation and environment—the **trade union**. Modern trade unions are workers' groups that may legally bargain with employers for better wages and working conditions.

Business people and industrialists bitterly opposed such workers' groups. They said trade unions would interfere with their right to run their own businesses in their own ways. Every European country in the early 1800s outlawed trade unions, which had not existed before the 1800s. Workers, however, fought to make the unions legal. In 1825 Britain took the lead in making certain trade unions legal.

In the mid-1880s, trade unions changed. Until then, most unions were made up of skilled workers—mechanics, carpenters, printers. After the mid-1880s, however, huge numbers of unskilled or semiskilled workers in whole industries, such as steel, banded together into countrywide unions. These new unions came into being after a series of long and bitter strikes in the 1880s and 1890s in Belgium, Britain, France, and Germany. When a dock workers' strike in 1889 shut down the port of **London**, business people realized that they could no longer ignore workers' demands for better working conditions.

Workers also tried to improve their lot by forming political parties. The socialists took the lead by founding the German Social Democratic party in 1875. Soon after, socialist parties like it appeared in Britain, France, and most other countries of western Europe. Many of the parties followed Marxist theory, though they ignored the revolutionary aspects. Wherever representative government and democracy were strong, workers used their parties to elect people who would work inside the system for reforms.

The countries of eastern Europe had no such parliaments. Autocratic governments there outlawed political parties and trade unions. Those countries had no orderly way to bring about reform, and it was there that Marxism remained strongly revolutionary.

An urban mass society grew.

The age of urban mass society brought new institutions and new ideas about government's role in society. Ordinary people achieved levels of education and mobility not thought of only a generation or two before.

Until about 1870 large numbers of Europeans could not read or write. Clearly, society needed people with at least a basic education to run modern factories and cities. So governments began to

ASSESS

1. What is a progressive income tax? (The rich pay more than the poor.)
2. Why is Florence Nightingale important? (opened nursing jobs to women)

OPTIONAL RETEACHING

Name some rights, benefits, and institutions (that we take for granted today) that began in the 19th and early 20th centuries. (suffrage, political parties, income taxes, trade unions) Students also may be assigned Activities reteaching page 167.

OPTIONAL ENRICHMENT

Ask interested students to research the life of Emmeline Pankhurst, militant leader of the woman suffrage movement in England. (average)

Students also may be assigned Activities enrichment page 168.

INDEPENDENT PRACTICE/ HOMEWORK

Assign the Section Review, the Chapter Review items, Activities page 166, or Workbook page 112.

CLOSURE

A lesson to all government leaders was retaught in the late 19th and early 20th centuries—the best way to avoid being overthrown is to reform from within. Western Europe learned the lesson well.

George Bellows' *The Cliff Dwellers* (1913) gives insight into crowded urban life. *(Los Angeles County Museum of Art; Los Angeles County Funds)*

set up public school systems for children between the ages of 6 and 14. Between 1871 and 1914, every Western country started a system of public education. At the same time, higher level schools grew in size and number. From them came engineers, doctors, teachers, technicians, and administrators to fill growing needs. Public education became the greatest single force in shaping public opinion and in teaching people how to live in an industrial civilization. Public education made a large reading public for the first time in history, and mass-circulation newspapers began to serve the new audience.

The cost of government rose.

At the same time that national governments were creating social security systems for workers, local governments found ways to make crowded cities more livable. Forward-looking mayors of industrial cities led the way.

New services. In Britain nearly every large town owned its gas and water supplies by 1900. The cities built schools, libraries, hospitals, museums, parks, and art galleries. City-run police and fire departments protected the people, and the cities lighted streets, collected garbage, and disposed of sewage. By 1914 most large cities on the continent had these services, as well as public markets, laundries, slaughterhouses, and employment agencies. Cities had to find a way for huge numbers of people to move cheaply and quickly from one part of the city to another. Streetcars came into use in the 1860s, at first, pulled by horses. Later, in the 1880s, electricity powered them. In very large cities, private companies and governments built underground railroads, or subways. London, in the 1860s, had the first subway. Boston built one in 1895, Paris in 1900, and New York in 1904. Many cities, especially in the United States, saved money by building elevated railroads.

Tax laws. The new national social security systems and city services required a large supply of money. Taxation was seen as the only way to get the large amounts needed. In 1870 no country in Europe had sales or income taxes. Money that governments needed came mostly from tariffs and from taxes on property. Reformers saw the need for tax money and favored a progressive income tax—a tax in which people with large incomes paid a higher percentage of their incomes in taxes than did people on small incomes. Although many people, mostly in the middle and upper classes, strongly opposed such taxes, European countries and the United States began to adopt them in 1911.

By 1914 the strong laissez-faire and Social Darwinist opinions of the early 1800s had faded. People still valued the freedom, dignity, and worth of the individual, but they came to believe that the state should look after the welfare of its people.

Section 5 Review

Identify suffrage, Susan B. Anthony, Reform Bill of 1832, trade unions, London

Main Ideas

1. What right did both men and women want in this period? How did universal suffrage change politics?
2. Name three social reforms of this period.
3. Why did workers form unions and parties?
4. Name some institutions of the new mass society?
5. Why did the cost of government rise?

Critical Thinking

Recognizing Values: How and why did middle-class attitudes about the responsibilities of government change in the 19th and early 20th centuries?

HIGHLIGHTS OF CIVILIZATION

Steam's Conquest of the Seas

James Watt's steam engine converted a trickle of water into a power that drove factories and revolutionized land transportation. This invention also profoundly altered travel by sea.

Before steam, ships were at the mercy of the winds and currents. Unforeseen delays frequently meant the loss of perishable cargoes.

Steam revolutionized water transportation, moving people and goods more directly, more quickly, and more cheaply than ever before. The development of transatlantic steamships illustrates the change. In a race held in April, 1838, two ships, the *Sirius* and the *Great Western*, competed to be the first steamship to cross the Atlantic Ocean under continuous steam power. The *Sirius*, a small ship, arrived first, but it had left England so loaded down with coal that there was little room for passengers. Even then, the captain had to burn the mast to keep up steam on the last day of the voyage. The *Great Western*, specifically designed for transatlantic travel, arrived soon after with fuel to spare. The *Great Eastern,* launched in 1858, was the most spectacular 19th-century steamship. This ship, powered by a four-cylinder James Watt engine, was 40 years ahead of its time, with room for 4,000 passengers and a double iron hull that was virtually indestructible. Although never a financial success, the *Great Eastern* was part of a revolution whose effects were felt in every corner of the world.

James Watt's steam engine (below) brought a revolution in water transportation illustrated by the Great Eastern steamship (left), launched in 1858.

HIGHLIGHTS OF CIVILIZATION
You may wish to point out that most 19th-century steamships used for ocean travel retained their masts and sails in case they ran out of fuel. It was not until the early 1900s that large ships without sails were built.

You may wish to share this newspaper account of the arrival in New York harbor of the *Great Western*. "This immense moving mass was propelled at a rapid rate through the waters of the Bay; she passed swiftly and gracefully around the *Sirius,* exchanging salutes with her destined anchorage in the East River."

The *Great Eastern* was especially designed for voyages from England around the tip of Africa to India and back to Europe. However, it was used instead for transatlantic travel, for which it was badly designed. As a passenger ship, it was a failure, but in 1866 it was used to lay the first successful transatlantic cable.

You may wish to share the following stanzas from a poem by Erasmus Darwin, written in 1789:

"Soon shall thy arm, unconquered steam afar
Drag the slow barge, or drive the rapid car;
Or on wide-waving wings expanded bear
The flying-chariot through the fields of air."

(from *The Botanic Garden, Pt. I.*)

Answers to Test Yourself

Key Terms, People, and Places
The key terms, people, and places tested here were introduced in the chapter sections and reviewed in the Section Reviews. For definitions see the page references at the appropriate Section Reviews. Also see the Glossary and Biographical Dictionary.

Main Ideas
The main ideas tested here were introduced in the sections of this chapter and reviewed in the Section Reviews. For answers to these questions, see the appropriate Section Reviews.

Critical Thinking
1. Students should present arguments that support the right and need to vote. For example, they may discuss the right to participate in one's government and to help decide the political and social future of one's community or country.
2. Students must weigh the theories and make their own decisions.

CHAPTER 28 REVIEW

Section Summaries

Section 1
The Industrial Revolution changed the Western world.
The Industrial Revolution began in Britain. Especially important were changes in the textile industry and in coal and iron production. Improved transportation knit regions more closely together.

Section 2
A second Industrial Revolution took place.
In Europe and North America, new industries appeared after the 1850s. Meanwhile, science and medicine developed a stream of new discoveries and theories.

Section 3
Urbanism and industrialism created many social problems.
Workers flocked from farms to cities, where there were crowded, unhealthy housing and poor working conditions. The middle class favored laissez-faire capitalism while building corporations and monopolies.

Section 4
Artists and thinkers responded to the Industrial Revolution.
Most of the arts felt the hold of romanticism until the mid-1800s. Then followed the literary realism of Dickens, the impressionist painting of Monet, the naturalism of Zola, and the post-impressionism of Van Gogh. Early socialists built model communities, but Karl Marx began a different form of socialism. After 1870 the standard of living rose higher than ever before.

Section 5
An age of urban mass society and politics began.
After 1850 a mass urban civilization came into being. Democracy took great strides forward with universal male suffrage and, later, legal and political rights for women. Labor unions became legal and gained members and power. Socialists reached their goals through reform laws.

Test Yourself

Key Terms, People, and Places
Identify the significance of each of the following:

Section 1
a. Industrial Revolution
b. cottage industry
c. mass production
d. James Watt
e. Liverpool

Section 2
a. Henry Bessemer
b. Orville and Wilbur Wright
c. Louis Pasteur
d. Charles Darwin
e. Social Dawinism

Review Dates

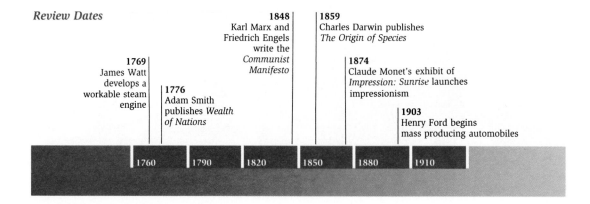

1769
James Watt develops a workable steam engine

1776
Adam Smith publishes *Wealth of Nations*

1848
Karl Marx and Friedrich Engels write the *Communist Manifesto*

1859
Charles Darwin publishes *The Origin of Species*

1874
Claude Monet's exhibit of *Impression: Sunrise* launches impressionism

1903
Henry Ford begins mass producing automobiles

1760 1790 1820 1850 1880 1910

Section 3
a. laissez-faire capitalism
b. Adam Smith
c. Thomas Malthus
d. Charles Dickens
e. John Stuart Mill

Section 4
a. romanticism
b. Ludwig van Beethoven
c. Émile Zola
d. socialism
e. cooperative movement
f. Karl Marx
g. class struggle

Section 5
a. suffrage
b. Susan B. Anthony
c. Reform Bill of 1832
d. trade unions
e. London

Main Ideas

Section 1
1. Name four conditions in Britain that favored industrialization.
2. What machines changed the textile industry?
3. How did coal and iron use become widespread?
4. How did transportation improve in the 1800s?

Section 2
1. What delayed industry's spread beyond Britain?
2. What were three new technologies of this time?
3. How did medical knowledge advance?
4. How did developments in biology change ideas?

Section 3
1. Describe the common working conditions.
2. Describe 19th-century Europe's class structure.
3. How did growing industry change capitalism?
4. Why did laissez-faire appeal to business leaders?
5. Name two famous people who objected to laissez-faire. What were their objections?

Section 4
1. Explain how the romantic movement was a response to its time.
2. Which movements followed romanticism? Why?
3. What were the goals of early socialists?
4. What made Marx think socialism was inevitable?
5. How were Marx's predictions wrong?

Section 5
1. What right did men and women fight for in this period? How did politics change?
2. What were three social reforms of this period?
3. How did unions and parties benefit workers?

4. What were some of the institutions of the new urban mass society?
5. What made the cost of government rise in the late 1800s and early 1900s?

Critical Thinking

1. Identifying Assumptions Voting rates have been very low in several recent presidential elections. How might you convince someone who chooses not to vote to exercise their hard-won right? Give several arguments that you might use.

2. Recognizing Values At a debate between the economists David Ricardo and John Stuart Mill, whom do you think you would support? Why? Support your answer with evidence.

Chapter Skills and Activities

Practicing Study and Research Skills
Using Problem-Solving Skills
In order to solve a problem, you must be able to define the problem accurately, identify its cause, and determine possible solutions. Many of the inventions, literature movements, and social policies of the Industrial Revolution arose as responses to problems in commercial or social areas. Identify one of these problems from the chapter, such as in the area of transportation or social inequality. Then (a.) write a sentence stating what the problem is, (b.) write another sentence identifying the cause or causes of the problem, then (c.) suggest one possible solution to the problem. Finally, (d.) compare your solution with how those people in history solved it.

Linking Past and Present

You have read in this chapter about the controversy that surrounded social changes. Controversy over reform is as strong today. Name two important social problems under debate in the national legislature.

Learning History Through Maps

Referring to the Atlas maps of Europe on pages 792–793, consider the advantages and disadvantages Britain faced as a developing industrial country because of its geography and location.

CRITICAL THINKING QUESTION LEVEL 1. easy;
2. average

Revolutions in Everyday Life and Politics

OVERVIEW

During the first half of the 19th century, liberalism and nationalism contributed to an independent Greece and Belgium and provided social, political, and economic reforms in Great Britain and France.

PLANNING CHART

Section	Text Pages	Key Concept	Suggested Teaching Time
1 Liberals and nationalists challenged political systems throughout Europe.	537–541	England took the lead in European reform in the first half of the 19th century.	Two days **More time?** Use *Source Reading 29A.*
2 The European balance of power shifted as Italy and Germany became unified nations.	541–544	The map of Europe changed and the power balance shifted when Italy and Germany became unified in 1870 and 1871.	One day **More time?** Use *Overhead Transparency 57.*
3 Democratic gains were made in western Europe.	544–547	As it had done earlier in the century, western Europe continued to press for reform between 1850 and 1914.	One day **Less time?** Discuss Sections 3 and 5 in one class period.
4 Reforms came slowly in Russia and nonindustrial Europe.	547–551	Russia and the rest of nonindustrial Europe lagged behind in matters of liberal and democratic reform.	One day
5 Democracy advanced in the United States, Canada, and Australia.	551–554	By 1914 the United States, Canada, and Australia had helped establish the Western world as the most democratically advanced region of the globe.	One day **More time?** Use *Source Reading 29B* or *Overhead Transparency 58.*

ANCILLARIES

Materials that may be used with this chapter to reinforce, reteach, enrich, and assess learning are pictured on the following pages.

Teacher's Resource File

ACTIVITIES

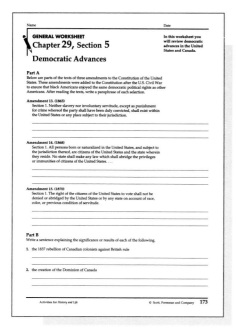

Section 1 Activity, p. 169

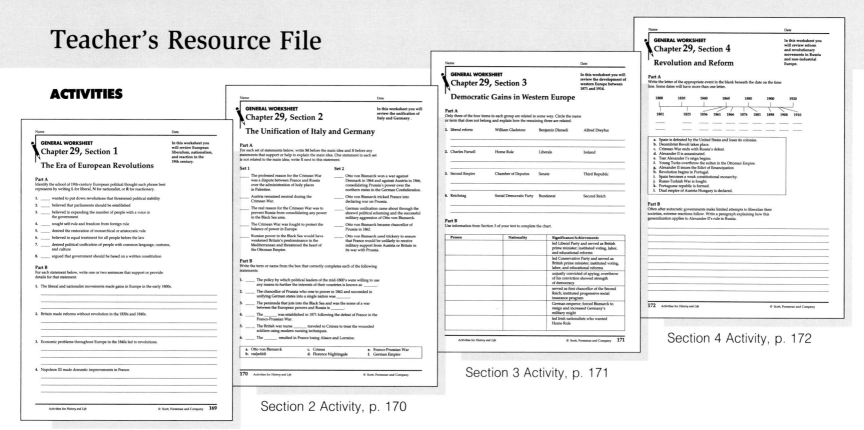

Section 2 Activity, p. 170

Section 3 Activity, p. 171

Section 4 Activity, p. 172

Section 5 Activity, p. 173

Chapter 29 Reteaching, p. 174

Chapter 29 Enrichment, p. 175

Teacher's Resource File

GEOGRAPHY SKILLS

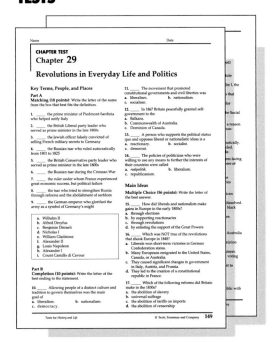

Chapter 29 Geography
Worksheet/Map, pp. 59–60

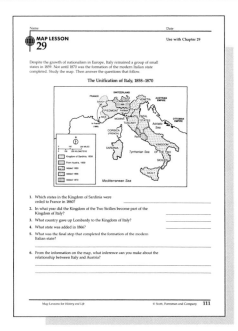

Chapter 29 Map Lesson, p. 111

TESTS

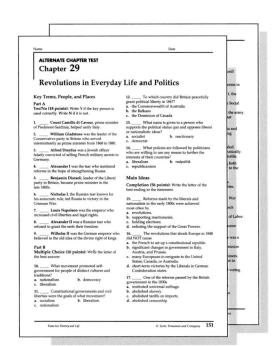

535c

Chapter Test, pp. 149–150

Alternate Chapter Test, pp. 151–152

Other Optional Ancillaries

WORKBOOK

WORKSHEET
Chapter 29, Section 1

In this worksheet you will review European liberalism, nationalism, and reaction.

Liberalism, Nationalism, Revolution

Part A
Complete each statement with the explanations given in your text.

1. The leaders of the Great Powers felt that they had to put down revolutions in any European country **because**

2. A liberal revolution broke out in France under Charles X **because**

3. Belgian nationalists and middle-class liberals revolted in 1830 **because**

4. In the 1830s the British reformed their voting laws and economic policies **because**

5. In the 1800s British working classes experienced extreme poverty **because**

6. Revolutions broke out in Europe in 1848 **because**

Part B
Describe the main goals of the Congress of Vienna and the Concert of Europe.

Section 1 Worksheet, p. 113

WORKSHEET
Chapter 29, Section 2

In this worksheet you will review the unification of Italy and Germany into national states.

The Unification of Italy and Germany

Part A
Number the events in each set in the order in which they happened.

Set 1
_____ Austria declared war on Italy.
_____ The Crimean War took place.
_____ The Kingdom of Italy was proclaimed.
_____ Most of northern Italy was united with Sardinia.
_____ Venetia and Rome came under Italian control, completing the unification of modern Italy.

Set 2
_____ The German Empire was formed.
_____ Otto von Bismarck became chancellor of Prussia.
_____ France declared war on Prussia.
_____ France was defeated by Prussia.
_____ Bismarck won wars against Denmark and Austria.

Part B
Identify the person described in each riddle.

1. I went to the Crimea to treat wounded soldiers in a war in which thousands of soldiers were needlessly wounded. I introduced modern nursing techniques that included rigid standards of cleanliness and effective organization. Who am I?

2. I led volunteer soldiers from all over Italy in the war against Austria. I urged my soldiers to continue fighting until all of Italy came under one Italian government. Who am I?

3. I was the chancellor of Prussia who believed strongly that Germany would not reach greatness through speeches and votes but "blood and iron." I led Prussia in victorious wars against Denmark, Austria, and France and am often credited with having brought about the unification of Germany. Who am I?

4. As prime minister of Piedmont-Sardinia, I recognized that the only way to drive the Austrians from northern Italy was with the help of foreign powers. For that reason, I made a secret pact with Napoleon III at the Paris peace conference at the end of the Crimean War. My mastery of realpolitik paved the way for the eventual unification of Italy. Who am I?

Section 2 Worksheet, p. 114

WORKSHEET
Chapter 29, Section 3

In this worksheet you will review democratic gains made between 1871 and 1914 in western Europe.

Democratic Gains in Western Europe

Part A
Write T if the statement is true and F if it is false. On the lines below, rewrite each false statement to make it true.

1. _____ Under Benjamin Disraeli and William Gladstone, Britain took few steps to extend voting rights.

2. _____ By 1891, Britain had established free and compulsory education.

3. _____ Irish Catholics had won the right to form and run their own government by the mid-1800s.

4. _____ Although Alfred Dreyfus was clearly a victim of anti-Semitism, the overthrowing of his conviction showed that in France the Republic was more powerful than the army.

5. _____ Otto von Bismarck instituted Europe's first progressive program of social insurance in an attempt to attract workers away from socialism.

6. _____ By 1890 the German emperors had had their fill of militaristic and nationalistic glory, and Wilhelm II decided to forego military and nationalist aims to pursue domestic reforms.

Part B
Write the letter of the correct description or definition from the box beside its name.

1. _____ Irish Free State
2. _____ Ulster
3. _____ anti-Semitism
4. _____ Bundesrat
5. _____ Chamber of Deputies and Senate
6. _____ Whigs
7. _____ Tories
8. _____ Reichstag

a. southern Ireland
b. prejudice against Jews
c. upper house of German legislature
d. Northern Ireland
e. French legislature in Third Republic
f. Conservatives in England
g. Liberals in England
h. lower house of German legislature

Section 3 Worksheet, p. 115

WORKSHEET
Chapter 29, Section 4

In this worksheet you will review reforms in non-industrial Europe and Russia.

Revolution and Reform

Part A
Write the letter of the correct name or term from the box beside its definition or identifying phrase.

1. _____ the 1825 attempt by intellectuals and army officers to overthrow the Russian government

2. _____ the Russian tsar who, despite the liberal ideals of his youth, ruled as an autocrat from 1801 to 1825

3. _____ act of 1861 that gave Russian serfs personal freedom and promised them land

4. _____ region between Europe and Russia that was home to many Slavic ethnic groups who wanted independence

5. _____ strict Russian tsar who ruled during the Crimean War, censored the press, took away academic freedoms, and sent enemies to Siberia

6. _____ money paid by freed Russian serfs to former landlords for the use of the land

7. _____ tsar who made reforms, including the abolishment of serfdom, in the hopes of strengthening Russia

a. Alexander I
b. Nicholas I
c. Alexander II
d. the Balkans
e. Decembrist Revolt
f. Edict of Emancipation
g. redemption tax

Part B
Write the letter of each effect from the box beside its cause.

1. _____ Russian intellectuals studied in France and learned democratic ideas; Russian army officers occupied France and were exposed to liberal ideas.

2. _____ Idealistic Russians attempted to overthrow the government in the Decembrist Revolt.

3. _____ The Russian army lost the Crimean War to the forces of more liberal societies.

4. _____ Alexander II freed the serfs but did little to improve their living conditions.

5. _____ Spain was defeated by the United States in the Spanish-American War of 1898.

6. _____ Despite European assistance, the Turkish government remained corrupt and inefficient.

7. _____ In the multi-ethnic Austrian-Hungarian Empire, Germans dominated in Austria, and Hungarians ruled in Hungary.

a. Alexander II instituted the liberal reforms of the 1860s.
b. Spain lost the remains of its once worldwide colonial empire.
c. People returned to Russia eager to implement liberal changes in government and society.
d. The Ottoman Empire disintegrated.
e. Other ethnic groups in Austria-Hungary, such as the Czechs, Romanians, Slovaks, and Serbs, longed for self-rule.
f. Tsar Nicholas I ruled Russia as a strict autocrat.
g. The peasants could not support their families and remained in grinding poverty.

Section 4 Worksheet, p. 116

WORKSHEET
Chapter 29, Section 5

In this worksheet you will review the advancement of democracy in the United States, Canada, and Australia.

Advances in Democracy

Part A
Below are several statements of opinion. On the lines below each statement, write a statement of fact about the same subject.

1. All Canadians should speak only the English language.

2. The arrival of immigrants to the United States between 1790 and 1860 brought nothing but confusion to America.

3. The process of industrializing America should have been delayed by 50 or 100 years to give people a chance to get used to territorial expansion.

4. During the 1860s the United States would have been better off allowing seceding states to leave the Union and begin their own independent nation.

5. The only reason that the North won the Civil War was that it believed in doing the right thing.

6. The United States, Canada, and Australia have nothing in common.

Part B
Write a paragraph describing how democratic political rights were extended in the United States.

Section 5 worksheet, p. 117

SOURCE READINGS

Source Reading 29A
Source Reading 29B

OVERHEAD TRANSPARENCIES

Overhead Transparency 57
Overhead Transparency 58

TEST GENERATOR

40 multiple-choice questions for Chapter 29

Revolutions in Everyday Life and Politics

1815–1914

1810	
1814	Congress of Vienna meets
1848	Revolutions shake Europe
1870	Italy becomes unified
1890	
1910	

It was March, 1848. In an Austrian chateau not far from Vienna, an old man was alone with his host. The old man played the "Marseillaise," the revolutionary French national anthem, again and again on a violin. The old man was Prince Metternich, who, until a few days before, had been one of the most feared and hated men in Europe. Now, after more than 40 years in the role of the Austrian foreign minister, he had lost power because of a bloody uprising in the Austrian capital of Vienna.

In many ways the events of 1848 grew from the French revolutionary ideals of liberty, equality, and fraternity. They became known all over Europe and gave rise to three movements: (1) liberalism, which stressed constitutional government and civil liberties; (2) democracy, which advocated giving the average citizen a voice in government; and (3) nationalism, which looked to give people of similar culture and traditions their own government.

The political history of 19th-century Europe is primarily the story of how these three movements changed governments. It is a story full of struggle. Governments feared radical changes and looked upon liberals and nationalists as dangerous radicals. Revolts occurred often, but most of them failed.

Although democracy was revolutionary in 1815, by 1914 it had become the most desired form of government. Because of nationalism, the political map of Europe in 1914 was quite different from the map of 1815. Two large nations—Germany and Italy—were born. The forces of liberalism, democracy, and nationalism also had a major impact on European civilization abroad, especially in the United States, Canada, and Australia.

Throughout the western world, these three forces revolutionized everyday life and politics. Nowhere in the world was the political consciousness of ordinary people more highly developed than it was in the west at the end of the 19th century.

The shape of Europe was drastically changed as a result of the meeting portrayed above of the Congress of Vienna in 1814. This painting is from an 1815 watercolor.

Reading Preview

In this chapter you will read how western political systems became more democratic between 1815 and 1914.

1. *Liberals and nationalists challenged political systems throughout Europe.*

2. *The European balance of power shifted as Italy and Germany became unified nations.*

3. *Democratic gains were made in western Europe.*

4. *Reforms came slowly in Russia and non-industrial Europe.*

5. *Democracy advanced in the United States, Canada, and Australia.*

1 | *Liberals and nationalists challenged political systems throughout Europe.*

After Napoleon was defeated, the people of Europe were sick of war and longed for peace. In 1814 the leaders of the countries who had won the war against France participated in peace talks at the **Congress of Vienna**. The main goals of this meeting were to settle conflicts among the Great Powers, a group made up of the five strongest powers of Europe—Britain, France, Prussia, Austria, and Russia—and to strike a political balance among these powerful states. To reach their goals, the Congress of Vienna first created small buffer states along the borders of France, which was still con-

BACKGROUND The Congress of Vienna was more like an extended party than a major international conference. As hosts, the Austrians staged lavish balls, hunts, and festivals. Also, Beethoven conducted the premiere of his *Seventh Symphony*.

1 *Lesson Plan*

Essential Learning Objectives

Students will learn to:

- identify what role nationalism played in creating an independent Greece and Belgium.

- analyze how liberalism contributed to economic and political reforms in Great Britain and France.

Europe in 1815

MAP STUDY This political map of Europe in 1815, after the Congress of Vienna, shows Europe divided into three general areas—western, central, and eastern. What three empires dominated eastern Europe in 1815?

sidered the main threat to the peace of Europe. Then Austria, Russia, Prussia, and Britain agreed to meet periodically to guard the Vienna settlement and to keep peace in Europe. This group, called the Concert of Europe, put forth the first international effort to try to solve shared problems.

Strong powers opposed liberalism and nationalism.

The leaders who met at the Congress of Vienna saw liberalism and nationalism as dangerous to their security. These leaders were considered to be **reactionary** because they reacted against liberal or nationalistic ideas they felt would upset the status quo. Nevertheless, liberalism and nationalism spread in Europe in the early 19th century. Both movements grew most rapidly in the cities, where the middle classes were gaining strength.

Aims of the liberals. As you read, **liberalism** was a movement that pushed for constitutional governments and civil liberties. Some European liberals wanted to keep the existing monarchies, but others wanted to form republics. However, all agreed on the need for parliaments that spoke for the people. These 19th-century liberals did not believe everyone should have a voice in government. Yet, by seeking to give a vote to every adult male who owned property, they aimed to broaden the base of government. Liberals believed that governments should be based on written constitutions and should protect the rights of people to speak, write, and gather freely.

ANSWER TO MAP STUDY The Russian, Austrian, and Ottoman empires

Aims of the nationalists. Although nationalists often favored liberal programs, the main goal of **nationalism** was to give people of distinct nationalities self-rule. Nationalists believed that all people who shared a language, customs, and culture had the right to form their own government. To do that, they needed self-determination—freedom from foreign rule. Nationalists felt that all true patriots should work for self-rule and for unification if their country had been divided politically.

Aims of the reactionaries. The men who drew up the Vienna settlement almost completely ignored liberal aims and nationalistic feelings of the people affected by their decisions. The stand of the Great Powers was stated publicly by Austria's Prince Metternich. He said that the Great Powers could rightly move to put down revolutions in any European country, because such revolutions threatened the stability of the entire continent. Besides crushing revolutions, Metternich and other European leaders also appointed rulers or carved political boundaries in flagrant disregard for the feelings of various nationalities.

Liberalism and nationalism made gains in the early 1800s.

Although reactionaries put up stiff opposition, liberal and nationalistic movements grew and made modest gains in the years after the Congress of Vienna. These movements met with some success in Greece, France, and Belgium in the early 1800s.

Nationalism in Greece. The Greeks, under the rule of the Ottoman Empire since the 15th century, longed to regain independence. In 1821 Greek nationalists rose against the Turkish government. Britain, France, and Russia eventually sided with the Greeks, hoping to speed the decline of the Ottoman Empire. Outnumbered by larger and better forces, the Turks lost. In 1830 Greece became an independent monarchy.

Liberalism in France. After the defeat of Napoleon, in 1814, Louis XVIII was named king of France. Although the new French government established a representative body, the king essentially held all power.

After the death of Louis XVIII in 1824, Charles X became the king. Charles X was quite reactionary. He tried to restore the power and wealth of the French aristocracy. He also ousted elected government officials who would not obey him and suppressed criticism of his policies. When a large number of liberals won seats in the Chamber of Deputies in the elections of 1830, Charles X simply tried to dissolve that governing body. This act was the final straw for the liberals of Paris. Revolution broke out, and Charles X went into exile in Britain.

The wealthy middle classes then became leaders in the revolution. In July, 1830, they offered the French crown to Louis Philippe [lü′ē fē lēp′], Duke of Orleans, who promised to honor the constitution of 1814. Louis Philippe's reign, called the July Monarchy, was a victory for the liberals. Censorship was ended, trial by jury was guaranteed, and more people were allowed to vote. However, voting was still limited to men who owned large amounts of property.

Nationalism in Belgium. As you have read, the Belgians were placed under Dutch rule by the Congress of Vienna in 1815. Unhappy with this arrangement and inspired by the success of the liberals in France, the Belgian people revolted in 1830. The Belgian nationalists and middle-class liberals declared Belgium a free country. They held national elections and drew up a constitution that was more liberal than any other in Europe at the time. In 1831 the Great Powers recognized Belgian independence under the stipulation that Belgium always remain neutral in any European conflict.

In France's revolution of 1830, the French middle class replaced Charles X with the more liberal king Louis Philippe.

1. Why did Belgium become independent? (People in Belgium did not want to be ruled by the Dutch.)
2. What part of Europe was slowest to experience liberal reform? (eastern Europe)

OPTIONAL RETEACHING

Rule three columns on the chalkboard and label them Political, Economic, and Social. With texts open, have students point out British reforms in each area.

OPTIONAL ENRICHMENT

1. Have interested students write a letter to the editor of the *London Times* dated December 1, 1831. The letter should either support or criticize the lowering of property requirements for male suffrage. (average)
2. Have capable students write a response to the following: The years following the Thirty Years' War saw the rise of absolutism. The years following the Napoleonic wars saw the rise of reactionary governments. Is it a general tendency in history that major wars are followed by reaction, not liberal reform? (challenging)
3. Also for enrichment:

 Source Reading 29A

INDEPENDENT PRACTICE/ HOMEWORK

Assign the Section Review, Activities page 169, or Workbook page 113.

CLOSURE

Liberalism and democratic reform took steps forward in the first half of the 1800s. A few nations, such as Belgium and Greece, won their independence. However, most liberal-led revolutions in 1848 were suppressed by reactionary governments.

Britain made reforms without violent upheaval.

Britain was the only major western European country to escape violent revolution in the 1830s. Nevertheless, under pressure from liberals, the British made major domestic reforms.

Voting reforms. The first important change the British Parliament made in voting laws was the Reform Bill of 1832, which you read about in Chapter 28. Political power no longer belonged only to the large landowners, but was extended to the middle classes as well.

However, many working people felt cheated by the 1832 Reform Bill, which did not give them the right to vote. Some joined a radical movement known as Chartism, which took its name from the People's Charter of 1838. The charter was a petition that called for broad reforms, including extending the right to vote to all men whether they owned property or not, abolishing the property qualification for eligibility to the House of Commons, and instituting the secret ballot for all elections. Between 1838 and 1848, the Chartists sent the House of Commons three petitions signed by millions of people. The petitions were rejected. Nevertheless, the push for these reforms continued, and within 50 years the reforms they called for all became law in Britain.

Economic reforms. The working classes in Britain not only pushed for reforms in voting laws, they also called for changes in economic policy. In Chapter 20 you read about mercantilism, which prescribed high tariffs to reduce the amount of foreign goods entering a country. In the 1800s Britain still retained their tariffs on imported grains, even though the country could not produce enough grain to feed the growing population. Thus, basic foods, such as bread, were quite expensive, causing severe hardship among the working classes.

Crop failures in the 1840s made the situation even worse. A group made up of middle- and working-class people was formed to push for abolition of the tariffs on grains, or, as they were known, the Corn Laws. This Anti–Corn Law League instituted a public campaign to pressure Parliament. As a result, Parliament ended the grain tariffs in 1846, and the price of grain dropped. This marked a turning point in English politics. For the

BACKGROUND In the next two decades, British patrols captured more than 1,000 slave ships and freed the Africans on board, allowing them to return to their homes.

first time, the middle and working classes won a big victory over the landowning upper classes, whose farm profits dropped without protective grain tariffs.

Abolition of slavery. Another issue of major importance to British reformers was slavery. They fought for slavery's abolition for two main reasons. First, they pointed out that slavery was immoral and "un-Christian." Second, they argued that it would be more profitable to develop Africa as a market for manufactured goods rather than use it as a source of slave labor. Because of the efforts of reformers, Parliament totally abolished slavery on British territory in 1833. The British government also gained permission from other European governments to permit British warships to seize slave ships of any nation found on the high seas.

Throughout Britain demonstrations of the kind below, led by the Anti-Corn Law League, helped to bring about the repeal of the Corn Laws in 1846.

Revolutions shook Europe in 1848.

The rumblings of the 1830s furthered the liberal cause in Europe, and west of the Rhine River, liberalism grew rapidly. East of the river, the reactionaries were firmly in power. However, economic problems throughout Europe in the 1840s led to revolutions on both sides of the Rhine.

In the mid-1840s, a business depression caused a serious loss of jobs all across Europe, from Britain to the Balkans. Potato blights swept from Poland to Ireland in 1845 and 1846, destroying an important food crop in these regions. In addition, the grain crops failed throughout Europe. Food was scarce and famine became widespread. Europeans who could manage the trip sought to escape these economic problems by emigrating to the United States, Canada, or Australia.

Violent revolts occurred in France, Italy, Austria, Prussia, and other states in the German Confederation. Although liberals won short-term victories in each of these countries, the reactionaries soon regained power. The only significant change in government occurred in France. There, King Louis Philippe was overthrown and a constitutional republic was set up, which permitted all adult males to vote. Louis Napoleon, nephew of Napoleon Bonaparte, was elected president in December, 1848. However, the Second Republic, as the new French government was called, proved to be short-lived. Within four years, Louis Napoleon had abolished the republic and proclaimed himself Napoleon III, Emperor of France.

Napoleon III (so named because his cousin, the son of Napoleon I, was technically the second Napoleon) had no outstanding ability in war or administration. However, he was a clever politician and could sway the public's feelings in any direction. Although he limited civil liberties and reduced legal rights, the French people supported their second emperor.

Napoleon III's popularity basically resulted from France's economic success during his reign. The railroads were expanded. The streets of Paris were broadened and beautiful parks built. For the peasants, Napoleon III set up model farms, and for the workers, he legalized labor unions. In addition, hospitals were built, and free medicine was distributed to the poorest classes.

BACKGROUND Had Napoleon III concentrated on domestic improvements, he might have gone down in French history as a great leader. Instead, he tried, but ultimately failed, to make France a great power in world politics. As you will read in the

Section 1 Review

Identify Congress of Vienna, reactionary, liberalism, nationalism, Napoleon III

Main Ideas

1. Compare and contrast the aims of liberalism and nationalism with the aims of reactionaries in 19th-century Europe.
2. How did liberals and nationalists make gains in Europe in the early 1800s?
3. What reforms did Britain make in the 1830s and the 1840s?
4. Why did revolutions shake Europe in 1848, and what were the results of these revolts?

Critical Thinking

Evaluating Sources of Information: In Britain in the 1830s the Chartists and members of the Anti–Corn Law League often clashed. Read the following passage. Which side do you think the writer is on? Whom is the writer addressing? Do you think the arguments the speaker makes are valid? Why or why not?

"And now they [the Parliament members who represented the middle classes] want to get the Corn Laws repealed—not for your benefit—but their own. 'Cheap Bread!' they cry. But they mean 'Low wages.' Do not listen to their cant and humbug. Stick to your Charter. You are veritable slaves without your votes."

<table><tr><td>2</td><td>The European balance of power shifted as Italy and Germany became unified nations.</td></tr></table>

The failure of the 1848 revolutions caused disillusionment among the European liberals and nationalists. As a result, a new kind of politician became prominent throughout Europe. These leaders were shrewd realists in their analyses of political situations and were willing to use any means, even force, to further the interests of their countries. Their policies were called ***realpolitik***, a German word meaning power politics. In *realpolitik*, war became a legitimate means for achieving political goals. The policy of *realpolitik* eventually led to instability that plagued Europe well into the 20th century.

next section, Napoleon III's inexperience in foreign policy would prove to be his downfall.

- Identify the causes of the Crimean War. Point out the results of the conflict, especially as it affected Russia.

- Discuss how Cavour, using *realpolitik*, was able to unify northern Italy. Point to problems in both French and Austrian policy in regard to Italy.

- Have the students list the steps in German unification. Show what role the Franco-Prussian War played in the unification.

GUIDED PRACTICE

Individually or in groups, alternately assign students to review the unification stories of either Italy or Germany. Have each group complete a time line of events.

BACKGROUND Fought in the fall of 1854, the Battle of Balaklava during the Crimean War was the inspiration for Alfred Lord Tennyson's poem "The Charge of the Light Brigade."

The Crimean War ended decades of peace between European nations.

The Crimean War, which began in 1853, was the first big armed clash in Europe after 1815. The professed reason for this war was a dispute between France and Russia over the administration of holy places in Palestine, which was under the jurisdiction of the weak Ottoman Empire. Actually, the conflict, which pitted French, British, Italian, and Turkish troops against Russian forces, was an attempt to prevent Russia from consolidating any power in the Black Sea. Such a shift in the balance of power would have weakened Britain's predominance in the Mediterranean and threatened the heart of the Ottoman Empire. Almost all fighting took place in the **Crimea**, the large peninsula that juts out into the Black Sea.

The invention of the telegraph in 1837 meant that for the first time news reports from foreign fronts could be rapidly dispatched. The European public was shocked by what they heard about the horrible conditions to which the soldiers were subjected and by the suffering of the wounded. **Florence Nightingale**, a British war nurse, traveled to the Crimea to treat the wounded soldiers. She introduced modern nursing techniques, including rigid standards of cleanliness and an organized medical staff.

The Crimean War was essentially a stalemate. When Austria, which had remained neutral, threatened to enter the war on the side of the British, French, Italians, and Turks in 1855, Russia sued for peace. In 1856 the warring countries gathered at Paris for a peace conference. The treaty that resulted hurt Russia in several ways. Most important was the ban on all battleships on the Black Sea. This development left Russia's southern border undefended, in effect, weakening Russia. Another important result of the peace conference in Paris was a secret pact France made with Italy to help oust Austria from two northern Italian states, paving the way for Italy's unification.

Italian nationalists fought to unify Italy.

As you can see on the map on page 543, Italy in the mid-1800s was divided into a number of separate states. Although Italian nationalists had been fighting for a united Italy for decades, they had met with little success. Austria controlled the two northern states of Lombardy and Venetia. The pope controlled the Papal States.

After the revolutions of 1848, the only success the Italian liberals and nationalists had was in establishing a strong constitutional monarchy in Piedmont and Sardinia. Under the leadership of Count **Camillo di Cavour** [kä vür'], the prime minister of the joined states of Piedmont-Sardinia, Italy eventually became unified.

A master of *realpolitik*, Cavour saw that the only way to drive the Austrians from northern Italy was

Florence Nightingale, at left, was an inspirational British nurse who worked in a Crimean war hospital such as the one below.

The Unification of Italy, 1858–1870

Kingdom of Sardinia 1858
From Austria 1859
Added 1860
Added 1866
Added 1870

MAP STUDY Italy was divided into small states for many years. What were the last two states to be added to the Italian union?

to enlist the help of foreign powers. It was Cavour who made the secret pact with Napoleon III of France at the Paris peace conference at the end of the Crimean War.

In April, 1859, after the Piedmont-Sardinia government refused Austria's ultimatum to reduce its army, Austria declared war. According to their pledge, France joined the Italian forces, and together they routed the Austrian forces from Lombardy. Revolutions broke out all over northern Italy. Napoleon III, fearful that all of Italy would actually be united and thus endanger France's security, made a separate peace with Austria. Never-

theless, the revolutions continued, and in 1860, all of northern Italy except Venetia was united with Sardinia.

Under the leadership of **Giuseppe Garibaldi** [gar′ə bôl′dē], volunteer troops from all over the peninsula continued the fight for a unified Italy. Together Garibaldi and Cavour succeeded in uniting most of the Italian States. In 1861, only a few months before Cavour died, the Kingdom of Italy was formally proclaimed. With the addition of Venetia and Rome, the unification of modern Italy was completed, as you can see on the map at left.

The German Empire was formed.

In Germany, as in Italy, unification came about mainly through the shrewd political scheming of one man. Cavour's counterpart in Germany was **Otto von Bismarck**, who became prime minister—or chancellor—of Prussia in 1862.

Find Prussia on the map on page 544. Notice that although it was divided into two parts, Prussia was the largest and strongest of the German states. The map on page 538, which shows Europe after the Congress of Vienna, indicates Prussia's only serious rival in the German Confederation was Austria, which held vast territory outside the Confederation. Prussia, under the leadership of Bismarck, was determined to increase its own strength and prestige at Austria's expense.

Bismarck believed that issues of the day would not be decided by speeches and votes, but "by blood and iron." Defying the authority of the liberal German parliament, he ordered taxes raised to strengthen and modernize the Prussian army. With his well-equipped, well-trained forces, Bismarck declared and won two wars, one against Denmark in 1864, the other against Austria in 1866. These wars illustrated Prussia's military superiority over Austria and consolidated Prussia's power over the northern states in the German Confederation.

Bismarck next turned his attention to the southern states in the German Confederation, which were distrustful of Prussia. He felt that the only way to bring the southern states to the northern side was by declaring war on France. Through a series of diplomatic maneuvers, Bismarck tricked Napoleon III into making secret agreements that would upset the balance of power, strengthening

Answers to Section 2 Review

Identify

Key Terms, People, and Places are defined on pages indicated in parentheses. Also see the Glossary and Biographical Dictionary. *realpolitik* (541), Crimea (542), Florence Nightingale (542), Camillo di Cavour (542), Giuseppe Garibaldi (543), Otto von Bismarck (543)

Main Ideas

1. It was the first big armed clash in Europe since 1815. Because of Russia's defeat, it could no longer be counted on to defend the existing balance of power in Europe.

2. In 1859 a united force of France and Piedmont-Sardinia was successful in routing the Austrians from Lombardy. By 1860 all of northern Italy had united with the kingdom of Piedmont-Sardinia. Under Giuseppe Garibaldi, most remaining Italian states joined the northern Italian states. In 1866 Venetia was ceded to Italy and in 1870 Rome came under Italian control, completing the unification.

3. During the Franco-Prussian War, Napoleon III's army was defeated and the French government fell. The harsh way the Germans dealt with the French at the end of this war led to great bitterness between France and Germany. The emergence of Germany as a strong nation caused a shift in the European balance of power, which created great tension.

Critical Thinking

Cavour's statement implies that individuals and nation-states are governed by different moral standards and that practicing lax moral standards in politics is acceptable. Accept students' opinions supported by reasonable explanations.

The Unification of Germany, 1865–1871

- Boundary, German Confederation of 1815
- Prussia, 1865
- Absorbed by Prussia, 1866
- Became member of Federation, 1867
- Became member of Empire, 1871

North Sea — SCHLESWIG, HOLSTEIN, MECKLENBURG, HANOVER, NETH., WESTPHALIA, *Ruhr R.*, BELG., *Rhine R.*, LUX., Frankfurt, LORRAINE, FRANCE, ALSACE, WÜRTTEMBERG, BAVARIA, SWITZ., BRANDENBURG, •Berlin, SAXONY, SILESIA, AUSTRIAN EMPIRE, EAST PRUSSIA, WEST PRUSSIA, RUSSIAN EMPIRE, *Baltic Sea*

0   100 MILES
0   100 KILOMETERS

MAP STUDY Like Italy, Germany was also divided. What were the first states to be absorbed by Prussia? What were the last states to become part of the empire, and when?

France while weakening Britain and Austria. Bismarck then revealed these secret deals to France's would-be allies. In this way Bismarck ensured that France would be unlikely to receive military support from Austria or Britain in a war against Prussia.

When a crisis developed between France and Prussia in 1870, Bismarck released the contents of a slightly altered telegram to the press. The telegram hinted that a volley of insults was exchanged between the French ambassador and the Prussian king, Wilhelm I. Both nations were outraged by this, and in July, 1870, France declared war on Prussia. The Franco-Prussian War lasted only six months, with Prussia the victor.

On January 18, 1871, the southern German states united with northern Germany to form the

BACKGROUND In the peace drawn up between France and the new Empire, France was forced to give two border provinces, Alsace and Lorraine, to Germany. Their harsh treatment at the hands of the Germans created lasting bitterness in France.

German Empire, under the rule of Kaiser Wilhelm I. Germany replaced France as the strongest nation in continental Europe. This shift in the balance of power created tensions that were not resolved until the next century.

Section 2 Review

Identify *realpolitik,* Crimea, Florence Nightingale, Camillo di Cavour, Giuseppe Garibaldi, Otto von Bismarck

Main Ideas

1. What was the significance of the Crimean War in European history?
2. How did the Italian states become united?
3. How did the unification of Germany affect France and the European balance of power?

Critical Thinking

Identifying Assumptions: Italy's Count Camillo di Cavour was quoted as saying, "If we did for ourselves what we do for our country, what rascals we should be." List at least two assumptions implied by Cavour's statement. Do you agree or disagree?

---

3 | *Democratic gains were made in western Europe.*

Between 1871 and 1914, the countries of western Europe developed socially, economically, and politically. Britain, France, and Germany were the leaders in these arenas.

Britain made many reforms.

Europe's economic, social, and political leader from 1871 to 1914 was Britain. For most of the time the reigning monarch was **Queen Victoria**. She became a symbol for an age of extensive political power and social well-being.

In the 1850s Britain's two main political parties—the Whigs and the Tories—changed their names to the Liberal party and Conservative party, respectively. **William Gladstone** led the Liberals, and **Benjamin Disraeli** [diz rā′lē], the Conservatives. As the two parties competed for power, Disraeli and Gladstone alternated in the job of prime minister from 1868 to 1880. After Disraeli died in 1881, Gladstone was prime minister until 1894.

Under Gladstone and Disraeli, both the Liberals and the Conservatives put forward bills to extend voting rights. By 1884 all male adults had gained the right to vote, property qualifications for membership in the House of Commons had been eliminated, and the secret ballot became law. Thus, the Chartists' demands, which had been outlined in the 1840s, were finally met. During this time labor unions gained more power, obtaining the legal right to hold strikes and to picket. A workmen's compensation law was also passed. State-run public schools were mandated. By 1891 education in Britain had become free and compulsory.

In contrast, in Ireland, which had been under the British yoke for centuries, there was little so-cial justice. In the 1700s the English passed harsh laws restricting the rights of Irish Catholics and confiscating their land. In the mid-1800s, the British Parliament began instituting some reforms in Ireland. The Irish Catholics were no longer required to pay taxes to the Anglican Church, and land reform measures gave the Irish more rights over the land they farmed.

Nevertheless, a movement for Irish freedom had grown in Ireland under a strong, charismatic leader, Charles Parnell. He promoted the cause of Home Rule—or self-rule—for Ireland. Parliament finally passed the Home Rule bill in 1914, but the largely Protestant northern Irish population of Ulster objected, fearing they would lose their rights without British protection. The issue of Irish self-rule was put aside during World War I. After the

This 1846 portrait shows the British Queen Victoria, her husband, Prince Albert, and five of their nine children. Victoria was known for her strong family values.

BACKGROUND Further reforms were made in Britain in the early 1900s. The Liberals passed laws that set up old-age pensions, unemployment insurance, and minimum wage laws. A graduated income tax also was instituted.

war, a compromise was reached. Southern Ireland, named the Irish Free State, became independent and Ulster, also called **Northern Ireland**, remained in the United Kingdom. However, the compromise was not acceptable to many Irish, and friction between Protestants and Catholics in Ulster has continued to this day.

France established the Third Republic.

After the fall of the Second Empire, with France's defeat in the Franco-Prussian War, the French set up the Third Republic in 1875. It had a two-house legislature, the Chamber of Deputies, elected by universal male suffrage, and the Senate, appointed by local officials. The Third Republic lasted until 1940—longer than any other French government since 1789.

Although it was resilient, the Third Republic was beset by problems from the beginning. Many French were royalists who wanted to bring back a monarchy. Some backed the successor to Louis XVIII, but others preferred the successor to Louis Philippe. The French public was also divided.

One of the most divisive issues in France at this time came over a military court ruling against a Jewish officer, Captain **Alfred Dreyfus**. In 1894 Dreyfus was tried and convicted of selling French military secrets to Germany. He was sentenced to life imprisonment in solitary confinement on Devil's Island, a notorious prison in French Guiana. However, information continued to be leaked to the Germans. Suspicion was cast on a royalist soldier as the source of the leak rather than Dreyfus, but the military court refused to reopen the case. Even after the royalist soldier admitted he was a spy, Dreyfus remained on Devil's Island. The public was deeply divided. The intellectuals, the socialists, and the supporters of the republic were in favor of a retrial. However, the army, the Church, and the royalists were against it.

The battle went on for more than a decade. Finally, in 1906 a civil court pardoned Dreyfus, finding him completely innocent of all charges. The overturning of the Dreyfus case was a victory for the Republic, which proved to be more powerful than the army. Although Dreyfus was clearly a victim of anti-Semitism—prejudice against Jews—the Third Republic's reversal of the case illustrated

the potential for justice in a democracy. In the period between 1871 and 1914, France was the major democratic republic in Europe.

The Second German Empire, though militaristic, instituted some reforms.

When Germany became unified at the end of the Franco-Prussian War, Kaiser Wilhelm I became head of the Second Empire or, in German, Reich [rīH]. The Second Reich had a constitution and a two-house legislature. The Reichstag [rīHs'täk'] was elected by universal male suffrage, and the Bundesrat [bùn'dəs rät] consisted of the German aristocracy.

Real power, however, was in the hands of the emperor and the head of the government whom he appointed, the chancellor. The first chancellor of the Second Reich was Otto von Bismarck. You have read that Bismarck was a shrewd leader in foreign affairs. He was no less shrewd in domestic affairs, shaping the emerging German state.

In the last half of the 19th century, Germany industrialized rapidly. This economic development increased Germany's prosperity. It also ushered in an era of political organization of the working classes. The emergence of a political party dedicated to socialism, the Social Democrat party, alarmed Bismarck. He feared that the party, popular with the working classes, would erode the emperor's power and perhaps even inspire revolutionary uprisings. Before the movement could gather momentum, Bismarck decided to try to nip it in the bud. He urged the legislature to pass laws against socialism, banned socialist publications, and put the leaders of the movement in prison.

Nevertheless, the Social Democrat party continued to grow in the 1880s. Bismarck next tried to draw workers away from socialism by making reforms. He instituted Europe's first progressive program of social insurance, which included sickness and accident insurance and liberal pensions. Although the socialist party continued to grow, Bismarck and the emperor remained firmly in power.

In 1888 Wilhelm I died and **Wilhelm II**, his grandson, became emperor at age 29. Kaiser Wilhelm II believed in the old idea of the divine right of kings. He saw in the experienced statesman Bismarck a threat to his authority. In 1890 Bismarck was forced to resign. An ambitious man, Wilhelm II sought to increase Germany's power. He glorified the army as a symbol of Germany's might.

Section 3 Review

Identify Queen Victoria, William Gladstone, Benjamin Disraeli, Northern Ireland, Alfred Dreyfus, Wilhelm II

Main Ideas

1. How did the Liberals and Conservatives work for reforms in Britain?
2. What groups clashed with each other in the Third Republic of France? What was the significance of the Dreyfus case?
3. What two methods did Bismarck use to fight socialism? Why did Wilhelm II clash with Bismarck?

Critical Thinking

Making Decisions: In most countries, a legal case cannot be retried once the verdict has been decided. An exception might be made if new evidence is discovered after the trial that might help the accused. If you were a judge in France in the years following Dreyfus' conviction, would you have agreed to a retrial? Explain your answer.

 Reforms came slowly in Russia and non-industrial Europe.

Although the nations of western Europe grew and changed rapidly in the late 1800s, growth and change came much slower to the non-industrial regions of Europe—Russia, Spain, Portugal, Italy, Austria-Hungary, and the Ottoman Empire. In these regions the rich and poor were sharply divided, and the middle class was small. Governments were either autocratic or unstable. Under these poor conditions, reforms came slowly.

Tsars opposed constitutional rule.

As you have learned, the government of Russia was headed by an autocratic ruler called the tsar. Throughout the 18th and early 19th centuries, the tsars ignored the deep desire of the Russian people for a better life. The nobles continually objected to

reforms that might weaken their power or limit their income. However, in the mid-1800s, the leaders of Russia realized that they had to begin making reforms.

The reign of Alexander I. Although the tsar **Alexander I** had professed liberal ideals in his youth, he did nothing to lessen the tsarist autocracy during his reign, from 1801 to 1825. However, Russian intellectuals, many of whom studied abroad in French universities, were exposed to the democratic ideals that swept Europe. Army officers who occupied France after Napoleon's defeat by the Russians also came in contact with these new ideas. Inspired and eager for change, these intellectuals and army officers formed secret societies that met to work for social change.

When Alexander died suddenly in December, 1825, these groups tried to topple the government. Although their uprising was easily put down, the Decembrist Revolt, named after the month in which it occurred, inspired later revolutionaries.

The reign of Nicholas I. After the revolt, **Nicholas I** became tsar. Shocked by the weak but definite current of revolution, he felt that the only way to keep charge of the government was to be a strict autocrat, in control of all power. As one of his officials stated, "The tsar is a father, his subjects are his children, and children ought never to question their parents." Nicholas censored the press and took away academic freedoms. He had police spies round up enemies and send them off to Siberia. Nicholas' government was also corrupt and inefficient. The cumbersome bureaucracy contributed to Russia's defeat in the Crimean War in 1856. Before the war concluded, Nicholas died, a bitter man.

The reign of Alexander II. The Russian defeat in the Crimean War led the new tsar **Alexander II** to believe that the only way to strengthen Russia was to institute reforms. He saw that the feudal institution of serfdom was holding Russia back economically, socially, and politically. As Alexander II told the nobles, "It is better to abolish serfdom from above than to wait until it begins to abolish itself from below."

In 1861 Alexander II issued the Edict of Emancipation. This act gave the serfs personal liberty and promised them land, which was to be owned

socialists, and intellectuals—who were for a retrial. The case showed that the Republic was more powerful than the army and showed the potential for justice in a republic.

3. He first urged the legislature to pass laws against socialism, banned socialist publications, and put Social Democrat leaders in prison. When this didn't work, Bismarck instituted some reforms called for by the socialists. Wilhelm II clashed with Bismarck because he thought the chancellor was a threat to his power.

Critical Thinking

Reasons for a retrial include the fact that information continued to leak to Germany even after Dreyfus was put in solitary confinement and that the royalist soldier confessed. Reasons for not granting a retrial include the fact that the royalist soldier should have been questioned before the time of the first trial, that the second information leak could have been independent of the first leak, and that retrials cast doubt on the military justice system.

4 *Lesson Plan*

Essential Learning Objectives

Students will learn to:

- explain why non-industrial countries in Europe lagged behind in social and political reforms.
- describe several examples of attempted democratic reforms in non-industrial Europe.

Ask the students why some countries provide social services and why some countries don't. Ask them for examples that fit these categories today. Point out that many countries in eastern Europe did not introduce social and economic reforms.

2 TEACH

- Write this generalization on the board: In non-industrial Russia, the 19th century was a tug-of-war between autocrats and reformers with the autocrats still on top in 1881. Have the students provide examples of this conflict.

- Briefly review events in Spain and Portugal. Have the students list reforms in these countries.

GUIDED PRACTICE

In Austria-Hungary and the Ottoman Empire, self-determination by ethnic groups was a key issue. Write the names of these ethnic groups on the board: Czechs, Romanians, Slovaks, Serbs, Bulgarians, and Bosnians. Ask the students which minority was found in each country.

collectively by members of the local villages. Although no longer in bondage, the former serfs found that they were often worse off than before. In many cases, the land they got was poor, and as it was increasingly subdivided among successive generations, the plots became so small, they could not support the family.

Alexander II made other reforms in Russia in the 1860s and 1870s. Trial by jury was instituted. More elementary schools were built, and poor children were allowed to go to high schools. A form of local self-government was also set up.

The reforms in government raised hopes that Alexander II might be convinced to accept a constitutional monarchy. However, the rise of revolutionary movements turned the tsar against further reform. In the closing years of his reign, Alexander II was as reactionary as Nicholas I had been. In 1880, however, he realized that his harshness was causing more harm than good, and he planned to introduce a national representative government.

However, before he could announce his plans, Alexander was assassinated in 1881. Alexander's death furthered the government's reactionary movement and intensified revolutionary zeal throughout Russia.

Spain and Portugal lacked stability.

Throughout the 1800s Spain was in turmoil. Although liberals worked to establish a constitutional government, the rich and powerful upper classes and the Catholic Church favored a reactionary monarchy. However, disagreements over the rightful successor to Spain's King Ferdinand VII, who died in 1833, led to bitter fighting among those who wanted to maintain the monarchy. For the rest of the century, Spain had no effective government, as liberals and groups of reactionary monarchists jostled for power.

Although Spain became a constitutional monarchy in 1876, only male property owners had the right to vote, and the government remained corrupt and ineffective. Spain, defeated by the United States in 1898, lost the remaining colonies in the once global Spanish Empire. With the country virtually bankrupt as the 20th century opened, Spain was faced with serious social, political, and economic problems that threatened to erupt violently.

Portugal, like Spain, was unstable during the 1800s. As in Spain, liberals and several groups of monarchists struggled for power. Although there was a clear succession of Portuguese kings and queens from the 1830s to the turn of the century,

DAILY LIFE

From 1815 to 1914, Vienna, Austria, enjoyed its Golden Age. Creativity and innovation were the highlights of this age, especially evident in the areas of music, theater, and architecture. Dancing to the charming waltzes of Johann Strauss (left) was all the rage, and women's dress (near right) became increasingly modern in style. In addition, coffee houses such as the Cafe Griensteidl (far right) attracted the artistic and intellectual elite of Vienna.

the government was unpopular. After the king and his son were assassinated in 1908, a revolution broke out and the Portuguese republic was formed in 1910. Nevertheless, in the early 20th century, Portugal failed to gain stability.

Minority groups threatened Austria-Hungary.

Austria-Hungary was a mixture of ethnic groups. Until 1866, when Austria suffered a humiliating defeat in a war with Prussia, the Austrians controlled all aspects of government in the empire. After that time, the Hungarians, the largest of the empire's other ethnic groups clamored for control of their own affairs. The Austrians acquiesced, and in 1866 the dual empire of Austria-Hungary was declared. Austria and Hungary each had its own government to rule on domestic affairs, but they combined forces for foreign policy.

The most serious problem the dual empire faced was the rising nationalism among ethnic minorities throughout Austria-Hungary. In Austria the Germans dominated all aspects of life—political, economic, and cultural. The Czechs, among the largest minorities within Austria, were proud of their rich history and heritage and wanted independence from Austria. In Hungary the Hungarians made up less than half the population, but they held complete control of the government. The other nationalities in the Austria-Hungary empire, including the Romanians, Slovaks, and Serbs, resented Hungarian control and longed for self-rule.

The Ottoman Empire began to disintegrate.

As you can see from the map on page 550, the Ottoman Empire sprawled over three continents in the early 1800s. It included people of numerous ethnic groups. The central government of Turkey held only loose control over the empire. As the tides of nationalism rose in the 19th century, the Ottoman Empire slowly disintegrated.

In the peace settlement at the end of the Crimean War in 1856, the Great Powers of Europe—Britain, France, Prussia, Austria, and Russia—pledged to protect the sovereignty of the Ottoman Empire. This agreement, they felt, would help uphold the balance of power and promote stability in Europe. However, the Turkish government was corrupt and inefficient, failing to institute liberal and nationalistic reforms demanded by various ethnics within the empire. The map on page 550

BACKGROUND The hostilities between nationalities in the Austria-Hungary government weakened the empire and led to its demise in the early 20th century.

549

 MAP STUDY The vast array of the nationalities within the Ottoman Empire contributed to its decline in the 1800s, as the map above details. What large peninsula was the center of the Ottoman Empire in 1914?

shows how over time, various areas of this far-flung empire gained independence. In most cases there was little the European powers could or cared to do to stop Turkey's gradual disintegration.

However, one region was of central importance to the European powers. Located in a strategically important position between Europe and Russia, the **Balkans** were a political hotspot. This region contained numerous Slavic ethnic groups who all wanted to form separate independent nations. The Russians, also Slavs, promoted nationalism in the Balkans. Austria-Hungary opposed Slavic nationalism, fearing that the large numbers of Slavic ethnic groups within its borders would become unruly should other Slavic groups achieve nationhood.

When the Turkish government failed to make governmental reforms promised after the Crimean War, one by one the Romanians, the Bulgarians, the Bosnians, and the Serbians in the Balkans all rebelled. In 1876 the Russo-Turkish War was fought, with Britain aiding the Turks and Russia aiding the Slavic rebels. Although Russia won the war, in the peace conferences that followed, the European powers limited Russian control in the Balkans. Austria-Hungary, Turkey, and Russia each gained influence over specific areas on the Balkan peninsula.

The protection Europe provided for the Ottoman Empire did little to encourage the Turkish sultan to strengthen his government. Rebellions continued throughout the empire. By 1908 the sultan was so weak that a successful revolution by a group known as the Young Turks toppled him from power. Although the Young Turks promised to reform the government, they were unsympathetic to the nationalistic feelings of ethnic groups under their domain. They instituted harsh measures to crush nationalism. As a result, the Balkan region remained a focus of international tension.

Section 4 Review

Identify Alexander I, Nicholas I, Alexander II, the Balkans

Main Ideas
1. Compare and contrast the reigns of the following tsars: Alexander I, Nicholas I, and Alexander II.
2. What groups in Spain and Portugal vied for power, preventing stable governments?
3. Discuss how ethnic groups weakened the government of Austria-Hungary.
4. How did the weaknesses of the Ottoman Empire affect Europe?

Critical Thinking
Analyzing Comparisons: In 1841 Russian Tsar Nicholas I likened the Ottoman Empire to a "sick man." Why do you think he made this comparison? Is it a valid comparison? Support your opinion with evidence.

5 *Democracy advanced in the United States, Canada, and Australia.*

The movements of liberalism, democracy, and nationalism that transformed Europe also affected the overseas extensions of European civilization. This was true not only in Latin America, as we saw in Chapter 27, but also in the major English-speaking countries of the United States, Canada, and Australia.

The United States grew rapidly.

The two most significant trends in the United States during the 19th century were rapid population growth and territorial expansion. Population increased dramatically because of the country's high birthrate and the arrival of millions of immigrants. In 1790 the United States had 4 million people, but by 1860 its population had jumped to 31 million, 1 million more than in Britain. The combined labor, energy, and skills of the immigrants, along with industrialization and technological impovement, contributed to the emergence of the United States as a dynamic world power in the 20th century.

Territorial expansion caused the United States to grow in area. As you can see from the map on page 553, the young republic expanded westward with amazing speed. The Louisiana Territory, purchased from France in 1803, doubled the size of the United States. In 1845 the nation annexed Texas, and in 1846 it acquired the Oregon Territory. In addition, after a war with Mexico in 1848, the United States took control of the huge area between Texas and the Pacific Coast. By 1860 the United States stretched all the way from the Atlantic to the Pacific. It was larger than any European country except Russia and was a treasure house of fertile land and mineral resources.

Civil war broke out.

The addition of new territory to the United States aggravated the bitter controversy of whether or not slavery should be allowed in the new lands. The southern states were for the expansion of slavery, but the northern states were against it.

When **Abraham Lincoln** was elected President after campaigning on a platform favoring the North, the South seceded—or withdrew—from the Union. Four years of civil war followed, the bloodiest conflict that any western nation had fought up to that time. The North won because of its overwhelming superiority in population, industrial resources, and wealth. As a result, slaves were freed, and the South remained part of the United States.

Americans pushed for reforms, and industry expanded.

The significance of the Civil War in world history is that the United States remained a large nation-state and did not split up into smaller countries. The country was committed to liberal and democratic principles in its political life and to private enterprise in its economic system. The ideal goals of American democracy were best stated by President Abraham Lincoln in his eloquent address at

3. Rising nationalism among ethnic minorities and growing resentment of outside control weakened the empire's government.
4. The rebellion of ethnic groups in the Balkans caused trouble in the Ottoman Empire. Other European nations with interests in this strategic region interfered, creating international tension.

Critical Thinking
The comparison could be made because Turkey was weak. The comparison might be considered valid, because lack of clarity in the designation of legal heirs can cause great conflict, similar to the tension created as the European powers divided the Ottoman Empire. It might be considered invalid because the Ottoman Empire could have made reforms or changes in the government that might have allowed it to become strong again.

5 *Lesson Plan*

Essential Learning Objective

Students will learn to describe liberal and democratic reforms that were made in the United States, Canada, and Australia in the late 19th and early 20th centuries.

1 FOCUS AND MOTIVATE

Direct the students to compare Atlas maps of the United States, Canada, and Australia. Discuss the effect of location, land area, and language on these countries. Tell the students that all three have a common political background.

- Concentrate first on the United States. Refer students to the territorial map on page 553. It tells the story of tremendous growth, from few cities on the Atlantic Ocean in 1790 to a world power 125 years later. As a class, ask students to list the various democratic reforms listed in the text on the chalkboard. Include rights gained by black Americans and unions.

- Have students recall the democratic reforms of 19th-century Canada and Australia. List them on the chalkboard. Point out that Australia was ahead of the United States in granting voting rights to women.

GUIDED PRACTICE

Ask students to list as many similarities as possible between the United States, Canada, and Australia. (The list could include that all: were once British colonies, had native populations, were about the same size, had a significant frontier experience, and were pioneers in democratic reform.)

From the Archives

The Emancipation Proclamation

Abraham Lincoln had long been opposed to slavery, but he was uncertain that it could be abolished within the framework of the Constitution of the United States. He eventually decided that since, in the Union view, the secession of the southern states was a rebellion that must be defeated by military force, freeing the slaves in rebel territory was "a fit and necessary war measure."

I, Abraham Lincoln, President of the United States, by virtue of the power in me vested as Commander-in-Chief. . . . do order and declare that all persons held as slaves within said designated States and parts of States are, and henceforward shall be, free; and that the Executive Government of the United States, including the military and naval authorities thereof, will recognize and maintain the freedom of said persons.

And I hereby enjoin upon the people so declared to be free to abstain from all violence, unless in necessary self-defense; and I recommend to them that, in all cases when allowed, they labor faithfully for reasonable wages.

Gettysburg in 1863: "government of the people, by the people, and for the people." To achieve these goals, reformers began working for the rights of black Americans, workers, and women, and for the expansion of other political rights in the 1800s such as the abolition of property rights as a requirement to vote. These struggles continued well into the 20th century.

Black rights. After the Civil War, two amendments were added to the Constitution—the 14th Amendment, which guaranteed black Americans all rights of citizenship, and the 15th Amendment, which guaranteed black men the right to vote. Even with these amendments, black Americans had to work against racial hatred and prejudice for many years before they were able to attain the full rights of citizenship as granted in the Constitution. Their struggle for equality continues today.

Labor rights. During the 1800s American workers began the struggle to improve their living and working conditions. In the half-century following the Civil War, rapid development transformed the United States into the world's industrial leader.

Industrialization required large numbers of workers, a need met in part by some 23 million immigrants who flooded into the United States between 1860 and 1910. They, as well as native-born Americans, flocked to the cities in search of jobs. As cities grew rapidly, factory workers faced long hours, low wages, and poor working conditions. Employers opposed efforts by workers to organize labor unions. They wanted to prevent workers from gaining the leverage of calling strikes and organizing collective bargaining.

Frequent violent clashes between workers and employers resulted. The workers persisted in their fight to unionize effectively, and in 1881 hundreds of small, independent unions joined together to form the American Federation of Labor (AFL).

Other political rights. During the 1800s groups of people worked to extend democracy by carrying out reforms at the government level. One example of a change that extended democracy was the 17th Amendment, which provided that senators be directly elected by the people instead of being chosen by state legislatures.

Another example was the 19th Amendment, which guaranteed voting rights to all women in the United States. Although both of these reforms were made in the 20th century, people began pushing for them in the mid-1800s. The efforts of the 19th-century reformers, in extending political rights to all citizens, helped make the United States one of the most advanced democracies in the world.

Canada developed as a bicultural nation.

North of the United States lay the British provinces known as Canada, which were ceded to Britain by France in 1763. After 1763 both French and British people settled in Canada. Gradually, the British population grew. First, many Americans loyal to

FROM THE ARCHIVES Henry Steele Commager, ed., *Documents of American History,* 9th ed. (Englewood Cliffs, New Jersey: Prentice-Hall, 1973), I, pp. 420–421. After signing the Emancipation Proclamation Lincoln declared, "I never, in my life, felt more certain that I was doing right than I do in signing this paper." Why would Lincoln or other people have doubts about this proclamation? (The Constitution did not give any president the power to free slaves.)

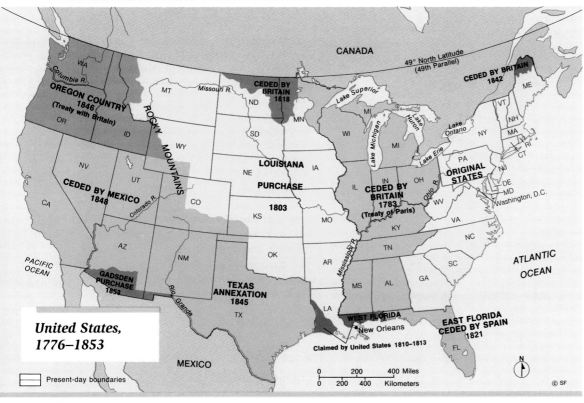

United States, 1776–1853

Present-day boundaries

MAP STUDY The map above shows the progress of territorial growth in the United States from 1776, when there were only the 13 original states, to 1853. What present-day states were carved out of the Louisiana Purchase of 1803?

Britain during the American Revolution arrived after the defeat of the British. Later, more British immigrants arrived.

In the early 1800s, conflict began to grow between Britain and the Canadian colonists, who wanted self-government like their American neighbors to the south. In 1837 some of the Canadian colonists rebelled against British rule. Although the rebellion was easily put down, the British government decided not to risk another war with an unruly colony and agreed to give Canada self-government.

In 1867 the **Dominion of Canada** was granted a constitution, though Britain retained control over foreign policy. The four provinces of Quebec, Ontario, Nova Scotia, and New Brunswick made up the original federal union, but by 1905 Canada had grown to include ten provinces and stretched from coast to coast.

The creation of the Dominion of Canada had worldwide significance. It was the first example of the peaceful granting of political liberty within a European colonial system. However, not all of Canada's struggles were resolved so equitably or peacefully. Antagonism between English and French Canadians, begun in the 1700s, continued throughout the 20th century, especially in the dominantly French-speaking province of Quebec.

3 | ASSESS AND CLOSE

ASSESS

1. What are the two cultures in Canada? (English and French)
2. What is the democratic significance of the 17th Amendment? (direct election of senators)

OPTIONAL RETEACHING

Explain that, like Canada and Australia, the United States has had a heavy European influence upon its history. Ask students to look at the territorial map and name those European nations that once claimed United States territory. (France, Britain, and Spain) Not shown are Russia, which once claimed Oregon Country; the Netherlands, which once controlled New York; and Sweden, which originally colonized Delaware. Students also may be assigned Activities reteaching page 174.

OPTIONAL ENRICHMENT

1. Have the students research the concept of dominion status for Canada. Use this information to create a time line on the Dominion of Canada. (average)
2. Students also may be assigned Activities enrichment page 175.
3. Also for enrichment:

Overhead Transparency 58

Source Reading 29B

INDEPENDENT PRACTICE/ HOMEWORK

Assign the Section Review, the Chapter Review items, Activities page 173, or Workbook page 117.

CLOSURE

Tell students that the democratic advances made in western Europe in the late 19th century were matched by the United States, Canada, and Australia. As in Europe, the gains did not come easily.

Answers to Section 5 Review

Identify
Key Terms, People, and Places are defined on pages indicated in parentheses. Also see the Glossary and Biographical Dictionary. Abraham Lincoln (551), Dominion of Canada (553), Commonwealth of Australia (554)

Main Ideas
1. in area and in population
2. The Civil War was fought over many issues, but one of the most emotional was the issue of whether slavery should be allowed in new U.S. territories. The North won the war, and the United States remained a united nation.
3. The 14th Amendment gave black Americans the rights of citizenship; the 15th Amendment gave them voting rights. In 1881 the American Federation of Labor was formed, which was a federation of numerous small, independent labor unions. The 17th Amendment provided direct election of Senators, and the 19th Amendment granted voting rights to U.S. women.
4. Canada gained self-government when the British government decided not to risk another war with a colony.
5. The European settlement of Australia began as a British penal colony in the late 1700s. In the mid-1800s, Britain stopped sending convicts and gave the colony some self-government. In 1901 the Commonwealth of Australia was formed.

Critical Thinking
The British would have been at a disadvantage trading with the South if protective tariffs raised the price of British goods. The British might have sought other sources of cotton.

Australia and New Zealand: Population Distribution

| · 50,000 people | * National capitals | · Other cities |

 MAP STUDY This modern-day map of Australia and New Zealand shows where people live today. Where did most people settle in Australia?

Australia developed slowly.

Located south of the equator between the Pacific and Indian oceans, Australia was an isolated continent. The earliest people of Australia were the Aborigines, the first of whom arrived about 40,000 years ago. A second wave of Aborigine settlers arrived 25,000 or 30,000 years ago. Scientists think that these people may have come to the continent by way of a temporary land bridge from New Guinea during glacial times. This second wave were the ancestors of today's Aborigines. When European settlers first arrived during the late 1700s, there were probably 300,000 Aborigines in all of Australia. Most lived in small groups because water was scarce and food was limited. They built no permanent villages and subsisted on hunting and gathering.

Although Dutch explorers were the first to visit Australia in 1606, the British were the first to found permanent settlements on the continent. The earliest British settlers were primarily convicts who served seven-year sentences and then were released. Most Australian settlers came from the British Isles. However, during the early 1800s, other settlers came from such European nations as Italy, Greece, Germany, and Yugoslavia. In the mid-1800s, Britain stopped deporting its convicts to Australia and gave the Australian colonies a degree of self-government.

The discovery of gold in 1851 quickened the pace of Australia's development, and by the end of the 19th century the Australian continent had nearly 4 million people. In 1901 the six Australian colonies formed a federal union that was called the **Commonwealth of Australia**, similar to the United States. Australia passed laws providing liberal social legislation and granted women the right to vote, years before such policies were adopted in Europe and the Americas. These reforms made Australia a pioneering democracy copied by other nations of the world. However, discrimination against the Aborigines remained strong.

Section 5 Review

Identify Abraham Lincoln, Dominion of Canada, Commonwealth of Australia

Main Ideas
1. In what ways did the United States grow during the 19th century?
2. What were the issues of the American Civil War, and what was the war's significance in world history?
3. Describe some of the reforms made in the United States to promote the rights of black Americans, labor rights, and the other political rights.
4. How did Canada develop into an independent nation?
5. Describe Australia's development from a colony to a democracy.

Critical Thinking
Predicting Effects: The Civil War in the United States was fought not only over the issues of slavery, but also over the issue of protective tariffs. The North wanted tariffs against cheap imported goods from Britain. Britain, however, was the South's main market for its cotton crop, so the South opposed high tariffs. What effect do you think high tariffs on British goods would have had on the southern economy? Explain your answer.

Medical Advances of the 19th Century

You may be surprised to learn that 19th-century physicians knew no more than ancient Egyptian doctors about relieving their patients' suffering during surgery. Fatal shock, brought on by the pain of surgery, was as common a killer in A.D. 1800 as in 1800 B.C.

However, in the early 19th century, the painkilling substance nitrous oxide was discovered. Commonly known as laughing gas, it was at first used

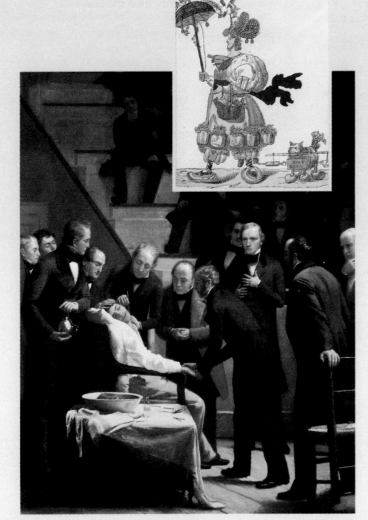

merely for entertainment. Those who inhaled it laughed uproariously. However, by the 1840s dentists and physicians realized that nitrous oxide and other similar gases could be used for anesthesia—as medicinal painkillers. The general adoption of anesthesia softened the brutal blow of 19th-century surgery.

Even with the reduction of pain and life-threatening shock, a person's chances of surviving an operation in the mid-1800s were still quite slim. Said one British physician, "A man laid on the table in one of our surgical hospitals is exposed to more chances of death than the English soldier on the field of Waterloo."

However, around 1865 an English surgeon named Joseph Lister began to understand the relationship between microorganisms and infection. Lister studied the work of the French scientist Louis Pasteur, who had discovered that airborne microorganisms caused food spoilage. Similar microorganisms, Lister theorized, must cause infection in open wounds. Lister developed a method of sterilization called antiseptic technique. Although this technique was modified over time, Lister introduced essential standards of cleanliness that made hospitals safer places to be in.

The introduction of anesthesia was an important U.S. medical contribution. William Thomas Morton first demonstrated the use of ether in surgery at Boston in 1846 (left). However, surgical infections took many lives until Lister developed antiseptic methods. The costumes for a woman and her dog were designed to ward off cholera in 19th-century Vienna (top left).

The following statement was made at the end of the 19th century by Sir William Osler, a famous British physician. Read the quote to the class and ask students to list the medical advances to which Osler is probably referring. (the development of anesthesia and of antiseptic technique)

"To us in the medical profession . . . whose work is with the sick and suffering, the great boon of this wonderful century is the fact that the leaves of the tree of Science have been for the healing of the nations."

Tell students that the pulling of some teeth and the amputation of limbs with badly infected wounds were common surgical procedures for thousands of years. Together, the introduction of anesthesia and the use of sterile (antiseptic) technique significantly reduced mortality from such common operations.

You may wish to ask students to find out when and where the first operation using nitrous oxide was performed. (In 1844 in Hartford, Connecticut, Dr. John Riggs performed the first operation—a tooth extraction—ever documented using nitrous oxide as an anesthesia.)

Ether was another gas used in 19th-century anesthesiology. The first painless amputation was performed with the aid of ether in 1846.

555

Answers to Test Yourself

Key Terms, People, and Places
The key terms, people, and places tested here were introduced in the chapter sections and reviewed in the Section Reviews. For definitions see the page references at the appropriate Section Reviews. Also see the Glossary and Biographical Dictionary.

Main Ideas
The main ideas tested here were introduced in the sections of this chapter and reviewed in the Section Reviews. For answers to these questions, see the appropriate Section Reviews.

Critical Thinking
1. Accept all answers students can defend. Other factors that might have contributed to the stability of democracy include: the lack of a rigid social hierarchy, the abundance of resources, and a fairly equitable distribution of wealth.
2. Students' responses should consider the advantages and disadvantages of such a government.

CHAPTER 29 REVIEW

Section Summaries

Section 1
Liberals and nationalists challenged political systems throughout Europe.
In the 1800s reactionaries opposed the aims of liberals and nationalists in Europe. Nevertheless, these movements made gains in Greece, Belgium, and France. Britain made reforms without violent upheaval. In 1848 revolutions occurred throughout Europe.

Section 2
The European balance of power shifted as Italy and Germany became unified nations.
In the late 19th century, political changes occurred in Europe. Italy and Germany were unified.

Section 3
Democratic gains were made in western Europe.
In the last half of the 19th century, Britain and France made liberal and democratic changes. The German government also became increasingly militaristic.

Section 4
Reforms came slowly in Russia and non-industrial Europe.
The tsars of Russia wavered back and forth about reforms. Unstable governments held back Spain and Portugal. Austria-Hungary did little to please its unhappy nationalities, and the Ottoman Empire weakened.

Section 5
Democracy advanced in the United States, Canada, and Australia.
The United States grew rapidly. Canada was the first British colony to peacefully achieve independence. Australia, outside the mainstream of European commerce, developed more slowly.

Test Yourself

Key Terms, People, and Places
Identify the significance of each of the following:

Section 1
a. Congress of Vienna
b. reactionary
c. liberalism
d. nationalism
e. Napoleon III

Section 2
a. *realpolitik*
b. Crimea
c. Florence Nightingale
d. Camillo di Cavour
e. Giuseppe Garibaldi
f. Otto von Bismarck

Section 3
a. Queen Victoria
b. William Gladstone
c. Benjamin Disraeli
d. Northern Ireland
e. Alfred Dreyfus
f. Wilhelm II

Section 4
a. Alexander I
b. Nicholas I
c. Alexander II
d. the Balkans

Review Dates

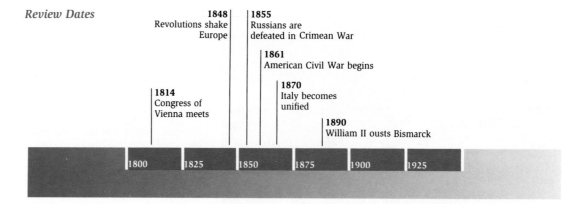

1814 Congress of Vienna meets

1848 Revolutions shake Europe

1855 Russians are defeated in Crimean War

1861 American Civil War begins

1870 Italy becomes unified

1890 William II ousts Bismarck

1800 | 1825 | 1850 | 1875 | 1900 | 1925

Section 5
a. Abraham Lincoln **c.** Commonwealth of
b. Dominion of Canada   Australia

Main Ideas

Section 1
1. How did the aims of liberals and nationalists differ from those of reactionaries in Europe?
2. What gains did liberals and nationalists make in the early 1800s in Europe?
3. Describe reforms Britain made in the 1830s and 1840s.
4. What were some of the causes of revolutions in 1848 and what were the results?

Section 2
1. Describe the significance of the Crimean War.
2. How did Italy become a united country?
3. How did the unification of Germany affect France and the European balance of power?

Section 3
1. How were reforms made by both Liberals and Conservatives in Britain?
2. How did various groups in France clash over the Dreyfus case?
3. How did Bismarck fight socialism? How did his goals clash with those of Wilhelm II?

Section 4
1. How were the reigns of Alexander I, Nicholas I, and Alexander II similar and different?
2. How did various groups in Spain and Portugal prevent stable governments?
3. What was the main problem of the empire of Austria-Hungry?
4. Discuss how the weaknesses of the Ottoman Empire affected Europe.

Section 5
1. How did the United States grow in the 1800s?
2. What was the main cause of the American Civil War and its significance in history?
3. What reforms were made in the United States to promote political rights?
4. Describe Canada's development in the 19th century.
5. How did Australia develop in the 19th century?

Critical Thinking

1. Assessing Cause and Effect Some historians believe that the United States, Canada, and Australia have been able to maintain democracies because democratic institutions were established from the start. Do you think this is a good explanation? What other causes might contribute to the stability of democracy?
2. Recognizing Values Consider the possibility of living under a dictatorship. Do you think you would be willing to do this if the ruler gave the people enough food, homes, and jobs?

Chapter Skills and Activities

Practicing Study and Research Skills
Interpreting political cartoons
Political cartoons convey an opinion about a political situation in a humorous or ironic way. Study this cartoon. The figure balancing on the tightrope represents the British prime minister Benjamin Disraeli. The figure on his back is the Turkish sultan. Summarize the ideas conveyed in this political cartoon.

Linking Past and Present
Do you think the spirit of idealism or the spirit of *realpolitik* dominates foreign relations today? Collect current examples from newspapers.

Learning History Through Maps
Refer to the political map on page 538 showing Europe in 1815. Compare this map to the one of German unification on page 544. How had Austria's status changed by 1871?

CRITICAL THINKING QUESTION LEVEL 1. challenging; 2. easy

Answers to Test Yourself

Key Terms and People
1. b
2. a
3. e
4. d
5. c

Key Dates
F, E, B, H, C, D, A, G

Key Places
A—Boston; E—Crimea; C—London;
B—Northern Ireland; D—Germany

Main Ideas
1. b
2. c
3. a
4. b
5. d

Critical Thinking
1. Students should compare the goals of the revolutions—liberty, equality, and democracy—with the changes that resulted. They should consider how much the revolutions affected our society today.
2. Students should note that industrial development is going on around the world, and that modern societies are now dependent upon much of the science and technology that was first developed during the 17th and 18th centuries. Some less positive effects include the widespread industrial pollution—from factories, cars, utilities, and so forth—that is contaminating the earth.

REVIEW

Summarizing the Unit

Chapter 26
Democratic Revolutions in England and North America

The intellectual drive of the 17th and 18th centuries to understand and improve society was called the Enlightenment. Such thinkers of the Enlightenment as John Locke, Montesquieu, Voltaire, and Jean Jacques Rousseau developed new ideas about liberty, democracy, and representative government, which helped bring about democratic revolutions. In England in the 1600s, the first of the democratic revolutions took place. The power of the Parliament grew at the expense of the English monarchy, and a new political system protected individual rights. Later, in 1776, England's American colonies successfully separated themselves from the English and established the United States of America.

Chapter 27
Revolutions in France and Latin America

The new democratic system that was based on the ideas of the Enlightenment and on the revolutionary experiences of England and North America was firmly planted in Europe by 1791. The French led the way for continental Europe, overthrowing their monarchy in 1792. These democratic ideals spread throughout Europe and to Latin America.

Chapter 28
The Industrial Revolution

During the 1800s new industrial methods, many resulting from the use of steam-powered machines, spread rapidly. New discoveries occurred in science and medicine as well as in literature, art, and music.

Chapter 29
Revolutions in Everyday Life and Politics

The political history of 19th-century Europe was primarily the story of how liberalism, democracy, and nationalism shaped governments and everyday life, and how they had influences around the world. In particular, Italy and Germany were both unified, and democratic advances were made in the United States. Canada, and Australia.

Using Writing Skills

This age of revolution represented a concerted attempt to improve the society of the time—through democratic government, technology, and social reform. Picture now your own society. How might it be improved or reformed to make it "perfect"? Consider how people would live, work, and act; whether there would be a need for laws and how these might be enforced; and how your society would be organized and governed.

Activity. Write a description of your idea of a perfect society. Remember to first use the prewriting techniques that you have learned to gather and organize your ideas. After you have completed your first draft, meet with a classmate to discuss each other's papers and suggest revisions. Follow the guidelines that you learned for revision in the Unit 6 Review. Then, write a final draft of your essay.

Test Yourself

Key Terms and People

Match each term or person with the correct definition.
1. believed people possessed natural rights to life, liberty, and property
2. set forth the principle of equality of all French citizens before the law
3. proved germs caused infectious diseases
4. believed in the idea of survival of the fittest
5. the belief in freedom from foreign rule

a. Code Napoleon
b. John Locke
c. nationalism
d. Charles Darwin
e. Louis Pasteur

Key Dates

Match the letters on the time line with the events for which they stand:

____ Revolutions shake Europe.
____ Mexico gains its independence.
____ The United States declares its independence.
____ Henry Ford begins mass producing automobiles.
____ Napoleon is crowned emperor of France.
____ The Congress of Vienna meets.
____ The English civil war begins.
____ Italy becomes unified.

Key Places

Match the letters on the map with the places described below:

____ where colonists rebelled against British taxes
____ peninsula where the first big armed clash in Europe after 1815 occurred
____ important urban center in Britain
____ mainly Protestant portion of Ireland
____ empire proclaimed in 1871

Main Ideas

1. The Enlightenment resulted in _____
a. a concern for the well-being of the rich.
b. a concern for the well-being of all people.
c. a stagnation in the development of the arts.
d. the loss of religious freedom.
2. Napoleon's greatest contribution was that _____
a. he created a more democratic government.
b. he permanently enlarged France's borders.
c. he created the basis of modern French law.
d. he established French colonies in the New World.
3. The American and French revolutions had long-range effects because _____
a. they led to the rise of modern nationalism.
b. they set up a new class system.
c. they discouraged economic growth.
d. they encouraged the belief that equality applied only to political rights
4. *Realpolitik* refers to the view that _____
a. war had a place in modern society.
b. war was a legitimate means for a country to further its own interests.
c. all adults should have the right to vote.
d. only people with property should be allowed to vote.
5. The first country in Europe to grant democratic gains to the people was _____
a. Germany.
b. Italy.
c. France.
d. Britain.

Critical Thinking

1. Making Hypotheses To what extent do you think the revolutions studied in this unit achieved the goals they set out to accomplish? Support your answer with evidence.
2. Predicting Effects In what ways is the Industrial Revolution still affecting our lives today? Give examples.

The Interval of Western Dominance

OVERVIEW

This unit covers the growth of Western imperialism, the two world wars, and the development of communist and nationalist movements.

ADDITIONAL TEACHING AIDS FOR UNIT EIGHT

Literature for the Teacher

Botting, Douglas. *The Aftermath: Europe.* New York: Time-Life, 1983.

Bushnell, John. *Mutiny Amid Repression: Russian Soldiers in the Revolution of 1905–1906.* Indiana University Press, 1985.

Fairbank, John K. *China Bound—50 Year Memoir.* New York: Harper & Row, 1982.

Harris, Joseph E. *Africans and Their History.* New York: New American Library, 1987.

Lehmann, Jean-Pierre. *The Roots of Modern Japan.* New York: St. Martins Press, 1982.

Lewis, David Levering. *The Race to Fashoda.* New York: Weidenfield & Nicolson, 1987.

Moorehead, Geoffrey. *India Britannica—Three Centuries of British Rule.* New York: Harper & Row, 1983.

Morrison, Wilbur. *Above and Beyond 1941–1945.* St Martins Press, 1983.

The Pacific War Remembered: an Oral History Collection. Edited by John Mason Jr. Annapolis: Naval Institute Press, 1986.

Shapiro, Leonard. *The Russian Revolutions of 1917.* Basic Books, 1984.

Literature for the Student

Barrington, Boardman. *Isaac Asimov Presents from Harding to Hiroshima.* New York: W. W. Norton, 1988. (average)

Elliott, John E. *Marx and Engels on Economics, Politics, and Society.* Glenview: Scott, Foresman and Co. 1981. (challenging)

Hobsbawn, Eric. *The Age of Empire 1875–1914.* Pantheon Books, 1987. (average)

Jenning, Patrick. *Pictorial History of World War I.* Longsmeadow Press, 1975. (easy)

Lifton, Betty Jean. *A Place Called Hiroshima.* Tokyo: Kodansha International Ltd., 1985. (easy)

Sheehan, Susan. *A Missing Plane.* G. P. Putnam's Sons, 1986. (average)

Stokesbury, James L. *A Short History of World War I.* Wm. Morrow, 1981. (challenging)

Audio-Visual Materials*

China: A Revolution Revisited. Video or film, 80 minutes, black and white, [Films, Inc.], 1971. Traces the events that happened in China from the last days of the Manchu Dynasty up to the revolution in 1949

Churchill and British History, 1874–1918. Video or film, 29 minutes, black and white, [Coronet], 1977

The Decline of Tsarism. Video, 30 minutes, color, [EB], 1986. Depicts the series of military

defeats and growing social unrest that resulted in the abdication of Tsar Nicolas II in 1917, ending the Romanov dynasty and leading to the Russian Revolution

The Maharajas: Imperialism by Conspiracy. Film, 25 minutes, color, [Centron], 1974. Depicts how the English East India Company made initial contact with India and used the force of its private armies to subdue hostile princes

The Mighty Continent—A View of Europe in the Twentieth Century. Film, 13 titles, two reels each, 53 minutes, color, [Time-Life], 1975.

The Outbreak of the First World War. Video, 29 minutes, color, [EB], 1987. Depicts the assassination of Ferdinand at Sarajevo and the series of international diplomatic maneuvers that ultimately led to World War I

The Price of Peace (1919–1918). Video, 24 minutes, color, [University of Illinois Film Center], 1983. Concentrates on the military capabilities of the United States in World War I

The Scramble for Africa. Video, 37 minutes, color. [EB], 1986. Depicts how 19th-century Britain, France, and Germany staked their

* For a complete listing of sources of audio-visual materials see page T30.

claims and pursued national glory through colonial expansion in Africa

The Triumph of the West: The Decline of the West. Video, 50 minutes, color, [Films, Inc.], 1987. Depicts how changes in Europe, the United States, and Russia and the emergence

of Japan as a superpower led to a loss of faith in Western civilization

World War II Series. Videos or films, 5 titles, 14 minutes each, color, [Coronet], 1985. "Fragile Peace, 1919–29," "Roots of Aggression, 1929–39," "Inevitable War, 1939–40," "The

Expanding Conflict, 1940–42," and "A World at War, 1942–45"

World War II, 1938–1945. Audio tapes, 10 cassettes with guide, [Encyclopedia Americana Audio Research Library], 1974.

OPTIONAL WRITING ASSIGNMENTS

1. You represent the British government and are in charge of explaining to the new viceroy of British India the duties and responsibilities of his new position. Write a letter to the viceroy giving a brief background on events which have led to this appointment. Your letter also should outline policies that should be followed in relations with the Indian people.

2. You are the editor of a German newspaper at the end of World War I. You have just learned the details of the Treaty of Versailles.

Write an editorial giving your opinion of the treaty. Use information about Germany and the treaty to make your opinion creditable.

3. You are the political adviser to Tsar Nicholas II. Write a report summarizing the causes of the unrest sweeping Russia in 1917. In addition, propose actions that the Czar should take to settle problems with the dissidents.

4. You are a British citizen opposed to the actions of Neville Chamberlain during the

Munich Conference in September, 1939. Write a letter to your local newspaper protesting the appeasement of Hitler. Your letter should contain references to past events to support your position, and you should propose actions which your country should take to stop Hitler's aggressions.

5. You are a news correspondent for a major United States radio network. Select one event during World War II and write a five-minute radio script describing the event.

UNIT TESTS
IN THE TEACHER'S RESOURCE FILE

Unit Test, pp. 177–178

Alternate Unit Test, pp. 179–180

FINE ART IN UNIT EIGHT

Fine art forms an integral part of the historical record of events portrayed in this textbook. A listing of the paintings, drawings, sculpture, historic photographs, architecture, and other works of fine art selected to illustrate this unit follows. Students may be asked to research the artists and their works and report their findings to the entire class. Students also may be asked to write one or more paragraphs describing what they see upon a detailed study of a work of art and what the artist was attempting to communicate.

The Interval of Western Dominance

Themes and Patterns   The political and economic revolutions in the West that you read about in Unit 7 ushered in a new phase of world history, an interval of Western dominance of the world. No civilization in history had ever been able to achieve worldwide political, military, and economic dominance. This dominance lasted only about 100 years, from the mid-1800s to the mid-1900s. During that time, however, the effects of the political and industrial revolutions were spread all around the globe. A true global economy came into existence, tied together by railroads and steamships, and linking all parts of the world through trade.

At the center of this network, and profiting most from it, were the nations of the West, particularly Britain, Germany, France, Belgium, the Netherlands, and the United States. Yet, by the mid-20th century, these nations fought two major wars among themselves that shattered their worldwide political and military dominance.

Wars often create new and unexpected problems. In Europe, World War I opened the door to revolution and communism in Russia. War also opened the way for dictatorship and militarism in Germany and Italy. When the German dictatorship embarked upon a policy of aggressive expansion, tensions exploded into World War II.

Meanwhile, the ideal of national independence spread in Asia, Africa, and the Middle East. Thus, nationalism, a doctrine that originated in 19th-century Europe, was transmitted to the rest of the world and became the single most powerful force of the 20th century.

The stark drama of an industrial landscape is shown in this 1940s painting of a factory by American artist Charles Sheeler. Industrialization has transformed the entire world.

Chapters in this Unit

30 The Surge of Imperialism

OVERVIEW

This chapter describes the expansion of imperial control by the industrialized nations to areas in many parts of the world.

PLANNING CHART

Section	Text Pages	Key Concept	Suggested Teaching Time
1 India lost its independence.	564–565	The decline of the Mughal Empire gave Britain the opportunity to make India the cornerstone of its Asian empire.	One day **More time?** Use *Overhead Transparency 59* or *Source Reading 30A*.
2 China and Japan reacted in opposite ways to imperialism.	566–570	China's weaknesses resulted in its division by Europeans; Japan avoided a similar fate by becoming an imperialist power itself.	One day **More time?** Use *Source Reading 30B*.
3 Many nations gained influence elsewhere in Asia and the Pacific.	570–572	Colonial powers gained greater control over Asian and Pacific areas and markets.	One day **Less time?** Include the material in Section 3 regarding European colonies in Southeast Asia with Section 2. Discuss the extension of United States influence in the Pacific with Section 5.
4 Africa was carved into many colonies.	573–577	European colonial divisions in Africa set the stage for later conflicts.	Two days
5 Intervention grew in Latin America.	577–578	Many Latin American nations became dependent on the industrial power of the United States.	One day **More time?** Use *Overhead Transparency 60*.

ANCILLARIES

Materials that may be used with this chapter to reinforce, reteach, enrich, and assess learning are pictured on the following pages.

Teacher's Resource File

ACTIVITIES

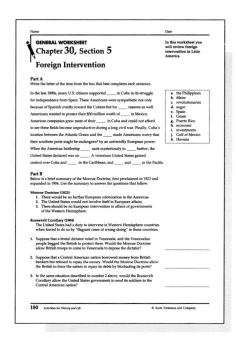

GENERAL WORKSHEET
Chapter 30, Section 1

In this worksheet you will review information about the British Empire in India.

The British in India

Part A
Write T if the statement is true and F if it is false. On the lines below, rewrite each false statement to make it true.

1. ___ The British Empire was small compared to the empires of France, Germany, and Italy.
2. ___ After the hold of the Mughal Empire on India weakened, the activities of the British East India Company extended British political control in India.
3. ___ Britain and France cooperated in their efforts to spread European rule overseas.
4. ___ The living standards of many Indians actually dropped during British rule.
5. ___ The British did not allow Indians to participate in government.

Part B
Write the letter of each effect from the box beside its cause.

1. ___ The hold of the Mughals over the Indian subcontinent weakened.
2. ___ The British defeated the French in the Seven Years' War.
3. ___ In 1857, rumors that the British were greasing rifle cartridges with beef and pork fat spread throughout British India.
4. ___ The British improved medical facilities and practices in India.
5. ___ The British introduced factory-made clothing to India.
6. ___ The power and possessions of the British East India Company grew.

a. The centuries-old Indian handicraft system was destroyed.
b. The sepoys rebelled.
c. The Indian population increased dramatically.
d. The British government passed the India Act of 1784.
e. The British moved into India to fill the vacuum of power.
f. The French were forced to give up imperial claims they had over Bengal.

Section 1 Activity, p. 176

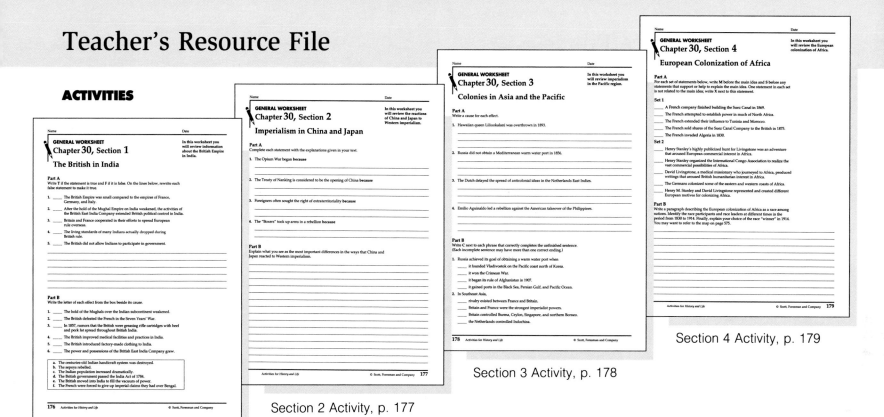

GENERAL WORKSHEET
Chapter 30, Section 2

In this worksheet you will review the reactions of China and Japan to Western imperialism.

Imperialism in China and Japan

Part A
Complete each statement with the explanations given in your text.

1. The Opium War began because
2. The Treaty of Nanking is considered to be the opening of China because
3. Foreigners often sought the right of extraterritoriality because
4. The "Boxers" took up arms in a rebellion because

Part B
Explain what you see as the most important differences in the ways that China and Japan reacted to Western imperialism.

Section 2 Activity, p. 177

GENERAL WORKSHEET
Chapter 30, Section 3

In this worksheet you will review imperialism in the Pacific region.

Colonies in Asia and the Pacific

Part A
Write a cause for each effect.

1. Hawaiian queen Liliuokalani was overthrown in 1893.
2. Russia did not obtain a Mediterranean warm water port in 1856.
3. The Dutch delayed the spread of anticolonial ideas in the Netherlands East Indies.
4. Emilio Aguinaldo led a rebellion against the American takeover of the Philippines.

Part B
Write C next to each phrase that correctly completes the unfinished sentence. (Each incomplete sentence may have more than one correct ending.)

1. Russia achieved its goal of obtaining a warm water port when
   ___ it founded Vladivostok on the Pacific coast north of Korea.
   ___ it won the Crimean War.
   ___ it began its rule of Afghanistan in 1907.
   ___ it gained ports in the Black Sea, Persian Gulf, and Pacific Ocean.

2. In Southeast Asia,
   ___ rivalry existed between France and Britain.
   ___ Britain and France were the strongest imperialist powers.
   ___ Britain controlled Burma, Ceylon, Singapore, and northern Borneo.
   ___ the Netherlands controlled Indochina.

Section 3 Activity, p. 178

GENERAL WORKSHEET
Chapter 30, Section 4

In this worksheet you will review the European colonization of Africa.

European Colonization of Africa

Part A
For each set of statements below, write M before the main idea and S before any statements that support or help to explain the main idea. One statement in each set is not related to the main idea; write X next to this statement.

Set 1
___ A French company finished building the Suez Canal in 1869.
___ The French attempted to establish power in much of North Africa.
___ The French extended their influence to Tunisia and Morocco.
___ The French sold shares of the Suez Canal Company to the British in 1875.
___ The French invaded Algeria in 1830.

Set 2
___ Henry Stanley's highly publicized hunt for Livingstone was an adventure that aroused European commercial interest in Africa.
___ Henry Stanley organized the International Congo Association to realize the vast commercial possibilities of Africa.
___ David Livingstone, a medical missionary who journeyed to Africa, produced writings that aroused British humanitarian interest in Africa.
___ The Germans colonized some of the eastern and western coasts of Africa.
___ Henry M. Stanley and David Livingstone represented and created different European motives for colonizing Africa.

Part B
Write a paragraph describing the European colonization of Africa as a race among nations. Identify the race participants and race leaders at different times in the period from 1830 to 1914. Finally, explain your choice of the race "winner" in 1914. You may want to refer to the map on page 575.

Section 4 Activity, p. 179

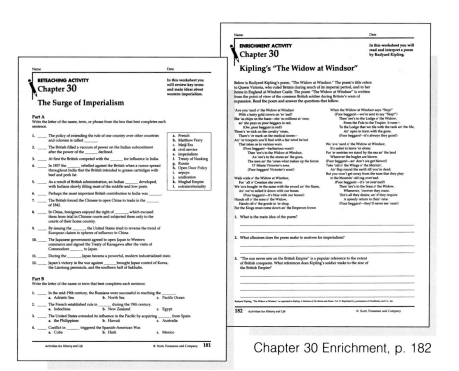

GENERAL WORKSHEET
Chapter 30, Section 5

In this worksheet you will review foreign intervention in Latin America.

Foreign Intervention

Part A
Write the letter of the item from the box that best completes each sentence.

In the late 1890s, many U.S. citizens supported ___ in Cuba in its struggle for independence from Spain. These Americans were sympathetic not only because of Spanish cruelty toward the Cubans but for ___ reasons as well. Americans wanted to protect their $50 million worth of ___ in Mexico. American companies grew most of their ___ in Cuba and could not afford to see these fields become unproductive during a long civil war. Finally, Cuba's location between the Atlantic Ocean and the ___ made Americans worry that their southern ports might be endangered by an unfriendly European power. When the American battleship ___ sank mysteriously in ___ harbor, the United States declared war on ___. A victorious United States gained control over Cuba and ___ in the Caribbean, and ___ and ___ in the Pacific.

a. the Philippines
b. Maine
c. revolutionaries
d. sugar
e. Spain
f. Guam
g. Puerto Rico
h. economic
i. investments
j. Gulf of Mexico
k. Havana

Part B
Below is a brief summary of the Monroe Doctrine, first proclaimed in 1823 and expanded in 1904. Use the summary to answer the questions that follow.

Monroe Doctrine (1823)
1. There would be no further European colonization in the Americas.
2. The United States would not involve itself in European affairs.
3. There should be no European intervention in affairs of governments of the Western Hemisphere.

Roosevelt Corollary (1904)
The United States had a duty to intervene in Western Hemisphere countries when forced to do so by "flagrant cases of wrong-doing" in these countries.

1. Suppose that a brutal dictator ruled in Venezuela, and the Venezuelan people begged the British to protect them. Would the Monroe Doctrine allow British troops to come to Venezuela to depose the dictator? ___
2. Suppose that a Central American nation borrowed money from British bankers but refused to repay the money. Would the Monroe Doctrine allow the British to force the nation to repay its debts by blockading its ports? ___
3. In the same situation described in number 2 above, would the Roosevelt Corollary allow the United States government to send its soldiers to the Central American nation? ___

Section 5 Activity, p. 180

RETEACHING ACTIVITY
Chapter 30

In this worksheet you will review key terms and main ideas about western imperialism.

The Surge of Imperialism

Part A
Write the letter of the name, term, or phrase from the box that best completes each sentence.

1. ___ The policy of extending the rule of one country over other countries and colonies is called ___.
2. ___ The British filled a vacuum of power on the Indian subcontinent after the power of the ___ declined.
3. ___ At first the British competed with the ___ for influence in India.
4. ___ In 1857 the ___ rebelled against the British when a rumor spread throughout India that the British intended to grease cartridges with beef and pork fat.
5. ___ As a result of British administration, an Indian ___ developed, with Indians slowly filling most of the middle and low posts.
6. ___ Perhaps the most important British contribution to India was ___.
7. ___ The British forced the Chinese to open China to trade in the ___ of 1842.
8. ___ In China, foreigners enjoyed the right of ___, which excused them from trial in Chinese courts and subjected them only to the courts of their home country.
9. ___ By issuing the ___, the United States tried to reverse the trend of European claims to spheres of influence in China.
10. ___ The Japanese government agreed to open Japan to Western commerce and signed the Treaty of Kanagawa after the visits of Commodore ___ to Japan.
11. ___ During the ___, Japan became a powerful, modern industrialized state.
12. ___ Japan's victory in the war against ___ brought Japan control of Korea, the Liaotung peninsula, and the southern half of Sakhalin.

a. French
b. Matthew Perry
c. Meiji Era
d. civil service
e. imperialism
f. Treaty of Nanking
g. Russia
h. Open Door Policy
i. sepoys
j. unification
k. Mughal Empire
l. extraterritoriality

Part B
Write the letter of the name or term that best completes each sentence.

1. ___ In the mid-19th century, the Russians were successful in reaching the ___.
   a. Adriatic Sea   b. North Sea   c. Pacific Ocean
2. ___ The French established rule in ___ during the 19th century.
   a. Indochina   b. New Zealand   c. Egypt
3. ___ The United States extended its influence in the Pacific by acquiring ___ from Spain.
   a. the Philippines   b. Hawaii   c. Australia
4. ___ Conflict in ___ triggered the Spanish-American War.
   a. Cuba   b. Haiti   c. Mexico

Chapter 30 Reteaching, p. 181

ENRICHMENT ACTIVITY
Chapter 30

In this worksheet you will read and interpret a poem by Rudyard Kipling.

Kipling's "The Widow at Windsor"

Below is Rudyard Kipling's poem, "The Widow at Windsor." The poem's title refers to Queen Victoria, who ruled Britain during much of its imperial period, and to her home in England at Windsor Castle. The poem "The Widow at Windsor" is written from the point of view of the common British soldier during Britain's wars of expansion. Read the poem and answer the questions that follow.

'Ave you 'eard o' the Widow at Windsor
  With a hairy gold crown on 'er 'ead?
She 'as ships on the foam—she 'as millions at 'ome,
  an' she pays us poor beggars in red.
(Ow, poor beggars in red!)
There's 'er nick on the cavalry 'orses,
  There's 'er mark on the medical stores—
An' 'er troopers you'll find with a fair wind be'ind
That takes us to various wars.
  (Poor beggars!—barbarous wars!)
Then 'ere's to the Widow at Windsor,
  An' 'ere's to the stores an' the guns,
The men an' the 'orses what makes up the forces
  O' Missis Victorier's sons.
  (Poor beggars! Victorier's sons!)

Walk wide o' the Widow at Windsor,
  For ' all o' Creation she owns.
We 've bought 'er the same with the sword an' the flame,
  An' we've salted it down with our bones.
  (Poor beggars!—it's blue with our bones!)
Hands off o' the sons o' the Widow,
  Hands off o' the goods in 'er shop,
For the Kings must come down an' the Emperors frown

When the Widow at Windsor says "Stop!"
  (Poor beggars!—we're sent to say "Stop!")
Then 'ere's to the Lodge o' the Widow,
  From the Pole to the Tropics it runs—
To the Lodge that we tile with the rank an' the file,
  An' open in form with the guns.
  (Poor beggars!—it's always they guns!)

We 'ave 'eard o' the Widow at Windsor,
  It's safest to leave 'er alone:
For 'er sentries we stand by the sea an' the land
  Wherever the bugles are blown.
  (Poor beggars!—an' don't we get blown!)
Take 'old o' the Wings o' the Mornin',
  An' flop round the earth till you're dead;
But you won't get away from the tune that they play
  To the bloomin' old rag over'ead.
  (Poor beggars!—it's 'ot over'ead!)
Then 'ere's to the Sons o' the Widow,
  Wherever, 'owever they roam.
'Ere's all they desire, an' if they require
  A speedy return to their 'ome.
  (Poor beggars!—they'll never see 'ome!)

1. What is the main idea of the poem?
2. What allusions does the poem make to motives for imperialism?
3. "The sun never sets on the British Empire" is a popular reference to the extent of British conquests. What references does Kipling's soldier make to the size of the British Empire?

Rudyard Kipling, "The Widow at Windsor" as reprinted in *Kipling: A Selection of His Stories and Poems*, Vol. 2. Reprinted by permission of Doubleday and Co., Inc.

Chapter 30 Enrichment, p. 182

Teacher's Resource File

GEOGRAPHY SKILLS

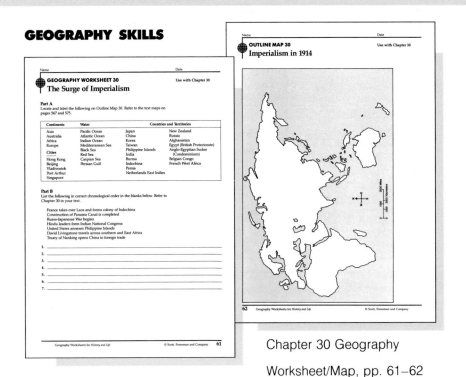

Chapter 30 Geography
Worksheet/Map, pp. 61–62

Chapter 30 Map Lesson, p. 112

TESTS

561c   Chapter Test, pp. 157–158

Alternate Chapter Test, pp. 159–160

Other Optional Ancillaries

WORKBOOK

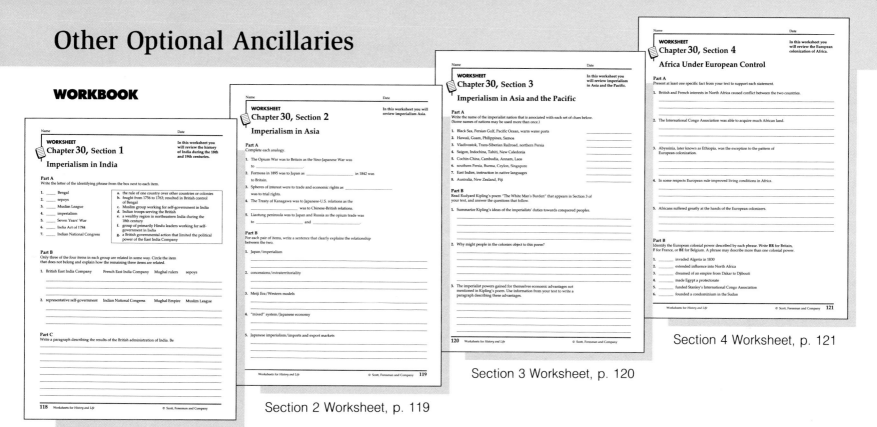

Section 1 Worksheet, p. 118

Section 2 Worksheet, p. 119

Section 3 Worksheet, p. 120

Section 4 Worksheet, p. 121

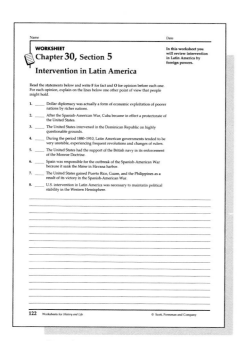

Section 5 Worksheet, p. 122

SOURCE READINGS

Source Reading 30A
Source Reading 30B

OVERHEAD TRANSPARENCIES

Overhead Transparency 59
Overhead Transparency 60

TEST GENERATOR

40 multiple-choice questions for Chapter 30

30

The Surge of Imperialism

1750–1914

1600

1700

1763   British take over India

1842   Treaty of Nanking forces China to open for trade

1900

2000

In the closing days of October, 1899, the lights burned on into the night in the East Wing of the White House. Unable to sleep, President William McKinley paced back and forth. He had a terribly difficult decision to make. During the summer American forces had captured the Philippine Islands from Spain. American opinion was sharply divided on whether we should annex the islands or set them free. In an interview given a few weeks later, McKinley explained how he made up his mind.

> When . . . the Philippines . . . dropped into our lap, I confess that I did not know what to do with them. I sought counsel from all sides . . . but got little help. . . . I walked the floor of the White House night after night until midnight . . . I went down on my knees and prayed Almighty God for light and guidance. . . . And one night late it came to me this way. . . . (1) that we could not give them back to Spain—that would be cowardly and dishonorable; (2) that we could not turn them over to France or Germany . . . that would be bad business and discreditable; (3) that we could not leave them to themselves—they were unfit for self-government . . . (4) that there was nothing left for us to do but to take them all, and to educate the Filipinos, and uplift and civilize and Christianize them, and, by God's grace, do the very best we could by them, as our fellow men for whom Christ also died.

The reasons given by McKinley for taking his country down the path of empire, was very much like those given by Britain, France, Germany, and other imperial powers to justify imperialism—that is, the rule of one country over other countries or colonies.

During the years from 1870 to 1914, several economic conditions led Western nations to become interested in colonies. First, rapid industrialism and a rising standard of living created the need for more raw materials. Second, competition among industrial countries led each to raise its tariffs on imports and to look

A Japanese print illustrates the naval battle that led to Russia's defeat in the 1905 Russo-Japanese War, when a victorious Japan emerged as a major power.

abroad for new export markets. Third, the less economically developed areas of the world offered opportunities for investment.

During the era of imperialism, a nation's greatness came to be measured by its colonial possessions. Among Europeans, national pride was mixed with religious and humanitarian motives. Missionaries, doctors, and colonial administrators believed they had a duty to "improve" the natives' lives. This attitude led to certain reforms in some areas, such as abolition of slavery and improvements in health and justice. Too often Europeans, however, who talked of noble purposes were more interested in profits and power.

Reading Preview

In this chapter you will read how the industrial nations embarked on imperialist ventures.

1. India lost its independence.

2. China and Japan reacted in opposite ways to imperialism.

3. Many nations gained influence elsewhere in Asia and the Pacific.

4. Africa was carved into many colonies.

5. Intervention grew in Latin America.

1 *Lesson Plan*

Essential Learning Objective

Students will learn to discuss factors that led to nationalist movements in India.

1 FOCUS AND MOTIVATE

As preparation for this section, ask students to recall what they learned in Chapter 23 about the rise and deterioration of the Mughal Empire. As the empire weakened, the British moved into India.

2 TEACH

Use a time line drawn across the chalkboard to illustrate the chronology of British rule in India. Clarify how Parliament ended the East India Company's control over India between 1784 and 1858. Explain the ways in which British rule helped to unify India and to raise health and literacy. Point out the negative aspects of British rule as well.

GUIDED PRACTICE

Direct students to list ways that British policies encouraged nationalism. (Students should grasp that the establishment of the Indian Civil Service and of English as the official language provided incentives for Indians to obtain British educations and thereby acquire liberal ideas.)

3 ASSESS AND CLOSE

ASSESS

How did Britain become the sole European power in India? (by defeating France in the Seven Years' War)

OPTIONAL RETEACHING

Hold a panel discussion to examine

1 *India lost its independence.*

Long before that fateful day when President McKinley cast his lot with American **imperialism**, the Great Powers of Europe had extended their rule over vast areas of Asia, Africa, and South America. Foremost among the holders of empire were the British whose proud boast was that the sun never set on their globe-girdling possessions. The most valuable of all of Britain's colonies was India, a land where British influence dated from the late 17th century.

The British took advantage of Mughal weakness.

As the hold of the Mughal Empire over the Indian subcontinent began to weaken, the British moved in to fill the vacuum. As you read in Chapter 23, after the death of Aurangzeb in 1707, the empire was torn with unrest. Within 40 years, it fell into chaos. By 1750 both the British East India Company and the French East India Company were active in India, operating there with the permission of the Mughal rulers. They had made several small settlements, which they rented from the local rulers. The trading companies had their own military forces that kept law and order in the settlements. In the absence of a strong local administration, these forces were also to be used to extend British political control.

During the 18th and 19th centuries, Britain and France were often at war with each other both in Europe and in their overseas empires. India was a frequent battleground. At first, the French were the winners. During the Seven Years' War (1756–1763), the British defeated the French. The British then became the masters of **Bengal**, a wealthy region in northeastern India. Bengal was the cornerstone of the British Empire in India.

The British East India Company's rule was limited.

The British government decided to eliminate the British East India Company's political power. The India Act of 1784 gave power over the company to a Board of Control whose president was a British cabinet member. The British government also chose the highest company official in India, the governor general. In 1814 Parliament took away the company's trade monopoly in India. In 1833 its China trade monopoly was also ended.

However, the British East India Company remained active. As the Mughal Empire fell apart, the company extended British control over more and more territory. It sometimes did this by conquering lands directly through the use of the company's own army, or it arranged alliances with local rulers who accepted company protection. By

Queen Victoria reigned from 1837 to 1901 when Britain reached the height of its imperial power. In 1876 she was proclaimed empress of India. Here she is shown writing, attended by an Indian servant.

the mid-19th century, nearly all of India had come under British control.

Indians resented British missionaries and policies, and they were alarmed by the aggressive expansion of the company in the mid-1800s. In 1857 a rumor spread among the sepoys [sē′poiz], Indian troops who served the British, that new rifle cartridges—the ends of which had to be bitten off—would be greased with beef and pork fat. Hindus regarded cows as sacred, and Muslims considered pigs unclean. Both groups were outraged. They rose in mutiny and slaughtered many Europeans. However, the **Sepoy Rebellion** did not have the support of the people, and the British were able to end the rebellion by late 1858.

As a result of the Sepoy Rebellion, the British Parliament abolished the East India Company in 1858 and transferred all of its activity and holdings to the British crown. The government created a new cabinet post, Secretary of State for India, and appointed a viceroy to rule within India. The British then divided India into two parts, British India, which was ruled directly by the British, and Indian India, which was ruled by Indian princes who were in charge of their own internal affairs.

In British India the viceroy had full power. He was aided by legislative and executive councils that included some Indians. All the members, however, were appointed rather than elected. An efficient Indian civil service developed, and though the British held all the top positions, Indians slowly filled most of the middle and lower posts.

British administration had mixed results.

Probably the most important contribution of the British in India was unification. Now almost all of the subcontinent had come under one authority. The use of English as the official language helped, since before this time, there had been no single language that all educated Indians could speak.

The British in India also suppressed organized bands of robbers, reduced the dangers of travel, and protected life and property. They outlawed suttee (the suicide of a widow on her husband's funeral pyre) and the killing of infant girls. They also improved medical facilities, added thousands of miles of railroad and telegraph lines, and built irrigation works throughout the countryside.

The picture had a dark side, too. Because of such changes, the population grew rapidly, and food production could not keep up with this growth. As a result, the living standard declined sharply for many. One poor harvest was enough to cause widespread famine. Because of its large population, poverty was and still is today a major problem in India.

Another heavy blow to the Indian economy was the end of the centuries-old handicraft system. With the growth of British industry, India became a market for cheap manufactured goods, especially cotton textiles. The Indians' handwoven cloth could not sell as cheaply as imported cloth, and, as part of their imperialist policies, the British forbade the Indians to sell their cloth to other countries. Thus, Indians were forced to depend more and more on agriculture to earn a living.

The seeds of a future independence movement were already being planted, however. During the 19th century, a small group of Indian intellectuals arose. Trained in British schools, they learned English history and language. What they learned about the liberal traditions of 19th-century Europe brought out their own desire for self-government. In 1885, therefore, a group of primarily Hindu leaders formed the **Indian National Congress**, and in 1906 a group of educated Muslims formed the **Muslim League**. Both groups worked for representative self-government for India. As a result, the strength of Indian nationalism grew steadily.

Section 1 Review

Identify imperialism, Bengal, Sepoy Rebellion, Indian National Congress, Muslim League

Main Ideas
1. How did the British gain control of India?
2. What changes did the British government make in the way the British East India Company operated?
3. How did British rule in India change after the Sepoy Rebellion? What were the results of British rule in India?

Critical Thinking
Recognizing Values: Judging from the brief description of British rule in this text, would you say that it was, on the whole, a positive or negative force? What values lead you to one conclusion or the other?

British East India Company, set up a new cabinet post, and appointed a viceroy to rule within India. Results were unification; improved public health, transportation, and communication; population increase with decline in living standards; decline of cloth industry; introduction of ideas of representative government.

Critical Thinking

Students may support British rule if they believe that national unity and modern ideas of social justice are most important. They may oppose it if they believe that people should have the right to follow their own customs.

Essential Learning Objectives

Students will learn to:

- discuss methods used in opening China to foreign influence.
- discuss the reactions of the Japanese to Western culture.
- describe the development of imperialism in Japan.

1 FOCUS AND MOTIVATE

Tell students to imagine that they are government officials in a country that does not allow foreign contact. Now contact has been made and a trade relationship has been suggested by a foreign power. Ask students to identify some possible reactions by the officials of the isolated nation. Write responses on the chalkboard. Direct students to compare their suggested responses with those of the governments of China and Japan, as they study this section.

2 China and Japan reacted in opposite ways to imperialism.

Following the age of exploration, the interest of Westerners in East Asia grew steadily. By the mid-19th century, both China and Japan were confronted with serious challenges to their independence and territorial integrity. A weakened China gradually succumbed to increasing pressures from the outside. Japan, however, effectively resisted those pressures and in a remarkably short time became itself an imperialistic power.

Foreign powers exploited China.

In China the power of the Manchu dynasty began to decline rapidly after 1800. (See Chapter 24.) By mid-century it was in serious trouble and faced open rebellion in many parts of the country. Just as its domestic problems were increasing, China faced strong pressure from the outside. Westerners stepped up pressure in an effort to increase their amount of trade with China. Frictions developed as the two very different civilizations came into closer contact.

The conflict known as the Opium War broke out in 1839. Basically, the Opium War grew out of the Manchu refusal to allow the British to establish regular trade with China. On the surface, however, the cause was opium. The British East India Company had been importing opium into China in return for Chinese tea and silk. Although there was a law against this importation, the Manchus had not enforced it for years. Many Chinese were becoming addicted to the drug, turning to robbery to get money to buy opium and neglecting their farms. Chinese leaders were concerned, and one day, a Chinese official seized a large amount of the drug and destroyed it. The British protested, but negotiations failed, and the two countries soon went to war.

The Opium War lasted three years. The Chinese, who had no navy, were no match for the British, and the conflict ended with the Treaty of Nanking in 1842. The Chinese ceded the southern port of **Hong Kong** to the British and paid damages for the opium they had destroyed. They also agreed to a lower tariff on trade. Most important, the

BACKGROUND The Treaty of Nanking was one of a series known as "unequal treaties," because China was repeatedly forced to give up more privileges without getting anything in return.

Chinese were forced to open five port cities to trade. The Treaty of Nanking thus marked the real opening of China, for soon after, other Western countries received similar trading rights.

Foreign traders, however, took advantage of the weakness of the Chinese government and often abused their trading rights. In 1856 war again broke out. This time, a combined British-French force attacked the Chinese capital, Beijing, forced the emperor to flee, and burned the beautiful summer palace. The treaties signed in 1858 and 1860 marked another defeat for the Chinese. The Manchus opened 11 more ports, legalized the opium trade, agreed to receive Western diplomats, and promised to protect Christian missionaries. China also had to give the right of **extraterritoriality** to foreigners; that is, foreigners were excused from trial in Chinese courts and subject only to the courts of their home country. Under Chinese law, it should be noted, a crime was the responsibility of a group and any group member could be punished. This custom was very different from Western ways.

The weakness of China was now clear to all, and foreign powers quickly moved in to carve up China. They set up **spheres of influence,** that is, regions where the economic interests of a certain country were supreme. Within its sphere, a country had rights to specific tracts of land called concessions. It controlled these concessions and enjoyed the right of extraterritoriality there. Russia, Germany, and France all gained concessions within China.

In the process of becoming a "Great Power" itself, the United States viewed with alarm the success of the European countries in obtaining exclusive trading rights in China. In 1899, in an effort to reverse the trend, the United States therefore issued the Open Door Policy. This policy urged countries having spheres of influence to allow all nations to compete in them on equal terms. Although several countries agreed on paper to the American plan, it had little real effect.

The Chinese deeply resented the exploitation and invasion of their country by foreigners. Their Manchu rulers held tightly to traditional Chinese customs and resisted change to Western ways. Many people joined the secret Society of Harmo-

Spheres of Influence in Asia, 1914

- ◯ British
- ● Portuguese
- ● French
- ● German
- ☐ Dutch
- ☐ Japanese
- ☐ American
- ☐ Russian

0   1000 Miles
0   1000 Kilometers

 MAP STUDY The map shows how foreign countries controlled much of Asia in 1914. Which countries controlled Burma? Korea? The Philippines?

2 TEACH

- Point out that China's government, like India's, was in decline at the time imperialistic contact began. Discuss events leading to the Opium War and China's loss of power in the treaties of Nanking of 1855 and 1860. Stress that China's inability to defend itself against attack was largely because China chose isolationism, which prevented industrial and military modernization.

- Discuss the reactions of Japanese officials to Perry's two visits. Point out that Perry's show of force and his dignified conduct impressed the Japanese. List the steps that Japan took that allowed it to avoid foreign domination.

GUIDED PRACTICE

Direct students to examine Japan's motives in becoming an imperialist power by comparing its actions with those of the Europeans. Refer to the map on page 567 to locate the areas the Japanese controlled by 1914. Be sure students grasp the significance of Japan's victory over Russia in 1905.

nious Fists—or "Boxers"—which opposed all Westerners. In 1900 the Boxers took up arms. They destroyed railroads, burned bridges, and killed Europeans. The Boxer Rebellion was quickly put down by a combined force of Europeans, Americans, and Japanese. Afterwards, stricter controls were placed upon the Chinese government. However, there remained a group of Chinese who believed that change in their own government was needed in order to get rid of European control. They began a revolutionary movement that spread rapidly through the country.

Japan opened its doors and adopted new ways.

As you learned in Chapter 24, during the Tokugawa Shogunate, Japan followed a policy of strict isolation from the rest of the world. By the mid-18th century, however, serious internal problems weakened Tokugawa rule and made the country less able to resist foreign influences. The first real break in the wall of isolation came in 1853 with the visit of an American fleet.

Since the early 1800s, American whaling ships had sailed in the northern Pacific, and clipper ships trading with China sailed near Japan. American shippers were interested in Japan because they needed ports where their vessels could stop for food, fuel, and water. They also wanted protection for their sailors. Those Americans who had been shipwrecked on Japanese shores had been badly treated.

In 1853 the American government sent Commodore **Matthew Perry** and a squadron of four ships to Japan. Perry brought a message from President Millard Fillmore, requesting that the Japanese open their country to foreign trade. Commodore Perry then left, promising to return the following spring for an answer.

In February, 1854, Commodore Perry returned with ten ships. He carried many presents for the Japanese officials—books, rifles, clocks, perfume, sewing machines, and even a small locomotive. The Japanese were impressed by the gifts and by Perry's dignity and show of force. They agreed to the Treaty of Kanagawa, which opened two Japanese ports to American ships, provided better treatment for shipwrecked sailors, and set up diplomatic relations between the two countries.

In 1858 a second treaty opened more ports. It also granted the right of extraterritoriality to Americans in Japan. Soon afterward, other Western nations worked out similar treaties, and the door seemed to be open for large-scale foreign influence in Japan.

Japan, however, did not go the way of China. Unlike the Chinese rulers, the Japanese decided that their country could survive only by adopting certain Western ways. One of the first changes was in the Shogunate itself. The Treaty of Kanagawa had caused antiforeign riots. The Tokugawas were blamed for these uprisings as well as for the poor conditions of the past hundred years. In 1867 powerful daimyo leaders forced the shogun to give up his powers. The next year the emperor was restored to a position of authority, and the capital was moved from Kyoto to Tokyo. Emperor Mutsuhito, a boy of 15, adopted Meiji [mā'jē], meaning "enlightened rule," as the name of his reign. His accession to the throne in 1868 is known as the Meiji Restoration.

During the 45 years of the **Meiji Era**, Japan became a powerful modern state, the first industrialized country in Asia. However, the enormous changes in political, social, and economic affairs were carefully controlled. Japanese leaders sent delegations to study all the major Western powers, and then adopted only what they thought would be good for Japan.

In 1871 the emperor abolished feudalism, and in 1889 he issued a constitution like that which Bis-

A Japanese artist captured the menacing alien quality of one of Commodore Perry's "Black Ships," as the Japanese called the American fleet in 1854.

marck had written for Germany. Although the constitution provided for a two-house legislature, the emperor remained supreme. Only the lower house was elected, and only about 1 percent of the people could vote. However, this number grew to about 20 percent in the next three decades.

Military leaders wielded great power in the government. The army and navy were strengthened. The army was based on the German model and the navy on the British.

Other changes were also made. Compulsory education was introduced, and illiteracy was almost wiped out. The government adopted new laws and a new judicial system, patterned after Western models. All foreign rights of extraterritoriality were eliminated by 1899.

Perhaps even more surprising than the political changes were those in economic life. Japanese leaders knew that Western strength was based on industrial power, so they pushed ahead with a major program to make Japan strong industrially. At the time of the Meiji Restoration in 1868, there were almost no factory workers in Japan. By 1900 there were half a million.

Because money for investment was scarce, the Japanese government gave loans to private businesses. The government also entered directly into the building of railroads, factories, shipyards, and telegraph and telephone systems. As a result, Japan developed a "mixed" system of private and government enterprise led by a few wealthy families who made up an economic ruling class.

Japanese ambitions led to imperialism.

In becoming a modern industrial state, Japan also became imperialistic. This, too, was part of its study of Western ways. Imperialism was at that time a respected philosophy among large segments of the Western world.

Japan had many reasons to justify its imperialism. First, a rapid rise in population resulted from better sanitation and medical services. In the Meiji Era alone, the population grew from about 30 million to more than 50 million. The nation did not grow enough food for its people. Second, Japan lacked raw materials and markets for its manufactured goods and viewed the Asian mainland as a solution for its difficulties. As early as 1876, the

During the Meiji period (1868–1912), the Japanese government encouraged industrialization. Above is a 1905 photograph of a silk weaving factory.

Japanese had obtained trading privileges in Korea. This angered the Chinese and led to the Sino-Japanese War of 1894–1895. By defeating China, Japan obtained its first major territory beyond its own borders, the island of Formosa (present-day Taiwan).

Japan had also gained control of the Liaotung [lyou'dùng] peninsula in Manchuria. However, backed by France and Germany, Russia forced Japan to return it to China. Soon afterward, Russia leased the Liaotung peninsula and its city of Port Arthur for itself through a treaty with China. This and other Russian moves in Korea angered Japan.

Talks between Japan and Russia over Korea and Manchuria broke down in 1904. Fighting began when Japan, without declaring war, attacked the Russian fleet at Port Arthur. Much to the surprise of the West, Japan won the Russo-Japanese War. This was the first time in modern history that an Asian country had defeated a European country. With the Treaty of Portsmouth (1905), Japan regained control of the Liaotung peninsula, won a sphere of influence in Korea, and took over the southern half of the Russian island of Sakhalin. Five years later, in 1910, Japan took complete control of Korea. Almost overnight, Japan had become a major world power.

OPTIONAL RETEACHING

Divide students into two groups, one representing the interests of the Chinese, the other representing the Western powers. Identify the key elements of extraterritoriality in a treaty between the two groups. Then have them negotiate a treaty that includes foreign legal authority in China.

OPTIONAL ENRICHMENT

1. Assign students to research and to report on the effects of the Russo-Japanese War on Russia. (average)
2. Assign students to research and to report on the provisions of the Treaty of Nanking regarding Hong Kong, the subsequent history of the colony, and its present status. (challenging)
3. Also for enrichment:

📖 *Source Reading 30B*

INDEPENDENT PRACTICE/ HOMEWORK

Assign the Section Review, Activities page 177, or Workbook page 119.

CLOSURE

Tell students that China and Japan followed different policies when dealing with Western powers. China tried to continue a policy of isolationism. Without westernization China was unable to create a modern military force that could defeat foreign attackers. Defeated by imperialist powers, China had to submit to foreign political and economic controls. Japan, on the other hand, chose to industrialize. Because its military strength grew, Japan defeated both China and Russia.

Identify

Key Terms, People, and Places are defined on pages indicated in parentheses. Also see the Glossary and Biographical Dictionary.
Hong Kong (566), extraterritoriality (566), spheres of influence (566), Matthew Perry (568), Meiji Era (568)

Main Ideas

1. The Manchu government agreed to open ports to foreign trade, give the right of extraterritoriality to foreigners, and began to lose control in the spheres of influence.

2. Commodore Perry opened Japan to foreign trade. The Japanese withdrew the Tokugawa Shogunate and the Meiji Era began. The Japanese studied Western methods, adopted new laws and industrialized.

3. Japan, imitating the West, viewed imperialism as a way to solve its need for food and markets. By 1910 it had gained control of Taiwan, the Liaotung peninsula, and Korea.

Critical Thinking

Japanese leaders understood that they would have to catch up with the West in technology and made major efforts to do so by developing a strong central government. The Chinese government, on the other hand, became weaker.

3 Lesson Plan

Essential Learning Objectives

Students will learn to:
- identify the areas in Southeast Asia that came under European control.
- explain the motivations of the Western powers in taking control of many Pacific islands.

Section 2 Review

Identify Hong Kong, extraterritoriality, spheres of influence, Matthew Perry, Meiji Era

Main Ideas

1. What did the foreign powers win from the Manchu government during the 19th century?
2. What events led Japan to become a modern industrial power?
3. Why did Japan become imperialistic? What territorial gains did it make by 1910?

Critical Thinking

Analyzing Comparisons: Japan succeeded in becoming an industrial nation by the late 1800s, but China failed to do so. How do you account for this difference?

---

3 Many nations gained influence elsewhere in Asia and the Pacific.

We have seen how India and China became victims of European imperialism. Thus, it should not be surprising that smaller countries in Asia, as well as many islands in the Pacific, also came under Western rule. In the Pacific region, however, imperialists found a new rival, the United States.

European powers expanded into several regions of Asia.

By stages, beginning with Ivan the Great and Ivan the Terrible, tsarist Russia expanded territorially to become a great land power. By the 19th century, Russia was a force to contend with in both Europe and Asia. The Russian dream of obtaining warm water ports was pursued intermittently and never given up. The goal might be achieved by gaining entrance to the Mediterranean through the Black Sea, by reaching the Persian Gulf through Persia, or by reaching the Pacific Ocean north of Korea. All three approaches were tried.

The effort to reach the Mediterranean was thwarted when Russia met defeat at the hands of France and England in the Crimean War, 1854–

1856, which you read about in Chapter 29. It was renewed again before 1914 and became a contributing factor in bringing on World War I. Russian efforts in Asia proved more fruitful, but again they were opposed by other Great Powers, notably Britain and Japan. When China was forced to open to Western exploitation in the mid-19th century, the Russians moved quickly to secure a large coastal area north of Korea where they founded the town of **Vladivostok** [vlad′ə vos′tok] in 1860, still Russia's main naval base in the Pacific.

In 1890 Russia began building the Trans-Siberian Railroad. China gave permission for the line to cross Manchuria and end at Port Arthur on the Liaotung peninsula. As you learned earlier, the Russians, however, lost control of the Liaotung peninsula to the Japanese after the Russo-Japanese War. This was a major blow to their imperialistic plans in that area. Meanwhile, Russian imperialists also moved into parts of Persia. This movement worried the British, who feared that Russia might reach the Persian Gulf and interfere with Britain's shipping route to India and the East. The British were also concerned that in Central Asia the Russians had reached the borders of Afghanistan, a position that also threatened India. In 1907 Britain and Russia signed an agreement promising that neither country would take over Afghanistan. In addition, Persia was divided into spheres of influence, with Russia controlling the north and Britain the south.

In Southeast Asia, Britain and France were the two chief rivals for territory. The French first moved into the area in the late 18th century. By the mid-1800s, however, hostile Asian feelings led to attacks on French missionaries. A French fleet attacked and captured Saigon in 1860. During the next 20 years, France took control of Cochin-China, Cambodia, and Annam. These areas had always paid tribute to China, which tried unsuccessfully to eject the French by force in the 1880s. In 1893 the French took over Laos [lä′ōs]. They grouped all these areas together to form the French colony of **Indochina**, an area a third larger than France itself. French rule in Indochina gradually transformed villagers into landless agricultural workers whose incomes came to depend on the rise and fall of world prices.

Queen Liliuokalani came to the Hawaiian throne in 1891. She tried to end American control of Hawaii but was overthrown in an American military coup.

Burma, meanwhile, had come under British influence. Conflicts along the Indian border had touched off small wars, and as the winner of these wars, Britain was able to take over more and more land. Burma was formally annexed (added) to India in 1885. Other possessions of the British in this area were Ceylon (present-day Sri Lanka), Singapore, and northern Borneo.

One other important European power in this region was the Netherlands, which controlled the East Indies. As with the British in India, a private trading company—the Dutch East India Company—ruled for many years. Then in 1798 the home government took over. It made the territory a colony called the Netherlands East Indies. The Dutch reaped handsome profits from their colony, which provided Europeans with spices, sugar, coffee, and tea. The Dutch built schools, but insisted

that instruction be given in native languages. This system preserved the many native cultures in the region. It also delayed the spread of anticolonial ideas such as nationalism and democracy.

Pacific islands came under foreign rule.

The 1800s saw the rapid development of ocean-going ships. This was followed by a vast increase in trans-Pacific commerce. For the first time in history, the Pacific Ocean became a major international waterway. Naturally, some of the thousands of islands in the Pacific became important refueling stations.

Britain, the leading naval power, gained control of Australia, New Zealand, and many Pacific islands. These included Fiji, southeastern New Guinea, and the southern Solomons. The Germans colonized the northern Solomons and northwestern New Guinea and bought some islands from Spain. Meanwhile, France secured Tahiti and annexed New Caledonia, a major source of nickel and chromium.

The United States, too, was interested in Pacific islands. During the 19th century, Americans and Europeans settled in the Hawaiian Islands, where they established missions and set up a thriving export trade in sugar. By the 1880s Americans dominated the government, although Hawaii was still technically independent.

In order to receive better trade benefits, Hawaiian sugar planters wanted the islands to become part of the United States. When the Hawaiian queen, **Liliuokalani** [lē lē'ü ō kä lä'nē], refused to support annexation, she was overthrown in 1893. In 1898 Congress took over the Hawaiian Islands, which became the 50th state of the United States in 1959.

Meanwhile, in the Spanish-American War of 1898, the United States acquired Guam and the Philippines, which had been Spanish possessions in the Pacific. With the U.S. victory over Spain, Filipino leaders expected independence for their country. The issue of the future of the islands was debated heatedly in Congress, the press, and by the American public. As we saw in the chapter introduction, President McKinley agonized over the question but in the end decided on annexation. The Filipino guerrilla leader, **Emilio Aguinaldo**

BACKGROUND The one area that escaped imperialism was Siam. Students might wish to read *The English Governess at the Siamese Court,* Mrs. Anna Leonowens's autobiographical account of her experiences at the court of King Morgkut during

the 1860s. The musical *The King and I* is based on these experiences.

571

1 FOCUS AND MOTIVATE

Have students find the Hawaiian Islands on a large world globe or wall map. Ask students to suggest reasons why these islands would have become important to the United States during the imperialist period. Students should recognize that the islands would have served as ports en route to colonies in Asia. Tell students that they will learn how other islands in the Pacific became part of the imperialistic plans of the West.

2 TEACH

- Explain Russia's need for warm water ports locating potential routes on the Asia and world maps in the Atlas. Discuss the problems encountered in each area.

- Chart on the chalkboard the areas colonized by Britain, France, the Netherlands, the United States, and Germany. Include dates, details of methods of rule, and conflicts.

GUIDED PRACTICE

Hand out outline maps of the world from the Geography Skills book. Direct students to color-code the colonial powers and their territories. Have students use matching colored lines to illustrate the sea routes between the European power and its colonies, and black lines to indicate the sites of Russia's attempted claims to ports.

3 ASSESS AND CLOSE

ASSESS

1. What European nations took over in Southeast Asia? (Britain, France, the Netherlands)
2. Which areas in the Pacific came under United States control? (Hawaii, the Philippines, Guam, Samoa)

Filipino prisoners of war are shown in this 1899 photograph taken during their fight against the United States for independence.

[ä gwē näl′dō], who had been fighting the Spanish, now led a rebellion against the American takeover. After three years of fierce fighting, the rebellion was crushed and the Philippines became an American possession.

While the debate over annexation was at its peak, Rudyard Kipling, the British poet of imperialism, urged the Americans on. In his poem, "The White Man's Burden," Kipling said what many in Europe and America at the time felt was an obligation to civilize "backward peoples."

> Take up the White Man's burden—
> Send forth the best ye breed—
> Go bind your sons to exile
> To serve your captives' need;
> To wait in heavy harness,
> On fluttered folk and wild—
> Your new caught, sullen peoples,
> Half-devil and half-child.
>
> Take up the White Man's burden—
> Ye dare not stoop to less—
> Nor call too loud on Freedom
> To cloak your weariness;
> By all ye cry or whisper.
> By all ye leave or do,
> The silent, sullen peoples
> Shall weigh your Gods and you.

Kipling's poem is a classical expression of ideas then current which have, in more recent times, caused understandable outrage on the part of Asians and others who have achieved independence. Africans and Asians were quick to point out that in many cases their culture was older than that of Europe and equally rich in its attainments.

American interests in the Pacific were not confined to Hawaii and the Philippines. In 1878 the United States secured rights to a naval base in Samoa, at the harbor of Pago Pago. The British and Germans contested the American arrangement with the Samoans, and in 1889 a three-way agreement was worked out. Ten years later, the islands were divided outright between Germany and the United States.

Section 3 Review

Identify Vladivostok, Indochina, Liliuokalani, Emilio Aguinaldo

Main Ideas

1. In what three areas did Russia seek a warm water port? Which parts of Asia came under French and Dutch rule?
2. Why did the Pacific islands attract imperialist powers in the 19th century? Which Pacific areas did the United States take over?

Critical Thinking

Analyzing Comparisons: Compare President McKinley's reasons for annexing the Philippines with the sentiments expressed by Kipling in "The White Man's Burden."

4 Africa was carved into many colonies.

Nowhere did imperial powers move with such speed and nowhere were the effects as pronounced as in Africa. In 1875 only a tenth was under European control. Within 20 years, however, only a tenth was free of such control.

France and Britain gained control of North Africa.

North Africa had been conquered by the Turks in the 15th century and made part of the Ottoman Empire. By the 19th century, however, Turkish power was declining, and the nations of Europe saw an opportunity to extend their influence.

One of the first important European moves into Africa was made by the French. They invaded Algeria in 1830, both for prestige and to stop Algerian pirates who attacked French ships. For many years, no other European state showed much interest in North Africa. However, in 1869 a French company finished building the **Suez Canal**, which linked the Mediterranean Sea to the Indian Ocean by way of the Red Sea. (See the map on page 575.) The Middle East again became, as it had been in ancient times, a major crossroads of world trade.

encountered a British force. The resulting crisis, which almost led to war between Britain and France, was resolved when the French government agreed to recall their troops.

In 1875 the British government bought a large bloc of shares in the Suez Canal Company. The canal was a vital link in Britain's lifeline to India, Australia, and New Zealand. When civil war broke out in Egypt in 1882, Britain sent in a military force and reduced the country to the status of a British **protectorate**, that is, a weaker country controlled and protected by a stronger one, particularly in foreign affairs.

The British next moved into the Sudan, hoping to acquire a solid belt of land from Cairo in the north to Cape Town in the south. In 1899, after major battles, Britain and Egypt made the Sudan a condominium, that is, an area they ruled jointly. However, Britain was the dominant power in this condominium.

Meanwhile, France had been actively developing Algeria and extending its influence over Tunisia and Morocco. The French soon gained control of much of Africa. (See map, page 575.)

Europeans explored the rest of Africa.

For centuries, only North Africa and the coasts of the rest of the continent were familiar to Europe-

Here are two rare photographs from Africa around 1900. Above is the sultan of Cameroon. At left is a family near Kampala, Uganda, making bark cloth.

advancing eastward in the area north of Korea. The French took Indochina; the Dutch took the East Indies.
2. The Pacific became a major international waterway when improvements were made in ship design. The United States took over Hawaii, Guam, the Philippines, and part of Samoa.

Critical Thinking
Both McKinley and Kipling saw Asians as "backward peoples," who were unfit to govern themselves. Both also point to education as a way of "uplifting" them. McKinley had a political and economic twist in his argument, suggesting that it was in the United States best interest to keep the Philippines out of other foreign nations' hands.

4 Lesson Plan

Essential Learning Objectives
Students will learn to:
- describe the conditions that enabled France and Britain to become powerful in North Africa.
- evaluate the effects of colonialism in Africa.

1 | FOCUS AND MOTIVATE

Tell students that Africa had remained almost free of European control until the late 1800s. Ask students to suggest reasons why European colonization of Africa took place later than in Asia or the Americas. (African states had restricted European traders to coastal areas during the years of the slave trade, which lasted until the late 19th century, and much of Africa was under Muslim control.)

- Using a large map of Africa or the Atlas map, point out the areas where France and Britain established control, explaining that the Ottoman Empire was in decline. Emphasize the extent of the territory France and Britain intended to conquer: France, Dakar to Djibouti; Britain, Cairo to Cape Town. Explain how these goals almost brought those nations to war in the Fashoda incident.

- Explain how Dr. Livingstone's writing prompted European interest in the African interior. Discuss how Stanley's explorations and the methods he used in obtaining land claims opened Africa to European colonization.

GUIDED PRACTICE

Direct students to use the maps of Africa on page 575 and in the Atlas to describe the type of geography that Stanley would have found in his explorations.

ASSESS

1. What were the first areas in Africa to come under European control? (France took Algeria and expanded across North Africa; Britain's interest in the Suez Canal led it to take control of Egypt and the Sudan.)
2. What events brought central Africa to the attention of the West? (Livingstone's writings, Stanley's search for him and his own explorations)

From the Archives

Competition for the Congo

In 1876 Leopold II, king of Belgium, organized a company to develop the Congo region of Africa. Other European nations, who were competing for the same resources and markets, called a meeting in Berlin to discuss countermeasures. The Berlin Conference (1884–1885) did recognize Leopold as the ruler of the Congo Free State but attempted to establish an agreement on free trade, missions, and rights of access to the region. Under this agreement the Congo was to be developed according to European ideas. The Africans were not consulted, and their interests were disregarded.

No power which exercises or shall exercise sovereign rights in the above-mentioned regions shall be allowed to grant therein a monopoly or favor of any kind in matters of trade. . . .

Christian missionaries, scientists, and explorers, with their followers, property, and collections, shall likewise be the objects of especial protection.

Freedom of conscience and religious toleration are expressly guaranteed to the natives, no less than to subjects and to foreigners. The free and public exercise of all forms of Divine worship, and the right to build edifices [buildings] for religious purposes, and to organize religious Missions belonging to all creeds, shall not be limited or fettered in any way whatsoever.

FROM THE ARCHIVES This excerpt is taken from a translation of the official proceedings appended to *The Belgian Congo and the Berlin Act* by Arthur B. Keith (Oxford: Clarendon Press, 1919), p. 304. Be sure that students can locate the Congo,

ans. In the mid-1800s, however, European explorers began to penetrate the interior of Africa south of the Sahara. One of the most famous and influential was David Livingstone, a Scottish medical missionary, who made several journeys across southern and East Africa between 1851 and 1873. His writings created widespread interest in Africa and aroused opposition to the still-flourishing slave trade.

Livingstone began his last journey in 1866 and was not heard from for several years. Many people feared that he was lost. In 1869 the *New York Herald* sent its best reporter, Henry M. Stanley, to Africa with orders to "find Livingstone." Stanley suffered many hardships in his search, but finally one day in 1871, he walked into a small village on Lake Tanganyika [tang'gə nyē'kə]. There stood a lone white man. In Stanley's words:

> I would have run to him, would have embraced him, only I did not know how he would receive me; so I walked deliberately to him, took off my hat, and said: 'Dr. Livingstone, I presume?' 'Yes,' he said with a kind smile, lifting his cap slightly. 'I thank God, Doctor, I have been permitted to see you.'

Stanley tried to persuade Livingstone to give up his work as missionary and explorer and return to Europe, but Livingstone refused and died in Africa two years later.

Meanwhile, Stanley became an explorer in his own right. During his journeys in Central Africa, he learned that Africa offered vast possibilities for commerce and returned to Europe to seek financial backing. With money from King Leopold II of Belgium, Stanley founded a private company called the International Congo Association.

The European powers divided Africa.

The International Congo Association rapidly began to acquire land along the Congo River. In this region were many peoples who lived by farming or cattle raising. Stanley returned to the area in 1879, and within a few years, he made more than 400 treaties with the chiefs of these peoples. Stanley did not explain to the chiefs that by placing their marks on bits of paper in return for guns and cloth, they were giving their land to the Congo Association. Stanley gained huge tracts of land by these methods. Much of this area came to be known as the Belgian Congo (present-day **Zaire**).

Other explorers also used Stanley's methods and obtained huge regions for their countries. As you can see from the map on the facing page, by 1914 only Liberia and Ethiopia remained independent.

The coming of Europeans brought mixed results

Belgium, and Berlin on a map. Ask them why matters relating to the Congo were being decided in Europe. (because European nations had the military and economic power to create colonies in "unclaimed areas" of Africa)

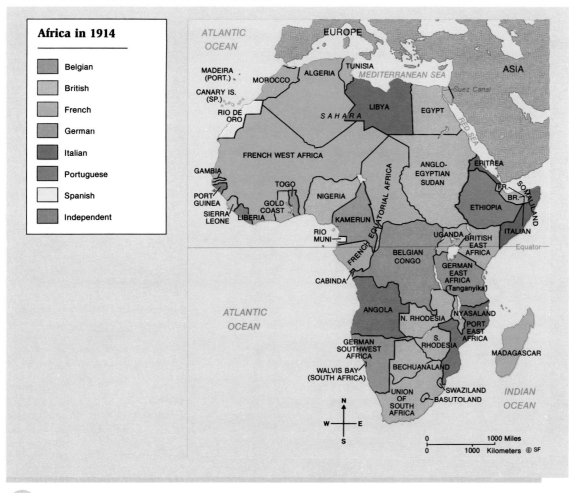

Africa in 1914

- Belgian
- British
- French
- German
- Italian
- Portuguese
- Spanish
- Independent

ATLANTIC OCEAN

EUROPE

ASIA

MADEIRA (PORT.)

MOROCCO   ALGERIA   TUNISIA

MEDITERRANEAN SEA

Suez Canal

CANARY IS. (SP.)

RIO DE ORO

LIBYA   EGYPT

SAHARA

RED SEA

FRENCH WEST AFRICA

ANGLO-EGYPTIAN SUDAN

ERITREA

GAMBIA

TOGO

PORT. GUINEA

GOLD COAST

NIGERIA

SIERRA LEONE   LIBERIA

KAMERUN

FR.   BR.

ETHIOPIA

SOMALILAND

RIO MUNI

FRENCH EQUATORIAL AFRICA

ITALIAN

UGANDA   BRITISH EAST AFRICA

Equator

CABINDA

BELGIAN CONGO

GERMAN EAST AFRICA (Tanganyika)

ANGOLA

N. RHODESIA

NYASALAND

PORT. EAST AFRICA

ATLANTIC OCEAN

GERMAN SOUTHWEST AFRICA

S. RHODESIA

MADAGASCAR

WALVIS BAY (SOUTH AFRICA)

BECHUANALAND

UNION OF SOUTH AFRICA

SWAZILAND   BASUTOLAND

INDIAN OCEAN

N
W   E
S

0   1000 Miles
0   1000 Kilometers © SF

🌐 **MAP STUDY** The map shows the European nations that ruled colonies in Africa in 1914. Which two nations held the most land?

in Africa. On the one hand, they did away with slavery and ethnic warfare in some areas. European help was also important in fighting disease and illiteracy and in building cities, roads, and industries.

On the other hand, Europeans cruelly exploited the Africans. Many were uprooted from their villages and compelled into forced labor. They were made to pay heavy taxes, and their lands were taken over. Some of the worst crimes took place in

the Belgian Congo, where European overseers inflicted brutal punishments in order to increase rubber production. Execution, whipping, and torture were common.

The brutal conditions improved in the 20th century. At the same time, a small westernized class of Africans slowly emerged. Resentful of their treatment at the hands of the Europeans, they formed the core of the nationalistic movements that gathered strength as the century advanced.

BACKGROUND France took a vast area on the Congo River and important colonies in West Africa. Germany gained slices of territory on the east and west coasts. The Italians made claims along the Red Sea. The British, too, were active in all parts of

Africa, and by the early 1900s Britain ruled more than a dozen African colonies. By 1914 most of Africa had been taken over by European powers.

575

A Key to History

GEOPOLITICS AND THE CARIBBEAN BASIN

Geopolitics is a way of thinking about the importance of geographic position, especially how it affects the control of resources and lines of communication and trade and military power. "Caribbean Basin" is a political term first used in World War II (1939–1945) to refer to the Caribbean Sea and all the lands in and around it. In the late 1980s, the Caribbean Basin held 41 nations and dependent territories with a population of more than 192 million people.

The Caribbean has always been important to the United States because of our trade with Latin America, the sea link between the Gulf states and the East Coast, and the defense of our southern seacoast. Its importance increased as the United States took a more dominant role in world affairs in the 1890s.

In 1897 an American naval officer, Alfred Thayer Mahan [mə han′] pointed out the similarities between the Caribbean and the Mediterranean Sea, which was once the center of Roman power. Both bodies of water had political and military importance, not only for the countries bordering them but also for the world at large.

The Caribbean became even more important with the completion of the Panama Canal in 1914, which linked the Atlantic and Pacific oceans. As you can see from the map, the sea lanes into and out of the Caribbean are confined in several places: the Florida Straits, the Yucatán Channel, the Galleons Passage, and the Panama Canal.

World War II demonstrated just how vulnerable the trade routes through the Caribbean were. In March of 1942 alone, German submarines in the Caribbean sank 19 Allied ships.

Since World War II, the sea lanes of the Caribbean have continued to be of major importance. Recognizing their mutual need for secure passage, the United States and other nations have worked to reconcile their diverse interests in the Caribbean Basin.

REVIEW

1. Why is the Caribbean so important to the United States?
2. In what ways is the Caribbean Basin like the Mediterranean Sea?
3. Define "geopolitics" and explain why it has special importance in relation to the Caribbean Basin.

What countries and dependencies border the Florida Straits? The Yucatán Channel? The Galleons Passage?

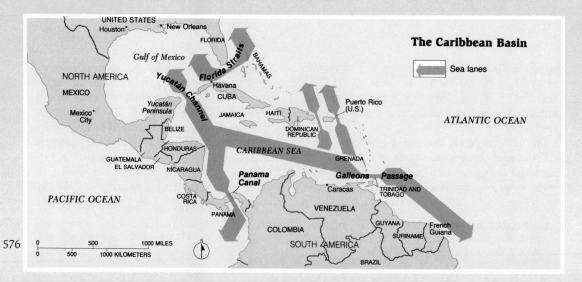

The Caribbean Basin

576

Section 4 Review

Identify Suez Canal, protectorate, Zaire

Main Ideas

1. How was North Africa affected by the decline of the Ottoman Empire and the construction of the Suez Canal?
2. What was the significance of the explorations of David Livingstone and Henry M. Stanley?
3. How did European imperialism affect the peoples of Africa?

Critical Thinking

Recognizing Cause and Effect: What conditions made it possible for Europeans to carve up Sub-Saharan Africa so quickly between 1875 and 1914?

 Intervention grew in Latin America.

In most of Africa, parts of Asia, and in the Philippines, the imperialist powers took over complete control of a country, governing it through agents sent out from London, Paris, St. Petersburg, and Washington. In Latin America, foreign intervention tended to be more economic than political. At times, however, military force was used to advance imperialist interests. **Economic imperialism** is a term frequently used to describe the relationship that developed between industrialized nations and Latin American nations, whose economic survival depended on trading raw materials for manufactured goods.

Foreign investments led to difficulties.

Latin American countries offered many important resources, including silver, gold, oil, rubber, platinum, tin, and copper. At the same time, most of these countries had weak governments, and American and European investors were quick to take advantage of this weakness. In the late 1800s, they spent billions of dollars to dig mines, sink oil wells, build railroads, and encourage public utilities. These developments improved conditions in the countries in which they were made, but they also caused major problems. Corrupt local officials often made dishonest deals with foreign investors.

Though the investors made huge profits, the majority of the population remained desperately poor.

Another problem was that Latin American governments tended to be very unstable. Revolutions often caused a change of rulers. The new governments sometimes took over foreign property without payment. When this happened, the foreigners called for help from their homelands.

The United States used the Monroe Doctrine to intervene.

The idea of large-scale European interference to protect their investments in Latin America worried the United States. The Monroe Doctrine of 1823, which was an American policy that European countries should not take over governments in the Western Hemisphere, had long been used by Americans—with the support of the British navy—to protect the Americas from European intervention. In the 1890s the United States used the Monroe Doctrine in other ways.

For one thing, the United States began to act as a negotiator in disputes between Latin American countries and European powers. More importantly, the United States now claimed that it had the right to intervene in Latin America itself to protect its own interests. The Spanish-American War of 1898 made this claim even clearer.

During the late 19th century, **Cuba** and **Puerto Rico** were swept by revolutions. These two colonies were all that remained of Spain's New World empire, and both islands wanted independence. The United States government supported this desire, and Americans were sympathetic toward the Cuban and Puerto Rican rebels, who were treated harshly by the Spanish. These American feelings were backed up by other facts: (1) Americans had invested $50 million in Cuba, (2) Cuba was the largest supplier of American sugar, and (3) Cuba was strategically important because it controlled the entrance to the Gulf of Mexico.

It was clearly in the interest of the United States that Cuba be friendly and stable. To many Americans, this meant that Cuba should be free of Spanish rule. Thus, when the American battleship *Maine* was mysteriously sunk in Havana harbor, Americans quickly blamed Spain and wanted to go to Cuba's aid. In 1898 the United States declared

5 *Lesson Plan*

Essential Learning Objective

Students will learn to explain why the policies of the United States led it to intervene in Latin American affairs.

1 FOCUS AND MOTIVATE

Point out to students that as European powers gained control in Asia and Africa, the United States felt it necessary to protect areas close to its own borders. Tell students to look for the ways the United States dealt with foreign involvement in Latin America as they study this section.

Explain how economic control followed the massive investments of U.S. and European businesses in Latin America. Chart on the chalkboard the chronology of U.S. intervention in Latin America.

GUIDED PRACTICE

Have students list motives of groups that supported U.S. entrance into the Spanish-American War.

3 ASSESS AND CLOSE

ASSESS

Why did Americans and Europeans invest heavily in Latin America? (to develop raw materials and resources)

OPTIONAL RETEACHING

Ask students to write a paragraph describing how the Monroe Doctrine was used to justify United States action in the Caribbean.

Students also may be assigned Activities reteaching page 181.

OPTIONAL ENRICHMENT

1. Students also may be assigned Activities enrichment page 182.
2. Also for enrichment:

 Overhead Transparency 60

INDEPENDENT PRACTICE/ HOMEWORK

Assign the Section Review, the Chapter Review items, Activities page 180, or Workbook page 122.

CLOSURE

Tell students that imperialism in Latin America more often took the form of economic rather than political control. Foreign investment caused exploitation and destabilization of nations.

---

war and defeated Spain in less than five months.

As a result of the Spanish-American War, the United States took over Puerto Rico, Guam, and the Philippine Islands. Although Cuba was allowed to set up an independent government, the United States placed several limits on the new government. The United States demanded the right to intervene in the foreign and domestic affairs of Cuba and to build naval bases on the island. In effect, Cuba became an American protectorate.

During the next 20 years, the United States actively intervened in Cuban affairs several times. Not until 1934 did the American government give up all such rights. Even then, the United States kept its naval base at Guantanamo [gwän tä′nä mō] Bay, which it still operates today.

Dollar diplomacy characterized the early 20th century.

In the 30 years after the Spanish-American War, American investments in Latin America reached new heights. The United States government worked closely with investors to get favorable terms for them. These joint efforts between government and business came to be referred to as the policy of dollar diplomacy.

Theodore Roosevelt, President from 1901 to 1909, was a major spokesman for dollar diplomacy. He strongly favored the canal that the United States planned to build across the Isthmus of Panama. This area, however, belonged to Colombia. When revolution broke out there in 1903, President Roosevelt sent American marines to the scene. They kept Colombian troops from putting down the Panamanian rebels. Three days later, the United States formally recognized the new Republic of Panama. The United States then arranged a perpetual lease on a canal zone 10 miles wide. Panama, like Cuba, became an American protectorate. The **Panama Canal**, which had important strategic value for the United States, was finished in 1914.

Meanwhile, in 1904 Roosevelt stated his famous Roosevelt Corollary to the Monroe Doctrine. The United States, he said, would be forced to take on the duties of international policeman in the Western Hemisphere. As a result of this policy, when the Dominican Republic went bankrupt in 1905,

the United States took over its customs collections and made sure that all its creditors were paid. In 1911 the United States also stepped into Nicaragua to set its finances in order and to protect American investments. In 1915 internal trouble broke out in Haiti, and American marines were sent to restore order. They remained in that country for almost 20 years.

Economic imperialism was an important factor influencing United States relations with its nearest Latin American neighbor, Mexico. A revolution in Mexico in 1910 endangered American investments, which by then amounted to billions of dollars. President Woodrow Wilson refused to recognize President Victoriano Huerta as the legitimate Mexican leader because he came to power with the assassination of his predecessor. In 1914 Wilson sent American marines to capture the Mexican port of Vera Cruz. War with Mexico was averted when Argentina, Brazil, and Chile offered to mediate between the United States and Mexico. The crisis passed, and the United States withdrew the marines. Although Wilson opposed economic imperialism and dollar diplomacy, his actions were frequently in support of American interests.

Many people in the United States did not support the policy of armed intervention in Latin America. They knew of the Latin American resentment toward the United States. Such feelings helped modify dollar diplomacy by the 1930s.

Section 5 Review

Identify economic imperialism, Cuba, Puerto Rico, Theodore Roosevelt, Panama Canal

Main Ideas

1. What conditions in Latin America invited economic imperialism?
2. How did the American government change the Monroe Doctrine in the 1890s? How did the United States keep control over Cuba after the Spanish-American War?
3. Give two examples of dollar diplomacy in the early 20th century.

Critical Thinking

Predicting Effects: What problems do you think European, Japanese, and American imperialism would create in the 20th century?

Indonesian Batik

On the Indonesian island of Java, batik [bə tēk′]—a distinctive and complex method of dyeing cloth—developed long before the Europeans arrived there in the 16th century. The Dutch, who controlled Java from the 1700s to the 1900s, sold cotton cloth imported from Holland to the Javanese. This ready-made fabric spurred the batik industry. The Dutch cloth had a much smoother surface than the hand-spun fabric that the Javanese had formerly used. Thus, delicate batiks with detailed designs could now be produced.

Batik involves painting with wax to create a design on undyed cloth.

When the cloth is dyed, the wax prevents the dye from soaking through to the fabric. To batik a blue butterfly on a yellow background, for example, the butterfly is painted with wax on undyed, white cloth. The cloth is then placed in a yellow dye bath. After the desired shade of yellow is achieved, the wax is scraped from the cloth, producing a white butterfly on a yellow background. To make the butterfly blue while maintaining the yellow background, the background is covered with wax and then the cloth is put into a blue dye bath. After the wax is scraped off for the second time, the blue butterfly appears.

For one piece of cloth, this process may be repeated more than a dozen times, creating intricate details and fine shades of color. Using this method, it may take an entire year to complete a batik two yards long. Such batiks, with their elegant patterns and graceful designs, have come to be prized as textile art throughout the world.

A Javanese woman draws with heated wax on cloth (below) to produce the finest batiks (left).

CHAPTER 30 REVIEW

Section Summaries

Section 1
India lost its independence.
In the mid-18th century, the British defeated the French in India and then took over more and more land at the expense of the weak Mughals. The British helped unify India, which resulted in the spread of both the English language and nationalism.

Section 2
China and Japan reacted in opposite ways to imperialism.
After the Opium War in 1839–1842, the British and other foreign powers began to divide China into spheres of influence. In 1854 the United States forced Japan to open its doors to foreign trade. Japan began a major modernization program.

Section 3
Many nations gained influence elsewhere in Asia and the Pacific.
The Russians gained influence in Manchuria, Mongolia, Central Asia, Persia, and Afghanistan. The French took over Indochina. The British added Burma to their empire in India. The Dutch ruled the East Indies. Britain, Germany, France, and the United States snapped up various Pacific Islands.

Section 4
Africa was carved into many colonies.
Africa was quickly divided up in the 1800s. The French and the British each took parts of North Africa. Meanwhile, explorers moved into the interior south of the Sahara. By 1914 all but Ethiopia and Liberia had lost their independence.

Section 5
Intervention grew in Latin America.
In Latin America, the United States played a dominant role, especially after the Spanish-American War of 1898. Economic imperialism influenced American relations with Mexico.

Test Yourself

Key Terms, People, and Places
Identify the significance of each of the following:

Section 1
a. imperialism
b. Bengal
c. Sepoy Rebellion
d. Indian National Congress
e. Muslim League

Section 2
a. Hong Kong
b. extraterritoriality
c. spheres of influence
d. Matthew Perry
e. Meiji Era

Review Dates

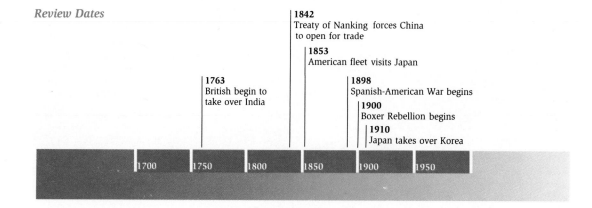

1842
Treaty of Nanking forces China to open for trade

1853
American fleet visits Japan

1763
British begin to take over India

1898
Spanish-American War begins

1900
Boxer Rebellion begins

1910
Japan takes over Korea

1700   1750   1800   1850   1900   1950

Section 3
a. Vladivostok **c.** Liliuokalani
b. Indochina **d.** Emilio Aguinaldo

Section 4
a. Suez Canal **c.** Zaire
b. protectorate

Section 5
a. economic imperialism **d.** Theodore Roosevelt
b. Cuba **e.** Panama Canal
c. Puerto Rico

Main Ideas

Section 1
1. By what means did the British gain control of India?
2. How did the British government change the way the British East India Company operated?
3. In what ways did British rule in India change after the Sepoy Rebellion? What were the effects of British rule in India?

Section 2
1. What concessions did the foreign powers gain from the Manchu government during the 19th century?
2. How did Japan become a modern industrial power?
3. For what reasons did Japan become imperialistic? Identify the territorial gains Japan made by 1910.

Section 3
1. Identify the three areas where Russia sought a warm water port. Which parts of Asia did the French and Dutch take over?
2. Why were imperialist powers attracted to Pacific islands in the 19th century? Which areas did the United States take over?

Section 4
1. How did the decline of the Ottoman Empire and the construction of the Suez Canal affect North Africa?
2. What was the importance of the explorations of David Livingstone and Henry M. Stanley?
3. How did imperialism affect Africans?

Section 5
1. What conditions led to economic imperialism?
2. How did the American government modify the Monroe Doctrine in the 1890s? How did the United States control Cuba after 1898?
3. Identify two examples of dollar diplomacy.

Critical Thinking
1. Analyzing Comparisons Using the text as your source of information, compare the motives of Britain, France, and Russia in taking over lands on the continents of Africa and Asia.

2. Identifying Assumptions Evaluate the impact of imperialism on the colonized countries. What did they gain or lose from it?

Chapter Skills and Activities

Practicing Study and Research Skills
Drawing Inferences
An inference is a conclusion drawn from facts that are known. For example, if you see dark clouds in the sky and hear the distant rumble of thunder, you will probably make the inference: "It will soon rain." You can make inferences based on what you know from experience as well as what you learn from reading or from maps, graphs, and other visual aids. Study the world population distribution map on pages 786–787 and the African political and physical maps on pages 796 and 797. Then make the inference required for each item below.
1. What reasons would you give for the lack of population in most of northern and southern Africa?
2. Why do Rwanda and Burundi have dense populations?
3. Why is the population of Egypt arranged in a line?

Linking Past and Present
The phrases "white man's burden" and "spheres of influence" are no longer stated as the official policies of modern governments. However, do you think that these ideas have disappeared, or do you think they still affect the way governments act today?

Learning History Through Maps
In the 18th and 19th centuries, the major powers divided Asia and the Pacific into spheres of influence. Judging from the map on page 567, how realistic do you think the dreams of the imperialists were? How would you have divided the world into spheres of influence?

CRITICAL THINKING QUESTION LEVEL 1. average; 2. challenging

Chapter

31 World War I

OVERVIEW

This chapter covers World War I, beginning
with the causes that led to war and ending
with the Versailles Treaty.

PLANNING CHART

Section	Text Pages	Key Concept	Suggested Teaching Time
1 Many factors together caused World War I.	583–586	A combination of factors, including industrialization, nationalism, competition for colonies, the building of alliances, and an arms race, led to war.	One day **More time?** Use *Overhead Transparency 61.*
2 Some forces promoted peace.	587	Economic and political cooperation, the establishment of international organizations, and the building of communication and transportation networks were forces that promoted peace.	One day **Less time?** Assign Section 2 to be read before class and teach it together with Section 3.
3 The Balkan crisis escalated.	588–590	Problems in the Balkans escalated, with the assassination of Archduke Ferdinand, pulling aligned nations into war.	One day **More time?** Use *Source Reading 31A.*
4 The world went to war.	590–596	The Allies fought the Central Powers in World War I, a war that was devastating to all nations involved.	Two days **More time?** Use *Source Reading 31B.*
5 The victors tried to build a lasting peace.	596–598	The victors of World War I, France, Britain, and the United States, created the harsh Versailles Treaty through which Germany lost much territory and wealth.	One day **More time?** Use *Overhead Transparency 62.*

ANCILLARIES

Materials that may be used with this chapter
to reinforce, reteach, enrich, and assess
learning are pictured on the following pages.

Teacher's Resource File

ACTIVITIES

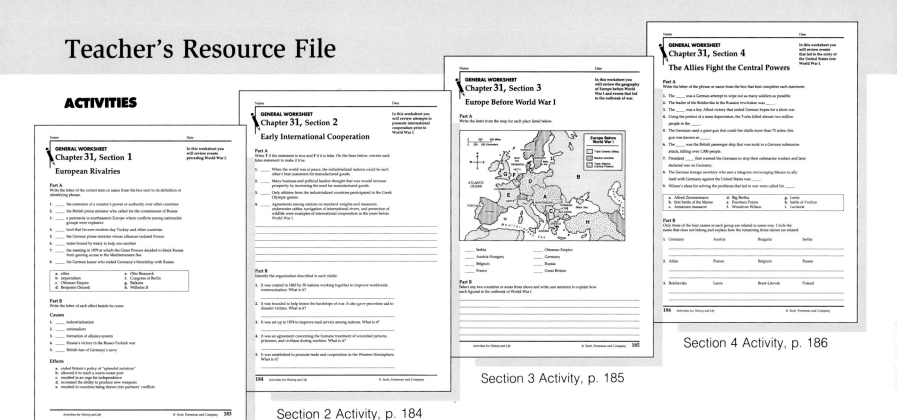

GENERAL WORKSHEET

Chapter 31, Section 1

European Rivalries

In this worksheet you will review events preceding World War I.

Part A

Write the letter of the correct term or name from the box next to its definition or identifying phrase.

1. _____ the extension of a country's power or authority over other countries
2. _____ the British prime minister who called for the containment of Russia
3. _____ a peninsula in southeastern Europe where conflicts among nationalist groups were explosive
4. _____ land that became modern-day Turkey and other countries
5. _____ the German prime minister whose alliances isolated France
6. _____ states bound by treaty to help one another
7. _____ the meeting in 1879 at which the Great Powers decided to block Russia from gaining access to the Mediterranean Sea
8. _____ the German kaiser who ended Germany's friendship with Russia

a. allies	e. Otto Bismarck
b. imperialism	f. Congress of Berlin
c. Ottoman Empire	g. Balkans
d. Benjamin Disraeli	h. Wilhelm II

Part B

Write the letter of each effect beside its cause.

Causes

1. _____ industrialization
2. _____ nationalism
3. _____ formation of alliance system
4. _____ Russia's victory in the Russo-Turkish war
5. _____ British fear of Germany's navy

Effects

a. ended Britain's policy of "splendid isolation"
b. allowed it to reach a warm-water port
c. resulted in an urge for independence
d. increased the ability to produce new weapons
e. resulted in countries being drawn into partners' conflicts

Section 1 Activity, p. 183

GENERAL WORKSHEET

Chapter 31, Section 2

Early International Cooperation

In this worksheet you will review attempts to promote international cooperation prior to World War I.

Part A

Write T if the statement is true and F if it is false. On the lines below, rewrite each false statement to make it true.

1. _____ When the world was at peace, the industrialized nations could be each other's best customers for manufactured goods.
2. _____ Many business and political leaders thought that war would increase prosperity by increasing the need for manufactured goods.
3. _____ Only athletes from the industrialized countries participated in the Greek Olympic games.
4. _____ Agreements among nations on standard weights and measures, underwater cables, navigation of international rivers, and protection of wildlife were examples of international cooperation in the years before World War I.

Part B

Identify the organization described in each riddle.

1. It was created in 1865 by 20 nations working together to improve worldwide communication. What is it?

2. It was founded to help lessen the hardships of war. It also gave peacetime aid to disaster victims. What is it?

3. It was set up in 1874 to improve mail service among nations. What is it?

4. It was an agreement concerning the humane treatment of wounded persons, prisoners, and civilians during wartime. What is it?

5. It was established to promote trade and cooperation in the Western Hemisphere. What is it?

Section 2 Activity, p. 184

GENERAL WORKSHEET

Chapter 31, Section 3

Europe Before World War I

In this worksheet you will review the geography of Europe before World War I and events that led to the outbreak of war.

Part A

Write the letter from the map for each place listed below.

_____ Serbia
_____ Austria-Hungary
_____ Belgium
_____ France
_____ Ottoman Empire
_____ Germany
_____ Russia
_____ Great Britain

Part B

Select any two countries or areas from above and write one sentence to explain how each figured in the outbreak of World War I.

Section 3 Activity, p. 185

GENERAL WORKSHEET

Chapter 31, Section 4

The Allies Fight the Central Powers

In this worksheet you will review events that led to the entry of the United States into World War I.

Part A

Write the letter of the phrase or name from the box that best completes each statement.

1. The _____ was a German attempt to wipe out as many soldiers as possible.
2. The leader of the Bolsheviks in the Russian revolution was _____.
3. The _____ was a key Allied victory that ended German hopes for a short war.
4. Using the pretext of a mass deportation, the Turks killed almost two million people in the _____.
5. The Germans used a giant gun that could fire shells more than 75 miles; this gun was known as _____.
6. The _____ was the British passenger ship that was sunk in a German submarine attack, killing over 1,000 people.
7. President _____ first warned the Germans to stop their submarine warfare and later declared war on Germany.
8. The German foreign secretary who sent a telegram encouraging Mexico to ally itself with Germany against the United States was _____.
9. Wilson's ideas for solving the problems that led to the war were called his _____.

a. Alfred Zimmermann	d. Big Bertha	g. Lenin
b. first battle of the Marne	e. Fourteen Points	h. battle of Verdun
c. Armenian massacre	f. Woodrow Wilson	i. Lusitania

Part B

Only three of the four names in each group are related in some way. Circle the name that does not belong and explain how the remaining three names are related.

1. Germany   Austria   Bulgaria   Serbia

2. Allies   France   Belgium   Russia

3. Bolsheviks   Lenin   Brest-Litovsk   Poland

Section 4 Activity, p. 186

GENERAL WORKSHEET

Chapter 31, Section 5

The Peace Settlement

In this worksheet you will review the Paris Peace Conference and the Treaty of Versailles.

Part A

Write the letter of the word or words that best complete each statement.

1. At the Paris Peace Conference, Woodrow Wilson upheld his _____, including the establishment of the _____.
2. George Clemenceau wanted Germany to _____.
3. Lloyd George wanted to destroy the _____.
4. Under the _____, France won back _____.
5. As a result of the Versailles Treaty, Poland became an _____.
6. Finland, Latvia, Lithuania, and Estonia were created from land lost by _____.
7. Present-day Turkey and the mandates for Syria, Iraq, Trans-Jordan, and Palestine were formed from the old _____.
8. The Polish Corridor gave Poland an outlet to the _____ and divided _____.

a. Russia	g. Ottoman Empire
b. Baltic Sea	h. Alsace and Lorraine
c. Fourteen Points	i. pay for war damages
d. Germany	j. independent nation
e. League of Nations	k. Versailles Treaty
f. German navy	

Part B

Use information from the text to complete each of the following sentences.

1. Clemenceau wanted to impose harsh terms on Germany **because**

2. The Germans agreed to sign the Versailles Treaty **because**

3. The United States could afford to be idealistic at Versailles **because**

Section 5 Activity, p. 187

RETEACHING ACTIVITY

Chapter 31

World War I

In this worksheet you will review key terms and main ideas about World War I.

Read the clues below and complete the crossword puzzle.

Across

5. 1879 alliance between Germany and Austria
6. a peninsula in southeastern Europe
8. a French city; site of a major battle
9. the Balkan nation in which the Austrian archduke was murdered
11. the German foreign secretary who sent a telegram urging Mexico to ally itself with Germany
12. the German kaiser who dismissed Bismarck
14. the German prime minister who isolated France
17. the extension of a country's power or authority over other countries
18. the Russian ruler who mobilized Russian troops following Austrian declaration of war on Serbia
19. the state on the Turkish-Russian border that suffered a massacre in 1915

Down

1. river where the battle that dashed Germany's hope for a quick victory in World War I took place
2. international games, revived in 1896
3. the United States President who hoped to make the world safe for democracy
4. opponents of the Central Powers
7. the heir to the Austrian throne who was killed in Sarajevo
10. the name of the peace treaty made by Wilson, Clemenceau, and Lloyd George
13. a British passenger ship sunk by German U-boats
15. a forest area in northern France where the armistice was signed
16. the empire from which Syria, Iraq, Trans-Jordan, and Palestine were created

Chapter 31 Reteaching, p. 188

ENRICHMENT ACTIVITY

Chapter 31

World War I and American Exports

In this worksheet you will interpret a graph to learn the effect of World War I on the American economy.

Use the graph to answer the questions below.

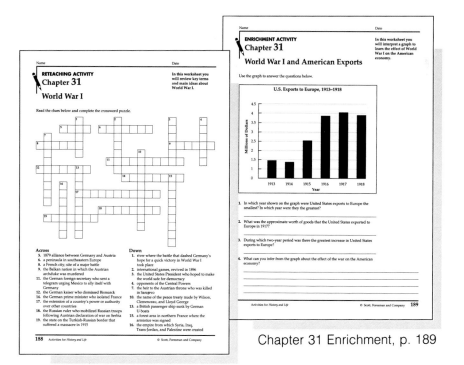

U.S. Exports to Europe, 1913–1918

1. In which year shown on the graph were United States exports to Europe the smallest? In which year were they the greatest?

2. What was the approximate worth of goods that the United States exported to Europe in 1917?

3. During which two-year period was there the greatest increase in United States exports to Europe?

4. What can you infer from the graph about the effect of the war on the American economy?

Chapter 31 Enrichment, p. 189

581b

Teacher's Resource File

GEOGRAPHY SKILLS

Chapter 31 Geography
Worksheet/Map, pp. 63–64

Chapter 31 Map Lesson, p. 113

TESTS

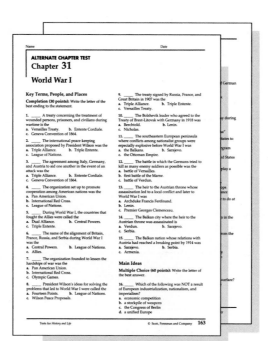

Chapter Test, pp. 161–162

Alternate Chapter Test, pp. 163–164

Other Optional Ancillaries

WORKBOOK

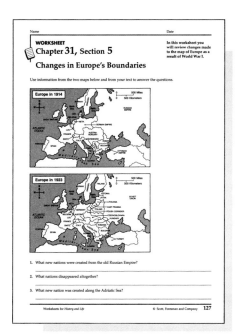

Section 1 Worksheet, p. 123

Section 2 Worksheet, p. 124

Section 3 Worksheet, p. 125

Section 4 Worksheet, p. 126

Section 5 Worksheet, p. 127

SOURCE READINGS

Source Reading 31A
Source Reading 31B

TEST GENERATOR

40 multiple-choice questions for Chapter 31

OVERHEAD TRANSPARENCIES

Overhead Transparency 61
Overhead Transparency 62

1900

1910

1914   World War I begins

1918   World War I ends

1920

1930

Chapter

31

World War I

1914 – 1920

A friend came to see me . . . he thinks it was on Monday, August 3 [1914]. We were standing at a window of my room in the Foreign Office. It was getting dusk, and the lamps were being lit in the space below on which we were looking. My friend recalls that I remarked on this [scene] with the words: "The lamps are going out all over Europe; we shall not see them lit again in our lifetime."

These were the sad words of Sir Edward Grey, the foreign secretary of Britain. Europe was heading into a long and costly war. This was to be the Great War that drew into it not only the major powers of Europe but those of America and Asia as well. The Great War, or World War I as it was later known, was global in scope, and it lasted for more than four years. Many think this conflict was the single most important event of the 20th century, since the end of the war signaled the beginning of Europe's decline as the center of world power and influence after 400 years of leadership.

World War I began simply as a local conflict between Austria and Serbia. The war soon escalated, however, into the first total war in history. Mass armies fought against one another. People at home, as well as the soldiers on the front, joined the war effort. Powerful nations employed weapons of mass destruction, such as airplanes, submarines, and poison gas.

By the time the war ended, millions of people on both sides had been killed. Britain and France had been severely weakened. The Hohenzollern dynasty in the German Empire, the Hapsburg dynasty in Austria, and the Romanov dynasty in Russia had each fallen apart. Communism had taken over in Russia, and anti-imperialism had grown stronger in Asia, the Middle East, and Africa. Finally, the United States had come forth as the most powerful nation in the world. Nobody in Europe in 1914 could have foreseen these results.

Charred trees loom over American soldiers trying to advance against entrenched German troops on the Western Front.

Reading Preview

In this chapter you will learn how the first total war began and changed the face of Europe.

1. Many factors together caused World War I.

2. Some forces promoted peace.

3. The Balkan crisis escalated.

4. The world went to war.

5. The victors tried to build a lasting peace.

1   *Many factors together caused World War I.*

Since 1870 European nations had undergone great change. By 1914 these nations had still not found a way to adjust to this change peacefully.

Industrialization and growing nationalism created new tensions.

One cause of the war may have been this inability to adjust to change. One such change that chal-

1   *Lesson Plan*
Essential Learning Objective

Students will learn to identify the tensions among nations that preceded World War I.

1   FOCUS AND MOTIVATE

Call students' attention to the fact that World War I began with a local conflict. Ask students to identify factors in the latter part of the 19th century that might have caused the local conflict to escalate into a war.

2   TEACH

- Discuss industrialization and nationalism as causes for the build-up of tensions prior to World War I. Ask students to explain why economic competition was destructive. Have them compare destructive with healthy types of competition, citing examples from the current world economy.

- Discuss the conflicts and wars that arose because of imperialist interests in Africa and Asia. Have students identify the nations that tried to retain colonies and those that tried to obtain them.

- List Germany's alliances on the chalkboard. (Dual Alliance—1879, Triple Alliance—1882, Reinsurance Treaty of 1887) Ask students to name the nations that had agreements with Germany and describe the terms of the alliances. Point out that Germany's action in allowing the alliance with Russia to lapse was a major faux pas, that Germany came to regret. Have students tell how this lapse changed the balance of power.

lenged Europe was the rapid spread of industrialization, especially in countries such as Germany. Newly industrialized nations faced stiff competition from one another for trade and markets for their goods. This economic competition came on top of rivalries that already existed for colonies and for allies (states bound by treaty to help each other).

Another change was the growth of intense nationalism. This urge for national power and independence took place among both the old and new powers. When a new nation—Germany, for example—tried to increase its power by building a strong navy, an older nation such as Britain saw the new nation's actions as a threat.

As a result, each country sought ways to insulate itself from enemy attack. Nations attempted to do this in three ways. First, they sought to control new colonies because many people thought that colonies added to a country's economic strength. Second, they tried to form alliances against possible enemies. Third, they worked to build armies, through the draft, and to stockpile weapons.

An armaments race thus began. Industrialization increased the capacity to mass produce new,

deadly weapons such as the machine gun, the tank, the airplane, and the submarine. These factors—industrialization, nationalism, competition for colonies, building of alliances, and an arms race—together set the stage for World War I.

Imperialism in Africa and Asia caused conflicts.

Many countries clashed in their efforts to gain territory and control of people in other parts of the world. As you learned in Chapter 30, this extension of a country's power or authority over other countries is known as imperialism. In Africa, for example, Germany threatened to take Morocco from France. A result of this threat was the first Moroccan crisis in 1905. Six years later the Germans again challenged French control in Morocco, but this time, Britain supported France and forced Germany to yield.

Britain also clashed with the descendants of Dutch settlers, known as the Boers, in South Africa. There Britain came out the winner after the Boer War in 1902.

In Asia Britain competed with Russia for territory. For centuries the Russians had been trying to

A Spanish cartoon from the 1870s shows the competition among European countries as a deadly game of billiards.

acquire a warm-water sea port. They needed an outlet to the sea that would be open all year because Russia's own coasts were blocked by ice most of the time. In 1877 Russia declared war on the Ottoman Empire (modern-day Turkey) in hopes of gaining such a port. After months of hard fighting, the Russians finally won this Russo-Turkish War. They were then in a position to reach the warm-water ports of the Mediterranean.

Britain was alarmed at these Russian gains. The Russian successes threatened British sea power in the Mediterranean and brought Russia close to the Suez Canal. For Britain, the canal was the vital link in the sea route to India, which was their colony. To protect the canal, the British prime minister, Benjamin Disraeli, asked for the help of other European countries. In July, 1878, representatives of all the Great Powers met at the Congress of Berlin. The most important result of the Congress was a decision to block Russia from further gains.

The actions taken at the Congress, however, did not halt Russia's drive for greater empire. Blocked in Europe and the Middle East, Russia in the 1890s turned to Manchuria. This move provoked Japan. The rivalry led in 1904 to the Russo-Japanese War you read about earlier, in which the Russians were defeated by Japan.

Germany's alliances divided Europe.

After France was defeated in the Franco-Prussian War of 1870–1871, the German prime minister, Otto von Bismarck, feared that the French might seek allies for a war of revenge. Bismarck was well known for his ruthlessness and effective military policy, his extraordinary political wisdom, and his diplomatic skills. He began to make alliances for Germany, mainly to isolate the French.

Bismarck's alliances. The most important alliance Bismarck made was with Austria in 1879. Called the Dual Alliance, it lasted until 1882, when Italy joined with Germany and Austria in a similar treaty, thus setting up the **Triple Alliance**. The members of the Triple Alliance promised that if any one of them should be attacked, all three would fight together.

Through very skillful diplomacy, Bismarck also brought Germany and Russia together. This alliance took the form of the Reinsurance Treaty of 1887. Germany promised to support Russia in certain matters concerning the **Balkans**, a peninsula in southeastern Europe where conflicts among nationalist groups were especially explosive. Find the Balkan peninsula on the map on page 586. In turn Russia promised to remain neutral if the French attacked Germany. These agreements accomplished Bismarck's basic plan to isolate France. No major country was left on the continent of Europe with whom France could make an alliance.

The Kaiser's alliances. In 1890, because of a dispute over foreign policy and internal politics with the young German Kaiser, Wilhelm II, Bismarck resigned from office. Putting an end to Bismarck's policy of friendship with Russia, the kaiser stopped making loans to the Russian tsar. He allowed the treaty between Germany and Russia to lapse and joined Austria in a promise to defend their common interests in the Balkans against the Russians.

The Russians now had to look to other major powers for alliances and loans. France eagerly grabbed the chance to ally itself with Russia since both countries feared Germany. France had made an amazing recovery from its defeat in the Franco-Prussian War, building a strong army and prospering once again. France could, therefore, loan Russia millions of francs. Russia used this money to purchase arms and build the Trans-Siberian Railroad. In 1894 France and Russia went a step further and signed a military alliance. Through these various alliances and feuds, Europe was split into two armed camps—on one side, Austria and Germany, and on the other, France and Russia.

Britain sought allies and expanded its navy.

Britain was in neither camp. Protected by its strong navy, Britain pursued a policy of "splendid isolation." Its rich colonies circled the earth, and its navy brought a feeling of security to the home islands and colonies. As long as no European nation threatened its interests, Britain did not want to be tied down to alliances.

By 1900, however, Britain decided that it needed allies. After all, Germany was building a merchant fleet and a navy to outstrip British sea power. In addition, Kaiser Wilhelm's warlike speeches and actions upset the British, who feared that an en-

ASSESS

1. Why did Russia declare war on the Ottoman Empire in 1877? (in the hope of gaining a warm-water port)
2. Who was Britain's prime minister in 1878? (Benjamin Disraeli)

OPTIONAL RETEACHING

Write statements explaining the main causes of World War I and the three ways in which major European nations sought to insulate themselves from enemies.

OPTIONAL ENRICHMENT

1. Assign students to research and describe in writing the accomplishments of Benjamin Disraeli. (average)
2. Have students research Bismarck's policies as German prime minister and describe which policies benefited the elite and which, the common people. (challenging)

INDEPENDENT PRACTICE/ HOMEWORK

Assign the Section Review, Activities page 183, or Workbook page 123.

CLOSURE

To summarize the lesson, tell students that industrialization, economic competition and search for new markets, nationalism, alliances between nations, and stockpiling of armaments were the major factors that led to World War I.

Europe in 1914

MAP STUDY Compare this map to the one on page 597. What happened to Poland, Serbia, and Montenegro as a result of the war?

emy blockade would put the island nation in danger of starvation. This fear was legitimate because Britain was forced to import most of its food. Thus, to keep control of the seas, the British felt that they had to build twice as many ships as the Germans. At the same time as this military tension was building, German industry was rivaling that of Britain. The two nations competed with one another in world economic markets, increasing the tension between them.

Because the British did not trust Germany, they decided to make an alliance with their old rival, France. In 1904, therefore, the British and French signed an agreement called the *Entente Cordiale* [äɴ tänt′ kôr dyàl′], which in French means "friendly understanding." By 1907 Russia joined France and Britain in the second of the great European alliances, the **Triple Entente**.

Section 1 Review

Identify Triple Alliance, Balkans, Triple Entente

Main Ideas
1. To what great changes did Europe have to adjust at the end of the 18th century? How did these changes affect relations between countries?
2. In which parts of the world were nations competing for territory?
3. Which countries did Germany gain as allies under Bismarck? How did that change under Kaiser Wilhelm II?
4. Why did Britain finally seek allies?

Critical Thinking
Recognizing Values: Why is it sometimes necessary for a country to change alliances and thus be in a position where it might end up fighting a country with which it was once allied?

586

2 Some forces promoted peace.

Although rivalries were building national tensions, economic and political cooperation between nations was also growing. These positive forces favored peace, but unfortunately, they could not stem the tide of war.

The world economy needed peace.

By the early 20th century, the nations and peoples of the world had become economically interdependent. European wealth and know-how had helped speed the economic growth of Asia, Africa, and the Americas. For example, Britain loaned money to help build the American railway system, as well as railroads in Argentina and eastern Europe.

Peace meant that raw materials could be bought and finished goods could be sold throughout the world. Large companies could set up offices, factories, and plantations in foreign countries. Telephones, telegraphs, and cables could be used for quick communication. Railroads and steamships could carry products anywhere without danger. Most important of all, the industrialized countries, though political and economic rivals, were also each other's best customers for manufactured goods. War would destroy the prosperity that came as a result of international trade. The possibility of an end to such prosperity encouraged many business and political leaders to work for world harmony.

International organizations were formed.

World organizations were another force working for peace. In 1865 twenty countries organized the International Telegraph Union to improve worldwide communication. Later, in 1874 the General Postal Union was formed to improve mail service between nations. International agreements also covered such matters as weights and measures, underwater cables, navigation of international rivers, and protection of wildlife. The Greek Olympic games, which had not been held since A.D. 394, were revived in 1896 at Athens, Greece. This event, held every four years, brought together people from nearly every country of the world.

In the Western Hemisphere, the Pan-American movement encouraged cooperation among American nations. Trade was promoted, and an organization called the **Pan American Union** was set up to help accomplish these goals.

In addition, the **International Red Cross** was founded to help lessen the hardships of war. The **Geneva Convention of 1864**—a treaty—was the first of several agreements concerning humane treatment of wounded persons, prisoners, and civilians during wartime. National Red Cross societies also gave peacetime aid to disaster victims and others.

Section 2 Review

Identify Pan American Union, International Red Cross, Geneva Convention of 1864

Main Ideas
1. How did the world economy depend on peace?
2. Give three examples of international cooperation before World War I began.

Critical Thinking
Making Comparisons: Describe the importance of the Olympics today. How do people in the participating nations feel about sending their finest athletes to such competitions? Do you think these same feelings applied to early Olympic contests? Why or why not?

Clara Barton founded the American Red Cross in 1881 and won U.S. support for the Geneva Convention.

3 Lesson Plan

Essential Learning Objective

Students will learn to list the causes and effects of events that led to World War I.

1 FOCUS AND MOTIVATE

Have students describe how the stage was set for World War I years before it began. (Nations built strong navies and armies, stockpiled weapons, and made alliances attempting to maintain or extend their spheres of interest.)

2 TEACH

• Discuss the reasons for tensions between Serbia and Austria-Hungary and events that led to war with Serbia. Elicit reasons Austria did not pursue diplomatic solutions to the conflict and ask for opinions as to whether the government of one nation is ever justified in interfering with that of another.

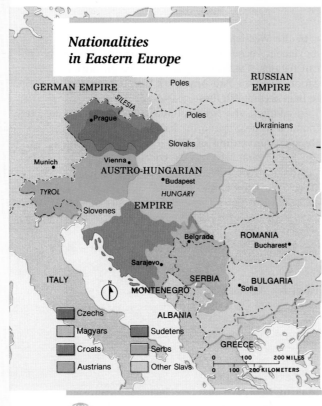

Nationalities in Eastern Europe

MAP STUDY Note the many peoples who lived in the Austro-Hungarian Empire. Which group was located on Serbia's northern borders?

3 The Balkan crisis escalated.

In spite of the growth of international organizations and economic prosperity, fear and suspicion spread among rival European countries between 1900 and 1914. Every great power—that is, Russia, Germany, Austria-Hungary, Britain, and France—believed that its own security depended on maintaining the alliance to which it belonged. In order to maintain a balance of power, therefore, each nation agreed to support the other members of each particular alliance if any member was attacked. Although this balance of power maintained peace for a time, the danger of a local conflict escalating into a general war was strong.

ANSWER TO MAP STUDY Serbians

Just such a local crisis broke out in the Balkan peninsula. The Balkans were known as the "powder keg of Europe" because tensions there threatened to ignite a major war. Quarrels continued between nationalist groups over internal boundaries, and nations outside the Balkans competed for control of the area.

The archduke of Austria was murdered.

By 1914 relations between **Serbia**, one of the Balkan nations, and Austria had reached a breaking point. Serbia, supported by Russia, wanted to unite with the Serbs living in the Austro-Hungarian Empire and create a Greater Serbia. Austria, supported by Germany, did not want Serbia cutting into its empire. Austria feared that if the Serbs did unite, the other minority Slavic groups in the empire would also demand self-rule. The empire would then collapse. Some Austrian leaders felt they had to destroy Serbia as an independent nation in order to stop the rising resistance to Austrian rule.

In June, 1914, **Archduke Francis Ferdinand**, heir to the Austrian throne, visited the Balkan city of **Sarajevo** [sär'ə yä'vō], hoping to ease the growing tensions. As Archduke Ferdinand rode through the streets in an open car, a young man sprang forward. He fired a gun and killed both the archduke and his wife, Sophie.

Count Leopold von Berchtold, the Austrian foreign minister, suspected that the Serbian government was responsible for the murder. Although his assumption was incorrect, he immediately took steps to stop Serbia from promoting anti-Austrian propaganda. He sent a letter to Kaiser Wilhelm II of Germany that was signed by the Austrian emperor. In the letter Berchtold asked for German help in order to stop Serbian agitation. The kaiser gladly agreed because he was eager to keep Austria as an ally. He also believed that the conflict could be kept within the Balkans. The kaiser's reply placed no limits on the amount of help Austria could expect from Germany. It became known as the "blank check."

With such strong support from Germany, Berchtold sent an ultimatum—an intimidating message—to Serbia on July 23, 1914. He warned that all anti-Austrian activities in Serbia must cease. He also said that Austro-Hungarian officials would be sent to Serbia to end such activities. Finally, all Serbian officials guilty of anti-Austrian propaganda should be dismissed from their government posts.

Austria declared war on Serbia in July, 1914.

Berchtold gave the Serbs 48 hours to reply. Should they refuse any part of the ultimatum, Berchtold was ready to go to war. He was sure that Austria could defeat Serbia in a local war. Furthermore, because Germany was such a strong country and was his ally, he believed other nations would be afraid to help Serbia.

The Serbs did agree to all of the Austrian demands except one. They refused to allow the Austro-Hungarian officials into their nation to end anti-Austrian propaganda. They felt that they would lose their independence if they agreed to this provision. Serbia then called on its ally Russia for help, and the Russians pledged their support. Thus, a local war was in danger of blowing up into a much larger conflict.

As tensions mounted, Sir Edward Grey, the British foreign secretary, tried to arrange talks between Serbia and Austria. Meanwhile, Berchtold convinced the Austrian emperor that war was the only way to deal with the Serbs. He paid no attention to Grey's proposals for peace. The German kaiser tried to keep the conflict from spreading, but German military leaders encouraged Berchtold toward war. On July 28, 1914, Austria declared war on Serbia.

Alliances brought other nations into the war.

Although the situation looked bleak, if the German kaiser had placed pressure on Austrian officials, a peaceful settlement might still have been achieved. Kaiser Wilhelm II urged Russia not to mobilize for war, but Russia ignored his request. Once the Russian army began to mobilize, other nations were forced to follow suit or be caught unprepared. This pressure to prepare for war precluded further tries at negotiation.

Russia. The Russians felt they should help their fellow Slavs, the Serbs. They also knew that a Serbian defeat would be a major blow to Russia's standing as a "Great Power." When France assured

This photograph shows Archduke Francis Ferdinand and his wife, Sophie, leaving the Senate House in Sarajevo. Five minutes later they were both assassinated. Their deaths set in motion the events that launched World War I.

Answers to Section 3 Review

Identify
Key Terms, People, and Places are defined on pages indicated in parentheses. Also see the Glossary and Biographical Dictionary.
Serbia (588), Archduke Francis Ferdinand (588), Sarajevo (588)

Main Ideas
1. to blame the Serbs, to seek German support, to put an end to anti-Austrian propaganda in Serbia
2. The British foreign secretary tried to arrange talks between Austria and Serbia; the German kaiser urged Russia not to mobilize.
3. to honor their alliances and preserve their right to call for help if needed, and to protect their standings as great powers; danger of local conflicts becoming widespread wars

Critical Thinking
Students may argue either position. They might think of the assassination as merely the match that ignited large amounts of fuel. However, this view is based on hindsight, and perhaps some events might have led to lasting peace.

4 Lesson Plan

Essential Learning Objectives
Students will learn to:
- describe World War I.
- identify factors that made World War I different from earlier wars.

Russia of its support, Tsar Nicholas II gave in to the advice of his war-hungry generals. He not only mobilized the army along Russia's border with Austria-Hungary, but also along the lengthy border with Germany.

Germany. News of Russian mobilization and French support caused alarm in Berlin, the German capital. It looked as if Germany would have to fight on two fronts—France on the west and Russia on the east. Germany at once demanded that Russia halt war moves and that France stay neutral, meaning it would not choose sides. These nations refused, so on August 1 Germany declared war on France. The Germans demanded that their troops be allowed to cross neutral Belgian frontiers on the way to the French front. Belgium refused and looked instead to Britain and France for help. Germany, however, ignored the refusal and sent its troops across Belgium anyway.

Britain. Although a member of the Triple Entente, Britain was not bound to help France or Russia in a war. However, in entering Belgium, Germany had broken a 75-year-old international treaty guaranteeing Belgium's neutrality. This violation angered Britain, which, like Germany, was a party to the treaty. German actions also aroused Britain's anger because the British feared that the Germans might try to gain control of the North Sea coast and thus threaten the British Isles. Therefore, on August 4, 1914, Britain declared war on Germany.

Section 3 Review

Identify Serbia, Archduke Francis Ferdinand, Sarajevo

Main Ideas
1. What was Austria's immediate response to the murder of its archduke?
2. What steps were taken to prevent a war between Austria and Serbia?
3. Why did other nations become involved in this conflict? Why was this dangerous?

Critical Thinking
Predicting Effects: Do you think that hostilities in Europe would have led to war if Archduke Francis Ferdinand had not been assassinated? Why or why not?

FROM THE ARCHIVES The excerpt is from *The Second Twenty Years at Hull House*, by Jane Addams (New York: Macmillan, 1930). Ask students if they agree with Jane Addams that war is equivalent to human sacrifice. Why do many people

From the Archives
A Voice for Peace in Time of War

Jane Addams (1860–1935), the founder of Hull House in Chicago, a famous settlement house for the poor, was deeply opposed to war. She helped found the Women's International League for Peace and Freedom in 1915 and served 15 years as its president. In recognition of her work, she became the first woman to receive the Nobel peace prize. Sometime later, Addams recalled her feelings as World War I broke out.

In our first horror against war we made an indictment [formal accusation] comparing warfare to human sacrifice. . . . It took the human race thousands of years to rid itself of human sacrifice; during many centuries it relapsed again and again in periods of national despair. So have we fallen back into warfare, and perhaps will fall back again and again, until in self-pity, in self-defense, in self-assertion of the right of life, not as hitherto, a few, but the whole people of the world, will brook [endure] this thing no longer.

4 The world went to war.

Only six nations were fighting at the start of the war in August of 1914. On one side were the four **Allies**—Britain, France, Russia, and Serbia. Opposing them were the two **Central Powers**—Germany and Austria. The strength of the Central Powers grew when the Ottoman Empire joined them in October, 1914, and Bulgaria a year later. Find these countries on the map on page 586.

Although Italy was an ally of Germany and Austria in the Triple Alliance, it felt no real friendship for Austria. When the war began, Italy declared that it would stay neutral. For several months both the Allies and the Central Powers tried to win Italy

seem to accept war, despite its horrors? (These questions call for free discussion in which all shades of opinion can be openly expressed.)

to their respective side. Finally, in April, 1915, after being promised territory in Austria and Africa should the Allies win, Italy joined the Allies.

In the meantime, Japan had joined the Allies in 1914. In addition, China declared war against Germany and Austria in 1917. By the end of the conflict, 31 nations had entered the war. World War I lasted more than four years and drew more than 61 million people into military service.

Nations the world over sought to lay the blame for this war on someone. Because Germany's kaiser hoped to make his nation the most powerful country in the world, the leaders of the Allied nations declared that Germany was chiefly at fault for World War I. Germany had encouraged Austria's dispute with Serbia by providing the Austrians with a blank check of support. Also, Germany had brought the other countries in by declaring war on France and by marching through neutral Belgium. Actually, each of the Allies and Central Powers had a reason for choosing war. All shared in the blame.

The war raged on two fronts.

By striking quickly through Belgium, Germany hoped to defeat France quickly and, therefore, minimize the danger of a two-front war. The highly trained German troops nearly reached Paris before the French stopped them. The French were aided by the Russians, who suddenly attacked Germany on its eastern front. This move by the Russians forced the Germans to shift large numbers of troops from west to east.

The western front. With the German forces diminished, the French were able to force the weakened Germans back at the Marne River. This deadly battle—known as the first battle of the Marne—was a key victory for the Allies. It ended German hopes that they could win this war quickly. For nearly three-and-a-half years, bitter fighting on the western front raged back and forth. The Allies and the Germans built trenches that zigzagged across the battlefront for more than 450 miles. The trenches were six to eight feet deep and only wide enough for two men to pass. Life for soldiers in the trenches was uncomfortable and tedious in the best of times and nightmarish during the worst times—when they were engaged in bat-

tle. The trench soldiers were exposed to the weather, surrounded by the smell of dead and rotting bodies, and plagued by rats. Separating the enemy trenches was a "no-man's land," an area covered with barbed wire. Below is a poem by the English writer Siegfried Sassoon, "Suicide in the Trenches," on the horror of the trenches:

> I knew a simple soldier boy
> Who grinned at life in empty joy,
> Slept soundly through the lonesome dark,
> And whistled early with the lark.
> In winter trenches, cowed and glum,
> With crumps and lice and lack of rum,
> He put a bullet through his brain.
> No one spoke of him again.
> You smug-faced crowds with kindling eye
> Who cheer when soldier lads march by,
> Sneak home and pray you'll never know
> The hell where youth and laughter go.

Defending from the trenches was easier than attacking. When one side decided to attack, its sol-

The German drive through Belgium shocked Americans, and U.S. war posters often alluded to German atrocities in that country.

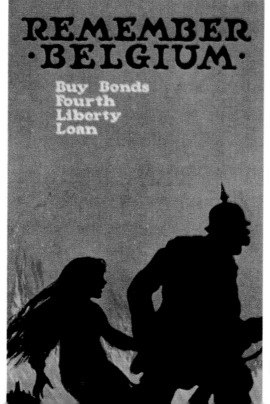

REMEMBER ·BELGIUM·

Buy Bonds
Fourth
Liberty
Loan

591

1 FOCUS AND MOTIVATE

Call attention to the fact that all of the European countries that entered World War I expected to be on the winning side. Ask students to give opinions as to why these nations held such an unrealistic point of view.

2 TEACH

• Have students add labels on the map they made in the last section for nations that entered World War I after 1914 and use color to indicate which countries were Allies and which made up the Central Powers. Elicit factors that led Italy to join the Allies rather than the Central Powers.

• Discuss why the war was fought on two fronts and which countries fought on the eastern and western fronts. Elicit reasons why Germany's strategy to defeat the French was unsuccessful. (Germany had to split its forces to fight the Russians in the east.) Have students explain why the first battle of the Marne and the battle of Verdun were significant. Compare the casualties of the Allies on the western front with their casualties on the eastern front and have students deduce why the Germans were able to inflict such heavy losses. (superior weapons) Elicit reactions to the slaughter of Armenian civilians by the Turks and ask for opinions on what other approaches the Turkish government might have used.

• Ask students to describe trench warfare and explain its advantages and disadvantages. What feelings are evoked by Sassoon's poem? What is its message?

- Discuss the events in Russia during World War I. Elicit students' opinions on the impact of the Russian revolution on Russian soldiers. Have students cite losses Russia incurred as a result of the war.

- Discuss how and why the battles and weapons of World War I were different from those in previous wars. Stress the fact that modern technology, new inventions, and mass production were the major reasons for the unprecedented number of lives lost during battles. Have students name the new technological inventions that created this new type of warfare. (submarines, airplanes, mines, torpedo boats, hand grenades, flame throwers, machine guns, giant guns that could shoot great distances, poison gas)

- Explain what events led the United States to join the Allies. Elicit opinions as to why the United States might have aided the Allies while claiming neutrality. Ask students to cite reasons for German submarine attacks on American ships.

- Discuss Germany's defeat. Have students speculate on whether the outcome of World War I would have been different without United States involvement. Have students explain what President Wilson hoped to accomplish by a peace settlement based on his Fourteen Points.

GUIDED PRACTICE

Have students write a couple of paragraphs explaining why all of the European countries were losers during World War I.

diers would climb out of the trenches, throwing grenades into the enemy's area and struggling through the barbed wire of the no-man's land. Meanwhile, enemy machine guns would wipe out line after line of attacking soldiers. The war went on and on this way, and the two sides were deadlocked. Fierce battles were fought, many soldiers were killed, but very little territory changed hands.

One of the most horrible battles of this war was the **battle of Verdun**, a German attempt to wipe out as many enemy soldiers as possible. The attacking Germans believed that killing large numbers of soldiers was the only way to stop the Allies. If the Allies did not have enough soldiers left to fight, they could not continue the war. The German commander chose the French city of Verdun for the site of this attack, believing that France would defend the city regardless of the consequences.

The French commander feared that losing Verdun would be too important a blow to French morale, so he chose to use as many men as needed to hold the city, eventually losing over 300,000 lives. The Germans lost almost as many men as the French did—about 280,000—and they finally called off the unsuccessful attack. The battle of Verdun is remembered as a symbol of the gross destructiveness of modern warfare.

The eastern front. The Russians kept a large part of the German army busy on the eastern front. The Russian invasion of East Prussia in 1914 drew German divisions from the western front. However, after the Germans made a successful counterattack, the Russians retreated. Further defeats took away the Russian will to fight. Russian losses, mounting into the millions, were even more staggering than those of the French and British. The Russians continued to resist the Germans and Austrians, but, for the most part, they could only manage to fight a defensive war.

In 1915 the British and French tried to send supplies to Russia but failed. Later in the year, Austria and Bulgaria defeated Serbia and occupied the country. This victory gave the Central Powers control of an unbroken line from Berlin, Germany, to Istanbul, Turkey.

A particularly brutal event of this period was the Armenian massacre of 1915. Armenia was then a state on the Turkish-Russian border, primarily under the control of the Ottoman Empire. When the war broke out, it was in a position of extreme danger—sitting between two enemies. The ruling Turks ordered the deportation of Armenians, using the pretext that the Armenians inhabited a war zone, that they were offering aid and comfort to the enemy, and that they were plotting a national uprising against the Ottoman Empire.

In carrying out the operation, the deportation became a massacre. Civilian men, women, and children and Armenian soldiers in the Ottoman army were tortured and slaughtered. Some were made to march hundreds of miles without food or water. Others were herded onto ships, believing that they were being rescued, only to be thrown into the Black Sea to drown. By 1918 almost 2 million Armenians had been murdered.

The Russian peace treaty. At the same time that Russian soldiers were fighting in the battlefields of World War I, the Russian people were fighting the tsar's forces in Moscow. As you will learn in Chapter 32, the tsar was overthrown in March, 1917, and the Bolsheviks [bōl′shə vikz] seized power in November.

After three years the Russians were sick of the war that had cost them so many lives and such severe food and fuel shortages. The Bolshevik leader, Vladimir Ilyich Ulyanov [ül yä′nôf], better known as **Lenin**, offered to make peace with the leaders of Germany. On March 3, 1918, the Bolsheviks and the Germans signed the Treaty of Brest-Litovsk. Through this treaty, Russia lost a third of its people, nine-tenths of its coal mines, and all of the immense oil fields in the Caucasus. As a result, Germany increased its power significantly. Even more importantly, Germany rushed its troops back to the west. The eastern front was secure.

Technology changed the whole character of war.

Since the dawn of history each generation has brought forth new weapons that have increased

British and German soldiers (right, top) walk back together after a battle. Life in the trenches (right) was grim and filthy. After 1916 tank warfare (right, inset) became standard practice.

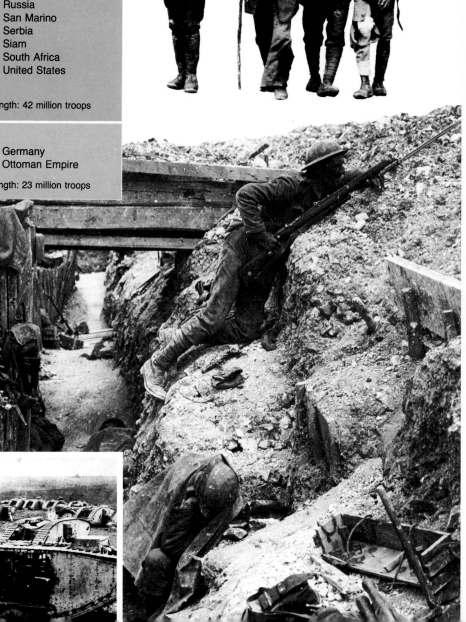

Combatants In World War I

The Allies

Australia	Japan
Belgium	Liberia
Brazil	Montenegro
Britain	New Zealand
Canada	Nicaragua
China	Panama
Costa Rica	Portugal
Cuba	Romania
France	Russia
Greece	San Marino
Guatemala	Serbia
Haiti	Siam
Honduras	South Africa
India	United States
Italy	

Maximum total mobilized strength: 42 million troops

The Central Powers

Austria-Hungary	Germany
Bulgaria	Ottoman Empire

Maximum total mobilized strength: 23 million troops

the horrors of war. Although the weapons of World War I pale in comparison to the nuclear weapons of today, the weapons used in 1914 were more powerful than ever before in history. For the first time, war was not based on face-to-face combat. Battles were fought in the air and under the sea, as well as on land and on the sea. Germany attacked British battleships with its new submarines called U-boats. Early in the war, both Germany and the Allies used airplanes for spying. By 1917 both had developed fighter and bomber planes. Each side bombed targets hundreds of miles from their home air bases.

During this war as well, the British introduced tanks. Later the Germans used them also. Sea and land mines, torpedo boats, hand grenades, flamethrowers, machine guns, and many other weapons were created or improved by technological advances. Giant guns, such as the German "Big Bertha," fired shells more than 75 miles. Poison gas, first used in battle by the Germans in 1915, caused vomiting and suffocation. The Allies soon began using poison gas also, and gas masks for soldiers became necessary equipment in the trenches.

Germany stepped up naval warfare.

During the first months of the war, the German navy caused tremendous damage to Allied shipping. Early in 1915 Germany stated that all the waters around the British Isles would be treated as a war zone. An enemy ship—even an unarmed merchant ship—found in this zone would be attacked. Britain fought back by ordering a blockade of Germany and seizing all goods headed for German ports.

By 1916 the British blockade caused a severe shortage of food supplies in Germany. Later in the year, however, Germany retaliated by building more submarines with which to attack British warships. With the help of these submarines, German light cruisers were able to slip through the blockade to raid ships on the Atlantic. Britain countered by building more warships and by developing depth charges, which were bombs used against submarines. Still, German naval warfare—especially submarine warfare—was very effective. By the early part of 1917, supplies of food and arms in Britain grew dangerously low.

This dramatic World War I poster is still used today to recruit American soldiers.

The United States joined the Allies.

Since August, 1914, the United States had tried to remain neutral. As the war dragged on, however, German submarines began attacking American ships that were carrying supplies to Britain and France. The Americans claimed that as neutrals, they had freedom of the seas and could go anywhere and sell supplies to anyone. The Germans, however, felt that they could not let vital supplies reach their enemies.

In 1915 and 1916, German submarine attacks caused the loss of hundreds of American lives. One submarine attack in particular—on a British passenger ship called the *Lusitania*—was considered an act of barbarism by many people. More than 1,000 people aboard the ship lost their lives, including 128 Americans. After the sinking of this ship, support for the British increased in the United States, and "Remember the *Lusitania*" became a popular slogan.

U.S. President **Woodrow Wilson** warned the Germans to stop the attacks. For a time the Germans agreed to relax their submarine attacks, hoping to keep the United States out of the war. However, when the British blockade squeezed off supplies to Germany, German leaders believed they had no choice but to resume submarine attacks. On January 31, 1917, Germany therefore announced "unrestricted submarine warfare," this meaning that all ships headed toward Britain and France would be attacked without warning. In the next two months, several U.S. ships were sunk.

Late in March, 1917, British agents intercepted a telegram sent to Mexico by Arthur Zimmermann, the German foreign secretary. The telegram encouraged Mexico to ally itself with Germany and help fight the United States. Besides financial aid, Zimmermann promised that Mexico would recover Texas, New Mexico, and Arizona when the Allies were defeated. German submarine warfare and the Zimmermann telegram raised pro-war feelings in the United States to a feverish pitch. President Wilson gave up his efforts to end the war through negotiation. Under the banner of Wilson's famous statement that "the world must be made safe for democracy," the United States entered the war, joining the Allies on April 6, 1917.

The tide turned for the Allies.

While Russia was crumbling, the first troops from the United States landed in France. German leaders tried desperately to win the war before the American army could get into action. Following the Brest-Litovsk treaty between Germany and the Soviet Union, they sent almost every German soldier to the western front. There they began a huge attack in the spring of 1918.

The British and French generals wanted to fill in their ranks with the arriving American soldiers, but U.S. General John Pershing, a brilliant military leader, said that the American troops should fight separately. He believed that when the Germans found out that a large, fresh American army was entering the war, it would hurt their morale. The Americans were trained for a fast, driving war, and Pershing refused to get involved in the slow trench warfare of the Allied armies. His strategies worked, and the Germans suffered heavy losses.

In the fall of 1918, German military leaders realized they could not win. One by one Germany's

allies quit. On November 3, German sailors mutinied at Kiel, a city and port in northwest Germany. Four days later a revolution broke out in Germany. A republic was founded, and the kaiser fled to Holland. Thus ended Hohenzollern rule and the Second German Reich.

Leaders of the new German government agreed to an armistice, which is an agreement to stop fighting. They asked that the peace settlement be based on President Wilson's **Fourteen Points**, which he had presented in a speech to Congress on January 8, 1918. These Fourteen Points outlined the President's ideas for solving the problems that had led to the war.

Wilson asked for an end to secret agreements, freedom of the seas in peace and war, the reduction of armaments, the right of nationality groups to form their own nations, and an association of nations to keep the peace. In other speeches Wilson called for a negotiated peace with reasonable

On the American home front, Girl Scouts collect peach pits. It took seven pounds of pits to make the filter for a gas mask.

3 | **ASSESS AND CLOSE**

ASSESS

1. Why did Germany invade Belgium? (to get to France)
2. Which Russian leader made many concessions to the Germans in the Treaty of Brest-Litovsk? (Lenin)

OPTIONAL RETEACHING

Have students outline in phrases World War I developments on the eastern front, on the western front, and in the warfare at sea. Have selected students use their outlines to describe the war orally in class.

OPTIONAL ENRICHMENT

1. Divide the class into two groups. Have one group represent the point of view of the Allies and the other group represent the point of view of the Central Powers in discussions of the following topics: the battles of the Marne and Verdun, the sinking of the *Lusitania,* and President Wilson's Fourteen Points. (average)
2. Assign interested students to read *All Quiet on the Western Front* by Erich Maria Remarque. Have students write a short synopsis of the novel that explains the writer's point of view toward war. (challenging)
3. Also for enrichment:

📖 *Source Reading 31B*

INDEPENDENT PRACTICE/ HOMEWORK

Assign the Section Review, Activities page 186, or Workbook page 126.

CLOSURE

Tell students that all of the nations who entered the war endured unprecedented losses and hardships. The Central Powers were holding their own until the United States entered the war. General Pershing's brilliant strategy rapidly ended the war.

595

Answers to Section 4 Review

Identify
Key Terms, People, and Places are defined on pages indicated in parentheses. Also see the Glossary and Biographical Dictionary.
Allies (590), Central Powers (590), battle of Verdun (592), Lenin (592), Woodrow Wilson (594), Fourteen Points (595)

Main Ideas
1. Russian attack on the eastern front forced Germany to shift troops away from the western front.
2. airplanes, submarines, mines, machine guns, giant long-distance guns, torpedo boats, hand grenades, flame throwers, poison gas
3. British blockades were causing shortages in Germany. Also, with naval blockades Germany could keep supplies from Britain.
4. German submarine attacks on American ships, sinking *Lusitania*, Zimmermann telegram to Mexico
5. The United States entered the war, Germany's allies quit fighting, German sailors mutinied, and a revolution broke out in Germany.

Critical Thinking
Both Germany and France tried to defeat Britain by cutting off their trade with other European countries. In both cases the blockading country also suffered severe shortages.

5 Lesson Plan

Essential Learning Objectives
Students will learn to:
- describe the terms of the Paris Peace Treaty.
- list the new nations formed by the treaty.

BACKGROUND The armistice was signed at 5 A.M. in the railroad car. Fighting halted at 11 A.M. that same day.

demands made on the losers. The Allies agreed to model the peace settlement on the Fourteen Points. However, some felt that Wilson's terms were too easy on Germany.

Early in the morning of November 11, 1918, the war ended. In a railroad car in the Compiegne [koɴ'pyen'] Forest in northern France, two German delegates met Allied officials to sign the armistice. The guns were silent.

Section 4 Review

Identify Allies, Central Powers, battle of Verdun, Lenin, Woodrow Wilson, Fourteen Points

Main Ideas
1. What prevented Germany from scoring a quick victory on the western front?
2. Describe some of the new military technologies introduced during World War I.
3. Why was naval warfare so important to Germany?
4. What were some of the factors that made the United States join the Allies?
5. List four factors that turned the tide for the Allies.

Critical Thinking
Analyzing Comparisons: How were Germany's actions against Britain similar to those France used in the Napoleonic Wars (as you learned in Chapter 27)? Why did this method fail both times?

---

5 The victors tried to build a lasting peace.

No previous war in the world's history had caused such widespread horror. More than 10 million troops were killed in battle, and 20 million more were wounded. Thirteen million civilians died from war-related famine, disease, and injuries. The cost of the war was estimated at more than $350 billion. Destruction was everywhere.

Three leaders dominated the Paris Peace Conference.

After the armistice had been signed, the Allied nations met in Paris to discuss peace terms. Contrary to Wilson's wishes, the defeated countries were not

---

allowed to send representatives to the peace conference. Thus, the so-called Big Three dominated the meeting: President Wilson; David Lloyd George, prime minister of Great Britain; and Georges Clemenceau [klem'ən sō'], premier of France.

Woodrow Wilson was an idealist. He stated the hopes of people everywhere when he said that the conflict had been fought "for . . . democracy . . . for the rights and liberties of small nations . . . for . . . free peoples . . . to make the world itself at last free." At the conference Wilson upheld his Fourteen Points. Above all, he wanted to see a **League of Nations**, an international association established to keep the peace. To get the others to agree, however, he had to make a compromise.

Georges Clemenceau, known as the "Old Tiger," had led France during the darkest hours of the war. He wanted Germany to pay for war damages because almost all the fighting in the West had been on French soil. Most of all he insisted that France be made safe from attack by Germany in the future. He wanted German power destroyed and sought to gain strong alliances with Britain and the United States. Clemenceau placed little faith in Wilson's proposed "League of Nations."

Lloyd George in turn wanted Germany's colonies for Britain. He also wanted the German navy destroyed. During the peace talks, he mediated between the idealism of Wilson and the severe terms of Clemenceau. When Wilson gave in on many details, including promising to protect France against

---

The treaty ending World War I was signed in the Hall of Mirrors at Versailles, depicted in this painting below. Seated in the center are Clemenceau (with mustache), Lloyd George (right), and Wilson (left).

Europe After World War I

 MAP STUDY European boundaries changed greatly after World War I. Compare this map to the one on page 586 and name four countries that were carved from the Austro-Hungarian Empire.

possible future German attack, Clemenceau and Lloyd George agreed to make the creation of the League of Nations part of the peace agreement, called the **Versailles Treaty**.

Germany lost territory and wealth in its defeat.

When the German delegation arrived to sign the Versailles Treaty, they found its terms harsher than they had expected. The Germans were out-raged at a war-guilt clause, which placed the entire blame for the war on Germany and its allies. They were also dismayed that many of Wilson's Four-teen Points were missing or had been weakened by changes. The first delegates from Germany re-fused to sign the treaty. To avoid occupation by Allied soldiers, however, a second German delega-tion signed it on June 28, 1919. Even though Ger-many signed the treaty, there was strong resent-ment over its harsh terms.

ANSWER TO MAP STUDY Austria, Hungary, Czechoslova-kia, and Yugoslavia; also parts of Poland, Italy, and Romania

597

ASSESS

What lands became mandates after World War I? (German colonies in Africa and in the Pacific)

OPTIONAL RETEACHING

Have students write a couple of paragraphs describing the outcome of the Versailles Treaty and explaining the reasons for its harsh terms.

Students also may be assigned Activities reteaching page 188.

OPTIONAL ENRICHMENT

Have students write a short paper on the League of Nations, its purpose, and its demise. (average)

Students also may be assigned Activities enrichment page 189.

INDEPENDENT PRACTICE/ HOMEWORK

Assign the Section Review, the Chapter Review items, Activities page 187, or Workbook page 127.

CLOSURE

Tell students that the harsh terms of the Versaille Treaty, which carved up Europe, included only a few of Woodrow Wilson's Fourteen Points.

Answers to Section 5 Review

Identify

Key Terms, People, and Places are defined on pages indicated in parentheses. Also see the Glossary and Biographical Dictionary. League of Nations (596), Versailles Treaty (597), mandates (598)

Main Ideas

1. U.S. President Wilson wanted a League of Nations set up. British Prime Minister George wanted Britain to take control of Germany's colo-

---

BACKGROUND Much of the land given to Poland through the Versailles Treaty had been taken from Poland by Germany in the 1700s.

In the treaty France won back the lost provinces of Alsace and Lorraine. The German territory west of the Rhine, called the Rhineland, was to become a buffer zone between the two enemies. It was to be occupied by Allied troops for at least 15 years. France was also given the rich coal mines of the Saar—located on the French-German border. The Saar was to be administered by the League of Nations, but after 15 years the Saarlanders could vote to have their region go back to the German government or remain under the French. In 1935 they voted to become a part of Germany again.

In March, 1917, Poland had become independent of Russia. Through the Versailles Treaty, it won a broad stretch of land from Germany. This region became known as the Polish Corridor. It gave Poland an outlet to the Baltic Sea. The Polish Corridor also divided Germany, isolating its province of East Prussia.

The Versailles Treaty gave German colonies in Africa and in the Pacific to the League of Nations. The League in turn placed them under the control of the Allied nations. These lands, known as mandates, were given mostly to Great Britain and France. (**Mandates** were lands that the League gave to certain nations to administer and develop.) Some mandates also went to Japan, South Africa, Australia, and New Zealand.

In the treaty the Allies required that Germany repay much of the cost of the war, or make reparations. They wanted an immediate payment of $5 billion in cash. Two years later they billed Germany for $32 billion, plus interest.

The treaty reduced German military power and permitted Germany an army of no more than 100,000 men. The navy was allowed only six warships, some other vessels, and no submarines or military airplanes.

The Germans were not alone in thinking such peace terms unjust. Even David Lloyd George doubted the justice of the Versailles Treaty. President Wilson hoped that his dream, the League of Nations, could correct the unjust treaty later.

New independent nations were formed.

Four empires had fallen apart in the course of World War I—the German, the Austro-Hungarian, the Ottoman, and the Russian. Based partly on se-

BACKGROUND Many people in the Middle East shifted from being under Ottoman rule to British or French rule.

BACKGROUND There were 3 classes of mandates, based on their ability for self-rule. A report on their administration was to be made once a year to the League.

cret agreements made during the war, the Allies drew up a series of peace treaties to divide up the territory. The Allies reorganized the land lost by Russia to Germany. From the western portion of the old Russian Empire came five new nations: Poland, Finland, Latvia, Lithuania, and Estonia.

The defeated Austro-Hungarian Empire was also divided into several new countries. Austria and Hungary became two independent republics, as did Czechoslovakia and Yugoslavia. Some Austro-Hungarian land also went to Poland, Italy, and Romania. See the map on page 597.

The Ottoman Empire, too, was divided up. Compare the map on page 586 with the map on page 597. Syria, Iraq, Trans-Jordan, and Palestine were created from the Ottoman Empire and then became mandates. The first was ruled by France, the other three by Britain. These mandates were promised independence at a future time.

The creation of the new states helped fulfill one of Wilson's Fourteen Points—the right of self-determination, or the right of peoples to form their own nations. However, redrawing the map of Europe again brought some groups under foreign control. For example, Austrians living in the Tyrol came under the rule of Italy. Other German-speaking Austrians (the Sudetens) were placed under Czechoslovakian rule. Some Germans lived in the new Polish Corridor, and many Hungarians came under Romanian control. Few of these peoples were happy about these changes, and their discontent was a dangerous sign for the future.

Section 5 Review

Identify League of Nations, Versailles Treaty, mandates

Main Ideas

1. Who were the major participants at the Paris Peace Conference? What were their goals?
2. Name at least three major terms that the treaty imposed on Germany.
3. Name four independent nations that were formed after the war.

Critical Thinking

Recognizing Values: Consider some reasons why Clemenceau and Wilson might have differed over the League of Nations.

The Automobile Revolution

The First Battle of the Marne caught the popular imagination because Paris taxicabs rushed 6,000 French soldiers to the front lines in a matter of hours. This spectacular troop movement represented the first major use of motorized transport in the history of warfare. In 1916 at the Battle of Verdun, motor convoys helped supply one-half million French troops and 150,000 draft animals at the fighting front and played a decisive role in the French victory. These wartime events pointed to one of the important technological changes of the 20th century—the automobile revolution.

Europeans pioneered in the development of the automobile in the late 19th century. However, an American industrialist, Henry Ford,

turned the automobile from a luxury item for the wealthy few to the accepted form of transportation for everybody. Ford did this by using assembly-line, mass-production methods to build cars that were reliable and inexpensive. Ford's famous Model T touring car first sold in 1908 for $850. By 1915 Ford's Detroit plant was producing a thousand Model T's a day, and the price fell to $440.

The automobile changed people's lives forever. An Indiana woman interviewed in the 1920s told how most people felt about the change: she said, "We'd rather do without clothes than give up the car."

A motor convoy approaches Verdun (below). Motorists jam a park in St. Louis in the 1920s (right).

nies. French Premier Clemenceau wanted Germany to pay damages.
2. Germany had to give Alsace and Lorraine back to France, German colonies in Africa and the Pacific were put under the control of the League of Nations, and Germany had to pay for war damages.
3. Answer can include four of the following: Poland, Finland, Latvia, Lithuania, Estonia, Austria, Hungary, Czechoslovakia, Yugoslavia.

Critical Thinking

France had been heavily damaged in the war. Being neighbors with Germany made France more vulnerable, so Clemenceau wanted power for France, not conversation. The United States was not as vulnerable so Wilson could be more idealistic about nations coming together to discuss differences openly.

HIGHLIGHTS OF CIVILIZATION

Ask for a show of hands to determine how many students agree with the woman in the interview. Then place two headings on the chalkboard, "Before Automobiles" and "After Automobiles." Encourage the students to speculate about the changes that accompanied the automobile revolution. (Items under "before" could include horses, streetcars, railroad, with positive and negative aspects of each. Some examples of negative aspects under horses: consume quantities of feed whether used or not, pollution from waste, dead carcasses; positive effect: manure used for fertilizer. Items under "after" could include more and better highways, garages, filling stations, growth of suburbs, shopping malls, drive-ins, Sunday drives, and automobile vacations, with their positive and negative aspects.)

Answers to Test Yourself

Key Terms, People, and Places

The key terms, people, and places tested here were introduced in the chapter sections and reviewed in the Section Reviews. For definitions see the page references at the appropriate Section Reviews. Also see the Glossary and Biographical Dictionary.

Main Ideas

The main ideas tested here were introduced in the sections of this chapter and reviewed in the Section Reviews. For answers to these questions, see the appropriate Section Reviews.

Critical Thinking

1. A country involved in an alliance is more secure in that it can turn to others for help. However, it also can get drawn into conflicts or wars that may not be in its best interests.

2. The Allies could have refused to get involved in the Austro-Serbian conflicts in the interests of peace. Through diplomacy they could have shown that they were not backing out on a commitment to an ally but rather were working to prevent a large-scale war.

Section Summaries

Section 1
Many factors together caused World War I.
In the early 20th century, national rivalries for trade and for colonies increased tensions. An arms race began that added further fuel to the fire. Nations tried to find security by forming alliances. Germany set up the Triple Alliance with Austria and Italy. France, Russia, and Britain formed the Triple Entente.

Section 2
Some forces promoted peace.
Along with more economic interdependence, political cooperation grew. Several new international organizations were formed, but fears and insecurities caused the mood for war to grow stronger than the desire for peace.

Section 3
The Balkan crisis escalated.
In 1914 the murder of Archduke Francis Ferdinand of Austria at Sarajevo led to war between Austria and Serbia. The war at once involved Russia, a friend of Serbia, and Germany, a partner of Austria. France and Britain joined Russia.

Section 4
The world went to war.
From 1914 to 1917, France and Britain fought bitterly against Germany on the western front. British and German naval blockades prevented trade and reduced food supplies in both countries. In 1917 the Bolsheviks gained control of Russia and made peace with Germany. That same year the United States entered the war because Germany had begun unrestricted submarine warfare and encouraged Mexico to attack the United States. Thousands of American soldiers joined the French and British, and together, forced the Central Powers to sue for peace.

Section 5
The victors tried to build a lasting peace.
President Wilson's Fourteen Points were not entirely acceptable to the other Allies. Agreement was reached, however, on the League of Nations. The major part of the Versailles Treaty took away German territory, wealth, and military strength. Other treaties set down the boundaries of new states. Some gained independence. Others were unhappily placed under foreign control. Four major empires ended and brought about the greatest change in the political map of Europe since 1815.

Review Dates

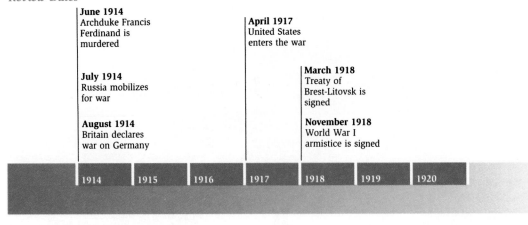

June 1914
Archduke Francis Ferdinand is murdered

July 1914
Russia mobilizes for war

August 1914
Britain declares war on Germany

April 1917
United States enters the war

March 1918
Treaty of Brest-Litovsk is signed

November 1918
World War I armistice is signed

| 1914 | 1915 | 1916 | 1917 | 1918 | 1919 | 1920 |

Test Yourself

Key Terms, People, and Places
Identify the significance of each of the following:

Section 1
a. Triple Alliance   **c.** Triple Entente
b. Balkans

Section 2
a. Pan American Union   **c.** Geneva Convention
b. International Red Cross   of 1864

Section 3
a. Serbia   **c.** Archduke Francis
b. Sarajevo   Ferdinand

Section 4
a. Allies   **d.** Lenin
b. Central Powers   **e.** Woodrow Wilson
c. battle of Verdun   **f.** Fourteen Points

Section 5
a. League of Nations   **c.** mandates
b. Versailles Treaty

Main Ideas

Section 1
1. How did industrialization and growing nationalism affect relations between countries?
2. Where did imperialistic interests clash around the world?
3. List the German allies under Bismarck.
4. How did German actions lead Britain to seek allies?

Section 2
1. How would war damage the world economy?
2. Name three prewar international ventures.

Section 3
1. How did Austria express its outrage at the murder of its archduke?
2. Who tried to prevent an Austro-Serbian war?
3. Why did this conflict draw in other nations?

Section 4
1. What weakened Germany on the western front?
2. How was this war different from any other before it?
3. How did naval war help Germany and Britain?

4. List three reasons why Wilson brought the United States into the war.
5. What finally brought the Central Powers to defeat?

Section 5
1. Who were the "Big Three"? What terms did each want in the peace treaty?
2. Name three penalties imposed on postwar Germany.
3. What were some of the new nations that were formed following World War I?

Critical Thinking

1. Predicting Effects Consider the pluses and minuses of forming an alliance. What might the effects be for a country entering an alliance?

2. Making Hypotheses Do you think something could have been done to avoid World War I? Explain.

Chapter Skills and Activities

Practicing Study and Research Skills

Recognizing a Historian's Interpretation
When you read a history book, you are learning the facts as seen by the author of the book. The writer knows many more facts, but he or she selects those that appear to be the most important and meaningful. The choice of facts is governed by the writer's outlook. For example, how might the Paris Peace Conference and Versailles Treaty be described by a Belgian historian who was a teenager during the war? How might a German historian of the same age interpret these events?

Linking Past and Present
The dangerous armaments race that began during the pre–World War I period continues today. Why may the race now be even more deadly?

Learning History Through Maps
Use the maps on pages 586 and 597 to find:
1. five new nations that were formed after the war from territories once included in the Russian Empire.
2. two key pieces of territory that Germany lost in Europe.

Practicing Study and Research Skills
The Belgian might write as a passive victim, having seen home and daily life upset and endangered for no reason. This person might be bitter toward the Germans or think that the treaty terms weren't harsh enough. A German historian might see the treaty as unjust and humiliating punishment or might see the whole period as one of national shame. He or she might try to justify German behavior.

Linking Past and Present
Nuclear weapons have the potential to destroy the whole planet. Countries known definitely to currently have nuclear weapons include the United States, Soviet Union, Britain, France, and China.

Learning History Through Maps
1. Poland, Finland, Latvia, Lithuania
2. the Saar, the Polish Corridor

CRITICAL THINKING QUESTION LEVEL 1. average;
2. challenging

32 The Soviet Union: The First Communist State

OVERVIEW

Widespread discontent, inadequate reform, and World War I led to the fall of tsarist Russia. In its place, Lenin created a communist nation and Stalin, at terrible human cost, forged it into the world's second largest industrial nation.

PLANNING CHART

Section	Text Pages	Key Concept	Suggested Teaching Time
1 The tsarist regime collapsed.	603–608	Widespread social unrest and discontent, coupled with a poorly managed war effort, led to the collapse of tsarist rule in Russia.	Two days **More time?** Use *Source Reading 32A.*
2 Bolsheviks took control of Russia.	608–611	Lenin overthrew the largely ineffective Provisional Government and established a communist state, the Soviet Union.	One day **More time?** Use *Overhead Transparency 63.*
3 Stalin created a totalitarian society.	613–614	Stalin ruthlessly killed and exiled peasants and political opponents in his effort to change the Soviet economy.	One day **More time?** Use *Source Reading 32B.*
4 The Soviet Union tried to protect its security.	615–616	Stalin tried to ensure national security through agreements with Western nations; failing this, he turned to Germany.	One day **More time?** Use *Overhead Transparency 64.* **Less time?** This section is relatively short. Summarize it for the class after completing Section 3.

ANCILLARIES

Materials that may be used with this chapter to reinforce, reteach, enrich, and assess learning are pictured on the following pages.

Teacher's Resource File

ACTIVITIES

Section 1 Activity, p. 190

Section 2 Activity, p. 191

Section 3 Activity, p. 192

Section 4 Activity, p. 193

Chapter 32 Reteaching, p. 194

Chapter 32 Enrichment, p. 195

Teacher's Resource File

GEOGRAPHY SKILLS

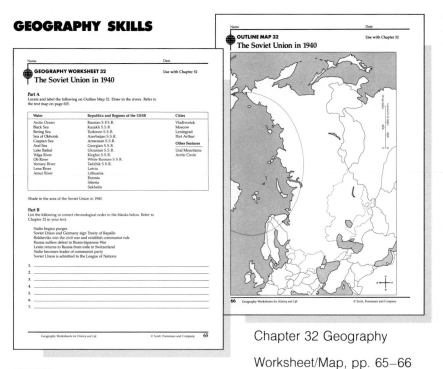

Part A
Locate and label the following on Outline Map 32. Draw in the rivers. Refer to the text map on page 615.

Water	Republics and Regions of the USSR	Cities
Arctic Ocean	Russian S.F.S.R.	Vladivostok
Black Sea	Kazakh S.S.R.	Moscow
Bering Sea	Turkmen S.S.R.	Leningrad
Sea of Okhotsk	Azerbaijan S.S.R.	Port Arthur
Caspian Sea	Armenian S.S.R.	
Aral Sea	Georgian S.S.R.	**Other Features**
Lake Baikal	Ukrainian S.S.R.	Ural Mountains
Volga River	Kirghiz S.S.R.	Arctic Circle
Ob River	White Russian S.S.R.	
Yenisey River	Tadzhik S.S.R.	
Lena River	Latvia	
Amur River	Lithuania	
	Estonia	
	Siberia	
	Sakhalin	

Shade in the area of the Soviet Union in 1940.

Part B
List the following in correct chronological order in the blanks below. Refer to Chapter 32 in your text.

Stalin begins purges
Soviet Union and Germany sign Treaty of Rapallo
Bolsheviks win the civil war and establish communist rule
Russia suffers defeat in Russo-Japanese War
Lenin returns to Russia from exile in Switzerland
Stalin becomes leader of communist party
Soviet Union is admitted to the League of Nations

1. _____
2. _____
3. _____
4. _____
5. _____
6. _____
7. _____

Geography Worksheets for History and Life   © Scott, Foresman and Company   **65**

---

66 Geography Worksheets for *History and Life*   © Scott, Foresman and Company

Chapter 32 Geography Worksheet/Map, pp. 65–66

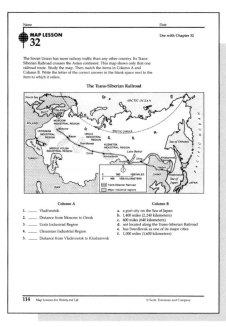

The Soviet Union has more railway traffic than any other country. Its Trans-Siberian Railroad crosses the Asian continent. This map shows only that one railroad route. Study the map. Then match the items in Column A and Column B. Write the letter of the correct answer in the blank space next to the item to which it refers.

The Trans-Siberian Railroad

Column A	Column B
1. _____ Vladivostok	a. a port city on the Sea of Japan
2. _____ Distance from Moscow to Omsk	b. 1,400 miles (2,240 kilometers)
3. _____ Urals Industrial Region	c. 400 miles (640 kilometers)
4. _____ Ukrainian Industrial Region	d. not located along the Trans-Siberian Railroad
5. _____ Distance from Vladivostok to Khabarovsk	e. has Sverdlovsk as one of its major cities
	f. 1,000 miles (1,600 kilometers)

114 Map Lessons for *History and Life*   © Scott, Foresman and Company

Chapter 32 Map Lesson, p. 114

TESTS

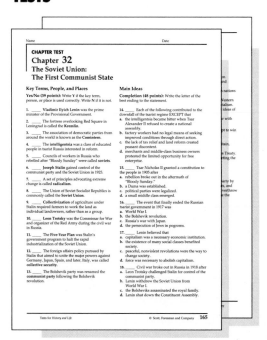

Key Terms, People, and Places
Yes/No (39 points): Write Y if the key term, person, or place is used correctly. Write N if it is not.

1. _____ **Vladimir Ilyich Lenin** was the prime minister of the Provisional Government.

2. _____ The fortress overlooking Red Square in Leningrad is called the **Kremlin**.

3. _____ The association of democratic parties from around the world is known as the **Comintern**.

4. _____ The **intelligentsia** was a class of educated people in tsarist Russia interested in reform.

5. _____ Councils of workers in Russia who rebelled after "Bloody Sunday" were called **soviets**.

6. _____ **Joseph Stalin** gained control of the communist party and the Soviet Union in 1925.

7. _____ A set of principles advocating extreme change is called **radicalism**.

8. _____ The Union of Soviet Socialist Republics is commonly called the **Soviet Union**.

9. _____ **Collectivization** of agriculture under Stalin required farmers to work the land as individual landowners, rather than as a group.

10. _____ **Leon Trotsky** was the Commissar for War and organizer of the Red Army during the civil war in Russia.

11. _____ The **Five-Year Plan** was Stalin's government program to halt the rapid industrialization of the Soviet Union.

12. _____ The foreign affairs policy pursued by Stalin that aimed to unite the major powers against Germany, Japan, Spain, and, later, Italy, was called **collective security**.

13. _____ The Bolshevik party was renamed the **communist party** following the Bolshevik revolution.

Main Ideas
Completion (48 points): Write the letter of the best ending to the statement.

14. _____ Each of the following contributed to the downfall of the tsarist regime EXCEPT that
a. the intelligentsia became bitter when Tsar Alexander II refused to create a national assembly.
b. factory workers had no legal means of seeking improved conditions other than direct action.
c. the lack of tax relief and land reform created peasant discontent.
d. merchants and middle-class business owners protested the limited opportunity for free enterprise.

15. _____ Tsar Nicholas II granted a constitution to the people in 1905 after
a. rebellion broke out in the aftermath of "Bloody Sunday."
b. a Duma was established.
c. political parties were legalized.
d. a small middle class emerged.

16. _____ The event that finally ended the Russian tsarist government in 1917 was
a. World War I.
b. the Bolshevik revolution.
c. Russia's war with Japan.
d. the persecution of Jews in pogroms.

17. _____ Lenin believed that
a. capitalism was a necessary economic institution.
b. the existence of many social classes benefited society.
c. peaceful, nonviolent revolutions were the way to change society.
d. force was necessary to abolish capitalism.

18. _____ Civil war broke out in Russia in 1918 after
a. Leon Trotsky challenged Stalin for control of the communist party.
b. Lenin withdrew the Soviet Union from World War I.
c. the Bolsheviks assassinated the royal family.
d. Lenin shut down the Constituent Assembly.

Tests for History and Life   © Scott, Foresman and Company   **165**

Chapter Test, pp. 165–166

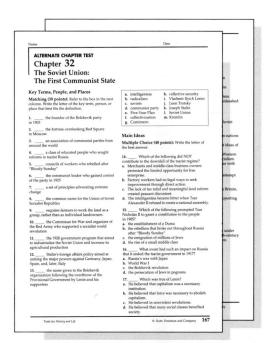

Key Terms, People, and Places
Matching (39 points): Refer to the box in the next column. Write the letter of the key term, person, or place that best fits the definition.

a. intelligentsia	h. collective security
b. radicalism	i. Vladimir Ilyich Lenin
c. soviets	j. Leon Trotsky
d. communist party	k. Joseph Stalin
e. Five-Year Plan	l. Soviet Union
f. collectivization	m. Kremlin
g. Comintern	

1. _____ the founder of the Bolshevik party in 1903

2. _____ the fortress overlooking Red Square in Moscow

3. _____ an association of communist parties from around the world

4. _____ a class of educated people who sought reforms in tsarist Russia

5. _____ councils of workers who rebelled after "Bloody Sunday"

6. _____ the communist leader who gained control of the party in 1925

7. _____ a set of principles advocating extreme change

8. _____ the common name for the Union of Soviet Socialist Republics

9. _____ requires farmers to work the land as a group, rather than as individual landowners

10. _____ the Commissar for War and organizer of the Red Army who supported a socialist world revolution

11. _____ the 1928 government program that aimed to industrialize the Soviet Union and increase its agricultural production

12. _____ Stalin's foreign affairs policy aimed at uniting the major powers against Germany, Japan, Spain, and, later, Italy

13. _____ the name given to the Bolshevik organization following the overthrow of the Provisional Government by Lenin and his supporters

Main Ideas
Multiple Choice (48 points): Write the letter of the best answer.

14. _____ Which of the following did NOT contribute to the downfall of the tsarist regime?
a. Merchants and middle-class business owners protested the limited opportunity for free enterprise.
b. Factory workers had no legal ways to seek improvement through direct action.
c. The lack of tax relief and meaningful land reform created peasant discontent.
d. The intelligentsia became bitter when Tsar Alexander II refused to create a national assembly.

15. _____ Which of the following prompted Tsar Nicholas II to grant a constitution to the people in 1905?
a. the establishment of a Duma
b. the rebellion that broke out throughout Russia
c. the emigration of millions of Jews
d. the rise of a small middle class

16. _____ What event had such an impact on Russia that it ended the tsarist government in 1917?
a. Russia's war with Japan
b. World War I
c. the Bolshevik revolution
d. the persecution of Jews in pogroms

17. _____ Which was true of Lenin?
a. He believed that capitalism was a necessary institution.
b. He believed that force was necessary to abolish capitalism.
c. He believed in nonviolent revolutions.
d. He believed that many social classes benefited society.

Tests for History and Life   © Scott, Foresman and Company   **167**

Alternate Chapter Test, pp. 167–168

601c

Other Optional Ancillaries

WORKBOOK

WORKSHEET
Chapter 32, Section 1
The Collapse of Tsarist Rule

In this worksheet you will review events leading to collapse of the tsarist regime in Russia.

Part A
Write the letter of the term from the box next to its definition or identifying phrase.

1. _____ council of workers
2. _____ national parliament created by the constitution of 1905
3. _____ massacre of unarmed workers by the tsar's troops in 1905
4. _____ class of educated people in Russia
5. _____ policy requiring that non-Russians use Russian language in public life
6. _____ mob attack against Jewish enclaves in Russia
7. _____ humiliating defeat for Russian imperialism
8. _____ radical Marxist group formed by Vladimir Ilyich Lenin

a. intelligentsia
b. Bolshevik party
c. soviet
d. pogrom
e. "Bloody Sunday"
f. "russification"
g. Duma
h. Russo-Japanese War

Part B
Write C next to each phrase that correctly completes the unfinished sentences. (Each incomplete sentence may have more than one correct ending.)

1. Actions of the last two tsars included
_____ tightening of censorship.
_____ religious persecution.
_____ banning of all political parties.
_____ brutal suppression of striking workers.
_____ land reform.

2. Alexander Kerensky's Provisional Government failed to win popular support because it
_____ supported the peasants in their seizure of estates.
_____ refused to carry out land reforms.
_____ continued Russian involvement in World War I.
_____ could not restore order in face of chaotic conditions.
_____ delayed free elections.

3. The constitution established in 1905
_____ set up the soviets.
_____ set up trade unions.
_____ legalized political parties.
_____ enabled reforms to take place over the tsar's objections.
_____ established the Duma.

4. Alexander II's refusal to establish a national assembly led
_____ some people to conclude that the tsarist government must be overthrown.
_____ some intelligentsia to embrace radicalism.
_____ to the establishment of legal political parties.
_____ to the formation of secret terrorist organizations.

128   Worksheets for History and Life   © Scott, Foresman and Company

Section 1 Worksheet, p. 128

WORKSHEET
Chapter 32, Section 2
The Bolshevik Revolution

In this worksheet you will review the process by which the Bolsheviks took control of Russia.

Part A
Write T if the statement if true and F if its is false. On the lines below, rewrite each false statement to make it true.

1. _____ In order to transform Russia into a communist society, all private property was taken over by the state.
2. _____ Lenin believed that force was necessary to abolish capitalism and establish a classless society.
3. _____ Lenin's establishment of a communist dictatorship helped end the civil war.
4. _____ The Allies sent troops to help overthrow the "Reds" because they wanted Russia to end its war with Germany.
5. _____ Even after World War I, the Allies tried to undermine the communists because they wanted to punish Lenin for his alliance with Germany.
6. _____ The communists finally won the civil war because they had a superior army and because the Russian people resented the Allied intervention.

Part B
Underline the term in parentheses that correctly completes each sentence.

1. After many long years of war, the communist government in 1921 (did/refused to) retreat from war communism.
2. Under the New Economic Policy, the state owned basic industries, and private enterprise in retail trade (was/was not) allowed.
3. Trotsky (supported/did not support) the idea of a socialist world revolution.
4. Stalin believed that the world revolution (would/would not) spread to other countries if the Soviet Union first developed its own socialism.
5. In 1925 Stalin's policy (was/was not) accepted at the 14th Party Congress.

Worksheets for History and Life   © Scott, Foresman and Company   129

Section 2 Worksheet, p. 129

WORKSHEET
Chapter 32, Section 3
The "Stalinization" of the Soviet Union

In this worksheet you will review the "Stalinization" of the Soviet Union.

Part A
Complete the chart with information from Section 3 of your text.

Stalin's Action	Purpose of Action
Collectivization of agriculture	To promote greater efficiency in food production
Forced export of foodstuffs	
Exile of some peasants to barren regions	
Abandonment of motto "to each according to his needs"	
Purges and public trials	

Part B
Describe how "Stalinization" affected each of the following aspects of Soviet life.

1. economic development

2. civil liberties

3. standard of living

4. artistic freedom

130   Worksheets for History and Life   © Scott, Foresman and Company

Section 3 Worksheet, p. 130

WORKSHEET
Chapter 32, Section 4
Soviet Foreign Policy Before 1939

In this worksheet you will review the Soviet Union's relations with other countries.

Part A
Number the events in the order in which they happened.

_____ The Soviet Union is admitted to the League of Nations.
_____ The Soviet Union aids anti-Franco forces in the Spanish Civil War.
_____ Germany and the Soviet Union sign the Treaty of Rapallo.
_____ The Soviets negotiate a non-aggression pact with Germany.
_____ France and England formally recognize the Soviet Union.
_____ The United States formally recognizes the Soviet Union.

Part B
Write the letter of each effect from the box beside its cause.

1. _____ Nazi promotion of anticommunist feeling
2. _____ formation of communist parties in most countries of the world
3. _____ 1922 Soviet-German treaty
4. _____ formation of Popular Front policy
5. _____ Chinese fear of communist control in 1927

a. Chinese rejection of Soviet help to unify China
b. closer ties between two "outcast" nations
c. an association of communist parties called the Comintern
d. Stalin's adoption of collective security policy
e. decreased emphasis on world revolution; increased support to nations struggling against dictatorships

Part C
Agree or disagree with the following statement: Stalin reversed his foreign policy objectives several times during the 1920s and 1930s. Explain your reasoning.

Worksheets for History and Life   © Scott, Foresman and Company   131

Section 4 Worksheet, p. 131

SOURCE READINGS

Source Reading 32A
Source Reading 32B

TEST GENERATOR

40 multiple-choice questions for Chapter 32

OVERHEAD TRANSPARENCIES

Overhead Transparency 63
Overhead Transparency 64

The Soviet Union: The First Communist State

1881–1939

1900	
1903	Lenin forms the Bolshevik party
1917	Tsarist regime collapses
1926	Stalin gains power
1930	
1940	

Dear comrades, soldiers, sailors, and workers! I am happy to greet in your persons the victorious Russian revolution, and greet you as the vanguard of the worldwide proletarian army. . . . Any day now the whole of European capitalism may crash.

The speaker was Lenin, a bald, stocky man, who had led the Russian Bolsheviks for more than ten years. Lenin, who was in exile in Switzerland when revolution broke out in 1917, returned secretly to Russia with the aid of the German High Command. The occasion for Lenin's speech was his arrival in Petrograd, the Russian capital, on April 16, 1917.

The Germans hoped that Lenin and his followers would undermine the Provisional Government of Russia. The Provisional Government had been set up in March 1917, after Tsar II was forced to give up his throne. In fact, German hopes were realized beyond anything they expected when Lenin and his followers seized power in November, 1917, and established the first communist state in history.

Thus, Russia experienced two revolutions in 1917. Together, they are known as the Russian Revolution. The first revolution was the collapse of the tsarist regime in March, 1917, and had nothing to do with the Bolsheviks. The second, or Bolshevik revolution, took place in November, 1917, when Lenin and his supporters overthrew the Provisional Government.

To understand why and how the two revolutions of 1917 occurred, two key questions must be answered. First, what conditions made revolution possible? Second, why did revolution break out in that particular year? The first question deals with long-range causes and the buildup of resentment against the tsarist regime. The second question deals with timing and the impact of World War I.

Once in power the Bolsheviks faced a great dilemma. According

Lenin calls upon workers to liberate the masses "from all slavery and exploitation" at a meeting held after the start of the 1917 Bolshevik revolution.

to Karl Marx, socialist revolutions were supposed to take place first in the most advanced industrial countries of Europe. Russia, however, was still an unindustrialized peasant country. Lenin solved the dilemma by revising Marxism to fit Russian conditions. He declared that a small Marxist party of revolutionaries could seize control in an undeveloped nation and then use the power of the state to industrialize.

The actual economic and social transformation of Russia took place during the regime of Joseph Stalin, Lenin's successor. Stalin used brute force and massive terror to force industrialization and collectivization of agriculture. In the process, he created a totalitarian dictatorship that took a terrible toll in human lives.

By 1939 the Soviet Union had become a major industrial power, with a strength that helped it survive the crisis of World War II. However, Stalin's methods left deep and painful scars that troubled Soviet society long after he was gone.

Reading Preview

In this chapter you will learn how the Russian Revolution led to the rise of the first communist state.

1. The tsarist regime collapsed.

2. Bolsheviks took control of Russia.

3. Stalin created a totalitarian society.

4. The Soviet Union tried to protect its security.

 The tsarist regime collapsed.

Long-range causes of the 1917 revolutions grew out of a dilemma that Russia faced at the end of the 19th century. While nations of western Europe industrialized and developed democratic govern-

1 *Lesson Plan*

Essential Learning Objectives

Students will learn to:

- describe the reasons for discontent in tsarist Russia before the revolution.
- explain the role of World War I in causing the revolution.

603

The Expansion of Russia, 1462–1917

- Before 1462
- 1462–1505
- 1506–1598
- 1599–1689
- 1690–1796
- 1797–1917
- Present-day boundaries

MAP STUDY The Russian Empire expanded in the 19th century. Was the area of expansion greatest east or west of the Caspian Sea?

ments, Russia remained a backward country with an outmoded, autocratic government. The tsars resisted most changes, and the Russian people were left with no effective means to gain reforms.

As discontent among the people grew, so did the threat of mass upheaval. Finally, this upheaval was triggered by a series of crises that snapped the links of loyalty to the tsars.

Discontent spread among peasants, workers, and the intelligentsia.

Russia in the 19th century was unlike any other country in Europe. It was a huge empire that stretched from Germany to the Pacific Ocean, more than twice the size of the United States today. Russia's population in 1900 was 130 million, with less than half of these people being Russians. The others were Byelorussians (White Russians), Ukrainians, and Poles and non-Slavic groups such as Latvians, Lithuanians, Estonians, Finns, Germans, Jews, Armenians, Georgians, Turkic peoples, Mongols, and many others.

Ruling over this vast empire with its different nationalities, languages, and religions were the Romanov tsars. The tsars were absolute autocrats who still believed in the divine right of kings long after that belief had gone out of fashion in western Europe. With an empire created through conquest, the tsars believed that only unlimited power could hold it together.

After 1881 tsarist regimes generally opposed major reforms that would improve conditions for the Russian people. This autocratic policy deepened resentment among the peasants, the workers, and the **intelligentsia**, which was a class of educated people interested in reform.

Peasant discontent. The most urgent need in Russia was for land reform. Much of the Russian population was made up of peasants who were illiterate and poverty-stricken. Until the 1850s most peasants were serfs. Although the serfs were emancipated in 1861, they were not given independent ownership of land. Emancipation therefore failed to create a class of independent farmers with incentive to improve agriculture. Consequently, Russian agriculture at the end of the 19th century was the most unproductive in all of Europe.

Generally, peasants worked on land assigned to them by their village commune, but few had enough land under this system to support their families. Burdened with debt and heavy taxes, many peasants leased extra land from large land-owners or worked for the landowners as laborers at low wages.

When the rural population began to grow rapidly in the late 19th century, competition to lease land intensified, and rents increased. This situation forced millions of peasants deeper into poverty. Because the tsarist regime provided no tax relief and proposed no meaningful land reform, discontent among the peasants became increasingly widespread.

Worker protests. There was also deep discontent among factory workers. Russia's industrial revolution did not begin until the 1890s and, as happened in western Europe, industrialization created a large new social class—the workers. By 1900 there were 3 million of these workers, who suffered low pay, long hours, and bad working conditions and lived in dismal shacks or huge communal barracks.

Unlike workers in western Europe, Russian workers had no legal ways to seek improvement through direct action. Trade unions were banned, and strikes were considered criminal activities. When a wave of strikes broke out in the 1890s to protest worsening conditions, the tsarist police brutally suppressed the protesters.

Since the government refused to grant worker reforms, strikes continued into the early 1900s in spite of police repression. This situation was particularly dangerous because, although workers made up only about 2 percent of the total population, they were concentrated in key cities such as St. Petersburg and Moscow. These cities were the nerve centers of the government, and any major uprising could paralyze the entire political system.

Intelligentsia unrest. Another important dissatisfied group was the intelligentsia. The intelligentsia included both women and men and came from a variety of social groups, such as government officials, nobles, writers, university students,

DAILY LIFE

Good company, music, and warm tea from a steaming samovar were among the simple pleasures of these peasants in the Russian countryside photographed in 1909 (far left). Life showed its darker side to the impoverished peasants in the city (left). A bourgeois woman attempted to stay "the slow death of creatures incessantly hungry" in this photograph from the 1870s.

On January 22, 1905, known as "Bloody Sunday," troops fired on unarmed workers petitioning the tsar. This event sparked the creation of the Duma.

doctors, lawyers, and other professionals. People in this educated class were strongly influenced by western European ideas of democracy. The intelligentsia began to work for basic political reform: a constitutional government instead of an autocracy, the right to express ideas freely without censorship, and the opportunity to participate in political decision making through a representative national assembly. In the 1860s, when Tsar Alexander II refused to establish a national assembly, members of the intelligentsia were bitterly disappointed. Some turned to **radicalism**, advocating extreme change. The radicals concluded that it was impossible to work for reform within the tsarist system and therefore believed that the tsarist government must be completely overthrown.

In the late 1800s, political parties in Russia were illegal. Therefore, many political organizations were formed secretly. Some of these secret organizations launched terrorist campaigns against the government and, in the early 1900s, assassinated hundreds of officials. Other groups were Marxist political parties that looked forward to the collapse of both capitalism and tsarism in Russia. The most radical of the Marxist groups was the Bolshevik party, formed in 1903 by **Vladimir Ilyich Lenin**. At the time, the Bolshevik party was quite small.

Crises and war weakened the tsar's power.

The last two tsars were Alexander III, who ruled from 1881 to 1894, and his son, Nicholas II, who was tsar until 1917. Neither of them made any effort at meaningful reform. In fact, both rulers tried to turn back the clock by ending some of the earlier reforms of Alexander II.

Under the last two tsars, censorship tightened, and religious persecutions increased. Many Jews were either terrorized or killed in mob attacks called pogroms [pō gromz']. Between 1882 and 1914, millions of Jews emigrated from Russia to seek a better life in the United States, Canada, and western Europe. Alexander III and Nicholas II also tried to "russify" non-Russians by forcing them to use the Russian language in schools and local government. The policy of "Russification" embittered many non-Russians such as Poles and Finns.

Meanwhile, Russia continued to play the role of

a Great Power by pushing for territorial expansion. Russian imperialism in East Asia soon brought a clash with Japan. By 1900 Russia dominated Manchuria and was eager to take over Korea, which Japan wanted to control. Thinking that Japan was militarily weak, Russia did not try to avoid war. With mounting unrest at home, one Russian official even welcomed "a little victorious war to stem the tide of revolution."

As you learned in Chapter 30, Japan struck first. In February, 1904, the Japanese fleet attached Port Arthur, a Russian naval base on the Liaotung peninsula. Russia was unprepared for war, and its army and navy suffered humiliating defeats during this conflict. The Russo-Japanese War ended in 1905 with a peace treaty that humiliated Russia.

The war with Japan was unpopular with the Russian people, partly because the war effort prevented much-needed reform at home. During the war, therefore, a revolution broke out, touched off by a violent event later called "Bloody Sunday"— January 22, 1905. On that day in St. Petersburg, a large group of unarmed workers carrying a petition to the tsar was fired upon by the tsar's troops. Several hundred people were killed in the square in front of the tsar's palace.

News of this act aroused fierce anger against the government, and strikes shut down railroads, the telegraph system, and government offices. Councils of workers called **soviets** sprang up in the

ASSESS
1. Who was Nicholas II? (last tsar of Russia)
2. What is a pogrom? (mob attack against Russian Jews)

cities to direct the rebellion. Crowds carried red banners and posters demanding reforms. (Red was the traditional color of revolutionary socialism.)

Shocked and frightened by this mass outburst, Tsar Nicholas II finally granted a constitution to the people in October, 1905. The tsar then called in loyal army troops to crush uprisings throughout the country. Under the constitution, a national parliament, known as the Duma [dü′mə], was set up, and both political parties and trade unions were legalized. It seemed that Russia had at last become a constitutional monarchy.

The Duma, however, had very limited powers. The first two Dumas, which met in 1906 and 1907, were dismissed by the tsar when members asked for reform. The third and fourth Dumas did pass some reforms, but members of these later Dumas actually represented interests of the wealthy more than the interests of peasants and workers.

The modest industrial growth in Russia during these years improved the lives of some workers, and a small middle class gradually developed. A limited land reform program allowed some landless peasants to become independent farmers. Nevertheless, discontent among workers and peasants remained strong because most of them were still poor and living in miserable conditions.

World War I ended the tsarist government.

When World War I broke out in 1914, Russia was forced to enter the war because of commitments to Britain and France but the nation was again unprepared to fight. As the conflict went on, government officials continually mismanaged the war effort, and many top military commanders proved to be incompetent. The Germans inflicted disastrous defeats in battle after battle, and Russian casualties rose by the millions. In the cities, food and fuel supplies ran low, and prices skyrocketed.

Throughout these crises Nicholas II was unable to rally the Russian people either to fight effectively or to produce adequate food and supplies. Instead of allowing the Duma to share in governing, the tsar accused the Duma of undermining his authority. After three years of constant hardship, morale among the Russian people and confidence in the government rapidly declined.

In March, 1917, severe food shortages led to street marches in Petrograd. (The capital, St. Petersburg, had been patriotically renamed Petrograd in 1914 in a wave of anti-German feeling.) The marches soon became riots as police and soldiers fought unruly mobs.

Within a few days, many soldiers, who were mostly young peasants, mutinied and joined the marchers. Soon government officials lost control, and the uprising became a revolution. Tsar Nicholas, at army headquarters near the battlefront, was forced to abdicate (resign) his throne, and tsarist authority collapsed throughout Russia.

The Duma quickly formed a cabinet of middle-class liberals and established a Provisional, or temporary, Government to rule until a national assembly could be elected to write a new constitution. Meanwhile, workers and soldiers in Petrograd formed a soviet, or council, to speak for their interests, as had been done in the 1905 revolution. Soviets also developed in other cities to replace local tsarist governments that had lost power.

The Provisional Government in Petrograd restored civil rights and promised free elections. However, it also continued Russian involvement in

At left is the imperial family. The golden eggs, made by Fabergé, the court jeweler, were Easter gifts from the tsar to his wife and mother.

BACKGROUND Nicholas abdicated on March 15 for himself and his only son, Alexis, in favor of Nicholas's brother, Michael. Michael, in turn, abdicated the following day, in effect, in favor of the Provisional Government.

607

OPTIONAL RETEACHING
Review how World War I helped trigger the revolution, and then write the following terms on the chalkboard: peasants, workers, intelligentsia, radicals, pogroms, Russification, Alexander III, Nicholas II, "Bloody Sunday," Bolshevik party, Vladimir Ilyich Lenin, soviets, the Duma, World War I, food shortages, riots, abdication, Provisional Government, Alexander Kerensky. Have students write the story of events leading to revolution in Russia incorporating as many of these items as possible.

OPTIONAL ENRICHMENT
1. Ask interested students to research Tsar Nicholas II. Why was he ineffectual in preventing the revolution? (average)
2. Pogroms caused many Russian Jews to flee from their country, with hundreds of thousands of them finding refuge in the United States. Encourage students to conduct interviews with Jewish families whose ancestors fled Russia because of pogroms. (challenging)
3. Also for enrichment:

 Source Reading 32A

INDEPENDENT PRACTICE/ HOMEWORK
Assign the Section Review, Activities page 190, or Workbook page 128.

CLOSURE
The tsar's failure to implement needed reforms and the poorly managed war effort led to the Bolshevik Revolution in 1917. The political chaos that followed the revolution left the door wide open for a strong leader who could provide immediate solutions to Russia's many problems.

Answers to Section 1 Review

Identify

Key Terms, People, and Places are defined on pages indicated in parentheses. Also see the Glossary and Biographical Dictionary. intelligentsia (604), radicalism (606), Vladimir Ilyich Lenin (606), soviet (606)

Main Ideas

1. Peasants' living conditions worsened in the late 19th century and the tsar provided no tax relief or land reform. Workers had no legal means to improve their conditions. The intelligentsia wanted constitutional government, freedom of expression, and political participation.

2. repeal of earlier reforms, censorship and religious persecution, Russification of non-Russians, defeat in the Russo-Japanese War, Bloody Sunday in Petrograd, weak Dumas

3. Russian involvement in World War I caused frequent crises, food shortages, and hardships that led to uprisings that turned into revolution.

Critical Thinking

The statement is only partially valid. The causes were very complex. Although lack of peasant and worker reforms fueled the revolution, these reforms probably would not have solved Russia's many problems under outdated tsarist rule.

2 Lesson Plan

Essential Learning Objectives

Students will learn to:

- describe the process by which Lenin seized control of Russia.
- explain shifts in Lenin's revolutionary economic program.

World War I, a decision that cost the new government much support among peasants and workers. The government also delayed free elections and refused to approve general land reform. These actions further weakened support, and peasants began to seize estates on their own and divide the land among themselves. As the Provisional Government failed to gain control, daily life in Russia became chaotic.

In July, 1917, Alexander Kerensky, a moderate socialist, became prime minister of the Provisional Government. Although he tried to restore order, he, too, failed to win the Russian people's support because he refused to stop the war or to carry out land reforms.

Section 1 Review

Identify intelligentsia, radicalism, Vladimir Ilyich Lenin, soviet

Main Ideas

1. Briefly describe the causes of discontent of the Russian peasants, workers, and intelligentsia.
2. Summarize the major events that seriously weakened tsarist rule.
3. What was the final blow that ended the tsarist regime?

Critical Thinking

Assessing Cause and Effect: Consider the following statement: "The main cause of the Russian Revolution was the tsar's refusal to grant reforms to peasants and workers." Is this a valid statement? Support your answer with evidence.

---

2 Bolsheviks took control of Russia.

Dissatisfaction with the policies of Alexander Kerensky's Provisional Government led more and more Russians to look to the Petrograd Soviet for leadership. As the Provisional Government became weaker and the Petrograd Soviet grew stronger, any party that gained control of the Soviet had the potential to topple the Provisional Government and seize control of the country.

BACKGROUND The Bolshevik revolution is also called the October Revolution. It took place in November, but Russia still followed the Julian calendar, which was 13 days behind the Gregorian calendar. In 1918 the Soviet Union switched to the

Lenin led the Bolshevik revolution.

The person who understood the ripe political opportunity in Russia better than anyone else was Lenin, leader of the Bolsheviks, the most radical of the socialist parties. Lenin, whose real family name was Ulyanov, was born in 1870 into a well-educated Russian family. His father was a respected school official, and his mother was the daughter of a doctor. Lenin was a bright and studious child who received high grades in school. Few would have predicted that he would later become one of the most influential revolutionaries of the 1900s.

As a young man, Lenin had planned to be a lawyer, but shortly after he entered the university, the tsarist authorities expelled him. In the eyes of the authorities, young Vladimir Ilyich Ulyanov was a dangerous person because his older brother, Alexander, had been executed for plotting to kill the tsar. Lenin then studied on his own, and, while earning a law degree, began reading the works of Karl Marx.

As you learned in Chapter 28, Marx was a 19th-century socialist philosopher who taught that capitalism would inevitably be overthrown by violent workers' revolutions. Lenin developed a firm belief in Marxism, and became convinced that force was necessary to abolish capitalism and establish a classless society. By the time Lenin was in his twenties, he was a determined revolutionary socialist. Because of his politics, he was forced to spend many years abroad as an exile.

After Lenin's return to Russia in April, 1917, he put all his energies into gaining power for the small Bolshevik party. Beginning in July, 1917, the Bolsheviks won broad support by promising peace to soldiers, land to peasants, and bread to workers. As the Bolsheviks won elections for representatives to the soviets, party strength increased. By the fall of 1917, the Bolsheviks had won control of the important Petrograd and Moscow soviets.

As part of their revolutionary activities, these soviets formed a workers' militia called the Red Guard. On November 6–7, 1917, the Red Guard, joined by pro-Bolshevik soldiers and sailors, seized the central government by force. The revolutionaries captured government buildings in the capital and stormed the Winter Palace, site of the Kerensky Provisional Government. All government min-

Gregorian calendar and now celebrates the October Revolution in November. The chart in Chapter 14 explains the background of various calendars in more detail.

BACKGROUND Kerensky fled to Paris and then moved to the United States in 1940. He remained in America until his death in 1970.

On November 7, 1917, the Red Guard stormed the Winter Palace in Petrograd, ending Kerensky's Provisional Government. This event launched the successful seizure of power by the Bolsheviks.

isters were arrested except Kerensky, who escaped and tried to fight against Lenin. With most of the Provisional Government leaders in prison, Kerensky failed to overcome the revolutionaries and soon fled the country.

After Lenin's successful and daring coup d'état, the Bolsheviks moved quickly to set up a party dictatorship. They also changed the name of the party to **communist party**.

The Communists faced many enemies.

As the undisputed leader of the communist party, Lenin became chief of state with unlimited power. He devoted his life to making Russia communistic by applying Marxist principles to Russian society.

In the early phase of this process, known as "war communism," all private property was taken over by the state. Industries, banks, railroads, and shipping were all placed under government ownership. Landholdings of the Orthodox Church were taken by the state, and **atheism**, which is disbelief in the existence of God, was encouraged.

To increase the food supply, peasants were allowed to farm the land they had seized for themselves. However, when the peasants tried to pre-vent food from being sent to the cities because people there could not pay for it, the Bolsheviks sent soldiers into farm villages to take the grain by force. This action again made the peasants become angry and bitter toward their government.

In 1918 a furious civil war broke out between the Bolsheviks, called the "Reds," and groups opposed to the revolution, called the "Whites." The war began in January, 1918, after Lenin used armed sailors to shut down the first freely elected Constituent Assembly in Russian history. Lenin took this action because the Bolsheviks did not have a majority in the assembly, and he was afraid of losing power.

Lenin wanted to establish a communist dictatorship, but many Russians, from socialists to monarchists, opposed and fought against the dictatorship. These counterrevolutionaries were joined by other nationalities, such as Ukrainians, Poles, Finns, Estonians, Latvians, and Lithuanians, who saw a chance to break away from Russian rule.

The civil war, which soon spread to almost every part of Russia, continued until 1920. Conditions created by this war were worse for Russia than those of World War I. Famine and disease killed thousands, and total casualties were in the

1 FOCUS AND MOTIVATE

Explain to students that Lenin, the leader of the communist revolution in Russia, accomplished the revolution with a Bolshevik party that, at the time of the revolution in 1917, numbered less than 1 percent of the Russian population.

2 TEACH

- Review Lenin's case against capitalism. As a follower of Karl Marx, Lenin believed that private ownership of business produced a greediness that would forever make workers the wage slaves of the owners. As students know from their study of the Industrial Revolution, there was reason for this kind of pessimism.

- Review the role of World War I in bringing on the Russian Revolution. Tell students that Lenin gained followers by convincing them that capitalist lust for profits had fueled the war.

- Remind students that the Russian Revolution was really two revolutions. Review the steps by which the Bolsheviks seized power in 1917.

- Discuss the Russian civil war. Have students answer these questions: Who was fighting against whom? What role did foreign nations play? Who won? Why?

GUIDED PRACTICE

Ask students to compare the communist program that Lenin put in place in 1918 (total takeover by the government of private property, seizure of church property, forced requisitioning of grain from the peasants) with the New Economic Policy (NEP) he introduced in 1921. Students should discover that Lenin took a small step back toward capitalism in 1921.

millions. Both sides committed terrible atrocities. Among the casualties were the former Tsar Nicholas II, his wife, and their five children. The entire family was shot by the Bolsheviks in 1918 at Ekaterinburg, a town along the route of the Trans-Siberian Railroad.

Meanwhile, Lenin led Russia out of World War I by signing a separate peace treaty with Germany—the treaty of Brest-Litovsk—in March, 1918. Britain and France, still desperately fighting to defeat Germany, wanted to bring Russia back into the war. Thus, the Allies sent troops and supplies to Russia to help the opposition overthrow Lenin. The

Leon Trotsky organized and led the Red Army during the Russian civil war. He issued the poster below warning Red troops to resist the Poles, French, and other anti-Soviet foreigners. The poster declares: "The Red Army will do its work, and nothing will stop it!"

БУДЬ НА СТРАЖЕ!

BACKGROUND After Nicholas's abdication, the royal family was eventually sent by the Bolsheviks to Ekaterinburg, a small town east of the Urals on the Trans-Siberian Railroad. During the Civil War, as troops opposing the Bolsheviks advanced

United States also sent troops to Russia but took no active part in the fighting. Japan, seeking to dominate eastern Siberia, occupied Vladivostok and other Pacific ports.

The Allies continued to take part in the Russian civil war even after an armistice with Germany ended World War I in November, 1918. Fearing that communism would spread to the rest of Europe, the Allies tried to destroy Lenin's regime. Faced with civil war and Allied intervention, the communist government seemed likely to fall.

Yet the communists finally defeated all their enemies. The opposition armies, widely scattered and uncoordinated, were unable to organize an effective military strategy. They were also unable to win over many Russian peasants because of the pro-landlord policy of the opposition generals. The Bolsheviks, on the other hand, had built up a superior army under **Leon Trotsky**, the Commissar for War. In addition, Allied intervention aroused Russian nationalism and drew the people into a more united front against the counterrevolutionaries.

All of these factors helped bring victory to the Bolsheviks, and by late 1920 communist rule in Russia was secure against its enemies. Still, the communist regime enjoyed no real popularity.

Marxist principles were modified.

To ease the strain of long years of war, the government in 1921 retreated from its policy of war communism and introduced instead the New Economic Policy (NEP). Under this program, the state still owned basic industries, but private enterprise in retail trade and small business was allowed. "Nepmen" (as small business people were called) did well under the new policy. The peasants were also more satisfied, because, except for a tax on surplus grain, they were free to grow and sell their produce as they wished.

Under Lenin the communists laid the base for a powerful dictatorship by building a strong, well-organized party. Communist leaders ensured that the communist party controlled the government and the economy and used force and terror to put down all enemies. The communists taught the ideas of Marx and Lenin to the people, and many Russians became workers for the state.

along the railway, it appeared that the family might be freed. Thus on July 16, the local Bolsheviks shot the family and threw their bodies down a mine shaft.

From the Archives

The First Soviet Constitution

The Russian Revolution transformed the old Russian Empire of the tsars into the Union of the Soviet Socialist Republics. Initially four republics joined in a treaty creating the Soviet Union. Later, in 1922, the First Congress of Soviets issued a declaration that, together with the treaty, served as the first constitution of the Soviet Union. A portion of the declaration explains the reasons for the creation of a federal union of the separate republics.

[The] war years have left their mark. The ruined fields, shut-down factories, destroyed productive forces, and exhausted economic resources inherited from the war render insufficient separate efforts by individual Republics to build the economy. It has proved impossible to restore the national economy while the Republics exist separately.

On the other hand, the instability of the international situation and the threat of new attacks necessitate the creation of a united front of the Soviet Republics in the face of the capitalist encirclement.

Finally, the very structure of Soviet power, which is international by its class nature, prompts the masses of working people of the Soviet Republics to take the road of uniting in one socialist family.

All these circumstances make it imperative for the Soviet Republics to unite in a federal state that is capable of ensuring both the security of its frontiers and economic advance on the home front, and the free national development of the peoples.

In 1922 the communist party created the Union of Soviet Socialist Republics (commonly called the **Soviet Union**) to take the place of the old Russian Empire. The Soviet Union then consisted of four republics, but after World War II it grew to include 15 republics.

FROM THE ARCHIVES The Russian text of the declaration is translated into English in *USSR: Sixty Years of Union, 1922–1982* (Moscow: Progress Publishers, 1982), p. 177 ff. What reasons made it necessary for the soviet republics to unite?

BACKGROUND Lenin was buried in a special mausoleum in Red Square, next to the Kremlin wall. It is a place of great reverence in Soviet society today, visited by many each year.

Stalin defeats Trotsky.

The death of Lenin in 1924 brought on a bitter fight for power between two strong communist leaders, Leon Trotsky and **Joseph Stalin**. Trotsky was a brilliant writer and speaker and the organizer of the Red Army. He was as well known as Lenin and was expected to become the new party leader. Joseph Stalin, whose real name was Joseph Djugashvili, was originally from Georgia, a region in the Caucasus Mountains. Stalin was not as well known as Trotsky, but he was a shrewd politician who used his post as party secretary to place supporters in key jobs.

The feelings of the times were on Stalin's side. The socialist world revolution that Trotsky supported was not occurring, and the idea had lost favor with Soviet leaders. Stalin, on the other hand, believed that the Soviet Union should develop itself as a "workers' paradise." Only after that goal was achieved, Stalin believed, could the world revolution spread to other countries.

In 1925 Stalin's policy was accepted at the 14th Party Congress, and by 1926 he was in control. Trotsky was dismissed from the communist party and exiled. In 1940 he was assassinated in Mexico by an agent of Stalin.

Section 2 Review

Identify communist party, atheism, Leon Trotsky, Soviet Union, Joseph Stalin

Main Ideas

1. Describe the major events that occurred in the Bolshevik revolution.
2. Who were the communists' main enemies inside and outside of Russia?
3. How did the Bolshevik government modify Marxist doctrine in 1921?
4. How did Stalin defeat Trotsky and become Lenin's successor?

Critical Thinking

Making Assumptions: When Stalin gained power in 1926, he argued that Russia should look inward and make itself a "worker's paradise" before leading a world revolution. Trotsky argued that Russia should look outward and create revolutions elsewhere in the world. What assumptions lay behind the thinking of these two leaders?

(1. Economic devastation, 2. Threat of attack, 3. International nature of communism) How does the last reason contain seeds for the Cold War? (suggests that other nations adopting communism join the USSR as an international force)

A MYSTERY IN HISTORY

In addressing the question of Lenin's loyalty to the revolution several incidents in his early life should be considered. When he was 17, his older brother Alexander was caught participating in a plot to kill the tsar. Before he was hanged, Alexander declared that his goal was to gain "political freedom" for the Russian people. The next year, when Lenin enrolled in the law school of Kazan University, he was expelled for taking part in a student meeting seeking more freedom for the students. "A quest for freedom" can thus be seen as a constant theme in Lenin's life, even if the means to that end might be open to some questions.

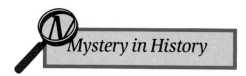

Mystery in History

WAS LENIN A GERMAN AGENT?

Vladimir Ilyich Lenin, creator of the Soviet Communist state, is regarded as the father of his country by people of the Soviet Union and is held in utmost respect. For Soviet citizens, Lenin was and still is a national hero who could do no wrong.

Ever since 1917, however, various people, some of them historians, have charged that Lenin was not the revolutionary leader he appeared to be. He did what he did, they say, only because he was paid by the Germans and followed German orders. This accusation has always been angrily denounced by the Soviet government as an outright lie.

Is there any evidence that Lenin really was a paid German agent? When World War II ended, the archives of the German government were opened to historians. There historians found definite proof that during World War I the German government had secretly sent money to support Lenin and the Bolsheviks, in hopes of undermining the Russian war effort.

Did receiving money from the Germans make Lenin a German agent? Some historians say it did and argue that the Germans not only financed Lenin, but also controlled his actions. Most historians, however, say that receiving financial aid from the Germans is no proof that Lenin carried out German orders.

These skeptics point out that, because the money came to Lenin from secret agents in Sweden and not directly from Germany, Lenin may not even have known its original source. Furthermore, they argue, one must remember that Lenin was a dedicated revolutionary. It made little difference to him where he got the money to support his revolutionary activities. His goal remained the same, and he always made his own decisions.

Although there is no way to be absolutely certain, most historians have come to the conclusion that Lenin was not a German agent. However, history leaves no doubt that German money did help Lenin carry out the most important revolution of the 20th century.

Lenin addresses a May Day rally in Red Square, 1919.

Stalin created a totalitarian society.

By the late 1920s, Stalin was clearly in charge of the communist party. Yet, until the mid-1930s, he was careful to consult others and to act modestly. Although Stalin was not officially the head of the government, in practice he was. Stalin's only title was general secretary of the communist party until 1941, when he became premier in addition to being party secretary.

Stalin developed the Five-Year Plans.

In 1928 the New Economic Policy (NEP) came to an end. Although Russia was still a backward country, the economy had improved. However, the Marxist dream of a classless society had not come true. The communist bureaucracy had replaced the tsarist bureaucracy, and a full range of economic classes still existed. Stalin, who felt that the Soviet Union would have to make drastic changes to catch up to the West economically, explained:

> We were fifty to a hundred years behind the advanced countries. We must make up this lag in ten years. Either we do this or they will crush us.

Thus Stalin instituted a government program called the First **Five-Year Plan**. It had two major goals: rapid industrialization and **collectivization** of agriculture. Collectivization meant requiring farmers to work the land as a group rather than as individual landowners. In theory, such farms would be more efficient because the peasants could share tractors and other farm machinery.

Stalin believed that the two goals could only be met by dictatorial controls because the huge amounts of money needed for new plants and factories would have to be squeezed out of the peasants against their will. Furthermore, the peasants would have to be forced to combine their small plots into large, collective farms. To raise money for industrialization, the peasants would be forced to sell their crops at very low prices to the government, which would then export most of the crops to buy machines for factories. In short, the peasants would have to pay the costs of industrialization. The government again abolished private landholding and other private enterprise.

Of course, most peasants strongly objected to giving up their land, tools, and livestock, and many burned crops and killed animals rather than give them to the government. Stalin crushed this opposition by sending uncooperative peasants to barren regions of the country, where many starved or died from the miserable living conditions. Other peasants were executed or sent to labor camps from which few returned.

In 1932 the government seized nearly all grain in the **Ukraine**—the region north of the Black Sea—and the north Caucasus, causing a devastating famine in those areas. Between 1932 and 1934, about 5 million peasants died from starvation. Despite such brutal methods, the government declared collectivization a success. By 1936 about 90 percent of the peasants belonged to nearly 250,000 collective farms scattered across the nation.

In 1933 the Second Five-Year Plan began but was held up by inefficiency and a shortage of skilled workers. Eventually, the Plan was enforced, and the Third Five-Year Plan went into effect in 1938 but was cut short by World War II. In the short span of 12 years, the Soviet Union had become a major industrial nation.

Soviet Life was "Stalinized."

Under Joseph Stalin, ordinary Russian citizens achieved some gains. The planned economy provided jobs for almost everyone, and factory production increased significantly. Efforts were made to wipe out illiteracy and to enable more people than ever before to receive free tuition and scholarships at universities. State medical care, old-age pensions, and insurance plans were put into effect. Women gained considerable, although not total, equality with men and were encouraged to enter the professions, especially medicine.

These positive results, however, did not hide the steady "Stalinization" of Soviet culture. In the early Stalin years, writers, artists, and scholars were allowed to work freely as long as they were not outspokenly anticommunist.

By the mid-1930s, party leaders decided that intellectuals had a role to play in developing Soviet communism. Thus, historians were required to glorify Russian heroes of the national past, and novelists had to portray all communists as pure

on religion, and the government continued to persecute the Orthodox Church and other religious groups.

613

3 Lesson Plan

Essential Learning Objectives

Students will learn to:
- explain Stalin's rationale for his Five-Year Plans.
- evaluate the Stalin record.

1 FOCUS AND MOTIVATE

This section focuses on the period that Joseph Stalin governed the Soviet Union. Some historians estimate that 20 million people died as a result of Stalin's policies. This is equivalent to all American high-school students today plus the entire population of the city of Chicago.

2 TEACH

- Ask students to describe the goals of the first Five-Year Plan (collectivization and rapid industrialization) and ask why Stalin believed the first necessitated the second. (Greater efficiency on the collective farms would mean more grain to sell abroad and more money to pour into industry.) Is this good logic? Who paid the heaviest price?

- In two columns on the chalkboard headed "Positive" and "Negative," ask the class to use their text to find positive and negative results of Stalin's domestic program from 1924–39. Have a volunteer record the findings on the chalkboard.

GUIDED PRACTICE

Ask groups of students to compare the following: Lenin's NEP and Stalin's Five-Year Plan; Athenian democracy and Stalinist Russia; Tsarist Russia and Stalinist Russia. Have students make notes that they use to discuss their comparisons.

ASSESS

1. What was collectivization? (group farming)
2. Why did Stalin conduct the purges? (to get rid of people he thought undesirable or uncooperative)

OPTIONAL RETEACHING

Write the following eight terms on the board: totalitarianism, Five-Year Plans, industrialization, collectivization, Stalinization, Kremlin, paranoia, and purges. Have students write one or more paragraphs that incorporate these terms in summarizing the Stalin years from 1924–1939.

OPTIONAL ENRICHMENT

1. Ask enterprising students to seek out and interview a Russian émigré, now living in America, who lived under Stalin. (average)
2. Ask an interested student to call or write a historian or journalist with knowledge of Russia to find out how Stalin is treated today in Soviet textbooks. (challenging)

INDEPENDENT PRACTICE/ HOMEWORK

Assign the Section Review, Activities page 192, or Workbook page 130.

CLOSURE

Russia advanced from fifth place in industrial output in 1913 to second place in 1938, behind only the United States. Much of the credit for this must go to Joseph Stalin. However, loss of basic freedoms under his regime was severe, and the cost in human life was horrendous.

Answers to Section 3 Review

Identify

Key Terms, People, and Places are defined on pages indicated in

---

idealists. Composers were forced to write songs and concert pieces that the common people could easily enjoy. These policies, of course, severely limited creativity among artists in all fields and led to general repression of innovative or independent artistic works.

Marxist theory was also changed to fit the needs of the state. The communist motto, "from each according to his ability; to each according to his needs," was dropped. Instead those citizens who obtained special training and skills were rewarded with higher salaries, bonuses, and social prestige because they were more valuable to the state than less skilled citizens.

Stalin became an absolute dictator.

In 1936, when the "Stalin Constitution" was adopted, communists everywhere boasted that the Soviet Union was now the most democratic country in the world. In practice, however, the new constitution was not democratic and did not protect even the most basic individual freedoms. Those who expected some loosening of totalitarianism were completely disappointed.

Eventually, Stalin became overwhelmingly suspicious of many of his old comrades from the revolution. Some historians believe that he suffered from paranoia—a severe form of mental illness. On the basis of false charges of treason, Stalin had hundreds of party leaders arrested by the secret police and tortured for admission of guilt. Stalin then staged mass public trials in Moscow from 1936 to 1938 at which most victims confessed and were executed at once.

The same things happened to countless other Soviet citizens, including army officers, government officials, scientists, writers, artists, and ordinary citizens. No one was immune from Stalin's

---

What's In a Name?

RED SQUARE Red Square was built in the late 1400s next to the eastern wall of the Kremlin, a huge citadel in the center of Moscow. The Russian name of the square is *Krasnaia Ploshchad*. The word *krasnaia* means both "red" and "beautiful" in Russian.

BACKGROUND Under the Stalin Constitution, the Communist party still held all political power, and behind the party, ruling the Soviet Union, was Stalin. No longer willing to be first among equals, Stalin's drive for absolute power could not be

---

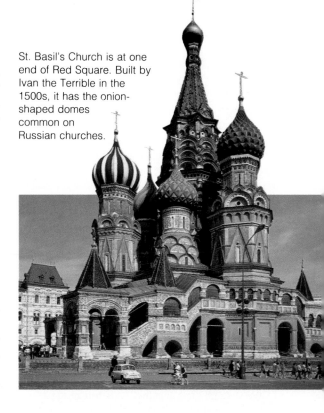

St. Basil's Church is at one end of Red Square. Built by Ivan the Terrible in the 1500s, it has the onion-shaped domes common on Russian churches.

purges, in which he eliminated millions of people he thought were undesirable or uncooperative with his policies. Huge numbers of people were sent to labor camps, never to be heard from again.

In the 1930s Stalin unleashed this reign of terror upon the Russian people. From his office in the **Kremlin**, the citadel overlooking Red Square, Joseph Stalin ruled as an absolute dictator.

Section 3 Review

Identify Five-Year Plan, collectivization, Ukraine, Kremlin

Main Ideas

1. Describe the goals of the Five-Year Plans. How were the Plans paid for?
2. Give examples of the "Stalinization" of Soviet life.
3. How did Stalin rule as an absolute dictator?

Critical Thinking

Recognizing Values: Stalin initiated Five-Year Plans that he claimed could only be successful under a dictatorship. What does this indicate about Stalin's values?

stopped. His picture and his name were constantly put before the public under the title "Great Marxist Leninist."

The Soviet Union, 1940

ARCTIC OCEAN

Bering Sea

Annexed by Soviet Union in 1939 and 1940

0   500   1000 MILES
0   500   1000 KILOMETERS

MAP STUDY   Compare this map to the one on page 604. In general, is the territory controlled by the Soviet Union the same as or different from that controlled by the Russian Empire?

4 The Soviet Union tried to protect its security.

As Stalin's dictatorship became locked in place within the Soviet Union, the Soviet leader looked outward. He took steps to establish the nation's security in the international community.

Other nations feared the spread of revolution.

Relations between the Soviet Union and the West were not friendly in the 1920s and 1930s. Given the earlier armed intervention of Britain, France, Japan, and the United States in their country, Soviet leaders understandably believed that the capitalists wanted to crush the communist nation. In fact, the Western democracies did fear Marxist ideas of worldwide revolution, but no government wanted to wage a war against the large and powerful Soviet Union.

The Soviet Union had not actually given up the Marxist idea of world domination and thus continued to encourage communism abroad. In the early 1920s, communist parties were founded in most countries of the world. These parties became members of the Communist International, called the **Comintern,** an association dominated by the

---

parentheses. Also see the Glossary and Biographical Dictionary.
Five-Year Plan (613), collectivization (613), Ukraine (613), Kremlin (614)

Main Ideas

1. Goals were rapid industrialization and collectivization of agriculture to increase farm production. To fund the plans, Stalin exported farm products confiscated from peasants.

2. All artistic works had to glorify communism and the state and be suitable for common people to enjoy. The communist motto was dropped, and citizens who were perceived to be particularly valuable to the state were more generously rewarded.

3. Stalin stifled individual freedoms and conducted purges that claimed the lives of millions of people.

Critical Thinking

It could be argued that Stalin would do anything he believed necessary to improve the lives of the Soviet people and make the country powerful and secure. Perhaps, however, Stalin valued power more than anything else.

4 Lesson Plan

Essential Learning Objective

Students will learn to:
describe Soviet foreign policies in the 1920s and 1930s.

1 FOCUS AND MOTIVATE

Explain that every nation has both domestic and foreign policies. Explore the meaning of domestic and ask students for examples of current U.S. domestic policies. Discuss foreign policy and also ask for examples.

Have students turn to the Atlas maps of Europe and Asia. Ask them what is usually the first foreign-policy concern of every nation. (national security) What major nations would students expect the Soviet Union to be most concerned about in the 1920s and 1930s? Remind students that Russia had suffered at the hands of the Japanese early in the century, had fought against Germany, and adjoined the world's most populous nation. (China).

GUIDED PRACTICE
Having identified Japan, Germany, and China as primary national security concerns, ask students to write a brief summary of Soviet foreign policy in the 1930s.

ASSESS
What was the Comintern? (the Communist International association)

OPTIONAL RETEACHING
Students may be assigned Activities reteaching page 194.

OPTIONAL ENRICHMENT
Students may be assigned Activities enrichment page 195, or:

 Overhead Transparency 64

INDEPENDENT PRACTICE/ HOMEWORK
Assign the Section Review, the Chapter Review items, Activities page 193, or Workbook page 131.

CLOSURE
After the ravages of Napoleon and the suffering of World War I, national security was a primary goal for Soviet leaders. Regrettably for the Russian people, the worst was yet to come.

Soviet Union. Although Stalin still favored building socialism in his own country, he used the Comintern as a worldwide propaganda tool.

The Soviet Union tried to win friends.

During the 1920s Germany was the only western European nation friendly to the Soviet Union. Both countries were outcasts—Germany because it was a defeated power in World War I, the Soviet Union because it was a communist state formed out of revolution. Thus in 1922 the two outcast nations signed the Treaty of Rapallo in which Germany formally recognized the Soviet Union and, in return, received full trading rights with the Soviets.

That same year a secret military agreement between the two countries was signed. Under this agreement German officers would help train the Red Army and, in exchange, Soviet factories would be used by the Germans to develop new weapons. This arrangement was a direct violation of the Versailles Treaty, signed at the end of World War I, which prohibited German rearmament.

Eventually, in spite of fears of communist revolution, most of the major powers set up diplomatic relations with the Soviet Union. Britain and France established diplomatic relations in 1924, and the United States followed suit in 1933. These actions created tentative ties between the West and the Soviets that would become stronger as World War II approached. Looking after its own best interests, the Soviet Union encouraged positive diplomatic relations with the West.

The Soviets also tried to gain a foothold in East Asia by supporting the Chinese Nationalist party in its effort to unify China. However, in 1927 the Chinese, afraid of communist control, rejected Soviet help. This rejection dealt a sharp blow to Stalin's aim of revolutionizing China.

Stalin failed to get collective security.

The 1930s saw a change in Soviet foreign policy. By 1934 the "Rapallo spirit" from the treaty with Germany was dead, and Hitler, now in command in Germany, actively promoted hatred of communism and of the Soviet Union. Japanese plans for conquest on the Asian mainland also worried the Soviet Union.

Faced with these dangers, Stalin felt that he had

no choice but to seek the good will of the Western democracies. Consequently, he advocated a foreign policy of **collective security**. This policy was aimed at uniting the major democratic powers such as the United States, Britain, France, and China against the aggressions of Germany, Japan, and, later, Italy.

In 1934 the Soviet Union was admitted to the League of Nations. At the same time, the Comintern slowed its efforts to incite world revolution. Stalin ordered communists in other countries to join with capitalists in the struggle against dictators such as Hitler in Germany and, later, Franco in Spain.

These orders were part of a so-called Popular Front policy, which was successful in several countries during the 1930s. For example, the Soviet Union sent military advisers and supplies to China in its fight against Japan during the 1930s. The Soviets also aided anti-Franco forces in the Spanish Civil War, which broke out in 1936.

Britain and France, however, remained distrustful of Stalin and did not become strong allies of the Soviet Union. Both Britain and France tried to appease Hitler and wanted to take no action with the Soviet Union that might antagonize the German leader. By the end of the 1930s, Stalin was forced to change his foreign policy and concede the failure of collective security. One result of this failure, which would have serious future consequences, was a nonaggression pact between the Soviet Union and Germany signed in 1939.

Section 4 Review

Identify Comintern, collective security

Main Ideas

1. What was Soviet foreign policy in the 1920s?
2. How did Stalin attempt to win friends among the major powers?
3. What was the outcome of Stalin's collective security policy?

Critical Thinking

Predicting Effects: What do you think might have happened if Britain, France, and the Soviet Union had signed a firm agreement to resist German aggression in the 1930s when it first happened?

The Ballets Russes

Against a backdrop of political turmoil in early 20th-century Russia, there blossomed a cultural and artistic movement of unusual vigor. The most prominent and energetic leader of this movement was an aristocratic intellectual named Sergei Diaghilev [syir gä′ dyä′gə ləf]. Under Diagiliev, the movement reached its highest expression in the form of a dance company, the Ballets Russes [ba lä rüs].

Although not an artist himself, Diaghilev had an enormous appreciation for all the arts and a tremendous talent for organizing. He hoped to dazzle Europe with the vitality of Russian art by combining painting, music, drama, and dancing

in one medium: ballet. In forming his dance company, Diaghilev brought together Russia's most original composers, musicians, painters, set and costume designers, choreographers (designers of dance movements), and dancers.

Even with the combined efforts of Russia's most lauded stars, the success of the Ballets Russes was not at all ensured. Although well respected in Russia, ballet was not held in high regard elsewhere in Europe. In fact, the Parisians would not allow Diaghilev to stage his ballets in the regal music hall, the Opéra. He had to rebuild a small theater to hold his "dancing performances."

However, on opening night the Ballets Russes melted all skepticism. Paris was enthralled by the sets, transported by the music, and dazzled by the dancing. The Russians not only raised ballet to high art in the eyes of Europe, they also gave new meaning to the word "beauty." Their fusion of the Russian arts revealed the essence of all art and brought a modern era of painting, music, and dance into the limelight.

A Russian maiden transforms herself into a beautiful bird to escape an evil sorcerer in The Firebird, *a ballet by Igor Stravinsky. Léon Bakst designed her costume (top left). Dancers Anna Pavlova and Vaslav Nijinsky (left) were celebrated for their extraordinary virtuosity.*

617

CHAPTER 32 REVIEW

Section Summaries

Section 1
The tsarist regime collapsed.
Russia in the late 19th century was a vast but undeveloped empire ruled by a tsarist autocracy. After 1881 the tsars generally opposed all reform, and, as a result, discontent became widespread among peasants, workers, and the intelligentsia. In 1917 the tsarist government collapsed, and a Provisional Government was set up.

Section 2
Bolsheviks took control of Russia.
The Provisional Government lost support and by November, 1917, Lenin and the Bolsheviks seized power. After strictly enforcing Marxist policy during the war years, Lenin, in 1921, permitted a less restrictive New Economic Policy (NEP), to improve the economy. The Soviet Union was established in 1922. Stalin defeated Trotsky, and in 1926 he gained control of the Soviet government.

Section 3
Stalin created a totalitarian society.
To rapidly modernize the Soviet Union, Stalin set up three Five-Year Plans for industrialization and collectivization of agriculture. Millions who protested Stalin's policies were eliminated by execution or exile to labor camps. Stalin assumed absolute dictatorial control by eliminating indivdual freedom and by purging political opposition.

Section 4
The Soviet union tried to protect its security.
In the 1930s the Soviet Union took a more active role in world affairs. The Soviets gained diplomatic recognition from some Western countries and attempted a policy of collective security to combat Hitler and other aggressors. That policy failed, and in 1939 Stalin signed a nonaggression pact with Hitler.

Test Yourself

Key Terms, People, and Places
Identify the significance of each of the following:

Section 1
a. intelligentsia   c. Vladimir Ilyich Lenin
b. radicalism   d. soviet

Section 2
a. communist party   d. Soviet Union
b. atheism   e. Joseph Stalin
c. Leon Trotsky

Section 3
a. Five-Year Plan   c. Ukraine
b. collectivization   d. Kremlin

Section 4
a. Comintern   b. collective security

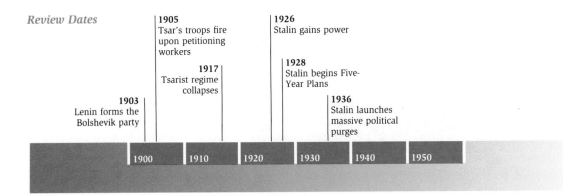

Review Dates

1903
Lenin forms the Bolshevik party

1905
Tsar's troops fire upon petitioning workers

1917
Tsarist regime collapses

1926
Stalin gains power

1928
Stalin begins Five-Year Plans

1936
Stalin launches massive political purges

| 1900 | 1910 | 1920 | 1930 | 1940 | 1950 |

Main Ideas

Section 1
1. What were the major grievances of peasants, workers, and the intelligentsia in Russia?
2. What major events and crises led to the weakening of tsarist rule?
3. What situation triggered the end of the tsarist regime?

Section 2
1. What sequence of events led to the Bolshevik coup d'état in 1917?
2. What enemies did the communists face inside and outside of Russia?
3. How was strict Marxist doctrine changed by the Bolsheviks in 1921?
4. How did Stalin defeat Trotsky and gain power?

Section 3
1. What were the goals of the Five-Year Plans? How were these plans financed?
2. Briefly describe Soviet life under "Stalinization."
3. What were the effects of Stalin's dictatorship?

Section 4
1. Describe the main elements of Soviet foreign policy in the 1920s.
2. Give examples of Stalin's efforts to win support among the major powers.
3. Why did Stalin's collective security policy fail?

Critical Thinking
1. **Predicting Effects**   What do you think might have happened to Russia if Lenin and the Bolsheviks had not seized power in 1917?
2. **Making Hypotheses**   If you were a writer or composer living in the Soviet Union under Stalin, how might you feel about the policies of the communist government?

Chapter Skills and Activities

Practicing Study and Research Skills

Identifying Primary and Secondary Sources
As you learned in the Chapter 19 Review, historical information falls into two basic categories, primary and secondary sources.

1. Identify each of the following as a primary or secondary source:
a. speech by Lenin
b. Stalin's 1936 constitution
c. a history of the Bolshevik revolution published in 1953
d. a copy of the New Economic Policy rules and regulations
e. a poem about the Russian civil war by a writer born in 1938
f. a textbook published in the Soviet Union
g. a biography of Leon Trotsky written by an American historian

2. Some of the most valuable modern historical sources are movies and other non-print materials. List some of these non-print sources, either primary or secondary, that are now common in everyday life.

Linking Past and Present
In the late 1980s, Mikhail Gorbachev, leader of the Soviet Union, initiated a policy of liberalization called *perestroika*. This policy attempted to give more economic and political power to local groups in Soviet society. For example, *perestroika* gave more decision-making power to Soviet citizens who ran local governments, factories, and collective farms. A priority of the new policy was increase in production of consumer goods.

Look in newspapers and magazines from the late 1980s to find out more about *perestroika* in Soviet political, economic, and social life. Make a chart comparing Gorbachev's policies in those areas with those of Stalin in the 1930s.

Learning History through Maps
Refer to the map of the Soviet Union on page 615 and answer the following questions:
1. How does the map help explain why the Soviet Union was concerned about Japanese aggression in the 1930s?
2. Use the map to explain why 14 of the republics are often referred to geographically and politically as "satellite" republics?
3. What areas were annexed by the Soviet Union in 1939 and 1940?

CRITICAL THINKING QUESTION LEVEL 1. average: 2. easy

Chapter 33 Nationalism, Revolution, and Dictatorship

OVERVIEW

This chapter covers the rise of nationalism in China, India, and the Middle East and of fascist dictatorships in Italy, Germany, and Japan.

PLANNING CHART

Section	Text Pages	Key Concept	Suggested Teaching Time
1 Chinese nationalists founded a republic.	621–623	A resentment of foreign influences and the corrupt Manchu dynasty led to the establishment of a republic and then to the rivalry between Chiang Kai-shek and Mao Zedong.	One day **Less time?** Assign Sections 1 and 2 to be read and discussed together.
2 Nationalists in India demanded independence.	624–625	Gandhi used civil disobedience and nonviolence to fight for India's freedom from Britain.	One day **More time?** Use the One-Day Play, *The Trial of Gandhi.*
3 Nationalists in the Middle East created new regimes.	625–628	Nationalist movements among Arabs, Turks, Iranians, and Jews tried to gain greater political independence.	One day **More time?** Use *Overhead Transparency 65* or *Source Reading 33A.*
4 Extreme nationalists in Europe and Japan established dictatorships.	628–632	Political and economic turmoil enabled fascist dictators to rise to power in Italy, Germany, and Japan.	Two days **More time?** Use *Overhead Transparency 66* or *Source Reading 33B.*

ANCILLARIES

Materials that may be used with this chapter to reinforce, reteach, enrich, and assess learning are pictured on the following pages.

Teacher's Resource File

ACTIVITIES

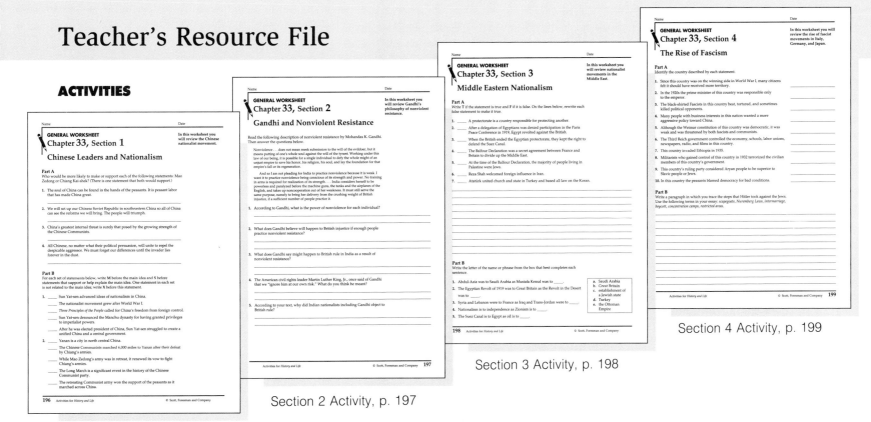

Section 1 Activity, p. 196

Section 2 Activity, p. 197

Section 3 Activity, p. 198

Section 4 Activity, p. 199

Chapter 33 Reteaching, p. 200

Chapter 33 Enrichment, p. 201

619b

Teacher's Resource File

GEOGRAPHY SKILLS

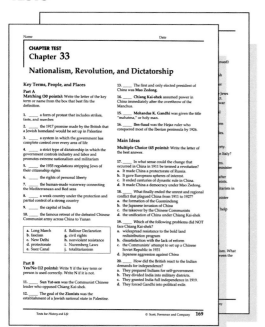

Nationalism, Revolution, and Dictatorship

Part A
Locate and label the following on Outline Map 33. Refer to the text map on page 627 and the Atlas maps on pages 792, 793, and 796.

Continents	Water	Countries	Cities
Europe	Suez Canal	Italy	Istanbul
Asia	Red Sea	Turkey	Rome
Africa	Mediterranean Sea	Germany	Ankara
	Black Sea	Egypt	Bonn
	Aegean Sea	England	London
		Ethiopia	

Part B
List the following in the correct chronological order in the blanks below. Refer to Chapter 33 in your text.

The Turkish Republic is formed
British soldiers fire on unarmed demonstrators in Amritsar
Chinese revolutionaries overthrow government
Mussolini attacks Ethiopia
Hitler becomes Führer of Germany
Chiang Kai-shek takes Beijing
Military leaders gain control in Japan
Palestine becomes mandate of Britain

1. _____
2. _____
3. _____
4. _____
5. _____
6. _____
7. _____
8. _____

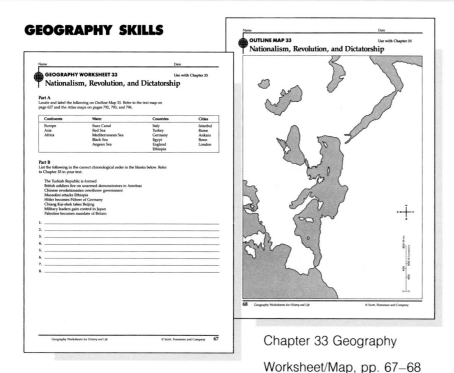

Nationalism, Revolution, and Dictatorship

Chapter 33 Geography
Worksheet/Map, pp. 67–68

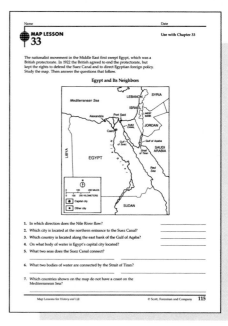

The nationalist movement in the Middle East first swept Egypt, which was a British protectorate. In 1922 the British agreed to end the protectorate, but kept the rights to defend the Suez Canal and to direct Egyptian foreign policy. Study the map. Then answer the questions that follow.

Egypt and Its Neighbors

1. In which direction does the Nile River flow? _____
2. Which city is located at the northern entrance to the Suez Canal? _____
3. Which country is located along the east bank of the Gulf of Aqaba? _____
4. On what body of water is Egypt's capital city located? _____
5. What two seas does the Suez Canal connect? _____
6. What two bodies of water are connected by the Strait of Tiran? _____
7. Which countries shown on the map do not have a coast on the Mediterranean Sea? _____

Chapter 33 Map Lesson, p. 115

TESTS

Nationalism, Revolution, and Dictatorship

Key Terms, People, and Places
Part A
Matching (30 points): Write the letter of the key term or name from the box that best fits the definition.

1. _____ a form of protest that includes strikes, fasts, and marches
2. _____ the 1917 promise made by the British that a Jewish homeland would be set up in Palestine
3. _____ a system in which the government has complete control over every area of life
4. _____ a strict type of dictatorship in which the government controls industry and labor and promotes extreme nationalism and militarism
5. _____ the 1935 regulations stripping Jews of their citizenship rights
6. _____ the rights of personal liberty
7. _____ the human-made waterway connecting the Mediterranean and Red seas
8. _____ a weak country under the protection and partial control of a strong country
9. _____ the capital of India
10. _____ the famous retreat of the defeated Chinese Communist army across China to Yunan

a. Long March	f. Balfour Declaration
b. fascism	g. civil rights
c. New Delhi	h. nonviolent resistance
d. protectorate	i. Nuremberg Laws
e. Suez Canal	j. totalitarianism

Part B
Yes/No (12 points): Write Y if the key term or person is used correctly. Write N if it is not.

11. _____ **Sun Yat-sen** was the Communist Chinese leader who opposed Chiang Kai-shek.
12. _____ The goal of the **Zionists** was the establishment of a Jewish national state in Palestine.

13. _____ The first and only elected president of China was **Mao Zedong**.
14. _____ **Chiang Kai-shek** assumed power in China immediately after the overthrow of the Manchus.
15. _____ **Mohandas K. Gandhi** was given the title "mahatma," or holy man.
16. _____ **Ibn-Saud** was the Hejaz ruler who conquered most of the Iberian peninsula by 1926.

Main Ideas
Multiple Choice (45 points): Write the letter of the best answer.

17. _____ In what sense could the change that occurred in China in 1911 be termed a revolution?
a. It made China a protectorate of Russia.
b. It gave Europeans spheres of interest.
c. It ended centuries of dynastic rule in China.
d. It made China a democracy under Mao Zedong.

18. _____ What finally ended the unrest and regional conflict that plagued China from 1911 to 1927?
a. the formation of the Guomindang
b. the Japanese invasion of China
c. the takeover by the Chinese Communists
d. the unification of China under Chiang Kai-shek

19. _____ Which of the following problems did NOT face Chiang Kai-shek?
a. widespread resistance to the bold land redistribution program
b. dissatisfaction with the lack of reform
c. the Communists' attempt to set up a Chinese Soviet Republic in 1931
d. Japanese aggression against China

20. _____ How did the British react to the Indian demands for independence?
a. They prepared Indians for self-government.
b. They divided India into military districts.
c. They granted India full independence in 1919.
d. They forced Gandhi into political exile.

Chapter Test, pp. 169–170

Nationalism, Revolution, and Dictatorship

Key Terms, People, and Places
Part A
Yes/No (30 points): Write Y if the key term or name is used correctly. Write N if it is not.

1. _____ **Nonviolent resistance** is a form of protest which includes strikes, fasts, and marches.
2. _____ The **Balfour Declaration** was a British promise to set up a Jewish homeland in Palestine.
3. _____ Under **totalitarianism** the federal government cannot interfere with the local government.
4. _____ **Fascism** is a type of dictatorship that places strict government rules on the people.
5. _____ The **Nuremberg Laws** gave citizenship rights to Jews in 1935.
6. _____ **Civil rights** are the rights of personal liberty.
7. _____ The **Suez Canal** is the human-made waterway that connects the Atlantic and Pacific.
8. _____ A **protectorate** is a country under the partial control of a stronger country.
9. _____ **New Delhi** is the capital of Turkey.
10. _____ The **Long March** was the retreat of the Chinese Communist army across China to Yunan.

Part B
Multiple Choice (12 points): Write the letter of the best answer.

11. _____ Who organized the Nationalist People's party and later was elected president of China?
a. Sun Yat-sen   b. Mao Zedong
c. Ibn-Saud

12. _____ Whose goal was it to establish a Jewish national state in Palestine?
a. the nationalists   b. the Nazis
c. the Zionists

13. _____ Who was the leader of the Chinese Communists and the Long March?
a. Sun Yat-sen   b. Mao Zedong
c. Ibn-Saud

14. _____ Who united China and formed a government recognized by the Western powers?
a. Sun Yat-sen   b. Mao Zedong
c. Chiang Kai-shek

15. _____ Who was given the title "mahatma," or holy man, by his followers?
a. Mustafa Kemal   b. Reza Shah Pahlavi
c. Mohandas K. Gandhi

16. _____ Who was the Hejaz ruler who conquered most of the Arabian peninsula by 1926?
a. Kemal Atatürk   b. Ibn-Saud
c. Reza Shah Pahlavi

Main Ideas
Completion (45 points): Write the letter of the best ending to the statement.

17. _____ The change that occurred in China in 1911 is called a revolution because
a. it made China a protectorate of Russia.
b. it gave Europeans spheres of interest.
c. it ended centuries of dynastic rule in China.
d. it made China a democracy under Mao Zedong.

18. _____ The unrest and regional conflict that plagued China from 1911 to 1927 was ended by
a. the formation of the Guomindang.
b. the Japanese invasion of China.
c. the takeover by the Chinese Communists.
d. the unification of China under Chiang Kai-shek.

19. _____ One problem that Chiang Kai-shek's government did NOT face was
a. widespread resistance to the bold land redistribution program.
b. dissatisfaction with the lack of reform.
c. the Communists' attempt to set up a Chinese Soviet Republic.
d. Japanese aggression against China.

20. _____ The British reacted to the Indian demands for independence by
a. preparing Indian leaders for self-government.
b. dividing India into military districts.
c. granting India full independence in 1919.
d. forcing Gandhi into political exile.

Alternate Chapter Test, pp. 171–172

ONE-DAY PLAYS

The Trial of Gandhi

Other Optional Ancillaries

WORKBOOK

WORKSHEET
Chapter 33, Section 1

In this worksheet you will review the nationalist movement in China.

Chinese Nationalism

Part A
Write the letter of each term or name from the box next to its identifying phrase.

1. _____ people who share a common history, language, and culture
2. _____ the desire for national independence and a strong national government
3. _____ special political and economic privileges granted to European nations in China
4. _____ the author of *Three Principles of the People*, which called for China's freedom from foreign control
5. _____ the Nationalist party leader who ordered an attack on Chinese Communists
6. _____ the Chinese Communists' 6,000-mile retreat to Yanan after their defeat by the Nationalist army.
7. _____ the Nationalist People's Party
8. _____ the Chinese Communist leader

| a. Chiang Kai-shek | c. Mao Zedong | e. nationalism | g. Guomindang |
| b. Sun Yat-sen | d. spheres of influence | f. national group | h. the Long March |

Part B
Write a brief answer to each of the following questions.

1. If you were Sun Yat-sen in 1910, what would you want most for China?

2. If you were Sun Yat-sen in the 1920s, what would be your greatest hope for your country?

3. If you were Chiang Kai-shek in the 1930s, what changes might you make in response to the common Chinese resentment of foreigners?

4. If you were Mao Zedong in retreat after the Long March, what might be your plans for the future?

5. If you were either a Communist or a Nationalist Chinese in 1937, how might you feel about the newly formed alliance with your political foe?

132 *Worksheets for History and Life* © Scott, Foresman and Company

Section 1 Worksheet, p. 132

WORKSHEET
Chapter 33, Section 2

In this worksheet you will review Gandhi's campaign for independence in India.

Indian Independence Movement

Part A
Complete each statement with the explanations given in your text.

1. Many Indians loyally supported the British war effort during World War I **because**

2. Gandhi opposed the Government of India Act of 1919 **because**

3. The British eventually consented to give India independence **because**

4. During the 1930s the British met with Indian leaders **because**

5. Full independence for India was not granted until 1947 **because**

Part B
During the Amritsar massacre, British soldiers opened fire on unarmed Indian demonstrators assembled in an open space surrounded by brick houses and a high wall. Write an editorial for an Indian newspaper denouncing the massacre but maintaining the principles of nonviolent resistance.

Worksheets for History and Life © Scott, Foresman and Company 133

Section 2 Worksheet, p. 133

WORKSHEET
Chapter 33, Section 3

In this worksheet you will review the Balfour Declaration and other important events promoting nationalism in the Middle East.

Nationalism in the Middle East

Part A
Write the letter of each phrase from the box next to the name of the country it identifies. A country may have more than one identifying phrase

1. _____ Egypt
2. _____ Palestine
3. _____ Turkey
4. _____ Saudi Arabia
5. _____ Iran

| a. country adjacent to the Suez Canal |
| b. Ibn-Saud's kingdom |
| c. Reza Shah Pahlavi's kingdom |
| d. the geographical focus of the Balfour Declaration |
| e. British protectorate that revolted |
| f. former home to 1.4 million Greeks |
| g. location of rich oil reserves |
| h. Kemal Atatürk's republic |
| i. a Muslim but not an Arab land |

Part B
The Balfour Declaration was a letter written in 1917 by the British foreign secretary, Arthur James Balfour, to a leading British Zionist, Lord Rothschild. The wording and intent of the document have been the subject of much debate. Read the following quotation from the Balfour Declaration and answer the questions below.

His Majesty's Government views with favour the establishment in Palestine of a National Home for the Jewish people, and will use their best endeavours to facilitate the achievement of this object, it being clearly understood that nothing shall be done which may prejudice the civil and religious rights of existing non-Jewish communities in Palestine, or the rights and political status enjoyed by Jews in any other country.

1. Where did the British government propose to establish a homeland for Jews? What group of people in the same place does the declaration seek to protect?

2. How might the British goals identified in question 1 be viewed as incompatible?

3. Why has this document been considered so controversial?

134 *Worksheets for History and Life* © Scott, Foresman and Company

Section 3 worksheet, p. 134

WORKSHEET
Chapter 33, Section 4

In this worksheet you will review the establishment of fascist dictatorships in Italy, Germany, and Japan.

Fascist Dictatorships

Part A
For each statement below, write two or three sentences that support or provide details for that statement.

1. The communist and fascist dictatorships that arose after World War I curtailed individual liberties in similar ways.

2. Fear of communism created Italian popular support for the Fascist party.

3. The Third Reich was a totalitarian state.

4. The Nazis systematically eliminated Jews from German national life.

Part B
Number the events in the order in which they happened.

_____ The Italian king invited Mussolini to become prime minister.
_____ A strong military clique gained power in Japan.
_____ The Weimar Republic was established in Germany.
_____ Hitler tried to seize power in Bavaria in the Beer Hall Putsch.
_____ Hitler became chancellor of the Third Reich.
_____ The Nuremberg Laws were passed.
_____ Hitler became Führer of Germany.

Worksheets for History and Life © Scott, Foresman and Company **135**

Section 4 Worksheet, p. 135

SOURCE READINGS

Source Reading 33A
Source Reading 33B

TEST GENERATOR

40 multiple-choice questions for Chapter 33

OVERHEAD TRANSPARENCIES

Overhead Transparency 65
Overhead Transparency 66

Chapter

33

Nationalism, Revolution, and Dictatorship

1911–1939

1900	
1911	Chinese revolutionaries overthrow the Manchu dynasty
1922	Mussolini becomes Italy's prime minister
1933	Hitler becomes Führer of Germany
1940	
1950	

Nationalism, or the desire for national independence and a strong national government, was originally a European idea. When empires were built, however (see Chapter 30), and nations all over the world lost their independence to imperialistic interests, the idea of nationalism spread far beyond Europe.

National groups—those who shared a common history, language, or culture—sought to create smaller, independent states out of the huge empires. By the beginning of the 20th century, a demand for independence was growing among Asians and Africans. In 1907, for example, one of the leaders of the Indian nationalist movement told the people of his country:

> The point is to have the entire control in our hands. I want to have the key of my house, and not merely be a stranger turned out of it. Self-government is our goal. . . .
>
> What the New party wants you to do is realize . . . that your future rests entirely in your own hands. If you mean to be free, you can be free.

A Chinese, African, Arab, or Jewish nationalist could just as easily have spoken those words. Each wanted to be free of outside control, in whatever form. In some areas nationalist revolutions broke out before World War I. In all areas, however, the war made the desire for independence stronger.

World War I also intensified the growth of nationalism in Europe. In its most extreme form, European nationalism expressed itself in the rise of a dictatorial, militaristic movement known as fascism. This movement grew out of the unsettled conditions brought on by World War I. The countries of Europe had poured their resources into the war and came out exhausted. The European countries in which fascist regimes came to power were Italy, Germany, and Spain. On the other side of the world, a similar regime came to power in Japan.

The Nazi party often organized dramatic mass rallies to create enthusiasm and support. Here 45,000 young men stand before their leader, Adolf Hitler.

Reading Preview

This chapter shows the struggle for power and self-rule around the globe in the early 20th century.

1. Chinese nationalists founded a republic.

2. Nationalists in India demanded independence.

3. Nationalists in the Middle East created new regimes.

4. Extreme nationalists in Europe and Japan established dictatorships.

 1 *Chinese nationalists founded a republic.*

As you learned earlier in this text, China was one of the oldest civilizations in Asia. It was never a European colony, but the ruling Manchu dynasty was weak because it rejected Western technology and opposed modernization. As a result, imperialist nations forced the rulers to give them more trading rights and territory. These conditions led to the growth of a nationalist movement.

During the late 1800s, China was forced to give up territory to Japan. At the same time, European

1 *Lesson Plan*

Essential Learning Objective

Students will learn to describe Sun Yat-sen's role in the Chinese revolution of 1911 and the struggle for power between Nationalists and Communists.

1 FOCUS AND MOTIVATE

Have students name three wars that China fought against foreign nations in the mid to late 1800s, explaining how China was exploited. (Opium Wars, the Boxer Rebellion, Sino-Japanese War; was forced to open Chinese ports to trade, legalize opium trade, excuse foreigners from trials by Chinese courts) Have students predict what effects these problems might have on China in the early 1900s.

2 TEACH

- Discuss the conditions that led to the revolution in China in 1911. Have students describe Sun Yat-sen's role in the revolution and his aims and accomplishments.

- Describe the struggle between the Nationalists and the Communists. Then ask students to cite some possible reasons why Western countries recognized Chiang's rather than Mao's government. (Chiang was not a Communist and was tolerant of special foreign trade rights.)

GUIDED PRACTICE

Have students identify three facts about the Long March.

Shortly after the death of the Manchu ruler Ci Xi (left), China became a republic led by Sun Yat-sen (right).

powers were establishing spheres of influence in China that gave them special political and economic privileges.

A revolution took place in China in 1911.

Young Chinese who resented this foreign influence organized secret societies to fight it. Among these nationalists was **Sun Yat-sen** [sŭn′yät′sen′]. Sun studied in Honolulu, Hawaii, for three years and later graduated from a medical college in the British colony of Hong Kong. Like other Chinese nationalists, Sun resented the Manchus for having made humiliating concessions to the imperialist powers. For many years he made plans to overthrow the weak but tyrannical Manchu dynasty.

His revolutionary activities forced him to flee China, so for 16 years he worked among Chinese communities abroad to organize the Guomindang [gwô′min dang′], or Nationalist People's party.

In 1911 Chinese revolutionaries overthrew the government. Sun then returned to China and struggled with regional leaders who did not want to give up their power to a central government. After ten years of conflict, Sun was elected president of China in 1921 and made plans to unify the country. The Western powers would not help Sun because he had criticized them for their imperialistic ambitions in China, so Sun turned to the Soviet Union for help. The Soviets sent him money, arms, and advisers.

Despite all of Sun's efforts, he succeeded in establishing a government only in the south, at Guangzhou (Canton). When Sun died in 1925, powerful regional leaders still controlled the rest of China, including the capital city of Beijing in the north.

However, Sun was a source of inspiration to his followers. Sun's writings became guides for reform. One book, *Three Principles of the People*, became a guide for the Guomindang. It called for nationalism and freedom from foreign control, government by the people and for the people, and economic security for all the Chinese.

Chiang Kai-shek united China under an official government.

Upon Sun's death his place was taken by **Chiang Kai-shek** [chyang′ kī′shek′], a young military officer. In 1926 Chiang led his army northward from Guangzhou toward Beijing—also hoping to unite China. However, Chiang had another concern. He was afraid that the communist wing of the Guomindang was becoming too strong. In 1927 he launched a surprise attack against the Chinese Communists, killing many of them. A small group of Chinese Communists led by **Mao Zedong** [mou′ dzu′dŭng] survived, and from that time on, the Nationalists and the Communists were bitter enemies engaged in a civil war.

In 1928 Chiang succeeded in taking Beijing and uniting China. Chiang's government was then recognized by the Western powers as the official government of China.

The new government faced many social and political problems.

The new government of Chiang Kai-shek had to deal with a number of difficult problems during its rule. One problem was growing dissatisfaction among the Chinese people over lack of reform. A second was an unsuccessful attempt by the Communists in 1931 to set up a Chinese Soviet Republic in southeastern China. A third was Japanese aggression against China in 1931 and a full-scale invasion in 1937.

Although Chiang's government was able to deal with the last two of these problems, they never did effectively solve the problem of the people's unrest. He was forced, however, to change the much-resented policies that had allowed foreign countries to acquire special trading rights and territory from China.

By 1931 the Chinese Communists had established 15 rural bases and had set up a rival government in southern and central China. Three years later, in 1934, Chiang's army forced the Communists to evacuate their bases. In response, Mao gathered his 90,000 followers and led these Chinese Communists on the **Long March**—a retreat from the battle that lasted for more than a year. They marched 6,000 miles (almost as far as from New York to California and back again) to Yanan, in north central China. Only half of those who started out survived the Long March, but the remaining Communists won the support of the peasants in Yanan and continued to fight against Chiang's armies.

When the Japanese invaded China in 1937, the Communists and Nationalists stopped their civil war and united temporarily to fight the Japanese. However, the differences between the Communists and Nationalists were too deep to make the alliance last, and civil war broke out again in 1945 after Japan's defeat.

Section 1 Review

Identify Sun Yat-sen, Chiang Kai-shek, Mao Zedong, Long March

Main Ideas
1. What caused revolution to break out in China?
2. What was Chiang Kai-shek's major accomplishment?
3. What problems did Chiang's new government face?

Critical Thinking

Analyzing Comparisons: In Sun Yat-sen's *Three Principles for the People,* he calls for a government for and by the people. Where do you think that Sun got this idea?

DAILY LIFE

Backbreaking work and hunger haunted the Chinese in the bitter decades before and after World War I. As the old order fragmented, employers forced brutal conditions upon workers, who would otherwise starve. The photograph at the far left, taken in 1918, shows a 14-year-old coal miner, who worked 12 hours a day 7 days a week. At the near left, people wait for food to be doled out by missionaries in the 1920s.

623

1 FOCUS AND MOTIVATE

Ask students how one group can resist control by another. Discuss which ways are violent or nonviolent.

2 TEACH

Compare Indian nationalists' aims with those of Chinese nationalists. Discuss why Gandhi's campaigns of nonviolent resistance were effective.

GUIDED PRACTICE

Have students write a paragraph describing events in India that led to eventual full independence in 1947.

3 ASSESS AND CLOSE

ASSESS

Why did India support Britain in World War I? (They hoped Britain would reward them with self-government.)

OPTIONAL RETEACHING

Have students list four ways in which Gandhi used nonviolent resistance.

OPTIONAL ENRICHMENT

1. Have students research Martin Luther King's methods of nonviolent resistance and compare them to Gandhi's methods. (challenging)
2. Also for enrichment:

 One-Day Play
The Trial of Gandhi

2 Nationalists in India demanded independence.

In the mid-19th century, the British took control of almost all of India. Within 50 years, however, Indian intellectuals began seeking self-government for India. Then came World War I.

Indian nationalists were disappointed after the war.

During World War I, India loyally supported Britain. Almost one million Indian soldiers fought on the side of the British, and wealthy Indian princes made large financial contributions to the war effort. Indians hoped their loyalty and support would be rewarded by self-government.

In 1917 Britain promised to give self-rule to India in several stages. At the end of the war, therefore, the Government of India Act of 1919 turned over certain governmental powers to India's provincial legislatures. However, the British reserved other, more important powers in the central government for themselves. Because of the act's limitations, most Indians were disappointed.

Gandhi, a believer in nonviolent resistance, led the Indian nationalists.

The widespread dissatisfaction found a spokesman in **Mohandas K. Gandhi** [gän′dē]. This remarkable nationalist leader had been educated in Britain as a lawyer. He then set up a successful law practice in South Africa, helping the Indians who lived there fight against discrimination. During World War I, Gandhi returned to India and became the champion of the oppressed and lowly. He led a very simple and self-sacrificing life, following the Hindu faith. Millions of Indians began to look up to him as a holy man, or **mahatma** [mə hät′mə]. Albert Einstein, the brilliant scientist, said of Gandhi: "Generations to come will scarcely believe that such a one as this walked the earth in flesh and blood."

Nonviolent resistance. Gandhi believed in the idea of **nonviolent resistance**—protest that didn't involve violence of any kind. He also used the tactic called civil disobedience, which is the deliberate and public refusal to obey a law in order to protest laws or policies that the protester considers unjust. Gandhi's approach of nonviolent resistance inspired many other leaders in later periods, including the Rev. Dr. Martin Luther King, Jr., in the fight for racial justice in the United States.

Gandhi's campaign for Indian independence. Gandhi strongly opposed the Government of India Act because it didn't give the Indian government enough independence. Millions of Indian people followed him in a nonviolent campaign of civil disobedience to force the British to give self-rule to India. Strikes, fasts, and protest marches were the "weapons" of Gandhi's campaign.

Not all Indian nationalists believed in nonviolent resistance, however. In 1919 there was a wave of murder, looting, and arson, and Indian-British relations were tense. That same year, in the city of Amritsar [əm rit′sər], British soldiers fired on unarmed demonstrators. Nearly 400 innocent people were killed, and 1,200 were wounded. Gandhi and his followers in the Indian National Congress were shocked at the behavior of the British. They became determined to win complete freedom for India.

During the 1920s and 1930s, Gandhi launched several campaigns of nonviolent resistance. One of his methods was to boycott, or refuse to buy, British-made goods. He also began a movement of "progressive nonviolent noncooperation," in which he led people to resist British authority. They refused to pay taxes. They returned all decorations and honors awarded by the British. They withdrew their children from government schools, and they boycotted the courts and the elections. The British arrested Gandhi several times and put him in jail.

While working for the independence of India, Gandhi tried to improve the lives of the untouchables, those Indians who belonged to the lowest caste. He also tried to bring about cooperation between Hindus and Muslims. Gandhi believed that injustice could be wiped out through love and patience.

India made progress toward independence in the 1930s.

Since 1857 the British had been able to keep order in India because the majority of the Indian people

BACKGROUND The phrases "nonviolent noncooperation" and "nonviolent disobedience" are other English translations sometimes used for Gandhi's plan.

respected and consented to the British authority. Gandhi's campaign of civil disobedience showed the British that this consent was no longer assured, and they could feel their authority crumbling. Thus, during the 1930s the British met with Indian leaders to gradually begin preparing India for self-government.

In 1935 the British Parliament passed a law that gave the Indian provinces self-government. From the capital of **New Delhi**, Indian members of the legislature then controlled all matters except those relating to defense and foreign affairs. However, because of the onset of World War II, full independence for India was not granted until 1947.

Section 2 Review

Identify Mohandas K. Gandhi, mahatma, nonviolent resistance, New Delhi

Main Ideas

1. Why were Indian nationalists disappointed after World War I?
2. What methods did Gandhi use to gain independence for India?
3. What progress was made toward Indian independence in the 1930s?

Critical Thinking

Making Hypotheses: Why do you think that Gandhi's campaign against the British was so effective, even though it was nonviolent?

Gandhi, in 1930, spins homemade thread, his symbolic challenge to the British textile industry.

---

3 Nationalists in the Middle East created new regimes.

Nationalist movements developed among Arabs, Turks, Persians (Iranians), and Jews in the Middle East. The Middle East, a modern political region, generally includes the North African and Asian countries of Turkey, Cyprus, Lebanon, Israel, Egypt, Jordan, Syria, Iraq, Iran, and the countries of the Arabian peninsula. Each group wanted its own independent country. Often the nationalist goal of independence went along with a desire for modernization.

Egyptian nationalists were the first in the region to challenge the Europeans.

The majority of people living in the Middle East are Arabs, those people whose native language is Arabic. Before World War I, none of them had total independence. They were controlled either by the French, the British, or the Ottoman Turks. World War I, however, weakened the rule of the British and French and ended that of the Ottomans. After the war, for example, several nonviolent underground movements challenged French rule in Tunisia, Algeria, and Morocco.

Since 1914, Egypt had been a protectorate of Britain. A **protectorate** is a country that is under the direct control of another, usually stronger country. After a delegation of Egyptian nationalists was denied permission to attend the Paris Peace Conference of 1919, Egypt rose up in revolt. Order was not restored until 1922, when the British agreed to end the protectorate. However, Britain kept the right to have troops in Egypt, to direct Egyptian foreign affairs, and to defend the all-important **Suez Canal**. This 118-mile, human-made canal connects the Mediterranean and Red seas and was crucial to the British because it shortened the route between Britain and India by 6,000 miles.

Arab leaders in the old Ottoman Empire sought self-government.

In the Middle East, Arab resentment against the corrupt rule of the Ottoman Turks had been building for a long time. When the Ottoman Empire entered World War I on the side of Germany, Britain

---

Answers to Section 2 Review

Identify

Key Terms, People, and Places are defined on pages indicated in parentheses. Also see the Glossary and Biographical Dictionary. Mohandas K. Gandhi (624), mahatma (624), nonviolent resistance (624), New Delhi (625)

Main Ideas

1. India supported Britain in the war, hoping to be rewarded with self-government. Britain gave only minor powers to India.
2. nonviolent resistance, including strikes, fasts, protest marches, boycotts, and other acts of civil disobedience
3. British gave Indian provinces self-government, and control of all but defense and foreign affairs to the Indian legislature.

Critical Thinking

British were sensitive to world opinion. Gandhi's boycotts affected Britain economically. Civil disobedience demonstrated that Indians no longer consented to British authority.

---

3 Lesson Plan

Essential Learning Objectives

Students will learn to:

• explain how many Middle East countries became part of the

British and French colonial empires.

identify Middle East countries that gained their independence after World War I.

Remind students of the spread of ideas that occurred when early empires were built. Ask them to cite examples of modern Western ideas that colonization might have spread to the Middle East. Discuss with students how these might have affected nationalist movements.

2 TEACH

- List the countries that France and England ruled as mandates. Ask students for reasons why Britain and France imposed their rule on the Middle East.

- Discuss Mustafa Kemal's role in Turkey's independence movement and political revolution. List these headings: Government, Religion, Law, Education, and Industrialization. Have students provide details of Kemal's reforms in each area.

- Compare the changes Reza Shah Pahlavi instituted with those of Kemal. Guide students to see that Kemal was more progressive in that he established a democracy while the Iranian shah ruled a despotic state.

- Have students cite the ways in which the Jewish nationalist movement was different from other nationalist movements. (international movement entailing a return to a homeland) Discuss the problems that the establishment of the Jewish state created for both Jews and Arabs.

tried to weaken Turkish power by winning over the Arabs disgruntled with Ottoman rule. In 1915 and 1916, Britain promised independence to the Arabs in hopes of sparking a rebellion against the Turks. In June, 1916, the Syrian and Arabian Arabs, supported by British arms and money, broke loose from the Ottoman Empire in the so-called Revolt in the Desert. The revolt weakened the already decaying Ottoman Empire.

When World War I ended, Arab leaders claimed self-government as their reward. It soon became clear, however, that Arab independence would be a victim of European power politics. During the war Britain and France had made a secret agreement to divide the Middle East region between themselves.

After the war the newly formed League of Nations divided up the region into mandates, which as you remember from Chapter 31, were lands once ruled by countries defeated in World War I. Syria and Lebanon were given to France. Iraq, Palestine, and Transjordan were given to Britain. The British and French drew boundaries to suit their own convenience and installed their own rulers in the mandates.

In the years that followed, Arab hostility toward European rule grew and the Europeans began to respond. The British gave Transjordan partial independence in 1928 and Iraq full independence in 1932. However, the British army stayed in both countries to protect Britain's interests there.

The collapse of the Ottoman Empire in 1918 also brought independence to several states in the Arabian peninsula. The most important of these independent states was the newly created kingdom of the Hejaz [hē jaz´]. Its ruler was Abdul-Aziz, commonly known as **Ibn-Saud** [ib´ən sä üd´]. Ibn-Saud conquered the warring Bedouin tribes and controlled nearly all of the peninsula by 1926. In 1932 Ibn-Saud changed the name of his kingdom to Saudi Arabia. A few years later, rich oil reserves were discovered there, adding to Saudi Arabia's power and prestige.

Kemal Atatürk arose as a new leader in Turkey.

Since Turkey had been on the losing side in World War I, it had to accept significant territorial losses as part of the peace settlement. Moreover, the Allies occupied various parts of Turkey, including the city of Istanbul. However, the Turks strongly resisted having their country occupied.

A new Turkish leader. In the early 1920s, a powerful army officer named Mustafa Kemal [müs´tä fä kə mäl´] became the leader of Turkish national resistance. Under Kemal's leadership the Turks drove out the Allied forces and regained control of Istanbul. For more security they moved the capital to the interior city of Ankara.

Kemal and his followers also carried out a successful political revolution. They overthrew the ruling sultan and in 1923 formed the Turkish Republic. Kemal was elected Turkey's first president and was given the name Atatürk [at´ə tėrk´], meaning "father of all the Turks," by the Turkish parliament in 1935, becoming **Kemal Atatürk**.

The Turkish Republic was much smaller than the Ottoman Empire had been. The new republic consisted mainly of the Anatolian peninsula, which is bounded on three sides by the Black, Aegean, and Mediterranean seas. The majority of the republic's people were Turks, but the Greeks, a people who had been living in the area since 1000 B.C., formed an important non-Turkish minority. Turkish nationalists considered the Greeks to be "foreigners," and fighting eventually broke out between the two groups. To settle the problem, 1.4 million Greeks were forced to move to Greece, and 400,000 Turks living in Greece were moved to Turkey. Uprooting so many people caused great hardship, but it gave Turkey and Greece more homogeneous populations.

Atatürk's program for reform. As president, Kemal Atatürk's main goal was to modernize Turkey. Under his leadership Turkey became the first traditional Islamic state in which church and state

What's in a Name?

ISTANBUL The name Istanbul comes from two words: *Islam*, referring to the Muslim religion, and *bul*, meaning "copious." Thus, Istanbul means the city "abounding in Islam."

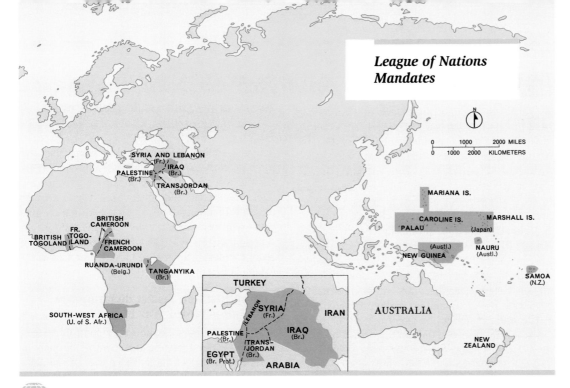

League of Nations Mandates

0   1000   2000 MILES
0   1000   2000   KILOMETERS

SYRIA AND LEBANON (Fr.)
IRAQ (Br.)
PALESTINE (Br.)
TRANSJORDAN (Br.)

BRITISH CAMEROON
FR. TOGO-LAND
BRITISH TOGOLAND
FRENCH CAMEROON
RUANDA-URUNDI (Belg.)
TANGANYIKA (Br.)
SOUTH-WEST AFRICA (U. of S. Afr.)

MARIANA IS.
CAROLINE IS.   MARSHALL IS.
PALAU   (Japan)
(Austl.)   NAURU (Austl.)
NEW GUINEA
SAMOA (N.Z.)

AUSTRALIA

NEW ZEALAND

TURKEY
LEBANON
SYRIA (Fr.)   IRAN
PALESTINE (Br.)   IRAQ (Br.)
TRANS-JORDAN (Br.)
EGYPT (Br. Prot.)
ARABIA

 MAP STUDY After World War I, the League of Nations established mandates to ready former German and Ottoman colonies for self-government. In the Middle East, which mandates did Britain gain? France? In Africa, which mandate was given to South Africa? Which countries received mandates over various Pacific islands?

were separated. The new republic tolerated all religions, and instead of the law of the Koran, the government adopted a law code modeled on the Napoleonic code.

Kemal's modernization affected people throughout Turkish society. Women gained the right to vote and to hold public office, and they were encouraged to become doctors, lawyers, and teachers. In addition, the government set out to reduce illiteracy and encourage industrialization through the development of mines, railroads, and factories. By the time Kemal Atatürk died in 1938, the nation of Turkey had moved a long way toward modernization of its economic and social structure.

Iran developed more slowly under the shah.

In 1921 an army officer named Reza Khan took over Iran, "Land of the Aryans." In 1925 he be-

came shah and changed his family name to Pahlavi, becoming Reza Shah Pahlavi. The shah was a strong nationalist and fought Soviet and British influence in Iranian affairs. Like Kemal Atatürk, the shah tried to modernize his country. He built schools, developed national resources, and supported the rights of women. However, the shah was also a harsh despot.

During World War II, the Iranians tried to remain neutral, but the Allies wanted to use the Trans-Iranian Railway to ship war supplies from Britain to the Soviet Union. When Reza Shah refused to cooperate, British and Soviet troops invaded Iran in 1941. They forced Reza Shah to abdicate, or abandon his throne. His son, Muhammed Reza Pahlavi, took command and signed a treaty that allowed the British and Soviets to use the railway and to keep troops in Iran until the end of the war.

ANSWER TO MAP STUDY Palestine, Transjordan, Iraq; Lebanon, Syria; South-West Africa; Japan, Australia, New Zealand

Answers to Section 3 Review

Identify

Key Terms, People, and Places are defined on pages indicated in parentheses. Also see the Glossary and Biographical Dictionary. protectorate (625), Suez Canal (625), Ibn-Saud (626), Kemal Atatürk (626), Zionists (628), Balfour Declaration (628)

Main Ideas

1. British ended their protectorate in Egypt but kept troops there to direct foreign affairs and defend the Suez Canal.
2. League of Nations made these lands French and British mandates, which later gained independence.
3. He established a new republic in Turkey and worked to modernize it—improving conditions for women, reducing illiteracy, and encouraging industrialization.
4. The shah sought to resist foreign influence and modernize Iran.
5. Arabs living there viewed Jews as intruders and feared economic and political domination.

Critical Thinking

They are all states under the control of another, stronger nation. All lack self-rule and self-determination.

The Jews established a homeland in Palestine.

As you learned earlier, both Jews and Arabs had lived in Palestine for many centuries. The country, however, had not been independent since the days of the Romans. Jewish nationalists, who called themselves **Zionists**, wanted to rebuild a Jewish state in Palestine, and some European Jews began to settle there in the late 1800s. To gain the support of the Zionists, in 1917 the British issued the **Balfour Declaration**, promising that a national home for the Jews would be established in Palestine. In 1920 when Palestine became a mandate of the British government, large-scale Jewish immigration began. Over the years immigrants started farms and industries and generally prospered.

The Arabs made up the larger part of the population in Palestine, and they were alarmed by these developments. They viewed the Jews as intruders and feared possible economic and political domination. As refugees fled from Nazi Germany in the 1930s and Jewish immigration increased, the Arabs turned to demonstrations and guerrilla warfare.

In guerrilla warfare bands of fighters who are not part of a regular army harass the enemy through small skirmishes, ambushes, and other forms of attack. The British failed to bring peace to the area during this period, and there is still not peace there today.

Section 3 Review

Identify protectorate, Suez Canal, Ibn-Saud, Kemal Atatürk, Zionists, Balfour Declaration

Main Ideas

1. What was the outcome of the challenge of the Egyptian nationalists?
2. When the Ottoman Empire was dissolved, what became of the Arab lands it had ruled?
3. What were the goals and accomplishments of Kemal Atatürk?
4. What were the goals of Reza Shah Pahlavi in the 1920s and 1930s?
5. What resistance did the Jews face in rebuilding their homeland in Palestine?

Critical Thinking

Analyzing Comparisons: What do mandates, protectorates, and colonies have in common?

4 *Extreme nationalists in Europe and Japan established dictatorships.*

In some parts of Europe and in Japan, the aftermath of World War I brought deep discontent. Extremist groups in these nations took advantage of widespread fears and frustrations to gain support for their own causes. They preached that national pride had to be restored and that the only way to accomplish this was through the bold actions of strong leaders. The goal of these extremists was to establish dictatorships.

Communist and fascist dictatorships arose after World War I.

A dictator is a person who seizes control of a government without getting that control through inheritance or free election. The power of the dictator is not limited by law or by the acts of any official body, such as the congress in the United States. After World War I, several major countries came under the rule of dictators. In Russia the communist dictatorship centered on government ownership of property and capital.

Another type of dictatorship, **fascism**, permitted private ownership of property and capital but placed strict government rules on the people and the economy. The term "fascism" did not refer to just any dictatorship, however. The word usually described a government that favored rule by a dictator, with strong control of industry and labor, and extreme nationalism and militarism.

Fascism arose first in Italy under the leadership of **Benito Mussolini** [mús′ə lē′nē], and later, similar forms of government appeared in Japan, Germany, and Spain. Neither communism nor fascism allowed opposing political parties to exist. Each type of government used censorship, denied **civil rights** (the rights of personal liberty), and took complete control of people's lives. Communism and fascism became the strongest anti-democratic movements in the world.

Mussolini gained power in Italy.

There was much unrest in Italy after World War I. The war had been much more expensive in money and lives than the people had expected, and many Italians were angry that Italy, though on the winning side, had received so little territory in the peace settlement. Italy also faced the same problems of economic slowdown, unemployment, and high prices that existed in other countries. By the end of 1920, the cost of living was eight times higher than it had been in 1914. Many people found it difficult even to buy bread. The government, which was split into many different parties, had no strong leaders or programs.

As unrest grew, many Marxist workers in the factories of northern Italy went on strike. The many strikes scared middle-class people who were afraid of a communist revolution. As a result, many Italians swung their support to the newly organized Fascist party, headed by Benito Mussolini, which was strongly anti-communist.

Mussolini's Fascist party. Mussolini had organized the Italian Fascist party shortly after the war ended. He took the name fascist from the Latin word *fasces.* It meant the bundle of rods bound around an ax that had become the symbol of authority during Roman times. The Fascist party was made up mainly of out-of-work men who had been

soldiers in the war. They wanted results in place of the do-nothing policies of the government. In addition, the Fascists were superpatriotic and had a strong devotion to Italy and to Mussolini, who was known as *Il Duce* [ēl′ dü′cha], "the leader."

The Fascists were a frightening group. They wore black shirts as uniforms, used the old Roman salute of the raised arm, and followed strict military discipline. They practiced violence and beat up, tortured, and sometimes killed political opponents.

At first Mussolini tried to gain political power legally through elections, but the Fascists did not win many votes. Therefore, in September, 1922, some 10,000 armed Fascists marched on Rome to take over the government. The king, afraid of a civil war, invited Mussolini to become prime minister. In the next nine years, Mussolini used every means, including terror, to make himself dictator of Italy. The Fascist party became the only legal party in the country, and the secret police arrested anyone who dared to criticize the Fascists.

Mussolini's conquest of Ethiopia. By 1930 the world depression had increased the problems within Italy. Although powerful, Mussolini felt that only a successful military move would enable him to keep his hold on Italy. Thus, in 1935, he attacked Ethiopia, then one of the four independent states left in Africa. Ethiopia had defeated Italy in 1896 when Italy attempted to enlarge Italian Somaliland, but in 1935, the Italians were armed with more advanced technology, including bombs, mustard gas, and tanks. The Italians

Benito Mussolini, in a characteristic strutting pose, addresses Italian troops in a training camp. They would soon leave for Africa and conquer Ethiopia.

quickly defeated the poorly equipped Africans. Mussolini was stronger than ever.

Military leaders won control in Japan.

In the 1920s democracy was making some progress in Japan, but the Japanese parliament held little power. It could not control the prime minister, who was responsible only to the emperor. In addition, military leaders were nearly independent of the government, and they were eager for more power. They disliked democracy and disagreed with Japan's moderate policy toward China. These militarists gained strength in parliament during the 1930s. They were supported by the farmers, who blamed democracy for bad conditions.

By 1930 the effects of the world depression were also deeply felt in Japan. The disruption caused by striking workers gave the militarists a chance to seize more power, and by late 1932 a strong military clique gained control. Their main goal was to build up the most powerful army and navy in East Asia. These military leaders terrorized the civilian members of the government, using murder to scare off political opposition and justifying their acts by declaring that they were glorifying Japan. Their nationalistic cause was supported by young men whose careers had been hurt by the depression. They also had the support of people with business interests in Manchuria who wanted a more aggressive policy toward China.

Hitler and the Nazi party rose to power in Germany.

Germany began the postwar years with a new national assembly that met in the city of Weimar [vī′mär] in January, 1919. The Weimar constitution included many democratic features: freedom of speech and religion, compulsory education of children, and a freedom of association that protected labor unions. However, the Weimar Republic was weak from the start, and Germany suffered from all the same economic problems that existed in other countries.

The Weimar Republic. The ruling group in the Weimar government was a coalition, or grouping, of socialist parties. Extremists on both the Right (fascists) and the Left (communists) threatened the ruling group. They blamed the coalition for ac-

From the Archives
Sigmund Freud and the Life of the Mind

As Adolf Hitler influenced political events of the 20th century, so Sigmund Freud [froid] (1856–1939) influenced the life of the mind. Freud was a Viennese doctor who revolutionized the way we think about ourselves by teaching that forces within us, of which we are largely unconscious, shape our lives. The excerpt below is from one of Freud's last works, written in 1930 as Hitler was rising to power.

The fateful question for the human species seems to me to be whether and to what extent their cultural development will succeed in mastering . . . the human instinct of aggression and self-destruction. It may be that in this respect precisely the present time deserves a special interest. Men have gained control over the forces of nature to such an extent that with their help they would have no difficulty in exterminating one another to the last man. They know this, and hence comes a large part of their current unrest, their unhappiness and their mood of anxiety.

cepting the hated Treaty of Versailles and declared that the socialists were traitors to their country. As the German economy grew weaker, people in Germany began to listen to these charges. To make matters worse, the most stable element in the German population, the middle class, had been all but ruined by the terrible inflation, or sharp increase in prices, of the postwar years.

In 1929 a worldwide depression began, and millions of Germans lost their jobs. The Weimar Republic seemed unable to help. The younger generation, disillusioned by this chaos, blamed the problems on the way their elders ran the country. Militarists also blamed the German defeat in World War I on liberals, pacifists, and Jews.

Many Germans had long felt deep-seated envy—and, even hatred—of the Jews, who made up less

FROM THE ARCHIVES The excerpt is from *Civilization and Its Discontents*, by Sigmund Freud, translated and edited by James Strachey (New York: W. W. Norton, 1961), p. 104. As anti-Semitism undermined the status of Jews, Freud, who

was Jewish, suffered marked indignities and frustrations in his career. He died in London, a refugee from Nazi Germany. Ask students to cite evidence that people are today attempting to master human aggression and self-destructive forces.

than one percent of the population. These Germans resented the fact that some Jews had achieved success as doctors, dentists, lawyers, authors, and musicians. It became popular to blame the Jews for Germany's troubles. Many Germans were willing to listen to anyone who made the Jews the scapegoats—the ones that were blamed for all the nation's ills. **Adolf Hitler** did just that.

Hitler was born in an Austrian village in 1889. During World War I, he enlisted in the German army. While in a hospital recovering from war injuries, news of the armistice and the German defeat reached him. He felt great anger and shame for his adopted country and came to hate the new German government, Jews, and anyone associated with the Versailles Treaty.

After the war Hitler joined a small political party, which in 1920 adopted the name of National Socialist German Workers' party, or Nazi party. Hitler helped draw up the program for the party, a set of goals that appealed to all discontented persons. He slowly began to build the party through public speeches. Hitler was an extremely talented public speaker and had a spell-binding effect on his audiences. Still, he was impatient for power.

In 1923 he tried, but failed, to seize power in Bavaria, a state in southwestern Germany, in what became known as the Beer Hall Putsch (revolution). As a result, Hitler was arrested for treason and sent to prison. While spending about a year in jail, he wrote the book *Mein Kampf*, which meant "My Struggle." The book was based on racist ideas

and presented Hitler's plan for aggression against other peoples and countries.

The Third Reich. In Germany, near the end of the 1920s, economic conditions became worse. Businesses failed, people lost jobs, and it took more and more money to buy less and less. More people began to vote for Nazi representatives in the Reichstag [rīHs'täk'], the German parliament, hoping that a new government would find new answers to these growing problems. By 1932 the Nazis were the largest political party in Germany.

In 1933 Hitler became chancellor (prime minister) of Germany, running a government known as the Third Reich [rīH]. (The First Reich, or empire, was begun by Charlemagne in 800 and was ended by Napoleon in 1806. The Second Reich began in 1871 with the unification of Germany and continued until 1918, when Germany was defeated in World War I.)

In 1934 Hitler stripped the Reichstag of all power. He also eliminated all political parties except the Nazis, outlawed trade unions, set up labor camps, and overturned laws he did not like. The Nazis seized control of the courts, industries, newspapers, police, and schools. Many children were taught to spy for the Nazis, even on their own parents. On August 2, 1934, Hitler became Führer [fy'rər], or leader, of Germany.

The "super race." The Nazis preached the idea of a "super race." According to the Führer, Germans were Aryans and were the "master race" or "super race." All other peoples, particularly Jews

Adolf Hitler gives the Nazi salute at a parade. Hitler was a spellbinding speaker who aroused widespread support for his racist and aggressive policies.

631

3 | ASSESS AND CLOSE

ASSESS

1. What African country did Mussolini defeat? (Ethiopia)
2. Name the type of government Germany had before Hitler came to power. (republic, or representative democracy)

OPTIONAL RETEACHING

Divide students into two teams. Have each team list as many aspects of people's lives as possible that a government can affect. Use these lists for a chart, comparing how these factors would be affected under a democracy and a totalitarian system.

Students also may be assigned Activities reteaching page 200.

OPTIONAL ENRICHMENT

1. Have students find and analyze a propaganda poster printed during or before a war, preferably World War II. Have them analyze the message of the poster. (average)
2. Ask students to research artists, entertainers, or writers in Germany during the years prior to World War II. Tell them to find out if or how their work was scrutinized or changed under Hitler. (challenging)
3. Students also may be assigned Activities enrichment page 201.
4. Also for enrichment:

 Overhead Transparency 66

 Source Reading 33B

INDEPENDENT PRACTICE/ HOMEWORK

Assign the Section Review, the Chapter Review items, Activities page 199, or Workbook page 135.

CLOSURE

Tell students that in the fascist dictatorships that arose in Italy, Germany, and Japan in the first third of the twentieth century, leaders controlled all aspects of human life and used a strong military to terrorize and kill.

Answers to Section 4 Review

Identify
Key Terms, People, and Places are defined on pages indicated in parentheses. Also see the Glossary and Biographical Dictionary.
fascism (628), Benito Mussolini (628), civil rights (628), Adolf Hitler (631), Nuremberg Laws (632), totalitarianism (632)

Main Ideas
1. Both dictatorships were ruled by a person who seized control without being elected or having inherited the office. However, the communist dictatorship centered on government ownership of property and capital, and the fascist dictatorship placed strict government rules on people.
2. The existing government was weak, the economy was poor, and the people were dissatisfied.
3. peasants who blamed democracy for bad conditions, young men whose careers had been hurt by the depression, and people with business interests in Manchuria
4. After World War I, Germany experienced inflation, unemployment, and bitterness about the Versailles Treaty. As discontent grew, so did the Nazi party. Hitler was a very effective public speaker, able to give voice to German frustrations. The idea of being a "super race" gave a sense of prestige to many Germans.

Critical Thinking
Dictators usually come to power under conditions of turmoil. When the existing government cannot provide security and stability, people will turn to a dictator who promises to provide these.

At this anti-Jewish rally in Berlin in 1935 (top), the banners read: "The Jews are our ruin." In Salzburg, in 1939, Nazi youths burn books by Jewish authors.

and Slavs, were inferior. According to the Nazi party, Jews were to be killed, and Slavs were to be made into slaves.

The Nazis thus began a carefully planned program to eliminate Jews from German national life. In 1935 the infamous **Nuremberg Laws** were passed, which took citizenship rights away from Jews. The laws forbade the intermarriage of Jews and gentiles (non-Jews). In addition, Jewish children were not allowed to attend German schools. The government also encouraged other Germans to boycott Jewish businesses and services.

By 1939 the Nazis had put tens of thousands of Jews into concentration camps and had eliminated all Jews from the economic life of Germany. The government took away the Jews' property and forced them to live in ghettos [get'ōs], sections of cities restricted to Jews.

Hitler's ideas of the German "super race" gave a sense of prestige to many Germans. They felt that Hitler was replacing weakness, defeat, and depression with strength, importance, and prosperity. Most Germans gladly accepted Hitler as their leader. Those who didn't were beaten up, imprisoned, murdered. Some of Hitler's opponents managed to leave Germany, but this became very difficult as the specter of war approached.

The military. The Third Reich prepared for war. As they did in Italy and Japan, fascists in Germany tried to mold the minds of their citizens through a program that glorified war. Textbooks were rewritten to show German military history in its best light, and the press and radio were censored to carry out that program.

Hitler believed that Germany must have "living space," that is, more territory for the German people. He began huge preparations for German expansion. Strict food-rationing laws were put into effect to make Germany self-sufficient in case of war. A highway system called the autobahn was built so that troops could move rapidly. In addition, a huge stockpile of arms was created.

German business leaders who in 1932 thought they could control Hitler found out too late that they could not. He had changed Germany into a police state. The government controlled every area of life—the economy, schools, labor unions, newspapers, radio, and films. Such a system of total control of a country is called **totalitarianism** [tō tal'ə ter'ē ə niz'əm].

Many people outside Germany also believed that their countries could deal with Hitler. They felt that he only wanted to return Germany to its rightful place among nations. Some people in democratic countries even admired Nazism for its discipline and its hostility to communism.

Section 4 Review

Identify fascism, Benito Mussolini, civil rights, Adolf Hitler, Nuremberg Laws, totalitarianism

Main Ideas
1. How are communism and fascism, described in this section, similar and different?
2. Why was Mussolini able to gain power in Italy?
3. Who supported the rise of the Japanese militarists in the 1930s?
4. How did Hitler come to power in Germany? How did his idea of a "super race" help him?

Critical Thinking
Making Hypotheses: It was said of Mussolini that he made "the trains run on time." Why would an Italian, faced with the chaotic conditions following World War I, want to support such a leader?

Nonviolent Resistance in Modern Times

Mohandas K. Gandhi's campaign of nonviolent resistance to British rule combined Indian traditions with Western techniques of political organization and publicity. Gandhi used a new word to describe nonviolent resistance—*satyagraha* [sə tya′grə hə]. The word comes from two Sanskrit words, *satya*, which means "insistence on truth"; and *agraha*, meaning "firmness" or "force." To Gandhi, this concept of "truth-force" or "love-force" involved converting an opponent by showing one's complete trust and love and by avoiding violence at all cost.

Hunger strikes, demonstrations, protest marches, and boycotts of government institutions and British goods were among the methods Gandhi and his followers used. Gandhi counted on the British sense of fair play to help him attain his goals. Eventually it did, although not without violence.

The Rev. Dr. Martin Luther King, Jr., applied techniques of nonviolent resistance to the U.S. civil rights movement. King used a boycott to end segregation on public buses in Montgomery, Alabama, in 1955–1956. In 1963 King led a massive march on Washington, D.C., to win laws ending racial discrimination and ensuring equal opportunities to black Americans in employment, education, and other areas of American life.

Indians formed a human blockade to thwart British rule (left). Rosa Parks (above) ignited the Montgomery, Alabama, bus boycott.

Gandhi compared the New Testament with the sacred Hindu text, the Bhagavad-Gita and said that Jesus' Sermon on the Mount "went straight to my heart ... [especially the] verses ... 'resist not evil: but whosoever shall smite thee on thy right cheek, turn to him the other also.'" Gandhi was also strongly influenced by the forms of nonviolence advocated by the Russian novelist Leo Tolstoy and the American essayist Henry David Thoreau.

Ask students if nonviolent resistance would work against any unjust government—for example, would it be as effective in a dictatorship as it would among democratic peoples? Have students explain their reasoning. (No; nonviolent resistance would be ineffective or impossible against a totalitarian government because it depends on a joint acceptance of certain basic rules; publicity is also necessary to gain public support, and this is impossible, too, under totalitarian rule.)

Answers to Test Yourself

Key Terms, People, and Places

The key terms, people, and places tested here were introduced in the chapter sections and reviewed in the Section Reviews. For definitions see the page references at the appropriate Section Reviews. Also see the Glossary and Biographical Dictionary.

Main Ideas

The main ideas tested here were introduced in the sections of this chapter and reviewed in the Section Reviews. For answers to these questions, see the appropriate Section Reviews.

Critical Thinking

1. Nonviolent activities by Dr. King and his followers include breaking laws that required black Americans to sit or stand in the back of buses, and sit-ins conducted at lunch counters that refused to serve blacks.

2. Students should discuss the "great man" theory, which says that important events might not happen without powerful, charismatic leaders. However, it must be the right person at the right time. A leader may be the product and symbol of the event as well as the person who caused it.

CHAPTER 33 REVIEW

Section Summaries

Section 1

Chinese nationalists founded a republic.

Nationalists in China resented the weak and corrupt Manchu dynasty. In 1911 they overthrew the Manchus and established a republic. The new leader was Sun Yat-sen. He was succeeded in 1925 by Chiang Kai-shek, who tried to unify the country. After 1927 he and the Chinese Communists, led by Mao Zedong, became bitter enemies. The two sides fought a civil war until 1937, when they united temporarily to fight the Japanese invaders.

Section 2

Nationalists in India demanded independence.

After World War I, Mohandas Gandhi led the Indian nationalists in their movement to become independent from Britain. He used civil disobedience and nonviolent resistance against British rule. During the 1930s Britain granted India limited self-government.

Section 3

Nationalists in the Middle East created new regimes.

After World War I, nationalist movements in the Middle East arose. Egypt gained independence in 1922 and was followed by Saudi Arabia and Iraq in the 1920s and 1930s. Turkey, the former center of the Ottoman Empire, became a republic in 1923. Its leader, Kemal Atatürk, began an intensive program of modernization. Iran, under Reza Shah Pahlavi, also started to modernize. Zionists wanted a national homeland for Jews in Palestine, and large-scale Jewish immigration began in the 1920s and 1930s. The Arabs in Palestine became alarmed.

Section 4

Extremist nationalists in Europe and Japan established dictatorships.

Unsettled conditions after World War I helped the rise of extremist nationalist movements. By 1922 Italy was a Fascist dictatorship under Benito Mussolini. By 1933 the world depression helped Adolf Hitler become the Nazi dictator of Germany. Militarists took control in Japan. Mussolini and Hitler both set up police states. They outlawed all political parties except their own. They built totalitarian systems in which the state controlled everything. Citizens had no rights. The aim of dictators such as Mussolini and Hitler was to expand their own power and that of the state.

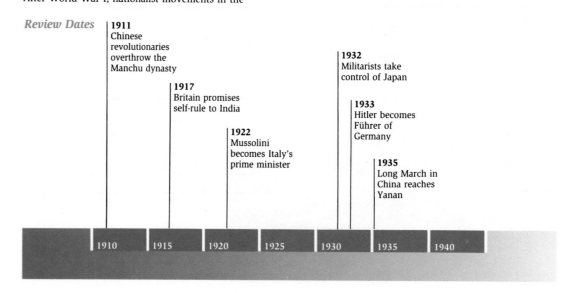

Review Dates

1911
Chinese revolutionaries overthrow the Manchu dynasty

1917
Britain promises self-rule to India

1922
Mussolini becomes Italy's prime minister

1932
Militarists take control of Japan

1933
Hitler becomes Führer of Germany

1935
Long March in China reaches Yanan

1910   1915   1920   1925   1930   1935   1940

Test Yourself

Key Terms, People, and Places
Identify the significance of the following:

Section 1

a. Sun Yat-sen

b. Chiang Kai-shek

c. Mao Zedong

d. Long March

Section 2

a. Mohandas K. Gandhi

b. mahatma

c. nonviolent resistance

d. New Delhi

Section 3

a. protectorate

b. Suez Canal

c. Ibn-Saud

d. Kemal Atatürk

e. Zionists

f. Balfour Declaration

Section 4

a. fascism

b. Benito Mussolini

c. civil rights

d. Adolf Hitler

e. Nuremberg Laws

f. totalitarianism

Main Ideas

Section 1

1. List some conditions in China that led to the revolution in 1911.

2. What did Chiang Kai-shek's rule accomplish for China?

3. Which forces weakened Chiang Kai-shek's government?

Section 2

1. How did the British disappoint Indian nationalists after World War I?

2. How did Gandhi work to gain independence and better living conditions for Indians?

3. What developments occurred concerning India's independence in the 1930s?

Section 3

1. How successful was Egypt's early struggle for independence?

2. How were the Arab lands treated after World War I?

3. What did Kemal Atatürk accomplish for his country?

4. Name two main objectives of Iran's ruler Reza Shah Pahlavi in the 1920s and 1930s.

5. Why did the Arabs feel threatened by the Jewish homeland in Palestine?

Section 4

1. Compare and contrast communist and fascist dictatorships.

2. What conditions in Italy allowed Mussolini to rule?

3. What groups supported the new Japanese military government?

4. Describe the atmosphere in Germany at the time Hitler became such a powerful leader.

Critical Thinking

1. **Recognizing Values** The values of Gandhi, expressed in this chapter, were picked up by civil rights leaders in the United States, including the Reverend Dr. Martin Luther King, Jr. Find two examples of activities or events of the United States' civil rights movement that go along with Gandhi's principles of nonviolent resistence.

2. **Predicting Effects** How important is a leader in a nationalistic struggle? What if Hitler had been Indian and Gandhi German?

Chapter Skills and Activities

Practicing Study and Research Skills

Developing Your Economics Vocabulary

Inflation and *depression* are two words used in this chapter to describe economic conditions that created unrest and discontent in several countries. Use a dictionary to define both these words. Then use an encyclopedia to learn about the ways these conditions affect people.

Linking Past and Present

Many of the conflicts that began in this chapter of history continue in the present. People are engaged in nationalistic struggles in many parts of the world. A well-known example is the conflict between the Israelis and the Palestinians in the Middle East. Based on what you've read in this chapter, what are the roots of this conflict?

Learning History Through Maps

Using the map on page 627 called "League of Nation Mandates," find four colonies under British control and three under French control.

CRITICAL THINKING QUESTION LEVEL 1. average; 2. easy

34 World Depression and World War II

OVERVIEW

This chapter explains the political, economic, and military backdrop of World War II and provides a description of the major fighting in the European and Pacific theaters.

PLANNING CHART

Section	Text Pages	Key Concept	Suggested Teaching Time
1 The world economy broke down.	638–640	The Great Depression was caused by a fall in agricultural prices, economic systems based on credit financing, and the stock market crash.	One day **More time?** Use *Overhead Transparency 67.*
2 Aggression destroyed an uneasy peace.	640–643	Fascist expansionism in China, Africa, Spain, and central Europe led France and Britain to develop the appeasement policy.	Two days **More time?** Use *Source Reading 34A.*
3 Total war engulfed the world.	645–648	The whole world is engulfed in war, with Germany and Japan winning major battles in the early years of World War II.	One day **Less Time?** Discuss part of Section 2 with this section.
4 The Allies were victorious.	648–652	Allied victories in the great sea battles of the Pacific theater and a two-front war in Europe led to the defeat of the Axis powers.	Two days **More time?** Use *Overhead Transparency 68, Source Reading 34B,* or the One-Day Play, *The Trial of Adolph Eichmann.*

ANCILLARIES

Materials that may be used with this chapter to reinforce, reteach, enrich, and assess learning are pictured on the following pages.

Teacher's Resource File

ACTIVITIES

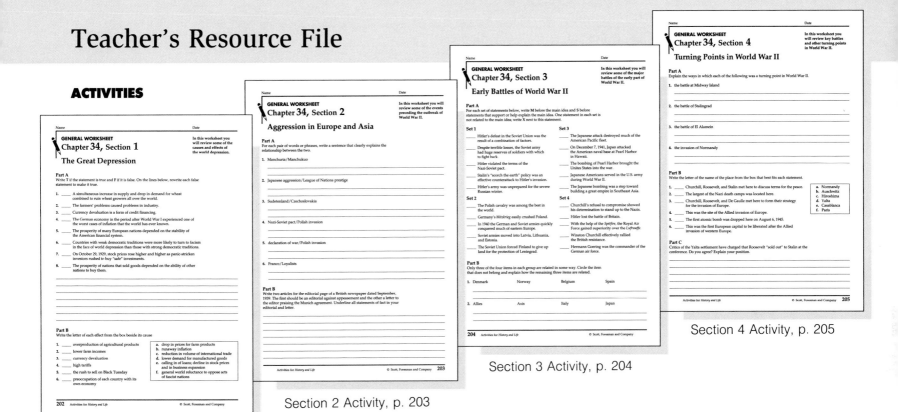

Section 1 Activity, p. 202

Section 2 Activity, p. 203

Section 3 Activity, p. 204

Section 4 Activity, p. 205

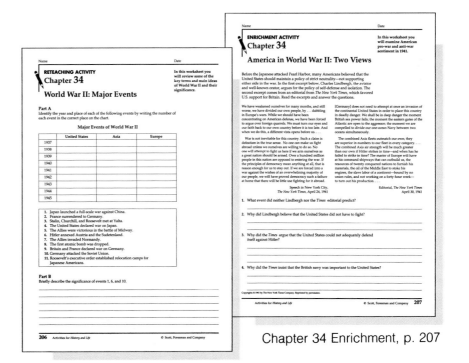

Chapter 34 Reteaching, p. 206

Chapter 34 Enrichment, p. 207

Teacher's Resource File

GEOGRAPHY SKILLS

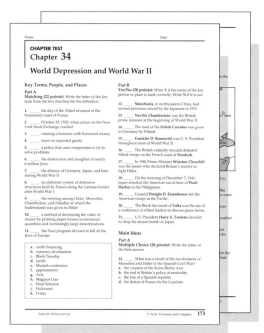

Chapter 34 Geography
Worksheet/Map, pp. 69–70

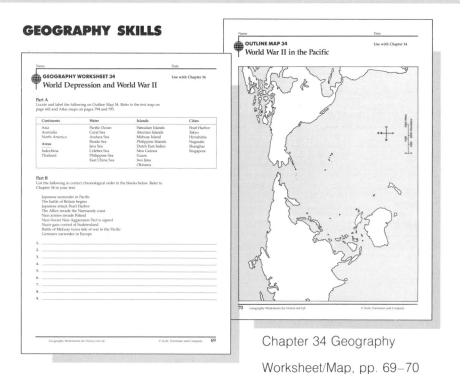

Chapter 34 Map Lesson, p. 116

TESTS

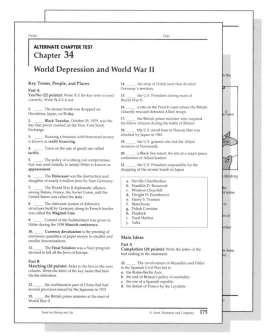

Chapter Test, pp. 173–174

Alternate Chapter Test, pp. 175–176

ONE-DAY PLAYS

The Trial of Adolph Eichmann

Other Optional Ancillaries

WORKBOOK

Name _____ Date _____

WORKSHEET
Chapter **34**, Section **1**

In this worksheet you will review some of the economic problems that led to world depression.

Causes of the World Depression

From the box below the diagrams, select the terms or phrases that best complete the missing parts of each chain. Use your completed diagrams to complete the following exercise.

Causes of the Great Depression

protective tariffs		
		"crash" of stock prices
	loss of revenue for farmers	decline in business production
default on loan payments	lower demand for manufactured goods	bankruptcy and unemployment

decrease in foreign trade	rush to sell stock	decrease in farm prices
loss of revenue	agricultural overproduction	

1. According to the chart, what was the immediate cause of the "crash" of stock prices?

2. Explain how a protective tariff—intended to protect a nation's producers—can sometimes cause producers to lose revenue.

3. Explain how a highly productive farm harvest could lead to lower, rather than higher, farm income.

4. Explain how farmers' problems also hurt manufacturers during the world depression.

136   Worksheets for History and Life   © Scott, Foresman and Company

Section 1 Worksheet, p. 136

Name _____ Date _____

WORKSHEET
Chapter **34**, Section **2**

In this worksheet you will review events leading to the outbreak of World War II.

Toward World War II

Part A
For each set, number the events in the order in which they happened.

1. ___ Germany attacked Austria.
   ___ The Rome-Berlin Axis was formed.
   ___ Japan joined Germany and Italy in alliance.
   ___ Hitler came to power in Germany.

2. ___ The League of Nations condemned Japan.
   ___ Japan seized several provinces in Manchuria.
   ___ The Chinese set up a new capital at Chongqing.
   ___ Japan launched a full-scale war against China.

3. ___ The Spanish set up a republic.
   ___ The Spanish Civil War began.
   ___ King Alfonso III of Spain was forced to abdicate.
   ___ The Loyalists were defeated.

4. ___ Stalin signed a pact with Hitler.
   ___ Britain and France declared war on Germany.
   ___ The Rome-Berlin-Tokyo Axis was formed.
   ___ Germany attacked Poland.

Part B
Use the following statistics to complete the bar graph showing the expansion of Germany. (For each bar you will have to add the area of the new territory to that previously annexed or seized.)

a. German territory, 1919 .... 101,500 square miles
b. annexation of Austria, March, 1938 .... + 32,400 square miles
c. annexation of the Sudetenland, Oct., 1938 .... + 10,800 square miles
d. seizure of Czechoslovakia, March, 1939 .... + 35,300 square miles
e. seizure of Polish Corridor, March, 1939 .... + 1,100 square miles

German Expansion, 1919-1939

German Territory (thousands of square miles): 100, 110, 120, 130, 140, 150, 160, 170, 180, 190

1919   March 1938   October 1938   March 1939

Worksheets for History and Life   © Scott, Foresman and Company   **137**

Section 2 Worksheet, p. 137

Name _____ Date _____

WORKSHEET
Chapter **34**, Section **3**

In this worksheet you will review World War II during the years 1940 and 1941.

World War II: The Dark Years

Part A
Support each statement with at least one specific example from your text.

1. World War II was more a global war than World War I had been.

2. Poland had little chance against the invading German army.

3. The battle of Britain was a turning point in the war.

4. President Roosevelt's decision to establish "relocation centers" for Japanese Americans remains controversial.

5. The American conversion to a war economy was one of the wonders of the industrial world.

Part B
Identify the country described by each phrase by writing **B** for Britain, **J** for Japan, **US** for the United States, **G** for Germany, and **USSR** for the Soviet Union.

___ attacked Finland
___ was isolationist for first two years of the war
___ broke a 1939 pact with the Soviet Union
___ planned to build an empire in Southeast Asia

___ was called by Hitler "a nation of shopkeepers"
___ was known for its *blitzkrieg*
___ inspired captive people everywhere by successfully resisting Hitler
___ entered the war after a surprise attack on a Pacific naval base

138   Worksheets for History and Life   © Scott, Foresman and Company

Section 3 Worksheet, p. 138

Name _____ Date _____

WORKSHEET
Chapter **34**, Section **4**

In this worksheet you will review events of the height and the end of World War II.

The Height and End of World War II

Part A
Complete each analogy.

1. El Alamein is to North Africa as Midway is to the _____.

2. The battle for Stalingrad is to the eastern front as the _____ is to the western front.

3. Casablanca is to war strategy as _____ is to peace terms.

4. General Douglas MacArthur is to "island-hopping" as _____ is to "Operation Overlord."

5. The "New Order" is to economic exploitation as _____ is to genocide.

6. May 8, 1945, is to Germany as August 10, 1945, is to _____.

Part B
Complete each statement with the explanations given in your text.

1. The Nazis subjected Slavic peoples to brutal wartime measures **because**

2. In July of 1942, the Germans began another offensive in the Soviet Union **because**

3. The battle of Stalingrad was significant **because**

4. Stalin was suspicious when England and France did not immediately open a second front in Europe **because**

5. In 1945 Stalin decided to end his policy of neutrality toward Japan **because**

Worksheets for History and Life   © Scott, Foresman and Company   **139**

Section 4 Worksheet, p. 139

SOURCE READINGS

Source Reading 34A
Source Reading 34B

OVERHEAD TRANSPARENCIES

Overhead Transparency 67
Overhead Transparency 68

TEST GENERATOR

40 multiple-choice questions for Chapter 34

CHAPTER INTRODUCTION

Have students read the introduction and call attention to the excerpt from Niemoller's speech. Ask students to explain what lesson they think Niemoller is trying to put forth. (People have a responsibility toward others.)

LOCATOR GLOBE

Call students' attention to the globe, which indicates the general area of the world discussed in this chapter. (Detailed maps appear on pages 642 and 650.)

TIME LINE

Have students use the time line to determine how many years World War II lasted. (6 years)

Chapter

34

World Depression and World War II

1929–1945

1920	
1929	Worldwide depression begins
1939	World War II begins
1945	Germany and Japan surrender
1950	
1960	

The legacy of World War I was not peace and cooperation. It was worldwide economic depression and global war. How did such terrible events occur so soon after World War I? During the 1920s nations as well as individuals chose to avoid and ignore the aproaching storm.

One such individual was Martin Niemoller, a prominent German minister, who was imprisoned as "Hitler's personal prisoner." He survived the concentration camps and later shared the lessons he had learned, making extensive speaking tours until his death in 1984. Niemoller is famous for a speech in which he described the price of ignoring reality:

> First they came for the socialists and I didn't speak out because I was not a socialist. Then they came for the Catholics but I was a Protestant and I didn't speak out. Then they came for the trade unionists and I didn't speak out because I was not a trade unionist. Then they came for the Jews and I didn't speak out because I was not a Jew. When they came for me there was no one left to speak for me.

However, even Martin Niemoller would argue that his jailer, Adolf Hitler, did not bring on World War II all by himself. There were other causes for the war. After World War I, the nations of Europe faced major problems in trying to return to their peacetime economies. Partly because of these problems, Britain and France could not agree on a common policy toward Germany. As a result, the restrictions against Germany in the Treaty of Versailles were not enforced. Hitler was quick to take advantage of Anglo-French disagreements to build up German power and follow an aggressive foreign policy. Mussolini sought to do the same for Italy. At a time when the world was already in the grip of the worst economic depression in history, both dictators created more crises. Tensions mounted.

636

Flames and smoke rise over the American airfield at Pearl Harbor, Hawaii. The surprise attack on December 7, 1941, brought the United States into World War II.

The world depression affected all nations, including Japan. As the depression deepened, Japan's export trade shrank and unemployment rose. Japanese militarists decided that Japan could survive as a major power only by conquering a vast empire in Asia. In this way, the problems and ambitions of Germany in Europe and Japan in Asia were linked together in causing a second great war in the 20th century.

More than 50 countries took part in World War II. The war lasted six years and was fought in Europe, Asia, North Africa, and across the Atlantic and Pacific oceans. An estimated 55 million people died in the conflict. When it finally ended, the victorious Allies divided Germany and stripped Japan of its empire.

Reading Preview

In this chapter you will learn about the Great Depression and World War II.

1. The world economy broke down.

2. Aggression destroyed an uneasy peace.

3. Total war engulfed the world.

4. The Allies were victorious.

Essential Learning Objectives

Students will learn to:

- describe the weaknesses of international markets during the 1920s.
- explain the causes of the Great Depression.

1 FOCUS AND MOTIVATE

Have students name goods, materials, and armaments that were needed during World War I. Ask them how the economy might change when a war is over. Have students think of commercial uses for military items.

2 TEACH

- Explain the relationship between oversupply and lower prices of wheat after World War I. Point out that lower prices result in decreased farm profits which leads to declines in machinery production and land value.

- Draw a flow chart to illustrate the effects of the 1929 stock market crash on world economies. Show how U.S. investors, banks, and businesses were connected to businesses in other countries. Help students deduce that the stock market crash led banks to call in their loans. Many companies then went bankrupt, causing great unemployment.

GUIDED PRACTICE

Direct students to list how countries tried to solve the effects of the world depression. (tried to become less dependent on world markets, raised tariffs, looked to government for help, created dictatorships) Also for guided practice:

Overhead Transparency 67

1 The world economy broke down.

By the 20th century, no nation possessed all the raw materials it needed, and none could produce all the manufactured goods its people wanted. Thus, through international trade, a world economic network came into existence. The prosperity of nations that sold goods depended on the ability of other nations to buy them. In 1929 that system broke down. However, there were major weaknesses in the world economy even before this time.

Agricultural prices fell during the 1920s.

One of the major economic weaknesses was in agriculture. After World War I, the high wartime demand for wheat fell. At the same time, the use of more advanced equipment and technology led to a huge increase of wheat production. As a result of the larger supply and lower demand, the world price of wheat dropped sharply. By 1930 a bushel of wheat cost less than it had in 400 years. Wheat growers all over the world were facing ruin.

The growers of other crops were also troubled by overproduction. World prices for cotton, corn, coffee, cocoa, and sugar fell. Planters in Brazil and other countries had to sell their crops at heavy losses. As a result of lower prices, farmers everywhere had less money to spend on manufactured goods. In addition, when depression struck other industries, the farmers' problems worsened because people had less money to spend on food.

Industrial recovery depended on loans.

A second major weakness in the world economy was that much of the industrial expansion of the late 1920s was paid for with borrowed money. Running a business with borrowed money is known as **credit financing**. An economic system based on credit financing will develop serious problems if the lenders demand repayment and the borrowers cannot pay. This was the kind of situation that developed in the 1920s. Many European countries, and Germany in particular, had received very large private loans from the United States.

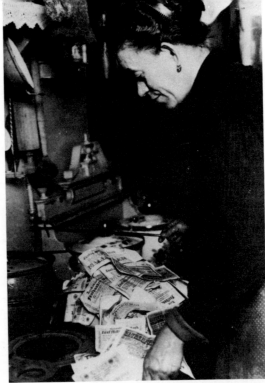

During the terrible inflation of the 1920s, some Germans burnt their worthless money as fuel because it had no other value.

Germany tried to solve its economic problems by **currency devaluation**, that is, by printing enormous quantities of paper money in larger and larger denominations. In 1918, for instance, four reichsmarks were worth about one dollar. By August, 1923, it took one million reichsmarks to equal the same dollar. A professional musician, who received a suitcase full of bills in payment for one concert, described his experience with the rapidly fluctuating reichsmark:

> On my way home, I passed a delicatessen and to relieve my hunger I spent half my fee on a couple of sausages. The next morning I saw in the paper that I could not even get one sausage for the other half of my fee.

If American lenders suddenly recalled their loans, industrial borrowers would not have enough money to buy raw materials and needed machinery to keep their factories going. Factories would close, industrial production would drop, and many people would be thrown out of work. Thus, the prosperity of Germany and the other European countries who had borrowed from the United States was insecure. It depended on the stability of the American financial system.

A financial crisis started a world depression.

On **Black Tuesday**—October 29, 1929—prices on the New York Stock Exchange began to drop very quickly. More than 16 million shares were offered for sale on that one day, and there were few buyers. Stock prices had been rising because many people had bought stocks in hopes of making quick fortunes. Suddenly these people began to fear that their gambles might not pay off. As they rushed to sell their stocks, prices "crashed."

The falling prices caused fear and panic in the business world. Banks called in their loans, and industries stopped expanding. American lenders recalled their loans from Europe. Businesses everywhere began to go bankrupt. Workers lost their jobs, banks failed, and prices dropped all over the world. Between 1929 and 1932, world manufacturing production fell by 38 percent. International trade shrank by more than 65 percent. As you can see from the table on this page, unemployment skyrocketed. By 1932 one of every four Britons and three of every ten Germans in the labor force

were out of work. It was the worst depression the world had ever known.

The world depression had important results.

Every country in the world felt the effects of the depression. Each thought it could help itself by becoming less dependent on the world market and by protecting home industries. Every country thus began raising its **tariffs**, that is, taxes on imported goods. The United States passed the highest tariff in its history in 1930. High tariffs further reduced international trade, since foreign borrowers could not get cash by selling in American markets. Without this cash, foreign borrowers found it almost impossible to pay off their loans.

The resulting problems of mass unemployment were so severe that people looked to their governments for help. Many Western governments began to take a much more active role in solving economic and social problems. In countries such as Italy and Germany with weak democratic traditions, the world depression encouraged the growth or consolidation of fascist dictatorships. Moreover, because the Western democracies were involved in their own problems, they were less willing to oppose acts of aggression by these fascist states.

Unemployment During the Depression, 1929–1939

	Belgium	Denmark	Germany	Great Britain	Netherlands	Sweden	United States
1929	2%*	16%	13%	11%	6%	11%	3%
1930	5	14	15	15	8	12	9
1931	15	18	23	22	15	17	16
1932	24	32	30	23	25	23	24
1933	20	29	26	21	27	24	25
1934	23	22	15	18	28	19	22
1935	23	20	12	16	32	16	20
1936	17	19	8	14	33	14	17
1937	14	22	5	11	27	11	14
1938	18	21	2	13	25	11	19
1939	19	18	—	12	20	9	17

*Percentages have been rounded off

The Great Depression began in the United States in 1929 with the stock market crash, and it quickly spread overseas. The chart at left shows the percentage of the work force unemployed from 1929 through 1939 in seven countries. The outbreak of war in 1939 marked the beginning of the end of the depression.

3 ASSESS AND CLOSE

ASSESS

How does currency devaluation affect buying power? (Devaluation decreases buying power.)

OPTIONAL RETEACHING

List on the chalkboard the results of high tariffs. Select students to add details to the problems higher tariffs created during the Great Depression.

OPTIONAL ENRICHMENT

1. Have students obtain newspaper articles on the 1929 stock market crash and write a summary of them. (average)
2. Assign a research report on the effect of currency devaluation on people's lives in Germany. (challenging)

INDEPENDENT PRACTICE/ HOMEWORK

Assign the Section Review, Activities page 202, or Workbook page 136.

CLOSURE

Tell students that all European economies were in distress before the stock market crash. The crash worsened economic conditions and brought poverty, hunger, and hopelessness.

Identify

Key Terms, People, and Places are defined on pages indicated in parentheses. Also see the Glossary and Biographical Dictionary.

credit financing (638), currency devaluation (638), Black Tuesday (639), tariffs (639)

Main Ideas

1. Wartime demand for wheat fell. Technology increased crop production, lowering prices.
2. Businesses and countries borrowed in order to expand. When repayment became difficult, Germany began to devalue its currency.
3. Many people had invested in the stock market to make a quick profit. When prices started to fall, investors tried to sell their stocks, but found no buyers. The economic crisis led to a worldwide depression.
4. Countries raised tariffs, reducing international trade. Unemployment shot up. Governments took a more active role in solving economic and social problems. Dictatorships arose.

Critical Thinking

Agree: Without foreign trade, foreign borrowers could not earn American dollars to pay off debts to American lenders. Foreigners could not earn dollars to buy American goods, deepening U.S. and foreign depressions. Disagree: Tariffs helped protect U.S. manufacturers and farmers against cheap foreign goods.

2 Lesson Plan

Essential Learning Objectives

Students will learn to:
- discuss how fascist governments expanded their power.

Section 1 Review

Identify credit financing, currency devaluation, Black Tuesday, tariffs

Main Ideas

1. Why did agricultural prices fall during the 1920s?
2. Why did industrial recovery depend on loans? What problems began to result from heavy borrowing?
3. Why did the price of stocks "crash" on October 29, 1929? What effects did this have on the United States and Europe?
4. What were the effects of the world depression?

Critical Thinking

Assessing Cause and Effect: Agree or disagree with the following statement and give reasons for your answer. "The United States made a serious mistake when it raised tariffs during the Great Depression because international trade dropped."

---

2 Aggression destroyed an uneasy peace.

As you learned in Chapter 33, the fascist governments of Germany and Italy glorified war and conquest. In direct violation of the Versailles Treaty, the dictators of these countries began to build up their military forces and make demands for additional territory. Tension built up among the European powers. Japan also felt threatened by rising Chinese nationalism and by the effects of the depression on its foreign trade. For a while, no effective action was taken against the moves of these dictatorships for fear that it would start another war. However, continued aggression finally destroyed the shaky peace and brought on a second world war.

Japan attacked China in 1931.

Inspired by dreams of becoming a great colonial power, Japanese militarists were determined to control China. In September, 1931, Japan seized several provinces in **Manchuria**, the northeastern part of China. (Find Manchuria on the map, page 650.) Some historians consider this action the true beginning of World War II. The Japanese trans-

formed Manchuria into a puppet state called Manchukuo [man'chü'kwō'], and despite League of Nations' demands, it refused to give up this territory, which was rich in natural resources. The Chinese retaliated by boycotting Japanese goods and cut imports from Japan by 94 percent. Japan tried to install local governments in China that would support Japan's expansion, but constant friction resulted.

In 1937 Japan launched a full-scale war against China. Shanghai, Nanjing, and other large cities fell to the Japanese, but the Chinese would not surrender. Instead, 50 million of them fled to the western part of China, taking machinery, farm equipment, and furniture in carts or on their backs. In 1938 they set up a new capital for China at Chongqing.

The League of Nations condemned the Japanese aggression, but its members were unwilling to use military force against Japan. Most countries were still suffering from the depression and did not want to damage their trade relations with Japan. Furthermore, countries like Britain and France that had suffered many casualties in World War I had a deep aversion to war. Outside of the League, the United States continued to follow its path of isolation. This refusal to take action dealt a heavy blow to the prestige of the League.

Hitler and Mussolini increased tension in Europe.

Adolf Hitler had come to power in 1933, and in 1935 he stated openly that he was rearming Germany. Later that same year, Italy's leader Mussolini attacked and conquered Ethiopia, as you learned in Chapter 33. In 1936 Hitler sent German troops into the Rhineland area northeast of France.

Hitler's moves were direct violations of the Versailles Treaty, and Mussolini's aggression was a challenge to the League of Nations. As with Japan, however, no effective action was taken against either dictator. Both France and Britain, the two strongest neighbors, wanted to avoid another conflict. Public opinion in both countries was strongly against war. Yet failure to act only encouraged the two dictators. Both Hitler and Mussolini realized that they could continue expansion without restraint from the Western democracies.

Fascism gained control in Spain in 1939.

Meanwhile, in 1931 the Spanish had forced the abdication of their monarch, King Alfonso XIII, and set up a republic. The new government tried to deal with the problems of poverty, illiteracy, and social unrest, but it failed to control a strong fascist faction that blocked the attempts to improve conditions. Led by General Francisco Franco, military chiefs revolted against the republic in 1936. The Spanish Civil War had begun. Franco's fascist forces were joined by other extreme nationalists.

Thousands of people, known as Loyalists, rushed to the defense of the Spanish republic. They were aided by the Spanish communists who felt that their best interests would be served by fighting fascism. Volunteers from other countries also helped the Loyalists. For a while they were successful, but they lacked sufficient arms.

As in the Rhineland crisis, Britain, France, and the other European states wanted to avoid a war. Therefore, they followed a policy of strict neutrality, as did the United States. Such policies stopped the democracies from helping the Loyalists. The Soviet Union was the only country to send military aid to the Loyalists.

Mussolini and Hitler, however, sent large amounts of arms and troops to help Franco. Finally, in March, 1939, Franco's forces gained control of Madrid, the Spanish capital. Franco installed a fascist dictatorship, thus ending the short-lived republic. The dictatorship would not end until the 1970s. Many people blamed the neutral policy of the democratic states for the rise of yet another fascist dictatorship in Europe.

Meanwhile, the Spanish Civil War brought Mussolini and Hitler closer together. In 1936, shortly after the war began, the two dictators worked out an agreement that they called the Rome-Berlin Axis. They hoped the world would turn around this axis. In 1940 Germany and Japan formed a diplomatic alliance, which Italy also joined. The alliance then became known as the Rome-Berlin-Tokyo Axis, or just **Axis**. Linked by this alliance, each of the three Axis powers felt that it could push its demands more aggressively.

Germany took over Austria and Czechoslovakia.

As you learned in Chapter 33, Hitler's goal was to expand the power of Germany until he controlled

A young girl (left) flees the Japanese bombing of Chongqing, 1939. Victims of the Spanish Civil War (below) flee for safety.

- examine how Britain, France, and Russia reacted to fascist aggression in the 1930s.

1 FOCUS AND MOTIVATE

Discuss why a country might invade another. (obtain natural resources, widen trade markets, and so on)

2 TEACH

- Discuss the Japanese seizure of Manchuria and its full-scale war against China. Have students identify the two factors that motivated Japan to go to war. (fear of rising Chinese nationalism, effect of the depression on Japan's foreign trade) Ask students to cite the actions of the Chinese in response to each conflict.

- Elicit reasons why the League of Nations failed to use force against Germany when Hitler sent troops to the Rhineland, against Italy when Mussolini conquered Ethiopia, and against Japan when it invaded China.

- Describe the events that led to the birth of two opposing political forces in Spain. Ask students to name the supporters of the Loyalists and of Franco's fascist forces.

- Identify the two countries Hitler took over—Austria and Czechoslovakia. Point out British and French reaction. Discuss with students possible reasons England and France chose appeasement over war against Hitler.

GUIDED PRACTICE

Have students compare the alignment of nations at the beginning of World War I with that at the beginning of World War II. Have students write statements telling how it was different and why it was different.

What type of government did the Spanish set up after the abdication of King Alfonso XIII? (a republic)

OPTIONAL RETEACHING

Draw a vertical time line on the chalkboard. Write the dates 1931, 1936, 1937, 1938, 1939, 1940 on the time line and have students name the events that took place at each time. (Japan invades Manchuria; Rome-Berlin Axis established, Spanish Civil War begins; full-scale war against China starts, Austria annexed; Munich conference held, Germans take Sudetenland; Hitler invades Poland, war declared on Germany; Rome-Berlin-Tokyo Axis established)

OPTIONAL ENRICHMENT

1. Ask students to find out the economic reasons for Japan's attack on China. Make sure students include Japan's economic limitations in their report. (average)
2. Also for enrichment:

 Source Reading 34A

INDEPENDENT PRACTICE/ HOMEWORK

Assign the Section Review, Activities page 203, or Workbook page 137.

CLOSURE

Tell students that Hitler and Mussolini increased tensions in Europe by rearming and by taking over territories. Franco increased tensions by involving Spain in a civil war. Japan, too, increased international tensions by starting a war against China. In spite of all these disquieting events, Britain and France tried to use diplomacy to avoid conflict. With the invasion of Poland, the price for peace became too high.

Axis Acquisitions, March, 1936–April, 1939

Annexed by Germany, March, 1936
Annexed by Germany, March, 1938
Annexed by Germany, September, 1938
Annexed by Germany, March, 1939
Annexed by Italy, 1936–1939

MAP STUDY This map shows the regions taken over by Germany and Italy in the late 1930s. Which areas did Germany annex between March, 1938, and March, 1939? Which area did Italy annex in 1936? 1939?

all of Europe. British and French leaders, however, refused to react forcefully to the Nazi aggression. They believed they could work out compromises to appease, or satisfy, Hitler. In this way they hoped to avoid another war. However, this policy of **appeasement** only proved to Hitler that he could take whatever land he wanted.

In March, 1938, Hitler invaded Austria and annexed, or added, the area of that country to Germany. Neither the British nor the French did anything more than protest this aggressive act.

Hitler's next target was Czechoslovakia. He claimed that the Czechs were oppressing the 3 million Germans living in a region called the Sudetenland. (Refer to the map above.) In the summer of 1938, Hitler demanded that the Sudeten Germans be given self-rule and threatened war if his demands were not met.

The Czechs turned to Britain and France for help, but the British, led by Prime Minister **Neville Chamberlain**, wanted to avoid war at all costs. To do this, Chamberlain made two trips to Germany

ANSWER TO MAP STUDY Austria, Sudetenland, Czechoslovakia; Ethiopia; Albania to talk to Hitler. The second time, Hitler increased his demands.

Chamberlain refused to accept the new terms and returned to London. He seemed to take a firm stand against Hitler. However, Hitler then announced, "This is the last territorial claim I shall make in Europe." He asked Chamberlain and French Premier Edouard Daladier [dä lä dyä′] to meet with him and Mussolini in Munich on September 29, 1938. They agreed. No representative from Czechoslovakia was invited to the meeting.

During the **Munich conference**, Chamberlain and Daladier agreed to the transfer of the Sudetenland to Hitler's control. Hitler promised he would take no more Czech territory. The Czechs had no choice but to give in. Six months later, however, Hitler took over the rest of Czechoslovakia.

This brutal action finally convinced Chamberlain and Daladier that Hitler could not be appeased. They realized that his real aim was to dominate all of Europe. They therefore gave up their policy of appeasement and decided to oppose any further German demands.

Germany attacked Poland and began World War II.

Hitler's next move was against Poland. The Treaty of Versailles had given Poland a corridor of land through Prussia. Note on the map on page 642 how this **Polish Corridor** divided Germany's territory. The Polish Corridor gave Poland an outlet to the Baltic Sea. Danzig, the port city of the corridor, had been declared an independent city under the protection of the League of Nations. About 90 percent of the corridor's population was Polish, but most of the people in Danzig were German.

In March, 1939, Hitler demanded that Danzig be given to Germany. He also said that the Nazis must be allowed to occupy a narrow strip of the corridor connecting Germany with East Prussia. Poland refused, and this time both Britain and France warned Hitler they would come to Poland's aid if he attacked it. The major question now was what the Soviet Union would do.

Britain and France knew that Poland could not be defended without Soviet help. Stalin, who had been ignored at the Munich conference, was not eager to join the democracies, who had long opposed the Soviet communist regime. Stalin wanted to protect his western frontiers and asked Britain and France for control over the countries in eastern Europe that bordered on the Soviet Union. For Britain and France, that was too high a price to pay for Soviet cooperation. However, Hitler was willing to pay such a price because he expected to conquer all the territory at a later time. He therefore made the Nazi-Soviet pact with Stalin, guaranteeing Stalin's neutrality in return for eastern Europe. With the danger of a two-front war gone, Hitler was free to strike at Poland. On September 1, 1939, he did. Two days later, Britain and France declared war on Germany. World War II had begun.

Section 2 Review

Identify Manchuria, Axis, appeasement, Neville Chamberlain, Munich conference, Polish Corridor

Main Ideas

1. Why did Japan invade China? Why didn't the League of Nations prevent it from doing so?
2. How did Hitler's actions in the Rhineland and Mussolini's in Ethiopia increase tensions in Europe?
3. What caused the downfall of the Spanish Republic?
4. How was Germany able to take over Austria and Czechoslovakia?
5. How did the German attack on Poland lead to the outbreak of World War II?

Critical Thinking

Recognizing Values: It was difficult for the governments of Britain and France to stop German expansion because their values differed from the government of Nazi Germany. Give examples of these differences.

A German military band plays in Prague after the German army occupies Czechoslovakia in March, 1939.

GEOGRAPHY

A Key to History

GEOPOLITICS AND NAZI EXPANSION

Adolf Hitler's quest for power was based in large part on a geopolitical theory that justified conquest and expansion. This theory was developed by Karl Haushofer, a retired general who taught geography at the University of Munich.

Haushofer's works on geopolitics described a nation as a living organism that has a life, a death, and a past from which it evolved. In order to live, he said, it must conquer other nations to gain needed *Lebensraum* [lă′bəns roum′], or "living space."

Through a series of conquests, Germany had evolved from a group

Where was Germany in relation to the Heartland? What was occurring in the Heartland in the 1920s and 1930s when Haushofer's theories became popular?

of small states to a large empire. Haushofer argued that to survive Germany must continue to conquer and expand.

Haushofer taught that control of the land areas of Eastern Europe and central Asia was the key to world conquest. He explained that whoever controlled the Heartland (an area extending from the southwestern Soviet Union to Mongolia) controlled the World Island (Europe, Asia, and Africa) and thereby controlled the world. Haushofer backed up this idea with statistics that showed that the Heartland had the potential to become the most important agricultural and industrial region in the world. The Heartland also provided a base from which armies could attack any country on its rim. He urged Germans to conquer all of Eastern Europe and the Soviet Union.

Haushofer held considerable influence during the Hitler regime. His theories were taught in the schools and popularized in the press. They justified Nazi expansion as "natural" and necessary growth. Some geographers opposed Haushofer's theories, arguing that a nation is not an organism and that geography can only influence, not determine, human behavior. However, these views were not popular in Nazi Germany.

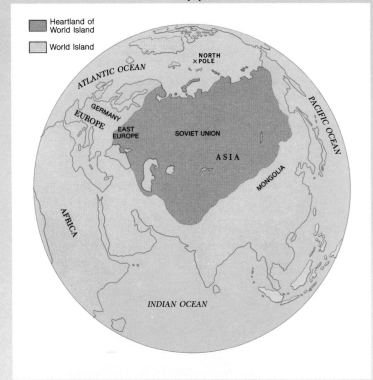

Heartland of World Island

World Island

REVIEW

1. Which continents make up the World Island?
2. Why did Germany need *Lebensraum*, according to Karl Haushofer?
3. If Haushofer was correct in asserting that the nation which controlled the Heartland would control the world, which nation today would be the leading world power?

3 Total war engulfed the world.

When war broke out in 1939, it was primarily a European conflict. For more than two years, most of the fighting took place in Europe and the North Atlantic Ocean. The United States maintained its neutrality, but it supplied war materials to the fighting democracies. At that time, the United States had only small armed forces and few modern weapons. It had almost no fighting ships or airplanes.

U.S. President **Franklin D. Roosevelt** was gradually able to change the public's opinion about isolation. As a result, the U.S. Congress authorized a two-ocean navy, enlargement of the air force, and, in 1940, passage of the Selective Service Act, which enabled the government to draft troops. When Japan attacked the United States in December, 1941, the war became worldwide. From that time on, there was heavy fighting in the Pacific, as well as in Asia and North Africa. Thus, World War II was much more truly a global war than World War I had been.

The Germans and Soviets conquered much of eastern Europe.

In attacking Poland, the Germans struck quickly. They launched a massive attack on Poland using mechanized armies in a new and terrifying form of warfare called a *blitzkrieg* [blits'krēg'], which means "lightning war." The Poles could not match the powerful German military force, with its panzer (armored) divisions and *Luftwaffe* (air force). The Polish air force was destroyed on the ground. The Polish cavalry, as one writer described it,

> . . . came riding on splendid horses; white-gloved officers signaled the charge, trumpets sounded, and sabers flashed in the sun. In a few minutes the cavalry lay in a smoking, screaming mass of men and horses.

In three weeks, Poland was totally crushed.

As part of the Nazi-Soviet pact, Stalin's armies moved into eastern Poland, Latvia, Lithuania, and Estonia. The Soviet Union then ordered Finland to give up some of its land near Leningrad. When Finland refused, the Soviet Union attacked it in November, 1939. By March, 1940, Finland was defeated and forced to surrender the land that the Soviet Union wanted for better protection of Leningrad. Soviet control of all these areas today dates from this time except for Nazi occupation in 1941–1944.

The Germans conquered western Europe.

After defeating Poland, Hitler made plans to crush France and Britain. First, he invaded and conquered Denmark and Norway in April, 1940. In May, he turned southward and overran the Netherlands and Belgium. By conquering Belgium, Hitler had bypassed France's major defenses along the **Maginot Line** [mazh'ə nō], an elaborate system of defensive structures built by France along the German border after World War I. The French army was cut to pieces, and in June, 1940, France surrendered. In the same month, Mussolini brought Italy actively into the war on the German side. The Axis forces were now in control of almost all of western Europe.

The defeated Allied troops were now trapped on the French coast at **Dunkirk**. The British formed a flotilla of naval vessels, fishing boats, yachts, barges, and tugboats and crossed the English Channel under fire from the German air force to rescue the British, French, and Belgian soldiers. More than 338,000 troops were saved as a result of this valiant effort.

The battle of Britain turned back the Nazis.

After the summer of 1940, Britain was left to stand alone against Germany. Britain had not been invaded since William the Conqueror had done so in 1066. However, Hitler believed that the British were weak, "a nation of shopkeepers." Therefore, he reasoned, the British would be willing to make a compromise peace. **Winston Churchill**, however, who had become prime minister in May, 1940, refused to make such a peace. Following Dunkirk he addressed Parliament and spelled out Britain's resolve:

> We shall defend our island whatever the cost may be. We shall fight on the beaches, we shall fight on the landing grounds, we shall fight in the fields, and in the streets, we shall fight on the hills; we shall never surrender.

Churchill's words inspired captive peoples everywhere with the hope that the British would somehow stand up to the Nazi war machine.

Hermann Gœring [gœ′ring], commander of the German air force, convinced Hitler that the Allied defeat on the continent had so weakened the British that they could be bombed into surrender. Mass bombings of Britain began in August, 1940, and for the next ten months, London suffered punishing nightly attacks that are known as the London blitz. During these months fierce air battles raged in the skies over Britain. With the help of a new device called radar and a fighter plane named the Spitfire, the Royal Air Force gradually gained

superiority over the *Luftwaffe*. By May, 1941, Hitler knew that he had lost the battle of Britain and that the British could not be defeated by air.

The battle of Britain, though it took place early in the war, is considered to be one of the major turning points of the war. Although the Germans still had the world's most powerful military force, they had failed to defeat a major opponent. Soon they would gain another major opponent, the Soviet Union.

Hitler attacked the Soviet Union in 1941.

Despite the Nazi-Soviet pact and against the advice of his generals, Hitler decided to invade the Soviet Union. He wanted to conquer this vast country because of its rich grain fields and its large supplies of oil, coal, and iron ore. Then he planned to turn back against Britain.

Before moving into the Soviet Union, Hitler conquered the Balkans and made alliances with Hungary, Romania, and Bulgaria. In early 1941 the Nazi forces also overran Greece and Yugoslavia.

In June, 1941, German forces swept into the Soviet Union. By December Germany had conquered

ЗАЩИТИМ РОДНУЮ МОСКВУ

The 1941 Russian war poster at left reads: "We will defend our Moscow." Below are the remnants of the Allied forces trapped at Dunkirk in June, 1940, awaiting rescue from the Nazis.

hundreds of thousands of square miles of territory. (See the map on page 650.) More than 3.5 million Soviet soldiers were killed or captured, and the Soviet Union lost almost its entire air force. The Germans were close to Moscow and had surrounded Leningrad. Leningrad held out against constant bombardment for almost three years, and nearly one million people died of starvation and disease in the besieged city.

Stalin did not believe that Hitler would break their 1939 pact and so was not fully prepared for war. However, despite terrible losses, the Soviet army still had huge reserves of manpower. Early in December, 1941, the Soviets launched a counterattack to drive the Germans back from Moscow. Stalin called upon his people to "scorch the earth." "The enemy," he declared, "must not be left a single engine, a single rail car, a single pound of grain, or a single gallon of fuel."

Hitler had made the same fatal mistake that another would-be conqueror, Napoleon, had also made: The invaders were not prepared for fighting in the severe Russian winter. The Germans had no antifreeze in their tanks and they wore their summer uniforms. As a result, thousands of Germans froze to death in the −30°F weather. The Soviets, prepared for winter fighting, halted the German army and forced it back from Moscow. "General Winter" had once again helped the Russians save their country from defeat.

Japan bombed Pearl Harbor and brought the United States into war.

On the morning of December 7, 1941, without warning or declaration of war, Japan attacked the American naval base at **Pearl Harbor** in Hawaii. The Japanese also attacked the U.S. possession of the Philippines, the British colony of Malaya, the Dutch East Indies, French Indochina, and other colonies in Southeast Asia. The Japanese planned to build a great empire in Southeast Asia that would supply Japan with oil, rubber, tin, and rice and provide a market for Japanese factory goods. Only the United States could stop Japan, because the European countries that had colonies in Asia were too busy fighting in Europe.

The Japanese surprise attack destroyed much of the American Pacific fleet. It also brought the

Millions of American women joined the wartime civilian labor force, providing workers for aircraft plants, shipyards, and other defense industries.

United States into the war. The United States declared war on Japan; then Germany and Italy declared war on the United States. By January 1, 1942, the United States, the Soviet Union, Britain, and 23 other nations had become allied to fight against Germany, Italy, Japan, and their allies. The war between the Axis and the Allies was now worldwide.

Two months after Pearl Harbor, President Roosevelt signed an executive order that resulted in the internment of 77,000 Japanese American citizens and 43,000 Japanese nationals living along the west coast of the United States. These citizens and aliens were spread among 26 "relocation centers" in 16 states across the country. As a result of this action, thousands were forced to sell their homes and businesses at short notice, causing financial ruin. The citizens among them were denied their basic constitutional rights. Most Japanese Americans were not allowed to return to their homes until the end of the war. The Japanese American relocation is still a disputed topic among Americans. In the late 1980s, the U.S. Congress voted to pay some reparations to Japanese Americans for their lost properties. However, the controversy still continues. Was this action a reasonable war measure, or should it be considered a gross violation of civil liberties?

In positive ways the American people proved themselves ready and willing to fight a worldwide conflict. Army and navy recruiting offices were flooded with volunteers, including the 350,000 women who served in the American armed forces.

3 | ASSESS AND CLOSE

ASSESS
1. Why didn't the London blitz work? (British air force gained superiority over the German *Luftwaffe*.)
2. Why did the Soviet Union invade Finland? (to force Finland to give up land near Leningrad)

OPTIONAL RETEACHING
Divide students into two groups. Have one group list the successes and defeats of the Axis powers and have the other group list the successes and defeats of the Allies.

OPTIONAL ENRICHMENT
1. Have students read and summarize newspaper articles on the bombing of Pearl Harbor. (average)
2. Ask interested students to research and write a report that compares Napoleon's invasion of Russia with Hitler's invasion. (challenging)

INDEPENDENT PRACTICE/ HOMEWORK
Assign the Section Review, Activities page 204, or Workbook page 138.

CLOSURE
Summarize the lesson by telling students that Hitler's miscalculation of the British will to fight, his unprepared invasion of Russia, and the United States entrance into the war were the three factors that caused the defeat of Nazi Germany.

Answers to Section 3 Review

Identify
Key Terms, People, and Places are defined on pages indicated in parentheses. Also see the Glossary and Biographical Dictionary.
Franklin D. Roosevelt (645), Maginot Line (645), Dunkirk (645), Winston Churchill (645), Pearl Harbor (647)

Main Ideas
1. The Germans launched a massive attack called a *blitzkrieg* against the unprepared Poles. The Soviets took over part of Poland and Finland and all of Estonia, Latvia, and Lithuania.
2. By June of 1940 Germany had conquered Denmark, Norway, the Netherlands, Belgium, and France.
3. The British won and Germany gave up attempts to conquer Britain.
4. Hitler wanted the Soviet's resources. Despite enormous losses, the Soviets pushed German forces back from Moscow.
5. Japan wanted to cripple the U.S. fleet so that Japanese expansion could continue. Bringing the United States into the war doomed Japan.

Critical Thinking
No. Americans were determined never to fight another foreign war. Others may say Yes. The United States was already on a partial war footing, and Americans would never have let the Germans and Japanese gain total control of the Atlantic and Pacific oceans.

Meanwhile, on the home front, women stepped in to fill jobs left by men in arms. They also took many newly created jobs in heavy industry and war plants where they built airplanes and fighting ships. The nation's conversion to a war economy was one of the wonders of the industrial world. By 1944, for example, one B-24 bomber was finished every 63 minutes at the Ford Willow Run plant near Detroit. The "arsenal of democracy" soon began to supply Britain and the Soviet Union with the arms, munitions, and equipment needed to halt the Axis.

Section 3 Review

Identify Franklin D. Roosevelt, Maginot Line, Dunkirk, Winston Churchill, Pearl Harbor

Main Ideas
1. How was Germany able to conquer Poland so quickly? What parts of eastern Europe did the Soviet Union take over?
2. What successes did the Germans achieve in western Europe in the early stages of the war?
3. What was the outcome of the battle of Britain?
4. Why did Hitler attack the Soviet Union? What was the outcome?
5. Why did Japan attack Pearl Harbor, and how did it affect the war?

Critical Thinking
Making Hypotheses: If the Japanese had not bombed Pearl Harbor, do you think the United States would have entered the war? Give reasons for your answer.

 ## The Allies were victorious.

The Axis powers reached the height of their expansion in the spring of 1942. The Japanese had created an empire that included much of China, all of Southeast Asia, and all of the islands of the western Pacific Ocean. (Refer to the map on page 650.) The Germans controlled Europe from Norway to North Africa and from the Atlantic coast to the gates of Moscow. Soon, however, the tide of battle slowly began to turn against the Axis powers.

Hitler implemented the Final Solution.

Both Japan and Germany forced their conquered peoples to work for them as slave laborers. As soon as they made conquests, the Nazis began to raid the economies of the subjugated countries for the benefit of Germany. This reorganization of Europe was called the "New Order." Thus, vast quantities of Soviet grain, French crops, and Romanian oil were shipped to Germany, and 7 million foreign workers were sent to Germany as slaves.

In the conquered lands, the Nazis used ruthless terror to control the local people. The horrors of Nazi rule were especially brutal aginst the Slavic peoples—Poles, Russians, Czechs, Yugoslavs—who were considered to be "inferior" peoples destined to serve the Nazis as slaves. More than 3 million people from the Soviet Union alone died in German prison camps.

As you learned in Chapter 33, Hitler's dream for world dominance included the creation of a race of superior beings, or "master race," called Aryans. According to Nazi ideas, most Germans were Aryans, but the population needed to be "purified" by the destruction of "defective" and "inferior" peoples. Gypsies and Jews were marked for total annihilation. Since the 1920s, Hitler had encouraged the already existing anti-Semitism in Germany in order to gain power and inflame the people with Nazi ideas. Jews were made the scapegoats for the signing of the Versailles Treaty and for every economic failure between the two wars. In the early years of the war, special Nazi execution squads, called the SS, shot hundreds of thousands of Jewish men, women, and children in Poland and the Soviet Union.

In 1942 the Nazis put into action a monstrous plan called the **Final Solution**, a carefully devised program to kill all the Jews of Europe. Deep inside Poland, special death camps equipped with poison gas chambers and cremating ovens were built especially to kill and dispose of the bodies of millions of people. The largest of these death camps was Auschwitz [oush'vits], where between 2 and 3 million Jews and hundreds of thousands of Poles, Russians, Czechs, Yugoslavs, Gypsies, and anti-Nazi Germans were brutally murdered.

In 1942 a young man, Filip Muller, like millions of his fellow prisoners, was jammed into a sealed cattle car and transported to Auschwitz. He was among the 10 percent of the prisoners singled out by the Nazis to work as slaves in the death camps. The rest were put to death. In his book, *Eyewitness Auschwitz: Three Years in the Gas Chambers*, Muller described these mass executions which took place on an hourly basis:

> There were 600 people crammed into the crematorium. The final SS man locked the door from the outside. Before long . . . sounds of coughing, screaming and shouting for help could be heard. . . . Sound ceased and in the silence each of us felt the horror of this terrible mass death.

Filip Muller was later moved to Treblinka, another death camp, and was liberated only in 1945. He had survived the worst of all Nazi programs—genocide, the murder of an entire people. By the end of the war, the Nazis had murdered nearly 6 million Jews. Jewish community life in Europe, which had existed since Roman times, was almost totally destroyed. This destruction and slaughter is remembered as the **Holocaust**.

The tide began to turn against the Axis.

In June, 1942, a great sea and air battle took place between the Japanese and the Americans at Midway Island in the North Pacific. (See the map on page 650.) When the battle ended, the Japanese had lost four large aircraft carriers and many airplanes and trained pilots. The United States was able to restore the naval balance it had lost at Pearl Harbor. Although the Axis powers still controlled most of the lands they had conquered, the tide of

At right is a photograph of Anne Frank, one of the millions of victims of Nazi atrocities. Below is a mass grave for some of these victims.

From the Archives

Anne Frank's Diary

Anne Frank was 13 years old when she began her diary. For the next two years, between 1942 and 1944, she recorded the events of a life in hiding with her family and four other Jews in an office building in Amsterdam. The diary, sometimes sorrowful but also full of good spirits, was left behind when the Gestapo discovered their hiding place. Anne was sent to a concentration camp where she died. The entry below is one of her last.

It's really a wonder that I haven't dropped all my ideals, because they seem so absurd and impossible to carry out. Yet I keep them, because in spite of everything I still believe that people are really good at heart. I simply can't build up my hopes on a foundation consisting of confusion, misery, and death. I see the world gradually being turned into a wilderness, I hear the ever approaching thunder, which will destroy us too, I can feel the sufferings of millions and yet, if I look up into the heavens, I think that it will all come right, that this cruelty too will end, and that peace and tranquillity will return again.

war began to shift in favor of the Allies. Several months later, the Americans began to push the Japanese out of their Pacific island strongholds.

A month after the battle of Midway, in July, 1942, the Germans began another offensive in the southern Soviet Union, which became another important turning point of the war. The German goal was to reach the Caucasus Mountains and gain control of the Soviet Union's chief food and oil supplies. By September, 1942, the Germans had reached the important city of Stalingrad on the

FROM THE ARCHIVES The excerpt is from *Anne Frank: The Diary of a Young Girl* (New York: Doubleday, 1952), p. 233. Ask interested students to report to the class on what Hitler's anti-Jewish decrees involved.

4 *Lesson Plan*

Essential Learning Objectives

Students will learn to:
- identify the Final Solution and the Holocaust.
- identify the events that led to the defeat of the Axis powers.

1 FOCUS AND MOTIVATE

Have students look at the map of Axis expansion by 1942 on page 650. Point out the areas held by the Axis and have students discuss various methods to defeat it. (armies and alliances from European theater; navies and air force from Pacific theater)

2 TEACH

- Describe Hitler's "New Order." Have students speculate as to how the use of slave labor affected the lives of peoples in the subjected countries. Guide students to conclude that Germany used forced labor and raided food crops, weapons, and oil because its own resources were limited.

- Discuss Nazi reasoning for the subjugation and killing of various groups of people. Have students cite possible reasons why the enslaved people and those facing certain death were unable to revolt. Ask students to explain what people today can learn from this abhorrent occurrence in history. Ask students to make suggestions for international safeguards against such occurrences.

- Chart and discuss the events that weakened the Axis powers after 1942. Guide the students to conclude that the Allies' superiority in the number of troops, resources, and armaments made defeat of the Axis

- powers a certainty once the United States entered the war.

- Explain the strategy for the invasion of Normandy. Have students identify the factors that made the invasion successful. Ask them to explain why Stalin questioned Roosevelt's and Churchill's motives for delaying the Normandy invasion.

- Discuss President Truman's reasons for using the atomic bomb in Japan. Ask students to give their opinions on whether Truman's desire to save American lives justified the use of atomic bombs.

Provide outline maps of Europe from the Geography Skills book. Have students draw in boundaries showing the division of Germany and control of Eastern Europe based on the Yalta conference.

ASSESS

1. Who planned the invasion of Normandy? (Churchill, Roosevelt, de Gaulle)
2. What country fought with the United States against Japan after February, 1945? (Soviet Union)

The Height of Axis Expansion, 1942

MAP STUDY The map above shows the extent of Axis conquests in late 1942. Judging from the map, did the Japanese occupy Australia? Burma? What made it difficult for U.S. ships to supply Britain and the Soviet Union?

Volga River. The Germans pounded the city, killing 40,000 civilians, but the Soviets fought ferociously and held on.

Although the German commander knew that he could not win the battle for Stalingrad, Hitler refused to let him retreat and save the army. The Soviets brought up fresh reserves, surrounded the Germans, and crushed them. In January, 1943, the Germans at Stalingrad surrendered, losing an army of more than 350,000 troops. From that time on, the Soviet Union took the offensive in eastern Europe, and Germany steadily retreated.

Another important turning point of the war came in North Africa. The aim of the German and Italian troops was to march east across North Africa to the Suez Canal and gain control of the rich oil fields of the Middle East. In October, 1942, they reached El Alamein [äl′ə mān], a town only 70 miles west of Alexandria, Egypt. However, the British stood their ground, then began a counterattack. By January, 1943, they had driven the Italians and Germans back 1,400 miles across North Africa. Meanwhile, in November, 1942, American and British troops landed in French Morocco and Algeria and pushed eastward. Squeezed from both

sides, more than 250,000 German and Italian troops surrendered in May, 1943.

After the North African victory, the path to southern Europe was open and the Allies invaded Sicily in July, 1943. Within two weeks, Mussolini was forced out of office and put in jail. A new government signed an armistice on September 8.

However, the new Italian government had little real control, and the Allied invasion met with stiff resistance from German forces. The Germans held northern Italy until early 1945.

The invasion of Normandy began the final push to Allied victory.

The Allied leaders realized that despite victories in Africa, Italy, and the Russian front, only an invasion of western Europe could bring about Nazi Germany's defeat. Stalin had been arguing for the opening of this second front ever since 1942. The longer it took to open a second front, the more suspicious Stalin became of the motives of Roosevelt and Churchill. As Stalin saw it, these two leaders of capitalist countries were deliberately delaying the opening of a second front to keep Nazi forces concentrated against the Soviet Union. Sta-

ANSWER TO MAP STUDY no; yes; German submarine concentrations

650

lin's suspicions remained with him even though, all through 1943, the United States sent the Soviet Union enormous quantities of American planes, guns, trucks, jeeps, clothing, food, and machinery. These supplies made an invaluable contribution to the Soviet war effort.

In January, 1943, Churchill and Roosevelt met in Casablanca to form the strategy for the invasion. Included in these plans was General Charles de Gaulle, leader of the Free French. During these meetings the participants agreed with Roosevelt's mandate that only an "unconditional surrender" from Germany would be acceptable.

The actual reason for the delay in opening the second front was that it took time to assemble all the necessary equipment and train all the troops for what would be the largest amphibious (sea-land) invasion in history. Complex plans had to be worked out carefully and in secret. By the spring of 1944, some 800,000 trained troops were ready in Britain. Ships and landing craft waited in anticipation at British ports.

At low tide in the early daylight hours of June 6, 1944, remembered as **D-day**, an enormous invasion force called "Operation Overlord," led by U.S. General **Dwight D. Eisenhower**, moved across the English Channel. The Normandy line of attack stretched 50 miles wide. A flotilla of 4,000 vessels carried the first line of infantry divisions to the five beaches—Utah, Omaha, Gold, Juno, and Sword—that had to be secured before the Allies could move deeper into the continent.

On the first day of the invasion, Allied casualties reached 11,000, including some 2,500 dead. After a week of fierce fighting, the Allies held the crucial strip of the Normandy beach. Within 100 days of D-day, 2.2 million Allied troops and 450,000 vehicles had been landed under fire on the heavily defended coast of France. No invasion force of this magnitude had ever been made before or since. In July the Allied armored divisions broke through the German lines and turned southward toward Paris. On August 25 the city was liberated. Now the forces from the west turned toward Berlin, as did the Soviets from the east.

A major conference was held at Yalta in February, 1945.

By February, 1945, victory in Europe was in sight for the Allies. To discuss peace terms, Roosevelt, Churchill, and Stalin met at **Yalta**, a Black Sea resort in the southern Soviet Union. They decided that Germany would be divided into four occupation zones controlled by each of the Allies, including France.

The most difficult problem for the Allies was control of eastern Europe. By the time of the Yalta

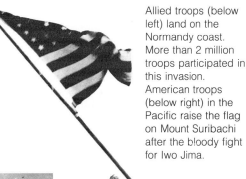

Allied troops (below left) land on the Normandy coast. More than 2 million troops participated in this invasion. American troops (below right) in the Pacific raise the flag on Mount Suribachi after the bloody fight for Iwo Jima.

OPTIONAL RETEACHING

Divide students into two groups. Have one team list the events that led to the defeat of the Japanese and the other list the events that led to the defeat of Germany. Have students describe the factors that ensured the defeat.

Students also may be assigned Activities reteaching page 206.

OPTIONAL ENRICHMENT

1. Have students read *Hiroshima* by John Hersey or *Anne Frank: The Diary of a Young Girl* and prepare an oral report on it for the class. (average)
2. Ask students to locate one of Bill Mauldin's cartoons from World War II and write an explanation of its message. (challenging)
3. Students also may be assigned Activities enrichment page 207.
4. Also for enrichment:

 Overhead Transparency 68

 Source Reading 34B

 One-Day Play
The Trial of Adolph Eichmann

INDEPENDENT PRACTICE/ HOMEWORK

Assign the Section Review, the Chapter Review items, Activities page 205, or Workbook page 139.

CLOSURE

Tell students that the Axis powers in Europe were defeated partly through the United States all-out effort in supporting the war through troops, armaments, and supplies to the Allies, and partly because the Germans were unable to sustain fighting on several fronts. The Japanese, on the other hand, finally were defeated through use of the atomic bomb, and the use of this weapon changed the nature of wars forever.

conference, Soviet armies were only 40 miles from Berlin and controlled almost all of eastern and central Europe. Roosevelt and Churchill feared that Stalin would impose communist dictatorships on the countries under Soviet control. They insisted that Stalin give them his promise that this would not happen.

Stalin promised that free elections would be held and independent governments would be set up in all the eastern European countries. Shortly after Yalta, however, it became clear that Stalin did not intend to honor his promise. (You will read about the division of Europe in Chapter 35.)

Throughout the war the Soviet Union had been neutral in the fight against Japan. However, in early 1945, Roosevelt believed that Soviet help was needed to end the war in East Asia quickly. At Yalta, Stalin promised to enter the war against Japan within 90 days after the war against Germany ended. He made this promise in return for territorial concessions in East Asia—at the expense of China. Looking toward the postwar world, the three leaders then made a pledge that when the war was over, a group to be called the United Nations would be established.

Germany and Japan surrendered.

A few weeks after Yalta, Soviet troops entered Berlin. German forces in Italy gave way to the Allies late in April. The final surrender of Germany took place on May 8, 1945. A few days earlier, Hitler had committed suicide. Mussolini had already been captured and shot by Italians. The Allied nations, too, had lost a leader. President Roosevelt had died on April 12, 1945. He was succeeded by his vice-president, **Harry S. Truman**.

Although the war in Europe was over, the war in East Asia continued. Following the brilliant strategies of U.S. General Douglas MacArthur, years of "island-hopping" had brought steady victory to American forces in the Pacific. Now Japan lay open to American invasion. Plans were laid for a direct assault on the islands of Japan. However, the United States wanted to avoid an invasion of Japan that would have meant the loss of hundreds of thousands of American troops. Instead, President Truman ordered that an atomic bomb be dropped on Japan.

In 1905 a German physicist named Albert Einstein had published a scientific paper that related matter to energy in a famous formula: $E = mc^2$ (energy equals mass times the velocity of light squared). This means that mass and energy are equivalent, and that a small amount of matter can be transformed into a huge amount of energy. Building on this discovery, scientists in the United States constructed an atomic bomb.

On August 6, 1945, the destructive force of 20,000 tons of dynamite destroyed most of the Japanese city of Hiroshima [hir'ō shē'mə]. This single atomic bomb wounded or killed more than 160,000 persons.

On August 9 another atomic bomb was dropped on Nagasaki [nä'gə sä'kē], Japan. On the same day, Soviet troops declared war on Japan and invaded the Japanese-held areas of Korea and Manchuria. On August 10, the Japanese surrendered. The Soviet action did not affect Japan's decision to surrender, but it did have, as you will see, far-reaching implications in the years to come.

Section 4 Review

Identify Final Solution, Holocaust, D-day, Dwight D. Eisenhower, Yalta, Harry S. Truman

Main Ideas
1. What was the purpose and result of the Final Solution?
2. How did the battles at Midway, Stalingrad, and El Alamein change the course of the war?
3. Why did the United States and Britain take so long to invade Normandy? What was the result of this invasion?
4. What were the terms discussed at the Yalta conference? What agreements would later be broken by Stalin?
5. What events led to the surrender of Germany and Japan?

Critical Thinking
Making Decisions: Some historians believe that President Truman knew that the Japanese were almost ready to surrender. However, in order to avoid heavy American losses that would have been unavoidable if the United States had mounted an invasion of Japan, President Truman ordered the bombing of Hiroshima and Nagasaki. Give an argument for and an argument against his action.

HIGHLIGHTS OF CIVILIZATION

The Dawning of the Nuclear Age

*If the radiance of a thousand suns
Were to burst at once into the sky,
That would be like the splendor of
  the Mighty One . . .
I am become Death,
The shatterer of worlds.*

These words from a sacred Hindu text came to the American scientist J. Robert Oppenheimer as he witnessed the test explosion of the first atomic bomb on July 16, 1945, over the desert near Alamagordo, New Mexico. A few weeks later, similar bombs would rain destruction over the Japanese cities of Hiroshima and Nagasaki, bringing World War II to a violent close.

The development of this terrible weapon was the work of the Manhattan Project—the code name for a secret, $2 billion U.S. research effort that took place between 1942 and 1945. Many of the physicists whose work made the bomb possible were new Americans, refugees from fascist Europe, including Albert Einstein; the Hungarians Leo Szilard and Edward Teller; and Enrico Fermi, an Italian who had won a Nobel Prize in 1938.

The scientists hoped their work would soon find peaceful applications. Still, the rising of the mushroom-shaped cloud that spelled the dawning of the atomic age filled many with doubt, regret, and fear. One writer recalled a passage from the Bible: "They have sown the wind, and they shall reap the whirlwind."

In 1934 Albert Einstein wrote $E = mc^2$, showing the relationship between energy and mass (left). In the late 1980s, nuclear power supplied 70 percent of France's electricity (below).

In addition to its New Mexico testing ground, the Manhattan Project involved theoretical work at universities in New York City, Chicago, and Berkeley, California; and manufacturing facilities at Oak Ridge, Tennessee, and Hanford, Washington, where radioactive material—the essential ingredient of an atomic bomb—was separated from its ore. Uranium 235 was used to make the bomb that was dropped over Hiroshima, and plutonium for the bomb used over Nagasaki. The first self-sustaining nuclear chain reaction that was the key to the success of the project was achieved in a field house at the University of Chicago on December 1, 1942.

In class discussion, list some of the positive and negative aspects of the nuclear age. (Positive aspects include possibility that nuclear weapons will act as a deterrent to war, source of huge amounts of energy, radioactive materials useful for medical purposes; negative aspects include possibility of accidental or deliberate total destruction, contamination from radioactive waste or nuclear accidents.)

Answers to Test Yourself

Key Terms, People, and Places
The key terms, people, and places tested here were introduced in the chapter sections and reviewed in the Section Reviews. For definitions see the page references at the appropriate Section Reviews. Also see the Glossary and Biographical Dictionary.

Main Ideas
The main ideas tested here were introduced in the sections of this chapter and reviewed in the Section Reviews. For answers to these questions, see the appropriate Section Reviews.

Critical Thinking
1. Students' answers might include the subjects of citizenship, national defense, racial purity, racism, and constitutional rights.
2. Students might answer that some people think nuclear weapons act as a deterrent against attack; others think they contribute to distrust among nations.

CHAPTER 34 REVIEW

Section Summaries

Section 1
The world economy broke down.
A world depression began in 1929 and became the worst in history. It occurred partly because of weaknesses after World War I in the world economy, especially agriculture. The world prices of wheat and other crops dropped, and many farmers faced ruin. When the New York stock market crashed, American lenders began to recall European loans. Businesses failed, and many people were thrown out of work. All countries raised their tariffs, and international trade fell sharply.

Section 2
Aggression destroyed an uneasy peace.
In the 1930s, the leaders of Nazi Germany, fascist Italy, and militaristic Japan made aggressive moves. Japan's military leaders attacked China. Hitler sent troops into the Rhineland. Mussolini conquered Ethiopia. In 1938 and 1939, Hitler annexed Austria and Czechoslovakia. On September 1, 1939, Germany attacked Poland, launching World War II.

Section 3
Total war engulfed the world.
By June, 1941, Hitler controlled almost all of central and western Europe, except Britain. He than attacked the Soviet Union. On December 7, 1941, Japan made a surprise attack on the American naval base at Pearl Harbor. The United States declared war on Japan, and Germany and Italy soon declared war on the United States. By early 1942 Japan had conquered a huge empire in Southeast Asia.

Section 4
The Allies were victorious.
Hitler set up a brutal "New Order" in Europe and began a policy of genocide. The tide of battle turned against Japan, Germany, and Italy in 1942–1943, after battles at Midway Island, Stalingrad, and El Alamein. Then in June, 1944, the Allies invaded Normandy. Germany surrendered in May, 1945, and Japan surrendered in August after the United States dropped atomic bombs on Hiroshima and Nagasaki.

Test Yourself

Key Terms, People, and Places
Identify the significance of each of the following:

Section 1
a. credit financing   c. Black Tuesday
b. currency devaluation   d. tariff

Section 2
a. Manchuria   d. Neville Chamberlain
b. Axis   e. Munich conference
c. appeasement   f. Polish Corridor

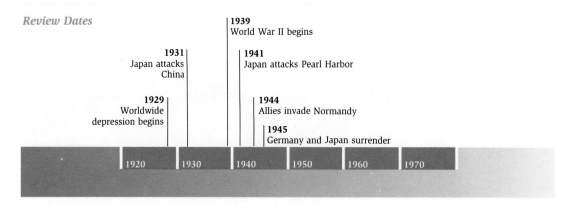

Review Dates

1929 Worldwide depression begins
1931 Japan attacks China
1939 World War II begins
1941 Japan attacks Pearl Harbor
1944 Allies invade Normandy
1945 Germany and Japan surrender

1920   1930   1940   1950   1960   1970

Section 3

a. Franklin D. Roosevelt
b. Maginot Line
c. Dunkirk
d. Winston Churchill
e. Pearl Harbor

Section 4

a. Final Solution
b. Holocaust
c. D-day
d. Dwight D. Eisenhower
e. Yalta
f. Harry S. Truman

Main Ideas

Section 1

1. What caused agricultural prices to fall during the 1920s?
2. Why did industrial recovery rely on loans? What problems occurred as a result of heavy borrowing?
3. What caused the price of stocks to "crash" on October 29, 1929? How did this affect the United States and Europe?
4. What was the impact of the world depression?

Section 2

1. Why did Japan invade China? Why was the League of Nations unable to prevent Japan from doing so?
2. How did Hitler's actions in the Rhineland and Mussolini's in Ethiopia lead to increased tensions in Europe?
3. Why did the Spanish Republic fail?
4. What permitted Germany to take over Austria and Czechoslovakia?
5. Why did the German attack on Poland lead to the outbreak of World War II?

Section 3

1. Why was Germany able to conquer Poland so quickly? What parts of eastern Europe were taken over by the Soviet Union?
2. What successes did Germany gain in western Europe in the early stages of the war?
3. What was the result of the battle of Britain?
4. Why did Hitler attack the Soviet Union? What was the result?
5. Why did Japan attack Pearl Harbor? What was its effect on the war?

Section 4

1. Describe the purpose and result of the Final Solution.

2. How did the battles at Midway, Stalingrad, and El Alamein affect the war?
3. Why did the United States and Britain delay in invading Normandy? What was the effect of this invasion?
4. What terms were discussed at the Yalta conference? Which of the agreements would Stalin later break?
5. Describe the events that led to the surrender of Germany and Japan.

Critical Thinking

1. **Analyzing Comparisons** During World War II, the Germans sent many people to death camps and other concentration camps. The United States sent many Japanese Americans to relocation centers, sometimes known as internment camps. What comparisons would you make between the two policies?
2. **Recognizing Values** Why do some people feel that nuclear weapons should be produced while others believe that they should be banned entirely?

Chapter Skills and Activities

Practicing Study and Research Skills

Using Oral History as a Source
Find out what it was like to live during the Great Depression or World War II. Ask older relatives or others to describe some of their experiences. Ask them to comment on how these experiences may have changed the way they conduct their lives today. Take notes on your interviews. Then write a report on what you learned from these interviews.

Linking Past and Present

The Holocaust, the direct attempt to kill all Jews on earth, was a crime that is hard to fathom today. However, there have been other attempts to do just the same thing. Use encyclopedias, newspapers, and magazines to find any similar "Final Solutions."

Learning History Through Maps

Compare the map of Axis acquisitions (page 642) with the political map of Europe in the Atlas (page 792). What changes do you see?

CRITICAL THINKING QUESTION LEVEL 1. average; 2. challenging

REVIEW

Summarizing the Unit

Chapter 30
The Surge of Imperialism
During the years from 1870 to 1914, Western nations became interested in colonies for raw materials, new export markets, and investment opportunities. Many nations also had religious or humanitarian reasons for their colonizing.

Chapter 31
World War I
World War I, which began as a conflict between Austria and Serbia, escalated into the first total war in history and signaled the beginning of Europe's decline as the center of world power. The United States emerged as the new world leader.

Chapter 32
The Soviet Union: The First Communist State
The Soviet Union emerged from World War I as the result of the March and October revolutions, known together as the Russian Revolution. The actual economic and social transformation of Russia however took place during the regime of Joseph Stalin.

Chapter 33
Nationalism, Revolution, and Dictatorship
Nationalism spread from Europe to Asia and Africa and intensified after World War I. In its most extreme form, nationalism expressed itself in the rise of a dictatorial, militaristic movements in Italy, Germany, and Japan.

Chapter 34
World Depression and World War II
After 1929, at a time when the world was in the grip of the worst economic depression in history, Britain and France were unable to respond to the crises created by the dictators Adolf Hitler and Benito Mussolini. Japanese militarists also pushed for expansion in China and Southeast Asia. World War II broke out in 1939 and was ultimately won by the Allies.

Using Writing Skills

Revising and polishing your work can turn a poor piece of writing into an excellent one. Proofreading—reading the piece carefully and marking errors to be corrected—is an important step in the revision process. Use a dictionary to check the spelling of any words about which you are uncertain. Make sure you use the correct punctuation and complete sentences.

Activity. Read the following story about U.S. President Harry Truman. Then, copy the story on a separate piece of paper, using the proofreaders' marks that you can find in most dictionaries or grammar textbooks to correct any errors that you find.

Harry Truman
Truman was a missouri farm boy and life-long democrat. Who had served in world war I and then returned home to fale as the owner of a mens clothing store. He went into politix wear, as a loyle. But honest member of the Democratic machine. He rose to become a county judge and later a united states senetur. After an undistingwished career. Truman emurged as the choise for the vicepresidenshul candidate 1944. After Franklin D Roosevelts death, Truamn assumed the presidentsy and went on to becme one of the outstanding U.S presidents

Test Yourself

Key Terms and People
Match each term or person with the correct definition.
1. region where the economic interests of a certain country were supreme
2. international association for keeping peace
3. the destruction of European Jews by the Nazis
4. 6,000-mile retreat of the Chinese communists
5. militaristic system of government ruled by a dictator, with strong control of industry and labor
a. fascism
b. spheres of influence
c. League of Nations
d. Holocaust
e. Long March

Key Dates

Match the letters on the time line with the events for which they stand:

1900 1910 1920 1930 1940 1950 1960

A B   C D   E   F   G

____ Hitler becomes Führer of Germany.
____ The Tsarist regime collapses.
____ The worldwide depression begins.
____ World War I begins.
____ Germany and Japan surrender.
____ Stalin gains power.
____ World War II begins.

Key Places

____ wealthy region controlled by the British
____ city where the Archduke Francis Ferdinand was assassinated
____ area thrown into famine when the Russian government seized its grain
____ independent country conquered by Mussolini
____ place where Germany's postwar fate was decided

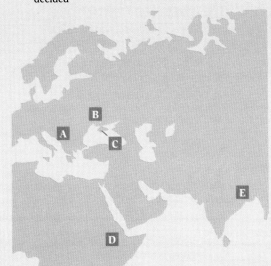

Main Ideas

1. Western nations became interested in colonies ____
a. only in Africa and Asia.
b. mainly to get rid of undesirable citizens.
c. primarily for cultural reasons.
d. largely for economic reasons.

2. Many historians believe that the Treaty of Versailles ending World War I caused ____
a. the conditions leading to World War II.
b. more permanent cooperation between nations.
c. economic stability in Europe
d. political stability in Europe.

3. The Soviet Union during the 1930s promoted ____
a. the rise of private businesses.
b. the growth of new political parties.
c. the collectivization of agriculture.
d. no relations with other countries.

4. Adolf Hitler was able to seize power in Germany because of ____
a. weakened economic conditions.
b. the desire to begin a war with Japan.
c. attacks on Germany by Poland.
d. fear of attack by the Russians.

5. The United States dropped the atomic bomb on Japan because ____
a. Truman thought the United States was losing the war.
b. Truman wanted to show he was a strong leader.
c. Truman wanted to avoid an American invasion of Japan.
d. Truman was carrying out Roosevelt's plan.

Critical Thinking

1. **Making Hypotheses** How do you think World War I might have been avoided? What conditions would have needed to be dealt with? Support your answer with evidence.

2. **Analyzing Comparisons** In what ways do you think Adolf Hitler and Benito Mussolini differed from Joseph Stalin? Support your answer with evidence.

The Era of Global Interdependence

ADDITIONAL TEACHING AIDS FOR UNIT NINE

OVERVIEW

This unit emphasizes global interdependence as it covers developments from 1945 to the present in Europe, Asia, Africa, the Middle East, and Latin America.

Literature for the Teacher

Carmack, Robert M. *Harvest of Violence: The Maya Indians and the Guatemalan Crisis.* Norman: University of Oklahoma Press, 1988.

Craig, Mary. *Lech Walesa and His Poland.* New York: Continuum, 1987.

Ehrmann, Henry W. *Politics in France* (4th Edition). Glenview: Scott, Foresman and Co., 1983.

Fusfeld, Daniel R. *The Age of the Economist* (5th Edition). Glenview: Scott, Foresman and Co., 1986.

Jones, Walter S. *The Logic of International Relations* (6th Edition) Glenview: Scott, Foresman and Co., 1988.

Knox, Donald. *The Korean War: Uncertain Victory.* San Diego: Harcourt Brace Jovanovich, 1988.

Keohane, Robert. O., and Joseph S. Nye. *Power and Interdependence* (2nd Edition). Glenview: Scott, Foresman and Co., 1989.

Lacey, Robert. *The Kingdom: Arabia and the House of Saud.* San Diego: Harcourt Brace Jovanovich, 1982.

Laffer, Arthur B., and Marc A. Miles. International *Economics in an Integrated World.* Glenview: Scott, Foresman and Co., 1982.

Lewis, Flora. *Europe: A Tapestry of Nations.* New York: Simon & Schuster, 1985.

Lieber, Robert J. *No Common Power: Understanding International Relations.* Glenview: Scott, Foresman and Co., 1988.

Palumbo, Michael. *The Palestinian Catastrophe.* London: Faber & Faber, 1987.

de Paor, Liam, *The People of Ireland.* South Bend: University of Notre Dame Press, 1986.

Taheri, Amir. *The Spirit of Allah: Khomeini and the Islamic Revolution.* Adler and Adler, 1986.

Woodruff, William. *Struggle for World Power.* St Martins Press, 1981.

Literature for the Student

Almond, Gabriel A., and G. Bingham Powell, Jr. *Comparative Politics Today: A World View.* Glenview: Scott, Foresman and Co., 1988. (challenging)

Art, Robert J., and Robert Jarvis. *International Politics, Anarchy, Force, Political Economy, and Decision-Making* (2nd Edition). Glenview: Scott, Foresman and Co., 1985. (challenging)

Avner, Yehuda. *The Young Inheritors: A Portait of Israel's Children.* Doubleday, 1982. (easy)

Barghoorn, Frederick C., and Thomas F. Remington. *Politics in the USSR* (3rd Edition), Glenview: Scott, Foresman and Co., 1986. (challenging)

Belcher, Wendy Laura. *Honey from the Lion: An African Journey.* New York: E. P. Dutton, 1988. (average)

Brown, Seyom. *New Forces, Old Forces, and the Future of World Politics.* Glenview: Scott, Foresman and Co., 1988. (challenging)

Dalton, Russell J. *Politics in West Germany.* Glenview: Scott, Foresman and Co., 1989. (challenging)

Henderson, Charles. *Marine Sniper.* New York: Berkeley Books, 1986. (average)

Howe, Russell Warren. *The Koreans: Passion and Grace.* San Diego: Harcourt Brace Jovanovich, 1988. (average)

The Illustrated History of the Vietnam War, Volumes 1–10. Bantam Books, 1987 paperback. (easy)

Karnow, Stanley. *Vietnam: A History, First Complete Account of the Vietnam War.* Viking Press, 1987. (average)

Kohler, Heinz. *Comparative Economic Systems.* Glenview: Scott, Foresman and Co., 1989. (challenging)

Lamb, David. *The Arabs: Journey Beyond the Mirage.* New York: Random House, 1987. (challenging)

McClure, Dr. John L. *Soldier Without Fortune.* New York: Dell Publishing Company, 1987. paperback. (easy)

Meyer, Carolyn. *Voices of South Africa.* San Diego: Harcourt Brace Jovanovich, 1988. (challenging)

Omer-Cooper, J. P. *History of Southern Africa.* London: James Currey, 1987. (challenging)

Pye, Lucian W. *China: An Introduction.* Glenview: Scott, Foresman and Co., 1984. (challenging)

Richardson, Bradley M. *Politics in Japan.* Glenview: Scott, Foresman and Co., 1984. (challenging)

Rose, Richard. *Politics in England: Change and Persistence* (5th Edition). Glenview: Scott, Foresman and Co., 1989. (challenging)

Rosenblum, Mort, and Doug Williamson. *Squandering Eden.* San Diego: Harcourt Brace Jovanovich, 1987. (average)

Rubinstein, Alvin Z. *Soviet Foreign Policy Since World War II: Imperial and Global.* Glenview: Scott, Foresman and Co., 1989. (challenging)

Townsend, James R., and Brantly Womack. *Politics in China* (3rd Edition). Glenview: Scott, Foresman and Co., 1986. (challenging)

Ziegler, David W. *War, Peace, and International Politics* (Fourth Edition). Glenview: Scott, Foresman and Co., 1987. (challenging)

Audio-Visual Materials*

China: The Middle Kingdom (Parts 1 and 2). Videos, 25 minutes each, color, [Journal]. A look at China from within—a discovery of its peoples' customs, ideals, and ways of life

End of the Tunnel: Vietnam. Video, 60 minutes, color, [University of Illinois Film Center], 1983. Documents the collapse of the South Vietnamese army

The First Vietnam War, 1946–1954. Video, 60 minutes, color, [University of Illinois Film Center], 1983. Covers the period of U.S. escalation of aid to the French

* For a complete listing of sources of audio-visual materials see page T30.

The Iron Curtain. Video or film, 32 minutes, color, [EB], 1983. Documents the current status of "behind the curtain" countries and divided Germany

The Korean War Series. Videos or films, 3 titles, 15 minutes each, color, [Coronet], 1988. "Aggression," "Escalation," and "Negotiation"

Japan Reaches for the Twenty-first Century. Film, 60 minutes, color. [Wetavision]. Looks at the Japanese of today as they prepare for the next century

Shalom in Action. Video, 55 minutes, color, [Journal]. Shalom Dance Company, in which every dancer has another "normal" profession—their stories give insight into Israeli history, geography, and culture

South Africa Today: A Question of Power. Video, 55 minutes, color, [Journal]. Two South African newspaper editors present opposing views on the complex problems facing the nation

The Triumph of the West: Capitulations. Video, 50 minutes, color, [Films, Inc.], 1987. Great challenges to the reign of Western culture, particularly in the Islamic world

Vietnam, The Ten Thousand Day War Series: The Bombing of Hanoi (Episode 20). Film, 26 minutes, color and black and white, [Heritage Visual], 1980. Analysis of the psychological basis of the United States limited bombing and its escalation

OPTIONAL WRITING ASSIGNMENTS

1. You are the U.S. Ambassador to the United Nations in 1959. Write a five-minute speech which you will deliver to the Security Council concerning the Hungarian uprising.

2. You are a student in the Soviet Union. Write a letter to a high school class in the United States. Your letter should discuss your daily life, changes that you see as a result of the leadership of Gorbachev, and your hopes for the future.

3. You were born in Japan in 1920 and migrated to the United States prior to World War II. You have just returned to Japan for your first visit since you left in 1940. Write a letter to a friend in the United States describing the changes which you notice and describe your feelings about these changes.

4. You are a State Department adviser for African affairs. Write a position paper outlining policies the United States should adopt relative to the government of South Africa and its policy of apartheid.

5. It is the year 2010. You are a reporter for a major news magazine. Your editor has asked that you research and write an article describing changes that have taken place in world affairs in the last 15 or 20 years. Your article should contain references to major changes in economics, politics, the military, and foreign affairs.

UNIT TESTS
IN THE TEACHER'S RESOURCE FILE

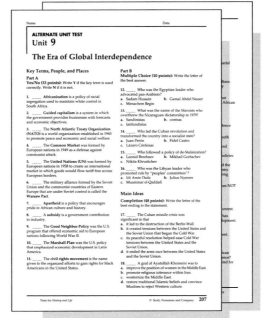

Unit Test, pp. 205–206

Alternate Unit Test, pp. 207–208

FINE ART IN UNIT NINE

Fine art forms an integral part of the historical record of events portrayed in this textbook. A listing of the paintings, drawings, sculpture, historic photographs, architecture, and other works of fine art selected to illustrate this unit follows. Students may be asked to research the artists and their works and report their findings to the entire class. Students also may be asked to write one or more paragraphs describing what they see upon a detailed study of a work of art and what the artist was attempting to communicate.

The Era of Global Interdependence

Themes and Patterns   We have now reached contemporary times, the half century following the end of World War II. Fifty-five centuries after humans created the first civilization in Sumer that you read about in Chapter 2, we have entered the era of global interdependence. Never before in world history have the destinies of all the world's peoples been so bound together as in these past 50 years.

   The evidence of interdependence is all around us. Economies are interlinked, and crises anywhere impact everywhere. For the first time in history, people face the ghastly possibility that all human life could be wiped out in a nuclear war. We now also know that the earth's resources are limited and that pollution caused by humans can seriously damage the quality of life for everyone on planet earth.

   The challenge for all of us is learning how to survive together, how to live harmoniously on a small, increasingly crowded planet. Looking back, we can see the era of global interdependence as the end result of all that has come before; looking ahead, we can see it as the beginning of a new age in the history of humanity.

Open heart surgery and other medical innovations are among the enormous technical advances of the period after World War II. These years brought many scientific achievements, such as computer technology and space exploration.

Chapters in This Unit

35 Europe, the Cold War, and the Superpowers

OVERVIEW

This chapter covers the development of the two superpowers, the Cold War, and European economic recovery.

PLANNING CHART

Section	Text Pages	Key Concept	Suggested Teaching Time
1 The Allies sought to restore peace.	661–664	The Allied Powers formed the United Nations to keep peace in the world and held the Nuremberg Trials to punish Nazi war criminals.	One day
2 A Cold War began in Europe.	664–667	Disagreements between the United States and the Soviet Union over the control of Germany and Eastern European countries led to the Cold War.	One day **More time?** Use *Overhead Transparency 69.*
3 The Soviet Union rebuilt its strength.	667–670	The Soviet Union recovered more slowly than other nations from World War II and, following the death of Stalin, pursued a policy of peaceful coexistence.	One day **More time?** Use *Source Reading 35A*
4 The United States experienced prosperity and social change.	671–673	The United States—the wealthiest and strongest nation on earth—became involved in two wars to prevent the spread of communism while people at home sought to rectify social and economic injustice.	One day **Less time?** Teach Sections 4 and 5 together, emphasizing prosperity and social change in both areas.
5 Western Europe became an economic giant.	673–676	Western Europe developed into a major economic power.	Two days **More time?** Use *Overhead Transparency 70* or *Source Reading 35B.*

ANCILLARIES

Materials that may be used with this chapter to reinforce, reteach, enrich, and assess learning are pictured on the following pages.

Teacher's Resource File

ACTIVITIES

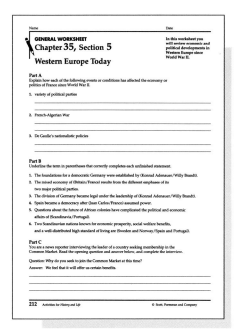

Section 1 Activity, p. 208

GENERAL WORKSHEET
Chapter 35, Section 1
Restoring the Peace

In this worksheet you will review the Nuremberg Trials and the United Nations.

Part A
Write the letter of the name from the box next to its identifying phrase.

1. _____ location of war crime trials from 1945 to 1949
2. _____ Nazi policy targeted at Jewish people
3. _____ site of infamous Nazi death camp
4. _____ nations with immense resources, population, and military strength
5. _____ site of a 1988 trial for a Nazi war criminal

a. genocide
b. Treblinka, Poland
c. Nuremberg
d. Israel
e. superpowers

Part B
Examine the cartoon and answer the questions that follow.

UNITED NATIONS

1. How does the cartoonist show support for the statement "It became possible for countries with small populations to block action in the General Assembly"?

2. What idea do you think the cartoon caption is trying to convey? Do you agree with this idea?

Section 2 Activity, p. 209

GENERAL WORKSHEET
Chapter 35, Section 2
The Cold War Heats Up

In this worksheet you will review the Cold War.

Part A
Write the letter of each effect from the box beside its cause.

1. _____ the 1949 merging of the American, French, and British occupation zones of Germany
2. _____ Britain's economic inability to support the anticommunist regime in Greece
3. _____ Truman Doctrine assistance
4. _____ the Soviet blockade of Berlin and the U.S. airlift of supplies
5. _____ formation of NATO

a. economic recovery of Western Europe
b. formation of Warsaw Pact
c. defeat of Soviet goals in Greece and Turkey
d. realization that neither superpower wanted war
e. formation of Federal Republic of Germany
f. establishment of the Truman Doctrine

Part B
Only three of the four items in each group are related in some way. Circle the item that does not belong and explain how the remaining three items are related.

1. Iron Curtain | weak Germany | reparations | Stalin

2. Truman Doctrine | NATO | Berlin airlift | Nuremberg trials

3. increased tariffs | Marshall Plan | spur to investment | increase in trade

4. Bulgaria | Hungary | Poland | Turkey

5. Versailles Treaty | Iron Curtain | satellite | puppet

Section 3 Activity, p. 210

GENERAL WORKSHEET
Chapter 35, Section 3
From Stalin to Gorbachev

In this worksheet you will review developments in the Soviet Union from 1945 to the present.

Part A
Complete each analogy.

1. *Perestroika* is to Mikhail Gorbachev as "peaceful coexistence" is to _____.
2. The Berlin Wall is to increased Cold War tensions as the _____ is to reduced tensions.
3. Hungary is to the year 1956 as _____ is to the year 1968.
4. "De-Stalinization" is to internal reform as the Five-Year Plan is to _____.

Part B
Complete the chart by writing the goal of each decision or action.

Decision or Action	Actor(s)	Year(s)	Goal of Action
the building of the Berlin Wall	Khrushchev	1961	
the halting of Soviet economic aid to Yugoslavia	Stalin	1948	
the Soviet decision to place missiles in Cuba	Khrushchev	1962	
the nuclear test ban treaty	Khrushchev and Kennedy	1963	
the repression of Soviet citizens critical of government	Brezhnev	1970s	

Section 4 Activity, p. 211

GENERAL WORKSHEET
Chapter 35, Section 4
Struggle and Triumph

In this worksheet you will review events related to the United States during the 1950s and 1960s.

Part A
For each statement below, write two or three sentences that support or provide details for that statement.

1. From 1945 to 1970, the United States flourished economically.

2. A revolution in civil rights took place in the United States after World War II.

3. The "temporary" division of Korea after World War II led to conflict during the 1950s.

Part B
Number the events in the order in which they happened.

_____ entry of Chinese troops into the Korean War
_____ United Nations condemnation of aggression in Korea and decision to send troops
_____ North Korean invasion of South Korea
_____ division of Korea at 38th parallel at end of World War II
_____ refusal of North Korea to hold reunification elections

Section 5 Activity, p. 212

GENERAL WORKSHEET
Chapter 35, Section 5
Western Europe Today

In this worksheet you will review economic and political developments in Western Europe since World War II.

Part A
Explain how each of the following events or conditions has affected the economy or politics of France since World War II.

1. variety of political parties
2. French-Algerian War
3. De Gaulle's nationalist policies

Part B
Underline the term in parentheses that correctly completes each unfinished statement.

1. The foundations for a democratic Germany were established by (Konrad Adenauer/Willy Brandt).
2. The mixed economy of (Britain/France) results from the different emphases of its two major political parties.
3. The division of Germany became legal under the leadership of (Konrad Adenauer/Willy Brandt).
4. Spain became a democracy after (Juan Carlos/Franco) assumed power.
5. Questions about the future of African colonies have complicated the political and economic affairs of (Scandinavia/Portugal).
6. Two Scandinavian nations known for economic prosperity, social welfare benefits, and a well-distributed high standard of living are (Sweden and Norway/Spain and Portugal).

Part C
You are a news reporter interviewing the leader of a country seeking membership in the Common Market. Read the opening question and answer below, and complete the interview.

Question: Why do you seek to join the Common Market at this time?
Answer: We feel that it will offer us certain benefits.

Chapter 35 Reteaching, p. 213

RETEACHING ACTIVITY
Chapter 35
The Era of Global Interdependence

In this worksheet you will review key terms and main ideas about the period after World War II.

Part A
Write T if the statement is true and F if it is false. On the lines below, rewrite each false statement to make it true.

1. _____ The United Nations charter gives every nation in the General Assembly the power to veto any decision.
2. _____ After World War II, the British economy became a mixture of free enterprise and socialism.
3. _____ The purpose of the Marshall Plan was to isolate the Soviet Union from the rest of Europe.
4. _____ The Common Market promotes the flow of goods by creating tariff-free borders.
5. _____ One result of the Korean War was the reunification of North and South Korea.
6. _____ West Germany's highly disciplined labor movement aided its economic recovery after World War II.

Part B
Write the letter of the name or term from the box next to its definition or identifying phrase.

1. _____ Eastern European counterpart of NATO
2. _____ containment policy that aided Turkey and Greece
3. _____ military alliance formed to prevent Soviet attack on Western Europe
4. _____ Churchill's term for what separated Western European countries from those under Soviet domination
5. _____ satellite nation invaded by Soviet Union
6. _____ total value of goods and services produced in a country in a given year
7. _____ event caused by troop movement across 38th parallel
8. _____ major victory for the American civil rights movement

a. Gross National Product
b. Hungary
c. Truman Doctrine
d. NATO
e. Iron Curtain
f. Warsaw Pact
g. 1954 Supreme Court decision
h. Korean War

Chapter 35 Enrichment, p. 214

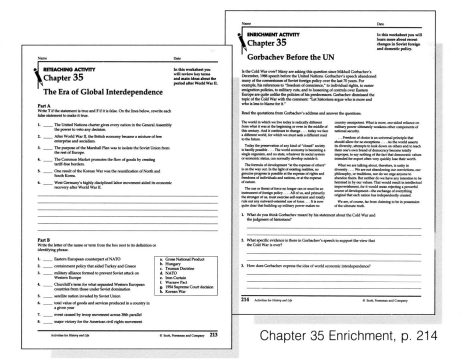

ENRICHMENT ACTIVITY
Chapter 35
Gorbachev Before the UN

In this worksheet you will learn more about recent changes in Soviet foreign and domestic policy.

Is the Cold War over? Many are asking this question since Mikhail Gorbachev's December, 1988 speech before the United Nations. Gorbachev's speech abandoned many of the cornerstones of Soviet foreign policy over the last 70 years. For example, his references to "freedom of conscience," to individual rights, to easier emigration policies, to military cuts, and to loosening of controls over Eastern Europe are quite unlike the policies of his predecessors. Gorbachev dismissed the topic of the Cold War with the comment: "Let historians argue who is more and who is less to blame for it."

Read the quotations from Gorbachev's address and answer the questions.

1. What do you think Gorbachev meant by his statement about the Cold War and the judgment of historians?

2. What specific evidence is there in Gorbachev's speech to support the view that the Cold War is over?

3. How does Gorbachev express the idea of world economic interdependence?

659b

Teacher's Resource File

GEOGRAPHY SKILLS

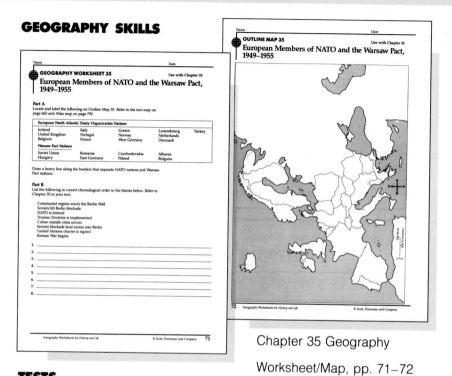

Chapter 35 Geography
Worksheet/Map, pp. 71–72

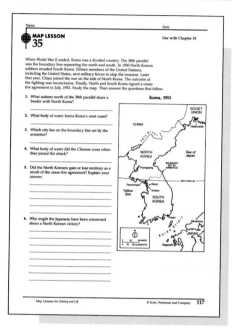

Chapter 35 Map Lesson, p. 117

TESTS

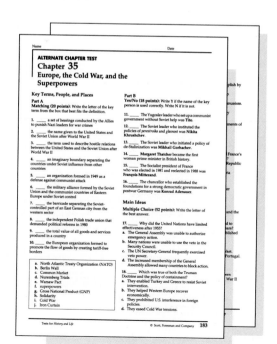

Chapter Test, pp. 181–182

Alternate Chapter Test, pp. 183–184

Other Optional Ancillaries

WORKBOOK

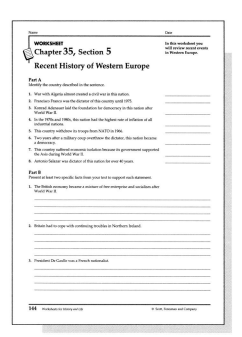

Section 1 Worksheet, p. 140

WORKSHEET
Chapter **35**, Section **1**

After World War II

In this worksheet you will review the emergence of the United States and the Soviet Union as superpowers and analyze the importance of the United Nations.

Part A
Complete each statement with the explanations given in your text.

1. By 1950 the United Nations Security Council was paralyzed **because**

2. After World War II, the Soviet Union and the United States became superpower nations **because**

3. Despite its limitations, the United Nations is a valuable organization **because**

Part B
Imagine that you are the head of a newly independent nation. You are deciding whether or not to join the United Nations. Make a list of three reasons for belonging to the United Nations. Below are some details about your country that may help you make your decision.

- Your nation is subject to severe droughts.
- You must negotiate with France over control of an island claimed by your country.
- Your country has little industry; it exports some foodstuffs.
- In the past your country has gone to war with two of its neighbors.
- One of your neighboring nations is ruled by a tyrant; many refugees have poured into your country.

140 Worksheets for History and Life   © Scott, Foresman and Company

---

WORKSHEET
Chapter **35**, Section **2**

The Cold War in Europe

In this worksheet you will review the Cold War.

Part A
Use information from your text to complete the chart.

Cold War Terminology

Term	Definition	Example(s)
Cold War		the Soviet blockade of Berlin and the U.S. airlift of food; the formation of NATO and the Warsaw Pact
satellite		Poland, Bulgaria, Hungary, Czechoslovakia, Romania, East Germany
	military aid program for nations threatened by armed minorities or outside pressures	U.S. aid to Greece and Turkey, the Berlin airlift, formation of NATO, Marshall Plan
blockade		

Part B
Write C next to each phrase that correctly completes the unfinished sentence. (Each incomplete sentence may have more than one correct ending.)

1. The Yalta agreement divided Germany into four zones jointly governed by
   ____ the Soviet Union.
   ____ the United States.
   ____ France.
   ____ Britain.
   ____ China.
2. After World War II, the Soviet Union wanted
   ____ heavy reparations from Germany.
   ____ favorable treaty terms for Italy.
   ____ economic assistance for Germany.
   ____ only friendly communist countries on its western border.

Worksheets for History and Life   © Scott, Foresman and Company   **141**

Section 2 Worksheet, p. 141

WORKSHEET
Chapter **35**, Section **3**

Soviet Cold War Policies

In this worksheet you will review Soviet foreign policy after 1945.

Part A
Identify the leader of the Soviet Union under whom the event took place by writing S for Stalin, K for Khrushchev, B for Brezhnev, and G or Gorbachev.

1. ____ launch of first satellite
2. ____ invasion of Czechoslovakia
3. ____ first nuclear test ban treaty
4. ____ introduction of *perestroika*
5. ____ de-Stalinization speech
6. ____ Hungarian uprising
7. ____ introduction of *glasnost*
8. ____ Yalta decisions and five-year plans
9. ____ U-2 incident
10. ____ outlawing of the labor union Solidarity
11. ____ building of Berlin Wall
12. ____ Cuban missile crisis
13. ____ establishment of Soviet domination over all countries of Eastern Europe

Part B
Fill in the blanks with the word or words that best complete each sentence.

No country suffered more from World War II than did the _____. Stalin wanted to restore the Soviet economy with two five-year plans that concentrated on rebuilding _____. Although _____ goods were scarce, the _____ increased. Stalin reimposed the harsh _____ controls of the 1930s and established Soviet domination of the countries of _____ Europe. However, _____, led by Josip Broz, who called himself _____, resisted Soviet control. Angered by this show of independence, Stalin cut off all Soviet _____ to that country.

142 Worksheets for History and Life   © Scott, Foresman and Company

Section 3 Worksheet, p. 142

WORKSHEET
Chapter **35**, Section **4**

Prosperity and Social Change

In this worksheet you will review events related to the United States during the 1950s and 1960s.

Part A
For each pair of words, write a sentence that clearly explains the relationship between the two.

1. segregation/civil rights movement

2. Mahatma Gandhi/Rev. Dr. Martin Luther King, Jr.

3. 1954 Supreme Court decision/schools

4. GNP/goods and services

5. Civil Rights Act of 1964/peaceful protest

6. GNP/prosperity

Part B
Some people believe that the Korean War accomplished almost nothing. Write an essay in which you agree or disagree with this point of view.

Worksheets for History and Life   © Scott, Foresman and Company   **143**

Section 4 Worksheet, p. 143

WORKSHEET
Chapter **35**, Section **5**

Recent History of Western Europe

In this worksheet you will review recent events in Western Europe.

Part A
Identify the country described in the sentence.

1. War with Algeria almost created a civil war in this nation.
2. Francisco Franco was the dictator of this country until 1975.
3. Konrad Adenauer laid the foundation for democracy in this nation after World War II.
4. In the 1970s and 1980s, this nation had the highest rate of inflation of all industrial nations.
5. This country withdrew its troops from NATO in 1966.
6. Two years after a military coup overthrew the dictator, this nation became a democracy.
7. This country suffered economic isolation because its government supported the Axis during World War II.
8. Antonio Salazar was dictator of this nation for over 40 years.

Part B
Present at least two specific facts from your text to support each statement.

1. The British economy became a mixture of free enterprise and socialism after World War II.

2. Britain had to cope with continuing troubles in Northern Ireland.

3. President De Gaulle was a French nationalist.

144 Worksheets for History and Life   © Scott, Foresman and Company

Section 5 Worksheet, p. 144

SOURCE READINGS

Source Reading 35A
Source Reading 35B

OVERHEAD TRANSPARENCIES

Overhead Transparency 69
Overhead Transparency 70

TEST GENERATOR

40 multiple-choice questions for Chapter 35

Europe, the Cold War, and the Superpowers

1945 – Present

1940	
1947	Marshall Plan helps Europe recover
1953	Stalin dies
1964	U.S. Civil Rights Act is passed
1970	
1980	

When World War II ended, the Allies agreed to divide Germany into four zones. Britain, France, the United States, and the Soviet Union each governed a zone. Germany's capital, Berlin, though located deep within the Soviet zone, was governed jointly by the four powers.

In June, 1948, the Soviet Union violated its agreement with the other three powers. In an attempt to force the American, British, and French authorities out of Berlin, the Soviets imposed a blockade on the city. Soviet troops and tanks prevented essential deliveries of food and other necessary supplies to the capital. The situation was dangerous. On June 25, 1948, the American military commander in Germany, General Lucius D. Clay, cabled a message to Washington:

> Conditions are tense. . . . Our troops and British are in hand and can be trusted. . . . Every [noncommunist] German leader . . . and thousands of Germans have courageously exposed their opposition to Communism. We must not destroy their confidence by any indication of departure from Berlin.

The Western Allies held firm. They airlifted food, clothing, and supplies into Berlin throughout the winter. Finally, in May, 1949, the Soviet government ended the blockade. The Berlin crisis ended, but it showed how far apart the Allies had moved since the end of World War II in 1945. Fear and rivalry had developed between the Allies, especially the United States and the Soviet Union. This rivalry came to be called the Cold War.

Meanwhile, Europe needed to rebuild after the devastation of World War II. As the United States experienced a period of prosperity and social change, Western Europe, with American assistance, made a remarkable recovery and in 20 years became an economic giant. Eastern Europe, controlled by Soviet-dominated

Children in West Berlin watch an American plane bring supplies to the citizens of the beleaguered city during the Berlin blockade of 1948–1949.

communist regimes, recovered less quickly. The Soviet Union rebuilt its shattered industrial base in record time but neglected agriculture and consumer goods for many years. Not until after Stalin's death in 1953 were efforts made to deal with those problems.

Reading Preview

In this chapter you will read how the Cold War began and how the United States and Western Europe prospered.

1. *The Allies sought to restore peace.*
2. *A Cold War began in Europe.*
3. *The Soviet Union rebuilt its strength.*
4. *The United States experienced prosperity and social change.*
5. *Western Europe became an economic giant.*

 The Allies sought to restore peace.

When World War II ended, the Allies created a new international peace-keeping organization to take the place of the unsuccessful League of Nations. They also brought Nazi leaders to trial for their crimes against humanity. Cooperation between the United States and the Soviet Union, however, became increasingly difficult to achieve as each nation assumed the new and complex role of superpower.

The Allied powers formed the United Nations.

During the summer of 1944, representatives from the United States, the Soviet Union, China, and Britain met in Washington, D.C., to plan the

- Outline and discuss the organization of the United Nations (UN). Ask students to identify the causes of the weaknesses of the Security Council and of the General Assembly. Have students discuss the UN's major value.

- Discuss the reasons for the Nuremberg Trials. Ask the students to identify the crimes committed by the Nazis who were put on trial. Point out the trial results.

GUIDED PRACTICE

Divide the class into American and Soviet teams to determine how they became superpowers. Guide each group by identifying economic, political, and military reasons.

Each member country of the United Nations has a representative in the General Assembly. The UN symbol, a globe encircled by olive branches, represents a peaceful world.

United Nations (UN). When the war ended, the plans became a reality, and in June, 1945, 50 nations signed the charter of the United Nations.

The UN charter created two major bodies—the General Assembly and the Security Council. The charter also established the Secretariat to administer the new organization, an International Court of Justice to hear disputes between nations, a Trusteeship Council to assist with colonies and mandates from the League of Nations, and an Economic and Social Council to improve social and health conditions throughout the world.

In the General Assembly, each member country had a representative. The Security Council, however, was limited. At first it had 11 members, but its membership increased to 15 in 1965. Five nations—the United States, the Soviet Union, France, Britain, and China—became permanent members of the Security Council. The other members of the Security Council were elected for two-year terms by the General Assembly. The chief responsibility of the Security Council was to keep peace in the world. An elected Secretary-General and staff administered the UN through the Secretariat.

Any one of the permanent members of the Security Council could veto any decision. Thus, if the permanent members disagreed, as the United States and the Soviet Union often did, the Security Council could not work effectively as a peace-keeping agency. The Soviets frequently used the veto in the Security Council, so by 1950 the council was paralyzed. The General Assembly then began to play a larger role. It gained the power to authorize emergency action on its own if the Security Council were blocked by a veto.

In the postwar years, the UN showed that it could play a significant peace-keeping role in places such as India, Pakistan, and Cyprus. It also played an important role in the creation of the new nation of Israel in 1948. However, the rivalry among Security Council members made it difficult for the UN to agree on several major issues. For example, the UN was powerless to aid Hungary when it attempted to free itself from Soviet control in 1956. It was also helpless when the Soviet Union invaded Czechoslovakia in 1968. The UN also failed to play a major role in the control of nuclear weapons and arms control.

As time passed, the UN developed in ways unforeseen in 1945. Membership in the General Assembly grew rapidly, especially after 1955 when 16 new countries were admitted in a single year. Many of the new members were former colonies

The United Nations relief program provides lunch for children in war-torn Greece in 1947.

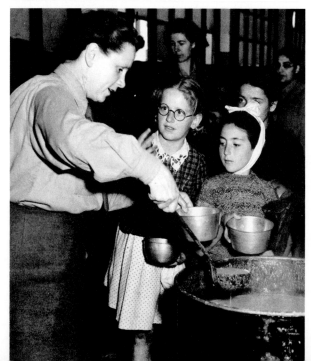

that had become independent nations. Neither the United States nor the Soviet Union could control how these nations voted in the General Assembly. It became possible for countries with small populations to block action in the General Assembly. As a result, the UN became less effective.

As it turned out, the major value of the United Nations was as a forum for discussion. It provided diplomats a channel for private meetings. The UN also provided nations the opportunity to jointly attack problems of world significance. For example, major successes were achieved in the eradication of certain diseases such as smallpox.

Nazi leaders were punished for atrocities at the Nuremberg Trials.

As the United Nations was being formed, the Allies faced another postwar problem. The Allied armies entering Germany in the last days of the war discovered shocking evidence of Nazi sadism and brutality. Dozens of concentration camps and slave labor camps were found in Germany, Poland, and Austria. As you learned in Chapter 34, these prisons had been used to confine and murder millions of European civilians because of their religion, ethnic background, or opposition to the Nazis.

The Jewish people, the main targets of a Nazi policy of genocide, had almost been destroyed. Nearly 6 million European Jews had died in the Holocaust, murdered by German soldiers or by special killing teams in death camps, such as Auschwitz and Treblinka. More than 5 million non-Jewish Poles, Russians, Gypsies, French, anti-Nazi political and religious leaders, and communists had also been killed. Countless others had been subjected to torture, starvation, sadistic "medical experiments," and other horrors.

To punish the German leaders for these atrocities as well as for other war crimes, the Allies conducted the **Nuremberg Trials** between 1945 and 1949. In all, 13 trials involving more than 200 defendants were held in the West German city. Most of the defendants were found guilty and were either imprisoned or sentenced to death.

Many other trials in Germany and elsewhere were conducted after the Nuremberg Trials. Some Nazi war crimes were still being tried in the late 1980s. John Demjanjuk, for example, a retired auto

From the Archives
The Universal Declaration of Human Rights

The Universal Declaration of Human Rights received United Nations approval in 1948. The articles below, along with 28 others, express what member nations felt the rights of individuals are.

Article 1. All human beings are born free and equal in dignity and rights. They are endowed with reason and conscience and should act towards one another in a spirit of brotherhood.

Article 2. Everyone is entitled to all the rights and freedoms set forth in this Declaration, without distinction of any kind, such as race, color, sex, language, religion, political or other opinion, national or social origin, property, birth or other status. Furthermore, no distinction shall be made on the basis of the political, jurisdictional, or international status of the country or territory to which a person belongs, whether it be independent, trust, non-self-governing or under any other limitation of sovereignty.

worker who lived illegally in the United States after the war, was convicted in 1988 by an Israeli court for having murdered hundreds of thousands of Jews at the death camp in Treblinka, Poland.

Two superpowers emerged after 1945.

When World War II ended, most of the strong nations of the prewar period had either been defeated or seriously weakened. These included Germany, Italy, Japan, France, Britain, and China. However, two nations—the United States and the Soviet Union—survived the war with such strength that no other nation could match them. Thus they came to be known as **superpowers**. Each of the two superpowers was a land giant that stretched across a continent. Each had a large population, possessed huge natural resources, and had immense military strength.

FROM THE ARCHIVES The excerpt is from The Universal Declaration of Human Rights, United Nations Publication No. 63.1.13 (New York: The United Nations, 1963). Compare the first two articles from this declaration with the provisions of the English Bill of Rights, the Declaration of Independence, and the Declaration of the Rights of Man and of the Citizen. (All three documents stress similar principles, but the UN Declaration applies to all people.)

Identify

Key Terms, People, and Places are defined on pages indicated in parentheses. Also see the Glossary and Biographical Dictionary.
United Nations (UN) (662), Nuremberg Trials (663), superpowers (663)

Main Ideas

1. Security Council and the General Assembly. Rivalry between the superpowers and frequent Soviet vetoes damaged the council. Many new members in the General Assembly meant action could be blocked by countries with small populations.
2. Nazi officers were placed on trial for war crimes.
3. Both the United States and the Soviet Union survived the war with great power and offered leadership to the world. Each mistrusted the other and reacted quickly if one tried to strengthen its security or influence.

Critical Thinking

The United States never joined the League, and even member nations ignored its decisions. Many more countries, including the United States, joined the UN. It sent peace-keeping troops to trouble spots. It also heard international disputes and tried to improve social and economic conditions.

2 Lesson Plan

Essential Learning Objective

Students will learn to identify the reasons for the rivalry between the United States and the Soviet Union.

The presence of two superpowers polarized international relations in the years after World War II. Each nation looked at the other as a rival or, at times, a dangerous enemy. When one of the superpowers sought to strengthen its security, the other saw the move as a threat. When one gained influence in some country, the other superpower saw that as a loss. This adversarial relationship between the two nations continued into contemporary times.

Section 1 Review

Identify United Nations (UN), Nuremberg Trials, superpowers

Main Ideas

1. Name the two major bodies of the United Nations. What damaged the effectiveness of each body?
2. What was the purpose of the Nuremberg trials?
3. What strengths did the superpowers have in common? In what ways were they rivals?

Critical Thinking

Analyzing Comparisons: Consider the similarities and differences between the League of Nations (Chapters 33 and 34) and the United Nations. What made the UN more successful than the League of Nations?

---

2 A Cold War began in Europe.

The term **Cold War** was first used by American journalists in 1948 to describe increasingly hostile relations between the Soviet Union and the United States. The hostility grew out of differences over how to treat Germany and Eastern Europe.

The Soviets wanted to control Eastern Europe and Germany.

Serious differences among the Allies appeared during the most important wartime meeting—the Yalta conference. As you learned in the last chapter, U.S. President Franklin D. Roosevelt, the British Prime Minister Winston Churchill, and Soviet leader Joseph Stalin met at Yalta in the Soviet Union in February, 1945. There, the three leaders pledged to support the establishment of governments in Eastern Europe representing the will of the people through free elections.

It soon became clear, however, that Stalin did not intend to keep his word. In a famous speech delivered in early 1946, Winston Churchill warned of the spread of communism in Eastern Europe:

> From Stettin in the Baltic to Trieste in the Adriatic, an iron curtain has descended across the Continent. . . . I do not believe that Soviet Russia desires war. What they desire is the fruits of war and the indefinite expansion of their power and doctrines.

After this speech, the countries under Soviet rule were referred to as "behind the **Iron Curtain**."

During the next two years, the Soviets installed puppet governments throughout Eastern Europe. By 1948 Romania, Bulgaria, Poland, Hungary, and Czechoslovakia were all under the domination of communist parties controlled by Moscow.

Meanwhile, the Allies' differences concerning Germany were even greater. Stalin wanted an extremely harsh peace treaty, one that would make it almost impossible for Germany to remain an industrial country. Stalin wanted to make sure that Germany would never again be strong enough, industrially or militarily, to threaten the Soviet Union. Roosevelt and Churchill thought that a severe treaty would cause a revolution in Germany.

History had shown these leaders the danger of punishing a defeated enemy too harshly. The Versailles Treaty, an extremely strict treaty that precipitated crippling inflation and economic chaos in Germany following World War I, had actually helped Hitler gather the support of the German masses in the 1930s. Hitler, as you learned in Chapter 33, had blamed the nation's woes on the treatment Germany had received at Versailles and convinced the people that revenge was in order.

Wanting to avoid a repeat of history, Churchill and Roosevelt firmly rejected Stalin's proposal. They also believed that a strong Germany would help prevent the spread of Soviet power in Europe. As you read in the chapter introduction, at the end of the war the three leaders compromised and agreed to a temporary plan: Germany was divided into four zones and jointly governed by the United States, the Soviet Union, Britain, and France.

CHANGES IN EUROPE AFTER WORLD WAR II

- Added to Soviet Union
- Added to Poland
- Added to Yugoslavia
- Added to Bulgaria
- ⋯⋯ Boundary of Allied occupation forces, withdrawn 1955

```
0    100   200   300 MILES
0  100 200 300 KILOMETERS
```

NORWAY
SWEDEN
FINLAND
North Sea
DENMARK
Baltic Sea
ESTONIA
LATVIA
LITHUANIA
EAST PRUSSIA
Danzig
SOVIET UNION
WHITE RUSSIA
NETHERLANDS
American Enclave
EAST GERMANY
British Zone
Soviet Zone
Berlin (Joint Occupancy)
BELG.
WEST GERMANY
LUX.
FRENCH Zone
FRANCE
American Zone
French Zone
POLAND
CZECHOSLOVAKIA
Soviet Zone
Vienna (Joint Occ.)
Amer. Zone
AUSTRIA
British Zone
RUTHENIA
BUCOVINA
BESSARABIA
SWITZERLAND
French Zone
HUNGARY
ROMANIA
(To France)
Trieste (Free City)
YUGOSLAVIA
Zadar
ITALY
PELAGOSA IS. (To Yugoslavia)
BULGARIA
SAZAN I. (To Albania)
ALBANIA
GREECE
DODECANESE IS. (To Greece)
Mediterranean Sea

 MAP STUDY What happened to Estonia, Latvia, and Lithuania as a result of World War II?

The German problem did not end with the temporary division of the nation. Distrust between the two superpowers increased as the nations debated the fate of Germany. The Soviet Union wanted heavy reparations from Germany to help rebuild its own country. It also wanted to make its occupation zone in Germany a satellite. (Satellite is a word used to describe the independent nations that came under Soviet control in the years following World War II.) British and American leaders, on the other hand, believed strongly that the economic fate of Europe depended heavily on Germany's ability to recover quickly.

The stalemate soon caused the "temporary" division of Germany to become more permanent. In 1949 West Germany—the American, British, and French zones—became, officially, the Federal Republic of Germany. East Germany—the Soviet zone—became the German Democratic Republic.

The rivalry between the United States and the Soviet Union increased.

The differences over Germany and Eastern Europe intensified the suspicion between the two superpowers. Their rivalry spread to other parts of Europe as each side tried to prevent the other from increasing its influence.

In 1947 one of the major trouble spots was in the eastern Mediterranean. The Soviet Union demanded that Turkey give up control of the Dardanelles, the strategic waterway that links the Black Sea and the Mediterranean. At the same time, in Greece, Soviet-backed rebels tried to overthrow a conservative government supported by Britain.

Although Britain had long guarded Western interests in the Mediterranean, the economically disabled nation announced that it could no longer afford to support the anticommunist regime in Greece. U.S. President Truman boldly stepped in to help. His words to the nation were, "We must not go through the Thirties again." To prevent this he proposed in March, 1947, what became known as

ANSWER TO MAP STUDY taken over by the Soviet Union; divided between the Soviet Union and Poland

665

1 **FOCUS AND MOTIVATE**

Ask students to explain why Stalin distrusted the United States during World War II. (He believed that the United States deliberately delayed sending ground forces to Europe so the Nazi forces would cause greater damage to his communist forces.)

2 **TEACH**

- List the Iron Curtain countries on the chalkboard and ask students to locate them on the map on page 665. Ask them to note their location in relation to the Soviet Union and infer why the Soviets chose to dominate those countries. Discuss Churchill's assessment of Soviet intentions. Ask students to name countries the Soviet Union tried to control.

- Explain why the Soviet Union proposed a harsh peace treaty for Germany. Ask students to explain what lesson Churchill and Roosevelt had learned from history that led them to reject the Soviet proposal. Compare the political and economic systems of East and West Germany.

- Discuss the reasons for the rivalry between the Soviet Union and the United States. Divide the chalkboard into three vertical sections titled Truman Doctrine, North Atlantic Treaty Organization, and Marshall Plan. Have students identify the ways the United States fought communist encroachment.

- Explain the need for economic aid in Europe. Have students cite reasons why the Soviet Union refused to let satellite countries participate in the Marshall Plan. Discuss the intent of the Marshall Plan. Ask students to give their conclusions on why the Marshall Plan was successful.

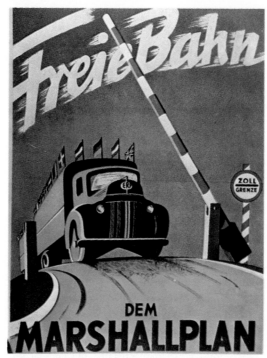

This West German poster says: "Clear the road for the Marshall Plan."

the Truman Doctrine. By terms of this doctrine, the United States promised not only to aid Greece, but also to support free peoples anywhere in the world who were "resisting attempted subjugation by armed minorities or by outside pressures." In effect Truman pledged to fight communism the world over. Truman's policy also became known as the policy of containment. This policy of containment would remain a cornerstone of U.S. foreign policy for many years to come.

Truman's containment policy enabled Turkey to resist Soviet pressure and also helped Greece defeat the Soviet-backed rebels who wanted to overthrow the government. Each of these situations illustrated clearly that the Soviet Union and the United States were not afraid to use force to accomplish their foreign policy goals. How much force were these nations willing to use? This question was put to a rigorous test in 1948 during the Berlin blockade, which you read about in the chapter introduction.

The peaceful ending of the Berlin blockade in 1949 showed that both the Soviet Union and the

United States wanted to avoid World War III. However, fears remained that Stalin planned to conquer Western Europe. These fears led to the **North Atlantic Treaty Organization (NATO),** formed in 1949 and made up of nine European nations plus the United States, Canada, and Iceland. These nations set up a NATO military force and agreed to defend each other if attacked. In 1955 the Soviet Union established its own military alliance, called the **Warsaw Pact**. The Warsaw Pact alliance included the Soviet Union and all the communist countries of Eastern Europe under Soviet control. It was then that Europe came to be divided into the two parts known as "Eastern Europe" and "Western Europe."

The Marshall Plan helped Western Europe recover.

Although the development of NATO and the policy of containment represented positive steps, Europe needed more than military aid and alliances to contain communism. Europe needed political stability, and that, in turn, required restoring its economic health.

When the guns fell silent in the spring of 1945, much of Europe lay in ruins. Millions of buildings from Britain to the Soviet Union had been destroyed. Entire cities had been reduced to rubble. Much of Europe's industrial capacity was in ruins, and its economic system had collapsed. Millions of displaced persons sought refuge and the chance to rebuild their shattered lives.

To help Europe recover, the United States launched the **Marshall Plan** in 1947. This was a broad program of economic aid offered originally to all European nations, including communist countries. Stalin saw the Marshall Plan as an attempt by the United States to penetrate Eastern Europe and undermine his control. He refused to let the satellite countries and the Soviet Union participate. Therefore, only Western European countries received Marshall Plan aid. The aid helped them rebuild their economies and preserve their democratic institutions. It also deepened the division between Eastern Europe and Western Europe.

The Marshall Plan had an amazing effect on the nations of Western Europe. Britain, Belgium, and several other nations recovered almost immediately. By 1950 West Germany's industrial output was greater than before the war. As tariffs fell and trade increased, the economic recovery of France and Italy leaped forward as well.

The determination of the citizens of Western Europe to rebuild their nations was remarkable. With the Marshall Plan aid acting as a spur to investment, all of Western Europe was on its economic feet by the early 1950s.

Section 2 Review

Identify Cold War, Iron Curtain, North Atlantic Treaty Organization (NATO), Warsaw Pact, Marshall Plan

Main Ideas
1. Why did the Soviet Union want to control Eastern Europe?
2. What was U.S. President Truman's response to Soviet intervention in Turkey and Greece in 1947?
3. How did the Marshall Plan help Western Europe recover from the war?

Critical Thinking
Analyzing Comparisons: As a defeated enemy in World War I, Germany was severely punished. After World War II, however, West Germany received very different treatment. Were the results better? Give reasons for your answer.

| 3 | *The Soviet Union rebuilt its strength.* |

No country suffered more from World War II than did the Soviet Union. Twenty million people lost their lives, and millions of others were left homeless. Thousands of factories, schools, and villages had been destroyed or severely damaged. The enormous task of rebuilding their nation faced the people of the Soviet Union.

Stalin reimposed harsh controls but failed to dominate Yugoslavia.

Stalin wanted to overcome all the wartime damage in only five years, between 1946 and 1950. In the next five years, 1951 to 1955, he pledged to ex-

pand production beyond prewar years. These two five-year plans concentrated on the rebuilding of industry, the basis of Soviet military strength. Agriculture and consumer goods were neglected.

Soviet output of steel, coal, and electricity increased during the Stalin years. Consumer goods, however, were scarcer than they had been in the 1920s, and agriculture was in even worse shape. By 1953 farm production was only 10 percent higher than it had been in 1914, three years before the Russian Revolution. Meanwhile, the population had grown by more than 20 percent.

To accomplish his goals, Stalin reimposed the harsh totalitarian controls of the 1930s. No one dared criticize official party policy. Thousands of people were killed or sent to forced-labor camps.

In order to protect the western borders of the Soviet Union, Stalin had brought all the countries of Eastern Europe under Soviet control. The one important exception was Yugoslavia. Led by Josip Broz, who called himself **Tito** [tē′tō], the Yugoslav communist party set up a communist government without Soviet help. Tito's independence angered Stalin. Determined to destroy Tito, in 1948 Stalin stopped all Soviet economic aid to Yugoslavia.

Tito, however, resisted Soviet control and obtained economic aid from the West. His greatest success was in holding the country together by suppressing the ethnic hatreds among the six republics and two provinces that made up the Yugoslav federation. In 1991, 11 years after Tito's death, the country fell into civil war. By January 1992 a UN-sponsored truce had been arranged, but it was clear, with the recognition of the independence of Croatia and Slovenia by much of Europe, that Yugoslavia had formally disintegrated.

Nikita Khrushchev showed both harshness and flexibility.

Stalin's death in 1953 touched off a struggle for power among the remaining leaders of the Soviet communist party. In 1956 **Nikita Khrushchev** won the struggle. Khrushchev rocked the communist world with a speech in February, 1956, that blamed Stalin for crimes against the Soviet people. **De-Stalinization**—the revision of Soviet admiration of Stalin—became official policy. This new policy brought other changes. Several forced-labor

BACKGROUND Stalin was buried beside Lenin in the mausoleum in Red Square until October, 1961, when his status was downgraded and his body was moved to a plain grave beside the Kremlin wall.

667

Ask students to explain the economic differences between capitalism and communism. Write responses on the chalkboard. (Capitalism: Private individuals or companies own businesses and compete with each other. Communism: The state owns land, factories, and other means of production.) Have students point out the strengths and weaknesses of both systems.

- Write Stalin, Khrushchev, and Brezhnev on the chalkboard. Have students list and discuss social, economic, and political developments under each leader. Have students cite factors that contributed to shortages of consumer goods in the Soviet Union. Ask them to give reasons why Soviet citizens did not express dissatisfaction over the suppression of freedoms until the 1960s and 1970s.

- List on the chalkboard and discuss the political crises that occurred under Stalin, Khrushchev, and Brezhnev. Have students discuss Khrushchev's and Brezhnev's satellite policy. Ask students to cite examples of reductions of tensions between the Soviet Union and the United States.

- Define *perestroika* and *glasnost*. Have students cite changes that Gorbachev instituted under his new policies. Discuss with students the outcome of these policies.

GUIDED PRACTICE

Have students write a paragraph giving their opinions on how Cold War tensions during Khrushchev's regime were detrimental to Soviet economic development.

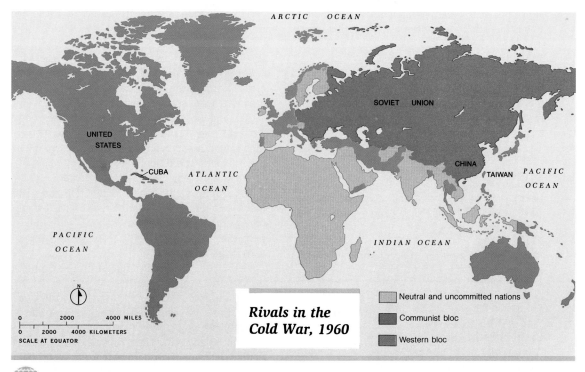

Rivals in the Cold War, 1960

Neutral and uncommitted nations
Communist bloc
Western bloc

MAP STUDY The map above shows the alignment of countries in the Cold War in 1960. Which bloc did Africa, India and most of Southeast Asia support in 1960?

camps were closed. Writers, artists, and composers enjoyed a little more freedom of expression. Cultural exchanges began with the West, and the Soviet Union welcomed tourists from abroad.

Khrushchev was the first of the post-Stalin leaders to recognize the need for reforms to make the highly centralized Soviet system more efficient and productive. Among the reforms instituted by Khrushchev were increased incentives for collective farmers and the delegation of more decision-making authority to factory managers in selected consumer goods industries.

In the late 1950s and early 1960s, clothing and television sets became more available in the Soviet Union, but farm production barely kept up with population growth. The main emphasis continued to be on heavy industry, weapons, and space technology. Under Stalin the Soviets had already devel-

oped the atom and hydrogen bombs. Under Khrushchev they launched Sputnik, the first satellite, in 1957. Four years later they put the first human into space.

Khrushchev's foreign policy had mixed results.

Generally Khrushchev showed greater understanding toward the satellite countries than Stalin had. He reestablished relations with Tito and made several compromises with Poland. Yet he also showed that his tolerance toward the Soviet satellites had its limits.

The Hungarian uprising and the U-2 incident. In October, 1956, an armed rebellion began in Hungary against the ruling Soviet-supported government. Khrushchev's troops quickly invaded the country and crushed the uprising.

ANSWER TO MAP STUDY Neither. They were neutral or uncommitted.

BACKGROUND Advanced students might like to study Imre Nagy, who led the Hungarian government that was formed in late October. The Soviets overthrew Nagy's government on November 4, 1956. Nagy was executed on June 17, 1958.

In his relations with the West, Khrushchev spoke of "peaceful coexistence," slowing the arms race, and banning the testing of nuclear weapons. Yet he also boasted that the Soviet Union would soon overtake the United States in all areas. In 1959 he became the first Soviet leader to visit the United States. However, in 1960 this relaxation of Cold War tensions ended when an American spy plane, the U-2, was shot down over the Soviet Union. Soviet outrage over the U-2 incident ended the brief thaw in the Cold War.

The Berlin Wall. Meanwhile, the Western sector of Berlin continued to be a major source of tension. As a showcase of prosperity and democracy deep inside communist East Germany, Berlin attracted 4,000 East German emigrés a week by 1960. In 1961, to stop this population drain, the communist regime built, practically overnight and without warning, a 25-mile barricade across the city and reinforced it with mines, booby traps, and heavily armed border guards. The barricade became known as the **Berlin Wall**. Khrushchev's goal was to get the Western powers to leave Berlin, something Stalin had failed to do in 1948–1949.

The Cuban missile crisis. In 1962 Khrushchev spread the Cold War to the Caribbean by installing missiles in Cuba, only 90 miles south of the United States. He hoped to use the missiles as a bargaining lever to gain concessions in Berlin. The President of the United States, John F. Kennedy, reacted quickly to the threat by demanding the missiles be removed.

After a week of frightening suspense, Khrushchev withdrew the missiles in exchange for a pledge that the United States would not invade Cuba. At first Americans felt pleased that they had won a diplomatic victory. However, an important outcome of this crisis was a major Soviet arms build-up that kept the arms race alive.

Reducing Cold War tensions. The peaceful resolution of the Cuban missile crisis was a turning point in the Cold War because it helped ease tensions between the Soviet Union and the United States. The two superpowers had come dangerously close to nuclear war, which neither wanted. As a result, in 1963 they set up an emergency "hot line" of direct communication between Moscow and Washington to reduce the danger of an acci-dental war. That same year, in another move to reduce tensions, the two superpowers and Britain agreed to ban the testing of nuclear weapons in the atmosphere, in outer space, and under water. Eventually, most of the other countries of the world also signed the nuclear test ban treaty.

Brezhnev continued the policy of peaceful coexistence and firm control of satellites.

Leonid Brezhnev, a colorless but tough-minded political personality, took over Khrushchev's position as first secretary of the communist party in 1964. In so doing, he became the new Soviet leader. Starting with Lenin, real power in the Soviet Union had been held by the first secretary, who was head of the communist party. Sometimes, as with Stalin, the first secretary also held an official government position as head of state. Brezhnev became president, and therefore the official leader of the Soviet Union, only in 1977. He held the two positions until his death in 1982.

Brezhnev, like Khrushchev, pursued the basic policies of peaceful coexistence and increased industrial potential of the Soviet Union. He also tried to improve the nation's agricultural productivity by allowing free enterprise on the private plots given to members of communes. Despite this improvement, the Soviet economic system still left much to be desired. Shortages, caused by poor central planning, forced Soviet citizens to wait in long lines at government stores for items such as meat and shoes. When available, these products were very expensive. The Soviet Union also had to import large amounts of grain to meet its food needs. The United States and other Western grain-producers supplied the Soviet Union with large quantities of grain.

Some Soviet citizens began to express open dissatisfaction with other aspects of the Soviet system. However, many critics were sent to prison, exiled, or confined to "psychiatric hospitals."

Brezhnev enacted a hard-line policy regarding Soviet satellites. In 1968, when Czechoslovakia tried to make its communist regime more democratic, Brezhnev saw the change as a dangerous threat to Soviet-style communism. He therefore sent Warsaw Pact troops into Czechoslovakia and restored hard-line communism.

Source Reading 35A

ASSESS

1. Under whose presidency did the Cuban missile crisis occur? (John F. Kennedy)
2. Why was the Berlin Wall built? (to stop the population drain from East Germany)

OPTIONAL RETEACHING

Divide students into four teams. Have each team choose a Soviet leader studied in this section and write on slips of paper the reforms, changes, or problems associated with that leader. Read each team's selection.

OPTIONAL ENRICHMENT

1. Have students give oral reports on newspaper or magazine articles describing the breakup of the Soviet Union. (average)
2. Assign interested students to read Chapter 5, Part I, or Chapter 1 or 6, Part II, of Aleksander I. Solzhenitsyn's *The Gulag Archipelago* and present oral reports on prison life in Soviet forced-labor camps. (challenging)
3. Also for enrichment:

INDEPENDENT PRACTICE/ HOMEWORK

Assign the Section Review, Activities page 210, or Workbook page 142.

CLOSURE

Tell students that economic recovery following World War II was slow and problem-ridden in the Soviet Union because of its inefficient centralized economy. Though production improved, Soviet leaders were unable to make communism work. Instead, Gorbachev's reforms unleashed long-simmering nationalist forces that ultimately led to the breakup of the Soviet Union.

Gorbachev began *perestroika* and *glasnost*.

In 1985 **Mikhail Gorbachev** [gor′bə chof′] became head of the communist party and decided that the political survival of the Soviet Union depended on reforming the economy. He therefore proclaimed a new policy of *perestroika* [per′es troi′kə]—restructuring—and *glasnost*—openness. It was a bold change to promote growth and free discussion.

Under *glasnost* Gorbachev permitted freedom of expression, called for the secret ballot, and encouraged more than one candidate for election to office. As a result, new political parties formed to challenge the communist party. In 1988 Gorbachev strengthened his own position by becoming president of the Soviet Union.

Gorbachev's policy of *perestroika*, however, did not work. He mistakenly believed only minor changes rather than radical reforms were needed to make the Soviet economy more productive. He also hesitated to completely replace the inefficient, centrally planned economy with a free market economy because of heavy opposition from conservative members of the communist party, who feared losing all their power. National elections in 1989 revealed that the communist party no longer had widespread popular support. Meanwhile, as the existing economic system rapidly broke down, severe shortages of food and consumer goods developed and inflation rose sharply.

The collapse of communism in Eastern Europe. To cut down on heavy military expenses, Gorbachev in 1989 moved to reduce Soviet military forces in Europe. He announced that the countries of Eastern Europe were free to follow their own paths.

Change occurred almost instantly, with Poland leading the way. As early as 1980, Polish workers had organized an independent trade union called **Solidarity,** which was headed by Lech Walesa. When free elections were held in June 1989, the Solidarity movement toppled the communist regime. Poland thus became the first nation in Eastern Europe to oust communism.

By the end of 1989, hard-line communist leaders had been forced out in East Germany, Czechoslovakia, Bulgaria, and Romania. Eastern Europe was free of communist power.

The end of the Soviet Union. Gorbachev's policies of *perestroika* and *glasnost* also ignited strong nationalist movements within the Soviet Union. The peoples of Estonia, Latvia, and Lithuania in the north demanded full independence, as did the people of Georgia in the south. Other nationalities fought among themselves over disputed territory, as did the Armenians and Azerbaijanis in the Caucasus. The Russian republic, the largest and most populous of the republics, elected its own Russian Congress and its own president, Boris Yeltsin, and declared its sovereignty in June 1990.

Gorbachev, fearing the complete breakup of the Soviet Union, proposed a new union treaty that would give real sovereignty to the republics. Hardliners in the Kremlin opposed the new treaty and on August 19, 1991, tried to seize power through a coup. The coup failed, largely because the plotters did not have the full support of the military and because Boris Yeltsin's popularity enabled him to defy their orders.

With conservative forces defeated, changes came with breathtaking speed. In November 1991 Estonia, Latvia, and Lithuania achieved complete independence. The following month, Russia, Ukraine, and Byelarus (formerly Byelorussia) declared the Soviet Union dead and formed a new Commonwealth of Independent States. They were joined by the remaining Soviet republics, except Georgia. Shortly after, Gorbachev resigned as president of the now shattered Soviet Union.

Section 3 Review

Identify Tito, Nikita Khrushchev, de-Stalinization, Berlin Wall, Solidarity, Mikhail Gorbachev

Main Ideas

1. What was Stalin's plan to rebuild the Soviet Union? What resistance in Yugoslavia did Stalin experience?
2. What new policies did Nikita Khrushchev follow?
3. Name five events that illustrate fluctuations in Cold War tensions during the rule of Nikita Khrushchev.
4. What policies did Brezhnev follow regarding peaceful coexistence and control of satellite countries?
5. What led to the breakup of the Soviet Union?

Critical Thinking

Identifying Assumptions: What assumptions did Gorbachev probably make when he instituted his policies of *glasnost* and *perestroika*?

4 The United States experienced prosperity and social change.

The United States emerged from World War II as the wealthiest and most powerful country on earth. It played a major role in world affairs even as important social changes took place at home.

The American economy was productive.

Unlike the Soviet Union, the United States mainland suffered no direct damage during World War II. Not only had the U.S. wartime economy expanded enormously to meet military needs, but it continued to grow rapidly after the war as well.

Americans in 1945 accounted for half the world's manufacturing output and about two-thirds of all global exports. Their standard of living in 1948 was twice as high as it was for the next wealthiest peoples—the British, the Swedes, and the Swiss.

During the next 25 years, the United States flourished economically as no nation in history had ever done. By 1970 the **Gross National Product (GNP)**—the total value of all goods and services produced in the country—was five times greater than it was in 1945. With only 6 percent of the world's population in 1970, the United States consumed more than half of the world's production. Only in the 1970s, when Western Europe and Japan made tremendous economic progress, did the gap with the American standard of living begin to narrow. Even so, the United States in the 1980s was still the world's wealthiest nation.

A revolution in civil rights took place.

Not all Americans shared the wealth. Perhaps as many as 10 percent lived in poverty. Black Americans, the largest minority group, suffered the most—from legal segregation in the south and social and economic discrimination in the north. They had the highest rates of unemployment, the lowest level of education, and the fewest opportunities for advancement of all Americans.

Beginning in the 1950s and 1960s, many Americans, both black and white, challenged the system of racial segregation and discrimination through the courts and by means of bus boycotts, sit-ins,

The Rev. Dr. Martin Luther King, Jr., leader of the civil rights movement, is shown with his wife, Coretta Scott King, and three of their four children.

and demonstrations. These organized and peaceful attempts to gain rights for blacks became known as the **civil rights movement.** In 1954 the Supreme Court ruled that segregated schools were unconstitutional. This was the civil rights movement's first major victory.

Religious leaders played an important, active role in the quest for civil rights. One particularly inspirational leader was **the Reverend Dr. Martin Luther King, Jr.,** a Baptist minister. A believer in nonviolence, the Rev. Dr. King later became the first black American to win the Nobel Peace Prize. He was greatly influenced by Mahatma Gandhi, who had led the fight for Indian independence through nonviolent protest. (See Chapter 33.) Beginning in the late 1950s, King led a series of peaceful protests and mass marches that stirred the conscience of millions of Americans. As a result, in 1964 Congress passed the Civil Rights Act, which prohibited discrimination in public services and in places of work. The following year it passed the Voting Rights Act, which guaranteed the right to vote to all black Americans. These civil rights

4 Lesson Plan

Essential Learning Objectives

Students will learn to:
- describe the civil rights revolution in the United States.
- cite reasons why the policy of containment led to war in Korea and Vietnam.

1 FOCUS AND MOTIVATE

Help students develop a list of components of a prosperous economy. Now add names of countries that would fit the definition developed by the class. Ask students to speculate about why the United States remained prosperous after World War II.

2 TEACH

- Discuss the growth of the United States economy between 1945 and 1970. Have students cite reasons why black Americans and other minorities did not share in U.S. wealth.

- Have students explain why the policy of containment was carried out in the Korean War and the Vietnam War.

GUIDED PRACTICE

Have students write a paragraph citing the effects of the civil rights movement on the rights of women and minority groups.

Whose nonviolent protests influenced the Rev. Dr. Martin Luther King, Jr.? (Mahatma Gandhi)

OPTIONAL RETEACHING

Write civil rights movement, nonviolent protest, Civil Rights Act, Voting Rights Act, and affirmative action on the chalkboard. Under each heading have the students write how each changed the lives of minorities in the United States. Ask the students to speculate how the civil rights movement changed attitudes of most Americans.

OPTIONAL ENRICHMENT

1. Have students obtain Martin Luther King's "I Have a Dream . . ." speech and summarize its message in writing. (average)
2. Ask interested students to read accounts of the Korean War. How were the political and military objectives different from World War II? (challenging)

INDEPENDENT PRACTICE/ HOMEWORK

Assign the Section Review, Activities page 211, or Workbook page 143.

CLOSURE

Tell students that the United States became involved in the Korean and Vietnam wars as a result of its containment policy. The civil rights revolution and changes in law began to correct economic and social discrimination at home.

---

victories were marred by a tragedy. In 1968 the Rev. Dr. Martin Luther King, Jr., was assassinated.

By the 1970s and 1980s, increasing numbers of black Americans were playing important roles in national, state, and local government. By the mid-1980s, for example, the nation had almost 250 black mayors and 6,000 black elected officials. In 1988 the Rev. Jesse Jackson challenged other leaders for the Democratic presidential nomination, winning widespread black support.

In addition to helping black Americans, the civil rights movement helped women and other minorities such as American Indians and Hispanic Americans. The Civil Rights Act of 1964, for example, also outlawed discrimination in employment on the basis of sex. Although not enforced at the time, this provision was to be of importance in the 1970s when the women's movement gained momentum.

By the end of the 1980s, many black and Hispanic Americans had achieved middle-class status. Women also found fewer barriers. Despite the progress in civil rights, however, many people still suffered from unemployment, poor housing, and lack of education. Civil rights leaders insisted that much work had yet to be done.

Containment prevented the spread of communism to South Korea.

At the same time as these changes were taking place in American society, the guiding principle of American foreign policy continued to be containment. That policy involved the United States in a major conflict, the Korean War.

Korea, like Germany, had been "temporarily" divided at the end of World War II, with the 38th parallel of latitude as the boundary line. The Soviet Union occupied the northern part of the country and the United States occupied the southern part. The Soviets installed a communist government in the north. They refused to accept a United States proposal to restore Korean unity by holding UN-supervised elections in all of Korea.

In June, 1950, in an effort to unify the country by force, North Korea invaded South Korea. The United Nations called the invasion an "act of aggression." During a Soviet boycott of the UN Security Council, the United States advocated that the UN take military action. Altogether 16 UN

Korea, 1953

MAP STUDY   Near what parallel, or line of latitude, was the boundary between North and South Korea drawn in the armistice agreement?

members sent troops to Korea—the largest number came from the United States.

UN troops pushed North Korean forces back north of the 38th parallel and toward the Yalu River, which separated Korea from China. To protect its border and to help the North Koreans, China sent 200,000 troops into Korea. They drove UN forces back south of the 38th parallel.

The Korean War continued until July, 1953. At that time, an armistice was signed, which left Korea divided along natural boundaries in almost the same way it had been before the Korean War began. The policy of containment, however, had suc-

ANSWER TO MAP STUDY 38th parallel

ceeded in preventing the expansion of communist power into South Korea.

Section 4 Review

Identify Gross National Product (GNP), civil rights movement, the Rev. Dr. Martin Luther King, Jr.

Main Ideas
1. Why did the United States have the world's highest standard of living after World War II?
2. What Supreme Court decision and major laws helped end segregation against Americans in the 1950s and 1960s?
3. Why did the United States fight in Korea after World War II? Why did the United States get involved?

Critical Thinking
Assessing Cause and Effect: In the 1950s and 1960s, both black and white Americans began to challenge racial segregation and discrimination through demonstrations, sit-ins, and boycotts. What were the long-range effects of these protests?

 Western Europe became an economic giant.

Western Europe recovered economically from World War II in about ten years. With a skilled and educated population, a wealth of raw materials, and a highly developed industrial system, Western Europe became one of the chief centers of industrial strength in the world.

Britain's economy mixed free enterprise and socialism.

The different emphases by Britain's two major political parties resulted in a mixed economic system. The Conservative party stressed free enterprise while the Labour party favored moderate socialism. A Labour party government was elected in 1945. During the next six years, the government placed the Bank of England, coal mines, iron and steel works, communications and transportation systems, and electric and gas utilities under public ownership. Four-fifths of the economy, however, remained in private hands.

The Labour government also started broad social programs that made major changes in British society. It created a welfare state—a state whose government provides for the welfare of its citizens through social services. Social services such as unemployment and old-age insurance, and free medical and health services for the entire population were launched. Income and inheritance taxes were also increased for the wealthy in order to redistribute wealth.

During the 1960s and 1970s, the British government made the educational system more democratic, promoted slum clearance programs, and constructed public housing. By 1980 Britain had more public housing than any other country in Western Europe, serving 35 to 40 percent of the nation's population.

Conservative leaders criticized the idea of a welfare state, but even though their party was voted back in office for 13 years (1951-1964), they did not change the basic features of the social security and health programs. Between 1964 and 1979, the two parties alternated in power.

When the Conservatives again won power in 1979, their leader, **Margaret Thatcher**, became the first woman prime minister in British history. Under her strong leadership, the Conservative party reduced the role of the central government, privatized industries, and curbed the power of the trade unions. When she resigned in 1990 because of continuing problems of low productivity, unemployment, and inflation, she had served for more than 11 years, longer than any 20th-century British prime minister. The new Conservative prime minister, John Major, also believed in free markets but paid more attention to problems of poverty.

Britain also had to cope with continuing troubles in Northern Ireland, a self-governing part of the United Kingdom since 1922. In 1969 violence broke out between the Protestant majority and the Roman Catholic minority there. The Catholics claimed that they were often discriminated against by the Protestant majority in social, political, and economic matters and demanded that Northern Ireland be annexed to the Republic of Ireland, where Catholics dominated. An extremist Catholic group called the Irish Republican Army (IRA) launched a campaign of terrorism, and that in turn skilled and educated population. Record responses on the chalkboard.

- List on the chalkboard the social programs that the Labour government instituted in Britain, the industries it nationalized, and the educational and housing changes it brought about. Have the students identify the major economic policies of Prime Minister Thatcher. Make certain the students understand how her policies differed from those of the Labour party.

- Compare Britain's economy with that of France. Have students identify the economic problems both countries had in common. Discuss why nationalization of industries and banks is favored by socialists.

- Have students cite De Gaulle's and Mitterand's strengths and weaknesses in running the French government.

- Have students list economic and political policies undertaken by Germany, Italy, Portugal, and the Scandinavian countries between 1955 and 1980.

- Discuss the nature of the Common Market as a trading bloc.

GUIDED PRACTICE

Have students write two summary statements, one about the political and one about the economic progress achieved by European nations after World War II.

Prime Minister Margaret Thatcher took a strong lead in reducing the role of the government in the British economy during the 1980s.

led to Protestant terrorism. Thousands of persons were killed, and the capital city of Belfast became a war zone, where ordinary citizens of both groups were randomly attacked and killed. The bloody fighting continued through the 1980s while the British and Irish governments tried to work out a peaceful solution. In 1985 they signed an agreement giving the Irish government an advisory role in Northern Ireland, but the violence continued.

France became a modern industrial democracy.

France's road to recovery and growth after World War II was rockier than it was for Britain because France lacked Britain's tradition of political stability. France had a variety of political parties, but no one party was able to gain a majority. As a result, the French government was run by a series of unstable governments. Sharp differences in policy often developed and caused old coalitions to fall apart and new ones to be formed. This was the atmosphere under which, in 1946, the Fourth Republic was created.

The problem turned critical in the 1950s when the government's costly struggle to preserve the French empire in Vietnam and Algeria bitterly divided the French. As you will read in Chapter 36, the French lost the struggle in Vietnam after eight years of fighting, and they withdrew from Vietnam in 1954. Later that same year a large-scale revolt broke out in Algeria.

The French-Algerian War was extremely unpopular with many French citizens and threatened France itself with civil war. In 1958 the French turned to their World War II hero, General Charles de Gaulle, to unify the country. A new constitution, approved by French voters, created the Fifth Republic with a far stronger presidency than before. It proved to be a much more stable political arrangement and has lasted to the present day. De Gaulle was elected president and moved to grant independence to Algeria in 1962.

Meanwhile, the French economy, assisted by the Marshall Plan, began to improve in the mid-1950s. Thus, the foundations for a modern industrial economic system were established. Like the British, the French developed a mixed economy. Industrial production grew rapidly, and French living standards rose.

With a stable government and a prosperous economy, France began to play an active and independent role in world affairs. President De Gaulle, a tall, proud, imperious man and an ardent French nationalist, refused to follow the American lead and developed an independent foreign policy. In 1966 he withdrew French troops from joint NATO command so that the French would have complete control over their military forces. De Gaulle maintained French membership in NATO, but he also insisted that France develop its own nuclear weapons and that his country make its own separate agreements with the Soviet Union.

De Gaulle left office in 1969, but his successors continued his independent policy in foreign affairs. However, like other industrial nations in the 1970s, France suffered from inflation, industrial slowdown, and unemployment. These problems led to the election of **François Mitterand**, a Socialist, as president in 1981.

Under Mitterand's leadership five major industrial groups and 39 banks were nationalized, that is, taken over by the government. When these actions failed to stimulate economic growth, Mitterand tried a new program of cutting taxes, reducing expenses for social programs, and shutting down some unprofitable socialized industries. By the mid-1980s, he had reduced inflation, but unemployment remained high, especially among the young. Still, Mitterand was reelected in 1988.

West Germany became Europe's most prosperous country.

Although West Germany had been devastated in 1945, it emerged during the 1950s as the most prosperous country in Europe. The foundations for strong, stable, democratic government were established by Germany's leader, Chancellor **Konrad Adenauer**, who was the dominating figure in postwar Germany. A powerful, strong-willed personality, Adenauer took office in 1949 at the age of 73. He governed West Germany shrewdly and skillfully for 14 years until 1963.

In 1969 a Socialist named Willy Brandt became chancellor. He succeeded in improving relations

This prosperous indoor mall in Dusseldorf, West Germany, reflects an international style that can be found in many cities around the world.

with Eastern Europe and the Soviet Union by accepting the division of Germany and the city of Berlin as permanent.

Economic growth continued to surge ahead and by the time Willy Brandt left office in 1974, West Germany was the strongest economic power in Western Europe.

What seemed permanent in 1974 collapsed so suddenly in 1989 and 1990 that it startled the world. When the Soviet leader, Mikhail Gorbachev, declared in 1989 that the peoples of Eastern Europe could follow their own paths of development without interference from the Soviet Union, Germans reacted by tearing down the Berlin Wall.

The hated communist regime of East Germany was swiftly toppled from power. In 1990 the two Germanies were dramatically reunited after a separation of 45 years. The task ahead was to rebuild the East's economy and to fully integrate it with that of the West.

Italy, Spain, and Portugal made progress, and Scandinavian countries prospered.

Italy in 1945 was in much the same condition as Germany. Severe fighting on Italian soil had destroyed many villages and towns. Much industry and many highways and rail lines had been ruined. The Italian economy was in chaos.

In 1946 Italian voters officially proclaimed their nation a republic and a democracy. The Italian royal family went into exile. A series of major reforms by the Italian government, along with Marshall Plan aid, helped the economy gain strength.

By the 1960s Italy had become a leading industrial power. In the 1970s and 1980s, however, Italy like the other industrial countries, had to grapple with high rates of inflation and unemployment.

Spain also faced difficulties after World War II. Still in the grip of the dictator Francisco Franco, Spain suffered from the economic isolation it had experienced because of Franco's support of the Axis powers during the war.

In the postwar years, recovery came slowly for Spain. By 1960, however, a major shift in the Spanish economy from agriculture to business and industry speeded Spanish economic growth.

In 1975 Franco died. Power was assumed by Juan Carlos de Bourbon, a member of the old Spanish royal family. In 1977 Spain held its first free election in 41 years. Despite an attempted

Identify

Key Terms, People, and Places are defined on pages indicated in parentheses. Also see the Glossary and Biographical Dictionary. Margaret Thatcher (673), François Mitterand (674), Konrad Adenauer (675), Common Market (676)

Main Ideas

1. The government took certain businesses out of the free enterprise system; it created the welfare system that offered social services for its citizens and increased taxes on the wealthy.

2. France lacked a tradition of political stability. In addition to economic weaknesses, it had problems with its colonies—Algeria and Vietnam.

3. Although defeated, West Germany benefited from the Marshall Plan. Under strong leadership it established a stable democracy.

4. Italy: a democratic republic. Spain: The dictator Franco still ruled; after his death power was assumed by the royal family and the country held free elections. Portugal: Dictator Antonio Salazar remained prime minister; in 1974 a military revolt made the country a democracy.

5. It provided tariff-free borders across member boundaries. By 1960 it had become the single largest trading bloc in the world.

Critical Thinking

Western Europe accepted economic aid from the Marshall Plan and the communist bloc did not, concentrating on rearmament and isolating itself. The Soviet Union insisted upon imposing communism, an inefficient economic system. The countries of Western Europe had freedom to select their governments and experiment with their economies.

---

coup in 1981, Juan Carlos remained king, and Spanish democratic government remained strong, with the Socialist Workers party in control.

Portugal, Spain's neighbor on the west, was not involved in the fighting of World War II. After the war's end, Portugal, which had long been aligned with Britain, became an important member of the Western bloc in Europe and a member of NATO.

During the 1950s opposition to Portugal's dictatorial government appeared, although Antonio Salazar [sä lə zär'], prime minister since 1932, remained in power. Uprisings by nationalists in Portugal's African colonies also created problems for the Salazar government. By the late 1960s, these conflicts had drained much of Portugal's resources away, with devastating effects on its economy.

In 1974 a group of military officers revolted against the government and seized power. Two years later, a new constitution was drawn up, and Portugal was again a democracy. Despite some political instability because of coalition governments, Portugal has remained a democracy. It also has made some economic progress in recent years.

The parliamentary governments of Denmark, Norway, and Sweden have long provided the political stability needed for economic prosperity. All three nations provide extensive social welfare benefits to their people, spreading a high standard of living to all income groups.

The economies of the Scandinavian countries grew tremendously after World War II. Socialist governments were in control throughout most of the postwar period. In the mid-1980s, the conservatives returned to power in Norway, but they retained the country's comprehensive welfare system. Like other highly industrialized nations, Norway and Sweden experienced some economic difficulties in the early 1980s. Prospects brightened with the drop in world oil prices in the mid-1980s and the development of Norwegian oil resources in the North Sea.

The European Common Market was formed.

In 1957 Belgium, France, Italy, Luxembourg, the Netherlands, and West Germany formed the European Economic Community, or **Common Market**.

The goal of this organization was to create an international market in which goods would flow unhampered by tariffs across the various borders. By 1962 the European Common Market was the single largest tariff-free trading bloc in the entire world.

Soon other countries wanted to join the Common Market. After long negotiations, Britain, Ireland, and Denmark entered in 1973. In 1980 Greece joined, and in 1986 Spain and Portugal were admitted, raising the total membership to 12.

In 1986 the Common Market accounted for more than one-third of all the world's imports and exports. This economic success led to the creation of the European Community (EC) in 1992, in which all economic barriers between member nations were eliminated. Even more dramatic was the announcement that the European Community and the European Free Trade Association would join together in 1993 to form the European Economic Area—a vast trading group of 380 million people in 19 countries. Together, these European nations would become an economic giant in which people, goods, and money would move freely.

Section 5 Review

Identify Margaret Thatcher, François Mitterand, Konrad Adenauer, Common Market

Main Ideas

1. Describe the economic system that developed in Britain after World War II.
2. Why was France's transition to a modern industrial democracy difficult?
3. Name several reasons why West Germany became Europe's most prosperous nation after World War II.
4. What type of governments did Italy, Spain, and Portugal gain after the war? Describe major governmental changes, if any, in the 1970s.
5. Why was the development of the Common Market important to Western Europe?

Critical Thinking

Recognizing Values: The countries of Western Europe achieved economic success but Eastern Europe and the Soviet Union either did not or took longer. What factors made the difference?

The Exploration of Space

On October 4, 1957, a Soviet rocket thrust *Sputnik I* into orbit around the earth. *Sputnik*—the word means "travel companion"—became the world's first artificial satellite. With its launch, the space age began. Since then the United States and the Soviet Union have raced to explore outer space through the launching of rockets, satellites, spacecraft, and space probes.

The Soviet Union put the first human, cosmonaut Yuri A. Gagarin, into orbit in April, 1961. Eight years later, in July, 1969, American astronauts landed on the moon. Neil Armstrong became the first human being to set foot on the moon, followed by Edwin Aldrin. Later ten other astronauts were landed on the moon in five separate missions.

The United States launched the first reusable space shuttle in 1981. However, the U.S. program was suspended in 1986 when an explosion shortly after liftoff killed seven persons. The program resumed in 1988, and the Soviets soon launched a similar shuttle.

Unmanned U.S. space probes are exploring the farthest reaches of the solar system, sending back to earth spectacular images of Jupiter, Saturn, Uranus, and Neptune. In July, 1988, the Soviet Union launched probes aimed at Mars, a preliminary to a planned U.S.-Soviet manned mission to Mars by 2010.

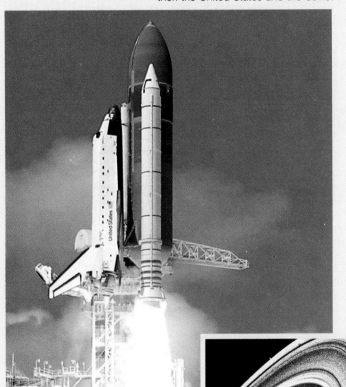

The space shuttle Discovery *thunders into earth orbit in 1988 from Kennedy Space Center at Cape Canaveral, Florida (far left). Voyager 2's astounding 1981 photograph helped prove Saturn's rings to consist largely of water ice (left). With luck, Voyager will transmit data from interstellar space until 2007.*

Students might be interested in knowing that one month after Sputnik I, a second Soviet satellite carried a small dog, Laika [lī′kə] ("barker") into outer space. The satellite re-entered the earth's atmosphere over the Caribbean Sea 2,366 revolutions later.

During the moon landings, the astronauts gathered samples of moon rocks, made surveys, and conducted experiments. Ask if anyone can name the third astronaut on the Apollo 11 flight, the one who stayed behind on the spacecraft Columbia. (Michael Collins) Videotapes of the first manned flight to the moon in 1969 might be shown in class if time permits. Students could also read a book about the space program, such as *First on the Moon: A Voyage with Neil Armstrong, Michael Collins, Edwin E. Aldrin, Jr.,* written with Gene Farmer and Dora Jane Hamblin (Boston: Little, Brown, 1970); *We Reach the Moon,* by John Noble Wilford (New York: The New York Times Company, 1969); *Flying to the Moon and Other Strange Places,* by Michael Collins (Sunburst, 1976); and *Liftoff,* by Michael Collins (Grove, 1988).

Ask students to speculate on the desirability of joint Soviet-U.S. space ventures. If necessary, point out that, in 1975, the United States and the Soviet Union conducted their first space mission called Apollo-Soyuz Test Project. A few years later the United States and Soviet Union conducted joint biological tests in space.

Key Terms, People, and Places
The key terms, people, and places tested here were introduced in the chapter sections and reviewed in the Section Reviews. For definitions see the page references at the appropriate Section Reviews. Also see the Glossary and Biographical Dictionary.

Main Ideas
The main ideas tested here were introduced in the sections of this chapter and reviewed in the Section Reviews. For answers to these questions, see the appropriate Section Reviews.

Critical Thinking
1. Possible answers: might discuss the age of the persons pursued, purpose of trying criminals, nature of crimes committed, difficulty in identifying people, concept of equal justice for all
2. Possible answers: might include a discussion of the purpose of the UN, its military strength, and its use as a forum for discussion

CHAPTER 35 REVIEW

Section Summaries

Section 1
The Allies sought to restore peace.
The rise of two superpowers, the United States and the Soviet Union, affected international relations in the postwar world. A new international organization, the United Nations, was created to keep the peace.

Section 2
A Cold War began in Europe.
After World War II, the competition between the Soviet Union and the United States led to the Cold War.

Section 3
The Soviet Union rebuilt its strength.
Economically, the Soviet Union suffered greatly from World War II, though militarily it was one of the strongest nations of the world in 1945. To secure its borders and to spread communism, it supported Soviet-style governments in Eastern Europe. However, in 1985 Mikhail Gorbachev ushered in a new era of change. He freed Eastern Europe to go its own way and began policies of restructuring and openness in Soviet society. By 1991 these policies had unleashed a surge of nationalism, which led to the breakup of the Soviet Union.

Section 4
The United States experienced prosperity and social change.
After World War II, the United States was the wealthiest and most powerful country on earth. It supported alliances, aid programs, the Korean War, and various policies to prevent communism from spreading. After 1954 the civil rights movement won equal rights for black Americans, other minorities, and women.

Section 5
Western Europe became an economic giant.
Britain became a welfare state, but later strengthened free enterprise. France gained a stable government. West Germany, Italy, Spain, and Portugal became democracies. The Scandinavian countries maintained welfare states and high standards of living.

Test Yourself

Key Terms, People, and Places
Identify the significance of each of the following:

Section 1
a. United Nations (UN)   **c.** superpowers
b. Nuremberg Trials

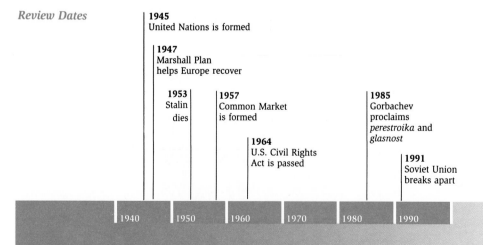

Review Dates

1945
United Nations is formed

1947
Marshall Plan
helps Europe recover

1953
Stalin
dies

1957
Common Market
is formed

1964
U.S. Civil Rights
Act is passed

1985
Gorbachev
proclaims
perestroika and
glasnost

1991
Soviet Union
breaks apart

1940   1950   1960   1970   1980   1990

Section 2
a. Cold War
b. Iron Curtain
c. North Atlantic
Treaty Organization (NATO)
d. Warsaw Pact
e. Marshall Plan

Section 3
a. Tito
b. Nikita Khrushchev
c. de-Stalinization
d. Berlin Wall
e. Solidarity
f. Mikhail Gorbachev

Section 4
a. Gross National
Product (GNP)
b. civil rights movement
c. the Rev. Dr. Martin
Luther King, Jr.

Section 5
a. Margaret Thatcher
b. François Mitterand
c. Konrad Adenauer
d. Common Market

Main Ideas

Section 1
1. Identify the two major bodies of the United Nations. What has weakened the effectiveness of each body?
2. Why were the Nuremberg Trials held?
3. Describe the strengths the superpowers have in common. How are they rivals?

Section 2
1. For what reasons did the Soviet Union want to control Eastern Europe?
2. How did President Truman respond to the Soviet intervention in Turkey and Greece in 1947?
3. In what ways did the Marshall Plan help Western Europe recover from the war?

Section 3
1. Describe Stalin's plan to rebuild the Soviet Union.
2. Identify Nikita Khrushchev's new policies.
3. What five events illustrate fluctuations in Cold War tensions during Nikita Khrushchev's rule?
4. What were Brezhnev's policies toward peaceful coexistence and communist satellites?
5. Identify *perestroika* and *glasnost*.

Section 4
1. For what reasons did the United States have the world's highest standard of living after World War II?
2. Describe the U.S. Supreme Court decision and major laws that helped end segregation.

3. Why did the United States fight in Korea between 1950 and 1953?

Section 5
1. How did Britain's economy develop after 1945?
2. Why was it difficult for France to become a modern industrial democracy?
3. Identify several reasons why West Germany became Europe's most prosperous nation after World War II.
4. What type of governments were formed in Italy, Spain, and Portugal after the war?
5. What was the significance of the Common Market?

Critical Thinking
1. Recognizing Values Should Nazi mass murderers and other war criminals still be sought for trial? Why?

2. Making Hypotheses Since populous countries such as the United States and the Soviet Union are greatly outnumbered by smaller nations, what might the effect be on world stability if the United Nations were disbanded or if the large countries withdrew?

Chapter Skills and Activities

Practicing Study and Research Skills
Seeing the Points of View of Others
Consider the history and geography of the Soviet Union and explain its policies toward Eastern Europe after World War II. Were these policies ultimately successful? Why or why not?

Linking Past and Present
The United States and the Soviet Union have many resources and strong defense systems. In what ways is Western Europe trying to become equally strong? Do you think it will succeed?

Learning History Through Maps
Compare the map on page 665 of Changes in Europe After World War II with the political map of Europe on page 792. Why do you think the countries of Eastern Europe had such importance for the Soviet Union?

CRITICAL THINKING QUESTION LEVEL 1. average; 2. challenging

36 The Assertion of Independence in Asia

OVERVIEW

This chapter covers Asia after World War II. European colonialism ended, governments struggled to build independent economies, and communist governments were established in China and Vietnam.

PLANNING CHART

Section	Text Pages	Key Concept	Suggested Teaching Time
1 Communists came to power in China.	681–686	Communist governments isolated China from the world, restructured its society, then reopened contacts to encourage technological development.	One day **Less time?** Teach Sections 1 and 3 in one day. Concentrate on the theme of communism, particularly efforts to ward off communist movements in Indonesia and the Philippines. **More time?** Use *Source Reading 36A.*
2 Postwar Japan and other Pacific Rim nations made remarkable progress.	686–688	Japan and other Pacific Rim nations made remarkable economic progress after World War II.	One day **More time?** Use *Overhead Transparency 71.*
3 Southeast Asian countries became independent.	689–693	After World War II the newly independent nations of Southeast Asia struggled to develop new, effective governments.	One day **More time?** Use *Overhead Transparency 72.*
4 South Asian countries faced major challenges.	693–696	Religious, social, and economic conflicts plagued the nations of South Asia as they attempted to form stable, independent governments after World War II.	One day **More time?** Use *Source Reading 36B.*

ANCILLARIES

Materials that may be used with this chapter to reinforce, reteach, enrich, and assess learning are pictured on the following pages.

Teacher's Resource File

ACTIVITIES

GENERAL WORKSHEET
Chapter 36, Section 1
China Under the Communists

In this worksheet you will review the history of China from 1949 to the present.

Part A
Complete each analogy.

1. Taiwan was to Nationalist China as mainland China was to _____.

2. Chiang Kai-Shek was to the Nationalists as _____ was to the Communists.

3. The commune system was to the _____ as the purge of intellectuals was to the "Great Cultural Revolution."

4. Border disputes were to increased Chinese-Soviet tensions as President Nixon's 1972 trip to China was to _____.

Part B
Give at least one example from the text to explain the ways in which China has made recent advances in each of the following areas.

1. agriculture

2. industry

3. science and technology

4. population growth

Section 1 Activity, p. 215

GENERAL WORKSHEET
Chapter 36, Section 2
Economic Success in Asia

In this worksheet you will review the economic development of Japan and other Pacific Rim countries.

Part A
Write one or two sentences explaining how each of the following helped Japan to become an economic giant after World War II.

1. the United States and other Western nations

2. Japan's democratic constitution

3. government policies encouraging savings

4. guided capitalism

Part B
Identify the country described by each phrase by writing SK for South Korea, T for Taiwan, HK for Hong Kong, and S for Singapore.

1. _____ has experienced student demonstrations protesting its authoritarian government

2. _____ first exported textiles, then steel, and most recently electronics and automobiles

3. _____ will experience a change of government in 1997

4. _____ like Hong Kong, serves as a major center of international trade and banking

5. _____ is a former British colony with one of the world's largest seaports

6. _____ has a mixed economy of private and state-owned companies

7. _____ is a British crown colony

8. _____ has had a government run by the Nationalist party since 1949

Section 2 Activity, p. 216

GENERAL WORKSHEET
Chapter 36, Section 3
Independence Movements

In this worksheet you will review the struggles of several Southeast Asian countries to become independent.

Part A
Write a sentence explaining why each occurrence below took place.

1. The European powers found it difficult to reestablish dominance in their Southeast Asian colonies after World War II.

2. The communist New People's Army gained the support of the peasants in rural areas of the Philippines soon after independence.

3. The United States sent money, advisers, arms, and troops to South Vietnam.

Part B
Use information from your text to complete the chart.

Theme	Definition	Example from Post-World War II Southeast Asia
Martial law	a state of emergency in which the military suspends civil liberties	
Puppet government		
Insurgency	a revolt against an established government, not as large or as organized as a revolution	
Military regime	dictatorship by a military clique	

Section 3 Activity, p. 217

GENERAL WORKSHEET
Chapter 36, Section 4
South Asia Since World War II

In this worksheet you will review the history of South Asian countries since World War II.

Part A
Write T if the statement is true and F if it is false. On the lines below, rewrite each false statement to make it true.

1. _____ The new country of Pakistan was composed of two distinct parts separated by 1,000 miles of Indian territory.

2. _____ The first prime minister of India was Mohandas Gandhi.

3. _____ Because of the "green revolution" in the 1950s, India has both solved the problem of undernourishment and produced food for export.

4. _____ Unlike India, Pakistan never has had a democratic election.

Part B
Present one or two specific facts from your text to support each statement.

1. India is a diverse nation.

2. Nehru favored a mixed system of free enterprise and moderate socialism.

3. Ethnic and religious conflicts have persisted in India.

4. India's constitution of 1950 called for important social reforms.

Section 4 Activity, p. 218

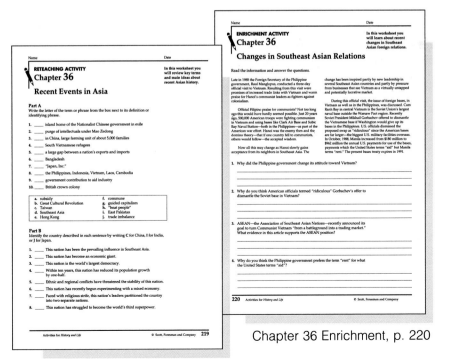

RETEACHING ACTIVITY
Chapter 36
Recent Events in Asia

In this worksheet you will review key terms and main ideas about recent Asian history.

Part A
Write the letter of the term or phrase from the box next to its definition or identifying phrase.

1. _____ island home of the Nationalist Chinese government in exile

2. _____ purge of intellectuals under Mao Zedong

3. _____ in China, large farming unit of about 5,000 families

4. _____ South Vietnamese refugees

5. _____ a large gap between a nation's exports and imports

6. _____ Bangladesh

7. _____ "Japan, Inc."

8. _____ the Philippines, Indonesia, Vietnam, Laos, Cambodia

9. _____ government contribution to aid industry

10. _____ British crown colony

a. subsidy	f. commune
b. Great Cultural Revolution	g. guided capitalism
c. Taiwan	h. "boat people"
d. Southeast Asia	i. East Pakistan
e. Hong Kong	j. trade imbalance

Part B
Identify the country described in each sentence by writing C for China, I for India, or J for Japan.

1. _____ This nation has been the prevailing influence in Southeast Asia.

2. _____ This nation has become an economic giant.

3. _____ This nation is the world's largest democracy.

4. _____ Within ten years, this nation has reduced its population growth by one-half.

5. _____ Ethnic and regional conflicts have threatened the stability of this nation.

6. _____ This nation has recently begun experimenting with a mixed economy.

7. _____ Faced with religious strife, this nation's leaders partitioned the country into two separate nations.

8. _____ This nation has struggled to become the world's third superpower.

Chapter 36 Reteaching, p. 219

ENRICHMENT ACTIVITY
Chapter 36

Changes in Southeast Asian Relations

In this worksheet you will learn about recent changes in Southeast Asian foreign relations.

Read the information and answer the questions.

Late in 1988 the Foreign Secretary of the Philippine government, Raul Manglapus, conducted a three-day official visit to Vietnam. Resulting from this visit were promises of increased trade links with Vietnam and warm praise for Hanoi's communist leaders as fighters against colonialism.

Official Filipino praise for communists? Not too long ago this would have hardly seemed possible. Just 20 years ago, 500,000 American troops were fighting communism in Vietnam and using bases like Clark Air Base and Subic Bay Naval Station—both in the Philippines—as part of the American war effort. Hanoi was the enemy then and the domino theory—that if one country fell to communists, others would follow—the accepted wisdom.

Now all this may change as Hanoi slowly gains acceptance from its neighbors in Southeast Asia. The change has been inspired partly by new leadership in several Southeast Asian countries and partly by pressure from businesses that see Vietnam as a virtually untapped and potentially lucrative market.

During this official visit, the issue of foreign bases in Vietnam as well as in the Philippines, was discussed. Cam Ranh Bay in central Vietnam is the Soviet Union's largest naval base outside the Warsaw Pact region. Recently Soviet President Mikhail Gorbachev offered to dismantle the Vietnam base if Washington would give up its bases in the Philippines. U.S. officials dismissed the proposed swap as "ridiculous" since the American bases are far larger—the biggest U.S. military facilities overseas. In October, 1988, Manila increased $180 million to $962 million the annual U.S. payments for use of the bases, payments which the United States terms "aid" but Manila terms "rent." The present bases treaty expires in 1991.

1. Why did the Philippine government change its attitude toward Vietnam?

2. Why do you think American officials termed "ridiculous" Gorbachev's offer to dismantle the Soviet base in Vietnam?

3. ASEAN—the Association of Southeast Asian Nations—recently announced its goal to turn Communist Vietnam "from a battleground into a trading market." What evidence in this article supports the ASEAN position?

4. Why do you think the Philippine government prefers the term "rent" for what the United States terms "aid"?

Chapter 36 Enrichment, p. 220

Teacher's Resource File

GEOGRAPHY SKILLS

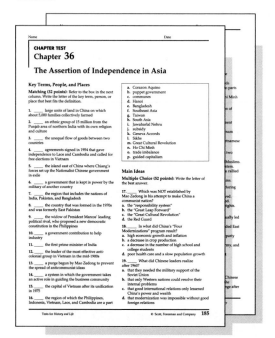

GEOGRAPHY WORKSHEET 36   Use with Chapter 36
The Assertion of Independence in Asia

Part A
Locate and label the following on Outline Map 36. Draw in the rivers. Refer to the text maps on pages 689 and 692.

Water	Cities	Countries, Territories, Areas	
Pacific Ocean	Ho Chi Minh City (Saigon)	China	Laos
Indian Ocean	Hanoi	Taiwan	Thailand
South China Sea	Manila	Philippines	Burma
Mekong River	Bangkok	Malaysia	India
	Phnom Penh	Indonesia	Singapore
		Vietnam	Hong Kong
		Cambodia (Kampuchea)	Australia

Draw in the 17th parallel.

Part B
List the following in correct chronological order in the blanks below. Refer to Chapter 36 in your text.

Communists establish People's Republic of China
India and Pakistan become independent nations
Singapore receives independence
Sikhs begin rebellion against Indian government
Mao begins "Great Cultural Revolution"
Vietnam conquers Cambodia
Corazon Aquino ascends to Philippine presidency
Vietnam is unified under communist rule

1. _____
2. _____
3. _____
4. _____
5. _____
6. _____
7. _____
8. _____

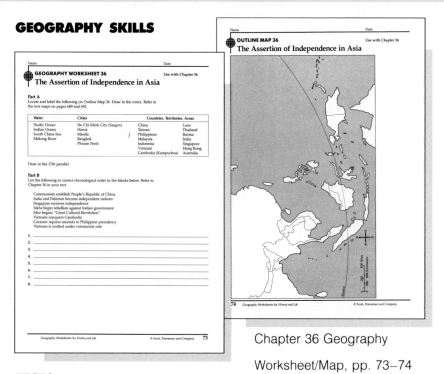

OUTLINE MAP 36   Use with Chapter 36
The Assertion of Independence in Asia

Chapter 36 Geography
Worksheet/Map, pp. 73–74

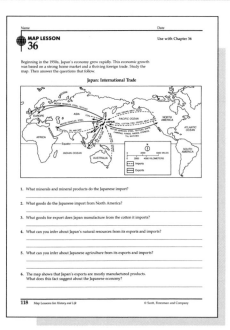

MAP LESSON
36   Use with Chapter 36

Beginning in the 1950s, Japan's economy grew rapidly. This economic growth was based on a strong home market and a thriving foreign trade. Study the map. Then answer the questions that follow.

Japan: International Trade

1. What minerals and mineral products do the Japanese import?

2. What goods do the Japanese import from North America?

3. What goods for export does Japan manufacture from the cotton it imports?

4. What can you infer about Japan's natural resources from its exports and imports?

5. What can you infer about Japanese agriculture from its exports and imports?

6. The map shows that Japan's exports are mostly manufactured products. What does this fact suggest about the Japanese economy?

Chapter 36 Map Lesson, p. 118

TESTS

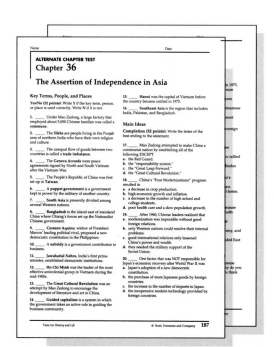

CHAPTER TEST
Chapter 36
The Assertion of Independence in Asia

Key Terms, People, and Places
Matching (32 points): Refer to the box in the next column. Write the letter of the key term, person, or place that best fits the definition.

1. _____ large units of land in China on which about 5,000 families collectively farmed
2. _____ an ethnic group of 15 million from the Punjab area of northern India with its own religion and culture
3. _____ the unequal flow of goods between two countries
4. _____ agreements signed in 1954 that gave independence to Laos and Cambodia and called for free elections in Vietnam
5. _____ the island east of China where Chiang's forces set up the Nationalist Chinese government in exile
6. _____ a government that is kept in power by the military of another country
7. _____ the region that includes the nations of India, Pakistan, and Bangladesh
8. _____ the country that was formed in the 1970s and was formerly East Pakistan
9. _____ the widow of President Marcos' leading political rival, who proposed a new democratic constitution in the Philippines
10. _____ a government contribution to help industry
11. _____ the first prime minister of India
12. _____ the leader of the most effective anti-colonial group in Vietnam in the mid-1900s
13. _____ a purge begun by Mao Zedong to prevent the spread of anticommunist ideas
14. _____ a system in which the government takes an active role in guiding the business community
15. _____ the capital of Vietnam after its unification in 1975
16. _____ the region of which the Philippines, Indonesia, Vietnam, Laos, and Cambodia are a part

a. Corazon Aquino
b. puppet government
c. communes
d. Hanoi
e. Bangladesh
f. Southeast Asia
g. Taiwan
h. South Asia
i. Jawaharlal Nehru
j. subsidy
k. Geneva Accords
l. Sikhs
m. Great Cultural Revolution
n. Ho Chi Minh
o. trade imbalance
p. guided capitalism

Main Ideas
Multiple Choice (52 points): Write the letter of the best answer.

17. _____ Which was NOT established by Mao Zedong in his attempt to make China a communist nation?
a. the "responsibility system"
b. the "Great Leap Forward"
c. the "Great Cultural Revolution"
d. the Red Guard

18. _____ In what did China's "Four Modernizations" program result?
a. high economic growth and inflation
b. a decrease in crop production
c. a decrease in the number of high school and college students
d. poor health care and a slow population growth

19. _____ What did Chinese leaders realize after 1960?
a. that they needed the military support of the Soviet Union
b. that only Western nations could resolve their internal problems
c. that good international relations only lessened China's power and wealth
d. that modernization was impossible without good foreign relations

Chapter Test, pp. 185–186

ALTERNATE CHAPTER TEST
Chapter 36
The Assertion of Independence in Asia

Key Terms, People, and Places
Yes/No (32 points): Write Y if the key term, person, or place is used correctly. Write N if it is not.

1. _____ Under Mao Zedong, a large factory that employed about 5,000 Chinese families was called a **commune**.
2. _____ The **Sikhs** are people living in the Punjab area of northern India who have their own religion and culture.
3. _____ The unequal flow of goods between two countries is called a **trade imbalance**.
4. _____ The **Geneva Accords** were peace agreements signed by North and South Vietnam after the Vietnam War.
5. _____ The People's Republic of China was first set up in **Taiwan**.
6. _____ A **puppet government** is a government kept in power by the military of another country.
7. _____ **South Asia** is presently divided among several Western nations.
8. _____ **Bangladesh** is the island east of mainland China where Chiang's forces set up the Nationalist Chinese government.
9. _____ **Corazon Aquino**, widow of President Marcos' leading political rival, proposed a new democratic constitution in the Philippines.
10. _____ A **subsidy** is a government contribution to business.
11. _____ **Jawaharlal Nehru**, India's first prime minister, established democratic institutions.
12. _____ **Ho Chi Minh** was the leader of the most effective anticolonial group in Vietnam during the mid-1900s.
13. _____ The **Great Cultural Revolution** was an attempt by Mao Zedong to encourage the development of literature and art in China.
14. _____ **Guided capitalism** is a system in which the government takes an active role in guiding the business community.
15. _____ **Hanoi** was the capital of Vietnam before the country became unified in 1975.
16. _____ **Southeast Asia** is the region that includes India, Pakistan, and Bangladesh.

Main Ideas
Completion (52 points): Write the letter of the best ending to the statement.

17. _____ Mao Zedong attempted to make China a communist nation by establishing all of the following EXCEPT
a. the Red Guard.
b. the "responsibility system."
c. the "Great Leap Forward."
d. the "Great Cultural Revolution."

18. _____ China's "Four Modernizations" program resulted in
a. a decrease in crop production.
b. high economic growth and inflation.
c. a decrease in the number of high school and college students.
d. poor health care and a slow population growth.

19. _____ After 1960, Chinese leaders realized that
a. modernization was impossible without good foreign relations.
b. only Western nations could resolve their internal problems.
c. good international relations only lessened China's power and wealth.
d. they needed the military support of the Soviet Union.

20. _____ One factor that was NOT responsible for Japan's economic recovery after World War II was
a. Japan's adoption of a new democratic constitution.
b. the purchase of more Japanese goods by foreign countries.
c. the increase in the number of imports to Japan.
d. the inexpensive modern technology provided by foreign countries.

Alternate Chapter Test, pp. 187–188

Other Optional Ancillaries

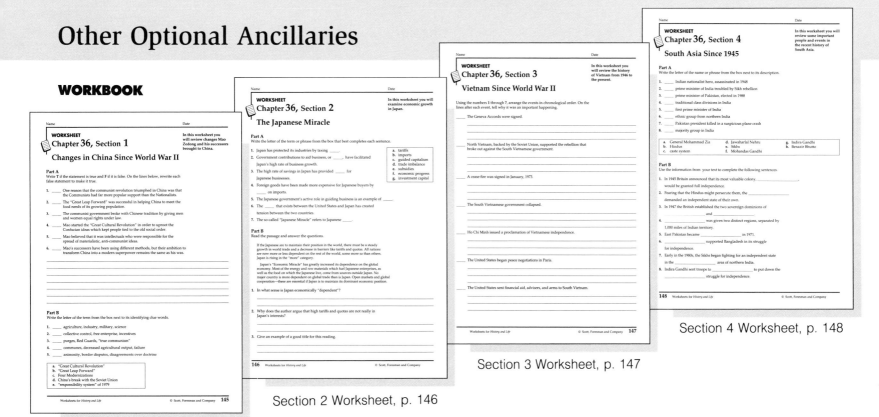

WORKBOOK

Section 1 Worksheet, p. 145

Section 2 Worksheet, p. 146

Section 3 Worksheet, p. 147

Section 4 Worksheet, p. 148

SOURCE READINGS

Source Reading 36A
Source Reading 36B

TEST GENERATOR

40 multiple-choice questions for Chapter 36

OVERHEAD TRANSPARENCIES

Overhead Transparency 71
Overhead Transparency 72

36

The Assertion of Independence in Asia

1945 – Present

1945

| 1947 | India and Pakistan become independent |

| 1949 | People's Republic of China is established |

| 1975 | Vietnam is unified under communist rule |

1980

1990

As the Cold War developed in Europe, important political developments took place in China, Japan, and India, as well as in many other Asian nations. An important change was the success of a communist revolution in China in 1949. The revolution, which ousted the ruling Nationalist Chinese government, marked the beginning of a new political order in China. The leader of the revolution, Mao Zedong, summed up how the victory was achieved.

> Fight, fail, fight again, fail again . . . till . . . victory; that is the logic of the people, and they . . . will never go against this logic. This is . . . Marxist law. The Russian people's revolution followed this law, and so has the Chinese people's revolution.

In the rest of Asia, the most significant change was the crumbling of the extensive Western and Japanese empires. The European powers and Japan were exhausted by World War II and no longer able to control their many Asian colonies, who were demanding their independence.

The assertion of independence transformed the role of Asia in world history. India emerged as the world's largest democracy, Japan developed as a leading industrial nation, and China struggled to become the world's third superpower.

Remarkable economic transformations took place in Asia, particularly among six countries that are part of the Pacific Rim. The six countries include two giants—China and Japan—and four smaller, newly industrialized countries—South Korea, Taiwan, Singapore, and Hong Kong. Some experts predict that the 21st century will be called "the Pacific Century" because the Pacific Rim's share of exports in the global market is expected to expand rapidly. Through the development of extensive trade ties with nations around the world, the Pacific Rim countries demonstrated how globally interdependent the world economy had become.

High population density is one of the challenges facing modern Asian nations today. Tokyo's Shinjuku subway station (above) is the busiest subway station in the world. About 3 million of Tokyo's commuters use the city's subway system daily.

Reading Preview

In this chapter you will read how Asian nations changed politically and economically after 1945.

1. Communists came to power in China.

2. Postwar Japan and other Pacific Rim nations made remarkable progress.

3. Southeast Asian countries became independent.

4. South Asian countries faced major challenges.

Communists came to power in China.

As you learned in Chapter 33, a struggle for control of China had been going on between Nationalists and Communists since the 1930s. Civil war once again erupted at the end of World War II.

A Communist revolution triumphed in China.

By 1949 the Communists, with far more popular support than the Nationalists, conquered most of

Essential Learning Objectives

Students will learn to:

- evaluate Mao Zedong's communist policies from 1949 to 1976.
- discuss China's relations with the world after 1960.

Remind students that China throughout its long history had experienced cyclical periods of poverty and food shortages, a result in part of its large population and its lack of modern technology. Ask students to suggest ways a government might solve such problems. Have students, as they study this section, identify the methods used by two leaders in China and how the people reacted.

681

- Clarify the time frame of this section by listing on the chalkboard policies that were begun by Mao (1949–1976) and Deng Xiaoping (1976–present).

- Explain how Mao came to power by winning the civil war against the Nationalists. List and discuss the changes made by Mao in creating a communist society in China: land ownership replaced by cooperatives, then communes; traditions weakened by attacking Confucian ideals; party loyalty strengthened by changing the family structure; women's status raised.

- Stress the ways in which opposition to these policies was dealt with. Point out the rationale behind the excesses of the Cultural Revolution in attempting to destroy old ideas and to control the direction of change.

- Emphasize the approach to change taken by Deng Xiaoping. Discuss the emphasis on individual and family responsibility used to increase food and industrial production.

GUIDED PRACTICE

Ask students to cite possible effects of the Chinese policy that permitted young Chinese to study in the United States, Europe, and Japan.

China. In October of that year, they proclaimed the birth of the People's Republic of China. This new government controlled the most populous country in the world, with about 600 million people.

Chiang Kai-shek and his remaining forces fled to the island of **Taiwan**, about 130 miles east of mainland China. There they set up the Nationalist Chinese government in exile, still claiming that it was the only legitimate government of China.

Like the government of the Soviet Union, the government of the People's Republic of China was a totalitarian dictatorship that crushed all opposition and exerted control over the personal lives of its people. In China all power was concentrated in the communist party's Central Committee, led by Chairman Mao. Millions of people who resisted the establishment of the communist regime were imprisoned or executed.

Mao was determined to transform China into a communist nation. Starting in 1949 Mao moved to win support of the peasantry by destroying the landlord class and redistributing private land as small farms to millions of former tenants and landless laborers. Mao's next step, a few years later, was to have all farmers form cooperatives. To do this peasants pooled their land and equipment, though they retained ownership, and shared the harvest according to what each contributed. Mao believed that the large cooperatives would be able to produce more food than small farms—an important goal because Mao wanted to build up Chinese industrial and military strength quickly. More food was needed to feed the growing numbers of people in cities and in the military.

The cooperatives, however, could not keep pace with the increased demand for food. Mao responded to this crisis by launching a program in 1957 called the "Great Leap Forward." One aim of this program was to increase food production by combining cooperatives into even larger units of 10,000 acres called **communes**. Each commune was made up of about 5,000 families.

The peasants hated the new commune system. They had to turn over work animals, equipment, and even small private plots to the communes and were not allowed to own anything except a few personal items. The leaders of the communes provided peasants with basic needs such as food and

Agricultural production has been one area in which the Chinese have made progress. Here commune workers harvest a crop of rapeseed, used primarily for cooking oil.

housing. In return, the peasants were expected to work the land and produce crops.

Under such a system, the peasants had little incentive to produce more than the minimum. As a result, crop production dropped drastically. Millions of people died from starvation, especially when bad weather and floods caused additional food shortages. In the end, the "Great Leap Forward" succeeded only in taking the nation a giant step backward.

The "Great Leap Forward" also set impossible goals in industrialization. Although the Soviet Union gave China industrial and technical aid, Mao's plans for industrialization failed. In Mao's haste to increase agricultural output and to industrialize, he had ignored an old Chinese proverb: "If you plant trees in the morning, don't expect to cut planks by nightfall."

Chinese society changed significantly.

Mao's determination to build a communist nation led him to attempt to change the traditional ways of Chinese society. To create complete loyalty to the communist state, Mao's regime tried to uproot the Confucian ideas that formed the base of Chinese life. The communists insisted that the party be more important than the family, the stronghold of traditional Chinese society, and that all people follow its doctrines. The communists also hoped to benefit from a change made in the legal status of women. In 1950 communist leaders introduced new marriage and divorce laws that freed women from arranged marriages and allowed them to choose their own husbands. Under the new laws, women were treated equally with men in divorce cases, and women's rights regarding children and property were protected.

The communist regime reasoned that women, once free from certain family obligations, would be more easily recruited as factory workers in industry. Although many women did become full-time salaried industrial workers, most continued to perform traditional family duties as well. In effect, women's responsibilities increased while men's duties remained the same.

The communists made changes in education as well. Mao and his advisers considered education the key to training good workers and loyal, obedient citizens. To achieve new education goals, most of the children of peasants and workers received at least an elementary education. At the high school and college level, the emphasis was on meeting the needs of industry through technical training. However, only a small percentage of students attended high school or college because there were too few teachers and resources.

Mao began a purge called the "Great Cultural Revolution."

By the mid-1960s, most Chinese had somewhat better living conditions than ever before. Food was rationed, but few people starved. Health conditions improved, and the average Chinese could buy a few small consumer goods, such as a bicycle or a sewing machine.

Given these modest improvements, Mao feared that the Chinese people were losing their revolutionary spirit. He feared that the Chinese might become "bourgeois," that is, merely interested in material possessions.

To remedy this situation, Mao took drastic action. He believed that the nation's interest in ma-

terialism could be traced to a group of intellectuals who had been spreading capitalistic, anticommunist ideas among the Chinese. In 1966 Mao began a purge, or cleaning out, of intellectuals, an extensive movement that became known as the "**Great Cultural Revolution**."

As part of this purge, university students, doctors, teachers, and other professionals were sent from cities into the countryside to do farm, mine, or factory work alongside the peasants. Mao also closed most of the nation's schools.

Mao organized 13 million teenagers into groups called the Red Guards. These teenagers, who were told that they were crusaders for a better China, launched parades, demonstrations, and terrorist attacks to support Mao's demand for a return to true communism. The Red Guards attacked teachers, government leaders, and factory managers, whom they accused of holding to "old ideas, old customs, and old habits."

The Red Guards terrorized people in cities and in the countryside. Eventually, however, many regional army commanders could no longer justify

During the Great Cultural Revolution, Chinese youth such as these below were encouraged to revere Mao as an infallible and almost superhuman figure.

China reevaluated its programs and policies.

By the time Mao Zedong died in 1976, China had made some progress in recovering from the terrible effects of the Great Cultural Revolution. The new leader of the communist party, Deng Xiaoping [dung'shyou'peng'], had larger ambitions than even Mao had entertained. Deng and his supporters hoped to make their country the world's third superpower by the year 2000. To reach this goal, they planned to modernize China's agriculture, industry, military force, and science and technology—a program called the "Four Modernizations."

Agriculture was the top priority of the "Four Modernizations" program because, without adequate food for the population, none of the other modernizations could succeed. In a remarkable departure from communist doctrine, the Chinese government in 1979 introduced an incentive program called the "responsibility system" to rural areas, where 80 percent of the Chinese lived.

Under the responsibility system, any crops grown by a family in excess of a state quota belonged to the family and could be consumed or sold in a free market. The farmers were also free to use their earnings to start small businesses.

The responsibility system was a success. Food production increased, and so did the income of China's farmers. By the end of the 1980s, China's agricultural system was a unique blend of collective control and free enterprise.

Success in agriculture encouraged China's leaders to apply similar methods to industry. In 1986 a plan was drafted that made managers of factories and businesses responsible for profits and losses. The plan also permitted small-scale private businesses to develop. In an effort to attract foreign investment, Chinese leaders invited investors from other countries to open factories in certain areas.

To speed modernization along, the Chinese government sent thousands of students to the United States, Europe, and Japan for technical training. These students returned to China with valuable technical skills that they could share with other Chinese. The modernization programs successfully led to such high rates of economic growth that by the end of the 1980s, China had to grapple with the problem of inflation.

the heavy-handed tactics of the Red Guards and so refused to obey orders from the central Chinese government. The order and unity that had been so painfully imposed by the communists after 1949 began to break down. Late in 1968 Mao realized that the Great Cultural Revolution was out of control, and stopped it by using the army to restore order. The Red Guard organization was disbanded, and schools were reopened.

FROM THE ARCHIVES The excerpt is from *On the Correct Handling of Contradictions Among the People*, February 27, 1957, as it appears in *Quotations from Chairman Mao Tsetung* (Peking: Foreign Languages Press, 1976), pp. 302–303. Is there anything inconsistent in the admonition to let "a hundred flowers bloom" and the expectation that questions in art and science "should be settled"? (Yes. It sounds like an agreed upon answer, one flower cultivated and 99 cast away.)

Another problem facing the Chinese government was massive population growth, which was the result of better health care introduced by the communist regime. Between 1949 and 1979, China's population doubled to reach more than one billion. Such massive population increases threatened to cancel out gains in food production.

Thus, in 1979 China became the first country in the world to launch a campaign to limit each family to only one child. The government also forced men and women to delay both marriage and childbirth. Within ten years, population growth was reduced by half. However, many Chinese disliked the new policy.

China's relations with the world changed after 1960.

Although the Soviet Union and China were both communist nations, a deep animosity existed beneath their superficial friendship. Joseph Stalin of the Soviet Union and Mao Zedong often disagreed about communist doctrine, and there were border disputes that continued to fester. In the late 1950s and early 1960s, divisions widened between the two communist powers. Finally, in 1963 China broke all ties.

A military confrontation between China and the Soviet Union then became a strong possibility. The two communist giants shared a 1,900-mile border, along which the Soviets stationed one million troops armed with modern weapons. Although China had one of the world's largest armies, the nation became increasingly wary of the Soviet presence in the late 1960s and early 1970s. China's weapons, though plentiful, were outdated and no match for the more sophisticated Soviet weapons.

China soon began to rethink its position in international relations. Could the nation accomplish its modernization goals if it were at odds with both the United States, with whom the Chinese clashed during the Korean War (1950–1953), and the Soviet Union? China's leaders thought not. If rapid modernization were to be successful, China would need cooperation from the industrialized nations.

These considerations led first to the People's Republic of China replacing Nationalist Taiwan in the UN in 1971, and then to the establishing of full diplomatic relations between China and the United States in 1979. By the late 1980s, China was carrying on large-scale trade with both the United States and Japan, as well as with the countries of Western Europe. China had emerged as an important economic and political power.

China's position was badly shaken in 1989. University students and young people launched a pro-democracy movement to protest restrictions on

Inspired by America's Statue of Liberty, the "Freedom Goddess" was erected by Chinese students in Beijing's Tiananmen Square in 1989 protests.

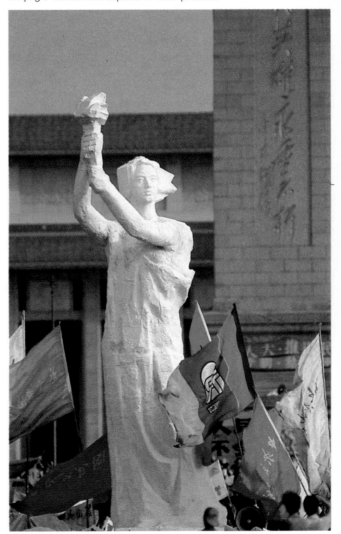

ASSESS

Why did Mao change his land reform program from the cooperative to the commune system? (Cooperatives could not supply the amounts of food needed by cities and the army.)

OPTIONAL RETEACHING

Direct students, in small groups, to write "government-planning statements" for increasing production in one of the four areas of modernization. Students should read their programs aloud to the class and discuss implementation priorities.

OPTIONAL ENRICHMENT

1. Have students locate and describe items imported from China. A trip to a department store or ads from magazines and catalogs should be helpful. (average)

2. Assign students to research and to report on the extent to which China's one-child policy has succeeded. Reports should include a discussion of possible long-term effects on the society. (challenging)

3. Also for enrichment:

📖 *Source Reading 36A*

INDEPENDENT PRACTICE/ HOMEWORK

Assign the Section Review, Activities page 215, or Workbook page 145.

CLOSURE

Tell students that Mao Zedong used repressive methods to restructure Chinese society into a communist state. Deng Xiaoping, on the other hand, used incentive programs to reward individual initiative to increase production. The goal of making China a world power led its leaders to reopen contacts with the United States, Europe, and Japan.

Identify

Key Terms, People, and Places are defined on pages indicated in parentheses. Also see the Glossary and Biographical Dictionary.

Taiwan (682), commune (682), Great Cultural Revolution (683)

Main Ideas

1. Mao Zedong distributed private land to small farmers who formed cooperatives.

2. Confucian traditions of family loyalty were undermined. Women were granted new rights. The education system was expanded.

3. It caused severe economic, social, and educational setbacks.

4. Four modernizations: agriculture, industry, military, and science and technology. The responsibility system was successful.

5. Chinese leaders realized that China must be involved with the rest of the world if modernization were to become a reality.

Critical Thinking

It is assumed that people are not motivated to work unless they receive some kind of personal gain for themselves or their families for their work.

2 Lesson Plan

Essential Learning Objectives

Students will learn to:

- identify the factors that led to Japan's postwar political and economic growth.
- describe the political systems and industrial development of Pacific Rim nations.

---

freedom of expression and the rampant corruption in all branches of government. Thousands of young people gathered on Tiananmen Square in Beijing as worldwide news media recorded the events. On June 4, 1989, hardline Communist leaders sent in troops and tanks. Thousands of people were shot and arrested. Worldwide public opinion condemned this brutal abuse of human rights but China's leaders countered that the drive to modernization required complete internal stability.

Section 1 Review

Identify Taiwan, commune, Great Cultural Revolution

Main Ideas

1. Describe Mao Zedong's first efforts to increase agricultural production in China.
2. How did Chinese society change under Mao's regime?
3. What were the effects of the Great Cultural Revolution on Chinese society?
4. What were the Four Modernizations? Give one example of a successful "modernization" program.
5. How did the attitude of Chinese leaders toward international relations change in the 1970s?

Critical Thinking

Identifying Assumptions: Consider the following statement: "Farm production in China increased under the responsibility system because people needed the incentive of personal gain to work hard and be more than minimally productive." What assumptions are being made in this statement?

---

2 Postwar Japan and other Pacific Rim nations made remarkable progress.

The East Asian nations of Japan, South Korea, Taiwan, Hong Kong, and Singapore all successfully completed post–World War II recovery and modernization plans. Japan's recovery and growth, in particular, is one of the most remarkable success stories in modern history.

Japan became a democracy.

As was the case in Europe, Japanese cities, factories, and railroads had been severely damaged or destroyed in the war, and the economy was in ruins. Many Japanese were hungry and homeless, with little hope of rebuilding their lives.

In 1945 Allied troops, mainly from the United States, occupied Japan. Led by an American general, Douglas MacArthur, the United States dismantled the Japanese military establishment since the treaty ending World War II forbade Japan from having a military. The Allies also tried Japanese leaders for war crimes and dissolved the large state-owned, Japanese companies.

The United States and other Western nations helped the Japanese restore their economy by providing modern technology at low cost. Western nations also began purchasing Japanese-made goods, which stimulated economic growth. Japan adopted a democratic constitution, which transferred power from the emperor to the people and renounced war as a means to achieve political objectives.

Unhampered by large military expenditures, Japan entered a period of unprecedented growth. Throughout the 1950s and 1960s, Japan's new democratic system became firmly established, and its economy grew rapidly. As foreign trade expanded, the Japanese standard of living soared.

Japan became an economic giant.

By the late 1980s, the Japanese population had reached 120 million. Japan was second in world industrial production, just behind the United States. It led the world in shipbuilding and ranked high in the production of cars and computers. Japan had achieved what some people called an economic miracle. The economic miracle was based not only on a strong home market, but even more on a thriving foreign trade.

Japan's economic progress depended largely upon the adaptive ability and productivity of the Japanese people and the unique factory production system they developed. For example, large firms hired people for life, an arrangement that created strong loyalty to the firm and provided a stable labor force. Although only one-third of Japanese workers were employed by the large firms, those firms produced most of the goods for export.

The Japanese government itself played an important role in improving the economy. In the 1950s the government established policies to encourage a high rate of savings among the Japanese. Japanese industries then borrowed from these savings to invest in new machinery and research for new products for export.

The government favored tariffs, or taxes, on imports and **subsidies**, or government contributions, to aid industry. At the same time, the Japanese government took an active role in guiding the business community. The government provided forecasts and economic objectives for business, targeting development in those areas it considered most desirable for economic growth. The system was a form of "**guided capitalism**" that some observers referred to as "Japan, Inc."

Although many women joined the workforce, they rarely got the better, high-paying jobs that were consistently given to men. This inequality existed despite the fact that women had legal equality with men and were often equally qualified. The Japanese tradition of male dominance, though weakening, was still strong.

Japan's economic strength affected its foreign policy.

The growth of Japan's trade and wealth, along with the nation's need for overseas markets and areas of investment, influenced Japan's foreign policy. For example, in the 1970s Japan and China, formerly two of the bitterest enemies, established a new trade relationship.

Relations with the United States also changed as tensions over trade developed. Japanese trade regulations prevented many American products from being sold in Japan. Yet Japanese exports to the United States, such as television sets, automobiles, and electronic equipment, increased dramatically in the 1980s. The unequal flow of goods, called a

Although more women have entered Japan's work force, their upward progress has been limited. These women work in fiber optics (left) and sales (below).

OPTIONAL RETEACHING

To help students grasp the political conditions in Pacific Rim countries, draw a long horizontal line on the chalkboard. Write "Political Freedom/Democracy" above the line, "More Freedom" at one end of the line and "Little Freedom" on the opposite end. Have students write the names of Pacific Rim countries in the appropriate place on the line. (China may also be included.)

OPTIONAL ENRICHMENT

1. Have students research and write reports on specific aspects of postwar Japan. Possible topics: The Japanese Constitution, The Role of the Emperor in a Democracy, Land Reform Under the Occupation, Japan's Rearmament. (average)
2. Also for enrichment:

 Overhead Transparency 71

INDEPENDENT PRACTICE/HOMEWORK

Assign the Section Review, Activities page 216, or Workbook page 146.

CLOSURE

Tell students that Allied occupation forces helped Japan develop a democracy and a strong economy that provided a high standard of living for its people. Other nations in the Pacific Rim also developed strong economies after World War II. Free market systems and an abundance of skilled workers who worked for relatively low wages contributed to their success.

trade imbalance, concerned United States manufacturers. Japan also realized that, because of its enormous wealth, it must assume a larger role in providing aid to other countries. In the late 1980s, Japan passed the United States as the world's leading foreign aid donor.

Smaller Pacific Rim countries had booming economies.

Besides Japan, four smaller countries of the Pacific Rim region achieved outstanding economic success in the 1970s and 1980s. South Korea, Taiwan, Hong Kong, and Singapore all became important manufacturing and trading centers. Each of these nations had to overcome two shared problems—high population density in a small area, and scarcity of natural resources. Leaders in each country overcame these problems by developing market-oriented economies and using a skilled labor force willing to work for low wages.

South Korea. In the 1950s South Korea began to build a broad base of industry and export products. Starting with textiles and clothing, South Korea expanded to steel production in the 1970s and electronics and automobiles in the 1980s. As the nation's economy grew and products were sent around the world, exports in the 1980s accounted for half of the country's economic activity.

Within South Korea, growing prosperity and rising living standards had political repercussions. By the late 1980s, middle-class South Koreans, often represented by university students, demanded that the longstanding authoritarian government allow genuine democratic reforms. Under pressure, the South Korean government began to move slowly toward reform.

Taiwan. Since 1949, when the Chinese Nationalists fled China, the Nationalist party has maintained political control of Taiwan. To remain in charge, the government refused to legalize rival parties and has restricted freedoms, particularly freedom of political expression.

Economically, Taiwan developed a mixed economy, with private companies existing along with state-owned companies. The private companies, however, became the driving force behind Taiwan's remarkable growth in industry and exports, especially of textiles and electronics.

Hong Kong. The island of Hong Kong, off the coast of mainland China, and nearby areas are a British crown colony. Since the 1950s Hong Kong has developed into an important international financial center and become a communications and transportation hub for East Asia. Light industries, such as textiles, clothing, electronics, fishing, and tourism, have also been part of Hong Kong's economic growth.

In 1997, when Britain's 99-year lease over Hong Kong expires, the People's Republic of China will reclaim sovereignty over the Hong Kong territory. Although it is not yet clear how this political change will affect Hong Kong, a 1985 agreement between Britain and China stated that the crown colony will be allowed to keep its capitalistic economic system for 50 years after the lease expires.

Singapore. Although geographically part of Southeast Asia, Singapore is included with the Pacific Rim countries because it, too, achieved success as a newly industrialized nation. In addition, its population is three-quarters Chinese. A former British colony, Singapore became a separate nation in 1965. With a parliamentary democracy, a free enterprise market economy, and one of the world's largest seaports, Singapore emerged in the 1980s as a major center of trade and banking.

Section 2 Review

Identify subsidy, guided capitalism, trade imbalance

Main Ideas

1. Give three reasons for Japan's economic recovery after World War II.
2. What factors contributed to making Japan an economic giant by the 1980s?
3. Describe Japan's foreign policy in the 1970s and 1980s.
4. How were the problems of high population density and scarcity of natural resources resolved by the Pacific Rim nations?

Critical Thinking

Assessing Cause and Effect: Consider the following statement: Japan's geographical features and population are major factors in its becoming an economic giant in the world. Give reasons why you agree or disagree with this statement. Support your answer with evidence.

Southeast Asia

- Commercial farming
- Subsistence farming
- Ranching
- Forests
- Lumbering
- Hunting, fishing, and gathering
- Mining
- Commercial fishing
- Urban land use
- National capitals
- Other cities

 MAP STUDY This map shows the political divisions of Southeast Asia, along with the economic uses of the region's land. What industry dominates the area's coastlines? What industry takes advantage of the region's forests?

<table>
<tr><td>3</td><td>Southeast Asian countries became independent.</td></tr>
</table>

Before World War II, most of **Southeast Asia** was divided among Europeans and Americans. After the war, these colonial empires dissolved.

Japan left local leaders in control.

During World War II, all of Southeast Asia was conquered by Japan and became part of the Japa-nese empire. Japanese rule lasted only three years, but in that period the Japanese allowed local lead-ers to take over important governmental posts. Near the end of the war, Japan trained local troops and officers to fight the Allies.

After the Japanese surrendered, and before the European powers could reestablish control, many of these popular local leaders proclaimed their countries to be independent. When European pow-ers brought in troops to reestablish dominance, conflict occurred.

ANSWER TO MAP STUDY commercial fishing; lumbering

In 1989 the government of Burma changed the official name of the country from Burma to Myanmar and the capital from Ran-goon to Yangon.

689

<table>
<tr><td>3</td><td>Lesson Plan</td></tr>
</table>

Essential Learning Objectives

Students will learn to:

- explain how policies developed during World War II led to the

breakup of colonial empires in Southeast Asia.
- describe the development and ramifications of dictatorships in several Southeast Asian nations.

Remind students that most of the countries of Southeast Asia had been European colonies since the late 19th century. Discuss why colonial areas would want to be independent and what problems they might have in building governments after achieving freedom. (Students should recognize that most colonial peoples had been given no opportunity to learn how to run governments.)

- Clarify events in the Philippines, Indonesia, and Vietnam by plotting events on a time line on the chalkboard. Use five-year increments from 1945 to the present.

- Discuss the policies of the government of North Vietnam toward the people of South Vietnam after unification of the country.

- Clarify the reasons for hostilities between Vietnam, Cambodia, and China despite their communist forms of government. Identify probable sites of border disputes for students on a wall map.

GUIDED PRACTICE

Help students identify possible reasons why the United States decided to aid South Vietnam beginning in the late 1950s. (Students should grasp that communist activities were also taking place in the Philippines and Indonesia at the time and that aiding South Vietnam was in line with the

Corazon Aquino, in her characteristic yellow dress, campaigns for the post of Philippine president, which she eventually won in 1986.

In some cases, however, independence came peacefully. The United States, faithful to a pre-war promise, granted independence to the Philippines in 1946. Britain granted independence to Burma, Malaysia, and Singapore over a period of several years. Thailand, though occupied by the Japanese during the war, quickly reestablished self-rule after the war.

The Philippines struggled to build democracy.

Despite a peaceful transition to independence, building stable democracies was often a difficult process, as was the case in the Philippines. Although a democratic constitution was adopted by the country in 1946, power and wealth in that nation was concentrated in a small elite class of people.

Most of the Philippine people were peasants who lived in rural poverty. During the 1950s the government tried to meet peasant demands for the breakup of large estates and the redistribution of land, but progress was slow. As a result, a communist insurgency movement called the New People's Army gained the support of the peasants. This popular force attacked government outposts and won control of isolated rural areas.

As fighting continued, Ferdinand Marcos, who was elected president of the Philippines in 1965, became increasingly authoritarian in his rule. Rather than give up office in 1972, Marcos declared martial law throughout the country and, backed by the army, arrested his political oppo-

nents. His actions ended democratic government in the Philippines. Marcos established a dictatorship, and through corrupt practices, accumulated enormous wealth for himself and his family. He was unable, however, to suppress the communist uprising or improve economic conditions, despite large amounts of military and economic aid from the United States.

Political opposition to President Marcos mounted in the 1980s. In 1983 his leading political rival Benigno Aquino [ä kē′nō] returned from a self-imposed exile, only to be assassinated as he arrived in the Philippines. Marcos' supporters were blamed for the assassination, which led to the political rise of Aquino's widow, **Corazon Aquino**. In 1986 she ran against Marcos in a fraudulent election. Although she was defeated, an outburst of demonstrations against Marcos led to the dictator's exile and Aquino's ascent to the presidency. As president of the Philippines, Aquino proposed a new democratic constitution and initiated social reforms and land redistribution. She also tried to halt the communist insurgency.

Indonesian independence led to military dictatorship.

Following a bitter war of independence from the Dutch, Indonesia faced many difficulties—a population that grew faster than the food supply, tumbling exports, increasing inflation, and rebellions against the new government. Indonesia's leader Sukarno, came to believe that democracy could not solve these problems quickly enough. In 1963 Sukarno, who was supported by the army, became absolute ruler for life. All Indonesian opposition political parties were banned.

Sukarno became increasingly procommunist, and Indonesian army leaders feared a communist takeover of the country. Consequently, in 1965 a military regime led by General Suharto took control of the Indonesian government. Anticommunist suppression became severe, and hundreds of thousands of Indonesians suspected of being communist were killed.

Indonesia has enormous natural resources and thus the potential for a stable economy. In addition to large reserves of oil, natural gas, and several minerals, the nation has immense timber and

BACKGROUND Ho Chi Minh's real name was Nguyen Tat Thanh. The assumed name means "Ho, the Seeker after Light."

rubber resources. However, under the military regime of General Suharto, only a privileged minority benefited from these riches. Almost half the Indonesians lived in extreme poverty.

Many people in Indonesia blamed the military rule of General Suharto for government corruption and mismanagement of the economy. Indonesians resented their continuous poverty, social injustices, and the authoritarian political system. However, General Suharto was reelected twice, in 1983 and 1987, and the army continued to dominate almost every phase of Indonesian life.

Vietnam, Laos, and Cambodia became independent.

After Japan was defeated in World War II, France tried to regain control of Laos, Cambodia (Kampuchea), and Vietnam. In 1946, however, pressure from anticolonial groups forced France to grant partial self-rule to Laos and Cambodia. The status of Vietnam, however, remained unsettled.

The division of Vietnam. In Vietnam the most effective anticolonial group was the Viet Minh [vē-yet′min], led by **Ho Chi Minh** [hō′chē′min′], a communist who had proclaimed independence for the Democratic Republic of Vietnam.

The French refused to recognize Ho Chi Minh's government, and fighting between the two groups began in 1954, ending in defeat for the French.

Later in that same year, agreements that were called the **Geneva Accords** were signed. The accords gave full independence to Laos and Cambodia and called for free elections in Vietnam. A temporary line drawn at the 17th parallel in Vietnam divided the nation into North and South Vietnam.

The promised elections were never held. Ho Chi Minh's communist government controlled North Vietnam, and an anticommunist government ruled South Vietnam. In 1957 a rebellion broke out against the South Vietnamese government. North Vietnam, backed by the Soviet Union, supported the rebellion because it wanted to bring all of Vietnam under communist rule.

The Vietnam War. In the Vietnamese civil war, the United States backed the government of South Vietnam by sending money, advisers, and arms. American leaders believed that providing this aid could prevent the spread of communism into other parts of Southeast Asia.

In the early 1960s, the United States began to send American troops to South Vietnam. By 1968 more than 500,000 Americans were fighting there. Yet, despite ever increasing American involvement in the war, the South Vietnamese government grew steadily weaker. Meanwhile, in the United States, public opposition to American involvement in the war gathered strength. Opponents of the war, many of whom were American college students,

At left, Saigon residents return to their destroyed homes, and below, a U.S. soldier wades across a murky swamp in Vietnam.

policy of containment set up by President Truman.)

3 | ASSESS AND CLOSE

ASSESS

1. What conditions caused the Philippine peasants to support the New People's Army? (a strong desire for land reform)
2. Why did Sukarno lose power in Indonesia? (He lost the support of army leaders because of his procommunist policies.)

OPTIONAL RETEACHING

Hand out outline maps of Southeast Asia from the Geography Skills book. Have students label each country with its name and the name in parentheses of its former colonial power. Students should use symbols or colors to indicate countries that
(a) fought wars for independence,
(b) gained independence peacefully,
(c) experienced communist activity. Students should make appropriate keys for their maps.

OPTIONAL ENRICHMENT

1. Have students use newspaper and magazine articles from 1986 to write a report describing the events that led to Corazon Aquino's presidency. (average)
2. Assign students to research and to write a report on the symbolism of the Vietnam Memorial in Washington, D.C. Ask students to discuss why many visitors find the memorial deeply moving. (challenging)
3. Also for enrichment:

 Overhead Transparency 72

INDEPENDENT PRACTICE/HOMEWORK

Assign the Section Review, Activities page 217, or Workbook page 147.

CLOSURE

Summarize the lesson by telling students that the newly independent nations of Southeast Asia, with little or no experience with self-government, were vulnerable prey for numerous dictatorial rulers and regimes.

Answers to Section 3 Review

Identify

Key Terms, People, and Places are defined on pages indicated in parentheses. Also see the Glossary and Biographical Dictionary. Southeast Asia (689), Corazon Aquino (690), Ho Chi Minh (691), Geneva Accords (691), Hanoi (692), puppet government (693)

Main Ideas

1. Many Asian countries proclaimed independence at the end of the war. When the European powers tried to regain control, conflict resulted.
2. Marcos lost support of the army. He was forced into exile and Aquino then became president.
3. high population growth, lack of development of natural resources, extreme poverty; military dictatorship
4. Independence from France came under the Geneva Accords.
5. After a 1978 war, Vietnam installed a puppet government in Cambodia. Guerrilla war against the regime continued until 1991 when a peace agreement was reached.

Critical Thinking

At the beginning of the war, it was believed that American aid could halt the spread of communism in

The Vietnam War, 1964–1975

- ✳ Major battles
- ▲ U.S. air bases

 MAP STUDY The Ho Chi Minh Trail, from North Vietnam to South Vietnam, passed through two other countries. Which countries were these?

called for the United States to withdraw its troops from Vietnam.

U.S. President Lyndon Johnson realized that public opposition would prevent him from committing the number of troops needed to win the war. As a result, the United States began peace negotiations in Paris in 1968. The talks failed, and public pressure to end the war escalated throughout the first term (1969–1972) of Johnson's successor, Richard Nixon.

In January, 1973, a cease-fire was finally signed, ending American fighting in Vietnam. More than 55,000 Americans lost their lives and billions of

dollars in aid were spent. In 1975 the South Vietnamese government collapsed, and Vietnam was unified under communist rule.

After nearly a decade of fighting, the United States had lost the war in Vietnam. The global significance of the defeat was that the world's leading superpower was not invincible. It became clear that there were limits to what the United States could achieve with its military power, especially in regional conflicts.

The unification of Vietnam. When Vietnam was unified, **Hanoi** [hä noi′] became the capital of the country. Saigon, the former capital of South Vietnam, was renamed Ho Chi Minh City. During 30 years of continuous war, Vietnam suffered much destruction. More than 2 million men, women, and children had been killed, and much of the countryside had been laid to waste.

The end of the war brought many changes to Vietnam. All political parties except that of the communists were banned, and thousands of South Vietnamese were sent to special reeducation camps. Other South Vietnamese were forced to go to remote camps as laborers, and thousands were sent to prison camps. The Vietnamese educational system was also reorganized to better serve the purposes of the communist state, and private enterprise was prohibited.

The harsh conditions imposed by Vietnamese leaders especially hurt the middle and upper classes. Beginning about 1978 thousands of people fled the country. Some tried to escape by boat to Malaysia, Thailand, and other Asian countries. Uncounted numbers of these refugees, known as "boat people," perished from piracy, exposure to weather, and starvation. Others eventually were able to settle in the United States, France, Germany, and Australia.

Vietnam gained control of Cambodia.

In 1975 a border war began between Cambodia (Kampuchea) and Vietnam. The Cambodian government was a tyrannical communist dictatorship that practiced mass murder, killing nearly 2 million of its 8 million people in an effort to impose a certain style of communism on the population.

Although Vietnam and Cambodia were both communist countries, they were also longstanding

BACKGROUND Cambodia became communist in 1975 after the Khmer Rouge ("Red Khmers") captured Phnom Penh, the capital. Led by Pol Pot, the communist government sent the entire urban population into forced labor camps in the jungles in order to purge them of "bourgeois thinking."

enemies. For several years, the Cambodians had launched raids across the Vietnamese border and seized villages that they claimed belonged to Cambodia. The Vietnamese counterattacked.

The war expanded, and late in 1978, the Vietnamese conquered Cambodia and installed a puppet government. A **puppet government** is one that is kept in power by military troops of another country. Soon, a fierce guerrilla war developed in Cambodia, with large numbers of Vietnamese troops fighting various Cambodian factions. Because of the constant fighting and danger, Cambodian refugees streamed into neighboring Thailand.

Talks began in the late 1980s to try to resolve the conflict. Fighting finally ended in 1991 when the rebel groups and the Vietnamese-backed Cambodian government agreed to a United Nations peace plan calling for democratic elections in 1993. After nearly two decades of constant war, Cambodia had been turned into one of the world's poorest countries. It had to deal with widespread devastation, 500,000 homeless people, and the return of 350,000 refugees.

Section 3 Review

Identify Southeast Asia, Corazon Aquino, Ho Chi Minh, Geneva Accords, Hanoi, puppet government

Main Ideas
1. What was the cause of conflict in European-controlled Asian countries after World War II?
2. Describe conditions that led to Corazon Aquino becoming president of the Philippines.
3. What are major problems in Indonesia? How was the country ruled under Sukarno and Suharto?
4. How did Cambodia, Laos, and Vietnam become independent nations?
5. Describe the relationship between Cambodia and Vietnam since the late 1970s.

Critical Thinking
Making Hypotheses: The United States became involved in a war in Vietnam, a country far away and unfamiliar to Americans. Looking back, the war is not seen as successful, yet its cost in lives and other resources was very high. Why do you think the United States took this action and what factors probably most affected the outcome? Support your answer with evidence.

4 South Asian countries faced major challenges.

The largest nations of **South Asia**—India, Pakistan, and Bangladesh—had long colonial histories. When World War II ended, India and Pakistan began to move toward independence, and Bangladesh followed in the 1960s.

India and Pakistan became independent nations.

The first major country in South Asia to be affected by the movement for independence was India, Britain's most valuable colony. In 1945 Britain announced that India would be granted full independence.

The problem of establishing a government was enormously complicated for India. About 400 million people, speaking 14 major languages and more than 1,000 other dialects and languages, were divided by extremes of wealth and poverty, deep religious differences, and a rigid caste system. The Muslims, constituting 25 percent of the population and fearing that the Hindus might follow a policy of persecution, demanded an independent state of their own. In 1946 bloody riots broke out, in which 12,000 people were killed.

In the face of these serious divisions, the British reluctantly accepted the idea of dividing India. On August 15, 1947, British leaders established two sovereign dominions—India and Pakistan. In 1949 India became a federal republic, which was mostly Hindu. Pakistan, mainly Muslim, became a republic in 1956.

Geographically and economically, partition was a highly artificial arrangement. Pakistan was given two distinct regions on either side of India, separated by 1,000 miles of Indian territory. These two regions possessed grain- and jute-producing areas and had a surplus of foodstuffs. India, on the other hand, had the factories needed to process raw materials, such as jute, but it had an inadequate food supply. In addition, the political boundaries of the two countries divided important canals and rivers between India and Pakistan.

Although many Muslims emigrated to Pakistan following partition, some 40 million more re-

Southeast Asia. Lack of understanding of the geography and culture of Vietnam and a lack of U.S. public support for the war were probably major factors in its unsuccessful outcome.

mixed economy. Discuss Nehru's accomplishments in agriculture and industry. Point out why most Indians do not benefit from the increased food production.

- Explain the details of Indira Gandhi's terms in office and clarify the basis for the Sikh hostility that led to her assassination.

- Describe the series of events leading to the election of Benazir Bhutto in 1988. Ask students to suggest reasons why her election was an important step for Pakistan.

- Clarify the similarities and differences between West Pakistan and East Pakistan (Bangladesh). Discuss reasons for the desire for independence in East Pakistan and the problems that still must be solved there.

Direct students to categorize the accomplishments of Nehru's government according to the goals he had set. Have them cite which goals were met and which failed, and suggest reasons for the failures.

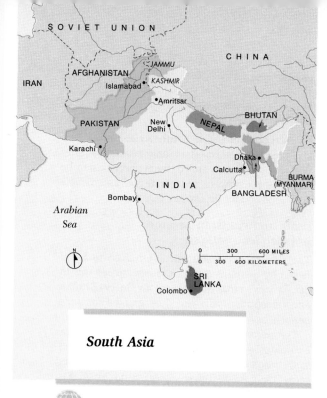

South Asia

MAP STUDY The map above shows South Asia. Which countries are in this region? Which is the largest?

mained in India. A large minority of Hindus also lived in Pakistan. Religious fanatics on both sides incited riots and committed horrible atrocities. In 1947 as many as one million people were massacred in Hindu-Muslim encounters. In 1948 when the Indian nationalist Mohandas Gandhi tried to quell the terrible riots, he was assassinated.

India chose a democratic form of government.

At the time of independence in 1947, the population of India was growing at a rate of about ten million people a year. Most Indians were poor, undernourished, and illiterate. Food shortages, even famine, were constant threats.

The nation chose to solve its problems under a democratic form of government. It adopted a parliamentary democracy and is governed under a constitution that took effect in 1950.

Through the capable leadership of **Jawaharlal Nehru** [jə wä′hər läl′ nā′rü], India's first prime

minister, democratic institutions were firmly established. Nehru, who led the nation until his death in 1964, had three goals—democracy, religious tolerance, and social and economic reforms.

Nehru was very concerned about India's widespread poverty and the fact that 40 percent of the people were without adequate food. In his view, the best way to improve the welfare of the people was through a mixed system of free enterprise and moderate socialism. Under Nehru's program, India's existing industries, farms, and commerce remained in private hands. However, new industrial projects such as steel mills, electric plants, and irrigation systems, were developed by the state. Through central planning, the government played a major role in economic development.

To make India self-sufficient in food production, Nehru's government in the 1950s financed major irrigation and flood control projects and redistributed land to farmers. During the 1950s the government directed a "green revolution," which was a program to increase the nation's agricultural production. Although the green revolution increased India's grain-producing capabilities, the nation's rapidly growing population barely allowed agricultural increases to keep pace.

As in agriculture, Nehru's goal in industry was to achieve self-sufficiency in manufactured goods. India, with an abundance of coal, oil, and iron ore—essential ingredients for industrial development—invested heavily to develop these valuable natural resources.

Important social reforms were also begun during Nehru's administration. India's constitution, which went into effect in 1950, gave women the right to vote. Later amendments also gave women equal rights with men in inheritance and ownership of property. Opportunities for women in education and business were expanded. The constitution also prohibited India's rigid caste system. Although the new law decreased discrimination, caste prejudices continued to divide Indian society.

Nehru's policies led to Indian accomplishments.

One of Nehru's major goals for India, agricultural self-sufficiency, was achieved in the 1970s. This goal was accomplished despite the nation's burgeoning population, which by the late 1980s exceeded 800 million people—almost double the number of people in 1947. By the late 1980s, India produced enough food to satisfy the needs of most of its people. In fact, the nation produced enough from its agricultural sector to enable it to export much of its produce.

Nehru's early efforts to industrialize the country also began to bear fruit in the 1970s and 1980s. Although India was still considered a developing nation because of its low gross national product, industrial production increased by more than 600 percent after 1950. Indian industries produced a variety of goods including automobiles, textiles, engines, and electrical appliances.

In spite of improvements in agricultural production and industrial development, many people in India were still underfed and undernourished. This situation existed because most increases in food production were on the nation's larger farms, those that specialized in raising produce for export. India's small farms, which supported about 75 percent of India's people, were largely unaffected by agricultural improvements and were still dependent upon India's seasonal monsoons.

India has yet to achieve firm political stability. One of the most troublesome problems India faces is the ethnic and regional conflicts that constantly threaten to splinter the nation. The difficulties of maintaining India's national unity became quite serious after Nehru's daughter, Indira Gandhi (no relation to Mohandas Gandhi), was elected prime

Indira Gandhi, India's prime minister before her assassination in 1984, speaks with her son Rajiv, who was assassinated in 1991 while campaigning.

minister in 1966. Although Gandhi promoted economic development, she also began to use authoritarian methods against her political opposition. In 1977, when widespread opposition arose against Gandhi's government, she was forced out of office. However, Gandhi's successors were ineffective, and she was reelected as prime minister in 1980.

During a second term as prime minister, Indira Gandhi faced political demands from several groups who had developed a strong ethnic consciousness. One such group was the 15 million **Sikhs** [sēks], who lived in the Punjab area of northern India. The Sikhs had their own religion—a blend of Islam and Hinduism—and a strong, distinctive culture. Early in the 1980s, some Sikhs began fighting for an independent national state. Indira Gandhi sent army troops against the rebellious Sikhs, and hundreds were killed in the armed conflict. In 1984 two of the prime minister's bodyguards, who happened to be Sikhs, assassinated her.

Indira Gandhi's son, Rajiv, was elected the new prime minister. He continued the policy of economic development, but in 1989 he was voted out of office. While campaigning for office in 1991, he, too, was assassinated.

A military dictatorship developed in Pakistan.

Pakistan suffered from political instability after gaining independence, allowing a military leader, General Mohammad Ayub Khan [ä yäb kän´], to seize control of the Pakistani government in 1958. Although he was dictatorial, the country remained relatively stable under his rule. Pakistan was an extremely poor country, with few railroads or roads and little industry. Nearly 80 percent of the people were farmers who barely made a living from small plots of land.

In the 1960s Pakistan enjoyed some economic progress when a land reform program began. Reforms in education and transportation followed, and a new constitution was written.

Despite these improvements, many Pakistanis were unhappy with their government, which continued to be dictatorial. Ayub's unpopularity grew as corruption flourished in his government, and he was forced out of office in 1969. Although a civil-

3 | ASSESS AND CLOSE

ASSESS
1. What are the majority religions in India and Pakistan? (Hinduism in India, Islam in Pakistan)
2. What type of government was established in India after independence? (a British-style parliamentary democracy)

OPTIONAL RETEACHING
Divide students into groups to act as government committees appointed to write laws or programs to solve India's problems: population growth, ethnic and language divisions, poverty, caste prejudices. Allow the entire class to discuss and vote on the proposed laws or programs.
Students also may be assigned Activities reteaching page 219.

OPTIONAL ENRICHMENT
1. Assign students to research and report on the environmental causes of flooding in Bangladesh. (average)
2. Assign students to research and report on Nehru's role in India's independence movement. (challenging)
3. Students also may be assigned Activities enrichment page 220, or:

 Source Reading 36B

INDEPENDENT PRACTICE/ HOMEWORK
Assign the Section Review, the Chapter Review items, Activities page 218, or Workbook page 148.

CLOSURE
Tell students that the nations of South Asia have faced many problems since gaining independence—famine, drought, political instability, religious

differences. Yet events within the last several decades—agricultural and industrial improvements in India and the election of Benazir Bhutto in Pakistan—give reason for optimism about the future of the region.

Pakistan's Benazir Bhutto, elected in 1988 as the first female leader of a Muslim nation, campaigns on her way to political victory.

ian was elected president for several years, in 1977 the military again seized power. General Mohammad Zia [zē′a] became president and set up a strict regime of martial law. However, government corruption continued, industrial development slowed, and government debt increased.

In 1988 General Zia died in a suspicious plane crash. In spite of widespread belief that the plane had been sabotaged by Zia's political enemies, no evidence of foul play was discovered.

Although the political future of Pakistan was unclear after Zia's death, political analysts suggested that Pakistan could possibly attain national unity in the near future. Evidence to support this optimism was seen in a ruling by Pakistan's supreme court in 1988 that legalized multi-party elections. Benazir Bhutto, the daughter of a former prime minister, won the first such election and became the first elected woman leader of a Muslim nation. However, she was forced out of office in 1990.

East Pakistan became Bangladesh.

In the late 1960s, East Pakistan became increasingly resentful of its ties with West Pakistan. Although both regions were Muslim, they were different in most other ways, especially in language and culture. Moreover, the West Pakistanis controlled the Pakistani economy, the army, and the government.

These conditions led East Pakistani leaders to demand control of taxes and the economy in their own region. The powers of the central government, these leaders argued, should be limited to foreign affairs and defense.

In effect, such demands would have made East Pakistan almost a self-governing unit, and West Pakistan refused to allow this. Thus, in 1971 West Pakistan attacked the rebellious eastern region, killing thousands of people and destroying much property. After this violence, the East Pakistanis declared independence and renamed their country **Bangladesh**. India supported Bangladesh by sending in troops. Within two weeks, West Pakistan was defeated, and Bangladesh was formed.

Bangladesh faced an uncertain future with many severe problems. Its capital city and other major cities and towns had been badly damaged in the war. The nation, with few natural resources and a large population, was forced to import millions of tons of rice and wheat each year to feed its people.

In the early 1990s, Bangladesh remained one of the poorest countries in the world, with a population of 113 million people in an area slightly smaller than the state of Wisconsin. Earnings from its major exports, jute and tea, were low and there seemed to be little possibility of industrialization in the near future. The nation's problems were compounded by terrible flooding, perhaps the worst to strike the area in a century.

Section 4 Review

Identify South Asia, Jawaharlal Nehru, Sikhs, Bangladesh

Main Ideas
1. Why was India partitioned into two countries?
2. Describe Nehru's policies for India.
3. What were the results of Nehru's policies for India?
4. How did the government of Pakistan form after independence?
5. What conditions led to the formation of Bangladesh?

Critical Thinking
Making Decisions: Faced with religious strife in India, British leaders decided to partition the country into two separate nations, India and Pakistan. If you had been in charge of India at that time, how might you have handled the problem? Support your decision with evidence.

HIGHLIGHTS OF CIVILIZATION

Japan's Rise to Economic Leadership

World Automobile Production

In millions of passenger cars in 1987

Japan

7.89

U.S.
7.09

West Germany
4.37

France
3.05

Italy
1.71

Spain
1.41

USSR
1.33

Britain
1.14

Source: Motor Vehicle Manufacturers Association. 1987

"The Japanese have set a breathless commercial pace for themselves and for the world. Can they maintain it?" This question, phrased in many different ways, has been asked many times over the years. When journalist Lance Morrow raised the query in 1983, Japan could look back on 25 years of rapid economic growth. At the same time, Japan faced new problems. Banking was beginning to take a dominant role in the Japanese economy and world financial markets, passing even the powerful Japanese industrial complex in importance.

In the 1850s, Japan had faced an economic crisis when Western nations sought to open its doors to foreign trade. The Meiji Restoration met this challenge aggressively by industrializing the Japanese economy along Western lines.

Spurred by Japan's industrial might (see graph), Tokyo's Stock Exchange has become the world's largest and most active (below).

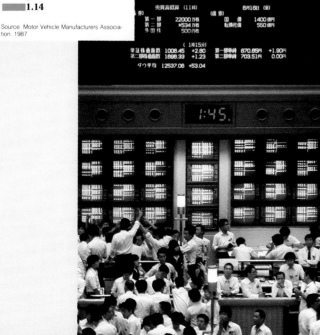

After World War II, Japan faced an even greater challenge as it attempted to restore its impoverished and devastated islands. With the help of the latest technology from the United States and other Western nations, Japan created a powerful economic empire based on electronics, steel production, and shipbuilding. By 1987 Japan had become the world's leading producer of automobiles. (See chart.)

Although the Japanese economy appeared stronger all the time, Japan faced yet another challenge. In each of Japan's major manufacturing industries—electronics, steel, shipbuilding, and automotives—companies were being threatened by other newly industrializing nations in Asia. Then Japanese leaders discovered a new source of strength in banking and finance.

To understand this development, one must realize that the value of Japanese money on the world market increased greatly during the 1980s. This meant that in 1989 the Japanese yen could be exchanged for two or three times as many dollars as in 1980. The strong yen meant that it was cheaper for the Japanese to purchase companies in other nations and let them manufacture the products for Japanese firms.

The new Japanese economy continued to have a strong home manufacturing base, but it also invested billions of dollars in the United States and in the industrialized nations of East Asia. This policy led to a higher level of economic integration in East Asia and to a leadership role for Japan in international banking and finance. Today a new generation of Japanese, as investors, managers, bankers, and financiers to the world, have found new ways to maintain that "breathless commercial pace" established by their predecessors.

HIGHLIGHTS OF CIVILIZATION

Many different reasons have been suggested to explain the economic miracle in Japan. The nation is only about the size of Montana, yet it has a population about one-half as large as the whole United States. It has only limited natural resources and only one-sixth of its land can be used for crops.

Most commentators, therefore, look to cultural traits to explain Japan's economic success. Some focus on the cooperation between government, business, and labor. Others point to a strong group loyalty based on a long tradition of isolation and the experience of losing World War II. Still others point out that Japan spends very little money on national defense.

A broader explanation points to the Japanese emphasis on the well-rounded individual dating back to the samurai. These warriors were expected to be experts in poetry and flower arranging as well as in warfare. In modern times this outlook on life shows up in careful attention to every detail, an appreciation of design, and a quest to do everything well.

James Fallows in a "Letter from Tokyo," (*Atlantic Monthly*, August, 1986, p. 19) emphasizes the Japanese ethic of hard work. Americans also work hard, he explains, but usually with a different motivation: "Americans work to make money and to win respect, but to some extent our culture says that you work hard so eventually you won't have to work . . . . They [the Japanese] work because that is their duty to a tight-knit, homogeneous society. They work . . . so as to keep on working."

Answers to Test Yourself

Key Terms, People, and Places
The key terms, people, and places tested here were introduced in the chapter sections and reviewed in the Section Reviews. For definitions see the page references at the appropriate Section Reviews. Also see the Glossary and Biographical Dictionary.

Main Ideas
The main ideas tested here were introduced in the sections of this chapter and reviewed in the Section Reviews. For answers to these questions, see the appropriate Section Reviews.

Critical Thinking
1. Agree: Large populations provide a competitive labor force willing to work for low wages, and location places these countries and territories in key positions to trade and interact with other Pacific Rim nations. Disagree: Labor force willing to work for low wages is important but location is not a major factor. The main reason for the economic success is the leadership of the countries and territories, which has developed huge markets in the western world and oriented products such as clothing and electronics to those western markets.
2. The recurring theme of struggle for independence even against strong odds shows that Asians strongly value guiding their own destiny under political systems of their choice.

CHAPTER 36 REVIEW

Section Summaries

Section 1
Communists came to power in China.
After World War II, civil war between Nationalists and Communists continued in China. In 1949 under Mao Zedong, the Communists won and established a new government in China. Mao's successors began a modernization program to develop the Chinese economy and improve foreign relations.

Section 2
Postwar Japan and other Pacific Rim nations made remarkable progress.
After losing World War II, Japan gradually developed its own democratic political system. Japan experienced tremendous economic growth. South Korea, Taiwan, Hong Kong, and Singapore also experienced phenomenal economic growth.

Section 3
Southeast Asian countries became independent.
The Philippines, under Corazon Aquino, struggled to build democracy and stability. Indonesia remained a poor country under the military rule of various dictators. A long civil war in Vietnam that involved the United States ended with Vietnam becoming a unified communist country in 1975. A war between Cambodia and Vietnam ravaged both nations.

Section 4
South Asian countries faced major challenges.
With independence, India split into two unfriendly nations—India, and Pakistan. India became a democracy and made progress in agriculture and industry. Pakistan remained unstable and underdeveloped. East Pakistan, renamed Bangladesh, became an independent nation in 1971.

Test Yourself

Key Terms, People, and Places
Identify the significance of each of the following:

Section 1
a. commune   c. Taiwan
b. Great Cultural Revolution

Section 2
a. subsidy   c. trade imbalance
b. guided capitalism

Section 3
a. Southeast Asia   d. Geneva Accords
b. Corazon Aquino   e. Hanoi
c. Ho Chi Minh   f. puppet government

Section 4
a. South Asia   c. Sikhs
b. Jawaharlal Nehru   d. Bangladesh

Review Dates

1947
India and Pakistan become independent

1949
People's Republic of China is established

1951
Japan's independence is restored

1966
Great Cultural Revolution begins in China

1975
Vietnam is unified under communist rule

1986
Corazon Aquino becomes ruler of the Philipines

1991
Peace comes to Cambodia

| 1940 | 1950 | 1960 | 1970 | 1980 | 1990 |

Main Ideas

Section 1

1. How did China first try to increase agricultural and industrial production under Mao Zedong?
2. What changes occurred during Mao's rule?
3. How did the Great Cultural Revolution affect China and her people?
4. Name the Four Modernizations and give an example of a successful modernization program in China.
5. Describe how China's leaders changed their attitude to foreign relations in the 1970s.

Section 2

1. Describe three main reasons behind Japan's economic recovery after World War II.
2. What were major factors behind Japan's great economic success in the 1970s and 1980s?
3. What was Japan's foreign policy in recent years?
4. In what ways did the countries and territories of the Pacific Rim respond to high population density and scarcity of natural resources?

Section 3

1. What was a major problem with independence in European-controlled countries after World War II?
2. What events led to Corazon Aquino becoming president of the Philippines?
3. Name the major problems of Indonesia. Describe the government under Sukarno and Suharto.
4. Explain how Cambodia, Laos, and Vietnam gained their independence.
5. What has happened in the relationship between Cambodia and Vietnam since the late 1970s?

Section 4

1. Explain why India was split into two countries.
2. What were Nehru's major goals for India?
3. Describe the effects of Nehru's policies on India.
4. What type of government did Pakistan have after gaining independence?
5. How did Bangladesh come to be independent?

Critical Thinking

1. Assessing Cause and Effect Consider the following statement: The main reasons that South Korea, Taiwan, Hong Kong, and Singapore have become economically successful in recent years are their large populations and advantageous locations. Explain why you agree or disagree with this statement. Support your opinion with evidence.

2. Recognizing Values A common theme throughout this chapter is the striving for independence that has taken place in former colonial nations of Asia. What does this theme tell you about the values of people in those nations?

Chapter Skills and Activities

Practicing Study and Research Skills

Reading Newspapers

The nations you have been reading about in this chapter are often in the news. Many important current events happened in the Pacific region as the countries there go through change and, in some cases, violence from war or from nature. News articles usually follow a basic plan. To get the most out of news articles, look first at the headline to gain clues about the main points of the news story. Then look for answers to the questions: *who? what? where?* and *when?*

   Check this week's newspapers. Photocopy or bring in an article about one of the countries discussed in this chapter. Underline what you think are the article's most important points. Then write a brief summary of the news story and express your opinion about the event and the way it was presented in the newspaper.

Linking Past and Present

The Vietnam War, though it ended in the 1970s, is still very much a part of our modern-day culture. Think about how the war is present in our lives by listing any recent movies, books, magazine or newspaper articles, or television shows that deal with the Vietnam War or its aftermath. What image of the war do these media pieces project? Are these images accurate?

Learning History Through Maps

Refer to the South Asia map on page 694. How does the map help explain the conflicts between East and West Pakistan?

CRITICAL THINKING QUESTION LEVEL 1. challenging; 2. easy

Answers to Chapter Skills and Activities

Practicing Study and Research Skills
You may want to collect articles from each student and categorize them according to political, economic, social, or religious topics. A good geography lesson is marking locations of countries mentioned in articles on a wall map.

Linking Past and Present
Students should consider their list of items, such as Rambo movies or articles about veteran concerns, and form a picture of the war in their minds. They should then use the information found in the chapter or other sources to decide whether the image is accurate.

Learning History Through Maps
The two regions are separated by 1,000 miles of Indian territory. East Pakistan was much smaller than West Pakistan and was probably less influential than the larger region.

Chapter

37 The Struggle for Self-Rule in Africa

OVERVIEW

This chapter describes conditions in African nations as they achieved independence and worked to form stable societies.

PLANNING CHART

Section	Text Pages	Key Concept	Suggested Teaching Time
1 Nationalism developed in Africa.	701–705	Changing world attitudes helped African nationalist movements, but independence did not solve problems resulting from colonial rule.	One day **More time?** Use *Overhead Transparency 73* or *Source Reading 37A.*
2 Africa's new nations began solving their problems.	706–710	Ethnic rivalries, sectionalism, and racial conflicts accompanied repressive government policies, and environmental disaster added to political unrest.	One day **More time?** Use *Overhead Transparency 74.*
3 The struggle for black rule reached southern Africa	712–714	Marxists prevailed in Angola and Mozambique, Britain aided leaders in Zimbabwe, and world pressure failed to end inequity in South Africa.	One day **More time?** Use *Source Reading 37B.*
4 North African nations became independent.	715–716	Algerian and other northern African nations gained independence threatened at times by Libya's attempts to extend its control in Africa.	One day

ANCILLARIES

Materials that may be used with this chapter to reinforce, reteach, enrich, and assess learning are pictured on the following pages.

Teacher's Resource File

ACTIVITIES

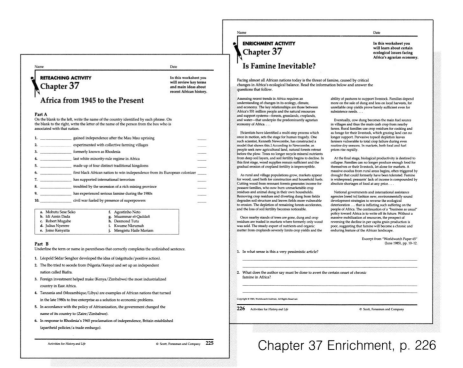

Section 1 Activity, p. 221

Section 2 Activity, p. 222

Section 3 Activity, p. 223

Section 4 Activity, p. 224

Chapter 37 Reteaching, p. 225

Chapter 37 Enrichment, p. 226

Teacher's Resource File

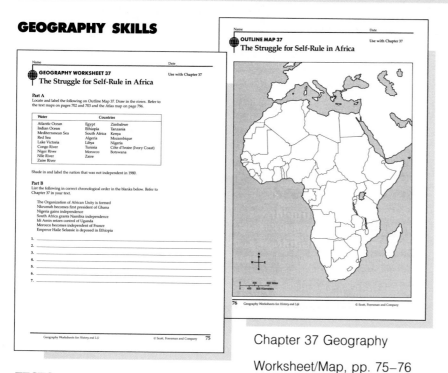

Chapter 37 Geography

Worksheet/Map, pp. 75–76

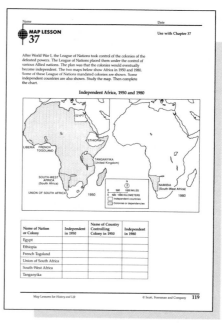

Chapter 37 Map Lesson, p. 119

TESTS

Chapter Test, pp. 189–190

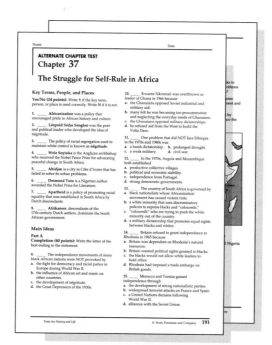

Alternate Chapter Test, pp. 191–192

Other Optional Ancillaries

WORKBOOK

WORKSHEET
Chapter **37**, Section **1**

In this worksheet you will review African culture and the growth of African nationalism.

African Culture and Nationalism

Write **T** if the statement is true and **F** if it is false. Rewrite each false statement to make it true.

1. _____ Négritude was a popular mass movement that originated among the urban poor in the late 19th century.
2. _____ As a general rule, the Europeans prepared their colonists for self-government by allowing them to play a role in the national governments.
3. _____ The Great Depression of the 1930s stimulated African nationalism.
4. _____ Because many Africans still identified themselves by their ethnic group or by their religion after nations were formed, conflicting loyalties often led to hostilities and civil wars.
5. _____ Nkrumah opposed Britain's plan concerning the independence of the Gold Coast.
6. _____ In reaction to criticism of his government, Nkrumah became increasingly intolerant and autocratic.
7. _____ Nkrumah was voted out of office because he had lost the confidence of the people.
8. _____ Ghana has enjoyed stable democratic government since Jerry Rawlings seized control of the government.

Worksheets for History and Life   © Scott, Foresman and Company **149**

Section 1 Worksheet, p. 149

WORKSHEET
Chapter **37**, Section **2**

In this worksheet you will review the history of seven African nations after they gained independence.

Recent African History

Part A
Complete each analogy.

1. Jomo Kenyatta is to free enterprise as Julius Nyerere is to _____.
2. Congo is to _____ as Tanganyika and Zanzibar are to Tanzania.
3. Lagos is to Nigeria as Abidjan is to _____.
4. Mengistu Haile Mariam is to Ethiopia as Idi Amin Dada is to _____.
5. Katanga is to Zaire as Biafra is to _____.
6. _____ is to oil as Zaire is to copper and cobalt.

Part B
Illustrate each general statement by an example from the recent history of one of the African countries discussed in Section 2.

1. The Soviet Union and Cuba have involved themselves in recent African affairs.

2. The existence of divided ethnic groups has complicated the internal political affairs of many African nations.

3. During the 1970s and 1980s, Africans faced an enormous crisis brought about by drought and famine.

4. Many African nations turned in the late 1980s toward free enterprise economies as a solution to some of their economic problems.

150 *Worksheets for History and Life   © Scott, Foresman and Company*

Section 2 Worksheet, p. 150

WORKSHEET
Chapter **37**, Section **3**

In this worksheet you will review the struggle for black rule in southern Africa.

Nationalism in Southern Africa

Part A
Identify each person described.

1. poet, medical doctor, and Marxist guerrilla leader who became the first president of Angola
2. the first president of Mozambique, who installed a communist system that nationalized private plantations and established state farms
3. the prime minister of Rhodesia, who unilaterally declared Rhodesia independent of Britain
4. a black South African lawyer who was arrested and jailed for organizing political protests
5. the Anglican archbishop of South Africa who was awarded the Nobel Peace Prize in 1985 for advocating peaceful change in South Africa

Part B
Complete each statement with the explanations given in your text.

1. Britain imposed a trade embargo on Rhodesia **because**

2. South Africa's decision to lift a few racial restrictions in the late 1970s did not appease the black majority **because**

3. A civil war broke out in Angola in the late 1970s **because**

4. In Rhodesia, Robert Mugabe and other black nationalist leaders opposed the government of Ian Smith **because**

5. In the 1970s and 1980s, Namibian nationalist guerrillas clashed with South African military units in Namibia **because**

Worksheets for History and Life   © Scott, Foresman and Company **151**

Section 3 Worksheet, p. 151

WORKSHEET
Chapter **37**, Section **4**

In this worksheet you will review recent independence movements in four North African nations.

Independence in North Africa

Part A
Use information from the text to complete each of the following sentences.

1. Most North Africans speak _____ and are of _____ or _____ descent.
2. In the North African countries, as in the Sub-Saharan states, the _____ religion predominates.
3. Algeria, Tunisia, and part of Morocco were colonies of _____.
4. Libya, which had been an _____ colony, was given its independence by the United Nations in 1951.
5. The _____ was formed to help solve inter-African disputes and to promote economic cooperation.
6. _____ were French settlers who came to Algeria in the 19th century.
7. _____ of Libya has been denounced by some nations for interfering in the affairs of other nations and for supporting international terrorists.
8. Algeria has had several border disputes with _____.

Part B
Identify the North African country described in each sentence by writing **L** for Libya, **M** for Morocco, **T** for Tunisia, and **A** for Algeria.

1. _____ Of all its North African colonies, France most wanted to keep this one.
2. _____ Its strong nationalist party worked peacefully for independence from 1934 to 1956.
3. _____ Terrorism, counterterrorism, and torture marked this nation's struggle for independence.
4. _____ Immediately after independence, this nation's large European community departed, allowing for land redistribution.
5. _____ Its government after independence tried to implement a policy of Islamic socialism.
6. _____ Its leader after independence banned political organizations and promoted people's committees.
7. _____ Its troops often have attempted to destabilize neighboring countries.
8. _____ This country had to gain independence from both France and Spain.

152 *Worksheets for History and Life   © Scott, Foresman and Company*

Section 4 Worksheet, p. 152

SOURCE READINGS

Source Reading 37A
Source Reading 37B

TEST GENERATOR

40 multiple-choice questions for Chapter 37

OVERHEAD TRANSPARENCIES

Overhead Transparency 73
Overhead Transparency 74

Chapter

37

The Struggle for Self-Rule in Africa

1945 – Present

1930	
1940	
1950	Four African countries are independent
1980	Fifty-one African countries are independent
1990	
2000	

One of the decisive developments after World War II was the birth of independent states in Africa. The determination to throw off European control was overpowering, a feeling dramatically expressed by the South African writer, Peter Abrahams, in his novel, *A Wreath for Udomo:*

> Mother Africa! Oh, Mother Africa, make me strong for the work I must do! Don't forget me in the many you nurse. I would make you great. I would have the world respect you and your children. I would have the sun of freedom shine over you once more.

As it turned out, the struggle for self-rule proved to be less difficult for most African countries than the task of maintaining national unity after independence was won. Like many of the developing nations in Latin America and Asia, the newly independent African nations had suffered greatly under colonial rule. Economically and politically the new nations had little experience to draw from as they set out on their own.

Soon the newly independent countries found enormous problems left behind by the colonial powers: widespread illiteracy, poor educational systems, rapid population growth, one-product economies, and impractical political divisions. In addition, the new nations had to deal with periodic droughts and the resulting famines.

Despite Africa's problems, the continent is a vitally important part of the global community. It is a treasure house for many of the world's rare and valuable minerals and is located next to some of the world's most important shipping lanes. In addition, its art, literature, and music influence the rest of the world. However, the challenge for African nations is to find ways to use the continent's enormous economic and human resources to improve the lives of its people.

Ghana's first president, Kwame Nkrumah (second from left) stands with other heads of state. From left to right are Nehru, Nasser, Sukarno, and Tito.

Reading Preview

In this chapter you will learn about the nations that formed in Africa after World War II.

1. Nationalism developed in Africa.

2. Africa's new nations began solving their problems.

3. The struggle for black rule reached southern Africa.

4. North African nations became independent.

1 Nationalism developed in Africa.

As you learned in Chapter 30, the acquisition of land in Africa by European nations proceeded swiftly in the late 1800s and early 1900s. By 1914 all of Africa, with the exception of Liberia and Abyssinia (now Ethiopia), had been partitioned by the European powers. (See the map in Chapter 30.) Gradually, a small group of westernized Africans emerged. Resentful of their treatment at the hands of the Europeans, they formed the core of nation-

1 Lesson Plan

Essential Learning Objectives

Students will learn to:

- discuss the effect of economic conditions on the spread of black nationalism in the African colonies.
- describe the negative consequences of colonial policies in Africa.

1 FOCUS AND MOTIVATE

Explain to students that, as had happened in other colonial areas such as the Americas and Asia, the peoples of Africa began to move toward independence. Tell students that there were 53 independent nations in Africa by the early 1990s. Discuss briefly the problems that newly independent areas might face. (Students should grasp that colonial rule was not concerned, usually, with preparing the people for self-government and that economies were organized for the benefit of the colonial power.)

2 TEACH

- Demonstrate the chronological development of nationalist movements in the 1920s and 1930s. Point out that demands for equal opportunity were partly the result of the Depression.

- Clarify how after World War II, colonial powers began to feel the expense of running their colonies at the same time that other countries (such as the United States and the Soviet Union) began to press for independence for colonies and access to resources.

- Emphasize the problems faced by new African nations at independence. (lack of experience in government, widespread illiteracy, lack of territorial unity because of conflicting ethnic groups) Point out that many of these problems resulted from colonial policies.

- Discuss those aspects of African culture that survived colonialism and how African textile design, art, and music became important in other nations.

GUIDED PRACTICE

Have students identify the stages that Ghana experienced as it moved toward independence. Students should recognize factors that were the result of colonial rule.

Nations Emerge in Africa, 1950–1980

1950

1965

Independent nations

Colonies or dependencies

🌐 **MAP STUDY** Namibia, the last colony in Africa, gained independence in 1990. Did most African countries gain independence before or after 1965?

alistic movements that gathered strength as the century advanced.

Black consciousness grew after World War I.

Early expressions of black pride and cultural nationalism came from a small group of educated black Africans in the British and French colonies during the 1920s and 1930s. One outstanding example was **Léopold Sédar Senghor**, a poet and political leader from the French colony of Senegal in West Africa. Senghor, who wrote in French, developed the idea of **négritude.** He and fellow black African intellectuals defined négritude as pride in the black race, black creativity, and African culture. They felt African cultures had an important contribution to make to the rest of the world. In his poem, "Le Kaya-Magan," Senghor described the essence of négritude:

. . . I . . . am the wellspring of joy . . . King of the moon, I make night one with day . . . Prince of the Rising Sun . . . my empire is that of . . . the great exiles from reason or from instinct . . . I am the movement of the tom-tom, strength of the future Africa.

Beginning in the 1930s, the nationalistic sentiments of Africa's black elite spread to the masses of ordinary people—the peasants and urban workers. These people, all of whom suffered greatly during the Depression, staged mass protests to demand improved living conditions and reforms in government. These protests were the beginnings of powerful mass movements for national independence.

World War II brought independence.

Soon after World War II, African leaders emerged who called for an end to colonial control. They wanted independence as soon as possible. To

BACKGROUND During the Great Depression of the 1930s, widespread unemployment among educated black Africans caused hostility toward well-paid Europeans who held most of the government jobs. Black Africans began to see foreign rule

as exploitation. Educated black Africans demanded change, formed political parties, and became leaders of unions, clubs, agricultural cooperatives, and non-Christian churches present before Europeans brought Christianity.

1980

achieve their goals, they created political parties and organized protests and strikes with widespread popular support. When elections were held to create new independent governments, the mass-based parties won, and their leaders came to power.

Independence movements swept across Africa with amazing success after World War II. England and France no longer wanted to pay to run their colonies, and other countries opposed colonialism and worked against it. In 1950 Africa had only four independent nations. By the early 1990s, there were 53 independent nations, almost a third of the total membership of the United Nations.

Independence left African nations facing many problems.

Sudden independence created difficulties for most of the new African nations. Under colonialism, people in African countries had been allowed to participate in government only at the local level, if at all. As a result, most new nations were not prepared for self-government. None of the new African states had strong traditions of political unity. Most had no common language other than their colonial language, usually French or English. Colonial governments had spent very little money on schools. Consequently, most citizens could not read or write, and only a few people had been able to get university educations.

During the 19th century, the European rulers who created the colonial political system paid little attention to African ways of life. Various ethnic groups who had nothing in common, such as the Ibo of southern Nigeria and the Hausa of northern Nigeria, were governed under one colonial unit only because it had been convenient for the European administrators. When colonial rule ended and new countries were formed, these artificial political units were kept together for two reasons. First, the new African leaders wanted to avoid border disputes. Second, no one wanted Africa to break up into very small, unworkable nations.

Besides creating often impractical political units, the colonial powers had largely neglected the development of areas that were poor in mineral resources or other valuable raw materials. Transportation systems, designed to move resources from the interiors of the colonies to the coasts in the most direct way possible, bypassed many centers of population. These areas would have greatly benefited from improved transportation systems. Routes connecting colonies also were generally not developed. These routes would have promoted intercolonial trade, which in turn, would have spurred economic growth and diversity.

Colonial governments had often encouraged their colonies to specialize in one cash crop or product. For example, Nigeria produced palm oil, and the Gold Coast (now Ghana) mined gold. This made it easier for the colonial power to make a profit, but it left new African nations' economies subject to severe price fluctuations.

Colonial governments inadvertently caused many of Africa's current population problems by limiting its economic activities to capital cities, most of which were located along the coasts. Traditional African cities within the interior were largely neglected. Thus, when many Africans

BACKGROUND After World War II, Britain and France changed their attitudes toward their colonies. The war had been costly to them, and they could no longer afford to maintain large colonial bureaucracies. In addition, the United States and the Soviet Union had emerged from the war as the new world superpowers. They did not approve of the old, exploitative colonial system. The colonial system also prevented the superpowers from having easy access to Africa's resources.

703

3 | ASSESS AND CLOSE

ASSESS

1. What was the goal of négritude? (pride in black culture, awareness of the contributions of Africans)
2. Which was the first black African country to achieve independence? (Gold Coast—or Ghana, as it was renamed)

1. Assign students to present to the class an art form of modern African origin. Students may wish to research the work of a poet, musician, or writer discussed in this section. (average)
2. Assign students to research and to report on the extent, purpose, and success of the Volta River Project in Ghana. (challenging)
3. Also for enrichment:

Summarize the lesson by telling students that demands for independence began as black consciousness grew among groups of educated Africans after World War I. The economic problems resulting from the Depression and World War II led some colonial powers to consider independence for their territories. Colonial rule had not prepared Africans for self-government: education, transportation, and agricultural development had been neglected. To solve these economic problems Africans have sought aid from both Western and communist countries.

started moving to cities after World War II, usually only one city in each country had to bear the whole burden of this population growth.

The effects of colonialism were not all negative, however. Colonial governments introduced modern forms of transportation and communication. Although education was largely neglected by colonial governments, Christian missionaries built many schools and churches. Many African leaders attended missionary schools, and hundreds of thousands of Africans converted to Christianity. Often Africans added their own unique African perspective to Christian ritual and beliefs.

African nations influenced art and music around the world.

Africa has always been a major source of cultural ideas, and today modern African nations continue to export artistic and musical products. For example, textiles from Côte d'Ivoire (Ivory Coast) are eagerly sought by people from other African countries and from Europe. Block prints, wax-resist (batik) prints, and tie-dyed cloth, often depicting African symbols and animals, inspire fashion designers worldwide. Artists from various African countries produce religious masks and complex tapestries that are prized by museums and private collectors.

Nigeria, Kenya, Senegal, and other African countries have been the source of critically acclaimed modern literature. Nigerian authors such as Chinua Achebe [chin′wə ə che′bē] and **Wole Soyinka** [wō′lā shō yin′kə] have written novels and poems, usually in English, which help make the contemporary African experience more understandable to both Africans and non-Africans. Their works cover a variety of themes about African life. In 1986 Soyinka was the first black to receive the Nobel Prize for Literature. His work is discussed on page 717.

Kenyan novelist Ngugi Wa-Thiongo's [en gü jē wu tē on′gō] early works dwelled on the problems of colonialism and the handicaps this system created for Africans. Ngugi has concentrated on writing criticisms of Kenyan failures since independence. The government jailed him several times for making these criticisms.

Traditional African music, especially that which

This silk textile from West Africa shows the kind of motifs that influenced European artists, such as Pablo Picasso and Georges Braque.

developed in the southern half of the continent, has influenced Western music for many centuries. Spirituals in the United States were originally developed by black Americans who were familiar with African musical patterns. Jazz, which began in the United States in the 1920s, incorporates rhythmic elements from the traditional music of West Africa. Blues, which developed from jazz, also uses several African musical techniques.

In the 1980s the American singer and composer Paul Simon traveled to Zimbabwe to compose and perform with a group of black South African musicians. Their traditional rhythms and harmonies, as well as some South African "township jive," became part of his album *Graceland*, a major international success. The troubled circumstances of black South Africans living under white rule influenced Simon's lyrics, as these lines from the song, 'Homeless,' demonstrate:

And we are homeless, homeless, homeless,
The moonlight sleeping on a midnight lake. . . .
Strong wind destroy our home
Many dead, tonight it could be you . . .
And we are homeless, homeless. . . .

Ghana led the way to independence for black Africa.

The first black African country to achieve independence was the Gold Coast, a British colony in West Africa. The new nation's first government gave the country the name **Ghana,** naming it after the famous Muslim kingdom that flourished in West Africa between the 9th and 11th centuries. (See Chapter 18.)

The first leader of Ghana, **Kwame Nkrumah** [kwä′mā en krü′mə], was one of the new generation of African leaders. He attended college in the United States and Britain, and after World War II, he returned to his homeland to lead the fight for independence.

In 1950 Nkrumah was arrested for his role in protests against Britain's gradual plan for independence. When national elections were held in 1951, he campaigned from jail. His nationalist party won the elections. Nkrumah was asked to form a cabinet and soon became prime minister of the colony. Finally, in 1957, the colony was granted its full independence. Nkrumah became its first president.

Kwame Nkrumah had ambitious development plans for Ghana's economy. He received aid from the West to build the Volta Dam, a dam designed to produce electricity for industry. However, he also received aid from China for state-run industries and from the Soviet Union for industrial and military aid. Many people thought that he was becoming too procommunist and neglecting the everyday needs of Ghanaians with his massive building projects. As criticism grew, Nkrumah restricted the press, jailed his opponents, and increased his own political power. In 1966 army officers took control while Nkrumah was visiting China. Nkrumah then fled to Guinea. He died in 1972.

The resulting military dictatorship tried to stabilize political and economic affairs, but failed. This lack of leadership led to coups in 1979 and again in 1981 by Jerry Rawlings, a military lieutenant. Although Rawlings helped Ghana recover some of its economic productivity, he came under increasing criticism in the early 1990s for not reintroducing elections and civilian rule more quickly.

Section 1 Review

Identify Léopold Sédar Senghor, négritude, Wole Soyinka, Ghana, Kwame Nkrumah

Main Ideas
1. What changes did World War I and the Great Depression bring to Africa?
2. What further changes did World War II bring?
3. Why was independence difficult for the newly formed African countries?
4. How do the arts in Africa influence people in other countries?
5. As the first black African country to achieve independence, what problems did Ghana have?

Critical Thinking

Analyzing Comparisons: Put yourself in the position of an African. Make a comparison between living under colonialism and independence. Give the positive and negative points of each way of life.

At left is the musical group Ladysmith, whose South African music attracted worldwide attention in the 1980s.

2 *Lesson Plan*

Essential Learning Objectives

Students will learn to:

- compare the economic and political development in Nigeria, Zaire, and East Africa.
- tell how political problems worsened Ethiopia's growing ecological tragedy.

1 FOCUS AND MOTIVATE

Discuss what students might already know about famine in Ethiopia. Tell students that they will learn about efforts to prevent future famine as they study this section. (Students should be aware that droughts caused crop failures in the Sahara region.)

2 TEACH

- Have students locate Nigeria on the Atlas map of Africa. Discuss the size of the population and its ethnic and religious make-up. Clarify how these differences resulted in civil war. Point out how oil prices affected Nigeria's present development.

- On the chalkboard, chart and clarify the specific events that followed independence in Uganda (ethnic conflicts, policies of Amin and Obote); in Kenya (initial violence in 1950s, progress under Kenyatta, potential for problems because of lack of good farmland and rapid population growth); in Tanzania (1964 merger, socialist policies, health services problems, movement toward free market system).

Below are oil workers in Port Harcourt, Nigeria. At right is a busy street in Lagos, Nigeria, clogged with heavy traffic.

2 Africa's new nations began solving their problems.

Ghana was not the only new African nation to experience political problems during the years following independence. The transition was difficult for most of the continent's countries.

Nigeria became the giant of black Africa.

A nation of about 119 million people, Nigeria is Africa's giant. Its diverse population belongs to more than 250 ethnic groups. The people in the north are generally Muslims. Those of the south are mostly Christians or members of other African religions. This immense cultural and religious diversity caused many difficulties in governing the new nation, including a bitter civil war between 1967 and 1970.

In the 1970s, however, Nigeria became one of the world's largest oil-producing nations. Although Nigeria began to develop new industries and improve agricultural methods and education, little of the wealth from oil production reached the average citizen. Governmental corruption and poor economic planning led to a growing public debt. A slump in world oil prices in the 1980s seriously affected the nation's economy. However, Nigeria continues to survive as a unified country with tremendous economic and cultural potential.

Three East African countries dealt with problems of independence.

After Nigeria gained independence in 1960, Britain turned to its colonies of Uganda, Kenya, and Tanzania. The British had tried to prepare these colonies for independence by establishing local legislative bodies modeled after Parliament. However, the growing black nationalism conflicted with Britain's timetable for independence.

Terror and rebellion in Uganda. The British colonial government, which had ruled Uganda since the 1890s, made little effort to rule the four traditional African kingdoms of Uganda as a unified state. When independence was won in 1962, these rival groups did not work well together, and soon the military took over to establish order. General **Idi Amin Dada,** who seized control in 1971, turned out to be one of the most brutal dictators in post-World War II Africa. During the eight years he was in power, Amin ruled through terror. Hundreds of thousands of Ugandans were arrested, tortured, and killed. Amin also allowed the economy to degenerate. About 50,000 Asians,

BACKGROUND Nigeria's first decade of independence was a violent period. Ethnic groups from the north competed with those from the south for control of the central government. An all-out civil war erupted in 1967. This conflict, which lasted until 1970, began when the Ibo tried to secede from Nigeria and set up an independent nation called Biafra. The war was a costly one for Nigeria. Especially devastated was the southeastern part of the nation, the home of many Ibo.

many of whom owned businesses in Uganda, were expelled. Capital from these businesses were distributed by Amin to loyal supporters. The formerly rich country became poverty-stricken.

In 1979 rebellious Ugandans, aided by the Tanzanian army, invaded the country and forced Amin into exile. The task of rebuilding the shattered nation was enormous. Fighting between ethnic groups caused the failure of several attempts to restore democracy. Finally, a military commander, Yoweri Museveni, took control in 1986. By the early 1990s, some economic stability had been restored, but democratic elections were repeatedly postponed.

Economic growth in Kenya. Kenyans had long lived in poverty under British rule. Toward the end of World War II, a group of Kenyans, mainly Kikuyus from central Kenya, organized a political party to work for reforms. When peaceful methods failed, a secret group formed, called the Mau Mau by the British.

In 1952 the Mau Mau began to use violent methods to achieve their goals. The British arrested and jailed thousands of Kenyan nationalists, including their leader, **Jomo Kenyatta.** Although Kenyatta and other nationalist leaders remained in jail until the early 1960s, the pressure for independence continued to mount. Finally, in 1963 Britain granted Kenya independence. Kenyatta was soon elected president, remaining in office until his death in 1978. Throughout his presidency, Kenyatta maintained a constitutional government and encouraged free enterprise.

Under Kenyatta's free-enterprise policies, agricultural production expanded, and tourism to Kenya's wild-game parks developed into a major industry. Foreign investment helped Kenya become the most industrialized country in East Africa.

Despite Kenya's progress, the nation's expanding economy could not keep pace with the rapidly growing population. Kenyatta's successor, Daniel T. Arap Moi, began to come under criticism in the early 1990s for jailing opposition leaders and refusing to permit multiparty democratic elections.

Socialism in Tanzania. In 1964 Tanzania [tan′zə nē′ə] became an independent nation when two former British colonies, Tanganyika and Zanzibar, merged. Britain had granted independence to Tanganyika in 1961 and to Zanzibar in 1963.

BACKGROUND Under Nyerere the goverment of Tanzania built sewage systems and brought electricity to many collective villages. Schools were also built and literacy increased to about 80 percent, the highest in Africa. New medical facilities

Africans still identified themselves mainly by their ethnic groups. These conflicting loyalties often led to hostilities.

Julius Nyerere [ni rer′e], a nationalist leader, was elected Tanzania's president. He remained in office for 20 years. Nyerere tried to pursue socialist goals of equality and communal ownership. He believed that Africans were more suited to socialism because of their traditional values of family and group concern. During Nyerere's rule the government invested large sums of money in the development of **collective villages,** or communes, and forced about 90 percent of Tanzania's farmers to move onto them.

Nyerere's attempt to collectivize Tanzanian agriculture did not succeed. Agricultural output dropped dramatically because Tanzanian farmers had little or no incentive to work the land properly. Without food to feed workers in the cities and cash crops to export, shortages developed of consumer goods, such as paper, soap, light bulbs, and fuel. Although Tanzanians often criticized neighboring Kenya as a capitalist "man-eat-man society," Kenyans joked about Tanzania as a socialist "man-eat-nothing society."

In 1985 Nyerere retired from office at the age of 65. His successor, Ali Hassan Mwinyi [mə wi′nē], turned away from much of Nyerere's socialism. He introduced many free-market policies, returned state-owned businesses to private hands, and stopped forcing people to live in the communal villages. Thus Tanzania became one of many African nations in the late 1980s to turn toward increased free enterprise as a solution to economic problems.

Jomo Kenyatta led the fight for Kenya's independence and served as its president from 1964 to 1978. He had played a major role in the rise of African nationalism since the 1920s.

improved health conditions somewhat, but Tanzania still needed more hospitals and doctors. In the late 1980s, Tanzania's 22 million people had only about 1,000 physicians and life expectancy was only 52 years.

• Point out how the Côte d'Ivoire's choice to retain ties with France eased the need for foreign investment capital. Discuss how Zaire's lack of preparation led to political breakdown after independence. Be sure that students grasp why Mobutu would have felt it necessary to stop Katanga's secession. (Profits from Katanga's mines were needed.)

• Identify the causes of food shortages in Ethiopia. (lack of rain, land abuse, government mismanagement, civil war). Clarify how the government of Ethiopia used the disaster against rebellious areas.

GUIDED PRACTICE

Have students list the resources of African nations. Point out which resources could be used in manufacturing processes, such as steel. Students should grasp the need for cooperation among African countries if they expect to develop these resources.

Sub-Saharan Africa: The Ten Most Populous Countries

Country	Population*	Capital	Percent Urban	Official Language(s)	Main Ethnic Groups
1. **Nigeria**	118,700,000	Abuja	28%	English	Hausa (21%), Yoruba (20%), Ibo (17%), Fulani (9%)
2. **Ethiopia**	50,000,000	Addis Ababa	15%	Amharic	Galla (40%), Amhara and Tigrai (32%), Sidamo (9%), Shankella (6%), Somali (6%)
3. **Zaire**	34,140,000	Kinshasa	34%	French	Mongo, Luba, Kongo, and Mangbetu-Azande (45%)
4. **South Africa**	30,190,000	Pretoria, Cape Town	56%	Afrikaans, English	Zulu, Xhosa, other African (70%), White (18%), Coloured (9%), Asian (3%)
5. **Tanzania**	24,800,000	Dar es Salaam	14%	Swahili	More than 100 peoples (99%)
6. **Kenya**	24,080,000	Nairobi	16%	Swahili, English	Kikuyu (21%), Luo (13%), Luhya (14%), Kelenjin (11%), Kamba (11%)
7. **Uganda**	17,000,000	Kampala	14%	English	Bantu, Nilotic, Nilo-Hamitic, Sudanic peoples (99%)
8. **Ghana**	14,900,000	Accra	40%	English	Akan (44%), Moshi-Dagomba (16%), Ewe (13%), Ga (8%)
9. **Mozambique**	14,900,000	Maputo	13%	Portuguese	Various Bantu peoples (100%)
10. **Côte d'Ivoire**	12,100,000	Abidjan	42%	French	Baule (23%), Bete (18%), Senufo (15%), Malinke (11%)

*Source: *Statesman's Year-Book 1991–1992*

Côte d'Ivoire found solutions to its urban problems.

Côte d'Ivoire [kōt dēv wär′], the official name of the Ivory Coast since 1986, was one of 12 French colonies to be granted independence by France in 1960. Unlike many other African nations that "Africanized" their place names and personal names, Côte d'Ivoire retained its French name and other links to France.

Like many other former colonies, Côte d'Ivoire had to deal with severe urban population problems caused by poor planning during colonial times. Unlike most other former colonies, however, Côte d'Ivoire has been quite successful in solving its urban problems. Evidence of this is apparent in **Abidjan,** the capital.

When Côte d'Ivoire gained independence, Abidjan had a population of about 300,000. By the late 1980s, the city's population had ballooned to more than 2 million. As in other African countries, many of Côte d'Ivoire's people moved to the capital because it offered jobs in industry and provided modern services unavailable in rural areas.

Over the years Abidjan achieved a reputation of a city that works. It has six-lane highways, modern skyscrapers, and a low unemployment rate. Generally, Abidjan has avoided many of the difficulties typical in other African cities, such as Lagos, Nigeria, and Kinshasa, Zaire. These problems include slums that are not serviced by electricity or water, and suffer from inadequate sewage systems and traffic jams caused by poorly planned streets.

ASSESS

1. What was the cause of Nigeria's civil war? (ethnic conflict)
2. How were the problems of drought and famine in the Sahara worsened by government policies? (Government mismanagement allowed grazing lands to be abused. In Ethiopia food shipments were kept from reaching rebel areas.)

The president of Côte d'Ivoire, Félix Houphuet-Boigny [hü fü ā′ bwän yē′], has received much of the credit for Abidjan's success, as well as that of his nation. Although Houphuet-Boigny led Côte d'Ivoire to independence from France in 1960, he has always maintained close economic ties with France and has encouraged foreign investment and free enterprise. Nevertheless, President Houphuet-Boigny, fearing the pressures of urbanization on Abidjan, built a new capital city, Yamoussoukro [yäm ü sük′rō], about 100 miles west of Abidjan.

Zaire's instability led to military dictatorship.

Belgian rule left Zaire totally unprepared for self-government in 1960. Independence was soon followed by mutiny in the army, ethnic feuds, riots, and looting. The rich mining province of Katanga [kə täng′ə], encouraged and supported by Western business interests, seceded.

Troops from the United Nations, made up mostly of Africans, restored order after two and a half years. During that time many people lost their lives. Among the fatalities was Patrice Lumumba, Zaire's first prime minister. When the UN forces withdrew, violence broke out again in Katanga. Finally an army officer, Joseph D. Mobutu, came to power in 1965, ended the rebellion, and set up a dictatorship.

One of Mobutu's policies was **Africanization.** In part, this meant encouraging pride in African culture and history, replacing European technicians with Africans, and changing European names to African ones. In line with this policy, the government changed the name of the country from Congo to Zaire [zä ēr′]. Joseph Mobutu changed his name as well to Mobutu Sese Seko [mō bü′tü se′sē se′kō].

Zaire had enormous economic potential. It had vast mineral deposits, especially copper and cobalt. Despite these resources, however, Zaire had a poor transportation system, which limited the amount of minerals it could sell on the world market.

In the 1980s political as well as economic problems besieged the nation. Mobutu increased his power and jailed many people who opposed his policies. He also spent large amounts of money on

DAILY LIFE

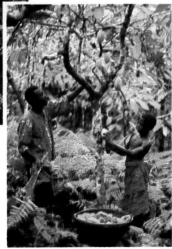

Africa is a land of immense variety and contrasts, and life everywhere has changed greatly in recent decades. Still, many Africans move everyday in settings much like those depicted in Côte d'Ivoire. In its ultramodern capital, Abidjan, shoppers can pick and choose from an overflowing cornucopia of fresh fruits and vegetables (far left), or they can buy imported canned goods at French supermarkets. Here too, as elsewhere, agriculture is a mainstay of the economy. Cacao (left) provides a bountiful harvest in rainforest areas.

Answers to Section 2 Review

Identify
Key Terms, People, and Places are defined on pages indicated in parentheses. Also see the Glossary and Biographical Dictionary.
Idi Amin Dada (706), Jomo Kenyatta (707), Julius Nyerere (707), collective villages (707), Abidjan (708), Africanization (709)

Main Ideas
1. ethnic conflicts, corruption, poor economic planning, slump in oil prices; political unity and great economic and cultural potential
2. Uganda had trouble unifying the four traditional kingdoms under one country. General Idi Amin Dada ruled through terror and his successors faced unrest and economic instability. Kenya followed free-enterprise policies and despite hunger problems, has been successful in economic areas. Tanzania formed a strict socialist government but met with many failures. Now it follows some free-enterprise reforms with good results.
3. It modernized Abidjan and built a new capital, Yamoussoukro, hoping that people will move there.
4. Lack of preparation for self-rule led to secession and war. Later, economic problems and a dictatorship made life difficult.
5. drought, famine, military dictatorship, and secessionist movement

Critical Thinking
Stability seems to derive from good government and economic development, such as enjoyed by Kenya and Côte d'Ivoire. Instability seems to be caused by poor economic planning, corruption, political repression, and ethnic conflict, such as experienced by Nigeria, Uganda, Tanzania, Zaire, and Ethiopia.

his own family and supporters. As the global recession caused a drop in demand for African raw materials, including copper and cobalt, Zaire's economy experienced serious problems. Rioting and army mutinies in the early 1990s weakened Mobutu's power and he was forced to consider reforms in the government.

Ethiopia suffered from drought, famine, and dictatorship.

During the 1970s and 1980s, Africans faced an enormous crisis brought about by drought and famine. The disaster was especially severe in the grazing regions south of the Sahara. From Mauritania to Ethiopia, millions of Africans suffered from lack of rainfall and food shortages. (To find the area of drought, refer to the Atlas map, page 796.) Abuse of the land, government inefficiency, problems from the colonial period, and civil war also contributed to the severity of the famine on the African continent. One country that suffered especially from drought and famine was Ethiopia.

Ethiopia is one of two African nations that maintained its independence during colonial times. Ethiopian history contains records of kings and emperors dating as far back as the 3rd century A.D. King Ezana, who ruled the kingdom in the 300s, made Christianity the official religion. In the 1970s Ethiopia was still ruled by an emperor, Haile Selassie. Christianity, although no longer the official religion, is followed by about half of Ethiopia's 42 million people. About 40 percent of Ethiopians are Muslim. The remainder follow other African religions.

Haile Selassie ruled Ethiopia harshly, and the population was mired in poverty. During a drought in 1972-1973, more than 200,000 people starved to death, but the government did little to help Ethiopians. After a wave of peasant revolts and strikes, the military staged a coup and deposed the emperor in September, 1974.

The new military government, under the leadership of Mengistu Haile Mariam, did not bring the reforms the people had expected. It restricted the press, executed large numbers of people who opposed it, introduced radical socialist economic policies, and adopted an anti-Western foreign policy.

Various ethnic and regional groups such as the Tigre and Eritreans, tried to secede and plunged Ethiopia into a brutal civil war.

Another famine soon followed in 1984–1985. Combined with the civil war, this famine claimed the lives of hundreds of thousands of Ethiopians. Western relief agencies provided massive food aid. However, some observers charged that Mengistu's government was using the famine for political purposes by forcibly relocating large numbers of secessionists and preventing aid from reaching areas that supported secessionists. In May 1991 Mengistu was forced to flee into exile. A temporary government made up of representatives from many of the groups in Ethiopia, including secessionists, took over and promised a return to democracy soon.

Western agencies have tried to help Ethiopia prevent future famines by improving transportation and introducing new plant strains and farming methods. In other parts of Africa, the causes of drought and famine, though not eliminated, are slowly being remedied. UN and Western aid agencies have encouraged reforestation, better grazing techniques, and improved farming techniques.

Section 2 Review

Identify Idi Amin Dada, Jomo Kenyatta, Julius Nyerere, collective villages, Abidjan, Africanization

Main Ideas
1. What problems faced Nigeria after independence? What strengths did it enjoy?
2. What problems did Uganda, Kenya, and Tanzania face after they gained independence?
3. How did Côte d'Ivoire try to solve its urban problems?
4. What problems did Zaire face after independence?
5. What catastrophes did Ethiopians suffer in the 1970s and 1980s?

Critical Thinking
Identifying Assumptions: You have studied the recent history of seven African nations. What factors seem to lead to a stable country? What factors seem to keep a country unstable?

GEOGRAPHY

A Key to History

AFRICA IN A WORLD SETTING

The African continent is a treasure house with the largest reserves of untapped natural and mineral resources in the world. Africa has the bulk of the world's diamonds, 90 percent of its cobalt, 50 percent of its gold and phosphate, and 40 percent of its platinum, as well as 30 percent of the uranium in the noncommunist world. The continent also has 40 percent of the world's potential hydroelectric power supply.

However, these resources are not evenly distributed. The map shows the location of major mineral resources and economic activity. Compare this map with the map of Africa in the Atlas to see which nations have what resources.

Millions of acres of untilled fertile farmland constitute another of Africa's rich resources—enough land to feed all of Africa and Western Europe. Africa has other assets as well. For example, its strategic location could allow it to control major oil shipping routes.

Despite all these assets, Africa's treasure house faces serious problems. Because the continent is still largely underdeveloped and is not industrialized, Africa's economy centers on extractive activities. In the extractive sector of an economy, workers derive products from nature, as by agriculture, mining, oil production, or lumbering. Substantially all of the raw materials Africa produces—minerals, oil, and forest products—are exported to other countries for processing and marketing. These other countries reap most of the profits. To achieve prosperity many African nations hope to construct their own refineries or other processing facilities that will provide more jobs within Africa.

REVIEW

1. What percent of the world's gold resources are found in Africa?
2. Define an extractive economy and explain why many African nations want to move toward processing their own raw materials.

Where is Africa's chromium found? Where is its oil located?

Legend

Symbol	Resource
⚒	Coal
● ○	Petroleum, natural gas
◗	Iron ore
+	Manganese
Ⅰ	Chromium
△	Copper
□	Aluminum
◙	Tin
▣	Cobalt
★	Uranium
⊗ ◑	Gold, platinum
⊞	Diamonds
▱	Phosphates

```
0   500  1000  Kilometers
0      500    1000  Miles
```
N

711

Essential Learning Objectives

Students will learn to:
- explain how Angola, Mozambique, and Zimbabwe gained their independence.
- examine the origin and policies of apartheid and how the international community has attempted to end it.

1 FOCUS AND MOTIVATE

Ask students to suggest reasons why majority rule is a key part of our system of government. Direct students to look for problems that took place in African nations as they sought to establish majority rule as they study this section.

2 TEACH

- Clarify that Angola and Mozambique did not become independent until the revolution in Portugal. Discuss the internal problems each nation experienced. Explain the purposes of wage incentives in improving production.

- Discuss Britain's role in aiding the black leadership in Zimbabwe through a trade embargo.

- List on the chalkboard the racial groups and their numbers in South Africa's population. Clarify the origin of each group. Emphasize the purpose of apartheid in keeping the races separate except for master-servant relationships.

- Illustrate the chronology of events in South Africa from 1931 to the present on a time line. Clarify the actions of the government in the "state of emergency." Discuss South Africa's control of Namibia.

---

3 The struggle for black rule reached southern Africa.

In the 1970s and 1980s, the spread of African nationalism led to independence movements in the southernmost part of the continent. This area included the Portuguese colonies of Angola and Mozambique, the British colony of Rhodesia, and the independent Republic of South Africa.

Angola and Mozambique fought for independence.

As you know, many African states gained independence in the early 1960s. However, Portugal refused to grant freedom to its colonies. As a result, in 1961 nationalist rebellions began in Portugal's two large African colonies—Angola on the west coast and Mozambique on the east coast. (Find these countries on the map on page 702.) Bloody fighting lasted for more than a decade. Finally, in 1974 a revolution brought a new socialist government to power in Portugal, and in 1975 it granted independence to Angola and Mozambique.

In Angola, Agostinha Neto [nä′tü], a poet and medical doctor as well as guerrilla leader, became Angola's first president. He had received Soviet aid during the struggle for independence and was a committed Marxist. Because of Neto's Marxist leanings, some Angolans did not support his presidency. Jonas Savimbi [sä vim′bē], another Angolan independence fighter, fought against Neto's government. Neto relied on Soviet-backed Cuban troops to help keep him in power. In turn, Savimbi depended on American and South African arms. The resulting 15 years of civil war severely hurt Angola. In 1991, with the Cold War ended, both sides agreed to peace.

Mozambique also experienced political and economic problems. Samora Machel [mä shel′], a Marxist, became head of the government in 1975. He soon installed a communist system, nationalizing private plantations. However, with mounting economic difficulties, Machel began to depart somewhat from strict Marxism. Wage incentives were reintroduced, and some of the plantations were returned to private owners. Machel died in 1986, but his successor continued the pro-Western reforms.

Black nationalists gained control in Zimbabwe.

In 1965 in the British colony of Rhodesia, a white minority of about 270,000 British settlers governed a black majority of 6 million. In that year white leaders demanded independence from Britain, but the British would not agree until political rights were first granted to blacks. Rhodesia's white prime minister, Ian Smith, refused and proclaimed Rhodesia's independence. The British then imposed a **trade embargo,** which made trade with Rhodesia illegal for British citizens and businesses. The embargo hurt Rhodesia's economy, but it did not immediately topple Smith's government.

Black Rhodesian nationalists began to fight a guerrilla war to overthrow the white-dominated Rhodesian government. Finally, after the loss of 20,000 lives, a cease-fire was arranged. In 1980 Robert Mugabe [mü gä′bē], one of the black nationalist guerrilla leaders, was elected prime minister, and the British granted independence to Rhodesia. Mugabe's government, which included whites, proclaimed the new independent state of Zimbabwe.

In the following decade, Zimbabwe's agricultural production soared. Regular elections, with limited opposition, kept Mugabe in power.

A white minority ruled South Africa.

At the southern tip of the continent, **South Africa** has long been the strongest African state, both economically and militarily. This highly industrialized nation is rich in valuable mineral resources, including diamonds and gold. Once a British colony, South Africa became fully independent in 1931.

Throughout its history, South Africa has been ruled by a white minority. After World War II, the white minority of about 4 million took complete political control over 15 million blacks and 3 million nonwhites, mainly Asians and "coloureds," as people of mixed racial descent are called in South Africa. Among whites, the dominant political leaders are the **Afrikaners** [af′rə kä′nerz]—descendants of 17th-century Dutch settlers.

The ancestors of most of South Africa's black population lived in the region long before whites

---

BACKGROUND The name "Zimbabwe" recalls the 13th-century city-state students read about in Chapter 18.

South Africa's Racial Homelands

 MAP STUDY The South African government has sought to move black citizens into designated "homelands." Name five homelands whose territories are divided into separate parcels.

began to build settlements in the region. Most of South Africa's black population is descended from the Nguni, Sotho, Venda, or Tsongo, who are Bantu peoples who settled in the area as early as A.D. 900.

In the 1940s and 1950s, the white Afrikaner government officially established the discriminatory policy of **apartheid** [ə pärt′hāt]. Apartheid is a policy of racial segregation used to maintain white control. Under this policy discriminatory laws prevented blacks and coloureds from living in the same communities as whites. They could not go to the same schools, ride on the same trains, or sit on the same park benches. They could not vote or own property, except in certain economically depressed areas.

The government strictly enforced these discriminatory laws, requiring hundreds of thousands of blacks and coloureds to give up their homes and move to desolate parts of the country that were designated as "homelands." You can see these areas on the map above. To go from one area of the country to another, the blacks and coloureds had to carry "passes" and identification cards and follow strict regulations. They were allowed to work only at low-paying jobs that white people did not want.

Although the policy of apartheid was made official in 1948, the principles and concepts behind this policy had existed ever since the Dutch began to settle in the region in the 1600s. Black South Africans never willingly accepted their position of inferiority under apartheid—official or not. In the 1950s and 1960s, they organized peaceful political protests but their leaders, such as the lawyer Nelson Mandela, were all arrested and jailed. Their political organization, the African National Congress (ANC), was outlawed.

GUIDED PRACTICE
Bring copies of a daily paper to class and have students find articles that might be censored if they lived in South Africa. Students should grasp that without access to news, individuals are isolated and unable to communicate effectively.

3 ASSESS AND CLOSE

ASSESS
What nations provided aid to the two sides in the Angolan civil war? (Cuba, Soviet Union, South Africa, United States)

OPTIONAL RETEACHING
Have students discuss South Africa's motives in attempting to overthrow the governments of Angola and Mozambique and in keeping control of Namibia. Students should grasp that Marxist governments might be seen as a threat to South Africa and that Namibia has valuable resources (diamonds and copper).

OPTIONAL ENRICHMENT
1. Assign students to research and to report on the effectiveness of the trade embargo against South Africa. Students might discuss the participation of the United States and other nations in this embargo. (challenging)
2. Also for enrichment:

📖 *Source Reading 37B*

INDEPENDENT PRACTICE/ HOMEWORK
Assign the Section Review, Activities page 223, or Workbook page 151.

CLOSURE
Tell students that independence in southern Africa came later than in other parts of Africa. Portugal's refusal to grant independence led to ten years of fighting. Freedom brought

713

Marxist governments to power that provoked further hostilities. Racial conflicts delayed independence in Zimbabwe, but the black majority gained power in 1980. South Africa's Afrikaner minority had enforced rigid segregation policies long before they were made official in 1948. Many nations joined trade embargoes to force South Africa to change its policies.

From the Archives

Peace and Justice

Archbishop Desmond Tutu (1931–), head of South Africa's Anglican Church, received the Nobel Peace Prize in 1984 for his role in opposing apartheid in South Africa. At the Nobel ceremony, he emphasized the importance of nonviolent means of securing justice.

There is no peace in southern Africa. There is no peace because there is no justice. There can be no real peace and security until there be first justice enjoyed by all the inhabitants of that beautiful land.

I have spoken extensively about South Africa, first because it is the land I know best, but because it is also a microcosm [miniature version] of the world and an example of what is to be found in other lands in differing degree—when there is injustice, invariably peace becomes a casualty. . . .

Let us work to be peacemakers. If we want peace, let us work for justice. Let us beat our swords into plowshares.

In the 1970s a wave of protests swept the country. As a result, in 1979 a few restrictions were lifted. Blacks were allowed into previously forbidden restaurants, and most sports were integrated. In 1984 two coloureds, but still no blacks, were included for the first time in South Africa's cabinet. However, the basic principles of "separate development" remained unchanged. Laws still prevented blacks from participating in politics and from freely living and working in the country. As a result, African resistance to the apartheid system continued, and riots and strikes became a common occurrence.

In 1986 the South African government declared a "state of emergency." Newspapers were closed, television news reports were censored, all political gatherings were forbidden; and people, including children as young as nine, were arrested and jailed for long periods without trial. In addition, public funerals for slain black leaders were prohibited.

World leaders protested these racist laws. In 1985 the Anglican archbishop **Desmond Tutu**, a black South African, was awarded the Nobel Peace Prize for advocating peaceful change in South Africa. Many countries, including the United States, instituted economic sanctions against South Africa.

In 1990 a new president, F. W. de Klerk, announced a set of reforms that included legalizing the ANC and other anti-apartheid groups. In addition, Nelson Mandela was freed, after 27 years of imprisonment. The stage was then set for further changes, including, observers hoped, the writing of a new constitution that would give political rights to all South Africans. Living conditions for blacks, however, did not change much, and there continued to be violent conflict between black and white factions struggling for power.

In 1990 South Africa also finally granted independence to its former League of Nations mandate, Namibia, previously called South-West Africa. Although all other former mandates had been given their independence in the 1960s, South Africa refused to grant independence to Namibia, which has important mineral resources. By 1990, however, South Africa gave in to the demands of Western nations and the UN for Namibia's independence.

Section 3 Review

Identify trade embargo, South Africa, Afrikaners, apartheid, Desmond Tutu

Main Ideas
1. How did Angola and Mozambique gain independence?
2. What events led to the establishment of Zimbabwe?
3. What have the black Africans in South Africa done to end the white minority rule in their country?

Critical Thinking
Predicting Effects: Trade embargoes have been used to bring about change in both Rhodesia (now Zimbabwe) and South Africa. What importance did that action play in Zimbabwe? Try to predict what the effects would be in South Africa.

FROM THE ARCHIVES Desmond Tutu's acceptance speech is reprinted in *UNESCO Courier,* (August, 1986), p. 11. When Tutu referred to beating "our swords into plowshares," he quoted an ancient Biblical image of peace used by two Hebrew prophets, Isaiah and Micah. Read the passage from Micah to the class (4:1–4). Ask students to suggest a place for a statue of a person beating a sword into a plowshare. (Such a statue by Russian Yevgeny Vuchetich is at the U.N.)

4 North African nations became independent.

In the decades following World War II, the North African countries of **Morocco,** Algeria, Tunisia, and Libya gained independence. These countries had much in common with Sub-Saharan African states, including the Muslim religion and historical trade ties.

However, the North African countries were different from Sub-Saharan African countries, too—in ethnicity, language, and economic ties. Almost all North Africans spoke Arabic and were of Arab or Berber descent. Throughout their history they had close cultural ties with the Middle East. Egypt, in particular, had had strong ties with Syria and other Middle Eastern countries, so it will be examined in the following chapter.

The North African nations followed different roads to independence.

When World War II ended, Algeria and Tunisia were still under the control of France. Morocco was under the control of both France and Spain. Libya had been a colony of Italy, which had been on the losing side of World War II. The Allies removed Libya from Italy's control, but they couldn't agree about what to do with it. Finally the United Nations gave Libya independence in 1951.

Independence did not come quite as easily for Morocco and Tunisia. Each of these nations needed to develop strong nationalistic parties to work for independence. Both finally won their independence in 1956, and during that same year Spain also gave up most of its Moroccan territory.

Algeria had a long and violent struggle for independence.

In contrast to Morocco and Tunisia, Algeria had a difficult struggle for independence because large numbers of French settlers had made Algeria their home. These settlers, who had come to Algeria in the 19th century, were called colons [kō lōNZ']. The colons had taken land from native Algerians and developed plantations that provided France with products it wanted, especially wine, citrus fruit, olives, and vegetables.

By the 1950s there were more than 1 million colons, many of whom had lived in Algeria for several generations, and 9 million Algerians. The colons owned 90 percent of the best farmland and were exempt from most taxes. The Algerians, meanwhile, were denied most civil rights, such as voting and trial by jury. They were even prohibited from conducting Muslim wedding ceremonies.

In 1954 a violent rebellion broke out. A nationalistic organization called the National Liberation Front (FLN) coordinated bombings and terrorist

The mild climate of northern Algeria enables people to enjoy a meal in an outdoor cafe.

4 *Lesson Plan*

Essential Learning Objectives

Students will learn to:
- compare the methods used to gain independence by north African nations.
- describe political and economic conditions in Algeria and Libya.

1 FOCUS AND MOTIVATE

Locate the nations of northern Africa on a large wall map, point out the similarities and differences between these nations and those of Sub-Saharan Africa and the Middle East. Emphasize the centuries of contact between the three areas.

2 TEACH

- Discuss the relationship between the French colons and native Algerians. Explain how the war between them ended, stressing the importance of De Gaulle's role. Clarify the causes of economic unrest in the 1980s.

- Explain the changes Qaddafi instituted in Libya and reasons for his attacks on other nations.

GUIDED PRACTICE

Distribute blank outline maps of Africa from the Geography Skills book and direct students to identify the areas that Qaddafi attempted to influence militarily or financially.

3 ASSESS AND CLOSE

ASSESS

In what ways is northern Africa similar to the Middle Eastern nations? (ethnic identity as Arabs, Arabic language, Islam, economic ties)

Answers to Section 4 Review

Identify
Key Terms, People, and Places are defined on pages indicated in parentheses. Also see the Glossary and Biographical Dictionary. Morocco (715), Muammar el-Qaddafi (716), Organization of African Unity (OAU) (716)

Main Ideas
1. These countries developed strong, successful nationalistic parties to win independence.
2. There were many French settlers in Algeria who had lived there for

attacks against the French. Eventually 500,000 French troops were brought in to suppress the independence struggle, but they did not succeed. In 1958 Charles de Gaulle came to power in France to deal with the problems. He negotiated a truce with the FLN, and in 1962 Algeria gained its independence.

After Algeria became independent, almost the entire colon community returned to France. This left a large amount of land for redistribution to Algerian farmers. The development of Algeria's oil and gas resources provided it with some money for industrialization. The government tried to maintain social services, such as education and housing, under a costly policy called Islamic socialism. However, its economic policies led to a decline in agricultural production, and many Algerians sought work in France.

The FLN dominated Algerian politics, outlawing opposition groups, until the late 1980s when it gave in to popular demands for democratic reforms. However, a fundamentalist party, Islamic Salvation Front, won the most votes in the 1991 elections. Fearing the establishment of an anti-democratic state, the army cancelled the results of the elections and took power. Algeria's move to democracy was stalled.

Algeria also had several problems with its neighbor, Morocco. One border dispute was settled by the **Organization of African Unity (OAU)** in 1970. The OAU is an organization of African nations formed in 1963 that promotes economic cooperation and settles inter-African disputes. Another dispute between Algeria and Morocco, involving the former Spanish colony, Western Sahara, remains unresolved.

Libya's Colonel Qaddafi interfered in many other nations.

When Libya became independent in 1951, it was ruled by King Idris, who came from a royal family recognized by only part of the country. The king was unable to gain widespread loyalty, and in the 1960s his unpopularity increased because he was pro-Western at a time when the West was supporting Israel in the Middle East.

In 1969, while King Idris was out of the country,

a group of military officers carried out a coup and deposed him. The leader of the young officers, Colonel **Muammar el-Qaddafi** [kä dä′fē], became the new head of state.

Qaddafi made many major changes in Libya. He took a distinct anti-Western position in all matters of foreign policy, though he also denounced the Soviet Union as atheistic (ungodly). Qaddafi banned political organizations and representative institutions because he said they were unfair. Instead he promoted rule by "peoples' committees" to which everyone had to belong. These committees managed all businesses, industries, and government services. Hundreds of people who opposed Qaddafi's policies were killed or went into exile abroad. Exile was not a safe haven for his opponents, however, as Qaddafi ordered the assassination of many of them.

Many world leaders denounced Qaddafi for interfering in the affairs of other nations and for his support of international terrorists. Several times he allowed Libyan troops to attack and cross into Egypt, Tunisia, and Chad. He supported at least two unsuccessful coup attempts in neighboring Sudan. He sent troops to help dictator Idi Amin in Uganda and funded anti-government Islamic groups in northern Nigeria. Such interference made Qaddafi unpopular with most African countries.

Section 4 Review

Identify Morocco, Muammar el-Qaddafi, Organization of African Unity (OAU)

Main Ideas
1. Describe the role of political parties in the drives for independence in Morocco and Tunisia.
2. Why was Algeria's struggle for independence violent?
3. Why did many nations denounce Muammar el-Qaddafi in the 1980s?

Critical Thinking
Making Hypotheses: Compare the goals of the OAU with those of the UN. What similar problems do they probably share?

HIGHLIGHTS OF CIVILIZATION

African Writers and Filmmakers

The traditional oral literature of Africa and family and religious values have shaped Africa's novels, plays, poetry, and films. Today, many talented African writers work in more than one literary art form. For example, Sembene Ousmane [sem be′nā üs′män] of Senegal, a novelist, is also the best known African filmmaker.

Wole Soyinka [wŏ′lā shō yin′kə], who won the Nobel Prize for Literature in 1986, is also a film producer but first and foremost a poet and playwright. Soyinka's style is evident in this excerpt from *Aké: The Years of Childhood*, which reconstructs the author's childhood in Aké, Nigeria, where his father was headmaster of the school. Soyinka, at age four and a half, had wandered from home. First a black police sergeant and then a white officer confront the lost boy.

The sergeant spun round on his heels, barked out some sentences in a very strange language to somebody hidden within the building. That person now came

out, smartly uniformed. The first thing that struck me about him was that he was albino. Then the next moment I realized that he was not an albino at all but a white man. . . .

Instinctively I backed one step towards the gate, but the man smiled, held out both hands in a gesture I did not quite understand, and approached. When he had come quite close, he bent down and, using the most unlikely accent I had ever heard asked,

"Kino o fe nibi yen?"

I knew the words were supposed to be in my own language but they made no sense to me, so I looked at the sergeant helplessly and said,

"I don't understand. What is he saying?"

The officer's eyes opened wide. "Oh, you speak English."

I nodded.

"Good. That is venhrry clenver. I was asking, what do you want? What can I doon for you?"

"I want to go home."

He exchanged looks with the Sergeant. "Well, that seems vum-vum-vum. And where is home?"

I could not understand why he should choose to speak through his nose. It made it difficult to understand him all the time but by straining hard, I could make sense of his questions. I told him that I lived in Aké. . . . "My father's name is Headmaster. Sometimes his name is Essay."

For some reason this amused him immensely, which I found offensive. There was no reason why my father's names should be the cause for such laughter.

Daily rituals are captured by Ancient Soi, a Kenyan artist, in this 1978 painting.

717

several generations and held power and land that they wanted to keep.
3. Qaddafi not only ruled his own country in a cruel way, but he also supported terrorism and tried to interfere with the governments of other African countries.

Critical Thinking

Both share the goals of international economic cooperation and the settlement of disputes. Both probably share the problems of getting independent countries to cooperate with each other.

HIGHLIGHTS OF CIVILIZATION

Encourage students to read the excerpt carefully and discuss the aspects of colonialism depicted in the relationship between the police officers and the lost boy. The language differences are one obvious subject for discussion as is the fact that the white officer, though well-meaning, offends Wole. Ask students to consider in particular the effects of colonialism on African writers, many of whom compose their works in the European language of the former colonial power. Soyinka, for example, writes in English except for poetry, which is composed in Yoruba. He has said that in Nigeria, "One is born to English. It's the language of the courts, the newspapers, the road signs." Ask students what impulses would lead a writer to compose different forms of literature in different languages.

Students can learn much about African cultures from *Aké: The Years of Childhood* (London: Rex Collings, 1981). An excellent anthology of contemporary African literature is *Black African Voices*, edited by James E. Miller, Jr., et al. (Glenview, Illinois: Scott, Foresman, 1970).

CHAPTER 37 REVIEW

Section Summaries

Section 1
Nationalism developed in Africa.
World War I, the Great Depression, and World War II brought many changes to Africa, including the rise of black nationalism. Ghana was the first colony to achieve independence in the post–World War II era.

Section 2
Africa's new nations began solving their problems.
Some African countries developed stable governments and growing economies. Others developed dictatorships. Several turned from socialism to a more capitalistic approach.

Section 3
The struggle for black rule reached southern Africa.
Independence came later for African nations in the south. Angola and Mozambique fought lengthy revolutions to achieve independence. Zimbabwe became independent after fighting a long guerrilla war. Fully independent since 1931, South Africa remained an oppressive and racist society that discriminated against black South Africans.

Section 4
North African nations became independent.
After World War II, Morocco, Tunisia, and Libya achieved independence fairly easily. Algeria had a hard struggle for freedom, but finally gained its independence after a war with France. Libya was ruled by Muammar el-Qaddafi, a dictator who supported international terrorism and anti-government groups in various African countries.

Test Yourself

Key Terms, People, and Places
Identify the significance of each of the following:

Section 1
a. Léopold Sédar Senghor   d. Ghana
b. négritude   e. Kwame Nkrumah
c. Wole Soyinka

Section 2
a. Idi Amin Dada   d. collective villages
b. Jomo Kenyatta   e. Abidjan
c. Julius Nyerer   f. Africanization

Section 3
a. trade embargo   d. apartheid
b. South Africa   e. Desmond Tutu
c. Afrikaners

Review Dates

1948 — South Africa officially establishes apartheid

1950 — Four African countries are independent

1954 — Ghana is granted independence

1963 — Organization of African Unity is founded

1980 — Fifty-one African countries are independent

1940   1950   1960   1970   1980   1990   2000

Section 4
a. Morocco   **c.** Organization of African
b. Muammar el-Qaddafi   Unity (OAU)

Main Ideas

Section 1
1. How did Africa change as a result of World War I and the Great Depression?
2. How did World War II bring further changes?
3. Why did newly independent African countries find freedom from colonialism difficult?
4. Describe some examples of African culture that have influenced people around the world.
5. What problems did Ghana have after becoming independent?

Section 2
1. Name problems that Nigeria faced after independence. What strengths does it enjoy?
2. Name one problem that Uganda, Kenya, and Tanzania faced after independence.
3. Name two major changes Côte d'Ivoire has made to solve its urban problems.
4. What problems did Zaire face after independence?
5. What catastrophes did Ethiopians suffer in recent years?

Section 3
1. Why did rebellions break out in Angola and Mozambique? What led to their success?
2. Why did Britain refuse to grant independence to Zimbabwe (Rhodesia)? How did it gain independence?
3. How have black South Africans shown their refusal to accept apartheid?

Section 4
1. How did political parties offer independence in Morocco and Tunisia?
2. Why did Algeria have a difficult struggle for independence?
3. What actions did Muammar el-Qaddafi take that made many countries denounce him?

Critical Thinking
1. Recognizing Values
Two terms, négritude and Africanization, have been introduced in this chapter to describe the black nationalistic feeling in Africa. How are they the same or different?
2. Identifying Assumptions
In Section 2 of this chapter, two different kinds of societies are described—one as "man-eat-man" and the other as "man-eat-nothing." Take each kind of "world" shown by these quotations and explain what you think each means.

Chapter Skills and Activities

Practicing Study and Research Skills
Working With Special Purpose Maps
You learned in this chapter that Africa is a treasure house of mineral resources. The map on page 711 shows Africa's major mineral resources. Use the political map on page 796 of the Atlas and the mineral map on page 711 to answer the following questions.
1. Which countries have major petroleum and natural gas deposits?
2. Are there any countries without major mineral resources indicated on the map? Does this mean they have no mineral resources?
3. Which countries have cobalt and copper?

Linking Past and Present
The system of apartheid in South Africa is one of the most oppressive in the world. Yet, until the 1950s and 1960s, the United States also had laws that excluded and discriminated against blacks. The U.S. civil rights movement helped to bring about more equality. Do you see any similarities in the pushes for change? What are the differences?

Learning History Through Maps
The three maps on pages 702 and 703 trace the history of independence in Africa from 1950 to 1980. Using these maps, answer the following questions.
1. How many independent countries were in Africa in 1950?
2. Between what years did Ghana become independent?
3. After independence some countries "Africanized" their names. What names did Rhodesia, Republic of Congo, and Bechuanaland use in 1980?

CRITICAL THINKING QUESTION LEVEL 1. average
2. easy;

38 Economic Growth and International Tension in the Middle East

OVERVIEW

This chapter covers the development of independence and economic growth in countries of the Middle East.

PLANNING CHART

Section	Text Pages	Key Concept	Suggested Teaching Time
1 A crossroads of people and ideas characterized the Middle East.	721–725	Language and religion have served to both unify and divide the people of the Middle East.	One day **Less time?** Combine the material on religious identities with the information on Islamic reform movements in Section 2. Discuss economic changes (Section 2) with political changes (Section 4). **More time?** Use *Overhead Transparency 75.*
2 Economic development brought social changes in the Middle East.	725–729	Wealth from oil reserves helped to accelerate modernization and urbanization in the Middle East.	One day
3 The Arab-Israeli conflict challenged the entire region.	729–731	The founding of Israel collided with the development of Arab nationalism.	One day **More time?** Use *Source Reading 38A.*
4 Political independence brought experiments with new types of governments.	732–736	Middle Eastern countries tried to meet the needs of their people by forming a variety of governments.	One day **More time?** Use *Overhead Transparency 76* or *Source Reading 38B.*

ANCILLARIES

Materials that may be used with this chapter to reinforce, reteach, enrich, and assess learning are pictured on the following pages.

Teacher's Resource File

ACTIVITIES

Section 1 Activity, p. 227

Section 2 Activity, p. 228

Section 3 Activity, p. 229

Section 4 Activity, p. 230

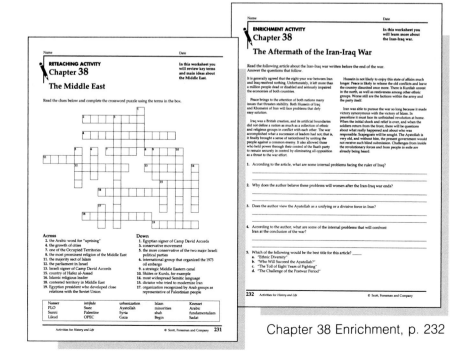

Chapter 38 Reteaching, p. 231

Chapter 38 Enrichment, p. 232

Teacher's Resource File

GEOGRAPHY SKILLS

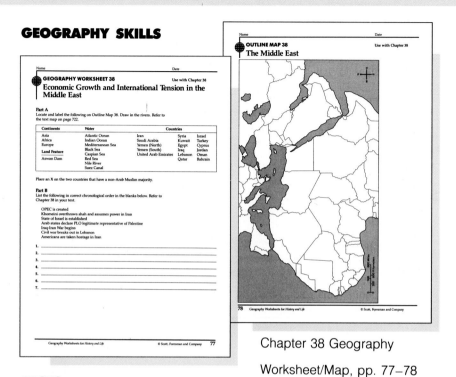

Chapter 38 Geography
Worksheet/Map, pp. 77–78

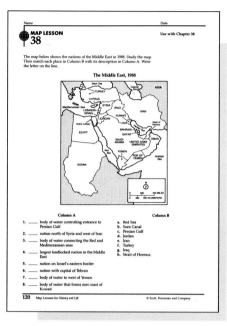

Chapter 38 Map Lesson, p. 120

TESTS

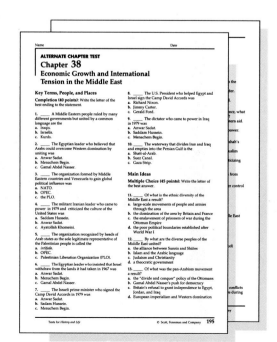

Chapter Test, pp. 193–194

Alternate Chapter Test, pp. 195–196

Other Optional Ancillaries

WORKBOOK

WORKSHEET

Chapter 38, Section 1

The Middle East

In this worksheet you will review the diverse cultures of the Middle East.

Part A
Choose words from the box to complete the chart.

Language Groups in the Middle East

Semitic — Indo-Iranian — Kurdish

Farsi | Arabic | Turkic | Hebrew

Complete the sentences.

1. The most widely spoken Semitic language in the Middle East is _____.
2. The Israelis and their Arabic neighbors are culturally related in that both speak _____ languages.
3. The second largest Middle Eastern language family is _____.
4. The principal language of Iran is _____.
5. A group of 5 million that has maintained a sense of identity as one people despite being ruled by four different governments has been unified by the _____ language.

Part B
Write C next to each phrase that correctly completes the sentence. (Each incomplete sentence may have more than one correct ending.)

1. The Middle East has been
___ the scene of the Iran-Iraq war of the 1980s.
___ the playing field for Soviet-Western power rivalries.
___ the birthplace of three major world religions.
___ a region where nations have enjoyed a long history of independence.

2. The concept of pan-Arabism
___ created the Sunni-Shiite split.
___ developed in response to Western imperialism.
___ espoused the policy of "divide and conquer."
___ viewed Arab unity as a way to prevent Western domination of Middle Eastern economies.

Worksheets for History and Life © Scott, Foresman and Company **153**

Section 1 Worksheet, p. 153

WORKSHEET

Chapter 38, Section 2

The Impact of Oil

In this worksheet you will review the impact of oil upon the Middle East.

Part A
Use the graph and table below and your text to complete the following exercises.

Estimated World Oil Production, 1986*

Arab OPEC		Non-Arab OPEC	
(Percent of World Production)			
Algeria	1.1%	Ecuador	0.5%
Iraq	3.2%	Gabon	0.3%
Kuwait	2.2%	Indonesia	2.2%
Libya	1.8%	Iran	3.2%
Qatar	0.6%	Nigeria	2.6%
Saudi Arabia	8.4%	Venezuela	3.0%
United Arab			
Emirates	5.1%		
Total	**22.4%**	**Total**	**11.8%**

1. Which Middle Eastern OPEC nations listed were among the original countries that founded OPEC in 1960?
2. Which OPEC nation produced the most oil in 1986?
3. How does the oil production of the Arab OPEC nations compare with that of the non-Arab OPEC nations? What significance might this have?

Part B
Write the letter of the item from the box that best completes each sentence.

The recent increase in oil production has brought both economic and social changes. For one thing, rapid _____ has occurred, often overwhelming local services. Women have benefited in that many now can find _____ in the cities. Ironically, this very improvement in women's rights has triggered a growth in Islamic _____. Some Westerners find it surprising that even modern Moslem women choose to wear the _____. Less surprising is the fundamentalist opposition to Western values such as _____. The clash between Western and _____ views is likely to continue.

a. fundamentalism
b. materialism
c. traditional
d. chadur
e. newly-created jobs
f. urbanization

*Data from "The Worldwide Report," by Oil and Gas Journal, December, 22-29, 1986.

154 *Worksheets for History and Life* © Scott, Foresman and Company

Section 2 worksheet, p. 154

WORKSHEET

Chapter 38, Section 3

Arab-Israeli Conflict

In this worksheet you will review the historic development of Arab-Israeli hostility.

Part A
Label the map with the letter of each item from the box.

Disputed Territories in the Middle East

A. Egypt
B. Jordan
C. Syria
D. Lebanon
E. Suez Canal
F. West Bank
G. Golan Heights
H. Jerusalem
I. Sinai Peninsula
J. Gaza Strip

Part B
Complete each statement with the explanations given in your text.

1. Jews came to Palestine after World War II **because**
2. The UN recommended that Palestine be partitioned **because**
3. After the 1948 war, many Arabs from Palestine became refugees in camps in the West Bank, Gaza, and nearby Arab countries **because**
4. An *intifada* broke out in the Occupied Territories in 1987 **because**
5. The Israelis did not want the Occupied Territories to become an independent Arab state **because**

Worksheets for History and Life © Scott, Foresman and Company **155**

Section 3 worksheet, p. 155

WORKSHEET

Chapter 38, Section 4

Political Development

In this worksheet you will review the recent history and important leaders of some Middle Eastern nations.

Part A
Identify the political leader who would be most likely to make or agree with each of the following statements by choosing the correct name from the box.

1. The Soviet Union is a useful ally. By cultivating Soviet friendship, one breaks the hold that the Western imperialists retain over our people.
2. Unity, freedom, and socialism are our goals.
3. Death to America! Down with all those who act in collusion with the great Satan!
4. Modernization is the key to prosperity. It is time for women to take their rightful places in society. Factories and schools will aid us to cast aside the backwardness of the past.
5. The Soviet military presence in Egypt and the eastern Mediterranean is deeply disturbing. The Soviets must leave!

| Anwar Sadat | Gamal Abdel Nasser | Muhammad Reza Pahlavi |
| Ayatollah Khomeini | Hafez al-Assad | |

Part B
Identify the country to which each phrase refers by writing IQ for Iraq, IR for Iran, IS for Israel, SA for Saudi Arabia, T for Turkey, and SY for Syria.

1. ___ in 1979 overthrew a monarchy that had taken steps to better the status of women
2. ___ faced international condemnation for its use of poorly armed, poorly prepared boys as combatants
3. ___ developed a multi-party democracy
4. ___ since 1963 ruled by Baath party
5. ___ returned to democracy between episodes of military intervention in government
6. ___ assumed a leadership role in OPEC
7. ___ intended to form a self-sufficient, agricultural society
8. ___ ruled by the iron hand of dictator Saddam Hussein

156 *Worksheets for History and Life* © Scott, Foresman and Company

Section 4 Worksheet, p. 156

SOURCE READINGS

Source Reading 38A
Source Reading 38B

TEST GENERATOR

40 multiple-choice questions for Chapter 38

OVERHEAD TRANSPARENCIES

Overhead Transparency 75
Overhead Transparency 76

719d

1945	
1948	Jews establish the state of Israel
1960	OPEC is formed
1979	A revolution overturns the Shah of Iran
1980	
1990	

Economic Growth and International Tension in the Middle East

1945–Present

In the years following World War II, many nations in the Middle East began to achieve true political independence. These nations started to separate themselves from the Western nations that had dominated the region during the first part of the 20th century. Along with political independence, social and technological changes also took place. Gamal Abdel Nasser, the popular leader of Egypt from 1954 to 1970, dramatically summed up the challenge facing his country and most of the Middle East in those years:

> Every people on earth goes through two revolutions—a political revolution by which it wrests the right to govern itself from the hand of tyranny and a social revolution involving the conflict of classes. . . . But as for us, the terrible experience through which our people is going is that we are having both revolutions at once.

Many of the changes the Middle East experienced in recent decades affected traditional living patterns. The role of women in society was altered. The poor and minorities in communities demanded more rights and services. In addition, new ideas and ideologies challenged values of the region's three principal religions—Judaism, Christianity, and Islam.

The Middle East also experienced international tensions during these decades. The establishment of the new state of Israel in 1948 left much of the Arab world bitter and both sides engaged in wars and threats of wars. The Iran-Iraq war of the 1980s demonstrated that political revolutions in one country could threaten the stability and peace of the whole region. The development of vast resources of oil vital to all industrial societies encouraged the Western powers and the Soviet Union to develop strategic interests in the region. These interests increased the tension in all regional conflicts.

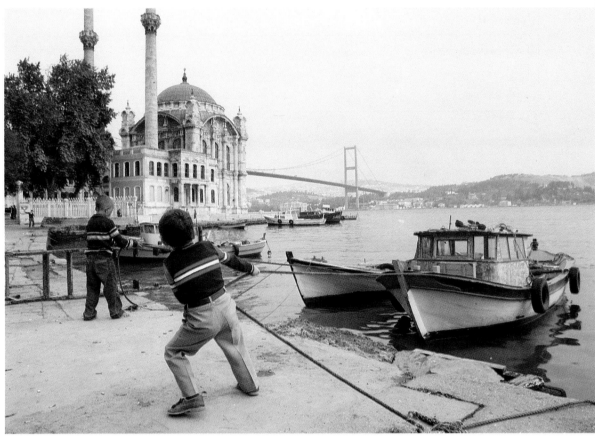

Young Turkish boys play around the Bosporus shore of an Istanbul suburb. The bridge in the background leads from Europe into Asian Turkey, symbolic of the role of the Middle East as a crossroads of peoples and cultures.

Reading Preview

In this chapter, you will learn how the Middle East has dealt with conflict and economic growth.

1. *A crossroads of people and ideas characterized the Middle East.*

2. *Economic development brought social changes to the Middle East.*

3. *The Arab-Israeli conflict challenged the entire region.*

4. *Political independence brought experiments with new types of governments.*

 A crossroads of people and ideas characterized the Middle East.

The Middle East is a region with a dry climate and few natural resources. However, the Middle East is also an area with enormous oil wealth and fertile soils, though most of the farmland is clustered along rivers or seacoasts.

Limited natural resources have played a significant role in the development of the Middle East. The climate of much of the region is hot and dry, similar to that of the American Southwest. Water is, therefore, a scarce and highly valuable resource.

721

1 *Lesson Plan*

Essential Learning Objective

Students will learn to explain the effect of religious and language differences on political conditions in the Middle East.

1 FOCUS AND MOTIVATE

Ask students to name the major world religions and the areas where they began. Guide students as necessary in recognizing that Judaism, Christianity, and Islam originated in the Middle East. Tell students to look for ways in which religion affects people's lives in the Middle East today as they study this section.

- Chart, on one-half of the chalkboard, the languages of the Semitic, Turkic, and Indo-Iranian language groups. List the Middle Eastern countries under the correct language group(s). Point out the countries that are represented in more than one group (Iran, Iraq, Syria).

- Next to the language-group chart, list Judaism, Christianity, Islam and the nations that follow these religions. Explain the sub-groups found in each religion (conservative and modern Judaism; Coptic, Maronite, and Greek Orthodox Christianity; Sunni and Shiite branches of Islam).

GUIDED PRACTICE

Hand out outline maps of the Middle East from the Geography Skills book. Direct students to label countries where Arabic is spoken and those that are predominantly Islamic. (Colors or letters can be used to symbolize language and religious groupings.) Complete maps by identifying the religions and languages of the non-Arab nations. Also for guided practice:

 Overhead Transparency 75

The Middle East

Commercial farming	Nomadic herding	◆ Mining	Little or no economic activity
Irrigated farming	Forests	Commercial fishing	✺ National capitals
Ranching	Lumbering	Urban land use	• Other cities

MAP STUDY The map above shows the political divisions and economic activities of the Middle East. What types of land use dominate the map's noncoastal areas? What mineral resource is found around the Persian Gulf?

Throughout the region rainfall is limited and, as a result, agriculture generally depends on irrigation. In addition, mineral resources, with the important exception of oil, are rare, thereby limiting industrial development.

Ethnic diversity is the result of a long history.

From the beginning of recorded history, there have been many large-scale movements of people and armies through the Middle East. As a result, the Middle East has evolved into a rich patchwork of peoples, many of whom maintain their ancient identities and cultures.

Most of the people of the Middle East speak a language that falls into one of three groups: Semitic, Turkic, or Indo-Iranian. The most widespread Semitic language is Arabic, which is spoken by about 177 million people in Egypt, Jordan, Lebanon, Iraq, Syria, Saudi Arabia, and the small na-

ANSWER TO MAP STUDY nomadic herding and little or no economic activity; oil tions of the Arabian peninsula. Another important Semitic language is Hebrew, spoken by Middle Eastern Jews, most of whom live in Israel.

The second largest Middle Eastern language family is Turkic. About half of all Turkic-speaking people live in Turkey, a nation of 55 million people. Turkic languages are also spoken in parts of Iran, Iraq, Cyprus, the Soviet Union, and China.

The third group of languages spoken in the Middle East is the Indo-Iranian family. The most prominent is Farsi, the principal language of Iran. In addition, some Middle East peoples speak other Indo-Iranian languages. Two examples are the Baluchis of eastern Iran and the Kurds.

The 5 million **Kurds** live divided among Iraq, Iran, Syria, and Turkey. The Kurdish language is part of the Kurds' sense of separate identity, a sense that has kept them unified as a people despite being ruled over by many different governments. Ever since the division of the Kurds at the end of World War I, they have engaged in rebellion against their four governments in an effort to establish an independent state for themselves.

Religious identities create unity and conflict.

The Middle East was the birthplace of three of the major world religions—Judaism, Christianity, and Islam. The three have important elements in common, such as their belief in one God and their emphasis on moral and ethical conduct. Over the centuries, however, disagreements among the religions about beliefs and authority have caused bitterness and conflict.

Although each of these religions plays an important role in the life of the Middle East, Islam is the most prominent today. About 93 percent of all people living in the Middle East are Muslim. Islam, as the majority religion, provides a spiritual and cultural unity to the Middle East, strongly influencing the arts, education, political organization, and family structure of almost all Middle Eastern states. Arabic, the language of the Koran and the predominant language in the region, also serves to unify the diverse peoples of the Middle East.

Some important differences have developed over time within Islam itself. For example, Muslims divided into two competing branches—the Sunnis

and the Shiites—in the mid-600s because of a dispute, which was never resolved, concerning who had the right to succeed Muhammad.

The Sunnis have remained a unified group and now include about 90 percent of the Muslim population. The Shiites, however, splintered into many rival sects, or divisions. In most Middle Eastern countries, the Sunni Muslims tend to be wealthier and in control of more political power than the Shiite minority. Such differences have led to clashes between the two groups, such as in Lebanon and Iraq, and are partially responsible for the recent war between Shiite Iran and Sunni Iraq.

Like the Muslims, the Christian population of the Middle East is also divided into many different denominations and sects. The Coptic Christians of Egypt and the Maronite Christians of Lebanon are the largest groups. Other groups include the Greek Orthodox Christians of Lebanon, Syria, and Turkey, as well as many other lesser-known sects.

Judaism also is practiced in differing forms. As you have learned, many Jews from around the world have migrated to Israel since World War II, bringing with them different ways of life. Some Jewish groups are so conservative that they will

The young woman below belongs to a rural Kurdish community in Turkey. The Kurds are divided among four Middle Eastern countries.

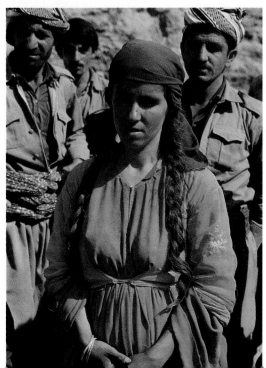

ASSESS

What language and religion is most common in the Middle East? (Arabic, Islam)

OPTIONAL RETEACHING

Ask one student to name a Middle Eastern nation, a second student, its language(s), and a third student its religion(s). Continue until all Middle Eastern nations have been named.

OPTIONAL ENRICHMENT

1. Assign students, individually or in pairs, to choose one Middle Eastern nation to research. Have students contribute information to a class chart showing the area, population, language and religious divisions of each nation. (average)
2. Have different students prepare written or oral reports on the origins and significant differences between the religious sects of either Islam, Christianity, or Judaism in the Middle East. (challenging)

INDEPENDENT PRACTICE/ HOMEWORK

Assign the Section Review, Activities page 227, or Workbook page 153.

CLOSURE

Summarize the lesson by telling students that the people of the Middle East share lands that once developed the world's first civilizations and three major religions. Differences in language and religious values in these nations today often cause conflicts and confrontation.

Middle Eastern Countries

Country	Population*	Religion	Official Language(s)	Main Ethnic Groups
Bahrain	486,000	Shiite (65%), Sunni (35%)	Arabic	Arab (73%), Asian (13%), Iranian (8%)
Cyprus	698,800	Greek Orthodox (78%), Muslim (18%)	Greek, Turkish	Greek (78%), Turkish (18%)
Egypt	50,700,000	Sunni (94%), Coptic Christian and other (6%)	Arabic	Egyptian (90%), Greek, Italian, Syro-Lebanese (10%)
Iran	53,920,000	Shiite (93%), Sunni (5%), Zoroastrian, Jewish, Christian, and Bahai (2%)	Persian. Kurdish, Turkish	Persian (63%), Turkish (13%), other Iranian (13%), Kurdish (3%), Arab (3%)
Iraq	17,060,000	Shiite (55%), Sunni (40%), Christian and other (5%)	Arabic, Kurdish	Arab (71%), Kurdish (18%), Turkish (2%), Assyrian and other (8%)
Israel	4,820,000	Jewish (85%), Muslim (11%), Christian and other (4%)	Hebrew, Arabic	Jewish (85%), Arab and other (15%)
Jordan	3,170,000	Sunni (92%), Christian (8%)	Arabic	Arab (98%)
Kuwait	2,040,000	Muslim (99%)	Arabic	Arab (78%), South Asian (9%), Iranian (4%)
Lebanon	2,800,000	Muslim (55%), Christian (45%)	Arabic	Arab (93%), Armenian (6%)
Oman	2,000,000	Muslim (100%)	Arabic	Arab (88%), Baluchi (4%), Persian (3%)
Qatar	371,863	Muslim (98%)	Arabic	Arab (45%), South Asian (34%), Iranian (16%)
Saudi Arabia	12,000,000	Muslim (100%)	Arabic	Arab (90%), Afro-Asian (10%)
Syria	11,300,000	Sunni (74%), Alawi, Druse, and other Muslim (16%), Christian (10%)	Arabic	Arab (90%), Kurdish, Armenian, and other (10%)
Turkey	50,670,000	Muslim (99%)	Turkish	Turkish (85%), Kurdish (12%)
United Arab Emirates	1,600,000	Muslim (96%), Christian, Hindu, and other (4%)	Arabic	South Asian (50%), Arab (42%), Westerners and East Asians (8%)
Yemen	12,000,000	Sunni Muslim (53%), Shiite Muslim (46%)	Arabic	Arab (87%), Afro-Arab (10%), Indian (2%)

*Source: Statesman's Year-Book 1991–1992

not attend movies on the Sabbath or stand in lines that contain both men and women. Others have adopted a more modern, secular lifestyle. This clash between traditional religious customs and modern secular lifestyles has been a continuing source of conflict in Israel.

Throughout the Middle East, governments have struggled with the issue of secularization, the idea that government and religion should be separate. In the United States, this concept is known as the separation of church and state. Nations within the Middle East have followed different courses with regard to secularization. Turkey, for example, established a government in which the Islamic authorities do not play a role, creating a secular government. Iran, on the other hand, established a theocracy—a government in which the ruler is also the Islamic religious leader.

Pan-Arabism grew in response to imperialism.

Imperialism also played a role in shaping the Middle East. As a result of World War I, the British and French divided Ottoman territories between themselves and ruled them as mandates of the League of Nations. Unlike the Ottomans, the Europeans followed a "divide and conquer" policy. They drew artificial borders that ignored the region's earlier unity and thereby created new tensions and conflicts.

Imperialism left the Middle East with other problems as well. To the Europeans, the region was mostly of strategic interest, and they made very little effort to develop it economically. Education and social welfare were also neglected. Democracy was neglected as well. The European rulers insisted on making the major political decisions, and as a result, the Middle Easterners were allowed little experience in democratic government.

Although Egypt, Jordan, and Iraq received independence from Britain before World War II, resentment toward Europeans lingered. Europeans remained unpopular because their troops remained stationed in large numbers throughout the Middle East during the war, and because the European powers refused to give independence to Palestine, Syria, and Lebanon.

Arab leaders, such as **Gamal Abdel Nasser** of Egypt, believed that if the Arabs could only unite, they could overcome not only the political domination of Britain and France, but the military, cultural, and economic domination of the Western world as well. This idea of Arab unity was called **pan-Arabism**. Over the years pan-Arabism has encountered both success and failure. Most Arab leaders, however, have chosen to work within the existing political structure rather than pursue the idea of one unified Arab nation.

Section 1 Review

Identify Kurds, Gamal Abdel Nasser, pan-Arabism

Main Ideas
1. List the three major language groups in the Middle East, and give an example of each.
2. How has the presence of Islam, Christianity, and Judaism in the Middle East brought both unity and conflict to the region?
3. Why did pan-Arabism arise in the Middle East?

Critical Thinking
Making Generalizations: Do you think a common language always makes people feel a sense of unity? Support your answer with evidence.

| 2 | *Economic development brought social changes to the Middle East.* |

Since World War II, much of the Middle East has experienced considerable economic growth. This growth was partly the result of the development of immense oil reserves, which gave many countries new income to invest in their economies. Some of the benefits of new wealth, however, were offset by rapidly growing populations and the cost incurred by wars.

Oil has made a significant impact on the Middle East.

Oil, the only mineral resource the Middle East possesses in large supply, has proven to be a very important asset for the region. The Middle East, which has 60 percent of the world's proven oil re-

GEOGRAPHY:
A KEY TO HISTORY

Teachers may want to emphasize how central the Indian Ocean has been to the Muslim World. The goal of every Muslim believer is to make a pilgrimage to Mecca at least once in a lifetime. Mecca itself is situated inland, a short distance from the Red Sea arm of the Indian Ocean.

Over the centuries millions of pilgrims sailed across the sea to reach Mecca. Of the thirty nations bordering the Indian Ocean, only three—Australia, Madagascar (Malagasy Republic), and South Africa—do not have significant Islamic populations. The four nations with the largest number of Muslims (Indonesia, Pakistan, Bangladesh, and India) all face the Indian Ocean.

Buddhism and Hinduism also are major religions in the region. Because of the great size of India's population, the number of Hindus in the region is about equal to the number of Muslims. Thus it would not be correct to call the Indian Ocean a Muslim ocean.

Answers to REVIEW

1. north-Asia, south-Antarctica, east-Australia, west-Africa
2. More than half of the world's people live within 2,000 miles of the mouth of the Ganges River on the Indian Ocean. The Ocean has also been a center of civilization and trade since the dawn of civilization.

Answer to MAP QUESTION

East Indies; Africa, Southwest Asia

A Key to History

THE CENTRALITY OF THE INDIAN OCEAN

Geographers often talk about particular places at the center of human activities. For example, the cities of Istanbul, Cairo, and New York are central places, partly because they are at the junction of transportation and communication routes. Oceans are not thought of in this sense, but they may have the same characteristics. The Indian Ocean is a good example.

Asia forms the northern boundary of the Indian Ocean. Africa lies to the west, and the East Indies and Australia are to the east. In the south, however, the ocean stretches all the way to the frozen coasts of Antarctica. Many of the nations

What islands separate the Indian and Pacific oceans? What land barriers separate the Indian Ocean and the Atlantic?

bordering the Indian Ocean have huge populations. Some scholars believe that the mouth of the Ganges River, which empties into the ocean at the 90° east meridian, should be at the center of world maps used to study history. More than half of the people in the world live within 2,000 miles of this central place.

One extension of the Indian Ocean, the Red Sea, separates Africa from Asia. The Red Sea extends to 30° north latitude, almost reaching the Mediterranean Sea. A canal connecting the two seas had been built in ancient times by the Egyptians and by Muslim engineers in the 7th century. The Suez Canal, for use by modern ships, was completed in 1869 and soon became one of the world's busiest waterways.

The Indian Ocean has served as a highway for the peoples of the world from the earliest period of human history. The Sumerians built the first vessels to sail this ocean. Later came the Egyptians, Persians, Indians, Arabs, and Chinese.

A Portuguese ship under Vasco da Gama rounded Africa and, guided by an Arab pilot, reached India in 1498. Within a few years, Europeans had established trading posts and colonies in the lands bordering the Indian Ocean. From this point on, trade has become truly global, but the Indian Ocean, surrounded by densely populated lands, continues to occupy a central position.

REVIEW

1. What lands border the Indian Ocean on the north, south, east, and west?
2. For what reasons do some scholars believe the Indian Ocean should be placed at the center of world maps?

serves, only recently realized the economic potential of this natural resource.

The change has been dramatic. Over the last 40 years, revenues from oil rose substantially as increased use of oil in industrial societies pushed the price of a barrel of oil upward. With more real income, Middle Eastern countries invested in their own economies. They built roads and communication networks and improved the housing and schools of their communities. In addition, they boosted agricultural production and promoted industrial manufacturing. Some countries with large oil reserves, such as Saudi Arabia and Kuwait, provided free education and medical care.

Along with working toward internal development, Middle Eastern countries also tried to use their valuable resources to gain political influence in the world. In 1960 Saudi Arabia, Kuwait, Iraq, and Iran joined with Venezuela to form the **Organization of Petroleum Exporting Countries (OPEC)**. In 1973, during a war between Israel and some of the Arab countries, OPEC was able to organize an embargo on the sale of oil. That is, they refused to sell their oil to Western nations until some effort was made to halt the war. In the years that followed, OPEC continued to try to set production limits and prices on oil and the Western nations continued to be dependent on OPEC oil.

From the 1960s to the 1980s, the Middle East experienced very rapid economic growth. Countries expanded and diversified their economies. The increase in economic activity led to more new jobs and new technologies. Education, though still not universal, became more attainable. Although the economy improved, longstanding social problems remained. For example, the increased wealth was not distributed evenly. In many countries peasants struggled for subsistence in isolated villages, and urban slums were neglected.

Middle East society reflects a wide variety of social patterns and experiences—both rural and urban. About 55 percent of the people of the Middle East make their living as farmers. Another 5 percent are nomadic pastoralists who depend on their animal herds, moving either from oasis to oasis or between the lowlands and the mountains with the changing seasons. The remaining 40 percent of the people live in cities.

Since World War II, the rapid growth of cities has placed a severe strain on the governments of the region. The population of some cities mushroomed in just a few decades. For instance, Amman, Jordan, which had 40,000 people in 1947, has about one million residents today. Other cities, such as Cairo, Egypt, have more than tripled their populations. This rapid growth sometimes overwhelmed such services as electricity, water, and housing.

Women's roles in Middle Eastern society changed.

As Middle Eastern countries diversified and urbanized their economies, their needs for workers changed. More skilled and educated people were needed to work in new jobs such as textile production, banking, and computer technology. These changing needs often benefited women..

Just as in the West, women were called upon to fill the new jobs created. Many women in the Middle East, especially Egyptians and Palestinians, therefore began to obtain higher education and modern job skills.

Against this backdrop of progress remains the conflicting role of women in the traditional religious value system of the Middle East. Islam, as interpreted by many Islamic scholars today, holds that women should be separate from men in most activities, including work and school.

Oil, the primary resource of the Persian Gulf nations, is being processed at the Kuwait Oil Complex, located in Ahmadi, Kuwait's main oil-producing area.

threat to traditional values and to their authority.)

OPTIONAL RETEACHING

Have students evaluate some of the major changes that took place in Middle Eastern nations from a modernist and a traditionalist point of view. (Example: the growth of industry, which led to more jobs for men and women, which went against values that taught that the sexes should be separated)

OPTIONAL ENRICHMENT

1. Have students research and report on the methods used in transporting oil from the Middle East. (average)
2. Have students research and prepare charts showing the value of items traded between the United States and the oil-producing countries of the Middle East over a period of years. (challenging)

INDEPENDENT PRACTICE/ HOMEWORK

Assign the Section Review, Activities page 228, or Workbook page 154.

CLOSURE

Summarize the lesson by telling students that since World War II many uses had been developed for petroleum-based products. These products became vital to the industrialized nations as well as to underdeveloped areas. Middle Eastern nations, as the principal producers of oil, gained great wealth. This wealth enabled governments to support education, industrialization, and internal development. Some leaders, especially traditionally oriented religious figures, opposed the various cultural changes that accompanied modernization.

Women's roles vary tremendously throughout the Middle East. These women above, in Cairo, Egypt, have chosen to wear traditional Islamic dress.

Although the Koran guarantees the right of women to own and inherit property, many Muslims believe that women should still hold what Westerners would consider a subservient position to men. According to these Muslims, women should be obedient to men, with their education considered less important. In addition, these people believe that women should not hold positions of political or religious authority over men.

Middle Eastern governments have dealt differently with the roles of women in their societies. Some governments, such as that of Egypt, have encouraged equal access to education for women, who can attend classes along with men. Under the conservative leadership of Saudi Arabia, however, women receive a strictly segregated education.

The types of clothing women choose to wear in the Middle East illustrate the variety of attitudes about women. In Iran, where the Islamic government has opposed many forms of Western materialism, women are made to cover their heads and clothing with a black cloth called a chadur. In other countries, women choose to wear Western-style dress.

However, some women, even in more socially permissive countries like Egypt, feel that Western dress is too revealing and materialistic. Many, especially younger women, now prefer to adopt a more conservative style of appearance, wearing a long, traditional-style gown with a scarf draped around their head. Some of these women believe that their action is a sign of their renewed commitment to the Islamic faith.

Islamic reform movements drew supporters.

Besides clothing, other areas of Middle Eastern life reflect conflict between Western and traditional views. Concern about their society's increased violence, corruption, and immorality led to the growth of a fundamental Islamic religious movement that advocated change.

In almost every country, religious organizations began to advocate change. Muslim activists and fundamentalists believed that a rejection of Western culture, along with a return to the basic Islamic beliefs and values, was necessary if the Middle East were ever to regain respect and influence in the world. Iran's **Ayatollah Khomeini** [ä′yä-tō′lə hō mā nē′], a militant leader who criticized the culture of the United States as that of the "Coca-cola and the miniskirt," explained in the following words:

> Muslims of the world . . . repel the treacherous superpowers from your countries and your abundant resources. . . . Rely on the culture of Islam, resist Western imitation and stand on your feet. Attack those intellectuals who are infatuated with the West and the East, and recover your true identity. Realize that intellectuals in the pay of foreigners have inflicted disaster upon their people and countries.

It should be noted that most Middle Easterners were only exposed to the most commercial aspects of Western culture. Most were therefore unfamiliar with the fundamental values of Western culture, such as our democratic rights and institutions.

Many fundamentalist Muslim reformers began to criticize their own governments for being too eager to acquire Western alliances, social values, and material goods. In Iran, for example, militant Muslim religious leaders, including the Ayatollah Khomeini, led masses of people in a revolution. In 1979 the revolutionaries overthrew the shah, who had become a very close ally of Western powers. The new leaders, who also objected to the unequal distribution of Iran's oil revenues, ushered in a strict Muslim government.

Section 2 Review

Identify OPEC, Ayatollah Khomeini

Main Ideas

1. What economic impact has oil had on the Middle East?
2. How have women's roles changed in the Middle East today?
3. Why is Islamic fundamentalism anti-Western?

Critical Thinking

Analyzing Comparisons: Compare the ideas and goals of Muslim fundamentalists to the ideas and goals of the Puritans you read about in Chapter 20.

3	*The Arab-Israeli conflict challenged the entire region.*

As you learned in Chapter 33, in 1945 Britain still controlled all of Palestine as a mandate under the League of Nations. Jewish refugees, mostly survivors of the Nazi Holocaust, began to pour into Palestine. These Jews viewed Palestine as their ancient Jewish homeland, and they believed that the persecution that they had endured for so long would end only when they lived in a country of their own.

Arab nationalism also grew after World War II, and Arabs once again demanded independence for Palestine. Because Jews made up only one third of the population of Palestine in 1945, an independent government that was based on a democratic vote would have meant a government dominated by Arabs. The Jews were opposed to living under this type of government.

The Jews declared Israel an independent state.

The British, who couldn't resolve the conflict, turned to the United Nations in 1947. The UN recommended that Palestine be partitioned and that Jerusalem be put under a UN trusteeship. The plan was accepted by the Jews but rejected by the Arabs. On the day the British left Palestine in 1948, the Jews proclaimed the state of **Israel** within their part of Palestine. Almost at once, seven Arab countries attacked Israel, and war followed. In 1949 the UN negotiated a cease-fire.

At the time of the cease-fire, the Israeli armies controlled more territory, including half of Jerusalem, than had been assigned to them in 1947. The UN partition plan had called for an Arab as well as a Jewish state in Palestine, but this part of the plan was never realized. In 1949 Transjordan took over the remainder of Palestine and Jerusalem, the area now known as the West Bank, and changed its name to Jordan. Egypt took responsibility for the Gaza Strip, a remaining part of Palestine along the Mediterranean. Locate these areas on the map on page 730.

During the 1948 war, several hundred thousand Palestinian Arabs fled their homes in what was then Israel. Many of these refugees were housed in makeshift camps run by the UN in the West Bank, the Gaza Strip, and nearby Arab countries. The fate of these displaced families continues to cause problems today.

Israel refused to allow the Palestinian refugees to return to their homes. Most of the Arab countries, except Jordan, also refused to give them citizenship and to help them resettle. As the years passed, the refugee camps thus became permanent

Yasser Arafat, the leader of the PLO since 1969, is seen here in his characteristic attire. Throughout his career, he has aroused much controversy.

Answers to Section 2 Review

Identify

Key Terms, People, and Places are defined on pages indicated in parentheses. Also see the Glossary and Biographical Dictionary. OPEC (727), Ayatollah Khomeini (728)

Main Ideas

1. new wealth, development projects, economic opportunities
2. more education, jobs, and political responsibility
3. Islamic fundamentalists believe that Western values are too materialistic and non-Muslim.

Critical Thinking

Both groups believed in a return to strict religious beliefs and practices, opposed materialism, and attacked governments that differed from them.

3 *Lesson Plan*

Essential Learning Objective

Students will learn to discuss the historical background of the positions of Palestinians and other Arabs and Israelis.

1 FOCUS AND MOTIVATE

Ask students to describe the meaning of the term, "homeland." Write responses on the chalkboard. Tell students that both the Israelis and the Palestinians claimed as their homeland the land now held by Israel.

2 TEACH

Draw a long time line across the chalkboard. Place the dates and events described from 1945 to 1987 on the time line. Pay special attention to the wars and conflicts of 1945, 1956, 1967, 1973, and 1987. Have students refer to the maps on pages 722 and 730 to locate areas involved in each conflict. (West Bank, Gaza Strip, Sinai, Suez Canal, Golan Heights)

GUIDED PRACTICE

Have students write sentences stating the positions of Sadat, Begin, and Carter as they may have been voiced at Camp David in 1979.

3 ASSESS AND CLOSE

ASSESS

What was the UN plan for Palestine in 1947? Why wasn't it followed? (The UN planned to separate the area into Jewish and Arab sections. Palestinians refused to accept the plan.)

OPTIONAL RETEACHING

Hand out four outline maps of the Middle East from the Geography Skills book. Direct students, in four groups, to prepare maps illustrating territorial claims in 1945, 1949, 1967, and 1987. Display the completed maps.

OPTIONAL ENRICHMENT

1. Have students write biographies of Sadat, Begin, or Carter. (average)
2. Have students prepare a report on one of the religious shrines within Israel of the Jews, Christians, or Muslims to illustrate arrangements that are in place to allow access to holy places. Places covered might include: The Dome of the Rock, Wailing Wall, tombs of Sarah and David, the Holy Sepulchre, Church of the Nativity. (challenging)
3. Also for enrichment:

 Source Reading 38A

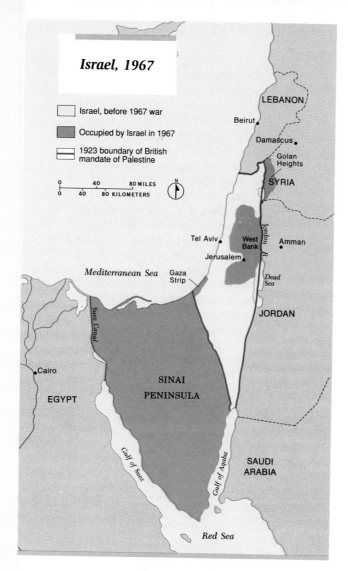

Israel, 1967

- ▢ Israel, before 1967 war
- ▨ Occupied by Israel in 1967
- ▭ 1923 boundary of British mandate of Palestine

LEBANON
Beirut
Damascus
Golan Heights
SYRIA
Tel Aviv
Jerusalem
West Bank
Amman
Gaza Strip
Dead Sea
JORDAN
Mediterranean Sea
Suez Canal
Cairo
EGYPT
SINAI PENINSULA
Gulf of Suez
Gulf of Aqaba
SAUDI ARABIA
Red Sea

MAP STUDY The map shows Israel in 1967. What four areas were occupied by Israel in 1967? Which of these lay outside the 1923 borders?

settlements. There were no jobs or farms, and few community services. The refugee settlements became centers of dissatisfaction and bases for violent attacks on Israel.

In 1964 the heads of the Arab states recognized the **Palestine Liberation Organization (PLO)** as the only legitimate representative of the Palestinian people. The PLO is an umbrella organization

BACKGROUND The oil embargo led by OPEC was lifted early in 1974, but by then OPEC had quadrupled the price of oil. The combined economic pressure of the embargo and the

ANSWER TO MAP STUDY Golan Heights, West Bank, Gaza Strip, and Sinai peninsula; Golan Heights and Sinai peninsula

for various Palestinian Arab guerrilla groups and service organizations. In addition, later that year the PLO received observer status at the UN to speak for Palestinian issues.

Arabs and Israelis continued to clash.

Since the establishment of Israel in 1948, the nation has constantly been on the brink of war with its Arab neighbors. The second war since 1948 between Israel and the Arab world broke out in 1956 when Egypt, under Nasser, took over the Suez Canal. Israel, Britain, and France, who depended on shipments through the canal, felt threatened by this action and attacked Egypt.

The third war began in 1967. Egypt, Syria, and Jordan began to mass their troops along the Israeli border. Israel, sensing an invasion, decided to strike first. In the ensuing war, known as the Six-Day War, the Israelis defeated the armies of the three Arab nations.

In the next few years, little progress was made toward peace. Egypt's new leader, **Anwar Sadat** [än'wär sä dät'], who came to power after Nasser's death in 1970, insisted that Israel withdraw from all the lands that it had taken in 1967. Israel refused to withdraw until the Arab states signed a peace treaty that recognized the state of Israel.

In an effort to regain the prestige and land they had lost in the Six-Day War, Egypt and Syria attacked Israel in 1973, starting the fourth major war. An oil embargo led by OPEC, along with Soviet threats of involvement in the war, eventually persuaded the United States to pressure Israel to agree to a cease-fire in October, 1973.

Egypt and Israel made peace.

In an effort to break the deadlock between Egypt and Israel, and to persuade Israel to return territory it occupied in Egypt, Egyptian President Sadat flew to Jerusalem in 1977 and called for peace before the Israeli parliament. The Israelis were cautious, but they agreed to meet with Sadat in the United States.

After lengthy discussions among President Sadat, Israeli Prime Minister **Menachem Begin** [me nä'kem bä'gin], and U.S. President Jimmy Carter, Egypt and Israel signed a peace treaty known as the Camp David Accords in 1979. Egypt

sudden sharp rise in oil prices hurt the economies of both industrialized and developing nations.

From the Archives

The Camp David Accords

The Framework for Peace signed at Camp David, Maryland, in 1978, provided a comprehensive basis for a peaceful settlement of a long series of wars between Israel and its Arab neighbors.

After four wars during 30 years, despite intensive human efforts, the Middle East, which is the cradle of civilization and the birthplace of three great religions, does not yet enjoy the blessings of peace. The people of the Middle East yearn for peace so that the vast human and natural resources of the region can be turned to the pursuits of peace and so that this area can become a model for coexistence and cooperation among nations.

thus became the first Arab country to formally recognize the legal existence of Israel. As part of this agreement, Israel returned all of the Sinai peninsula to Egypt. Many people hailed Sadat's leadership as an act of courage, and he and Begin shared the Nobel Peace Prize of 1978.

The other Arab states, however, felt that Sadat had betrayed Arab unity by trading the recognition of Israel for Egyptian territory, leaving the Palestinian people to struggle alone for a solution to their problem. Egypt was, therefore, expelled from the Arab League and was not readmitted until after Sadat's death.

The Palestinian problem remained unresolved.

When the Israeli army occupied the West Bank and Gaza Strip in 1967, the Israeli government took over all the land that remained of the former mandate of Palestine. The Palestinian Arabs did not flee from their towns and villages, as they had in 1948, and Israel did not try to formally annex the area to Israel. The Israeli army sought to maintain law and order in the Occupied Territories, as these lands were called. The Arabs living in the

FROM THE ARCHIVES The official text is conveniently reprinted in *The Middle East,* 5th edition, (Washington: Congressional Quarterly, 1981), p. 254 ff. Point out that only Egypt and Israel signed the Camp David Accords in 1978.

increasing the number of Jews in the area. By the early 1990s, however, there were more than 1.5 million Arabs in the West Bank and Gaza Strip, and only about 60,000 Jewish inhabitants.

Occupied Territories had no political rights. They felt frustrated by the lack of solutions to their grievances, and they desired national independence and self-government.

In 1987 discontent among Palestinian Arabs turned into an open rebellion, or *intifada* in Arabic. Men, women, and children joined in strikes and stonings of Israeli soldiers. Despite arrests by the Israeli army, demonstrations continued.

In addition, the Israelis could not agree on how they should deal with the Occupied Territories. On the one hand, their annexation would mean a large number of discontented Arabs would become part of the Israeli state. On the other hand, to allow an independent Arab state to form on the West Bank would pose a threat to Israel's security.

For many years the PLO opposed Israel's very existence, pursuing a policy of terrorism to achieve that goal. However, in 1988 Yasser Arafat, the PLO leader, announced a change in the organization's policy. It recognized Israel's right to exist and renounced terrorism. Arafat hoped that this new policy, combined with pressure on Israel from the *intifada*, would persuade Israel to recognize an independent Palestinian state in the Occupied Territories. As the Cold War eased, the United States also hoped for a settlement of the Palestinian problem and persuaded Syria, Lebanon, Jordan, Palestinian representatives, and Israel to meet in Madrid, Spain, in 1991. These meetings opened the way for new negotiations for Middle East peace.

Section 3 Review

Identify Israel, Palestine Liberation Organization (PLO), Anwar Sadat, Menachem Begin

Main Ideas
1. How did the Arab states and the United Nations react to the desire of the Israelis to establish a Jewish state?
2. Why could the Israelis and Palestinians not agree on peace?
3. What was agreed upon in the Camp David Accords?
4. What caused the *intifada*?

Critical Thinking
Making Decisions: If you were a peace negotiator sent to the Middle East, how would you try to get the Arabs and Israelis to make peace?

INDEPENDENT PRACTICE/ HOMEWORK
Assign the Section Review, Activities page 229, or Workbook page 155.

CLOSURE
Tell students that after the establishment of the state of Israel in 1948, armed conflict became a way of life between Israel and the Arab nations on its borders. Egypt was the first Arab nation to recognize Israel in 1979. Disagreements about the political future of the Palestinians in the Occupied Territories led to strikes, demonstrations and deportations. Israelis themselves were divided over the disposition of these areas.

Answers to Section 3 Review

Identify
Key Terms, People, and Places are defined on pages indicated in parentheses. Also see the Glossary and Biographical Dictionary.
Israel (729), Palestine Liberation Organization (PLO) (730), Anwar Sadat (730), Menachem Begin (730)

Main Ideas
1. The Arab states wanted independence for Palestine and would not agree to a Jewish state there. The UN would have divided Palestine between Jews and Arabs.
2. The Arabs refused to recognize Israel, and Israel refused to give up occupied territories.
3. Egypt recognized Israel, and Israel returned the Sinai to Egypt.
4. Palestinian Arabs in Occupied Territories wanted independence.

Critical Thinking
Students should consider the history and situations of both groups, and their needs and alliances.

Lesson Plan

Essential Learning Objective

Students will learn to describe the development and type of each of the political systems in the Middle East.

1 FOCUS AND MOTIVATE

Ask students to name and describe the basic power structures of different types of government. Remind students, if necessary, of the basic concepts of theocracy, monarchy, dictatorship, and democracy. Direct students to look for ways that the governments discussed in this section responded to conditions in their countries.

2 TEACH

- Chart the political developments in each Middle Eastern nation covered in this section. Clarify the ways in which each government dealt with problems.

- Emphasize the causes of the Iranian revolution. Check to be sure students grasp why people would oppose change in favor of retaining traditional values. Discuss the policies of the revolutionary government toward the United States and reasons for the war between Iran and Iraq.

- Explain that Israel chose a democratic government because many of its people had knowledge of European systems. Turkey's successful modernization and secularization encouraged political awareness in its people.

---

4 Political independence brought experiments with new types of governments.

For the Middle East, political independence following World War II brought both new responsibilities and new desires. Minorities demanded more rights, sometimes violently, and more citizens wanted to participate in government. As a result, civil war and separatist movements plagued several countries. In addition, nations quarreled with one another over borders and ideology. During this period of turmoil, however, many nations experimented with governments that would be more responsible to their people or more effective in accomplishing national goals than pre-independence governments had been.

Egypt, Syria, and Iraq experienced strong leadership.

The nations of the Middle East came to independence without much experience in democracy. In some cases, such as in Egypt, strong popular leaders emerged who established a government that was at least partly responsive to the wishes of the people. Other countries, such as Syria and Iraq, turned to dictatorships in order to establish order and encourage progress in their communities.

Egypt. In 1952 a group of young Egyptian army officers overthrew the corrupt Egyptian monarchy, which had cooperated closely with the West. They then declared Egypt a republic. In 1954 one of these leaders, Colonel Gamal Abdel Nasser, became prime minister and later, president.

Nasser was committed to using all of his personality and power to make Egypt a strong independent nation. To help Egypt's poor, Nasser sought a more equal distribution of wealth. He promoted land reforms, encouraged industrialization, and developed the country's natural resources. The Aswan Dam, completed in 1970, was one of Nasser's major accomplishments. It was built to generate electricity for industry and to provide regular irrigation for agriculture. To help Egypt's international position, and to counterbalance Western influence, he developed close relations with the Soviet Union and other Eastern-bloc countries.

Anwar Sadat became Egypt's next president. He was concerned about the strong Soviet military presence in Egypt and their naval build-up in the eastern Mediterranean. In a dramatic policy shift, Sadat ordered all Soviet military personnel to leave Egypt in 1972. Thereafter Egypt shifted its allegiance toward the United States and signed the Camp David Accords with Israel.

Syria. Syria became independent in 1946, ending 25 years of French control. During their rule, the French divided ethnic and religious groups and prevented the formation of any democratic political institutions.

Because of this and other reasons, the first years of Syrian independence were a time of political instability. In 1963, however, a group known as the Baath party gained control of the government and ruled as a dictatorship. The party's goals were summed up in its slogan: "(Arab) unity, freedom, and socialism." The Baath party had strong support in the Syrian army, which had always played an important role in Syrian politics. In 1970 a general, Hafez al-Assad, became president, ruling Syria with an iron hand.

The Baath leaders adopted a socialist program that involved government control of all aspects of the economy. Their goal was state ownership of the means of industrial production and the redistribution of agricultural land. Although the domestic economy was a major concern for the Baath government, military expenditures were severe drains on national finances. A significant part of Syria's military spending has gone toward maintaining the presence of the Syrian army in war-torn Lebanon.

Besides foreign conflict, Syria's government faced serious problems at home in the late 1980s. A major challenge came from Islamic fundamentalists within Syria. A fundamentalist organization, called the Sunni Muslim Brotherhood, carried out more than 300 political assassinations in 1981. Although President Assad was able to keep Syria united through all the turmoil, it was at the cost of dictatorship and the absence of free expression.

Iraq. Iraq was one of the new states created after World War I. With the League of Nations mandate, Britain obtained control of Iraqi oil fields, second in size only to those of Saudi Arabia. How-

GUIDED PRACTICE
Ask students to identify the type of government in each nation and describe how problems are handled in that system. Also for guided practice:

 Overhead Transparency 76

ever, Britain was not able to create a strong united nation from the many different religious and ethnic groups that still make up Iraq's population to this day.

The various Iraqi governments that controlled the country after it gained independence in 1932 were equally unable to form a unified nation. After a succession of coups, the Arab socialist Baath party in Iraq, which is related to the Baath party in Syria, came to power in 1968, and has since remained in control. No opposition to the Baath party is allowed, and since 1979 one man, **Saddam Hussein** [hü sān′], has been a dictator.

The Iraqi socialist Baath party advocated nationalization of industry, land reform, and the introduction of extensive social services. One of its social programs, a national literacy program, was a major success. Following its economic goal of nationalization of industry, Iraq nationalized the Iraq Petroleum Company in 1972. With rich oil revenues, which increased fivefold in the 1970s, the Iraqi government undertook development projects.

The Iraqi government, however, also chose war as a policy. In 1980 Iraq attacked its neighbor Iran in order to seize control of access to the Gulf for its oil exports. Iraq ultimately wanted to become the dominant power in the Persian Gulf. A costly war followed, ending in 1988 with no additional territory for Iraq. Then in 1990 Iraq invaded its neighbor Kuwait in order to seize control of Kuwait's rich oil fields. Many nations objected to this act of aggression. The United States took the lead in assembling an international military force of more than 500,000 men and women. In a military assault known as Desert Storm, Iraq was driven from Kuwait in 1991.

Iraq's economy was severely damaged by these wars, but Saddam Hussein was able to remain in power. However, Iraq lost respect and friends among Arab nations and the world community. Allegations that Iraq used chemical weapons against Iran and dissident Iraqis, as well as plans for constructing nuclear weapons, concerned its neighbors. Saddam Hussein's bid to become the dominant power in the Middle East appeared to have failed.

Another difficulty Iraq faced was its Kurdish minority, which has attempted repeatedly to form its own Kurdish state. Kurdish dissidence increased during the Iran-Iraq war and following the Persian Gulf war, but Kurdish goals of independence remained frustrated.

A revolution convulsed Iran.

Iran is one of three non-Arab states in the Middle East. As you read in Chapter 33, Muhammad Reza Pahlavi became shah in 1941 and tried to modernize Iran in a very short time. Investing money from large oil profits, the shah began a program of reform and industrial development in 1960. He built

The Ayatollah Khomeini (below right) commanded a fanatical following (below left), who supported such moves as the taking of American hostages.

factories, schools, and highways, and advocated an ambitious program of land reform. He also emancipated women from some of the traditional Muslim restrictions, such as wearing the veil, and gave them the right to vote. An economic boom began in Iran, but the new wealth it created was distributed very unequally.

In addition, the shah was a cruel dictator. Thousands of Iranians were arrested and tortured to death by his secret police for criticizing the shah's policies and for wanting a greater say in the government. In the midst of this turmoil, the shah began a program of enormous military spending in the mid-1970s, with the intent of making Iran the strongest power in the Persian Gulf area. High inflation resulted, and unrest mounted.

The strongest opposition to the shah's government came from Muslim religious leaders. These religious leaders saw their authority being undermined by civil courts, which had replaced those run by the Muslim clergy. In addition, they believed that the shah's programs of modernization and his emancipation of women threatened traditional religious values.

Early in 1979 opposition to the shah's government peaked, and violent demonstrations forced the shah to flee Iran. The monarchy was overthrown, and a revolutionary government took command. Under the Ayatollah Khomeini, a new Islamic republic was established. Elections were held for a representative parliament, but candidates had to be approved by religious leaders.

The new government resorted to mass arrests and executions of opponents. Since the United States had supported the shah's government, America was denounced by the new regime as "the great Satan." In late 1979 militants seized the American embassy in Tehran and took more than 50 Americans hostage. After prolonged negotiations, the hostages were freed in early 1981 after 444 days in captivity.

Iraq and Iran disputed their borders.

In 1980 Saddam Hussein, the president of Iraq, suddenly attacked Iran. Hussein believed that he could take advantage of the weakness that resulted from Iran's struggle to regain internal stability after its revolution. Iraq's aim was to gain control of a waterway, called the **Shatt-al-Arab** [shät′əl-ä′räb], that divided the two countries and emptied into the Persian Gulf. Iran put up a fierce resistance, and by the late 1980s as many as 500,000 Iranians and 500,000 Iraqis had been killed.

Disruption of oil shipping in the Persian Gulf drew other powers into the conflict and threatened world peace. The United States sent its navy to the Persian Gulf to protect oil tankers and engaged in naval combat with the Iranians and Iraqis several times. The war proved to be the longest and most costly in lives and money of any war since World War II. A cease-fire was agreed upon in 1988, and the United Nations led negotiations to determine ownership of the Shatt-al-Arab.

Although Iran lost no territory, it suffered a loss of prestige as a result of the war. Its policy of sending hundreds of thousands of poorly armed and prepared young recruits into the front lines of the war, where large numbers of them were killed, was seen by other nations as cruel and pointless. In addition, Iran stubbornly pursued the war for many years in an effort to export its revolutionary Islamic ideas. Many Sunni nations besides Iraq, such as Saudi Arabia and Kuwait, were threatened by this attempt to export revolution and instability. Iran's revolution became discredited throughout much of the Middle East.

Israel, Turkey, and Lebanon worked for stability.

Democratic experiments in the Middle East have not always been successful. In the years since World War II, however, Israel developed a multiparty democracy, Turkey repeatedly returned to democracy between episodes of military intervention, and Lebanon struggled with a parliamentary coalition government.

Israel. The founders of Israel drew their inspiration both from the Jewish faith and from the political experience of Western democracies. They quickly established a democratic government based upon the Western European parliamentary model. Since 1948, a wide variety of political opinions have been expressed by Israel's dozens of political parties. At any one time, as many as 14 political parties have been represented in the parliament, the Knesset [knes′et].

3 | ASSESS AND CLOSE

ASSESS

1. What was a common need of poor farmers in most countries of the Middle East? (land redistribution)

2. What was the cause of the Iran-Iraq War? (Iraq attacked Iran to gain control of the Shatt-al-Arab waterway and to become the major power in the Persian Gulf.)

The Israeli city of Tel Aviv has mainly modern architecture. About 40 percent of the Middle East population now lives in rapidly growing cities.

During the 1980s the government of Israel was divided between the two opposing parties and their philosophies—the moderately socialist Labor party and the more conservative Likud. These two principal parties—with the support of the many smaller splinter groups—struggled to gain power and form a lasting government.

Throughout the 1980s, elections gave neither party a majority vote. By the early 1990s, however, Labor was forced to become part of a coalition government in which the Likud party held the upper hand. Likud pursued austere economic policies and an aggressive foreign policy, which included the invasion of southern Lebanon because of continuing terrorist attacks.

Turkey. Turkey, with a non-Arab population of more than 53 million, is the largest country in the Middle East. It is of major strategic importance because of its location. It shares a border with the Soviet Union and also controls the straits between the Black and Mediterranean seas. As a member of NATO, Turkey is also a vital link in Western Europe's defense system.

As you learned in Chapter 33, Turkey, like its neighbors, went through a period of rapid modernization under Kemal Atatürk. Before this period, the majority of Turkey's population had been rural, traditionally Muslim, and conservative.

Following Kemal Atatürk, Turkish leaders pushed programs of modernization and secularization, a domestic policy that continued after World War II. Modernization made the average Turk literate and politically aware. Urbanization proceeded at a rapid rate and individual expectations rose. The economy, however, could not keep pace. Although Turkey had some rare minerals and a modest industrial base, the country lacked the oil that propelled many of its neighbors' economies in the 1970s. As the price of oil increased, Turkey's economy suffered and many Turks migrated.

With chronic unemployment and inflation caused by Turkey's lagging economy, political and social turmoil developed. Groups opposed to the government at times turned to violence. Since World War II, the military intervened in the government three times in order to maintain order,

OPTIONAL RETEACHING

Guide a class discussion on how the governments of Syria or Iraq might become more democratic. (Students should grasp that internal conflicts make it difficult to achieve peaceful compromise needed in a democratic system. Education and high standards of living might enable the growth of democratic processes.)
Students also may be assigned Activities reteaching page 231.

OPTIONAL ENRICHMENT

1. Assign a group of students to make a chart that includes the following information on Middle Eastern nations: Form of government, Language(s), Religion(s), Literacy rate, Per capita income, Life span, Birthrate. (average)
2. Assign students to prepare reports on the extent to which land reforms have been successful in Egypt, Syria, and Iraq. (challenging)
3. Students also may be assigned Activities enrichment page 232, or:

 Source Reading 38B

INDEPENDENT PRACTICE/ HOMEWORK

Assign the Section Review, the Chapter Review items, Activities page 230, or Workbook page 156.

CLOSURE

Tell students that the leaders of Egypt, Syria, and Iraq often used strong methods to maintain order and to implement change. This in part was because during their periods under colonial rule, people in these countries did not develop democratic traditions. Fundamentalists rebelled against forced westernization in Iran and established an Islamic republic. Democracies were established in Israel and Turkey. Saudi Arabia's monarchy used its control of the nation's oil wealth to provide education, health benefits, and jobs in industry.

most recently in 1980. Each time, however, the military restored civilian rule.

Lebanon. This Middle Eastern country has struggled to form a stable government that fairly represents each of its many Muslim and Christian factions. During the 1970s Lebanon's government was a successful republic, but in the late 1970s, competing religious groups brought on a civil war.

By that time, the Muslims had grown to be more than 40 percent of the Lebanese population. When they were denied more representation in the Maronite Christian-dominated government, the Muslims refused to participate in either the government or the Lebanese army. Instead, the Muslims formed their own army. Eventually, each of the many religious sects had their own private, well-supplied soldiers. Lebanon became an armed camp of warring factions, and the government was unable to function as a stabilizing influence. Civil war ravaged the country, and law and order broke down. In 1982 Israel occupied southern Lebanon to restore order there, and in 1989 Syria sent its army into the rest of Lebanon to end the civil war. These foreign armies remained into the 1990s.

Saudi Arabia remained a monarchy.

Historically one of the most isolated areas in the world, the Arabian peninsula became an important focus of world attention in the 20th century. The peninsula is dominated by oil-rich Saudi Arabia. Smaller states, also rich in oil, make up the other one-tenth of the peninsula.

Political unification of Saudi Arabia in 1932 coincided with the discovery of its enormous oil reserves. Vast wealth in the form of oil revenues poured into the country and drastically altered what had been a traditional society. In the course of a few decades, Saudi Arabia's population became 80 percent urban. Most Saudis, however, did not share equally in their country's new oil wealth. The Saudi royal family remained firmly in control of these riches. It invested in modern cities and new industries such as steel mills and petrochemical plants. The Saudi government also invested in education and universal health care.

With its vast wealth, Saudi Arabia became a leader in the Arab world, rivaling even Egypt. Strongly opposed to the state of Israel, the Saudis gave gener-

A Lebanese student walks along a street patrolled by a Syrian soldier in Shiite South Beirut. Much of the city was destroyed in the long civil war.

ous financial aid to the PLO until relations cooled when the PLO sided with Iraq during the Persian Gulf war in 1990–1991. Saudi Arabia strongly opposed Iraq's invasion of Kuwait, which had brought on the war, and provided military bases and financial support for the U.S.-led international military operation against Iraq, Desert Storm.

Section 4 Review

Identify Saddam Hussein, Shatt-al-Arab
Main Ideas
1. How did Egypt, Syria, and Iraq benefit from strong leadership?
2. Why were the Muslim fundamentalists in Iran against the shah?
3. What were the results of the Iran-Iraq war?
4. In what ways did Israel, Turkey, and Lebanon try to achieve political stability?
5. How has Saudi Arabia's monarchy used its wealth to strengthen its nation?

Critical Thinking
Making Hypotheses: Imagine that you are a fundamentalist leader in Saudi Arabia or Iran, working to isolate your people from Western influence. Do you think that your mission is possible in our modern world? Support your hypothesis with evidence.

HIGHLIGHTS OF CIVILIZATION

Desert Agriculture

Someday the arid regions of the Middle East, once considered the granary of the world, may again be renowned for agriculture. In the past 30 years, Middle Eastern scientists have developed new technologies to boost the agricultural production of their hot, dry region.

For example, drip irrigation, which can increase crop yields in dry regions, was pioneered in Israel. In a drip irrigation system, plastic tubes feed a steady trickle of water directly to plants. Newly developed strains of traditional Middle Eastern crops—wheat, barley, lentils, and chickpeas—can withstand drought and tolerate salty soil.

Middle Eastern scientists are also experimenting with thin layers of asphalt about three feet beneath the surface of the soil, which can prevent irrigation water from draining below the level of crops' roots. Hydroponics is raising agricultural production particularly around the Persian Gulf. With this technique plants are not grown in soil but instead suspended in a nutrient-rich solution of water. All of these new agricultural techniques can help make the deserts of the Middle East bloom again.

Drip irrigation in Egypt (right) and an Israeli cotton harvest (below) show new farming methods in dry lands.

Answers to Test Yourself

Key Terms, People, and Places
The key terms, people, and places tested here were introduced in the chapter sections and reviewed in the Section Reviews. For definitions see the page references at the appropriate Section Reviews. Also see the Glossary and Biographical Dictionary.

Main Ideas
The main ideas tested here were introduced in the sections of this chapter and reviewed in the Section Reviews. For answers to these questions, see the appropriate Section Reviews.

Critical Thinking
1. The Middle East, with its tremendous reserves of oil, has tried to use its oil wealth to politically influence nations around the world, especially through OPEC.
2. Answers should include specific examples from the chapter. Among the causes are different religious beliefs, disputes over land, the desire of leaders for power, greed, and factional fights.

Section Summaries

Section 1
A crossroads of people and ideas characterized the Middle East.
Limited natural resources has played a significant role in the development of the Middle East. Rainfall is scarce and mineral resources, with the exception of oil, are rare. Three major language groups exist—Semitic, Turkic and Indo-Iranian. Three major world religions—Judaism, Christianity, and Islam—were born in the Middle East, of which Islam is the most prominent today. Besides religion, European imperialism also shaped the Middle East by creating artificial boundaries and preventing local economic and political development. The idea of Arab unity, pan-Arabism, developed as a reaction to Western domination.

Section 2
Economic development brought social changes to the Middle East.
Oil, the only mineral resource the Middle East possesses in large supply, has permitted many countries to invest in their own economies and increase their political power. However, many social problems still remain such as an uneven distribution of wealth, the rapid growth of urban areas, and the limited role of women in society. As a result, religious groups advocating a return to basic Islamic beliefs as a rejection of Western materialism have grown stronger in recent years.

Section 3
The Arab-Israeli conflict challenged the entire region.
After Israel declared its independence in 1948, many surrounding Arab states long refused to recognize its legitimacy. War has erupted several times, leaving many Palestinian Arabs as refugees. In 1964 the PLO was formed to try to replace Israel with an Arab state. In 1979 Egypt signed a peace treaty with Israel and became the first Arab country to formally recognize Israel. By 1987 discontent among Palestinian Arabs living in refugee camps on lands occupied by Israel turned into an open rebellion.

Section 4
Political independence brought experiments with new types of governments.
In 1956 Egypt, under Gamal Abdel Nasser, turned for support to the Soviet Union, but his successor, Anwar Sadat, established better relations with the United States. Civil war between the various Christian, Muslim, and PLO factions wracked Lebanon after 1975. Syria and Iraq both became socialist countries under the rule of dictators. Turkey modernized but faced economic and political problems. A violent revolution in Iran replaced the dictatorial shah with an Islamic dictatorship led by the Ayatollah Khomeini. Saudi Arabia became one of the world's richest nations with its oil wealth.

Review Dates

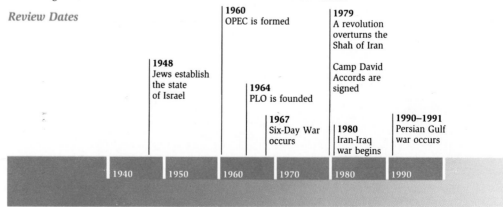

1948 Jews establish the state of Israel

1960 OPEC is formed

1964 PLO is founded

1967 Six-Day War occurs

1979 A revolution overturns the Shah of Iran

Camp David Accords are signed

1980 Iran-Iraq war begins

1990–1991 Persian Gulf war occurs

1940 | 1950 | 1960 | 1970 | 1980 | 1990

Test Yourself

Key Terms, People, and Places
Identify the significance of each of the following:

Section 1
a. Kurds
b. Gamal Abdel Nasser
c. pan-Arabism

Section 2
a. OPEC
b. Ayatollah Khomeini

Section 3
a. Israel
b. Palestine Liberation Organization (PLO)
c. Anwar Sadat
d. Menachem Begin
e. Algiers

Section 4
a. Saddam Hussein
b. Shatt-al-Arab

Main Ideas

Section 1
1. Identify the three major language groups in the Middle East, and give an example of each.
2. In what ways has the presence of Islam, Christianity, and Judaism in the Middle East brought both unity and conflict to the region?
3. For what reason did pan-Arabism arise?

Section 2
1. What has been the economic impact of oil on the Middle East?
2. In what ways have women's roles changed in the Middle East today?
3. For what reason is Islamic fundamentalism anti-Western?

Section 3
1. What was the reaction of the Arab states and the United Nations to the desire of the Jews to establish the state of Israel?
2. Why were the Israelis and Palestinians unable to agree on peace?
3. What was decided upon in the Camp David Accords?
4. What caused the *intifada*?

Section 4
1. In what ways did Egypt, Syria, and Iraq benefit from strong leadership?

2. What caused the Muslim fundamentalists in Iran to oppose the Shah?
3. What were the outcomes of the Iran-Iraq war?
4. How did Israel, Turkey, and Lebanon try to achieve political stability?
5. How has the monarchy in Saudi Arabia used its wealth to strengthen its nation?

Critical Thinking
1. **Assessing Cause and Effect** In what ways has the Middle East had a profound effect on the world because of its enormous oil supply? How has the region used its oil strength politically? Support your answer with evidence.
2. **Making Generalizations** For what reasons in history or in the present have wars started? Give some examples from the chapter.

Chapter Skills and Activities

Practicing Study and Research Skills
Using the *Readers' Guide to Periodical Literature*
As you learned in the Chapter 17 Review, the *Readers' Guide to Periodical Literature,* found in many libraries, is a useful tool with which to locate magazine articles for researching a subject. As with a card catalog, however, you may not always find your topic in the *Readers' Guide* on the first try. You may have to follow the *Readers' Guide*'s hints. For example, if you look up the general topic of "Middle East," you will find a list of related topics to check, such as Israel, Iran-Iraq war, and so forth. Select a topic concerning the Middle East and find the names and sources of three separate articles listed in the *Readers' Guide.*

Linking Past and Present
What do you think is the greatest problem from the past hindering the development of peace in the Middle East in the future? Why?

Learning History Through Maps
Compare the map of Israel, 1967, on page 730 with the political maps of Asia and Africa in the Atlas on pages 794 and 796. What comparisons would you make between the historical and current maps?

CRITICAL THINKING QUESTION LEVEL 1. average; 2. easy

OVERVIEW

This chapter describes the social and economic problems hampering development in Latin America today and the conflict and repression that have come with the efforts to build modern nations.

PLANNING CHART

Section	Text Pages	Key Concept	Suggested Teaching Time
1 Inequities in Latin America were inherited from the past.	741–744	Historical inequities coupled with population growth have created social pressures and demands for land and jobs.	One day
2 Changes took place in Mexico and Cuba.	744–746	Revolutions brought a degree of economic development to Mexico and a new dictatorship to Cuba.	One day **Less time?** Combine Sections 2 and 4 in a lesson on the revolutionary movements in Latin America. **More time?** Use *Source Reading 39A.*
3 Latin Americans struggled to become self-sufficient.	746–749	Argentina, Chile, and Brazil experienced years of oppressive military rule and, finally, hopeful signs of progress.	One day **More time?** Use *Overhead Transparency 77* or *Source Reading 39B.*
4 Central America became engulfed in conflict.	749–753	Guerrilla wars against dictators ravaged Nicaragua and El Salvador and brought United States involvement.	One day
5 Latin America's relations with the world changed.	753–756	Latin America's relations with the United States and the world became more complex.	One day **More time?** Use *Overhead Transparency 78.*

ANCILLARIES

Materials that may be used with this chapter to reinforce, reteach, enrich, and assess learning are pictured on the following pages.

Teacher's Resource File

ACTIVITIES

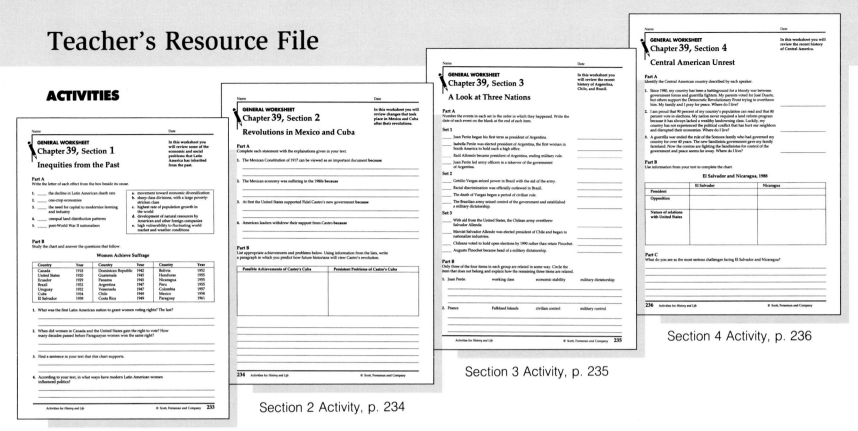

Section 1 Activity, p. 233

Section 2 Activity, p. 234

Section 3 Activity, p. 235

Section 4 Activity, p. 236

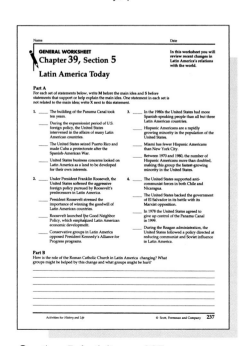

Section 5 Activity, p. 237

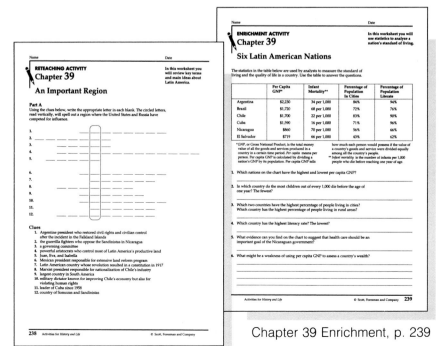

Chapter 39 Reteaching, p. 238

Chapter 39 Enrichment, p. 239

Teacher's Resource File

GEOGRAPHY SKILLS

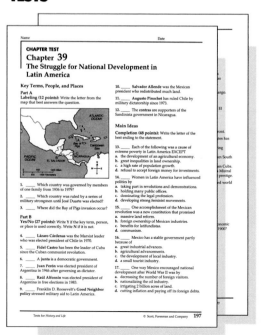

GEOGRAPHY WORKSHEET 39 Use with Chapter 39
Latin America Today

Part A
Locate and label the following on Outline Map 39. Draw in the rivers. Refer to text map on page 743.

Continents	Water	Countries and Territories	
North America	Atlantic Ocean	Mexico	El Salvador	Peru
South America	Pacific Ocean	Cuba	Nicaragua	Bolivia
	Caribbean Sea	Haiti	Costa Rica	Paraguay
Region	Gulf of Mexico	Dominican Republic	Panama	Chile
Central America	Amazon River	Grenada	Colombia	Argentina
		Jamaica	Venezuela	Uruguay
		Guatemala	Guyana	United States
		Belize	Suriname	Puerto Rico
		Honduras	Brazil	French Guiana
			Ecuador	Falkland Islands

Part B
List the following in correct chronological order in the blanks below. Refer to Chapter 39 in your text.

Allende is killed by military coup in Chile
Mexican revolution overthrows Porfirio Díaz
Juan and Eva Perón seize power in Argentina
Sandinistas take control of Nicaragua; Somoza is overthrown
Revolution in Cuba brings Fidel Castro to power
United States channels military aid to the Salvadoran government

1. ___
2. ___
3. ___
4. ___
5. ___
6. ___

Geography Worksheets for History and Life   © Scott, Foresman and Company   **79**

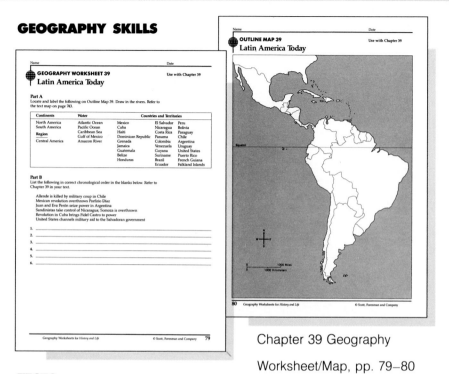

OUTLINE MAP 39 Use with Chapter 39
Latin America Today

80 Geography Worksheets for History and Life   © Scott, Foresman and Company

Chapter 39 Geography
Worksheet/Map, pp. 79–80

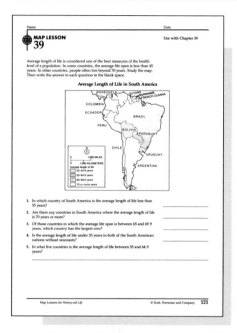

MAP LESSON 39 Use with Chapter 39

Average length of life is considered one of the best measures of the health level of a population. In some countries, the average life span is less than 45 years. In other countries, people often live beyond 70 years. Study the map. Then write the answer to each question in the blank space.

Average Length of Life in South America

1. In which country of South America is the average length of life less than 55 years?
2. Are there any countries in South America where the average length of life is 70 years or more?
3. Of those countries in which the average life span is between 65 and 69.9 years, which country has the largest area?
4. Is the average length of life under 55 years in both of the South American nations without seacoasts?
5. In what five countries is the average length of life between 55 and 64.9 years?

Map Lessons for History and Life   © Scott, Foresman and Company   **121**

Chapter 39 Map Lesson, p. 121

TESTS

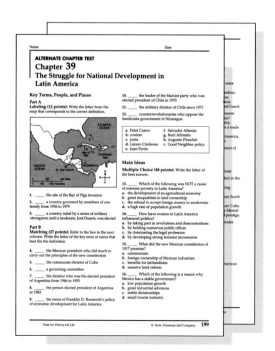

CHAPTER TEST
Chapter 39
The Struggle for National Development in Latin America

Key Terms, People, and Places
Part A
Labeling (12 points): Write the letter from the map that best answers the question.

1. ___ Which country was governed by members of one family from 1936 to 1979?
2. ___ Which country was ruled by a series of military strongmen until José Duarte was elected?
3. ___ Where did the Bay of Pigs invasion occur?

Part B
Yes/No (27 points): Write Y if the key term, person, or place is used correctly. Write N if it is not.

4. ___ **Lázaro Cárdenas** was the Marxist leader who was elected president of Chile in 1970.
5. ___ **Fidel Castro** has been the leader of Cuba since the Cuban communist revolution.
6. ___ A **junta** is a democratic government.
7. ___ **Juan Perón** was elected president of Argentina in 1946 after governing as dictator.
8. ___ **Raúl Alfonsín** was elected president of Argentina in free elections in 1983.
9. ___ Franklin D. Roosevelt's **Good Neighbor policy** stressed military aid to Latin America.

10. ___ **Salvador Allende** was the Mexican president who redistributed much land.
11. ___ **Augusto Pinochet** has ruled Chile by military dictatorship since 1973.
12. ___ The **contras** are supporters of the Sandinista government in Nicaragua.

Main Ideas
Completion (48 points): Write the letter of the best ending to the statement.

13. ___ Each of the following was a cause of extreme poverty in Latin America EXCEPT
a. the development of an agricultural economy.
b. great inequalities in land ownership.
c. a high rate of population growth.
d. refusal to accept foreign money for investments.
14. ___ Women in Latin America have influenced politics by
a. taking part in revolutions and demonstrations.
b. holding many public offices.
c. dominating the legal profession.
d. developing strong feminist movements.
15. ___ One accomplishment of the Mexican revolution was a new constitution that promised
a. massive land reform.
b. foreign ownership of Mexican industries.
c. benefits for latifundistas.
d. communism.
16. ___ Mexico has a stable government partly because of
a. great industrial advances.
b. agricultural advancements.
c. the development of local industry.
d. a small tourist industry.
17. ___ One way Mexico encouraged national development after World War II was by
a. decreasing the number of foreign visitors.
b. nationalizing the oil industry.
c. irrigating 2 billion acres of land.
d. cutting inflation and paying off its foreign debts.

Tests for History and Life   © Scott, Foresman and Company   **197**

Chapter Test, pp. 197–198

ALTERNATE CHAPTER TEST
Chapter 39
The Struggle for National Development in Latin America

Key Terms, People, and Places
Part A
Labeling (12 points): Write the letter from the map that corresponds to the correct definition.

1. ___ the site of the Bay of Pigs invasion
2. ___ a country governed by members of one family from 1936 to 1979
3. ___ a country ruled by a series of military strongmen until a moderate, José Duarte, was elected

Part B
Matching (27 points): Refer to the box in the next column. Write the letter of the key term or name that best fits the definition.

4. ___ the Mexican president who did much to carry out the principles of the new constitution
5. ___ the communist dictator of Cuba
6. ___ a governing committee
7. ___ the dictator who was the elected president of Argentina from 1946 to 1955
8. ___ the person elected president of Argentina in 1983
9. ___ the name of Franklin D. Roosevelt's policy of economic development for Latin America

10. ___ the leader of the Marxist party who was elected president of Chile in 1970
11. ___ the military dictator of Chile since 1973
12. ___ counterrevolutionaries who oppose the Sandinista government in Nicaragua

a. Fidel Castro	f. Salvador Allende
b. contras	g. Raúl Alfonsín
c. junta	h. Augusto Pinochet
d. Lázaro Cárdenas	i. Good Neighbor policy
e. Juan Perón	

Main Ideas
Multiple Choice (48 points): Write the letter of the best answer.

13. ___ Which of the following was NOT a cause of extreme poverty in Latin America
a. the development of an agricultural economy
b. great inequalities in land ownership
c. the refusal to accept foreign money to modernize
d. a high rate of population growth
14. ___ How have women in Latin America influenced politics?
a. by taking part in revolutions and demonstrations
b. by holding numerous public offices
c. by dominating the legal profession
d. by developing strong feminist movements
15. ___ What did the new Mexican constitution of 1917 promise?
a. communism
b. foreign ownership of Mexican industries
c. benefits for latifundistas
d. massive land reform
16. ___ Which of the following is a reason why Mexico has a stable government?
a. low population growth
b. great industrial advances
c. stable dictatorships
d. small tourist industry

Tests for History and Life   © Scott, Foresman and Company   **199**

Alternate Chapter Test, pp. 199–200

Other Optional Ancillaries

WORKBOOK

Section 1 Worksheet, p. 157

Section 2 Worksheet, p. 158

Section 3 Worksheet, p. 159

Section 4 Worksheet, p. 160

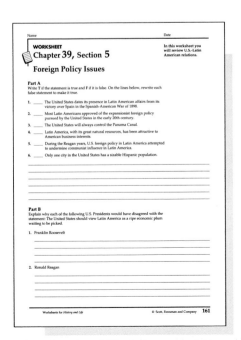

Section 5 Worksheet, p. 161

SOURCE READINGS

Source Reading 39A
Source Reading 39B

OVERHEAD TRANSPARENCIES

Overhead Transparency 77
Overhead Transparency 78

TEST GENERATOR

40 multiple-choice questions for Chapter 39

Chapter

39

1945

1947 — Women get the right to vote in Argentina

1959 — Castro takes power in Cuba

1979 — Sandinista revolution wins power in Nicaragua

1980

1990

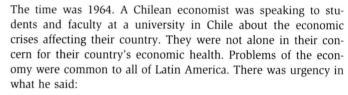

The Struggle for National Development in Latin America

1945–Present

The time was 1964. A Chilean economist was speaking to students and faculty at a university in Chile about the economic crises affecting their country. They were not alone in their concern for their country's economic health. Problems of the economy were common to all of Latin America. There was urgency in what he said:

> If the economy of Latin America continues to grow at the rate of 1 percent a year, it would take us 70 years to double the present per capita income . . . . To achieve the present per capita income of the United States, we would have to wait almost 200 years . . . . Latin America must accelerate its rate of development, for the needs of our peoples are so pressing that their satisfaction cannot wait the passage of several generations.

The desire and impatience for a better life have been powerful forces in Latin America in recent years. To understand this drive, we need to recall why Latin America suffers from such an economic dilemma.

In the late 1800s and early 1900s, the United States and many industrialized European nations began to pursue imperialistic interests around the globe. Latin America, a vast area rich in many resources, became a prime target for imperialism. Many Latin American nations supplied raw materials to industrial nations. In exchange, Latin America received the manufactured goods and capital that it needed for development.

With imperialism, Latin America became more and more dependent on foreign markets, products, and investment. Moreover, the money that did come into the region went to a very small minority of landowners and business people who largely neglected the needs of the rest of the people. As a result, Latin America developed into a region of many very poor people and a few very rich.

740

Glass skyscrapers glimmer in the warm Mexican sunshine. Bustling urban centers have grown up all around Latin America in recent years.

Reading Preview

In this chapter you will learn how the struggle for national development has unfolded in Latin America.

1. *Inequities in Latin America were inherited from the past.*
2. *Changes took place in Mexico and Cuba.*
3. *Latin Americans struggled to become self-sufficient.*
4. *Central America became engulfed in conflict.*
5. *Latin America's relations with the world changed.*

BACKGROUND Peninsulares, the Spanish-born rulers, made up the upper class. Below them were the creoles, the colonial-born white aristocracy. Finally, at the lowest level of society were

 Inequities in Latin America were inherited from the past.

The 20th century has been a turbulent period for much of Latin America. Contributing to this instability have been economic and social inequities inherited from the past, along with a high rate of population growth.

Extremes of wealth and poverty existed throughout Latin America.

Serious inequality existed among the peoples of Latin America throughout the 19th century. One reason for the poverty was that Latin American nations did not develop strong, industrialized econ-

the Indians, Africans, and people of mixed ancestry. Illiteracy, disease, and poverty were a way of life for most of them.

- Explain how one-product economies and foreign control of resources prevented local investment in Latin American industries. Students should understand that foreign ownership draws profits out of countries.

- Point out that land ownership by a few latifundistas kept most Latin American farm workers poor.

- List improvements in Latin America that led to a decline in the death rate. Stress that better health practices enabled more children to live to adulthood and to have children of their own. Ask students to tell what happened as large numbers of peasants sought better lives in the cities.

- Discuss the traditions that prevented women from open participation in Latin America. Point out the areas in which women have begun to be heard. (political demonstrations and revolutionary movements)

GUIDED PRACTICE

Ask students to compare life in U.S. and Latin American cities. Guide students in grasping that city governments in the United States use tax revenues from businesses and residents to pay for services. Latin American countries lack the industrial base and middle-class taxpayers of cities in industrialized nations.

BACKGROUND After World War II, a strong nationalistic movement developed in various countries throughout Latin America. The goal was to have a more independent economy omies. Most of the nations had agricultural economies based on the export of only one major agricultural product, such as sugar, bananas, or wood. Others relied on mining one mineral resource, such as tin, copper, or oil.

One-product economies can be unreliable. Prices for that product may drop or bad weather may ruin a crop and destroy the major source of income for a whole season. Without a reliable source of foreign income, most Latin American governments could not afford to modernize their farming methods or develop industries that would provide new jobs for people.

Moreover, most Latin American natural resources were developed by American and other foreign companies. For example, American companies controlled copper mining in Chile and banana production in Honduras. Although Latin Americans needed foreign capital, they deeply resented the foreign control.

Some of Latin America's most serious difficulties were caused by the great inequalities in landownership. Since the 17th and 18th centuries, most of

and a fairer distribution of wealth. The leaders of this movement said that rapid modernization and economic diversification offered the only hope of improving living conditions.

the area's productive land has been in the hands of a small group of upper-class creoles called the **latifundistas** [lä tē fün dē′stäs]. For years these powerful aristocrats refused to redistribute land to the landless poor. At the end of World War II, a few wealthy landowners held 60 percent of the land. Yet, 80 percent of all the farm workers were without land. Rural poverty was widespread.

Population growth increased social pressures.

Latin American countries have also had to grapple with the highest rate of population growth in the world. In 1930 the population of Latin America was 104 million. By the late 1980s, it had grown to about 450 million. By the year 2000, the population is expected to reach more than 600 million.

Ironically, the population explosion was caused mainly by a decline in the death rate, the result of better sanitation, epidemic control, and other public health measures. Birthrates, however, did not decline. Many Latin Americans have long valued large families. Roman Catholicism, the faith of most Latin Americans, reinforced this value, as did the economic need for more workers.

Rapid population growth created enormous social pressures. Many peasants believed they could escape the crushing poverty in the country by moving to the biggest city in their country and finding jobs. Millions settled in shantytowns,

Mineral resources form the base of many Latin American economies. Miners (above left) work in a Bolivian tin mine. Wells (below left) pump oil in Venezuela.

MAP STUDY Latin America encompasses Mexico, Central America, and South America—those regions of the Americas in which most of the people speak Spanish or Portuguese. What is the largest South American country? What immense river flows here?

ASSESS

1. Why do one-product economies not have dependable sources of income? (Falling world prices or bad weather can cause a loss of income for a year or more.)

2. What group owns most of the best land in Latin America? (the latifundistas, descendants from colonial times of upper-class creoles)

OPTIONAL RETEACHING

Draw vertical lines to divide the chalkboard into three large sections. Label the sections: Past, Present, and Future. Direct students to identify conditions in Latin America's past that led to problems today and to suggest changes that might bring improvements in the future.

OPTIONAL ENRICHMENT

1. Assign students to research and prepare a chart illustrating the size of populations of Latin American nations and of each nation's largest cities. (average)

2. Ask for volunteers to research and prepare written reports on industrial development in Latin American nations of their choice. Major products and exports should be included. (challenging)

INDEPENDENT PRACTICE/ HOMEWORK

Assign the Section Review, Activities page 233, or Workbook page 157.

CLOSURE

Tell students that many of Latin America's problems developed from conditions in colonial times. Traditions and economic need encouraged the large

which were poor residential sections, filled with crudely built houses, that began to ring cities such as Mexico City, Mexico, and Buenos Aires, Argentina. These peasants lived in flimsy shacks without running water or electricity, and with no sewage disposal or garbage collection. It is not hard to understand why these areas came to be known as *ciudades perdidas* (lost cities) in Mexico or *villas miserias* (misery towns) in Argentina.

BACKGROUND Land reform has been one of the major issues in most of the countries of Latin America because agriculture is the chief occupation in the region.

Women achieved rights and goals slowly.

Another inequity from Latin America's past was the dominance of men in public life and the arts. As in the United States, large numbers of women did not begin to enter the professions and gain status as teachers, professors, dentists, doctors, lawyers, artists, and writers until the 20th century. In most of Latin America, women did not get the right to vote until the 1930s and 1940s.

ANSWER TO MAP STUDY Brazil; the Amazon River

families that today seek better lives in the shantytowns around cities. Women have taken part in revolutions and political demonstrations demanding change and better conditions.

2. Lesson Plan

Essential Learning Objective
Students will learn to evaluate how well Mexican and Cuban revolutionary governments succeeded.

1 FOCUS AND MOTIVATE

Tell students that successful revolutions against dictators took place in Mexico in 1911 and in Cuba in 1959. Ask students to name demands that a new revolutionary government might face. (industrial development, jobs,

From the Archives

Living on the Edge

Jacinta [ha sēn'ta] Vegas, born in northern Peru, moved to Lima to search for a better life. Here she described how she supported herself and four children there in 1968.

I work for two days a week, and make two dollars a day. For three months during the summer I have work every day, and on top of that I get an annual bonus of twelve dollars . . .

We moved to this shed four years ago, and we own the site, it's a good shed, very solid, fresh bamboo mats in the walls. And two rooms! . . .

We spend about 20 or 40 cents a day. We eat porridge made from pea-meal or oatmeal. On Sundays, we eat porridge made with flour. Sometimes we manage rice and stewed vegetables. Never meat.

Latin American women, however, have influenced politics in ways other than by holding office. They participated in key demonstrations in Argentina and Chile in the 1970s and took part in revolutionary movements in Mexico, Cuba, and Nicaragua. Although Latin American women have not developed as strong a feminist movement as women have in the United States and Europe, their importance in public life, the professions, and the arts has increased in recent years.

Section 1 Review

Identify latifundistas
Main Ideas
1. What were the main weaknesses of most Latin American economies?
2. How did population growth affect Latin American cities?
3. How did Latin American women influence politics?

Critical Thinking
Predicting Effects: What would you expect to happen politically in countries where a few people control all the land and the vast majority have nothing?

FROM THE ARCHIVES The excerpt is from *The Shadow: Latin America Faces the Seventies*, by Sven Lindquist, translated by Keith Bradfield (Harmondsworth, England: Penguin, 1972), as found in *Documents in World History*, Vol. II (New York: Harper

2 Changes took place in Mexico and Cuba.

The buildup of social and economic tensions caused frequent political upheavals in Latin America, which often resulted in one military ruler replacing another. The upheavals in Mexico and Cuba, however, went far beyond a change in the government.

A social revolution transformed Mexico.

One of the most significant Latin American revolutions of the 20th century began in Mexico in 1911. Revolutionaries overthrew Porfirio Díaz [dē'äs], a long-time dictator who had protected the interests of the upper classes. The most important result of the revolution was a new constitution. The constitution, approved in 1917, called for universal suffrage (the right to vote), massive land reform, benefits for laborers, and restrictions on foreign ownership of land and natural resources. Putting many of these principles into practice remains a challenge today.

The Institutional Revolutionary Party (PRI), organized in the 1920s, has been in power since its formation. Throughout the 1920s and 1930s, the elected presidents of Mexico were army generals who did little to implement the social and economic reforms called for in the constitution.

The real breakthrough for reform came in 1934, when **Lázaro Cárdenas** [kär'THā näs] was elected president. Cárdenas was a dynamic young Indian from a poor family who did more to carry out the revolutionary principles of the new constitution than any other president of Mexico. During the six years he was in office, he broke up many large estates and distributed more than twice as much land to poor peasants than had been done by all previous administrations combined. Cárdenas' administration also started rural schools, taught the peasants better farming methods, and piped water into remote villages.The Cárdenas government also took control of the oil wells.

Mexico promoted national development.

After World War II, Mexico irrigated more than 2.5 million acres of land. Advanced farming tech-

& Row, 1988), pp. 191–192. Direct students' attention to the speech of the Chilean economist quoted at the opening of the chapter. Ask students for opinions as to how the excerpt by Gacinta Vegas reflects the economist's words.

niques used on this land helped Mexico grow sufficient food to feed its people for the first time.

In the mid-1950s, Mexico accelerated its industrial development. Within ten years it was producing its own iron, steel, chemicals, and electrical goods. Government development of a large tourist industry, concentrated along Mexico's Pacific coast and in the Yucatán peninsula, also strengthened the Mexican economy.

As a result of these efforts, by the mid-1970s Mexico had the fastest-growing economy in the Americas. Huge new oil discoveries promised even greater economic possibilities. More than a fourth of the Mexican people were now in the middle class, and Mexico had one of the most stable governments in Latin America.

In the 1980s, however, declining oil prices made it difficult to finance social programs. Mexico's foreign debt grew to one of the largest in the world, the country suffered from high unemployment, and inflation climbed to 159 percent by 1987. Many Mexicans felt the ruling PRI had become corrupt and incompetent.

Nevertheless, the PRI candidate, Carlos Salinas de Gortari, won the presidential election in 1988. His policy was to modernize the economy by privatizing state-owned companies. In 1991 Mexico signed a free-trade treaty with the United States in hopes of creating a stronger economic base.

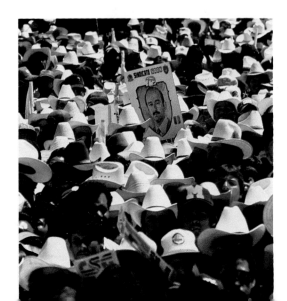

Revolution made Cuba a communist state.

The second country where revolution caused significant change was Cuba. The country was transformed from a corrupt dictatorship under Fulgencio Batista [bä tēs′tä] to a communist dictatorship led by **Fidel Castro** [kas′trō].

Castro was born in 1927, the son of a successful Spanish immigrant family. While studying law in Havana, Castro became involved in student politics, became a radical, and turned against the Batista regime. Arrested and then released from jail, he fled to Mexico in 1955. In December, 1956, he returned to Cuba with a small band of followers. For two years Castro led a guerrilla war from a remote mountain hideout. Batista reacted with a policy of repression so intense that he lost public support. On New Year's Eve, 1958, Batista fled into exile, and a week later, Castro and his forces entered Havana in triumph.

After the revolution, Castro promised free elections, democratic government, and far-reaching social and economic reforms. At first, Castro had the support of the United States. However, he lost this support when, in an attempt to consolidate his power, he failed to hold free elections, seized properties belonging to U.S. citizens, banned criticism of the Cuban government, and jailed and executed opponents. Thousands of refugees, mostly members of Cuba's middle class, escaped to the United States and other nations.

Some of these Cuban refugees, with the help of the U.S. government under President John F. Kennedy, tried to invade Cuba in order to topple Castro from power. However, their landing at the Bay of Pigs in Cuba in 1961 did not achieve any support among the local Cuban population. As a result, the **Bay of Pigs invasion** failed miserably. The invasion further strained the bad relations between Cuba and the United States, leading to an end to diplomatic relations.

Shortly afterward, Castro declared Cuba a socialist state, thus receiving economic and military aid from the Soviet Union. In 1962 the Cuban missile crisis (see Chapter 35) soured relations with the United States even further. Castro continued to anger the U.S. government by supporting guerrilla fighters and terrorist groups in some African and Latin American countries.

2. Assign students to research and report on Cuban trade arrangements with the Soviet Union. (challenging)

3. Also for enrichment:

 Source Reading 39A

INDEPENDENT PRACTICE/ HOMEWORK

Assign the Section Review, Activities page 234, or Workbook page 158.

CLOSURE

Tell students that revolution in Mexico led to far-reaching changes in land distribution, industrial production, and improved living standards. In Cuba revolution brought about a controlled economy under a communist dictatorship. Living standards were raised, but freedom was sacrificed.

Answers to Section 2 Review

Identify

Key Terms, People, and Places are defined on pages indicated in parentheses. Also see the Glossary and Biographical Dictionary.
Lázaro Cárdenas (744), Fidel Castro (745), Bay of Pigs invasion (745)

Main Ideas

1. a new constitution calling for universal suffrage, land reform, benefits for laborers, restriction on foreign ownership of land and resources

2. It irrigated land, improved farming, and developed industries.

3. communist dictatorship; promised free elections, democratic government, social and economic reform; improved health, housing, education

Critical Thinking

Perhaps Castro feared that such policies would unleash an internal revolution or that Gorbachev was straying too far from orthodox communist principles.

One of Castro's major goals was to make Cuba a strong industrial nation. However, the island nation of Cuba did not have adequate natural resources or trained people to develop its industry, so in 1963 Castro put aside that goal and turned to a program of producing as much sugar as possible. Sugar harvests, though, constantly fell short of Castro's goals.

Castro's government transformed Cuba into a socialist state. It took control of all factories, mines, and banks and confiscated large and medium-sized farms. It also provided better housing, more schools, and better medical care for workers and rural people.

Freedom of expression, however, was severely limited and human rights were abused. In 1980 more than 120,000 refugees fled the country, many to south Florida.

By early 1991 the Cuban economy was plagued by waste, inefficiency, and low productivity. Cuba faced its worst economic crisis in 30 years when Cuba's chief supporter, the Soviet Union, rejected communism, drastically reduced its aid, and stopped bartering low-priced Soviet oil for high-priced Cuban sugar. Castro, however, clung to Marxism and refused to allow major market reforms or democratic elections.

Section 2 Review

Identify Lázaro Cárdenas, Fidel Castro, Bay of Pigs invasion

Main Ideas

1. What did the social revolution in Mexico accomplish?
2. How did Mexico promote national development after World War II?
3. What kind of government was put in place after the Cuban revolution? What did the government promise? What did it achieve?

Critical Thinking

Making Hypotheses: In the late 1980s, Castro was one of the most conservative communist leaders in the world. He denounced the policies of *perestroika* and *glasnost,* introduced by the Soviet leader, Mikhail Gorbachev, and refused to allow them in Cuba. What might explain Castro's behavior?

---

3 *Latin Americans struggled to become self-sufficient.*

Unlike Mexico and Cuba, other Latin American countries did not experience full-fledged revolutions. However, unrest, discontent, and political violence arose from time to time, leading to a situation in which military dictatorships took control. The gross human rights violations imposed by these military dictatorships, involving torture and brutality, have caused an outcry among humanitarians all over the world.

Unrest and dictatorships troubled Argentina.

In 1943 a group of army officers, led by Colonel **Juan Perón**, seized power in Argentina. By settling strikes and making friends with labor leaders, Perón built an effective power base from which to run for office. Elected president in 1946 with the overwhelming support of Argentina's workers, Perón rewarded them with higher wages, paid holidays, pension plans, and health benefits.

Perón appointed his wife, Eva, to the post of Minister of Social Welfare. In 1947, largely through her efforts, Argentinian women were given the

Juan and Eva Perón had extravagant plans but left Argentina in shatters.

right to vote. Eva Perón also distributed government funds for education and relief and collected money from labor and business that was used to help orphans, the aged, and other needy persons.

Juan Perón started to industrialize Argentina, but there was not enough money to pay for his grandiose programs. Meanwhile, he neglected agriculture. This neglect hurt Argentina, one of the world's leading exporters of beef and grain. The world price of beef fell, and Argentina's income declined even more. Inflation then became a problem, destroying the gains workers had made. As unrest among the people grew, Perón's dictatorship became harsher. He attacked the Roman Catholic Church and suppressed newspapers. Dissenters were often jailed, tortured, or exiled. Perón was forced into exile in Spain in 1955.

From 1955 to 1973, one military dictatorship after another tried to solve Argentina's problems of high inflation and rising unemployment. None succeeded, not even the brief return of Perón and his second wife, Isabel, who were in the presidency between 1973 and 1976. The military took over again in 1976 and set up a brutal dictatorship in which at least 9,000 people in the opposition were arrested and then "disappeared," presumably killed.

Economic conditions did not improve. To divert attention, the military regime went to war with Britain in 1982 over control of the Falkland Islands and suffered a humiliating defeat. Free national elections were then held in 1983 and a civilian, Raúl Alfonsín, won the presidency. He restored civil rights but inflation continued. In 1989 Carlos Menem, a Peronist, was elected president. He cut spending and privatized state industry, but charges of corruption and involvement in the drug trade marred his administration.

Chile experienced economic and political changes.

Chile was another South American nation that experienced political unrest. Chile is rich in minerals, and mining is the leading industry. Chile is one of the world's largest producers of copper, which provides much of the country's foreign income.

In Chile, as in most other South American nations, land and industry have been in the hands of

General Augusto Pinochet, here dressed in full military attire, ruled Chile under a harsh military dictatorship for many years.

a small number of wealthy landowners and powerful business groups. Chile has suffered from rural poverty, labor unrest, and inflation. When the world price of copper dropped, these conditions worsened.

In 1970 **Salvador Allende** [ä yän′ dä], the leader of a Marxist party, was elected president, facing widespread discontent. Allende's government nationalized many large industries and copper mines, many of them owned by companies in the United States. It also took over the large landed estates and organized them into state farms. These programs disrupted the economy and created resentment among the middle and upper classes. The United States intervened against the Allende government by halting loans and private investment while continuing to send aid to the Chilean military. In 1973, with the approval and aid of the United States, the Chilean army seized control of the government. During the takeover President Allende was killed.

Between 1973 and 1990, Chile was ruled by a military dictatorship headed by General **Augusto Pinochet** [pē nō chet′]. A small group of officers led by Pinochet held tight control of both government and its citizens. Thousands of Chileans who

industries. However, inflation, rising taxes, and shortages of consumer goods led to widespread discontent.

1 FOCUS AND MOTIVATE

Ask students to define the conditions that are necessary for a successful democracy to exist. (Citizens vote in free elections and hold office, the majority rules with protections for the rights of the minority.) Remind students that the Latin American nations often wrote democratic constitutions modeled on that of the United States. Have students watch for circumstances that have made it difficult for the nations discussed in this section to establish functioning democracies.

2 TEACH

- Describe how Perón won and then lost the support of the workers. Discuss the events that led to the return of civil government in Argentina.

- Discuss Allende's actions. Explain which groups were angered and how this led to his overthrow. Describe the methods used by the Pinochet regime, and explain the significance of the 1988 vote.

- Emphasize Brazil's wealth of land and resources. Point out ways that industry and agriculture were diversified.

Sprawling urban shantytowns, such as this one, serve as unreliable and unsanitary shelter for millions of Latin America's poor.

opposed the government were jailed, tortured, or killed. Concentration camps were set up, the national congress dissolved, civil liberties abolished, and political parties banned.

Pinochet's economic policies, however, were successful. Inflation fell and living standards rose, although not all people benefited. Teachers, civil servants, and skilled laborers did not share in the prosperity. In the 1980s Pinochet's government moved away from kidnappings, murder, and widespread torture of political opponents, but it still restricted freedom of speech and used terror and intimidation against selected critics of the regime. No open elections had been permitted in Chile since 1973.

When General Pinochet asked Chileans to vote in a plebiscite in 1988 on whether they wanted his regime to remain in power for another eight years, the majority decided against Pinochet. In 1989 a civilian, Patricio Aylwin, won election and in 1990 took office as Chile's new president.

Brazil moved toward rapid modernization.
Brazil is the fifth largest country in the world. As you can see from the map on page 743, Brazil covers almost half of South America's landmass. It also contains more than half of South America's people. With millions of acres of unused land, the world's largest reserves of iron ore, and the tenth most productive economy in the world, Brazil has the potential to become a powerful nation.

Like many other countries in Latin America, Brazil depended for many years on the export of one agricultural product—coffee. As a result, the government was dominated by powerful coffee growers. In 1930, however, a rancher and politician named Getúlio Vargas [jā tū′lyō vàr′gəs] seized power with the support of the Brazilian army. Vargas, who made himself a dictator, wanted to reduce Brazil's dependence on the coffee industry. He therefore began programs of industrialization and encouraged the growing of crops other than coffee beans.

Vargas improved conditions for laborers, promoted elementary education, and restricted child labor. When he died in 1954, Brazil was well along the road to an industrial revolution—with large new factories to produce iron, steel, automobiles, and textiles. In the decade after Vargas' death, Brazil had several civilian presidents who continued his program of modernization. During this period the new capital city of Brasília [brə zē′lyə] was built in the interior of the country. (Find Brasília on the map of South America on page 790.

Much of Brazil's modernization depended upon huge foreign loans, and the country went deeply into debt. Prices rose quickly, and the government had difficulty repaying the loans. In addition, dishonesty and corruption became a serious problem in the Brazilian government. In 1964 the Brazilian army once again seized control of the government and established a military dictatorship. Until 1985 a series of high-ranking military officers led the Brazilian government. They crushed dissent, imposed censorship, and terrorized opponents. In 1985 a civilian was elected president.

Today Brazil is a land of great contrasts. The nation's 145 million people lead remarkably different lives. About half of all Brazilians are black or of mixed ancestry and about half of them are white, along with a small Asian population. The upper and middle classes, who live mostly in the cities and are primarily white, have benefited most from the nation's rapid change to an industrial economy. Crowded around the outskirts of those cities, however, are millions of less fortunate Brazilians. Most of these people are black or of mixed ancestry. Many live in sprawling slums with no electricity, no running water, and no sewage systems. They have few schools and are for the most part unemployed.

Some Brazilians say that blacks and mixed peoples are unable to improve their situations because of racial discrimination. Although racial discrimination has been outlawed in Brazil since 1951, many blacks say that a white social code effectively discriminates against them in employment, education, and other areas. These blacks say that although discrimination is often difficult to prove, statistics show that blacks generally eat less well, get less education, earn less, and die earlier than

whites. Brazil has made progress in modernization, yet it still faces the major problem of raising the standard of living among millions of Brazilians of black and mixed ancestries.

Section 3 Review

Identify Juan Perón, Salvador Allende, Augusto Pinochet

Main Ideas
1. What form of government has been dominant in Argentina? What problems continue to arise?
2. What economic and political changes have occurred in Chile since 1970?
3. How has Brazil attempted to modernize its economy?

Critical Thinking
Making Decisions: Imagine that you are a loan officer at a large American bank. Would you loan more money to Argentina or Brazil to help them develop further and improve the economy in their countries?

4 Central America became engulfed in conflict.

As you read earlier, Central America gained its independence from Spain in the early 19th century. Since that time Central America has been an area of instability and conflict. In the 20th century, the United States has often sent troops there to protect its economic and strategic interests.

Economic and social problems hindered Central America's development.

Central America has in recent years become a crisis point in the Western Hemisphere. Stretching some 1,300 miles, this lush, tropical region is made up of seven nations: Guatemala, Belize, Honduras, El Salvador, Nicaragua, Costa Rica, and Panama.

All the nations in Central America have faced the same problems. Limited industrial capacities, unequal land distribution, and dependence on a few export crops have contributed to the area's economic and political difficulties. Although con-

BACKGROUND Brazil's army rulers placed a higher priority on economic and social development than on the rights of a democratic government. They permitted a small amount of democracy by allowing the Brazilian parliament to meet. Despite

frequent rallies and demonstrations demanding an end to military rule, the army remained firmly in control until 1985.

have all been scarred by their years under military dictatorships and their unstable economies. Still, each country now has taken steps away from political repression and toward economic diversification.

4 Lesson Plan
Essential Learning Objectives

Students will learn to:
- identify the social and economic problems that are common in Central America.
- understand the roots and the repercussions of the conflicts in Nicaragua and El Salvador.

Ask students why events in Central America were, and still are, important to the United States. (trade, alliances, anticommunism, geographical closeness, strategic location to the Panama Canal) Tell students that the United States has intervened in the political affairs of Central American nations with some frequency. Direct students to look for areas of special interest to the United States as they study this section.

- Locate and identify the nations of Central America on the map on page 750. Point out Nicaragua, Honduras, El Salvador, and Costa Rica. Discuss the ways in which the problems in these areas were similar to those of other Latin American nations. Emphasize Costa Rica's uniqueness in escaping class and economic conflicts.

- Discuss the rule of General Somoza, pointing out the mixture of social reform and corruption that marked his regime in Nicaragua.

- Explain the symbolism of the use of Sandino's name by the revolutionary force that overthrew Somoza. Discuss U.S. motives in aiding the contras and point out that such aid resulted in controversy within the United States.

- Point out the extent to which political conditions in El Salvador seemed to improve. (political parties allowed, elections held, reforms begun)

Mexico, Central America, and the West Indies

MAP STUDY Central America includes the countries on the land bridge between Mexico and South America. Name these countries. The West Indies, nearby, includes the islands in the Caribbean Sea. What countries lie on the two largest islands in the West Indies?

ditions have improved somewhat since the 1950s, many problems remain.

Land reform, for example, placed more land in the hands of small farmers but did not increase production. Most small farmers couldn't afford the machinery and fertilizers that were needed to farm their land profitably. Other farm families received plots that had extremely poor soil or that were not suitable for farming, limiting production.

For most of their history, the peoples of Central America have also faced serious health and literacy problems. A shortage of doctors (except in Costa Rica and Panama) has made common health problems such as malnutrition worse. Illiteracy and lack of schools heighten the difficulties of many Central American rural residents. Although some progress has been made, millions of children have little or no opportunity to attend school.

BACKGROUND Deaths among infants and young children are very common throughout Central America. In parts of the region, almost 50 percent of all children die before the age of five. Malnutrition is also a major problem. In Guatemala, for example, almost 35 percent of the population does not get the food it needs to be healthy.

Like many people in South America, most Central Americans are poor, especially the mestizos—persons of mixed European and Indian ancestry—and Indians. The average Honduran, for example, makes only enough to barely survive. Most people must simply cope with poor living conditions, low incomes, and no health care.

One important exception to this pattern is found in Costa Rica. This country was never heavily populated and never had a wealthy class of landowners. It became, instead, a nation of family-sized farms with few landless peasants in the countryside and with prosperous retail businesses in the cities. These conditions have made a significant difference to Costa Rico's economic and social development. In the 1980s, 90 percent of Costa Rican people could read, and 80 percent voted. The voter-participation rate has been one of the highest in the world. Overall, Costa Rica has been a stable, democratic society.

Continuing social and economic difficulties have often caused political turmoil in Central America. The struggles pit conservative landowners and business people, on the one hand, against small farmers, laborers, and peasants, on the other. The military, usually a conservative force, has often seized control of the government and imposed its will on the people. Opponents of these governments have increasingly responded with guerrilla attacks, terrorism, and revolution.

Around 1900 events in Central America became more important to the United States. Goals of U.S. policy were to protect the Panama Canal and the sea lanes of the Caribbean. Over the years U.S. policy goals broadened. Maintaining trade with the region became important, as was preventing too much Soviet influence. However, with the end of the Cold War in 1989–1990, the Soviets greatly reduced their influence. The end of civil war in both Nicaragua and El Salvador also heralded a new era in U.S. relations.

Dictatorships have plagued Nicaragua.

A long series of rulers with unlimited authority controlled **Nicaragua** from about 1850 until 1936. Twice during that time the threat of civil war endangered U.S. economic interests in Nicaragua. U.S. marines were sent in 1912 and again in 1926 to intervene and to support the ruling government. During the second intervention, a rebel leader named Augusto César Sandino [sän dē′nō] conducted guerrilla raids against both the Nicaraguan government of President Juan Sacasa and the American troops.

After the U.S. marines left in 1933, Sandino threw his support to President Sacasa. Sandino, who had been declared an "outlaw" by the United States, was assassinated in 1934.

In 1936 General Anastasio Somoza, the commander of Nicaragua's National Guard, or army,

GUIDED PRACTICE

Have students write one or more paragraphs explaining why, in their opinion, the United States should or should not have supported the contras of Nicaragua.

At right, colorful paper kites are flown above a Guatemalan cemetery where crowds of poor villagers gather during the Catholic holy days. Most Central Americans are Catholic.

ASSESS

1. What group controlled Nicaragua from the 1930s to 1979? (the Somoza family)
2. What reforms did the government of El Salvador make in the 1980s? (Land and businesses were nationalized; free elections were held.)

OPTIONAL RETEACHING

Ask students to identify conditions in Nicaragua and El Salvador that led the United States to become involved.

OPTIONAL ENRICHMENT

1. Assign students to research and prepare charts comparing the seven nations of Central America, using almanacs or current encyclopedias. Information should include area, population, exports, per capita income, life expectancy, and type of government. (average)
2. Assign students to research and report on the Arias Peace Plan for which the president of Costa Rica, Oscar Arias, won the Nobel Peace Prize in 1987. A discussion of attempts to carry out the plan should be included. (challenging)

INDEPENDENT PRACTICE/ HOMEWORK

Assign the Section Review, Activities page 236, or Workbook page 160.

CLOSURE

Tell students that the nations of Nicaragua and El Salvador, like many other Latin American countries, have suffered from a lack of industrial development, a need for land reform, illiteracy, and poverty. Efforts to overthrow dictatorial and often corrupt governments resulted in revolutionary wars. The United States became involved in attempting to stop Marxist groups from gaining power.

forced Sacasa from office. Because the commander of the National Guard could not be a candidate for the presidency, Somoza resigned his military position. He was immediately elected president and within a few days reassumed his leadership of the National Guard.

Although elected, Somoza was in reality a dictator with total power. He supported some social reforms, including women's suffrage and improvements in education and public health, but his administration was corrupt and ruthless. Through changes in the Nicaraguan constitution by the legislature, which he controlled, Somoza remained in office for 20 years.

Anastasio Somoza was assassinated in 1956, but he was immediately replaced as president by his son, Luis Somoza. Eleven years later, in 1967, Luis Somoza's younger brother, Anastasio Somoza, replaced him as president. All three Somozas became rich at the expense of the common people of Nicaragua. The National Guard and friends and relatives of the Somozas enjoyed special favors and privileges while the Somozas ruled.

Sandinistas seized power in Nicaragua.

In the 1960s the Sandinista Front of National Liberation—a Marxist group named after Sandino, the rebel leader of the 1920s and 1930s—began guerrilla attacks against the unpopular Somoza government. As Somoza attempted to use the National Guard to wipe out the rebels, the **Sandinistas** grew stronger. With aid from Cuba, Costa Rica, Mexico, and Honduras, the Sandinistas launched a full-scale war against Somoza and the National Guard. Despite appeals from the United States for reform, Somoza refused to alter his policies or to negotiate with the Sandinistas.

In June of 1979, the Sandinistas began their final offensive. On July 17, 1979, Somoza fled to the United States, and the Sandinistas took control of Nicaragua. A five-person revolutionary **junta**—a governing committee—became the governing body of the country. Once in control the Sandinistas redistributed nearly half of Nicaragua's farmland from the rich to the poor. The Sandinistas took control of many other parts of the Nicaraguan economy. Political parties, although allowed to exist, were heavily repressed.

Because of these actions and because the economy did not improve, the revolutionaries lost the support of many Nicaraguans who had backed them during the revolution. Some of this opposition came from the Moskito Indians, whom the Sandinistas had tried to remove from their homes along the Coco River in northeastern Nicaragua.

As opposition to Nicaragua's new government grew, disillusioned Nicaraguans joined several groups that made up the **contras**, or counterrevolutionaries. Working from base camps in Honduras, the contras received aid from the United States Central Intelligence Agency (CIA) and other sources solicited by the Reagan administration. The contras repeatedly launched guerrilla raids and attacks against Sandinista units in the Nicaraguan countryside.

The Sandinista junta responded to U.S. criticism by holding elections in late 1984. Daniel Ortega [ôr-tā' gə], the leader of the Sandinista junta, was elected president. Restrictions on freedom of speech and the press continued, and so did attacks from the contras in the countryside. The United States, showing its opposition to the Sandinista government, ordered an embargo on trade with Nicaragua—meaning that they refused to do business with Nicaragua. This embargo was very damaging to the Nicaraguan economy because the United States was Nicaragua's chief trading partner. Looking for help where he could find it, Ortega developed closer ties with the Soviet Union and received shipments of arms. The United States became increasingly concerned about growing Soviet influence in Central America.

In 1990 there was a dramatic turnaround. In national elections, the opposition candidate Violeta Chamorro won an upset victory over Daniel Ortega and became the new president. Her goals were to work for a transition to democracy and to promote the country's economic recovery. President Bush lifted the U.S. embargo, promised economic aid, and helped disband the contras.

Revolution swept El Salvador.

El Salvador is another Central American nation that has been troubled by political violence. During most of the 20th century, this small nation was ruled by a series of military strongmen, usually

Daniel Ortega, president of Nicaragua, used a striking mural of the Sandinista hero Augusto César Sandino as a backdrop for a 1985 speech.

placed into power by a coup d'état, a sudden seizure of political power.

During the 1960s staged elections were held in which military candidates always won the presidency. Political parties were permitted, however, and they remained competitive with one another. After the election in 1977 of another general, Carlos Romero, many opposition groups joined revolutionary forces.

In 1979 a revolution swept Romero from office. In 1980 a four-man Revolutionary Government Council was established. This body carried out the responsibilities previously given to the president and legislature. José Napoleón Duarte [dü ar′tā], a moderate, was named president of the Revolutionary Government Council.

The Council began a major reform program early in 1980. All farms or estates, 1,250 acres or more in size, were expropriated, that is, taken from private owners for public use. Banks and certain export industries were nationalized. Redistribution of the expropriated land to landless farmers was planned.

Despite these moves, a Marxist opposition group, the Democratic Revolutionary Front, launched a guerrilla war in the El Salvadoran countryside. An offer of amnesty for guerrillas willing to surrender resulted in several hundred fighters laying down their arms. The Revolutionary Government Council also established an electoral commission and promised free elections for the legislature and the presidency. The guerrillas, however, continued to attack government troops and facilities. During this warfare, tens of thousands of Salvadorans were killed. Although the promised elections took place and Duarte became president, the war continued to rage.

Duarte died of cancer in 1989. The new president, Alfredo Cristiani, sought to end the crisis. Conservatives opposed a policy of national reconciliation. The guerrillas refused to stop fighting unless the government ended repression and made political changes. Finally, UN-sponsored negotiations led to a formal peace agreement in 1992, ending 12 years of civil war.

Section 4 Review

Identify Nicaragua, Sandinistas, junta, contras, El Salvador

Main Ideas
1. What are some of the economic and social problems in Central America?
2. Why was the Somoza dictatorship unpopular in Nicaragua?
3. Why didn't the United States support the Sandinistas?
4. What did the new revolutionary government of El Salvador promise?

Critical Thinking
Analyzing Comparisons: How are the political events in Nicaragua and El Salvador similar? How are they different?

5 *Latin America's relations with the world changed.*

Latin American countries have long hoped to decrease their dependency on the world's industrialized nations. As these nations searched for economic solutions to their problems, their role in world affairs changed dramatically.

5 *Lesson Plan*

Essential Learning Objective
Students will learn to describe Latin America's worldwide economic and cultural influence.

2 TEACH

- List the chronology of U.S.–Latin American relations from the 1930s to the 1980s. Emphasize the focus of each period.

- Identify the areas of the U.S. in which many Hispanic Americans live. Stress that Hispanic Americans are not necessarily immigrants. Puerto Ricans, for example, are U.S. citizens by birth (Jones Act, 1917).

- Discuss the importance of trade between Latin America and Europe and Japan.

GUIDED PRACTICE

Ask students why the pope would feel a special concern for the oppressed in Latin America. (Catholicism is predominant religion.)

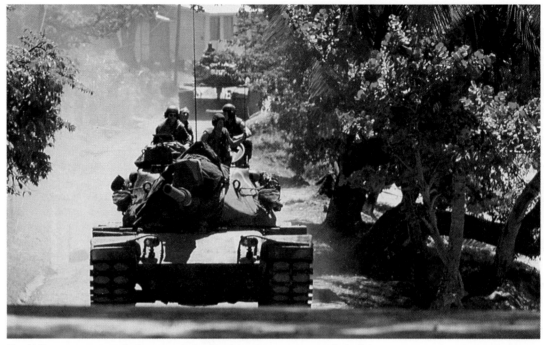

The U.S. government actively supported anticommunist governments in Latin America in the 1980s. U.S. soldiers are shown above coming to the aid of anticommunist forces in Grenada in November, 1983.

The United States developed vital interests in Latin America.

During the 1930s the United States, under President Franklin D. Roosevelt, softened the expansionist foreign policy that it had begun in 1898. President Roosevelt stressed the importance of winning good will in Latin America and launched the **Good Neighbor policy.** This policy emphasized economic development in Latin America, partly as a strategy to ward off the influence of Nazi Germany.

The idea of good neighborliness was extended under President John F. Kennedy in the early 1960s, with his Alliance for Progress program. The Alliance tried to promote economic development and social reform. However, conservative groups in Latin America opposed social reforms, and the program failed.

In the 1970s and 1980s, the U.S. government, particularly under the two terms of President Ronald Reagan, became fearful of the extension of communist influence in Latin America. As a result,

the United States supported anticommunist forces in Chile, El Salvador, Nicaragua, and Grenada. In 1987 the Iran-contra scandal shook the Reagan administration with allegations of the illegal transfer of funds from an arms deal with Iran to the Nicaraguan contra forces.

Late in 1989 the U.S. government, now led by President George Bush, faced a challenge in Panama. General Manuel Noriega, a military dictator who had thwarted free elections, was indicted in U.S. courts on drug charges. As tensions grew between Panama and the United States, Bush believed that the safety of Americans living in Panama was threatened and sent in a military invasion force. Noriega's government was overthrown, and the general was brought to the United States to be tried on drug charges.

Hispanic culture in the United States expanded.

Another aspect of United States relations with Latin America has been the growth of Hispanic culture in the United States. In the early 1990s, the United States had more Spanish-speaking people—more than 20 million—than any Latin American country except Mexico, Argentina, and Colombia. New York City alone had more than 1.5 million Hispanic Americans, most of whom came from Puerto Rico and other parts of the Caribbean. San Antonio, Los Angeles, Miami, and Chicago also had large Hispanic-American populations. Many of Los Angeles' and San Antonio's Hispanic Americans came from Mexico, and most of Miami's Hispanic-American population came from Cuba.

Between 1970 and 1980, the Hispanic-American population more than doubled, making this group the fastest growing minority in the United States. Demographers—people who study changes in population groupings—say that Hispanic Americans will become the nation's largest minority by the year 2020. The increase in population has drawn substantial attention in the political and business world.

Latin America gained greater world attention.

Latin America's position in world affairs began to change in the 1960s as Western European nations and Japan began to compete with the United States as major investors and traders. The investments of these other countries made Latin America dependent on a variety of nations rather than being solely dependent on the United States.

Countries such as Mexico, Brazil, Argentina, and Venezuela borrowed heavily from abroad to speed up their industrial development. When the world price of oil and other export commodities fell in the early 1980s, however, these nations could not keep up with their payments to repay the loans. Throughout much of Latin America, high foreign debt has left a toll on the environment. To pay off their debt, countries have tried either to industrialize rapidly, which often polluted their cities, or to boost agricultural production, which led to the destruction of rainforests.

DAILY LIFE

In recent years Hispanic culture has become more visible in the United States, influencing such areas as fashion, food, music, and architecture. For example, designer Ofelia Montejano (far left) has carried the jewel tones of her Mexican heritage into her fashions. In addition, Latin cuisine or its North American cousin, Tex-Mex, has become a staple for many Americans, as glorified in this delicious spread at New York City's Cafe Iguana (near left).

Gabriel García Marquez, left, and Gabriela Mistral, right, are two highly respected Latin American writers who both won the Nobel Prize for literature. Mistral, who won in 1954, was the first Latin American to receive a Nobel Prize.

Latin America's debt crisis shows how interdependent the world is. Mexico alone had borrowed from more than 1,400 banks in the United States and Europe. Brazil had borrowed from more than 1,100 foreign banks. Their loans amounted to so much money that, if they had not been able to pay back their loans—an event that was avoided by setting up new loan terms—many of these banks would have failed. These failures would have hurt the whole world's financial system.

Although political and economic events in Latin America during the 1980s were front-page news all around the world, other events were equally important. Culturally, Latin America gained much prestige during the 1980s through recognition of writers such as Gabriela Mistral, a Chilean poet, and Gabriel García Márquez, a Colombian novelist. Márquez won the Nobel Prize for literature in 1982. Latin American music also contributed to American jazz and other popular music in this era.

The Roman Catholic Church in Latin America has played an important role in the drive for human rights by actively calling for social reform and opposing repressive military regimes in Latin America. Pope John Paul II visited many Latin American nations in the 1980s, asking dictators to hold free elections and to halt human rights violations. The Church traditionally has defended the political systems that are in power. This new role of calling for reform has made the Church an important force for change in Latin America and has attracted worldwide attention.

Section 5 Review

Identify Good Neighbor policy

Main Ideas

1. In what ways has the United States been involved in Latin America since the 1930s?
2. What is the fastest growing minority in the United States? What do demographers predict for this group?
3. Name two ways that Latin America has gained worldwide attention.

Critical Thinking

Predicting Effects: How do you think having such a large Hispanic population will affect the United States?

756

HIGHLIGHTS OF CIVILIZATION

Latin American Literature

Latin America has produced some of the finest writers of our time. Their works develop universal themes, at once classical and familiar. These themes are expressed in passages of lyric beauty, striking imagery, and humor that frequently jolt the reader with a shock of recognition.

Four Latin American writers have won the Nobel Prize for literature: Gabriela Mistral of Chile (1945), Miguel Angel Asturias of Guatemala (1967), Pablo Neruda of Chile (1971), and Gabriel García Márquez of Colombia (1982). Many other writers have established worldwide reputations, including Jorge Luis Borges [bor häs′] and Alfonsina

The Mexican painter and muralist Diego Rivera drew Mother and Child *in 1926.*

Storni of Argentina, Carlos Fuentes [fwän′tās] of Mexico, and Isabel Allende [ä(l) yän′dā] of Chile.

Gabriela Mistral (1889–1957) was a teacher in rural schools, a diplomat, and a poet. The love of a mother for her child is a constant refrain in Mistral's poetry, as in the following lines from "Children's Hair."

> Soft hair, hair that has all the softness in the world, how could I be happy dressed in silk, if I did not have you in my lap? Each passing day is sweet and nourishing only because of those hours when it runs through my hands.

A nostalgia for a past golden age pervades the work of Gabriel García Márquez (1928–). His 1988 novel *Love in the Time of Cholera* is set in a stagnant tropical port at the turn of the century. García Márquez described its ruined landscape:

> Independence from Spain and then the abolition of slavery precipitated the conditions of honorable decadence in which Dr. Juvenal Urbino had been born and raised. The great old families sank into their ruined palaces in silence. Along the rough cobbled streets that had served so well in surprise attacks and buccaneer landings, weeds hung from the balconies and opened cracks in the whitewashed walls of even the best-kept mansions, and the only signs of life at two o'clock in the afternoon were languid piano exercises played in the dim light of siesta. Indoors, in the cool bedrooms saturated with incense, women protected themselves from the sun as if it were a shameful infection, and even at early Mass they hid their faces in their mantillas.

HIGHLIGHTS OF CIVILIZATION

Gabriela Mistral's poem "Children's Hair" is from *Selected Poems of Gabriela Mistral,* translated by Langston Hughes (Bloomington: Indiana University Press, 1957), p. 65. The excerpt by Gabriel García Márquez is from *Love in the Time of Cholera* (New York: Alfred A. Knopf, 1988), p. 17.

Ask students to describe the mood evoked in each passage. (serene, peaceful, loving; silent, withdrawn, isolation from the world) Ask students if they think the authors are writing in response to the mood or politics in their countries. (Opinion: Yes, Mistral is trying to find the softness and love in a brutal world; Márquez is evoking a place that is immune from the terrible troubles of the world.)

757

CHAPTER 39 REVIEW

Section Summaries

Section 1
Inequities in Latin America were inherited from the past.
Latin America entered the 20th century with a history of extreme wealth and extreme poverty. Most of the land belonged to a small group of wealthy people, and those without land had little chance of escaping poverty. Meanwhile, a population explosion created many new social and economic problems.

Section 2
Changes took place in Mexico and Cuba.
The 1917 Mexican revolution produced a progressive constitution, but changes were slow in coming. Social reform and industrial development moved ahead, but declining oil prices created foreign debt. In Cuba Fidel Castro led a revolution in 1959—promising free elections and democratic government. Castro, however, eventually lost the support of the United States and declared Cuba a socialist state. Castro received massive Soviet aid, but such help fell sharply after the breakup of the Soviet Union in 1991.

Section 3
Latin Americans struggled to become self-sufficient.
After a long history of harsh dictators, Argentina is today under civilian control but has one of the highest foreign debts in the world. In Chile Salvador Allende, who became president in 1970, was overthrown by the Chilean army and replaced by Augusto Pinochet, a harsh military dictator. In Brazil a military dictator seized power in 1930. He began to industrialize and to encourage the growing of crops other than coffee. Today Brazil has moved toward both these goals, but the country is still burdened with an enormous national debt and sprawling slums.

Section 4
Central America became engulfed in conflict.
Limited industrial capacity, unequal land distribution, and dependence on only a few export crops have contributed to the area's difficulties. Serious health problems and illiteracy are also common. Most Central American nations were ruled by dictators for much of the 20th century. In recent years political violence has been particularly intense in Nicaragua and El Salvador.

Section 5
Latin America's relations with the world changed.
Although its presence is often resented, the United States has a strong interest in the Panama Canal as well as in the economic potential of Latin America. Meanwhile, Latin American culture is being recognized internationally, especially in the area of literature. In addition, the Hispanic population in the United States is growing at a rapid rate.

Review Dates

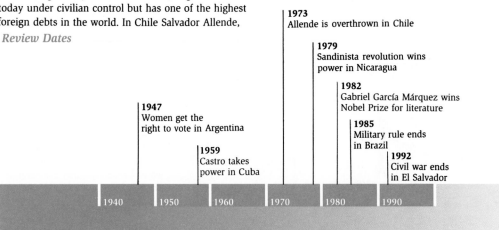

1973 Allende is overthrown in Chile

1979 Sandinista revolution wins power in Nicaragua

1982 Gabriel García Márquez wins Nobel Prize for literature

1985 Military rule ends in Brazil

1992 Civil war ends in El Salvador

1947 Women get the right to vote in Argentina

1959 Castro takes power in Cuba

1940   1950   1960   1970   1980   1990

Test Yourself

Key Terms, People, and Places
Identify the significance of each of the following:

Section 1
a. latifundistas

Section 2
a. Lázaro Cárdenas   c. Bay of Pigs invasion
b. Fidel Castro

Section 3
a. Juan Perón   c. Augusto Pinochet
b. Salvador Allende

Section 4
a. Nicaragua   d. contras
b. Sandinistas   e. El Salvador
c. junta

Section 5
a. Good Neighbor policy

Main Ideas

Section 1
1. What were the most important problems facing Latin American economies?
2. Why is there so much poverty in the cities?
3. Name two ways that Latin American women became active in politics.

Section 2
1. What social changes were written into the new Mexican constitution?
2. How did Mexico move toward national development?
3. What form of government did Castro put in place?

Section 3
1. What kind of leaders and economic challenges have dominated Argentina?
2. In Chile how was Pinochet different from Allende?
3. What steps has Brazil taken toward modernization?

Section 4
1. What economic and social problems plague most Central American economies?
2. How did the United States respond to the Sandinistas in Nicaragua?
3. What did the Sandinistas do after the revolution?
4. What changes did Duarte try to make in El Salvador?

Section 5
1. For what reasons did the United States become interested in Latin America in the early 1900s?
2. How does the growth in number of Hispanic Americans compare with that of other minority groups?
3. What has brought Latin America to the public eye?

Critical Thinking

1. **Making Hypotheses** Sandino, the Nicaraguan rebel leader, was considered an "outlaw." What other leaders were considered outlaws? Why?

2. **Assessing Cause and Effect** Considering what you have read in this and earlier chapters, why do you think that so many Latin American countries are challenged with instability?

Chapter Skills and Activities

Practicing Study and Research Skills

Recognizing Bias
When reading about recent history or current events, one of the most important skills you need is the ability to recognize bias. A biased statement or term is one based on emotion or prejudice instead of on a rational consideration of facts.

Popular opinion was strongly divided over the proper role of the United States in the Nicaraguan war. In this debate there were two labels for the faction that opposed the Sandinistas. Some called them "contras" (or counterrevolutionaries); others called them "freedom fighters." What bias is revealed in each label?

Linking Past and Present
The inequities in Latin America existed long before the 19th and 20th centuries. So did the three social ranks of peninsulares, creoles, and mestizos. When did these inequities begin?

Learning History Through Maps
Using the map on page 750, find the country of Panama. Why do you think that the Panama Canal would be of significant interest to the United States?

CRITICAL THINKING QUESTION LEVEL 1. challenging; 2. average

---

40 An Interdependent World

OVERVIEW

Chapter 40 examines two sets of problems—the economic gap between the West and developing countries and environmental concerns that confront us all.

PLANNING CHART

Section	Text Pages	Key Concept	Suggested Teaching Time
1 The world has become economically interdependent.	761–764	International economic interdependence brought into focus the vast distance between Western market economies and economically developing nations.	One day **More time?** Use *Overhead Transparency 79* or *Source Reading 40A.*
2 Our global society faces many environmental challenges	764–769	The environment has been under siege for more than a century and shows signs of serious injury.	One day **Less time?** Read Section 1 aloud in class and proceed to discuss Section 2 at greater length .
3 Futurists predict what the world will be like.	770–772	Malthusians, expansionists, and ecologists predict the future, which really lies in our collective hands.	One day **More time?** Use *Overhead Transparency 80* or *Source Reading 40B.*

ANCILLARIES

Materials that may be used with this chapter to reinforce, reteach, enrich, and assess learning are pictured on the following pages.

Teacher's Resource File

ACTIVITIES

Examine the graph and answer the questions that follow.

The World's GNP

1. Why might other countries be concerned about the economic policies of the United States?

2. What does this chart suggest about the possibility that the Soviet Union will economically surpass the United States and other Western nations within this century?

3. How does this chart support your text's description of the world economy?

Section 1 Activity, p. 240

GENERAL WORKSHEET
Chapter **40**, Section **2**

Environmental Issues

In this worksheet you will review the adverse effects of several environmental conditions.

Part A
Complete each chain of events by using the terms from the box.

| burning of certain types of coal | → | | → | destruction of ecosystems in rivers and forests |

| clearing of forests and gathering of wood | → | | → | decline in world supply of oxygen |

| overgrazing, poor irrigation systems, overuse of agricultural land | → | | → | decline in world food supply; increase in uninhabitable land acreage |

| acid rain | desertification | deforestation |

Part B
Examine the cartoon and check any statements below that the cartoon supports.

PESTICYCLE

____ Technology has led to environmental problems.
____ The term "pesticycle" refers to a single action by human beings.
____ Global warming is a gradual process.
____ People should be concerned with preservation of the environment.
____ Eventually people will pay for their careless interference with nature.
____ A single action can have many consequences.

Section 2 Activity, p. 241

GENERAL WORKSHEET
Chapter **40**, Section **3**

Three Futurist World Views

In this worksheet you will review the three world views described in your text: Malthusian, expansionist, and ecological.

Part A
Read the description of the three futurist world views in the center column. Identify each view in the first column, and write one strategy advanced by each group in the third column.

World View	Description	Proposed Strategy for the Future
	a pessimistic view that holds that modern society is too complex to deal with its problems	
	an optimistic view that predicts that science and technology will solve problems	
	a view that holds that the world and its parts are interconnected	

Part B
Use the above chart and your text to answer the following questions.

1. What would be the purpose of the world government advanced by the Malthusians?

2. How would an expansionist respond to the Malthusian prediction about nature's inability to meet humanity's demands on its resources?

3. What do you see as the major differences between the expansionist and ecological points of view?

Section 3 Activity, p. 242

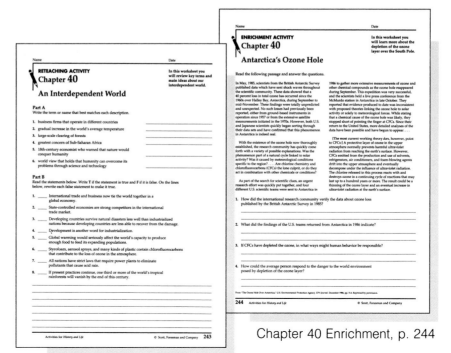

RETEACHING ACTIVITY
Chapter **40**

An Interdependent World

In this worksheet you will review key terms and main ideas about our interdependent world.

Part A
Write the term or name that best matches each description.

1. business firms that operate in different countries
2. gradual increase in the world's average temperature
3. large-scale clearing of forests
4. greatest concern of Sub-Saharan Africa
5. 18th-century economist who warned that nature would conquer humanity
6. world view that holds that humanity can overcome its problems through science and technology

Part B
Read the statements below. Write T if the statement is true and F if it is false. On the lines below, rewrite each false statement to make it true.

1. ____ International trade and business now tie the world together in a global economy.
2. ____ State-controlled economies are strong competitors in the international trade market.
3. ____ Developing countries survive natural disasters less well than industrialized nations because developing countries are less able to recover from the damage.
4. ____ Development is another word for industrialization.
5. ____ Global warming would seriously affect the world's capacity to produce enough food to feed its expanding populations.
6. ____ Styrofoam, aerosol sprays, and many kinds of plastic contain chlorofluorocarbons that contribute to the loss of ozone in the atmosphere.
7. ____ All nations have strict laws that require power plants to eliminate pollutants that cause acid rain.
8. ____ If present practices continue, one third or more of the world's tropical rainforests will vanish by the end of this century.

Chapter 40 Reteaching, p. 243

ENRICHMENT ACTIVITY
Chapter **40**

Antarctica's Ozone Hole

In this worksheet you will learn more about the depletion of the ozone layer over the South Pole.

Read the following passage and answer the questions.

In May, 1985, scientists from the British Antarctic Survey published data which have sent shock waves throughout the scientific community. These data showed that a 40 percent loss in total ozone has occurred since the 1960s over Halley Bay, Antarctica, during September to mid-November. These findings were totally unpredicted and unexpected. No such losses had previously been reported, either from ground-based instruments in operation since 1957 or from the extensive satellite measurements initiated in the 1970s. However, both U.S. and Japanese scientists quickly began sorting through their data sets and have confirmed that this phenomenon in Antarctica is indeed real.

With the existence of the ozone hole now thoroughly established, the research community has quickly come forth with a variety of possible explanations. Was the phenomenon part of a natural cycle linked to solar activity? Was it caused by meteorological conditions specific to the region? . . . Are chlorine chemistry and chlorofluorocarbons (CFCs) the lone culprit, or do they act in combination with other chemicals or conditions?

As part of the search for scientific clues, an urgent research effort was quickly put together, and four different U.S. scientific teams were sent to Antarctica in 1986 to gather more extensive measurements of ozone and other chemical compounds as the ozone hole reappeared during September. This expedition was very successful, and the scientists held a live press conference from the McMurdo station in Antarctica in late October. They reported that evidence produced to date was inconsistent with proposed theories linking the ozone hole to solar activity or solely to meteorological forces. While stating that a chemical cause of the ozone hole was likely, they stopped short of pointing the finger at CFCs. Since their return to the United States, more detailed analyses of the data have been possible and have begun to appear. . . .

[The most current working theory does, however, point to CFCs] A protective layer of ozone in the upper atmosphere normally prevents harmful ultraviolet radiation from reaching the earth's surface. However, CFCs emitted from the production and use of solvents, refrigerators, air conditioners, and foam-blowing agents drift into the upper atmosphere and eventually decompose under the influence of ultraviolet radiation. The chlorine released in this process reacts with and destroys ozone in a continuing cycle of reactions that may last up to a hundred years or more. The result could be a thinning of the ozone layer and an eventual increase in ultraviolet radiation at the earth's surface.

1. How did the international research community verify the data about ozone loss published by the British Antarctic Survey in 1985?

2. What did the findings of the U.S. teams returned from Antarctica in 1986 indicate?

3. If CFCs have depleted the ozone, in what ways might human behavior be responsible?

4. How could the average person respond to the danger to the world environment posed by depletion of the ozone layer?

From "The Ozone Hole Over America," U.S. Environmental Protection Agency, EPA Journal, December 1986, pp. 3-6. Reprinted by permission.

Chapter 40 Enrichment, p. 244

Teacher's Resource File

GEOGRAPHY SKILLS

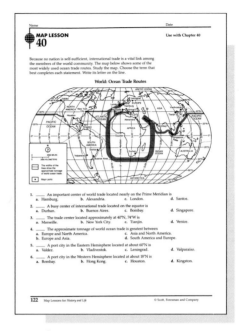

Chapter 40 Geography
Worksheet/Map, pp. 81–82

Chapter 40 Map Lesson, p. 122

TESTS

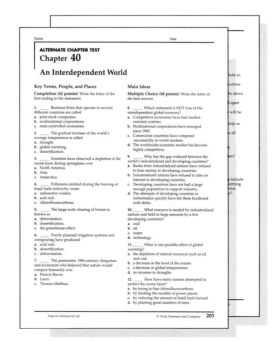

Chapter Test, pp. 201–202

Alternate Chapter Test, pp. 203–204

Other Optional Ancillaries

WORKBOOK

Section 1 Worksheet, p. 162

Section 2 Worksheet, p. 163

Section 3 Worksheet, p. 164

SOURCE READINGS

Source Reading 40A
Source Reading 40B

TEST GENERATOR

40 multiple-choice questions for Chapter 40

OVERHEAD TRANSPARENCIES

Overhead Transparency 79
Overhead Transparency 80

40

An Interdependent World

1945 – Present

1970

1980

1987   International leaders meet to save ozone layer

1988   INF Treaty calls for destruction of intermediate-range nuclear missiles

1990

2000

To many thinkers, the 20th century has been a period notable for its abrupt, dramatic changes. Perhaps the most significant change has been the emergence of our interdependent, global society—a society whose members have become more dependent upon one another economically, politically, and culturally than ever before in history.

Our global society developed for a variety of reasons. The most important reason, however, is the global economy that has emerged since World War II. In the global economy of the 20th century, international trade brings Middle East oil to Japan, Japanese automobiles to the United States, U.S. computers to Europe, and European manufactured goods to Africa. With the aid of the computer, corporations with headquarters in one nation keep in close contact with their branches in other countries. Banks from industrialized nations loan money to developing countries in Latin America, Africa, and Asia. The nonpayment of these loans may well cause the failure of these banks in the United States, Western Europe, and Japan.

The enormous advances in science and technology that have occurred in the 20th century have not solved all of humanity's problems. Indeed they have caused quite a few of their own. Environmental concerns have begun to weigh heavily on the minds of many people, concerns that are demanding an immediate response. The world's air, water, and soil are becoming contaminated with poisons and nuclear wastes; deserts are advancing into once arable land; and vast rainforests are disappearing—all at an incredibly rapid pace.

What will be the consequences if we fail to meet the many challenges that our interdependent world presents? What does the future hold for us in a world where a crisis in one part of the world affects nations on the opposite side of the globe?

The electronic telephone switching equipment shown in this photograph symbolizes the complex communication network that links all parts of the globe.

Reading Preview

In this chapter you will learn about the challenges that face the modern world.

1. *The world has become economically interdependent.*
2. *Our global society faces many environmental challenges.*
3. *Futurists predict what the world will be like.*

The world has become economically interdependent.

The most striking aspect of interdependence is its economic dimension. Although the world is politically divided into more than 150 independent nations, economically it has become one vast integrated system. The growing population of the world has also had an impact upon the world's economic system.

- Ask why an American or West German corporation might build a factory in Taiwan or Brazil. Discuss labor costs and tax breaks. Is this in the best interest of the developing nation? (Pros: Jobs and foreign capital come into the nation. Cons: Big profits are taken out of the nation, leading to charges of labor exploitation.)

- Have students look at the world map in the Atlas and note that North America, Europe, and Japan are all north of the Tropic of Cancer; in contrast, the bulk of developing nations are to the south. Ask students why certain writers in recent years have written about the new "war" between the North and the South.

- population projections show that in the year 2000, of the largest 43 cities in the world, 31 will be in developing nations. Mexico City (28 million), São Paulo (25 million), Seoul (22 million), and Bombay (15 million) will be in the top five.

- Ask students to consider the pros and cons of allowing developing nations to default on a portion of their international debt.

- Explain how high-priced oil provided a false collateral for loans to oil-producing countries, such as Mexico. (When the price of oil fell, such countries were unable to pay their debts and both they and their creditors suffered.)

GUIDED PRACTICE

Using the Atlas, ask students to list developed nations south of the Tropic of Cancer and less developed nations north of the Tropic of Cancer. Does

---

From the Archives

The Poor Are Wonderful People

Mother Teresa (1910–) is a Roman Catholic nun who was born in Albania and has spent most of her life working with the poor in India. In 1949 she founded the Missionaries of Charity to serve the poor, first in India, then in other parts of the world. She received the Nobel Peace Prize for her work in 1979. In the following passage, Mother Teresa tells why she wanted to help the poor.

Our poor are very great people, very lovable people. We don't know them, that's why we can't love them. And if we don't love them, we can't serve them. That's why I beg you: try to find your poor here, first in your own home. Don't allow anybody to be lonely, to feel unwanted, unloved, but especially your own, especially your neighbor. . . .

There is no great difference in the reality of one country or another, because it is always people you meet everywhere. They may look different or be dressed differently, or may have a different education or position. But they are all the same. They are all people to be loved. They are all hungry for love. . . .

[The poor] are great people! They are very lovable people!

Business and trade circled the globe.

The interdependence of the global economy has been most evident in areas of business and trade. A key development of the 1980s was the rapid emergence of **multinational corporations**, business firms of the industrialized nations that operated in a number of different countries.

From the 1960s to the 1980s, major companies from the United States, Western Europe, and Japan located their factories wherever labor was cheap and local governments were willing to grant financial benefits such as tax breaks. These conditions were found primarily in developing countries. The

FROM THE ARCHIVES Mother Teresa of Calcutta, *My Life for the Poor* (New York: Harper & Row, 1985), 71–72, 82. Note how Mother Teresa approaches her work: First we must know people, which leads to loving them, and then to serving them.

---

growth of American, European, and Japanese multinational corporations ushered in an era of global business. International trade now ties the world together in a global economy.

Another dimension of the global economy was that it was based on a highly competitive worldwide market in which the most successful competitors were nations with market-oriented economic systems. By contrast, the state-controlled communist economies were so badly managed and inefficient, they could not compete in the international market. Few would buy their poorly manufactured goods. The communist nations therefore earned little money to buy advanced technology from the Western countries and Japan.

When a great wave of popular uprisings swept away all the communist regimes of Eastern Europe in 1989, each of these countries moved to establish market economies. The Soviet Union itself began to dismantle its centrally planned economy and to grope toward creating private enterprise, a trend that accelerated with the breakup of the Soviet Union in 1991. In these efforts to transform their economies, the countries of Eastern Europe and the former Soviet Union looked to the leading industrialized nations for assistance. These events made clear that communism as an economic system was an enormous failure, and a major restructuring of the global economy would continue into the 21st century.

The gap widened between rich and poor countries.

The global economy also put into sharp focus a grimmer side of interdependence—the tremendous contrast in the levels of well-being between the economically developed and the underdeveloped countries of the world. About half of the world's population lived in the poor countries of Asia, Africa, and Latin America. Yet these nations produced very little of the world's total output of goods and services.

In the urban areas of the developing nations in Africa, South America, and Asia the challenges of a growing population were severe. In these areas one found many of the contradictions of our modern world: wealth and poverty, abundance and hunger, modern technology and unemployment.

Why do you think she advocates knowing and loving people before serving them? (Answers will vary, but a central point is that service to "people in general" runs the danger of becoming superficial and self-serving.)

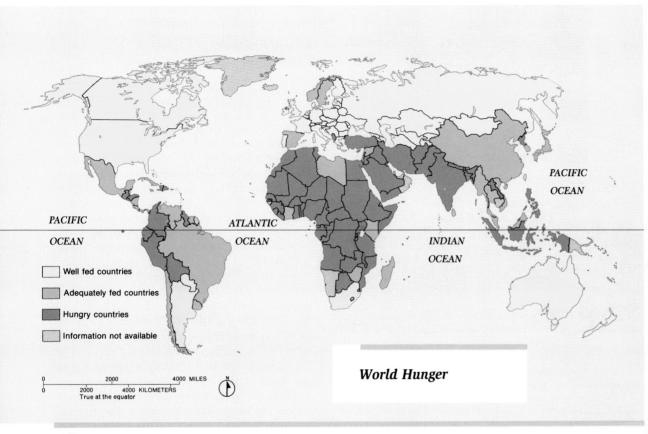

PACIFIC
OCEAN

PACIFIC
OCEAN

ATLANTIC
OCEAN

INDIAN
OCEAN

- ☐ Well fed countries
- ☐ Adequately fed countries
- ■ Hungry countries
- ☐ Information not available

0   2000   4000 MILES
0 2000 4000 KILOMETERS
True at the equator

N

World Hunger

 MAP STUDY   World hunger is a continuing problem everywhere on earth. Which continent has the most widespread problem of hunger?

This poverty created a variety of other social and health problems. Many poor countries struggled to grow enough food to feed their burgeoning populations. Often these same nations faced natural disasters that served to make a terrible situation worse. These disasters were often intensified by the efforts of developing countries to raise cash to pay back loans to Western nations.

Some economists argued that the only way for the less developed nations to solve their problems was to industrialize their economies. Many developing countries tried to do this by borrowing large sums of money from the West. However, when the

fruits of industrialization did not provide these countries with enough money to cover their debts, they were placed in a perilous economic situation. They were faced with a dual problem—a lack of sufficient industrialization to achieve economic health and enormous unpaid debts to the West that left them strapped for working capital to further industrialize their economies.

In addition, many people in these developing countries faced the difficult challenge of finding a way to use the material technology of the industrialized West without sacrificing the cultural and moral strength of their people. Some people, such

ANSWER TO MAP STUDY Africa

the economic generalization about North and South hold? Also for guided practice:

 Overhead Transparency 79

3 | ASSESS AND CLOSE

ASSESS
What do developing nations risk losing when they industrialize? (unique cultures, ample resources, a relative lack of environmental problems)

OPTIONAL RETEACHING
Write the following terms on the chalkboard: multinational corporations, North-South gap, underdeveloped world debt, economic interdependence. Ask pairs of students to alternate using each term in a question and response.

OPTIONAL ENRICHMENT
1. Using a current almanac, look up the population of the world's cities and prepare a bar graph locating by name and nation the world's 30 most populous cities. (average)
2. Also for enrichment:

 Source Reading 40A

INDEPENDENT PRACTICE/ HOMEWORK
Assign the Section Review, Activities page 240, or Workbook page 162.

CLOSURE
Speaking of the 13 American colonies, Benjamin Franklin once said that we must hang together or surely we will all hang separately. There is a lesson in this for today's world.

The sharp contrast between rich and poor is shown by the well-stocked American supermarket (top) and a famine-stricken region in Sudan.

as the rulers of Iran, chose to respond to this challenge by completely and openly rejecting the culture of the West.

In this interdependent global economy, however, a few developing nations did have one natural resource that the Western industrialized nations needed—oil. Without oil, the economies of the industrialized nations would grind to a halt. As a result, the Soviet Union and the West vied for influence in the Middle East, an area rich in oil. During the oil boycott of the 1970s, scenes of cars stretching for blocks around U.S. gas stations as Americans waited for their allotment of gas showed the power that some developing nations had over the industrial nations of the world.

The global economy brought together the rich and poor nations of the world. No one nation could exist independently any longer. In the modern world, the economies of the richest nations on earth were strongly tied to the economies of the poorest nations.

Section 1 Review

Identify multinational corporations
Main Ideas
1. How did the rise of multinational corporations affect the global economy?
2. How did some economists think that the gap between rich and poor nations should be lessened? What important resource did some developing nations have that the industrialized nations needed?

Critical Thinking
Recognizing Values: Many people around the world believe that the West has come to favor material well-being at the expense of spiritual values, such as devotion to religion, learning, concern for others, and a close-knit family life. Do you think spiritual values can be preserved in a strongly materialistic society? Explain your answer.

---

2 Our global society faces many environmental challenges.

The future of our global society will depend upon our ability to find creative, long-term solutions to a variety of issues. Besides the economic and population challenges discussed earlier, the declining health of the environment and the world's increasing demands for energy will present challenges.

Environmental issues will challenge scientists in the coming decades.

Technology and industrialization, the products of human ingenuity, have given us many comforts. However, they have also caused a wide variety of environmental problems. Scientists have identified a wide spectrum of environmental issues facing the world today. The four most significant are global warming, air and water pollution, deforestation, and desertification.

Global warming. Many scientists believe that global warming is the most significant environmental issue in the world today. **Global warming** is the gradual increase in the world's average temperature. The main cause of a possible warming trend is the release of large amounts of carbon dioxide into the earth's atmosphere. Carbon dioxide, a heavy odorless gas, is formed when any fuel containing carbon is burned. Coal and oil, two of the world's most widely used fossil fuels, contain large amounts of carbon.

The role of carbon dioxide in the environment is not all negative. The gas plays a dual role in the heating and cooling of the earth. It allows the warming rays of the sun to pass through the earth's atmosphere to heat the earth, thereby creating a livable environment. However, excessive amounts of carbon dioxide trap the warm air, preventing the heat from escaping. The heat builds up, and as a result, the earth becomes a "greenhouse" where higher global temperatures occur.

The effects of higher global temperatures could be serious. Among the possible effects are an increase in drought and a rise in both the temperature and level of the oceans. Long droughts would seriously affect world food production, which in turn would cause worldwide physical and economic hardship. Increases in the level of the oceans, caused by the melting of the polar ice caps in the event of higher temperatures, would endanger coastal communities. Major port cities, such as New York, Buenos Aires, and Hong Kong, would be submerged beneath the sea.

Acid rain eats away treasures of the past, like this 19th-century statue on a Chicago museum. The original model for this statue, on a building on the Acropolis in Athens, has also been ruined by air pollution.

Scientists and environmentalists believe that we can prevent a global warming trend, but only if actions are taken immediately to reduce the amount of fossil fuels burned. Legislation in the United States and other countries already has helped reduce the amount of carbon dioxide put into our atmosphere. For example, the United States passed strict emissions standards for automobiles in the 1970s. The United States also passed automobile fuel efficiency laws to ensure that cars burn less fuel per mile. Although these laws are helpful, scientists warn that even stricter laws will be needed in the coming years.

Many nations of the world have also taken action to halt another troubling environmental problem—the thinning of the ozone layer. Teams of scientists have been studying the earth's ozone layer for some time. Since 1979, scientists have observed a gradual depletion of the ozone layer over **Antarctica** during the springtime. By 1987, this "hole" was twice the size of the United States.

Some scientists believe that the loss of ozone in the atmosphere is of major concern to our health. Many predict that further decline in the ozone layer will lead to more health problems through excessive exposure to the sun's rays, which can cause skin cancer and other ailments.

The loss of ozone is attributed to production of chlorofluorocarbons—chemicals used in aerosol sprays, refrigeration, and many kinds of plastic and styrofoam products. Therefore, many nations, including the United States, have taken action to ban chlorofluorocarbons. In September, 1987, leaders from countries around the world met to tackle this problem. Their goal was to ban the use of chlorofluorocarbons worldwide.

Air and water pollution. A second major environmental issue is air and water pollution. Water pollution is caused by the seepage of garbage, sewage, toxic chemicals, and radioactive wastes into oceans, rivers, and lakes. Such seepage contaminates or kills off fish and makes water unsafe to drink. Air pollution is caused by automobile-exhaust fumes as well as by smoke, gas, and particles from furnaces in factories, homes, and office buildings that burn oil and coal.

Indirectly, and less obviously, the burning of fossil fuels also causes acid rain. **Acid rain** is largely produced by the burning of certain types of coal. When the emissions produced by burning coal enter the upper atmosphere, they sometimes change into highly acidic compounds. When the conditions are right, the acid returns to earth in the form of rain.

Acid rain has damaged the forests of much of Europe, Canada, and the northeastern United States. Although the overall effects of acid rain on ecosystems are not entirely understood, environmentalists believe that acid rain has the potential to harm fish that live in streams and microorganisms found in soil that perform important functions in the food chain. Acid rain has also been responsible for damaging thousands of buildings and statues, especially those made of limestone.

In recent years many governments have taken positive steps to reduce the emission of particles that cause acid rain. In West Germany, for example, the government passed strict laws in the early 1980s that required all of its power plants to be fitted with special cleaners that eliminate pollutants which cause acid rain. However, such equipment is very costly.

Deforestation. The third major environmental issue facing the world is the large-scale clearing of forests, especially tropical forests in the Amazon Valley, Southeast Asia, and Central Africa. In general, **deforestation** is the result of a combination of land-clearing for farms and gathering of wood by farmers for fuel. Commercial lumbering, to a lesser degree, is also causing deforestation.

Some experts predict that if present practices continue, one-third of the world's tropical forests will vanish by the year 2000. Other experts believe that all of the world's tropical rainforests could be gone by the turn of the century unless the deforestation is halted.

The loss of the world's tropical forests would cause a decline in the world's supply of oxygen. Forests, like other plant life, recycle carbon dioxide and produce oxygen. Environmentalists estimate that tropical forests currently produce about 40 percent of all the oxygen that we breathe. Large-scale deforestation could also intensify the greenhouse effect by allowing a build-up of carbon dioxide in the atmosphere.

In the 1980s, environmentalist groups around the world called for action to prevent further deforestation. As a result, some nations, especially Brazil, began programs to restrict the practice.

Desertification. A fourth major environmental issue is the gradual advance of desert land, known as **desertification.** Although it is of greatest concern in sub-Saharan Africa, desertification is also a problem in other areas. In the 1980s and early 1990s, desertification affected parts of western China, India, Pakistan, Iran, Iraq, Saudi Arabia, North Africa, Peru, Chile, and northern Mexico.

Desertification, particularly in the Sahara, is largely the result of human activities, such as deforestation, poorly planned irrigation systems, and overgrazing of sheep and cattle. These practices have helped allow the desert to spread.

A Brazilian couple seeks to build a new life on cleared land in the vast rainforest. However, rainforest land is not well suited to farming, since soil nutrients are rapidly exhausted once the land is cleared.

Some nations are in danger of becoming unlivable because of desertification. For example, the people of Mali, a country that lies mainly south of the Sahara, must begin each day by shoveling away the night's accumulation of sand from their doorsteps. The people are not free to migrate to more livable regions, because modern political boundaries make such migration difficult.

Efforts to stop desertification greatly intensified in the 1980s and early 1990s, thanks largely to the work of environmental groups that have made people more aware of this problem. Measures so far include the planting of trees to help prevent erosion of the soil as well as prohibiting the grazing of livestock in certain areas.

Worldwide energy needs are increasing rapidly.

Because of a combined population explosion and demand for higher living standards throughout the world, some experts believe that the global energy supply will have to be tripled by the year 2000 to meet our growing needs. Currently, most of the world's supply of energy needs are met by coal, petroleum, natural gas, uranium, and hydroelectric power. Hydroelectric power, which is harnessed by dams hooked up with water turbines and generators, is an almost inexhaustible resource, given the earth's plentiful supply of water. Coal and nuclear sources will also be available for centuries. Petroleum and natural gas, however, are resources that very well could be exhausted within the next century.

The petroleum and natural gas situation seems to imply that coal, hydroelectric power, and nuclear power will have to take up the slack in the years to come. Each of these resources, however, has its limitations, and indeed, some very serious drawbacks. Coal, for example, may be turned into liquid or gas to perform many of the same functions as petroleum or natural gas. Although the technology does exist to do this, the costs are high and refineries needed to liquify or gasify coal are expensive to build. In addition, the pollutants emitted from the burning of coal are hazardous to the environment.

Hydroelectric power is a renewable source of energy that has the potential for creating substan-

Each day the residents of this village must sweep away the sand that has blown against their homes, an effect of the spread of the Sahara.

tially more electrical power than it is currently producing. In the United States, about 5 percent of all energy is supplied by hydroelectric power. Worldwide, about 1 percent of all energy needs is supplied by hydroelectric power.

Some hydroelectric plants are able to produce even more power than fossil fuel or nuclear power stations. The Itaipu [ē tī′pü] Dam power plant, for example, jointly owned by Brazil and Paraguay, will be one of the world's largest hydroelectric plants when it is completed in the 1990s.

Although hydroelectric power represents a clean, almost inexhaustible source of energy, it has some drawbacks. First, hydroelectric power relies upon the presence of moving water. Many of the world's suitable locations already have power plants in place. Second, costs associated with building hydroelectric plants are very high. Some nations with potential sites, such as those in Asia, Africa, and South America, do not have the economic resources needed to build the plants. Third, hydroelectric plants have been known to create various environmental problems. At times, fish and other wildlife have been destroyed. In several cases the filling of reservoirs behind dams has triggered earthquakes. In addition, damage to a dam can release uncontrolled torrents of water.

Nuclear power, another energy source that could fill the void left by the depletion of fossil fuels, has long been the most controversial source of energy. Nuclear power's adherents believe that it is the world's solution to the energy crisis. Its

3 | ASSESS AND CLOSE

ASSESS

1. What is the greenhouse effect? (trapping of warm air by excessive carbon dioxide)
2. What is destroying the ozone layer? (chlorofluorocarbons)

OPTIONAL RETEACHING

Ask students to identify what environmental problem would likely be ameliorated by each of the following government actions: annual vehicle emissions test, ban on chlorofluorocarbons, limits on commercial lumbering, limits on power plant emissions, planting of trees and fencing of livestock.

OPTIONAL ENRICHMENT

1. Encourage interested students to investigate waste-disposal practices in their community. A phone call to the sanitation department or the local government is a good starting place. (average)
2. One of the biggest sticking points when negotiating for nuclear arms reduction is verification. Ask interested students to research what verification procedures were established by the 1988 INF treaty. (challenging)

INDEPENDENT PRACTICE/ HOMEWORK

Assign the Section Review, Activities page 241, or Workbook page 163.

A MYSTERY IN HISTORY

Scientists meeting in Toronto in September, 1988, concluded that the earth's temperature rose one degree in the last century because of the greenhouse effect. If the trend continues, some concluded, there could be another 3- to 9-degree increase in the next century.

One problem with the data, however, is that many of the readings are from urban regions, which are warmer, wetter, and cloudier than surrounding rural areas because of pollution. Some scientists point to this factor as well as several others to question the data. "There is nothing in the climate record to suggest clearly what the trend will be in the next century," concluded David Phillips of Canada's Atmospheric Environment Service. (quoted in the *Chicago Tribune,* September 29, 1988).

Ask students to look for articles relating to the greenhouse effect. Not all the evidence points to a warming trend. For example, the Scripps Institute of Oceanography in 1988 predicted a cooling trend on the basis of a drop in temperatures of the ocean surface off equatorial South America. See "Big Chill for the Greenhouse," *Time,* October 31, 1988, p. 90.

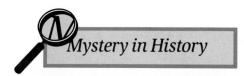

Mystery in History

COMING: FIRE OR ICE?

The human race did not begin to flourish until the continental icecaps retreated about 10,000 years ago. As the last Ice Age ended, the earth gradually warmed. Until recently, many scientists had expected that another Ice Age might occur in the distant future. The massive continental glaciers had, after all, advanced and receded at least four times in the past 1.5 million years and many times before that. Perhaps, they conjectured, our civilization would end up buried in ice.

In the 1980s, however, a series of atmospheric events suggested that the earth might get warmer before the next Ice Age occurred. The warmer temperatures were expected to result from the greenhouse effect—the trend toward global warming because of the increase of carbon dioxode and other gases in the earth's atmosphere. Worldwide fossil-fuel burning releases such gases into the air so rapidly that the earth's

Is there a global warming trend? Will the world shiver in the grip of glacial ice? Or will none of the disasters some scientists predict occur?

ecosystems cannot always restore the balance as they were meant to. As a result, the gases rise in the atmosphere and act as a greenhouse, trapping heat from the sunlight as it is reflected back into space.

In the late 1980s, according to one study, worldwide temperatures rose higher than at any time during the preceding 130 years in which careful records have been kept. Another study of 2,000 weather stations in the 20th century also indicated a trend toward warmer climates.

These trends could mean severe changes in our atmosphere. Higher average temperatures would mean a gradual warming of the oceans and the melting of the remaining glaciers and polar icecaps. As the ice melted, the meltwater would flow into the world's oceans, raising the sea level and flooding the coastal cities. The whole pattern of climates around the world would change.

No one, of course, knows if these changes will occur, and many scientists believe there is no evidence to indicate a warming trend. In earth science a trend is measured in thousands of years, not decades. Some scientists point to periods in the past when the earth got noticeably cooler after severe volcanic eruptions spewed forth ash and gases, darkening the skies and shielding the earth from some of the sun's rays.

Human beings have no control over the forces deep within the earth that cause volcanoes. These same forces, for example, could conceivably push up the continents as the weight of the ice was removed during a prolonged melting period. A similar rebound from the retreat of the last glacier can still be measured in parts of North America. Our earth, after all, is a dynamic place, constantly in motion, continually changing. That is the essence of its mysterious ways.

critics claim, however, that its continued use will result in serious long-term problems for the environment and for human life.

Although many people still think that nuclear power is our best long-term energy choice, the high hopes for nuclear power as a solution to growing worldwide demand for energy suffered some setbacks in the 1980s. One setback was that construction costs soared so high that many nations, including the United States, had to cut back sharply on plans to build more nuclear plants. Another setback was a series of nuclear reactor accidents. These accidents, which occurred in various countries around the world, intensified protests against the use of nuclear power.

The threat of nuclear war continues to worry our global society.

Despite widespread reservations about nuclear power, the greatest fears about nuclear technology were not about its peaceful uses, but about the frightening consequences of using nuclear weapons in war. For about 20 years after the nuclear explosions at Nagasaki and Hiroshima, nuclear weapons were concentrated mainly in the hands of the two superpowers—the United States and the Soviet Union—though Britain also had nuclear arms. Other countries, however, believed that nuclear weapons were necessary for their national security. As a result, by 1968 both France and China had developed nuclear bombs. In 1974 India also exploded a nuclear device.

By the 1980s there was evidence that South Africa, Israel, and Pakistan were also producing nuclear weapons. Experts predicted that in the 1990s as many as 20 countries would have their own atomic weapons. This prospect increased the danger of nuclear weapons being used by small nations in regional conflicts. That was why in 1991 the UN sent an international inspection team to Iraq after its defeat in the Gulf war to make sure Iraq did not have the capability of producing weapons of mass destruction.

For most of the post-World War II period, the greatest danger of a nuclear war stemmed from the arms race between the two superpowers. By the early 1970s, each had enough nuclear weapons to destroy one another and to contaminate the rest of the world with radiation. The fear of that happening kept the two nations from using their nuclear weapons, but they came dangerously close, especially during the Cuban missile crisis of 1962 that you read about in Chapter 35.

After that the United States and the Soviet Union began to work for arms control. Negotiations went very slowly because both sides were so suspicious of each other. For nearly 30 years the two superpowers concentrated on working out detailed arms control agreements. One of the most significant was the Intermediate Nuclear Forces (INF) Treaty, which both sides signed in 1988. For the first time, both superpowers agreed to destroy a whole class of nuclear weapons (intermediate-range missiles).

In 1991 U. S. President George Bush departed from this negotiating procedure when he dramatically announced that the United States on its own would reduce its arsenal of tactical (short-range) nuclear weapons. Shortly afterward Soviet leader Mikhail Gorbachev declared that the Soviet Union would reduce its tactical nuclear arms as well. The world seemed a bit safer, but the breakup of the Soviet Union in 1991 marked a new period of uncertainty over the control of nuclear arms.

Section 2 Review

Identify global warming, Antarctica, acid rain, deforestation, desertification

Main Ideas

1. Name two major environmental problems confronting the world. What steps must be taken to solve these problems?
2. What are the major fossil fuels the world now depends upon for most of its energy needs? What is likely to happen to the supply of these fuels during the next century.
3. Why does the possibility of nuclear war continue to pose a threat? What positive steps have been taken to prevent nuclear war?

Critical Thinking

Predicting Effects: Do you think that many of the problems described in this section can be solved? Give reasons for your answers.

Essential Learning Objectives

Students will learn to:

- describe three possible scenarios for the 21st century.
- consider the lessons of history and what gave rise to the ideas, cultures, and problems of today.

Draw three globe-sized circles on the chalkboard. In the first write 200 million to represent the number of people who lived on earth at the time of Jesus. Explain to students that these people drove no cars, built no nuclear power plants, and discarded no chlorofluorocarbon-laden styrofoam cups. In the second circle write 5 billion to represent the people on earth in the late 1980s. They drove more than 400 million cars, had more than 500 nuclear reactors, and were using enough chlorofluorocarbons to create a hole in the ozone layer the size of the United States. In the third circle draw a question mark. This lesson concerns the third circle.

- Review with students the three futuristic world views presented in this last section—Malthusian, expansionist, and ecological. On the chalkboard, list the more salient attributes of each. Show how each view places humankind in a different relationship with nature—the conquered, the conqueror, and the coexister.

- Explore the implications of a less materialistic culture. Draw a smallish circle in the middle of the chalkboard and write "25% fewer cars" inside. Draw several rays extending out from

The global problems you read about in Section 2 are indeed immense. Yet people in every generation back to the australopithecines have had to endure trying times. History shows us that human ingenuity and spirit have triumphed over adversity time and time again.

Many futurists—people who use scientific methods to theorize about the future—believe that there is good reason to be very optimistic about life in the next few decades. Other futurists are less optimistic, and still others are downright pessimistic. We will look at three of these futuristic views and their societal strategies. Although no one knows which view, if any, will prevail, each is logical and very possible. Keep in mind as you read that there are also many other points of view besides those discussed.

The Malthusian world view paints a depressing picture of society's future.

The Malthusian world view is named after **Thomas Malthus**, the pessimistic 18th-century English clergyman and economist whom you read about in Chapter 28. Malthus believed that the problems of his time were the result of humanity's predestined need to alter nature through science and technology. This "tampering" with nature, as Malthus saw it, was responsible for problems such as overpopulation and an ever increasing need to satisfy physical wants. Eventually, Malthus theorized, human intervention would push nature to its limits and thus bring forth disaster.

Today's Malthusians believe that modern society, with its insatiable thirst for technological and scientific improvements, has become far too complex to effectively deal with its many problems. To support this belief, they point to the growing inefficiency of our cities and their inability to deal with increasingly complex problems such as pollution and overpopulation. This inefficiency, the Malthusians maintain, eventually will spell doom for our global society in one form or another.

The solutions proposed by the Malthusians are quite drastic. They call for huge population reduc-

Traffic chokes this highway in Bangkok, Thailand, a city of some 5 million people. As elsewhere, gridlock ties up many streets in Asian cities.

tions in all nations, but especially in the developing nations. They also feel that people must use fewer resources, limit material consumption, and redistribute the world's wealth. Finally, they believe that a world government should be formed. This government would oversee the implementation of all of these programs.

The expansionist world view paints an optimistic picture of society's future.

Unlike the Malthusians, the expansionists are extremely optimistic about the future. They believe that humanity is capable of overcoming many of its problems through science and technology. Although expansionists believe that the world is out of balance, they say that historically our world has often been imbalanced and that we have always found a way to right ourselves.

The expansionist world view has its roots in various Western sources. One is the widespread use of scientific experiments to gain knowledge and mastery of the physical world. As you learned in Chapter 22, Francis Bacon, the 16th-century English philosopher, stressed experimentation as an essential part of what became known as the scientific method. The expansionist world view can also be tied to the Enlightenment's belief in the power of reason and rational behavior. Yet another source for the development of the expansionist world view was 19th-century industrialization, which raised living standards dramatically and helped to equate "progress" with the satisfaction of material wants.

Because expansionism worked in the past, its believers contend that it will continue to work in the future. They reject the Malthusian forecasts as both hysterical and inaccurate. For example, they say that technology has so far increased food production to keep pace with population increases. They point out that earlier Malthusian forecasts of resource depletion were wrong.

Expansionists are convinced that growth can continue in the underdeveloped nations and enable them to move into the industrial age. Meanwhile, the developed countries will be able to continue on their course, a course that is leading them into a post-industrial age in which the emphasis will be to provide services rather than goods.

The expansionists foresee the development of many alternative sources of energy in the next few decades. They forecast that new breakthroughs in nuclear, thermonuclear, and solar energy technology will provide an almost indefinite supply of power. Such limitless energy can be used to manufacture synthetic metals and to fuel the technology for colonizing other planets, where the process of expansion can begin once again. New energy sources will also help us solve many environmental problems. Most importantly, the expansionists predict, technology will enable us to eliminate world poverty.

The ecological world view is neither optimistic nor pessimistic.

Unlike Malthusians or expansionists, people who hold an ecological world view are neither optimistic or pessimistic about the prospects for our future world. Believers in this world view hold that the world is a unified system whose parts are connected and interacting. Unlike the Malthusians and the expansionists, who believe that either nature or humanity will eventually "conquer" the other, advocates of the ecological world view believe that humanity cannot stand apart from nature. People are an inseparable part of the vast ecosystem. Therefore, they can never conquer the environment, but will stand or fall with it because the universe is one unitary whole.

The ecological world view has both non-Western and Western roots. These roots include Taoism's message about the balance of nature and humanity's need to live in harmony with it. Recall that in Chapter 8 you learned that Taoism grew out of the teachings of the Chinese philosopher Laozi [lou′dzu′]. In the West, this world view finds support both from the Judeo-Christian view of God's plan for humanity and from 19th-century socialist views about replacing competition with cooperation in the development and the use of the world's resources.

New technology includes solar parabolic dishes that generate power for a town in Australia.

the primary circle to secondary circles. Ask students what changes might result from a 25% cutback of U.S. cars. (unemployment in Detroit, reduced global warming, decline in travel-related businesses, and so on) Point out that measures to conserve resources will have serious implications.

GUIDED PRACTICE

Have students list their predictions about what life in the 21st century will be like. Have students compare their views with those stated in the text. Classify and list students' views on the chalkboard. Poll students as to how many agree with each view. Also for guided practice:

 Overhead Transparency 80

3 ASSESS AND CLOSE

ASSESS

1. What solutions do Malthusians offer for world problems? (huge population reductions and limiting of consumption)
2. Why do we think of the expansionists as optimistic? (because they expect new developments in science and technology to solve the world's problems)

OPTIONAL RETEACHING

Have students make diagrams (similar to a family tree) that show the three future visions discussed in this chapter and the historical/philosophical linkages that contributed to each.

Students also may be assigned Activities reteaching page 243.

OPTIONAL ENRICHMENT

1. Have students survey friends and family members as to their visions for the future. Write a short report showing results. (average)

The ecological world view has two major objectives. The first is to conserve the earth's natural resources for future generations. The second is to develop ways to distribute resources to all of the world's people. According to this view, the resources needed by all people—basic standards of nutrition, health, shelter, and education—should be made available on a global scale. To accomplish these goals, some holders of the ecological world view believe that an international organization such as the United Nations should be given the authority to manage and distribute the world's resources. Others believe, however, that the specific uses of major resources should be left in the hands of national, state, and local governments rather than a world government as suggested by the Malthusians. Smaller governments, they argue, would ensure that cultural and community uniqueness is not lost.

Holders of the ecological world view have their own unique strategies for solving world problems. Unlike the Malthusians, they do not call for radical population reductions. Yet neither do they promote the technological expansion suggested by the expansionists. Rather, they believe in selective growth. Ideally, they believe, overall population growth would decrease in the developing countries in the decades ahead. This reduction would be achieved through educational programs designed to improve standards of living. Meanwhile, the industrial nations would plan to have a smaller output of goods and a larger output of services.

In the ecological world view, the world of the future will be one that emphasizes a simpler, less materialistic lifestyle. This in turn would involve a fundamental shift to values appropriate for meeting tomorrow's challenges.

The world views described here are three different ways of thinking about the future. Many other viewpoints also exist. The evolution of society in the next few decades is almost certain to be filled with many unforeseen surprises.

The future holds promise and challenge for humanity.

After 5,000 years of recorded history, what are the prospects for humanity? Whatever the future may bring, we cannot expect a world where all human problems are solved. Such a state of affairs is neither possible nor desirable. The human race has progressed by facing challenges. This is perhaps history's greatest lesson. Although history cannot reveal the future for us, it can inspire us to meet the challenges and avoid the pitfalls that have occurred in the past.

We can learn from the past, although the lessons history teaches are often indirect. Mistakes are repeated that a knowledge of the past could have prevented. Hitler repeated Napoleon's mistake by invading Russia. The mistakes that followed World War I led to World War II. In both cases it can be argued that the parallels were inexact, and they were. However, the warning signals were there, and they were ignored. History offers many such examples of faulty judgment and ensuing calamity. Yet it also provides far more examples, little noticed and often unrecorded, of the triumph of human reason and the advancement of social justice and human kindness. The Israelite prophets, the Greek and Chinese philosophers, the Roman jurists, Christian and Islamic scholars, 18th-century rationalists, 19th-century inventors, and 20th-century physicists and medical researchers all moved civilization forward. There is every reason to believe that your generation will mark out paths for the 21st century along the high road of civilization, and you will leave the world better than you found it.

Section 3 Review

Identify Thomas Malthus

Main Ideas
1. Why do the Malthusians have little hope for the future?
2. What do the expansionists believe will be the key to finding solutions to the world's major problems?
3. Describe the historical development of the ecological world view. Why is this view neither optimistic or pessimistic?
4. Give two examples of lessons that can be learned from history.

Critical Thinking

Making Decisions: Which view of humanity's future most closely parallels your own? Give reasons for your viewpoint.

Scientific Advances of the 20th Century

Science and technology have transformed life in the 20th century, and they will undoubtedly continue to transform life in the 21st. Two technologies of immeasurable potential are fiber optics and superconductors.

Fiber optics involves encoding electronic messages as light signals and sending these signals through threads of thin glass. By cutting the costs of materials, improving reception, and saving energy, fiber optics has cut communications costs.

This same technology may someday be used to speed up already high-speed computers. It may also be helpful in developing a new type of computer that can give us insights into the way the human brain works.

Superconductors—materials that can transmit electric current at high speeds—are currently used in particle accelerators for subatomic research and in medical research. However, so far the uses of superconductors have been limited, because scientists have not yet found a superconducting material that works except at extremely low temperatures.

Nevertheless, the supercooled superconductors, like fiber optics, may soon change our lives. They may speed up the work of computers and be employed as extremely sensitive sensors for earthquake detection and brain research. In a decade or two, frictionless trains, levitated above tracks lined with superconductors, could whiz along smoothly at speeds well above 100 miles an hour. Superconductors could also be used in the transmission and storage of electricity, potentially conserving tremendous amounts of energy.

University of Colorado scientists are developing optical technology for industrial use and for world markets (top left). A researcher in Massachusetts is heating metal alloys in a bank of furnaces to make superconducting wire (left).

HIGHLIGHTS OF CIVILIZATION

Scientific and technological advances have caused rapid changes in our 20th-century world. We can be sure that they will continue to have a large impact on our lives in the 21st century.

Currently in the United States, most long- and intermediate-distance phone calls are carried by optical fibers. Only the most local of local calls are carried by the relatively bulky and slow copper wires.

The costs of supplying refrigeration to maintain the frigid temperatures that superconductors need to operate usually offset the cost benefits of conducting electricity without resistance.

In early 1989 the highest temperatures at which superconductivity had been achieved were between 110 and 120K (Kelvin), which is about $-262°F$ to $-244°F$. Scientists use the Kelvin scale, which measures absolute zero as the temperature at which substances have absolutely no kinetic energy. This temperature corresponds to $-273°C$ $(-460°F)$.

The practical uses of fiber optics and superconductors are just now being envisioned. Superconductivity found its most important application in the 1980s in the field of medical diagnosis. Magnetic resonance imaging uses superconducting materials in the presence of powerful magnetic fields to provide sharp images of the various layers of tissue in the body.

CHAPTER 40 REVIEW

Section Summaries

Section 1
The world has become economically interdependent.
The world has become one vast integrated economic system. Multinational corporations emerged that helped connect the world together. Market-oriented economic systems surpassed communist countries with their state-controlled economies. The gap between the economically developed and the developing countries widened. The developing countries did not have enough industrialization to achieve economic health, and they had enormous unpaid debts to the West. Some oil-producing countries were able to influence the economies of the industrialized nations.

Section 2
Our global society faces many environmental challenges.
The question of survival has taken on great importance. Changes in the environment caused by global warming, air and water pollution, deforestation, and desertification have caused scientists to look for creative solutions to improve the environment. Increased energy needs have forced scientists to search for additional ways to increase the world's power supply without harming the environment. Fears exist over the use of nuclear technology which can be used peacefully for energy

and destructively for military conflicts. This threat of nuclear war has forced countries to work together to provide a safe environment.

Section 3
Futurists predict what the world will be like.
Futurists provide a varied view of the future. Those who followed Thomas Malthus believed that people would push nature to its limits and thus bring forth disaster. Malthusians today believe that modern society has become too complex to deal effectively with its many problems. Unlike the Malthusians, the expansionists are optimistic about the future, feeling that humanity is capable of overcoming problems through science and technology. Unlike Malthusians or expansionists, those who hold an ecological world view believe that the world is a unified system whose parts are connected and interacting. People are an inseparable part of the vast ecosystem. The needs of all people should be decided on a global scale.

Test Yourself

Key Terms, People, and Places
Identify the significance of each of the following:
Section 1
a. multinational corporations

Review Dates

1968
France and China develop nuclear bombs

1972
United States and Soviet Union sign Strategic Arms Limitation Treaty

1963
United States and Soviet Union ban above-ground nuclear tests

1974
India explodes a nuclear device

1988
INF Treaty calls for destruction of intermediate-range missiles

1950　1960　1970　1980　1990　2000

Section 2

a. global warming   **d.** deforestation

b. Antarctica   **e.** desertification

c. acid rain

Section 3

a. Thomas Malthus

Main Ideas

Section 1

1. In what ways did the rise of multinational corporations affect the global economy?

2. Describe the way that the gap between rich and poor nations might be lessened. What important natural resource did some developing nations have that industrialized nations needed?

Section 2

1. Describe two major environmental problems that face the world. Identify steps that could be taken to solve these problems.

2. What major fossil fuels does the world now depend on for most of its energy? What might happen to the supply of these fossil fuels in the 21st century?

3. Why does the possibility of nuclear war still pose a threat? Identify the positive steps that have been taken to prevent nuclear war.

Section 3

1. Why do the Malthusians have little hope for the future?

2. Describe what the expansionists think could be the key to finding solutions to major global problems.

3. Describe the background of the ecological world view. Why is this view neither optimistic nor pessimistic?

4. What are two examples of lessons that people can learn from history?

Critical Thinking

1. Making Hypotheses   Why is it so difficult for many developing nations to provide goods and services for their citizens?

2. Predicting Effects   Many environmental problems that face us today can probably only be solved by international cooperation. Do you think it is possible to get countries to work together to achieve the necessary solutions? If so, how could international cooperation be achieved?

CRITICAL THINKING QUESTION LEVEL 1. challenging; 2. average

Chapter Skills and Activities

Practicing Study and Research Skills

Developing Criteria for Making Judgments

Making an intelligent decision about any problem requires a set of criteria, or standards, for judgment. For example, to decide what to wear to school, one criteria you would certainly consider is the day's weather. Assume that you must make the choice in the situation described below. Select four criteria from the list that would be most important in helping you make a choice.

size (area)	land use
population	traditions
population density	customs
latitude	political situation
elevation	economic system
landforms	transportation
weather	type of government
climate	per capita GNP
natural resources	language(s) spoken
natural vegetation	literacy rate
water bodies	

As president of your country, you decide to build a new nuclear power plant. Doing so, you hope, will help develop a poorer section of your country. What four criteria will guide you in choosing the location for your new power plant? Write a paragraph explaining your choices.

Linking Past to Present

How does the way that you live today differ from the way that your great-grandparents lived in 1900 in relation to health, education, consumer goods, and vocational opportunities? How will your great-grandchildren's lives in the year 2080 probably differ? Give examples.

Learning History Through Maps

Compare the map of World Hunger on page 763 with the World Population Distribution map on pages 786–787. What generalizations can you make about the well-fed countries? The hungry countries?

Answers to Chapter Skills and Activities

Practicing Study and Research Skills

population density, elevation, landforms, political situation

Linking Past and Present

In 1900 many things we take for granted (antibiotics, high school education, TVs, cars, ready-made clothes, radios) didn't exist, and most people were farmers. Have students give ideas for the future, such as living on other planets, global warming trend, overcrowded cities, famine, high living standard for all.

Learning History Through Maps

Of the well-fed countries, only Europe is densely populated; of the hungry ones, not all are densely populated.

UNIT NINE

REVIEW

Summarizing the Unit

Chapter 35
Europe, the Cold War, and the Superpowers
When World War II ended, the Allies' cooperation deteriorated into fear and rivalry. This rivalry, primarily between the United States and Western Europe on one side, and the Soviet Union on the other, became known as the Cold War.

Chapter 36
The Assertion of Independence in Asia
After World War II, many important political changes took place in Asia. The Chinese Communists assumed power in China, and most colonies sought and achieved independence. In addition, Japan and some other Asian countries experienced remarkable economic growth.

Chapter 37
The Struggle for Self-Rule in Africa
After World War II, many newly independent African nations experienced economic and political difficulties. Some countries enjoyed political stability and growth in the postwar era, but widespread drought led to great suffering.

Chapter 38
Economic Growth and International Tension in the Middle East
After 1945 most nations in the Middle East achieved political independence. Social and political changes led to increased regional and international tension, including four wars between Israel and its Arab neighbors.

Chapter 39
The Struggle for National Development in Latin America
Latin America continued to experience a wide gulf between its rich and poor in the years following World War II. Rapid population growth and high foreign debt led to economic and political problems for many countries.

Chapter 40
An Interdependent World
The 20th century emerged as a period of global interdependence. Countries no longer existed in isolation, and instead their economies and cultures were increasingly interrelated. Worldwide environmental problems developed.

Using Writing Skills

In the last eight unit reviews, you have practiced three steps in the writing process—prewriting, writing, and revising. The last and final step is presenting, in which you share or present your writing to an audience of one or more. This step is sometimes called publishing.

   Activity. To master the presenting step, first divide into small groups and select a topic that interests you which concerns the world as a whole. Some possible topics might be women's roles around the world, international trade, the disappearing rainforests, or waste recycling. Then, gather information about that topic. Finally, decide how you'd like to present your information—designing and making a bulletin board, producing and acting in a television news broadcast or play, publishing a special magazine issue, or writing a group letter to your representative in congress. Use your creativity.

Test Yourself

Key Terms and People
Match each term or person with the correct definition.
1. the total value of all goods and services produced in a country
2. India's first prime minister
3. policy of racial segregation
4. political organization of oil producers
5. dictator of Argentina who emphasized industry
a. Juan Perón
b. apartheid
c. GNP
d. OPEC
e. Jawaharlal Nehru

Key Dates

Match the letters on the time line with the events for which they stand:

1940 1950 1960 1970 1980 1990 2000

AB CD E F G H

___ The U.S. Civil Rights Act is passed.
___ INF Treaty calls for the destruction of intermediate-range nuclear weapons.
___ The People's Republic of China is established.
___ Vietnam is unified under communist rule.
___ Jews establish the state of Israel.
___ Iran-Iraq war begins.
___ Fidel Castro takes power in Cuba.
___ Ghana is granted independence.

Key Places

Match the letters on the map with the places described below:

___ the modern Jewish state
___ impoverished Muslim country hurt by flooding
___ country with a policy of apartheid
___ waterway that was a cause of the Iran-Iraq war
___ country in which the Sandinistas hold power

Main Ideas

1. Cooperation between the Allies and the Soviet Union ended with _____
a. the use of the atomic bomb on Japan.
b. the blockade of Berlin.
c. the Nuremberg Trials.
d. the bombing of Pearl Harbor.
2. After World War II, Japan _____
a. spent fortunes rebuilding its military.
b. became a leading agricultural producer.
c. developed new markets for its goods.
d. became a communist country.
3. After gaining independence, India adopted _____
a. a colonialist government.
b. a communist government.
c. an Islamic government.
d. a democratic government.
4. South Africa faced international attention because _____
a. the government harbored terrorists.
b. many people migrated to South Africa.
c. the government was well integrated.
d. the government followed a policy of apartheid.
5. A situation that has not been a serious problem for Latin American economies is _____
a. a dependence on a single product.
b. long-term social inequalities.
c. a low rate of population growth.
d. a high rate of population growth.

Critical Thinking

1. Making Hypotheses After World War II, many countries banded together in organizations and alliances such as NATO and OPEC to work toward their common goals. What benefits to members could arise from working in such international organizations? Would there be any difficulties?
2. Making Decisions Over the past 40 years, the gap between rich and poor nations has widened tremendously. Imagine that you are a leader of a prosperous country in the world today. What policies might you institute to lessen this division?

EPILOGUE

The Challenge of Living in an Interdependent World

In getting to the present, we have seen human existence move from a condition of relative isolation to one of global interdependence. As you read in the opening introduction, this is one of the central themes of world history. Along the way to interdependence, the human community has gone through many changes. The story of those changes makes up the substance of history.

Many historians say that the rate of change speeded up as contacts between peoples increased. The closer we moved to our own time, the more numerous were the connections and the more frequent the changes. This process explains why Part One of this book covered many thousands of years, while Part Two covered only 1,000 years, and Part Three just 500 years.

As you read in the introduction to Part Three, the main themes of the past 500 years were the rise of the West to a position of world dominance, the creation of a global economy, and the emergence of an interdependent world. The great breakthroughs that enabled the West to gain its position of world dominance were the industrial and political revolutions of the late 18th and early 19th centuries. These revolutions gave the Western nations superior technology, strong economies, great military strength, and highly organized political states. Without them, world dominance would have been impossible.

In extending their control around the globe, the Western nations brought into being an economic system in which they supplied the world with manufactured goods and the rest of the world supplied them with raw materials. In the 20th century, all the nations of the world became so economically dependent on one another that we can speak of an age of true interdependence. It is also an age in which science and technology, along with Western ideas of democracy, nationalism, capitalism, and socialism have been spread widely around the globe. The result is that the 20th century has seen more major change than any previous century.

The 21st century will be even more interdependent, and we can be certain that the pace of change will continue to quicken. The marvels of the computer and the microchip, the impact of global telecommunications and trade, are fast producing tomorrow's world.

Sculpted in Hungary around 7,000 years ago, the clay man on the facing page holds a sickle, an advanced tool for that time. Today modern technology includes complex robot hands like the one above.

ATLAS AND REFERENCE SECTION

* Map Update
1. The Union of Soviet Socialist Republics broke apart in 1991. Lithuania, Latvia, Estonia were recognized as independent nations in September 1991. The Commonwealth of Independent States was formed on December 1991 by the independent nations of Armenia, Azerbaijan, Byelarus, Kazakhstan, Kyrgyzstan, Moldova, Russia, Tajikistan, Turkmenistan, Ukraine, Uzbekistan. Georgia was not a member as of early 1992.
2. North and South Yemen were reunified as the Republic of Yemen in May 1990.
3. The former Yugoslavian republics of Slovenia and Croatia were recognized as independent countries by the European Community January 1992. Croatia's boundaries, however, remain in flux.

CONTENTS

UNDERSTANDING MAP PROJECTIONS

Most world maps in use today are not entirely accurate because of a basic property of the earth's surface—it is curved. How then do mapmakers show the surface of the earth, which is a three-dimensional sphere, on a two-dimensional piece of paper?

To look at the problem, think of the earth as an orange with the continents outlined on the peel. To transfer the image from the orange to a sheet of paper, you would first cut the orange and take off the peel. Then, you would stretch and tear the peel to get it to lie flat on the paper. As a result, the map would have interruptions where the tears occur and distortion where the peel is stretched.

Map projections are scientific attempts to solve or reduce the problem of distortion, which changes the size and shape of continents. Many different map projections have been developed, each with distinct advantages and disadvantages.

Three of the most common world map projections are shown at right. The Robinson projection, shown at top and used for world maps throughout *History and Life,* comes closest to reality in terms of both size and shape. There is some distortion in relative size, though, near the poles in order to more fairly represent the shapes of continents in the middle and low latitudes. The Mercator, at center, has the advantage of true directions and accurate shapes of land and water. However, it seriously distorts the size of land near the poles. The interrupted projection, at bottom, shows the true relative size of the earth's landmasses, but it distorts distances, especially across water.

Robinson Projection

Mercator Projection

Interrupted Projection

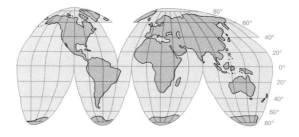

ATLAS

The World: Political

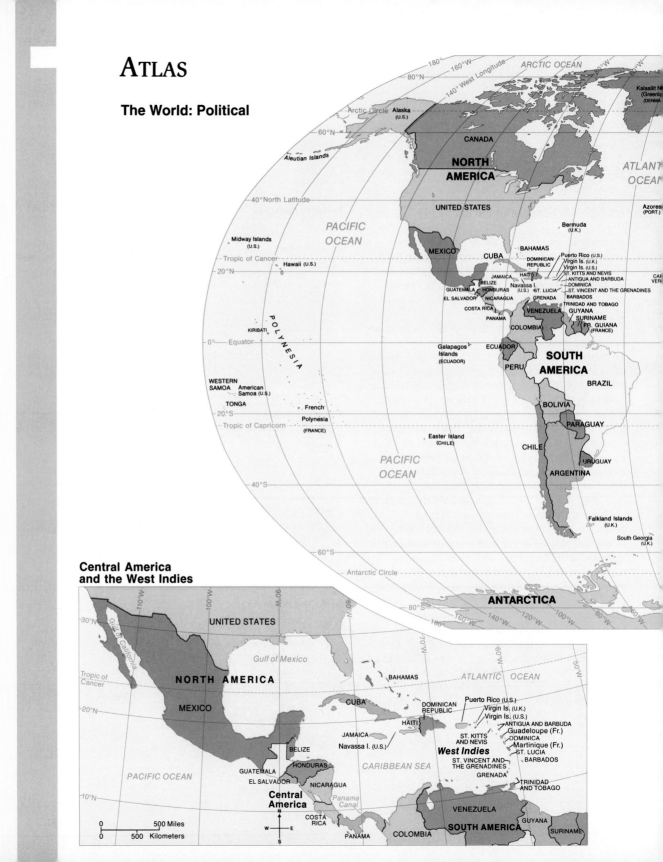

Central America and the West Indies

500 Miles

500 Kilometers

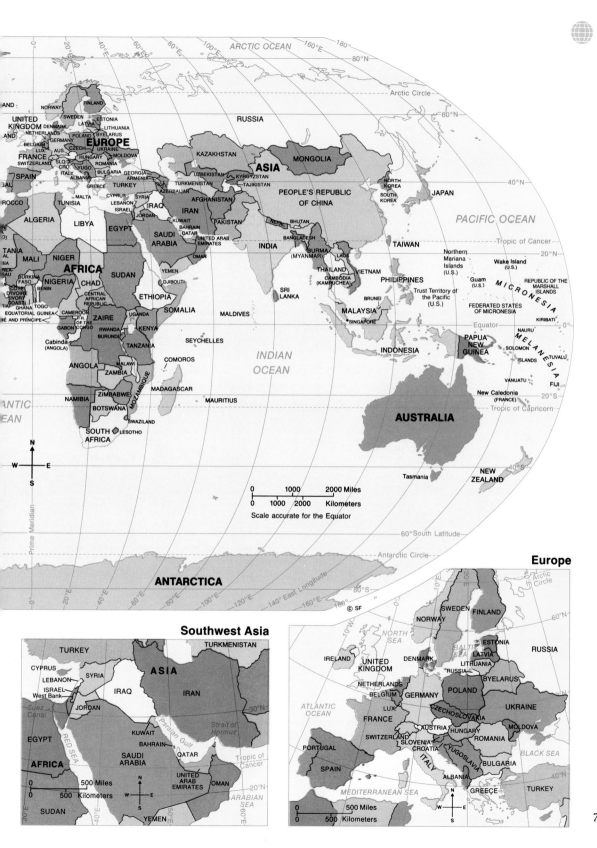

ARCTIC OCEAN

EUROPE

ASIA

RUSSIA

KAZAKHSTAN

MONGOLIA

PEOPLE'S REPUBLIC
OF CHINA

NORTH
KOREA

SOUTH
KOREA

JAPAN

PACIFIC OCEAN

UNITED
KINGDOM

NORWAY
SWEDEN FINLAND
DENMARK
NETHERLANDS
ESTONIA
LATVIA
LITHUANIA
POLAND BYELARUS
GERMANY
FRANCE
LUX.
BELGIUM
AUS. CZECH UKRAINE
SWITZERLAND SLO. HUNGARY MOLDOVA
ITALY CRO.
SPAIN YUGO. ROMANIA
ALBANIA BULGARIA GEORGIA
GREECE TURKEY ARMENIA
MALTA CYPRUS AZERBAIJAN
TUNISIA LEBANON SYRIA
ISRAEL
JORDAN IRAQ
MOROCCO

UZBEKISTAN KYRGYZSTAN
TURKMENISTAN TAJIKISTAN

ALGERIA LIBYA EGYPT
AFGHANISTAN

IRAN
PAKISTAN

KUWAIT
BAHRAIN
QATAR
SAUDI
ARABIA
UNITED ARAB
EMIRATES
OMAN

NEPAL BHUTAN

BANGLADESH

BURMA
(MYANMAR)

INDIA

TAIWAN

Tropic of Cancer

Northern
Mariana
Islands
(U.S.)

Wake Island
(U.S.)

REPUBLIC OF THE
MARSHALL
ISLANDS

AFRICA

TANIA
MALI NIGER
BURKINA
FASO
NIGERIA CHAD
SUDAN
YEMEN
DJIBOUTI

ETHIOPIA

SOMALIA

THAILAND
CAMBODIA
(KAMPUCHEA)
VIETNAM
LAOS

PHILIPPINES

SRI
LANKA

MALDIVES

BRUNEI

MALAYSIA
SINGAPORE

Guam
(U.S.)

Trust Territory of
the Pacific
(U.S.)

FEDERATED STATES
OF MICRONESIA

M I C R O N E S I A

KIRIBATI

GUINEA-
BISSAU
GUINEA
SENEGAL
CÔTE
D'IVOIRE
(IVORY
COAST)
GHANA TOGO
BENIN
EQUATORIAL GUINEA
SÃO TOMÉ AND PRÍNCIPE
GABON
P.R.
OF THE
CONGO
CAMEROON
CENTRAL
AFRICAN
REPUBLIC
ZAIRE
UGANDA
RWANDA
BURUNDI
KENYA

Cabinda
(ANGOLA)

TANZANIA

SEYCHELLES

Equator

NAURU
SOLOMON
ISLANDS

TUVALU

INDONESIA

PAPUA
NEW
GUINEA

M E L A N E S I A

ANGOLA
ZAMBIA
MALAWI
MOZAMBIQUE
ZIMBABWE
NAMIBIA
BOTSWANA
MADAGASCAR

COMOROS

INDIAN
OCEAN

MAURITIUS

VANUATU

FIJI

New Caledonia
(FRANCE)

20°S

Tropic of Capricorn

AUSTRALIA

SOUTH
AFRICA
SWAZILAND
LESOTHO

N
W E
S

0   1000   2000 Miles
0 1000 2000 Kilometers
Scale accurate for the Equator

Tasmania

NEW
ZEALAND

40°S

Prime Meridian

60°South Latitude

Antarctic Circle

ANTARCTICA

© SF

Europe

Arctic
Circle

SWEDEN FINLAND

NORWAY

NORTH
SEA

IRELAND

UNITED
KINGDOM

DENMARK

BALTIC
SEA

ESTONIA
LATVIA
LITHUANIA

RUSSIA

RUSSIA

BYELARUS

60°N

NETHERLANDS
BELGIUM
GERMANY
LUX.
POLAND

UKRAINE

ATLANTIC
OCEAN

FRANCE

SWITZERLAND
AUSTRIA
SLOVENIA
CROATIA

CZECHOSLOVAKIA

HUNGARY
MOLDOVA
ROMANIA

PORTUGAL

ITALY

YUGOSLAVIA
BULGARIA

BLACK SEA

SPAIN

ALBANIA

GREECE

TURKEY

40°N

N
W E
S

MEDITERRANEAN SEA

0   500 Miles
0   500 Kilometers

Southwest Asia

TURKEY

TURKMENISTAN

CYPRUS
LEBANON
West Bank
ISRAEL
JORDAN

SYRIA

ASIA

IRAQ

IRAN

Suez
Canal

EGYPT

RED SEA

Persian Gulf

Strait of
Hormuz

KUWAIT

BAHRAIN
QATAR

Tropic of
Cancer

AFRICA

SAUDI
ARABIA

UNITED
ARAB
EMIRATES

OMAN

30°N

20°N

N
W E
S

0   500 Miles
0   500 Kilometers

SUDAN

YEMEN

ARABIAN
SEA

783

The World: Physical

Land Elevation

Feet		Meters
10,000		3,000
5,000		1,500
2,000		600
500		150
0		0
Below Sea Level		Below Sea Level

Ice-covered land

International boundaries

0   500   1000   1500 Miles

0   500 1000 1500   Kilometers

Scale accurate for the Equator

ARCTIC OCEAN

BARENTS SEA

ICELAND

NORTH SEA

BALTIC SEA

NORTH EUROPEAN PLAIN

ALPS

EUROPE

URAL MTS.

Ob R.

Lena R.

Arctic Circle

60°N

Lake Baikal

CAUCASUS MTS.

BLACK SEA

CASPIAN SEA

ASIA

GOBI (DESERT)

SEA OF JAPAN

40°N

MEDITERRANEAN SEA

PLATEAU OF TIBET

HIMALAYAS

Huang

Yangtze

EAST CHINA SEA

PACIFIC OCEAN

ATLAS MTS.

SAHARA (DESERT)

ARABIAN DESERT

THAR DESERT

Ganges

Indus

Tropic of Cancer

20°N

RED SEA

Nile R.

ARABIAN SEA

Bay of Bengal

SOUTH CHINA SEA

PHILIPPINE ISLANDS

AFRICA

Congo R.

Lake Victoria

INDIAN OCEAN

Equator

0°

MADAGASCAR

ATLANTIC OCEAN

KALAHARI DESERT

AUSTRALIA

GREAT VICTORIA DESERT

20°S

Tropic of Capricorn

40°S

N
W — E
S

Prime Meridian

60°South Latitude

Antarctic Circle

ANTARCTICA

80°S

20°E 40°E 60°E 80°E 100°E 120°E 140°E East Longitude 160°E 180°

© SF

785

The World: Population Distribution

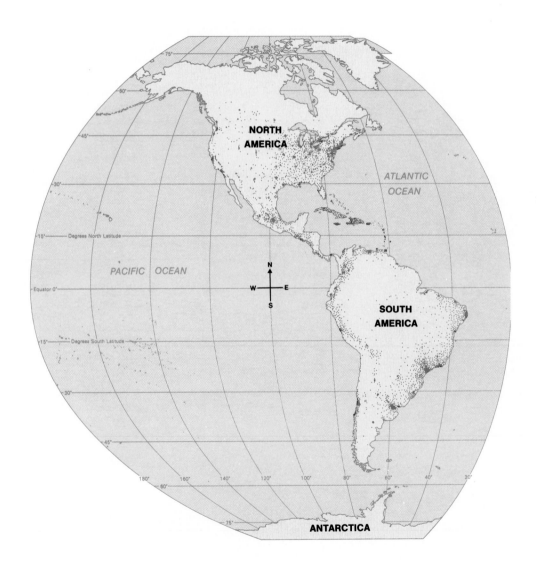

· 100,000 people

NORTH AMERICA

ATLANTIC OCEAN

PACIFIC OCEAN

75°
90°
45°
30°
15° · Degrees North Latitude
Equator 0°
15° · Degrees South Latitude
30°
45°
60°
75°

180° 160° 140° 120° 100° 80° 60° 40° 20°

N
W · E
S

SOUTH AMERICA

ANTARCTICA

North America
Political

— International boundaries
⊛ National capitals
• Other cities

0 250 500 Miles
0 250 500 Kilometers

North America
Physical

Land Elevation

Feet		Meters
14,000		4,000
7,000		2,000
1,500		500
700		200
0		0
Below Sea Level		Below Sea Level

▲ Mountain peaks

☐ Ice caps

White lines represent international boundaries

0 250 500 Miles

0 250 500 Kilometers

ASIA

BERING SEA

Bering Strait

ARCTIC OCEAN

Pt. Barrow

BROOKS RANGE

BEAUFORT SEA

ALASKA PENINSULA

ALASKA RANGE

Mt. McKinley

Kodiak I.

Gulf of Alaska

COAST MOUNTAINS

Alexander Arch.

Queen Charlotte Is.

Vancouver I.

Puget Sound

Mt. Rainier

ROCKY MOUNTAINS

GREAT PLAINS

N. CASCADES

COAST RANGES

SIERRA NEVADA

GREAT BASIN

Great Salt Lake

Mt. Whitney

DEATH VALLEY

MOJAVE DESERT

GRAND CANYON

COLORADO PLATEAU

Conception Pt.

30°North Latitude

Eugenia Pt.

BAJA CALIFORNIA

Cape San Lucas

Gulf of California

SIERRA MADRE WEST

SIERRA MADRE EAST

CENTRAL PLATEAU

Mt. Orizaba

ISTHMUS OF TEHUANTEPEC

YUCATÁN PENINSULA

CENTRAL AMERICA

ISTHMUS OF PANAMA

Panama Canal

SOUTH AMERICA

Equator 0°

Great Bear Lake

Great Slave Lake

Lake Athabasca

Reindeer Lake

Victoria I.

Queen Elizabeth Is.

Baffin Bay

Baffin I.

Davis Strait

Kalaallit Nunaat (Greenland)

Iceland

Hudson Bay

UNGAVA PENINSULA

LABRADOR

LABRADOR SEA

CANADIAN SHIELD

Saskatchewan R.

Lake Winnipeg

Lake of the Woods

Superior

Michigan

Huron

Erie

Ohio

Omaha

CENTRAL PLAINS

INTERIOR PLAINS

BLACK HILLS

Missouri

Platte

Snake R.

Arkansas

OZARK PLATEAU

Red R.

Rio Grande

Mississippi

COASTAL PLAIN

Gulf of Mexico

Okeechobee

FLORIDA PENINSULA

Cape Canaveral

Cape Hatteras

Chesapeake Bay

APPALACHIAN MTS.

PIEDMONT

COASTAL PLAIN

Champlain

Cape Cod

Long I.

Newfoundland

Gulf of St. Lawrence

LAURENTIAN SHIELD

ATLANTIC OCEAN

Bermuda Is.

Tropic of Cancer

Bahama Is.

Cuba

West Indies

Greater Antilles

Jamaica

Navassa I.

Hispaniola

Puerto Rico

Leeward Is.

Lesser Antilles

Windward Is.

CARIBBEAN SEA

L. Nicaragua

PACIFIC OCEAN

N
W E
S

789

NORTH AMERICA

CARIBBEAN SEA

CENTRAL
AMERICA

10° North Latitude

Barranquilla
Cartagena
Maracaibo
Valencia
Caracas

Orinoco R.

VENEZUELA

Ciudad Guayana

Georgetown

GUYANA

Paramaribo
Cayenne

Medellín

SURINAME

FRENCH
GUIANA
(Fr.)

ATLANTIC

OCEAN

Coco Is.
(Costa Rica)

Bogotá

Cali

COLOMBIA

Equator

Quito

Galápagos Is.
(Ecuador)

ECUADOR

Amazon R.

Belém

Guayaquil

Manaus

Iquitos

Trujillo

PERU

BRAZIL

Recife

10° South Latitude

Callao
Lima

Salvador

PACIFIC

OCEAN

Cuzco

Arequipa

La Paz

Brasília

BOLIVIA

Sucre

Belo Horizonte

Tropic of Capricorn

Antofagasta

PARAGUAY

São Paulo
Rio de Janeiro
Santos

Asunción

Tucumán

N

W   E

S

30°S

Córdoba

Pôrto Alegre

Valparaíso
Santiago

Rosario

URUGUAY

Buenos Aires
Montevideo
La Plata

Concepción

ARGENTINA

Bahía Blanca

40°S

Falkland Is.
(U.K.)

Punta Arenas

0   200   400   600 Miles

0   200   400   600
Kilometers

South America
Political

———— International boundaries
⊛ National capitals
• Other cities

NORTH AMERICA

CENTRAL
AMERICA

CARIBBEAN SEA

GUAJIRA PENINSULA

-10° North Latitude

Lake Maracaibo

Coco Is.

L L A N O S

Angel Falls

GUIANA HIGHLANDS

*ATLANTIC
OCEAN*

-Equator 0°

Galápagos Is.

▲ *Mt. Chimborazo*

Marajó I.

A M A Z O N

Gulf of Guayaquil

B A S I N

Aguja Point

A N D E S

*Cape São
Roque*

Mt. Huascarán ▲

-10° South Latitude

M O U N T A I N S

MATO GROSSO PLATEAU

São Francisco

10°S

PACIFIC

OCEAN

▲ *Mt. Ancohuma*

Lake Titicaca

B R A Z I L I A N

-20°S

ATACAMA DESERT

H I G H L A N D S

GRAN CHACO

-Tropic of Capricorn-

M O U N T A I N S

Cape Frio

Iguaçu Falls

20°S

N

W   E

S

-30°S

A N D E S

P A M P A S

30°S

Mt. Aconcagua ▲

Río de la Plata

Colorado

-40°S

Blanca Bay

San Matías Gulf

Chiloé I.

South America

Physical

P A T A G O N I A

Gulf of San Jorge

Land Elevation

Feet		Meters
14,000		4,000
7,000		2,000
1,500		500
700		200
0		0
Below Sea Level		Below Sea Level

0	200	400	600 Miles
0	200	400	600 Kilometers

Strait of Magellan

Falkland Is.

50°S

Strait of Magellan

▲ Mountain peaks

Tierra del Fuego

Cape Horn

791

White lines represent
international boundaries

Europe

Political

— International boundaries
⊛ National capitals
• Other cities

ARCTIC OCEAN

ICELAND
⊛ Reykjavik

NORWEGIAN SEA

ATLANTIC OCEAN

Faeroe Is. (Den.)

Shetland Is. (U.K.)

Hebrides Is. (U.K.)

Orkney Is. (U.K.)

SCOTLAND
Glasgow •

NORTH SEA

NORTHERN IRELAND • Belfast
UNITED KINGDOM
REPUBLIC OF IRELAND
• Dublin
• Manchester
ENGLAND
WALES
London •

NORWAY
• Bergen
⊛ Oslo

Orust I.— (Sweden)

SWEDEN
• Stockholm ⊛

FINLAND
Helsinki ⊛
• St. Petersburg

⊛ Tallinn
ESTONIA

Riga ⊛
LATVIA

RUSSIA
⊛ Moscow

Volga River

DENMARK
⊛ Copenhagen
BALTIC SEA

LITHUANIA
Vilnius ⊛
RUSSIA

• Minsk ⊛
BYELARUS

NETHERLANDS
The Hague ⊛ • Amsterdam
• Hamburg

• Berlin
GERMANY

Vistula River

⊛ Warsaw
POLAND

Essen • • Dortmund
BELGIUM
Brussels ⊛ • Düsseldorf
LUXEMBOURG
Luxembourg ⊛
• Bonn

Kiev ⊛
UKRAINE

Elbe River
Oder River

• Paris

Seine River
Loire River
Rhine River

⊛ Prague
CZECHOSLOVAKIA

Dnieper River

Bay of Biscay

• Munich

Danube River

Vienna ⊛

MOLDOVA
Kishinev ⊛

FRANCE

Zurich • LIECHTENSTEIN
Vaduz •
Bern ⊛ SWITZERLAND

⊛ Budapest
HUNGARY

AUSTRIA

ROMANIA

• Bordeaux

Ljubljana ⊛ • Zagreb
SLOVENIA CROATIA

Belgrade ⊛
Bucharest ⊛

BLACK SEA

Rhône River
Garonne River

Milan • Po River
• Turin • Genoa

Danube

SAN MARINO
⊛ San Marino

YUGOSLAVIA

⊛ BULGARIA
Sofia ⊛

Ebro River

• Marseille

Monaco •
MONACO

ITALY

• Naples

Istanbul •

PORTUGAL
• Madrid

⊛ Andorra la Vella
ANDORRA

Corsica (Fr.)
VATICAN CITY ⊛⊛ Rome

ALBANIA
• Tirana

TURKEY
40°N

⊛ Lisbon

SPAIN
• Barcelona

Sardinia (It.)

GREECE

ASIA

Tagus River

• Córdoba

Balearic Is. (Sp.)

N
W ⊛ E
S

Athens •

Crete (Gr.)

Guadalquivir River

Gibraltar (U.K.)

• Palermo

Sicily (It.)

MALTA ⊛ Valletta

MEDITERRANEAN SEA

AFRICA

| 0 | 200 | 400 Miles |
| 0 | 200 | 400 |

Kilometers

Europe
Physical

Land Elevation

Feet		Meters
14,000		4,000
7,000		2,000
1,500		500
700		200
0		0
Below Sea Level		Below Sea Level

— International boundaries

☐ Ice caps

ARCTIC OCEAN

North Cape

BARENTS SEA

NORWEGIAN SEA

KOLA PENINSULA

WHITE SEA

SCANDINAVIAN PENINSULA

Gulf of Bothnia

Lake Onega

Lake Ladoga

Gulf of Finland

Iceland

Arctic Circle

ATLANTIC OCEAN

Shetland Is.

Hebrides Is.

Orkney Is.

BALTIC SEA

Volga River

NORTH SEA

Great Britain

British Isles

Ireland

IRISH SEA

NORTH EUROPEAN PLAIN

Dnieper River

North Latitude

English Channel

Thames River

RUHR VALLEY

Vistula River

Oder River

Elbe River

Seine River

BRITTANY PENINSULA

Loire River

Rhine River

Danube River

CARPATHIAN MTS.

Dniester River

W   E
N
S

Bay of Biscay

Gironde River

CENTRAL MASSIF

ALPS

Po River

HUNGARIAN BASIN

TRANSYLVANIAN ALPS

Danube River

BLACK SEA

10° West Longitude

PYRENEES

DINARIC ALPS

BALKAN MTS.

ADRIATIC SEA

BALKAN PENINSULA

ASIA

IBERIAN PENINSULA

Corsica

APENNINES

APENNINE PENINSULA

Sardinia

Balearic Is.

TYRRHENIAN SEA

PINDUS MTS.

AEGEAN SEA

Tagus River

Guadalquivir River

of Gibraltar

IONIAN SEA

Sicily

Crete

Malta

MEDITERRANEAN SEA

AFRICA

0	200	400 Miles
0	200	400 Kilometers

Asia
Political

⊛ — International boundaries
⊛ National capitals
• Other cities

	500	1,000 Miles
0		
0	500	1,000
		Kilometers

Asia
Physical

Land Elevation

Feet	Meters
14,000	4,000
7,000	2,000
1,500	500
700	200
0	0
Below Sea Level	Below Sea Level

International boundaries

1,000 Miles

1,000 Kilometers

500

500

Africa
Political

— International boundaries
✦ National capitals
• Other cities

| 0 | 400 | 800 Miles |
| 0 | 400 | 800 | Kilometers |

796

© SF

EUROPE

ASIA

ATLANTIC
OCEAN

Azores

Madeira Is.

Canary Is.

Cape
Verde

MEDITERRANEAN SEA

ATLAS MOUNTAINS

Strait of Gibraltar

Gulf of
Sidra

Suez Canal

S A H A R A

AHAGGAR
PLATEAU

TIBESTI
MOUNTAINS

LIBYAN DESERT

NUBIAN
DESERT

Tropic of Cancer

40°North Latitude

RED SEA

20°N

S A H E L

GEZIRA

Gulf of Aden

ETHIOPIAN
HIGHLANDS

SOMALI PENINSULA

Senegal River

HORN
OF
AFRICA

GREAT RIFT
VALLEY

Mt. Cameroon

Ubangi   River

Volta River

Gulf of Guinea

São Tomé

Cape
Lopez

CONGO
BASIN

Lake
Albert

Lake
Turkana

Mt. Kenya

Lake
Victoria

Mt. Kilimanjaro

Equator

ATLANTIC

OCEAN

Zanzibar

Kasai River

KATANGA
PLATEAU

Lake
Tanganyika

Cape
Delgado

Comoro Is.

Lake
Nyasa
Lake
Malawi

Mozambique Channel

Madagascar

Zambezi

Lake
Kariba

NAMIB DESERT

OKAVANGO
SWAMP

Victoria
Falls

Tropic of Capricorn

KALAHARI
DESERT

Limpopo River

Orange River   Vaal River

DRAKENSBERG RANGE

GREAT KARROO

Cape of
Good Hope

N
W   E
S

INDIAN

OCEAN

797

Africa
Physical

Land Elevation
Feet		Meters
14,000		4,000
7,000		2,000
1,500		500
700		200
0		0
Below
Sea Level		Below
Sea Level

International boundaries

0	400	800 Miles
0	400	800

Kilometers

Australia and Oceania
Physical-Political

Land Elevation

Feet	Meters
14,000	4,000
7,000	2,000
1,500	500
700	200
0	0
Below Sea Level	Below Sea Level

— International boundaries
⊛ National capitals
· Other cities
▲ Mountain peaks

798

HISTORICAL REFERENCE

World Population Growth, 8000 B.C. – A.D. 2000

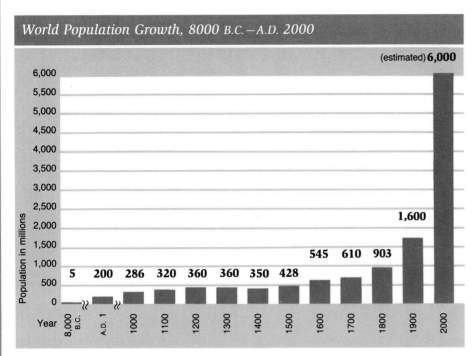

Estimates vary regarding the world's population at various dates. This graph is useful mainly for showing the great increase in population growth that occurred after A.D. 1800. That is when the Industrial Revolution began in Europe and the United States. Major advances in farming, food distribution, sanitation, and medical knowledge in the 19th and 20th centuries led to the tremendous increase in human population in recent years.

World Religions Today

Religion	North America[1]	South America	Europe[2]	Asia[3]	Africa	Oceania[4]	Totals
Total Christian	260,924,600	197,642,000	334,467,100	103,740,700	147,400,400	18,781,100	1,062,955,900
Roman Catholic	142,433,400	186,660,800	178,000,400	57,300,100	57,950,100	5,230,600	627,575,400
Eastern Orthodox	5,650,600	351,200	45,100,000	2,340,000	8,800,200	390,100	62,632,100
Protestant[5]	112,840,600	10,630,000	111,366,700	44,100,600	80,650,100	13,160,400	372,748,400
Jewish	7,610,700	738,600	4,110,200	4,290,700	229,400	73,900	17,053,500
Muslim[6]	1,580,900	405,100	20,200,600	378,100,100	153,220,400	87,000	553,594,100
Zoroastrian	2,700	2,600	14,000	228,200	1,100	1,000	249,600
Shinto	45,000	—	—	32,000,000	—	—	32,045,000
Taoist	32,000	13,000	13,500	20,000,000	800	2,900	20,062,200
Confucian	99,000	58,000	440,000	157,500,000	2,000	18,000	158,117,000
Buddhist	330,000	240,000	240,000	248,770,100	15,000	23,700	249,618,800
Hindu	310,000	635,000	440,000	458,600,000	850,000	325,000	461,160,000
Totals	270,934,900	199,734,300	359,925,400	1,403,229,800	301,719,100	19,312,600	2,554,856,100
Population[7]	395,365,000	262,963,000	766,325,000	2,777,385,000	536,589,000	24,458,000	4,763,085,000

(1) Includes Central America and West Indies. (2) Includes communist countries where it is difficult to determine religious affiliation. (3) Includes areas in which persons have traditionally enrolled in several religions, as well as China, with an official communist establishment. (4) Includes Australia, New Zealand, and islands of the South Pacific. (5) Protestant figures outside Europe usually include "full members" (adults) rather than all baptized persons and are not comparable to those of ethnic religions or churches counting all adherents. (6) According to the Islamic Center, Wash., D.C., there are 1 billion Muslims worldwide. (7) United Nations data, midyear 1984.

Early Civilizations

Major States and Empires, c. 500 B.C.

Major States and Empires, c. A.D. 200

Major States and Empires, c. 1200

Islamic world

Major States and Empires, c. 1500

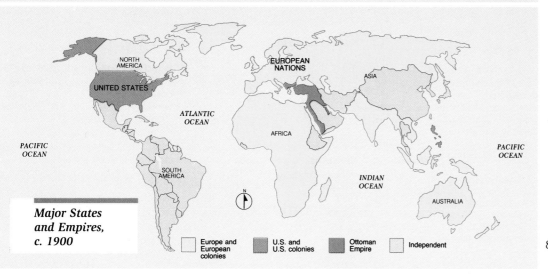

Major States and Empires, c. 1900

Europe and European colonies   U.S. and U.S. colonies   Ottoman Empire   Independent

LIST OF RULERS

Roman Empire

	Year rule began
Augustus	27 B.C.
Tiberius	A.D. 14
Caligula	37
Claudius	41
Nero	54
Galba	68
Galba; Otho, Vitellius	69
Vespasian	69
Titus	79
Domitian	81
Nerva	96
Trajan	98
Hadrian	117
Antoninus Pius	138
Marcus Aurelius and Lucius Verus	161
Marcus Aurelius (alone)	169
Commodus	180
Pertinax; Julian	193
Septimius Severus	193
Caracalla and Geta	211
Caracalla (alone)	212
Macrinus	217
Elagabalus	218
Severus Alexander	222
Maximinus	235
Gordian I and Gordian II; Pupienus and Balbinus	238
Gordian III	238
Philip (the Arab)	244
Decius	249
Gallus and Volusian	251
Aemilian	253
Valerian and Gallienus	253
Gallienus (alone)	258
Claudius (the Goth)	268
Quintillus	270
Aurelian	270
Tacitus	275
Florianus	276
Probus	276
Carus	282
Carinus and Numerianus	283
Diocletian	284
Diocletian and Maximian	286
Galerius and Constantius	305
Galerius, Maximinus II, Severus	306
Galerius, Maximinus II, Constantine, Licinius, Maxentius, Daia	307
Constantine and Licinius	314
Constantine (the Great)	324
Constantine II, Constans, Constantius II	337
Constantius II and Constans	340
Constantius II	350
Julian II (the Apostate)	361
Jovian	363

The Divided Empire

Valentinian (West) and Valens (East)	364
Valentinian with Gratian (West) Valens (East)	367
Gratian with Valentinian II (West) Valens (East)	375
Gratian with Valentinian II (West) Theodosius (East)	378
Valentinian II (West) and Theodosius (East)	383
Theodosius	394
Honorius (West) and Arcadius (East)	395
Honorius (West) and Theodosius II (East)	408
Valentinian III (West) and Theodosius II (East)	423
Valenentian III (West) and Marcian (East)	450
Maximus (West), Avitus (West); Marcian (East)	455
Avitus (West), Marcian (East)	456
Majorian (West), Leo (East)	457
Severus II (West), Leo (East)	461
Anthemius (West), Leo (East)	467
Olybrius (West), Leo (East)	472
Glycerius (West), Leo (East)	473
Nepos (West), Leo II (East)	474
Romulus Augustulus (West) and Zeno (East)	475
End of Roman Empire in West. Odoacer takes over.	476

England and Great Britain

Saxons and Danes

	Years of reign
Alfred the Great	871–900
Ethelred the Unready	978–1016
Canute	1016–1035
Harold I	1035–1040
Hardicanute	1040–1042
Edward the Confessor	1042–1066
Harold II	1066

Normans

William the Conqueror	1066–1087
William II	1087–1100
Henry I	1100–1135
Stephen	1135–1154

Plantagenets

Henry II	1154–1189
Richard I (the Lion-Hearted)	1189–1199
John	1199–1216
Henry III	1216–1272
Edward I	1272–1307
Edward II	1307–1327
Edward III	1327–1377
Richard II	1377–1399

Lancaster and York

Henry IV	1399–1413
Henry V	1413–1422
Henry VI	1422–1461
Edward IV	1461–1483
Edward V	1483
Richard III	1483–1485

Tudors

Henry VII	1485–1509
Henry VIII	1509–1547
Edward VI	1547–1553
Mary I	1553–1558
Elizabeth I	1558–1603

Stuarts

James I	1603–1625
Charles I	1625–1649
Charles II	1660–1685
James II	1685–1688
William III and Mary II	1689–1694
William III (alone)	1694–1702
Anne	1702–1714

Hanoverians

George I	1714–1727
George II	1727–1760
George III	1760–1820
George IV	1820–1830
William IV	1830–1837
Victoria	1837–1901
Edward VII	1901–1910

Windsors (name adopted 1917)

George V	1910–1936
Edward VIII	1936
George VI	1936–1952
Elizabeth II	1952–

France

Capetians

Hugh Capet	987–996
Robert II (the Pious)	996–1031
Henry I	1031–1060
Philip I (the Fair)	1060–1108
Louis VI (the Fat)	1108–1137
Louis VII	1137–1180
Philip II Augustus	1180–1223
Louis VIII	1223–1226
Louis IX	1226–1270
Philip III	1270–1285
Philip IV	1285–1314
Louis X	1314–1316
Philip V	1316–1322
Charles IV	1322–1328

Valois

Philip VI	1328–1350
John	1350–1364
Charles V	1364–1380
Charles VI	1380–1422
Charles VII	1422–1461
Louis XI	1461–1483
Charles VIII	1483–1498
Louis XII	1498–1515
Francis I	1515–1547
Henry II	1547–1559
Francis II	1559–1560
Charles IX	1560–1574
Henry III	1574–1589

Bourbons

Henry IV	1589–1610
Louis XIII	1610–1643
Louis XIV	1643–1715
Louis XV	1715–1774
Louis XVI	1774–1792

After 1792

Napoleon I	1804–1814
Louis XVIII (Bourbon)	1814–1824
Charles X (Bourbon)	1824–1830
Louis Philippe (Orléans)	1830–1848
Napoleon III	1851–1870

Russia

Ivan III (the Great)	1462–1505
Basil III	1505–1533
Ivan IV (the Terrible)	1533–1584
Theodore I	1584–1598
Boris Godunov	1598–1605
Theodore II	1605
Basil IV	1606–1610

Romanovs

Michael	1613–1645
Alexius	1645–1676
Theodore III	1676–1682
Ivan V and Peter I	1682–1689
Peter I (the Great) alone	1689–1725
Catherine I	1725–1727
Peter II	1727–1730
Anna	1730–1740
Ivan VI	1740–1741
Elizabeth	1741–1762
Peter III	1762
Catherine II (the Great)	1762–1796
Paul	1796–1801
Alexander I	1801–1825
Nicholas I	1825–1855
Alexander II	1855–1881
Alexander III	1881–1894
Nicholas II	1894–1917

Mali and Songhai

Sundiata	1230
Uli	1255
Wati	1270
Khalifa	1274
Abu-Bakr	1274
Sakura	1285
Qu	1300
Muhammad	1305
Musa I	1307
Magha I	1337
Sulayman	1341
Qasa	1360
Mari Jata II	1360
Musa II	1374
Magha II	1387
Sandaki	1388
Mahmud	1390–?

Sonni Dynasty of Songhai

Sonni Silman Dandi	?–1464
Sonni Ali	1464
Sonni Baro	1492–1493

Askia Dynasty of Songhai

Askia Muhammad	1493
Musa	1528
Muhammad Benkan	1531
Ismail	1537
Ishaq I	1539
Dawud I	1549
al-Hajj	1582
Muhammad Bana	1586
Ishaq II	1588
Muhammad Gao	1591

Inca Empire

Manco Capac	c.1100
Sinchi Roca	
Lloque Yupanqui	
Mayta Capac	
Capac Yupanqui	c.1200
Inca Roca	
Yahuar Huacac	
Viracocha	
Inca Urcon	1438
Pachacuti	1438
Topa Inca Yupanqui	1471
Huayna Capac	1493
Huascar	1526–1532
Atahualpa	1530–1533
Topa Hualpa	1533
Manco Inca Yupanqui	1533
Sayri Topa	1545
Titu Cusi Yupanqui	1560
Topa Amaru	1571–1572

Aztec Empire

Acamapichtli	1372
Huitzilihuitl	1391
Chimalpopoca	1415
Itzcoatl	1426
Montezuma I	1440
Axayacatl	1468
Tizoc	1481
Ahuitzotl	1486
Montezuma II	1502
Cuitlahuac	1520
Cuauhtemoc	1520–1521

FACTS ABOUT COUNTRIES[1]

Flag	Country or Dependency	Capital	Area	Population[2]	Major or Official Languages	Important Products
	Afghanistan	Kabul	250,000 (mi^2) 647,497 (km^2)	16,000,000	Pushtu, Dari Persian	carpets, natural gas, fruit, salt, coal, wheat
	Albania	Tirana	11,099 28,748	3,000,000	Albanian	minerals, metals, olives, cereals, tobacco, lumber
	Algeria	Algiers	919,591 2,381,741	25,000,000	Arabic, French	wheat, barley, petroleum, wine, fruit, iron ore
	Andorra	Andorra la Vella	175 453	51,000	French, Spanish	livestock, tobacco, cereals, potatoes, iron ore
	Angola	Luanda	481,351 1,246,700	10,000,000	Bantu languages, Portuguese	coffee, diamonds, cotton, oil, fish, iron ore
	Antigua and Barbuda	St. Johns	171 442	85,000	English	cotton, clothing, rum, molasses, sugar, bananas
	Argentina	Buenos Aires	1,068,297 2,766,889	33,000,000	Spanish	meat, wool, hides, wheat, corn, fruit, vegetables
	Armenia[3]	Yerevan	11,490 29,800	3,300,000	Armenian, Russian	almonds, cotton, livestock, minerals, machinery
	Australia	Canberra	2,967,895 7,686,848	17,000,000	English	wheat, wool, livestock, metal ores, coal, bauxite
	Austria	Vienna	32,374 83,849	8,000,000	German	lumber, metal products, paper, textiles, food
	Azerbaijan	Baku	33,430 86,600	7,100,000	Azerbaijani, Russian	cotton, fruit, grain, oil, steel, iron ore
	Azores (PO)	Ponta Delgada	902 2,335	253,600	Portuguese	farm products, fish, fruit, grains
	Bahamas	Nassau	5,380 13,935	256,000	English	pharmaceuticals, salt, fish, lobsters, rum
	Bahrain	Manama	254 659	486,000	Arabic, English, French	petroleum products, fish, aluminum processing
	Bangladesh	Dhaka	55,598 143,998	113,000,000	Bengali, English	jute goods, tea, fish, leather, seafood, hides
	Barbados	Bridgetown	166 431	260,000	English	clothing, molasses, rum, sugar, fish, lime
	Belgium	Brussels	11,781 30,513	10,000,000	Dutch, French	precious stones, iron and steel products
	Belize	Belmopan	8,867 22,965	193,000	English, Spanish	molasses, rice, lumber, livestock, fish, fruit
	Benin	Porto-Novo	43,483 112,622	5,000,000	French, others	palm oil, cotton, cocoa beans, fish, iron ore
	Bermuda (UK)	Hamilton	20 53	59,000	English	perfumes, petroleum products, pharmaceuticals
	Bhutan	Thimphu	18,147 47,000	1,000,000	Dzongkha, Nepali	lumber, fruit, coal, vegetables, cement
	Bolivia	La Paz, Sucre	424,163 1,098,581	6,000,000	Spanish, Quechua, Aymara	petroleum, tin, gold, lead, zinc, coffee
	Botswana	Gaborone	231,804 600,372	1,000,000	English, Setswana	livestock, diamonds, copper, nickel, salt

(PO) Portugal   (UK) United Kingdom

[1] includes countries with populations over 30,000; flags are based on most recent information available at time of publication.

[2] Source: *Statesman's Year-Book 1991–1992*

[3] The Soviet Union broke apart in 1991. Lithuania, Latvia, and Estonia were recognized as independent nations in September 1991. The Commonwealth of Independent Nations was formed in December 1991 by the independent nations of Armenia, Azerbaijan, Byelarus, Kazakhstan, Kyrgyzstan, Moldova, Russia, Tajikistan, Turkmenistan, Ukraine, and Uzbekistan. Georgia was not a member as of early 1992.

Flag	Country or Dependency	Capital	Area	Population	Major or Official Languages	Important Products
	Brazil	Brasília	3,286,473 (mi²) 8,511,965 (km²)	156,000,000	Portuguese	iron ore, steel, motor vehicles, coffee, sugar
	Brunei	Bandar Seri Begawan	2,226 5,765	267,000	Malay, English, Chinese	petroleum, rubber, lumber, rice, pepper, bananas
	Bulgaria	Sofia	42,823 110,912	9,000,000	Bulgarian	farm products, minerals, machinery, equipment
	Burkina Faso	Ouaga-dougou	105,869 274,200	9,000,000	French, others	livestock, cotton, peanuts, sesame, grains
	Burma[1]	Rangoon[2]	261,216 676,552	39,000,000	Burmese	teak, rice, sugar, precious stones, rubber
	Burundi	Bujumbura	10,747 27,834	6,000,000	Kirundi, French	cotton, hides, tea, coffee, bananas, grain
	Byelarus	Minsk	80,134 207,600	10,300,000	Byelorussian, Russian	flax, grain, livestock, potatoes, peat, machinery
	Cambodia	Phnom Penh	69,898 181,035	8,000,000	Khmer	fish, rubber, paper, timber, rice, sugar
	Cameroon	Yaoundé	183,568 475,442	12,000,000	English, French, others	cotton, coffee, cocoa beans, tea, rubber
	Canada	Ottawa	3,851,791 9,976,139	27,000,000	English, French	motor vehicles, machinery, lumber, metal ores
	Canary Islands (SP)	Las Palmas	2,808 7,273	1,615,000	Spanish	fish, fruit, grains, wine, vegetables, sugar
	Cape Verde	Praia	1,557 4,033	369,000	Portuguese	fish, shellfish, salt, bananas, coffee, sugar
	Central African Republic	Bangui	240,534 622,984	3,000,000	French, Sango	coffee, diamonds, cocoa beans, lumber, cotton
	Chad	N'Djamena	495,752 1,284,000	6,000,000	French, Arabic, others	livestock, cotton, rice, animal products, fish
	Chile	Santiago	292,256 756,945	13,000,000	Spanish	paper, lumber, copper, iron, nitrates, fish
	China	Beijing	3,705,390 9,596,961	1,110,000,000	Mandarin Chinese, others	farm products, petroleum, minerals, metals
	Colombia	Bogotá	439,735 1,138,914	33,000,000	Spanish	petroleum, coffee, sugar, cotton, textiles
	Comoros	Moroni	719 1,862	503,000	Arabic, French	vanilla, copra, cloves, perfume essences, sugar
	Congo	Brazzaville	132,046 342,000	2,000,000	French, Lingala, Kokongo	lumber, petroleum, cocoa beans, palm oil, sugar
	Costa Rica	San José	19,575 50,700	3,000,000	Spanish	livestock, sugar, cocoa beans, coffee, palm oil
	Croatia	Zagreb	21,829 56,538	4,700,000	Croato-Serbian	grain, livestock, timber, coal, petroleum, cement
	Cuba	Havana	44,218 114,524	11,000,000	Spanish	sugar, rice, citrus, tobacco, nickel, fish
	Cyprus	Nicosia	3,572 9,251	698,800	Greek, Turkish	cereals, citrus, grapes, potatoes, copper, cement
	Czechoslo-vakia	Prague	49,370 127,869	15,600,000	Czech, Slovak, Hungarian	iron and steel, machinery, beer, wheat, potatoes
	Denmark	Copenhagen	16,629 43,069	5,100,000	Danish	machinery, textiles, dairy products, clothing

(SP) Spain   [1]officially, Myanmar   [2]officially, Yangon

Flag	Country or Dependency	Capital	Area	Population	Major or Official Languages	Important Products
	Djibouti	Djibouti	8,494 (mi²) 22,000 (km²)	484,000	Arabic, French, Afar, Somali	salt, livestock, hides
	Dominica	Roseau	290 751	81,200	English, French patois	cocoa beans, lime juice, bananas, pumice, fruit
	Dominican Republic	Santo Domingo	18,816 48,734	7,200,000	Spanish	coffee, tobacco, bauxite, nickel, sugar, cocoa
	Ecuador	Quito	109,483 283,561	10,500,000	Spanish, Quechua	bananas, coffee, cocoa beans, fish, petroleum
	Egypt	Cairo	386,659 1,001,449	50,700,000	Arabic	cotton, textiles, chemicals, rice, petrochemicals
	El Salvador	San Salvador	8,124 21,041	5,200,000	Spanish	cotton, coffee, sugar, livestock, lumber, rice
	Equatorial Guinea	Malabo	10,830 28,051	417,000	Spanish, Fang, Bubi	lumber, coffee, cocoa beans, bananas, fish
	Estonia	Tallinn	17,413 45,100	1,600,000	Estonian, Russian	fish, peat, grain, livestock, vegetables, paper, shale
	Ethiopia	Addis Ababa	471,776 1,221,900	50,000,000	Amharic, others	hides, coffee, oilseeds, fruits, vegetables, metals
	Fiji	Suva	7,056 18,274	727,000	Fijian, Hindi, English	copra, sugar, gold, lumber, bananas, ginger
	Finland	Helsinki	130,128 337,032	4,970,000	Finnish, Swedish	lumber, paper, manufactured goods, glassware
	France	Paris	211,207 547,026	56,180,000	French	machinery, clothing, farm products, textiles
	French Guiana (FR)	Cayenne	35,135 91,000	93,500	French, Creole	shrimp, rice, lumber, gold, bauxite, sugar
	French Polynesia (FR)	Papeete	1,544 4,014	188,800	French, Polynesian languages	coconuts, citrus, bananas, sugar, vanilla, pearls
	Gabon	Libreville	103,346 267,667	1,220,000	French, Bantu languages	coffee, petroleum, lumber, manganese, iron ore, gold
	Gambia	Banjul	4,361 11,295	875,000	English, others	fish, peanuts, cotton, grains, livestock
	Georgia	Tbilisi	26,900 69,700	5,500,000	Georgian, Russian	grain, vegetables, coal, manganese, steel, timber
	Germany[1]	Berlin	137,838 357,000	79,000,000	German	precision instruments, chemicals, motor vehicles
	Ghana	Accra	92,099 238,537	14,900,000	English, others	lumber, petroleum, gold, manganese, cocoa beans
	Greece	Athens	50,944 131,944	10,000,000	Greek	textiles, minerals, fish, fruit, cotton, tobacco
	Greenland[2] (DE)	Godthab	840,000 2,175,600	56,558	Danish, Greenlande	metallic ore, fish, fish products, seals
	Grenada	St. George's	133 344	110,000	English	cocoa beans, citrus, fish, nutmeg, bananas, sugar
	Guadeloupe (FR)	Basse-Terre	687 1,779	336,000	French, Creole	fruits, vegetables, sugar, vanilla, cocoa beans, fish
	Guam (US)	Agana	212 549	130,400	Chamorro, English	palm oil, fish, copra, citrus, bananas, sugar
	Guatemala	Guatemala	42,042 108,889	9,000,000	Spanish, Indian languages	cotton, sugar, livestock, bananas, coffee, lumber
	Guinea	Conakry	94,925 245,857	6,700,000	French, Fulani, others	bauxite, fruit, coffee, iron ore, rice, bananas

(DE) Denmark   (FR) France   (US) United States
[1]East Germany reunified with West Germany 10/3/90.
[2]officially, Kalaallit Nunaat

Flag	Country or Dependency	Capital	Area	Population	Major or Official Languages	Important Products
	Guinea-Bissau	Bissau	13,948 (mi²) 36,125 (km²)	966,000	Portuguese	peanuts, palm oil, fish, shrimp, lumber, coconuts
	Guyana	Georgetown	83,000 214,969	990,000	English, Hindi, Urdu	bauxite, aluminum, sugar, rice, shrimp, coffee
	Haiti	Port-au-Prince	10,714 27,750	5,700,000	French, Creole	coffee, sugar, rice, textiles, bauxite
	Honduras	Tegucigalpa	43,277 112,088	4,400,000	Spanish, Indian languages	bananas, coffee, sugar, lumber, livestock
	Hong Kong (UK)	Victoria	403 1,045	5,760,000	Chinese, English	textiles, clothing, electronic goods, cameras, shoes
	Hungary	Budapest	35,919 93,030	10,590,000	Hungarian	consumer goods, tools, machinery, wheat, fruit
	Iceland	Reykjavik	39,768 103,000	253,500	Icelandic	fish, livestock, dairy products, chemicals
	India	New Delhi	1,269,339 3,287,590	843,930,000	Hindi, others	clothing, textiles, jute, machinery, cars, steel
	Indonesia	Jakarta	788,421 2,042,012	179,100,000	Bahasa Indonesia, others	petroleum, tin, lumber, rubber, tea, rice
	Iran	Tehran	636,293 1,648,000	53,920,000	Farsi, Kurdish, Azerbaijani	wheat, petroleum, livestock, textiles, cement
	Iraq	Baghdad	167,925 434,924	17,060,000	Arabic, Kurdish	petroleum, cement, livestock, cotton, textiles
	Ireland	Dublin	27,136 70,283	3,540,000	Irish, English	chemicals, dairy products, textiles, machinery
	Israel	Jerusalem	8,019 20,770	4,820,000	Hebrew, Arabic	citrus, chemicals, clothing, machinery, food products
	Italy	Rome	116,303 301,225	57,600,000	Italian	clothing, shoes, textiles, machinery, foods, cars
	Ivory Coast (Côte d'Ivoire)	Abidjan	124,503 322,463	12,100,000	French, others	lumber, coffee, cocoa beans, sugar, cotton
	Jamaica	Kingston	4,244 10,991	2,400,000	English	bauxite, bananas, sugar, citrus, rum, cocoa beans
	Japan	Tokyo	143,750 372,313	123,260,000	Japanese	cars, metal products, textiles, electronics
	Jordan	Amman	37,737 97,740	3,170,000	Arabic	phosphates, fruits, olives, copper, sulfur
	Kazakhstan	Alma-Ata	1,049,155 2,717,300	16,700,000	Kazakh, Russian	cotton, grain, livestock, metal ores, oil, coal, steel
	Kenya	Nairobi	244,960 582,646	24,080,000	Swahili, Bantu languages, English	livestock, coffee, tea, hides, cement, sugar
	Kiribati	Bairiki	281 728	66,250	English, Gilbertese	copra, fish, mother-of-pearl, phosphates
	Korea, North	Pyongyang	46,540 120,538	22,420,000	Korean	chemicals, minerals, rice, wheat, cement
	Korea, South	Seoul	38,025 98,484	42,800,000	Korean	machinery, steel, clothing, footwear
	Kuwait	Kuwait	6,880 17,818	2,040,000	Arabic, English	petroleum, shrimp, fertilizer
	Kyrgyzstan	Bishkek	76,640 198,500	4,400,000	Kirghiz, Russian	livestock, rice, sugar beets, wheat, hemp, fruit, tobacco, machinery
	Laos	Vientiane	91,429 236,800	4,050,000	Lao	lumber, tin, coffee, textiles, fruits, rice

(UK) United Kingdom

807

Flag	Country or Dependency	Capital	Area	Population	Major or Official Languages	Important Products
	Latvia	Riga	24,595 (mi²) 63,700 (km²)	2,700,000	Latvian, Russian	barley, oats, livestock, timber, machinery
	Lebanon	Beirut	4,015 10,400	2,800,000	Arabic, French	textiles, fruits, lumber, jewelry, cotton, tobacco
	Lesotho	Maseru	11,720 30,355	1,720,000	English, Sesotho	livestock, diamonds, hides, wool, wheat
	Liberia	Monrovia	43,000 111,800	2,440,000	English, others	lumber, iron ore, gold, cocoa beans, coffee, fish
	Libya	Tripoli	679,359 1,759,540	4,000,000	Arabic	petroleum, olives, dates, barley, citrus fruit
	Lithuania	Vilnius	25,170 65,200	3,700,000	Lithuanian, Russian	grain, potatoes, sugar beets, timber, machinery
	Luxembourg	Luxembourg	998 2,586	378,400	Luxembourgish, German, French	chemicals, steel, oats, barley, potatoes, wheat
	Macao (PO)	Macao	6 16	440,000	Chinese, Portuguese	manufactured goods, fish, electronic goods, clothing
	Madagascar	Antananarivo	226,657 587,041	11,440,000	Malagasy, French	chromium, graphite, cloves, cotton, coffee
	Malawi	Lilongwe	45,747 118,484	7,980,000	English, Chichewa	fish, tobacco, peanuts, fertilizer, textiles
	Malaysia	Kuala Lumpur	127,316 329,749	17,810,000	Malay, Chinese, Tamil, English	petroleum, lumber, tin, rubber, palm oil, textiles
	Maldives	Male	115 298	214,139	Divehi	coconuts, fish, millet, breadfruit, vegetables
	Mali	Bamako	478,764 1,240,000	9,090,000	French, others	fish, livestock, cotton, peanuts, textiles, rice
	Malta	Valletta	122 316	354,900	Maltese, English	manufactured goods, ships, textiles, fruits
	Marshall Islands	Majuro	70 183	40,609	English, others	copra, tortoise shell, mother-of-pearl, fish
	Martinique (FR)	Fort-de-France	425 1,102	359,000	French, Creole	bananas, rum, sugar, pineapples, vegetables
	Mauritania	Nouakchott	397,953 1,030,700	1,970,000	Arabic, French	copper, iron ore, dates, cereals, vegetables
	Mauritius	Port Louis	790 2,045	1,082,000	English, others	molasses, sugar, tea iron ore, rice, fish
	Mexico	Mexico City	761,601 1,972,547	81,140,000	Spanish, Indian languages	cotton, petroleum, corn, livestock, coffee, minerals
	Micronesia	Kolonia	280 726	108,600	English, others	copra, fish, handicrafts
	Moldova	Kishinev	13,000 33,700	4,400,000	Moldavian (Romanian), Russian	grain, sugar beets, steel, clothing, machinery
	Mongolia	Ulaanbaatar	604,247 1,565,000	2,095,000	Mongolian	livestock, wheat, oats, footwear, minerals
	Morocco	Rabat	172,413 446,550	24,500,000	Arabic, Berber, French, Spanish	phosphates, citrus, carpets, chemicals
	Mozambique	Maputo	309,494 801,590	14,900,000	Portuguese, Bantu languages	cotton, cashew nuts, sugar, copra, tea
	Namibia	Windhoek	318,259 824,292	1,290,000	Afrikaans, English, others	sheepskins, diamonds, uranium, copper, lead

(FR) France   (PO) Portugal

808

Flag	Country or Dependency	Capital	Area	Population	Major or Official Languages	Important Products
	Nepal	Katmandu	54,362 (mi²) 140,797 (km²)	18,000,000	Nepali, Newari	rice, lumber, grain, sugar, jute, cotton
	Netherlands	Amsterdam, The Hague	16,041 41,548	14,890,000	Dutch	manufactured goods, foods, flower bulbs
	Netherlands Antilles (NE)[1]	Willemstad	308 800	192,866	Dutch	phosphates, sugar, fruits, vegetables, fish
	New Cale-donia (FR)	Nouméa	7,358 19,058	164,173	French, Melane-sian languages	nickel, coffee, copra, chrome, iron, cobalt
	New Zealand	Wellington	103,736 268,676	3,390,000	English, Maori	lumber, dairy products, wool, manufactured goods
	Nicaragua	Managua	50,193 130,000	3,750,000	Spanish, Indian languages	coffee, cotton, sugar, chemicals, livestock
	Niger	Niamey	489,189 1,267,000	7,450,000	French, Hausa, others	coal, iron, uranium, peanuts, livestock
	Nigeria	Abuja	356,667 923,768	118,700,000	English, others	petroleum, lumber, tin, cotton, palm oil
	Norway	Oslo	125,182 324,219	4,200,000	Norwegian, Lapp	petroleum, lumber, fish, ships, chemicals
	Oman	Muscat	105,000 271,950	2,000,000	Arabic	petroleum, fish, asbestos, dates
	Pakistan	Islamabad	310,402 809,943	105,400,000	Urdu, English, others	cotton, rice, fish, sugar, leather
	Panama	Panama City	29,761 77,082	2,320,000	Spanish, English	bananas, sugar, rice, coffee, lumber, corn
	Papua New Guinea	Port Moresby	178,259 461,691	3,800,000	Melanesian lan-guages, English	cocoa beans, copra, lumber, copper, rubber
	Paraguay	Asunción	157,047 406,752	4,160,000	Spanish, Guarani	livestock, tobacco, cotton, oilseeds, lumber
	Peru	Lima	496,222 1,285,216	22,330,000	Spanish, Quechua, Aymara	coffee, cotton, sugar, fish, copper, silver
	Philippines	Manila	115,830 300,000	60,500,000	Pilipino, English, others	lumber, sugar, textiles, coconuts, tobacco
	Poland	Warsaw	120,725 312,677	37,930,000	Polish	machinery, textiles, coal, iron, steel
	Portugal	Lisbon	35,552 92,082	10,300,000	Portuguese	cork, fish, wine, olives, textiles
	Puerto Rico (US)	San Juan	3,435 8,897	2,134,000	Spanish, English	chemicals, clothing, fish, electronic goods, sugar
	Qatar	Doha	4,247 11,000	371,863	Arabic	petroleum, fish, steel
	Réunion (FR)	Saint-Denis	969 2,510	50,082	French, Creole	sugar, beans, vanilla, molasses, rum, bananas
	Romania	Bucharest	91,699 237,500	23,000,000	Romanian, Hungarian, others	lumber, petroleum, coal, machinery, minerals
	Russia	Moscow	6,592,800 17,075,000	148,000,000	Russian	gas, petroleum, coal, iron ore, grain, machinery
	Rwanda	Kigali	10,169 26,338	6,710,000	Kinyarwandu, French	coffee, tea, beans, potatoes, livestock
	St. Christopher and Nevis	Basseterre	100 258	43,410	English	molasses, sugar, cotton, salt, fish, spices

(FR) France   (NE) Netherlands   (US) United States
[1]Aruba became independent from the Netherland Antilles in 1986 and is now an autonomous member of the Netherlands. (Capital: Oranjestad; Population: 62,500)

Flag	Country or Dependency	Capital	Area	Population	Major or Official Languages	Important Products
	St. Lucia	Castries	238 (mi²) 619 (km²)	146,600	English, French patois	bananas, coconuts, fish, cocoa beans, spices
	St. Vincent and the Grenadines	Kingstown	150 390	113,950	English	bananas, arrowroot, copra, nutmeg, sugar
	Samoa, American (US)	Pago Pago	76 198	32,297	Samoan, English	tuna, pet food, fish meal, handicrafts
	Samoa, Western	Apia	1,093 2,831	163,000	Samoan, English	copra, cocoa beans, lumber, bananas
	São Tomé and Príncipe	São Tomé	372 964	115,600	Portuguese	copra, palm oil, cocoa beans, lumber, bananas
	Saudi Arabia	Riyadh	829,996 2,149,690	12,000,000	Arabic	petroleum, cement, dates, chemicals, livestock
	Senegal	Dakar	75,750 196,192	7,170,000	French, Wolof, others	phosphates, fertilizer, peanut oil, cotton, fish
	Seychelles	Victoria	108 280	67,378	English, French	copra, vanilla, fish, livestock, cinnamon
	Sierra Leone	Freetown	27,699 71,740	4,140,000	English, Mende, others	coffee, cocoa beans, fish, ginger, peanuts, sugar
	Singapore	Singapore	224 581	2,690,000	English, Chinese, Malay, Tamil	manufactured goods, fish, electronic goods, textiles
	Slovenia	Ljubljana	7,819 20,251	1,900,000	Slovenian	wheat, maize, potatoes, timber, lignite, steel
	Solomon Islands	Honiara	10,983 28,446	308,796	Melanesian languages, English	lumber, fish, copra, rice, palm oil, spices
	Somalia	Mogadishu	246,199 637,657	6,260,000	Somali	spices, iron ore, livestock, bananas, peanuts
	South Africa	Capetown, Pretoria	471,443 1,221,037	30,190,000	Afrikaans, English, Bantu languages	gold, diamonds, uranium, wool, fruits, chrome
	Spain	Madrid	194,896 504,782	39,540,000	Spanish, Catalan, Galician, Basque	footwear, fruit, vegetables, cars, clothing
	Sri Lanka	Colombo	25,332 65,610	16,810,000	Sinhala, Tamil, English	rubber, tea, graphite, petroleum, spices, fish
	Sudan	Khartoum	967,495 2,505,813	25,560,000	Arabic, others	livestock, peanuts, copper, cotton, sesame seeds
	Suriname	Paramaribo	63,251 163,820	416,839	Dutch, Surinamese, English	aluminum, bauxite, citrus, lumber, shrimp, sugar
	Swaziland	Mbabane	6,704 17,363	681,059	English, Siswati	coal, iron ore, citrus, cotton, livestock, sugar
	Sweden	Stockholm	173,731 449,964	8,500,000	Swedish	lumber, motor vehicles, machinery, iron and steel
	Switzerland	Bern	15,941 41,288	6,700,000	German, French, Italian	precision instruments, dairy products, chemicals
	Syria	Damascus	71,498 185,180	11,300,000	Arabic	clothing, fruits, vegetables, cotton, petroleum
	Tajikistan	Dushanbe	55,240 143,100	5,300,000	Tajik, Russian	grain, livestock, clothing, coal, lead, oil, sulphur, zinc
	Taiwan	Taipei	13,885 35,961	20,300,000	Mandarin Chinese	electrical machinery, footwear, textiles, citrus
	Tanzania	Dar es Salaam	364,898 945,087	24,800,000	Swahili, Bantu languages, English	diamonds, cashews, sisal, cloves, coffee, tea

810

(US) United States

Flag	Country or Dependency	Capital	Area	Population	Major or Official Languages	Important Products
	Thailand	Bangkok	198,456 (mi²) 514,000 (km²)	55,900,000	Thai, Chinese	rubber, tapioca, tin, rice, textiles, lumber
	Togo	Lomé	21,925 56,785	3,400,000	Ewe, Mina, others	coffee, cocoa beans, rice, phosphates, cotton, iron
	Tonga	Nuku'alofa	290 751	95,200	Tongan, English	coconuts, bananas, vanilla, pineapples, papayas, fish
	Trinidad and Tobago	Port-of-Spain	1,981 5,130	1,240,000	English, Hindi	ammonia, fertilizer, petroleum, sugar, rice
	Tunisia	Tunis	63,379 164,152	7,750,000	Arabic, French	textiles, phosphates, olive oil, fertilizers
	Turkey	Ankara	301,381 780,576	50,670,000	Turkish	fruits, textiles, foods, livestock, cotton, nuts
	Turkmenistan	Ashkhabad	186,400 488,100	3,600,000	Turkmen, Russian	cotton, livestock, grain, oil, clothing, vegetables
	Uganda	Kampala	91,343 236,880	17,000,000	English, Swahili, others	cotton, coffee, tea, tobacco, sugar, textiles
	Ukraine	Kiev	171,770 445,000	51,800,000	Ukrainian, Russian	grain, sugar beets, livestock, coal, steel, chemicals
	United Arab Emirates	Abu Dhabi	32,278 83,600	1,600,000	Arabic, others	petroleum, fish, pearls, dates, tobacco, fruits
	United Kingdom	London	92,247 244,100	57,240,000	English, Welsh, Gaelic	chemicals, foods, iron and steel, motor vehicles
	United States of America	Washington, D.C.	3,615,105 9,363,123	249,630,000	English	aircraft, chemicals, machinery, grain, fruits
	Uzbekistan	Tashkent	172,741 447,400	20,300,000	Uzbek, Russian	cotton, livestock, rice, coal, cement, clothing
	Uruguay	Montevideo	68,037 176,215	3,110,000	Spanish	livestock, wool, leather, textiles, wheat, rice
	Vanuatu	Port-Vila	5,700 14,763	142,630	Bislama, English, French	fish, copra, cocoa beans, livestock
	Venezuela	Caracas	352,143 912,050	9,250,000	Spanish	petroleum, iron ore, coffee, cocoa beans
	Vietnam	Hanoi	127,242 329,556	65,000,000	Vietnamese	coal, minerals, fruits, vegetables, rice, rubber
	Virgin Islands (US)	Charlotte Amalie	133 344	106,000	English	manufacturing, petroleum refining, fruits, sugar
	Yemen[1]	Sanaa	203,850 527,970	12,000,000	Arabic	coffee, cotton, wheat, fish salt, dates, cotton
	Yugoslavia[2]	Belgrade	98,766 255,804	24,110,000	Serbo-Croatian, Croato-Serbian, Slovenian	processed foods, lumber, chemicals, shoes, fruits
	Zaire	Kinshasa	905,563 2,345,409	34,140,000	French, Bantu languages	copper, diamonds, cobalt, petroleum, coffee
	Zambia	Lusaka	290,584 752,614	8,500,000	English, Bantu languages	cobalt, lead, zinc, cotton, chemicals
	Zimbabwe	Harare	150,803 390,580	9,370,000	English, Shona, Sindebele	cotton, fruits, sugar, copper, chrome, nickel

(US) United States
[1]Yemen reunified as the Republic of Yemen May 1990.
[2]Yugoslavia broke apart when Slovenia and Croatia were recognized as independent countries by European Community January 1992.

Glossary/Biographical Dictionary

Salvador Allende

Pronunciation Key

a	hat	i	it	oi	oil
ā	age	ī	ice	ou	out
ä	far	o	hot	u	cup
e	let	ō	open	u̇	put
ē	equal	ô	order	ü	rule
ėr	term				

ch	child		a in about
ng	long		e in taken
sh	she	ə =	i in pencil
th	thin		o in lemon
ᴛʜ	then		u in circus
zh	measure		

The key to the pronunciation of foreign sounds is on page 835 of the index.

A

Abbas, Shah (1557–1629), one of Persia's greatest kings, who ruled from 1587 to 1629 (p. 429)

Abbasid dynasty [ab′ə sid], *n.* in 750, the dynasty established by the Abbasids after the overthrow of the Umayyad rulers of the Islamic Empire. (p. 257)

Abidjan [ab′i jän′], *n.* capital of Côte d'Ivoire, formerly the Ivory Coast, in the southeastern part of the country. (p. 708)

Abraham [ā′brə ham] (c. 1800 B.C.), (in the Bible) the ancestor of the Hebrews; the founder of Judaism. (p. 45)

absolute monarch, *n.* a ruler who has complete authority over the government of a country and the lives of the citizens of that country. (p. 398)

acid rain, *n.* rain containing a dilute solution of sulfuric and nitric acid, created by pollutants given off during the burning of fossil fuels. (p. 765)

Act of Supremacy [sə prem′ə sē], *n.* (in England) in 1534, the act issued by Parliament that made Henry VIII head of the Anglican Church of England. (p. 393)

Adenauer [ad′n ou′ər], Konrad (1876–1967), German statesman, first chancellor of West Germany from 1949 to 1963. (p. 675)

Aegean Sea [i jé′ən], *n.* sea between Turkey and Greece; an arm of the Mediterranean Sea. (p. 60)

Aeschylus [es′kə ləs] (525–456 B.C.), Greek tragic poet and dramatist; considered by many to be the father of tragedy. (p. 83)

Africanization, *n.* in Zaire, the policy of President Mobutu to encourage pride in African culture and history. (p. 709)

Afrikaners [af′rə kä′nerz], persons born in South Africa of European, especially Dutch, descent; Boers. (p. 712)

Age of Reason, *n.* an intellectual, social, and political movement in Europe characterized by rational thinking, beginning in the 17th century and reaching its highest point in the 18th century; also called the Enlightenment. (p. 416)

agriculture [ag′rə kul′chər], *n.* science, art, or occupation of cultivating the soil, including the production of crops and the raising of livestock; farming. Agriculture developed during the Neolithic period. (p. 11)

Aguinaldo [ä gē näl′ dō], **Emilio** (1870?–1964), Philippine leader against Spain and later, after the Spanish-American war, against the United States. (p. 571)

Akbar [ak′bär] (1542–1605), Mughal ruler of India from 1556 to 1605. (p. 430)

alchemy [al′kə mē], *n.* the chemistry of the Middle Ages, which combined science, magic, and philosophy. Alchemy tried to find a means of changing cheaper metals into gold and silver and to discover a universal remedy for disease. (p. 279)

Alexander (the Great) (356 B.C.– 323 B.C.), king of Macedonia from 336 B.C. to 323 B.C. He conquered the Greek city-states and the Persian empire. (p. 72)

Alexander I (1777–1825), tsar of Russia from 1801 to 1825. (p. 547)

Alexander II (1818–1881), tsar of Russia from 1855 to 1881. He abolished serfdom. (p. 547)

Allende [ä yän′dā], **Salvador** (1908–1973), leader of the Marxist party in Chile and president of the country from 1970 to 1973. (p. 747)

Allies [al′īz], *n., pl.* the countries that fought against Germany, Austria-Hungary, Turkey, and Bulgaria in World War I, including Britain, France, Russia, Serbia, and the United States. (p. 590)

Almoravids [al′mə rä′vidz], *n., pl.* in the 11th century, a group of Muslim Berbers who lived in the northwestern part of ancient Ghana. (p. 328)

alphabet [al′fə bet], *n.* the letters of a language, arranged in their usual order, not as they are in words; a set of letters or characters representing sounds, used in writing (from the first two letters of the Phoenician alphabet— "aleph" and "bet") (p. 44)

Amin [ä mēn′] **Dada, Idi** (1925–), Ugandan general and dictator of Uganda from 1971 to 1979. (p. 706)

Anglo-Saxons [ang′glō sak′səns], *n., pl.* the Germanic tribes that invaded England in the 400s and 500s and ruled most of England until the Norman Conquest in 1066. (p. 183)

Antarctica [ant′ärk′tə kə], *n.* continent around or near the South Pole. (p. 765)

Anthony [an′thə nē], **Susan B.** (1820–1906), American leader in the movement for women's suffrage. (p. 530)

Susan B.
Anthony

Vasco de
Balboa

apartheid [ə pärt′hāt], *n.* policy of racial segregation used to maintain white control, especially as practiced by law in South Africa. (p. 713)

appeasement [ə pēz′mənt], *n.* the policy of giving in to the demands of another, especially the demands of a potential enemy. (p. 642)

aqueducts [ak′wə dukts], *n., pl.* artificial channels or large pipes for bringing water from a distance; structures that support such channels or pipes. (p. 107)

Aquinas [ə kwī′nəs], **Saint Thomas** (1225?–1274), Italian philosopher and theologian of the Roman Catholic Church; author of *Summa Theologica.* (p. 207)

Aquino [ä kē′nō], **Corazon** [kō′rä-sôn′] (1933–   ), Philippine political leader, president of the Philippines since 1986. (p. 690)

arabesque [ar′ə besk′], *n.* an elaborate design of flowers, leaves, geometrical figures, and so forth, originating in the Islamic world; Turks and Persians created many of these designs. (p. 282)

Arabic [ar′ə bik], *n.* the Semitic language of the Arabs, related to Hebrew, now spoken chiefly in the Arabian peninsula, Iraq, Syria, Jordan, Lebanon, and North Africa. (p. 272)

Archimedes [är′kə mē′dēz] (287?–212 B.C.), Greek mathematician, physicist, and inventor, who first stated the principles underlying specific gravity and the use of the lever. (p. 85)

Aristophanes [ar′ə stof′ə nēz] (448?–385 B.C.), Greek writer of comedies. (p. 83)

Aristotle [ar′ə stot′l] (384–322 B.C.), Greek philosopher and scientist, student of Plato and the tutor of Alexander the Great. (p. 81)

Asoka [ə sō′kə] (?–232 B.C.), Indian emperor (273–232 B.C.), of the Mauryan dynasty, who gave India unity, peace, and a responsible government; responsible for spreading Buddhism throughout the Eastern Hemisphere. (p. 126)

Atahualpa [ä′tä wäl′pä] (1500?–1533), the last ruler of the Inca Empire in Peru, murdered by the Spaniards under Pizarro. (p. 455)

atheism [ā thē′iz′əm], *n.* disbelief in the existence of God. (p. 609)

Athens [ath′ənz], *n.* capital of Greece, in the southeastern part. In ancient times, a Greek city-state famous for its art and literature. (p. 66)

Attila [at′l ə] (A.D. 406?–453), leader of the Huns in their invasions of Europe; defeated by the Romans and Goths in 451. (p. 183)

Australia, Commonwealth of, *n.* formed in 1901, a federal union of six Australian colonies similar to the United States, associated with the United Kingdom of Great Britain and Northern Ireland. (p. 554)

australopithecines [ô′strə lō pith′-ə sēns′], *n., pl.* group of extinct primates whose fossil remains have been found in various parts of the world, especially in southern and eastern Africa; early prehumans. (p. 7)

Avignon [à vē nyôn′], *n.* city in southeastern France, the residence of the popes from 1309 to 1377. (p. 388)

Axis [ak′sis], *n.* Germany, Italy, and Japan, and their allies, during World War II. (p. 641)

Aztecs [az′teks], *n., pl.* a highly civilized American Indian people who ruled a large empire in central Mexico before its conquest by the Spaniards in 1521. (p. 335)

B

Bacon [bā′kən], **Francis** (1561–1626), English essayist, statesman, and philosopher who advocated scientific experimentation. (p. 410)

Bacon [bā′kən], **Roger** (1214?–1294), English philosopher and pioneer of modern science. (p. 208)

Baghdad [bag′dad], *n.* capital of Iraq, in the central part, on the Tigris River; formerly the capital of the Islamic Empire under the Abbasid dynasty. (p. 258)

Balboa [bal bō′ə], **Vasco de** [vä′skō dä] (1475?–1517), Spanish explorer who was the first European to visit the Pacific Ocean, in 1513; he also established the first successful Spanish settlement on the American mainland. (p. 375)

Balfour Declaration, *n.* in 1917, the British-issued declaration promising the Jews a national homeland in Palestine. (p. 628)

Balkans [bol′kəns], *n., pl.* a peninsula in southeastern Europe, extending south into the Mediterranean Sea; the Balkan states consist of countries on the Balkan peninsula which contained numerous Slavic ethnic groups. (pp. 550, 585)

Bangladesh [bäng′glə desh′], *n.* country in South Asia, on the Bay of Bengal, in the Commonwealth of Nations; formerly the Pakistani province of East Pakistan. (p. 696)

Bay of Pigs invasion, *n.* in 1961, a failed attempt by Cuban refugees, with some assistance from the United States, to invade Cuba and remove Cuban leader Fidel Castro from power. (p. 745)

Beethoven [bā′tō vən], **Ludwig van** [lüd′vig vän] (1770–1827), German composer whose symphonies and chamber music laid the groundwork for romantic music. (p. 526)

Menachem
Begin

Simón
Bolívar

Begin [bā′gin], **Menachem** [menä′kem] (1913–   ), Israeli political leader, prime minister of Israel from 1977 to 1983. (p. 730)

Beijing [bā jing′], *n.* the modern-day capital of China in the northeast part of the country; established by the Jin dynasty. (p. 294)

Benedict [ben′ə dikt], **Saint** (A.D.480?–543?), Italian monk who founded the Benedictine order. (p. 186)

Bengal [ben gôl′], *n.* former province of India, in the northeastern part, now divided into West Bengal (a part of India) and East Bengal (formerly a part of Pakistan and, since 1972, the country of Bangladesh). In the 18th and 19th centuries, Bengal was the cornerstone of the British Empire in India. (p. 564)

Benin [bə nēn′], *n.* a forest state of ancient Africa, located in what is now southern Nigeria. (p. 333)

Bering Strait [bir′ing], *n.* the narrow strip of water between the Bering Sea and the Arctic Ocean which separates North America from Asia. Scientists believe that this strait was once a land bridge over which many separate migrations of peoples crossed into the Americas. (p. 162)

Berlin Wall, *n.* barricade erected in the divided city of Berlin by the East German government to stop the flow of emigrés into West Berlin. (p. 669)

Bessemer [bes′ə mər], **Sir Henry** (1813–1898), English engineer who invented the Bessemer process, a method of making a good grade of steel. (p. 519)

Bible [bī′bəl], *n.* the collection of sacred writings of the Christian religion comprising the Old and New Testaments; the form of the Old Testament accepted by the Jews. (p. 45)

Bill of Rights, *n.* the first ten amendments to the Constitution of the United States, adopted in 1791, which include a declaration of fundamental rights held by United States citizens. (p. 486)

Bill of Rights of 1689, *n.* part of the Revolution Settlement passed by the English Parliament and agreed to by William and Mary, guaranteeing the fundamental rights of the people of England. (p. 481)

Bismarck [biz′märk], **Otto von** (1815–1898), German prince and statesman who united the German States into an empire in 1871. (p. 543)

Black Death, *n.* the bubonic plague that spread through Europe and Asia in the 1300s, carried along trade routes by caravans and travelers from infected areas. One-fourth to one-half of the entire population of Europe is believed to have died of the Black Death between 1348 and 1370. (p. 205)

Black Tuesday, *n.* October 29, 1929, the day during which the prices on the New York Stock Exchange began to drop very quickly, signaling the beginning of the Great Depression. (p. 639)

Boccaccio [bō kä′chē ō], **Giovanni** [jō vä′nē] (1313–1375), Italian humanist poet and prose writer. (p. 358)

Bolívar [bō lē′vär], **Simón** [sēmōn′] (1783–1830), Venezuelan general and statesman, who led revolts against Spanish rule in South America. Bolivia is named after him. (p. 503)

Bonaparte [bō′nə pärt], **Napoleon** [nə pō′lē ən] (1769–1821), French general and emperor of France from 1804 to 1815. (p. 498)

Boniface VIII [bon′ə fās], **Pope** (1294–1303), head of the Catholic Church who declared that the Pope had absolute power over everything and everyone on earth. (p. 388)

Boston [bô′stən], *n.* seaport and capital of Massachusetts, on the Atlantic. (p. 485)

bourgeoisie [bùr′zhwä zē′], *n.* (in France before the Revolution) the upper level of the Third Estate consisting of wealthy city-dwellers, such as lawyers, doctors, merchants, and manufacturers; the middle class. (p. 493)

Boyle [boil], **Robert** (1627–1691), English scientist and philosopher credited with being the first person to use the scientific method in chemistry. (p 415)

British East India Company, *n.* private company set up by the British government in 1600 to establish trading posts and promote trade. (p. 378)

bronze [bronz], *n.* a reddish-brown metal made by melting together the right amounts of tin and copper. (p. 16)

Buddhism [bü diz′əm], *n.* religion based on the teachings of Buddha which maintains that right living will enable people to attain nirvana, a condition free from all desire and pain. (p. 125)

bureaucracy [byù rok′rə sē], *n.* system of government by groups of officials; concentration of power in government bureaus. (p. 235)

Byzantine Empire [biz′n tēn′], *n.* eastern part of the Roman Empire after its division in A.D. 395. The Byzantine Empire ended with the capture of its capital, Constantinople, by the Turks in 1453. (p. 231)

Caesar [sē′zər], **Julius** (102–44 B.C.), Roman general, statesman, and historian. (p. 99)

caliph [kā′lif], *n.* the former title of religious and political heads of some Muslim states. Also, calif. (p. 254)

Fidel Castro

Charlemagne

Winston Churchill

Cc

Calvin [kal'vən], **John** (1509–1564), French leader of the Protestant Reformation at Geneva. (p. 391)

Canaanites [kā'nə nīts], *n., pl.* Semitic people who settled along the eastern coast of the Mediterranean; conquered by the Arameans and ancient Jews about 1200 B.C. (p. 43)

Canada, Dominion of, *n.* in 1867, establishment of Canada as a self-governing country within the British Commonwealth; Canada was allowed a constitution, but Britain retained control over foreign policy. (p. 553)

capitalism [kap'ə tə liz'əm], *n.* an economic system based on the ownership of land, factories, and other means of production by private individuals or groups of individuals who compete with one another to produce goods and services offered on a free market for profit. (p. 354)

Cárdenas [kär'ᴛнā näs], **Lázaro** (1895–1970), Mexican political leader and president of Mexico from 1936 to 1940. (p. 744)

Carolingian Renaissance [kar'ə lin'jē ən ren'ə säns'], *n.* a great revival of learning which took place during the reign of Charlemagne. (p. 188)

Carthage [kär'thij], *n.* city and seaport of ancient times in North Africa, founded by the Phoenicians. It was destroyed by the Romans in 146 B.C., rebuilt in 29 B.C., and finally destroyed by the Arabs in A.D. 698. (p. 96)

caste system [kast], *n.* rigid and complex social structure into which Hindus are divided. By tradition, a Hindu is born into a caste and cannot rise above it within this lifetime. (p. 123)

Castro [kas'trō], **Fidel** (1927–   ), Cuban revolutionary and premier of Cuba since 1959. (p. 745)

Catherine the Great (1729–1796), empress of Russia from 1762 to 1796, she made many territorial conquests; Catherine II. (p. 404)

Cavaliers [kav'ə lirs'], *n. pl.* people who supported Charles I of England in his struggle with Parliament from 1640 to 1649. (p. 480)

Cavour [kä vur'], **Camillo Benso di** [kä mē'lō ben'sō dē] (1810–1861), Italian statesman, a leader in unifying Italy. (p. 542)

Central Powers, *n., pl.* Germany and Austria-Hungary during World War I, sometimes also including their allies Turkey and Bulgaria. (p. 590)

Cervantes [sər van'tēz], **Miguel de** [mē gel' ᴛнā] (1547–1616), Spanish writer, author of *Don Quixote.* (p. 366)

Chamberlain [chām'bər lən], **Neville** (1869–1940), British statesman, prime minister of Great Britain from 1937 to 1940. (p. 642)

Champlain [sham plān'], **Samuel de** (1567?–1635), French explorer who founded Quebec and was the first French governor of Canada. (p. 378)

Chandragupta Maurya [chun'drə gùp'tə mä'ùr yə] (?–?286 B.C.), Indian emperor and founder of the Mauryan Empire. (p. 126)

Chang River [chäng], *n.* river flowing from Tibet through central China into the East China Sea, the longest river in China. Also known as the Yangtze. (p. 137)

Charlemagne [shär'lə mān] (A.D. 742–814), king of the Franks from A.D. 768 to 814 and emperor of the Holy Roman Empire from A.D. 800 to 814. (p. 187)

Chaucer [chô'sər], **Geoffrey** (1340?–1400), English poet, author of *The Canterbury Tales.* (p. 209)

Chiang Kai-shek [chyang' kī'shek'] (1886–1975), Chinese general and political leader, president of Nationalist China in 1948, and of its government on Taiwan from 1950 to 1975. (p. 622)

Children's Levy, *n.* recruiting system of the Ottoman Empire; every five years thousands of boys were chosen from the conquered non-Muslim peoples of the empire and taken to Istanbul where they were converted to Islam, educated, and trained for either the army or the state bureaucracy. (p. 426)

China, *n.* a country in eastern Asia whose civilization developed along the Huang River. (p. 36)

Christianity [kris'chē an'ə tē], *n.* the religion based on the teachings of Jesus Christ as they appear in the Bible; Christian religion. (p. 179)

chronicles [kron'ə kəls], *n., pl.* records of events in the order in which they took place; history; stories. (p. 186)

Churchill [chėr'chil], **Winston** (1874–1965), British statesman and writer, prime minister of Great Britain from 1940 to 1945 and from 1951 to 1955. (p. 645)

city-state, *n.* an independent state consisting of a city and the territories depending on it. (p. 22)

civil rights, *n., pl.* the rights of a citizen, especially the rights guaranteed to all citizens of the United States, regardless of race, color, religion, or sex; the rights of personal liberty. (p. 628)

civil rights movement, *n.* organized attempts to gain rights for black Americans which began in the 1950s and 1960s in the United States. (p. 671)

classical culture, *n.* the blend of Greek and Roman culture that formed the roots of Western civilization. (p. 105)

class struggle, *n.* a conflict between divisions of society, especially between capital and labor. (p. 528)

Clovis [klō'vis] (A.D. 465?–511), king of the Franks from A.D. 481 to 511; founder of the Merovingian dynasty. (p. 186)

Christopher
Columbus

Code Napoleon, *n.* Napoleon's legal code which established the principle of equality of all citizens before the law and modernized the French legal system. (p. 499)

Colbert [kôl ber′], **Jean** (1619–1683), French statesman and financier during the reign of Louis XIV. (p. 399)

Cold War, *n.* after World War II, the contest for power between the communist nations headed by the Soviet Union and the nations of the West headed by the United States. (p. 664)

collective security, *n.* the guarantee by a group of countries of the security of each country in the group; the maintenance of peace by collective action against a country attacking any nation in the group. (p. 617)

collectivization [kə lek′ti vī zā′-shən], *n.* the process of transferring ownership from individuals to the state or all the people collectively; in agriculture, requiring farmers to work the land as a group rather than as individual landowners. (p. 613)

Columbus [kə lum′bəs], **Christopher** (1451?–1506), Italian navigator in the service of Spain who sailed to America in 1492, making its existence known to Europeans. (p. 373)

Comintern [kom′in tèrn′], *n.* the Communist International, an association composed of communist parties from all countries and dominated by the Soviet Union. (p. 615)

Commercial Revolution, *n.* changes in the European economy brought about by an increase in money and trade from the colonies overseas; result was the growth of capitalism and deep poverty for the lower classes. (p. 379)

common law, *n.* law based on custom and usage and confirmed by the decisions of judges, as distinct from statute law. (p. 219)

Common Market, *n.* an association of Belgium, France, Italy, Luxembourg, the Netherlands, and West Germany, established in 1958 to eliminate tariffs among its members and to have a common tariff for external commerce; European Economic Community. Britain, Denmark, and Ireland joined the Common Market in 1973, Greece in 1981, Spain and Portugal in 1985. (p. 676)

commune [kom′yün], *n.* a political division made up of groups of collective farmers or workers. (p. 682)

Communist Party, *n.* the name given the Bolshevik party after Lenin's successful coup d'état in 1917. (p. 609)

condottieri [kon′dôt tye′rē], *n., pl.* leaders of private bands of soldiers in Italy around the 1300s and 1400s. (p. 356)

Confederation of the Rhine, *n.* group of 38 states that Napoleon placed under his protection after he defeated the Austrians and Russians; he imposed modernizing reforms including the establishment of religious freedom and the abolition of serfdom. (p. 500)

Confucius [kən fyü′shəs] (551 B.C.–479 B.C.), *n.* Chinese philosopher and moral teacher. His followers combined his teachings with religious ideas to make a religion called Confucianism. (p. 141)

conquistadors [kon kēs′tə dôrz], *n., pl.* Spanish conquerors in North or South America during the 1500s. (p. 454)

Constantinople [kon′stan tə-nō′pəl], *n.* former name of Istanbul; the capital of the Byzantine Empire and later the capital of Turkey. (p. 184)

contras [kon′tras], *n., pl.* guerrillas or rebels, especially those in Nicaragua, fighting a government established by revolution; counter-revolutionary. (p. 752)

cooperative movement, *n.* movement based on Robert Owen's socialist ideas; stores and factories were set up in which members shared in the profits and losses. (p. 527)

Copernicus [kə pėr′nə kəs], **Nicolaus** (1473–1543), Polish astronomer who demonstrated that the earth rotates on its axis and that the planets revolve around the sun. (p. 410)

Cordova [kôr′də və], city in southern Spain; a learning center for scholars during the golden age of Muslim culture, from 900 to 1100. (p. 255)

Cortés [kôr′tez], **Hernando** [er-nän′dō] (1485–1547), Spanish soldier who conquered Mexico. (p. 454)

cottage industry, system of production in which workers make products at home with an agreement with someone who agrees to sell the products. (p. 514)

Counter Reformation, *n.* the reform movement within the Roman Catholic Church during the 1500s and 1600s designed to counter the effects of the Reformation. (p. 393)

credit, *n.* money in a person's account. As money was used more during the Middle Ages, a merchant could deposit money in one city, get a receipt, and collect the money in another city. (p. 205)

credit financing, *n.* a system of running a business with borrowed money. (p. 638)

creoles [krē′ōlz], *n., pl.* children born in Latin America whose parents were born in Spain. (p. 459)

Crimea [krī mē′ə], *n.* peninsula in the southwestern part of the Soviet Union in Europe, on the north coast of the Black Sea. (p. 542)

Cro-Magnon people [krō mag′-nən], group of prehistoric people who lived in southwestern Europe about 25,000 years ago. Considered of the same species as mod-

Oliver
Cromwell

Leonardo
da Vinci

Charles Dickens

ern human beings, they used stone and bone implements; some were skilled artists. (p 8)

Cromwell [krom′wel], **Oliver** (1599–1658), English general, statesman, and Puritan leader, Lord Protector of the Commonwealth from 1653 to 1658. (p. 480)

Crusaders [krü sā′dərs], *n., pl.* people who took part in any of the Crusades to recover the Holy Land from the Muslims. (p. 201)

Cruz [krüz], **Juana Inés de la** (1651–1695), a Mexican nun who became the greatest lyric poet of the Spanish colonial period. (p. 464)

Cuba [kyü′bə], *n.* country on the largest island in the West Indies, south of Florida. (p. 577)

cuneiform [kyü nē′ə fôrm], *n.* the wedge-shaped writing used by the Sumerians and later adopted by other ancient peoples of the Fertile Crescent. (p. 23)

currency devaluation, *n.* the printing of enormous quantities of paper money in larger and larger denominations, making money worth less. (p. 638)

Cuzco [küs′kō], *n.* city in southern Peru, once the capital of the Inca empire. (p. 337)

Cyrillic alphabet [si ril′ik], *n.* an alphabet now used for Russian and many other Slavic languages, which is a modern form of an ancient Slavic alphabet named for St. Cyril, an apostle to the Slavs in the A.D. 800s, who is traditionally supposed to have invented it. (p. 236)

da Gama [də gam′ə], **Vasco** [vas′kō] (1469?–1524), Portuguese navigator who discovered a route from Europe to India by sailing around southern Africa. (p. 373)

daimyo [dī′myō], *n., pl.* feudal nobles of Japan; the word means "great name." (p. 317)

Damascus [də mas′kəs], *n.* capital of Syria, in the southwestern part; one of the world's oldest cities. (p. 255)

Danube [dan′yüb], *n.* river flowing from southern West Germany through Austria, Czechoslovakia, Hungary, Yugoslavia, Bulgaria, Romania, and the Soviet Union into the Black Sea. (p. 182)

Darwin [där′wən], **Charles Robert** (1809–1882), English naturalist who formulated the theory of evolution through natural selection. (p. 521)

da Vinci [də vin′chē], **Leonardo** (1452–1519), Italian painter, musician, sculptor, architect, engineer, and scientist. (p. 360)

D-day, *n.* June 6, 1944, the day when the Allies landed in France in World War II. (p. 651)

Declaration of the Rights of Man and of the Citizen, declaration passed by the French National Assembly on August 27, 1789, proclaiming the "inalienable rights" of the French people. (p. 495)

deforestation [de fôr′ist ā shən], *n.* the large-scale process of clearing forests for farms, fuel and lumber. (p. 766)

Delhi [del′ē], *n.* city in northern India, former capital of India; center of the most important Muslim kingdom from 1206 to 1526. (p. 263)

democracy [di mok′rə sē], *n.* a government run by the people who live under it, either in a direct or indirect fashion. (p. 64)

Descartes [dā kärt′], **René** [rə nā′] (1596–1650), French philosopher and mathematician. (p. 410)

desertification [di zėrt′ə fə kā′shən], *n.* deterioration of arid land into desert, caused by a change in climate or by overuse by people and animals. (p. 766)

despot [des′pət], *n.* monarch having unlimited power; absolute ruler. (p. 50)

despotism [des′pə tiz′əm], *n.* government ruled by someone with unlimited power. (p. 105)

de-Stalinization, *n.* the revision of Soviet admiration of Stalin that became official policy after 1956 in the Soviet Union. (p. 667)

Diaspora [dī as′pər ə], *n.* in the first and second centuries A.D., communities outside Judea where many Jews lived, including Alexandria, Damascus, and Babylon; the scattering of the Jews after their captivity in Babylon. (p. 104)

Dickens [dik′ənz], **Charles** (1812–1870), English writer whose novels described the plight of the poor. (p. 524)

Disraeli [diz rā′lē], **Benjamin** (1804–1881), Earl of Beaconsfield; British statesman and novelist, prime minister in 1868 and from 1874 to 1880. (p. 544)

Dominic [dom′ə nik], **Saint** (1170–1221), Spanish priest who founded an order of preaching friars in 1215 and an order of nuns in 1206. The Dominicans stressed vows of poverty and missionary work among the people. (p. 200)

Donatello [don′ə tel′ō] (1386?–1466), Italian sculptor. (p. 362)

dowry [dou′rē], *n.* money or property that a woman brings to the man she marries. During the Middle Ages, every upper class father tried to provide a dowry for his daughter. (p. 198)

Dreyfus [drā′fəs], **Alfred** (1859–1935), French army officer of Jewish birth who was convicted of treason in 1894, but was proved innocent in 1906. (p. 546)

Dunkirk [dun′kərk], *n.* seaport in northern France from which British forces crossed the English Channel to escape German forces in 1940. (p. 645)

dynasty [dī′nə stē], *n.* succession of rulers who belong to the same family. (p. 27)

Dwight D.
Eisenhower

Elizabeth I

E

economic imperialism, *n.* the domination of another nation's economic structure without actually taking governmental control; this relationship frequently developed between industrialized nations and Latin American nations. (p. 577)

Edo (Tokyo) [ē'dō], *n.* former name of Tokyo, capital of Japan, in the central part, on southeastern Honshu. (p. 447)

Egypt, *n.* country in northeastern Africa, located along the Nile River; the cradle of an ancient civilization. (p. 26)

Eisenhower [ī'zn hou'ər], **Dwight David** (1890–1969), American general, the 34th President of the United States, from 1952 to 1960. (p. 651)

Elizabeth I [i liz'ə bəth] (1533–1603), queen of England from 1558 to 1603; the daughter of Henry VIII and Anne Boleyn. (p. 393)

El Salvador [el sal'və dôr], *n.* country in west Central America. (p. 752)

empire [em'pīr], *n.* group of countries or states under one ruler or government. (p. 29)

encomienda [en'kō mē en'də], *n.* in the Latin American colonies, the system of forced labor used by the Spanish settlers, generally employing the conquered Indian populations and imported African slaves. (p. 460)

Enlightenment, *n.* a philosophical movement in Europe in the 1700s that emphasized rationalism, intellectual freedom, and freedom from prejudice and superstition in social and political activity. (p. 473)

epics, *n., pl.* long narrative poems that tell the adventures and achievements of one or more great heroes, written in a digni-fied, majestic style, and often giving expression to the ideals of a nation or race. (p. 123)

Epicurus [ep'ə kyūr'əs] (342?–270 B.C.), Greek philosopher who taught that pleasure is the highest good, but that true pleasure depends on self-control, moderation, and honorable behavior. (p. 82)

Erasmus [i raz'məs], **Desiderius** (1466?–1536), Dutch scholar and religious teacher, a leader of the Northern Renaissance. (p. 364)

Euclid [yü'klid] (c. 300 B.C.), Greek mathematician who wrote a famous book on geometry. (p. 85)

Euripides [yū rip'ə dēz'] (480?–406? B.C.), Greek dramatist. (p. 83)

extraterritoriality [ek'strə ter'ə-tôr'ē al'ə tē], *n.* the privilege of having freedom from the jurisdiction of the country that a person is in; ambassadors have certain extraterritorial privileges. (p. 566)

F

fascism [fash'iz'əm], *n.* the principles or methods of a government or a political party favoring rule by a dictator, with strong control of industry and labor by the central government, great restrictions upon the freedom of individuals, and extreme nationalism and militarism. (p. 628)

Fertile Crescent, *n.* crescent-shaped strip of land extending from the eastern shore of the Mediterranean to the Persian Gulf; known for the great fertility of its soil in ancient times. The first urban civilations arose here. (p. 16)

feudalism [fyü'dl iz'əm], *n.* the social, economic, and political system of western Europe in the Middle Ages. Under this system vassals gave military and other services to their lord in return for his protection and the use of his land. (p. 195)

feudal state [fyü'dl], *n.* an area ruled by a noble who gets his authority from the king; in return, the noble owes the king allegiance and military help to keep order and the protect the kingdom. (p. 138)

Final Solution, *n.* during World War II, the Nazi-devised program to kill all the Jews in Europe. (p. 648)

Five Nations, *n.* confederation formed around the year 1400 by five Iroquois Indian groups to support their common interests; this union remained quite strong until the 1700s. (p. 341)

Five Pillars, *n.* name given the five duties of a good Muslim as found in the Koran. (p. 252)

Five-Year Plan, *n.* government plan instituted by Stalin; its two major goals were rapid industrialization and collectivization. (p. 613)

Flanders [flan'dərz], *n.* region in northern Europe. For many years, France and England fought for this area. It is now divided among Belgium, France, and the Netherlands. (p. 223)

Florence [flôr'əns], *n.* city in central Italy, famous for its art. (p. 354)

foot-binding *n.* in China, the process whereby a little girl's feet were tightly wrapped and gradually bent until the arch was broken and the toes were pushed under. The resulting small feet were considered beautiful, as well as a sign of wealth. This process was outlawed in the 20th century. (p. 299)

Fourteen Points, *n.* presented in a speech to Congress on January 8, 1918, by President Woodrow Wilson, the Fourteen Points outlined his ideas for solving the problems that had led to World War I. (p. 595)

Francis [fran'sis], **Saint** (Saint Francis of Assisi) (1181?–1226), Italian founder of the Franciscan

Mohandas
Gandhi

William E.
Gladstone

order of friars which stressed vows of poverty and gentleness to all creatures. (p. 200)

Francis Ferdinand [fran′sis fėrd′n-and], **Archduke** (1863–1914), archduke of Austria whose assassination contributed to the outbreak of World War I. (p. 588)

Franklin [frang′klən], **Benjamin** (1706–1790), American statesman, author, scientist, printer, and inventor. (p. 415)

Frederick the Great [fred′ər ik] (1712–1786), third king of Prussia, from 1740 to 1786; Frederick II. (p. 402)

G

Galileo [gal′ə lā′ō] (1564–1642), Italian astronomer, physicist, mathematician, and inventor, whose discoveries formed the basis for modern physics. (p. 411)

Gandhi [gän′dē], **Mohandas** [mō-hän′dəs] **K.,** (1869–1948), Hindu political, social, and religious leader in India, known as "Mahatma Gandhi." (p. 624)

Ganges River [gan′jez′], *n.* river flowing across northern India and Bangladesh into the Bay of Bengal. It is regarded as sacred by the Hindus. (p. 119)

Garibaldi [gar′ə bôl′dē], **Giuseppe** [jü zep′ä] (1807–1882), Italian patriot and statesman. (p. 543)

Geneva Accords, *n., pl.,* agreements signed in 1954 after the French defeat in Indochina; the accords gave full independence to Laos and Cambodia, called for free elections in Vietnam, and, at the 17th parallel, divided Vietnam into North and South Vietnam. (p. 691)

Geneva Convention of 1864, *n.* an international agreement establishing rules for the treatment of prisoners of war, the wounded, and so forth, first formulated at Geneva, Switzerland. (p. 587)

Genghis Khan [jeng′gis kän′] (1162–1227), Mongol conqueror of central Asia. (p. 242)

Ghana [gä′nə], *n.* country in West Africa, a member of the Commonwealth of Nations; formerly the Gold Coast, a British colony. (p. 705)

Ghana (ancient) [gä′nə], *n.* ancient African kingdom which began developing about the year 500 and became a leading trade center; it flourished until 1235; located far to the north of modern Ghana. (p. 327)

Gilbert, William (1540–1603), English physician and physicist known for his studies of magnetism. (p. 415)

glaciation [glā′shē ā′shən], *n.* the process of covering with ice or glaciers. (p. 9)

Gladstone [glad stōn′], **William Ewart** (1809–1898), British statesman who was prime minister four times. (p. 544)

global warming, *n.* the gradual increase in the world's average temperature, mainly caused by the release of large amounts of carbon dioxide into the atmosphere. (p. 764)

Glorious Revolution, in 1688, the English Parliament invited Mary and William of Orange, the Protestant daughter and son-in-law of King James II, to replace the Catholic ruler on the throne. James II fled without fighting. (p. 481)

Good Neighbor Policy, *n.* a diplomatic policy, first sponsored by the United States in 1933, to encourage friendly relations and mutual defense among the nations of the Western Hemisphere. (p. 755)

Gorbachev [gôr′bə chof], **Mikhail** [mē kə ēl′], (1930–), Soviet political leader, 1985–1991. (p. 670)

Gracchus [grak′əs], **Gaius** [gī′yəs] (153?–121 B.C.), Roman political and social reformer, brother of Tiberius. (p. 99)

Gracchus [grak′əs], **Tiberius** [tī-bir′ē əs] (163?–133 B.C.), brother of Gaius, who shared in the effort to bring political and social reform to Rome. (p. 99)

Great Cultural Revolution, *n.* a movement begun in China in 1966 by Mao to purge the intellectuals and reestablish the people's revolutionary spirit. (p. 683)

Great Schism [siz′əm], *n.* a disagreement in 1378 which split the Papacy; the French cardinals elected a French Pope who remained in Avignon and the Italian cardinals elected an Italian Pope who ruled at Rome. In 1417 a single Pope was elected in Rome. (p. 388)

griots [grē′ōz], *n., pl.* in early West Africa, the special group of men who were the professional record keepers, historians, and political advisers to chiefs. (p. 160)

Gross National Product (GNP), *n.* the total value of all goods and services produced in a country. (p. 671)

guided capitalism, *n.* a form of capitalism in which the government takes an active role in guiding the business community by providing forecasts and economic objectives for business, targeting development in desirable areas, and so forth. (p. 687)

guilds [gilds], *n., pl.,* (in the Middle Ages) organizations of merchants in towns or of persons in a particular trade or craft, formed to keep standards high, promote their business interests, protect themselves, and prevent competition. (p. 206)

Guptas [gup′təs], *n., pl.* a Hindu dynasty that ruled India from the A.D. 300s to 500s. The reign of the Guptas is sometimes called the golden age of Hindu culture. (p. 129)

Gutenberg Bible [güt′n bėrg′], *n.* possibly the first European book printed with movable type, finished about 1455. (p. 364)

Henry
VIII

Adolf
Hitler

H

Habeas Corpus Act [hā′bē əs
kôr′pəs], *n.* law passed by Parliament in 1679, which stated that
the government could not arrest
or imprison any person without
showing a good, legal reason. (p.
480)

haiku [hī′kü], *n.* a brief poem of
three lines, containing five syllables in the first line, seven in the
second, and five in the third. (p.
314)

Haiti [hā′tē], *n.* country in the
western part of the island of Hispaniola, in the West Indies; former name of Hispaniola. (p. 462)

hajj [haj], *n.* pilgrimage to Mecca,
required of every Muslim at least
once in his or her life. (p. 272)

Hammurabi [ham′ù rä′bē] (c.
1700 B.C.), *n.* king of Babylon,
who brought all of southern Mesopotamia under one rule and
made a famous code of laws,
called the Code of Hammurabi.
(p. 25)

Hanging Gardens (of Babylon),
n., pl. in the ancient city of Babylon, the lush roof-top gardens regarded by the Greeks as one of
the seven wonders of the world.
(p. 49)

Hangzhou [häng′jō′], *n.* seaport in
eastern China, set up as the capital by the Song emperor when he
was forced to flee south by the
Jins in the 12th century (p. 294)

Hannibal [han′ə bəl] (247–183?
B.C.), Carthaginian general who
fought the Romans and invaded
Italy. (p. 97)

Hanoi [hä noi′], *n.* capital of Vietnam, in the northern part of the
country. (p. 692)

Hapsburg [haps′bèrg′], *n.* member
of a German princely family
prominent since about 1100. The
Hapsburgs were rulers of the Holy
Roman Empire from 1438 to 1806,
of Austria from 1804 to 1918, of

Hungary and Bohemia from 1526
to 1918, and of Spain 1516 to
1700. (p. 394)

Harun al-Rashid [hä rün′ äl rä-
shēd′] (A.D. 763?–809), caliph of
Baghdad from A.D. 786 to 809. He
is the leading character of The
Arabian Nights. (p. 257)

Harvey [här′vē], **William** (1578–
1657), English physician who discovered that blood circulates
through the body. (p. 416)

Hausa [hou′sə], *n.* a people who
lived in city-state trading centers
in what is now northern Nigeria.
(p. 436)

heliocentric system [hē′lē ō-
sen′trik], *n.* theory developed by
Copernicus in which the sun was
the center of the solar system,
and the earth and the planets
moved around it; sun-centered
system. (p. 410)

Hellenistic Age [hel′ə nis′tik], *n.* a
time of great economic growth
and of cultural exchange between
the East and the West, following
Alexander the Great's death in
323 B.C., and lasting nearly 200
years. (p. 74)

Henry II (1133–1189), king of England from 1154 to 1189 and first
of the Plantagenet line of kings.
(p. 219)

Henry VIII, (1491–1547), king of
England from 1509 to 1547 and
the father of Edward VI, Mary I,
and Elizabeth I. He established
the Anglican Church of England
with himself as head. (p. 392)

Henry the Navigator (1394–1460),
prince of the Portuguese royal
family, who promoted the navigational sciences through the founding of a naval school in the 15th
century. (p. 373)

Herodotus [hə rod′ə təs] (484?–
425? B.C.), Greek historian called
the father of history. (p. 83)

hibachi [hi bä′chē], *n.* large earthenware pot that burned charcoal
and was used to heat Japanese
houses. (p. 320)

hieroglyphics [hī′ər ə glif′iks], *n.*
system of writing using pictures,
characters, or symbols standing
for words, ideas, or sounds.
(p. 31)

Hijra [hi′jər ə], *n.* name given to
Muhammad's journey from Mecca
to Medina in A.D. 622. This journey is so important to Muslims
that it marks the beginning of the
Muslim calendar. (p. 251)

Himalayan Mountains [him′ə-
lā′ən], *n., pl.* mountain system
extending about 1,600 miles from
the Pamirs in Pakistan eastward
through India, Nepal, Brutan, and
the southern Chinese border. Its
highest peak is Mount Everest. (p.
118)

Hinduism [hin′dü iz′ əm], *n.* the
dominant Indian religion; parts of
Hinduism consist of the caste system and the worship of one God,
Brahman, with many faces. (p.
121)

Hippocrates [hi pok′rə tēz′] (460?–
377? B.C.), Greek physician, called
the father of medicine. (p. 85)

Hitler [hit′lər], **Adolf** (1889–1945),
German National Socialist (Nazi)
leader, born in Austria, dictator of
Germany from 1933 to 1945. (p.
631)

Hobbes [hobz], **Thomas** (1588–
1679), English philosopher; author of the classic book, *Leviathan*, published in 1651. (p. 398)

Ho Chi Minh [hō′ chē′ min′],
(1890?–1969), Vietnamese political leader, president of North
Vietnam from 1954 to 1969. (p.
691)

Hohenzollren [hō′ən zol′ərn], *n.*
member of a German princely
family, prominent since the Middle Ages. The kings of Prussia
from 1701 to 1918 and emperors
of Germany from 1871 to 1918
were Hohenzollerns. (p. 400)

Holocaust, *n.* the systematic annihilation by the Nazis of about 6
million European Jews from 1933
to 1945. (p. 649)

Holy Land, *n.* Palestine; especially the parts of Palestine where Jesus lived and died. (p. 260)

Holy Roman Empire, *n.* a loosely organized empire in western and central Europe regarded both as the continuation of the Roman Empire and as the earthly form of a territory whose spiritual head was the Pope. It began with the coronation of Otto the Great (A.D. 962) or, according to some, with the coronation of Charlemagne (A.D. 800) and ended when Francis II renounced the imperial crown (1806). (p. 226)

hominids [hom′ə nids], *n.* a family of primates that includes human beings. (p. 7)

Homo erectus [hō′mō i rek′təs], *n.* an extinct species of prehistoric human beings of the Pleistocene period. (p. 7)

Homo sapiens [hō′mō sā′pē enz], *n.* the species including all existing races of human beings. (p. 7)

Hong Kong [hong′ kong′], *n.* British crown colony on the southeastern coast of China; Hong Kong was ceded to the British in 1842 after the Opium War. (p. 566)

Huang River [hwäng], *n.* river in China flowing from north central China into the Yellow Sea; Yellow River. (p. 137)

Huguenots [hyü′gə nots], *n., pl.* French Protestants of the 1500s and 1600s. (p. 396)

humanism [hyü′mə niz′əm], *n.* any system of thought or action concerned with human interests and values; study of the humanities; literary culture. (p. 357)

Hundred Years' War, *n.* series of wars between England and France from 1337 to 1453. (p. 223)

hunter-gatherers, *n., pl.* people who rely entirely on hunting wild animals and gathering roots, berries, fruits, and nuts for their existence. (p. 9)

Hussein [hü sān′], **Saddam** (1937–), political leader in Iraq and president of the country since 1979. (p. 733)

Huygens [hī′gənz], **Christian** (1629–1695), Dutch physicist, mathematician, and astronomer; he built the first useful pendulum clock in 1656. (p. 413)

I

Iberian peninsula [ī bir′ē ən], *n.* a peninsula in southwestern Europe bordered by the Mediterranean Sea and the Atlantic Ocean and containing the nations of Spain, Portugal, and Andorra. (p. 224)

Ibn Batuta [ib′ən bä tü′tä] (1304?–1378?), Muslim traveler who journeyed throughout the Muslim world, as well as China, during the 14th century. He left many accounts of his 75,000 miles of travels which are valuable sources of information about the time. (p. 275)

Ibn Khaldun [ib′ən kal dün′] (1332–1406), Muslim scholar from Tunis; he applied philosophical ideas to history. (p. 280)

Ibn-Saud [ib′ən sä üd′] (1880–1953), king of Saudi Arabia from 1932 to 1953; also known as Abdul-Aziz. (p. 626)

Ice Age *n.* the era from about 1.5 million B.C. to about 8000 B.C., during which there were at least four long periods when the polar ice caps extended across the continents. (p. 9)

icons [ī′knoz], *n., pl.* pictures or images of Jesus Christ, angels, or saints, usually painted on wood or ivory, and venerated as sacred in the Orthodox Church. (p. 239)

ideographic [id′ē ə graf′ik], *adj.* having to do with an ideograph, a graphic symbol that represents a thing or an idea directly, without representing the sounds of the word for the thing or idea. (p. 166)

Idris Alooma [id′ris ə lü′mə], ruler of Kanem-Bornu in the central Sudan in Africa, from 1580 to 1617. (p. 435)

imperialism [im pir′ē ə liz′əm], *n.* policy of extending the rule or authority of one country over other countries and colonies. (p. 564)

Incas [ing′kəs], *n., pl.* an ancient people of South America who had a highly developed culture and ruled a large empire in Peru and other parts of South America before it fell to the Spaniards in the 1500s. (p. 337)

Indian National Congress, *n.* a group of mainly Hindu leaders formed in 1885 to work for representative self-government in India. (p. 565)

Indochina [in′dō chī′nə], *n.* peninsula in southeastern Asia comprising Burma, Cambodia (Kampuchea), Laos, Malaya, Singapore, Thailand, and Vietnam; in the 19th century, the French colony in southeastern Asia composed of Cochin-China, Cambodia, Annam, and Laos. (p. 579)

Indonesia [in′də nē′zhə], *n.* country in the East Indies that includes Java, Sumatra, Kalimantan, Celebes, West Irian, and smaller islands, formerly belonging to the Netherlands. (p. 275)

Industrial Revolution, *n.* the change from an agricultural to an industrial society and from home manufacturing to factory production, especially the one that took place in England from about 1750 to about 1850. (p. 514)

Indus Valley, *n.* the area along the Indus River in what is now Pakistan and western India, where an ancient civilization flourished between 2500 B.C. and 1500 B.C. (p. 34)

inflation [in flā′shən], *n.* a sharp increase in prices resulting from a great expansion of the money supply. (p. 105)

Jesus

Joan
of Arc

Inquisition [in′kwə zish′ən], *n.* court appointed by the Roman Catholic Church in the 1200s to discover and suppress heresy; abolished in the 1800s. (p. 225)

intelligentsia [in tel′ə jent′sē ə], *n., pl.,* educated people interested in reform; the intellectuals of a country. (p. 604)

interest [in′tər ist], *n.* money paid for the use of money, usually a percentage of the amount invested, borrowed, or loaned. (p. 203)

International Red Cross, *n.* an international organization to care for the sick and wounded in war, and to relieve suffering caused by floods, fire, diseases, and other calamities. (p. 587)

Intolerable Acts, *n., pl.* laws passed by the British Parliament to punish the American colonists for the "Boston Tea Party." These laws included the closing of Boston harbor and the repeal of the charter of the Massachusetts colony. (p. 485)

Iron Curtain, *n.* an imaginary wall or dividing line separating the Soviet Union and the countries under Soviet control or influence from other nations after World War II. (p. 664)

irrigation [ir′ə gā′shən], *n.* the process of supplying crops with water by using ditches, by sprinkling, and so forth. (p. 13)

Isfahan [is′fə hän′], *n.* city in western Iran; built by Shah Abbas, it was the capital of Persia until the 1800s. (p. 429)

Islam [is′ləm], *n.* the religion of the Muslims, based on the teachings of Muhammad as they appear in the Koran; there is only one God, Allah, and Muhammad is his prophet. (p. 251)

isolationism [ī′sə lā′shə niz′əm], *n.* principle or policy of avoiding political alliances and economic relationships with other nations. (p. 443)

Israel [iz′rē əl], *n.* country in southwestern Asia, on the Mediterranean Sea, including the major part of Palestine; the ancient land and kingdom of the Jews. (p. 729)

Istanbul [is′tän bül′], *n.* city in northwestern Turkey, on the Bosporus; formerly Constantinople. (p. 426)

Ivan the Great [ī′vən] (1440–1505), grand duke of Muscovy from 1462 to 1505; Ivan III. (p. 243)

Ivan the Terrible (1530–1584), grand duke of Muscovy from 1533 to 1547, and tsar of Russia from 1547 to 1584; Ivan IV. (p. 243)

J

Janissary Corps [jan′ə ser′ē], *n.* an elite division of the Sultan's guard, which existed from the 1300s until 1826, and was selected from the Children's Levy. (p. 427)

Japan [jə pan′], *n.* country made up of four large islands and many smaller ones, in the western Pacific east of the Asian mainland. (p. 309)

Jefferson [jef′ər sən], **Thomas** (1743–1826), American statesman, third President of the United States, from 1801 to 1809. He wrote the Declaration of Independence. (p. 486)

Jerusalem [jə rü′sə ləm], *n.* capital of Israel, in the eastern part. Formerly the capital of Palestine; a holy city to Jews, Christians, and Muslims. (p. 201)

Jesus [jē′zəs] (6 B.C.?–A.D. 29?), *n.* founder of the Christian religion. The name means "God of Salvation." (p. 178)

Jin dynasty [chin], *n.* Manchurian nomads who overran China, captured the Song emperor, and by 1127 had established an empire in northern China. (p. 290)

Joan of Arc (1412–1431), French heronie who led armies against the invading English and saved the city of Orleans. She was condemned as a witch and burned to death. In 1920 she was made a saint. (p. 223)

joint-stock company, *n.* a company in which an individual could gain part ownership by buying shares of stock whose value was dependent on the company's profits. The Dutch East India Company and the British East India Company were joint-stock companies. (p. 381)

Judaism [jü′dē iz′əm], *n.* religion of the Jews, based on the teachings of Moses and the prophets as found in the Bible, and on the interpretations of the rabbis. (p. 45)

junta [jun′tə, hun′tə], *n.* political or military group holding power after a revolution. (p. 752)

Justinian [ju stin′ē ən] (A.D. 483–565), emperor of the Byzantine or Eastern Roman Empire, from 527 to 565. During his reign a famous code of laws was compiled. (p. 232)

K

Kabuki [kä bü′kē], *n.* a form of Japanese drama with song and dance, a flamboyant style of acting, and rich decor and costuming. It dates from the 1600s. (p. 448)

Kalahari [kä′lä här′ē], *n.* a large desert and plateau region in southern Africa. (p. 152)

Kamikaze [kä′mē kä′zē], *n.* a Japanese word meaning "Divine Wind," given to the typhoon that destroyed Kublai Khan's invading forces in 1281. The name "kamikaze" was revived during World War II to recognize Japanese suicide pilots. (p. 317)

Jomo
Kenyatta

Kublai
Khan

Vladimir Ilyich
Lenin

Kanem-Bornu [kä′nem bor′nü], *n.* in the 1500s, the strongest Muslim state of the central Sudan in Africa. (p. 435)

Kangxi [käng′shē] (1654–1722), Chinese emperor from 1661 to 1722, the longest reign in Chinese history. (p. 444)

Kemal Atatürk [kə mäl′ at′ə-tėrk′], **Mustafa** [müs tä fä′] (1881–1938), first president of Turkey, from 1923 to 1938, who had overthrown the Turkish Sultan and formed the Turkish Republic in 1923. (p. 626)

Kenyatta [ken yä′tə], **Jomo** (1893–1978), Kenyan political leader, president of Kenya from 1964 to 1978. (p. 707)

Kepler [kep′lər], **Johann** [yō′hän] (1571–1630), German astronomer who developed three laws of planetary motion in which he described the oval path, called an ellipse, of the planets. (p. 411)

Khomeini [hō mä nē′], **Ayatollah Ruhollah** [ä′yä tō′lə rü hō′lə] (1900–1989), Iranian religious and political leader. (p. 728)

Khrushchev [krüsh chôf′], **Nikita** [ni kē′tə] **S.** (1894–1971), Soviet statesman, premier of the Soviet Union from 1958 to 1964. (p. 667)

Kiev [kē′ef], *n.* a city on the Dnieper River in the southwestern Soviet Union. Once the capital of the first Russian state, now the capital of the Ukrainian S.S.R. (p. 239)

Kilwa, *n.* former coastal marketplace in Africa, close to the gold fields of the kingdom of Zimbabwe, that became a rich city-state. (p. 330)

King [king], **Reverend Martin Luther, Jr.** (1929–1968), American Baptist minister who led a nonviolent movement to end racial discrimination in the United States; first black American to win the Nobel Peace Prize. (p. 671)

Koran [kô rän′], *n.* the sacred book of the Muslims. It consists of revelations of Allah to Muhammad and is the standard by which Muslims live. (p. 251)

Korea [kô rē′ə], *n.* former country on a peninsula in east Asia, divided into North Korea and South Korea after World War II. (p. 303)

Kremlin [krem′lən], *n.* citadel of Moscow, where the chief offices of the Soviet government are located. (p. 614)

Kublai Khan [kü′blī kän′] (1216?–1294), Mongol emperor from 1259 to 1294; the first Mongol ruler of China (1260–1294). (p. 300)

Kumbi-Saleh [kum′bē sä′lə], *n.* twin cities that made up the capital of ancient Ghana in Africa. (p. 327)

Kurds [kerds], *n., pl.* a nomadic Muslim people living chiefly in Kurdistan, an extensive plateau and mountainous region in southwestern Asia now divided among Turkey, Iran, Iraq, and Syria. (p. 723)

Kush, *n.* ancient African kingdom that developed along the Nile River in what is now Sudan. It flourished from about 750 B.C. to A.D. 350. (p. 158)

Kyoto (Heian-Kyo) [kyō′tō], *n.* city in central Japan; formerly the capital and at one time known as Heian-kyo. (p. 314)

L

laissez-faire capitalism [les′ā fer′], *n.* principle that trade, business, and industry should operate with a minimum or complete absence of regulation and interference by government. (p. 524)

Laozi [lou′dzu′] (604? B.C.–531? B.C.), Chinese philosopher whose teachings have formed the basis of a religion known as Taoism. (p. 141)

las Casas, Bartolome de (c. 16th century), a Spanish priest who spoke out against the cruel treatment of the Indians in the Latin American colonies and was chosen by Charles V to be "Protector of the Indians". (p. 460)

latifundistas [lä tē fün dē′stäs], *n.* in Latin America, a small group of upperclass creoles who have controlled most of the productive land since the 17th and 18th centuries. (p. 742)

Latin America, *n.* South America, Central America, Mexico, and most of the West Indies. The lands get this name from the predominance of Latin languages spoken there. (p. 462)

Lavoisier [lä vwä zyä′], **Antoine** [än twän′] (1743–1794), French chemist who discovered oxygen. (p. 415)

League of Nations, *n.* association of many countries, established in 1920 to promote international peace and cooperation; dissolved on April 18, 1946, and the United Nations assumed some of its functions. (p. 596)

Lebanon [leb′ə nən], *n.* country in the Middle East, at the eastern end of the Mediterranean, north of Israel; ancient site of the Phoenician city-states. (p. 43)

Leeuwenhoek [lā′vən hŭk], **Anton van** [än′tôn vän] (1632–1723), Dutch scientist who was the first to study blood cells and microorganisms through magnifying lenses (a microscope). (p. 416)

Left, *n.* political label for persons representing political and social change; changes sought vary from country to country. (p. 505)

Lenin [len′ ən] **Vladimir Ilyich** (1870–1924), Russian communist leader, the founder of the Soviet government and its first premier, from 1918 to 1924. (p. 592, 606)

liberalism [lib′ər ə liz′əm], *n.* liberal principles and ideas; belief in progress and reform. (p. 538)

Liliuokalani

Louis XIV

Niccolo
Machiavelli

Liliuokalani [lē lē′ü ō kä lä′nē] (1838–1917), Hawaiian queen from 1891 to 1893; she opposed Hawaii's annexation by the United States and was overthrown. (p. 571)

Lincoln [ling′kən[, **Abraham** (1809–1865), 16th President of the United States, from 1861 to 1865, during the Civil War. (p. 551)

lineage [lin′ē ij], *n.* descent in a direct line from a common ancestor. (p. 159)

Liverpool [liv′ər pül], *n.* seaport in western England. (p. 517)

Locke [lok], **John** (1632–1704), English philosopher during the Age of Reason. (p. 475)

loess [les], *n.* a fine, rich, yellowish-brown soil, usually deposited by the wind. (p. 37)

London [lun′dən], *n.* capital of the United Kingdom of Great Britain and Northern Ireland, in southeastern England, on the Thames River. (p. 531)

Long March, *n.* in 1934–1935, the 6,000-mile retreat of the Chinese Communists led by Mao Zedung; a retreat from the advancing army of Chiang Kai-shek. (p. 623)

Louis IX. See Saint Louis.

Louis XIV [lü ē′] (1638–1715), king of France from 1643 to 1715, called "Louis the Great"; his motto was "L Etat, c est moi" (I am the state). (p. 399)

Louis XVI (1754–1793), king of France from 1774 to 1792, guillotined during the French Revolution. (p. 493)

Luther [lü′thər], **Martin** (1483–1546), leader of the Protestant Reformation in Germany. (p. 389)

Macao [mə kou′], *n.* seaport on a peninsula off the southern coast of China; Portuguese colony that includes this peninsula and two small islands nearby. (p. 443)

Macedonia [mas′ə dō′nē ə], *n.* ancient country in southeastern Europe, north of Greece; at one time ruled by Alexander the Great. (p. 72)

Machiavelli [mak′ē ə vel′ē], **Niccolo** [nē′kō lō′] (1469–1527), Italian statesman and writer who advised that rulers use craft and deceit to maintain their authority. (p. 356)

Magellan [mə jel′ən], **Ferdinand** (1480?–1521), Portuguese navigator. His ship was the first to sail around the world. (p. 375)

Maginot Line [mazh′ə nō], *n.* an elaborate system of defensive structures built by France along the border with Germany after World War I. The German army outflanked it in 1940. (p. 645)

Magna Carta [mag′nə kär′tə], *n.* the great charter which the English barons forcibly secured from King John at Runnymede on June 15, 1215. The Magna Carta provided a basis for guaranteeing the personal and political liberties on the people of England, and placed the king under the rule of the law. (p. 220)

mahatma [mə hät′mə], *n.* in India, a wise and holy person. (p. 624)

Mahmud of Ghazni (971?–1030), leader of one of the many Muslim warrior tribes that invaded India from the 10th to the 12th centuries. (p. 263)

Mali [ma lē], *n.* a province in ancient Africa that became a medieval kingdom. It reached its greatest importance in the 1300s. (p. 284)

Malinche [mä lēn′chā] (c. 16th century), a female Aztec slave, given to Cortés and used by him as a translator, diplomat, and informant. (p. 454)

Malthus [mal′thəs], **Thomas** (1766–1834), English clergyman and economist. (p. 524)

Manchuria [man chùr′ē ə], *n.* region in northeast China, including several provinces of China. The seizure of this area in September,

1931, by Japan is considered by many to be the start of World War II. (p. 640)

Manchus [man′chüs], *n., pl.* a people of Manchuria who conquered China in 1644 and ruled until 1912. (p. 443)

Mandate of Heaven, *n.* Chinese theory of government; rulers were expected to govern justly and to look after the well-being of the people. If a king did not do this, he would lose favor with the gods and could be overthrown. (p. 139)

mandates [man′dāts], *n., pl.* former German colonies in Africa and the Pacific region that the League of Nations gave to certain Allied nations to administer and develop. (p. 598)

manorial system [mə nôr′ē əl], *n.* during the Middle Ages, the agricultural system that was centered on self-contained estates called manors. Part of the manor was set aside for the lord and the rest divided among the peasants, who paid the owner rent in goods, services, or money. If the lord sold the manor, the peasants or serfs were sold with it. (p. 196)

Mansa Musa [män′sə mü′sə], one of ancient Mali's most famous Muslim rulers, named for the prophet Moses. (p. 284)

Mao Zedong [mou′ dzu′dùng] (1893–1976), Chinese Communist leader, chairman of the Chinese Communist Party from 1945 to 1976. (p. 622)

Marathon [mar′ə thon], **battle of,** *n.* decisive victory for the Athenians over the Persians in 490 B.C. After the battle, a runner ran twenty-six miles to Athens with news of the victory. (p. 69)

Marco Polo [mär′kō pō′lō] (1254?–1324?), Italian merchant who wrote about his travels in Asia. (p. 301)

Marshall Plan, *n.* plan adopted by the United States for giving financial aid to European nations after

Mao
Zedong

Karl
Marx

World War II; named after George Catlett Marshall who proposed it. (p. 666)

Marx [marks], **Karl** (1818–1883), German political philosopher, writer on economics, and advocate of socialism; author of *Das Kapital.* (p. 528)

mass production, the making of goods in large quantities, especially by machinery. (p. 516)

Maya [mī′yə, mä′yə], *n., pl.* the ancient American Indian people of Central America and Mexico. The Maya had a highly developed civilization from about A.D. 300–900. (p. 164)

Mecca [mek′ə], *n.* the religious capital of Saudi Arabia, in the western part. Birthplace of Muhammad. Muslims turn toward Mecca when praying and go there on pilgrimages. (p. 251)

Meiji Era [mā′jē], *n.* the 45-year period in Japan which began in 1868 with the accession to the throne of Emperor Mutsuhito and during which Japan became the first powerful, industrialized, modern state in Asia. (p. 568)

Menes [mē′nēz] **King,** (c. 3100 B.C.), the ruler of Upper Egypt, who united his kingdom with the kingdom of Lower Egypt to form the world's first national government. (p. 27)

mercantilism [mėr′kən ti liz′əm], *n.* the economic system of Europe in the 1500s and 1600s, which favored a balance of exports over imports; it regulated a nation's agriculture, industry, and trade with that end in view. (p. 381)

Mesolithic period [mes′ə lith′ik], *n.* the middle part of the Stone Age, lasting from about 8000 B.C. to about 6000 B.C.; the Middle Stone Age. (p. 8)

Mesopotamia [mes′ə pə tā′mē ə], *n.* the ancient name for the eastern portion of the Fertile Crescent, lying between the Tigris and Euphrates rivers. (p. 22)

Messiah [mə sī′ə], *n.* Hebrew word meaning "anointed one", the expected leader and deliverer of the Jewish people; in Christian use, Jesus. (p. 179)

mestizos [mə stē′zōs], *n., pl.* people of mixed descent, especially the children of Spanish soldiers and Indian women in Latin America. (p. 459)

Mexico City [mek′sə kō], *n.* capital of Mexico, in the central part; originally the Aztec capital Tenochtitlán. (p. 455)

Michelangelo [mī′kə lan′jə lō] (1475–1564), Italian sculptor, painter, architect, and poet. (p. 362)

middle class, *n.* class of people who are socially and economically between the very wealthy class and the class of unskilled laborers and unemployed people. Also known as the bourgeoisie. (p 206)

Middle East, *n.* region extended from Sudan, Egypt, and Turkey in the west to Iran in the east, and including Iraq, Israel, Jordan, Syria, and Saudi Arabia. (p. 11)

Middle Passage, *n.* the name given to the worst part of the slave trade—the sea voyage from Africa to America—during which the slaves were kept in unclean conditions and given small amounts of food; many slaves died during the voyage (p. 335)

Mill, John Stuart (1806–1873), English economist and philosopher, who championed the idea of personal liberty. (p. 524)

millets [mil′itz], *n., pl.* in the Ottoman Empire, the groups into which the population was divided according to their religion. Each millet had its own religious head who collected taxes and administered justice, as well as its own laws and courts. (p. 427)

Ming dynasty [ming], *n.* the ruling Chinese dynasty from 1368 to 1644, known for exquisitely decorated ceramics and paintings. (p. 441)

Minoan [mi nō′ən], *n.* the civilization that prospered on Crete from about 3500 to 1400 B.C. (p. 60)

missionaries [mish′ə ner′ēs], *n., pl.* people who want to advance religious ideas and often wish to convert, or change, others to their faith. (p. 460)

Mitterrand [mē tə rän′], **François** [frän swä′] (1916–   ), French political leader, president of France since 1981. (p. 674)

Monet [mō nä′], **Claude** [klōd] (1840–1926), French painter, leader of the French impressionist movement. (p. 526)

Mongols [mong′gəls], *n., pl.,* an Asian people, now inhabiting Mongolia and nearby parts of China and Siberia; rulers of Russia from the 13th to the 15th centuries. (p. 242)

monotheism [mon′ə thē is′əm], *n.* doctrine or belief that there is only one God. (p. 31)

Monroe Doctrine, *n.* doctrine that European nations should not interfere with American nations or try to acquire more territory in the Western Hemisphere. The Monroe Doctrine came from President Monroe's message to Congress on December 2, 1823. (p. 503)

monsoons [mon sünz′], *n., pl.* seasonal winds of the Indian Ocean and southern Asia, blowing from the southwest from April to October and from the northeast during the rest of the year. (p. 119)

Montesquieu [mon′tə skyü], **Baron de La Brede et de** [də lä bred′ ä də] (1689–1755), French philosopher and writer. His real name was Charles de Secondat. (p. 475)

Montezuma [mon′tə zü′mə] (1480–1520), Aztec emperor of Mexico from 1502 to 1520, defeated by Cortés. (p. 455)

Moors [mùrs], *n., pl.* Muslim people of mixed Arab and Berber ancestry, living in northwestern

Benito
Mussolini

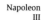

Napoleon
III

Africa. In the A.D. 700's, the Moors conquered Spain. They were driven out in 1492. (p. 255)

More, Thomas (1478–1535), English statesman and author, canonized in 1935. (p. 364)

Morocco [mə rok'ō], *n.* country in northwestern Africa. (p. 715)

mosaics [mō zā'iks], *n., pl.* decorative art made of small pieces of stone, glass, or wood, of different colors, inlaid to form a picture or design. (p. 239)

Moscow [mos'kou], *n.* capital of the Soviet Union and the Russian Soviet Federated Socialist Republic, in the western part of the Soviet Union; once a city-state in Russia. (p. 243)

Moses [mō'ziz] (c. 1300 B.C.), (in the Bible) the great leader and lawgiver of the Jews, who led them out of Egypt. (p. 45)

mosque [mosk], *n.* a Muslim place of worship. (p. 253)

Mt. Fuji [fü jē], *n.* extinct volcano in south Japan, near Tokyo. It is the highest mountain in Japan. (p. 310)

Mozart [mōt'särt], **Wolfgang Amadeus** [vôlf'gäng ä'mä-dā'üs], (1756–1791), Austrian composer who wrote over 600 musical compositions. (p. 478)

Mughals [mu'gulz], *n., pl* Muslim conquerors of India who came from Central Asia in the 1500s and maintained a strong empire until the 18th century. (p. 432)

Muhammad [mú ham'əd] (A.D. 570?–632), Arab prophet, founder of Islam, the religion of the Muslims. Also, Mohammed, Mahomet. (p. 251)

multinational corporations, *n., pl.* business firms with branches in many nations. (p. 762)

Munich conference [myü'nik], *n.* in 1938, meeting among Germany, France, Italy, and Great Britain, during which the Munich Pact was signed, turning over the Sudetenland (a part of Czechoslovakia) to Germany. (p. 643)

826

Murasaki, Lady (c. 978), *n.* a Japanese woman, author of *The Tale of Genji,* one of the first novels. It is a literary classic that is still read and studied. (p. 314)

Muslim League, *n.* in India, a group of educated Muslims formed in 1906 to work for representative self-government. (p. 565)

Muslims [muz'ləms], *n., pl.* people who believe in and follow the teachings of Muhammad; followers of the religion of Islam. (p. 194)

Mussolini [mùs'ə lē'nē], **Benito** (1883–1945), leader of the Italian Fascists and prime minister of Italy from 1922 to 1943. (p. 628)

Mycenaeans [mī'sə nē'ənz], *n., pl.* people from the Caspian Sea region, who invaded the Greek peninsula about 1900 B.C. and established a flourishing civilization. (p. 62)

mythology [mi thol'ə jē], *n.* group of myths relating to a particular country or person. (p. 62)

N

Nantes [nants; French naNt], **Edict of,** *n.* decree granting religious toleration to Huguenots, signed in 1598 by Henry IV and cancelled in 1685. (p. 397)

Napoleon III [nə pō'lē ən] (1808–1873), Louis Napoleon, president of France from 1848 to 1852 and emperor from 1852 to 1870; the nephew of Napoleon I. (p. 541)

Nasser [nä'sər], **Gamal Abdel** [gə-mäl' ab'dəl] (1918–1970), Egyptian political leader, president of the United Arab Republic from 1958 to 1970. (p. 725)

nation [nā'shən], *n.* a people occupying the same country, under the same government, and usually speaking the same language. (p. 215)

National Assembly, *n.* in 1789, the assembly formed in France by members of the Third Estate of the Estates-General; they attempted to gain some political power for the middle classes without overthrowing the French king. (p. 494)

nationalism [nash'ə nə liz'əm], *n.* patriotic feelings or efforts; desire and plans for national independence. (p. 216, 539)

Neanderthal people [nē an'dər-thôl], prehistoric people who lived in caves in Europe, North Africa, and western and central Asia in the early Stone Age. (p. 8)

Nebuchadnezzar [neb'yə kəd nez'-ər] (?–562 B.C.), king of Babylon from 605 to 562 B.C. He established the Chaldean Empire (also known as the Neo-Babylonian Empire). (p. 49)

negritude [neg'rə tüd], *n.* a concern with and pride in the black race, black history, black creativity, and African culture. (p. 702)

Nehru [nā'rü], **Jawaharlal** [jə-wä'hər läl'], (1889–1964), prime minister of India from 1947 to 1964. (p. 694)

Neolithic period [nē'ə lith'ik], *n.* the last part of the Stone Age, from about 6000 B.C. to about 3000 B.C.; the New Stone Age. This period was marked by the beginning of agriculture and the use of polished stone weapons and tools. (p. 8)

New Delhi, *n.* capital of India, in the northern part, just south of the city of Delhi. (p. 625)

New Testament, *n.* the second of the two principal divisions of the Bible, which contains the life and teachings of Jesus recorded by His followers. (p. 178)

Newton [nüt'n], **Sir Issac** (1642–1727), English mathematician, physicist, and philosopher, who discovered the law of gravitation. (p. 412)

Nicaragua [nik ə rä'gwə], *n.* country in Central America, north of Costa Rica. (p. 751)

Florence
Nightingale

Nicholas I [nik′ə ləs] (1796–1855), tsar of Russia from 1825 to 1855. (p. 547)

Niger River [nī′jər], *n.* a river flowing from west Africa into the Gulf of Guinea. (p. 153)

Nightingale [nīt′n gāl], **Florence** (1820–1910), English nurse who worked to improve nursing and hospital sanitation. (p. 542)

Nineveh [nin′ə və], *n.* capital of ancient Assyria. Its ruins are on the Tigris River, opposite Mosul in northern Iraq. (p. 49)

Nkrumah [en krü′mə], **Kwame** [kwä′mä] (1909–1972), prime minister of Ghana from 1957 to 1960, president from 1960 to 1966. (p. 705)

nomad [nō′mad], *n.* member of a tribe that moves from place to place to have food or pasture for its livestock. This way of life developed during the Neolithic period. (p. 12)

nonviolent resistance, *n.* protest that does not involve violence of any kind. (p. 624)

North Atlantic Treaty Organization (NATO), *n.* an alliance of sixteen Western nations providing for joint military cooperation, originally formed in 1949 with twelve nations. (p. 666)

Northern Ireland, *n.* self-governing district in northeastern Ireland that voted not to join the Republic of Ireland; a part of the United Kingdom of Great Britain and Northern Ireland. (p. 546)

Northwest Passage, *n.* sea route from the Atlantic Ocean to the Pacific Ocean along the north coast of North America. (p. 376)

Nuremberg Laws [nùr′əm bèrg′], *n., pl.* laws passed in Germany in 1935 by the Nazi government which took citizenship rights away from Jews. (p. 632)

Nuremberg Trials, *n., pl.* after World War II, trials held between 1945 and 1949 in the West German city of Nuremberg to punish German leaders for war crimes. (p. 663)

Nur Jahan (?–1645), Persian-born wife of Mughal Emperor Jahangir of India; she often ruled in her husband's absence, unusual for a wealthy woman of her time. (p. 431)

Nyerere [ni rer′e], **Julius** (1921–), nationalist leader and president of Tanzania from 1964 to 1985. (p. 707)

O

Obas [ō′bəs], *n., pl.* the kings of the ancient African kingdom of Benin; they ruled from about the 11th century to the 18th century. (p. 333)

Octavian [ok tā′vē ən] (63 B.C.–A.D. 14), grandnephew and heir of Julius Caesar; the first emperor of Rome, from 27 B.C. to A.D. 14. The Roman Senate gave him the honorary title of Augustus meaning "the Majestic." (p. 101)

Omar Khayyam [ō′mär kī′yäm′] (1050?–1123?), Persian poet, astronomer, and mathematician who wrote *The Rubaiyat.* (p. 280)

OPEC [ō′pek] **(Organization of Petroleum Exporting Countries)** *n.* an organization started in 1966 by several oil-producing countries in an effort to set production limits and prices on oil. (p. 727)

Organization of African Unity (OAU), *n.* an organization of African nations formed in 1963 to promote economic cooperation and settle inter-African disputes. (p. 716)

Orthodox Church [ôr′thə doks], *n.* group of Christian churches in eastern Europe, western Asia, and Egypt that honor the patriarch of Constantinople; Greek Orthodox Church; Eastern Orthodox Church; Eastern Church. (p. 233)

Otto the Great (A.D. 912–973), king of Germany from A.D. 936 to 973 and emperor of the Holy Roman Empire from A.D. 962 to 973. (p. 226)

P

Padua [paj′ü ə], *n.* city in northeastern Italy. (p. 416)

Paleolithic period [pā′lē ə lith′ik], *n.* the earliest part of the Stone Age, which lasted from about 2 million B.C. to about 8000 B.C.; the Old Stone Age. Paleolithic tools were crudely chipped out of stone. (p. 8)

Palestine [pal′ə stīn], *n.* region or country in southwest Asia between the Mediterranean Sea and the Jordan River; a name applied since ancient times to the land of the Jews. Palestine is often called the Holy Land and in the Bible is called Canaan. It is now divided chiefly between Israel and Jordan. (p. 178)

Palestine Liberation Organization (PLO), *n.* an Arab political group formed in 1964 to work for the creation of a Palestinian state as a homeland for the Arab people who originally lived in Palestine and their descendants. (p. 730)

Panama Canal, *n.* canal cut across the Isthmus of Panama to connect the Atlantic and Pacific oceans, built and formerly controlled by the United States. (pp. 578, 754)

Pan American Union, *n.* organization of twenty-one American republics formed in 1890 to promote mutual cooperation and peace. (p. 587)

pan-Arabism, *n.* the idea or concept of Arab unity. (p. 725)

Paracelsus [par′ə sel′səs] (1493–1541), Swiss alchemist and physician. (p. 416)

Paris [par′is], *n.* capital and largest city of France, in the northern part, on the Seine River. (p. 206)

Parliament [pär′lə mənt], *n.* in Great Britain, the national lawmaking body, consisting of the House of Lords and House of Commons; council or congress that is the highest lawmaking body in other countries. (p. 220)

827

Louis
Pasteur

Rembrandt
van Rijn

Pasteur [pa stèr′], **Louis** (1822–1895), French chemist who discovered the means of immunization against rabies and developed pasteurization, the process of heating milk at a high temperature to destroy harmful bacteria. (p. 520)

patricians [pə trish′əns], *n., pl.* members of the nobility of ancient Rome, composed of the families descended from the original body of Roman citizens. (p. 92)

Patrick [pat′rik], **Saint** (A.D. 389?–461?), British missionary and bishop who converted Ireland to Christianity; the patron saint of Ireland. (p. 185)

patriotism [pā′trē ə tiz′əm], *n.* love and loyal support of one's country. (p. 216)

Pax Romana [paks′ rō′mä nä], *n.* "Roman Peace"; the first two centuries of the Roman Empire from 27 B.C. to A.D. 180. (p. 102)

Pearl Harbor, *n.* United States naval base near Honolulu, on the south coast of Oahu, bombed by the Japanese on December 7, 1941, causing U.S. entry into World War II. (p. 647)

Peloponnesian War [pel′ə pə nē′shən], *n.* beginning in 431 B.C., the struggle of the Sparta-led city-states of ancient Greece against Athens. This war led to the defeat of Athens in 404 B.C. (p. 71)

peninsulares [pā nēn′sü lä′räs], *n.pl.* in the Spanish American colonies, the name given by the colonists to the Spanish-born officials. (p. 459)

Pericles [per′ə klēz′] (490? B.C.–429 B.C.), Athenian statesman, orator, and military commander, under whose leadership ancient Athens reached its peak of culture and power. (p. 70)

Perón, Juan (1895–1974), Argentine army officer who became president and dictator of Argentina from 1946 to 1955 and from 1973 to 1974. (p. 746)

Perry, Matthew C. (1794–1858), American naval officer who arranged a treaty between the United States and Japan and opened Japan to American trade. (p. 568)

Persian Empire [pèr′zhə n], *n.* ancient empire in western and southwestern Asia conquered by Alexander the Great in 334–331 B.C. (p. 69)

Persian Gulf [pèr′zhən], *n.* gulf of the Arabian Sea, between Iran and the peninsula of Arabia. (p. 275)

Peshawar [pə shä′wər], *n.* a city in what in now northern Pakistan, near the Kyber Pass; once the capital of the Kushan kings. (p. 128)

Peter the Great (1672–1725), tsar of Russia from 1682 to 1725, who was responsible for "westernizing" the country; Peter I. (p. 402)

Petrarch [pē trärk] (1304–1374), Italian poet, famous for his sonnets. (p. 358)

pharaoh [fer′ō], *n.* the title of any of the kings of ancient Egypt; from the Egyptian word meaning "royal house". (p. 27)

Pinochet [pē nō chet′], **Augusto** (1915–   ), military dictator of Chile 1973–1990. (p. 747)

Pizarro [pi zär′ō], **Francisco** (1471–1541), Spanish explorer who conquered Peru and the Inca Empire. (p. 455)

Plato [plā′tō] (427?–347? B.C.), Greek philosopher, the pupil of Socrates and the teacher of Aristotle. (p. 81)

plebeians [pli bē′əns], *n., pl.* the common people of ancient Rome, usually small farmers and tradespeople. (p. 92)

polis [pō′lis], *n.* in early Greek society, a settlement established by a clan for protection from outside attackers. (p. 64)

Polish Corridor, *n.* the strip of land giving Poland an outlet to the Baltic Sea through Prussia and the seaport city of Danzig as de-

creed by the Treaty of Versailles at the end of World War I. Great Britain and France entered World War II when Germany invaded Poland allegedly to regain the Corridor. (p. 643)

polytheism [pol′ē thē iz′əm], *n.* belief in more than one god. (p. 31)

Pope [pōp], *n.* the supreme head of the Roman Catholic Church. The position of Pope evolved from the Bishop of Rome. (p. 181)

porcelain [pôr′sə lin], *n.* a very fine earthenware, usually having a translucent white body and a transparent glaze; china. (p. 296)

potlatch [pot′lach′], *n.* a ceremonial festival among certain American Indians of the northern Pacific coast at which they gave away valuable objects to display their wealth. (p. 341)

potter's wheel, *n.* a rotating horizontal disk set upon a vertical axle; wet clay is thrown on the disk, or wheel, and molded into dishes, vases, pots, and so on. (p. 16)

Protagoras [pro tag′ər əs] (481?–411? B.C.), Greek philosopher and teacher, one of the Sophists. (p. 80)

protectorate [prə tek′tər it], *n.* a weak country under the protection and partial control of a strong country. (pp. 573, 625)

Prussia [prush′ə], *n.* former duchy and kingdom in northern Europe which became the most important state in the confederation of German states united by Bismarck in 1871. It is now divided among East Germany, West Germany, Poland, and the Soviet Union. (p. 400)

Ptolemy [tol′ə mē], Claudius (c. A.D. 100), Greek mathematician, astronomer, and geographer at Alexandria. (p. 112)

Puerto Rico [pwer′tō rē′kō], island in the eastern part of the West Indies, a self-governing commonwealth under the protection of the United States. (p. 577)

Cardinal
Richelieu

Maximilien
de Robespierre

Franklin D.
Roosevelt

Punic Wars [pyü′nik], *n. pl.* the three major wars fought by Carthage and Rome between 264 and 146 B.C. for control of the western Mediterranean. (p. 97)

puppet government, *n.* a government that is kept in power by military troops of another country. (p. 693)

purdah [per′də], *n.* the Muslim custom of keeping women hidden from men or strangers. (p. 266)

Pyrrhic victory [pir′ik], *n.* victory won at too great a cost; from Pyrrhus, king of Epirus, who defeated the Roman armies but lost so many men in doing so that he could not attack Rome itself. (p. 94)

Pythagoras [pə thag′ər əs] (582?–500? B.C.), Greek philosopher, religious teacher, and mathematician. (p. 85)

Q

el-Qaddafi [kä dä′fē], **Muammar** [mü ä mär′äl], (1942–), Libyan political leader since 1970. (p. 716)

Qian Long [chyen′ lung′] (1736–1795), last of the great Manchu emperors of China; reigned 1736 to 1795. (p. 444)

R

radicalism [rad′əkə liz′əm], *n.* principles and practices of radicals; support or advocacy of extreme changes or reforms, especially in politics. (p. 606)

Raphael [raf′ē əl] (1483–1520), Italian painter of the Renaissance period. (p. 361)

al-Razi [rä′zē] (860?–925?), 9th century Muslim physician from Persia, the author of many scientific works; known as Rhazes in the West. (p. 277)

reactionary [rē ak′shə ner′ē], *adj.* having to do with or favoring a return to a previous, usually more conservative, state of affairs. *-n.* person who favors reaction, especially in politics. (p. 538)

realpolitik [rä äl′pō li tēk′], *n.* power politics; political realism; practical politics. (p. 541)

Reconquista [rä kon kēs′tə], *n.* reconquest; a series of campaigns to drive the Moors out of Spain and Portugal, ending in 1492. (p. 225)

Reformation [ref′ər mā′shən], *n.* the religious movement in Europe in the 1500s that aimed at reform within the Roman Catholic Church but led to the establishment of Protestant churches. (p. 390)

Reform Bill of 1832, in Britain, bill giving seats in the House of Commons to the emerging industrial towns, thereby allowing the new business class a share of political power. (p. 530)

reincarnation [rē′in kär nā′shən], *n.* the rebirth of the soul in a new body. (p. 122)

Rembrandt van Rijn [rem′brant vän rīn′] (1606–1669), Dutch Renaissance painter and etcher. (p. 366)

republic [ri pub′lik], *n.* nation or state in which the citizens elect representatives to manage the government, which is usually headed by a president. (p. 93)

Restoration [res′tə rā′shən], *n.* in England, the reestablishment of the monarchy in 1660 under Charles II; period from 1660 to 1688 during which Charles II and James II reigned. (p. 480)

Rhine [rīn], *n.* river flowing from central Switzerland through West Germany and the Netherlands into the North Sea. (p. 182)

Richard the Lion-Hearted (1157–1199), king of England from 1189 to 1199; also, "Richard Coeur de Lion" and Richard I. (p. 260)

Richelieu [rish′ə lü; French rē shə lyœ′], **Cardinal** (1585–1642), French cardinal and statesman who virtually controlled France from 1624 to 1642. His real name was Armand Jean du Plesis; also, Duc de Richelieu. (p. 398)

Right, *n.* political label for persons representing conservatism, a belief that political and social structures work well the way they are and should generally be left alone. (p. 505)

Robespierre [rōbz′pyer], **Maximilien de** (1758–1794), one of the chief leaders of the French Revolution and of the Reign of Terror. (p. 496)

Roman Catholic, of, having to do with, or belonging to the Christian Church that recognizes the pope in Rome as the supreme head. (p. 186)

romanticism [rō man′tə siz′əm], *n.* style of literature, art, and music prevalent during the Romantic Period (1798–1870) when freedom of form, individualism, love of nature, and humanitarianism were championed. (p. 525)

Rome [rōm], *n.* capital of Italy, on the Tiber River; ancient city in the same place, the capital of the Roman Empire. (p. 92)

Roosevelt [rō′zə velt], **Franklin Delano** (1882–1945), the 32nd President of the United States from 1933 to 1945, the longest period served by one person. (p. 645)

Roosevelt [rō′zə velt], **Theodore** (1858–1919), the 26th President of the United States, from 1901 to 1909. (p. 578)

Roundheads [round′heds′], *n., pl.* Puritans who supported the Parliament in England during the civil wars from 1642 to 1652. The Roundheads wore their hair short in contrast to the long curls of their opponents, the Cavaliers. (p. 480)

Jean Jacques
Rousseau

William
Shakespeare

Rousseau [rü sō′], **Jean Jacques** (1712–1778), French philosopher who wrote about government and education. (p. 475)

sacraments [sak′rə mənts], *n., pl.* any of certain religious ceremonies of the Christian Church, considered especially sacred, such as baptism. (p. 199)

Sadat [sä dät′], **Anwar** [än′wär] (1918–1981), president of Egypt from 1970 to 1981. (p. 730)

Safavid dynasty [sä fä′vid], *n.* Shiite Muslim dynasty which arose in Persia (present-day Iran) in the 1500s and maintained a rivalry with the Ottoman Empire for several centuries. (p. 428)

Sahara [sə her′ə], *n.* the world's largest desert, in North Africa, extending eastward from the Atlantic to the Nile Valley and southward from the Mediterranean Sea to the Sudan. (p. 152)

St. Louis [lü ē′] (1214–1270), king of France from 1226 to 1270; he led Crusades to the Holy Land and was later made a saint. (p. 222)

St. Petersburg [sānt pē′tərz bèrg′], *n.* former capital of Russia under the tsars, built by Peter the Great. (p. 402)

Saladin [säl′ə dən] (1137?–1193), sultan of Egypt and Syria from about 1175 to 1193. He captured Jerusalem and defeated the crusaders led by Richard I of England. (p. 260)

samurai [sam′ú rī′], *n.* the military class in feudal Japan, consisting of the retainers of the great nobles. (p. 316)

Sandinistas, *n., pl.* in Nicaragua, a Marxist group named after Sandino, a rebel leader of the 1920s and 1930s; Sandinista Front of National Liberation. Sandinistas controlled the Nicaraguan government from 1979 to 1990. (p. 752)

San Martín [sän′ mär tēn], **José de** (1778–1850), creole soldier who led armies against the Spanish in Argentina, Chile, and Peru. (p. 503)

Sarajevo [sär′ə yä′vō], *n.* city in central Yugoslavia, scene of the assassination of the Austrian archduke Francis Ferdinand in 1914, which brought on World War I. (p. 588)

Sea of Japan, *n.* part of the Pacific Ocean between Japan and the Asian mainland; a barrier to invaders and a lane for travel between Japanese islands. (p. 310)

Sejong, King (reigned 1419–1451), Korean ruler of the Yi dynasty, who instituted many social reforms and established the Hall of Talented Scholars. (p. 304)

Senghor [saN gôr′], **Léopold Sédar** (1906–), poet and political leader from Senegal in West Africa. (p. 702)

Sepoy Rebellion [sē′poi], *n.* a rebellion of the sepoys, the native Indian soldiers, against the British and other Europeans, 1857 to 1858. (p. 565)

Serbia [sèr′bē ə], *n.* former kingdom in southeastern Europe, now part of Yugoslavia. (p. 588)

serfs [sèrfs], *n., pl.* (in the feudal system) slaves who could not be sold off the land, but passed from one owner to another with the land. (p. 195)

Shakespeare [shāk′spir], **William** (1564–1616), English poet and dramatist. (p. 366)

Shatt-al-Arab [shät′əl ä′räb], *n.* waterway in southeastern Iraq, flowing into the Persian Gulf. It is formed by the joining of the Tigris and the Euphrates rivers. (p. 734)

Shi Huangdi [shèr′ hwäng′dē′] (c. 259 B.C.–210 B.C.), strong emperor of the Quin dynasty who subdued and unified the Chinese states. His name means "first supreme emperor." (p. 142)

Shiites [shē′īts], *n., pl.* members of the sect of Islam which believes that Muslim leadership passed from Muhammad to his son-in-law. Most of the Shiites live in Iran and Iraq. (p. 257)

Shinto [shin′tō], *n.* the native religion of Japan, primarily the worship of nature deities and ancestral heroes. (p. 311)

shogun [shō′gun], *n.* the former hereditary commander in chief of the Japanese army. The shoguns were the real rulers of Japan for hundreds of years until 1867. (p. 316)

Shona [shō′nə], *n.* a group of Bantu people who established the kingdom of Zimbabwe in Africa beginning in the 11th century. (p. 332)

Siddhartha Gautama [sid′är′thə gô′tə mə] (563 B.C.–483 B.C.), a religious teacher of northern India and the founder of Buddhism; known as the Buddha, a title meaning "The Enlightened One." (p. 124)

Sikhs [sēks], *n., pl.,* members of a religious sect of northwestern India, founded in the early 1500s as a blending of Islam and Hinduism. (p. 695)

silent trade, *n.* type of trading conducted in Africa between the North and West Africans in which one group presented their goods for trade and then withdrew a half-day's journey from the trade site and waited while the other group presented what they considered fair payment; there was no verbal or visual communication, only signaling with drums. This was described by the 10th century Arab geographer al-Masudi. (p. 326)

Silk Road, *n.* during the Han dynasty, a caravan trading route running along the Great Wall of China, through the deserts and mountains of Central Asia, to the Mediterranean Sea. (p. 144)

Joseph
Stalin

Silla [shē′lə], *n.* a Korean kingdom that gained control over the entire peninsula in 668, unified the country, and established the Silla dynasty. During the Silla dynasty's rule (668–935), Korea experienced a Golden Age. (p. 303)

Slavs [slävs], *n., pl.* groups of peoples in eastern, southeastern, and central Europe whose languages are related. Russians, Poles, Czechs, Slovaks, Bulgarians, and Yugoslavs are Slavs. (p. 239)

Smith, Adam (1723–1790), Scottish political economist; wrote the first major explanation of laissez-faire capitalism. (p. 524)

social contract, *n.* theory of John Locke's whereby the people set up a government and in doing so give it the power to protect their natural rights; agreement between the people and the government. (p. 475)

Social Darwinism, *n.* a theory popular in the 19th and 20th centuries, based on Darwin's laws, which stated that society was structured on the basis of survival of the fittest; the poor and downtrodden became so because they were not fit to survive. (p. 521)

socialism [sō′shə liz′əm], *n.* theory or system of social organization in which the major means of production and distribution are owned, managed, or controlled by the government, by associations of workers, or by the community as a whole. (p. 527)

Socrates [sok′rə tēz′] (469?–399 B.C.), Athenian philosopher whose teachings were written down by his disciple Plato; his type of persistent questioning has come to be known as the Socratic method. (p. 80)

Solidarity [sol′ə dar′ə tē], *n.* independent trade union formed by Polish workers in 1980 that demanded political reforms. (p. 670)

Song dynasty [song], *n.* dynasty that ruled China from A.D. 960 to 1279; Chinese culture advanced

during this period and for a time China was united. (p. 293)

Songhai [song′hī], *n.* province of ancient Ghana whose king established the Songhai Empire in 1468; its capital, Gao, was located not far from Timbuktu. (p. 328)

Sophists [sof′ists], *n., pl.,* a group of teachers of rhetoric, philosophy, and ethics in ancient Greece. (p. 80)

Sophocles [sof′ə klēz′] (495?–406? B.C.), Greek tragic poet and dramatist. (p. 83)

South Africa, *n.* country at the southern tip of South Africa; formerly Union of South Africa. (p. 712)

South Asia, *n.* the Asian continent south of the Himalaya Mountains, including India, Pakistan, Bangladesh, Nepal, and Sri Lanka. (p. 693)

Southeast Asia, *n.* region in Asia including Malaysia, the countries of Indochina, the islands of Indonesia, and sometimes, the Philippines. (p. 689)

soviet [sō′vē et], *n.* an elected assembly concerned with local government, especially in the Soviet Union; council of workers. (p. 607)

Soviet Union, *n.* the common name for the Union of Soviet Socialist Republics, a union of fifteen republics in eastern Europe and western and northern Asia; broke apart 1991; Lithuania, Latvia, Estonia recognized as independent nations, September 1991; Commonwealth of Independent States formed December 1991 by Armenia, Azerbaijan, Byelarus, Kazakhstan, Kyrgyzstan, Moldova, Russia, Tajikistan, Turkmenistan, Ukraine, Uzbekistan. Georgia not a member as of early 1992. (p. 611)

Soyinka [shō yin′kə], **Wole** (1934–), Nigerian author; in 1986, he became the first black African to receive the Nobel Prize for Literature. (p. 704)

Spanish Armada [är mä′də], *n.* the Spanish fleet sent to attack England in 1588 but defeated in the English Channel. (p. 396)

Spanish Inquisition, *n.* court appointed by the Roman Catholic Church to suppress heresy, but used by the Spanish to root out both religious and political dissent; the Spanish Inquisition became infamous for persecution and terror. (p. 395)

Sparta [spär′tə], *n.* important city-state located on the Peloponnesus peninsula in ancient Greece; noted for its soldiers and military-like society. (p. 67)

specialization of labor, the practice of dividing work so that those people most skilled in a particular task perform only that task, while others specialize in other jobs. (p. 12)

spheres of influence, *n.* regions within a country where the economic interests of a foreign country are supreme; within its sphere, the foreign country has special rights and controls. (p. 566)

Stalin [stä′lin], **Joseph** (1879–1953), Soviet political leader, dictator of the Soviet Union from 1929 to 1953. (p. 611)

Stoics [stō′iks], *n., pl.* members of an ancient Greek school of philosophy founded by Zeno. This school taught that virtue is the highest good and that one should be free from passion and unmoved by life's happenings. (p. 82)

subcontinent [sub kon′tə nənt], *n.* a landmass or region that is very large, but smaller than a continent. (p. 117)

subsidy [sub′sə dē], *n.* grant or contribution of money, especially one made by a government. (p. 687)

Suez Canal [sü ez′], *n.* canal across the Isthmus of Suez, connecting the Mediterranean Sea to the Indian Ocean via the Red Sea. (pp. 573, 625)

suffrage [suf′rij], *n.* the right to vote. (p. 529)

Sun
Yat-sen

Margaret
Thatcher

Sufi order [su fē], *n.* ascetic Muslim sect practicing a form of mysticism that began in Persia in the 9th century. (p. 281)

Suleiman the Magnificent [sü lā-män'] (1494?–1566), sultan of the Ottoman Empire at the height of its power, from 1520 to 1566. (p. 426)

sultan [sult'n], *n.* an Arabic word meaning "ruler"; usually the ruler of a Muslim country. (p. 260)

Sundiata [sun'dē ä'tə] (c. 1200), in Africa, leader of the Ghana province of Mali; he conquered the Ghana king and established the empire of Mali. (p. 328)

Sunnis [sún'ēz], *n., pl.* members of the sect of Islam that believes in the traditional part of Islamic law based on Muhammad's acts and sayings, as well as the Koran. (p. 257)

Sun Yat-sen [sún' yät'sen'] (1866–1925), Chinese revolutionary leader and statesman who worked to establish the republic of China. (p. 622)

superpowers, *n., pl.* nations so great or so strong that their actions and policies greatly affect those of smaller, less powerful nations. (p. 663)

Swahili [swä hē'lē], *n.* a Bantu language containing many Arabic and Indian words, spoken in much of eastern Africa and parts of Zaire. (p. 330)

T

Taiwan [tī'wan], *n.* island country off southeastern China; since 1949, the seat of the Chinese nationalist government; Nationalist China. (p. 682)

Taizong [tī'dzung'] (600–649), Chinese emperor (627–649) of the Tang dynasty, who consolidated the empire and concentrated on the peaceful development of China. (p. 145)

Taj Mahal [täj' mə häl'], *n.* a tomb, or taj, of white marble at Agra, in northern India; built in the 1600s by Mughal emperor Shah Jahan to honor his deceased wife. (p. 433)

Tamerlane [tam'ər lān] (1333?–1405), Turko-Mongol conqueror of most of southern and western Asia; also, Timur. (p. 264)

Tamils [tam'əlz], *n., pl.* people of southern India who are descendants of the ancient Dravidians and speak the Dravidian language known as Tamil. (p. 128)

Tang dynasty [täng], *n.* a Chinese dynasty from A.D. 618 to 907, under which China extended toward central Asia, Buddhism gained its political influence, printing was established, and poetry reached its finest development. Also T'ang. (p. 144)

tariffs [tár'ək], *n., pl.* duties or taxes that a government charges on imported or exported goods. (p. 639)

Tarik [tár'ək] (c. 8th century), Berber commander, who, in 711, led a combined Arab and Berber army into Spain, defeated the Christian Visigothic kingdom and established Muslim rule. (p. 255)

Thatcher [thach'ər], **Margaret** (1925–   ), British political leader, prime minister 1979–1990; the first woman prime minister in British history. (p. 673)

theocracy [thē ok'rə sē], *n.* government in which a god is recognized as the supreme civil ruler and in which religious authorities rule the state as the god's representatives. (p. 30)

Thucydides [thü sid'ə dēz'] (460?–400? B.C.), Greek historian; author of *History of the Peloponnesian War.* (p. 84)

Timbuktu [tim buk'tü], *n.* city in present-day central Mali; its official name is Tombouctou; the cultural center of the ancient kingdom of Mali. (p. 284)

Tito [tē'tō], **Marshal** (1892–1980), Yugoslav communist leader, president of Yugoslavia from 1953 to 1980. His real name was Josip Broz. (p. 667)

Tokugawa Shogunate [tō kü gä'wā], *n.* the third and final period of Japan's feudal age, lasting from 1603–1868. (p. 447)

Torah [tôr'ə], *n.* the entire body of Jewish law and tradition; also the first five books of the Old Testament. (p. 47)

Tordesillas [tôrd ə sē'əs], **Treaty of,** *n.* treaty of 1494 between Spain and Portugal setting up an imaginary line of demarcation for New World land claims. All newly discovered lands west of the line were to go to Spain, while Portugal held lands east of the line. (p. 374)

Tories [tôr'ēs], *n., pl.* members of a British political party that favored royal power and the established church and opposed change; supporters included lower nobility and gentry who were loyal to the king. (p. 480)

totalitarianism [tō tal'ə ter'e ə-nez'əm], *n.* methods of a government controlled by one political group which suppresses all opposition, often with force, and which controls many aspects of its citizens' lives. (p. 632)

Toussaint l'Ouverture [tü san' lü ver tyr'], **Pierre Dominique** (1743–1803), Haitian general and political leader who led a revolt and established a government in Haiti. (p. 462)

Tower of Babel, (in the Bible) a high tower whose builders hoped to reach heaven. God punished them by changing their language into several new and different languages so that they could not understand one another and could not finish the tower; believed by some to be the temple-tower, or ziggurat, built by Nebuchadnezzar in honor of a Chaldean god. (p. 49)

Harry S.
Truman

Queen
Victoria

trade embargo, *n.* restrictions put on a country's commerce, or trade, with other countries. (p. 712)

trade imbalance, *n.* the unequal flow of goods that sometimes occurs between countries. (p. 688)

trade unions, *n., pl.* workers' groups that may legally bargain with employers for better wages and working conditions. (p. 531)

Triple Alliance, *n.* union formed by a treaty bringing together Germany, Austria and Italy toward the end of the 19th century; the three countries agreed to help each other if any one of them was attacked. (p. 585)

Triple Entente [än tänt'], *n.* a European alliance established at the beginning of the 20th century by France, Great Britain, and Russia. (p. 586)

Trotsky [trot'skē], **Leon** (1879–1940), leader in the Russian Revolution and Soviet minister of war from 1918 to 1925. He was later exiled and was assassinated in Mexico. (p. 610)

Troy, *n.* a city situated in what is now Turkey, important to trading in the ancient world. (p. 63)

Truman [trü'mən], **Harry S** (1884–1972), the 33rd President of the United States who served from 1945 to 1953. (p. 652)

Trung Sisters (C.A.D. 40), two Vietnamese noblewomen who headed the most famous rebellion against harsh Chinese rule in A.D. 39. They led Vietnamese troops into battle against a more powerful Chinese army and, though defeated, are looked upon today as national heroes. (p. 303)

Tutu [tü tü], **Desmond** (1931–   ), South African Anglican archbishop and Nobel Peace Prize winner. (p. 714)

typhoons [tī füns'], *n., pl.* violent cyclones or hurricanes occurring in the western Pacific Ocean, chiefly during the period from July to October. (p. 310)

U

Ukraine [yü krān'], *n.* the region north of the Black Sea, in the Soviet Union. (p. 613)

Umayyad dynasty [ū mī'yad]. *n.* Muslim dynasty founded in Syria in 661 which began a caliphate that lasted until 750 and under which the Islamic Empire was born. (p. 255)

United Nations (UN), *n.* a worldwide organization established in 1945 to promote world peace and economic and social welfare. It has over 150 member countries and is headquartered in New York City. (p. 662)

United States Constitution, *n.* the written set of fundamental principles by which the United States is governed. (p. 486)

United States of America, *n.* country in North America made up of 50 states, the District of Columbia, Puerto Rico, and other possessions, extending from the Atlantic to the Pacific and from the Gulf of Mexico to Canada; Alaska lies west and northwest of Canada and Hawaii is an island group in the Pacific. (p. 485)

universities [yü'nə vèr'sə tēs], *n., pl.* institutions of higher education usually including schools of law, medicine, education, business, and so on, as well as (in the United States) a college of liberal arts and a graduate school. (p. 207)

Uthman dan Fodio [uth'mən dan fō'dē ō] (?–1817), African leader of the Fulani's political and religious revolution against the Hausa between 1804 and 1809; builder of the Fulani Empire in Africa. (p. 436)

V

Venice [ven'is], *n.* city on the northeast coast of Italy with many canals in place of streets; at one time an Italian city-state. (p. 354)

Verdun [vər dun'], **battle of,** *n.* World War I battle during which France and Germany each lost about 280,000 soldiers; the battle took place in and around the French city of Verdun in northeastern France, on the Meuse River. (p. 592)

Vergil [vèr'jəl] (70–19 B.C.), Roman poet, author of the *Aeneid*. Also, Virgil. (p. 110)

Versailles Treaty, *n.* peace treaty ending World War I, signed by the Allies and Germany on June 28, 1919, in the city of Versailles in northern France. (p. 597)

Vesalius [və sā'lē əs], **Andreas** (1514–1564), Flemish physician who was a pioneer in the study of human anatomy. (p. 416)

viceroy [vīs'roi], *n.* person ruling a country or province as the deputy of the sovereign; governor. (p. 458)

Victoria [vik tôr'ē ə], **Queen** (1819–1901), ruler of Great Britain from 1837 to 1901. (p. 544)

Vienna, Congress of, *n.* in 1814, peace talks involving the countries that had defeated Napoleon and France; the main objectives were to settle conflicts among the Great Powers (Britain, France, Prussia, Austria, and Russia), and to establish a political balance among them. (p. 537)

Vietnam [vē et'näm'], *n.* country in southeast Asia under China's rule from 100 B.C. to A.D. 900 and later made part of French Indochina. From 1954 to 1976 it was divided into two countries, North Vietnam and South Vietnam. (p. 303)

Vikings [vī'kings], *n., pl.* Norsemen; the Scandinavian seafarers who raided the coasts of Europe during the A.D. 700s, 800s, and 900s, conquered parts of England, France, Russia, and other countries, and explored distant lands that may have included North America. (p. 194)

George
Washington

Orville
Wright

Vladivostok [vlad′ə vos′tok], *n.* seaport on the Sea of Japan in the southeastern Soviet Union; founded by the Russians in 1860. (p. 570)

Voltaire [vol tar′], **Francois Marie Arouet de** (1694–1778), French satirical and philosophical writer. (p. 475)

W

Wang Anshi [wäng′ än′shėr′] (A.D.?–1086), *n.* minor official during the Song dynasty who became prime minister in 1069 and instituted broad reforms in government and financial policy. (p. 299)

Warsaw Pact, *n.* a military alliance between the Soviet Union and the communist countries of Eastern Europe under Soviet control, established in 1955. (p. 666)

Wars of the Roses, *n.* from 1455 to 1485, wars for the throne in Great Britain between two branches of the English royal family—the House of York whose emblem was the white rose, and the House of Lancaster whose emblem was the red rose. Henry Tudor of the House of Lancaster won the throne and established the Tudor dynasty. (p. 221)

Washington [wosh′ing tən], **George** (1732–1799), commander in chief of the American army in the Revolutionary War; first President of the United States (1789 to 1797). (p. 485)

Waterloo [wô′tər lü], *n.* the site of the battle in which Napoleon I was finally defeated in 1815; town in Belgium, near Brussels. (p. 501)

Watt [wot], **James** (1736–1819), Scottish engineer and inventor who perfected the steam engine. (p. 517)

Whigs [hwigs], *n., pl.* members of a British political party of the late 1600s to early 1800s who favored reforms, progress, and parliamentary rather than royal power, and opposed the Tory party. (p. 480?)

Wilhelm II [vil′helm] (1859–1941), last emperor of Germany, from 1888 until he abdicated the throne in 1918. He was known as Kaiser Wilhelm. (p. 546)

William the Conqueror (1027?–1087), duke of Normandy who conquered England at the battle of Hastings in 1066 and was king of England from 1066 to 1087. (p. 217)

Wilson [wil′sən], **(Thomas) Woodrow** (1856–1924), the 28th President of the United States (1913 to 1921). (p. 594)

Wright [rīt], **Orville** (1871–1948), American inventor who, with his brother Wilbur, perfected the airplane and made the world's first flight in a motor-powered plane in 1903. (p. 520)

Wright, Wilbur (1867–1912), American inventor who with his brother Orville, made the world's first successful flight in a motor-powered plane at Kitty Hawk, North Carolina, in 1903. (p. 520)

Wu Di [wü′ dē′] (156 B.C.–87 B.C.), *n.* Chinese emperor (140 B.C.–87 B.C.), of the Han dynasty, who extended the empire south to Vietnam and west to Central Asia and brought an era of peace to most of Asia. (p. 143)

X

Xi River [shē], *n.* river in south China, where trading centers developed. (p. 137)

Y

Yalta [yol′tə], *n.* seaport and winter resort in south Crimea, on the Black Sea; the site of a major Allied conference during World War II. (p. 651)

Yaroslav [yü ru slaf′] (c. 11th century), ruler of Kievan Russia from 1019 to 1054; he established Russia as a European power. Also known as Yaroslav the Wise. (p. 241)

Yucatán peninsula [yü′kə tan′], *n.* peninsula of southeast Mexico and north Central America. The Maya culture developed there about 500 B.C. (p. 164)

Z

Zaire [zä ir′], *n.* country in central Africa, formerly the Belgian Congo. (p. 574)

Zhou dynasty [jō], *n.* a Chinese dynasty that ruled from about 1027 B.C. to about 256 B.C., noted as the era of the philosophers Confucius, and Lao-tse. (p. 138)

ziggurat [zig′ů rat], *n.* an ancient temple in the form of a great pyramid with each story smaller than that below it. (p. 22)

Zimbabwe [zim bä′bwä], *n.* ancient African kingdom with gold fields and flourishing trade; present-day Zimbabwe includes the area of the historic Zimbabwe kingdom. (p. 330)

Zionists [zī′ə nists], *n., pl.* people who support or favor Zionism, the movement that started in the 1800s to set up a Jewish national state in Palestine and that now seeks to help maintain and develop the state of Israel; Jewish nationalists. (p. 628)

Zola [zō′lə], **Émile** [ā mēl′] (1840–1902), French novelist, one of the naturalist writers. (p. 526)

INDEX

Pronunciation Key

The Index tells you where to find maps *(map)*, illustrations *(illus.)*, charts, diagrams, and definitions. Pronunciations are respelled in the familiar Thorndike Barnhart pronunciation key in the *Scott, Foresman Advanced Dictionary* which is shown below. For many foreign words in *History and Life*, the pronunciation given is not the local pronunciation but an Anglicized version, one acceptable to educated Americans.

Some words and names, taken from foreign languages, are spoken with sounds that do not otherwise occur in English. Symbols for these sounds are given in the key as "foreign sounds."

a hat	oi oil	ch child
ā age	ou out	ng long
ä far	u cup	sh she
e let	ú put	th thin
ē equal	ü rule	ᴛʜ then
ėr term		zh measure
i it		a in about
ī ice		e in taken
o hot	ə =	i in pencil
ō open		o in lemon
ô order		u in circus

Foreign Sounds

Y as in French *du*.
Pronounce (ē) with the lips rounded as for (ü).

à as in French *ami*.
Pronounce (ä) with the lips spread and held tense.

œ as in French *peu*.
Pronounce (ā) with the lips rounded as for (ō).

N as in French *bon*.
The N is not pronounced, but shows that the vowel before it is nasal.

Abacus, 295, *illus.* 295
Abbas, Shah [1557–1629], 428–429
Abbasid (ab′ə sid) dynasty, 257–259, 273, 277, 279, 280
Abdul-Aziz (Ibn Saud) 1880–1953, 626
Abidjan (ab′i jän′), Côte d'Ivoire (5°26′N/3°58′W), 708
Aborigines (Australia), 554
Abraham, 45
Abrahams, Peter, 700
Absolutism, 398–404
Abu Bakr (ä′bü bäk′ər) [573–634], 248, 254
Abyssinia, 701
Academy, in Athens, 81
Achebe, Chinua, 704
Achilles (ə kil′ēz), 63
Acid rain, 765–766, *illus.* 765

Acre, 202
Acropolis (ə krop′ə lis), 67, *illus.* 66
Actium, battle of (31 B.C.), 101
Adams, John, 472–473
al-Adawiyya, Rabiah, 280
Adenauer, Konrad, 675
Adrianople, battle at, 183
Aegean (i jē′ən) **civilization,** 60–63, *map* 60
Aegean Sea (Europe 37°N/25°E), 58, 60, *map* 60
Aeneid [i nē′id], 63, 110–112
Aeschylus (es′kə ləs) [525–456 B.C.], 83
Afghanistan: ancient, 128; Arab Muslims in, 256; Russian imperialism and, 570
Africa, ancient, *illus.* 154: art of, 160–161, *illus.* 161; government in, 159–160; kingdoms of, *map* 160; Kush, kingdom of, 157–158; languages in, 160; migrations within, 159, *map* 160; religion in, 160; societies of, 155–160
Africa, modern: *map* 152; art and music of, 704, 717, *illus.* 704; ancient civilizations in, 150–161; colonialism in, 704; daily life in, 709; and deforestation, 766; and desertification, 766–767; drought and famine in, 710, *map* 796; economies in, 703; empires in West, 325–329; Ethiopia and, *map,* 642; Europeans in, 334–335; filmmakers from, 717; forest states in, 333–335; geography, impact of, 152–155; imperialism in, 573–575, *map* 575, 584; independence movements in, 700–717, *maps* 702–703; Islamic Empire in, 283–284; kingdoms in East, 329–332; languages in, 703; leaders of, *illus.* 701; literature of, 704; nations [1950–1980], *map* 704; and North African independence, 715–716; population problems in, 704; Portuguese in, 373, 676; resources of, 711, *map* 711; as Roman province, 98; slave trade and, 380, *map* 380; southern, 712–714; Sub-Saharan, 708; trade routes in, *map* 326; vegetation regions, *map* 152; West Africa, 435–436; writers from, 717
African Americans. *See* Black Americans
Africanization, Mobutu, Joseph, and, 709
African National Congress (ANC), 713
African slaves, in Latin America, 461–462, *illus.* 460
Afrikaners (af′rə kä′nerz), 712
Agamemnon (ag′ə mem′non), 83
Age of Reason, 416. *See also* Enlightenment
Agincourt (aj′in kôrt), **battle of** [1415], 223
Agriculture (*see also* Farming): in Africa, ancient, 155–157; in Age of Exploration, 382; in Americas, ancient, 162–163; in Brazil, 748; in Bronze Age, 16; in China, 684, *illus.* 682; in China, ancient, 37; collectivization of, 613; desert, 735; early, 17; of Egypt, ancient, 26; and Great Depression, 638; in Greece, ancient, 65; of Indus Valley civilization, 35; in Islamic Empire, 273, 274; in Middle Ages, 196–197, *illus.* 199; in Middle East, 737; Native American, 342; in Neolithic period, 11–12, 13–14; potato and, 414; in Rome, ancient, 99
Aguinaldo (ä′gē näl′dō), **Emilio** [1870?–1964], 572
Ahura Mazda, 50
Airplane, 520; in World War I, 594
Air pollution, 765–766
Aix-la-Chapelle (āks′lä shä pel′), 188
Akbar (ak′bär) [1542–1605], 430; architecture of, 433
Ake: The Years of Childhood, 717
Akhenaton (äk ə nä′tn) [1375?–1362 B.C.], 31
Akkadian Empire, *map* 22–23
Alawi, 257

Albuquerque, Afonso de, 377
Alchemy, 279
Aldrin, Edwin, 677
Alemanni, 182, *map* 182
Alexander I, of Russia [1775–1825], 500, 547
Alexander II, of Russia [1818–1881], 547
Alexander III, of Russia [1845–1894], 606
Alexander of Novgorod (Alexander Nevsky), 243
Alexander the Great [356 B.C.–323 B.C.], 72–74, *illus.* 74: empire of, *map* 73; and India, 126
Alexandria, Egypt, 74, 85, 112
Alfonso XIII, of Spain [1886–1914], 641
Algebra, 279
Algeria: French in, 573, *map* 575; independence of, 715–716; war with France, 674
Alhambra (al ham′brə), **Spain,** 285
Ali, 248; Shiite followers of, 257
Allah, 251, 252
Allende (ä yān′dā), **Salvador** [1908–1973], 747
Alliance for Progress, 757
Alliances, before World War I, 485, 585–586
Allied powers, and United Nations, 661
Allies: in World War I, 590; in World War II, 645, 647, 648, 649–652
Almoravids (al′mə rä′vidz), 328
Alphabet: Cyrillic, 236–237; Egyptian, ancient, 32; Greek, 92; kana, as Japanese, 314; Korean, 304; Phoenician, 32, 44; Phoenician-derived, 45; Roman, 188; runes as, 185; Sanskrit, 123–124
Alphonso I, of Portugal [1112–1185], 225
Alsace-Lorraine, 598
Altamira, cave of, 4
Amazon Valley, and deforestation, 766, *illus.* 766
Amendments, to U.S. Constitution, 486: and senatorial elections, 552; and slavery, 552; and women's voting rights, 486
American Federation of Labor (AFL), 552
American Indians. *See* Indian, American; Native Americans
American Revolution, impact of, 505–508
Americas (*see also* Central America; Columbus, Christopher; Exploration, Age of; Latin America; North America; South America): civilizations, ancient, in, 162–166; diseases brought into, 380; empires and cultures in, 324, 335–342; Maya civilization in, 164–166, *map* 336; Native Americans in, 162–163
Amin (ä mēn′) Dada, Idi [1925–   ], 706–707
Amman, Jordan, 727
Amon-Re (ä′mon rā′), 31, 32
Amphibious invasion, 651
Amritsar (əm rit′sər), India, 624
Anabaptists, 392
Analects, 141
Anatomy, 416
Angkor Wat, temple of, 129
Angles, 182, 183, 186, *map* 182. *See also* Anglo-Saxons
Anglican Church, 393
Anglo-Saxons: British invasions by, 183–184
Angola, 710, 712, *map* 702
Auguisciola, Sofonisba (sō′fō nēz′bä äng-gwē′shō lä) [1532–1625], 362
Annam, 570
Anne, of England [1665–1714], 482, *illus.* 482
Anglican Church, 479
Antarctica (90°S/0°E): ozone layer depletion, 765

835

I i

849

and Marathon, battle of, 69
Spartan, 68
Spheres of influence, 566, 570, *map* 567
Spice trade, 377
Spinning jenny, 514
Spinning mule, 514
Spirit of Laws, The [1748], 475
Spitfire, 646
Splendid isolation, 585
Spring and Autumn period, in China, 138
Sputnik, 668, 677
Sri Lanka (*see also* Ceylon), Indian influence on, 129
Stalin (stä′lin), **Joseph** [1879–1953], 603, 611: and China, 685; and Nazi-Soviet pact, 643; and Yalta conference, 651–652; 664
Stalingrad, battle of, 649
Stamp Act, *illus.* 485
Stanley, Henry M. [1841–1904], 574
Stanton, Elizabeth Cady [1815–1902], 530
State of nature, 476
State of Prisons in England and Wales, The [1777], 477
Steam engine, 412, 512, 517
Steamships, 533
Steel, 518–519
Stephenson, George [1781–1848], 517
Steppe region, *map* 302
Steward, in medieval Europe, 197
Stock certificates, *illus.* 523
Stock market crash [1929], 639
Stoicism (stō′ə siz′əm), 81–82, 178
Stoics, 82, 103
Stone Age, 8: advances in, 12; Middle (Mesolithic), 8, 11, *illus.* 13; New (Neolithic), 8, 11, 14; Old (Paleolithic), 8
Stonehenge, 15, *illus.* 15
Straits, strategic, 240, *map* 240
Strategic Arms Limitation Treaty (SALT I), 769
Strauss, Johann [1804–1849], 548
Streetcars, 532
Stuart family, in England, 479, 482
Sturm und Drang, 525
Subcontinent, India as, 117–118
Submarine, in World War I, 594, 595
Sub-Saharan Africa (*see also* Africa), populous countries in, 708
Subway, 532
Sudan: ancient, 158, 325; British in, 573, *map* 575; Kanem-Bornu in, 435
Sudetenland, 642
Sudetens, 598
Suez Canal (Egypt 29°58′N/32°31′E), 573, 730, and Egyptian nationalism, 625; before World War I, 585
Suffrage: male, 529–530; women's, 530
Sufi orders, 280, 281
Suharto (sü′här′tō′) [1921–   ], 690–691
Suicide in the Trenches, 591
Suiko, empress of Japan, 313
Sukarno (sü kär′nō′), **President** [1901–1970], 690
Suleiman (sü′lä män′) **I, the Magnificent** [1495?–1566], 426
Sulla (sul′ə), **Lucius** [138–78 B.C.], 99
Sultan, 260
Sumer, 20, *map* 22–23
Sumerians (sü mir′ē ənz), 22–25: and Indian Ocean, 724; mathematics of, 39, *illus.* 39; religion of, *illus.* 21
Summa Theologica, 208
Sundiata (sùn′dē ä′tə) [c. 1200], 328
Sun Goddess, Japanese worship of, 311
Sun King (Louis XIV), 399
Sunna, 254
Sunni Muslims, 248, 257, 428, 723

Sunni Muslim Brotherhood, 732
Sun Yat-sen (sun′ yät′sen′) [1867–1925], 622, *illus.* 622
Superconductors, 773
Superpowers, 663–664, 665–666
Super race, 631
Suriname (sùr′ ə nam), 383
Survival of the fittest, 521, 524
Susa (sü′sə) (Persian Empire), 50
Suttee (su tē′), 431, 565
Swahili (swä hē′lē) **culture,** 330–331, *map* 330
Sweden, 676: Great Northern War and, 404; nationalism in, 225; and Thirty Years' War, 397
Swift, Jonathan [1667–1745], 477–478
Synchronic thinking, 434
Syracuse, ancient Greece, coin from, *illus.* 64
Syria, 724, 725: under Alexander the Great, *map* 73; Arabs and, 254; Arameans, 44; as mandate, 598; nationalism in, 626; political independence in, 732; and Six-Day War, 730, *map* 730; role in Lebanon, 736, *illus.* 736
Szilard, Leo, 653

T

Tacitus (tas′ə təs) [55?–120?], 90, 112, 176
Taghaza (tə gä′zə), Africa, 326
Tahiti, 571
Taiwan, (Asia 23°30′N/121°E) 682, 688
Taizong (tī′dzung′) [600–649], 145
Taj Mahal (täj′ mə häl′), 433, *illus.* 423; *map* 433
Tale of Genji, 308, 314
Tamerlane [c. 1336–1405], 264
Tamils (tam′əlz), 128
Tanganyika (tang′gə nyē′kə), 707
Tang (tang) **dynasty,** 144–146, *illus.* 298: Chinese expansion under, 145, *map* 145
Tanka, 314
Tanks, in World War I, 594, *illus.* 593
Tanzania (tan′zə nē′ə), 707
Taoism (dou′iz′əm), 141–142, 771; symbols of, 142
Tariffs, and Great Depression, 639
Tarik, 255
Tarquin family (Etruscan), 92–93; Tarquin the Proud [534–510 B.C.], 93
Taxation without representation, and Magna Carta, 220
Taxes, and social reforms, 532
Technology (*see also* Industrial Revolution; Inventions; Science and technology) 763, 764: in China, 295; and exploration, 372–373, *illus.* 372; and Industrial Revolution, 518–519; in Middle Ages, 205, 208; solar parabolic dishes and, *illus.* 771; in World War I, 592–594
Tel Aviv, Israel, *illus.* 735
Telegraph, 519; invention of [1837], 542
Telemann, Georg Philipp [1681–1767], 405
Telephone, 519, *illus.* 518, 759
Telescope, 411, 412, 413, 417, *illus.* 417
Telford, Thomas [1757–1834], 517
Teller, Edward, 653
Temperature, study of, 413
Ten Commandments, 46, 47, 51
Ten Lost Tribes of Israel, 46
Tenno, Jimmu, 311
Tenochtitlán (tä nōch′ tē tlän′) (Mexico City), 336, 455, *illus.* 454
Tetzel, Johann [1465?–1519], 389–390
Texas, annexation of by U.S., 551

Textiles: from Côte d'Ivoire, 704; and Industrial Revolution, 514–516
Thailand, 690, *map* 689: Cambodian refugees, 693; Indian influence on, 129
Thatcher, Margaret [1925–   ], 673, *illus.* 674
Thebes (thēbz), 28: Philip of Macedonia and 72
Theocracy (thē ok′rə sē), Egypt, ancient, as 30; in Iran, 725
Theodora (thē′ə dô′rə) **Empress** [?–548], 233, 236, *illus.* 236
Theodoric (thē od′ər ik), Emperor [454?–526], 184
Theodosius (thē′ə dô′shē əs) I [346?–395], 105, 180
Thermopylae (thər mop′ə lē), 69, *map* 60
Theseus (thē′sē əs), 61
Third Estate, 493, 494
Third Reich (rīн), 631
Third Republic (France), 546
Third Rome, 230, 244
Thirty Years' War [1618–1648], 397
Thor, 182
Three Principles of the People, 622
Thucydides (thü sid′ə dēz′) [460?–400 B.C.], 84
Thuluth (thü′ləth) **script,** 267
Thutmose (thüt′mō sə) **III, King of Egypt** [ruled c. 1450 B.C.], 29; empire of, *map* 22–23
Tiahuanaco (tē′ə wä nä′kō), 337; culture of, 337
Tiananmen Square, 686, *illus.* 685
Tiberius (tī bir′ē əs) [42 B.C.–A.D. 37], 99, 103
Tiber River, 102
Tibet, plateau of, 136, *map* 136
Tigris-Euphrates (tī′gris) **rivers,** 3, 48, *map* 22
Tigris-Euphrates river system civilization (*see also* Mesopotamia), 20, *map* 22–23
Timbuktu (tim buk′tü), (Tombouctou, Mali 16°50′N/3°W), **Africa,** 276, 284, 328, 329, *illus.* 328
Time of Troubles, 244, 402
Titian (tish′ən), 361, *illus.* 362
Tito (tē′tō) (Josip Broz) [1892–1980], 667
Titus, arch of, *illus.* 104
Tiw (tē′ü), 182
Tlaloc (tlä′lok), 337
Toju, Nakae [1608–1648], 446
Tokugawa (tō kü gä′wä) **Shogunate, Japan** [1603–1868], 316, 319, 441, 445–448, 567, 568: women in, 446
Tokyo, Japan, 447, *illus.* 681; as Japanese capital, 568
Toltec (tol′tek) **peoples,** 164
Tom Jones, 478
Torah, 47, 51, *illus.* 51
Tordesillas, Treaty of [1494], 374
Tories, in England, 480–481
Totalitarianism (tō tal′ə ter′ē ə niz′əm): in Nazi Germany, 632; in Russia, 613–614
Tours, battle of, 255
Toussaint L'Ouverture (tü saɴ′ lü er tyr′), **Pierre Dominique,** 462, 502, *illus.* 462
Tower of Babel, 49
Towns, in Middle Ages, 202–206
Toynbee, Arnold, 90
Trade: and Age of Exploration, 371–374; and Byzantine Empire, 237; with Central America, 751; in China, ancient, 139–140, 144, communist, 686, Ming dynasty, 442, *map* 444, 19th century, 566, Song dynasty, 297; in Constantinople, 240; and Crusades, 202; and discovery of Americas, 379–380; and

W

ACKNOWLEDGMENTS

Quoted Material

xxii Allen Johnson, *The Historian and Historical Evidence*. New York: Charles Scribner's Sons, 1926, p. 21. **xxii** Natalie Zemon Davis, "History's Two Bodies," *The American Historical Review*, Vol. 98, No. 1, February 1988. **xxiii** Bernard Norling, *Towards a Better Understanding of History*. South Bend, IN: University of Notre Dame Press, 1960, p. 42. **xxiii** Paul Gagnon, *Democracy's Untold Story: What World History Books Neglect*. Washington, D.C.: American Federation of Teachers, 1987, p. 28. **xxiii** Sherman Kent, *Writing History*. New York: Appleton-Century Crofts, 1941. p. 1. **25** From "The Holy Priestess of Heaven" from *Inanna-Queen of Heaven and Earth* by Diane Wolkstein and Samuel Noah Kramer. Copyright © 1983 by Diane Wolkstein and Samuel Noah Kramer. Reprinted by permission of Harper & Row, Publishers, Inc. **31** From *The Book of the Dead*, Oliver J. Thatcher, ed., *The Ideas That Have Influenced Civilization*, Milwaukee, 1901. **38** "Poem of a Shang House" from *The Ancient Worlds of Asia* by Ernst Diez, translated by W. C. Darwell, 1961. Reprinted by permission of Paul Zsolnay Verlag. **51** W. Gunther Plaut, ed., *The Torah: A Modern Commentary*. New York: Union of Hebrew Congregations, 1981. **58** From *The History of the Peloponnesian War* by Thucydides, edited by Sir Richard Livingstone (New York: Oxford University Press, 1966). **63** *The Odyssey of Homer: Newly Translated Into English Prose*. New York: Oxford University Press, 1932. **80** *The Works of Aristotle*, Volume II. Chicago: Encyclopaedia Britannica, Inc., 1952. **113** Dana Carleton Munroe, *A Source Book of Roman History*. Boston: D.C. Heath & Company, 1904. **122** From the *Bhagavad Gita* trans. by Sr. Edwin Arnold, (Boston, 1885). **124** From *History of the World: Early Civilizations*, p. 73, (New York: Golden Press, 1966). **125** Richard A. Gard, ed., *Buddhism*. New York: George Braziller, 1961. **126** Quoted in Percival Spear, *India: A Modern History*, (Ann Arbor; University of Michigan Press, 1961). **131** From "Malavika and Agnimitra" by Kalidasa in *Ancient Poetry from China, Japan & India*, rendered into English verse by Henry W. Wells. Copyright © 1968 by the University of South Carolina Press. Reprinted by permission. **141** Reprinted by permission of Macmillan Publishing Company Inc., and Unwin Hyman Ltd. from *The Analects of Confucius* by Arthur Waley. Copyright 1938 by Unwin Hyman Ltd.; copyright renewed. **161** D. T. Niane, *Sundiata: An Epic of Old Mali*, trans. by G. D. Pickett. London: Longmans, Green & Co., Ltd., 1969. **176** From *The Complete Works of Tacitus*, Translated from the Latin by Alfred John Church and William Jackson Broadribb. Ed. Moses Hadas. (New York: Random House, Inc., 1942) p. 716. **211** Henry Adams, *Mont-Saint-Michel and Chartres*. Boston: Houghton Mifflin Company, 1905. **224** From *The Trial of Jeanne d'Arc*, translated by W. P. Barrett. Reprinted by permission of Routledge & Kegan Paul Ltd., London. **230** Marcus Nathan Adler, trans. *Itinerary of Benjamin of Tudela*. (New York: Philipp Feldheim, Inc.) **236** *Procopius*, Vol. I, trans., Henry B. Dewing, Loeb Classical Library (Cambridge: Harvard University Press, 1914), pp. 231–233. **237** From Anna Comnena, *Alexiade*, ed. B. Leib (Paris, 1967), Vol. I, pp. 123–125. **239** Samuel H. Cross and Olgerd P. Sherbowitz-Wetzor (trans. and ed.), *The Russian Primary Chronicle* (Cambridge: Harvard University Press, 1930, 1958). **242** Serge A. Zenkovsky, trans., *Medieval Russia's Epics, Chronicles, and Tales*. New York: E.P. Dutton, 1963. **242** The Koran, trans. by M. N. Pickthall in *The Meaning of the Glorious Koran* (New York: Mentor Classics, 1956), pgs. 438–439. Reprinted by permission of George Allen and Unwin Ltd., London. **277** Marcus Nathan Adler, Trans., *Itinerary of Benjamin of Tudela*. New York: Philipp Feldheim, Inc. **252** From *The Meaning of the Glorious Koran* by M. M. Pickthall. Reprinted by permission of Unwin Hyman Ltd. **280** From *Rabi'a the Mystic and Her Fellow Saints in Islam* by Margaret Smith. Cambridge, England: Cambridge University Press, 1928. Reprinted by permission of Cambridge University Press, New York. **280** From *A Literary History of the Arabs* by Reynold A. Nicholson (Cambridge University Press, 1966). **280** Edward Fitzgerald, trans., *Rubaiyat of Omar Khayyam*. Boston: Houghton Mifflin, 1898. **285** Desmond Stewart, *Great Ages of Man, A History of the World's Culture: Early Islam*. New York: Time-Life Books, 1967. **296** Quoted in Elizabeth Seeger, *The Pageant of Chinese History*. London: Longman Group Limited, 1934, 1937. **297** Patricia Buckley Ebrey, ed., *Chinese Civilization and Society: A Sourcebook*. New York: The Free Press, 1981. **305** Okakura Kakuzo, *The Book of Tea*. New York: Dodd, Mead & Company, Inc., 1906. **308** James A. Murdoch, *History of Japan I*. London: Routledge & Kegan Paul Ltd., 1964. **311** From *An Outline History of Japan* by Herbert H. Gowen. Copyright 1939 by Appleton-Century Co. Inc., renewed 1955 by Herbert H. Gowen. Reprinted by permission of E. P. Dutton, a division of Penguin Books USA Inc. **314** Tanka poem from *The Manyoshu*. Copyright © 1965 Columbia University Press. **324** From *Narrative of Travels and Discoveries in Northern and Central Africa, In The Years 1822, 1823, and 1824* by Major Denham, Captain Clapperton and Doctor Oudney. London: John Murray, 1826, p. 63. **329** From *Ancient African Kingdoms* by Margaret Shinnie. New York: St. Martin's Press, Inc., 1965. **331** From the translation in *The Ethiopian Observer*, 2, Vol, 5, 1960. **333** Thomas Hodgkin, *NIGERIAN PERSPECTIVES: An Historical Anthology*. London: Oxford University Press, 1960. **343** "Oracle xv" from *Yoruba Poetry* by Bakare Gbadamosi and Ulli Beier, The Ministry of Education, Ibadan, 1959. **351** Niccolo Machiavelli, *The Prince*, trans. by Robert M. Adams. New York: W. W. Norton & Company, 1977. **370** Hakluyt Society, *Works Issued by the Hakluyt Society*, 196 vols. London: 1847–1951. **374**

Henry Steele Commager, ed., *Documents of American History*, Vol. I to 1898. Englewood Cliffs, NJ: Prentice-Hall, Inc., 1973. **396** Sir Simonds D'Ewes, *The Journals of All the Parliaments during the Reign of Queen Elizabeth*. London, 1682. **405** Percy M. Young, *Masters of Music: Mozart*. New York: David White Company, 1966. **408** Niccolo Machiavelli: *The Prince*, trans. by Robert M. Adams. New York: W. W. Norton & Company, 1977. **413** H. S. Thayer, trans., *Newton's Philosophy of Nature: Selections From His Writings*. New York: Hafner Publishing Company, 1953. **417** Stillman Drake, trans., *Discoveries and Opinions of Galileo*. New York: Doubleday, 1957. **432** From *Sources of Indian Tradition*, Second Edition, Vol. I, edited and revised by Ainslie T. Embree. Copyright © 1988 Columbia University Press. Used by permission. **440** Jonathan D. Spence, *Emperor of China: Self-Portrait of K'ang-hsi*. New York: Vintage Books, 1975, p. 65. **445** E. Backhouse and J. O. P. Bland, *Annals & Memoirs of the Court of Peking*. Boston: Houghton Mifflin Co., 1914. **446** Ryusaku Tsunoda, Wm. Theodore de Bary and Donald Keene, *Sources of Japanese Tradition*. New York: Columbia University Press, 1958, p. 381. **448** David John Lu, *Sources of Japanese History, Vol. I*. New York: McGraw-Hill Book Company, 1974. **449** Donald Keene, *Nō: The Classical Theatre of Japan*, introduction by Ishikawa Jun. Tokyo: Kodansha International Ltd., 1966. **452** Bernard Diaz del Castillo, *The True History of the Conquest of Mexico*, trans. by Maurice Keating, 1800. **458** From *Letter to a King: A Peruvian Chief's Account of Life Under the Incas and Under Spanish Rule* by Huaman Poma, edited by Christopher Dilke. Copyright © 1978 by Christopher Dilke. Reprinted by permission of Unwin Hyman Ltd. **464** H. W. Janson, *History of Art: A Survey of the Major Visual Arts from The Dawn of History to the Present Day*. New York: Harry N. Abrams, Inc., 1962. **464** From Eduardo Galeano, *Memory of Fire: 1. Genesis*, translated by Cedric Belfrage. Copyright © 1985 by Cedric Belfrage. Reprinted by permission of Pantheon Books, a Division of Random House, Inc. **474** John Locke, *Of Civil Government*. London: J. M. Dent & Sons, Ltd., 1924. **487** Paul Delarue and Marie-Louise Tenèze, *Le Conte populaire français*, Vol. I. Paris, 1976. **503** Lecuna and Bierck, *Selected Writings of Bolivar, I*. 512 Quoted in Paul Joseph Mantoux, trans. by Marjorie Vernon, *The Industrial Revolution in the Eighteenth Century*. New York: Harper & Row, 1961. **528** From *The Marx-Engels Reader*, edited by Robert C. Tucker. Copyright © 1972 by W. W. Norton & Company, Inc. Reprinted by permission. **552** Abraham Lincoln, *The Emancipation Proclamation*, January 1, 1863. **555** Otto L. Bettmann, Ph.D., *A Pictorial History of Medicine*. Springfield, Illinois: Charles C. Thomas, 1956. **574** *General Act of the Conference of Berlin*, signed February 26, 1885. **582** Viscount Grey of Fallodon, *Twenty-Five Years*, Vol. II (New York: Frederick A. Stokes Company, 1925), p. 20. **590** Jane Addams, *The Second Twenty Years at Hull-House*. New York: The Macmillan Company, 1930. **591** "Suicide in the Trenches" from *The Collected Poems* by Siegfried Sassoon. Copyright 1918, 1920 by E. P. Dutton & Co. Copyright 1936, 1946, 1948 by Siegfried Sassoon. All rights reserved. Reprinted by permission of Viking Penguin, a division of Penguin Books USA, Inc., and G. T. Sassoon. **596** Woodrow Wilson, *War and Peace: Presidential Messages, Addresses, and Public Papers (1917–1924)*, ed. Ray Stannard Baker and William E. Dodd (New York: Harper & Brothers, 1927). **602** Quoted in N. N. Sukhanov, *The Russian Revolution, 1917: A Personal Record*, Joel Carmickael, ed. New York: Oxford University Press, 1955, p. 273. **611** Cited in *Great Soviet Encyclopedia*, 3rd ed., Vol. 14. 1973. **611** *USSR: Sixty Years of the Union, 1922–1982*. Moscow: Progress Publishers, 1982. **620** Bal Gangadar Tilak, *His Writings and Speeches* (Madras, India: Ganesh & Co., 1923). **630** Sigmund Freud, *Civilization And Its Discontents*, trans. by James Strachey. New York: W. W. Norton & Company, 1961. **633** Louis Fischer, *The Life of Mahatma Gandhi*. New York: Harper & Row, Publishers, Inc., 1950. **636** Otto Friedrich, BEFORE THE DELUGE: A PORTRAIT OF BERLIN IN THE 1920's. New York: Harper & Row, 1972, p. 140. **645** Robert Wernick, BLITZKRIEG. New York: Time-Life Books, 1977. **649** Filip Müller, EYEWITNESS AUSCHWITZ: THREE YEARS IN THE GAS CHAMBERS. New York: Stein and Day Publishers, 1979, pp. 33–34. **649** Excerpt from *Anne Frank: The Diary of A Young Girl* by Anne Frank. Copyright 1952 by Otto H. Frank. Reprinted by permission of Doubleday, a division of Bantam, Doubleday, Dell Publishing Group, Inc. and Vallentine, Mitchell & Co. Ltd. **660** Lucius D. Clay, *Decision in Germany* (New York: Doubleday & Co., Inc., 1950). p. 360. **663** *The Universal Declaration of Human Rights*, United Nations Publication No. 63.1.13. New York: The United Nations, 1949, pp. 33–38. **684** *Quotations from Chairman Mao Tsetung*. Peking: Foreign Languages Press, 1976. **697** Lance Morrow, "All the Hazards and Threats of Success: After their miracle, the Japanese fear 'advanced nations' disease.'" *Time*, August 1, 1983, p. 25. **704** Lyrics from "Homeless" by Paul Simon. Copyright © 1986 by Paul Simon. Used by permission of Warner/Chappell Music, Inc. All rights reserved. **717** Premier Gamal Abdul Nasser, *Egypt's Liberation: The Philosophy of the Revolution*. Washington, D.C.: Public Affairs Press, 1955. **731** *Presidential Documents: Weekly Compilation of Presidential Documents*, Vol. XIV, p. 1523. U.S. Government Printing Office. **740** Albert Baltra Cortés, "Neustra América y sus problemas," pp. 3–27. Translated by the editor, Benjamin Kreen in "The Crisis of Latin America," LATIN AMERICAN CIVILIZATION: THE NATIONAL ERA, Volume 2, Third Edition. Boston: Houghton Mifflin Company, 1974, p. 439. **744** From Sven Lindqvist, *The Shadow: Latin America Faces the Seventies*, translated by Keith Bradfield. Copyright © 1969 by Sven Lindqvist. Reprinted by permission of Bonnier Fakta Bokforlag AB, Stockholm. **757** Gabriel García Márquez, *Love in the Time of Cholera*, trans. by Edith Grossman. New York: Alfred A. Knopf, 1988. **757** From "Children's Hair" from *Selected Poems of Gabriela Mistral*, translated by Langston Hughes. Copyright © 1957 by Indiana University Press. Reprinted by permission of

Joan Daves. **762** From *My Life for the Poor* by Mother Teresa of Calcutta. Edited by Jose Luis Gonzalez-Balado and Janet N. Playfoot. Copyright © 1985 by Jose Luis Gonzalez-Balado and Janet N. Playfoot. Reprinted by permission of Harper & Row, Publishers, Inc.

Illustrations

Unless otherwise acknowledged, all photos are the property of Scott, Foresman and Company. Page positions are as follows: (T) top, (B) bottom, (L) left, (R) right, (C) center, (INS) insert COVER AND FRONTISPIECE: SCALA/Art Resource, NY **xxiv** Courtesy of the Trustees of the British Museum **1L** The Avery Brundage Collection/Photo: Laurie Platt Winfrey, Carousel Inc. N.Y. **1C** Lepsius, DENKMÄLER . . . 1860 **1R** Robert Frerck/Odyssey Productions, Chicago **2** Photo: Mario Ruspoli, From "The Cave of Lascaux, The Final Photographs" © 1986 Bordas Publishing, S.A., Paris, Published 1987 Harry N. Abrams, Inc. NY **5** Alexander Marshack **8** The Cleveland Museum of Natural History **10** American Museum of Natural History **11** Alexander Marshack **12** Photo: Mario Ruspoli, From "The Cave of Lascaux, The Final Photographs" © 1986 Bordas Publishing, S.A., Paris, Published 1987 Harry N. Abrams, Inc. N.Y. **13L** National Museum of Denmark **13R** Oriental Institute, The University of Chicago, Courtesy Iranian Prehistoric Project **14** Israel National Museum, Jerusalem **15** Georg Gerster/COMSTOCK INC. **17T** Ankara Archeological Museum **17C** Oriental Institute, The University of Chicago **17B** The Iraqi Museum, Baghdad/Photo: Aldo Durazzi **21** Oriental Institute, The University of Chicago **23** Robert Harding Picture Library Ltd., London **24L** The Louvre, Paris **24TR** Oriental Institute, The University of Chicago **24BR** Courtesy of the Trustees of the British Museum **26** Robert Harding Picture Library Ltd., London **28** AP/Wide World **29** Robert Harding Picture Library Ltd., London **30L** Brian Brake, Hilleison Agency/Photo Researchers **30R** Lee Boltin **35ALL** National Museum, New Delhi **36** Robert Harding Picture Library Ltd., London **37** Freer Gallery of Art, The Smithsonian Institution, Washington, D.C. **39T** Courtesy of the Trustees of the British Museum **39B** The Metropolitan Museum of Art, Rogers Fund, 1930 **43** Scala/Art Resource, N.Y. **46** Egyptian National Museum, Cairo/Photo: Barry Iverson **51L** Art Resource, NY **51R** Israel National Museum, Jerusalem **56** National Archaeological Museum, Athens/Photo: François René Roland, Paris **59** Scala/Art Resource, NY **61** Hirmer Fotoarchiv, Munich **62** Museo Archeologico Del Piero, Greece/Photo: Nimatallah/Artephot-Ziolo, Paris **64** Courtesy, Museum of Fine Arts, Boston **66** Ray Manley/Shostal Associates **67** Angora Museum, Athens **68** Courtesy of the Trustees of the British Museum **71L** Villa Giulia Museum, Rome **71R** The Metropolitan Museum of Art, Fletcher Fund, 1931 **74** Naples National Museum/Photo: Raymond V. Schoder, S.J. **75** Robert Frerck/Odyssey Productions, Chicago **79** Courtesy of the Trustees of the British Museum **81** Alinari/Art Resource, NY **82** Mary Evans Picture Library **83** Courtesy of the Trustees of the British Museum **84** Maurice Newcombe **85** University Prints, Boston **86** The Louvre, Paris/Photo: Raymond V. Schoder, S. J. **89** Robert Llewellyn **91** David Hiser/Photographers/Aspen **92** Scala/Art Resource, NY **93** Scala/Art Resource, NY **95** The Louvre, Paris/Giraudon/Art Resource, NY **97** Courtesy of the Trustees of the British Museum **98** Alinari/Mansell Collection **100** Alinari/Art Resource, NY **101** Courtesy of the Trustees of the British Museum **103** A. M. Van Der Heyden **104** A. M. Van Der Heyden **106** The Metropolitan Museum of Art, Rogers Fund **107L** Robert Frerck/Odyssey Productions, Chicago **107TR** Courtesy of the Trustees of the British Museum **107BR** Staatliches Saalburgmuseum **108** Eric G. Carle/Shostal Associates **109** Italian State Tourist Office, N.Y. **110T** G. Barone/FPG **110B** Alinari/Art Resource, NY **111** New York Public Library, Astor, Lenox and Tilden Foundations, Rare Book and Manuscripts Division/Photo: Laurie P. Winfrey, Carousel-NY **113** National Gallery of Art, Washington, D.C./ Samuel H. Kress Collection **117** Nelson Gallery of Art/Atkins Museum, Kansas City, Mo. **119** Robert Frerck/Odyssey Productions, Chicago **122** The Metropolitan Museum of Art, Eggleston Fund, 1927 **123** By courtesy of the Victoria & Albert Museum **124** By courtesy of the Victoria & Albert Museum **126** Robert Frerck/Odyssey Productions, Chicago **128** Dr. Robert G. Thompson **131** Martin Hürlimann **135** Four by Five **137** Lowell Georgia/Photo Researchers **139** Courtesy The Chinese Embassy, Washington, D.C./Photo: Seth Joel **140** The British Library **143** Paulus Leeser Photography, Inc. **147T** Courtesy Kodansha Ltd. Publishing **147B** Nelson Gallery of Art/Atkins Museum, Kansas City, Mo. **151** © Richard Sloan, Shadow of the Ruins, Private Collection **153** Bruno Barbey/Magnum Photos **154** K. Iowambo/Sygma **156** Courtesy Jan Kanter **157** Murray Roberts **158** Courtesy of The Newberry Library, Chicago **159** Jonathan Blair **161** National Museum, Lagos, Nigeria/Photo: Dirk Bakker **163** The Smithsonian Institution **165** Munson-Williams-Proctor Institute, Utica **167** © Jake Rajs/Image Bank **172** Mehmet Biber/Photo Researchers **173L** Wan-go H.C. Weng **173C** Giraudon/Art Resource, N.Y. **173R** Werner Forman **174** Trinity College, Dublin **177** Aldo Durazzi **180** The Metropolitan Museum of Art, Cloisters Collection **181** A. Nogues/Sygma **183T** Courtesy of the Trustees of the British Museum **183B** Courtesy of the Trustees of the British Museum **184** Deutsches Archaologisches Institut, Rome **189** Courtesy The Vatican Collections, Rome **193** Harley Ms. 4379, Fol. 23/The British Library **198** from BOUTELL'S HERALDRY, revised by C. W. Scott Giles, O.B.E., Frederick Warne & Co., London. Revised edition, 1958) **199** Rheinisches Nationalmuseum **200** BARGELLO: Scala/Art Resource, NY **203** Bibliothèque De L'Arsenal Service/Photographique, Bibliotheque Nationale **204** The Pierpont Morgan Library, New York. M. 399 F. 10v **206** French Government Tourist Office **208** Musée Conde, Chantilly/